Brazil

Regis St Louis

Gary Chandler, Gregor Clark, Aimée Dowl

Bridget Gleeson, Robert Landon, Kevin Raub,

MANAUS (p644)
Gateway to jungle trips along the mighty Amazon, the once-glorious city has teeming markets and Amazonian culture

PANTANAL (p413)
Verdant wonderland with fantastic wildlife viewing coupled with trekking, horseback riding and boat trips

BONITO (p428)
One of Brazil's top ecotourism destinations with river snorkeling, forest-backed waterfalls and surreal caverns

IGUAÇU FALLS (p328)
More than 250 spectacular waterfalls surrounded by Atlantic rain forest

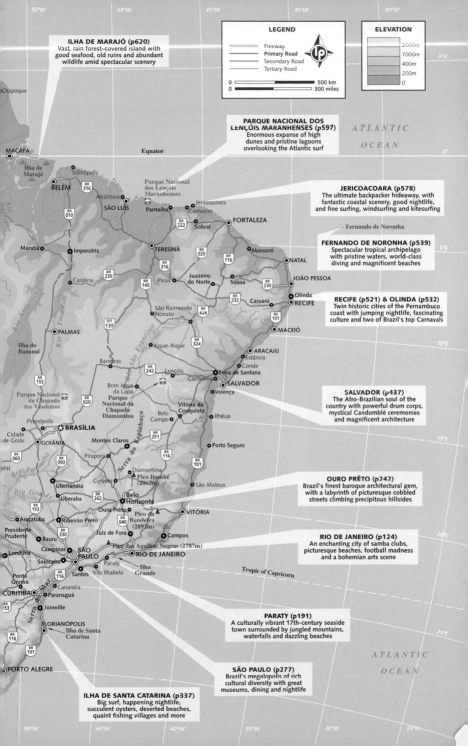

LEGEND

Freeway
Primary Road
Secondary Road
Tertiary Road

0 ——— 500 km
0 ——— 300 miles

ELEVATION

2000m
1000m
400m
200m
0

ILHA DE MARAJÓ (p620)
Vast, rain forest–covered island with good seafood, old ruins and abundant wildlife amid spectacular scenery

PARQUE NACIONAL DOS LENÇÓIS MARANHENSES (p597)
Enormous expanse of high dunes and pristine lagoons overlooking the Atlantic surf

JERICOACOARA (p578)
The ultimate backpacker hideaway, with fantastic coastal scenery, good nightlife, and fine surfing, windsurfing and kitesurfing

FERNANDO DE NORONHA (p539)
Spectacular tropical archipelago with pristine waters, world-class diving and magnificent beaches

RECIFE (p521) & OLINDA (p532)
Twin historic cities of the Pernambuco coast with jumping nightlife, fascinating culture and two of Brazil's top Carnavals

SALVADOR (p437)
The Afro-Brazilian soul of the country with powerful drum corps, mystical Candomblé ceremonies and magnificent architecture

OURO PRÊTO (p242)
Brazil's finest baroque architectural gem, with a labyrinth of picturesque cobbled streets climbing precipitous hillsides

RIO DE JANEIRO (p124)
An enchanting city of samba clubs, picturesque beaches, football madness and a bohemian arts scene

PARATY (p191)
A culturally vibrant 17th-century seaside town surrounded by jungled mountains, waterfalls and dazzling beaches

SÃO PAULO (p277)
Brazil's megalopolis of rich cultural diversity with great museums, dining and nightlife

ILHA DE SANTA CATARINA (p337)
Big surf, happening nightlife, succulent oysters, deserted beaches, quaint fishing villages and more

On the Road

REGIS ST LOUIS Coordinating Author
Researching Rio de Janeiro during Carnaval (p77) has its perks. That's me as a pirate marching along with the Caprichosos de Pilares samba school during our celebratory dance through the Sambódromo.

GREGOR CLARK Unexpected surprises lurk around every corner in Brazil. En route to the historical town of Biribiri (the true aim of this excursion), we stopped spontaneously at a roadside waterfall. Next thing I knew my friends were motioning me over to see these cliff paintings. We finally reached Biribiri at sunset.

GARY CHANDLER That's me on a huge sand bar in the Rio Tapajós, one of countless beaches that emerge during the Amazon's dry season. You can't swim at most river beaches because of stingrays (aka 'wish you-were-dead fish' because of their sting), but it's still great to relax on the sand after a long hot day in the forest.

AIMÉE DOWL Brazil is well known as a wildlife wonderland and an easy place to make friends. On this day at the Parque de Aves near Foz do Iguaçu (p329), I got to appreciate both.

ROBERT LANDON I love to fly into São Paulo and look out on the vast forest of high-rise buildings spreading to every horizon. But this trip, I also fell for Jardim Botânico (p291), the city's under-appreciated botanical gardens. They offer a delightfully leafy, impeccably tended respite from the urban chaos.

BRIDGET GLEESON Arriving in Maceió, I was surrounded by skyscrapers and traffic, so I was relieved when I first laid eyes on the colorful old-fashioned *jangadas* (sailboat of the Northeast) sailing out to the coral reef (p508). I waded into the water and hopped onto one; 10 minutes later I was floating blissfully in the clear green sea.

KEVIN RAUB There is no rest for the wicked while on a Lonely Planet research sojourn – we 're even on the clock underwater! This is Buraco das Cabras, a dive site in Fernando de Noronha (p541), taken on the last dive of my advanced scuba course. I'm attempting to interview one of these cute little xiras, but they were fiercely tight-lipped and quicker than greased lightning! Passed my course, though.

PAUL SMITH I am standing in one of the exact centers of South America in Parque Nacional da Chapada dos Guimarães (p409). If you think that South America can only have one exact center then you're almost certainly right, but tell that to the residents of Cuiabá who insist the Centro Geodésico is located there!

For full author biographies see p744.

Brazil Highlights

The world's fifth-largest country has an astounding array of natural and cultural wonders, with soulful coastal cities, wildlife-filled rain forests and Unesco World Heritage sites all jockeying for attention in the vast Brazilian landscape. Traveling in Brazil can mean so many things, from bouncing over surreal dune-covered national parks to snorkeling through undersea wonders off reef-fringed islands. There are historic Northeastern cities full of Afro-Brazilian rhythms, picture-book colonial towns and awe-inspiring scenery – thundering waterfalls, Amazonian rain forest, Pantanal wetlands – that resemble nowhere else on earth.

Brazil's highlights are many, and make for some tough decisions when planning itineraries. For a few ideas, authors and travelers share what they love most about the country here. Share your highlights at www.lonelyplanet.com/brazil.

JOHN PENN

1 PÃO DE AÇÚCAR, RIO DE JANEIRO

Most travelers who've done it agree: the most memorable – if slightly terrifying – way to the top isn't by cable car, but by ropes, sturdy shoes and plenty of perspiration expended climbing up Sugarloaf's kinder, gentler backside (p152). But no matter how you reach the rocky 396m-high clifftop, breathtaking views over the Cidade Maravilhosa (Marvelous City) – and a well-deserved caipirinha – await.

Regis St Louis, Lonely Planet Author

PANTANAL

The Pantanal (p413) is a stunning marshy wilderness positively teeming with wildlife. The region is South America's answer to the African savannas and one of the continent's most fantastic natural attractions, best viewed from a boat or canoe.

**Paul Smith,
Lonely Planet Author**

TOM BOYDEN

2

JOHN MAIER JR

3

RIO'S NIGHTLIFE

No place quite captures the soul of Rio de Janeiro as does Lapa (p174). Mixing on the cracked sidewalks and battered back lanes are rich and poor, straight and gay, pimps and prostitutes, *malandros* (con artists), musicians, artists, gringos and the assorted characters that have long called Lapa home. The energy on the streets is palpable – infused by the enchanting rhythms of samba spilling out of old-fashioned dance halls and festive, open-sided bars.

Regis St Louis, Lonely Planet Author

CRAIG PERSHOUSE

4

IGUAÇU FALLS

The ultimate natural spectacle, Iguaçu Falls (p328) lures visitors with its first tier of cascades and continues to dazzle them with a seemingly endless theater of tumbling water. The finale comes at the bottom of the aptly monikered Devil's Throat, which spits you out thoroughly drenched. Stay back if you want to stay dry!

Aimée Dowl, Lonely Planet Author

VIVIANE PON

5 CARNAVAL, RIO DE JANEIRO

Sure there are reasons not to come to Carnaval (p76), like the jacked-up prices at hotels and the big crowds all over town. But then again, where else can you dance through the streets for days on end, following pounding drum corps and 30-piece marching bands surrounded by costumed merrymakers bent on celebrating life to the fullest? The big parade is sheer spectacle; it's magnificent to see from the stands, but the best way to experience it is to join a samba school, don a crazy costume and dance though the Sambódromo.

Regis St Louis, Lonely Planet Author

JANE SWEEN

6 PARQUE NACIONAL DA CHAPADA DOS GUIMARÃES

Not taking your camera to Chapada dos Guimarães (p409) is a crime. The area is made up of some of the most stunning scenery you are ever likely to see, from the craggy Cidade de Pedra, to the jaw-dropping Véu de Noiva waterfall. My advice is to make sure you have a big enough memory card or you'll find yourself reluctantly deleting some memorable shots.

Paul Smith, Lonely Planet Author

THE PELOURINHO, SALVADOR

It's sensory overload as you step into the Pelourinho (p443): the sound of beating drums wafts out of the open windows of candy-colored colonial buildings, vibrantly attired *baianas* (Bahian aunts) beckon you into their restaurants with 'free caipirinha' tickets, children tug at your shirtsleeves asking for coins and a couple of capoeiristas (practitioners of capoeira) draw a crowd on the Terreiro de Jesus. It's chaotic, colorful and unique – it's no wonder Michael Jackson chose this Unesco site as the setting for his controversial music video, *They Don't Care About Us*.

Bridget Gleeson, Lonely Planet Author

JOHN MAIER JR

OURO PRÊTO

With more ups and downs than a roller coaster, Ouro Prêto's 18th-century streets (p242) veer precipitously between one baroque masterpiece and the next. From gold town to state capital, revolutionary hotbed to Unesco World Heritage site, this colonial gem has been at the center of the action for over 300 years.

Gregor Clark, Lonely Planet Author

BRUCE BI

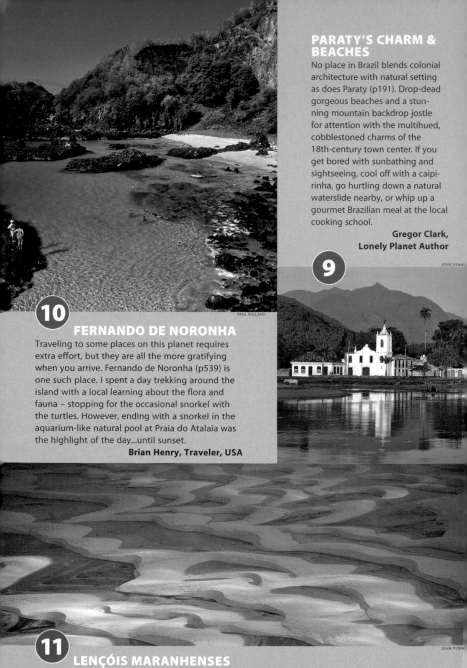

PARATY'S CHARM & BEACHES

No place in Brazil blends colonial architecture with natural setting as does Paraty (p191). Drop-dead gorgeous beaches and a stunning mountain backdrop jostle for attention with the multihued, cobblestoned charms of the 18th-century town center. If you get bored with sunbathing and sightseeing, cool off with a caipirinha, go hurtling down a natural waterslide nearby, or whip up a gourmet Brazilian meal at the local cooking school.

**Gregor Clark,
Lonely Planet Author**

9

JOHN PENN

PAUL BIGLAND

10

FERNANDO DE NORONHA

Traveling to some places on this planet requires extra effort, but they are all the more gratifying when you arrive. Fernando de Noronha (p539) is one such place. I spent a day trekking around the island with a local learning about the flora and fauna – stopping for the occasional snorkel with the turtles. However, ending with a snorkel in the aquarium-like natural pool at Praia do Atalaia was the highlight of the day...until sunset.

Brian Henry, Traveler, USA

JOHN PENN

11

LENÇÓIS MARANHENSES

I was not prepared for the stunning sandscapes of Parque Nacional dos Lençóis Maranhenses (p597), where translucent blue lagoons are the only blemish on a never-ending horizon of windswept dunes. Near Atins, I visited an isolated lagoon and had it all to myself for as long as I wanted. Were it not for the research of this book, I'd still be there, in my own little travel dream.

Kevin Raub, Lonely Planet Author

OLINDA

Before visiting Olinda (p532), I wasn't sure if I would like it. But then I found myself fascinated by the colored houses and their uniqueness – the city on the hill turned out to be one of the most beautiful places I have ever seen. And just when I thought it couldn't get any better, I was introduced to the perfect view over a camarão (shrimp) lunch from one of the city's hilltop restaurants. Olinda totally exceeded my expectations!

Mara Czaja, Traveler, Germany

SHANIA SHEGEDYN

12

JERICOACOARA

For three days we waited for the threatening thunderstorm clouds and gray skies to clear so we could get a view from the top of Sunset dune in Jericoacoara (p578). On our last night, as the sun was going down, the skies cleared. We made our way to the top with a crowd of locals and travelers from around the world. We watched as the sun slowly dipped below the horizon and the sky melted into an amazing kaleidoscope of colors that I'll never forget. It was well worth the wait!

Todd Adamson, Traveler, USA

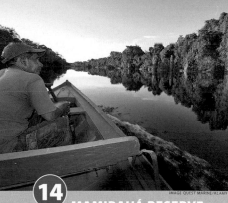

IMAGE QUEST MARINE/ALAMY

14

TIM HUGHES

13

MAMIRAUÁ RESERVE

Our first evening 'spotlighting' tour at the reserve (p662) had us cruising down the Amazon on a clear, dark night, gazing into the two red eyes of countless caiman stretched out along the shore. On our second, rain poured down upon us, punctuated by claps of thunder and bolts of lightning. We could see fewer glowing pairs of eyes, but there were no doubt hundreds of caiman nearby. A Far Side caption kept coming to me: 'Mmmm. Tourist Dinner Cruise for the Crocs!'

Judyth Reichenberg, Traveler, USA

JUNGLE TRIP FROM MANAUS

My flight from the USA arrived at 4am; by 6 I was on my way into the jungle, by 10 I was canoeing through a flooded forest, and by 2pm I was conked out in a hammock overlooking the river. That's one great thing about trips from Manaus (p644): instant gratification.

**Gary Chandler,
Lonely Planet Author**

15

JOHN BORTHW

JOHN MAIER JR

16

ILHA DE SANTA CATARINA

A combo of world-class beaches and a world-famous party scene attracts throngs of beautiful people to Florianópolis and other towns on this southern island (p337). Long stretches of clean, smooth sand are ideal for simple sun-worshipping, and shores battered by endless summer waves lure surfers and kitesurfers. Brazil's biggest surf competition is also held here. When you've had enough of the water, hit the nightlife, which is as good as anything you'll find in Miami or Ibiza.

Aimée Dowl, Lonely Planet Author

ANDRE SEALE/SPECIALIST STOCK/COR

17

BONITO

Ever wondered what it feels like to be a fish? Snorkeling the Rio da Prata, one of countless breathtaking aquatic attractions in the 'waterworld' that is Bonito (p428), will give you a first-hand experience of the daily life of a dourado, the personality of the piraputanga and the problems faced by a pacu.

Paul Smith, Lonely Planet Author

MICAH WRIGHT

18 ILHA GRANDE

Thanks to its fabulous isolation, Ilha Grande (p186) served for decades as a prison and leper's colony. Spared from development by this unusual history, its jungle-clad slopes and dozens of beaches are some of the best preserved in all of Brazil. With no motor vehicles to spoil the party, this is one clean, green island – a true nature lover's paradise.

Gregor Clark, Lonely Planet Author

CHRIS SCHMID/EYEMAGE MEDIA/ALAMY

19 MORRO DE SÃO PAULO

Your 10-passenger speedboat careens over ripples and waves, practically airborne at times, as the village of Morro de São Paulo (p467) recedes behind you. Off in the distance, you see heads bobbing in the aqua-blue sea; shortly you realize they're snorkelers exploring the natural pools beside a coral reef and drinking cold *cerveja* (beer) at a rustic floating bar. Before the sun sets, you'll see tropical fish through your face mask, sample savory raw oysters and wander the quiet streets of an island village.

Bridget Gleeson, Lonely Planet Author

TIRADENTES

The colonial town of Tiradentes (p257) is so well preserved, and its natural setting so appealing, you could be excused for feeling like you've wandered onto a movie set. Cobbled lanes, flower-draped walls and some stunning colonial architecture make every step a delight – even more if you like to hike. The surrounding mountains are threaded with trails, and Tiradentes' hyperactive restaurant scene means you'll always have a good dinner to come home to.

Gregor Clark, Lonely Planet Author

20

SÃO PAULO'S JARDINS NEIGHBORHOOD

In general, São Paulo has lousy street life. Everything is designed around the car. But the leafy Jardins district (p286) is a wonderful exception. When I have downtime in Sao Paulo, it is definitely my favorite place to meet a friend for a leisurely lunch or *kaffeklatch* (coffee and chat), then a wander around Rua Oscar Freire and Alameda Lorena. The shops and restaurants here are constantly reinventing themselves in beautiful ways.

Robert Landon, Lonely Planet Author

21

THE CHURCHES OF PENEDO

Walking down a steep cobble-stone hill on a steamy afternoon in Penedo (p514), you'll feel like you've stumbled into a town that's not listed in guidebooks. Filled with charming open-air plazas, colonial architecture in every pastel shade imaginable and strikingly decorative churches, Penedo still holds a quiet air of days gone by.

**Bridget Gleeson,
Lonely Planet Author**

22

JOHN PENNOCK

WWW.AMAZONTREECLIMBING.COM

23

AMAZON TREE CLIMBING

I thought the experience would be centered around being at the top of the tree and looking over the rain forest. But the climb itself is just as stunning (p657). You can literally see each layer of the rainforest...I just kept looking over at my husband and kids in awe thinking, 'Are we really here?'

Lori Jensen, Traveler, USA

BRUCE BI

24

BRASÍLIA

When you are faced with the 'logical' layout of Brazil's capital city (p377) for the first time, it takes you a few days to accept just how illogical you really are. Fortunately you don't need a 'logical' mind to appreciate the architectural wonders of the city, epitomized by the remarkable Praça dos Trés Poderes, which is at its best after dark when moody street lighting gives it an otherworldy glow.

Paul Smith, Lonely Planet Author

SÃO MIGUEL DAS MISSÕES

Just another reason why it's worth lingering in southern Brazil, where history elegantly rises from the earth in the eerie Jesuit ruins at Sao Miguel das Missões (p372). These remnants of Brazil's troubled and fascinating colonial history are off the beaten path, but well worth the ride over the rolling hills reaching toward Paraguay.

Aimée Dowl, Lonely Planet Author

GOLDEMBERG FONSECA DE ALMEIDA FROM DOURADOS BR

25

SÃO LUÍS & ALCÂNTARA

The colonial combo of side-by-side neighbors São Luís (below; p589) and Alcântara (p596) sees both providing a perfect compliment to each other: big city São Luís, with its tiled-facades in various stages of decay, are a stunning but gritty Iberian urban fabric; the anecdote lies across the sea in Alcântara, where tranquility looms over an more impressively preserved village, a snail's-pace place where colors and cobblestones are the most pressing worry.

**Kevin Raub,
Lonely Planet Author**

DIEGO LEZAMA

26

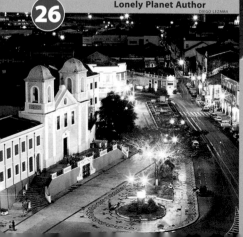

CRISTIANO BURMESTER/AL

27

ILHABELA

Nowhere else in Brazil is quite like Ilhabela (p307). It is so many things at once. Most of all it's a stunningly beautiful island where nature has been extremely well preserved. You can still hike over wild mountain trails to reach deserted beaches. Yet its restaurants and cafés have an urban sophistication, as if a few seeds from trendy São Paulo have sprouted in the middle of the Atlantic rain forest.

Robert Landon, Lonely Planet Author

Contents

Regional Map Contents

Amazon Region p603

Ceará, Piauí & Maranhão p566

Paraíba & Rio Grande do Norte p547

Pernambuco p522

Sergipe & Alagoas p500

Bahia p435

Mato Grosso & Mato Grosso do Sul p403

Brasília p378

Goiás p390

Minas Gerais p233

Espírito Santo p221

São Paulo State p271

Rio de Janeiro State p185

Rio de Janeiro p131

Paraná p316

Santa Catarina p337

Rio Grande do Sul p359

Destination Brazil

One of the world's most captivating places, Brazil is South America's giant, a dazzling country of powdery white-sand beaches, pristine rain forests and wild, rhythm-filled metropolises. Brazil's attractions extend from enchanting, frozen-in-time colonial towns to dramatic landscapes of red-rock canyons, thundering waterfalls and idyllic tropical islands. Add to that, Brazil's biodiversity: legendary in scope, its diverse ecosystems boast the greatest collection of plant and animal species found anywhere on earth.

Brazil offers big adventures for travelers with budgets large and small. There's horseback riding in the Pantanal, kayaking flooded forests in the Amazon, ascending rocky cliff tops to breathtaking views, whale-watching off the coast, surfing stellar breaks off palm-fringed beaches and snorkeling crystal-clear rivers or coastal reefs – all part of the great Brazilian experience. No less entrancing is the prospect of doing nothing, aside from sinking into warm sands and soaking up a glorious stretch of beach, caipirinha – Brazil's national cocktail – in hand.

Brazil's most famous celebration, Carnaval, storms though the country's cities and towns with hip-shaking samba and *frevo*, dazzling costumes and carefree joie de vivre, but Brazilians hardly regulate their passion for revelry to a few weeks of the year. Wherever there's music, that carefree lust for life tends to appear – whether dancing with Cariocas at Rio's atmospheric samba clubs or following powerful drumbeats through the streets of Salvador. There's the dancehall *forró* of the Northeast, twirling *carimbó* of the Amazon, scratch-skilled DJs of São Paulo and an endless variety of regional sounds that extends from the back-country *sertanejo* to reggae-loving Maranhão.

With so much going for them, it's no wonder that Brazilians say 'Deus e Brasileiro' (God is Brazilian). How else to explain the treasure chest of natural and cultural riches sprinkled all across the country? Pride in the great national bounty has only grown in recent years, during an unprecedented period of prosperity. GDP growth is way up – averaging 5% annually since 2000. Inflation – that beast that long crippled Brazil's economy – appears at last tamed. According to the government, some 19 million Brazilians have risen into the middle class during this period. Low unemployment levels, record numbers of new jobs and widespread growth across diverse sectors of the economy show that Brazil is at last living up to its promise, made back in the mid-20th century, to be 'the great land of the future'.

Many Brazilians – and international observers alike – credit former President Lula with the success of their nation. The son of a poor, illiterate peasant family from Brazil's drought-prone Northeast, Luíz Inácio 'Lula' da Silva seemed an unlikely candidate for Brazil's highest office. He had worked as a shoeshine boy, peanut seller and a mechanic before finding his calling as a trade-union leader and activist; his popularity and later political success helped him become Brazil's first president with working-class roots.

'The most popular politician on earth,' as US President Obama joshingly described Lula in 2009, certainly left office as one of Brazil's most popular elected officials. During his two-term administration, Lula guided Brazil onto the world stage, helping the nation win the rights to host the 2014 FIFA World Cup, and played a key role in securing the 2016 Summer Olympics for Rio. His diplomacy extended beyond sports – negotiating with Turkey, for example, a nuclear-fuel swap deal for Iran.

Despite the odd scandal associated with his party PT (Workers' Party), Lula enjoyed stratospheric approval ratings (80% in early 2010). Critics,

FAST FACTS

Population: 201 million

Annual population growth: 1.17%

Life expectancy at birth: 69 years (men), 76 years (women)

GDP: R$3.69 trillion

Inflation rate: 4.2%

Number of free condoms distributed annually: 500 million

Monthly minimum wage: R$510

Infant mortality per 1000 live births: 22 (USA: 6)

Unemployment: 7.3% (USA: 10%)

Adult literacy: 88.6%

however, say that much of the success stems from the prudent economic policies – including the creation of Brazil's now rock-solid currency, the real – by his predecessor, Henrique Cardoso.

The enormous growth in agribusiness has played a substantive role in the economy. (Brazil is the world's largest exporter of beef and the largest producer of coffee, oranges and sugarcane; and it's among the top three global producers for soy and corn.) China's continued growth, and more importantly, its demand for Brazilian commodities, has also been a factor.

Rising oil prices and a growing acceptance of human-produced climate change has made plant-based biofuel an important topic around the globe. In Brazil, biofuel's success is a result of three decades of effort and billions spent on incentives. Brazilian ethanol, made from energy-efficient sugarcane (eight times more efficient than fuel made from US corn), provides 40% of the country's fuel. The success of Brazil's ethanol program is increasingly seen as a model for other countries.

'Brazilian ethanol... (eight times more efficient than fuel made from US corn) provides 40% of the country's fuel'

Energy remains a hot topic in Brazil – particularly since the discovery, between 2007 and 2010, of vast oil reserves stretching more than 800km offshore. Estimates show these oil fields could be among the largest on earth, and they could potentially transform the nation into one of the world's top energy exporters. Brazil is also a major producer of hydroelectric power (the massive Itaipu dam alone provides 20% of Brazil's energy supply and 94% of Paraguay's), and privatization has led to improvements in the grid. Electricity rationing, not uncommon at the turn of the millennium, seems largely a thing of the past. Dozens of new hydroelectric projects are in the works including Brazil's newest but controversial Belo Monte dam in the Amazon.

The boom in industry and Brazil's ongoing development hasn't been good news for everyone. As chief stewards of the largest rain forest on the planet, Brazil has worried environmentalists with projects such as the Belo Monte dam, which will permanently flood 450 sq km of Amazonian forest to create it. Cash-cow crops such as soy and sugarcane continue to bring destruction to old-growth forests. Some innovative green solutions, however, are gaining traction – including the possibility of paying landowners not to cut down their trees.

For most Brazilians, deforestation takes a backseat to the more apparent social ills of violence and poverty, afflicting so many parts of the nation. Lula's antipoverty measures did help many of the worst-off. His *Bolsa Família* (family grant) program brought hardship relief to some 12 million families (more than 40 million Brazilians), though critics say it does little to redress the underlying roots of poverty.

The proliferation of favelas (shantytowns) still looms large in the national consciousness, though even there change has come. Lula's enormous Growth Acceleration Program (PAC), which earmarked billions of reais for infrastructure, has brought improvements – running water, sanitation, roads and housing – to some of Brazil's poorest favelas. At the same time, 'pacification' programs are attempting to drive out drug traffickers and replace them with a police presence and a permanent sense of security inside these struggling communities.

How all of this plays out will undoubtedly be very different at the dawn of 2011, when a new president takes power. He or she has very big shoes to fill.

Getting Started

Before you go to Brazil, find out whether you need a visa. Many nationalities require them, including citizens from the USA, Canada and Australia. See p712 for more details.

If you're going to Carnaval in Rio, Salvador or Olinda, secure hotel reservations as far in advance as possible. That also holds true for Rio's Reveillon (New Year's Eve) or if you're hitting other major festivals (p28); bookings are often easily done over the internet. During the busy summer season (December to March), it's also wise to book ahead.

Brazil is a large country, with vast distances between destinations. If you plan to visit a number of regions, consider purchasing a Brazil Airpass (p719), which allows you between four and nine in-country flights at a set rate. These tickets must be purchased outside the country.

WHEN TO GO

There is never really a bad time to visit Brazil, but whether you want to party like a rock star or escape the masses may help deciding when to go. Brazil's high season coincides with the northern-hemisphere winter, running from December to March. This is when the country fills with both foreign visitors and vacationing Brazilian families (school holidays run from mid-December to Carnaval, usually in February). Hotel rooms cost about 30% higher at this time and you'll face more crowds, though this is also the most festive time in Brazil. Brazil's low season runs from May to September. With the exception of July, which is also a school-holiday month, this is the cheapest and least-crowded time to visit the country – though it can be deserted in some resort areas and cold in the South.

Depending on where you go, weather may be a significant factor in your travel plans. In Rio the humidity can be high in summer, with temperatures hovering around 28°C (82°F), but can often reach 35°C (95°F) or higher. Rainfall is another factor, with October to January being the wettest months. In winter Rio temperatures hover around 23°C (73°F), with a mix of both rainy and superb days.

On the Northeast coast, from Bahia to Maranhão, temperatures are a bit warmer year-round than in Rio – with days reaching 31°C (88°F) – but due to a wonderful tropical breeze and less humidity, it's rarely stifling. The rainy

See Climate Charts (p701) for more information.

> **DON'T LEAVE HOME WITHOUT...**
>
> - Getting your visa, if you need one (p712).
> - Learning a few Portuguese words and phrases (p741).
> - An appetite for steak, seafood, caipirinhas, *agua de côco* (coconut water) and fresh tropical fruits (p85).
> - A yellow-fever vaccine (p728), if planning a trip to the Amazon. You may want to take medication against malaria as well (p726).
> - A waterproof jacket.
> - A strong insect repellent (p730).
> - Binoculars for wildlife watching.
> - Travel insurance (p705).
> - Sunscreen, sunglasses and a hat.

season runs from about mid-December to July, though even then you'll encounter gorgeous days.

The Amazon region (the North) is one of the world's rainiest places and rainfall occurs most frequently from December to May, making travel exceedingly difficult at this time. The rest of the year the region still receives plenty of rain, though showers tend to last only an hour or two.

The Pantanal also has rainy and dry seasons; try to go during the dry season (mid-April to late September). The rest of the year, the wetlands receive tremendous rainfall, washing out roads and making travel a formidable challenge.

The South has the most extreme temperature changes, and during the winter months (June to August), Rio Grande do Sul, Santa Catarina, Paraná and São Paulo have temperatures between 13°C (55.4°F) and 18°C (64.4°F). In some towns, the occasional snowfall is even possible. As elsewhere along the coast, summer is quite hot, and you'll have lots of company on the beach.

COSTS & MONEY

Brazil, with its booming economy and strong real, is one of Latin America's most expensive countries. Travelers who have visited the country in years past will notice a substantial increase in the costs of food, lodging and just about everything else (but the beach is still free).

How much to budget depends on where you stay and how much ground you plan to cover. Some cities, such as Rio, have grown particularly pricey since 2005. Rural and less-visited destinations are often significantly cheaper. Bus travel costs about R$8 (US$4.60) per hour of distance covered. Flights,

---

TRAVELING RESPONSIBLY

Since our inception in 1973, Lonely Planet has encouraged our readers to tread lightly, travel responsibly and enjoy the serendipitous magic independent travel affords. International travel is growing at a jaw-dropping rate, and we still firmly believe in the benefits it can bring – but, as always, we encourage you to consider the impact your visit will have on both the global environment and the local economies, cultures and ecosystems.

Sustainable travel is possible within Brazil, but with the increasing use of 'eco' splashed about, it can be hard to separate the green from the greedy (see p766) for tips on finding ecofriendly hotels). With a little research – and a healthy sense of adventure – your trip can have a positive impact on the local economy while not damaging the environment.

For more detailed information on the wider environmental issues facing Brazil, and how these are being tackled, see p120.

Getting There & Away

By necessity, most people fly into Brazil. To combat the heavy environmental costs associated with air travel, consider offsetting your carbon emissions (p717). Once in Brazil, flights will prove tempting if you're traveling great distances, but there are other options, including riverboats in the Amazon, buses and even a few rare train lines.

Slow Travel

Slow travel is getting back to basics. Skip the long plane journey in favor of traveling locally, focusing your trip on a region in Brazil such as Bahia or Maranhão. You can always come back and cover another part of the country. And once you get to where you are going, hike, bike and paddle your way to that off-track destination. We're not saying that you should never take planes, taxis or buses. When necessary, take that bus or taxi ride. It directly benefits the Brazilian economy, so you'll know your carbon footprint is going directly toward putting dinner on the plates of locals. You can also take an organized tour (p120) based on sustainable itineraries, or you can volunteer your time (p713).

which sometimes run fare specials, might not cost much more for long hauls. Decent accommodations and particularly rental cars (which cost about R$100 per day) can quickly eat up a budget.

If you're frugal, you can travel on about R$100 (US$60) a day – paying around R$40 for accommodations, R$30 for food and drink, plus bus travel, admission to sights and the occasional entertainment activity. If you just stay in hostels and plan to lie on a beach, eating rice, beans and cheap lunch specials every day, you may scrape by on R$75 a day.

If you stay in reasonably comfortable hotels, eat in nicer restaurants, go out most nights and book the occasional flight or guided excursion, you'll probably spend upwards of R$250 a day (more if traveling solo). If staying overnight at very comfortable guesthouses in resort areas, eat at the best restaurants and not stint on excursions or nightlife can easily spend upwards of R$500 a day.

Lastly, during the December-to-February holiday season, lodging costs are higher than at other times of the year. During Carnaval accommodations prices double or triple (and four-night minimum stays are typically required), but a month or so afterwards, the prices drop to low-season rates. Another thing to remember: resort areas near major cities – such as Búzios near Rio and Morro de São Paulo near Salvador – are often packed on summer weekends. There will be fewer crowds – and sometimes lower prices – if you visit during the week.

Brazil is fair value for solo travelers, as long as you don't mind staying in hostels. Otherwise, a single room generally costs about 75% of the price of a double room.

Accommodations & Food

Your tourist dollar can go a long way to supporting Brazilians if you choose your accommodations carefully. Stay clear of chain hotels and all-inclusive resorts in Brazil's larger cities and beach towns. These places are often owned by foreign investors who take all the profits out of the country. You're much better off staying in family-run pousadas (guesthouses), where your money will remain in the hands of the local people.

In terms of food, Brazil requires some tough choices to be made. Although Brazilian beef is top notch, the explosion of cattle farming continues to fuel the destruction of the Amazon's rain forest, with old-growth forests cleared to make way for pastures. A growing number of cafés and restaurants serve organic and vegetarian fare, and we've included these options where available. Also avoid major fast-food chains, as these have played a significant role in fueling the country's deforestation.

Responsible Travel Organizations

Brazil has no certification system to identify the 'green-ness' of accommodations and tour operators. However, there is one national organization, **Abeta** (www.abeta.com.br), which is a collection of adventure and ecotourism operators, who maintain certain guidelines for safety and promote sustainable initiatives. Visit its website for a list of its 200-plus members. Environmentally responsible organizations working in Brazil include the following:

- **Rainforest Alliance** (www.rainforestalliance.org)
- **ResponsibleTravel.com** (www.responsibletravel.com)
- **Sustainable Travel International** (www.sustainabletravelinternational.org)

For a list of sustainable businesses and organizations (including tour operators, restaurants and accommodations) in Brazil, see p766.

TRAVEL LITERATURE

Brazil on the Rise, by Larry Rohter (2010), paints an insightful portrait of the nation's politics and culture, detailing the great changes that have transformed Brazil into a rising superpower. Rohter served as the *New York Times* bureau chief in Rio for 14 years.

The Lost City of Z: A Tale of Deadly Obsession in the Amazon, by David Grann (2009), relates the final journey in 1925 of Percy Fawcett, one of the last great Victorian adventurers on his quest to find the lost city of El Dorado deep in the Amazon. Grann's retraces Fawcett's journey, creating a page-turner that is equal parts adventure story, biography and travelogue.

Don't Sleep, There are Snakes: Life and Language in the Amazonian Jungle, by Daniel Everett (2008), is an engrossing story about Everett's many years living and studying the extraordinary Pirahã people in the Amazon, and the profound influence they had on his own life.

A Death in Brazil, by Peter Robb, is a fascinating travelogue published in 2004. Robb, who spent 20 years in Brazil, explores four centuries of Brazilian history, while detailing his own modern-day travels, creating a compelling portrait of the country.

'David Grann retraces Fawcett's journey, creating a page-turner that is equal parts adventure story, biography and travelogue.'

Travelers' Tales Brazil, edited by Scott Doggett and Annette Haddad, is a fine anthology of tales of travel and life in Brazil. The excellent 2nd edition (2004) includes contributions from writers such as Diane Ackerman, Joe Kane, Petru Popescu and Alma Guillermoprieto.

How to Be a Carioca, by Priscilla Ann Goslin, is highly recommended for anyone planning to spend time in Rio. Her tongue-in-cheek descriptions of the Carioca (residents of Rio) lifestyle are spot on. Don't miss the hilarious 'essential vocabulary' section for mastering the local lingo.

The Capital of Hope: Brasília and Its People, by Alex Shoumatoff, is an engaging portrait of Brasília, informed by the author's interviews with government workers and the capital's first settlers.

Peter Fleming's *Brazilian Adventure* is about the young journalist's expedition into Mato Grosso in the 1930s – a wild region then – in search of vanished explorer Colonel Fawcett. What Fleming found is less important than the telling, written with wry humor.

For a fascinating journey from the Andes through Brazil and on to the Atlantic Ocean in the 19th century, read *Exploration of the Valley of the Amazon*, by William Lewis Herndon. This recently republished volume is a vivid account of the people and local cultures Herndon encountered, along with observations of the plants, animals and geography of the Brazilian landscape.

After serving as US president, winning the Nobel Peace Prize and surviving an assassin's bullet, Theodore Roosevelt explored parts of Brazil and wrote the great adventure story *Through the Brazilian Wilderness*.

Although not specifically about Brazil, Redmond O'Hanlon's hilarious *In Trouble Again: A Journey Between the Orinoco and the Amazon* tells of his fretful journey through Latin America.

Also not solely about Brazil is Peter Matthiessen's *The Cloud Forest*, a captivating account of a 30,000km journey across the South American wilderness from the Amazon to Tierra del Fuego.

Moritz Thomsen's *The Saddest Pleasure: A Journey on Two Rivers* is an engaging book about the author's experiences in South America, including journeys through Brazil and along the Amazon.

Running the Amazon, by Joe Kane, is the story of the 10 men and one woman who, in 1986, became the first expedition to cover the entire length of the Amazon River, from the Andes to the Atlantic, on foot and in rafts and kayaks.

TOP 10

FESTIVALS & EVENTS

1 Carnaval, Shrove Tuesday and the days preceding it, February or March, Rio de Janeiro (p77), Salvador (p80) or Olinda (p83)

2 Semana Santa (Holy Week), March or April, Ouro Prêto (p246) or Cidade de Goiás (p393)

3 Festa do Divino Espírito Santo (p394), 50 days after Easter, Pirenópolis

4 Boi-Bumbá (p660), late June, Parintins

5 Bumba Meu Boi (p594), late June to second week of August, São Luís

6 Festa da NS de Boa Morte (p461), mid-August, Cachoeira

7 Folclore Nordestino (p534), late August, Olinda

8 Círio de Nazaré (p611), second Sunday in October, Belém

9 Oktoberfest (p349), mid-October, Blumenau

10 Reveillon and Festa de Iemanjá (p159), December 31, Rio de Janeiro

FILMS & DOCUMENTARIES

1 *Orfeu Negro* (1959)

2 *Pagador de Promessas* (1962)

3 *Dona Flor & Seus Dois Maridos* (1976)

4 *Bye Bye Brasil* (1980)

5 *Pixote* (1981)

6 *Central do Brasil* (1998)

7 *Madame Satã* (2002)

8 *Cidade de Deus* (City of God; 2002)

9 *House of Sand* (2006)

10 *Tropa de Elite* (2007)

MUSIC ALBUMS

1 *A Tábua de Esmeralda*, Jorge Ben

2 *Alfagamabetizado*, Carlinhos Brown

3 *Chega de Saudade*, João Gilberto

4 *Construção*, Chico Buarque

5 *Bossa Negra*, Elza Soares

6 *Clube da Esquina*, Milton Nascimento

7 *Elis & Tom*, Elis Reginas and Antonio Carlos (Tom) Jobim

8 *Refazenda*, Gilberto Gil

9 *Samba Meu*, Maria Rita

10 *Tropicália: Ou Panis Et Circensis*, Caetano Veloso, Gilberto Gil et al

INTERNET RESOURCES

Brazilian Embassy in London (www.brazil.org.uk) Excellent country lowdown, with links to dozens of local tourism sites in Brazil.

Brazzil (www.brazzil.com) In-depth articles on the country's politics, economy, literature, arts and culture.

Gringoes (www.gringoes.com) Articles written by anglophones living in Brazil.

Hip Guide to Brazil (www.brazilmax.com) Guide to Brazilian culture and society; good, selective articles and links.

Lonely Planet (www.lonelyplanet.com) Summaries on Brazil travel, the popular Thorn Tree bulletin board, online accommodation booking and links to other resources.

Terra Brasil (http://vidaeestilo.terra.com.br/turismo) Portuguese-language travel site with useful information on cities, beaches, ecotourism and more.

Events Calendar

Home to the world's best street parties, Brazil has much more up its sleeve than just Carnaval. Lively festivals and events happen throughout the year, all across the country. More festivals are described in the destination chapters.

JANUARY

LAVAGEM DO BONFIM   2nd Thu in Jan
In Salvador, this equal-parts Catholic and Candomblé fest features a ritual washing of the church steps followed by all-night music and dancing (p448).

SOMMERFEST   mid-Jan–mid-Feb
Blumenau's German-themed Oktoberfest is so popular that they also throw another version of it in mid summer (p350).

FEBRUARY–MARCH

FESTA DE IEMANJÁ   Feb 2
On Praia Rio Vermelho in Salvador, Candomblé groups pay homage to the *orixá* Iemanjá, goddess of the sea and fertility, followed by a lively street party (p448).

CARNAVAL   5 days preceding Ash Wednesday
The famous bacchanalian event happens nationwide in February or March and is liveliest in Rio, Salvador and Olinda, with parades, costumes and round-the-clock merrymaking (p76).

APRIL–MAY

SEMANA SANTA   Week preceding Easter
In Ouro Prêto, Holy Week is a colorful event of processions and streets 'painted' with flowers (p247). Other well-known Holy Weeks happen in Congonhas (p253) and Cidade de Goiás (p393).

**FESTA DO DIVINO
ESPÍRITO SANTO**   50 days after Easter
Popularly known as Cavalhadas, this old-fashioned folk festival in Pirenópolis comprises medieval tournaments, dances and festivities, including mock battles between Moors and Christians (p394).

JUNE

SÃO PAULO PRIDE   early Jun
It's official, São Paulo throws the largest gay pride parade on earth, attracting more than three million people to this massive parade (p294).

**RIO DAS OSTRAS JAZZ &
BLUES FESTIVAL**   early Jun
Located 170km east of Rio, Rio das Ostras boasts one of Brazil's best jazz and blues fests amid a lovely tropical beach setting.

BUMBA MEU BOI   Jun 13-30
Maranhão's magnificent mythic bull festival has African, Indian and Portuguese roots and features singing, dancing, poetry and countless ox costumes (p565).

BOI-BUMBÁ   last Fri, Sat & Sun of Jun
In Parintins in the Amazon, this popular traditional folk festival recounts the death and resurrection of an ox, with music and dancing (p660).

JULY–AUGUST

FEST ITÁLIA   mid-Jul
Italians have made many cultural contributions to the south, including this vibrant Blumenau fest featuring a week of wine, pasta and music (p350).

**FESTIVAL LITERÁRIA INTERNACIONAL
DE PARATI**   early Aug
This important literary festival brings together celebrated authors from around the world, plus film screenings, exhibitions and musical performances (p193).

FOLCLORE NORDESTINO   late Aug
Olinda's highly recommended fest celebrates music and folklore from across the Northeast (p534).

SEPTEMBER–OCTOBER

RIO INTERNATIONAL
FILM FESTIVAL late Sep-early Oct
Rio's international film festival – Latin America's biggest – features more than 200 films from all over the world, shown at some 35 theaters (p159).

BIENAL DE SÃO PAULO Oct-Dec
This major art event occurs in even numbered years (next in 2012 and 2014) and showcases the work of over 120 artists from around the globe (p287).

CÍRIO DE NAZARÉ 2nd Sun in Oct
Belém's enormous annual event brings one million to the streets to take part in the procession of one of Brazil's most important icons (p611).

OKTOBERFEST mid-Oct
This beer-drinking extravaganza in Blumenau is the best place to connect to southern Brazil's German roots (p349).

NOVEMBER–DECEMBER

MACEIÓ FEST 3rd week of Nov
Maceió's biggest bash of the year is much like Carnaval, with street parades, outlandish costumes, bars that are open 24 hours and a general joie de vivre among the populace, but is held in November (p508). At this time, the locals head to the beaches.

CARNATAL 1st week of Dec
The country's biggest 'off-season Carnaval' is this Salvador-style festival held in Natal in December. It features raucous street parties and pumping *trios elétricos* (bands playing atop mobile speaker-trucks; p556).

REVEILLON Dec 31
Some two million revelers, dressed in white, pack the sands of Copacabana Beach in Rio, where music concerts and fireworks ring in the New Year (p159).

Itineraries
CLASSIC ROUTES

RIO & THE SOUTHEAST   Three Weeks

Gorgeous beaches, rain-forest-covered islands and colonial towns are just some of the things you'll experience on a trip around the Southeast.

Spend a few days discovering **Rio** (p124) and its beaches, restaurants and incredible music scene before heading to **Ilha Grande** (p186), an island blanketed by rain forest and ringed by beaches. Next is **Paraty** (p191), a beautifully preserved colonial town. **Ilhabela** (p307) is another car-free island of beaches, forests and waterfalls. Stop in **São Paulo** (p277) for high culture, including the nation's best museums and restaurants. Then take in a bit of friendly Mineira hospitality, good restaurants and a burgeoning arts scene in **Belo Horizonte** (p234).

Head to exquisite **Ouro Prêto** (p242), **Diamantina** (p261) and **Tiradentes** (p257), some of Brazil's finest colonial gems. Visit the hiker's paradise of **Parque Nacional de Caparaó** (p271); further east, relish the dramatic beauty (and natural pools) of **Pedra Azul** (p231) state park. Afterwards, continue to the coast, for wave-frolicking and feasting on *moqueca* (seafood stew) in relaxed **Guarapari** (p227). Further south are equally stunning beaches, including chic **Búzios** (p214), lovely but less glitzy **Arraial do Cabo** (p211) and surf-loving **Saquarema** (p210).

On the way back to Rio, detour north to **Petrópolis** (p202), a cool mountain retreat. Great hiking is nearby at **Parque Nacional da Serra dos Órgãos** (p207).

This 2300km trip begins and ends in Rio de Janeiro. The circular route passes through picturesque coastal towns, beach-lovers' getaways, surfing spots, idyllic islands, magnificent gold-mining towns and South America's largest metropolis.

BEST OF BRAZIL
Three Months

On this epic trip you'll experience the rhythm infused towns of the Northeast, the jungles of the Amazon and the biodiversity of the Pantanal, with beaches, tropical islands and historic towns thrown into the mix.

From **São Paulo** (p277), head east to Rio, stopping at glorious beaches such as **Ubatuba** (p304), **Trindade** (p197) and **Paraty-Mirim** (p197). Spend a couple of days in fabulous **Rio** (p124).

From there head north, via bus or plane to **Salvador** (p437), the country's Afro-Brazilian gem. Further up the coast visit pretty **Olinda** (p532), then catch a flight from **Recife** (p521) to the spectacular archipelago of **Fernando de Noronha** (p539).

Back on the mainland, travel north, stopping in the backpackers' paradise of **Jericoacoara** (p578) en route to the surreal dunes in the **Parque Nacional dos Lençóis Maranhenses** (p597), a stark contrast to the colonial beauty of **Alcântara** (p596). To the west lies **Belém** (p606), a culturally rich city near the lush island of **Ilha de Marajó** (p620). Catch a boat up the Amazon (or fly) to **Manaus** (p644), where you can arrange jungle trips.

From Manaus, fly to **Brasília** (p377) to take in its stunning architecture, then visit **Parque Nacional da Chapada dos Veadeiros** (p399). Next head to Cuiabá, gateway to both the breathtaking canyons of **Chapada dos Guimarães** (p409) and the fantastic wildlife watching in the **Pantanal** (p413). Head south via Campo Grande (another Pantanal gateway) to **Bonito** (p428) for crystal-clear rivers, lush forests and caves. Continue south to the awe-inspiring **Iguaçu Falls** (p328). Before completing the circle, explore the secluded beaches and charming Germanic towns around **Florianópolis** (p339).

This 12,500km (!) reveals Brazil in all her captivating complexity from wild nights to wildlife with a survey of pristine islands, storybook towns, steamy jungles and more. To really do Brazil justice, you'll need at least six months.

BAHIA & THE NORTHEAST   Six Weeks

Those looking for the soul of Brazil would do well to focus on the Northeast. A confluence of music, history and culture amid spectacular natural scenery makes for an unforgettable journey.

Begin south of Porto Seguro in the pretty towns of **Arraial d'Ajuda** (p484) and **Trancoso** (p486), both blessed with great guesthouses and restaurants, a laid-back nightlife and access to endless walks on the beach. Contine north to **Itacaré** (p473), a lively town with great surf. Then head on to rhythm-filled **Salvador** (p437), Bahia's most vibrant and colorful city. From there, catch a boat to **Morro de São Paulo** (p467), an island with enchanting beaches and a laid-back vibe.

Detour west to **Parque Nacional da Chapada Diamantina** (p496) for crisp mountain streams, panoramic views and an endless network of trails. Back on the coast, **Olinda** (p532) is one of Brazil's best-preserved colonial cities. From Olinda's buzzing neighbor **Recife** (p521), fly out to **Fernando de Noronha** (p539), an exquisite archipelago of rich marine life and splendid beaches.

Returning to the mainland, visit beautiful and laid-back **Praia da Pipa** (p560), then hit the spectacular coastline stretching from **Natal** (p553) to **Jericoacoara** (p578), including the **Genipabu Dunes** (p555). West of Jericoacoara, **Parque Nacional dos Lençóis Maranhenses** (p597) is a striking landscape of dunes, lagoons and beaches. The final stops are reggae-charged **São Luís** (p589) and the untouristy colonial gem of **Alcântara** (p596).

This 4500km trip takes you from gorgeous tropical beaches to culturally rich colonial cities. Porto Seguro, with its many flight connections, is a good gateway. Those with extra time can easily spend three or more months exploring this vibrant region.

ROADS LESS TRAVELED

WATERWAYS OF THE AMAZON   Six Weeks

Few places ignite the imagination like the Amazon. The largest forest on the planet has astounding plant and animal life. Surprising to many visitors, these wetlands also contain historic cities, beautiful river beaches and one of the most important archaeological sites in South America.

Begin in **Belém** (p606), a culturally rich city at the mouth of the great river. From here explore the forest-covered island of **Ilha de Marajó** (p620) or head northeast to **Algodoal** (p618), a rustic fishing hamlet in a splendid setting.

Get a hammock and travel by boat up the Amazon River. Stop in **Monte Alegre** (p632) to see ancient rock paintings, the oldest-known human creations in the Amazon. Upstream is **Santarém** (p623), a pleasant city with many nearby attractions. Across the river, **Alenquer** (p632) is near beautiful, rarely visited countryside. Also reachable is the virgin rain forest of the **Floresta Nacional (FLONA) do Tapajós** (p627) and **Alter do Chão** (p629), a picturesque lagoon with white-sand beaches.

Continue upriver to **Manaus** (p644), Amazonia's largest city and its center for arranging jungle trips or visits to the **Reserva Xixuaú-Xipariná** (p659). You can also travel to **Santa Elena de Uairén** (p674), Venezuela, for treks up **Mt Roraima** (p675). West of Manaus lies the fairly unexplored **Parque Nacional do Jaú** (p659).

You'll see an incredible variety of wildlife at the **Mamirauá Reserve** (p662), outside of **Tefé** (p660). From there, continue by river to **Tabatinga** (p664), and into **Leticia** (p665) in Colombia for excursions into the **Parque Nacional Natural Amacayacu** (p669) or for stays at jungle lodges along the **Rio Javari** (p669).

This 3900km trip begins in Belém, and travels mostly by boat along the world's mightiest river. Several detours include Belém to Ilha de Marajó, and Manaus to Santa Elena de Uairén in Venezuela.

SOUTHWARD BOUND
Three Weeks

One of Brazil's most overlooked regions has gorgeous islands and beaches, unexplored national parks and fascinating towns with largely European roots.

Start in **Foz do Iguaçu** (p328) to gaze at the most impressive waterfalls on the planet. Take short day trips to Argentina and Paraguay to get a taste of lush rain forests before heading east (by overnight bus or quick flight) to **Curitiba** (p316), a cosmopolitan city with an environmentally responsible design. Perhaps visit **Parque Estadual Marumbi** (p322), a paradise for climbers and nature lovers. Next, take the scenic train ride to **Paranaguá** (p323), a sleepy waterfront town that's the jumping-off point to car-free **Ilha do Mel** (p324). The forest-covered island has lovely beaches and low-key guesthouses, and is skirted by some pretty trails.

Next head to **Blumenau** (p348) and nearby **Vale Europeu** (p350), where Pomerode, Timbó and Nova Trento boast Teutonic architecture, blond-haired residents and a local brew more Bavarian than Brazilian. Head back east to the coast to **Porto Belo** (p354), with its picturesque beaches and excellent diving. Continue south to **Ilha de Santa Catarina** (p337), a forest-covered gem of sand dunes, sparkling beaches, pretty lagoons and sleepy fishing villages.

On into Rio Grande do Sul, stretch the dramatic canyon and waterfalls of **Parque Nacional de Aparados da Serra** (p370). Inland, it's worth detouring to the Italian-immigrant town of **Bento Gonçalves** (p364), gateway to the rolling vineyards of the Serra Gaucho.

Head east to **Santo Ângelo** (p371), which leads on to the Jesuit missions. From there you can visit **São Miguel das Missões** (p372), **São João Batista** (p372) and numerous other holy sites; true grail-seekers can even cross the border into **Paraguay** or **Argentina** (p373) for a look at even more haunting Jesuit missions.

This 1600km trip begins in Foz do Iguaçu and travels through Brazil's southernmost states. Highlights include forested islands, mountainous national parks, Bavarian-style towns, idyllic beaches and historic missions. At trip's end, go to Porto Alegre for a flight to Rio or São Paulo.

TAILORED TRIPS

WATCHING WILDLIFE   Six Weeks

Brazil contains an astounding variety of fauna and flora with incomparable settings for spying wildlife. Winter (June to September) is probably the best time to go. Despite its urban facade, Rio boasts enticing natural attractions such as **Parque Nacional da Tijuca** (p150) home to coatis, ocelots, three-toed sloths and various species of monkeys. Yet more simians (including howler monkeys) can be spotted on **Ilha Grande** (p186).

Sea turtles are making a comeback in Brazil, and you might see hatchlings in places such as **Praia do Forte** (p463) and **Mangue Seco** (p466). Whale-watching is unrivalled in certain parts of Brazil, includ-ing the offshore reef of **Parque Nacional Marinho de Abrolhos** (p491) and **Praia do Rosa** (p355), though by far the best place to see aquatic life is **Fernando de Noronha** (p539). **Bonito** (p428), with its crystal-clear rivers, makes for some great snorkeling among river fish, including meter-long catfish. Nearby canyons are home to numerous scarlet macaws.

High on any naturalist's list should be the **Pantanal** (p413), where river otters, caimans, monkeys, jaguars, anacondas and capybara, plus numerous bird species are all part of the mix. The **Amazon region** (p602), of course, has many places to see Brazil's wild side, from spotting river dolphins around **Santarém** (p623) to glimpsing toucans outside of **Manaus** (p644).

AROUND BRAZIL IN 80 MEALS   Four Weeks

Brazil has a long history of immigration and cultural diversity. A way of experiencing this is through its cuisine. Food lovers should linger in **São Paulo** (p296) and sample dishes such as *camarões à paulista* (marinated shrimp). Although Cariocas didn't invent *feijoada* (bean-and-meat stew), they serve it with finesse, making **Rio** (p165) an essential stop (hint, it's served on Saturdays). *Churrascarias* (barbecued-meat restaurants) are widespread in **Porto Alegre** (p362) and other *gaúcho* cities; it's also the place to try *erva mate*, a tealike beverage. Other southern delights are the vineyards near **Bento Gonçalves** (p365) and the German restaurants of **Blumenau** (p350). **Minas Gerais** (p87) has its own cuisine, and **Ouro Prêto** (p248) is a good place to try *tutu á mineiro* (mashed black beans and manioc), served with meat dishes. Tasty fish is found in the Central West. Don't miss *dourado, pacu* or *pintado* – available in **Bonito** (p431) among other places. The Northeast has many addictive Afro-Brazilian dishes including *moqueca* (spicy fish stew) and *acarajé* (bean-and-shrimp fritters). **Salvador** (p451) is its cu-linary capital. The Amazon's diversity doesn't end at the waterline. Wonderful dishes such as *tacacá* (a spicy soup) and many delicious fish, including *surubim, tambaquí,* and the prized *tucunaré,* warrant the trip to **Belém** (p613).

History

Brazil's population, the fifth biggest in the world, reached its lands from Africa, Asia, Europe and other parts of the Americas – diverse origins that have created one of the planet's most racially mixed societies. How they came, intermingled and developed the unique Brazilian identity that charms visitors today is a rough-and-tumble story of courage, greed, endurance and cruelty, eventually yielding a fitful progress towards the democracy the country now enjoys.

BEFORE THE PORTUGUESE

For a fascinating look at the history of the Amazon, its indigenous peoples, explorers and stunning biodiversity, read *The Tree of Rivers: The Story of the Amazon* (2008) by John Hemming.

By the time the Portuguese rolled up in AD 1500, what is now Brazil had already been populated for as long as 12,000 years. But unlike the Incas, Brazil's early inhabitants never developed a highly advanced civilization and they left few clues for archaeologists to follow. One of the few certainties is that it wasn't the Portuguese who discovered *terra brasilis*.

It's generally believed that the early inhabitants of the Americas arrived from Siberia in waves between about 12,000 and 8000 BC, crossing land now submerged beneath the Bering Strait, then gradually spreading southward over many millennia. Researchers in the remote Serra da Capivara in the Northeastern state of Piauí (p589) have found some of Brazil's earliest evidence of human presence. The oldest traces of human life in the Amazon region can be seen on a detour from a river trip between Santarém and Belém: a series of rock paintings estimated to be 12,000 years old near Monte Alegre (p632). Other remnants of early civilizations can be found on the Ilha de Marajó (p620 and p632) at the mouth of the Amazon, and at the Gruta da Lapinha (p242) in Minas Gerais.

By the time the Portuguese arrived, there were probably between two and four million people in what's now Brazil.

CABRAL & CHUMS

Pedro Álvares Cabral died largely forgotten in 1520. His likeness adorns those rarely seen Brazilian one-cent coins.

The course of Brazilian history was changed forever in 1500, when a fleet of 12 Portuguese ships carrying nearly 1200 men rolled up near what is today Porto Seguro.

The fleet, ostensibly bound for East Africa and Asia to set up trading posts, had headed west after passing the Cape Verde Islands, off the coast of West Africa. Increasingly it is thought that, far from having been simply blown off course, the Portuguese already had reason to suspect there was a large landmass across the southern Atlantic, which would make such a giant detour worthwhile. Whatever the motive, on April 22, 1500, Pedro Álvares Cabral and his gang stepped for the first time onto Brazilian soil. Their indigenous reception committee was ready and waiting.

TIMELINE

c 12,000 BC	1494	1500
Early inhabitants of the Americas arrive from Siberia in waves between about 12,000 and 8000 BC, crossing land now submerged beneath the Bering Strait, then gradually spreading southward over many millennia.	The two dominant empires of the time sign the treaty of Tordesillas, dividing newly discovered lands in the New World between Spain and Portugal. The eastern half of South America will 'belong' to Portugal.	Portuguese explorer Pedro Álvares Cabral makes landfall around present-day Porto Seguro and claims possession of the land – believed at first to be an island – for the Portuguese crown.

'There were 18 or 20 men,' marveled scribe Pero Vaz de Caminha in a letter back to the Portuguese king. 'They were brown-skinned, all of them naked, without anything at all to cover their private parts. In their hands they carried bows and arrows.'

The festivities didn't last long. Having erected a cross and held Mass in the land they baptized Terra da Vera Cruz (Land of the True Cross), the Portuguese took to the waves once again. With lucrative spice, ivory and diamond markets in Asia and Africa to exploit, Portugal had bigger fish to fry elsewhere. It wasn't till 1531 that the first Portuguese settlers arrived in Brazil.

BRAZIL'S INDIGENOUS PEOPLE

For Brazil's *índios* (indigenous people), April 22, 1500 marked the first chapter in their gradual extermination. Sixteenth-century European explorers along the Amazon encountered large, widespread populations; some were practicing agriculture while others were nomadic hunter-gatherers. Coastal peoples fell into three main groups: the Guarani (south of São Paulo and in the Paraguai and Paraná basins inland), the Tupi or Tupinambá (along most of the rest of the coast) and the Tapuia (peoples inhabiting shorter stretches of coast in among the Tupi and Guarani). The Tupi and Guarani had much in common in language and culture. A European adaptation of the Tupi-Guarani language later spread throughout colonial Brazil and is still spoken by some people in Amazonia.

Over the following centuries a four-front war was waged on the indigenous way of life. It was a cultural war, as well as a physical, territorial and biological one. Many *índios* fell victim to the *bandeirantes* – groups of roaming adventurers who spent the 17th and 18th centuries exploring Brazil's interior, pillaging *índio* settlements as they went. Those who escaped such a fate were struck down by the illnesses shipped in from Europe, to which they had no natural resistance. Others were worked to death on sugar plantations.

If the *bandeirantes* were responsible for the physical destruction of the indigenous population, it was the Jesuits who began their cultural destruction, outlawing their traditions and customs and settling them in *aldeias* (missions), though at the same time they did oppose *índio* slavery and attempted to protect the indigenous from the *bandeirantes*.

By the start of the 21st century Brazil's indigenous population had dwindled to somewhere between 350,000 and 600,000, the majority of them in the relatively isolated Amazonian forests. See the boxed text, p38, for more on how they are surviving.

DIVIDING THE LAND

Thirty years after Brazil's 'discovery,' Portugal's King João III decided it might actually be worth settling there after all. The first settlement sprang up at São Vicente, when a fleet of five ships carrying some 400 men docked near what is now the port of Santos.

In Portuguese, the term *índios* (Indians) is not considered offensive, and is even used by indigenous groups to describe themselves. The term for someone from India is *indiano*. Spanish and English make no such differentiation.

French philosopher Jean-Jacques Rousseau based his optimistic view of human nature (the noble savage) in part on early Portuguese descriptions of natives who were 'innocent, mild and peace-loving'.

1534–36	1549	1550
Hoping to develop the land into colonies and bring back wealth, the Portuguese crown divides Brazil into 14 captaincies and doles them out to rich nobles. Only two captaincies prove successful.	The king sends Tomé de Sousa to be the first governor of Brazil, to centralize authority and save the few remaining captaincies. Sousa founds the city of Salvador, which will remain Brazil's capital for over two centuries.	Facing a shortage of labor (as *índios* die from introduced European diseases), Portugal turns to the African slave trade; open-air slave markets flourish in the slowly growing colony.

BRAZIL'S ÍNDIOS TODAY

When the Portuguese arrived in 1500, there were, by the most common estimates, between two and four million *índios* (indigenous people) already living in Brazil, in over 1000 different tribes. Five centuries later there are an estimated 400,000 to 600,000 *índios* left, living in a little over 200 tribes. Slavery, diseases, armed conflict and loss of territory all took a savage toll on Brazil's native peoples, to the point where in the 1980s *índio* numbers were under 300,000 and it was feared they might die out completely. Since then there has been a marked recovery in the indigenous population, partly thanks to international concern about groups such as the Yanomami, who were threatened with extermination by disease and violence from an influx of gold prospectors into their lands. Government policy has become more benign and huge areas of Brazil are now Terra Indígena (Indigenous Land). Just over 1 million sq km – more than 12% of the whole country – is now either officially registered as Indigenous Land or in the process of registration.

Indigenous Lands remain state property, but their indigenous inhabitants are granted permanent possession and exclusive use, meaning that this 12% of national territory is reserved for about 0.25% of the national population. Unsurprisingly, there are those who think this is too much and fail to respect *índio* rights to these lands. Disputes between indigenous groups and loggers, miners, homesteaders, hunters, road builders and reservoir constructors are still common, and sometimes violent.

It's thought there may still be over 60 uncontacted tribes, mostly small groups in the Amazon forests – home to about 60% of Brazil's *índios* (and almost all of the existing Indigenous Lands).

Most of Brazil's *índios* still live traditional lifestyles, hunting (some still with blowpipes and poisoned arrows) and gathering and growing plants for food, medicine and utensils. Their homes are usually made of natural materials such as wood or grass. Ritual activity is strong, body- and face-painting is prevalent, and most indigenous people are skilled in making pottery, basketry, masks, headdresses, musical instruments and other artisanry with their hands. None of those known to the outside world are truly nomadic. Indigenous Lands generally have an exemplary record of environmental conservation because their inhabitants continue to live sustainable lifestyles.

The largest tribes include the Tikuna on the upper Rio Solimões in Amazonia (around 32,000 strong), the Yanomami in the hills straddling the Brazil–Venezuela border, and the Guarani, of whom some 46,000 are scattered around southern Brazil, with further members in Argentina, Paraguay and Bolivia. At the other extreme, a handful of tribes are on the verge of extinction.

Índios in Amazonia have generally had more luck in holding onto their territory and avoiding cultural disintegration. Many Guarani, in the southern parts of Brazil, live on lands too small to support them, and they suffer from a high suicide rate.

In an attempt to ward off the ambitions of other European countries, the king divided the Brazilian coast into 14 captaincies, each with about 250km of coastline and also lands stretching inland to the west. These territories were awarded to *donatários*, minor gentry favored by the king. It was hoped that, through settlement, the long coastline could be secured at minimal cost.

1621	1624	1637
The Dutch West India Company sets up shop in Northeastern Brazil, heralding the beginning of the Dutch presence in Brazil. Its goal: to wrest control of the colony from Portugal.	The Dutch invade Salvador, capturing and ransacking the city in a lightning two-day attack. They control the city for a year before Portuguese troops finally repel them.	The charismatic Dutch Prince Maurice of Nassau becomes governor of New Holland. Headquartered in Recife, Maurice helps Dutch extend control over Northeastern Brazil, from Bahia to Maranhão.

The settlers' lives were made difficult by the climate, hostility from the indigenous population and competition from the Dutch and French. Four captaincies were never settled and four destroyed by *índios*. Only Pernambuco and São Vicente were profitable.

In 1549 the king sent Tomé de Sousa to be the first governor of Brazil, to centralize authority and save the few remaining captaincies. Sousa was joined by some 1000 settlers; among them Portuguese officials, soldiers, exiled prisoners, New Christians (converted Jews) and the first six Jesuit priests. The city of Salvador was founded as Sousa's base, and remained Brazil's capital until 1763, when Rio de Janeiro took over.

SUGAR & SLAVERY

Brazil didn't boast the ivory and spices of Africa and the East Indies, and the only thing that had interested the Portuguese in the early years after they had found it was a rock-hard tree known as *pau brazil* (brazilwood), which yielded a valuable red dye. Merchants began sending a few ships each year to harvest brazilwood and take it back to Europe, and the colony changed its name to Brazil in tribute to the tree. Alas, the most accessible trees were rapidly depleted, and the *índios* soon stopped volunteering their labor. But after colonization in 1531, the settlers soon worked out that Brazil was a place where sugarcane grew well. Sugar came to Brazil in 1532 and hasn't left since. It was coveted by a hungry European market, which used it for medicinal purposes, to flavor foods and even in wine.

These days sugar is as popular as ever in Brazil. You can sip it on the beach in the form of a *caldo de cana* (sugarcane juice). You can neck it in one of Brazil's many *pé-sujo* (dirty-foot) bars as a shot of *cachaça* (white spirit made from sugarcane). You can pour copious amounts into your coffee, as do most Brazilians, and you can even run your car on it.

Perhaps envisaging Brazil's sugarcoated future, the colonists turned to this new industry. They lacked just one thing: a workforce.

The Slave Trade

Initially the Portuguese seemed to hit it off with Brazil's natives. There was even an exchange of presents between Cabral's men and the *índios* on the beach, with a Portuguese sombrero swapped for feather headdresses. Relations cooled when the Portuguese started enslaving their neighbors for work on the sugarcane plantations. Yet, for a variety of reasons the Portuguese felt the *índios* didn't make great slaves and turned instead to Africa's already existing slave trade.

African slaves started to pour into Brazil's slave markets from about 1550. They were torn from a variety of tribes in Angola, Mozambique and Guinea, as well as the Sudan and Congo. Whatever their origins and cultures, their destinations were identical: slave markets such as Salvador's Pelourinho

The Brazilian NGO Instituto Socioambiental has heaps of fascinating information on the indigenous population, in English and Portuguese, at www.socioambiental.org.

The first bishop of Brazil, Bishop Pêro Fernandes Sardinha, was shipwrecked off the coast of Alagoas in 1556, then ceremonially killed and eaten by the local Caeté people.

1644–1654	1650s	1695
Prince Maurice of Nassau is called back to Holland. The Portuguese wage war over the following decade, pushing the Dutch back to Recife; they surrender in 1654, ending Holland's presence in Brazil.	Communities of runaway slaves, called *quilombos*, flourish in the countryside, eventually becoming targets by *bandeirantes*. Hundreds of these informal communities will later become towns following abolition in the late 19th century.	Palmares, the largest *quilombo* in Brazil's Northeast – and home to more than 20,000 inhabitants – is finally destroyed following decades of attacks by Portuguese troops.

(p443) or Belém's Mercado Ver-o-Peso (p608). By the time slavery was abolished in Brazil in 1888, around 3.6 million Africans had been shipped to Brazil – nearly 40% of the total that came to the New World.

Africans were seen as better workers and less susceptible to the European diseases that had proved the undoing of so many *índios*. In short, they were a better investment. Yet the Portuguese didn't go out of their way to protect this investment. Slaves were brought to Brazil in subhuman conditions: taken from their families and packed into squalid ships for the month-long journey to Brazil.

Visitors to the beaches of Porto de Galinhas (p536), near Recife, might not pick up on the area's grim past. Even after abolition, slave traders continued to smuggle in slaves, often packed into a ship's hull under crates full of *galinhas* (chickens).

> The northeastern tip of Brazil is nearer to Africa than it is to far southern or western Brazil.

Masters & Slaves

For those who survived such ordeals, arrival in Brazil meant only continued suffering. A slave's existence was one of brutality and humiliation. Kind masters were the exception, not the rule, and labor on the plantations was relentless. In temperatures that often exceeded 30°C (86°F), slaves were required to work as many as 17 hours each day, before retiring to the squalid *senzala* (slave quarters), and with as many as 200 slaves packed into each dwelling, hygiene was a concept as remote as the distant coasts of Africa. Dysentery, typhus, yellow fever, malaria, tuberculosis and scurvy were rife; malnutrition a fact of life. Syphilis also plagued a slave population sexually exploited by its masters.

> One of Brazil's great folk heroes is Chico Rei, an African king enslaved and brought to work in the mines, but who managed to buy his freedom and later the freedom of his tribe.

Sexual relations between masters and slaves were so common that a large mixed-race population soon emerged. Off the plantations there was a shortage of white women, so many poorer white settlers lived with black or indigenous women. Brazil was already famous for its sexual permissiveness by the beginning of the 18th century.

Aside from the *senzala*, the other main institution of the sugar plantation was the *casa grande* ('big house') – the luxurious mansion from which the masters would control their slaves.

Resistance & the Quilombos

Resistance to slavery took many forms. Documents of the period refer to the desperation of the slaves who starved themselves to death, killed their babies or fled. Sabotage and theft were frequent, as were work slowdowns, stoppages and revolts.

Other slaves sought solace in African religion and culture. The mix of Catholicism (made compulsory by slave masters) and African traditions spawned a syncretic religion on the sugar plantations, known today as Candomblé. The slaves masked illegal customs with a facade of Catholic

1696	1727	1750
News of the discovery of gold in Brazil reaches Lisbon. The finds, located in the present-day states of Minas Gerais, Mato Grosso, Goiás and southern Bahia, will bring tens of thousands of migrants in ensuing years.	The first coffee bean arrives in Brazil.	After years of negotiations with the Spanish, the Portuguese win the Treaty of Madrid, which hands over 6 million sq km to the Portuguese and puts Brazil's western borders largely where they are today.

BRAZIL'S TOP HISTORICAL SITES

Brazil has some fascinating places to delve into history, from the 11,000-year-old rock paintings at Monte Alegre in the Amazon (p632) to the 1960s-era futurism of Brasília (p377). Rio is packed with heritage sites (see p146), while other top destinations lie scattered around the country.

- **Museu Imperial, Petrópolis** (p203) The stunning summer palace of Dom Pedro II In Petrópolis, and the cool mountain retreat of the Portuguese royal court.
- **Minas de Passagem, near Ouro Prêto** (p249) Descend into an early-1700s-era mine where black slaves worked and died.
- **Igreja de Santa Efigênia dos Pretos, Ouro Prêto** (p245) An 18th-century church built by and for slaves, who prayed to black saints that they wouldn't die in the nearby mines.
- **São Miguel das Missões, Rio Grando do Sul** (p372) The Unesco World Heritage site is home to the mystical ruins of an 18th-century Jesuit settlement.
- **Basílica do Bom Jesus de Matosinhos, Congonhas** (p252) The magnificent sculptural masterpiece created in 1800 by Aleijadinho, a great artist and sufferer of leprosy.
- **Forte Defensor Perpétuo, Paraty** (p193) A weathered 1703 fort built to defend the town of Paraty – a colonial gem – from pirates.
- **Museu da Imigração Japonesa, São Paulo** (p286) A fine place to discover the early history of São Paulo's countless Japanese immigrants.
- **Vale dos Vinhedos, near Bento Gonçalves** (p365) Germans and later Italians left deep roots here, in the heart of Brazil's wine-growing region.
- **Museu Afro-Brasileiro, Salvador** (p443) An excellent place to connect to the centuries of Afro-Brazilian heritage that have so deeply enriched the country.
- **Teatro Amazonas, Manaus** (p646) The lavish 1896 opera house is a symbol of the great wealth of the Amazon's rubber barons

saints and rituals. The martial art *capoeira* (see p455) also grew out of the slave communities.

Many slaves escaped from their masters to form *quilombos*, communities of runaway slaves that quickly spread across the countryside. The most famous, the Republic of Palmares, which survived through much of the 17th century, was home to some 20,000 people. Palmares was a network of *quilombos* covering a broad tract of lush tropical forest straddling the border of Alagoas and Pernambuco states. Under their leaders Ganga Zumba and his son-in-law Zumbi, its citizens became pioneers of guerrilla warfare, repeatedly fending off Portuguese attacks between 1654 and 1695. Eventually Palmares fell to a force of *bandeirantes* from São Paulo.

As abolitionist sentiment grew in the 19th century, many (unsuccessful) slave rebellions were staged, the *quilombos* received more support and

1750s	1763	1789
Gold (and later diamonds) begin to define the colonial economy. In Minas Gerais the population explodes from 30,000 in 1710 to 500,000 by the end of the century.	With gold flowing from the mines of Minas Gerais through Rio de Janeiro, the city grows wealthy and swells in population to 50,000; the Portuguese court transfers the capital of Brazil from Salvador to Rio.	The first organized movement toward independence springs to life. Tiradentes and 11 other conspirators organize the Inconfidência Mineira to overthrow the Portuguese. The plot is quickly foiled, however, and Tiradentes is executed.

ever-greater numbers of slaves fled the plantations. Only abolition itself, in 1888, stopped the growth of *quilombos*. Over 700 villages that started as *quilombos* remain today. Some were so isolated that they remained completely out of contact with white Brazilians until the last couple of decades.

Quilombo (directed by Cacá Diegues) is an epic history flick in which the vast Palmares *quilombo* – a community of runaway slaves led by the legendary Zumbi – is reconstructed in Rio's Baixada Fluminense.

COLONIAL RIVALS

It's hard to picture what Brazil would have been like under French or Dutch rule. Tom Jobim might have composed a track about the *Meisje* from Ipanema; Brazilians might be tucking into frogs' legs and not *feijoada* (bean-and-meat stew) every Sunday. For a time, such outcomes were a distinct possibility.

Technically, the 1494 Treaty of Tordesillas divided the New World between Spain and Portugal. An imaginary line, running north–south from roughly the mouth of the Amazon to what is now Santa Catarina, was drawn on the map. Land to the east became Portuguese territory; land to the west fell under Spanish control.

But the line proved very imaginary indeed. As any traveler brave enough to venture into the further reaches of Mato Grosso will discover, enforcing such a vast border running through thick jungles and swamps was never a particularly viable idea. Brazil's borders remained in flux until as late as 1930.

Over the years, Portugal repeatedly ignored the frontier in an attempt to squeeze more land out of its rivals. France and Holland also had their eyes on Brazil's green and lucrative land.

The French

In 1555 three boatloads of French settlers landed on a small island in Rio's Baía de Guanabara. Obviously liking what they found, the French decided to try to incorporate parts of southern Brazil into their ever-growing empire. Antarctic France would be its name.

Things didn't go to plan – a few years later the *franceses* were expelled by the Portuguese, who landed near Praia Vermelha, at the foot of Sugarloaf mountain. It was here that Estácio de Sá founded the city of São Sebastião do Rio de Janeiro on March 1, 1565.

Rio de Janeiro got its name because its Portuguese discoverers arrived in January (Janeiro), 1502, and thought that Guanabara Bay on which it lies was the mouth of a river *(rio)*.

The French made another brief attempt to claw Brazilian soil from the Portuguese, further north, in 1612, when they founded the city of São Luís, which took its name from France's then king, Louis XIII. Three years later, the Portuguese sent the French packing once again.

The Dutch

The challenge from Holland proved harder to shake off. The Dutch West India Company (DWIC), set up in 1621, was much more than a simple trading business. Its business, in fact, was war, and its goal was to take Brazil's Northeast from the Portuguese.

1807	1815	1822
Napoleon invades Portugal and the Portuguese prince regent (later known as Dom João VI) and his entire court of 15,000 flee for Brazil. The royal coffers shower wealth upon Rio.	Having fallen hard for Brazil, Dom João VI declares Rio the capital of the United Kingdom of Portugal and Brazil. The same year, a mounting financial crisis forces the king to return to Portugal.	Left in charge of Brazil after his father Dom João VI returns to Portugal, the prince regent Dom Pedro I declares independence from Portugal and crowns himself 'emperor' of Brazil.

The Dutch bombardment of Salvador began on the morning of May 9, 1624. By the following day, the invading force of 3000 men from 26 ships had captured and ransacked the city. Salvador's return to Portuguese hands was almost as quick; it was just a year before a combined force of 12,000 Spanish and Portuguese troops evicted the Dutch. But five years later the Dutch were back, storming the cities of Olinda and Recife and making Recife the capital of New Holland. In 1637 a Dutch prince, Maurice of Nassau, was brought in to govern the colony. Educated at university back home in, among other things, good manners, Nassau was a definite hit with the locals. His policy of freedom of worship, which left Brazil's Catholics to their own devices despite the Protestant invasion, brought a definite stability to the region.

The Dutch extended their control over much of Northeastern Brazil, from the São Francisco river in Bahia to Maranhão. That Brazilians didn't go on to become Dutch speakers is largely down to the exit of Nassau, who returned to Holland in 1644 after a series of disagreements with the boys from the DWIC. New Holland had hardly waved its ruler goodbye when violent uprisings broke out, designed to uproot the Dutch. The following decade saw a series of bloody clashes in the Northeast: two crucial battles, in which the Portuguese came out victorious even though outnumbered, took place in 1648 and 1649. The Dutch were driven back into Recife and eventually surrendered in 1654, drawing a line under Holland's part in Brazilian history.

THE BANDEIRANTES & THE GOLD RUSH

The *bandeirantes*, too, were keen to make inroads into Brazil. These bands of explorers roamed Brazil's interior in search of indigenous slaves, mapping out undiscovered territory and bumping off the odd indigenous community along the way.

The *bandeirantes* took their name from the trademark flag-bearer who would front their expeditions. During the 17th and 18th centuries, group after group of *bandeirantes* set out from São Paulo. The majority were bilingual in Portuguese and Tupi-Guarani, born of Portuguese fathers and indigenous mothers. They benefited from both indigenous survival techniques and European weaponry.

By the mid-17th century they had journeyed as far as the peaks of the Peruvian Andes and the Amazon lowlands. It was the exploits of these discoverers that stretched Brazil's borders to their current extent. In 1750, after four years of negotiations with the Spanish, their conquests were secured. The Treaty of Madrid handed over 6 million sq km to the Portuguese and put Brazil's western borders more or less where they are today.

The *bandeirantes* were known for more than just their colorful flags. Protected from *índio* arrows by heavily padded cotton jackets, they waged an all-out war on Brazil's natives, despite the fact that many of them had indigenous mothers. Huge numbers of *índios* fled inland, searching for shelter

Three worthwhile history books in English are Thomas E Skidmore's *Brazil: Five Centuries of Change* (2009); Robert Levine's *The History of Brazil* (1999); and Boris Fausto's *A Concise History of Brazil* (1999).

1831	mid 1830s	1835
Brazil's first homegrown monarch, Dom Pedro I, proves incompetent and abdicates the throne. His son Pedro II takes power in 1840 and ushers in a long period of growth and stability.	The coffee bush, which flourishes in the soil of Rio de Janeiro province, plays a major role in the colony's economy. *Fazendas* (ranches) spring up around the Southeast as Brazil becomes a major coffee exporter.	Inspired by the successful Haitian Revolution some years earlier, Brazilian slaves in Salvador stage an uprising – Brazil's last big slave revolt – which narrowly fails.

in the Jesuit missions. But there were few hiding places – it is thought the *bandeirantes* killed or enslaved well in excess of 500,000 *índios*.

Gold

'As yet we have no way of knowing whether there might be gold, or silver or any kind of metal or iron [here],' reported Pero Vaz de Caminha to his king in 1500.

Though it wasn't discovered until nearly two centuries later, there certainly was gold in Brazil. Unsurprisingly, it was the *bandeirantes* who, in between decapitating *índios*, discovered it in the Serra do Espinhaço in Minas Gerais.

For part of the 18th century Brazil became the world's greatest gold 'producer,' unearthing wealth that helped build many of Minas Gerais' historic cities. The full title of Ouro Prêto (p242), one of the principal beneficiaries of the gold boom, is actually Vila Rica de Ouro Prêto (Rich Town of Black Gold).

Other wild boomtowns such as Sabará (p251), Mariana (p249) and São João del Rei (p253) sprang up in the mountain valleys. Wealthy merchants built opulent mansions and bankrolled stunning baroque churches, many of which remain to this day.

Gold produced a major shift in Brazil's population from the Northeast to the Southeast. When gold was first discovered, there were no white settlers in the territory of Minas Gerais. By 1710 the population had reached 30,000, and by the end of the 18th century it was 500,000. An estimated one-third of the two million slaves brought to Brazil in the 18th century were sent to the goldfields, where their lives were often worse than in the sugar fields.

But the gold boom didn't last. By 1750 the mining regions were in decline and coastal Brazil was returning to center stage. Many of the gold-hunters ended up in Rio de Janeiro, which grew rapidly.

> With great mineral wealth flowing out of Brazil, it's no surprise that piracy surged during the epoch. Islands such as Ilha Grande (p186), with its sheltered bays and fresh water supply, made convenient launch pads on gold-laden Portuguese vessels.

TIRADENTES

As if the French and Dutch hadn't been enough to deal with, Brazil's Portuguese rulers also faced threats from within. During the 18th century calls for independence grew ever stronger and in 1789 the first organized movement came to life.

In charge was Joaquim José da Silva Xavier – a dentist from Ouro Prêto known as Tiradentes (Tooth Puller). With 11 other conspirators – all outraged by attempts to collect taxes – Tiradentes began talks about how best to uproot the Portuguese.

Though the plotters earned themselves a grand name – the Inconfidência Mineira – their plans were quickly foiled. All 12 were arrested and sentenced to death and, although a royal pardon was eventually issued exiling the rebels to Angola and Mozambique, it came too late for Tiradentes, who was hanged in Rio de Janeiro in 1792. As a warning to other would-be rebels the authorities sliced up his body and displayed the parts across Minas Gerais. His head

1865	1888	1889
Brazil, allied with Uruguay and Argentina, wages the 'War of the Triple Alliance' on Paraguay. It proves South America's bloodiest conflict, killing hundreds of thousands (and wiping out half of Paraguay's population).	Slavery is abolished in Brazil, the last country in the New World to do so. The law is signed into effect by Princesa Isabel, admired by many blacks as their benefactress.	A military coup, supported by Brazil's wealthy coffee farmers, overthrows Pedro II. The monarchy is abolished and the Brazilian Republic is born. Pedro II goes into exile in Paris and dies a few years later.

was put on show in Ouro Prêto, his house destroyed and salt scattered on the ground outside so that nothing would grow there. According to one version of events, soldiers formally recorded the event on a manuscript – using Tiradentes' blood as ink.

Tiradentes became a national martyr – a symbol of resistance – and during the later Vargas era, a museum in his honor was opened in Ouro Prêto's old town hall.

DOM JOÃO VI

Brazil became a temporary sanctuary to the Portuguese royal family in 1807. Running scared from Napoleon, whose army was at that moment advancing on Lisbon, some 15,000 court members fled to Rio de Janeiro, led by the prince regent, Dom João.

Like so many *estrangeiros* (foreigners) arriving in Brazil, the regent fell in love with the place and granted himself the privilege of becoming the country's ruler. He opened Rio's Jardim Botânico (Botanical Gardens; p142) to the public in 1822, and they remain there to this day in the upmarket Jardim Botânico neighborhood.

Even after Napoleon's defeat at Waterloo in 1815, Dom João showed no sign of abandoning Brazil. When his mother, Dona Maria I, died the following year, he became king and declared Rio the capital of the United Kingdom of Portugal and Brazil. Brazil became the only New World colony ever to have a European monarch ruling on its soil.

> The hilarious film *Carlota Joaquina – Princesa do Brasil* is about a Spanish princess married to the future Dom João VI, who flees with the entire Portuguese court to Brazil to escape Napoleon.

INDEPENDENCE

Independence eventually came in 1822, 30 years after the Inconfidência Mineira. Legend has it that, on the banks of São Paulo's Ipiranga river, Brazil's then regent, Dom João's son Pedro, pulled out his sword, bellowing, '*Independência ou morte!*' (Independence or death!). With the same breath he declared himself Emperor Dom Pedro I.

The Portuguese quickly gave in to the idea of a Brazilian empire. Without a single shot being fired, Dom Pedro I became the first emperor of an independent Brazil. The *povo brasileiro* (Brazilian people), however, were not as keen on Pedro as he was about their newly born nation. From all accounts he was a blundering incompetent, whose sexual exploits (and resulting string of love children) horrified even the most permissive of Brazilians. After nine years of womanizing he was forced to abdicate, leaving his five-year-old son, Dom Pedro II, to take over.

A period of crisis followed: the heir to the throne was, after all, just a child. Between 1831 and 1840 Brazil was governed by so-called *regências* (regencies), a time of political turmoil and widespread rebellions. The only solution was the return of the monarchy and a law was passed to declare Dom Pedro II an adult, well before his 18th birthday.

> Brazil is the only country in the New World that was both the seat of an empire (when the Portuguese king came here) and an independent monarchy (when Dom Pedro I declared independence).

1890	1890s	1897
Demand for rubber skyrockets with the start of the automobile industry in the US. Brazil, the world's only natural exporter until 1910, fuels boom times in Amazonian cities like Belém and Manaus.	With slavery abolished Brazil opens its borders to immigrants to meet its labor needs. Tens of thousands arrive each year from Italy, Portugal, Spain, Germany and later Japan and other countries.	Some 20,000 refugees and former soldiers settle on the barren hillside of Morro da Providência just outside of downtown Rio de Janeiro. This becomes the country's first favela.

Aged just 15, Dom Pedro II received the title of Emperor and Perpetual Defender of Brazil, precipitating one of the most prosperous spells in the country's history, barring the war with Paraguay in 1865. Invaded by its neighbor, Brazil teamed up with Argentina and Uruguay and thrashed the Paraguayans back across the border.

Paraguay was left crippled – its population slashed to just 200,000, of whom around 180,000 were women. Brazil, too, suffered heavily: around 100,000 men died, many of them slaves sent to war in the place of wealthier Brazilians.

ABOLITION & THE REPUBLIC

Since the 16th century, slavery had formed the backbone of a brutally unequal society in Brazil. 'Every dimension of our social existence is contaminated,' lamented abolitionist Joaquim Nabuco in 1880.

To undo something so deeply ingrained into the Brazilian way of life was never likely to be easy. Brazil prevaricated for nearly 60 years before any sort of resolution was reached. The 19th century was punctuated by a series of halfhearted legislative attempts to lay the slave industry to rest. Repeatedly such laws failed.

Slave trafficking to Brazil was banned in 1850, but continued clandestinely. Another law, in 1885, freed all slaves over the age of 65. The lawmakers had obviously forgotten that the average life expectancy for a slave at this time was 45. Not until May 13, 1888 – 80 years after Britain had freed its slaves – was slavery itself officially banned in Brazil. Unsurprisingly, this didn't make a huge immediate difference to the welfare of the 800,000 freed slaves, who were largely illiterate and unskilled. Thousands were cast onto the streets without any kind of infrastructure to support them. Many died, while others flooded to Brazil's urban centers, adding to the cities' first slums. Still today, blacks overall remain among the poorest and worst-educated groups in the country.

Not far out of the door behind slavery was the Império Brasileiro. In 1889 a military coup, supported by Brazil's wealthy coffee farmers, decapitated the old Brazilian empire and the republic was born. The emperor went into exile, where he died a couple of years later.

A military clique ruled Brazil for the next four years until elections were held, but because of ignorance, corruption, and land and literacy requirements, only about 2% of the adult population voted. Little changed, except that the power of the military and the now-influential coffee growers increased, while it diminished for the sugar barons.

FULL OF BEANS

The first coffee bean found its way into Brazil in the 18th century. The responsible party was, they say, an army officer called Francisco de Mello Palheta, who had journeyed to French Guiana and came back brandishing a handful of coffee beans – a gift from a lover he had left behind. On ar-

The bloodiest and most radical of the 1830s revolts was the Cabanagem War in Pará. Rebels held Belém for a year before being evicted and decimated by government troops.

A book about the relationship between slaves and masters on Pernambuco's sugar plantations, Gilberto Freyre's *The Masters and the Slaves* (1933), revolutionized Brazilian thinking about the African contribution to Brazilian society.

'Order and Progress,' the slogan on Brazil's flag, comes from French philosopher Auguste de Comte (1797–1857), whose elevation of reason and scientific knowledge over traditional religious beliefs was influential on the young Brazilian republic.

1920	1930	1937
The rubber boom goes bust as the Dutch and English plant their own rubber trees in the East Indies. Brazil's monopoly on the world rubber market deflates.	Getúlio Vargas comes into power. Inspired by European fascists, President Vargas presides over an authoritarian state, playing a major role in Brazilian politics until his fall from power in 1951.	Getúlio Vargas announces over the radio that Brazilians now have a new constitution for what he calls the 'Estado Novo' (New State); he passes minimum wage laws in 1938, expands the military and centralizes power.

rival back in Brazil, the beans were swiftly planted, thus beginning another Brazilian love-hate affair – with *café*.

Whatever the truth, the coffee industry eventually grew into a huge success. By 1889 coffee accounted for two-thirds of Brazil's exports.

Coffee growers filled the gap left in Brazil's export market by the decline of its sugar industry since the 1820s. Unable to compete with the newly mechanized sugar mills in the West Indies, sugar exports plummeted. Coffee, meanwhile, flourished, and coffee plantations soon took up vast tracts of land in São Paulo and Minas Gerais states.

Although coffee was the making of many millionaires in the southern states, it was also the cause of great suffering. The coffee *fazendas* (ranches) in many ways replicated the Northeastern sugar plantations: slaves worked inhuman hours in cramped and fetid conditions. In Rio many such estates have now opened their doors to the public, and provide a chilling insight into Brazilian *escravidão* (slavery). After abolition in 1888, the workforce changed, but the conditions did not.

A masterpiece of Brazilian literature, *Rebellion in the Backlands* vividly describes the Canudos massacre. Author Euclides de Cunha witnessed the end of Canudos as a correspondent for a São Paulo newspaper.

OPEN BORDERS

In the final decade of the 19th century, Brazil opened its borders. Millions of immigrants – from Italy, Japan, Spain, Germany, Portugal and elsewhere – streamed into Brazil to work on the coffee *fazendas,* and to make new lives in the rapidly growing cities, especially Rio and São Paulo, adding further textures to Brazil's ethnic mixture and confirming the shift of Brazil's economic center of gravity from the Northeast to the Southeast. When you tuck into a pizza in São Paulo's Bela Vista district or sample a *pastel chinês* (Chinese pastry) at one of Rio's many street-corner snack bars, it is more than likely to be this generation of border hoppers you have to thank.

Over the next century, immigrants continued to flood into Brazil. The country became a haven for Jews fleeing persecution at the hands of the Nazis, as well as Nazis looking to avoid being put on trial for war crimes. Arabs, universally known as *turcos* by the Brazilians, also joined the influx of newcomers. Many of the traders you'll meet at Rio de Janeiro's Rua Uruguaiana flea market hail from the Middle East.

The first favela (slum or shantytown) appeared on Rio's landscape in 1897, but it wasn't until 1994 that the communities (which today number over 600) were included on maps.

RUBBER

Toward the end of the 19th century the Amazon region was the scene of another Brazilian economic boom: that of the *Hevea brasiliensis*, the rubber tree.

Demand for rubber rocketed in 1890 with the invention of the pneumatic tire and the start of the automobile industry in the US. The rubber price shot up, bringing huge wealth to the main Amazonian cities of Belém and Manaus. Manaus' spectacular opera house, the Teatro Amazonas (p646), opened in 1896, was one fruit of the rubber boom. Rubber production reached its peak in 1912, when latex exports made up nearly 40% of Brazil's export revenue.

1938	1942	1950
Lampião, the last great *cangaçeiro* (bandit of the Northeast), is ambushed and killed by police. He and his gang would later be mythologized as folk heroes (Robin Hood types) in the feudal Northeast hinterland.	Initially maintaining neutrality, Brazil enters WWII on the side of the Allies, providing raw materials (including rubber, quartz and other materials), plus 25,000 troops (the only Latin American nation to do so).	Newly constructed Maracanã Stadium in Rio de Janeiro plays center stage in the FIFA World Cup. Brazil dominates until the final, when before 200,000 fans (a still-held world record), it suffers a stunning loss to Uruguay.

THE ORIGINS OF THE FAVELA

The end of the 19th century may have brought an end to slavery, but newly freed blacks weren't welcomed into a new and equitable society. They faced enormous obstacles finding work and a place to live. Some of the newly freed fled to *quilombos*, which were runaway slave communities that sprang up throughout Brazil, including on forested areas outside of Rio; there was even a small *quilombo* in present-day Leblon.

Freed slaves weren't the only group struggling for survival at the end of the 19th century. In the Northeast, terrible droughts in the 1870s and '80s, coupled with the decline of the sugar industry, brought economic devastation. Offering a vision of hope, messianic movements became popular among Brazil's poor. The most famous was that of Canudos. Its leader, Antônio Conselheiro (Antônio the Counselor), had wandered for years through the backlands preaching and prophesying the appearance of the Antichrist and the end of the world, defending the poor and antagonizing the authorities. He railed against the new republican government and in 1893 eventually settled with his followers at Canudos, in the interior of northern Bahia. Within 1½ years Canudos had grown to a city of 35,000.

The republican government sensed plots in Canudos to return Brazil to the monarchy. Miraculously, the rebels first defeated a force of state police, and then two subsequent attacks by the federal army. Hysterical demonstrations in the cities demanded that the republic be saved from the rebels. That's when a federal force of 8000 well-supplied soldiers – many of whom hailed from Rio – eventually took Canudos after vicious, hand-to-hand, house-to-house fighting. It was a war of extermination that nearly wiped out every man, woman and child from Canudos; the settlement was then burned to the ground to erase it from the nation's memory.

The soldiers and their wives – some of whom were survivors taken from the Canudos massacre – returned to Rio, where they were promised land in exchange for their victory. The government, however, reneged on the promise. The soldiers, who had camped out in front of the Ministry of War, then occupied the nearby hillside of Morro da Providência. Oddly enough, as the first tenants put up makeshift shelter and settled in, they came across the same hardy shrub they found in the arid lands surrounding Canudos. Called 'favela,' this plant caused skin irritations in all who come in contact with it – according to some accounts, the protective shrub even helped repel the army's initial invasions. Soon hillside residents began calling their new home the Morro da Favela (perhaps in hopes that the plant would have protective benefits for those who took part in the war), and the name caught on. Soon the word favela was used to describe the ever-increasing number of informal communities appearing around Rio, which quickly gathered a mix of former slaves and poverty-stricken inhabitants from the interior, who came to the city seeking a better life.

As with all booms, the bust had to come. The British may have given Brazil one of its greatest gifts in football, but they also stole one of Brazil's greatest assets. In 1876 Englishman Henry Wickham had smuggled 70,000 rubber-tree seeds out of Amazonia on a chartered freighter to Kew Gardens in London. Seedlings quickly found their way to the British colonies in Southeast Asia,

1954	1958	1960
Following an explosive political scandal, the military calls for the resignation of President Getúlio Vargas. He pens a melodramatic letter then shoots himself through the heart at his Rio palace.	Still reeling from defeat eight years earlier, Brazil wins its first soccer World Cup. The team catapults to victory over Sweden, largely on the skills of a precocious 17-year-old unknown by the name of Pelé.	President Juscelino Kubitschek spearheads the creation of a new capital. Architects Oscar Niemeyer and Lúcio Costa (and countless workers) play a starring role in building hypermodern Brasília from scratch in just 41 months.

where large rubber plantations were established. When the plantations started to yield in 1910, the price of latex plummeted on the world market. The Brazilian rubber boom blew out in spectacular fashion.

MILK & COFFEE POLITICS

On November 15, 1894, Prudente de Morais became Brazil's first directly elected civil president. At this time Brazil was dominated by land-owning families from two states: Minas Gerais and São Paulo. These groups controlled national politics, and Brazil's presidents came almost without exception from these states of milk and coffee respectively. Each state was dominated by a series of rural landowners known as *coronéis* (colonels), who controlled the local political, judicial and police systems through friends and family in all the important public posts.

Such political bias was reflected in the electoral system. Ballots were not secret and those who voted against the ruling powers suffered reprisals. Fraud was common: many people would vote more than once and, from time to time, even the dead found the power to vote.

Disillusioned with the dominance of this wealthy few, a new movement among the military, known as *tenentismo*, began to form in opposition to the small oligarchies of Minas and São Paulo.

The world-famous Copacabana Beach was the scene of the first rebellion. On July 5, 1922, 18 tenants set out from the fort of Copacabana (p143) and clashed with government troops. Just two of the *tenentes* – Eduardo Gomes and Siqueira Campos – survived, the latter giving his name to the metro station a few blocks from the beach.

For another eight years Brazil's coffee farmers continued to enjoy the status of political untouchables, but the Wall St bust of 1929 changed everything. The coffee market all but dried up, prices plummeted and many of Brazil's powerful coffee farmers were left ruined. The economic and political upheaval soon translated into revolution.

GETÚLIO VARGAS, POPULIST DICTATOR

The Vargas era began in 1930 when members of the newly formed Liberal Alliance party decided to fight back after the defeat of their candidate, Getúlio Vargas, in the presidential elections. The revolution kicked off on October 3 in Rio Grande do Sul and spread rapidly through other states. Twenty-one days later President Júlio Prestes was deposed and on November 3 Vargas became Brazil's new 'provisional' president.

The formation of the Estado Novo (New State) in November 1937 made Vargas the first Brazilian president to wield absolute power. Inspired by the fascist governments of Salazar in Portugal and Mussolini in Italy, Vargas banned political parties, imprisoned political opponents and censored artists and the press.

Read about one man's recent bicycle journey across the Amazon (traveling the length of the Transamazônica) on Amazon Pilgrim (http://amazonpilgrim.com).

Brazzil Magazine (www.brazzil.com) focuses a cynical eye on Brazilian history, politics and culture.

1962	1963	1964
Twenty Brazilian musicians perform in a highly successful Carnegie Hall concert, bringing bossa nova (and Tom Jobim's much-hummed *Girl from Ipanema*) onto the world stage.	Brazilian filmmakers create a new movement with the birth of Cinema Novo, in highly expressive and often experimental films that tackle Brazil's social problems. Director Glauber Rocha leads the way with *Black God, White Devil*.	President Goulart is overthrown by a military coup – with strong evidence of US involvement. So begins the era of dictatorship, with generals running the show for the next 20 years.

Despite this, many liked Vargas. The 'father' of Brazil's workers, he created Brazil's minimum wage in 1938. Each year he introduced new labor laws to coincide with Workers' Day on May 1, to sweeten the teeth of Brazil's factory workers.

Like any fascist worth his salt, Vargas began WWII siding with Hitler's Third Reich. Mysteriously, an offer of US investment to the sum of US$20 million in 1942 led Vargas to switch allegiances. The National War Memorial in Flamengo – a huge concrete monument and museum, which represents a pair of hands begging the skies for peace – today pays testament to the 5000 Brazilians who served in Europe.

Vargas, of course, wasn't exactly practicing what he preached. The glaring contradiction of someone fighting for democracy in Europe and maintaining a quasi-fascist state back home soon became impossible. After WWII, the military forced him to step down.

Yet he remained popular and in 1951 was elected president – this time democratically. But Vargas' new administration was plagued by the hallmark of Brazilian politics – corruption. For this, a young journalist called Carlos Lacerda attacked him incessantly. In 1954 Vargas' security chief sent two gunmen to assassinate Lacerda at his home in Copacabana. The troublesome scribe was only slightly wounded but an air force major was killed, precipitating a huge scandal. Amid calls from the military for his resignation, Vargas responded dramatically. He penned a note saying 'I leave this life to enter into history,' and on the following morning, August 24, 1954, fired a single bullet through his own heart.

HEY BIG SPENDER!

Juscelino Kubitschek de Oliveira, whose tongue twister of a name swiftly earned him the *apelido* (nickname) JK, was elected president in 1956. 'Fifty years' progress in five' had been his election promise. His critics responded with 'Forty years' inflation in four.' Sadly for JK, the second assessment came closer to the mark, despite an 80% increase in industrial production during his term.

Kubitschek's lasting legacy was the building of Brasília, Brazil's love-it-or-hate-it capital, located slap bang in the center of the country as a symbol of national unity and a catalyst for the development of the interior. Though the construction of such a city was written into the 1891 constitution, it was Kubitschek who, quite literally, made the idea concrete. The windswept, shadeless streets of Brasília were inaugurated with much fanfare on April 21, 1960.

As if Kubitschek hadn't made enough enemies by taking the honor of capital city from the 'Marvelous City' of Rio de Janeiro, his successor, Jânio Quadros, went one step further. He tried to outlaw bikinis on Brazil's beaches, a serious affront to Brazilian popular culture. Quadros also made

The website of the Brazilian embassy in London (www.brazil.org.uk) has lots of interesting tidbits about Brazil, including a breakdown of its often baffling political system.

Austrian author Stefan Zweig, who fled the Nazis, settled in Brazil and fell in love with his adopted country. His book *Brazil, Land of the Future* (1941) is an idealistic vision of the nation.

July, 1968	December, 1968	1968
Caetano Veloso, Gilberto Gil and other musicians release the album *Tropicália: ou Panis et Circencis*, and *tropicália* is born. It's a highly experimental movement in music and art that takes aim at the military dictatorship.	The government passes the repressive Ato Institutional 5 law, which purges opposition legislators, judges and mayors from public office; most political parties are banned. Protests erupt nationwide; over 100,000 take to the streets in Rio.	Despite the politically repressive atmosphere, the Brazilian economy booms, averaging an incredible 10% growth for the next six years. Rapid income growth continues into the 1970s.

the even worse mistake of irritating the military by decorating Che Guevara in a public ceremony in Brasília. This triggered plots among the right-wing military and after seven months in office Quadros resigned, claiming 'occult forces' were at work.

THE GENERALS TAKE OVER

Quadros' vice-president, a leftist by the name of João Goulart, took power. Though Goulart didn't demonstrate an overt aversion to *fio dental* (dental-floss bikinis), the military wasn't keen on him either. In 1964 he was over-thrown in a so-called *revolução* (revolution) – really a military coup, believed to have received backing from the US government. President Lyndon Johnson did nothing to dampen such theories when he immediately cabled his warm-est wishes to the new Brazilian administration.

Brazil's military regime was not as brutal as those of Chile or Argentina – a reality that led to the somewhat unkind saying, 'Brazil couldn't even or-ganize a dictatorship properly.' Yet for the best part of 20 years, freedom of speech was an unknown concept and political parties were banned. The Lei de Segurança Nacional (National Security Law) of 1967 tightened the noose on political dissidents, who were often tortured, murdered or – perhaps worse – thrown into Brazilian jails.

The dictatorship coincided with one of the most culturally rich periods in Brazilian history, but a generation of composers and academics were ex-iled for their opposition to the regime – among them sociologist Fernando Henrique Cardoso (who would go on to become president) and musician Gilberto Gil (who decades later would become culture minister in the Lula government).

A draconian censorship law known as the Ato Institucional 5 (AI-5) marked the height of repression in 1968. In response, Brazil's middle-class student movement came to life. In June 1968 the streets of Rio de Janeiro hosted a mass demonstration, known as the Passeata dos cem mil (March of the 100,000), against the dictatorship. Many in the Catholic Church, which had broadly supported the coup, also turned against the government, inspired by Liberation Theology.

Perversely during a time of such repression, the Brazilian economy flour-ished. Year after year in the late 1960s and early 1970s, the economy grew by over 10%, as Brazil's rulers borrowed heavily from international banks. But in the absence of rural land reform, millions moved to the cities, where favelas filled up the open spaces.

During this time, Brazil's obsession with 'megaprojects' was born. Under the quick-spending regime, construction began on numerous colossal (and mostly ill-fated) plans, including the Transamazônica highway, the Rio-Niterói Bridge and the Ilha do Fundão, which was to house Rio's Federal University.

Set during the military dictatorship, Bruno Barreto's film *Four Days in September* (1998) is based on the 1969 kidnapping of the US ambassador to Brazil by leftist guerrillas.

According to the 1.5-million-member Movimento Sem Terra (MST; Landless Workers' Movement), half the arable land in Brazil is controlled by just 1.6% of landowners.

1968–1972	1972	1979–80
Veloso and Gil jailed for several months then released and exiled to London, where they continue performing. Other outspoken critics are less fortunate, suffering torture from the regime. The repression continues to the 1980s.	The era of megaprojects and skyrocketing deficits begins, with the opening of the 5300km Trans-Amazonian high-way. It cost nearly US$1 billion, but never achieved its goal (thankfully, say environmental-ists) of colonizing the Amazon.	The consistent decline of work-ers' wages leads to strikes by workers across the country. Unions lead the call for justice and young workers join with in-tellectuals and activists to form Brazil's Workers' Party (PT).

THE WORKERS ORGANIZE

By the late 1970s, the economic boom was dying and opposition to the regime began to spread from the educated middle class to the working class. A series of strikes in the São Paulo car industry signaled the intent of the militant new workers' movement. At the helm was Luíz Inácio 'Lula' da Silva, who famously lost one *dedo* (finger) in a factory accident but made up in charisma for what he lacked in the finger department.

The Partido dos Trabalhadores (PT; Workers' Party), Brazil's first-ever mass political party to speak for the poor, grew out of these strikes. Though grass-roots metalworkers formed the PT's base, the party's broad membership extended to some of Brazil's leading left-wing academics, among them literary critic Antonio Candido and historian Sérgio Buarque de Holanda, whose book *Raízes do Brasil* (The Roots of Brazil) remains a defining work in Brazilian scholarship. In January 1980 the PT's first manifesto declared the need to 'build an egalitarian society, where there are neither exploited nor exploiters.'

First came the *abertura* (opening), a slow, cautious return to civilian rule between 1979 and 1985. With popular opposition gathering force, the military announced gradual moves toward a democratic Brazil. Political prisoners and exiles were granted amnesty. Six new political parties – of which the PT was one – emerged. The tail end of this *abertura* was marked by the *direitas já* (elections now) movement, which called for immediate and direct presidential elections.

DEMOCRACY & DEBT

In 1985 a presidential election took place, but the only voters were the members of the national Congress, which caused the PT to boycott such an indirect vote. Unexpectedly, Tancredo Neves, opposing the military candidate, came out on top, and millions of Brazilians took to the streets to celebrate the end of military rule.

Immediately a spanner was thrown in the works: Neves died from heart failure before he could assume the presidency. His vice-presidential candidate, the whiskered José Sarney, took over.

Sarney – who had supported the military until 1984 – held office until 1989, a period in which runaway inflation helped Brazil rack up a gargantuan foreign debt. By 1990 the external debt stood at a crippling US$115 billion. Sarney's stint as president proved a sad rebuttal of his catchphrase, *'tem que dar certo'* (it has to work out). Virtually nothing did – though he can claim to have implemented one crucial law: Brazil's illiterate, previously excluded from the political system, were at last permitted to vote.

In the 1989 direct presidential election, the first ever that could be called democratic, it was a Northeastern political climber by the name of Collor who was victorious, beating Lula, the PT's candidate, by the smallest of

---

Although it's set in Britain in the future, Terry Gilliam's dystopian film *Brazil* (1985) pulls themes from real 1980s Brazil, and other military dictatorships, showing an Orwellian world of crushing bureaucracy.

From 1987 to 1997, Brazilians suffered devastating hyperinflation, averaging 2000% annually. This meant rent doubled every 10 weeks, credit cards charged 25% a month interest and food and clothes went up 40% a month.

The government-run Bolsa Família gives small stipends (R$22 per child, maximum R$66) to parents in exchange for keeping their children in school and making sure they receive prescribed vaccinations.

1984	1985	1985
As the military dictatorship nears its end, the Movimento Sem Terra (MST; Landless Workers' Movement) – an organization calling for land reform – is founded. The fringe organization of 6000 families grows to more than 1.5 million today.	Following a cautious period of *abertura* (opening), Brazil holds an indirect presidential election. Tancredo Neves wins a surprise victory and millions of Brazilians take to the streets to celebrate the end of military rule.	Jubilation is cut short when Neves dies of heart failure before taking office. His vice-presidential candidate José Sarney takes power, but proves unable to handle the rampant inflation and huge debt left by his predecessors.

margins – and only after the powerful Globo TV network had helped to sabotage Lula by screening his ex-lover claiming he had tried to force her to have an abortion 16 years before.

A TROUBLED ADMINISTRATION

Fernando Collor de Mello, former governor of the small state of Alagoas, had a certain superficial charisma and a talent for manipulating TV, and came from a background of established influence – his father was a media boss, his grandfather had been a minister under Getúlio Vargas and his wife hailed from a landowning clan with powerful political ties in Alagoas.

Collor revolutionized consumer laws – when you see a 'best before' date on a tub of Brazilian margarine, it's him you have to thank. 'Sell by' dates, however, couldn't save him from disgrace. An ever-lengthening list of scandals involving Collor and his intimate associate PC Farias – alleged corruption on a vast scale, alleged drug deals, family feuds – led to a congressional inquiry, huge student protests and eventually the president's impeachment.

Though out of office, 'Fernandinho' managed to avoid a prison sentence, receiving little more than an eight-year ban from politics. Found not guilty of 'passive corruption' by the Supreme Court in 1994, he moved to Miami, where he remained for five years. In 1998 Collor returned to Brazil, and after several unsuccessful attempts to re-enter Brazilian politics was elected to Congress as a senator for Alagoas.

BRAZIL'S BOOM DAYS

Following Collor's impeachment, Vice-President Itamar Franco found himself in the hot seat. Despite his reputation as an eccentric, his administration was credited with competence and integrity. Franco's greatest achievement was to stabilize Brazil's violently erratic economy, introducing a new currency, the real. Pegged to the US dollar, the real caused inflation to plummet from a rate of over 5000% in late 1993 to under 10% in 1994.

The Plano Real sparked an economic boom that continues to this day, though it was his successor, former finance minister Fernando Henrique Cardoso, who presided through the mid-1990s over a growing economy and record foreign investment. He is often credited with laying the groundwork that put Brazil's hyperinflation to bed, though often at the neglect of social problems.

Come the 2002 election, Lula, at the fourth time of asking, toned down his socialist rhetoric, campaigned with the slogan 'Lulinha, Peace and Love,' swapped his jeans for suits, and promised to repay Brazil's international debts. This, and the PT's corruption-free reputation, won over enough of the electorate's middle ground – and the media giant Globo – to give Lula a convincing victory over the center-right candidate Jose Serra. For the first time ever, Brazil had a government on the left of the political spectrum and

Bye-Bye Brasil is a classic Brazilian film that follows a traveling circus across Brazil's Northeast, charting the profound changes in Brazilian society that characterized the second half of the 20th century.

The documentary *They Killed Sister Dorothy* (2008), directed by Daniel Junge, paints a compelling portrait of the US missionary nun Dorothy Stang and the indigent farmers she helped to protect.

Australian Peter Robb weaves the whole of Brazil's history, and most of its literature, into his account of the alleged widespread corruption of the Collor de Mello regime, *A Death in Brazil* (2003).

1988	**1994**	**1994**
Amazonia rubber-tappers' leader and environmentalist Chico Mendes is murdered by a local rancher and his son. The public outcry following Mendes' death forces the government to create extractive reserves.	Following the impeachment of President Collor, Vice-President Itamar Franco takes power. He introduces a new currency, the real, which stabilizes the economy and ushers in an economic boom.	In Rio de Janeiro the Favela-Bairro project is unveiled. Over the next decade, US$180 million will be spent providing neglected communities with access to decent sanitation, health clinics and public transportation.

WORLD CUP DREAMS

Bringing the World Cup back to Brazil has long been a dream of the football-crazed nation. In 2007, the dream became reality when FIFA announced that Brazil had won the rights to host the World Cup in 2014. The South American giant last staged the big sporting event in 1950, when Brazil lost in the dramatic final against Uruguay before 200,000 fans in Rio's Maracanã Stadium (which has since been modified to hold smaller crowds). The unforgettable day of infamy was later called 'maracanazo' and is still in common parlance.

Brazil, the most successful football nation in the history of the games (with five World Cup victories), will become the fifth country to host the event twice. Unlike in 1950, when games were largely held in the South and Southeast, the 2014 World Cup is scheduled to be staged all across the country in 12 different cities: Belo Horizonte, Brasília, Cuiabá, Curitiba, Fortaleza, Manaus, Natal, Porto Alegre, Recife, Rio de Janeiro, Salvador and São Paulo. Normally host nations hold the event in only eight to 10 cities, but because of Brazil's great size and its number of significant cities, FIFA granted an exemption.

Much work and expense lies ahead with stadium construction and remodeling. Another huge sum is earmarked for infrastructure projects, including upgrading ports, highways and 10 of the host cities' airports (most importantly Rio's and São Paulo's) to cope with the huge influx of fans – an estimated 500,000 visitors. In January 2010, Brazil drew up a list of projected spending (two years after it was scheduled to), declaring that the federal government would spend US$7.4 billion on transport, infrastructure and oversight and that Brazilian states and municipalities in charge of hosting matches will spend US$3.9 billion on stadiums and facilities.

As of early 2010, Brazil had already fallen behind on its construction schedules, and FIFA had grown increasingly worried that Brazil wouldn't be ready in time for the big event. There is even speculation that Brazil will have to cut its host cities from 12 down to eight or 10. But no matter how it pans out in the end, Brazil is likely to throw a spectacular World Cup – if only for the animation of its fans and for the huge parties that will accompany the event.

Rio for its part will play a starring role in the 2014 World Cup, hosting both the opening match and the final; it will play an even bigger role two years later when it hosts the Summer Olympics. For more details on preparations in the Cidade Maravilhosa, see p126.

The Accidental President of Brazil, by Fernando Henrique Cardoso, is an elucidating memoir by one of Brazil's most popular presidents, a former sociology professor vaulted into power.

a president who really knew what poverty was like. One of 22 children born to a dirt-poor illiterate farm-worker from Brazil's stricken Northeast, Lula had worked as a shoeshine boy, then a mechanic, then a trade-union leader.

His accession initially alarmed investors, who had envisioned a left-leaning renegade running the economy amok. In fact, he surprised friends and foes alike with one of the most financially prudent administrations in years, while still addressing Brazil's egregious social problems.

Lula managed Brazil's budget prudently enough to repay the country's entire US$15 billion debt to the International Monetary Fund (IMF) ahead of schedule in 2005. Lula's antipoverty program of Fome Zero (Zero Hunger) collapsed under poor management, though its successor Bolsa Família

2002	2003	2005
After four unsuccessful attempts, Luíz Inácio 'Lula' da Silva is elected president. The former union leader serves a moderate first term, despite upper-class fears of radical agendas. Brazil wins its fifth World Cup title.	President Lula launches the Bolsa Família program of cash payments to 11 million of Brazil's poorest families. The social program is credited with reducing poverty by 27% during Lula's first term.	American missionary nun Dorothy Stang is murdered by a local rancher. Her strong support of indigent farmers' rights and for protecting the rain forest earned her the nickname 'Angel of the Amazon'.

(Family Purse) did bring hardship relief to more than 11 million families – about one-fifth of the population.

In 2006, Lula's popularity and commitment to social issues helped him sail to victory. He made employment a top priority. According to government reports, during Lula's two-term administration an astounding 14 million jobs were created – 11 million in the 'formal economy'. Lula also raised the minimum wage by 25%, which had an immediate impact on many working families, while the percentage of Brazilians living in 'extreme poverty' went from 20% to 11%. Add to that the estimate of some 19 million Brazilians entering the middle class during Lula's two terms.

Unfortunately, Lula's administration had some setbacks, including a wide-reaching corruption scandal in 2005 that saw a number of his PT party members resigning in disgrace, though the scandal never quite touched the president – his approval rating reached 90% at one point. Meanwhile, urban violence continued to rage in slum areas, though even blighted favelas saw some improvements over the last decade, with projects helping to bring sewer systems, transportation and other essential infrastructures to some of Brazil's poorest urban communities. Meanwhile, the economic disparity between rich and poor still remains shockingly wide.

As Lula prepared to leave office in 2010, Brazil's economic prosperity was clear. Brazil became a net foreign creditor (as opposed to debtor) for the first time in 2008 and the country weathered the economic recession at the end of the decade better than any other developing country. By 2020, São Paulo is expected to be the 13th richest city in the world. Despite all the good economic news, many in the middle class and intellectuals believe Lula is merely sailing on the glory of policies and successes originally initiated by his predecessor, Cardoso. As Lula hands the reins off to his successor, Brazil's future looks bright, but as history has proved, administration change always keeps Brasileiros guessing.

Two recent books look at one of Brazil's most popular presidents: Richard Bourne's *Lula of Brazil: The Story So Far* (2008), and *Lula and the Workers Party in Brazil* (2003) by Sue Branford.

In 2009, the Brazilian real was the best-performing currency in the world having rallied more than 100% against the US dollar since President Lula took office in 2003.

2005	2006	2007
Brazil repays its entire debt to the International Monetary Fund (IMF) – US$15 billion – ahead of schedule. Lula presides over good economic times, with low inflation, a raised minimum wage and surging growth rates.	Despite a cash-for-votes corruption scandal in his party, Lula is reelected president. During his second (and final) term, which ends in 2010, Lula presides over continued economic growth, and he enjoys record-high approval ratings.	Rio erupts in celebration when Brazil wins the right to host the 2014 FIFA World Cup, and will showcase the world's most famous football tournament for the first time in 64 years. Two years later, Rio is named as the host city for the 2016 Olympics.

The Culture

THE NATIONAL PSYCHE

Brazilians are known for lively celebrations (Carnaval is but one manifestation), which generally becomes more animated the further north you go. This joie de vivre can be seen in football matches, on the beaches, in the samba clubs and on the streets. The flip side of this trait is *saudade*, that woeful manifestation of homesickness, longing or deep regret, given much play on old bossa nova records.

In a land of profound diversity, the Brazilians themselves exhibit some deep contradictions. A landscape of beaches, mountains and forests that is universally praised receives incredible destruction (the Amazon) – and indifference – from its citizens; Brazilian racial harmony is a widely accepted ideal, yet blacks are egregiously underrepresented in the government and suffer the lion's share of poverty; Carnaval is a time of wild freedom, while sexual repressiveness lurks the rest of the year.

Perhaps owing to the incredible diversity of the population, it's possible to find Brazilians who profess to be Catholics while also attending a Candomblé ceremony (p62) from time to time, who believe in science and market economies while nurturing beliefs in mystics and fatalism.

Contradictions are most severe in the social-class system, where you can find poor and rich living in close proximity, often separated by nothing more than a highway. It's not surprising then that violence is such a prevalent facet of Brazilian society. Nearly every Carioca (Rio resident) and Paulistano (São Paulo city resident) has a horror story of getting mugged. The response is often one of resignation and 'What can be done?'.

Indeed, there is much resignation in the national character. Some suggest this is a holdover from the military dictatorship that ruled people's lives for 20 years (from 1964–84), creating a docile public. But Brazilians have been a nonconfrontational people since the beginning of the republic. Brazil was the only country in Latin America to gain its independence without spilling a drop of blood, and slavery ended in 1888 (the last in the Americas) without battles or violent showdowns.

In a country noted for its bureaucracy (the legacy of the dictatorship), Brazilians have to put up with serious inefficiencies. This has led to some rather creative solutions to one's problems. There's the official way of doing something, and then there's the *jeitinho*, that characteristically Brazilian way around it. A few friends, and a bit of good humor, can go a long way.

LIFESTYLE

Constructing a portrait of the typical Brazilian is a complicated task, given the wide mix of social, cultural and economic factors in play. One thing that everyone agrees on is the huge chasm separating rich from poor.

The country's middle and upper class live in comfortable apartments or houses, with all the trappings of the first world, including good health care in private clinics, cars, vacation homes and easy access to the latest gadgets and trends (though prices for luxury goods are much higher here, eg 16GB iPhones without a plan cost R$1850). The wealthiest send their children to private schools and abroad to university. Maids are common – even among middle-class Brazilians – and some families have chauffeurs and cooks. Depending on where one lives in the country, crime is likely to be of high concern. Those who can take extra precautions, opting for high-security buildings or even hiring bodyguards.

Meeting Brazilians: one kiss on each cheek for ladies (start at the left – her right); a handshake between gents. The same holds true when bidding goodbye.

Many uncontacted indigenous groups still live in the Amazon. In 2007, 89 Metyktire suddenly emerged in a village in Pará, the first time this particular group (feared dead) had been encountered since 1950.

Somewhere below the elite are working-class folks struggling to put food on the table and pay the rent; the children tend to live at home until they are married. Couples tend to marry younger.

At the bottom of the socioeconomic ladder are *favelados* (slum dwellers), who live in self-constructed housing (usually boxy concrete or brick dwellings) in crowded makeshift communities. Ranging in size from a few thousand inhabitants to well over 50,000, favelas are found in nearly every urban area in Brazil. Most residents have electricity and running water, though open sewers run through many favelas. Many favelas are also built on hillsides, making them susceptible to landslides during heavy rains. Access to education, adequate health care, transportation and other essential infrastructure can often be limited, though this is slowly changing under government-funded favela improvement schemes. The favelas are often 'governed' by drug lords and their gangs, who are frequently the communities' only benefactors. They often try to paint themselves as 'Robin Hood' types, complete with pithy slogans about peace and justice. Dangers to residents come during gun battles with police or when rival gangs move in.

How to Be a Carioca, by Priscilla Ann Goslin, is a humorous portrait of the Rio dweller, with tongue-in-cheek riffs on beach-going, driving, soap operas, football and Carioca slang.

In the countryside, conditions for the poor can be even worse. Unequal land distribution dating back to the colonial era means that thousands of homeless rural families are left to squat on vacant land or work long hours as itinerant laborers for low wages.

Former President Lula, who grew up among such poverty, has made some improvements in bringing relief to the neediest. His raising of the minimum wage by 25% and the creation of Bolsa Família (Family Grant) has helped millions of Brazilians; some 10.4 million Brazilians have emerged from poverty-level conditions in the past 10 years, according to a UN report published in 2010.

ECONOMY

If you haven't heard by now, Brazil is booming. One of the four BRIC countries (along with Russia, India and China), Brazil was highlighted by economists at the turn of the century as a developing country with enormous economic potential. Since then, Brazil's growth has reached stratospheric heights, with an ever-expanding presence in world markets that has helped make Brazil Latin America's biggest economy – by a wide margin.

Brazil fared relatively well during the global financial crisis of 2008–09. The nation suffered a mild recession in 2009, with GDP contracting by 0.2% – the first time its economy contracted in 17 years. In 2010, however, the economy was already on the rebound (indeed, it was one of the first emerging markets to begin a recovery), with Brazilian Finance Minister Guido Mantega predicting over 5% growth during the course of the year.

THE LOVE MOTEL

Something of a Brazilian institution, the love motel provides a discreet meeting place for a rendezvous. Visited by all rungs of society, love motels are found in every part of the country. Some are designed with lavish facades – decked out to resemble medieval castles, Roman temples or ancient pyramids – while others blend more subtly into the landscape. Inside, rooms come standard with mirror-covered ceilings, heart-shaped beds, rose-tinted lighting, Jacuzzis, televisions loaded with porn channels, dual-headed showers and a bedside menu of sex toys (and food). In many countries, love motels scream seediness, but in Brazil they are viewed as colorful but perfectly acceptable places. People need a place for their liaisons – they might as well have a laugh and a bit of fun while they're at it.

The recovery indeed was strong: in the first four months in 2010, Brazil created 962,000 new formal-sector jobs – the highest figure ever recorded. Sales of computers and cars are booming, construction is up, and more and more flights (and even a few airlines) have appeared in recent years as more cash-flush Brazilians take to the skies. Brazil also has a strong industrial sector, accounting for 26% of GDP, and is involved in a wide range of industries including automobiles, aircraft, computers, steel and petrochemicals. Oil and other natural resources have also boosted the economy – in particular the massive underwater oil fields discovered in 2007 that could hold more than nine billion barrels of oil. The discovery has helped transform Brazil's state-owned Petrobras into a global player.

Despite his left-leaning roots, Lula ran a fiscally conservative administration, focusing on improving the public-debt ratio, and also attracting investment.

The growth has been particularly strong in agribusiness, which employs about 20% of the country's 95-million-strong workforce and has led to record trade surpluses in recent years. Today Brazil is the world's biggest exporter of sugar, coffee, orange juice, soy and beef, and a major producer of corn, cotton and other crops.

While Brazil has rarely been a source of innovation, it has put technology to creative uses in recent years – most notably in the realm of biofuel. During the oil crisis in the 1970s, Brazil transformed its sugarcane into an alternative fuel: ethanol. See the boxed text, p122 for the lowdown.

Economic management has been good, but public debt still remains high, which strains government finances and threatens social security and other important safety nets. This is one of the key issues in Brazil's continued economic health for the future: maintaining sufficient growth to generate employment and reducing government debt. Environmentalists also point out that Brazil's growth in agribusiness has led to the continued destruction of the rain forest. The high price for soybean products, for instance, has led to huge tracts of forest being chain-sawed to make way for fields, a practice with enormously damaging implications for Brazil's environment. See the boxed text, p98 for some dramatic new strategies underway.

POPULATION

Brazil is the world's fifth most populous country, but it also has one of the smallest population densities, with around 24 people per sq km. Most of Brazil's population lives along the coast, particularly in the South and Southeast, home to 75% of the country's inhabitants. Until the mid-20th century, Brazil was largely a rural country – today, its population is more than 70% urban. The population in cities has exploded in the last half-century, though growth is slowing.

The Northeast has the highest concentration of Afro-Brazilians, with Salvador as its cultural capital. In the Amazon live Caboclos (literally 'copper-colored'), the mixed descendants of indigenous peoples and the Portuguese. In the South is the most European of the Brazilian population, descendants of Italian and German immigrants. Overall the population is 54% white, 6% black, 39% mixed and 1% other (including Japanese, Arabs and indigenous groups).

While there is much more mixing between races, Brazil is a long way from being a color-blind society. Afro-Brazilians make up the bulk of low-paid workers, and are far more likely to live in favelas than in middle-class neighborhoods. More than 60% of Afro-Brazilians live in poverty. Afro-Brazilians die younger than whites, earn less and have a greater risk of going to prison. Only 6% of university students are black – though a new quota system

Greater São Paulo had 2.2 million residents in 1950, compared to 20 million today.

The 1979–83 droughts in the Northeast were among the worst the country has ever experienced, leaving between 250,000 and one million people dead.

launched in 2003 (and still bogged down in Congress) aims to create more opportunities for young Afro-Brazilians. A black political representative or even a high-ranking black employee is a rarity – clear examples of the lack of opportunities for blacks in Brazil.

The indigenous population today numbers between 400,000 and 600,000, comprising 200 tribes – a fraction of the estimated two million or more in Brazil at the time of European arrival. Customs and beliefs vary widely from tribe to tribe – as do the strengths of these traditions in the face of expulsion from traditional lands, declining numbers, missionary activity and other influences. Brazil's largest groups of *índios* (Indians; indigenous people) include the Tikuna on the upper Rio Solimões (numbering 20,000 or more), the Yanomami in northwestern Amazonia (more than 11,000), and the 30,000 or so Guarani in the Central West and South.

After centuries of genocidal attacks, slavery, dispossession and death from imported diseases, Brazil's indigenous population is growing again but still faces a host of problems. Most of them live in the Amazon rain forest, and therefore the threats that the rain forest faces – logging, mining, ranching, farming, roads, settlements, dams, hydroelectric schemes – also threaten the *índios* whose way of life depends on it.

Survival International (www.survival-international.org) is a good source of information on indigenous Brazilians.

MULTICULTURALISM

Brazilian identity has been shaped not only by the Portuguese, who provided its language and main religion, but also by native *índios*, Africans and the many immigrants over the years from Europe, the Middle East and Asia.

Indigenous culture, though often ignored or denigrated by urban Brazilians, has helped shape modern Brazil and its legends, dance and music. Many indigenous foods and beverages, such as tapioca, manioc (cassava), potatoes, maté and guaraná (a shrub whose berry is a stimulant; also a popular soft drink) have become staples.

The influence of African culture is also evident, especially in the Northeast. The slaves imported by the Portuguese brought with them their religion, music and cuisine, all of which have become a part of Brazilian identity.

Brazil had several waves of voluntary immigration. After the end of slavery in 1888, millions of Europeans were recruited to work in the coffee fields. The largest contingent was from Italy (some one million arrived between 1890 and 1920), but there were also many Portuguese and Spaniards, and smaller groups of Germans and Russians.

The Ukrainian community in Brazil numbers 550,000, the majority of whom live in the South. Prudentópolis is a city of Orthodox churches and Slavic features, with 75% of the population of Ukrainian descent.

Immigration is only part of the picture when considering Brazil's diversity. Brazilians are just as likely to mention regional types, often accompanied by their own colorful stereotypes. Caboclos, who are descendents of the *índio*, live along the rivers in the Amazon region and keep alive the traditions and stories of their ancestors. *Gaúchos* populate Rio Grande do Sul, speak a Spanish-inflected Portuguese and can't quite shake the reputation for being rough-edged cowboys. By contrast, Baianos, descendents of the first Africans in Brazil, are stereotyped for being the most extroverted and celebratory of Brazilians. Mineiros (residents of Minas Gerais state) are considered more serious and reserved than Brazil's coastal dwellers, while Sertanejos (residents of the backlands – called *sertão* – of the Northeast) are dubbed tough-skinned individuals with strong folk traditions. Cariocas (residents of Rio city) are superficial beach bums according to Paulistanos (residents of São Paulo city), who are often denigrated as being workaholics with no zeal for life – a rivalry that anyone who's lived in LA or New York can understand.

Japanese immigration began in 1908, and today São Paulo has the world's largest Japanese community outside of Japan.

Today there are dozens of terms to describe Brazilians' various racial compositions, and it is not uncommon for apparently white Brazilians to have a mix of European, African and indigenous ancestors. Yet, despite appearances of integration and racial harmony, underneath is a brutal reality. Although blacks and mulattoes account for 45% of the population, they are sorely underrepresented in government and business, and often see little hope of rising out of poverty. The indigenous are even more openly discriminated against, continuing a cycle that began with the genocidal policies of the first Europeans.

SPORTS

For insight into what's happening in the Brazilian football scene – from player news to upcoming matches – visit http://en.sambafoot.com.

Brazil's selection to host the 2014 World Cup has given a huge psychological boost to the nation, which hasn't staged the massive event since 1950. Brazil plans to spend US$1 billion on the big event and hopes to attract half a million visitors (see the boxed text, p54). The other big sporting news is Rio's winning bid for the Summer Olympics in 2016. Although it's still years away, enormous preparations are already underway (see the boxed text, p126).

Football (Soccer)

Football (*futebol* to Brazilians) was introduced in the 1890s when a young student from São Paulo, Charles Miller, returned from studies in England with two footballs and a rule book and began to organize the first league. It quickly became the national passion, and Brazil is the only country to have won five World Cups. The rest of the world acknowledges that Brazilians are among the best footballers, and Brazilians are, to put it mildly, insane about the sport.

No one goes to work on big international game days, a situation that the government – which is prepared to spend whatever it takes to win a World Cup – laments. Since Brazil's unexpected loss to France in the 1998 World Cup final, some of the shady business that goes on behind the soccer scenes has started to come to light, and parliamentary commissions have investi-

---

BRAZILIAN FOOTBALL: THE CLUBS

Apart from a couple of short breaks for the Christmas–New Year holiday and Carnaval, professional club competitions go on all year. If you get a chance, see a game live; there's no experience quite like it. Keep in mind that five new stadiums are under construction and some listed here may be closed for upgrades in preparation for the World Cup in 2014. Check with the local tourist office for the latest game and stadium information.

Club	Home city	Stadium (capacity)	Jerseys
Bahia	Salvador	Pituaçu (34,000)	white
Botafogo	Rio de Janeiro	João Havelange (45,000)	black & white stripes
Corinthians	São Paulo	Pacaembu (40,000)	white; black collar
Cruzeiro	Belo Horizonte	Mineirão (90,000)	blue
Flamengo	Rio de Janeiro	Maracanã (80,000)*	red; black hoops
Fluminense	Rio de Janeiro	Maracanã (80,000)*	red, green & white stripes
Grêmio	Porto Alegre	Olímpico (50,000)	blue, black & white stripes
Internacional	Porto Alegre	Beira-Rio (60,000)	red
Palmeiras	São Paulo	Parque Antarctica (32,000)	green
Santa Cruz	Recife	Arruda (66,000)	white; black & red hoops
Santos	Santos	Vila Belmiro (26,000)	white
São Paulo	São Paulo	Morumbi (80,000)	white; red & black hoops
Sport	Recife	Ilha do Retiro (50,000)	red & black hoops
Vasco da Gama	Rio de Janeiro	São Januário (35,000)	white; black slash

*Games likely to be held at João Havelange stadium while Maracanã is being renovated.

gated corruption in football. The fans may criticize the way football is run, but nothing dims their intense passion for the game itself.

Until recently, most of the best players left Brazil for more lucrative contracts with European clubs. Since 2008, however, many big Brazilian stars have returned home to play for more adoring fans and not insubstantial salaries. Ronaldo, who returned from AC Milan to play for São Paulo's Corinthians, earned US$10 million on licensing and new sponsorship in 2009. Other Brazilian stars to return in recent years include Adriano (who left Inter Milan to play for Flamengo), Robinho (left Man United to play for Santos), Edmilson (left Villareal to join Palmeiras), Frederico Chaves Guedes (aka 'Fred,' who left Lyon to play for Fluminense) and Roberto Carlos (a former Real Madrid player who now plays for Corinthians).

Brazilian footballers play in some pretty far-flung destinations, including Albania, India, Botswana, Iran, Liechtenstein, Indonesia and even the Faroe Islands.

Volleyball

Volleyball is Brazil's second sport (both men's and women's teams were ranked number one in 2010 according to the *Federation Internationale de Volleyball's* world ranking). A natural for the beach, it's also a popular spectator sport on TV. A local variation you'll see on Rio's beaches is *futevôlei* (volleyball played without hands), only for the most talented of players.

MEDIA

Brazil has a vigorous media, and anything vaguely controversial – whether political or social in nature – will garner serious attention by the Brazilian press. There is substantial press freedom today, although the nation does have some antiquated press laws left over from the military dictatorship (for instance 'crimes of opinion,' ie published articles that besmirch the names of government officials, are criminal offences).

Today Brazil's most successful media conglomerate is Rede Globo, the world's third-largest TV network (behind NBC and CBS) and watched by more than 120 million people daily. TV is by far the biggest form of media in Brazil, though radio is also popular (with thousands of radio stations nationwide), and there are hundreds of dailies across the country.

Until the 1990s, the media and political demagogues worked hand in hand. Shortly after radio arrived in Brazil in the 1930s, President Getúlio Vargas initiated weekday transmissions of the *Voice of Brazil* as a means of distilling government propaganda to the people. The rise of Brazil's great media mogul Roberto Marinho – who went on to found Globo – was largely assisted by his decision not to criticize the fascistic regimes of the military government from 1964 to 1984. Other newspapers simply foundered if anything remotely critical of the government was published.

For information on press freedom in Brazil and other countries, visit www.rsf.org, the website of the international watchdog association, Reporters Without Borders (available in English, Spanish and French).

RELIGION

Officially, Brazil is a Catholic country and claims the largest Catholic population of any country in the world. But Brazil is also noted for the diversity and syncretism of its many sects and religions, which offer great flexibility to their followers.

Brazil's principal religious roots have been the animism of the indigenous people, Catholicism, and African cults brought by the blacks during the period of slavery. The colonists prohibited slaves from practicing their religions, just as they forbade music and dance for fear that they would reinforce the group identity of the captives. Religious persecution led to religious syncretism: to avoid persecution the slaves gave Catholic names and identities to all their African gods. This was generally done by finding the similarities between the Catholic images and the *orixás* (deities) of Candomblé. Thus the slaves worshiped their own deities behind representations of Catholic saints.

In the 19th century Brazil wrote freedom of religion into its constitution, but the African cults continued to suffer persecution for many years. Candomblé was seen by white elites as charlatanism that displayed the ignorance of the poorest classes. But the spectrum of religious life was gradually broadened by the addition of *índio* animism to Afro-Catholic syncretism, and by the increasing fascination of whites with the spiritualism of Kardecism.

Today large numbers of converts are being attracted to Evangelical Christianity, to the Afro-Brazilian cults, and to spiritualist or mystic sects.

Christianity

Catholicism retains its status as Brazil's official religion, but is declining in popularity. Many people now merely turn up to church for the basics: baptism, marriage and burial. Evangelical Christianity, however, is booming. All over Brazil, especially in poorer communities where people are most desperate, you will come across simple, recently built churches full of worshippers. Sometimes there will be two or three rival Evangelical churches on the same street, going by names such as the Assembléia de Deus (Assembly of God), Igreja Pentecostal Deus é Amor (God is Love Pentecostal Church) and even the Igreja do Evangelho Quadrangular (Church of the Quadrangular Gospel). In one, worshippers may be moaning and speaking in tongues, in another they'll simply be listening to the stern words of a preacher.

Note: In this book you will find the abbreviation NS used for 'Nossa Senhora' (Our Lady) or 'Nosso Senhor' (Our Lord), for example NS do Pilar.

Afro-Brazilian Cults
CANDOMBLÉ

Sacred Leaves of Candomblé, by Robert Voeks, is a nonacademic work on cultural anthropology and ethnobotany. Voeks explores medicinal plants used in Candomblé and the survival of Afro-Brazilian religion in Brazil.

Candomblé is the most orthodox of the religions brought from Africa by the Nago, Yoruba and Jeje peoples. Candomblé is an African word denoting a dance in honor of the gods, and is a general term for the religion. Afro-Brazilian rituals are directed by a *pai de santo* or *mãe de santo* (literally saint's father or mother – the Candomblé priests) and practiced in a *casa de santo* or *terreiro* (house of worship). This is where the initiation of novices takes place as well as consultations and rituals. The ceremonies are conducted in the Yoruba language.

The religion centers upon the *orixás*. Like the gods in Greek mythology, each *orixá* has a unique personality and history. Although *orixás* are divided into male and female types, there are some that can switch from one sex to the other, such as Logunedé, son of two male gods, Ogun and Oxoss, or Oxumaré, who is male for six months of the year and female for the other six months. (Candomblé, not surprisingly, is much more accepting of homosexuality and bisexuality than other religions.)

Candomblé followers believe that every person has a particular deity watching over them – from birth until death. A person's *orixá* can be identified when a *pai* or *mãe de santo* makes successive throws with a handful of *búzios* (shells), in a divination ritual known as Jogo dos Búzios (Casting of Shells). The position of the shells is used to interpret one's luck, one's future and one's past relationship with the gods.

To keep themselves strong and healthy, followers of Candomblé give food or other offerings to their respective *orixá*. The offering depends on the *orixá's* particular preferences. For example, to please Iemanjá, the goddess or queen of the sea, one should give perfumes, white and blue flowers, rice and fried fish. Oxalá, the greatest deity, the god and owner of the sun, eats cooked white corn. Oxúm, god of fresh waters and waterfalls, is famous for his vanity. He should be honored with earrings, necklaces, mirrors, perfumes, champagne and honey. Whichever god is receiving the offering, Exú must first be appeased, as he serves as the messenger between the individual and the god. Exú, incidentally, likes *cachaça* (high-proof sugarcane alcohol) and other alcoholic drinks, cigarettes and cigars, strong perfumes and meats.

In Bahia and Rio, followers of Afro-Brazilian cults turn out in huge numbers for the festival held during the night of December 31 and on New Year's Day. Millions of Brazilians go to the beach at this time to pay homage to Iemanjá. Flowers, perfumes, fruits and even jewelry are tossed into the sea to please the mother of the waters, or to gain protection and good luck in the new year.

UMBANDA & QUIMBANDA (MACUMBA)

Umbanda (white magic) is a mixture of Candomblé and spiritualism with Angolan/Bantu roots. The ceremony, conducted in Portuguese, incorporates figures from all the Brazilian ethnicities: Prêto Velho (the old black slave), O Caboclo (an *índio* – in this context) and other *índio* deities, O Guerreiro (the white warrior), and so on. Umbanda is less structured than Candomblé, and rituals vary from region to region. Some sects tend toward practices found in Kardecism (contacting spirits, seances), while others feature more straightforward praying or preaching by the *pai* or *mãe de santo*.

Quimbanda, a form of black magic, is the evil counterpart to Umbanda. Its rituals involve lots of blood, animal sacrifice and nasty deeds, and it's technically illegal. The religion is also known as Macumba.

Kardecism

During the 19th century, Allan Kardec, the French spiritual master, introduced spiritualism to Brazilian whites in a palatable form.

Kardec's teachings, which incorporated some Eastern religious ideas into a European framework, are now followed by a small percentage of Brazilians. Kardecism emphasizes parlor seances, multiple reincarnations and speaking to the dead. Kardec's writings on his teachings include *The Book of Spirits* and *The Book of Mediums*.

Other Cults

A few indigenous rites have become popularized among Brazilians without being incorporated into Afro-Brazilian cults. The cults União da Vegetal (in Brasília, São Paulo and the South) and Santo Daime (centered in Acre and Amazonas states) are both based on consumption of the hallucinogenic drink *ayahuasca*, which has been used for centuries by indigenous peoples of South America. *Ayahuasca* aside, these cults are very straight, dictating that moral behavior and dress follow strict codes. The government tolerates the use of *ayahuasca* in these religious ceremonies, and tightly controls its production and supply.

The cult of Santo Daime was founded in 1930 in Rio Branco, Acre, by Raimundo Irineu Serra, a rubber tapper who had been initiated into the use of *ayahuasca* by *índios* on the Acre–Peru border. In visions he received instructions to set up a base near Rio Branco to spread the doctrine of *ayahuasca*. The name Santo Daime comes from the wording of the cult's prayers, '*Dai-me força, dai-me luz…*' ('Give me strength, give me light…'). Santo Daime and União da Vegetal together have between 10,000 and 20,000 members. Santo Daime's two major communities are Ceú do Mapiá in Amazonas and Colônia Cinco Mil, near Rio Branco.

The Brasília area, believed by some to be especially propitious for supernatural contact, has syncretic cults that can be visited near the city in Vale do Amanhecer (Valley of the Dawn) and Cidade Eclética (Eclectic City) – see the boxed text, p383.

Serge Bramly's *Macumba* provides a fascinating portrait of the religion; the highlights are interviews with Maria José, a *mãe de santo* (saint's mother), who explains the philosophy, history and practice of Macumba.

For info on the relationship between psycho-active plants and mystical experiences, read the excellent *Cleansing the Doors of Perception*, written by Huston Smith, one of the great scholars on world religions.

WOMEN IN BRAZIL

Brazil had one of the earliest feminist movements in Latin America, and women were among the first in the region to gain the right to vote, in 1932. Today there is a growing number of feminist NGOs, dedicated to educating women about their legal rights and family planning, while also training police how to handle cases of domestic violence. In Brasília there's even a feminist lobby (Feminist Center for Studies and Advising); it has a Portuguese-language website, www.cfemea.org.br.

Domesticas (Maids), the first film by Fernando Meirelles, delves into the lives of five women who work as *domesticas*, creating a compelling portrait of Brazil's often overlooked underclass.

In spite of advances, many *machista* (chauvinist) stereotypes persist, and women are still sorely underrepresented in positions of power. Only about 12% of senators and 9% of deputies in the lower house are women, which is one of the lowest figures in Latin America (where women on average make up 24% of the legislature). Should Lula's handpicked female successor Dilma Rousseff win the presidential election, it could be a major impetus for breaking down barriers for women.

In other spheres, women represent 40% of the workforce – a huge leap from decades past but still below the average in Latin America (where women comprise 52% of the workforce). Unfortunately, the wage gap remains high, with men earning 30% more than women of the same age and income level.

Benedita da Silva: An Afro-Brazilian Woman's Story of Politics and Love is the memoir of Brazil's first Afro-Brazilian female senator, detailing her rise from the favelas to becoming an important political voice.

Instances of domestic abuse are frighteningly common (one report stated that every 15 seconds a woman is beaten in Brazil). In response, the first women's police station opened in 1990 specifically to handle violence against women. Today there are more than 250 women's police stations, largely staffed by female police officers.

Women receive 120 days of paid maternity leave (men receive seven days of paternity leave). Abortions are still illegal in Brazil (except in cases of rape and maternal health risks), and an estimated one million are performed each year, often with substantial health risks. More than 200,000 women each year are hospitalized from clandestine abortions.

ARTS
Music & Dance

Few countries in the world can compete with Brazil's rich musical heritage. Music here is a deeply ingrained part of life, a form of both celebration and escape, and is heard everywhere. Perhaps because of its African roots, Brazilian music is a collective community act, a *festa* (party), and is virtually inseparable from dancing.

MORE TV, LESS CHILDREN

Despite a strong religious culture that condemns family planning, the birth rate in Brazil has declined significantly in the last 30 years – going from an average of 4.3 births per woman in 1980 (from a more startling 6.3 in 1963) to 2.2 in 2010. This precipitous drop is similar to that found in China, yet Brazil has never had a government-promoted policy on family planning.

Curiously, a study in 2009 made a correlation between low fertility rates and the availability of the Globo TV signal. It suggested that one of the main game-changers in the realm of declining birth rates was the *telenovela*, or Brazilian soap opera. These enormously popular shows champion female characters who either have no children or very few children (one or two). The TV or *telenovela* influence is also found to impact divorce rates and in the preponderance of children named after characters on the shows. In a society where TV has long filled the place of books and newspapers, the social impact of the shows can't be discounted. After one show that featured a young girl preparing for chemotherapy, over 20,000 bone-marrow donations were prompted in the following month.

Shaped by the mixing of varied influences from three continents, Brazilian popular music has always been characterized by great diversity. The *samba canção* (samba song), for example, is a mixture of Spanish bolero with the cadences and rhythms of African music. Bossa nova was influenced by samba and North American music, particularly jazz. *Tropicália* mixed influences ranging from bossa nova and Italian ballads to blues and North American rock. Brazil is still creating new and original musical forms today.

SAMBA, PAGODE & CHORO

The birth of modern Brazilian music essentially began with the birth of samba, first heard in the early 20th century in a Rio neighborhood near present-day Praça Onze. Here, Bahian immigrants formed a tightly knit community in which traditional African customs thrived – music, dance and the Candomblé religion. Local homes provided the setting for impromptu performances and the exchange of ideas among Rio's first great instrumentalists. Such an atmosphere nurtured the likes of Pixinguinha, one of samba's founding fathers, as well as Donga, one of the composers of 'Pelo Telefone,' the first recorded samba song (in 1917) and an enormous success at the then-fledgling Carnaval.

Samba continued to evolve in the homes and *botequims* (bars with table service) around Rio. The 1930s are known as the golden age of samba. By this point, samba's popularity had spread beyond the working-class neighborhoods of central Rio, and the music evolved at the same time into diverse, less-percussive styles of samba. Sophisticated lyricists such as Dorival Caymmi, Ary Barroso and Noel Rosa popularized *samba canção*, melody-driven samba laid over African percussion. (For insight into Noel Rosa's poetically charged and tragically brief life, check out the 2006 film *Noel: Poeta da Vila.*) Songs in this style featured sentimental lyrics and an emphasis on melody (rather than rhythm), foreshadowing the later advent of cool bossa nova. Carmen Miranda, one of the big radio stars of the 1930s, would become one of the first ambassadors of Brazilian music.

The 1930s were also the golden age of samba songwriting for Carnaval. *Escolas de samba* (samba schools or clubs), which first emerged in 1928, soon became a vehicle for samba songwriting, and by the 1930s samba and Carnaval would be forever linked. Today's theme songs still borrow from that golden epoch.

Great *sambistas* (samba singers) continued to emerge in Brazil over the next few decades, although other emerging musical styles diluted their popularity. Artists such as Cartola, Nelson Cavaquinho and Clementina de Jesus made substantial contributions to both samba and styles of music that followed from samba.

Traditional samba went through a rebirth a little over a decade ago with the opening of old-style *gafieiras* (dance halls) in Lapa. Today, Rio is once again awash with great *sambistas*. Classic *sambistas* such as Alcione and Beth Carvalho still perform, while rising stars such as Teresa Christina and Grupo Semente are intimately linked to Lapa's rebirth. Other talents to look out for on Rio's stages include Thais Villela, a rising star on the Lapa scene, and Diogo Nogueira, the deep-voiced samba son of legendary singer João Nogueira. Another singer carrying on the tradition of her father is Mart'nália, daughter of samba legend Martinho da Vila. Check out her 2006 album *Menino do Rio*.

Another popular artist still active in Rio is Maria Rita, the talented singer and songwriter whose voice is remarkably similar to that of her late mother, Elis Regina – one of Brazil's all-time greats. Although Rita's work often falls

For an excellent overview of Brazilian music, from the great funk albums of the '60s to more recent talents, visit www.slip cue.com/music/brazil /brazillist.html. The site www.allbrazilianmusic .com is also useful.

Journalist, author and former dancer Alma Guillermoprieto vividly captures life in Rio's Mangueira *favela* and preparation for the big Carnaval parade in her well-written book *Samba*.

into the Música Popular Brasileira (MPB) camp, her 2007 album *Samba Meu Samba Meu* is still her best, with a brilliant collection of sambas.

Pagode is a style that branched off from samba and emerged in Rio in the 1970s. This informal, backyard-party samba features the *cavaquinho* (a small four-string guitar, a relative of the ukulele) and a few informal percussion instruments. The style is relaxed, rhythmic and melodic and enjoys widespread popularity. Beth Carvalho (also the queen of *samba canção*), Jorge Aragão and Zeca Pagodinho were pioneer *pagode* singers and are still going strong.

Choro is a slightly more distant relative of samba. Characterized by its jazzy sound, melodic leaps and sometimes rapid-fire tempo, *choro* is mostly instrumental music and highly improvisational. It's played on the *cavaquinho* or guitar alongside a recorder or flute. The flutist Pixinguinha (1898–1973) is one of the great legends of *choro*, while today's lions include Paulinho da Viola and Paulo Moura, a saxophonist and master of *choro* rhythms.

The Brazilian Sound, by Chris McGowan and Ricardo Pessanha, is a well-illustrated, readable introduction to Brazilian music, with insight into regional styles and musicians (big-name and obscure). Useful discography included.

BOSSA NOVA

In the 1950s came bossa nova (literally, new wave), sparking a new era of Brazilian music. Bossa nova's founders – songwriter and composer Antônio Carlos (Tom) Jobim and guitarist João Gilberto, in association with the lyricist-poet Vinícius de Moraes – slowed down and altered the basic samba rhythm to create a more intimate, harmonic style. This initiated a new style of playing instruments and of singing.

Bossa nova's seductive melodies were very much linked to Rio's Zona Sul, where most bossa musicians lived. Songs such as Jobim's 'Corcovado' and Roberto Meneschal's 'Rio' evoked an almost nostalgic portrait of the city with their quiet lyricism. Bossa nova was also associated with the new class of university-educated Brazilians, and its lyrics reflected the optimistic mood of the middle class in the 1950s.

By the 1960s bossa nova had become a huge international success. The genre's initial development was greatly influenced by American jazz and blues, and over time the bossa nova style came to influence those musical styles in turn. Bossa nova classics were adopted, adapted and recorded by such musical luminaries as Frank Sinatra, Ella Fitzgerald and Stan Getz, among others.

Bossa Nova: The Story of the Brazilian Music that Seduced the World, by Ruy Castro, is an excellent book that captures the vibrant music and its backdrop of 1950s Rio.

In addition to the founding members, other great Brazilian bossa musicians include Marcos Valle, Luiz Bonfá and Baden Powell, whose talented son Marcel Powell carries on the musical tradition. Bands from the 1960s such as Sergio Mendes & Brasil '66 were also quite influenced by bossa nova, as were other artists who fled the repressive military dictatorship to live and play abroad. More recent interpreters of the seductive bossa sound include the Bahian-born Rosa Passos and the Carioca Paula Morelenbaum.

TROPICÁLIA

One of Brazil's unique artistic movements, emerging in the late 1960s, *tropicália* was a direct response to the dictatorship that held power from 1964 to 1984. Leading the movement were Caetano Veloso and Gilberto Gil, making waves with songs of protest against the national regime. (Gil, ironically, is today's much-loved Minister of Culture.) In addition to penning defiant lyrics, *tropicalistas* introduced the public to electric instruments, fragmentary melodies and wildly divergent musical styles. In fact, the *tropicalistas'* hero was poet Oswald de Andrade, whose 1928 *Manifesto Antropofágico* (Cannibalistic Manifesto) supported the idea that anything under the sun could be devoured and recreated in one's music. Hence, the movement fused elements of American rock and roll, blues, jazz and British psychedelic styles into bossa nova and samba rhythms.

Important figures linked to *tropicália* include Gal Costa, Jorge Ben Jor, Maria Bethânia, Os Mutantes and Tom Zé. Although *tropicália* wasn't initially embraced by the public, who objected to the electric and rock elements (in fact, Veloso was booed off the stage on several occasions), by the 1970s its radical ideas had been absorbed and accepted, and lyrics of protest were ubiquitous in songwriting of the time.

While 'pure' *tropicália* bands aren't around anymore, the influence can still be heard in the music of groups such as AfroReggae, one of Rio's leading funk bands.

MÚSICA POPULAR BRASILEIRA (MPB)

Música Popular Brasileira (MPB) is a catchphrase to describe all popular Brazilian music after bossa nova. It includes *tropicália*, *pagode*, and Brazilian pop and rock. All Brazilian music has roots in samba; even in Brazilian rock, heavy metal, disco or pop, the samba sound is often present.

MPB first emerged in the 1970s along with talented musicians such as Edu Lobo, Milton Nascimento, Elis Regina, Djavan and dozens of others, many of whom wrote protest songs not unlike the *tropicalistas*. Chico Buarque is one of the first big names from this epoch, and is one of Brazil's best songwriters. His music career began in 1968 and spanned a time during which many of his songs were banned by the military dictatorship – in fact his music became a symbol of protest during that era.

Jorge Ben Jor is another singer whose career, which began in the 1960s, has survived up to the present day. Highly addictive rhythms are omnipresent in Ben Jor's songs, as he incorporates African beats and elements of funk, samba and blues in his eclectic repertoire. The celebratory album *África Brasil* and his debut album, *Samba Esquema Novo* (with recognizable hits such as 'Mas, Que Nada!'), are among his best.

Salvador-born Carlinhos Brown continues to make immeasurable contributions to Brazilian music, particularly in the realm of Afro-Brazilian rhythms. Some of his best work uses elements from *merengue*, Candomblé and James Brown–style funk. In addition to his popular percussion ensemble Timbalada, he has some excellent albums of his own (notably *Alfagamabetizado*).

> *Tropical Truth: A Story of Music and Revolution in Brazil*, by Caetano Veloso, describes the great artistic experiment of *tropicália* in 1960s Brazil. Although digressive at times, Veloso captures the era's music and politics.

BRAZILIAN ROCK, POP & HIP-HOP

MPB tends to bleed into other genres, particularly into rock and pop. One artist who moves comfortably between genres is Bebel Gilberto (the talented daughter of João Gilberto), who blends bossa nova with modern beats on jazz-inflected bilingual albums like *All in One* (2009). Rio-born Marisa Monte is popular at home and abroad for her fine singing and songwriting. Mixing samba, *forró* (popular music of the Northeast), pop and rock, Marisa has been part of a number of successful collaborations in the music world, most recently with Arnaldo Antunes and Carlinhos Brown to create the hit album *Tribalistas* (2003). Other notable young singers who hail from a bossa line include Roberta Sá (with an excellent live album *Pra se Ter Alegria*, 2009) and Fernanda Porto (whose music is often described as drum 'n' bossa, a blend of electronica and bossa grooves – check out her 2009 album *Auto-Retrato*).

The expat singer-songwriter and performance artist Cibelle incorporates a mix of pop, folk and Brazilian sounds in her lush (mainly English-language) recordings, such as those on *The Shine of Dried Electric Leaves* (2006). She came to prominence as the main vocalist on Suba's noteworthy album *São Paulo Confessions* (1999). An emerging star both at home and abroad, Céu sings dreamlike melodies with elements of *tropicália*, samba, reggae and jazz (indeed, she's hard to peg on her two well-received albums, the latest of which is *Vagarosa*, released in 2009).

> The sensually charged lambada dance craze swept Brazil in the late '80s. It even made a brief international appearance, spurred by laughably bad films such as *Lambada* and *The Forbidden Dance*.

Brazilian hip-hop emerged from the favelas of Rio and São Paulo sometime in the 1980s. Breakout rap artists such as Racionais MCs, from São Paulo, touched a nerve with hard-edged lyrics about life in the *favelas* and in jails. Their 1998 album *Sobrevivendo no Inferno* (Surviving in Hell) sold more than a million copies – a record for independent releases in Brazil. One of the best on the scene today is Marcelo D2 (formerly of Planet Hemp), impressing audiences with albums like *A Procura da Batida Perfeita* (2005) and *Meu Samba é Assim* (2006).

Well known outside of Brazil is Seu Jorge, who starred in the film *Cidade de Deus* (as well as singing brilliant Portuguese versions of Bowie songs on Wes Anderson's film *The Life Aquatic*). His best solo work is *Cru* (2005), an inventive hybrid of hip-hop and ballads, with politically charged beats. The Carioca rapper MV Bill is a man with a message. His songs focus on youth facing the ever-present threats of drugs and violence. He's even written a book *(Falcão – Meninos do Tráfico)* and created a network of youth centers in Rio that offer kids – who might otherwise be on the street – classes in dancing, music and art.

Derived more from English than Amrican rock, this is the least Brazilian of all Brazilian music. Homegrown talents include the group Legião Urbana from Brasília, a national favorite even after the death of its lead singer in 2007. Skank, O Rappa, Os Paralamas Sucesso and the Rio-based Barão Vermelho are other essential names. The versatile and original Ed Motta, from Rio, injects soul, jazz and traditional Brazilian music into rock.

In other genres, indie-rock favorite Los Hermanos is among the best bands competing for airtime. Check out its excellent album *Ventura*. Vanguart, fitting somewhere in the folk-rock genre, is also a group to watch. Its self-titled debut album (2007) channels samba, blues and classic rock. Other recent successes include the saucy girl-band Cansei de Ser Sexy (Tired of Being Sexy), whose 2006 self-titled album blends '80s new wave and electro-pop and features irreverent lyrics (sung in English) and up-tempo beats.

For a more detailed history of Brazilian music, check out Chris McGowan and Ricardo Pessanha's recently updated *The Brazilian Sound* (2008). McGowan's blog, with links to Brazilian artists, is also worth checking out: http://thebraziliansound.blogspot.com.

THE IPOD 25: SOUNDS FROM BRAZIL

One of the world's great music cultures, Brazil has an astounding array of talented musicians. A list of our favorite songs could easily fill this chapter, but we've limited our highly subjective pick to 25 songs from 25 different artists.

- 'Por Você' – Barão Vermelho
- 'Sampa' – Caetano Veloso
- 'Alvorado' – Cartola
- 'Samba de Orly' – Chico Buarque and Toquinho
- 'Aguas de Março' – Elis Regina (written by Tom Jobim)
- 'Hoje é Dia da Festa' – Elza Soares
- 'Namorinho de Portão' – Gal Costa
- 'Quilombo, o El Dorado Negro' – Gilberto Gil
- 'Desafinado' – João Gilberto
- 'Mas Que Nada' – Jorge Ben Jor
- 'A Procura da Batida Perfeita' – Marcelo D2
- 'Encanteria' – Maria Bethânia
- 'Novo Amor' – Maria Rita
- 'Carinhoso' – Marisa Monte (written by Pixinguinha)
- 'Ultimo Desejo' – Noel Rosa
- 'Besta é Tu' – Novos Baianos
- 'Panis et Circenses' – Os Mutantes
- 'Lanterna dos Afogados' – Os Paralamas do Sucesso
- 'Beira Mar' – Raimundo Fagner and Zeca Baleiro
- 'Funk Baby' – Seu Jorge
- 'Acenda o Farol' – Tim Maia
- 'Garota de Ipanema' – Tom Jobim
- 'Aquarela do Brasil' – Toquinho (written by Ary Barroso)
- 'Não me deixe só' – Vanessa da Mata
- 'Felicidade' – Vinícius de Moraes

REGIONAL MUSIC

The Northeast has perhaps the most regional musical and dance styles. The most important is *forró*, a lively, syncopated music centered on the accordion and the *zabumba* (an African drum). Although a few artists, such as Luiz Gonzaga and Jackson do Pandeiro, have achieved national status, *forró* was long dismissed by urbanites as unsophisticated. The film *Eu, Tu, Eles* (Me, You, Them) has brought down-home *forró* back to center stage, aided in part by Gilberto Gil singing the hit *Esperando na Janela*.

Another type of distinctive regional music is the wonderful Bumba Meu Boi festival sound from São Luís, Maranhão (see the boxed text, p594). There is also *frevo*, a frenetic, samba-related, Carnaval-based music specific to Recife and neighboring Olinda.

The *trio elétrico*, also called *frevo baiano*, began more as a result of a change in technology rather than in music. It started as a joke when, during Carnaval in Salvador in the 1950s, a group of musicians spearheaded by innovative musical talents Dodo and Osmar (aka Adolfo Nascimento and Osmar Alvares Macedo) got on top of a truck and played *frevo* with electric guitars. The *trio elétrico* is not necessarily a trio, but it's still the backbone of Salvador's Carnaval, when trucks piled high with speakers – with musicians perched on top – drive through the city surrounded by dancing mobs. It was popularized when Caetano Veloso began writing songs about the *trio elétrico*. Another important element of Carnaval on the streets of Salvador is the *bloco afro* (Afro-Brazilian percussion group). Filhos de Gandhi and Grupo Olodum are the most famous of these – Filhos has deep African roots and is strongly influenced by Candomblé; Olodum invented samba-reggae.

Mangue beat (also known as *mangue bit*), from Recife, combines folkloric and regional styles with international influences as diverse as hiphop, neo-psychedelic and *tejano* (instrumental folk music with roots in northern Mexico and southern Texas). The early leaders of the genre were Chico Science and Nação Zumbi – the title of whose 1996 masterpiece, *Afrociberdelia*, kind of summed up what its music was about. Chico Science died in a 1997 car crash, but Nação Zumbi has gone forward without him, and other bands such as Mestre Ambrósio and Mundo Livre S/A continue to carry the *mangue* torch.

Axé is a label for the profuse samba/pop/rock/reggae/funk/Caribbean fusion music that emerged from Salvador in the 1990s. Taking its cue from Salvador's older Carnaval forms, *axé* was popularized by the powerful, flamboyant Daniela Mercury. Other exponents include the groups Ara Ketu and Chiclete com Banana. At its best it's great, superenergetic music – hear Daniela sing 'Toda Menina Baiana' (Every Bahian Girl) – but some bands overcommercialized it at the end of the '90s.

The influence of Brazilian indigenous music was absorbed and diluted, as was so much that derived from Brazil's indigenous cultures. The *carimbó* music of the Amazon region (where the majority of *índios* live today) is influenced primarily by the blacks of the coastal zones.

'The trio elétrico is... still the backbone of Salvador's Carnaval'

Cinema

Brazil has a prolific film industry, though much of what it makes doesn't venture beyond the country's borders. *Lula, O Filho do Brasil* (Lula the Son of Brazil, 2010), directed by Fábio Barreto, is one of the nation's most recent high-profile films (and to date its costliest at R$17 million). The biopic of outgoing president Lula from shoeshine boy to union leader wasn't well received at home (some critics complained of a whitewashing of some darker episodes in Lula's life), though it may fare better abroad.

Beyond Ipanema (2009), written and directed by Béco Dranoff and Guto Barra, is an excellent documentary about one of Brazil's most important exports: music. Featuring interviews with Caetano Veloso, Seu Jorge, Bebel Gilberto, David Byrne and many others, the film explores the influence of Brazilian music on the world stage.

One of the most talked-about films of recent years is the 2007 *Tropa de Elite* (Elite Squad), which depicts police brutality in the favelas; it also makes a very clear link between middle-class college kids who buy drugs and the deaths of young children in the favelas who are recruited by drug lords to help meet the demand for cocaine and other substances. It was made by José Padilha, the acclaimed director of the disturbing documentary *Bus 174* (2002), which depicts a high-profile bus hijacking that took place in Rio de Janeiro in 2000.

Set in 1970 during the height of the military dictatorship *O Ano em Que Meus Pais Saíram de Férias* (The Year My Parents Went on Vacation; 2006), directed by Cao Hamburger, is a poignant coming-of-age story. Brazil's official Oscar entry for best foreign film in 2007 tackles complex issues with sensitivity in the story of one young boy left adrift in a working-class neighborhood of São Paulo. Political repression, the World Cup of 1970 and Jewish culture all form the backdrop of Hamburger's remarkably well-made film.

The beautifully set *Casa de Areia* (House of Sand, 2005), directed by Andrucha Waddington, follows three generations of women as they struggle on the dramatic but desolate landscape in Maranhão. It stars real-life mother and daughter Fernanda Montenegro and Fernando Torres, with Seu Jorge in a supporting role.

Slightly more uplifting is *Dois Filhos do Francisco* (The Two Sons of Francisco, 2005), based on the true story of two brothers – Zeze and Luciano di Camargo – who overcame their humble origins to become successful country musicians. Despite some unfortunate melodrama, the film has merit, including a curious soundtrack created under the direction of Caetano Veloso.

Made by two Americans, *Favela Rising* (2005) is a documentary that shows favela life through the eyes of Anderson Sá, founder of the Grupo Cultural Afro Reggae (Afro-Reggae Group) and symbol of hope for many poor children growing up in the favela. In the film, Sá, who turned his life around after involvement in gangs, starts a music school for youths, creating a grass-roots movement that spreads to other favelas.

For a trip back to Rio's Lapa of the 1930s, check out Karim Aïnouz's compelling *Madame Satã* (2002). Rio's gritty red-light district of that time (which hasn't changed much in the last 75 years) is the setting for the true story of Madame Satã (aka João Francisco dos Santos), the troubled but good-hearted *malandro* (con artist), transvestite, singer and capoeira master who was synonymous with Lapa's bohemianism.

Eu, Tu, Eles (Me, You, Them), Andrucha Waddington's social comedy about a Northeasterner with three husbands, was well received when it was released in 2000. It has beautiful cinematography and a score by Gilberto Gil that contributed to the recent wave of popularity of that funky Northeastern music, *forró*.

One of Brazil's top directors, Fernando Meirelles, earned his credibility with *Cidade de Deus*, the 2002 film based on a true story by Paolo Lins. The film, which showed brutality and hope coexisting in a Rio favela, earned four Oscar nominations. More importantly, it brought much attention to the urban poor in Brazil. Following his success with *Cidade de Deus*, Meirelles went Hollywood with *The Constant Gardener* (2004), a conspiracy film shot in Africa.

Rio de Jano is a colorful documentary about French cartoonist Jean le Guay, aka Jano, who came to Rio and made marvelous work of the Cariocas. Look for the book in Rio's bookstores.

Turistas, about evil Brazilians stealing organs from well-toned foreign kids, upset many Brazilians, who complained about egregious misrepresentations. Urban violence, Brazil has. Organ harvesters, not the last time we checked.

Walter Salles is one of Brazil's best-known directors, whose Oscar Award–winning *Central do Brasil* (Central Station; 1998) should be in every serious Brazilianist's film library. The central character is an elderly woman who works in the main train station in Rio writing letters for illiterates with families far away. A chance encounter with a young homeless boy leads her to accompany him into the real, unglamorized Brazil on a search for his father. Salles' film *Diarios de Motocicleta* (The Motorcycle Diaries; 2004) chronicles the historic journey of Che Guevara and Alberto Granada across South America. Some of Salles' best works came earlier. In fact, his first feature film, *Terra Estrangeiro* (Foreign Land), shot in 1995, holds an important place in the renaissance of Brazilian cinema.

Hector Babenco is another top Brazilian director. *Carandiru* (2003) is an inside look at São Paulo's hellish state penitentiary of the same name. Based on the real-life experiences of a doctor who worked inside the prison, *Carandiru* garnered a number of film-festival awards, including the Cannes Palme d'Or. Even more powerful is Babenco's earlier film, *Pixote* (1981), which shows life through the eyes of a homeless child who gets swept from innocent waif to criminal by the currents of the underworld. Babenco went on to direct international Hollywood hits *Kiss of the Spider Woman* (1985) and *Ironweed* (1987). *The Past* (2007), his latest release, stars Gael García Bernal in a twisted post-love story set in Argentina (where Babenco grew up before becoming a Brazilian naturalized citizen).

Brazilian Cinema, edited by Randal Johnson and Robert Stam, provides a fascinating overview of the great movements that have shaped the industry, exploring Cinema Novo, tropicalism, anthropophagy and other important influences.

The English-made film *The Mission* (1986) depicts life in the early colonial days and the brutal relationship between Guarani and the vying world powers of Portugal and Spain. It was shot around Iguaçu Falls and features spectacular cinematography.

Dealing with Brazil's more recent troubles is Bruno Barreto's *O Que é Isso Companheiro* (released as *Four Days in September* in the US, in 1998). Set during the dictatorship, it was based on the 1969 kidnapping of the US ambassador to Brazil by leftist guerrillas.

Carlos Diegues' *Bye Bye Brasil* (1980) is another important Brazilian film. The first major film produced after the end of the dictatorship, it chronicles the adventures of a theater troupe as it tours the country, witnessing the profound changes in Brazilian society in the second half of the 20th century. Diegues also directed *Orfeu* (1999), a lackluster remake of the Camus classic.

Prior to the dictatorship, which stymied much creative expression in the country, Brazil was in the grip of Cinema Novo. This 1960s movement focused on Brazil's bleak social problems, and was influenced by Italian neorealism. One of the great films made during this epoch was the 1962 *O Pagador de Promessas* (The Payer of Vows), a poetic story about a man who keeps his promise to carry a cross after the healing of his donkey. It won the Palme d'Or at the Cannes film festival. Another great pioneer of Cinema Novo is the director Glauber Rocha. In *Deus e o Diabo na Terra do Sol* (Black God, White Devil; 1963), Rocha explored the struggle, fanaticism and poverty of Northeastern Brazil. It's one of the great films of the period.

Going back in time, we reach *Orfeu Negro* (Black Orpheus), Marcel Camus' 1959 film, which opened the world's ears to bossa nova by way of the Jobim and Bonfá soundtrack. Music aside, the film did a clever job recasting Ovid's original Orpheus-Eurydice myth in the setting of Rio's Carnaval (a fertile ground for mythmaking).

Neorealism was one of the earliest movements affecting Brazil cinema, and *O Cangaceiro* (The Brigand, 1953) by Lima Barreto was perhaps the first Brazilian film to receive international recognition. The film chronicles the adventures of a roving band of outlaws, and was inspired by the Northeast's most infamous outlaw, Lampião.

Literature

Carioca author Paulo Coelho, whose books have sold more than 100 million copies, is one of the world's most widely read novelists. While critics tend to knock his simplistic New Age spiritual fables, books such as *The Pilgrimage* (1987), *The Alchemist* (1988) and *The Witch of Portobello* (2006) have struck a nerve with his global fan base, bringing him rock-star fame.

A writer of 'actual' rock-star fame is talented singer and songwriter Chico Buarque. The author of two rather mediocre novels, Buarque seemed to jump the fence successfully in his third effort, *Budapest* (2003), an engaging and meditative novel of love and language set in Budapest and Rio.

A far different worldview is presented in works from the detective genre, with popular novels finally available in English. Often called the Raymond Chandler of Brazil, Luis Alfredo Garcia-Roza writes hard-boiled page-turners, often set in his Copacabana neighborhood. To explore the noir side of Rio check out his novels *Southwesterly Wind* (2004) and *Window in Copacabana* (2005). Patrícia Melo is another Brazilian crime novelist (and playwright), who's received praise from both readers and academics for her smart, psychologically complex thrillers. Among her best works are *The Killer* (1998) and *Inferno* (2002).

Brazil's most famous writer is Jorge Amado, who died in August 2001. Born near Ilhéus in 1912, and a longtime resident of Salvador, Amado wrote colorful romances about Bahia's people and places. His early work was strongly influenced by communism. His later books are lighter in subject, but more picturesque and intimate in style. The two most acclaimed are *Gabriela, Clove and Cinnamon*, which is set in Ilhéus, and *Dona Flor and Her Two Husbands*, set in Salvador. *Tent of Miracles* explores race relations in Brazil, and *Pen, Sword and Camisole* laughs its way through the petty worlds of military and academic politics. *The Violent Land* is an early Amado classic.

Clarice Lispector (1920–77), one of Latin America's great 20th-century novelists, is surprisingly little known outside the country. Her existentialism-influenced writings focus on human isolation, alienation and moral doubt, and convey a deep understanding of women's feelings. The short-story collections *Family Ties* and *Soulstorm* are among her best works.

Joaquim Maria Machado de Assis, another Carioca, is widely regarded as Brazil's greatest writer. The son of a freed slave, Assis worked as a typesetter and journalist in late-19th-century Rio. A tremendous stylist with a great command of humor and irony, Assis had a sharp understanding of human relations, which he used to great effect in his brilliantly cynical works. He used Rio as the background for most of the works he produced in the late 19th century, such as *The Posthumous Memoirs of Bras Cubas* (1881) and *Quincas Borba* (1891).

Without a word wasted, Graciliano Ramos (1892–1953) tells of peasant life in the *sertão* in his best book, *Barren Lives*. The stories are powerful portraits. Also read anything you can find by Mário de Andrade (1893–1945), a leader of the country's 1920s artistic renaissance. His comic *Macunaíma*, which pioneered the use of vernacular language in Brazilian literature and was a precursor of magical realism, could only take place in Brazil.

Themes of repression and violence gained prominence starting in the late 1960s with the advent of military dictatorship. The bizarre and brutal *Zero*, by Ignácio de Loyola Brandão, was banned by the military government until a national protest lifted the prohibition. *Tower of Glass*, five stories by Ivan Ângelo, is all São Paulo: an absurdist 1970s look at big-city life where nothing that matters, matters. João Ubaldo Ribeiro's *Sergeant Getúlio* is a story of a military man in Brazil's Northeast. No book tells better of the sadism, brutality and patriarchy that run through Brazil's history. Ribeiro's *An Invincible*

Tristes Tropiques, by Claude Lévi-Strauss, is both a well-written travelogue and one of the most important anthropological studies of some of Brazil's indigenous peoples.

An Anthology of Twentieth-Century Brazilian Poetry (1972) is a fine introduction to Brazilian poets. It's edited by American poet Elizabeth Bishop, who planned a short trip to Santos and ended up staying 15 years.

Memory (which, like *Sergeant Getúlio*, was translated into English by the author himself) is a hugely popular 400-year saga of two Bahian families from opposite ends of the social spectrum.

Márcio Souza is a modern satirist based in Manaus. His biting humor captures the frightening side of the Amazon, and his imaginative parodies of Brazilian history reveal the stupidity of personal and official endeavors to conquer the rain forest. Do your best to obtain *Mad Maria* (a historical novel about the Madeira–Mamoré railway) and *Emperor of the Amazon* if you're going to Amazonia.

Dinah Silveira de Queiroz's *The Women of Brazil* is about a Portuguese girl who goes to 17th-century Brazil to meet her betrothed. Another author of interest is Joyce Cavalcante, who emerged in the 1990s as a writer able to express the experience of women in modern Brazil as well as the enduring social problems of the Northeast. Her *Intimate Enemies* is a tale of corruption, violence and polygamy, told with humor.

Aluísio Azevedo was one of the first in history to bring attention to the harrowing life in Rio's *favelas*. *Slum* brings rich characters and naturalistic scenery to life in this fascinating story from the 1890s, republished in the US and Europe.

Inferno, by Patrícia Mello, is a chilling novel about a boy's ascent to the top of Rio's cocaine trade. The author had never set foot in a favela before writing it, creating controversy.

Painting & Visual Arts

Brazil's best-known contemporary artist outside the country is the photographer Sebastião Salgado. Noted for his masterful use of light, the black-and-white photographer has earned international acclaim for his highly evocative photos of migrant workers and others on the fringes of society. Genesis, his latest project, will take him to the Galapagos Islands, the Himalayas, the Namibian desert, the glaciers of Argentina and other remote regions as he films the peaceful integration of man and nature – a kind of 'planetary anthropology,' as he described it.

Ernesto Neto is another top figure in Brazil's contemporary art scene. His installations – some massive enough to fill an exhibition space – are made of membranelike fabric, sculpted into a wild assortment of shapes, from disturbingly anthropomorphic pieces to subterraneanlike labyrinths, and he often brings the viewer into his work.

One of Neto's inspirations is Hélio Oiticica (1937–80), one of the most significant figures of the avant-garde of the '60s and '70s. He's best known for interactive works such as his *Cosmococa,* an installation that invited viewers to lie on sand covered with plastic sheeting, while watching a projection in which lines of cocaine were arranged across a photo of Marilyn Monroe.

Sebastião Salgado's *Workers* ranks among the great photographic portrait books of our time. Salgado shows the toil of laborers in powerful images captured in Spain, France, South Dakota and the gold mines of Brazil.

Although she's sometimes associated with the *tropicália* movement, Lygia Clark (1920–88) had an art career spanning three decades. Her earliest pieces were monochrome constructivist paintings of the 1950s; in the '60s, her work became more conceptual, morphing finally into highly experimental explorations of sensory perception, ultimately entering a kind of psycho-therapeutic realm.

Prior to the experimental era of constructivism and the avant-garde, European art was the principal influence on Brazilian artists, and movements such as neoclassicism, romanticism and impressionism were also observed in Brazil. One of the great neorealists of the 20th century was Cândido Portinari (1903–62). Early in his career he made the decision to paint only Brazil and its people. Strongly influenced by Mexican muralists such as Diego Rivera, he fused indigenous, expressionist influences with a sophisticated, socially conscious style.

The 18th century was the era of Brazilian baroque art. Wealth provided by the gold rush helped talented artists to realize their full potential. The acknowledged genius of this period was the sculptor and architect Antônio Francisco Lisboa (1738–1814), better known as Aleijadinho (see the boxed text, p252, for information on his life and works).

Brazil's earliest artists were colonial painters in Jesuit and Benedictine missionaries, who brought European sensibility to churches and sacred objects. The 17th-century Dutch invasion in the Northeast brought with it some important Flemish artists, such as Frans Post, who painted the flora and fauna in their tropical surroundings.

Architecture

Salvador, capital of colonial Brazil from 1549 to 1763, has managed to preserve many outstanding Renaissance and baroque buildings. A special feature of its old town, where more than 600 buildings and monuments have been

ARCHITECT OF THE CENTURY

'I deliberately disregarded the right angle and rationalist architecture designed with ruler and square to boldly enter the world of curves and straight lines offered by reinforced concrete… This deliberate protest arose from the environment in which I lived, with its white beaches, its huge mountains, its old baroque churches, and the beautiful suntanned women.' – *The Curves of Time: The Memoirs of Oscar Niemeyer* (2000)

Oscar Niemeyer, who turned 100 in 2007, clearly drew inspiration from his hometown of Rio de Janeiro. Considered one of the great pioneers of modernism, Niemeyer left a lasting legacy with his sculptural and evocative designs. Born in Rio's Laranjeiras neighborhood, he spent his youth exploring the city's bohemian side before finding his calling in the firm of well-known Brazilian architect Lúcio Costa in the 1930s. His early works were also influenced by French modernist Le Corbusier, who served as a consultant on projects like the modernist skyscraper of the Palácio Gustavo Capanema in Rio, completed in 1943. Following WWII he gained international recognition for his work as one of the principal architects for the headquarters of the United Nations.

By the 1950s he had proven himself as one of Brazil's most visionary architects, and for President Juscelino Kubitschek he was the ideal choice for his ambitious project of planning a city in the middle of nowhere. The design for the nation's new capital, Brasília, would become Niemeyer's most important legacy, working with urban planner Lúcio Costa and landscape architect Burle Marx. Brasília has its critics – some of whom decry a city designed for automobiles and buildings rather than pedestrians; others criticize the regimented design of the city into sectors and its lack of an organic mix of work and play sites that are intrinsic to most other Brazilian cities. In its defense, Brasília is still considered one of the world's most audacious urban-design projects. Its wild, airplane-shaped street plan has many iconic buildings, including Niemeyer's crown-shaped cathedral, Palácio da Alvarado (the president's residence) and the National Congress.

The whole city was completed in just three years. Yet Niemeyer wouldn't be around to bask in the success. Following the 1964 military coup, his membership in the Communist Party turned him into a persona non grata. He went into exile in Paris, where he continued his architecture practice (designing among other buildings the headquarters for the French Communist Party). In 1984, with the military dictatorship in its last throes, he returned to Brazil and picked up where he left off, designing masterpieces such as the Museu do Arte Contemporânea (p152) in Niterói. As of 2010, Niemeyer still worked every day from his office, a studio on the top floor of a highrise on Av Atlântica, with a stunning view of Copacabana Beach.

Other great works of Niemeyer's include the landmark buildings inside the Parque do Ibirapuera (p287) in São Paulo, the stunning eye-shaped Museu Oscar Niemeyer (p318) in Curitiba and the wild Museu de Arte de Pampulha (p237) in Belo Horizonte. Also currently under construction is the Caminho de Niemeyer (Niemeyer Way), in Niterói (p151) opposite Rio de Janeiro, which will house a series of beautifully sited buildings overlooking the bay.

The Curves of Time: The Memoirs of Oscar Niemeyer is recommended for those interested in the art and life of Brazil's great architect (from exile in Paris to romps with Henry Miller).

restored since 1992, are the many brightly colored houses, often decorated with high-quality stucco.

Olinda is essentially an 18th-century city. Its architectural wealth and unique atmosphere stem from its 20 baroque churches and many convents, chapels and houses with red-tile roofs. In São Luís the entire street plan of the late-17th-century heart of the city survives, along with many historic buildings, including fine mansions with colorful tiled facades.

The 18th-century mining towns of Minas Gerais also harbor architectural riches from the colonial era. The crown jewel is Ouro Prêto, the focal point of the 18th-century gold rush, which is adorned with the greatest concentration of fine baroque buildings in Brazil, many of them designed or embellished by the genius of Brazilian baroque, Aleijadinho. Lovely Ouro Prêto is joined on the World Heritage List by Diamantina, founded by 18th-century diamond hunters. Other Minas towns, such as Tiradentes and São João del Rei, also have baroque works.

Brazil's architecture in the 19th and early 20th centuries was much influenced by French styles. Neoclassical tastes yielded grandiose, monumental constructions such as Rio de Janeiro's Museu Nacional de Belas Artes (p148) and Amazonian rubber-boom palaces such as Manaus' Teatro Amazonas (p646) and Belém's Teatro da Paz (p608). Art nouveau style arrived around the turn of the 20th century: an outstanding example in Rio is the interior of the Confeitaria Colombo (p168).

The 1930s was the era of art deco, as exemplified by Rio's central railway station and statue of Cristo Redentor (Christ the Redeemer; p145), the buildings along Belém's Av Presidente Vargas and many apartment buildings in Rio de Janeiro. The 1930s also saw the emergence of a new generation of Brazilian architects, led by Oscar Niemeyer (see the boxed text, p74) and influenced by the modernist ideas of Le Corbusier.

Many other talented architects emerged in the second half of the 20th century. Lina Bo Bardi (1914–92), born in Rome, immigrated to Brazil following WWII and was highly active in Brazil's intellectual life. Her first project was São Paulo's Casa de Vidro (Glass House; 1951), a Zenlike cube atop slender columns that melds into the surrounding landscape. She went on to expand on the idea of weight and levity in her design for the Museu de Arte de São Paulo (MASP; p287), a bold design featuring two huge red concrete frames that suspend the interior glass structure above the ground. She remained active in the design world until the 1990s, both as a practitioner and a theorist, collaborating in numerous projects. Her many admirers remark on her 'anthropological architecture,' design based on a respectful attitude toward the user.

One of Brazil's most active contemporary architects is Paulo Mendes da Rocha (b 1929). In 2006, the São Paulo-based architect won the Pritzker prize (the Nobel of the architecture world) for his 'deep understanding of the poetics of human space.' Part of the avant-garde group of 'brutalist' architects in São Paulo, Mendes da Rocha designs with simple materials and forms that could be readily and easily constructed. There's also an ethical dimension to his work that focuses on the harmony between indoor and outdoor space. His work can be seen in São Paulo's Praça do Patriarca, a revitalized public space crowned with a curved steel canopy that appears to float overhead.

When Brazil Was Modern: A Guide to Architecture: 1928–1960, by Lauro Cavalcanti, is a well-illustrated guide to the 30-odd architects who made important contributions to Brazil's modern landscape.

The comprehensive book Brazil's Modern Architecture is written by a variety of Brazilian architects and critics, discussing the high modernism of the mid-20th century plus more recent projects.

Carnaval

One of the world's largest parties, Carnaval – in all its colorful, hedonistic bacchanalia – is celebrated with verve in practically every town and city in Brazil. Although Carnaval is ostensibly just five days of revelry, from the Friday to the Tuesday preceding Ash Wednesday, the festivities can begin weeks in advance – as is the case in Rio. It can also happen out of season – notably in Natal, Maceió, Recife and São Luís. Some towns dispense with Ash Wednesday altogether and keep the party rolling – for a full week in Porto Seguro and even longer in Olinda.

Carnaval in Brazil takes a few different forms and features a multitude of rhythms – samba in Rio, *axé* and *afoxé* in Salvador, *frevo* and *maracatu* in Recife – although drinking, dancing and the general air of joie de vivre are hallmarks no matter the destination. Rio and São Paulo both host massive all-night parades, complete with Technicolor floats and vast assemblages of drummers and dancers moving through custom-built stadiums before tens of thousands. Salvador's Carnaval happens on the streets, with huge trucks packed with speakers and topped with well-known bands, playing to massive crowds as they move through the city. In Olinda, the historic center becomes center stage for Carnaval, with giant puppets, festival-goers in costume and bands playing a wide mix of highly danceable beats.

Porto Alegre, Florianópolis, Ouro Prêto, São Luís, Corumbá and many other cities all throw down respectable bashes – with live bands (and *cachaça*, a sugarcane alcohol) keeping the crowds buzzing through the night. For those looking for something more low-key, resort areas such as Búzios, Ilha Grande, Paraty, Ilhabela, Arraial d'Ajuda and Jericoacoara are a few places to enjoy the merriment of Carnaval without the jaw-dropping crowds of better-known fests.

No matter where you go, you'll need to reserve accommodation well in advance. You'll also have to steel yourself for the higher prices charged everywhere. Accommodations double or even triple their rates and minimum stays (four to seven nights) are usually required.

Carnaval! by Barbara Maudlin is a handsome coffee-table book with vivid photographs of Carnaval celebrations around the world – from Bulgaria to Brazil.

Rio's excellent insider website www.ipanema .com has loads of up-to-date info on Carnaval events about town.

HISTORY

Carnaval, like Mardi Gras, originated from various pagan spring festivals. During the Middle Ages, these tended to be wild parties until tamed, in Europe, by both the Reformation and the Counter-Reformation. But not even the heavy hand of the Inquisition could squelch Carnaval in the Portuguese colony, where it came to acquire *índio* (indigenous) costumes and African rhythms.

Some speculate that the word *carnaval* derives from the Latin *carne vale*, meaning 'goodbye meat,' owing to the 40 days of abstinence (from meat and other worldly pleasures) that Lent entails. To compensate for the deprivation ahead, sins are racked up in advance with wild parties in honor of King Momo, the king of Carnaval.

CARNAVAL DATES

The following are the Carnaval dates (Friday to Shrove Tuesday) in coming years:

- **2011** March 4 to 8
- **2012** February 17 to 21
- **2013** February 8 to 12
- **2014** February 28 to March 4

CARNAVAL IN RIO DE JANEIRO

If you haven't heard by now, Rio throws an exceptional party, with music and dancing filling the streets for days on end. The culmination of the big fest is the brilliantly colorful parade through the Sambódromo, with giant mechanized floats, pounding drummers and whirling dancers – but there's lots of action in Rio's many neighborhoods for those seeking more than just the stadium experience.

Out-of-towners add to the mayhem, joining Cariocas in the street parties and costumed balls erupting throughout town. There are free live concerts throughout the city (near the Arcos do Lapa, on Largo do Machado and on Praça Floriano, among other places), while those seeking a bit of decadence can head to the various balls about town. Whatever you do, prepare yourself for sleepless nights, an ample dose of caipirinhas (cane-liquor cocktails) and samba, and mingling with joyful crowds spilling out of the city.

To get more information on events during Carnaval, check *Veja* magazine's *Veja Rio* insert (sold on Sunday at newsstands) or visit **Riotur** (Map p134; ☎ 0xx21-2541 7522; www.rioguiaoficial.com.br; Av Princesa Isabel 183; ☼ 9am-6pm Mon-Fri), the tourist organization in charge of Carnaval.

> Get a close-up look at Carnaval preparations at Cidade do Samba (Samba City; http://cidadedosam barj.globo.com; Rua Rivadávia Correa 60, Gamboa), which is where the top samba schools assemble the Carnaval floats.

CARNAVAL ON THE STREETS

In recent years, these street parties have exploded in popularity. Joining the *bandas* and *blocos* (street parties) is one of the best ways to have the Carioca experience. These marching parades consist of a procession of brass bands (in the case of *bandas*) or drummers and vocalists (in the case of *blocos*) followed by anyone who wants to dance through the streets. In 2000 there were only a handful of these events happening around town. In 2010 there were over 400 street parties, filling every neighborhood in town with the sound of pounding drums and old-fashioned Carnaval songs – not to mention thousands of merrymakers. For many Cariocas, this is the highlight of Carnaval. You can don a costume (or not), learn a few songs and join in; all you have to do is show up – and for Zona Sul fests, don't forget to bring your swimsuit for a dip in the ocean afterwards.

For complete listings, pick up a free *Carnaval de Rua* guide from Riotur. It's wise to confirm dates and times before heading out.

> For a complete rundown on the latest Carnaval info in Rio, including street parties, samba schools and balls, visit www.rio-carnival.net.

Banda de Ipanema (Praça General Osório, Ipanema; ☼ 4pm 2nd Sat before Carnaval, Carnaval Sat & Carnaval Tue) This long-standing *banda* attracts a wild crowd, complete with drag queens and others in costume. Don't miss it.

Banda de Sá Ferreira (cnr Av Atlântica & Rua Sá Ferreira, Copacabana; ☼ 4pm Carnaval Sat & Sun) This popular Copacabana *banda* marches along the ocean from Posto 1 to Posto 6.

Banda Simpatia é Quase Amor (Praça General Osório, Ipanema; ☼ 2pm 2nd Sat before Carnaval & Carnaval Sun) Another Ipanema favorite, with a 50-piece percussion band.

Barbas (cnr Ruas Assis Bueno & Arnoldo Quintela, Botafogo; ☼ 1pm Carnaval Sat) One of the oldest *bandas* of the Zona Sul parades through the streets with a 60-piece percussion band.

Bloco do Bip Bip (Rua Almirante Gonçalves 50, Copacabana; ☼ 6pm Carnaval Fri & 5pm Carnaval Tue) Meets in front of the old samba haunt Bip Bip (p174).

Carmelitas (cnr Rua Dias de Barros & Ladeira de Santa Teresa, Santa Teresa; ☼ 2pm Carnaval Fri & 8am Carnaval Tue) Crazy mixed crowd (some dressed as Carmelite nuns) parades through Santa Teresa's streets.

Céu na Terra (Curvelo, Santa Teresa; ☼ 8:30am Carnaval Sat) Follows along the *bonde* (streetcar line) on a memorable celebration through Santa Teresa en route to Largo das Neves.

Cordão do Bola Preta (cnr Rua Evaristo da Veiga & Rua 13 de Maio, Centro; ☼ 8am Carnaval Sat) The oldest and biggest *banda* still in action. Costumes are always welcome, especially those with black-and-white spots.

Many of Rio's *blocos* have
bawdy, whimsical names,
such as *Rola preguiçosa*
(Lazy phallus), *Que merda
é essa?* (What shit is
this?) and *Você naõo vale
nada, mas eu gosto de
você* (You're worthless,
but I like you).

Dois Pra Lá, Dois Pra Cá (Carlinho de Jesus Dance School, Rua da Passagem 145, Botafogo;
👁 2pm Carnaval Sat) This fairly long march begins at the dance school and ends at the Copacabana Palace.

Monobloco (Ave Rio Branco, Centro; 👁 8am 1st Sun after Carnaval) Rise and shine! This huge
bloco attracts upwards of 400,000 revelers who, nursing hangovers (or perhaps still inebriated)
gather in Centro for a final farewell to Carnaval.

Suvaco de Cristo (Rua Jardim Botânico, Jardim Botânico; 👁 8am Sun before Carnaval) Very
popular *bloco* (which means 'Christ's armpit' – in reference to the open-armed Redeemer looming
overhead), it also meets on Carnaval Saturday, but doesn't announce the time (to avoid overcrowd-
ing), so ask around.

CARNAVAL BALLS

Carnaval balls are giant, often costumed, parties with live music and dancing,
and an ambience that runs the gamut between staid and formal to wild and
tawdry. The most famous ball is held at the Copacabana Palace (p163). It's
a black-tie affair, and tickets run R$1100 to R$3200.

Popular, less pricey balls (around R$40) are held at Rio Scenarium (p175/)
and at **Scala** (Map p132; ☎ 2239 4448; Av Afrânio de Melo Franco 296, Leblon). The most
extravagant gay balls are found at Le Boy (p177). These are all good places
to don a costume.

Tickets go on sale about two weeks beforehand, and the balls are held
nightly during Carnaval. The *Veja Rio* insert in *Veja* magazine has details.

The classic film *Orfeu
Negro* (Black Orpheus;
1959) cleverly sets the
Orpheus-Eurydice myth in
the setting of a Rio *favela*
(shantytown) during
Carnaval. The bossa nova
soundtrack is excellent.

SAMBA-SCHOOL PARADES

The highlight of any Carnaval experience is attending (or participating in)
a parade at the Sambódromo. There before a crowd of some 30,000 (with
millions more watching on TV), each of 12 samba schools has its 80 minutes
to dance and sing through the open Oscar Niemeyer–designed stadium. The
pageantry is not simply eye candy for the masses. Schools are competing for
top honors in the parade, with winners announced (and a winner's parade
held) on the Saturday following Carnaval.

Here's what to expect: each school enters the Sambódromo with amped
energy levels, and dancers take things up a notch as they dance through
the stadium. Announcers introduce the school, then the lone voice of the
puxador (interpreter) starts the samba. Thousands more voices join him
(each school has 3000 to 5000 members), and then the drummers kick in,
200 to 400 per school, driving the parade. Next come the main wings of the

---

JOINING A SAMBA SCHOOL

Those who have done it say no other part of Carnaval quite compares to donning a costume
and dancing through the Sambódromo before roaring crowds. Anyone with the desire and a
little extra money to spare can march in the parade. Most samba schools are happy to have foreigners join one of the wings. To get the ball rolling, you'll need to contact your chosen school
in advance; they'll tell you the rehearsal times and when you need to be in the city (usually a
week or so before Carnaval). Ideally, you should memorize the theme song as well, but it's not
essential (you can always lip sync). For a list of samba schools and contact information, see p176.

The biggest investment, aside from the airfare to Rio, is buying a *fantasia* (costume), which will
cost upwards of R$600. If you speak some Portuguese, you can contact a school directly; many
Rio travel agencies can also arrange this. One recommended outfit is **Rio Charm** (www.riocharm
.com.br), which brings travelers together to parade with a Grupo A school (which some say is less
formal and more fun). Costumes cost around R$400.

Those seeking an insider's perspective on samba schools should read Alma Guillermoprieto's
excellent book, *Samba*.

school, the big allegorical floats, the children's wing, the celebrities and the bell-shaped *baianas* (women dressed as Bahian aunts) twirling in elegant hoopskirts. The *baianas* honor the history of the parade itself, which was brought to Rio from Salvador da Bahia in 1877.

Costumes are fabulously lavish, with 1.5m feathered headdresses; long, flowing capes that sparkle with sequins; and rhinestone-studded G-strings. The whole procession is also an elaborate competition. A handpicked set of judges chooses the best school on the basis of many components, including percussion, the *samba do enredo* (theme song), harmony between percussion, song and dance, choreography, costumes, story line, floats and decorations. The dance championship is hotly contested, with the winner becoming not just the pride of Rio but all of Brazil.

The Sambódromo parades start with the *mirins* (young samba-school members) on the evening of Carnaval Friday, and continue on through Saturday night when the Group A samba schools strut their stuff. Sunday and Monday are the big nights, when the Grupo Especial – the 12 best samba schools in Rio – parade: six on Sunday night, and six more on Monday night. The following Saturday, the six top schools do it again in the Parade of Champions, which generally has more affordable tickets than on the big nights. Each event starts at 9pm and runs until 4am.

Most visitors stay for three or four schools, and come to see their favorite in action (every self-respecting Carioca has a school they support, just as they have a favorite football team). If you're really gung-ho, wear your school's colors and learn the theme song (the words are found on each of the school's websites) so you can sing along when it marches through the Sambódromo.

Tickets

Getting tickets at legitimate prices can be tough. **Llesa** (http://liesa.globo.com), the official samba-school league, begins selling tickets in December or January, most of which get immediately snatched up by travel agencies then later resold at higher prices. Check with Riotur (p77) about where you can get them, as the official outlet can vary from year to year. At face value, tickets run from R$110 to R$300, though you'll probably have to pay about twice that (or more) if you buy just before Carnaval. The best sectors, in order of preference, are sectors 9, 7, 11, 5 and 3. The first two (9 and 7) have great views and are in the center, which is the liveliest place to be.

By Carnaval weekend, most tickets are sold out, but there are lots of scalpers. If you buy a ticket from a scalper (no need to worry about looking for them – they'll find you!), make sure you get both the plastic ticket with the magnetic strip and the ticket showing the seat number. The tickets for different days are color-coded, so double-check the date as well.

If you haven't purchased a ticket but still want to go, during Carnaval you can show up at the Sambódromo at around midnight. This is when you can get grandstand tickets for about R$30 from scalpers outside the gate. Make sure you check which sector your ticket is for. Most ticket sellers will try to pawn off their worst seats.

And if you can't make it during Carnaval proper, there's always the cheaper Parade of Champions the following Saturday.

Getting to the Sambódromo

Don't take a bus to or from the Sambódromo (Map p140). It's safer to take a taxi or the metro (Praça Onze or Central stations), which runs around the clock during Carnaval until 11pm Tuesday. It's also a great opportunity to check out the paraders commuting in costume.

In each of Rio's samba schools, the Rainha da Bateria, or 'queen of the rhythm section,' is often a well-known actor or pop star, and costumes can run upwards of R$50,000.

Portela holds the most Carnaval victories among Rio's samba schools, with some 21 titles.

Passistas are a samba school's best dancers. They roam the parade, stopping to show off fancy footwork along the way. The women are dressed in wild, revealing outfits, and the men usually hold tambourines.

Make sure you indicate to your taxi driver which side of the stadium you're on. If you take the metro, remember your stop depends on where your seats are. For sectors 2, 4 and 6, exit at Praça Onze. Once outside the station, turn to the right, take another right and then walk straight ahead (on Rua Júlio Carmo) to sector 2. For sectors 4 and 6, turn on Rua Carmo Neto and proceed to Av Salvador de Sá. You'll soon see the Sambódromo and hear the roar of the crowd. Look for signs showing the entrance to the sectors. If going to sectors on the other side (1, 3, 5, 7, 9, 11 and 13), exit at Central station. You'll then have to walk about 700m along Av Presidente Vargas until you see the Sambódromo.

OPEN-AIR CONCERTS

Lapa becomes a major focal point during Carnaval. In front of the Arcos do Lapa (Map p138), the Praça Cardeal Câmara transforms into an open-air stage, with concerts running through Carnaval. About half a dozen different bands play each night (samba, of course) during this event, which is called Rio Folia. The music starts at 10pm and runs past 2am, though revelers pack Lapa until well past sunrise.

SAMBA-SCHOOL REHEARSALS

King Momo is slimming down these days. Following the heart attack of several of Rio's portliest Momos (weighing over 200kg), the city seems to be losing its taste for obese Carnaval kings.

Around August or September, rehearsals start at the *escolas de samba* (samba schools or clubs). Some schools begin as early as July. Rehearsals usually take place in the *favelas* (shantytowns) and are open to visitors. They're fun to watch, but go with a Carioca for safety. Mangueira and Salgueiro are among the easiest schools to get to. See p176 for a complete listing of samba schools.

CARNAVAL IN SALVADOR

Although Rio's Carnaval hogs all the attention, Salvador hosts its own magnificent bash. In fact, this is one of the largest Carnavals in Brazil, attracting over two million revelers at last count.

Carnaval in Salvador usually kicks off Thursday night, with the mayor handing King Momo the keys to the city at Campo Grande (though in recent years it's happened at Praça Castro Alves). It all comes to an end on Ash Wednesday, with a handful of street parades giving a final afternoon send-off.

You can find lots of information on Salvador's Carnaval on the handy website www.bahia-online.net.

As elsewhere in Brazil, music plays a key role in the celebration, and in Salvador that means *axé*, an Afro-Bahian musical genre that incorporates a wide range of sounds, from samba-reggae and *forró* (a Northeastern two-step) to calypso and fast-passed *frevo* (a fast, syncopated, brass-band beat). It's the undisputed pop anthem during Carnaval in Salvador, and in many other parts of the Northeast.

TRIOS ELÉTRICOS & BLOCOS

The other integral element for the Salvadoran party is the *trio elétrico* – a long, colorfully decorated truck that's covered with oversized speakers. Small stages perch up top, with a band pumping out the rhythms as the *trio slooowly* winds through town. Hundreds of thousands line the streets of the parade route, packing in tightly – indeed, moving freely becomes a Sisyphean task.

Each *trio* is the centerpiece of a *bloco*, the gathering of revelers that surrounds the trucks. Those who want to be a part of the *bloco* pay anywhere from R$100 to upwards of R$700 (depending on the popularity of the *bloco*); this gives access to the *cordão*, the safer, roped-off area guarded by security personnel that surrounds the trio. *Bloco* members receive an *abadá*, an outfit (usually T-shirt and shorts) that identifies them as part of the group.

Those who don't want to pay to join a *bloco* can always choose to *fazer pipoca* (be popcorn) in the street. Once you get over the initial crush of the surrounding crowds, you can enjoy a wide variety of music and be spared the hassle involved with picking up the *abadá*. For details on staying safe during Carnaval, see the boxed text on p448.

You can also escape some of the madness by buying a day in a *camarote*, the walled-off, roadside bleachers with their own facilities. Head to the tourist office for information on *camarote* tickets.

AFOXÉS & BLOCOS AFROS

Sprinkled between each of the *bloco*s – and densely concentrated in the Pelourinho, where there are no *trio elétrico*s – are *afoxés*, groups that parade to the rhythms, songs and dances found in Candomblé (the polytheistic Afro-Brazilian religion). Years ago, *afoxé* groups would perform a ritual in the *terreiro* (house of worship) before hitting the streets. Today, this is not mandatory, and in fact many *afoxé* members don't worship the *orixás* (the gods that the groups celebrate).

One of the most famous *afoxé* groups around today is the **Filhos de Gandhy** (Sons of Gandhi; www.filhosdegandhy.com.br), founded in 1949. Although Gandhi was not born in Brazil, the *bloco's* founding members felt he was an important symbol of peace; their nonviolent approach earned the *bloco* respect in the eyes of the authorities, which took a largely repressive stance toward Afro-Brazilian culture in the early 20th century. The *bloco* also helped pave the way for numerous other *afoxés*. Today, the Filhos are now the largest *afoxé*, with over 10,000 members. They wear blue-and-white outfits with white turbans, shimmering sashes and blue-and-white beaded necklaces. Like some other *afoxés*, the group plays the serene rhythms of *ijexá*, and sprays the crowd with perfume.

The assortment of *blocos afros* also play an intrinsic role in the Carnaval festivities in Salvador. These are groups that celebrate African or Afro-Brazilian heritage in both costumes and themes – like the *bloco* Malê de Balê, named in homage to the Malê Revolt. Some of the better-known *blocos*

Bahia's favorite literary son, Jorge Amado, features Carnaval in some of his best known stories, such as *Dona Flor and Her Two Husbands*, which opens during Salvador's riotous fest.

BAHIA'S BEST BLOCOS

Some of the well-known stars in Salvador's Carnaval occasionally headline a *bloco* – including Daniela Mercury, whose samba-reggae hit from 1992 earned her nationwide attention. Since then, she's remained a significant presence during Carnaval. Another big-name performer appearing from time to time is Ivete Sangalo, a pop starlet who cranks out both the good and the bad. Meanwhile, luminaries like Caetano Veloso and Gilberto Gil, both from Bahia, shouldn't be missed if they perform during Carnaval. Veloso's 1969 song *Atrás do trio-elétrico* ('Behind the trio-elétrico') introduced much of Brazil to this genre of music.

Top-name *bloco*s of Salvador include the following:

Alerta Geral One of the only samba *bloco*s in Salvador's Carnaval, Alerta Geral often headlines great *sambistas* (samba singers) like Jorge Aragão.

Ara Ketu This *bloco afro* celebrates Yorubá heritage and always has top-notch bands playing for it.

As Muquiranas Gay and straight men alike don their finest knickers and parade as women in this ribald, fun-loving *bloco*.

Os Mascarados High-quality music courtesy of founder Margareth Menezes, one of the top Afro-Bahian singers performing today.

Nana Banana Usually headed by the band Chiclete com Banana, one of Bahia's most popular *axé* groups, with tens of thousands of followers.

Timbalada Founded by talented musician Carlinhos Brown, it features a percussion-based group whose members paint themselves up to resemble African warriors.

such as Ilê Aiyê (still around today) arose in the 1970s during the dawn of black pride in Brazil and, indeed, having African ancestry is a requirement to join Ilê Aiyê's *bloco*.

The most famous *bloco afro* performing today is **Olodum** (http://olodum.uol.com .br), a group widely credited for creating samba-reggae during Carnaval in 1986. Today the powerful drum corps parades with some 200 drummers, a handful of singers and thousands of costumed members. Olodum also performs throughout the year in the Pelourinho, and has gained international recognition in years past. It's played with Paul Simon (on the *Rhythm of the Saints* album) and Michael Jackson (in the song and Spike Lee–directed video 'They Don't Care About Us'). As a side note, Olodum has a strong social-service component, teaching inner-city school children a variety of arts and academic courses.

PARADE ROUTES

There are three main Carnaval circuits: the beachside Barra to Rio Vermelho circuit (where most tourists hang out), the narrow Campo Grande to Praça Castro Alves circuit, and the Pelourinho (no *trios* here, mostly concerts and parading drum corps). Some neighborhoods also hold their own parties. Bahiatursa and Emtursa (see p441) publish a schedule of events with a route map.

BARRACAS

Another unique feature of Salvador's Carnaval is the ever-present *barraca* (tent) – the go-to place for caipirinhas, *batidas* (fruit-filled cocktails), beer and other drinks. Thousands of *barracas* cover the city during Carnaval, many with their own sound systems, and they add to the general good cheer.

CARNAVAL IN OTHER CITIES

Most foreign travelers tend to join the party in Rio or Salvador, but there are scores of other places to wrack up a few sins Brazilian-style before Ash Wednesday (or perhaps the week after) brings the revelry to a close.

RECIFE

The underrated Carnaval in Recife ranks among Brazil's most colorful festivals, and purists claim it's the best Carnaval in the country. The appeal: Recife's celebration is a highly participatory event with an infectious euphoria and fabulous dancing. People don't sit and watch here, they join in – Carnaval groups and spectators don elaborate costumes and dance for days.

CARNAVAL THROUGHOUT THE YEAR

If you can't make it to Brazil during Carnaval, you can still join the party by hitting one of the so-called out-of-season Carnavals.

Carnatal Natal's huge out-of-season Carnaval (p556) is the country's biggest and kicks off in the first week of December, with extensive street parties and Salvador-style *trios elétricos*.

Recifolia Recife throws not one but two Carnavals. The second happens late October or November.

Fortal Half a million revelers celebrate Carnaval street-party style at Fortaleza's big bash in the last week of July (p571).

Marafolia The massive Salvador-style party in São Luís (p594) takes place in mid-October.

Maceió Fest Maceió's Carnaval (p508) features drinking, dancing and music-filled trucks, and happens in the third week of November.

Carnaval Recife-style also features music, dance and costumes that incorporate obvious African, indigenous and European elements: groups dress as African royalty and their ministers, enacting various sagas of war and peace while singing their lines to processional rhythms; others dress as stylized *índios* and dance to flutes and percussive beats; while still others take on the finery of the Portuguese court, all the while dancing and performing.

The music played in Recife's Carnaval is particularly diverse, including Rio-style samba, *forró* (a Northeastern two-step), *maracatu* (a slow heavy Afro-Brazilian rhythm), *frevo* (a syncopated, hyperfast brass-band beat, with lightning dance steps to match), *mangue* (an aggressive blend of hard rock, hip-hop and traditional Northeast styles such as *maracatu*). You'll also find rock and reggae, plus other regional sounds, such as Salvador-style *axé*, *pagode* (an informal type of samba) and *choro* (a more distant relative of samba, mostly instrumental and highly improvisational).

Galo da Madrugada, which is claimed, probably correctly, to be the largest Carnaval *bloco* in the world, brings over one and a half million people cramming onto the streets of central Recife for the official Saturday-morning Carnaval opening (see p526). For more information on the different styles of music and costumes of Recife, see the boxed text on p526.

In Rio state, Paraty has its own odd version of the party, more akin to Woodstock than Carnaval, as hundreds of young revelers cover themselves in mud and dance through the streets.

OLINDA

Neighboring Olinda also throws an excellent Carnaval, and it's so close to Recife that you could fête Carnaval in both cities. Olinda's revelry lasts a full 11 days and has a spontaneity and inclusiveness rarely found in big-city Carnavals.

There are organized Carnaval events, including balls, a night of *maracatu* and a night of *afoxé*, but everything else happens in impromptu fashion on the streets. The official opening events – with all the pomp and ceremony of the Olympic Games – commence with the parade of As Virgens do Bairro Novo, a *bloco* of more than 400 'virgins' (men in drag), and awards for the most beautiful, the most risqué and the biggest prude.

Fabulously costumed groups of musicians and dancers, some thousands strong, parade right through the day from early morning to evening, with spectators joining them to dance *frevo* and *maracatu* through the narrow streets. It's playful and very lewd. Five separate areas have orchestras (as the bands call themselves) playing nonstop from 8pm to 6am every night. For schedules, see www.olinda.pe.gov.br.

In an effort to combat AIDS and promote safe sex, the Brazilian government distributes over 500 million condoms during Carnaval each year – some 55 million in Rio alone.

PORTO SEGURO

Porto Seguro hosts the second-largest Carnaval in Bahia after Salvador, and it shares many features with its bigger neighbor to the north. *Trios elétricos* topped with *axé*-pumping bands cruise the main drag, and folks can join in the *blocos* by purchasing an *abadá*. Meanwhile, open-air concerts take place on beaches and on the main plazas, with music and dancing day and night. The celebration lasts a few days longer than most. Festivities wrap up on the Saturday after Ash Wednesday, which gives a full week of celebration; it also means some high-profile bands playing in Salvador finish up in Porto Seguro. Prices in this resort town tend to be lower than elsewhere, and the vibe is more peaceful and laid-back than in bigger cities.

FLORIANÓPOLIS

Carnival in the south may lack the Afro-Brazilian heritage and folkloric customs of the north, but the celebration can be a great time nonetheless. Florianópolis hosts one of the biggest and best bashes of the South, and it's increasingly one of Brazil's most gay-friendly Carnavals, after Rio.

Much of the action happens in the center, with concert stages sprinkled around town. On Saturday night, the city's five samba schools parade Rio-style through Floripa's open-air Sambódromo (also called the Passarela Nêgo Quirido). Tickets are inexpensive, but buy early to avoid long queues. On Sunday afternoon, men dressed as women parade in the *bloco* dos Sujos, one of Floripa's best-loved *bloco*s. Other samba-playing *bloco*s celebrate the rest of the night. On Monday evening, the city hosts its **Pop Gay Festival**, attracting thousands of gay revelers, many in outrageous costumes. Other gay events happen on Praia Mole.

In addition to events throughout Florianópolis, the beaches and towns of Ilha de Santa Catarina host their own parties, which always attract a festive crowd.

SÃO PAULO

Brazil's biggest city doesn't have much of a reputation as a party town during Carnaval – most Paulistas flee the urban jungle for the coast. The lack of crowds and lower prices, however, certainly appeal to some. São Paulo has only a handful of street parties, but it does throw a spectacular Rio-style parade in its own Sambódromo. Sampa's samba schools parade on Friday and Saturday nights (Rio's big nights are Sunday and Monday), and ticket prices are cheaper than in Rio. Outside of the parade, most of the Carnaval action happens in bars and nightclubs, with costumed balls and other special events.

Food & Drink

In Brazil, eating is, like so many other things, another pretext for pleasure-taking. There is no such thing as Brazilian haute cuisine per se, but the food tastes damned good just about anywhere you go. Even more remarkable is the cultural know-how about what, where, when and how to eat.

This *arte de comer bem* (art of eating well) has nothing to do with either fussiness, *á francesa*, or pseudoscientific taboos, *á americana*. Brazilians simply understand that the body feels better when it's kept hydrated with fruit and water while at the beach, or that a fattening little snack and a few sips of strong, hot coffee or ice-cold beer make the ride home from work infinitely more pleasant.

The food is as syncretic as the country itself. The most basic 'Brazilian' meal can include Portuguese olive oil, native manioc, Japanese sushi, African okra, Italian pasta, German sausage and Lebanese tabbouleh. Still, the cuisine can be reduced to three delightful principles: generosity, freshness and simplicity.

First, you should plan for some of the largest portions on the planet – a single main course can leave two people stuffed. It's hard to go hungry here, even on a modest budget. As for freshness, the fertile soil and luxuriant climate ensure that a stunning variety of produce is available at all times. Many of the local fruit and vegetable names have no translation simply because they exist nowhere else. Packaged foods are generally frowned upon, and farm animals are rarely pumped full of hormones, if only because of the prohibitive cost.

Given the richness and variety of fresh ingredients, Brazilians generally eat their food neat. They feel no need for fancy sauces or rarefied cooking processes. Meat is coated in salt and set on the grill, while veggies are steamed and served straight up. Simply add a drizzle of olive oil and a bit of salt to taste. That said, there are complex regional dishes that are well worth their careful preparation.

Travelers are often surprised to learn that Brazilians tend to eschew spicy food. In fact, restaurants rarely include pepper shakers as part of the normal table service, though it's generally available upon request, as is hot sauce. There are exceptions, of course, especially in the Northeast, where the burn of *malagueta* pepper laces many dishes.

One thing, though, you can be sure of – in Brazil, you're going to eat exceedingly well.

STAPLES & SPECIALTIES

Just as there's no 'typical' Brazilian face, there's no single Brazilian cuisine. Foodies prefer to say it's a conglomeration of regional cuisines, each itself a hybrid of ethnic cuisines adapted to local conditions. That said, here follows a description of a typical Brazilian meal – available just about anywhere you go.

Certainly, the meal will include *arroz e feijão* (rice and beans), the principle staples of the Brazilian diet. Each is cooked with garlic and onions. To the rice add tomatoes, and to the beans add bay leaves and perhaps some bacon. On top of the beans, sprinkle *farofa* – manioc flour sautéed in butter, perhaps with bits of egg or bacon.

Grilled meats, known as *churrasco* or *grelhadas,* are the meal's crowning glory: chicken, beef or pork is dredged in salt and grilled over an open fire. A green salad or sautéed or steamed vegetables (beets, carrots, green beans, broccoli or kale) round out the main course. French fries, usually served in great quantities, are also hugely popular, though you might go even more local and ask for fried manioc – a crunchy delight.

Maria-Brazil.org (www .maria-brazil.org/brazil ian_recipes.htm) has a very good section on Brazilian food, including easy-to-follow recipes and a guide to shopping in the country's supermarkets and street fairs.

Yara Roberts' handsomely photographed *The Brazilian Table* provides recipes for scores of delicious-sounding Brazilian dishes; she also delves into the cultural heritage of Brazilian cooking.

Delightful Brazilian Cooking, by Eng Tie Ang and Martine Fabrizio, has a range of Brazilian recipes that tend to be healthy as well as straightforward to execute.

BRAZIL'S TOP 10

The following is a highly subjective list of our favorite dining spots in Brazil.

- **Zuka** (p167) Rio de Janeiro.
- **Le Gite d'Indaiatiba** (p195) Paraty.
- **Maní** (p298) São Paulo.
- **Atelier das Massas** (p363) Porto Alegre.
- **ZUU a.Z.d.Z** (p386) Brasília.
- **Restaurant Solar do Unhão** (p452) Salvador.
- **Aipim** (p485) Arraial d'Ajuda.
- **Parati** (p504) Aracaju.
- **Oficina do Sabor** (p535) Olinda.
- **Cafeteria do Largo** (p652) Manaus.

A digestive pause is followed by *sobremesa* (dessert), which could include either fresh or preserved fruit, a pudding enlivened with coconut or passion fruit, deliciously creamy cakes, caramel (aka *doce de leite*) in several forms, or the flanlike *quindim*. The meal only comes to a conclusion with the consumption of a strong, sweet shot of coffee – Brazilian, of course.

Note that, except in higher-end restaurants, food is generally served family-style – that is, with generous helpings on communal plates. Also, all the dishes (except dessert) are served at once – there are no formal courses.

Bahia & the Northeast

Looking to reproduce Brazilian dishes you've tried on your travels? *The Art of Brazilian Cookery*, by Dolores Botafogo, is the classic text on Brazilian cuisine, with recipes adapted for North American and European cooks.

Brazilian restaurants outside of Brazil tend to serve, more specifically, Bahian cuisine, perhaps because it's the most obviously exotic. It developed in the kitchens of the region's slave-based sugar plantations, and its African origins reveal themselves in the three main ingredients: coconut milk; the spicy *malagueta* pepper; and *dendê* oil, a reddish-orange extraction of West African palm, which is deliciously distinctive though it can also be very hard to digest for those who are unused to it. The delicious stew known as *moqueca* includes all three, plus meat or seafood, and is a classic Bahian specialty. On the streets of Bahia you can't escape the smell of *acarajé* – fritters made with brown beans and shrimp fried in *dendê* oil.

By contrast, the much drier inland areas of the Northeast known as the Sertão produce a very different cuisine. Perhaps the most famous ingredient is *carne seca* or *carne de sol,* both of which consist of beef that has been salted and dried to preserve it against the region's punishing heat. Squash, which manages to survive in difficult growing conditions, is also very popular.

The Amazon

Cookbrazil.com (www .cookbrazil.com) offers a range of classic Brazilian recipes, from appetizers through desserts. There are also commentaries by readers who have made the recipes and offer their tips.

Amazonian cuisine is strongly influenced by the region's native Tupi people, who live largely on manioc, freshwater fish, yams and beans, and exotic fruit. *Caldeirada* is a popular fish stew not unlike bouillabaisse, and *pato no tucupí* is a regional favorite made with duck, garlic, *jambú* herb and the juice of both lemons and manioc roots. *Jacaré* (caiman meat) is another delicacy.

The Central West

Occupying the prairie-like cerrado, the Central West is dominated by sprawling *fazendas* (ranches) that produce pork and beef, as well as staples such as corn, rice, kale and manioc. The region's rivers offer up the meaty *dourado* fish, the *pintado* (a type of catfish), and, of course, the infamous piranha. Recipes tend to be simple but delicious, relying on the freshness of local ingredients.

Rio, São Paulo & the Southeast

The mountainous state of Minas Gerais offers the most distinctive regional cuisine of the Southeast. Pork is particularly popular, as is the kalelike *couve*, which is sautéed in oil with garlic and onions. *Frango ao molho pardo* (chicken stewed in its own blood with vegetables) sounds gruesome but tastes delicious. *Queijo minas* is a soft, vaguely sweet white cheese that, when served with *goiabada* (guava paste), makes a refreshing dessert.

São Paulo is the gastronomic capital of Brazil, thanks to high levels of disposable wealth and a large Italian community that places a high social value on refined eating. Here you'll find temples of fine dining as well as humble ethnic restaurants that reflect the city's dazzling number of immigrant communities, among whom the Japanese deserve special mention. Forming the largest colony outside of Japan, they have made sushi popular throughout Brazil. Note that pizza baked in a wood-burning oven is a Sunday-night tradition.

Rio doesn't have its own cuisine per se, but as the adopted home of Brazilians of all stripes, it offers excellent food from every region. As the former colonial capital, the Portuguese influence is less adulterated here than elsewhere, evidenced by the popularity of *bacalhau* (codfish). *Feijoada*, a bean-and-meat stew served with rice, *farofa*, kale and sliced orange, is the city's contribution to the national cuisine. Because it takes a few hours to cook as well as digest, it is traditionally served on Saturday. Food in Rio tends be lighter than elsewhere, at least in the upscale places in the Zona Sul neighborhoods such as Ipanema, where the body beautiful is held in higher esteem than gastronomic delight. Expect lots of delicious (and often quite creative) salads and sandwiches.

The South

Italian and German food rules the day in the South. The country's love affair with pasta and beer began here – both have become Brazilian staples. Expect to see lots of sausage and sauerkraut in the German enclaves of Joinville and Blumenau. Brazilian wine, whose quality improves year by year, comes from grapes lovingly imported from Italy and planted in the accommodating soil of Rio Grande do Sul.

> Experts trace Brazil's present-day love of very sweet desserts to Moorish origins, via the Arab occupation of Portugal.

> In Brazil, St John the Baptist (São João) is considered a protector of the corn crop, and his saint's day on June 24 is often celebrated with a profusion of corn dishes.

> You'll find a nice summary of Brazilian cuisine, plus easy-to-follow recipes for select classic dishes, at www .sallybernstein.com.

TRAVEL YOUR TASTEBUDS

Acarajé Eat these Bahian fritters, made of brown beans and dried shrimp, as soon as they've been fished from a spattering pot of *dendê* (palm) oil.

Açaí This addictive, deep-purple, vitamin-rich berry from the Amazon is a staple of both Tupi people and Rio bodybuilders.

Cafezinho A small shot of Brazilian coffee that should be strong as the devil, hot as hell and sweet as love.

Caipirinha The divine national cocktail is made with limes, sugar, ice and *cachaça* (a high-proof sugarcane alcohol).

Feijoada completa Plan for a long, digestive nap after indulging in this stew of black beans and well-larded meat and sausage.

Jambú This Amazonian herb makes the tongue tingle, then go slightly numb.

Picanha Not to be confused with piranha, Brazil's favorite cut of beef comes from the cow's rump; it's eaten pinkish, salty and fresh from the grill.

Piranha Take a bite out of this flesh-eater; the meat is delicious, but beware of sharp bones.

As in Argentina, the pampas (grassy plains) of the far south were long dominated by *gaúchos* – Brazilian cowboys who taught the region to love beef above all other meats. *Churrasco* is better here than anywhere else in the country. In fact, throughout Brazil it is considered a mark of a good grill restaurant that its meat carvers are *gaúchos* (which also used to describe natives of Rio Grande do Sul). The region preserves another cowboy tradition – *erva maté* tea (see the boxed text, p364).

Joaquim Machado de Assis, Brazil's greatest 19th-century writer, was also a famous gourmand. Cooking and eating are essential ingredients of his eerily postmodern novels.

Pan-Brazilian Fusion

Like much of the world, Brazil has undergone a kind of culinary renaissance in the last decade. One result has been a new, high-end, pan-Brazilian fusion cuisine. It begins with a renewed excitement about native ingredients, from the Amazonian fruits of the north to the grass-fed beef of the south. Up-and-coming chefs fuse these with cordon bleu and other classic European cooking methods to create novel, often exquisite, combinations. Asian and Arab influences are also evident, especially in São Paulo, home to the largest Japanese and Lebanese communities outside their respective countries. Indeed, São Paulo is in many ways the capital of this new Brazilian-fusion cuisine, though it is quickly spreading to the more prosperous enclaves around the country.

DRINKS
Nonalcoholic Drinks
JUICES

Brazilians consider avocado a fruit rather than a vegetable (which it technically is), and it is most commonly consumed as a juice with a healthy dose of sugar.

Brazilian *sucos* (juices) are divine. Staples include known quantities such as orange, lime, papaya, banana, passionfruit, carrot, beet, pineapple, melon, watermelon and avocado. Then there are the Amazonian fruits that hardly exist outside Brazil. The berrylike *açaí* is prized for its nutritional value and addictive taste, while guaraná (a type of berry) is loaded with caffeinelike stimulants. They defy translation, as do *graviola, cupuaçu* and *fruta do conde*.

Caldo de cana is extracted directly from lengths of sugarcane, usually with a machine that's a hand-cranked, multicogged affair. *Agua de côco* (coconut juice) is available anywhere that it's hot and where there are people. With a few strokes of a butcher's knife, vendors open a hole large enough for a straw. It sounds touristy but it's not – the juice is high in electrolytes, and Brazilians value its hydrating properties.

In Rio, where juice is a way of life, corner bars can offer 30 or 40 different varieties, made from fresh fruit and vegetables or from pulp. Request them *sem açúcar e gelo* or *natural,* if you don't want sugar and ice. Juices often have water mixed in; this is almost certain to be purified but if you're worried about it, ask for juices mixed with *suco de laranja* (orange juice) instead of water, or for a *vitamina* (juice with milk). Orange juice is rarely adulterated.

CAFFEINE

Capital amassed by São Paulo's coffee barons, plus the creation of infrastructure (including trains and port facilities) for the exporting of coffee, fueled the city's startlingly rapid industrialization, beginning in the 1880s.

Brazilians like their coffee to be really strong, really hot and 'as sweet as love.' In the morning they take it with milk *(café com leite)*. For the rest of the day, it's *cafezinhos,* regular coffee served either in a drinking glass or an espresso-sized coffee cup and often presweetened. It is sold in stand-up bars, and dispensed free in large thermoses in restaurants, at hotel reception desks and in offices to keep the general population perky the whole day through. Espresso is increasingly available in more upscale establishments, and just about everywhere in São Paulo, which boasts a highly evolved coffee culture.

A good cup of tea is harder to come by, but *erva maté* (called simply *maté*) is a potential alternative. It's available throughout the country and is usually served cold and cloyingly sweet. Only in the state of Rio Grande do Sul is it drunk hot (see the boxed text, p364).

Made from an Amazonian berry, guaraná 'champagne' rivals Coca Cola as Brazil's favorite soft drink. It's served cold, carbonated and sweet, and it's reputed to have all sorts of health-giving properties.

Alcoholic Drinks

BEER

Brazilians enjoy their beer served *bem gelada* (icy cold). In general, a *cerveja* refers to a 600ml bottled beer, a 'longneck' is a 300ml bottle, and a *cervejinha* is a 300ml can. Antárctica (ant-*okt*-chee-kah) and Brahma are the best national brands. Keep your eyes peeled for regional brands, including delicious Devassa from Rio, Bohemia from Petrópolis, Cerpa from Pará, Cerma from Maranhão and the tasty Serramalte from Rio Grande do Sul. For thicker palates, try the stoutlike Caracu or Xingu, sweet black beers from Santa Catarina.

Chope (*shop*-ee) is a pale-blond pilsner draft that's lighter and generally superior to canned or bottled beer. Antárctica and Brahma produce the two most widespread versions. In big cities you may even find *chope escuro*, a kind of light stout. Key phrase: *Moço, mais um chope, por favor!* (Waiter, another draft, please!). Many a Brazilian evening is whiled away in plastic chairs at plastic tables set up pell-mell on sidewalks and terraces, the empty bottles and glasses left to pile up as a sort of badge of honor.

CACHAÇA

Also called *pinga* or *aguardente, cachaça* is a high-proof sugarcane alcohol produced and drunk throughout the country. It can be cheaper than water (literally) or as dear as whiskey, and yes, price definitely signals a difference in taste and effect (and aftereffect!). Velho Barreiro, Ypioca, Pitú, Carangueijo, and São Francisco are some of the better labels.

The caipirinha is the unofficial Brazilian national drink. Ingredients are simple – *cachaça* with crushed lime, sugar and ice – but the results are sublime when sipped in the cool of an evening. You can replace the *cachaça* with vodka (to make a *caipirosca*) or sake (to create *caipisakes*) and the lime with a variety of fruit, including passion fruit, pineapple, strawberries, kiwi, the cherrylike *pitanga*.

Batidas are made with cachaça and fresh fruit juice – and are often blended to creamy, frothy perfection. They're somewhat akin to daiquiris.

CELEBRATIONS

Brazilians love to eat (then again, who doesn't?), and holidays and celebrations are another excuse for the hearty consumption of both food and alcohol. Any day off from work is an occasion for *churrasco*. Many of the gastronomic traditions are borrowed wholesale from European and American culture: turkey at Christmas, chocolate at Easter, champagne at the New Year, iced cakes for birthdays and weddings. In addition, pork and lentils augur good luck at the New Year, and during the winter feast days known as Juninas (June saints' days), *cachaça* is spiced with cinnamon, cloves and ginger and served warm. Despite the cultural importance of Carnaval, there is not a specific cuisine – alcohol trumps food.

WHERE TO EAT & DRINK

Eating out in Brazil can mean fried treats at the corner *lanchonete* (snack bar or greasy spoon); a lunchtime *prato feito* (ready-to-eat hot meal including rice, beans, a meat dish and salad) at a *bar* (pub) or *botequim* (working man's restaurant); a gorge session at a sit-down *rodízio* (all-you-can-eat) restaurant; or à la carte dining on white linen.

Unable to grow grapes, Italian immigrants to Espírito Santo made wine out of *jabuticaba*, a purplish-black grapelike fruit that grows out of a rain forest tree's trunk rather than on a vine.

GlobalGourmet.com (www.globalgourmet .com/destinations/ brazil/) provides a good introduction to the history and culture of Brazilian cuisine, as well as clearly outlined recipes.

FEIJOADA *Regis St Louis*

Brazil's national dish, *feijoada* is a delicious stew of black beans slowly cooked with a great variety of meat, including dried tongue and pork offcuts, seasoned with salt, garlic, onion and oil. The stew is accompanied by white rice and finely shredded kale, fried *farofa* (manioc flour) and pieces of orange.

The popular myth is that *feijoada* originated in the kitchens of African slaves, who had to make the most of otherwise unsavory cuts of pork and beef. Others argue that the recipe is essentially a Portuguese invention adapted to Brazilian climes. Kale, a typical accompaniment, is certainly a Portuguese favorite. Fried *farofa*, on the other hand, was inherited from Brazil's indigenous peoples. Certainly it began life as a humble dish, though it has long been adopted by the middle and upper classes as 'classically' Brazilian.

Ingredients

6 cups dried black beans
¼ kg smoked ham hocks
¼ kg Brazilian *lingüiça* (Brazilian sausage; substitute chorizo or sweet sausage)
¼ kg Brazilian *carne seca* or lean Canadian (loin-cut) bacon
1kg smoked pork ribs
(the intrepid can add one each of a pork ear, foot, tail and tongue)
2 bay leaves
salt and black pepper
3 garlic cloves, minced
1 large onion, chopped
3 tablespoons olive oil
4 strips smoked bacon
orange slices to garnish
rice, *farofa*, kale or collard greens to serve
hot sauce (optional) to serve

Preparation

After soaking beans overnight, bring them to the boil in 3L of water and then keep them on low to medium heat for several hours, stirring occasionally. Meanwhile, cut up the ham hocks, *lingüiça* and *carne seca* into 3cm or 4cm chunks, separate the pork ribs by twos and place them all in a separate pan full of water and bring to the boil. After the first boil, empty out the water and add the mixture, along with the bay leaves and salt and pepper, to the beans. As the pot simmers, in a separate pan sauté the garlic and onion in olive oil, adding in the smoked bacon. Take two ladles of beans from the pot, mash them and add to the frying pan. Stir around, cook for a few more minutes, then add frying-pan contents to the pot; this will thicken the mixture. Simmer for another two to three hours, until the beans are tender and the stock has a creamy consistency. Remove bay leaves and serve over rice with *farofa* and kale or collard greens. Garnish with fresh orange slices. Add hot sauce as desired.

To eat quickly and well, head to a *por-kilo* restaurant, which serves food by weight, and costs from R$30 to R$50 per kilogram. Offerings generally include fresh salads and veggies, rice, beans, grilled meat and fish, plus regional specialties. It's a great option for travelers, as you don't have to decipher a menu. Try to get there early (noon for lunch or 7pm or 8pm for dinner), when offerings are freshest and available in abundance.

Churrascarias are generally *rodízio*-style and include a salad bar, plus, at higher-end places, meat that's brought to your table fresh from the grill and carved for you. Prices vary wildly, from R$25 to R$90 for the all-the-meat-you-can-eat experience. *Rodízio* restaurants serving pizza and *massa* (pasta) are also popular and cost between R$15 and R$26.

Lone travelers will be made to feel at home wherever they go. If you want to strike up a conversation, head to the closest corner bar or food stand, where bonhomie is almost certain to abound.

Unless service was extraordinary, tipping is not necessary – your bill will include a 10% service charge. In restaurants frequented by tourists, count your change and make sure your check is itemized: *Pode discriminar?* (Can you itemize?). There is no pressure to turn a table – you can linger as long as you like just about anywhere you go.

Quick Eats

In Brazil, you're never far from a *lanchonete,* where you can get *salgadinhos* (savory snacks, usually fried) – also known as *tira-gostos* and *petiscos* – for around R$2. Try *quibe,* which is cracked wheat stuffed with spiced meat then deep-fried – it's both delectable and rib-sticking. *Pasteis* (dough filled with meat, cheese or seafood then deep-fried) are unbeatable when eaten piping hot. *Pão de queijo* (a concoction of cheese and tapioca dough) is also deliciously ubiquitous.

For a few more reais, you can get a *sanduiche,* a term that covers a multitude of hot sins, from the *X-tudo* (cheeseburger with everything) to the dependable *misto quente* (toasted ham-and-cheese sandwich). Cold sandwiches, usually on crustless white bread, are called *sanduiche natural.*

VEGETARIANS & VEGANS

Vegetarianism is very much a minority activity in Brazil. Many Brazilian waiters consider *sem carne* (without meat) to include such 'vegetable' groups as chicken, pork and animal fats, so be very clear when ordering in restaurants. Beware especially the typical black-bean dishes, which are often flavored with meat.

Most cities offer a few all-vegetarian options, though, but where this is neither convenient nor possible, head to a *por-kilo* restaurant – they usually offer at least half a dozen different salad, vegetable and bean dishes. For a list of some of the finer vegetarian eateries in Rio, see p166.

EATING WITH KIDS

Brazilians love children, and except at the finest establishments you will find that yours will be welcome wherever you go, as long as the kids are reasonably well behaved. Note that bratty behavior is little tolerated by Brazilian parents, who consider a quick swat far more constructive than a mere time-out.

Familiar food is available for unadventurous palates just about anywhere you go, from burgers and pizza to grilled-cheese sandwiches. Prepackaged baby food is generally available from supermarkets, though not from corner stores.

HABITS & CUSTOMS

Brazilians tend to have a small *café da manha* (breakfast; often shortened to *café*) of coffee with milk and a sweet or savory baked good; a big *almoço* (lunch) any time from noon to 2pm; a hearty *lanche* (late-afternoon snack) of a *salgadinho* with juice, coffee or beer; and a light *jantar* (dinner) of soup and/or sandwiches or a smaller recapitulation of lunch, usually sometime around 9pm or even later.

Extended families religiously gather for Sunday lunch, the most important meal of the week. It can last until 5pm or later and may seamlessly blend into *lanche* and *jantar.* Snacking is perfectly acceptable at any time of the day or night, as is a quick shot of ultrasweet coffee.

Eat Smart in Brazil, by Joan and David Peterson, provides an excellent introduction to Brazil's culinary history, some classic recipes and an extensive and very useful glossary.

The indigenous Maué so revere guaraná – an Amazonian fruit whose caffeine-packed seed resembles the human eye – that its plant is said to have given birth to the tribe's founder.

Açaí, the Amazonian berry, now widely available in smoothies outside of Brazil, has high levels of fiber, omega-6 acids, potassium and vitamins C and E; its much-touted antioxidant properties, however, are exaggerated.

DOS & DON'TS

Brazilians are casual about many things. Table manners are not one of them. Where possible, avoid eating with your hands – middle-class Brazilians often eat sandwiches with a knife and fork, and no one eats pizza with their hands. If you dine in someone's home, bring a small gift such as wine or flowers – or win permanent friends with a liter of duty-free whiskey.

Smoking is no longer acceptable in restaurants or bars. Brazilians love their cell phones – you can make or receive a quick call on any occasion except the most formal.

COOKING COURSES

For a deeper understanding of Brazilian table manners as well as other matters of custom and etiquette, check out *Brazil – Culture Smart!* by Sandra Branco.

Based in the colonial town of Paraty, the **Academy of Cooking & Other Pleasures** (http://chefbrazil.com) offers five-day courses with respected chef and educator Yara Roberts and includes cooking classes as well as *cachaça* tasting, visits to local farms and more.

You can learn how to prepare some iconic Brazilian dishes (eg *moqueca* and *feijoada*) and expert caipirinhas at a half-day class in English offered by Cook in Rio (see p157). Best of all, you get to eat the fruits of your labors.

In Salvador, Senac (p447) is another fine place for travelers to learn the art of Brazilian cooking.

EAT YOUR WORDS

Use the following guide to help you order correctly and better understand – and enjoy – the dishes once they arrive. For pronunciation guidelines, see the Language chapter, p732.

Menu Decoder

MENU BASICS

almoço	ow·*mo*·so	lunch
arroz	a·*hoz*	rice
aves	*a*·ves	poultry
azeite	a·*zay*·te	olive oil
bebida	be·*bee*·da	drink
café da manha	ka·*fe* da ma·*nyang*	breakfast
carne	*kar*·ne	meat (usually beef)
churrasco	shoo·*has*·ko	barbecue
comida caseira	ko·*mee*·da ka·*zay*·ra	home-style cooking
comida por kilo	ko·*mee*·da porr *kee*·lo	pay-by-weight buffet
dendê	deng·*de*	reddish palm oil
entrada	eng·*tra*·da	first course, appetizer
farinha de mandioca	fa·*ree*·nya de mang·dee·o·ka	manioc flour; the staple food of Brazil's *índios* (indigenous people) before colonization and the staple for many Brazilians today, especially in the Northeast and Amazon
farofa	fa·*ro*·fa	garnish of manioc flour sautéed with butter
feijão	fay·*zowng*	bean
frutos do mar	*froo*·tos do marr	seafood
grelhadas	gre·*lya*·das	grilled meat or fish
lanche	*lang*·she	hearty, late-afternoon snack
lanchonete	lang·sho·*ne*·te	snack bar
molho	*mo*·lyo	sauce
peixe	*pay*·she	fish

por-kilo	porr-*kee*-lo	per kilogram; used for self-serve restaurants
prato	*pra*-to	main course
prato feito	*pra*-to *fay*-to	literally 'made plate'; plate of the day; typically, an enormous and cheap meal
pratos típicos	*pra*-tos tee-pee-kos	local dishes
refeição	he-fay-*sowng*	meal
refeição comercial	he-fay-*sowng* ko-merr-*syow*	meal/serving of various dishes (normally comes with enough food for two to share)
rodízio	ho-*dee*-zyo	smorgasbord, usually with lots of meat
sobremesa	so-bre-*me*-za	dessert

MAIN DISHES

barreado	ba-rre-*a*-do	a mixture of meats and spices cooked in a sealed clay pot for 24 hours and served with banana and *farofa;* the state dish of Paraná
bobó de camarão	bo-*bo* de ka-ma-*rowng*	manioc paste flavored with dried shrimp, coconut milk and cashew nuts
canja	*kang*-zha	soup made with rice and chicken broth
carne de sol	*kar*-ne de sol	tasty, salted meat, grilled and served with beans, rice and vegetables
casquinha de siri	kas-*kee*-nya de *see*-ree	stuffed crab
cozido	ko-*zee*-do	a meat stew heavy on vegetables
feijoada	fay-zho-*a*-da	bean-and-meat stew served with rice and orange slices, traditionally eaten for Saturday lunch
frango ao molho pardo	*frang*-go ow *mo*-lyo *par*-do	chicken pieces stewed with vegetables and the blood of the bird
moqueca	mo-*ke*-ka	Bahian fish stew cooked in a clay pot with *dendê* oil, coconut milk and spicy peppers
pato no tucupí	*pa*-to no too-koo-*pee*	roast duck flavored with garlic, juice of the manioc plant and *jambú;* a favorite in Pará
pirarucu ao forno	pee-ra-hoo-*koo* ow *forr*-no	a preparation of Brazil's most famous fish from the rivers of Amazonia, in which the fish is oven-cooked with lemon and other seasonings
tutu á mineira	too-*too* a mee-*nay*-ra	savory black-bean mash typical of Minas Gerais
vatapá	va-ta-*pa*	a seafood dish of African origins with a thick sauce of manioc paste, coconut and *dendê* oil
xinxim de galinha	sheeng-*sheeng* de ga-*lee*-nya	pieces of chicken flavored with garlic, salt and lemon

Food Glossary

FRUIT & VEGETABLES

abacate	a·ba·*ka*·te	avocado
abacaxí	a·ba·ka·*shee*	pineapple
açaí	a·sa·*ee*	gritty, deep-purple forest berry
acerola	a·se·*ro*·la	acidic, cherry-flavored fruit; a megasource of vitamin C
alface	ow·*fa*·se	lettuce
alho	*a*·lyo	garlic
batata	ba·*ta*·ta	potato
beterraba	be·te·*ha*·ba	beetroot
caju	ka·*zhoo*	fruit of the cashew plant
carambola	ka·rang·*bo*·la	starfruit
cenoura	se·*no*·ra	carrot
cupuaçu	koo·poo·*a*·soo	acidic, slightly pearlike fruit
fruta do conde	*froo*·ta do *kong*·de	sugar-apple fruit
goiaba	go·*ya*·ba	guava
graviola	gra·vee·*o*·la	custard apple
jaca	*zha*·ka	jackfruit
laranja	la·*rang*·zha	orange
limão	lee·*mowng*	lime or lemon
maçã	ma·*sang*	apple
mamão	ma·*mowng*	papaya
mandioca	mang·dee·*o*·ka	manioc, cassava (also known as *aipim*)
manga	*mang*·ga	mango
maracujá	ma·ra·koo·*zha*	passion fruit
melancia	me·lang·*see*·a	watermelon
melão	me·*lowng*	honeydew melon
morango	mo·*rang*·go	strawberry
pupunha	poo·*poo*·nya	a fatty, vitamin-rich Amazonian fruit taken with coffee
uva	*oo*·va	grape

SNACKS

acarajé	a·ka·ra·*zhe*	Bahian fritters made of brown beans and dried shrimp fried in *dendê* oil
empadão	eng·pa·*downg*	a tasty pie, typical of Goiás, made from meat, vegetables, olives and eggs
quibe	*kee*·be	cracked wheat stuffed with spiced meat then deep-fried
pão de queijo	powng de *kay*·zho	balls of cheese-stuffed tapioca bread
pastel	pas·*tel*	thin square of dough stuffed with meat, cheese or fish, then fried
salgadinhos	sow·ga·*dee*·nyos	savory snacks; also *salgados*
salgados	sow·*ga*·dos	savory snacks; also *salgadinhos*

MEAT, FISH & DAIRY

camarão	ka·ma·*rowng*	shrimp
carne	*kar*·ne	meat in general, also beef; also known as *bife* and *carne de vaca*

carneiro	karr-*nay*-ro	lamb
dourado	do-*ra*-do	meaty freshwater fish
frango	*frang*-go	chicken
leite	*lay*-te	milk
ovos	*o*-vos	eggs
porco	*porr*-ko	pork
queijo	*kay*-zho	cheese
requeijão	he-kay-*zhowng*	cream cheese
siri	*see*-ree	crab
talnha	*tai*-nya	a meaty but tender local fish

DESSERT

arroz doce	a-*hoz do*-se	rice pudding
bolo	*bo*-lo	cake
brigadeiro	bree-ga-*day*-ro	*doce de leite* covered with chocolate
cocada	ko-*ka*-da	baked coconut treat
doce de leite	*do*-se de *lay*-te	creamy milk-and-sugar concoction
goiabada	go-ya-*ba*-da	sweet guava paste
pavé	pa-*ve*	creamy cake
quindim	*keen*-deem	egg-based sweet
sorvete	sorr-*ve*-te	ice cream

DRINKS

agua	*a*-gwa	water
aguardente	a-gwarr-*deng*-te	firewater, rotgut; any strong drink, but usually *cachaça*
batida	ba-*tee*-da	blended drink
cachaça	ka-*sha*-sa	sugarcane spirit
café	ka-*fe*	coffee
caipirinha	kai-pee-*ree*-nya	drink made from *cachaça* and crushed citrus fruit, such as lemon, orange or *maracujá*
cerveja	serr-*ve*-zha	beer
chope	*sho*-pe	draft beer
erva maté	*err*-va *ma*-te	popular tea of southern Brazil
guaraná	gwa-ra-*na*	soft drink made from Amazonian berry
pinga	*peen*-ga	another name for *cachaça*
refrigerante	he-free-zhe-*rang*-te	soft drink
suco	*soo*-ko	juice
vitamina	vee-ta-*mee*-na	juice with milk

Environment

Brazil boasts some of the most astounding plant and animal life on earth. It's home to the world's largest rain forest, as well as some of the greatest wetlands – not to mention stunning beaches.

More known species of plants (over 55,000), freshwater fish (around 3000), amphibians (775) and mammals (522) are found in Brazil than in any other country in the world. Brazil ranks third for the number of birds (over 1700) and fifth for reptiles (633). Around 10 to 15 million types of insect fly, hop and wriggle their lives away here too. About a quarter of the mammals in Brazil, more than one-third of the reptiles and over half the amphibians occur nowhere else – and new species are being discovered all the time, including 14 types of monkey since 1990.

Unfortunately, Brazil is also renowned for the destruction of its natural environment; all of its major ecosystems are threatened and over 200 animal species are endangered. Conservation, however, remains one of the hot topics of the day, and protecting Brazil's natural wonders is increasingly seen as pivotal for Brazil's future. Travelers can play an important role by supporting genuinely sustainable businesses and organizations. See the GreenDex (p766) for a list of green options across the country.

The Nature Conservancy website (www.nature .org) includes portraits of Brazil's major ecosystems and information on the country's endangered species.

THE LAND

Brazil is the world's fifth-largest country (after Russia, China, Canada and the USA). Its 8.5 million sq km occupy almost half of South America and it borders every country in the continent except Chile and Ecuador.

Away from the generally narrow coastal plains, southern, southeastern and northeastern Brazil are composed chiefly of low, hilly country broken by occasional dramatic escarpments, with some mountain ranges, such as the Serra do Espinhaço and Serra do Mar, rarely exceeding 2000m in elevation. Many southern and southeastern rivers flow inland to join the Paraná, the Uruguay or Paraguay, big waterways flowing southward toward the Rio de la Plata (River Plate), between Uruguay and Argentina.

The National Geographic documentary *Amazon: Land of the Flooded Forest* explores this unique region, where water and land life intermingle for six months of the year.

At the heart of the country spreads a broad, elevated plain, the Planalto Brasileiro, broken by several small mountain ranges but with an average altitude of only about 500m. Apart from the great Rio São Francisco, which empties into the Atlantic north of Salvador, most rivers here flow north to the enormous, low-lying Amazon Basin. There they feed the mighty Amazon, along with hundreds of other tributaries originating in the Andes, in the mountains along the Brazil–Venezuela border and in the Guyana Shield further east. Pico da Neblina (3014m) on the Venezuelan border is Brazil's highest peak.

Brazil has five principal biomes (major regional plant and animal groupings): Amazonia, Atlantic rain forest, caatinga (semiarid land), cerrado (the central savanna) and the wetlands of the Pantanal.

Amazonia

Covering over 4 million sq km – almost half the country – Brazilian Amazonia incorporates 30% of the world's tropical forest. It's home to around 45,000 plant species (some 20% of the world total), 311 mammals (about 10% of the world total), 1000 bird species (15%), 1800 types of butterfly and around 2000 species of fish (in contrast, Europe has about 200). The forest still keeps many of its secrets: to this day, major tributaries of the Amazon river remain unexplored, thousands of species have not yet been classified and dozens of human communities have avoided contact with the outside world.

Including a further 2 million sq km in neighboring countries, the entire Amazon Basin holds 20% of the world's freshwater and produces 20% of the world's oxygen. Unfortunately, deforestation remains a serious threat, with around 10,000 sq km of forest felled each year.

Rain forests can occur in areas where more than 2000mm of rain falls annually and where this rainfall is spread over the whole year. In the Amazon, half the rain comes from damp trade winds blowing in from the Atlantic Ocean and the rest results from vapor released by Amazonia's own soil and trees – much of which is recycled rain. Humidity is always greater than 80%, and temperatures range constantly between 22°C (72°F) by night and 31°C (88°F) by day.

The Smithsonian Atlas of the Amazon is a treat for anyone who falls under the spell of Amazonia – 150 maps, 300 photos and lots of fascinating information.

FLOODPLAIN & DRY LAND

Seasonal rainfall patterns mean that the water levels of the Amazon river and its tributaries rise and fall at different times of the year. This produces dramatic alterations in the region's geography. Water levels routinely vary by 10m to 15m between low and high marks; during high-water periods, areas totaling at least 150,000 sq km (about the size of England and Wales together) are flooded.

THE STATES OF BRAZIL

IT PAYS NOT TO CUT IT DOWN

Deforestation is a major contributor to global warming, accounting for 17% of the world's carbon dioxide (CO_2) emissions (more than the world's planes, cars, trucks and ships combined) and 70% of the emissions in Brazil. How to keep the forests from being felled is the big challenge – and one that can play a pivotal role in climate change. Deforestation adds CO_2 to the atmosphere through fires and machinery used to cut down trees, and it also destroys the living plants that absorb carbon emissions from cars and factories around the planet.

One simple but dramatic new strategy under way is to pay landowners to preserve the forests on their property. Controversial though it may be, a growing number of scientists, environmentalists and politicians say that cash payments are the most effective way to stop the felling of tropical forest and if successful could play a major role in limiting global warming.

More technologically innovative solutions – biofuels, wind and solar energy – tend to garner all the attention in regard to climate change, but keeping a forest intact yields a remarkably simple environmental payback: a property owner reduces the emissions on his land to zero.

Encouraging people not to hack down forests and plant lucrative crops such as soy or corn or raise cattle is a daunting task in Brazil, particularly in the Amazon and in Mato Grosso, where previous government policy encouraged development of the land – clearing the forests and creating farmland. This Brazilian policy encouraged settlement through cheap land and housing subsidies, some of which are still in existence today. Indeed, in the 1970s, to be eligible for loans to buy seed and tractors, farmers had to clear 80% of their land.

Globalization has created huge opportunities for growers from Brazil – who alongside Indonesia lead the world in the felling of their rain forests each year. Trees are chopped down to help feed the growing population across the globe and its increasing appetite for beef. Today Mato Grosso is Brazil's leading producer of soy, beef and corn, all of which are exported across the globe by multinational companies.

To incentivize the preservation of forests (cleared farm land in Mato Grosso yields over US$1200 an acre, after all), policy makers advocate a wide range of strategies, including direct payments to landowners to keep forests standing, along with indirect subsidies, like higher prices for soy and beef produced without clear-cutting the land.

In recent years, Brazil with a grant from Norway created the **Amazon fund** (www.amazonfund.org), which provides financial incentives for the preservation of rain forest. Partnered with **Amazônia Association** (www.amazonia.org), it aims to establish more reserves (currently it has over 1820 sq km) where the local natives are co-owners and work to preserve the land in exchange for preservation of their local culture and education, economic and health benefits for their families.

New laws are also playing a role in preserving the forest. National laws stipulate that 80% of every tract in the upper Amazon, and 50% in more developed regions, must remain forested. Enforcement for such enormous territory, however, is difficult.

Of course, the importance of rain forests goes far beyond just their 'carbon sequestering' abilities. Blessed with astounding biodiversity, tropical forests have a far greater concentration of different plant and animal species than most other ecosystems. Of the 250,000 species of higher plants known to science, 45,000 can be found in the Amazon rain forest. This reservoir of genetic diversity is an incredibly vital source of food and medicine; a quarter of the medicines used in the developed world contain elements extracted from tropical forests. The Amazon rain forest has already given us rubber, manioc (cassava) and cocoa, as well as antimalarial drugs, cancer drugs and hundreds of other medicinal plants. A cure for AIDS, breast cancer or the common cold might be lurking somewhere in its flora or fauna. The destruction of such a storehouse would be an incalculable loss.

The regularly inundated floodplains of the 'white-water' (actually creamy-brown) rivers flowing down from the Andes are known as *várzea* and sustain forests up to 20m tall. Many of the trees have elevated roots. *Igapó* is the common name for forests flooded by the darker waters of the Rio Negro basin. It's particularly fascinating to boat through a flooded forest because you move along at treetop level and can get closer to the wildlife.

Forests on *terra firme* (higher land, not subject to flooding) typically grow to 30m in height. Here are found the Brazil nut tree and valuable hardwoods such as mahogany, which prefer a drier environment.

On the waters themselves live aquatic plants, such as the giant *Victoria amazonica* water lily (named after Britain's Queen Victoria and up to 2m in diameter) and even floating islands with amphibious grasses.

FOREST LAYERS
The rain forest is stratified into layers of plant and animal life. Most of the animal activity takes place in the canopy layer, 20m to 30m above ground, where trees compete for sunshine, and butterflies, sloths and the majority of birds and monkeys live. Here hummingbirds hover for pollen, and macaws and parrots seek out nuts and tender shoots. A few tall trees reaching up to 40m, even 50m, poke above the canopy and dominate the forest skyline. These 'emergent trees' are inhabited by birds such as the harpy eagle and toucan and, unlike most other rain-forest plants, disperse their seeds by wind.

The dense foliage of the canopy layer blots out sunlight at lower levels. Below the canopy is the understory. Epiphytes (air plants) hang at midlevels and below them are bushes, saplings and shrubs growing up to 5m in height. Last is a ground cover of ferns, seedlings and herbs – plants adapted to very little light. Down here live ants and termites, the so-called social insects. The *saubas* (leaf-cutter ants) use leaves to build underground nests for raising fungus gardens, while army ants swarm through the jungle in huge masses, eating everything in their path. Insects, fungi and roots fight for access to nutrients, keeping the forest floor quite tidy. At ground level it's cooler than in the canopy, averaging about 28°C (82°F), but humidity is higher, at about 90%.

The forest's soils are typically shallow. Many trees have buttress roots that spread over wide patches of ground to gather more nutrients.

Atlantic Rain Forest
Brazil's 'other' tropical rain forest, the Mata Atlântica (Atlantic rain forest), is actually older than the Amazon forest and evolved independently. It once extended along the country's southeast-facing coast, from Rio Grande do Norte to Rio Grande do Sul. Today, three-quarters of Brazil's population and all its main industrial cities are located in what used to be the Mata Atlântica, and only 7% of the original forest remains.

Along the coast, there are still long stretches of this luxuriant forest. Some areas boast what may be the highest biodiversity levels on earth. It also contains many unique species – 21 of its 26 primate types are found only here, as are more than 900 of its 2000-plus kinds of butterflies, and many of its 600-plus bird species. Unsurprisingly, many of these species are endangered, including the four types of lion tamarin and the two woolly spider monkeys (the largest primates in the Americas).

The Atlantic rain forest's distinctive flora – more than half of its tree species exist nowhere else – includes large trees such as brazilwood, ironwood, Bahian jacaranda and cedar, as well as many rare tree ferns. The 20,000 plant species here, half of them endemic, account for 8% of the world total. Unesco recognized the Mata Atlântica's importance in 1999 when it placed 33 separate areas in Paraná, São Paulo, Espírito Santo and Bahia states, totaling 5820 sq km, on the World Heritage List.

Caatinga
Caatinga is semiarid land, with hardy vegetation composed mainly of cacti and thorny shrubs adapted to a shortage of water and extreme heat – the natural environment of much of the interior of the Northeast region, the

Amazônia (www.amazonia.org.br) is a superb resource for Amazonia news and other information in both English and Portuguese.

The Amazon Basin averages between 130 and 250 rainy days a year, depending on exactly where you are.

In *The Last Forest: The Amazon in the Age of Globalization*, authors Mark London and Brian Kelly revisit the river basin 25 years after writing an earlier book on it, and conclude all is not yet lost.

sertão. Rainfall (300mm to 800mm a year) is irregular, and often torrential when it comes (in the first half of the year). Most rivers rising here are dry for half the year. Despite this, the caatinga harbors surprising biodiversity. When it does rain, the trees break into leaf and the ground turns green. 'Islands' of humidity and fertile soils around the mountain ranges are known as *brejos*. Caatinga is a habitat unique to Brazil, although less than one-tenth of it is in its natural state.

Wood and coal from the caatingas are a primary energy source for many of the region's more than 20 million inhabitants, and also fuel hungry brick-works and steel industries. Centuries of cattle ranching, and more recent ill-advised attempts at irrigated, pesticide-aided agriculture, have devastated large areas of caatinga. Some 40,000 sq km of caatinga were desertified in the last 15 years of the 20th century.

Cerrado

Cerrado covers the central high plains of Brazil – 2 million sq km in a rough triangle from southern Minas Gerais to Mato Grosso to southern Maranhão, nearly a quarter of the country in all. Typical cerrado is open savanna grass-land dotted with trees, though it can edge into scrub, palm stands or even fairly thick forest. Over 800 bird species are known to live here and plant diversity is great – 10,000 species, of which 45% are found nowhere else in the world. Many plants are used to produce cork, fibers, oils, handicrafts, medicines and food. Medicinal plants native to cerrado include arnica and golden trumpet.

Despite the cerrado's size, it is severely threatened. Only about 20% has intact original vegetation, and with deforestation running at about 30,000 sq km a year, some researchers fear the cerrado will disappear completely by 2030. Less than 1% is under environmental protection.

Pantanal

The Pantanal is a vast swampy wetland in the center of South America, about half the size of France – some 210,000 sq km spread across Brazil, Bolivia and Paraguay. It's the largest inland wetland on earth, and 140,000 sq km of it lies in Brazil, in the states of Mato Grosso and Mato Grosso do Sul.

During the wet season, from October to March, the waters from the higher surrounding lands run into the Pantanal, inundating as much as two-thirds of it for half the year. The Pantanal, though 2000km upstream from the Atlantic Ocean, is only 100m to 200m above sea level and drains very slowly. Its chief outlet is the Rio Paraguai, which ultimately drains into the Atlantic Ocean via the Rio de la Plata. Waters reach their highest levels, up to 3m above dry-season levels, around March in the northern Pantanal, but not until about June in the south.

This seasonal flooding has made systematic farming impossible, severely limiting human impact on the area, and it creates an enormously rich feed-ing ground for wildlife. The Pantanal is still one of Brazil's wildest regions. It is the best area to head in all Brazil if you want to see wildlife, boasting greater visible numbers of animals and at least as much variety of creatures as Amazonia, with which it shares many species. The Pantanal supports approximately 650 bird species, 300 fish species, up to 190 mammals and 170 reptile species including iconic creatures like the giant anaconda, the jaguar, the puma, the giant anteater, the hyacinth macaw, the giant otter, and the black howler and brown capuchin monkeys – and somewhere between 10 and 35 million caimans. The most visible mammal is the capybara, the world's largest rodent, which is often seen in family groups or even large herds.

One hectare (10,000 sq meters) of well-conserved caatinga can be home to 200 different ant species.

John Kricher's *A Neotropical Companion*, while not specific to Brazil, is a good introductory text for neotropical ecology and explains many of the forest's intricacies in straightforward terms.

A superb guide for travelers visiting the Pantanal is *Brazil: Amazon and Pantanal* by David L Pearson and Les Beletsky. It's accessible and informative, identifying wildlife, plants, environmental threats and conservation issues.

The floodwaters replenish the soil's nutrients, the waters teem with fish, and the ponds provide ecological niches for many animals and plants. In the dry season the lagoons and marshes dry out and fresh grasses emerge on the savanna, while hawks and caimans compete for fish in the shrinking ponds.

With cerrado to the east, Amazon rain forest to the north and spots of Atlantic rain forest to the south, Pantanal vegetation – an estimated 3500 plant species – is a mishmash of savanna, forest, meadow and even, on some of the highest points, caatinga.

Despite threats to its ecosystems, the Pantanal is still generally well conserved and the region provides a secure habitat for reduced populations of threatened species such as the hyacinth macaw, giant otter, marsh deer, jaguar and maned wolf.

Other Environmental Zones

The mountainous regions of southern Brazil were once covered by coniferous forests that were dominated by the prehistoric-looking, 30m- to 40m-high *araucária* (Paraná pine) tree. The *araucária* forests have been decimated by timber cutters and now survive only in scattered areas such as the Aparados da Serra national park, generally at altitudes above 500m.

Apart from the cerrado, grasslands occur chiefly in Brazil's far north (northern Roraima) and far south (Rio Grande do Sul). Unlike the cerrado, which has a consistent scattering of medium to tall trees, the Roraima grasslands have only low trees and bushes, while the *campos do sul* (southern fields), on the rolling southern pampas, generally have no trees except where interspersed with patches of woodland.

WILDLIFE

Brazil's teeming flora and fauna make it one of the planet's best destinations for nature lovers. For more details on some of Brazil's best-known animal species, see p105.

Mammals

ANTEATERS, ARMADILLOS & SLOTHS

Zoologists group these animals together in the edentate order. Edentate means 'toothless,' and while that's not strictly true of sloths, these creatures feed chiefly on plants and insects.

The giant anteater (up to 2m long) lives off termites and ants. Its meat is prized in some areas of Brazil, and it's a threatened species. The collared or lesser anteater, up to 1.4m long, is yellow and black, mainly nocturnal and often climbs trees.

Sloths have strong arms and legs, and spend most of their time hidden (and sleeping) in trees. You have a good chance of seeing some if you get a bit off the beaten track in Amazonia: from a moderate distance they look like clumps of vegetation high in trees. The species you're most likely to see is the brown-throated three-toed sloth.

Brazil's several species of armadillo are mainly nocturnal and widely distributed.

COATIS & RACCOONS

The widespread coati is one of the carnivorous animals that you're most likely to come across – possibly as a pet, for it's easily tamed. Its distant relative, the crab-eating raccoon, with a ringed tail and black eye mask like the North American raccoon, is found in Amazonia, the Pantanal and in between, always near water, where it seeks out its diet of crabs, fish, mollusks and small amphibians.

For 15 years Mark Plotkin devotedly tracked down Amazonian witchdoctors to understand some of their encyclopedic knowledge of medicinal plants. His *Tales of a Shaman's Apprentice* is a travelogue and adventure story too.

A good field guide to the animals of tropical Brazil is *Neotropical Rainforest Mammals* by Louise Emmons.

The giant ground sloth, which grew to the size of an elephant, once inhabited much of Brazil. It was easy prey for prehistoric hunters and was presumably hunted to extinction 10,000 years ago.

DEER, PECCARIES & TAPIRS

In the Pantanal, most people see at least a few deer. The biggest, which is active by day, is the marsh deer, whose antlers can grow to 60cm long. Other species – some found as far north as Amazonia – include the pampas deer, which lives more out in the open than most other deer, and the small (60cm to 70cm long) gray brocket deer and red brocket deer.

Peccaries, which look like small wild boars, are fairly widely distributed in forests. They live in groups, are active by day and feed on fruit, roots, carrion and small animals. The collared peccary, around 1m long and weighing 20kg, is named for the light-colored semicircle below its neck and is found in groups of 10 to 50. The slightly bigger white-lipped peccary travels in groups of 50 or more, chewing and trampling everything in its path.

The large Brazilian tapir (up to 300kg) is found in forests across the country and rarely strays far from mud, which it uses to keep cool and control parasites.

One River: Explorations and Discoveries in the Amazon Rain Forest by Wade Davis reflects on the importance of the Amazon and its contents to the planet as a whole.

DOGS, FOXES & WOLVES

The maned wolf is commonly hunted and is a threatened species. It is russet-colored, fox-faced and long-legged, grows to about 1m long (plus tail) and has a mane of darker hair on the back of the neck. It inhabits cerrado and the Pantanal. Other Brazilian members of the dog family include the crab-eating fox and the bush dog, both also present in cerrado and the Pantanal. They are pretty rare and you'll be lucky if you see any of these three.

DOLPHINS, MANATEES & WHALES

In the captivating *Journey of the Pink Dolphins*, Sy Montgomery recounts some magical experiences with these amazing inhabitants of Amazonian waterways.

On many rivers in the Amazon Basin you should catch glimpses of the pink dolphin. It's most often seen where tributaries meet larger rivers, and is most active in the early morning and late afternoon. Sightings are tantalizing – and getting good photos virtually impossible – as the dolphin surfaces unpredictably, for just a second or so at a time, to breathe. Often it won't even lift its head above the surface. The pink dolphin has a lumpy forehead, a long beak and no dorsal fin (just a ridge). Adults are 1.8m to 2.5m long, weighing 85kg to 160kg.

Amazonian rivers are also home to the gray dolphin, a bit smaller than the pink and often found together with it. Unlike the pink dolphin, the gray also inhabits the sea, in coastal waters from Florianópolis to Panama. When it surfaces it usually lifts its head and part of its body out of the water.

Larger than the dolphin is the Amazon manatee, a slow-moving vegetarian that is illegally hunted for its meat and in danger of extinction. Prospects are even poorer for the marine West Indian manatee, of which there are just 500 left in coastal waters from the state of Alagoas northward.

Seven whale species occur off Brazil's coasts, with good sightings off Praia do Rosa (p355) between June and October. The rare humpback whale breeds in the same months in the Parque Nacional Marinho de Abrolhos (p491), off the coast of southern Bahia.

Amazonian myth has it that the pink dolphin can turn itself into a handsome man able to seduce young women.

FELINES

Many visitors dream of sighting a wild jaguar, but few have the luck of seeing one in the wild. The elusive and splendid jaguar is widely but thinly distributed in Brazil, occurring in Amazonia, the Pantanal, the cerrado and such easterly national parks as Caparaó (p271), Ilha Grande (p186), Monte Pascoal (p488), Chapada Diamantina (p496) and Chapada dos Veadeiros (p399). Jaguars hunt at night, covering large distances. They prey on a wide variety of animals, in trees, water and on the ground, including sloths, monkeys, fish, deer, tapirs, capybaras and agoutis – but rarely people.

The puma, almost as big as the jaguar and similarly elusive, is the same beast as North America's cougar or mountain lion. As well as preying on deer, it sometimes attacks herds of domestic animals, such as sheep or goats.

Brazil's four smaller wildcats are also widely but sparsely distributed and rarely seen. Three have markings similar to the jaguar. The largest of the three (up to 1.4m long with tail and weighing 15kg) is the ocelot; next biggest is the margay; and then the oncilla. The jaguarundi is probably more often seen than any other Brazilian feline, because it's active by day. A good swimmer, it's also known as the otter-cat, and is similar in size to the margay, with a uniformly colored coat, which may be black, brown or gray.

The Brazilian version of the yeti is the Mapinguari, a legendary animal of the Amazon that grows to 2m, is covered in red hair and can rip apart palm trees.

MARMOSETS & TAMARINS

Around 20 species of marmoset and tamarin, which are small – often very small – primates, are found in Brazil. Some are fairly common, but the four species of lion tamarin, inhabitants of the Atlantic rain forests and with a resemblance to miniature lions, are all endangered. The golden lion tamarin exists only in the Reserva Biológica Poço das Antas in Rio de Janeiro state (within earshot of interstate Hwy BR-101). A campaign to save this species – a squirrel-sized creature with a brilliant orange-gold color – has, amazingly, brought its population up from about 100 in the 1970s, to above 1000 now, and the golden lion tamarin has left the critically endangered list.

MONKEYS

About 80 of the world's approximately 300 primate species (which also include marmosets and tamarins) are found in Brazil, many of them unique to the country. Southeast Brazil's two species of woolly spider monkey (see p272), the southern *muriqui* and northern *muriqui*, with their thick brown fur, are the largest primates in the Americas and both are endangered, the northern species critically so and down to a population of under 300.

Howler monkeys are known for their distinctive roar. They live in groups of up to 20 that are led by a single male. In Amazonia you're most likely to encounter the red howler monkey. Further south, including in the Pantanal, the black howler monkey is the local species. The brown howler monkey inhabits the small remaining areas of the Mata Atlântica.

The two types of uakari monkey, the black-headed and the bald, inhabit Amazonian flooded forest. The bald uakari has a red or pink bald head and thick, shaggy body fur ranging from chestnut-red to white (giving rise to the popular names red uakari and white uakari). Bald uakaris are threatened, but if you happen to visit the Mamirauá Reserve (Reserva de Desenvolvimento Sustentável Mamirauá; p662) you stand a good chance of seeing the very distinctive white uakari.

The bald uakari's red complexion and lack of head hair have earned it the nickname *macaco-inglês* (English monkey).

RODENTS

In addition to the world's largest rodent, the widespread capybara, you might also encounter smaller rodents – but still up to 60cm or 70cm long – including the paca and various species of agouti.

Reptiles

CAIMANS

Relatives of the alligator, caimans survived a devastating bout of poaching for their skins in the 1980s. The most common type is the yacare caiman or Paraguayan caiman. Amazonia has four species, the most common being the spectacled caiman – the one you may get to handle on nighttime expeditions. Caimans lay eggs in nests of leaves and stalks, and these are vulnerable to predators such as coatis and lizards; the hatched young are prey for herons and storks.

MAN BITES PIRANHA

Why are people scared of piranhas? The fish should be frightened of us, as humans eat piranhas a billion times more often than piranhas eat people. They're reasonably tasty, if a bit small and bony. A standard activity on an Amazon jungle trip is catching your own piranha lunch. You'll be taken by canoe to a promising spot and given a simple fishing rod constructed of cane, line and hook, and small chunks of meat for bait. Put a piece of bait onto the hook, drop it into the water, and – presto – free lunch. For the piranhas, that is, which will nibble the bait right off your hook without getting caught.

Your more-skilled local companions, however, will catch half a dozen of them without even trying – and *these* will be your lunch.

A piranha is not just a piranha, of course. It could be any of about 40 species of the *Serrasalmo* genus. Piranhas are found in the basins of the Amazon, Orinoco, Paraguay and São Francisco rivers and in the rivers of the Guianas. Some live on seeds and fruits, some on other fish, and only a handful of species are potentially a risk to larger creatures. These types are most dangerous when stuck in tributaries, meanders or lakes that get cut off from main rivers in the dry season. When they have eaten all the other fish, the piranhas will attack more or less anything, including wounded mammals entering their waters. The scent of blood or bodily fluids in the water can whip a shoal into a feeding frenzy. Confirmed accounts of human fatalities caused by piranhas are extremely few, but plenty of Amazonian river folks have scars or missing fingers to testify just how sharp and vicious those little triangular teeth can be.

SNAKES

In addition to the well-known anaconda, other constrictor snakes include the boa constrictor, which is 3m to 5m long, generally brown patterned and lives off small animals in varied and widespread habitats; and the handsome green-and-white emerald tree boa. A number of other snakes live in trees, but most are harmless.

Although it is rare to encounter a venomous snake in the wild, Brazil still has quite a few species of them, including rattlesnakes, vipers and coral snakes. The most dangerous in the Pantanal is Wied's lancehead, a gray-black-and-white-patterned viper up to 70cm long that sometimes hides in houses; its bite can be fatal if not treated quickly. Also to be steered clear of is the highly poisonous Brazilian coral snake, with its rings of red, black and white. It lurks under rocks or logs and only bites when it feels threatened. The various false coral snakes are, lucky for them, nearly impossible to distinguish from the real thing.

TURTLES

Endangered sea turtles are making a comeback on the turtle-nesting beaches from Santa Catarina state to Ceará. The Tamar Project, founded in 1980, does an impressive job of protecting them (see the boxed text on p464 for more on Tamar and sea turtles). Brazil is also home to several species of river turtle, spread throughout the country and mostly not endangered.

Fish

Amazonia is home to at least 2000 freshwater fish species, and the Pantanal to around 300 species. The biggest Amazonian fish is the enormous pirarucu, or arapaima, which can weigh well over 100kg. Its red and silvery-brown scale patterns are reminiscent of Chinese paintings. The pirarucu is a voracious hunter of other fish, and a rich food source for humans. To try to preserve the shrinking population, catching it is banned if it's less than 1.5m in length or during the October-to-March spawning season.

(Continued on page 113)

BRAZILIAN WILDLIFE GUIDE

Home to an astounding assortment of creatures great and small, Brazil is one of the world's great destinations for wildlife watching. Brazilian rain forests, wetlands, grasslands and coastal waters teem with life. Scarlet macaws, pink river dolphins, spider monkeys, capybara, sea turtles, three-toed sloths and jaguars are just a handful of the thousands of animal species that make Brazil such a biodiversity hot spot. And visiting the habitats of Brazil's wildlife attractions usually means big adventure: canyon descents, boat journeys down the Amazon, canopy walks through treetops and horseback rides across the surreal landscape of the Pantanal.

MAMMALS

Brazil has more mammals than any other country on the planet. Some of its most famous species – such as jaguars and maned wolves – are rarely spotted. Others, including coati, capybara and many monkey species can, with luck, be sighted on wildlife outings. For information about water-dwelling mammals see p110.

JOHN HAY

PAUL KENNEDY

① Jaguar

The largest American feline is thinly distributed across Amazonia, the Pantanal, the cerrado (a type of savanna) and easterly national parks. Yellow with black spots, jaguars can grow to 2.5m long, including tail, and males can weigh 120kg. They're solitary, nocturnal and are unusually good swimmers.

② Capybara

The widespread capybara is the world's largest – and arguably most endearing – rodent at 1m long and weighing up to 70kg. At home on land or in water, these giant guinea-pig-like creatures travel in herds and are easily seen in the Pantanal.

③ Capuchin Monkey

The lithe capuchins are named for the hair atop their heads, which resembles monks' cowls. They're dispersed over almost the whole country – even in Rio de Janeiro – living in groups of up to 20.

④ Sloth

True to their name, sloths move very slowly. They hang upside down from branches, feeding on leaves, sleeping up to 18 hours a day and descending to the ground to excrete just once a week. Surprisingly, they're good swimmers. Your best chance of seeing one is in the Pantanal or the Amazon.

⑤ Howler Monkey

Howler monkeys are more easily heard than seen; their roar (not really a howl) carries many kilometers. They're stocky and are found in groups 10m to 20m high in trees. Take heed: howler monkeys will pelt you with their excrement if they feel threatened.

⑥ Squirrel Monkey

The most common primates in Amazonia, squirrel monkeys have pale faces, dark nose areas, big ears and long tails. They move in small, noisy groups. The black spider monkey grows up to 1.5m long and has long thin limbs and a prehensile tail.

⑦ Coati

The carnivorous and widespread coati is furry and cute, and is the size of a small or medium-sized dog. It has a long brown-and-yellow-ringed tail, and a long flexible snout that noses around for food on the ground or up in trees.

⑧ Giant Anteater

The giant anteater can grow well over 2m long. It tears open ant and termite nests with its sharp claws and laps up as many as 35,000 termites a day with its probing sticky tongue. You're most likely to see the giant anteater in cerrado habitat.

⑨ Brazilian Tapir

Found in most forested parts of the country, the Brazilian tapir is shy and nocturnal. The tapir spends its evenings foraging for leaves, fruit and roots with its long snout. It's related to the horse and weighs up to 300kg.

BIRDS

There is a plentiful range of fantastically colorful birds in almost every region of Brazil, making the country a major destination for birding trips. An astounding 1700-plus species of birds can be seen in Brazil – more than in Europe and North America combined. Bring top-quality binoculars!

RALPH HOPKINS

❶ Toucan
Among the best-known of Latin American birds, toucans have huge rainbow-colored (but mostly hollow) beaks, enabling them to reach berries at the end of branches. They fly with surprising agility and live at forest tree-top level across Brazil.

❷ Scarlet Ibis
The spectacular scarlet ibis is a deep-pink-colored, 50cm long water-loving bird that's found in flocks along parts of the Northeast coast and on the Ilha de Marajó, at the mouth of the Amazon River.

❸ Macaw
Icons of the tropical rain forest, macaws are colorful and charismatic New World parrots. They often travel in pairs, covering up to 25km a day foraging for food. When flying, they can be distinguished by their straight-arrow body shape.

❹ Harpy Eagle
Brazil's most emblematic bird of prey is this rare and enormously powerful eagle, which weighs up to 10kg and has a wingspan of up to 2.5m. Found chiefly in Amazonia, it enjoys a diet of monkeys, sloths and other medium-sized animals.

❺ Hummingbird
These beautiful little birds, with their dazzling iridescent colors, may be seen all over Brazil. They flit rapidly, almost insectlike, from one spot to the next, and can even fly backwards. The lyrical Brazilian name for them is *beija-flor* (flower kisser).

❻ Jabiru
The tall (1.4m) black-headed and scarlet-necked jabiru has become a symbol of the Pantanal, but is also found in Amazonia. You'll see them flapping inelegantly along waterways or standing motionless ready to jab for fish with their long beaks.

❼ Trogon
This family of medium-sized, brightly colored (sometimes iridescent) birds with long tails includes the celebrated quetzals. You may see trogons perching and flying at medium heights in tropical forests.

❽ Greater Rhea
The biggest Brazilian bird (*ema* in Portuguese) is found in the cerrado and the Pantanal. It can grow up to 1.4m tall and weigh some 30kg. Its sizable wings spread while running to function like sails.

AQUATIC LIFE

Brazil's swirling rivers and lush coastline harbor an impressive array of aquatic life. Sure there are flesh-eating fish in the Amazon, but you'll also find river- and ocean-dwelling dolphins, brilliantly hued tropical fish, river otters, oversized but graceful manatees and seven whale species that pass near the coast.

2

3

JENNY & TONY ENDERBY

① Giant Otter

The endangered giant otter can measure 2m from nose to tail tip. This highly social animal inhabits lakes and calm rivers in forests from Amazonia to the Pantanal, usually in family groups of six to eight.

② Pink Dolphin

One of the world's five freshwater cetaceans, the pink dolphin – and it really is pink – lives only in the Amazon and Orinoco Rivers and their tributaries. It has tiny eyes and is almost blind but has a highly evolved sonar system.

③ Southern Right Whale

These massive mammals can be 18m long and can weigh more than 60 tons. You can best see them off the Santa Catarina coast between June and October, when hundreds migrate north from Antarctica in search of a warmer, calmer place to spawn.

④ Spinner Dolphin

The Fernando de Noronha archipelago is a good site for observing large groups of spinner dolphins, small marine dolphins less than 1.8m long. They gather by the hundreds in the bays at sunrise.

⑤ Amazon Manatee

The Amazon manatee is a large, slow-moving vegetarian that averages a length of 3m and a weight of 500kg. It feeds on grasses and floating vegetation and is illegally hunted for its meat by riverbank dwellers. The manatee is consequently in danger of extinction.

⑥ Pirarucu

The king of Amazonian fish is the beautiful and enormous pirarucu, which can grow to 3m long and weigh well over 100kg. Unusually, the male protects the young for up to the first six months of their lives.

⑦ Piranha

The infamous carnivorous fish is abundantly present in the Amazon, but contrary to popular belief is quite fearful of humans. Largely scavengers, piranhas range in size from 15cm to 26cm and mostly eat fish, plants and insects.

REPTILES & AMPHIBIANS

Lovers of serpents and scaly, cold-blooded creatures have plenty to celebrate in Brazil. Here you'll find both the much revered and mythologized anaconda as well as the stealthy black caiman. Those who prefer smaller, cuddlier creatures can head for the coast, where baby sea turtles make their crucial first journey into the ocean.

LEE FOSTER

❶ Caiman

Brazil has several species of caiman, close relatives of the alligator. They eat fish, amphibians, crustaceans and some birds. The biggest is the black caiman, which can reach over 5m long. It's best seen in Amazonia and the Pantanal.

❷ Anaconda

The infamous anaconda coils around its victims to crush and suffocate them, then eats them whole. Anacondas grow up to 10m long and can live in water or on land and are considered common in the Pantanal.

❸ Sea Turtle

Five of the world's seven species of sea turtle are found along Brazil's coasts. The loggerhead, hawksbill, green, olive ridley and leatherback are all protected under the Tamar project (p464), and if you're lucky you might be able to see hatchlings.

TOM BOYD

❹ Poison Dart Frog

These colorful and tiny Amazonian amphibians are renowned for the powerful toxins they secrete. Their bright hues and ostentatious patterns warn would-be predators of their lethal composition. Some tribes use the frogs' venom in their own medicines. The Yanomami and some other tribes use the venom in hunting.

(Continued from page 104)

The most important food fish of central Amazonia is the little jaraqui, which swims in shoals of thousands. Another food fish, the tambaqui, is of the same family as piranhas. The rotund tambaqui can reach 1m in length and weigh up to 25kg. Normally it lives on nuts (which it can crack with its jaws) and seeds, but when the waters recede it can turn carnivorous.

Amazonia harbors at least 100 species of catfish, named for the long bristles that help them search for food on river bottoms. One aggressive catfish, the piraíba, grows up to 3m long and weighs as much as 200kg. It will even attack water birds. The dourado, up to 1m long with pale-gold sides, is common in the Pantanal as well as Amazonia, and is a popular dish in restaurants throughout the country.

You will hear about the infamous candiru in Amazonia. There are many species of these small catfish, most of them pretty obnoxious. The really infamous type is one of the *Vandellia* genus, about 5cm long. This little charmer normally lives inside the gills of other fish to suck their blood, but is attracted to urine and reputedly able to wriggle up humans' urinary tracts, where it lodges itself with sharp spines and can only be removed by surgery. The belief that it can actually swim up a stream of urine to get inside you is almost certainly false, but it's probably not a good idea to urinate in Amazonian waters just the same. Locals wear clothing to exclude the candiru in areas where it's known.

Other best-avoided inhabitants of Brazilian freshwaters include the stingray (*arraia* in Portuguese) and the electric eel (Portuguese: *poraquê*). The stingray lives on river floors and can inflict deep, painful cuts with the barbs in its tail. The electric eel, growing up to 2.75m long, is capable of a 600-volt discharge to stun its prey and could potentially kill a human with a volley of electric pulses.

Much sought after in Amazonia, both for its delicious taste and its famous fighting qualities as a sport fish, is the peacock bass (Portuguese: *tucunaré*). Growing to 50cm or more, it has a peacocklike 'eye' spot on its tail. Also sought – for home aquariums the world over – are the tiny but brightly colored tetra fishes. These come from the murky *igapós* (flooded Amazon forests), where they would doubtless go unseen if more demurely pigmented.

Birds

With its diverse habitats and extraordinary number of species, Brazil is a major hot spot for bird-watchers.

BIRDS OF PREY

Much like great cats, birds of prey command respect and are always an object of fascination. Brazil has around 40 species of eagle, hawk, falcon, kite, caracara and kestrel, some quite common, and they're not very easy to tell apart.

The largest bird of prey in the Americas is the ferocious harpy eagle, with claws bigger than human hands. It eats sizable mammals (including monkeys) and nests at least 25m above the ground in large jungle trees. Although a few harpies still inhabit Mata Atlântica, the bird is found chiefly in Amazonia.

The crested caracara is common in many areas – it's 50cm to 60cm long with a 1.2m or 1.3m wingspan. Its broad diet includes fish dying from a lack of oxygen as Pantanal ponds dry up, and animals that have been run over on roads or burnt in forest fires. Also common in Amazonia and the Pantanal are the yellow-headed caracara, about 40cm long, and the black-collared

---

The pirarucu has gills but they are basically useless. It breathes with lungs instead, and has to surface for air about every 10 minutes or it will drown.

Bird-watchers might want to pack *A Field Guide to the Birds of Brazil* (2009) by Ber van Perlo, an excellent and compact bird-identification guide, with 187 color plates covering Brazil's 1700-plus species.

hawk, a reddish-brown fish-catcher, with a white head and chest, that reaches lengths of 45cm. The osprey, or fishing eagle, is bigger (55cm to 60cm; wingspan 1.45m to 1.7m), with a darker brown body.

HUMMINGBIRDS

In Brazil there are dozens of species of these often striking jewel-like little birds, known as *beija-flores* (flower-kissers), and they occupy an important role in Brazilian art and folklore, often mentioned in music and poetry. Even one of Rio's best-known samba schools is called Beija-Flor.

PARROTS

These are the kinds of bird that have come to symbolize tropical rain forests, and people travel from all over the world to see some of Brazil's dozens of species. These charismatic, colorful birds have strong, curved beaks that they use to break open seeds and nuts and they also eat soft clay to temper the acidity of their other foods.

Hummingbirds beat their wings up to 80 times a second, allowing them to hover while extracting pollen from flowers – making a light humming noise as they do.

The name scarlet macaw is given to two large, gloriously colored species – *Ara chloroptera*, also called the red-and-green macaw, which grows up to 95cm long, with blue-and-green wings and a red-striped face; and *Ara macao*, which is a bit smaller with blue-and-yellow wings. The latter bird is restricted to Amazonia, but the red-and-green macaw also inhabits the Pantanal, cerrado and even caatinga. The blue-and-yellow macaw, about 85cm long, is also widely distributed. The yellow covers its underside, the blue its upper parts.

Unfortunately, macaws' beautiful plumage makes them a major target for poachers. Poaching contributed greatly to the decline of the endangered hyacinth macaw, the world's largest parrot (1m long). This gorgeous bird, deep blue with splashes of yellow, is down to a wild population of about 3000 and conservationists are struggling to bring it back from the brink. Its range extends from Pará state to the Pantanal; the recently established Parque Nacional das Nascentes do Rio Parnaíba (p567) in Piauí state is a good place to see it.

TOUCANS

Among the most colorful groups of Latin American birds are toucans, which despite their large beaks are able to fly with a surprising agility. Toucans live at forest treetop level and are often best seen from boats.

A Field Guide to Medicinal and Useful Plants of the Upper Amazon, by James L Castner, combines clear photos, accurate descriptions and intriguing details on Amazonia's huge wealth of medicinal plants.

Brazil's biggest is the toco toucan, whose habitat ranges from Amazonia to the cerrado to the Pantanal. Around 55cm long, including its bright orange beak, the plumage is black except for a white neck area. In Amazonia you may see the white-throated toucan or the yellow-ridged toucan. Both are fairly large birds, with black beaks.

WATERFOWL

Highly visible birds in the Pantanal and Amazonia include herons, egrets, storks, ibises, spoonbills and their relatives. The tiger heron, with its brown and black stripes, is particularly distinctive. The sight of hundreds of snowy egrets gathering in a waterside rookery looks like a sudden blooming of white flowers in the treetops.

Of the storks, one of the most striking is the tall black-headed and scarlet-necked jabiru found in the Pantanal and Amazonia. In the Pantanal, also look for the similarly sized maguari stork, which is mainly white with a pinkish face, and the smaller wood stork, with its black head and beak with a curved end. The beautiful pink roseate spoonbill is another Pantanal resident. The spectacular scarlet ibis lives in flocks along the Northeast coast.

Kingfishers fly across or along rivers as boats approach. The biggest species is the 42cm-long ringed kingfisher, which is predominantly bright turquoise with a rust-colored underside.

Plants

Brazil's history and future are inextricably tied to its forests and nature. So close is this association that the country even gets its name from the brazilwood (*pau brasil*) tree, which the early Portuguese explorers cut and exported as fast as they could for a valuable red dye found in its core.

The last ice age did not reach Brazil and the rain forests have never suffered long droughts, so the area has had an unusually long period of time to develop plant species that are found nowhere else in the world. Although some of these long-evolved species have been destroyed in the last 30 years through heavy deforestation, there remains an impressive range of flora in Brazil – from over 200 species of delicate orchids and the world's largest variety of palms (390) to 90m-tall hardwood trees.

Though estimates run at around 45,000, it would be impossible to determine an exact number of plant species in the Amazon, let alone in the whole of Brazil, as new plants are being discovered all the time and, unfortunately, others are disappearing with frightening frequency. The great majority of the plants in Brazil's rain forests are trees – estimated at some 70% of the total vegetation. Many rain-forest trees look similar even though they are of different species, but a trained eye can distinguish more than 400 species of tree per hectare in some areas.

One of the most economically important trees is the rubber tree, which grows in the wild or on sustainable plantations for the large-scale production of latex. Another sustainable forest product is the nut from the Brazil nut tree, a good snack if you are able to get the shell off without having a nervous breakdown. Mahogany trees are the most prized of Brazilian hardwoods and, despite being protected, are still often felled and sold (usually within Brazil).

Many edible fruits also grow in the rain forest, so many in fact that a number of them only have names in Portuguese. Some of the more popular fruits, including *açaí, acerola and cupuaçu,* can be found at juice bars throughout the country. Guaraná berries, containing a stimulant similar to caffeine, are also making their way into energy drinks the world over.

Outside the rain forests the plant life is quite different. In some of the drier parts of the country it may seem that the only plants are palm trees, shrubs or thorny cacti.

NATIONAL PARKS & PROTECTED AREAS

Much of Brazil is, officially at least, under environmental protection. Over 1000 areas, covering some 1.3 million sq km (around 15% of the whole country), are protected. Some of these are run by the federal government, some by state governments and some by private individuals or nongovernmental organizations (NGOs).

The amount of protected territory continues to grow. At least 20 new national parks have been created since the late 1990s. In 2006 the Amazonian state of Pará announced it was giving protected status to 150,000 sq km of rain forest, much of it virgin forest. A senior researcher from the Brazilian sustainability institute Imazon hailed the move as 'the greatest effort in history toward the creation of protected areas in tropical forests.'

Unfortunately, the degree of protection that Brazil's protected areas actually receive is erratic and in some cases practically nonexistent. The federal government's environmental agencies, the Instituto Chico Mendes de Conservação da Biodiversidade (ICMBio) and the Instituto Brasileiro do

The greatest number of different tree species ever found in 1 hectare (10,000 sq meters) was 476, recorded in an area of Atlantic rain forest in the hills of Espírito Santo state.

A Brazil nut tree takes 10 years to reach maturity and can produce more than 450kg of nuts per year.

Wade Davis' *The Lost Amazon: The Photographic Journey of Richard Evans Schultes* is a fascinating biography of Richard Evans Schultes, a Harvard ethnobotanist and expert in sacred hallucinogens. It includes Schultes' black-and-white photos.

PARKS, RESERVES & LANDSCAPES OF BRAZIL

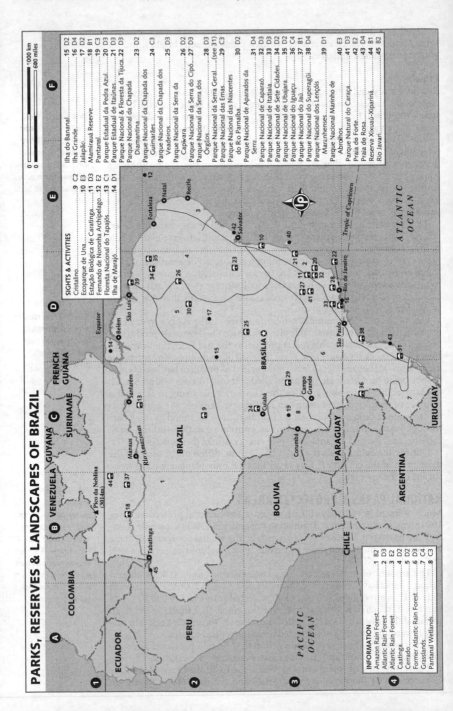

INFORMATION	
Amazon Rain Forest	1 B2
Atlantic Rain Forest	2 D3
Atlantic Rain Forest	3 E2
Caatinga	4 D2
Cerrado	5 D2
Former Atlantic Rain Forest	6 D3
Grasslands	7 C4
Pantanal Wetlands	8 C3

SIGHTS & ACTIVITIES	
Cristalino	9 C2
Ecoparque de Una	10 E3
Estação Biológica de Caratinga	11 D3
Fernando de Noronha Archipelago	12 E2
Floresta Nacional do Tapajós	13 C1
Ilha de Marajó	14 D1
Ilha do Bananal	15 D2
Ilha Grande	16 D4
Jalapão	17 D2
Mamirauá Reserve	18 B1
Pantanal	19 C3
Parque Estadual da Pedra Azul	20 D3
Parque Estadual de Itaúnas	21 D3
Parque Nacional & Floresta da Tijuca	22 D3
Parque Nacional da Chapada Diamantina	23 D2
Parque Nacional da Chapada dos Guimarães	24 C3
Parque Nacional da Chapada dos Veadeiros	25 D3
Parque Nacional da Serra da Capivara	26 D2
Parque Nacional da Serra do Cipó	27 D3
Parque Nacional da Serra dos Órgãos	28 D3
Parque Nacional da Serra Geral	(see 31)
Parque Nacional das Emas	29 C3
Parque Nacional das Nascentes do Rio Parnaíba	30 D2
Parque Nacional de Aparados da Serra	31 D4
Parque Nacional de Caparaó	32 D3
Parque Nacional de Itatiaia	33 D3
Parque Nacional de Sete Cidades	34 D2
Parque Nacional de Ubajara	35 D2
Parque Nacional do Iguaçu	36 C4
Parque Nacional do Jaú	37 B1
Parque Nacional do Superagüi	38 D4
Parque Nacional dos Lençóis Maranhenses	39 D1
Parque Nacional Marinho de Abrolhos	40 E3
Parque Natural do Caraça	41 D3
Praia do Forte	42 E2
Praia do Rosa	43 D4
Reserva Xixuaú-Xipariná	44 B1
Rio Javari	45 B2

Meio Ambiente e dos Recursos Naturais Renováveis (IBAMA; Brazilian Institute of the Environment & Renewable Natural Resources), have limited budgets that allow limited protection against illegal logging, ranching, settlement and poaching happening on millions of hectares of federally protected lands.

Terras Indígena (Indigenous Lands) occupy about 12% of Brazilian territory, nearly all in the Amazon. Though not explicitly dedicated to nature conservation, their inhabitants tend to use them with minimal environmental impact.

Where to Go

Brazil is a huge country and its flora and fauna are scattered across vast regions. Plan ahead to take in areas that meet your interests in nature. The table on p119 lists highlight areas for getting up close with natural Brazil.

SOUTHEAST

Many national parks in this region cover mountainous terrain, with some of Brazil's highest peaks, and make for spectacular hiking and climbing. Vegetation ranges from lush Mata Atlântica to *araucária* forest and cerrado.

SOUTH

Abundant wildlife is a big attraction of the Superagüi and Iguaçu national parks – and also of the Argentine Parque Nacional del Iguazú on the other side of the Iguaçu Falls. The Aparados da Serra and Serra Geral national parks contain stunning canyons and rock formations.

CENTRAL

If you're keen to see animals in the wild, don't miss the Pantanal, which has the greatest concentration of fauna in the New World – visible to the most casual observer in the Pantanal's open spaces. The Chapada dos Veadeiros and Chapada dos Guimarães national parks have gorgeous scenery with spectacular waterfalls, canyons and deep valleys. Parque Nacional das Emas is Brazil's best-preserved tract of cerrado, with abundant visible wildlife, including the *emas* (rheas) for which it's named.

NORTHEAST

The Northeast's natural highlights range from the escarpments, peaks, waterfalls and rivers of the Parque Nacional da Chapada Diamantina (a great hiking area) to the vast dune fields of the Parque Nacional dos Lençóis Maranhenses. Marine attractions rank high here too, with two national marine parks, Fernando de Noronha and Abrolhos. The Fernando de Noronha archipelago, 350km out into the Atlantic, abounds in dolphins, sea turtles and bird life and has some of the world's best diving, snorkeling and beaches.

The government-backed Tamar Project (see the boxed text on p464), protecting Brazil's five sea-turtle species, has 21 stations along Brazil's coasts, mainly in the Northeast. The headquarters, which you can visit, is at Praia do Forte, Bahia.

NORTH

The Amazon region, with its dense jungles and countless rivers, is easily Brazil's richest for wildlife and plant diversity, but getting to see the best of it is a challenge. The further you get from sprawling, urban Manaus, the more wildlife you're likely to see. On a trip of less than five days from Manaus you will probably see pink and gray river dolphins, caimans, piranhas, a fair variety of birds and a few monkeys, but it won't be the teeming jungles

The Iguaçu Falls, along with other scenic Brazilian locations, featured in the James Bond movie *Moonraker* (1979) and the Oscar-winning *The Mission* (1986) with Robert de Niro and Jeremy Irons.

Jacques Cousteau's two movies about the Amazon, *Amazon – River of the Future* and *Amazon – Journey to a Thousand Rivers*, follow the great oceanographer over this extraordinary ecosystem.

BRAZIL'S TOP PROTECTED & NATURAL AREAS

Area	Features
Cristalino	state park & private reserve on southern edge of Amazon rain forest
Ecoparque de Una	private Mata Atlântica reserve with rare golden-headed lion tamarin
Estação Biológica de Caratinga	Mata Atlântica, half world population of endangered muriqui (largest American primate)
Fernando de Noronha archipelago	fabulous marine park on islands 350km from Natal
Floresta Nacional do Tapajós	lush Amazonian rain-forest preserve
Ilha de Marajó	island in the mouth of the Amazon
Ilha do Bananal	huge river island in Tocantins
Ilha Grande	tract of virgin Mata Atlântica, just off coast of Rio state
Jalapão	beautifully diverse area of eastern Tocantins
Mamirauá Reserve (Reserva de Desenvolvimento Sustentável Mamirauá)	Amazonian floodplain reserve with excellent ecotourism program
Pantanal	vast wetlands that are the best place to see wildlife in Brazil
Parque Estadual da Pedra Azul	dramatic 1822m blue-tinged rock-formation with natural pools and surrounding forest
Parque Estadual de Itaúnas	sand dunes, beaches, Tamar Project turtle preserve
Parque Nacional & Floresta da Tijuca	Mata Atlântica & mountains right in Rio
Parque Nacional da Chapada Diamantina	large mountainous park in Bahia with gorgeous landscape, waterfalls, rivers
Parque Nacional da Chapada dos Guimarães	waterfalls, canyons, bizarre rock formations
Parque Nacional da Chapada dos Veadeiros	high-altitude cerrado with sublime landscapes, near Brasília
Parque Nacional da Serra da Capivara	park in southern Piauí with thousands of prehistoric paintings & amazing rock formations
Parque Nacional da Serra do Cipó	mountains, waterfalls & cerrado, near Belo Horizonte
Parque Nacional da Serra dos Órgãos	mountains & cliffs, 86km from Rio
Parque Nacional da Serra Geral	spectacular canyons, adjoining Aparados da Serra national park
Parque Nacional das Emas	fantastic cerrado preserve with rheas
Parque Nacional das Nascentes do Rio Parnaíba	recently (2002) created park of cerrado savanna and red-rock escarpments
Parque Nacional de Aparados da Serra	stunning canyons, *araucária* forests, in Rio Grande do Sul
Parque Nacional de Caparaó	highest mountains in southern Brazil
Parque Nacional de Itatiaia	ruggedly beautiful mountainous park, 150km from Rio
Parque Nacional de Sete Cidades	unique rock formations in Piauí
Parque Nacional de Ubajara	small Ceará park with large caves, lush vegetation, dramatic escarpments
Parque Nacional do Iguaçu	Brazilian side of the international waterfalls park
Parque Nacional do Jaú	one of the world's largest tracts of protected tropical rain forest; no infrastructure
Parque Nacional do Superagüi	large area of coastal Mata Atlântica
Parque Nacional dos Lençóis Maranhenses	enormous expanse of sand dunes & clear rain pools, near coast
Parque Nacional Marinho de Abrolhos	marine park 80km off the Bahia coast, coral reefs
Parque Natural do Caraça	variety of terrain, from Mata Atlântica to wild mountain vegetation
Praia do Forte	ecological beach resort, headquarters of Tamar Project
Praia do Rosa	beach town in Santa Catarina, whale sanctuary
Reserva Xixuaú-Xipariná	remote ecotourism project, 1½-day boat trip from Manaus
Rio Javari	area near Peruvian border with some pristine rain forest

Activities	Best time to visit	Page
viewing birds, butterflies, monkeys, swimming, kayaking, abseiling	any	p412
hiking, wildlife, endangered species	any	p479
wildlife, hiking	any	p272
diving, snorkeling, hiking, surfing, dolphin- and turtle-watching	any	p539
boat trips, wildlife, rare plants	any	p627
wetlands, hiking, wildlife	any	p620
bird- and animal-watching, boat trips, fishing	any	p642
swimming, hiking, diving, flora & fauna	any	p186
wildlife, hiking, camping	any	p642
viewing wildlife & plants, boat trips, hiking	any	p662
wildlife, hiking, safaris, horseback riding, boating	Apr-Oct	p413
hiking, horseback riding, swimming	any	p231
wildlife, swimming, hiking, turtle-watching	Sep-Mar to see turtles hatching	p222
hiking, great views	any	p150
hiking, trekking, climbing	any	p496
hiking, safaris	any	p409
hiking, swimming, canyoning, rappelling, Jeep tours	Apr-Oct	p399
hiking, archaeology	any, cooler Nov-Mar	p589
hiking, camping, climbing	any	p265
climbing, hiking	May-Oct for hiking	p207
hiking, camping	any	p370
wildlife, hiking	any	–
viewing rare wildlife, hyacinth macaws	Apr-Jul	p567
hiking	any	p370
hiking, climbing, camping	Feb-Oct	p271
hiking, climbing, wildlife	any	p201
hiking, cycling, swimming, archaeology	any	p588
hiking	any	p583
wildlife	any	p332
rare flora & fauna, boat trips	any	p659
abundant wildlife, rare flora, hiking, beaches	any	p328
hiking, swimming, wildlife	any	p597
whale-watching, marine & bird life	any	p491
hiking, swimming	any	p266
hiking, cycling, turtle-viewing	any	p463
whale-watching, surfing	Jun-Oct	p355
rare flora & fauna, boat trips	any	p659
wildlife, jungle, boat trips, hiking	any	p669

you might have imagined. Further afield – and harder to reach and more expensive to visit – the Mamirauá Reserve, Parque Nacional do Jaú, Reserva Xixuaú-Xipariná, Ilha do Bananal, the Rio Javari and the Cristalino area offer much greater variety and abundance of visible wildlife.

ORGANIZED TOURS

Operators specific to single localities are covered in the regional chapters in this book. You can find other reputable companies offering organized tours and adventure-based activities by browsing the listings of Abeta (www.abeta.com .br), a collective of adventure and ecotourism operators, who maintain certain guidelines for safety and promote sustainable initiatives. The following are some of the companies offering a wider range of trips.

Andarilho da Luz (www.andarilhodaluz.com.br) Based in Belo Horizonte, this recommended outfit has tours all over Brazil and is particularly recommended for Minas Gerais trips.

Brazil Ecojourneys (www.brazilecojourneys.com) Recommended southern Brazil specialist with whale-watching, and off-the-beaten-track hiking expeditions in the Serra Geral and Mata Atlântica.

Brazil Ecotravel (www.brazil-ecotravel.com) Offers a huge variety of tailor-made trips for wildlife-watching, adventure activities and more.

Ecotour Expeditions (www.naturetours.com) US-based outfit offers unique riverboat journeys up the Amazon.

Field Guides (www.fieldguides.com) Well-established, US-based birding-tour operator. It runs over a dozen specialized bird-watching tours in Brazil with expert guides.

Focus Tours (www.focustours.com) Highly rated birding- and nature-tour firm using English-speaking naturalist guides. Destinations include the Pantanal, Chapada dos Guimarães, Cristalino, the Emas and Itatiaia national parks, and the Parque Natural do Caraça.

Tropical Nature Travel (www.tropicalnaturetravel.com) Part of a nonprofit organization promoting conservation through ecotourism. It offers Amazonia, Pantanal and cerrado trips using some of Brazil's best ecolodges.

Victor Emanuel Nature Tours (www.ventbird.com) A highly professional US-based birding-tour company, with a number of experienced guides.

ENVIRONMENTAL ISSUES

Sadly, Brazil is as renowned for its forests as it is for destroying them. At last count more than one-fifth of the Brazilian Amazon rain forest had been completely destroyed. Though rapid deforestation in the Amazon slowed after a swath of jungle the size of Greece was cleared between 2000 and 2006, 2008 proved a disturbing year: on top of the 12,000 sq km that were

---

SUSTAINABLE TOUR OPERATORS

Half the tourism businesses anywhere in Brazil promoting natural attractions seem to have those three letters 'eco' in their names. And the rest have them in their propaganda. Especially in Manaus and the Pantanal, hosts of rival 'eco' operators are eager to snap you up for 'ecotours' of the jungles, rivers, lakes or wetlands. Some of these are reputable and dependable, some are just out for a quick buck, and a few will scam you. As you attempt to pick one, weighing up costs, quality, reliability, comfort and all the other factors, it's worth remembering the definition of ecotourism as provided by the International Ecotourism Society: 'Responsible travel to natural areas that conserves the environment and improves the well-being of local people.' A guiding principle of genuine ecotourism is that it benefits resident human communities too and thus encourages them to look after the local environment. If possible, give your business to an ecotourism venture run by the community itself.

For tips on choosing a responsible guide, see the boxed texts, p416 and p658.

For a list of environmentally responsible businesses in Brazil, see p766.

razed, an additional 25,000 sq km was lost to fires and logging, according to Brazil's National Institute of Space Research. Recent surges in commodities (driven by China) and a sharp rise in worldwide biofuels interest, along with the passing of a controversial road-paving law that gives the go-ahead to the long-fought paving of the 765km BR-319 between Manaus and Porto Velho, ensure the Amazon remains a threatened environment.

Deforestation in Brazil was accelerated rapidly by the military government in the 1970s as it attempted to develop Amazonia with the ambitious Plano de Integração Nacional. Long roads, such as the 2500km of the Transamazônica highway from Aguiarnópolis (Tocantins state) to Labrea (Amazonas), were constructed through the jungle. Thousands left Brazil's drought-stricken Northeast to build homesteads in the newly cleared forest.

A turning point, of sorts, was the 1988 assassination of Chico Mendes, a leader among the rubber tappers and a prominent opponent of rain-forest destruction (see the boxed text on p692). The incident focused international attention on the plight of the Brazilian rain forest and its poorer inhabitants, and helped spur the creation of sustainable reserves.

In recent years, Brazil has created millions of hectares of new protected areas, and today more than 20% of Brazilian Amazonia is covered by parks and reserves, with a further 25% set aside as indigenous territory, which tends to be at least equally well conserved. Deforestation still occurs inside protected areas – but at only one-seventh of the rate outside protected areas. Protected status usually decreases the value of land, making it less attractive to illegal land-grabbers and speculators.

The land grab, however, continues to plague the Amazon. In many cases small-scale settlers have been forced off their land, and hundreds have been murdered for resisting this. The state of Pará, where only one-third of land is officially registered, is particularly notorious. According to the Brazilian Catholic Church more than 500 people have been killed in such land disputes in Pará since 1986 – among them, in 2005, American missionary Dorothy Stang, who campaigned against exactly this kind of illegal land grabbing.

Meanwhile, big development projects continue apace in the Amazon. In 2010 the government gave the green light to the creation of a massive hydroelectric installation – Belo Monte – on the Rio Xingu in Pará. It's slated to flood an estimated 500 sq km of the Amazon, affecting around 12,000 people according to Brazil's environmental agency Ibama. Work on the estimated US$10 billion project is slated to begin in 2015. When complete it will be the world's third-largest hydroelectric dam, producing around 11,000 megawatts of electricity.

Smaller hydroelectric installations are also in the works. In coming years, the government plans to build over 200 small hydroelectric dams across the country in hopes of both generating electricity and driving economic development.

Sustainability Initiatives

Some of the most promising environmental initiatives are those that make conservation act in the interests of the local populace and ensure the sustainable use of resources. Community ecotourism projects are growing in popularity. Extractive reserves also play a key role in the forest. These are protected areas used by those who depend on subsistence agriculture and traditional extractive activities, such as rubber tapping, fruit or nut collecting, or fishing.

Hopes for less destructive logging practices have been raised by international certification schemes, such as those implemented by the Forest Stewardship Council. Such schemes seek to certify timber that has been produced by sustainable methods, something that is increasingly demanded

The Burning Season: The Chico Mendes Story (1994) stars Raul Julia as Mendes and is a quick way to get an overview of this man's important life and legacy.

Conservation International's website, www .conservation.org, covers various aspects of ecotourism and the global conservation movement, including CI's extensive work in Brazil.

For sustainable forestry and sustainable tourism initiatives in Brazil, check the Rainforest Alliance (http://rainforest -alliance.org).

by domestic and international consumers of Brazilian timber. This type of consumer demand encourages reduced-impact logging, whereby forestry areas are divided into blocks to be exploited on a rotating basis and given time to regenerate. At the same time, the largest specimens of valuable tree species are left standing in order to reseed the block, and care is taken to minimize damage to trees that are not being felled. Some major Brazilian home-supply stores and a number of international stores carry certified lumber. However, it's also true that most illegal timber from the Amazon stays in Brazil, a large proportion of it being used in the construction industry in the south of the country.

Other Issues

The deforestation of the Amazon hogs the headlines and is undoubtedly the number-one environmental issue for Brazil, but other ecosystems are also under severe pressure. The Atlantic rain forest, older than the Amazon forest and once a quarter of its size, is now down to just 7% of its original area.

SUGAR POWER, SWEET OR SOUR?

At least one pump at almost every Brazilian gasoline station bears the name of a fuel as yet uncommon elsewhere in the world. Beside the pumps for various grades of gasoline and diesel, there are pumps labeled Álcool Comum, and they're usually among the busiest on the forecourt. This fuel alcohol, known in English as ethanol, is widely considered Brazil's big lucky break in the field of energy. Since 2003, when new 'flex-fuel' cars – able to run on any combination of gasoline and ethanol – were developed in Brazil, they have sold like hot cakes. By 2009 flexible-fuel cars represented more than 90% of new car sales during the year, and ethanol accounted for 50% of transport fuel.

Álcool, made from sugarcane, gives fewer kilometers per liter than gasoline but is cheaper, so overall it works out more economical for drivers. It's also considered better for the environment. It still yields carbon-dioxide emissions such as gasoline – but a comparable amount of carbon dioxide is absorbed from the atmosphere by the growth of the plants from which the fuel is processed, greatly reducing the fuel's contribution to greenhouse gases.

Brazil has been producing ethanol for more than 30 years, with record growth in recent years. As of 2010, the nation was producing some 25 billion liters of ethanol annually, representing around 38% of the world's total. It has suddenly found itself the world leader in a commodity that looks set to boom worldwide. As countries across the world attempt to reduce their dependence on expensive, polluting fossil fuels, biofuels (made from living organisms or their waste) such as ethanol look like being a big part of the future.

The US is a bigger ethanol producer than Brazil (the two countries account for nearly 90% of world production), but Brazil is the biggest exporter at around 4 billion liters in 2009. And it has rapidly expanded the area of sugarcane plantations – covering around 78,000 sq km by 2010. Brazil has built scores of new distilleries to turn the cane into motor fuel, with dozens of new plants slated for construction as this book went to press.

Unfortunately, ethanol is not the win-win solution to the world's fuel needs that its fans claim. The carbon absorbed by the growing plant may cancel the carbon emitted by the fuel, but the fuel's production also consumes large amounts of fossil fuel through fertilizer and fungicide use, the distillation process and transport. On this score, Brazil has a big advantage over the US, where ethanol is made chiefly from corn (maize) and burns up about seven times as much fossil fuel in its production than Brazilian sugarcane ethanol. By some estimates US-produced corn ethanol may not even reduce overall carbon dioxide emissions at all.

Environmentalists also fear that Brazilian rain forest will be felled to make way for sugar plantations, and that chemical runoffs from the plantations – chiefly in Brazil's central highlands – will damage the Pantanal and Amazon ecosystems. Responding to this concern, President Lula proposed in 2007 that new plantations be located only on already degraded land without native vegetation.

The Pantanal wetlands also face serious threats, including the rapid spread of intensive soy, cotton and sugarcane farming on Brazil's central plains, which are the source of most of the Pantanal's water. The sugarcane is the raw material of ethanol motor fuel (see the boxed text, p122), whose international growth has led to the creation of dozens of new ethanol distilleries in Mato Grosso do Sul. Herbicides, fertilizers and other chemicals from the plantations drizzle their way into Pantanal waters, and forest clearance on the plains leads to erosion and consequent silting of Pantanal rivers. The growing cities around the Pantanal (many of which lack adequate waste treatment plants) and ongoing industrial development also pose serious risks to this region.

The International Ecotourism Society (www .ecotourism.org) is a great source of ideas, news, facts and recommendations on sustainable travel the world over, Brazil included.

On Brazil's coasts, growth of cities and burgeoning tourism developments threaten many delicate coastal marine ecosystems despite the creation of protected areas on extensive tracts of land and sea.

Environmental Organizations

The following organizations are among those working actively to protect Brazil's environment. Strategies range from campaigns to save a single animal species to lobbying in Brasília and pressuring institutions to stop financing destructive 'megaprojects' – building long-distance roads through rain forest, flooding large areas for hydroelectricity, planting vast areas of bush with chemically fertilized soybeans.

Some groups concentrate primarily on research, while others can arrange volunteer work. The following organizations are based in Brazil:

The Brazilian research institute Imazon (www .imazon.org.br) reports on various aspects of Amazon ecology.

Amazônia (www.amazonia.org.br) Amazônia is an Amazon monitoring and information program. The website is a terrific resource.

Conselheiro Brasileiro de Manejo Florestal (www.fsc.org.br) Brazilian representative of the Forest Stewardship Council, working for sustainable forestry via a certification scheme.

Instituto de Pesquisa Ambiental da Amazônia (IPAM; www.ipam.org.br) An environmental research institute and pressure group, IPAM is dedicated to sustainable development in Amazonia and organizes environmental education and training around Brazil.

Instituto do Homem e Meio Ambiente da Amazônia (Imazon; www.imazon.org.br) This research organization promotes sustainable development with an eye on both social and environmental concerns in the Amazon.

Instituto Socioambiental (ISA; www.socioambiental.org) ISA campaigns and lobbies for Brazil's indigenous peoples and environment. It publishes books and maps, and has several offices around Brazil.

SOS Mata Atlântica (www.sosmatatlantica.org.br) Works for the protection of the Atlantic rain forest.

Tamar Project (Projeto Tamar; www.tamar.org.br, in Portuguese) Tamar is the official Brazilian government project to protect sea turtles. Working with local communities, Tamar has seven visitor centers and 21 stations that protect over 1000km of coastline. National coordination is done from the Rio Vermelho branch, at Praia do Forte, 50km north of Salvador.

Other international organizations working on sustainable initiatives in Brazil:
Conservation International (www.conservation.org)
Environmental Defense (www.environmentaldefense.org)
Friends of the Earth (www.foe.co.uk)
Greenpeace (www.greenpeace.org)
Nature Conservancy (www.nature.org)
Rainforest Action Network (www.ran.org)
Rainforest Alliance (http://rainforest-alliance.org)
Rainforest Foundation (www.rainforestfoundation.org)
Survival (www.survival-international.org)
World Wildlife Fund (www.wwf.org)

Rio de Janeiro City

Be warned: Rio's powers of seduction can leave you with a bad case of *saudade* (indescribable longing) when you leave. Planted between lush, forest-covered mountains and breathtaking beaches, the Cidade Maravilhosa (Marvelous City) has many charms at her disposal.

Although joie de vivre is a French invention (as is the bikini), it's the Cariocas (Rio dwellers) who've made it their own. How else to explain the life-lusting zeal with which the city's inhabitants celebrate their days? While large-scale festivities such as Carnaval make Rio famous, there are countless occasions for revelry – Saturday at Ipanema Beach, a *festa* (party) in Lapa, football at Maracanã, or an impromptu *roda de samba* (samba circle) on the sidewalks of Leblon, Copacabana or any other corner of the city. Music is the meeting ground for some of Brazil's most creative artists and nets an audience as diverse as the city. This is another of Rio's disarming traits: its rich melting pot of cultures. Cariocas they may call themselves, but the city's enticing variety of cuisines speaks volumes about its history of immigration.

The spectacular landscape is another of Rio's shameless virtues. Verdant mountains and white-sand beaches fronting deep blue sea offer a range of adventure: surfing great breaks, hiking through Tijuca's rain forests or rock climbing up the face of Pão de Açúcar (Sugarloaf).

The downside to Rio is its crime rate and alarming social inequalities. Yet despite her many problems, most visitors arrive home already dreaming of their return.

HIGHLIGHTS

- Watch the sunset, caipirinha in hand, over at lovely **Ipanema Beach** (p130)
- Celebrate with King Momo – and millions of others – at **Carnaval** (p76)
- Take the cog train up Corcovado for stunning views beneath the open-armed **Cristo Redentor** (p145)
- Find the perfect beat at a samba club in **Lapa** (p175), Brazil's most musically charged neighborhood
- Admire the Cidade Maravilhosa from eagles' nest heights atop **Pão de Açúcar** (p144)

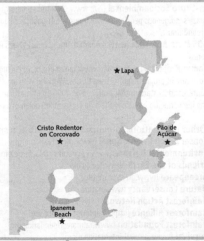

★ Lapa

Cristo Redentor
on Corcovado
★

Pão de
Açúcar
★

Ipanema
Beach
★

■ TELEPHONE CODE: 0XX21   ■ POPULATION: 6.2 MILLION   ■ AREA: 1182 SQ KM

HISTORY

The Tamoio people were living on the land surrounding the Baía de Guanabara when Gaspar de Lemos sailed from Portugal for Brazil in May 1501 and entered the huge bay in January 1502. Mistaking the bay for a river, Lemos named it Rio de Janeiro. The French, however, were the first Europeans to settle along the great bay in 1555. After a brief alliance with the Tamoio – who hated the Portuguese for their cruelty – the French were expelled in 1567. The Portuguese victors then drove the Tamoio from the region in another series of bloody battles.

By the 17th century, the Tamoio had been wiped out. Those who weren't taken into slavery died from disease. Other indigenous groups were 'pacified' and taken to live in settlements organized by the Jesuits. The Portuguese had set up a fortified town on the Morro Castelo in 1567 and, by the 17th century, Rio became Brazil's third-most important settlement (after Salvador da Bahia and Recife-Olinda). African slaves streamed in and the sugar plantations thrived. Even more slaves arrived to work in the gold mines of Minas Gerais during the 18th century.

In 1807 Napoleon's army marched on Lisbon. Two days before the invasion, 40 ships carrying the Portuguese prince regent (later known as Dom João VI) and his entire court of 15,000 set sail for Brazil. When the prince regent arrived in Rio, his white Brazilian subjects celebrated wildly, dancing in the streets. He immediately took over the rule of Brazil from his viceroy.

Dom João fell in love with Brazil. Even after he became king of Portugal, he remained and declared Rio the capital of the United Kingdom of Portugal, Brazil and the Algarve. This made Brazil the only New World colony to ever have a European monarch ruling on its soil.

At the end of the 19th century the city's population exploded because of European immigration and internal migration (mostly of ex-slaves from the declining coffee and sugar regions). By 1890 Rio boasted more than a million inhabitants, a quarter of them foreign-born, and the city spread rapidly.

The early 1920s to the late 1950s were Rio's golden age. With the inauguration of the grand hotels (the Glória in 1922 and the Copacabana Palace in 1924), Rio became a romantic, exotic destination for Hollywood celebrities and international high-society people who came to play and gamble at the casinos and dance or perform in the nightclubs.

Rio continued to change. Three large landfill projects were undertaken to ease the strain on a city restricted by its beautiful surroundings. The first was to become Aeroporto Santos Dumont, near Centro. The second resulted in Flamengo Park, and the third expanded the strand at Copacabana.

Rio remained the political capital of Brazil until 1960, when the government moved to Brasília. During the 1960s, modern skyscrapers rose in the city, and some of Rio's most beautiful buildings were lost. During the same period, the favelas (shantytowns) of Rio grew to critical mass with immigrants from poverty-stricken areas of the Northeast and the interior, swelling the number of Rio's urban poor. The Cidade Maravilhosa began to lose its gloss as crime and violence increased.

The final decade of the military dictatorship that ruled Brazil from 1964 to 1985 was not kind to Rio. There were numerous protests during that period (notably in 1968 when some 100,000 marched upon Palácio Tiradentes). Even Rio's politicians opposed the military regime, which responded by withholding vital federal funding. The administration was forced to tighten its belt, and infrastructure deteriorated as the city's coffers dried up.

As Rio entered the new millennium, social problems continued to plague the city, with violence continuing to take thousands of lives – particularly in the favelas. Rio's middle and upper classes seemed mostly resigned to life behind gated and guarded condos, while poverty and violence surged in the slums nearby.

As a result of a worsening situation, Brazilian officials began to take a new approach. President Lula, aware of the link between poverty and crime, announced in 2007 that Rio's favelas would receive US$1.7 billion to invest in running water, sanitation, roads and housing.

Pulling people out of poverty has long been one of Lula's overarching goals, and Brazil has had marked success in achieving this, with 10.4 million people leaving poverty-level conditions since 2001. The city for its part continues to focus on bringing these dramatic improvements to other slums in the city, setting a goal of reaching 100 favelas by 2011 and the entire city by 2016.

OLYMPIC FEVER

Cynics have already started fanning the flames, saying that Rio, with its social problems and aging infrastructure, won't be able to pull off a smooth Olympic games. The city, however, has already started asking the tough questions and seems determined to show the world it can throw down a memorable Olympics, as well as play its part in showcasing the FIFA World Cup (see p54).

Rio certainly has its work cut out. The city will need a total of 34 separate venues to host the Olympic events; 18 are already in place, nine new permanent venues will be built and seven temporary ones (including four built on Copacabana Beach). Maracanã, set to become the star of the Olympics, will host the opening and closing ceremonies; it's currently undergoing a US$280 million renovation in preparation for the event (and for the 2014 World Cup, where it will also play a starring role).

Rio needs to add a massive number of hotel rooms; an estimated 48,000 are needed to cope; Rio has only 22,000. Brazil's pitch to the IOC floated the idea of housing people on six cruise ships (a logistical challenge), plus building a 20,000-room Olympic village in Barra. The IOC said it would have to pay 'particular attention' to these ideas.

Transportation, no small consideration on Rio's bus-clogged avenues, is a critical factor, and the city is considering a full gamut of ideas – from building aerial trams over the mountains (a green but ultimately impractical idea) to extending the metro to Barra (not going to happen by 2016), and implementing dedicated bus lanes to create 'surface metros' (the most likely scenario). Rio must also upgrade its airports.

Other parts of the city will receive a makeover in preparation for the games, including the port – which has an unsavory reputation for crumbling buildings, squatters and crime.

The projected cost of the Olympics is a staggering US$14.4 billion. The return? A São Paulo business school estimated the games would pump US$51 billion into the economy through to 2027. More immediately, the games would add 120,000 jobs through 2016.

Even if the games don't go perfectly, visitors will probably find enough redeeming features (caipirinhas on Ipanema Beach, colorful matches at Maracanã) along the way to find the overall experience worthwhile.

Speaking of 2016, this is the year that seems to be on everyone's minds – at least when they're not thinking of 2014. The great moment for Rio – and Brazil – seems just over the horizon as it prepares to host first the FIFA World Cup, followed two years later, by the Summer Olympics (see p126).

ORIENTATION

Rio is a city of unusual urban diversity, with beaches, mountains, skyscrapers and the omnipresent favelas all woven into the fabric of the landscape. The city itself can be divided into two zones: the Zona Norte (North Zone), which consists of industrial, working-class neighborhoods, and the Zona Sul (South Zone), full of middle- and upper-class neighborhoods and Rio's well-known beaches. Centro, Rio's business district and the site of its first settlement, marks the boundary between the two, and a number of the important museums and colonial buildings are there.

The parts of Rio you are most likely to explore stretch along the shore of the Baía de Guanabara and the Atlantic Ocean. South from Centro are the neighborhoods of Lapa, Glória, Catete, Flamengo, Botafogo and Urca – where the striking peak of Pão de Açúcar dominates the landscape. Further south lie the neighborhoods of Copacabana, Ipanema and Leblon, the only stops for many travelers to the city.

Other areas of interest include the quaint, colonial neighborhood of Santa Teresa, on a hill overlooking Centro, and the looming statue of Cristo Redentor (Christ the Redeemer), atop Corcovado in Cosme Velho, from where there are fabulous views of both zones of the city.

Aside from the bus station, Maracanã Football Stadium and the international airport, most travelers have few reasons to visit the Zona Norte.

Rio de Janeiro's international airport, Aeroporto Galeão (also called Aeroporto Tom Jobim), is 15km north of the city center. Santos Dumont airport, used by a few domestic flights, is by the bayside in the city center,

1km east of Cinelândia metro station. Rio's central bus station, Rodoviária Novo Rio, lies about 5km northwest of Centro. For information on getting into town from the bus station or from the airports, see p181.

Maps

If you need something more detailed than the maps available at the tourist office, Guia Quatro Rodas publishes several useful maps, including an excellent city map of Rio de Janeiro (R$15), as well as their encyclopedic *Ruas Rio de Janeiro* (R$20). Both are updated annually and available at most newsstands.

INFORMATION
Bookstores

Argumento (Map p132; ☎ 2239 5294; Rua Días Ferreira 417, Leblon; ☼ 10am-midnight) Small selection of foreign-language books and magazines. Has a café in back.
Café Arlequim (Map p138; ☎ 2215 5795; Praça XV de Novembro 48, Centro) Combination bistro/bookstore/music shop, inside the Paço Imperial.
Letras e Expressões Ipanema (Map p132; ☎ 2521 6110; Rua Visconde de Pirajá 276; ☼ 8am-midnight); Leblon (Map p132; ☎ 2511 5085; Av Ataúlfo de Paiva 1292; ☼ 24hr) Foreign-language books and magazines, plus an internet café at each branch.
Livraria da Travessa Av Rio Branco (Map p138; Av Rio Branco 44, Centro); Sete de Setembro (Map p138; ☎ 3231 8015; Rua Sete de Setembro 54, Centro; ☼ 9am-8pm Mon-Fri, 9am-2pm Sat); Shopping Leblon (Map p132;

☎ 3138 9600; Afrânio de Melo Franco 290); Rua Visconde de Pirajá (Map p132; ☎ 3205 9002; Rua Visconde de Pirajá 572, Ipanema) Books and periodicals, CDs and an excellent café at the Ipanema branch.
Livraria Prefácio (Map p136; ☎ 2527 5699; Rua Voluntários da Pátria 39, Botafogo) Occasionally hosts readings in its back café.
Nova Livraria Leonardo da Vinci (Map p138; ☎ 2533 2237; Av Rio Branco 185, Centro) One of Rio's best collections of foreign-language books.

Cultural Centers

Entry to each of the following is free.
Casa de Cultura Laura Alvim (Map p132; ☎ 2267 1647; Av Vieira Souto 176, Ipanema) Ipanema's beachside cultural center has a cinema, gallery space and a small café.
Casa França-Brasil (Map p138; ☎ 2332 5120; www.casafrancabrasil.rj.gov.br; Rua Visconde de Itaboraí 78, Centro; ☼ 10am-8pm Tue-Sun) Opened in 1990, this cultural center hosts Franco-Brazilian exhibitions. A lovely indoor-outdoor bistro is attached.
Centro Cultural Banco do Brasil (Map p138; ☎ 3808 2020; www.cultura-e.com.br; Rua Primeiro de Março 66, Centro; ☼ 10am-8pm Tue-Sun) One of Rio's best cultural centers, with excellent exhibitions, a film series and lunchtime and evening concerts.
Centro Cultural Carioca (Map p138; ☎ 2242 9642; www.centroculturalcarioca.com.br; Rua do Teatro 37, Centro; ☼ 11am-8pm Mon-Fri & 4:30-8:30pm Sat) On Praça Tiradentes, this cultural center hosts musical groups along with dance recitals and ongoing exhibitions.

RIO IN...

Two Days

Start your day off with a refreshing glass of *açaí* (berry-like fruit) at a neighborhood juice bar and head to lovely **Ipanema Beach** (p130). For lunch, stroll up the sands to Leblon and grab a bite on restaurant-packed **Rua Días Ferreira** (p166), followed by window-shopping on the streets of Leblon and Ipanema. In the afternoon, go to Praia do Arpoador, one of Rio's best places to watch the sunset. Have dinner at one of Lagoa's **lakeside kiosks** (p142). On day two, visit **Pão de Açúcar** (p144), followed by a stroll around **Urca** (p144). Around lunchtime, ride the **bonde** (tram; p149) to Santa Teresa and dine at **Bar do Mineiro** (p171) or another classic Santa spot. In the evening, go to a samba club in **Lapa** (p175) for Rio's best music scene.

Five Days

On your third day, do something active – hire a bike for a ride along the beachfront or go hiking in **Parque Nacional da Tijuca** (p150). In the evening, dine in one of Ipanema's great **restaurants** (p165). On day four, explore the old streets of **Centro** (p146), stopping in some of its excellent museums and historic churches, and joining the happy-hour crowd at open-air bars on **Travessa do Comércio** (p148). On your last day, rise early for a stroll along Copacabana Beach, stopping for a bite at a beach-front **kiosk** (p168). Afterwards, take the cog train up Corcovado to see **Cristo Redentor** (p145) for outstanding views. Have dinner that night in **Yorubá** (p169) or **Porcão Rio's** (p170).

Centro Cultural Laurinda Santos Lobo (Map p138; ☎ 2224 3331; Rua Monte Alegre 306, Santa Teresa; ☺ 9am-5pm Tue-Sun) Built in 1907, this large mansion occasionally hosts exhibitions and open-air concerts.

Fundição Progresso (Map p138; ☎ 2220 5070; Rua dos Arcos 24, Cinelândia; ☺ 9am-6pm Mon-Fri) This former foundry stages avant-garde exhibitions and performances.

Instituto Moreira Salles (Map p131; ☎ 3284 7400; www.ims.com.br; Rua Marquês de Sao Vicente 476, Gávea; admission free; ☺ 1-8pm Tue-Sun) A beautiful cultural center that hosts impressive exhibitions. Leafy gardens and a café lie next door.

Emergency

Report robberies to the **tourist police** (Map p132; ☎ 2332 2924; Rua Humberto de Campos 315, Leblon; ☺ 24hr).

Other useful numbers:
Ambulance (☎ 192)
Fire department (☎ 193)
Police (☎ 190)

Internet Access

Internet cafés charge R$4 to R$8 per hour.
@Onze (Map p136; Rua Marquês de Abrantes 11; ☺ 9am-11pm)
Central Fone Centro (Map p138; basement level, Av Rio Branco 156; ☺ 9am-9pm Mon-Fri, 10am-4pm Sat); Ipanema (Map p132; Rua Teixeira de Melo 47; ☺ 9.30am-8pm)
Fone Rio (Map p134; Rua Constante Ramos 22, Copacabana; ☺ 8am-midnight)
Jasmim Mango (Map p138; Rua Pascoal Carlos Magno 143, Santa Teresa; ☺ 10am-10pm Wed-Mon)
Letras e Expressões Ipanema (Map p132; Rua Visconde de Pirajá 276; ☺ 8am-midnight); Leblon (Map p132; Av Ataúlfo de Paiva 1292; ☺ 24hr)
Locutório (Map p134; Av NS Copacabana 1171, Copacabana; ☺ 8am-2am)
Tele Rede (Map p134; Av NS de Copacabana 209A, Copacabana; ☺ 8am-2am)

Internet Resources

www.ipanema.com Dubbed 'the insider's guide to Rio,' this website has excellent up-to-date city info.
www.rioguiaoficial.com.br Riotur's comprehensive website.
www.riotimesonline.com Online English weekly for news and current events.

Media

Rio's main daily papers are *Jornal do Brasil* (www.jbonline.com.br) and *O Globo* (www.globo.com.br). Both have entertainment

and event listings, particularly strong on Thursday and Sunday. The national publication *Veja* has a *Veja Rio* insert, which details weekly entertainment options (it comes out on Sunday).

Medical Services

For medical emergencies, the best hospital for foreigners is the **Clínica Galdino Campos** (Map p134; ☎ 2548 9966; www.galdinocampos.com.br; Av NS de Copacabana 492, Copacabana; ☺ 24hr), with high-quality care and multilingual doctors.

There are scores of pharmacies in town, a number of which stay open 24 hours:
Drogaria Pacheco Av NS de Copacabana 115 (Map p134; Av NS de Copacabana 115, Copacabana; ☺ 24hr); Av NS de Copacabana 534 (Map p134; Av NS de Copacabana 534, Copacabana; ☺ 24hr); Rua Visconde de Pirajá (Map p132; Rua Visconde de Pirajá, Ipanema)
Farmácia do Leme (Map p134; Av Prado Júnior 231, Copacabana; ☺ 24hr)
Farmácia Piauí (Map p132; ☎ 2274 8448; Av Ataúlfo de Paiva 1283, Leblon; ☺ 24hr)

Money

ATMs and banks can be found throughout the city; a number are marked on the maps. Banco do Brasil, Bradesco, Citibank and HSBC are the best banks to try when using a debit or credit card (HSBC charges the lowest withdrawal fees). Even though many ATMs advertise 24-hour service, these '24 hours' usually fall between 6am and 10pm. On Sundays and holidays, ATM access ends at 3pm. Money changing is speedier at *casas de câmbio* (exchange offices) than at banks. At the airport, international ATMs and money exchange are located on the 3rd floor of arrivals.

IPANEMA

Find other *câmbios* scattered along Rua Visconde de Pirajá, about two blocks east and west of Praça NS de Paz.
Citibank (Map p132; Rua Visconde de Pirajá 459A, Ipanema) ATM and money exchange.
HSBC (Rua Vinícius de Moraes 71) ATM.

COPACABANA

Câmbios can be found on Av NS de Copacabana, near the Copacabana Palace hotel. The following are also on the main streets of Copacabana, as well as other ATMs; see Map p134.
Banco do Brasil (Av NS de Copacabana 264)
Banco do Brasil (Av NS de Copacabana 1274) ATM.

Casa Universal (Av NS de Copacabana 371) A recommended *câmbio*.
Citibank (Av NS de Copacabana 828) ATM.
HSBC (Av Princesa Isabel 186) ATM.

CENTRO

A number of exchange offices can be found on either side of Av Rio Branco, several blocks north of Av Presidente Vargas. Other options include the following, located on Map p138:
Banco do Brasil (Rua Senador Dantas 105) ATM.
Casa Aliança (☎ 2224 4617; Rua Miguel Couto 35C) A recommended *câmbio*.
Citibank (Rua da Assembléia 100) Has ATM and money exchange.
HSBC (Av Rio Branco 108) ATM.
HSBC (Praça Floriano 23)

Post

Most *correios* (post offices) open from 8am to 6pm Monday to Friday, and on Saturday until noon. Any mail addressed to Posta Restante, Rio de Janeiro, Brazil, ends up at the **main post office** (Map p138; Rua Primeiro de Março 64, Centro).

Other post office branches include the following:
Botafogo (Map p136; Praia de Botafogo 324, Botafogo)
Copacabana (Map p134; Av NS de Copacabana 540, Copacabana)
Ipanema (Map p132; Rua Prudente de Morais 147, Ipanema)

Telephone

For local phone calls – and other calls within Brazil – you will need to buy a *cartão telefônico* (phone card; R$5 to R$20). These cards are available from newsstands. See p709 for more info. Many internet cafés (p128) offer international calling service, and Skype is also widely available.

Tourist Information

Riotur is Rio's tourism agency. It has a tourist information hotline called **Alô Rio** (☎ toll-free in Brazil 0800-285 0555, 2542 8080; ☒ 9am-6pm). The helpful receptionists speak English. Riotur's useful multilingual website, www.rioguiaoficial.com.br/en, is also a good source of information.

All of the Riotur offices distribute maps and the excellent (and updated) quarterly *Rio Guide*, listing the major events of the season.

You'll find information kiosks at the following locations:
Copacabana (Map p134; ☎ 2541 7522; Av Princesa Isabel 183; ☒ 9am-6pm Mon-Fri) Has the most helpful staff.

Copacabana Beach Kiosk (Map p134; Av Atlântica near Rua Hilário de Gouveia; ☒ 8am-10pm)
Galeão airport Terminal 1 (Domestic Arrival Hall; ☎ 3398 3034; ☒ 7am-11pm); Terminal 2 (International Arrival Hall; ☎ 3398 2245; ☒ 6am-11pm)

Travel Agencies

Andes Sol (Map p134; ☎ 2275 4370; Av NS de Copacabana 209, Copacabana) A good multilingual agency.
Blame It on Rio 4 Travel (Map p134; ☎ 3813 5510, in USA 917-254-4867; www.blameitonrio4travel.com; Rua Xavier da Silveira 15B, Copacabana) Excellent travel agency run by a friendly and knowledgeable US expat.
Casa Aliança (Map p138; ☎ 2109 8900; www.casaalianca.com.br; Rua Miguel Couto 35B, Centro)
Guanatur Turismo (Map p134; ☎ 2548 3275; Rua Dias da Rocha 16A, Copacabana; www.guanaturturismo.com.br) Sells bus tickets to some domestic and international destinations.

DANGERS & ANNOYANCES

Rio gets a lot of bad international press about violence, and unfortunately it's not all hype. The crime rate is high, and tourists are sometimes targeted. To minimize your risk of becoming a victim, you should take some basic precautions. First off: dress down and leave expensive (or even expensive *looking*) jewelry, watches and sunglasses at home.

Copacabana and Ipanema beaches have a police presence, but robberies still occur on the sands, even in broad daylight. Don't ever take anything of value with you to the beach. Late at night, don't walk on any of the beaches. Lapa and Santa Teresa are other areas well worth visiting but have their share of crime. Avoid walking around empty streets; it's safest to stick to well-trafficked areas. Santa Teresa is liveliest on Saturdays and Sundays.

Buses are well-known targets for thieves. Avoid taking them after dark, and keep an eye out while you're on them. Take taxis at night to avoid walking along empty streets and beaches. That holds especially true for Centro, which becomes deserted in the evening and on weekends, and is better explored during the week.

Get in the habit of carrying only the money you'll need for the day, so you don't have to flash a wad of reais when you pay for things. Cameras and backpacks attract a lot of attention. Consider using disposable cameras while you're in town; plastic shopping bags also nicely disguise whatever you're carrying. Maracanã football stadium is worth a visit,

SUNDAY SUNNY SUNDAY

Many museums in Rio are free on Sunday, making it a good day to pack in your sightseeing. If the weather is simply too lovely for staying indoors, head to the shore. On Sundays the beachfront road running from Leblon to Leme closes to traffic (until 6pm). Cyclists, joggers and skaters fill the seaside lanes; further north, the road through Parque do Flamengo also closes to traffic.

but take only your spending money for the day and avoid the crowded sections. Some travelers prefer going with a tour group (p178).

If you have the misfortune of being robbed, slowly hand over the goods. Thieves in the city are only too willing to use their weapons.

Scams

A common beach scam is for one thief to approach you from one side and ask you for a light or the time. While you're distracted, the thief's partner grabs your gear from the other side.

SIGHTS

The once mighty 'capital of the Brazilian empire' (as one Portuguese king called it), Rio has much more than just pretty beaches. From the bohemian lanes of old Santa Teresa to the village-like charm of Urca, Rio's colonial streets, magnificent churches and leafy plazas provide urban wanderers with days of exploration.

Rio's historic center, its lake (Lagoa Rodrigo de Freitas), the lush Jardim Botânico (Botanical Gardens) and the Atlantic rain forest still trimming many parts of the city make for some fascinating exploring. There are also the fantastic overlooks from Pão de Açúcar (Sugarloaf) and Cristo Redentor, tranquil islands in the bay, wildly beautiful beaches to the west, and vibrant markets, with vendors peddling everything from vintage samba recordings to tangy *jabuticaba* (a native fruit).

Ipanema & Leblon

Truly among the world's most enchanting addresses, Ipanema and Leblon are blessed with a magnificent beach and open-air cafés, bars and restaurants scattered along tree-lined streets. Here you'll find a mix of wealthy Cariocas, young and old, gay and straight.

Ipanema acquired international fame in the early '60s as the home of the bossa nova character 'The Girl from Ipanema.' It became the hangout of artists, intellectuals and wealthy liberals, who frequented the sidewalk cafés and bars. After the 1964 military coup and the resulting crackdown on liberals, many of these bohemians were forced into exile. During the '70s, Leblon became the nightlife center of Rio. The restaurants and bars of Baixo (Lower) Leblon, on Av Ataúlfo de Paiva, between Rua Aristídes Espínola and Rua General Artigas, were the meeting points for a new generation of artists and musicians. Evenings continue to be very animated here, even though the heart of Rio's nightlife has moved to Lapa.

IPANEMA & LEBLON BEACHES

The beaches of Ipanema and Leblon (Map p132) are one long beach, separated by the Canal and park Jardim do Alah. *Postos* (posts) further subdivide the beach into diverse areas. **Posto 9**, right off Rua Vinícius de Moraes, is **Garota de Ipanema**, which is where Rio's most lithe and tanned bodies tend to migrate. The area is also known as the **Cemetério dos Elefantes** because of the old leftists, hippies and artists who hang out there. The beach in front of Rua Farme de Amoedo, also called **Bolsa de Valores** and **Crystal Palace**, is the gay section, while **Posto 8** is mostly the domain of favela kids. **Arpoador**, between Ipanema and Copacabana, is Rio's most popular surf spot. Leblon attracts a mix of single Cariocas, as well as families from the neighborhood. **Posto 10** is for sport lovers, with ongoing volleyball games. **Baixo Bebê**, between posts 11 and 12, is a meeting spot for affluent parents with children.

Whatever spot you choose, you'll enjoy cleaner sands and sea than those found in neighboring Copacabana. Keep in mind that if you go on Saturday or Sunday, it gets very crowded. Incidentally, the word *ipanema* is an indigenous word for 'bad, dangerous waters' – an apt description given the strong undertow and sometimes oversized waves crashing on the shore. Be careful, and swim only where the locals do.

A few fishermen, casting out to sea, mingle with couples admiring the view stretching down Leblon and Ipanema Beaches, as seen from the lookout known as **Mirante do Leblon**, at the west end of Leblon Beach.

(Continued on page 142)

RIO DE JANEIRO

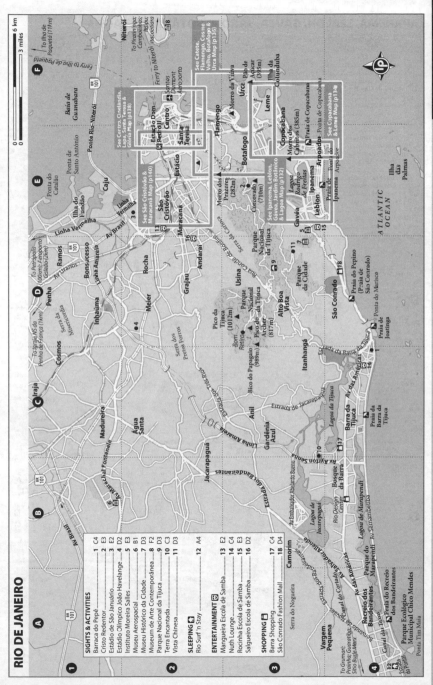

SIGHTS & ACTIVITIES	
Barraca do Pepê	1 C4
Cristo Redentor	2 E3
Estádio de São Januário	3 E2
Estádio Olímpico João Havelange	4 D2
Instituto Moreira Salles	5 E3
Museu Aeroespacial	6 B1
Museu Histórico da Cidade	7 D3
Museum de Arte Contemporânea	8 F2
Parque Nacional da Tijuca	9 D3
Terra Encantada	10 C3
Vista Chinesa	11 D3

SLEEPING 🛏	
Rio Surf 'n Stay	12 A4

ENTERTAINMENT 🎭	
Mangueira Escola de Samba	13 E2
Nuth Lounge	14 C4
Rocinha Escola de Samba	15 E3
Salgueiro Escola de Samba	16 D2

SHOPPING 🛍	
Barra Shopping	17 C4
São Conrado Fashion Mall	18 D4

See Centro, Cinelândia, Lapa, Santa Teresa & Glória Map (p139)

See São Cristóvão & Maracanã Map (p140)

See Catete, Flamengo, Cosme Velho, Botafogo & Urca Map (p135)

See Ipanema, Leblon, Gávea, Jardim Botânico & Lagoa Map (p132)

See Copacabana & Leme Map (p134)

IPANEMA, LEBLON, GÁVEA, JARDIM BOTÂNICO & LAGOA

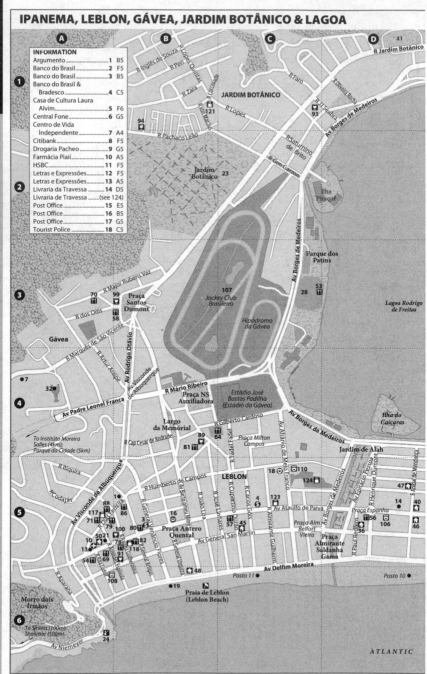

INFORMATION

Argumento	1 B5
Banco do Brasil	2 F5
Banco do Brasil	3 B5
Banco do Brasil & Bradesco	4 C5
Casa de Cultura Laura Alvim	5 F6
Central Fone	6 G5
Centro de Vida Independente	7 A4
Citibank	8 F5
Drogaria Pacheo	9 G5
Farmácia Piaí	10 A5
HSBC	11 F5
Letras e Expressões	12 F5
Letras e Expressões	13 A5
Livraria da Travessa	14 D5
Livraria de Travessa	(see 124)
Post Office	15 E5
Post Office	16 B5
Post Office	17 G5
Tourist Police	18 C5

SIGHTS & ACTIVITIES

Baixo Bebê	**19** B6
Casa do Caminho	
Language Centre	**20** F5
Dive Point	**21** A5
Escolinha de Vôlei	**22** E6
Jardim Botânico	**23** C2
Mirante do Leblon	**24** A6
Museu Amsterdam Sauer	**25** E5
Museu H Stern	**26** E5
Paddle Boats	**27** F3
Parque Brigadeiro Faria	
Lima	**28** C3
Parque da Catacumba	**29** F3
Parque Garota de	
Ipanema	**30** H6
Parque Lage	**31** D1
Planetário	**32** A4
Special Bike	**33** G5

SLEEPING

Arpoador Inn	**34** H6
Bonita	**35** G5
Che Lagarto Ipanema	**36** D5
Everest Rio	**37** E5
Hostel Harmonia	**38** F5
Hotel Fasano	**39** G6
Hotel San Marco	**40** F5
Hotel Vermont	**41** F5
Ipanema Beach House	**42** E5
Ipanema Hotel Residência	**43** F5

Ipanema Inn	**44** E5
Lemon Spirit Hostel	**45** C5
Mar Ipanema	**46** D5
Margarida's Pousada	**47** D5
Marina All Suites	**48** B6
Rio Hostel - Ipanema	**49** G5
Ritz Plaza Hotel	**50** A5
Sol Ipanema	**51** F5
Yaya Hotel	**52** F5

EATING

00	(see 32)
Arab da Lagoa	**53** C3
Armazém do Café	**54** A5
Bazzar	**55** E5
Benkei	**56** D5
Bibi Crepes	**57** C5
Braseiro da Gávea	**58** B3
Brasileirinho	(see 63)
Bráz	**59** E1
Cafeína	**60** F5
Capricciosa	**61** F5
Carretão	**62** G5
Casa da Feijoada	**63** G5
Cobal do Leblon	**64** C4
Delírio Tropical	**65** F5
Felice Caffé & Gelateria	**66** G6
Frontera	**67** G5
Galitos Grill	**68** F5
Garcia & Rodrigues	**69** A5
Guimas	**70** A3
HortiFruti	**71** A5
Koni Store	**72** F5
Laffa	**73** F5
Lagoa Kiosks	(see 53)
Lagoa Kiosks	**74** F3
New Natural	**75** F5
Olympe	**76** E1
Polis Sucos	**77** F5
Prima Bruschetteria	**78** E5
Sushi Leblon	**79** A5
Talho Capixaba	**80** B5

Universo Orgânico	(see 81)
Vegetariano Social Clube	**81** B4
Vezpa Pizzeria	**82** B5
Via Sete	**83** E5
Yögoberry	**84** F5
Zazá Bistro Tropical	**85** F5
Zona Sul Supermarket	**86** B5
Zona Sul Supermarket	**87** G5
Zuka	**88** A5

DRINKING

Academia da Cachaça	**89** B4
Bar D'Hotel	(see 48)
Bar Lagoa	**90** F4
Bar Veloso	**91** B5
Baretto-Londra	(see 39)
Barthodomeu	**92** F5
Caroline Café	**93** C1
Cobal de Leblon	(see 64)
Da Graça	**94** B1
Devassa	**95** F5
Drink Café	(see 53)
Empório	**96** E5
Galeria Café	**97** G5
Garota de Ipanema	**98** F5
Hipódromo	**99** B3
Jobi	**100** B5
Palaphita Kitch	**101** F4
Shenanigan's	**102** F5
Tô Nem Aí	**103** F5

ENTERTAINMENT

00	(see 32)
Baronneti	**104** E5
Cafeína	(see 60)
Cineclub Laura Alvim	(see 5)
Dama de Ferro	**105** F4
Estação Ipanema	**106** D5
Jockey Club Brasileiro	**107** C3
Melt	**108** A6
Nuth Club (Lagoa)	**109** E4
Scala	**110** C5
Vinícius Piano Bar	**111** F5

SHOPPING

Espaço Brazilian Soul	**112** E5
Forum	**113** E5
Gilson Martins	**114** E5
Havaianas	**115** G5
Hippie Fair	**116** G5
Isabela Capeto	**117** A5
Lidador	**118** B5
Lidador	**119** E5
Maria Oiticica	**120** E5
O Sol	**121** B1
Osklen	**122** E5
Rio Design Center	**123** C5
Shopping Leblon	**124** C5
Toca do Vinícius	**125** F5
Urucum Art & Design	(see 106)

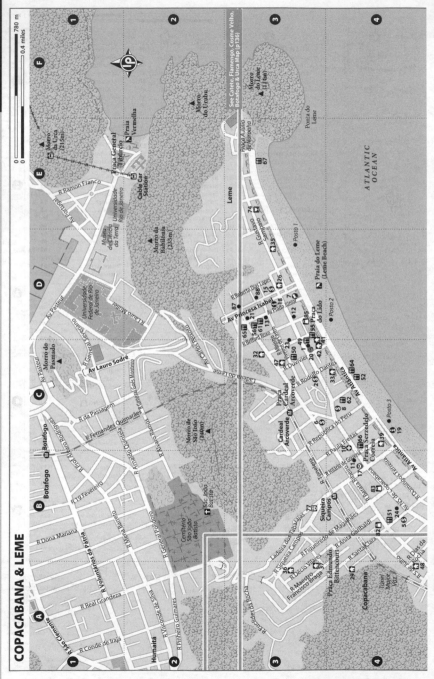

COPACABANA & LEME

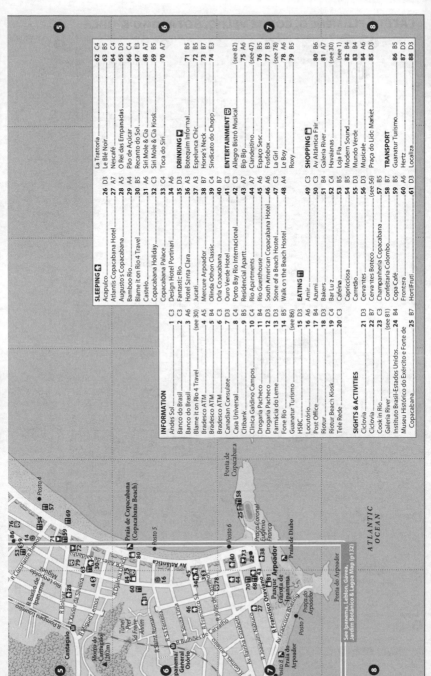

INFORMATION
Andes Sol 1 C3
Banco do Brasil 2 C3
Banco do Brasil 3 A6
Blame It on Rio 4 Travel .... (see 30)
Bradesco ATM 4 A5
Bradesco ATM 5 B4
Bradesco ATM 6 C3
Canadian Consulate 7 D3
Casa Universal 8 C4
Citibank 9 B5
Clinica Galdino Campos 10 C4
Drogaria Pacheco 11 B4
Drogaria Pacheco 12 B5
Farmácia do Leme 13 D3
Fone Rio 14 B5
Guanatur Turismo .... (see 86)
HSBC 15 D3
Locutório 16 A6
Post Office 17 B4
Riotur 18 D3
Riotur Beach Kiosk 19 C4
Tele Rede 20 C3

SIGHTS & ACTIVITIES
Ciclovia 21 D3
Ciclovia 22 B7
Cook in Rio 23 C3
Galeria River 24 B4
Instituto Brasil–Estados Unidos .... (see 81)
Museu Histórico do Exército e Forte de
   Copacabana 25 B7

SLEEPING
Acapulco 26 D3
Atlantis Copacabana Hotel 27 A7
Augusto's Copacabana 28 A5
Bamboo Rio 29 A4
Blame It on Rio 4 Travel 30 B5
Castelo 31 A6
Copacabana Holiday 32 C3
Copacabana Palace 33 C4
Design Hotel Portinari 34 A6
Fantastic Rio 35 D3
Hotel Santa Clara 36 A3
Jucati 37 A3
Mercure Arpoador 38 B7
Olinda Othon Classic 39 C4
Orla Copacabana 40 B7
Ouro Verde Hotel 41 C3
Porto Bay Rio Internacional 42 C3
Residencial Apart 43 A7
Rio Apartments 44 A7
Rio Guesthouse 45 A6
South American Copacabana Hotel ... 46 A6
Stone of a Beach Hostel 47 C3
Walk on the Beach Hostel 48 A4

EATING
Amir 49 C3
Azumi 50 C3
Bakers 51 B4
Bar Luz 52 C4
Cafeína 53 B5
Capricciosa 54 B5
Carretão 55 D3
Cervantes 56 D3
Cervantes Boteco .... (see 56)
Champanheria Copacabana 57 B5
Confeitaria Colombo 58 B7
Copa Café 59 B5
Frontera 60 A6
HortiFruti 61 D3

La Trattoria 62 C4
Le Blé Noir 63 B5
Nescafé 64 C4
O Rei das Empanadas 65 D3
Pão de Açúcar 66 C4
Recanto do Sol 67 E3
Siri Mole & Cia 68 A7
Siri Mole & Cia Kiosk 69 B5
Toca do Siri 70 A7

DRINKING
Botequim Informal 71 B5
Espelunca Chic 72 B5
Horse's Neck 73 B7
Sindicato do Chopp 74 E3

ENTERTAINMENT
Allegro Bistrô Musical .... (see 82)
Bip Bip. 75 A6
Clandestino .... (see 47)
Espaço Sesc 76 B5
Fosfobox 77 B3
La Girl .... (see 78)
Le Boy 78 A6
Roxy 79 B5

SHOPPING
Av Atlântica Fair 80 B6
Galeria River 81 A7
Havaianas .... (see 30)
Loja Fla .... (see 1)
Modern Sound 82 B4
Mundo Verde 83 B4
Musicale 84 A6
Praça do Lido Market 85 D3

TRANSPORT
Guanatur Turismo 86 B5
Hertz 87 D3
Localiza 88 D3

CATETE, FLAMENGO, COSME VELHO, BOTAFOGO & URCA

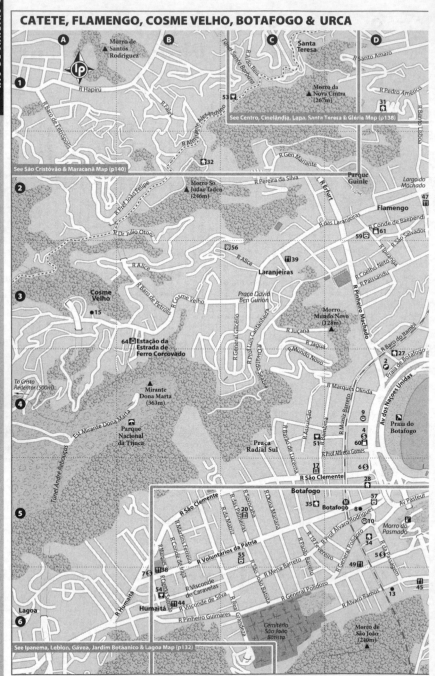

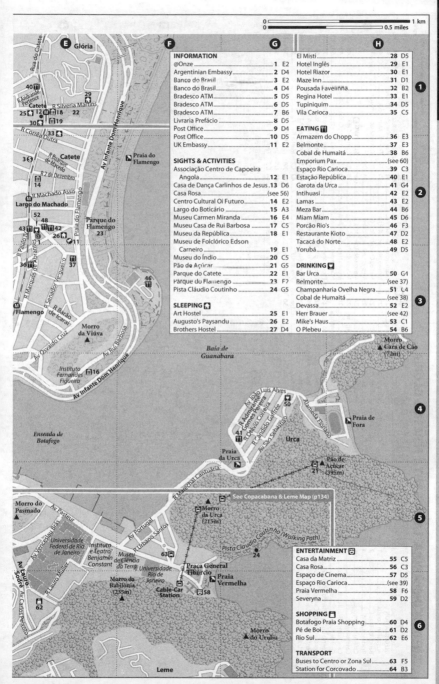

INFORMATION
@Onze	**1** E2
Argentinian Embassy	**2** D4
Banco do Brasil	**3** E2
Banco do Brasil	**4** D4
Bradesco ATM	**5** D5
Bradesco ATM	**6** D4
Bradesco ATM	**7** B6
Livraria Prefácio	**8** D5
Post Office	**9** D4
Post Office	**10** D5
UK Embassy	**11** E2

SIGHTS & ACTIVITIES
Associação Centro de Capoeira Angola	**12** E1
Casa de Dança Carlinhos de Jesus	**13** D6
Casa Rosa	(see 56)
Centro Cultural Oi Futuro	**14** E2
Largo do Boticário	**15** A3
Museu Carmen Miranda	**16** E4
Museu Casa de Rui Barbosa	**17** C5
Museu da República	**18** E1
Museu de Folclórico Edson Carneiro	**19** E1
Museu do Índio	**20** C5
Pão de Açúcar	**21** G5
Parque do Catete	**22** E1
Parque do Flamengo	**23** F2
Pista Cláudio Coutinho	**24** G5

SLEEPING
Art Hostel	**25** E1
Augusto's Paysandu	**26** E2
Brothers Hostel	**27** D4

El Misti	**28** D5
Hotel Inglês	**29** E1
Hotel Riazor	**30** E1
Maze Inn	**31** D1
Pousada Favelinha	**32** B2
Regina Hotel	**33** E1
Tupiniquim	**34** D5
Vila Carioca	**35** C5

EATING
Armazem do Chopp	**36** E3
Belmonte	**37** E3
Cobal de Humaitá	**38** B6
Emporium Pax	(see 60)
Espaço Rio Carioca	**39** C3
Estação República	**40** E1
Garota da Urca	**41** G4
Intihuasi	**42** E2
Lamas	**43** E2
Meza Bar	**44** B6
Miam Miam	**45** D6
Porção Rio's	**46** F3
Restaurante Kioto	**47** D2
Tacacá do Norte	**48** E2
Yorubá	**49** D5

DRINKING
Bar Urca	**50** G4
Belmonte	(see 37)
Champanharia Ovelha Negra	**51** L4
Cobal de Humaitá	(see 38)
Devassa	**52** E2
Herr Brauer	(see 42)
Mike's Haus	**53** C1
O Plebeu	**54** B6

ENTERTAINMENT
Casa da Matriz	**55** C5
Casa Rosa	**56** C3
Espaço de Cinema	**57** D5
Espaço Rio Carioca	(see 39)
Praia Vermelha	**58** F6
Severyna	**59** D2

SHOPPING
Botafogo Praia Shopping	**60** D4
Pé de Boi	**61** D2
Rio Sul	**62** E6

TRANSPORT
Buses to Centro or Zona Sul	**63** F5
Station for Corcovado	**64** B3

CENTRO, CINELÂNDIA, LAPA, SANTA TERESA & GLÓRIA

0 — 600 m
0 — 0.4 miles

INFORMATION
Australian Consulate 1 D5
Banco do Brasil 2 C5
Bradesco ATM 3 C4
Café Arlequim ....(see 38)
Casa Aliança 4 C3
Casa França-Brasil 5 D3
Central Fone 6 C4
Centro Cultural Banco do Brasil ...(see 20)
Centro Cultural Carioca 7 B4
Centro Cultural Laurinda Santos
  Lobo 8 A7
Citibank 9 C4
French Consulate 10 D5

Fundição Progresso ....(see 24)
HSBC 11 D5
HSBC 12 C4
Jasmin Mango 13 C3
Livraria da Travessa 14 C3
Livraria da Travessa 15 D3
Main Post Office 16 C4
Nova Livraria Leonardo da Vinci ...17 D5

Centro Cultural Banco do Brasil 20 D3
Centro de Arte Hélio Oiticica 21 B4
Escadaria do Selarón 22 C6
Espaço Cultural da Marinha 23 D3
Fundição Progresso 24 C7
Igreja de NS da Glória do Outeiro 25 D7
Igreja de NS de Candelária 26 C3
Igreja São Francisco da Penitência
  & Convento Santo Antônio 27 C4
Ilha Fiscal 28 E2
Largo da Guimarães 29 B7
Macuco Rio ....(see 30)
Mar do Rio ....(see 30)
Marlin Yacht Tours 30 E7

US Consulate 17 D5

SIGHTS & ACTIVITIES
Angola N'Golo (Capoeira) ....(see 73)
Bonde to Santa Teresa 18 C5
Catedral Metropolitana 19 C5

Mosteiro de São Bento 31 C2
Museu Histórico Nacional 32 E4
Museu Chácara do Céu 33 B6
Museu de Arte Moderna 34 D6
Museu de Arte Sacra ....(see 19)
Museu do Bonde 35 B7
Museu Nacional de Belas Artes 36 D5
Núcleo de Dança Renata Peçanha 37 B4
Paço Imperial 38 D4
Parque das Ruínas 39 B7
Parque do Flamengo 40 D6
Petrobras Building 41 C5
Pier Mauá ....(see 30)
Pink Fleet 42 B7
Praça Floriano 43 D5
Praça XV de Novembro 44 D3

Real Gabinete Português de Leitura .45 B4
Theatro Municipal 46 C5
Travessa do Comércio 47 D3

SLEEPING ☆
Cama e Café 48 A7
Camping Clube do Brasil 49 C5
Casa Áurea 50 A8
Casa Mango Mango 51 B6
Castelinho 38 ....52 A7
Hotel Marajó 53 C6
Hotel Sa ta Teresa 54 A7
Mama Ruisa 55 B7
Rio Hostel 56 B6
Solar de Santa 57 B7
Terra Brasilis 58 B6

Praça Mauá

Gamboa

Saúde

Centro

Lapa

Santa Teresa

Glória

Cinelândia

Baía de Guanabara

Santos Dumont Aeroporto

See São Cristóvão & Maracanã Map (p140)

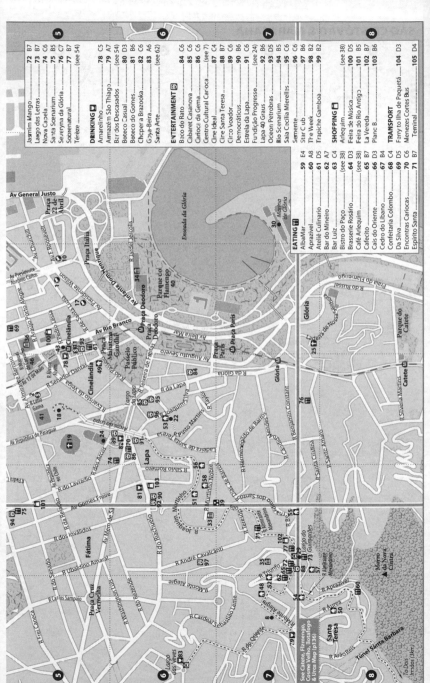

Jasmim Mango 72 B7
Largo das Letras 73 B7
Nova Capela 74 C6
Santa Scenarium 75 B5
Se:eyna da Glória 76 C7
Soonenatural 77 B7
Térèze .... (see 54)

DRINKING
Amarelinho 78 C5
Armazém São Thiago 79 A7
Bar dos Descasados .... (see 54)
Boteco Casual 80 D3
Boteco do Gomes 81 B6
Chcper a Brazooka 82 C6
Goya-Beira 83 A6
Santa Arte .... (see 62)

ENTERTAINMENT
Baco do Rato 84 C6
Cabaret Casanova 85 C6
Carioca da Gema 86 C6
Centro Cultural Carioca .... (see 7)
Cine Ideal 87 C4
Cine Santa Teresa 88 B7
Circo Voador 89 C6
Democráticus 90 B6
Estrela da Lapa 91 C6
Fundição Progresso .... (see 24)
Lapa 40 Graus 92 B6
Oceon Petrobras 93 D5
Rio Scenarium 94 B5
Sala Cecília Meirelles 95 C6
Semente 96 C6
Star C ub 97 B6
Tre Week 98 B2
Trapiche Gamboa 99 B2

SHOPPING
Arlequim .... (see 38)
Feira de Música 100 D5
Feira do Rio Antigo 101 B5
La Vereda 102 B7
Planc B. 103 B6

TRANSPORT
Ferry to Ilha de Paquetá 104 D3
Menezes Cortes Bus
  Terminal 105 D4

EATING
AlbaMar 59 E4
Aprazível 60 A8
Ateliê Culinário 61 D5
Bar do Mineiro 62 A7
Bar Luiz 63 C4
Bistro do Paço .... (see 38)
Brasserie Rosário 64 D3
Café Arlequim .... (see 38)
Cafecito 65 B7
Cais do Oriente 66 D3
Cedro do Líbano 67 B4
Confeitaria Colombo 68 C4
Da Silva 69 D5
Encontras Cariocas 70 C6
Espírito Santa 71 B7

SÃO CRISTÓVÃO & MARACANÃ

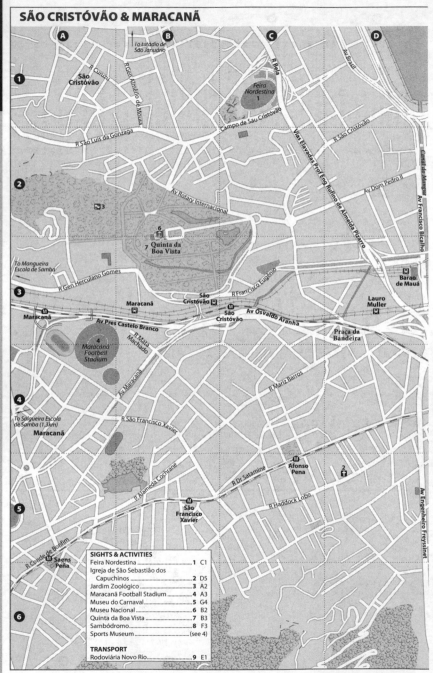

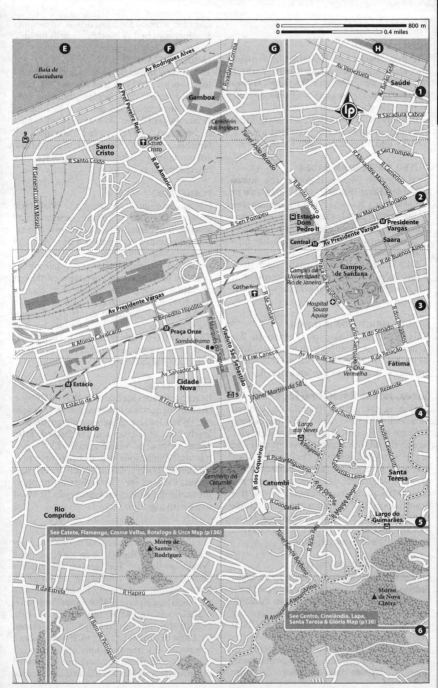

(Continued from page 130)

MUSEU H STERN

The headquarters of H Stern, the famous jeweler, contains the **Museu H Stern** (Map p132; ☎ 2274 8897; www.hstern.com.br; Rua Visconde de Pirajá 490; admission free; ☺ 9am-6pm Mon-Fri, 9am-2pm Sat), an interesting fine-jewelry museum.

If you're in the market for it, the adjoining store has an array of finely crafted jewelry, watches and other accessories for sale.

MUSEU AMSTERDAM SAUER

Next door to Museu H Stern, the **Museu Amsterdam Sauer** (Map p132; ☎ 2512 1132; www.amsterdamsauer.com; Rua Garcia D'Ávila 105; admission free; ☺ 9am-7pm Mon-Fri, to 4pm Sat) also houses an impressive collection of precious stones – over 3000 items in all. It also has two life-size replicas of mines.

Like H Stern, the Amsterdam Sauer store is the place to lay down some serious cash if you're looking for precious gems or well-made accessories.

PARQUE GAROTA DE IPANEMA

This small park (Map p132) next to the Arpoador rock features a tiny playground, a concrete area popular with skaters and a lookout with a view of Ipanema Beach.

Gávea, Jardim Botânico & Lagoa

Beginning just north of Ipanema and Leblon, these well-heeled neighborhoods front Lagoa Rodrigo de Freitas, a picturesque saltwater lagoon ringed with a walking/cycling trail and dotted with lakeside kiosks. The other big draw here is the royal garden (Jardim Botânico) that gave the neighborhood its name. Here you'll find stately palms, rare orchids and colorful flowering plants. Aside from its natural attractions, these neighborhoods have some excellent restaurants, trendy bars, a planetarium and the city's horseracing track.

LAGOA RODRIGO DE FREITAS

One of the city's most picturesque spots, **Lagoa Rodrigo de Freitas** (Map p132) is encircled by a 7.2km walking/cycling path. Bikes are available for hire (R$10 per hour) from stands along the east side of the lake, as are paddle boats (R$20 per half hour). For those who prefer caipirinhas (drinks made from sugarcane spirit, crushed lime, sugar and ice) to plastic swan boats, the **lakeside kiosks** on either side of the lake offer alfresco food and drinks, sometimes accompanied by live music on warm nights.

JARDIM BOTÂNICO

The exotic **Jardim Botânico** (Map p132; ☎ 3874 1808; www.jbrj.gov.br; Rua Jardim Botânico 920, Jardim Botânico; admission R$5; ☺ 8am-5pm), housing over 8000 plant species, was designed by order of Prince Regent Dom João in 1808. It's quiet and screne on weekdays and blossoms with families and music on weekends. A pleasant outdoor café overlooks the gardens. Take insect repellent.

PLANETÁRIO

Gávea's stellar attraction, the **Planetário** (Planetarium; Map p132; ☎ 2274 0046; www.rio.rj.gov.br/planetario, in Portuguese; Av Padre Leonel Franca 240; museum only adult/child R$8/4, museum & planetarium show adult/child R$16/8; ☺ 9am-5pm Tue-Fri, 3-6pm Sat & Sun) features a museum, a *praça dos telescópios* (plaza of telescopes) and two state-of-the-art operating domes, each capable of projecting over 6000 stars on its walls. Visitors can also take a peak at the night sky (free) through the telescopes on Tuesday, Wednesday and Thursday from 7:30pm to 8:30pm (6:30pm to 7:30pm in winter). Periodically, the Planetário hosts live Sunday concerts.

PARQUE LAGE

Beautiful **Parque Lage** (Map p132; ☎ 3257 1819; www.eavparquelage.rj.gov.br in Portuguese; Rua Jardim Botânico 414; ☺ 9am-5pm) has English-style gardens, a lovely café, little lakes and the **Escola de Artes Visuais** (School of Visual Arts), which often hosts art exhibitions and an occasional performance. Native Atlantic rain forest surrounds Parque Lage. This is the starting point for challenging hikes up Corcovado (it's best to go with a guide).

PARQUE DA CATACUMBA

On the edge of the lake (but across the busy road), this **park** (Map p132; Av Epitácio Pessoa, Lagoa; ☺ 8am-5pm Tue-Sun) and sculptural garden added some new adventure activities in 2010, including a 7m-high rock-climbing wall (R$15), a zipline (R$10), rappelling down a 30m rockface (R$40) and a canopy walk (R$30) through the treetops. It's operated by **Lagoa Aventuras** (☎ 4105 0079; www.lagoaaventuras.com.br). It's free to simply stroll through the park, and there's a short but steep trail (15-minute walk) to the Mirante do Sacopã, which offers scenic views from a height of 130m above Lagoa.

PARQUE DA CIDADE & MUSEU HISTÓRICO DA CIDADE

The 19th-century mansion on the lovely grounds of the **Parque da Cidade** (Map p131; admission free; ☉ 7am-6pm) now houses the **Museu Histórico da Cidade** (City History Museum; ☎ 2512 2353; Estrada de Santa Marinha 505, Gávea; admission R$6; ☉ 10am-4pm Tue-Fri, 10am-3pm Sat & Sun), which portrays Rio from its founding in 1565 to the mid-20th century. The museum also has exhibitions of furniture, porcelain, photographs and paintings by well-known artists.

INSTITUTO MOREIRA SALLES

The beautiful **Instituto Moreira Salles** (Map p131; ☎ 3284 7400; www.ims.com.br in Portuguese; Rua Marquês de Sao Vicente 476, Gávea; admission free; ☉ 1-8pm Tue-Sun), next to the Parque da Cidade, contains an archive of more than 80,000 photographs, many portraying the old streets of Rio. The gardens, complete with artificial lake and flowing river, were designed by Brazilian landscape architect Burle Marx. There's also a craft shop and a café serving lunch and afternoon tea.

Copacabana & Leme

Framed by mountains and deep blue sea, Rio's most beautiful beach curves 4.5km from end to end. No longer a symbol of Rio's glam, Copacabana is a fascinating but chaotic place, its art-deco buildings, aging beachfront hotels and tree-lined side streets form the backdrop to a wildly democratic mix of tourists, elderly middle-class Cariocas, and favela dwellers (who live in the hillsides surrounding the neighborhood). Despite its faults (crime for one), the neighborhood has its charms – old-school *botecos* (small, open-air bars), eclectic restaurants, vibrant street life, and the handsome beach still entrance many visitors.

The name Copacabana comes from a small Bolivian village on Lake Titicaca. Historians believe a statue of the Virgin Mary (Our Lady of Copacabana) was brought to Rio and consecrated inside a small chapel near Arpoador. Copacabana remained a small fishing village until Túnel Velho opened in 1891, connecting Copacabana with the rest of the city. The construction of the neoclassical Copacabana Palace hotel in 1923 heralded Copacabana's golden era as a tropical getaway for the rich

and fabulous. Copacabana remained Rio's gem until the 1970s, when the area began the fall into decline.

COPACABANA & LEME BEACH

A magnificent confluence of land and sea, the long, scalloped beach of Copacabana and Leme (Map p134) always has a flurry of activity stretching its length: overamped footballers singing their team's anthem, Cariocas and tourists lining up for caipirinhas at kiosks, favela kids showing off their football skills, and beach vendors picking their way through the mass of bronzed bodies.

As in Ipanema, each group stakes out its stretch of sand. Leme is a mix of older residents and favela kids, while the area just west of the Copacabana Palace is the gay and transvestite section, known as the Stock or Stock Market – easily recognized by the rainbow flag. Young football and *futevôlei* (volleyball playcd without hands) players hold court near Rua Santa Clara. Posts 5 and 6 are a mix of favela kids and Carioca retirees, while the beach next to Forte de Copacabana is the unofficial *posto de pescadores* (fishermen's post). In the morning, you can buy the fresh catch of the day.

The beach is lit at night and there are police in the area, but it's still not wise to walk there after dark – stay near the liveliest beach kiosks when venturing out. Av NS de Copacabana is also sketchy – watch out on weekends, when the shops are closed and few locals are around.

MUSEU HISTÓRICO DO EXÉRCITO E FORTE DE COPACABANA

Built in 1914, on the promontory of the former Our Lady of Copacabana chapel, the Forte de Copacabana (Copacabana Fort) was one of Rio's premier defenses against attack. You can still see its original features, including walls up to 12m thick, defended by Krupp cannons. The several floors of exhibits in the fort's **museum** (Map p134; ☎ 2521 1032; cnr Av Atlântica & Rua Francisco Otaviano, Copacabana; admission R$4; ☉ 10am-4pm Tue-Sun), tracing the early days of the Portuguese colony to the mid-19th century, aren't the most tastefully presented, but the view alone warrants a visit. There's a lovely café overlooking Copacabana.

Botafogo

A largely middle-class residential area, Botafogo lacks the sensuality of Ipanema and the decadence of Copacabana, but it's one of Rio's most traditional neighborhoods. It boasts some fine, small museums, excellent theaters, quaint bookstores, neighborhood bars and a welcome shortage of high-rise buildings.

The area attained prominence in the late 1800s when the Portuguese court arrived in Brazil. Dom João VI's wife, Carlota Joaquina, had a country villa built in Botafogo with convenient access to Baía de Guanabara, one of her favorite bathing spots. With royalty established in the area, many mansions were constructed, some of which still stand – as schools, theaters and cultural centers.

MUSEU DO ÍNDIO

Featuring multimedia exhibitions on Brazil's northern tribes, the small **Museu do Índio** (Map p136; ☎ 2286 8899; www.museudoindio.org.br; Rua das Palmeiras 55, Botafogo; admission R$3, free Sun; ☾ 9am-5:30pm Tue-Fri, 1-5pm Sat & Sun) provides an excellent introduction to Brazil's indigenous people. Next to native food and medicinal plants, the four life-size dwellings in the courtyard were built by four different tribes. The museum contains an archive of more than 14,000 objects, 50,000 photographs and 200 sound recordings.

MUSEU CASA DE RUI BARBOSA

This **house museum** (Map p136; ☎ 3289 4600; www.casaruibarbosa.gov.br, in Portuguese; Rua São Clemente 134; admission R$2; ☾ 9am-5:30pm Tue-Fri, 2-6pm Sat & Sun) and former home of renowned Brazilian journalist and diplomat Rui Barbosa contains his library and personal belongings, along with an impressive archive of manuscripts and first editions of other Brazilian authors. Barbosa played a major role in shaping the country's socioeconomic development in the early 20th century.

Urca

The tranquil, shady streets of Urca offer a pleasant escape from the urban bustle of other parts of the city. An eclectic mix of building styles and manicured gardens lines its streets, with local residents strolling among them. Along the sea wall, which forms the northwestern perimeter of Pão de Açúcar, fishers cast for dinner as couples lounge beneath palm trees, taking in views of Baía de Guanabara and Cristo Redentor off in the distance. Tiny Praia Vermelha, in the south,

has one of Rio's finest beach views. A lovely walking trail begins from here.

Although it was the site of one of the first Portuguese garrisons in the region, almost 300 years elapsed before Urca developed into a residential neighborhood. Today it holds the distinction of being one of the safest and – in spite of Pão de Açúcar being in its midst – least discovered by foreign visitors.

PÃO DE AÇÚCAR

Seen from the peak of **Pão de Açúcar** (Sugarloaf; Map p136; ☎ 2461 2700; Praça General Tibúrcio, Urca; adult/child R$44/22; ☾ 8am-7:50pm), Rio is undoubtedly the most beautiful city in the world. There are many good times to make the ascent, but sunset on a clear day is the most rewarding.

A visit to Pão de Açúcar is a must, but if you can, avoid it from about 10am to 11am and 2pm to 3pm, when most tourist buses arrive. Avoid cloudy days as well. Two cable cars connect to the summit, 396m above Rio. The first ascends 220m to **Morro da Urca**. From here, you can see Baía de Guanabara and the winding coastline; on the ocean side of the mountain is Praia Vermelha. Morro da Urca has its own restaurant, souvenir shops, a playground, an outdoor theater and a helipad (for helicopter tours, see p158).

The second cable car goes up to Pão de Açúcar. At the top, the city unfolds beneath you, with Corcovado mountain and Cristo Redentor off to the west, and Copacabana Beach to the south. If the breathtaking heights unsteady you, a drink stand serves caipirinhas or *cerveja* (beer). The two-stage cable cars depart every 30 minutes.

Those who'd rather take the long way to the summit should sign up with one of the granite-hugging climbing tours offered by various outfits in Rio (see p152).

PRAIA VERMELHA & PISTA CLÁUDIO COUTINHO

Beneath the shadow of Morro da Urca, the narrow **Praia Vermelha**, in a small, calm bay, has superb views of the rocky coastline from the shore. Its coarse sand, unlike that of any other beach in Rio, gives the beach the name *vermelha* (red).

A paved 2km path, **Pista Cláudio Coutinho** (Map p136; ☾ 6am-sunset) winds along the southern contour of Morro da Urca. It's a lush area, shaded by trees, with the waves crashing on the rocks below. Keep an eye out for families of small *micos* – capuchin monkeys with ringed tails. About 300m along the path, there's a small unmarked trail that leads up to Morro da Urca. Pão de Açúcar can also be climbed – but it's not recommended without climbing gear.

Flamengo

Flamengo was once Rio's finest residential district, but lost its glitter after the tunnel to Copacabana opened in 1904. Today, Flamengo maintains its largely residential roots. Along tree-shaded sidewalks, old-school restaurants and historic bars lie beside fragrant juice bars and Música Popular Brasileira–playing internet cafés. Flamengo also boasts the large Parque do Flamengo, which fronts a scenic beach (too polluted for swimming).

PARQUE DO FLAMENGO

The result of a landfill project that leveled São Antônio hill in 1965, **Parque do Flamengo** (Map p136 and Map p138) now spreads all the way from downtown Rio through Glória, Catete and Flamengo, and on around to Botafogo. Cyclists and inline skaters glide along the paths winding through the park, while the many football fields and sports courts are framed against the sea. On Sunday and holidays, the avenues through the park are closed to traffic (from 7am to 6pm), bringing a welcome calm to the verdant park.

Designed by famous Brazilian landscaper Burle Marx (who also landscaped Brasília), the park features some 170,000 trees of 300 different species. In addition there are several museums in the park, including the Museu de Arte Moderna (p147) and the Museu Carmen Miranda.

MUSEU CARMEN MIRANDA

Although Carmen Miranda is largely forgotten in Hollywood, the once-great Brazilian singer still has her fans, and has become a cult icon among Rio's gay community. In addition to photographs and music of her era, the tiny **Museu Carmen Miranda** (Map p136; ☎ 2551 2597; facing Av Rui Barbosa 560, Flamengo; admission free; 10am-5pm Tue-Fri, 1-5pm Sat) displays the starlet's iconographic costumes and jewelry.

Cosme Velho

Cosme Velho lies west of Laranjeiras and is one of the city's most visited neighborhoods –

if only for the statue of Cristo Redentor soaring above its streets.

CRISTO REDENTOR

Atop Corcovado (which means 'hunchback'), **Cristo Redentor** (Christ the Redeemer; Map p131 ☎ 2558 1329; Rua Cosme Velho 513, Cosme Velho; adult/child R$36/18; 8:30am-6:30pm) gazes out over Rio, a placid expression on his well-crafted face. The mountain rises straight up from the city to 710m, and at night, the brightly lit, 38m-high statue is visible from nearly every part of the city – all 1145 tons of the open-armed redeemer.

The view from the top of Corcovado provides a spectacular panorama of Rio and its surroundings. Corcovado lies within Parque Nacional da Tijuca. The most memorable way to the top is by cog train (Map p136; departures every 30 minutes). For the best view, sit on the right-hand side going up. There's also a road going up to the base of the monument. A private car or taxi will go only as far as Paineiras car park, from which you must transfer to an authorized van to go the 2km further to the top (R$15 per person). Be sure to choose a clear day to go up.

LARGO DO BOTICÁRIO

The brightly painted houses on the picturesque square of **Largo do Boticário** (Map p136; Rua Cosme Velho 822) date from the early 19th century. Largo do Boticário was named in honor of the Portuguese gentleman – Joaquim Luiz da Silva Souto – who once ran a *boticário* (apothecary) utilized by the royal family.

Catete & Glória

Like Flamengo, these twin districts flourished in the mid-19th century, when their location at the outskirts of the city made them desirable places to live. The area's star attraction is the Palácio do Catete (now the Museu da República), the republic's seat of power before the capital was transferred to Brasília.

IGREJA DE NS DA GLÓRIA DO OUTEIRO

This tiny **church** (Map p138; ☎ 2557 4600; www.outei rodagloria.org.br; Praça Nossa Senhora da Glória 135; 9am-noon & 1-4pm Mon-Fri, 9am-noon Sat & Sun) commands lovely views over Parque do Flamengo and the bay. Considered one of the finest examples of religious colonial architecture in Brazil, the church dates from 1739 and became the favorite of the royal family upon their arrival in 1808.

HISTORICAL SITES

Paço Imperial (p148) The former imperial palace was home to the royal family when they arrived from Portugal.

Praça XV (Quinze) de Novembro (p148) Named after the date Brazil declared itself a republic (November 15, 1822), this plaza has witnessed a lot of historical action, including the crowning of two emperors and the abolition of slavery.

Travessa do Comércio (p148) This narrow alley is a window into colonial Rio, with 18th-century buildings converted into bars and restaurants.

Museu Histórico Nacional (p147) Set in the 18th-century royal arsenal, this museum houses Rio's best assortment of historical artifacts.

Jardim Botânico (p142) Prince Regent Dom João VI insured the city would have no shortage of green spaces, and ordered this verdant garden planted in 1808.

Museu da República (p146) Formerly known as the Palácio do Catete, this mansion was Brazil's presidential home from 1896 to 1954. Getúlio Vargas was the last president to live here, and committed suicide in one of the upstairs rooms.

Praça Floriano (p148) Centro's picturesque main square has long been the meeting ground for popular demonstrations, including student uprisings against the military dictatorship in the 1960s and victory celebrations following World Cup finals.

Garota de Ipanema (p172) Famed drinking spot where Tom Jobim and Vinícius de Moraes penned *The Girl from Ipanema*, whose international success introduced the world to bossa nova.

MUSEU DA REPÚBLICA

Located in the Palácio do Catete, the **Museu da República** (Map p136; ☎ 3235 2650; www.museudarepub lica.org.br, in Portuguese; Rua do Catete 153, Catete; admission R$6, free on Wed; ☽ 10am-5pm Tue-Fri, 2-6pm Sat & Sun) has a good collection of art and artifacts from the Republican period. Built between 1858 and 1866 and easily distinguished by the bronze condors on the eaves, the palace was home to the president of Brazil from 1896 until 1954, when President Getúlio Vargas killed himself. The bedroom in which the suicide occurred is eerily preserved on the 3rd floor.

Behind the Palácio lies **Parque do Catete**, a small, nicely landscaped park with shade-covered walks and a pond.

MUSEU DE FOLCLÓRICO EDSON CARNEIRO

Next door to the Palácio do Catete, this **museum** (Map p136; ☎ 2285 0441; Rua do Catete 179, Catete; admission free; ☽ 11am-6pm Tue-Fri, 3-6pm Sat & Sun) provides an excellent introduction to Brazilian folk art. Its collection includes Candomblé costumes, ceramic figurines and religious costumes used in festivals, though our favorite exhibits are the delightful, mechanized scenes (the circus, bull riders, samba show, rubber tree workers).

CENTRO CULTURAL OI FUTURO

Boasting 200 sq m of exhibition space spread over six floors, the **Centro Cultural Oi Futuro** (Map p136; ☎ 3131 6060; www.oifuturo.org.br; Rua 2 de Dezembro 63; admission free; ☽ 11am-8pm Tue-Sun) features multimedia installations focusing on architecture, urban design and video art. The top-floor auditorium of this cultural center has a regular line-up of film screenings and concerts. The 1st floor functions as a library where visitors can peruse art books and design mags; a listening station has eclectic music.

Centro & Cinelândia

Rio's bustling commercial district, Centro is a blend of high-rise office buildings with remnants of its grand past still present in looming baroque churches, wide plazas and cobblestone streets.

Many pedestrian-only areas crisscross Centro. The most famous of these is known as **Saara**, a giant street bazaar crammed with discount stores. In the last century, Saara attracted an influx of immigrants from the Middle East, and still has a few authentic Lebanese restaurants. Saara extends between Ururguaiana metro station and Campo de Sanatana.

At the southern edge of the business district, Cinelândia's shops, bars, restaurants and movie theaters are popular day and night. The bars and restaurants get crowded at lunch and after work, when street musicians sometimes wander the area.

CENTRO CULTURAL DO BANCO DO BRASIL

Housed in a beautifully restored building dating from 1906, the **Centro Cultural do Banco**

do Brasil (CCBB; Map p138; ☎ 3808 2020; www.cultura-e.com.br, in Portuguese; Rua Primeiro de Março 66; admission free; ☺ 10am-9pm Tue-Sun) is one of Brazil's best cultural centers, with a cinema, two theaters and some of the city's best (and free) exhibitions. There's always something going on at CCBB – visit the website for listings.

CENTRO DE ARTE HÉLIO OITICICA
This avant-garde **museum** (Map p138; ☎ 2242 1012; Rua Luís de Camões 68; admission free; ☺ 11am-6pm Tue-Fri, 11am-5pm Sat & Sun) is set in a 19th-century neoclassical building that originally housed the Conservatory of Music and Dramatic Arts. Today, the center displays permanent works by the artist, theoretician and poet Hélio Oiticica, as well as bold contemporary art exhibitions, well-tuned to Oiticica's progressive aesthetics.

ESPAÇO CULTURAL DA MARINHA
On the waterfront, the **Espaço Cultural da Marinha** (Map p138; ☎ 2104 5592; Av Alfred Agache s/n; admission free; ☺ noon-5pm Tue-Sun) is a sailor's delight. Moored along the dock are the *Riachuelo* submarine and the *Bauru* (a small WWII destroyer), which have been turned into floating museums. You'll also find a 19th-century vessel used by Dom João VI, countless ship models, and maps and navigational instruments charting the history of imperial and Brazilian navigation. The boat tour to Ilha Fiscal (p151) leaves from here.

IGREJA SÃO FRANCISCO DA PENITÊNCIA & CONVENTO SANTO ANTÔNIO
Overlooking the Largo da Carioca is the baroque **Igreja São Francisco da Penitência & Convento Santo Antônio** (Map p138; ☎ 2262 0197; Largo da Carioca 5; admission R$2; ☺ church 8am-6pm daily, convent 9am-noon & 1-4pm Tue-Fri), dating from 1726. Recently restored to its former glory, the church's sacristy has blue Portuguese tiles and an elaborately carved altar made out of jacaranda wood. It also has a roof panel by José Oliveira Rosa depicting St Francis receiving the stigmata. The church's statue of Santo Antônio is an object of great devotion to many Cariocas in search of a husband or wife.

IGREJA DE NOSSA SENHORA DE CANDELÁRIA
The construction of the original church to Our Lady of Candelária (dating from the late 16th century), on the present site, was credited to a ship's captain who had almost been shipwrecked at sea. Upon his safe return he vowed to build a church to her. A later design led to its present-day grandeur, which rated **Igreja de NS de Candelária** (Map p138; ☎ 2233 2324; Praça Pio X; ☺ 8am-4pm Mon-Fri, 9am-1pm Sat & Sun) among the largest and wealthiest churches of Imperial Brazil. The interior is a spectacular combination of baroque and Renaissance styles. The ceiling above the nave features six large panels that depict the romanticized version of the sea captain's journey and the subsequent origin of the church. The cupola, fabricated entirely from limestone shipped from Lisbon, is one of its most striking features.

MOSTEIRO DE SÃO BENTO
Another fine colonial gem, the **Mosteiro de São Bento** (Map p138; ☎ 2206 8100; Rua Dom Gerardo 68; guided visits R$8; ☺ 7am-6pm) was built between 1617 and 1641 on Morro de São Bento, one of the four hills that once marked colonial Rio. The simple facade hides a baroque interior richly decorated in gold. Among its historic treasures are wood carvings designed by Frei Domingos da Conceição and paintings by José Oliveira Rosa. On Sunday, the High Mass at 10am includes a choir of Benedictine monks singing Gregorian chants. To reach the monastery from Rua Dom Gerardo, go to number 40 and take the elevator to the 5th floor.

MUSEU DE ARTE MODERNA
At the north end of Parque do Flamengo, the **Museu de Arte Moderna** (MAM; Map p138; ☎ 2240 4944; www.mamrio.org.br, in Portuguese; Rua Jardel Jercolis; adult/child R$8/4; ☺ noon-6pm Tue-Fri, to 7pm Sat & Sun) is immediately recognizable by the striking postmodern edifice designed by Alfonso Eduardo Reidy. The landscaping by Burle Marx is no less impressive. After a devastating fire in 1978 that consumed 90% of its collection, the museum is finally back on its feet and now houses 11,000 permanent works, including pieces by Brazilian artists Bruno Giorgi, Emiliano Di Cavalcanti and Maria Martins. You'll find excellent photography and design exhibits, and the cinema hosts regular film festivals throughout the year.

MUSEU HISTÓRICO NACIONAL
Housed in the colonial arsenal, which dates from 1764, the impressive **Museu Histórico Nacional** (Map p138; ☎ 2550 9224; www.museuhistorico nacional.com.br; off Av General Justo; adult/child R$6/3, free

Sun; ⏰ 10am-5:30pm Tue-Fri, 2-6pm Sat & Sun) contains over 250,000 historic relics relating to the history of Brazil from its founding to its early days as a republic. The museum is located near Praça Marechal Âncora and features many well-designed displays, from gilded imperial coaches and the throne of Dom Pedro II to massive oil paintings depicting the horrific combat in the war with Paraguay. There's some attention paid to Brazil's indigenous population and to curious relics such as the writing quill that Princess Isabel used to sign the document abolishing slavery in Brazil and a full-sized model of a colonial pharmacy.

MUSEU NACIONAL DE BELAS ARTES
Rio's **Museu Nacional de Belas Artes** (Map p138; ☎ 2240 0068; Av Rio Branco 199; adult/child R$5/2, free on Sun; ⏰ 10am-6pm Tue-Fri, noon-5pm Sat & Sun) houses more than 18,000 original paintings and sculptures, some of which date back to works brought over from Portugal by Dom João VI in 1808. One of its most important galleries is the Galeria de Arte Brasileira, with 20th-century classics such as Cândido Portinari's *Café*. Other galleries display Brazilian folk art, African art and furniture, as well as contemporary exhibits. Guided tours are available in English (call ahead).

PAÇO IMPERIAL
Built in 1743, the **Paço Imperial** (Imperial Palace; Map p138; ☎ 2215 2622; cnr Praça XV de Novembro & Rua Primeiro de Março; free admission; ⏰ noon-6pm Tue-Sun) hosts worthwhile multimedia exhibitions. Originally built as a governor's residence, it later served as the home to Dom João and his family when the Portuguese royals fled Napoleon and transferred the throne to the colony. In 1888 Princesa Isabel proclaimed the Freedom from Slavery Act from the palace's steps. In addition to exhibitions, there are several restaurants, and a café and music store on the 1st floor.

Adjoining the Paço is the **Praça XV (Quinze) de Novembro**, the broad plaza where Brazil's two emperors (Pedro I and Pedro II) were crowned. It was later the site of the deposition of Emperor Pedro II in 1889.

TRAVESSA DO COMÉRCIO
Beautiful two-story colonial townhouses line the narrow cobblestone street of **Travessa do Comércio** (Map p138; near Praça XV de Novembro). The archway known as Arco de Teles leading into the area was once a part of an old viaduct running between two buildings. Today, the street contains half a dozen restaurants and drinking spots that open onto the streets. It's a favorite spot for Cariocas after work.

PRAÇA FLORIANO
The heart of modern Rio, **Praça Floriano** (Map p138; Av Rio Branco) comes to life at lunchtime and after work when the outdoor cafés are filled with beer drinkers, samba musicians and political debate. The square is also Rio's political marketplace. There's daily speechmaking, literature sales and street theater. Most city marches and rallies culminate here on the steps of the old Câmara Municipal (Town Hall), in the northwest corner of the plaza.

REAL GABINETE PORTUGUÊS DE LEITURA
Built in the Manueline Portuguese style in 1837, the gorgeous **Real Gabinete Português de Leitura** (Portuguese Reading Room; Map p138; ☎ 2221 3138; Rua Luís de Camões 30; admission free; ⏰ 9am-6pm Mon-Fri) houses over 350,000 works, many dating from the 16th to the 18th centuries. It also has a small collection of paintings, sculptures and ancient coins.

THEATRO MUNICIPAL
Built in 1905 in the style of the Paris Opera, the magnificent **Theatro Municipal** (Municipal Theater; Map p138; ☎ 2332 9191; Rua Manuel de Carvalho; www.theatromunicipal.rj.gov.br; guided tour R$10; ⏰ 10am-11:30am & 2-3:30pm Thu-Sat) is the home of Rio's opera, orchestra and ballet. If you can't attend a performance here, you can come for a guided tour of the theater.

Lapa
Formerly a residential neighborhood of the wealthy, Lapa had its best days before the 20th century, and its mansions are now sadly neglected. Today Lapa recalls decades of dereliction in the minds of some Cariocas, while others cite the cultural renaissance happening here. Undoubtedly, Lapa is the center of a vibrant bohemian scene in Rio, with dozens of music clubs, bars and old-fashioned restaurants scattered along its avenues.

On weekend nights, revelers pack the neighborhood's samba clubs, its streets and the wide plaza in front of the Arcos do Lapa, the neighborhood's prominent landmark. Narrow tracks course over the 64m-high structure, carrying the famous *bonde* (tram) to and from Santa Teresa (see p149).

CATEDRAL METROPOLITANA

The enormous cone-shaped **Catedral Metropolitana** (Map p138; ☎ 2240 2669; Av República do Chile 245, Lapa; admission free; ☺ 7am-5:30pm) was inaugurated in 1976 after 12 years of construction. Among its sculptures, murals and other works of art are four breathtaking stained glass windows, which stretch 60m to the ceiling.

The small **Museu de Arte Sacra** (Museum of Sacred Art) in the basement contains a number of historical items, including the baptismal font used at the christening of royal princes and the throne of Dom Pedro II. The cathedral can accommodate up to 20,000 worshippers.

ESCADARIA SELARÓN

An ever-expanding installation, the **Escadaria Selarón** (Selarón Staircase; Map p138; btwn Rua Joaquim Silva, Lapa & Rua Pinto Martins, Santa Teresa), leading up from Rua Joaquim Silva, became a work of art when Chilean-born artist Jorge Selarón decided to cover the steps with colorful mosaics. A dedication to the Brazilian people, the 215 steps are a vivid riot of color. In the morning, you can often find him at work, and he welcomes visitors to bring tiles from other countries, which he'll then add to the Lapa landscape.

FUNDIÇÃO PROGRESSO

Once a foundry for safes and ovens, the **Fundição Progresso** (☎ 2220 5070; Rua dos Arcos 24, Lapa; admission free; concerts R$10-50; ☺ 9am-6pm Mon-Fri) today hosts avant-garde exhibitions, performances and popular samba parties during the summer.

Santa Teresa

Set on a hill overlooking the city, the cobbled streets and aging mansions of Santa Teresa are a vision of days long past. Named after the Carmelite convent founded here in 1750, Santa Teresa was the uppermost residential neighborhood in the 19th century, when Rio's upper class lived here and rode the *bonde* (tram) to work in Centro. During the 1960s and 1970s many artists and bohemians moved into Santa Teresa's mansions, initiating a revitalization process that still continues. Throughout the year, impromptu festivals and street parties fill the air, making it one of Rio's most exciting neighborhoods.

The neighborhood's ongoing restoration has led to an influx of boutique hotels, restaurants and cafés, and some have compared Santa Teresa to Paris' Montmartre. Yet this rugged neighborhood is unlikely to ever completely lose its edginess, if only for the omnipresent favelas spreading down the hillsides. Be cautious when walking around Santa Teresa, and avoid deserted streets. The best time to explore is on Saturday or Sunday when the neighborhood is at its liveliest.

BONDE

The **bonde** (Map p138; ☎ 2240 5709; station at Rua Lélio Gama 65, Centro; fare R$0.60; ☺ departures every 30min, 7am-10pm) that travels up to Santa Teresa from Centro is the last of the historic streetcars that once crisscrossed the city. Its clatter through the cobbled streets has made it the icon for bohemian Santa Teresa. The tram travels over the Arcos do Lapa and up Rua Joaquim Murtinho before reaching Largo do Guimarães. From there, one line (Paula Matos) takes a northwestern route, terminating at Largo das Neves. The longer route (Dois Irmãos) continues from Largo do Guimarães uphill and southward before terminating near the water reservoir at Dois Irmãos.

MUSEU CHÁCARA DO CÉU

The former mansion of art patron and industrialist Raymundo Ottoni de Castro Maya is now the **Museu Chácara do Céu** (Map p138; ☎ 3970 1126; Rua Murtinho Nobre 93, Santa Teresa; admission R$6, free Wed; ☺ noon-5pm Wed-Mon), with a small collection of modern art. In addition to works by Portinari, Di Cavalcanti, and a good assortment of European and Asian works, the museum displays furniture and Brazilian maps dating from the 17th and 18th centuries. Beautiful gardens surround the museum, with fine views of Centro and Baía de Guanabara. Sadly, four of the museum's most valuable paintings were stolen during an armed robbery in 2006.

PARQUE DAS RUINAS

The **Parque das Ruinas** (Map p138; ☎ 2252 1039; Rua Murtinho Nobre 169, Santa Teresa; admission free; ☺ 8am-8pm Tue-Sun) contains the ruins of the mansion that belonged to Brazilian heiress Laurinda Santos Lobo. Her house was a meeting point for Rio's artists and intellectuals for many years until her death in 1946. The real reason to come here is for the excellent view from up top. There's a small outdoor café and occasional open-air concerts are held here.

Greater Rio

To the west of Centro lie some of Rio's big-name attractions, including the Sambódromo, the Maracanã Football Stadium and the Feira Nordestina, one of Brazil's wildest markets. You'll also find the Quinta da Boa Vista, a large park containing the Museu Nacional and the Jardim Zoológico (zoo). These latter sites lie in São Cristóvão, which in the 19th century was home to the nobility, including the monarchs themselves. It has since become one of the most populous suburbs in Rio.

To the east of Centro lies Rio's scenic bay. Unfortunately, it's too polluted for swimming, but it makes a fine setting for sailing out to Ilha de Paquetá or Niterói. For cruises on the bay, see p158.

SÃO CRISTÓVÃO & AROUND
Sambódromo

The epicenter of Rio's Carnaval, the **Sambódromo** (Map p140; Rua Marquês de Sapucaí, Cidade Nova) was designed by Oscar Niemeyer and completed in 1984. The small **Museu do Carnaval** (Map p140; free admission; 🕙 11am-5pm Tue-Sun) has information on the history of Rio's samba schools, and you can try on costumes, but aside from that, there isn't much to see when the parades aren't happening.

Feira Nordestina

The enormous **Feira Nordestina** (Map p140; ☎ 3860 9976; www.feiradesaocristovao.com.br, in Portuguese; Campo de São Cristóvão, São Cristóvão; admission R$1; 🕙 10am-4pm

---

PARQUE NACIONAL DA TIJUCA

The Floresta da Tijuca (another name for Parque Nacional da Tijuca) is all that's left of the Atlantic rain forest that once surrounded Rio de Janeiro. In just 15 minutes you can go from the concrete jungle of Copacabana to the 120-sq-km tropical jungle of **Parque Nacional da Tijuca** (Map p131). A more rapid and dramatic contrast is hard to imagine. The forest is an exuberant green, with beautiful trees, creeks and waterfalls, mountainous terrain and high peaks. It has an excellent, well-marked trail system. Candomblistas (devotees of the Candomblé religion) leave offerings by the roadside, families have picnics and serious hikers climb the 1012m to the summit of **Pico da Tijuca**.

The heart of the forest is the Alto da Boa Vista area, which has many lovely natural and artificial features. Among the highlights of this beautiful park are several waterfalls (**Cascatinha Taunay**, **Cascata Gabriela** and **Cascata Diamantina**), a 19th-century chapel (**Capela Mayrink**) and numerous caves (**Gruta Luís Fernandes**, **Gruta Belmiro** and **Gruta Paulo e Virgínia**). Also in the park is a pleasant picnic spot (**Bom Retiro**) and several restaurants, which are near the **Ruínas do Archer**, the ruins of Major Archer's house).

The park is home to many different bird and animal species, including iguanas and monkeys, which you might encounter on one of the excellent day hikes you can make here. Maps can be obtained at the small artisan **shop** (🕙 7am-9pm), just inside the park entrance.

The entire park closes at sunset. It's best to go by car, but if you can't, catch a number 221, 233 or 234 bus. Alternatively, take the metro to Saens Peña then catch a bus going to Barra da Tijuca and get off at Alto da Boa Vista. The best route by car is to take Rua Jardim Botânico two blocks past the Jardim Botânico (heading east from Gávea). Turn left on Rua Lopes Quintas and then follow the Tijuca or Corcovado signs for two quick left turns until you reach the back of the Jardim Botânico, where you turn right. Then follow the signs for a quick ascent into the forest and past the **Vista Chinesa** (get out for a good view) and the **Mesa do Imperador**, both of which offer some fantastic views of Rio's mountainous seascape. As soon as you seem to come out of the forest, turn right onto the main road and you'll see the stone columns at the entrance of Alto da Boa Vista on your left after a couple of kilometers. You can also drive up to Alto da Boa Vista by heading out to São Conrado and turning right up the hill at the Parque Nacional da Tijuca signs.

Warning: There have been occasional reports of armed robberies within the park. Most Cariocas recommend going on weekends when there are more people around. Also see p152 for companies that lead hikes in the area.

Tue-Thu & 10am Fri to 10pm Sun) is not to be missed. The fair (32,000 sq meters with 658 stalls) showcases the culture from the Northeast, with *barracas* (stalls) selling Bahian dishes as well as beer and *cachaça* (sugarcane spirit), which flows in great abundance. Bands perform *forró* (popular music of the Northeast), samba and Música Popular Brasileira (MPB). On Friday, the fair turns into a huge party that runs nonstop until Sunday.

Maracanã Football Stadium

For a quasi-psychedelic experience, go to a *futebol* match at **Maracanã** (Map p140; ☎ 2334 1705; Av Maracanã, São Cristóvão; admission R$15-100) at Brazil's temple to football (soccer). Matches here rate among the most exciting in the world, particularly during a championship game or when local rivals Flamengo, Vasco da Gama, Fluminense or Botafogo go head-to-head.

Games take place year-round and generally happen on Saturday or Sunday (starting at 4pm or 6pm) or on Wednesday and Thursday (around 8:30pm). At research time, the stadium was closed for renovations for the 2014 FIFA World Cup. The stadium should reopen in late 2012. See also p178.

Maracanã's **sports museum** (admission R$20; 9am-5pm Monday to Friday except game days) has photographs, posters, cups and the uniforms of Brazilian sporting greats, including Pelé's famous No 10 shirt. There's also a store where you can buy football shirts. Enter the north entrance, through gate 15 off Rua Mata Machado.

Quinta da Boa Vista

The residence of the imperial family until the Republic was proclaimed, today **Quinta da Boa Vista** (Map p140; General Herculano Gomes, São Cristóvão; 9am-5pm) is a large and busy park with gardens and lakes. On weekends it's crowded with football games and families from the Zona Norte. The former imperial mansion houses the **Museu Nacional** (Map p140; ☎ 2562 6900; admission R$3; 10am-4pm Tue-Sun). In addition to Etruscan ceramics, Egyptian mummies and stuffed prehistoric animals, the museum contains a small Brazilian section with relics from the country's early indigenous people.

The **Jardim Zoológico** (Map p140; ☎ 2569 2024; adult/child R$6/3; 9am-4:30pm Tue-Sun), Rio's zoo, is 200m west of Boa Vista. It boasts a medium-sized collection of Brazilian mammals and endangered species. Highlights include the tropical-bird aviary (the gardens are a good place for birdwatchers) and the Nocturnal House, offering visitors a close-up view of sloths, bats and other creatures of the night.

BAÍA DE GUANABARA
Ilha Fiscal

The lime-green, neo-Gothic palace of **Ilha Fiscal** (Map p138; ☎ 2233 9165; admission R$10; tours 1pm, 2:30pm & 4pm Tue-Sun), sitting in the Baía de Guanabara, looks like something out of a fairy tale. It was designed by engineer Adolfo del Vecchio and was the location of the last Imperial Ball on November 9, 1889. Today it's open for guided tours, which leave from the Espaço Cultural da Marinha (p147), north of Praça XV (Quinze) de Novembro.

Ilha de Paquetá

Ilha de Paquetá (off Map p131), in the Baía de Guanabara, was once a popular tourist spot and remains a pleasant escape from the city's bustle. There are no cars on the island. Transport is by foot, bicycle (with hundreds for rent) or horse-drawn carts. There's a certain decadent charm to the colonial buildings, unassuming beaches and businesses catering to local tourism. The place gets crowded on weekends.

Go to Paquetá for the boat ride through Rio's famous bay and to see Cariocas at play – especially during the Festa de São Roque, which is celebrated with fireworks, a procession and music on the weekend following August 16.

Boats leave from near the **Praça XV (Quinze) de Novembro** (Map p138) in Centro. The **ferry** (☎ 0800 704 4113) takes 70 minutes and costs R$9 return. There are nine departures daily, the most useful being 7:10am, 10:30am and 1:30pm.

NITERÓI

East of Rio, the city of Niterói's principal attraction is the famous Museu do Arte Contemporânea (MAC). The cruise across the bay, however, is perhaps just as valid a reason for leaving Rio. The ferry costs about R$5.60 return and leaves from Praça XV de Novembro in Centro; it's usually full of commuters. Once you reach the dock, the immediate area is a busy commercial district, full of pedestrians and crisscrossing intersections. From here catch a bus to the MAC or to one of the beaches – or get back on the ferry and head back.

Museu do Arte Contemporânea

Designed by Brazil's most famous architect, Oscar Niemeyer, the **Museu do Arte Contemporânea** (MAC; Map p131; ☎ 2620 2400; www .macniteroi.com.br, in Portuguese; Mirante da Boa Viagem s/n, Niterói; admission R$4; ⏰ 11am-6pm Tue-Sun) is a curvilinear building with breathtaking views, but the exhibitions inside aren't always very notable. To get here from the Niterói ferry terminal, turn right as you leave and walk about 50m across to the bus stop in the middle of the road; a 47B minibus will drop you at the museum door.

BEACHES EAST OF NITERÓI

A number of beaches lie just east of Niterói. The ones closest to town are too polluted for swimming, but as you continue out, you'll reach some pristine beaches – Piratininga, Camboinhas, Itaipu and finally **Itacoatiara**, the most fabulous of the bunch. Framed by two looming hills on either side and backed by vegetation, the white sands of Itacoatiara seem a world removed from the urban beaches of Rio. *Barracas* sell scrumptious plates of fish, and there are also food stands overlooking the beach. The surf is strong here – as evidenced by the abundance of surfers – so swim with caution. To get here, you can take bus 38 from the ferry terminal (R$4, 50 minutes) or any bus labeled 'Itacoatiara.' If you're traveling in a group you can negotiate a return fare with a taxi driver.

BARRA DA TIJUCA & WEST OF RIO

Ten kilometers west of Leblon, Barra da Tijuca (Barra) is the Miami of Rio, with malls and shopping centers set against the tropical landscape. At 12km long, the lovely beach here is the city's longest. Beyond this, the region gets less and less urban. Some of Rio's most beautiful beaches lie out this way (see the boxed text, p153 for details). Further west begins Brazil's gorgeous coastal road that travels through the region known as the Costa Verde (p186).

Praia da Barra da Tijuca

The best thing about Barra is **Praia da Barra da Tijuca** (Map p131). It's a long, scenic beach with blue sea lapping at the shore; the first few kilometers are filled with bars and seafood restaurants.

The young and beautiful hang out in front of *barraca* number 1 – also known as the Barraca do Pepê, after the famous Carioca

hang gliding champion who died during a competition in Japan in 1991.

The further west you go the more deserted it gets, and the stalls turn into trailers. It's calm on weekdays and crazy on hot summer weekends. For other beaches to the west, see opposite.

Sítio Burle Marx

The enormous 350,000-sq-meter estate, **Sítio Burle Marx** (off Map p131; ☎ 2410 1412; Estrada da Barra de Guaratiba 2019, Guaratiba; admission R$5; ⏰ 9:30am & 1:30pm, by advance appointment only) was once the magnificent home of Brazil's most famous landscape architect, Roberto Burle Marx. The beautifully lush gardens of the estate, 22km west of the city, easily warrant a visit. Strolling the verdantly landscaped area allows visitors the chance to see and smell thousands of exotic plant species from both Brazil and abroad. A lovely 17th-century Benedictine chapel, along with Burle Marx's original farmhouse and studio, completes the idyllic setting.

ACTIVITIES

Given the mountains, beaches and forests in their backyard, it's not surprising that Cariocas are an active bunch. The coastline brings an array of options: jogging, hiking, walking, cycling and surfing. The mountains offer their own allure: you can hang glide off them or rock climb up them. Great hiking trails through Atlantic rain forest lie just outside the city.

Walking & Jogging

Good walking and jogging paths in the Zona Sul include Parque do Flamengo (Map p138), which also has workout stations. Around Lagoa Rodrigo de Freitas (Map p132), a 7.5km track provides a path for cyclists and joggers. Along the seaside, from Leme to Barra da Tijuca, there's a bike path and footpath. On Sunday, the road is closed to traffic from 7am to 6pm. The road skirting through Parque do Flamengo is also closed on Sundays.

Located between the mountains and the sea at Praia Vermelha in Urca is the Pista Cláudio Coutinho (p144). It's closed to bicycles but open to walkers and joggers from 7am until 6pm daily, and is very secure because of the army post nearby.

Hiking & Climbing

Aside from access to nearby national parks such as Parque Nacional da Serra dos Órgãos

BEACHES WEST OF RIO

Although Copacabana and Ipanema are Rio's most famous stretches of sand, there are many stunning beaches in the area, some in spectacular natural settings. For surfing possibilities, see p154.

Pepino/São Conrado

The first major beach you'll reach heading west of Leblon is **Praia do Pepino** (Map p131) in São Conrado. Pepino is a beautiful beach, and is less crowded than Ipanema. It's also where hang gliders like to lounge when they're not soaring overhead.

Recreio dos Bandeirantes

Although it gets crowded on weekends, **Recreio dos Bandeirantes** (Map p131) is almost deserted during the week. The large rock acts as a natural breakwater, creating a calm bay. The 2km-long stretch of sand is popular with families.

Prainha

The secluded 700m-long **Prainha** (off Map p131) lies just 6km past Recreio. It's one of the best surfing beaches in Rio, so it's always full of surfers. Waves come highly recommended here.

Grumari & Guaratiba

The most isolated and unspoiled beach close to the city, **Grumari** (off Map p131) is quiet during the week and packed on weekends with Cariocas looking to get away from city beaches. It is a gorgeous setting, surrounded by mountains and lush vegetation.

From Grumari, a narrow road climbs west over a jungle-covered hillside toward **Guaratiba**. West of here is a good view of the **Restinga de Marambaia** (the vegetation-rich strip between the beach and the mainland), closed off to the public by a naval base. Cariocas enjoy eating lunch at several of the seafood restaurants in the area.

Fairly regular S020 buses run along the beach avenues of Copacabana, Ipanema and Leblon to São Conrado and Recreio dos Bandeirantes. You can also take the **surf bus** (www.surfbus.com.br), which makes four return trips daily from Largo do Machado metro station near Flamengo out to Prainha via Copacabana, Ipanema, Leblon, São Conrado, Barra de Tijuca, Recreio dos Bandeirantes and Macumba. For Grumari and Guaratiba, you'll need your own wheels.

(p207) and Parque Nacional de Itatiaia (p201), Rio has many trails through the rain forest of Floresta da Tijuca (p150). Visitors can also take part in hikes around Corcovado, Morro da Urca, Parque Lage and other areas. It's advisable to go with a guide for a number of reasons – to avoid getting lost and robbed are top of the list. Group outings can also be a good way to meet Cariocas.

Rio is also the center of rock climbing in Brazil, with hundreds of documented climbs within an hour's drive. You can also try your hand at the rock-climbing wall in **Parque da Catacumba** (p142). Avid climbers who want to keep fit might want to stay in **Tupiniquim Hostel** (p163), which also has a climbing wall. Parque da Catacumba also offers rappelling, ziplining and canopy walks.

Rio Hiking (☎ 2552 9204, 9721 0594; full-day tour from R$150; www.riohiking.com.br) Founded by a mother-

and son team of outdoor enthusiasts, Rio Hiking offers a wide variety of hikes. Popular treks go up Pico da Tijuca (the highest point in the national park), Pedra da Gávea, Pão de Açúcar and Corcovado. Cycling, rafting, kayaking and rappelling trips can also be arranged.

Rio Adventures (☎ 2705 5747; www.rioadventures .com; full-day hiking/climbing/rafting tours from R$150/250/250) Offering a range of outdoor activities, Rio Adventures leads hikes through Tijuca National Park, including short treks up Pico Tijuca and Pedra Bonito. It also offers sightseeing tours, rock climbs (Pão de Açúcar, Corcovado and Pico da Tijuca), rafting excursions (to Paraibuna River, 175km northwest of Rio) and parachuting and paragliding trips.

Crux Ecoadventure (☎ 3474 1726, 9392 9203; www .cruxecoaventura.com.br) This reputable outfit offers a range of climbing excursions, including ascents up Pão de Açúcar. Other possibilities: rappelling down waterfalls, full-day hikes through Floresta da Tijuca, and cycling and kayaking trips.

Climb in Rio (☎ 2245 1108; www.climbinrio.com) Navigating more than 400 routes around Rio (50 up Pão de Açúcar alone) and the state, this is a good outfit for climbing junkies. There are half- and full-day climbs as well as multiday mountain ascents. It also offers climbing courses.

Cycling

There are over 74km of bike paths around Rio, including those around Lagoa Rodrigo de Freitas (p142), along Barra da Tijuca and the oceanfront from Leblon to Leme. This last path also connects to Praia de Botafogo and Parque do Flamengo, running all the way to Centro. In the Tijuca forest, a 6km cycle path runs from a waterfall (Cascatinha) to a museum (Açude). On Sundays the beach road from Leblon to Leme closes to traffic, as does the road through Parque do Flamengo.

You can rent bikes from a stand along the east and west sides of Lagoa Rodrigo de Freitas for R$10 per hour. A few other places to rent bikes:

Ciclovia (Map p134; ☎ 2275 5299; Av Prado Júnior 330; per hr/day R$9/50; 🕑 9am-7pm Mon-Fri, 9am-4pm Sat) Free delivery to hotels in the Zona Sul.

Special Bike (Map p132; ☎ 2513 3951; Rua Visconde de Pirajá 135B, Ipanema; per hr/day R$15/45; 🕑 9am-7pm Mon-Fri, to 3pm Sat)

Hang Gliding

If you weigh less than 100kg (about 220lb) and can spare R$250, you can do the fantastic tandem hang glide off 510m-high Pedra Bonita – one of the giant granite slabs that tower above Rio – onto Praia do Pepino in São Conrado. No experience is necessary; tandem riders are secured in a kind of pouch attached to the kite.

Flights typically last around 10 to 20 minutes, depending on weather and wind conditions. You can usually fly on all but three to four days per month, and conditions during winter are even better. If you schedule for an early flight, you have more flexibility to accommodate weather delays. Prices include pick-up and drop-off from your hotel. Travel agents also book tandem flights, but tack on their own fee. To cut out the middlemen, call direct.

Delta Flight in Rio (☎ 9693 8800; www.deltaflight. com.br) With more than 20 years experience, Ricardo Hamond has earned a solid reputation as a safety-conscious and extremely professional pilot; he has flown more than 12,000 tandem flights.

Just Fly (☎ 2268 0565; www.justfly.com.br) Paulo Celani is a highly experienced tandem flyer with over 6000 flights to his credit.

SuperFly (☎ 3322 2286; www.riosuperfly.com.br) Ruy Marra, founder of SuperFly, has more than 25 years of flying experience and is an excellent tandem glider pilot.

Tandem Fly (☎ 2422 6371, 3322 5817, 2493 4324; www.riotandemfly.com.br) Three experienced pilots run this tandem flight outfit. They also give lessons for those wanting to fly solo.

Surfing

Rio has some fine options when it comes to surfing, with some great breaks just outside the city. If you're not ready to leave the Zona Sul, Praia do Arpoador, between Copacabana and Ipanema, draws large flocks of surfers. Better breaks lie further west in Barra, Joátinga, Prainha and Grumari. Across the bay, Itacoatiara also has good breaks. For transportation to the western beaches, grab your board and hop on the **Surf Bus** (☎ 8702 2837; www.surfbus.com.br; R$4), a bright yellow-orange bus that makes four return trips daily (beginning at 7am) from Largo do Machado metro station (near Flamengo) to Prainha, with stops at beaches along the way.

If you don't have a board, you can hire or buy one in Arpoador at **Galeria River** (Map p134; Rua Francisco Otaviano 67, Arpoador; rental per day R$30), a commercial center full of surf shops and boutiques.

Beginners who want to learn to surf can take classes through informal *escolinhas* (schools) off Ipanema Beach and off Barra. You can also stay at the **Rio Surf 'N Stay** (Map p131; ☎ 3418 1133; Rua Raimundo Veras 1140, Recreio dos Bandeirantes; www.riosurfnstay.com) in Recreio dos Bandeirantes, which offers lessons (in English) and overnight accommodation.

You'll find more detailed information on all the breaks around Rio on www.wannasurf .com. If you can read Portuguese, check out www.riosurfpage.com.

Volleyball & Other Beach Sports

Volleyball is Brazil's second most popular sport (after football) and a natural activity for the beach. A local variation of the sport, seen on Rio's beaches, is *futevôlei*. It's a cross

---

CAPOEIRA IN RIO

The only surviving martial art native to the New World, capoeira was invented by Afro-Brazilian slaves about 400 years ago (see p455). In Rio you can see musicians and spectators arranged in the *roda de capoeira* (capoeira circle) at the weekly **Feira Nordestina** (p150) in São Cristóvão.

Those interested in taking classes can try one of the following. Note that all classes are in Portuguese.

Angola N'Golo (Map p138; ☎ 3770 7256; www.angolangolo.com; Rua Almirante Alexandrino, Santa Teresa; per class/month R$20/80; ☼ 7-10pm Mon & Wed, 10am-1pm Sat) Next to Largo das Letras.

Associação Centro de Capoeira Angola (Map p136; ☎ 9954 3659; www.ccarj.com; Rua do Catete 164, Catete; per class/month R$25/100)

Casa Rosa (Map p136; ☎ 8874 8804; www.casarosa.com.br; Rua Alice 550, Laranjeiras; classes per month R$60)

Fundição Progresso (Map p138; ☎ 3356 2382; www.fundicao.org; Rua dos Arcos 24, Lapa)

---

between volleyball and football – with no hands allowed.

Usually played on the firm sand at the shoreline, *frescobol* involves two players, each with a wooden racquet, hitting a small rubber ball back and forth as hard as possible.

Those interested in improving their volleyball game – or just meeting some Cariocas – should pay a visit to Pelé at **Escolinha de Vôlei** (Map p132; ☎ 9702 5794; www.peledapraia.com) near Rua Garcia D'Ávila, on Ipanema Beach. Pelé, who speaks English, has been giving volleyball lessons since the late 1990s. Lessons are in the morning (from about 8am to 11am) and in the afternoon (5pm to 7pm). Look for his large Brazilian flag on the beach.

Diving

Dive Point (Map p132; ☎ 2239 5105; www.divepoint.com .br, in Portuguese; Shop 2, Av Ataúlfo de Paiva 1174, Leblon; 2-tank dives from R$150) offers diving courses and tours around Rio's main beaches and Cagarras Island (in front of Ipanema), as well as trips to Angra dos Reis and Búzios.

One of several dive operators in the Marina da Glória, **Mar do Rio** (Map p138; ☎ 2225 7508; www .mardorio.com.br, in Portuguese; shop 16, Marina da Glória, Av Infante Dom Henrique, Glória) offers two-tank dives (R$120) on Saturday and Sunday, departing at 8:30am and returning at 2:30pm. It also offers night dives twice a month. Less-experienced divers can opt for one of the courses, including a five-day PADI-certified basic course.

Fishing

The Marina da Glória has a number of boating outfits, although **Marlin Yacht Tours** (Map p136; ☎ 2225 7434; www.marlinyacht.com.br; Marina da Glória, Av Infante Dom Henrique, Glória) has the largest fleet – including schooners, sailboats and motor-

boats. Here you can hire a vessel for a sailing, fishing or diving adventure, creating your own itinerary. Prices aren't cheap, so it's best to gather a group.

WALKING TOUR

A mélange of historic buildings and aging skyscrapers, the center of Rio is an excellent place to discover the essence of the city away from its beaches and mountains. Among the hustle and bustle of commerce, you'll find fascinating museums, atmospheric bars and theaters, open-air bazaars and the antique stores set near old samba clubs. This tour is best done during the week, as the center gets deserted (and unsafe) on weekends.

Start at **Praça Floriano** (**1**; p148), which is the heart of modern Rio. Praça Floriano comes to life at lunchtime and after work when the outdoor cafés fill with Cariocas. The neoclassical **Theatro Municipal** (**2**; p148) overlooking the plaza is one of Rio's finest buildings.

On the east side of Av Rio Branco, facing Praça Floriano, is an open-air music market, **Rua Pedro Lessa (3)**, where you can browse the record and CD stalls. Next to it is the **Centro Cultural Justiça Federal** (**4**; ☎ 2510 8846; Av Rio Branco 241; admission free; ☼ noon-7pm Tue-Sun), which hosts changing contemporary exhibitions. The solid **Biblioteca Nacional** (**5**; ☎ 2262 8255; Av Rio Branco 219; admission free; ☼ noon-8pm Mon-Fri) is on the other side of Rua Pedro Lessa, while north on Av Rio Branco is another historic building, today hosting the **Museu Nacional de Belas Artes** (**6**; p148). Head inside to see works of some of Rio's best 19th-century painters.

Now cross Av Rio Branco and walk in front of the Theatro Municipal, then take a left down Av 13 de Maio. Cross Av Almirante Barrosoa and you're in the **Largo da Carioca (7)**, a

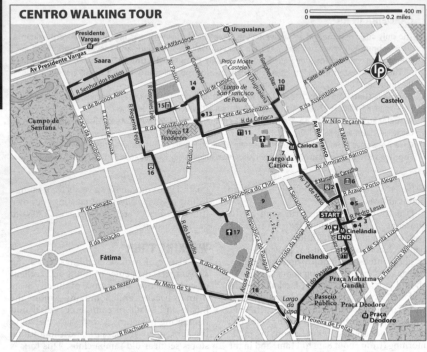

CENTRO WALKING TOUR

WALK FACTS

Start: Praça Floriano
End: Amarelinho
Distance: 4km
Duration: 3 hours, depending on breaks

pedestrian area that gets packed with vendors during the week. Up on the hill is the recently restored **Convento Santo Antônio** (**8**; p147). The original church here was started in 1608, making it one of Rio's oldest.

Gazing south from the convent, you'll notice the **Petrobras building** (**9**), whose boxlike metal chassis seems to cast an ominous shadow over the area. Behind it is the concrete-loving Catedral Metropolitana.

Come back down from the convent and take a left on Largo da Carioca, a right on Rua Sete de Setembro and a left on Rua Gonçalves Dias and stop in the **Confeitaria Colombo** (**10**; p168) for a serving of caffeine, cake and art nouveau. Head back to Rua da Carioca. Along this street, you'll find an array of old shops, a slice out of 19th-century Rio. **Bar Luiz** (**11**;

p170), at number 39, makes a fine stop for a bite or a *chope* (draft beer).

At the end of the block, turn right onto the hustle of **Praça Tiradentes** (**12**). On opposite sides of the square are the Teatro João Caetano and the Teatro Carlos Gomez, historic buildings that still stage some excellent music, dance and theater performances. Around the corner is the **Centro Cultural Carioca** (**13**; p127). Stop in here to see what's on musically for the evening. Just up from the theater is the **Real Gabinete Português de Leitura** (**14**; p148), with a lovely collection of books. For a taste of modern art, cross Av Passos and visit the avant-garde **Centro de Arte Hélio Oiticica** (**15**; p147).

Afterwards, continue walking west to Rua Gonçalves Ledo and then take a right. When you reach Rua da Alfândega turn left. This will take you into the heart of Saara, a long-standing neighborhood bazaar packed with shops and pedestrians. Walk, shop and snack as far as Campo de Santana. Make a U-turn there and proceed back along Rua Senhor dos Passos. Take a right on Rua Regente Feijó. When this street ends take a short left and then a right and head down Rua do Lavradio. This street is famous for its antique shops set in the colorful 19th-century buildings. A number of great nightspots, such as **Rio Scenarium** (**16**; p175), feature excellent samba bands playing in restored colonial buildings.

When you reach Av República do Chile take a left and stop in the **Catedral Metropolitana** (**17**; p149) for a glimpse of the church's marvelous stained-glass windows. When you leave, head back to Rua do Lavradio for more window shopping. When you reach Av Mem de Sá, take a left and follow the road around the curve as you pass beneath the **Arcos do Lapa (18)**. This is Rio's big samba center at night, with clubs and old-school bars scattered all over the neighborhood. When you reach the Largo da Lapa, a small plaza along which a restaurant and a few samba clubs are scattered, take a left and walk along Rua do Passeio. You'll have great views of the arches from here. In two more blocks you'll be back to where you started. When you reach Praça Floriano, stop in at **Ateliê Culinario** (**19**; p170) or **Amarelinho** (**20**; p173) for a *chope* or juice, a refreshing cap to the walk.

COURSES
Dance

Given the resurgent popularity of dance-hall samba throughout the city, it's not surprising that there are a number of places where you can learn the moves – then practice them – in Lapa.

Casa de Dança Carlinhos de Jesus (Map p136; ☎ 2541 6186; www.carlinhosdejesus.com.br, in Portuguese; Rua Álvaro Ramos 11, Botafogo) At this respected dance academy, Carlinhos and his instructors give samba, forró, salsa and hip-hop classes in the evenings from about 7pm to 10pm.

Centro Cultural Carioca (Map p138; ☎ 2252 5751; www.centroculturalcarioca.com.br, in Portuguese; Rua do Teatro 37, Centro; 4-week course, meeting twice per week R$70; ☺ noon-8pm Mon-Sat) An excellent place to take classes. Its large dance hall hosts live samba parties on Friday.

Fundição Progresso (Map p138; ☎ 2220 5070; www.fundicaoprogresso.org, in Portuguese; Rua dos Arcos 24, Lapa) Offers classes in dancing (African styles, as well as salsa, tango and samba), as well as percussion, acrobatics and capoeira. Courses typically cost R$150 for the month.

Núcleo de Dança Renata Peçanha (Map p138; ☎ 2221 1011; 2nd fl, Rua da Carioca 14, Centro) A large upstairs studio on the edge of Lapa, this dance academy offers classes in forró, samba and other styles. Twice-weekly classes cost about R$75 per month.

Rio Samba Dancer (☎ 8229 2843; http://riosamba dancer.com; 90-min private lesson per person R$30-40) English-speaking dance instructor Hélio Ricardo offers private one-on-one dance classes (in samba or forró), and he will even take you out to dance places around town where you can practice your new moves (R$80 per person including dance lesson, R$100 for couples).

Language

Most language institutes charge high prices for group courses. You can often find a private tutor for less. Hostels are a good place to troll for instructors, with ads on bulletin boards posted by native-speaking language teachers available for hire. One organization that offers competitively priced classes is **Casa do Caminho Language Centre** (Map p132; ☎ 2267 6552; www.casadocaminho-languagecentre.org; site 403, Rua Farme de Amoedo 75, Ipanema), which offers intensive group classes – three hours a day for five days for R$320, or 60 hours of class time over a month for R$820. Profits go toward the Casa do Caminho (www.casadocaminhobrasil.org) orphanages in Brazil.

The respected **Instituto Brasil-Estados Unidos** (IBEU; Map p134; ☎ 2548 8430; www.ibeu.org.br; 5th fl, Av NS de Copacabana 690, Copacabana) has three different levels of classes. Each meets two hours a day, four times weekly over four weeks and costs R$1220.

COOK IN RIO

At long last, travelers finally have the opportunity to take a locally run cooking course, **Cook in Rio** (Map p134; ☎ 8761 3653; www.cookinrio.com; Rua Ronald Carvalho 154, Copacabana), which teaches aspiring chefs how to make some of Brazil's most famous dishes. Each one-day class runs from 11am to 4pm and includes the preparation of either *moqueca* (seafood stew) or *feijoada completa* (multi-dish black bean and pork stew) along with appetizers and side dishes, dessert and a masterful caipirinha. The best part is that you'll get to devour your creations afterwards. Courses cost R$120 per person, including the cost of food and drinks.

RIO FOR CHILDREN

Brazilians are very family-oriented. Some hotels let children stay free, although the age limit varies. Babysitters are readily available and most restaurants have high chairs.

Lonely Planet's *Travel with Children* gives a lot of good tips and advice on traveling with kids in the tropics.

There's plenty of good spade and sand-bucket fun to be had on Rio's beaches, particularly Leblon's *posto* 12, known as Baixo Bébe for its mini-playground and all the moms and tots around. Other amusement for kids includes the shows and exhibits at the **Planetário** (p142), the animals of **Jardim Zoológico** at Quinta da Boa Vista (p151), the impressive ships at **Espaço Cultural da Marinha** (p147), and the mechanized displays at the **Museu de Folclórico Edson Carnerio** (p146). You can also hire bikes (including big, shaded four-seaters) and visit the playground near the bike stand at **Lagoa Rodrigo de Freitas** (p142).

In addition, children may also enjoy the following sights:

Terra Encantada (Map p131; ☎ 2421 9444; www .terra-encantada.com.br, in Portuguese; Av Ayrton Senna 2800, Barra da Tijuca; adult/child R$40/20; ☺ 2-9pm Thu-Sun) The Enchanted Land includes Cabhum, a 64m, 100km/h free fall, and Ressaca, a toboggan ride that goes over a waterfall, among many other rides.

Museu Aerospacial (Map p131; ☎ 2108 8954; www .musal.aer.mil.br, in Portuguese; Av Marechal Fontenele 2000, Campo dos Afonsos; admission free; ☺ 9am-3pm Tue-Fri, 9:30am-4pm Sat & Sun) Has expositions on Santos Dumont (the Brazilian father of aviation) and the role of Brazil's air force in WWII. There's lots of old planes, including replicas of Santos Dumont's planes: the *14 Bis* and the *Demoiselle*.

TOURS
Favela Tours

Aurélio Rio Guide (☎ 3592 0445, 7828 6382; www .aurelioguide.com; per person R$60) Run by a longtime resident, Aurélio shows an authentic side of Rocinha, going up by moto-taxi (a ride on the back of a motorcycle) then descending through the narrow lanes and alleys, stopping en route to meet local residents (Aurélio is well known here).

Be a Local (☎ 9643 0366; www.bealocal.com.br) Offers daily trips into Rocinha (you'll ride up by moto-taxi, and walk back down), with stops along the way (R$65 per person). It also organizes a night out at a *baile* (dance) funk party in Castelo das Pedras on Sunday (R$60).

Marcelo Armstrong (☎ 3322 2727; www.favelatour .com.br; per person R$65) The pioneer of favela tourism,

Marcelo takes small groups to visit the favelas of Rocinha and Vila Canoas near São Conrado, where he does an excellent job explaining the social and political context of the favela in relation to greater Rio de Janeiro. Marcelo's outfit donates a portion of its profits to favela social projects.

City Walking Tours

If you're looking for a longer guided hike, see p152.

Cultural Rio (☎ 9911 3829; www.culturalrio.com.br; 4hr tour per person from R$110) Run by the quirky Carlos Roquette, this tour offers visitors an in-depth look at social and historical aspects of Rio de Janeiro. Itineraries include a night at the Teatro Municipal, colonial Rio, baroque Rio, imperial Rio and a walking tour of Centro. Professor Roquette has been in business for over 20 years.

Bay Tours

Macuco Rio (Map p138; ☎ 2205 0390; www.macucorio .com.br; Marina de Glória, Glória; cruise R$100) Macuco's high-velocity 28-seat speedboat offers two trips daily. Tours circle the bay or head to Cagarras Archipelago, for bird- and possibly dolphin-spotting.

Marlin Yacht Tours (Map p138; ☎ 2225 7434; www .marlinyacht.com.br; Marina da Glória, Glória; cruise R$50-80) Marlin offers several tours aboard large 30-person schooners to Cagarras Island, stopping for a beach swim along the way. It also offers a sunset cruise and sailing and diving trips.

Pink Fleet (Map p138; ☎ 2555 4063; www.pinkfleet com.br; Marina da Glória, Glória; cruise R$80) Runs two-hour weekend cruises to all of Rio's best water-accessible attractions in a German-made luxury cruise ship (skip the nonincluded, unmemorable meal).

Other Tours

All of the following outfits, except for Santa Teresa Tour include round-trip transportation from your hostel/hotel in the price.

Be a Local (☎ 9643 0366; www.bealocal.com; per person R$60-90) Popular with backpackers, Be a Local offers group tours with a younger, edgier flavor. It offers favela tours, outings to football matches at Maracanã and trips to evening favela parties.

Brazil Expedition (☎ 9998 2907; www.brazilexpedi tion.com; city tours R$85) The friendly English-speaking guides from Brazil Expedition run a variety of traditional tours around Rio, including trips to Cristo Redentor, nightlife tours in Lapa, game-day outings at Maracanã and favela tours.

Helisight (☎ 2511 2141; www.helisight.com.br; per person 6min/30min R$150/520) Offering helicopter tours since 1991, Helisight has eight different itineraries, all giving a close-up view of Cristo Redentor and gorgeous views over the city. There is a three-person minimum.

Jeep Tour (☎ 2108 5800; www.jeeptour.com.br; tours from R$85) Travels to the Parque Nacional da Tijuca in a large, open-topped jeep. The tour includes a stop at the Vista Chinesa, then on to the forest for an easy hike and a stop for a swim beneath a waterfall, before making the return journey.

Rio by Jeep (☎ 9693 8800; www.riobyjeep.com; tours from R$95) A recommended outfit offering jeep tours.

Santa Teresa Tour (☎ 2507 4417; www.santateresa tour.com.br; tours without/with transport R$35/75) Offers two daily culture and architecture tours through Rio's most historic neighborhood.

FESTIVALS & EVENTS

Aside from Carnaval (p76), there are many other exciting events happening throughout the year.

Dia de São Sebastião (January 20) The patron saint of the city is commemorated with a procession that carries his image from the Igreja de São Sebastião dos Capuchinos (see Map pp140-1; Rua Haddock Lobo 266) in Tijuca to the Catedral Metropolitana (Map p138), where it's blessed in a Mass celebrated by the archbishop of Rio.

Dia da Fundação da Cidade (March 1) The founding of the city by Estácio de Sá in 1565 is commemorated with a Mass in the church of its patron saint, São Sebastião.

Sexta-Feira da Paixão (March or April) Good Friday is celebrated throughout the city. The most important ceremony is a reenactment of the Stations of the Cross under the Arcos do Lapa, carried out by more than 100 actors.

Festas Juninas (June) The June Festival is one of the most important folkloric festivals in Brazil. In Rio, it's celebrated in various public plazas throughout the month, primarily on June 13 (Dia de Santo Antônio), June 24 (Dia de São João) and June 29 (Dia de São Pedro).

Portas Abertas (www.artedeportasabertas.com.br; a weekend in July) Santa Teresa's artists open their studios and the neighborhood becomes a living installation in this twice-yearly event.

Festa de São Pedro do Mar (July 13) The fishing community pays homage to its patron saint in a maritime procession. Decorated boats leave from the fishing district of Caju, 2km north of Centro, and sail to the statue of São Pedro in Urca.

Festa de NS da Glória do Outeiro (August 15) A solemn Mass is held in the Igreja de NS da Glória do Outeiro, which is ablaze with decorated lights, with a procession into the streets of Glória to mark the Feast of the Assumption. This festival includes music and colorful stalls set up in the Praça NS da Glória. Festivities start at 8am and continue all day.

Dia de Independência do Brasil (September 7) Independence Day is celebrated with a big military parade down Av Presidente Vargas. It starts at 8am at Candelária and terminates just west of Praça Onze, north of the Sambódromo.

Rio International Film Festival (www.festivaldorio. com.br, in Portuguese; September and October) The festival is one of the biggest in Latin America. Over 200 films from all over the world are shown at some 35 theaters. The festival usually runs for 15 days from the last week of September through to the first week of October.

Rio Jazz Festival (October) Features three nights of great music. National and international acts present a wide variety of music – not just jazz. Dates vary from year to year.

Festa da Penha (October and November) This is one of the largest religious and popular festivals in the city. It takes place every Sunday in October and the first Sunday in November, at Igreja NS da Penha de França, Largo da Penha 19 in Penha. It's very lively.

Reveillon & Festa de Iemanjá (December 31) New Year's Eve (Reveillon) in Rio is celebrated by millions of people. Tons of fireworks explode in the sky over Copacabana. New Year's Day coincides with the festival of Iemanjá, the sea goddess. Wearing white, the faithful carry a statue of Iemanjá to the beach and launch flowers and other offerings into the sea.

SLEEPING

Rio has a wide mix of lodging options, including boutique hotels, hostels, B&Bs and plenty of cookie-cutter high-rise accommodations along Copacabana. Here's the lowdown on where to stay: if you want to be in the heart of the action and don't mind paying for it, stay in Ipanema or Leblon, with beautiful beaches, and excellent restaurants, shopping and nightlife. If you don't want to pay a premium for those neighborhoods, opt for busier Copacabana, where you can find less pricey options while still being near the beach (and a short taxi or bus ride to Ipanema). For an alternative to beach culture, take a peek at Santa Teresa's colonial guesthouses. The neighborhood is also close to the fantastic music scene of Lapa. Other neighborhoods along the metro line (Botafogo, Flamengo and Catete) generally have cheaper options than the beachside southern neighborhoods.

The best way to save money on lodging is by booking online. You can save anywhere from 30% to over 50% off the rack rates by booking through reliable Rio booking agencies such as www.ipanema.com and www .riocharm.com.br.

Hotel rates are 30% higher during summer (December to mid-March) and prices double or triple for New Year's Eve and Carnaval, when most places, including hostels, require four-day (or more) minimum bookings.

Keep in mind that many hotels add in a combined 15% service and tax charge, though cheaper places don't generally bother with this.

Ipanema & Leblon

Ocean views with access to Rio's loveliest beaches, restaurants and bars make Ipanema and Leblon a magnet among travelers. Not surprisingly, prices here are higher than elsewhere. There are a great many hostels here and plenty of high-end options, but not much in-between.

BUDGET

Che Lagarto Ipanema (Map p132; ☎ 2512 8076; www.chelagarto.com; Rua Paul Redfern 48, Ipanema; dm/d from R$40/120) Che Lagarto's Ipanema branch is a five-story hostel, with tiny, basic rooms and not much common space – aside from the pricey bar on the 1st floor. Great location.

Rio Hostel – Ipanema (Map p133; ☎ 2287 2928; www.riohostelipanema.com; Casa 1, Rua Canning 18, Copacabana; dm/d R$40/130; 💻) The friendly Rio Hostel is set in a small villa on a peaceful stretch of Ipanema. It has clean rooms, an airy top-floor deck with hammocks and a small front veranda.

Bonita (Map p132; ☎ 2227 1703; www.bonitaipanema.com; Rua Barão da Torre 107, Ipanema; dm R$40-50, d with/without bathroom R$180/160; 🍴 💻 📶 🐾) This converted house has history – it's where bossa nova legend Tom Jobim lived from 1962 to 1965 and wrote some of his most famous songs. Rooms are clean but simply furnished and open onto a shared deck overlooking a small pool and outdoor lounge.

Ipanema Beach House (Map p132; ☎ 3202 2693; www.ipanemahouse.com; Rua Barão da Torre 485, Ipanema; dm/d R$45/140; 💻 🐾) This lovely converted two-story house has six- and nine-bed dorms (with three-tiered bunk beds). There are also several private rooms, spacious indoor and outdoor lounge spaces, a small bar and a pool.

Lemon Spirit Hostel (Map p132; ☎ 2294 1853; www.lemonspirit.com; Rua Cupertino Durão 56, Leblon; dm/d/tr R$45/160/195; 🍴 💻 📶) Leblon's first hostel, Lemon Spirit boasts an excellent location one block from the beach. The dorm rooms (nine beds in three-tier bunks) are clean and simple, there's also a tiny courtyard and a small bar-lounge space that's a good spot for meeting other travelers.

Hostel Harmonia (Map p132; ☎ 2523 4905; www.hostelharmonia.com; Casa 18, Rua Barão da Torre 175,

Ipanema; dm R$50; 💻) Run by three Swedes, Hostel Harmonia is one of the best choices on Ipanema's hostel row, with a good traveler vibe. The rooms have two-toned wood floors, with six beds in each room.

MIDRANGE & TOP END

Margarida's Pousada (Map p132; ☎ 2239 1840; margaridacarneiro@hotmail.com; Rua Barão da Torre 600, Ipanema; s/d/tr from R$130/200/220; 🍴 💻 📶) For those seeking a smaller, cozier atmosphere than the high-rise hotels provide, this excellently located Ipanema guesthouse is a good option. You'll find 11 pleasant, simply furnished rooms scattered about the low-rise building. Margarida also operates a secluded guesthouse in Jardim Botânico.

Yaya Hotel (Map p132; ☎ 3813 3912; www.yayario.com; Rua Farme de Amoedo 135, Ipanema; s/d/tr R$130/180/240; 🍴) A good alternative to high-rise hotels, Yaya has eight rooms with wood floors and walls and a clean, bright appearance set in a converted house on a quiet street. The downside: the rooms share four bathrooms.

Hotel Vermont (Map p132; ☎ 3202 5500; www.hotelvermont.com.br; Rua Visconde de Pirajá 254, Ipanema; s/d/tr R$210/230/300; 🍴) One of the few no-frills hotels in Ipanema, the Vermont offers guests basic accommodations. Although the place received a slight makeover in recent years, the rooms are nothing fancy – clean but not spotless, with tile floors and elderly bathrooms.

Hotel San Marco (Map p132; ☎ 2540 5032; www.sanmarcohotel.net; Rua Visconde de Pirajá 524, Ipanema; s/d from R$212/229; 🍴 💻 📶) It's all about location if you stay at the San Marco. Rooms are clean but cramped, and the green bedspreads aren't winning any style awards. There are even a couple of coffin-sized 'economy' rooms that run R$173/193 for a single/double.

Ipanema Inn (Map p132; ☎ 2523 6092; www.ipanemainn.com.br; Rua Maria Quitéria 27, Ipanema; d R$212-330; 🍴) Ipanema Inn is a simple hotel with nice touches. The rooms have woodblock prints on the walls, off-white tile floors and modern bathrooms with big tubs.

Arpoador Inn (Map p132; ☎ 2523 0060; www.arpoadorinn.com.br; Rua Francisco Otaviano 177, Ipanema; d with/without ocean view R$455/244; 🍴) This six-story is the only hotel in town that doesn't have a busy street between it and the beach. The rooms are small and basic, but the brighter, prettier 'deluxe' rooms have glorious ocean views.

Ipanema Hotel Residência (Map p132; ☎ 3125 5000; www.ipanemahotel.com.br; Rua Barão da Torre 192, Ipanema;

d from R$330; 🔲 🔲) This high-rise apart-hotel
has large apartments, with kitchen units,
lounge areas and pleasantly furnished bedrooms. Each is furnished differently, so try
looking at a few before committing.

Mar Ipanema (Map p132; ☎ 3875 9190; www.mar
ipanema.com.br; Rua Visconde de Pirajá 539, Ipanema; d R$359-
449; 🔲) This reliable hotel in Ipanema has
trim, modern rooms with decent beds, good
lighting, tidy wooden floors and an inviting
color scheme. There's no view, though.

Everest Rio (Map p132; ☎ 2525 2200; www.everest
.com.br; Rua Prudente de Morais 1117, Ipanema; s/d from
R$380/409; 🔲 🛜) Just a block from the beach,
Everest Park has comfortable rooms with large
windows and modern bathrooms. Deluxe here
means more space; the best rooms – Luxo
Superior – have a view of the lake.

Sol Ipanema (Map p132; ☎ 2525 2020; www.sol
ipanema.com.br; Av Vieira Souto 320, Ipanema; s/d R$375/415,
with ocean view R$465/520; 🔲 🖥 🛜 🔲) The tall,
slender Sol Ipanema features rooms decorated in warm hues, with dark wood furnishings and good lighting. Deluxe rooms face
the ocean.

Ritz Plaza Hotel (Map p132; ☎ 2540 4940; www
.ritzhotel.com.br; Av Ataúlfo de Paiva 1280, Leblon; s/d from
R$380/420; 🔲 🔲) The newly renovated Ritz
Plaza has stylish rooms and common areas
that give the place a boutique feel. The one- or
two- bedroom suites all have kitchen units,
balconies – some with partial ocean views –
art on the walls, good lighting and spotless
bedrooms.

Marina All Suites (Map p132; ☎ 2172 1100; www
.marinaallsuites.com.br; Av Delfim Moreira 696, Leblon; ste from
R$777; 🔲 🖥 🔲) Marina All Suites offers style
and comfort with ocean views. Elegantly furnished suites have decent sound systems and
space enough for you to host your own small
parties. The rooftop pool, lounge space and
2nd-floor restaurant and lounge Bar D'Hotel
attracts the beautiful crowd.

Hotel Fasano (Map p132; ☎ 3202 4000; www.fas
ano.com.br; Av Vieira Souto 80, Ipanema; d from R$1250;
🔲 🖥 🛜 🔲) Designed by Philippe Starck,
the ultra-stylish Fasano is the top destination
for celebutantes when they come to Rio. It has
a great location and a much-touted seafood
restaurant and bar. If you book here, make
sure you get a room with an ocean view.

Copacabana & Leme
Copacabana, particularly Av Atlântica, is
packed with hotels. Quality and price varies

considerably, and many places are in dire need
of an update.

BUDGET
Stone of a Beach hostel (Map p134; ☎ 3209 0348; www
.stoneofabeach.com.br; Rua Barata Ribeiro 111, Copacabana;
dm R$30-39, d R$90-120; 🔲 🖥 🛜 🔲) This popular
full-service hostel has basic dorms (with six to
18 beds) amid a friendly, party atmosphere.
The small rooftop pool with adjoining bar
and restaurant (serving inexpensive meals
nightly) is a good place to meet other travelers, and there are loads of activities for solo
backpackers.

Bamboo Rio (Map p134; ☎ 2236 1117; www.bam
boorio.com; Rua Lacerda Coutinho 45, Copacabana; dm R$32-
39, d R$120-140; 🔲 🖥 🛜 🔲) Set in a converted
villa, Bamboo Rio is a friendly, comfortable
hostel with tidy air-conditioned dorm rooms
(sleeping from five to 12), ample lounge space,
a tiny pool and an inviting bar area.

Walk on the Beach hostel (Map p134; ☎ 2545
7500, www.walk-on-the-beach.com; Rua Dias da Rocha 85,
Copacabana; dm R$35-45; 🖥) In an unsigned
two-story house on one of Copacabana's
rare quiet streets, this nicely designed hostel
offers fan-cooled dorms (each with three to 12
beds). It has a lounge room and a small bar,
and maintains a low-key vibe.

Castelo (Map p134; ☎ 2521 5130; www.castelohostel
.com.br; Rua Saint Roman 20, Copacabana; dm/d R$35/100;
🖥) The aptly named Castelo occupies a beautifully converted castle-like mansion (built in
the 1920s) on a quiet stretch of Copacabana.
Here you'll find huge dorms with single beds
(no bunks) and polished wood floors, plus
spacious common areas.

MIDRANGE
Jucati (Map p134; ☎ 2547 5422; www.edificiojucati.com
.br; Rua Tenente Marones de Gusmão 85, Copacabana; s/d/tr/q
R$130/160/190/220; 🔲) Overlooking a leafy park,
the unmarked Jucati doesn't offer much in the
way of atmosphere, though it does have large,
simply furnished apartments with slate floors
and small kitchens.

Residencial Apartt (Map p134; ☎ 2522 1722; www
.apartt.com.br; Rua Francisco Otaviano 42, Arpoador; s/d ste
R$138/217) This old-fashioned all-suites hotel
doesn't have much charm about it, but the
price and location are excellent. The basic
one-bedroom suites come with small kitchen
units, a gloomy lounge room (with cable
TV) and a bedroom with adequate natural
lighting.

LONG-TERM RENTALS

If you're planning to stay in Rio for longer than a few nights, you might consider renting an apartment, which is often a better value than staying in a hotel. Nightly rates start around R$120 for a studio apartment; rates rise significantly during Carnaval and New Year's Eve.

Aurélio Rio Guide (☎ 7828 6382; www.aureliorioguide.com) Aurélio rents Ipanema and Copacabana apartments, as well as a house in Búzios.

Blame it on Rio 4 Travel (Map p134; ☎ 3813 5510; www.blameitonrio4travel.com; Rua Xavier da Silveira 15B, Copacabana) Run by an expat from New York, this professional agency rents apartments and runs a full-service travel agency.

Copacabana Holiday (Map p134; ☎ 2542 1525; www.copacabanaholiday.com.br; Rua Barata Ribeiro 90A, Copacabana) Specializes in Copacabana.

Fantastic Rio (Map p134; ☎ 2543 2667; http://fantasticrio.br.tripod.com; Apt 501, Av Atlântica 974, Leme) Multilingual Peter Corr rents modest one-bedrooms to spacious four-bedrooms with beach views.

Rio Apartments (Map p134; ☎ 2247 6221; www.rioapartments.com; Rua Rainha Elizabeth 85, Copacabana) A Swedish-run outfit with many apartment rentals in the Zona Sul.

Hotel Santa Clara (Map p134; ☎ 2256 2650; www.hotelsantaclara.com.br; Rua Décio Vilares 316, Copacabana; s/d from R$155/175) Up the street from a neighborhood park lies the Santa Clara, with its whitewashed exterior and blue shutters. The rooms in back are a little gloomy, while the upstairs rooms are best, with wood floors, antique bed frames, a writing desk and a balcony.

TOP END

Atlantis Copacabana Hotel (Map p134; ☎ 2521 1142; www.atlantishotel.com.br; Rua Bulhões de Carvalho 61, Copacabana; d R$210-260; 💻 🏊) In a good location between Copacabana and Ipanema, the Atlantis has clean, cheaply furnished rooms (with views above the 9th floor). There's a modest pool and sauna on the roof.

Ouro Verde Hotel (Map p134; ☎ 2543 4123; www.dayrell.com.br; Av Atlântica 1456, Copacabana; s R$200-260, d R$230-280; ❄ 🏊) One of the most reasonably priced hotels on the beachfront, Ouro Verde has spacious, old-fashioned rooms with aging carpets and bathrooms. The ocean view however (at least in the luxo rooms), is outstanding.

Augusto's Copacabana (Map p134; ☎ 2547 1800; www.augustoshotel.com.br; Rua Bolívar 119, Copacabana; s/d/tw R$205/228/250; ❄ 🏊) Augusto's plays off the kitschy ancient Rome theme in common areas. The rooms, meanwhile, are fairly straightforward with a light and airy feel, and modern bathrooms. Some have balconies (but no views). The biggest rooms end in 1 or 8.

Acapulco (Map p134; ☎ 3077 2000; www.acapulcohotel.com.br; Rua Gustavo Sampaio 854, Leme; s/d from R$215/240; ❄ 🛜) On a quiet street one block from the beach, Acapulco has modern, streamlined rooms with colorful duvets and curtains. It also has a handful of suites for those seeking a bit more room.

South American Copacabana Hotel (Map p134; ☎ 2227 9161; www.southamericanhotel.com.br; Rua Francisco Sá 90, Copacabana; s/d from R$216/238; ❄ 💻 🏊) Solid value for its trim, modern rooms, this 13-story hotel is a short stroll to both Copacabana and Ipanema beaches. Rooms are set with pressed-wood floors, colorful bedspreads and a touch of artwork on the walls.

Orla Copacabana (Map p134; ☎ 2525 2425; www.orlahotel.com.br; Av Atlântica 4122, Copacabana; d R$248-313; ❄ 🛜 🏊) The Spanish-owned Orla Copacabana has attractive, understated rooms, but the beach-facing location is the real draw. Avoid the dark and cramped standard rooms, and try for a deluxe room with an ocean view.

Olinda Othon Classic (Map p134; ☎ 2159 9000; www.othon.com.br; Av Atlântica 2230, Copacabana; d with/without ocean view from R$342/270; ❄ 🛜) Overlooking Copacabana Beach, the Olinda Othon is indeed a classic. Its marble lobby, complete with chandeliers, Oriental carpets and grand piano has an Old-World charm, although its rooms are modern. The best of the bunch face the ocean and are worth the extra *reais*.

our pick **Rio Guesthouse** (Map p134; ☎ 2521 8568; www.rioguesthouse.com; Rua Francisco Sá 5, Copacabana; d R$300-450; ❄ 🛜) On the top floor of a high-rise overlooking Copacabana Beach, this small guesthouse offers handsomely decorated rooms in a welcoming setting. There's also a sunny patio with views of the beach.

Design Hotel Portinari (Map p134; ☎ 3222 8800; www.hotelportinari.com.br; Rua Francisco Sá 17, Copacabana; d from R$320; ⊠) This stylish 13-story hotel has artfully lit rooms with comfortable beds, big windows and tile floors. The top-floor restaurant is decorated with tropical plants and has fine views through the floor-to-ceiling windows.

Mercure Arpoador (Map p134; ☎ 3222 9600; www .mercure.com.br, in Portuguese; Rua Francisco Otaviano 61, Copacabana; s/d ste R$367/397; ⊠ ⊠) The dapper all-suites Mercure Arpoador has rooms with white leather sofas that open into beds, modern kitchenettes, TVs with stereo and DVD player, ambient lighting and comfortable bedrooms. All have verandas – though there's no view.

Porto Bay Rio Internacional (Map p134; ☎ 2546 8000; www.portobay.com.br; Av Atlântica 1500, Copacabana; d/ste from R$480/850; ⊠ ⌨ ⊠) One of Copacabana's top beachfront hotels, Porto Bay has elegant rooms with fluffy duvets, light hardwoods, stylish furnishings and simple artwork. Big windows let in lots of natural light, and most rooms have balconies.

Copacabana Palace (Map p134; ☎ 2548 7070; www .copacabanapalace.com.br; Av Atlântica 1702, Copacabana; d from R$785; ⊠) The city's most famous hotel, the Palace has hosted heads of state and rock stars. The dazzling white facade dates from the 1920s, when the hotel became a symbol of the city. Inside you'll find a range of rooms, a wonderful pool and excellent restaurants.

Botafogo

Botafogo, with its growing number of hostels, has some of the best budget options in the city. Though lacking beach access, Botafogo is an authentic slice of Rio, with old-school *botecos* and lively nontouristy restaurants hidden on the tree-lined streets,

El Misti (Map p136; ☎ 2226 0991; www.elmistihostel .com; Praia do Botafogo 462, Casa 9; dm R$29-40, s R$40, d R$110-130; ⌨) Located along Botafogo's hostel row, El Misti is popular for its cheap dorms (with triple bunk beds) and lively atmosphere.

Tupiniquim (Map p136; ☎ 2244 1286; www.tupini quimhostel.com.br; Rua São Manoel 19; dm R$30-35, d with/ without bathroom R$100/80; ⊠ ⌨ ⊠) Tupiniquim offers plenty of amusement for travelers seeking something beyond just a cheap bed for the night. There's a rock-climbing wall, pingpong, pool table, table football, record player, book- and DVD library and an enclosed patio with barbecues several nights a week.

Vila Carioca (Map p136; ☎ 2535 3224; www.vilacari oca.com.br; Rua Estácio Coimbra 84; dm/d from R$32/110; ⊠ ⌨ ⊠) On a peaceful tree-lined street, this low-key and welcoming hostel has six- to 15-bed dorms in an attractively decorated house. The common areas are a fine spot to mingle with other travelers.

Brothers Hostel (Map p136; ☎ 2551 0997; www .brothershostel.com; Rua Farani 18; dm/d with HI card from R$37/120, without HI card from R$47/140; ⊠ ⌨ ⊠) In a handsomely converted house, Brothers Hostel has airy, meticulously clean rooms and common areas, with polished wood floors and tall ceilings – with a maximum of eight beds to a room. The rock-loving bar brings together Cariocas and foreign travelers.

Flamengo & Catete

These middle-class neighborhoods have affordable options if you don't mind hopping on the metro to reach the beach.

Art Hostel (Map p136; ☎ 2205 1983; www.arthostelrio .com; Rua Silveira Martins 135, Catete; dm R$29-45, s/d from R$50/90; ⌨ ⊠) On a quiet street off busy Rua do Catete, this long, narrow three-story hostel attracts an alternative, somewhat bohemian crowd. Dorm rooms pack from four up to 14 beds. The main art-filled lounge becomes an exhibition and performance space (poetry readings, art shows) twice a month.

Hotel Riazor (Map p136; ☎ 2225 0121; www.hotel riazor.com.br; Rua do Catete 160, Catete; s/d R$75/90; ⊠) The colonial facade of the Riazor hides worn quarters short on style. The equation here is simple: bed, bathroom, TV, air-con, and a door by which to exit the room and explore the city. You'll find a mix of travelers and lost souls at this hotel.

Maze Inn (Map p136; ☎ 2558-5547; www.jazzrio.info; Casa 66, Rua Tavares Bastos 414, Favela Tavares Bastos; s/d from R$80/100) Set in Tavares Bastos, one of Rio's safest favelas, the Maze Inn is a fantastic place to overnight – for those looking for an alternative view of Rio. The rooms are uniquely decorated with original artworks (for sale) by English owner and Renaissance man Bob Nadkarni, while the veranda offers stunning views of the bay and Pão de Açúcar.

Hotel Inglês (Map p136; ☎ 2558 3052; www.hotelin gles.com.br; Rua Silveira Martins 20, Flamengo; s/d R$120/150; ⊠ ⌨) Boasting a colonial facade, the Inglês has a range of simple rooms, the best have high ceilings and windows overlooking leafy Parque do Catete. The rooms in back are cramped.

Augusto's Paysandu (Map p136; ☎ 2558 7270; www.paysanduhotel.com.br; Rua Paissandu 23, Flamengo; s/d R$149/165; ✖) Set on a quiet street lined with imperial palm trees, the Paysandu is an affordable and decent option in Flamengo. The hotel's best rooms feature high ceilings, good natural light and space to stretch out.

Regina Hotel (Map p136; ☎ 3289 9999; www.hotelregina.com.br; Rua Ferreira Viana 29, Flamengo; s/d R$172/190, with balcony R$188/210; ✖ ☐) The renovated Regina boasts 117 rooms, each with a bright modern appearance, with wood or tile floors and sparkling bathrooms. Front-facing rooms (luxos) have sizeable balconies for catching a breeze off the bay.

Santa Teresa & Lapa

A growing number of budget and midrange hotels have opened in Santa Teresa in recent years, drawing travelers to this intriguing, arts-loving neighborhood. Do take care when walking around, day or night, as security is still an issue.

BUDGET
Pousada Favelinha (Map p136; www.favelinha.com; Rua Antonio Joaquim 13, Morro do Pereirão da Silva; dm/d R$35/75) Located in Favela Pereirão da Silva, this clean, attractive guesthouse has four double rooms and a five-bed dorm, all with balconies and stunning views. While the Pereirão da Silva is one of Rio's more peaceful favelas, this place isn't for everyone – some love it; some don't. Visit the website for directions.

Terra Brasilis (Map p138; ☎ 2224 0952; www.terrabrasilishostel.com; Rua Murtinho Nobre 156, Santa Teresa; dm R$35-40, d R$130-150; ☐ 🛜) Near the Parque das Ruinas, this peacefully set guesthouse has a mix of dorms (sleeping six to 12) and doubles, all with wood floors and French doors that open onto a veranda overlooking the city. The breezy patio with bar is a fine place to nurse a drink.

Rio Hostel (Map p138; ☎ 3852 0827; www.riohostel.com; Rua Joaquim Murtinho 361, Santa Teresa; dm R$37, d R$120-140; ✖ ☐ 🛜 🛋) A favorite among travelers, Rio Hostel has handsomely designed rooms, a cozy lounge and a backyard patio. The spirit of bonhomie prevails with barbecues and occasional jam sessions by guests and local musicians.

Casa Mango Mango (Map p138; ☎ 2508 6440; www.casamangomango.com; Rua Joaquim Murtinho 587; dm R$40, d R$140-220; ✖ ☐ 🛜 🛋) In an atmospheric 19th-century mansion, this friendly guest-

house has a wide range of uniquely furnished rooms (some without windows, others with gorgeous views) and a lush garden and patio. Has excellent breakfasts.

Hotel Marajó (Map p138; ☎ 2224 4134; Rua Joaquim Silva 99, Lapa; s/d/tw R$55/60/80; ✖) A few paces from the Selarón steps, this basic hotel rents simple, fairly clean rooms, all with air-con. The best rooms are quite sunny; the worst are rather gloomy.

Casa Áurea (Map p138; ☎ 2242 5830; www.casaaurea.com.br; Rua Áurea 80, Santa Teresa; dm R$65, s/d with shared bathroom R$110/140, s/d with bathroom R$160/190; ✖ ☐ 🛜) Set on a quiet street, this handsome two-story house has been converted into a simple guesthouse with pleasant, airy rooms and a small garden with hammocks out back.

MIDRANGE & TOP END
our pick **Cama e Café** (Map p138; ☎ 2225 4366; www.camaecafe.com.br; Rua Progresso 67, Santa Teresa; d from R$95) Cama e Café is a B&B network that links travelers with local residents. There are several dozen colonial houses to choose from, with accommodations ranging from modest to lavish – indeed the best rooms are antique-filled suites set inside castle-like mansions with verandas and lush gardens.

Castelinho 38 (Map p138; ☎ 2252 2549; www.castelinho38.com; Rua Triunfo 38, Santa Teresa; s/d from R$170/220; ✖) Castelinho has spacious rooms with high ceilings, wood floors and a light, airy design. It's set in a mid-19th-century mansion and has an outdoor terrace with a garden and lounge space.

Solar de Santa (Map p138; ☎ 2221 2117; www.solardesanta.com; Ladeira do Meireles 32, Santa Teresa; d with/without bathroom R$480/255; ✖ 🛋) Set in a converted colonial mansion, this marvelous four-room guesthouse has beautifully designed rooms that open onto a veranda with splendid views.

Mama Ruisa (Map p138; ☎ 2242 1281; www.mamaruisa.com; Rua Santa Cristina 132, Santa Teresa; d from €230; ✖ 🛋) Mama Ruisa aims for bohemian chic in its seven spacious, uniquely designed guestrooms set in a lavishly decorated colonial house.

Hotel Santa Teresa (Map p138; ☎ 2221 1406; www.santateresahotel.com; Rua Almirante Alexandrino 660, Santa Teresa; d from R$750; ✖ ☐ 🛜 🛋) Probably the finest boutique hotel in Rio, the Santa Teresa has artfully designed rooms, an award-winning restaurant, a full-service spa, a stylish bar and a pool with fine views over the city.

EATING

Rio has an impressive array of restaurants, serving Brazilian regional cuisine along with international and fusion fare. In general, Ipanema and Leblon boast Rio's best dining scene, though every neighborhood has its gems.

You can eat on the cheap (try per-kilo places and juice bars), but it's worth splashing out for a meal once and a while (dinner for two averages R$80 to R$120) to enjoy fantastic cuisine in some beautiful settings. Among Rio's quintessential dining experiences: feasting at a *churrascaria* (all-you-can-eat barbecued-meat restaurant), dining alfresco beside the lake in Lagoa, joining the fashion parade at a sidewalk café in Ipanema, chowing on local favorites at a neighborhood *boteco* and lingering over the sweeping views from a restaurant patio high-up in Santa Teresa.

Self-caterers should check out Rio's *feiras* (produce markets); see p179.

Ipanema & Leblon

By day, Ipanema's busy cafés and juice bars fill with bronze bodies heading to and from the beach, while at night its tree-lined streets make a picturesque setting for open-air dining. Leblon's Rua Días Ferreira and Ipanema's Rua Garcia D'Ávila are packed with dining options.

For fresh tropical fruits, visit the *feiras*, which are on Monday on Rua Henrique Dumont (Ipanema), Tuesday on Praça General Osório (Ipanema), Thursday on Rua General Urquiza (Leblon) and Friday on Praça NS de Paz (Ipanema). On Sunday, the Hippie Fair, in Praça General Osório (Ipanema), has a stall in the southeast corner of the plaza where you can buy tasty Northeastern cuisine. Don't miss it.

BUDGET

Cheap Eateries

Koni Store (Map p133; ☎ 2521 9348; Rua Maria Quitéria 77, Ipanema; hand roll R$7-10; 🕑 11am-3am Sun-Wed, to 6am Thu-Sat) This bright orange *Japazilian* hot spot has exploded in Rio – 15 outlets since opening in late 2006. They do fresh tuna or salmon in sushi cones *(temaki)*, the best of which is salmon with crunchy wasabi peas and shoestring leeks.

Galitos Grill (Map p132; ☎ 2287 7864; Rua Farme de Amoedo 62; mains R$10-20; 🕑 noon-10pm) A handy spot in the neighborhood is this open-sided purveyor of roast chicken. Grab a seat at the counter and enjoy tasty lunch specials (around R$10), whipped up in a hurry.

Bibi Crepes (Map p132; ☎ 2259 4948; Rua Cupertino Durão 81, Leblon; crepes R$11-16; 🕑 noon-1am) It serves over two dozen sweet and savory crepes, as well as design-your-own salads (chose from 40 different toppings).

Delírio Tropical (Map p132; ☎ 3201 2977; Rua Garcia D'Ávila 48, Ipanema; salads R$12-16; 🕑 9am-9pm) Delírio Tropical serves 16 different varieties of salad along with soups and hot dishes (veggie burgers, grilled salmon). The open layout has a pleasant, casual vibe, with big windows overlooking the street.

Cafés & Juice Bars

Polis Sucos (Map p132; ☎ 2247 2518; Rua Maria Quitéria 70, Ipanema; juices R$3-6, snacks R$3-8; 🕑 7am-midnight) Serving 40 or so juices, Polis Sucos is a great place to get your vitamins, and you can pair those tangy beverages with sandwiches (vegetarian, chicken, filet mignon).

Armazém do Café (Map p132; ☎ 2259 0170; Rua Rita Ludolf 87B, Leblon; snacks R$4-8; 🕑 9am-midnight) Dark wood furnishings and the scent of freshly ground coffee lend an authenticity to this Leblon coffeehouse. Armazém also serves snacks and desserts.

Prima Bruschetteria (Map p132; ☎ 2222 2222; Rua Rainha Guilhermina 95, Leblon; bruschettas R$5-8; 🕑 noon-midnight) New in 2010, Prima showcases an Italian delicacy not often seen in these parts, with fresh, imaginative ingredients appearing atop its char-grilled bread. You'll also find salads, antipasto plates and risottos.

Universo Orgânico (Map p132; ☎ 3874 0186; store 105, Rua Conde Bernadotte 26, Leblon; juices R$7, snacks R$6-12; 🕑 8am-7pm Mon, to 9:30pm Tue-Sat, 11am-8pm Sun) In the back of a small shopping gallery, Universo Orgânico whips up delicious fruit and veggie shakes – such as the carrot, ginger, apple and linseed combo – plus veggie burgers and savory nonmeat *salgados* (snacks).

Cafeína (Map p132; ☎ 2521 2194; Rua Farme de Amoedo 43, Ipanema; sandwiches R$12-24; 🕑 9am-8pm Sun & Mon, 8am-11:30pm Tue-Sat) This popular café, in the heart of Ipanema, has outdoor tables for enjoying coffees and freshly made sandwiches, flavorful salads, quiche and some very rich desserts.

Quick Eats & Self Catering

HortiFruti (Map p132; ☎ 2512 6820; Rua Días Ferreira 57, Leblon; 🕑 8am-8pm Mon-Sat, to 2pm Sun) Leblon's popular indoor fruit and vegetable market, with other groceries too.

Zona Sul Supermarket (Map p132; ☎ 2259 4699; Rua Dias Ferreira 290, Leblon; ❤ 24hr, closed midnight Sun to 7am Mon) The best branch of Rio's supermarket chain stocks plenty of freshly baked breads, imported cheeses, wine, prosciutto and more. There's also a handy location facing Praça General Osório.

Vezpa Pizzeria (Map p132; ☎ 2540 0800; Av Ataúlfo de Paiva 1063, Leblon; slice R$5-8; ❤ noon-4am) Vezpa is a recommended New York–style by-the-slice pizza place, with around a dozen varieties on hand.

Yogoberry (Map p132; ☎ 3281 1512; Rua Visconde de Pirajá 282, Ipanema; small/medium yogurt R$6/8; ❤ 10am-10pm) Fueling Rio's frozen yogurt craze, Yogoberry comes in just two flavors: *natural* (plain) and *chá verde* (green tea), but the fresh fruit toppings – melon, peach, strawberry – turn it into a delicacy.

Laffa (Map p132; ☎ 2522 5888; Rua Visconde de Pirajá 175, Ipanema; sandwich small/large R$9/14; ❤ 11:30am until late) A new hit on the street-food scene is Laffa, a lively little eatery where harried staff whip up satisfying, piping-hot grilled lamb or turkey shawarmas, falafel sandwiches or exotic inventions such as strawberry and Nutella wraps.

Talho Capixaba (Map p132; ☎ 2512 8760; Av Ataúlfo de Paiva 1022, Leblon; sandwiches R$12-24; ❤ 8am-10pm) This tiny deli and gourmet grocer has pastas, salads, antipasti and excellent sandwiches (charged by weight) made from quality ingredients. Take away or dine inside or on the sidewalk tables.

MIDRANGE & TOP END

Felice Caffè & Gelateria (Map p132; ☎ 2522 7749; Rua Gomes Carneiro 30, Ipanema; mains R$18-40; ❤ noon-midnight Mon-Fri, 10am-midnight Sat & Sun) Felice serves gourmet sandwiches (grilled veggies, steak, thick burgers), juicy grilled dishes, bountiful salads, and rich Italian-style ice cream, pulled from the highly enticing front counter.

Vegetariano Social Club (Map p132; ☎ 2540 6499; Rua Conde de Bernadotte 26L, Leblon; lunch buffet R$20-24; ❤ noon-midnight Mon-Sat, to 5:30pm Sun) On Saturday vegetarians can sample Brazil's signature dish at this Zenlike spot when tofu *feijoada* is served. At other times, VSC serves a small (10-dish) lunch buffet, while the more elaborate evening à la carte menu features risottos, *yakisoba*, heart-of-palm stroganoff and other inventive dishes.

> ### RIO'S TOP VEGETARIAN OPTIONS
>
> **Bistro do Paço** (p170) Centro.
> **Frontera** (p167 and p168) Ipanema & Copacabana.
> **La Trattoria** (p168) Copacabana.
> **Le Blé Noir** (p169) Copacabana.
> **New Natural** (p166) Ipanema.
> **Prima Bruschetteria** (p165) Leblon.
> **Vegetariano Social Club** (p166) Leblon.

New Natural (Map p132; ☎ 2287 0301; Rua Barão da Torre 167, Ipanema; per kg R$36-39; ❤ 8am-10pm) Featuring an excellent lunch buffet with many vegetarian options, the New Natural has fresh pots of soup, rice, veggies and beans.

Brasileirinho (Map p132; ☎ 2513 5184; Rua Jangadeiros 10, Ipanema; mains R$24-42; ❤ noon-2am) This rustically decorated restaurant serves good, traditional Mineiro cuisine. Favorites include *tutu a mineira* (mashed black beans with manioc), *carne seca* (dried and salted beef) and *picanha* (rump steak).

Via Sete (Map p132; ☎ 2512 8100; Rua Garcia D'Ávila 125, Ipanema; mains R$26-42; ❤ noon-midnight) Via Sete serves a good selection of salads, grilled vegetable wraps, as well as heartier fare such as grilled tuna and a high-end steak burger, using mostly organic ingredients. The restaurant's front patio is a prime people-watching spot.

Bazzar (Map p132; ☎ 3202 2884; Rua Barão da Torre 538, Ipanema; mains R$26-40; ❤ lunch & dinner) On a quiet, tree-lined street, Bazzar is a handsomely designed contemporary restaurant, serving unique dishes such as grilled *namorada* (a type of perch) with whole grain rice, citrus and pesto, and lamb with polenta and mushrooms. It has outdoor seating in front.

Garcia & Rodrigues (Map p132; ☎ 3206 4100; Av Ataúlfo de Paiva 1251, Leblon; mains R$28-50; ❤ 8am-midnight) This French restaurant has a lovely deli where you'll find fresh bakery items, imported cheeses, salads, wines and desserts.

Zazá Bistrô Tropical (Map p132; ☎ 2247 9101; Rua Joana Angélica 40, Ipanema; mains R$29-50; ❤ dinner) French-colonial decor and delicately spiced cuisine await those venturing inside this charming converted house in Ipanema. Inventive combinations, blending East and West, match the seductive mood inside. Upstairs, diners lounge on throw pillows, with candles glowing along the walls. Those who prefer fresh air can dine on the porch out front.

Capricciosa (Map p132; ☎ 2494 2212; Rua Vinícius de Moraes 134, Ipanema; small/large pizzas from R$36/45; ☾ dinner) This trendy spot serves a huge variety of tasty thin-crust pizzas.

Benkei (Map p132; ☎ 2540 4829; Rua Henrique Dumont 71, Ipanema; all-you-can-eat R$36-48; ☾ dinner Mon, lunch & dinner Tue-Sun) This casual Japanese restaurant is a favorite haunt for after-the-beach meals on weekends. Benkei does have a menu, though nearly everyone here comes for the all-you-can-eat sushi buffet, with a wide variety of rolls and sashimi, plus miso soup.

Frontera (Map p132; ☎ 3289 2350; Rua Visconde de Pirajá 128, Ipanema; per kg R$42-46; ☾ 11:30am-11pm) Frontera offers more than 60 dishes at its delectable lunch buffet, featuring a mouth-watering assortment of grilled meats, baked casseroles and seafood pastas, plus salads, fresh fruits, grilled vegetables and desserts.

our pick **Zuka** (Map p132; ☎ 2249 7550; Rua Dias Ferreira 233, Leblon; mains R$45-80; ☾ dinner Mon, lunch & dinner Tue-Sun) One of Rio's best restaurants, Zuka prepares delectable mouth-watering cuisine – zingy ceviche or the confection-like delicacy of Zuka's original foie gras to start, followed by rack of lamb with passion fruit, grilled fish of the day with *mandoquinha* purée and many other imaginative dishes.

Sushi Leblon (Map p132; ☎ 2512 7830; Rua Días Ferreira 256, Leblon; dinner for 2 R$75-150; ☾ lunch & dinner) Leblon's premier sushi destination, Sushi Leblon boasts creative additions to its award-winning sashimi, including grilled *namorado* (a type of perch) with passion fruit *farofa* (manioc flour sautéed with butter) and sea-urchin ceviche.

Casa da Feijoada (Map p132; ☎ 2247 2776; Rua Prudente de Morais 10B, Ipanema; feijoada R$50; ☾ noon-11:30pm) At this longstanding institution, any day is fine to sample the rich, black bean and salted pork dish. The *feijoada* is served with the requisite orange slices, *farofa* and grated kale, all of which pair nicely with a caipirinha.

Gávea, Jardim Botânico & Lagoa

During summer, live music fills the air at open-air restaurants around Lagoa Rodrigo de Freitas. Gávea has a few lively dining and drinking spots around Praça Santos Dumont, while Jardim Botânico has a sprinkling of eateries on Rua JJ Seabra and Rua Pacheco Leão.

Braseiro da Gávea (Map p132; ☎ 2239 7494; Praça Santos Dumont 116, Gávea; mains R$18-30; ☾ 11am-midnight Mon-Sat) Extremely popular with the weekend crowd, this open-air bistro serves large portions of its popular steak, pot roast and fried chicken.

Arab da Lagoa (Map p132; ☎ 2540 0747; Parque dos Patins, Av Borges de Medeiros, Lagoa; platter for 2 R$50; ☾ 10am-1am) One of numerous outdoor restaurants on the lake, this popular spot serves traditional Middle Eastern specialties such as hummus, baba ghanoush, tabbouleh, *quibe* and tasty thin-crust pizzas.

Bráz (Map p132; ☎ 2535 0687; Rua Maria Angélica 129, Jardim Botânico; pizzas R$28-43; ☾ dinner) Perfect crusts and super-fresh ingredients are two of the components that make Bráz the best pizza place in town.

00 (Zero Zero; Map p132; ☎ 2540 8041; Planetário, Av Padre Leonel Franca 240, Gávea; mains from R$30; ☾ 8pm-late) Inside Gávea's planetarium, 00 is a sleek restaurant-lounge that serves Brazilian cuisine with Asian and Mediterranean accents. After dinner, have a few cocktails and stick around: some of Rio's best DJs spin at parties here.

Guimas (Map p132; ☎ 2259 7996; Rua José Roberto Macedo Soares 5, Gávea; mains R$36-50; ☾ noon-1am) A classic open-air *boteco* with creative flair, Guimas has been going strong since the late 1990s. Winning dishes include the *bacalhau à bras* (codfish mixed with potatoes, eggs and onions) and the juicy *picanha no sal grosso* (grilled rump steak).

Olympe (Map p132; ☎ 2539 4542; Rua Custódio Serrão 62, Lagoa; mains R$44-82; ☾ dinner Mon-Sat, lunch Fri) One of Rio's best chefs, Claude Troisgros continues to dazzle guests with unforgettable meals at his award-winning restaurant. Originally from France, Troisgros mixes Old-World with new in ever inventive combinations. The setting is in a lovely house on a tree-lined street.

Copacabana & Leme

Copacabana has everything from award-winning dining rooms to charming bistros from the 1950s. Although the open-air restaurants along Av Atlântica have nice views, the food isn't so hot, and things get a little seedy at night.

For fresh fruits, visit Copacabana *feiras*, which happen on Wednesday on Rua Domingos Ferreira, Thursday on Rua Belford Roxo and Rua Ronald de Carvalho, and Sunday on Rua Décio Vilares. Supermarkets include **Pão de Açúcar** (Av NS de Copacabana 497, Copacabana; ☾ 24hr) and the fruit-filled **HortiFruti** (Map p134; Av Prado Junior 277; ☾ 8am-8pm Mon-Sat, 8am-2pm Sun).

THE KIOSKS OF COPACABANA

In recent years Copacabana Beach has seen a new crop of flashy kiosks, allowing punters to get a decent meal (the kitchens are cleverly concealed underground), an ice-cold draft beer or gourmet snacks without ever leaving the sand.

Here are a few current favorites:

- **Siri Mole & Cia kiosk** (Map p134; near Rua Bolívar; ⊙ 10am-midnight Tue-Sun, from 3pm Mon) Serving snacks such as *acarajé* (R$10) or heartier Bahian dishes, just like its sit-down restaurant (p169), plus delicious tropical cocktails.

- **Bar Luiz** (Map p134; near Copacabana Palace; ⊙ 8am-1am) Famed for its refreshing ice-cold *chope*, Bar Luiz also has good *bolinhos de bacalhau* (codfish balls, R$28 for 10), *salada de batata* (potato salad) and other appetizers.

- **Nescafé** (Map p134; near Copacabana Palace; ⊙ 8am-1am) Serves nearly 20 varieties of savory or sweet crepes (around R$15), plus breakfast options and, of course, caffeinated drinks.

- **Recanto do Sol** (Map p134; near Praça Julio de Noronha; ⊙ 24hr) At the northeast end of the beach, this peacefully set kiosk serves small plates of sardines and fresh fish (R$20), as well as strong caipirinhas.

- **Champanheria Copacabana** (Map p134; near Rua Constante Ramos; ⊙ 10am-midnight Sun-Thu, till 2am Fri & Sat) An upscale option for those who simply can't gaze across the sea without sipping champagne cocktails (R$12) and eating *ciabatta* with sardines and capers (R$11).

BUDGET
Cheap Eateries

O Rei das Empanadas (Map p134; ☎ 3258 3003; Rua Barata Ribeira 48; empanadas R$2.50-3.50; ⊙ 9am-11pm) Piping hot empanadas are baked fresh throughout the day and come in a dozen varieties, including *carne picante* (spicy beef), *camarão* (shrimp) or dessert options (banana with chocolate).

Cervantes (Map p134; ☎ 2275 6147; Av Prado Júnior 335B, Copacabana; sandwiches R$12-18; ⊙ noon-late Tue-Sun) This Copacabana institution gathers a mixed crowd who feast on trademark steak-and-pineapple sandwiches. Fussy waiters are quick to the tap when your *chope* runneth dry. Around the corner, at Rua Barato Ribeiro 7, is Cervantes' stand-up *boteco*, good for a meal in a hurry.

Toca do Siri (☎ 2267 0894; Av Rua Raul Pompeia 6; acarajé R$15; ⊙ noon-midnight Tue-Sun) Around the corner from Siri Mole & Cia is their smaller, cheaper and more casual boteco, best known for tasty *acarajé* (spicy shrimp-filled croquettes) and other Bahian specialties.

Cafés & Dessert Shops

Cafeína (Map p134; ☎ 2547 8651; Rua Constante Ramos 44, Copacabana; pastries R$2-4; ⊙ 8:30am-11:30pm Tue-Sat, 9am-8:30pm Sun & Mon) A few blocks from the beach, Cafeína is a pleasant indoor and outdoor spot that serves good coffee, sandwiches, salads and a variety of baked goods.

Bakers (Map p134; ☎ 2256 7000; Rua Santa Clara 86B, Copacabana; sandwiches R$14-24; ⊙ 9am-8pm Mon-Fri, to 6:30pm Sat, 9am-5pm Sun) Behind shiny countertops are tasty banana Danishes, apple strudels and flaky croissants, plus gourmet sandwiches, salads and quiches.

Confeitaria Colombo (Map p134; ☎ 3201 4049; Forte de Copacabana, Praça Coronel Eugênio Franco, Copacabana; mains R$15-30; ⊙ 10am-8pm Tue-Sun) Located inside the Forte de Copacabana (admission R$2), this café has shady outdoor tables with magnificent views of Copacabana Beach.

MIDRANGE & TOP END

Frontera (Map p134; ☎ 3202 9050; Av NS de Copacabana 1144, Copacabana; per kg R$36-47; ⊙ 11am-11pm) Much like its Ipanema branch (p167), Frontera spreads an excellent lunch buffet. At night it serves all-you-can-eat crepes and pizzas for under R$20 per person.

La Trattoria (Map p134; ☎ 2255 3319; Rua Fernando Mendes 7A, Copacabana; mains R$22-44; ⊙ lunch & dinner) This casual but festive Italian trattoria has been a neighborhood favorite for over 30 years. Seafood pasta dishes are particularly recommended.

Copa Café (Map p134; ☎ 2235 2947; Av Atlântica 3056, Copacabana; mains R$26-48; ⊙ 7pm-1am Mon-Sat) Facing the beach, this sleek, lounge-like place has black wood floors, white bar stools, an open layout and electronic music. The menu features high-end bistro fare: risottos, seared tuna steaks and gourmet burgers – the house specialty.

Amir (Map p134; ☎ 2275 5596; Rua Ronald de Carvalho 55C, Copacabana; mains R$28-45, all-you-can-eat R$33-45; ☻ lunch & dinner) Serving some of Rio's best Middle Eastern dishes, this enticing two-story restaurant near the beach offers consistently good plates of hummus, *kaftas* (savory meatballs), falafel and salads. Daytime crowds come for the buffet (R$33/45 on weekdays/weekends), while at night it's à la carte.

Azumi (Map p134; ☎ 2541 4294; Rua Ministro Viveiros de Castro 127, Copacabana; plates R$30-60; ☻ dinner Tue-Sat) This low-key sushi bar is a favorite among the *nisei* (second-generation Japanese) community. Azumi's *sushiman* (sushi chef) masterfully prepares delectable sushi and sashimi. The tempuras and soups are also excellent.

Carretão (Map p134; ☎ 2542 2148; Rua Ronald de Carvalho 55, Copacabana; all-you-can-eat R$30; ☻ 11:30am-midnight) It's all about the meat at this inexpensive *churrascaria*. There is another branch in Ipanema, at Rua Visconde de Pirajá 112.

Le Blé Noir (Map p134; ☎ 2287 1272; Rua Xavier da Silveira 15A, Copacabana; mains R$30-48; ☻ dinner) Flickering candles, subdued conversation and tasty crepes (over 50 varieties) make this popular restaurant a real date-pleaser.

Capricciosa (Map p134; ☎ 2255 2598; Rua Domingos Ferreira 187, Copacabana; pizzas from R$36; ☻ dinner) This stylish spot serves tasty thin-crust pizzas.

Siri Mole & Cia (Map p134; ☎ 2267 0894; Rua Francisco Otaviano 50, Copacabana; mains R$70-95; ☻ dinner daily, lunch Tue-Sun) Rated one of Rio's best Bahian restaurants, Siri Mole & Cia serves outstanding *vatapá* (manioc paste with coconut and seafood), *moqueca de camarão* (shrimp stew) and *ensopada de peixe* (fish and coconut milk stew). Stop in on Saturday (before 5pm) for the all-you-can-eat seafood buffet (R$58).

Botafogo & Urca

Cobal de Humaitá (Map p136; Rua Voluntários da Pátria 446, Botafogo; ☻ closed Sun) This place is a fruit and flower market by day, with lively cafés and restaurants that open at night.

Meza Bar (Map p136; Rua Capitão Salomão 69, Botafogo; tapas R$10-25; ☻ 6pm-1am) Botafogo's see-and-be-seen hot spot serves up delectable, Brazilian-slanted tapas to a sophisticated and trendy crowd. Creative cocktails and delightful staff round out the fun here.

Emporium Pax (Map p136; ☎ 2559 9713; 7th fl, Praia de Botafogo 400, Botafogo; mains R$18-30; ☻ noon-8:30pm) One of many eateries at Botafogo

Praia Shopping, Emporium Pax offers spectacular views of Pão de Açúcar and Baía de Guanabara. As well as salads, pastas and tasty desserts, the lunch buffet draws in the shoppers and film-goers.

Garota da Urca (Map p136; ☎ 2541 8585; Av João Luís Alves 56, Urca; mains R$20-40; ☻ noon-2am) Overlooking the small Praia da Urca, this neighborhood restaurant serves standard Brazilian fare, but the stunning views from the open-air veranda are the real draw.

Miam Miam (Map p136; ☎ 2244 0125; Rua General Goés Monteiro 34, Botafogo; mains R$22-30; ☻ 8pm-1am Mon-Sat) This stylish place features a unique brand of 'comfort food', which means bruschetta with pesto and tapenade, endive salad with gorgonzola, pepper crusted tuna with lentil ragout and other inventive dishes. Don't miss the creative cocktail menu.

Yorubá (Map p136; ☎ 2541 9387; Rua Arnaldo Quintela 94, Botafogo; mains for 2 R$80-95; ☻ 7-11pm Wed-Fri, 2-11pm Sat, noon-6pm Sun) Candlelit Yorubá looks as if it's always ready for the arrival of an *orixá* (deity of Candomblé). And if the goddess Iemanjá were to pay a surprise visit, she'd find heavenly plump shrimp and rich coconut milk blended to perfection in *babão de camarão*, and outstanding *moqueca* (Bahian fish stew).

Flamengo & Catete

On weekend nights, the restaurants and bars lining Rua Marquês de Abrantes crowd with neighborhood diners. In Catete, the streets near Largo do Machado have a few popular outdoor restaurants.

Tacacá do Norte (Map p136; ☎ 2205 7545; Rua Barão de Flamengo 35, Flamengo; tacacá R$12; ☻ 9am-10pm Mon-Sat, to 7pm Sun) The fragrant and tasty Amazonian soup known as *tacacá* is made of manioc paste, *jambu* (a Brazilian vegetable) leaves, and fresh and dried shrimp – and this is one of the few places in Rio to try it.

Espaço Rio Carioca (Map p136; ☎ 2225 7332; www .espacoriocarioca.com.br; Rua Leite Leal 45, Laranjeiras; mains R$14-35; ☻ 3-10pm Mon-Fri, noon-10pm Sat & Sun; ☎) This large multilevel space just west of Catete, has a ground-level bookstore, an upstairs bistro with a terrace and a café that hosts live music four nights a week. The bistro menu features salads, sandwiches and heartier daily specials (pastas, risotto, grilled steak).

Estação República (Map p136; ☎ 2225 2650; Rua do Catete 104, Catete; per kg R$35-40; ☻ 11am-11pm) Estação's buffet table is a neighborhood institution. Featuring an extensive selection of salads, meats, pastas and vegetables, it's easy to indulge without breaking the bank.

Armazem do Chopp (Map p136; ☎ 2557 4052; Rua Marquês de Abrantes 66, Flamengo; mains R$20-30; ☽ noon-midnight) In a barnlike structure above the street, Armazem do Chopp is a neighborhood favorite for its tasty grilled dishes and traditional Brazilian fare. At night, its open-air front deck is a lively place for ice-cold drafts.

Lamas (Map p136; ☎ 2556 0799; Rua Marquês de Abrantes 18A, Flamengo; mains R$20-40; ☽ dinner) This classic restaurant opened in 1874 and, in spite of the mileage, dishes here hold up well. You can't go wrong with grilled *linguiça* (garlicky pork sausage) or filet mignon.

Intihuasi (Map p136; ☎ 2225 7653; Rua Barão do Flamengo 35D, Flamengo; mains R$28-46; ☽ noon-3pm & 7-11pm Tue-Sat, noon-5pm Sun) Colorfully decorated with Andean tapestries and artwork, Rio's only Peruvian restaurant serves excellent ceviches, *papas rellenas* (meat-filled potatoes), seafood soups and other classic dishes from the Andes.

Restaurante Kioto (Map p136; ☎ 2556 9880; 3rd fl, Rua Ministerio Tavares Lira 105, Flamengo; all-you-can-eat lunch/dinner R$33/40; ☽ noon-midnight) Hidden on a street behind Largo do Machado this simple, well-concealed restaurant is worth seeking out when craving a sushi feast that won't break the bank.

Porção Rio's (Map p136; ☎ 2554 8535; Av Infante Dom Henrique, Flamengo; all-you-can-eat R$78; ☽ 11:30am-midnight) Set in Parque do Flamengo with a stunning view of Pão de Açúcar, this is one of Rio's best *churrascarias*. Arrive early, both to score a good table and to see the view before sunset.

Centro

Rio's busiest neighborhood has everything from greasy lunch counters to French bistros, with ethnic and vegetarian fare, juice bars and *churrascarias*. Most restaurants open only for lunch on weekdays. Many pedestrian-only areas throughout Centro (such as Rua do Rosário) are full of restaurants, some spilling onto the sidewalk, others are hidden on upstairs floors, all of which make restaurant-hunting something of an art. Areas worth exploring include Travessa do Comércio just after work, when the restaurants and cafés fill with chatter. The cafés and restaurants around Praça Floriano are also popular gathering/quaffing spots.

BUDGET & MIDRANGE

Bistro do Paço (Map p138; ☎ 2262 3613; Praça XV de Novembro 48; mains R$10-24; ☽ 11am-7:30pm Mon-Fri, noon-7pm Sat & Sun) Inside the Paço Imperial, this airy lunchtime spot serves fresh salads, tasty sandwiches and piping hot quiches, with decent vegetarian options

Cedro do Líbano (Map p138; ☎ 2224 0163; Rua Senhor dos Passos 231; mains R$14-62; ☽ 11am-5pm) Along a bustling pedestrian strip, this 70-plus-year-old institution serves traditional Lebanese cooking: *quibes*, *kaftas* and lamb.

Café Arlequim (Map p138; ☎ 2220 8471; Paço Imperial, Praça XV de Novembro 48, Centro; mains R$14-28; ☽ 9am-8pm Mon-Fri, 10am-6pm Sat) In the middle of a book and music shop, this small, lively café is a fine spot to refuel, with Italian (Illy) coffee, sandwiches, salads, quiche, lasagna and desserts.

Brasserie Rosário (Map p138; ☎ 2518 3033; Rua do Rosário 34, Centro; mains from R$18; ☽ 8am-8pm Mon-Fri, 10am-5pm Sat) Set in a handsomely restored 1860s building, this atmospheric bistro has a hint of Paris. Croissants, *pain au chocolat* (chocolate croissant) and other bakery items fill the front counters, while the restaurant menu features roast meats and fish, soups, baguette sandwiches and the like.

Ateliê Culinario (Map p138; ☎ 2240 2573; Praça Floriano, Cinelândia; mains R$18-25; ☽ noon-10pm Mon-Fri) Ateliê Culinario serves up decent Brazilian fare on its open-air terrace to a festive crowd. Outdoor tables open onto Praça Floriano, which is a lively gathering spot on weekday evenings. At weekends, it stays opens during film screenings at the Odeon next door.

Bar Luiz (Map p138; ☎ 2262 6900; Rua da Carioca 39, Centro; mains R$20-45; ☽ 11am-11pm Mon-Sat) A festive air fills this 1887 brewpub as diners get their fill of traditional German cooking (potato salad and smoked meats), along with ice-cold drafts on tap.

Confeitaria Colombo (Map p138; ☎ 2505 1500; Rua Gonçalves Dias 34, Centro; mains from R$24, desserts from R$4; ☽ 8am-8pm Mon-Fri, 10am-5pm Sat) Stained-glass windows, brocaded mirrors and marble countertops create one of the most lavish settings for coffee, a meal or most importantly dessert – including an excellent *pastel de nata* (custard tart).

TOP END

Da Silva (Map p138; ☎ 2524 1010; 4th fl, Av Graça Aranha 187, Centro; all-you-can-eat R$40, after 2pm R$30; ☽ noon-4pm Mon-Fri) Hidden inside the Clube Ginástico

Português, this large, simply decorated restaurant offers one of Rio's best lunch buffets. Portuguese in flavor, Da Silva has delicious salads, steaks and seafood, along with an enormous variety of addictive *bacalhau* dishes and other baked dishes.

Cais do Oriente (Map p138; ☎ 2203 0178; Rua Visconde de Itaboraí 8, Centro; mains R$33-46; ✆ lunch daily, dinner Tue-Sat) Brick walls lined with tapestries stretch high to the ceiling in this almost cinematic 1870s mansion. Set on a brick-lined street hidden from the masses, Cais do Oriente blends West with East in dishes such as filet steak and sesame tuna.

AlbaMar (Map p138; ☎ 2240 8378; Praça Marechal Âncora 186; mains R$43-68; ✆ noon-6pm) With a heralded new chef at the helm, AlbaMar has reinvented itself as a one of Rio's top seafood destinations. Top picks are fresh oysters, grilled seafood with vegetables and *moqueca* dishes. The old-fashioned green gazebo-like structure offers excellent views of the Baía de Guanabara and Niterói.

Santa Teresa & Lapa

Santa Teresa has superb views, while Lapa has an unrivaled music scene, and both are excellent places to discover a mix of new and old-fashioned eating and drinking haunts.

BUDGET

Cafecito (Map p138; Rua Pascoal Carlos Magno 121, Santa Teresa; sandwiches R$10-22; ✆ 10am-10pm Tue-Sun) A few steps above street level, this open-air café serves imported beers, desserts, cocktails (caipirinhas and mojitos), tapas plates and gourmet sandwiches (with ingredients such as smoked trout, artichoke hearts, prosciutto).

Jasmim Mango (Map p138; ☎ 2242 2605; Largo do Guimarães 143, Santa Teresa; mains R$13-25; ✆ 10am-11pm) Well-placed beside the *bonde* stop, Jasmim Mango is a charming spot to linger over sandwiches, quiches, pastas, pizzas and desserts. There's an airy patio in back and several computers on the 2nd floor for checking email.

MIDRANGE & TOP END

Encontras Cariocas (Map p138; ☎ 2221 0028; Av Mem de Sá 77, Lapa; pizzas R$14-30; ☎ 6pm-5am Wed-Sun) This late-night pizza parlor is a good place to stop in while exploring Lapa's music scene. You'll find 24 pizza varieties amid old-fashioned charm – high wooden ceilings, brick walls and warm lighting.

Largo das Letras (Map p138; ☎ 2221 8992; Rua Almirante Alexandrino 501, Santa Teresa; pizzas R$15-25; ✆ 2-10pm Tue-Sat, 2-8pm Sun) Directly above the Largo do Guimarães *bonde* stop, this low-key café, bookstore and cultural spot (with capoeira classes four nights a week) has outdoor tables where neighborhood crowds enjoy decent pizzas (served from 5pm onwards). There's live music from Wednesday to Sunday.

Santa Scenarium (Map p138; ☎ 3147 9007; Rua Lavradio 36, Lapa; mains R$16-25; ✆ 11:30am-midnight) This atmospheric restaurant on Lapa's antique row serves grilled meats and other Brazilian staples, as well as cold beer, appetizers and sandwiches (such as the popular filet mignon on ciabatta). There's live music most nights.

Nova Capela (Map p138; ☎ 2252 6228; Av Mem de Sá 96, Lapa; mains R$18-50; ✆ 11am-late) Nova Capela serves traditional Portuguese cuisine. *Cabrito* (goat) is very popular. It stays open late into the night, and fills with a garrulous mix of neighborhood regulars, party kids and assorted characters who stumble in off the street.

Bar do Mineiro (Map p138; ☎ 2221 9227; Rua Paschoal Carlos Magno 99, Santa Teresa; mains for 2 R$50-60; ✆ 11am-1am Tue-Sun) Photographs of old Rio cover the walls of this old-school *boteco* in the heart of Santa Teresa. The *feijoada*, served daily, is tops. Other popular dishes include *pasteis* (savory pastries) filled with *abóbora* (pumpkin) or *carne-seca*. Strong caipirinhas will help get you in the mood.

Espírito Santa (Map p138; ☎ 2508 7095; Rua Almirante Alexandrino 264, Santa Teresa; mains R$27-38; ✆ noon-6pm Mon & Wed, to midnight Thu-Sat, to 10pm Sun) Espírito Santa is set in a beautifully restored mansion in Santa Teresa, with sweeping views from its back patio. The cuisine is no less amazing: the chef expertly prepares rich meat and seafood dishes from the Amazon.

our pick Sobrenatural (Map p138; ☎ 2224 1003; Rua Almirante Alexandrino 432, Santa Teresa; mains for 2 R$70-85 ✆ noon-midnight Mon-Sat) The exposed brick and old hardwood ceiling set the stage for feasting on the *frutos do mar* (seafood). Lines gather on weekends for grilled fish and *moqueca*. During the week, stop by for lunchtime specials.

Aprazível (Map p138; ☎ 3852 4935; Rua Aprazível 62, Santa Teresa; mains around R$40; ✆ noon-1am Thu-Sat, noon-7pm Sun) Hidden on a winding road high up in Santa Teresa, Aprazível has beautiful views and a lush garden setting. The menu features gourmet Brazilian fare. Unfortunately, it's often booked by tour groups, so reserve ahead.

Térèze (Map p138; ☎ 3380 0220; Hotel Santa Teresa, Rua Almirante Alexandrino 660, Santa Teresa; mains R$55; ☺ noon-5pm daily, 7pm-midnight Mon-Sat) Térèze provides a memorable dining experience, from the inventive menu (char-grilled octopus with couscous salad, black risotto with seafood, macadamia-crusted veal tenderloin), to the suggested wine pairings and the superb views over the city. Even the design is green – tables and artwork are made from reclaimed lumber and recycled materials.

Barra & Greater Rio

Outside the city limits one can find fresh seafood in open-air spots overlooking the coast.

Bira (off Map p131; ☎ 2410 8304; Estrada da Vendinha 68A, Barra de Guaratiba; mains for 2 R$95-125; ☺ noon-6pm Thu & Fri, noon-8pm Sat & Sun) Splendid views of Restinga de Marambaia await diners who make the trek to Bira, about 45 minutes outside of the city. On a breezy, wooden deck, you can feast on *moquecas*, sea bass, shrimp and crabmeat pastries.

Tia Palmira (off Map p131; ☎ 2410 8169; Caminho do Souza 18, Barra de Guaratiba; set lunch R$60; ☺ 11:30am-5pm Tue-Sun) A venerable destination for 40 years, Tia Palmira wins fans with its seafood *rodízio*. Plate after plate of *vatapá* (a seafood dish with a thick sauce of manioc paste, coconut and *dendê* or palm oil), crabmeat, grilled fish, shrimp pastries and other fruits of the sea come to your table until you can eat no more.

DRINKING

Leblon and Ipanema offer flashy nightspots, as well as old-school watering holes. A youthful bar scene draws revelers to Gávea, while scenic Lagoa draws mostly couples. Centro's narrow pedestrian streets attract drinkers during weekday cocktail hours, while a mix of old and new clutters the streets of Lapa and Santa Teresa.

Ipanema & Leblon

Academia da Cachaça (Map p132; ☎ 2239 1542; Rua Conde de Bernadotte 26G, Leblon; ☺ noon-1am Sun-Thu, to 2am Fri & Sat) Along with traditional Brazilian cooking, this indoor-outdoor spot serves over 500 varieties of *cachaça*. For a treat (and/or a bad hangover), try the passion-fruit *batida* (*cachaça* and passion-fruit juice).

Bar Veloso (Map p132; ☎ 2274 9966; Rua Aristides Espínola, Leblon; ☺ 11am-3am) The open-sided

Bar Veloso attracts a young, good-looking crowd who spill out onto the sidewalk on busy weekends.

Baretto-Londra (Map p132; ☎ 3202 4000; Av Vieira Souto 80, Ipanema; ☺ 7pm-2am Mon-Thu, to 4am Fri & Sat) Inside Hotel Fasano, Rio's glammiest bar has a loungey atmosphere, an A-list crowd and pricey drinks (beer R$16, martinis R$26).

Barthodomeu (Map p132; ☎ 2247 8609; Rua Maria Quitéria 46, Ipanema; ☺ noon-2am) Barthodomeu is a friendly bar that has *boteco* charm – open-sided, wood tables, minimal decor and piping hot appetizers, including tasty mini-*moquecas* (seafood stew).

Cobal de Leblon (Map p132; Rua Gilberto Cardoso, Leblon; ☺ closed Mon) Leblon's popular market features a number of open-air bars and restaurants, and it's a great spot to catch a football match on game day.

Devassa (Map p132; ☎ 2522 0627; Rua Prudente de Moraes 416, Ipanema; ☺ noon-2am) Devassa makes its own creamy brews, serving them up to chatty Cariocas at this bar and restaurant chain. The choices: *loura* (pilsner), *sarará* (wheat beer), *ruiva* (pale ale), *negra* (dark ale) and *Índia* (IPA).

Empório (Map p132; ☎ 3813 2526; Rua Maria Quitéria 37, Ipanema; ☺ 8pm-4am) A young mix of Cariocas and gringos stirs things up over cheap cocktails and blaring music at this battered Ipanema favorite.

Garota de Ipanema (Map p132; ☎ 2523 3787; Rua Vinícius de Moraes 49, Ipanema; ☺ 10:30am-2:30am) The famed spot where Tom Jobim and Vinícius de Moraes wrote *A Garota de Ipanema* (The Girl from Ipanema) draws a mix of tourists and locals. It serves excellent *picanha Brasileira*, a skillet of sizzling sliced sirloin.

Jobi (Map p132; ☎ 2274 0547; Av Ataúlfo de Paiva 1166, Leblon; ☺ 9am-4am) A favorite since 1956, Jobi is one of Leblon's most traditional drinking spots. Grab a seat by the sidewalk, order a cold beverage and watch the night unfold.

Shenanigan's (Map p132; ☎ 2267 5860; Rua Visconde de Pirajá 112A, Ipanema; ☺ 6pm-3am Mon-Fri, 2pm-3am Sat, to 2am Sun) Cariocas and sunburnt gringos mix it up over games of pool and darts at this Irish pub. Live bands play occasionally.

Gávea, Jardim Botânico & Lagoa

Bar Lagoa (Map p132; ☎ 2523 1135; Av Epitácio Pessoa 1674, Lagoa; ☺ 6pm-2am Mon-Fri, noon-2am Sat & Sun) Overlooking the lake, Bar Lagoa is one of the neighborhood's classic haunts. A youthful air pervades the ever-crowded tables.

Caroline Café (Map p132; ☎ 2540 0705; Rua JJ Seabra 10, Jardim Botânico; ◷ 6pm-3am Sun-Thu, to 4am Fri, 7pm-4am Sat) This scenic indoor-outdoor spot is a major date spot (it's mostly couples).

Da Graça (Map p132; ☎ 2249 5484; Rua Pacheco Leão 780, Jardim Botânico; ◷ noon-2am Tue-Thu & Sun, to 3am Fri & Sat) Colorful Da Graça is one of Jardim Botânico's liveliest bars, with a festive and colorfully kitsch decor and sidewalk tables packed on weekends.

Drink Café (Map p132; ☎ 2239 4136; Parque dos Patins, Av Borges de Medeiros, Lagoa; live-music charge R$5; ◷ 5pm-2am Mon, 9am-2am Tue-Sun) One of several, open-air restaurants along the lake, the Drink Café hosts live jazz and bossa nova most nights.

Hipódromo (Map p132; ☎ 2274 9720; Praça Santos Dumont 108, Gávea; ◷ 8pm-3am) Hipódromo is one of several bars in the area responsible for the local residents' chronic lack of sleep. A young college-age crowd celebrates here most nights.

Palaphita Kitch (Map p132; ☎ 2227 0837; Av Epitácio Pessoa, Lagoa; ◷ 6pm-3am) A great spot for a sundowner, Palaphita Kitch is an open-air, thatched-roof wonderland with rustic bamboo furniture, flickering tiki torches, and a peaceful setting on the edge of the lake. Has creative (and pricey) cocktails.

Copacabana & Leme

Copa's beach kiosks (p168) are also a fine destination for an afternoon or early-evening drink.

Botequim Informal (Map p134; ☎ 3816 0909; Rua Domingos Ferreira 215, Copacabana; ◷ noon-1am) An anchor of the newly emerging nightlife stretch known as Baixo Copa, Botequim Informal is a lively drinking spot with an elevated open-sided deck, frothy drafts and tasty appetizers

Espelunca Chic (Map p134; ☎ 2236 4090; Rua Bolívar 17A, Copacabana; ◷ 5pm-3am) This inviting open-sided drinking spot (which means 'chic dump') attracts a fifty-fifty blend of neighborhood locals and tourists who stumble upon it from nearby hotels.

Horse's Neck (Map p134; ☎ 2525 1232; Sofitel Rio de Janeiro, Av Atlântica 4240, Copacabana; ◷ noon-2am) Ocean breezes and potted palms give a tropical vibe to this 2nd-floor hotel bar with lovely views across Copacabana Beach.

Sindicato do Chopp (Map p134; ☎ 2541 3133; Av Atlântica 514, Leme; ◷ 11am-3am) With a peaceful beachfront location, this casual bar is a relaxing and largely local spot to enjoy a draft or a filling meal.

Botafogo & Urca

Cobal do Humaitá (Map p136; Rua Voluntaírios da Pátria, Botafogo) A large food market on the western edge of Botafogo (technically in Humaitá), the Cobal transforms into a festive nightspot when the sun goes down, complete with live music and open-air eating and drinking.

Bar Urca (Map p136; ☎ 2295 8744; Rua Cândido Gaffré 205, Urca; ◷ 8am-11pm Mon-Sat, to 8pm Sun) This simple neighborhood bar and restaurant is in a marvelous setting near the waterfront. At night patrons take a seat along the seaside wall as waiters bring cold drinks and appetizers.

Champanharia Ovelha Negra (Map p136; ☎ 2226 1064; Rua Bambina 120, Botafogo; ◷ 5:30-11:30pm Mon-Fri) One of Rio's best happy-hour scenes, Ovelha Negra serves tasty appetizers and 40 different varieties of champagne and *prosecco* (Italian sparkling white wine).

O Plebeu (Map p136; ☎ 2286 0699; Rua Capitão Salomão 50, Botafogo; ◷ 11:30am-4am Mon-Sat, 11:30am-9:30pm Sun) In the liveliest stretch of Botafogo, O Plebeu is a welcoming, open-sided two-story bar with tables spilling onto the sidewalk and a 2nd-floor balcony.

Flamengo & Catete

Belmonte (Map p136; ☎ 2552 3349; Praia do Flamengo 300, Flamengo; mains R$18-36; ◷ 7am-late) This wildly popular *boteco*, a chain started by a poor Northeasterner in the '50's, Belmonte serves up well-chilled *chope* until late into the night. Thursday is currently the liveliest night to go.

Devassa (Map p136; ☎ 2556 0618; Rua Senador Vergueiro 2; ◷ noon-1am) A particularly inviting branch of the Devassa network, this bar is set on a shaded square, and serves the usual Devassa hits, including great drafts.

Herr Brauer (Map p136; ☎ 2225 4359; Rua Barão do Flamengo 35; ◷ noon-midnight Tue-Sun, noon-4pm Mon) Dedicated to the great beers of the world, this tiny drinking den has earned admirers for its Belgian and German beers.

Centro & Cinelândia

Amarelinho (Map p138; ☎ 2240 8434; Praça Floriano 55, Cinelândia; ◷ 11am-2am) With tables spilling onto Praça Floriano, Amarelinho is a popular spot for lunch and that ever-important after-work drink.

Boteco Casual (Map p138; ☎ 2232 0250; Travessa do Comércio 26; ◷ 11am-midnight Mon-Fri; 11am-6pm Sat) On weeknights, Cariocas pack the sidewalk tables at this popular bar – one of several low-key open-air spots on the pedestrian-only Travessa do Comércio.

Santa Teresa & Lapa

Armazém São Thiago (Map p138; ☎ 2232 0822; Rua Áurea 26, Santa Teresa; ☟ noon-midnight Mon-Sat, to 10pm Sun) Still referred to by everyone as the 'Bar do Gomes', this historic, but still hole-in-the-wall drinking establishment features a few stand-up tables and a counter. It doesn't look like much but crowds pack this place on weekends, with punters spilling onto the sidewalks.

Bar dos Descasados (Map p138; ☎ 2222 2755; Rua Almirante Alexandrino 660, Santa Teresa; ☟ noon-midnight) Inside the Hotel Santa Teresa (p164), this stylish bar with outdoor seating has lovely views over the city (looking north) and decadent cocktails (including a caipirinha made with tangerines grown on the property) It's usually empty during the week and a livelier destination, mostly for couples, on weekends.

Boteco do Gomes (Map p138; ☎ 2531 9717; Rua do Riachuelo 62, Lapa; ☟ 7am-1am) In Lapa, this *boteco* has the look of an old-time bar with brick walls, art-deco light fixtures, and tile floors. A mix of musicians, students and Lapa hangabouts gather for a drink at stand-up tables in front or in the roomier back dining area.

Choperia Brazooka (Map p138; ☎ 2224 3235; Rua Mem de Sá 70, Lapa; ☟ 6pm-2am Tue-Wed, 6pm-5am Thu-Sat) This popular four-story beer house has lots of nooks and crannies where you can while away the night over ice-cold drafts and tasty appetizers. The 20- and 30-something crowd packs this place, so arrive early to score a table.

Goya-Beira (Map p140; ☎ 2221 4863; Largo das Neves 13, Santa Teresa; ☟ 6pm-midnight Sun-Thu, to 2am Fri & Sat) Small but charming, Goya-Beira faces peaceful Largo das Neves, with the occasional tram rattling by. The open-sided bar draws a vibrant mix on weekends. It's fine to arrive and leave by tram, but it's unsafe to walk here from Largo do Guimarães – take a taxi instead.

Mike's Haus (Map p138; ☎ 2509 5248; Rua Almirante Alexandrino 1458A, Santa Teresa; ☟ noon-midnight Tue-Sun) This German-style pub serves frothy German beers and filling pub grub. It's a bit off the beaten path, so plan on sticking around before moving on.

ENTERTAINMENT
Music & Dancing

Rio's music scene features some incredibly talented performers playing in atmospheric settings to a democratic crowd. Lapa is the heart

of samba, and its old clubs are a must-see for visitors. The widest assortment of music venues is along Av Mem de Sá. In the summer, the city hosts its **Noites Cariocas** (www.noitescariocas .com.br) big parties at Pier Mauá, just north of Centro that have seen the likes of Caetano Veloso, Jorge Ben Jor and other big names.

LIVE MUSIC
Lapa

Beco do Rato (Map p138; ☎ 2508 9574; Rua Morais e Vale 5, Lapa; admission free; ☟ 8pm-3am Tue-Fri) One of Lapa's classic samba spots, this small outdoor bar has excellent live groups playing to a laidback crowd. Friday nights are particularly recommended.

Circo Voador (Map p138; ☎ 2533 5873; www.circo voador.com.br, in Portuguese; Rua dos Arcos, Lapa; admission R$30-50) In a curvilinear building behind the Arcos da Lapa, this concert space hosts big names like Chico Buarque and Jorge Ben Jor as well as up-and-coming bands playing rock, ska, funk and samba.

Estrela da Lapa (Map p138; ☎ 2507 6686; Av Mem de Sá 69, Lapa; admission R$15-30; ☟ 7pm-1am Mon, 9pm-2am Tue-Sun) Inside a restored 19th-century mansion, Estrela da Lapa has an eclectic music scene and hosts bands playing *choro*, blues and hip-hop. On weekends, shows are followed by a DJ who keeps the dance floor going until late.

Fundição Progresso (Map p138; ☎ 2220 5070; www .fundicao.org, in Portuguese; Rua dos Arcos 24, Lapa; admission R$20-35) Inside this enormous old factory are several stages that host some of the best concerts and arts events in Lapa.

Semente (Map p138; ☎ 9781 2451; Rua Joaquim Silva 138, Lapa; admission R$15-25; ☟ 8pm-2am Sat-Thu) This tiny bar hosts up-and-coming samba and *choro* groups and is a more authentic space to find samba's soul. Sunday and Monday nights are current picks.

Other Locations

Allegro Bistrô Musical (Map p134; ☎ 2548 5005; www .modernsound.com.br; Modern Sound, Rua Barata Ribeiro 502, Copacabana; admission free; ☟ 9am-9pm Mon-Fri, to 8pm Sat) The small café in Copacabana's excellent music store, Modern Sound, features live music most nights of the week, typically from 5pm to 9pm.

Bip Bip (Map p134; ☎ 2267 9696; Rua Almirante Gonçalves 50, Copacabana; ☟ 8pm-midnight) A neighborhood institution, Bip Bip has been hosting samba jams for more than 15 years. The ambience is simple: just a breadbox-sized storefront with tables spilling onto the sidewalk. Current schedule: samba on Thursday and Sunday at 8pm, Choro on Tuesday and Wednesday at 8:30pm and Bossa Nova on Monday at 9pm.

Casa Rosa (Map p136; ☎ 2557 2562; Rua Alice 550, Laranjeiras; admission R$15-25; ☑ 11pm-5am Fri & Sat, 7pm-2am Sun) One of Rio's best nightspots, the Casa Rosa has a large outdoor patio between several dance floors, where different bands play throughout the night.

Espaço Rio Carioca (Map p136; ☎ 2225 7332; www .espacoriocarioca.com.br; Rua Leite Leal 45, Laranjeiras; ☑ 3-10pm Mon-Fri, noon-10pm Sat & Sun; admission R$10-20) This creative space (equal parts bookstore, café and bistro), hosts live music from Wednesday to Saturday (MPB, jazz), beginning around 8:30pm.

Maze Inn (Map p136; ☎ 2558 5547; www.jazzrio.info; Casa 66, Rua Tavares Bastos 414, Catete; admission before/after 10pm R$10/20; ☑ 10pm-3am 1st Fri of month) This once-a-month event is well worth attending if you're in town. It's set in the guesthouse of the same name (p163) high up in Tavares Bastos (Rio's safest favela). There's a fun mix of Cariocas and expats, with good live jazz and fantastic views.

Praia Vermelha (Map p136; ☎ 2275 7292; Praça General Tibúrcio, Urca; admission R$6-12; ☑ noon-midnight Mon-Sat) Perched over the beach of the same name, Praia Vermelha has gorgeous views of Pão de Açúcar looming overhead. By night, jazzy MPB bands play from 6pm onward, making for an enviable open-air setting. The food, unfortunately, is less spectacular.

Severyna (Map p136; ☎ 2556 9398; Rua Ipiranga 54, Laranjeiras; admission R$10; ☑ 11:30am-2am) At night this barnlike dining hall hosts live bands playing *forró* and other music from Northeastern Brazil. Shows begin around 8pm.

Vinícius Piano Bar (Map p132; ☎ 2523 4757; Rua Prudente de Morais 34, Ipanema; admission R$30-40) Billing itself as the 'temple of bossa nova,' Vinícius Piano Bar has been an icon in the neighbor-hood since the late '80s. The small, intimate upstairs music space hosts a fine assortment of jazz and bossa nova groups.

SAMBA CLUBS

Gafieiras (dance halls) are a big attraction in Lapa. Here you'll find restored colonial buildings hiding dance floors and large samba bands – along with their many admirers.

Carioca da Gema (Map p138; ☎ 2221 0043; Av Mem de Sá 79, Lapa; admission R$20-25; ☑ closed Sun) One of the first to bring samba back to Lapa, this small, colorful club hosts an excellent line-up of bands and a good mixed crowd that packs the dance floor most nights.

Centro Cultural Carioca (Map p138; ☎ 2252 6468; www.centroculturalcarioca.com.br; Rua do Teatro 37, Centro; admission R$20-30; ☑ 7pm-1am Mon-Thu 8:30pm-2am Fri & Sat) This restored theater, on Praça Tiradentes, books top samba groups throughout the year, and it's a historic setting in which to hear – and dance to – live music.

Democráticus (Map p138; ☎ 2252 4611; Rua do Riachuelo 91, Lapa; admission R$20-40; ☑ 10pm-4am Wed, 11pm-4am Thu-Sat, 8pm-midnight Sun) This spacious 19th-century dance hall has an enormous dance floor and a long stage, covered with musicians. For an authentic slice of Rio's old-fashioned love of samba, Democráticus is hard to beat.

Lapa 40 Graus (Map p138; ☎ 3970 1338; Rua Riachuelo 97, Lapa; admission R$5; ☑ 6pm-4am) This impressive multistory music venue and pool hall has tables for lounging on the 1st floor, pool tables on the 2nd floor, and a small stage and dancing on the top floor (admission to shows is R$5 to R$30).

Rio Scenarium (Map p138; ☎ 3147 9005; Rua Lavradio 20, Lapa; admission R$15-25; ☎ 7pm-2:30am Tue-Sat) Perhaps Rio's most beautiful nightspot, Rio Scenarium has three antique-filled floors, with balconies overlooking the stage on the 1st floor. Talented samba bands play to a dance-happy crowd, about half of whom are tourists.

TICKET MATTERS

When entering most samba clubs and live-music bars (plus self-serve restaurants) you'll be handed a ticket, which is used to track your consumption throughout the evening. When you're ready to move on, you'll pay a cashier for the goods (and possibly an admission fee). The cashier will then give you another ticket to pass onto the door attendant as you exit. It's all wonderfully Brezhnevian – but saves you the trouble of having to cough up every time you order a cocktail. Don't lose that ticket, as you may be charged R$100 or more. You'll see this system in many areas of Brazil.

Trapiche Gamboa (Map p138; ☎ 2516 0868; www .trapichegamboa.com.br, in Portuguese; Rua Sacadura Cabral 155, Gamboa; admission R$12-20; ☼ 7pm-2am Tue-Thu, to 3am Fri, 9pm-4am Sat) Another charming live samba joint, Trapiche Gamboa is set in a multistory colonial edifice in Gamboa (just north of Centro) and has a welcoming vibe, with samba musicians gathering around a table on the ground floor, and dancers spilling out around them. It's best reached by taxi (around R$25 from the Zona Sul).

SAMBA SCHOOLS

Starting around September, in preparation for Carnaval, most big samba schools open their rehearsals to the public. These are large dance parties, and provide a good chance to mingle with Cariocas. Schools typically charge R$5 to R$30 at the door (prices are higher the closer you are to Carnaval). Many samba schools are in the favelas, so use common sense when going.

You can visit the samba schools on a tour (see p158) or you can go by yourself: you can catch a taxi there, and there are always cabs outside the schools waiting to take people home. It's a good idea to confirm that the rehearsals are on before heading out. Following is a list of some of the more popular samba schools, rehearsal days and contact information. The most popular schools for tourists are Mangueira and Salgueiro.

Beija-Flor (☎ 2791 2866; www.beija-flor.com.br; Pracinha Wallace Paes Leme 1025, Nilópolis; ☼ 9pm Thu)

Grande Rio (☎ 2671 3585; www.granderio.org.br; Rua Almirante Barroso 5-6, Duque de Caixas; ☼ 10pm Fri)

Imperatriz Leopoldinense (☎ 2560 8037; www .imperatrizleopoldinense.com.br; Rua Professor Lacê 235, Ramos; ☼ 8pm Sun)

Mangueira (Map p131; ☎ 2567 4637; www.mangueira .com.br; Rua Visconde de Niterói 1072, Mangueira; ☼ 10pm Sat)

Mocidade Independente de Padre Miguel (☎ 3332 5823; www.mocidadeindependente.com.br; Rua Coronel Tamarindo 38, Padre Miguel; ☼ 10pm Sat)

Porta da Pedra (☎ 3707 1518; www.unidosdoporto-dapedra.com.br; Av Lúcio Tomé Feteiro 290, Vila Lage, São Gonçalo; ☼ 8pm Wed)

Portela (☎ 2489 6440; Rua Clara Nunes 81, Madureira; ☼ 10pm Fri)

Rocinha (Map p131; ☎ 3205 3318; www.academi cosdarocinha.com.br; Rua Bertha Lutz 80, São Conrado; ☼ 10pm Sat)

Salgueiro (Map p131; ☎ 2238 0389; www.salgueiro .com.br; Rua Silva Teles 104, Andaraí; ☼ 10pm Sat)

Unidos da Tijuca (☎ 2518 3957; www.unidosdatijuca .com.br; Clube dos Portuários, Rua Francisco Bicalho 47, Cidade Nova; ☼ 10pm Sat)

Vila Isabel (☎ 2578 0077; www.gresunidosdevilaisabel .com.br; Av 28 de Setembro 382, Vila Isabel; ☼ 10pm Sat)

NIGHTCLUBS

Flyers advertising dance parties can be found in music stores and clothing shops in Ipanema and Leblon, and in the surf shops in Galeria River shopping center, near Praia de Arpoador. Some clubs give a discount if you've got a flyer.

00 (Zero Zero; Map p132; ☎ 2540 8041; Planetário, Av Padre Leonel Franca 240, Gávea; admission R$20-50; ☼ 10pm-4am Thu-Sun) Housed in Gávea's planetarium, 00 (Zero Zero) is a restaurant by day, sleek lounge by night. With an outdoor patio and some of Rio's best DJs, 00 has a solid reputation in the fashion-literate party crowd.

Baronneti (Map p132; ☎ 2522 1460; Rua Barão da Torre 354, Ipanema; admission R$20-35; ☼ 11pm-5am Tue-Sun) One of Ipanema's few nightclubs, Baronneti has a sleek and trim interior with two dance floors. Given its prime Zona Sul location, you'll find a young, well-heeled crowd here. Eclectic DJs and fruity cocktails keep the fans returning.

Casa da Matriz (Map p136; ☎ 2266 1014; www.casada matriz.com.br, in Portuguese; Rua Henrique de Novaes 107, Botafogo; admission R$10-25; ☼ 11pm-4am Mon & Thu-Sat) Artwork lines this space in Botafogo. With numerous rooms to explore (lounge, screening room, dance floors) this old mansion embodies the creative side of the Carioca spirit.

Clandestino (Map p134; ☎ 3209 0348; Rua Barata Ribeiro 111, Copacabana; admission R$10-30; ☼ 11pm-5am Wed-Sat) Next door to Stone of a Beach hostel, Clandestino brings together Cariocas and backpackers, with an urban underground vibe, courtesy of DJs spinning hip-hop and funk and art films playing on a screen in the background.

Fosfobox (Map p134; ☎ 2548 7498; Rua Siqueira Campos 143, Copacabana; admission R$10-25; ☼ 11pm-4am Thu-Sat) This subterranean club is hidden under a shopping center near the metro station. Good DJs spin everything from funk to glam rock, and the crowd here is one of Rio's more eclectic.

Melt (Map p132; ☎ 2249 9309; Rua Rita Ludolf 47A, Leblon; admission R$10-30; ☼ 10pm-3am) The sinewy Melt club is one of those places that couldn't possibly be anywhere but Leblon. Models and their admirers lie draped around the candle-lit lounge, while wait staff glide between the

GAY RIO

Rio has been a major destination for gay travelers since the 1950s. Back then the action was near the Copacabana Palace – and remnants of the past are still there (look for the rainbow-hued flag). Today, however, the party has mostly moved on, with the focal point of the GLBT (gay, lesbian, bisexual, transgender) scene, especially for visitors, in Ipanema. The gay beach sits at the end of Rua Farme de Amoedo (again, look for the rainbow flag), while bars and cafés of nearby streets – Rua Teixeira de Melo and Rua Farme de Amoeda have a sprinkling of gay bars and cafés.

Nightlife

For more info on what's happening around town, check out www.riogayguide.com.

Cabaret Casanova (Map p138; ☎ 2221 6555; Av Mem de Sá 25, Lapa; ⏰ Fri & Sat) This is one of Rio's oldest clubs, featuring a good mixed crowd, drag queens and slightly trashy music.

Cafeína (Map p132; ☎ 2521 2194; Rua Farme de Amoeda 43, Ipanema; ⏰ 8am-11:30pm) A popular Ipanema café that attracts a mix of gays and straights.

Cine Ideal (Map p138; ☎ 2252 3460; www.cineideal.com.br, in Portuguese; Rua da Carioca 62, Centro; ⏰ Fri & Sat) An old movie theater, and now an electronic music club, Ideal has an outdoor terrace with views of old Rio.

Dama de Ferro (Map p132; ☎ 2247 2330; www.damadeferro.com.br, in Portuguese; Rua Vinícius de Moraes 288, Ipanema; ⏰ Tue-Sat) This club boasts one of the best electronic-music scenes in town but no one goes until very late.

Fosfobox (Map p134; ☎ 2548 9478; basement level, loja 22A, Rua Siqueira Campos 143, Copacabana; ⏰ Tue-Sun) This small underground club has live alternative bands, a mixed crowd and easygoing ambience.

Galeria Café (Map p132; ☎ 2523 8250; www.galeriacafe.com.br; Rua Teixeira de Mello 31, Ipanema; ⏰ Thu-Sat) This bar with a mixed crowd has lovely decor.

La Girl (Map p134; ☎ 2247 8342; www.lagirl.com.br, in Portuguese; Rua Raul Pompéia 102, Copacabana; ⏰ Mon, Fri & Sat) This lesbian club has a great atmosphere.

Le Boy (Map p134; ☎ 2513 4993; www.leboy.com.br, in Portuguese; Rua Raul Pompéia 102, Copacabana; ⏰ Tue-Sun) Open since 1992, Le Boy is Rio's gay temple. There are theme nights with drag shows and go-go boys.

Star Club (Map p138; Buraco Da Lacraia; ☎ 2242 0446; Rua André Cavalcante 58, Lapa; ⏰ Thu-Sat) You'll find glamorous and trashy visitors, bizarre drag shows, karaoke, a dark room and other attractions.

Tô Nem Aí (Map p132; ☎ 2247 8403; Rua Farme de Amoeda 57, Ipanema; ⏰ noon-3am) On Ipanema's gayest street, this popular bar is a great after-beach spot.

The Week (Map p138; ☎ 2253 1020; Rua Sacadura Cabral 154, Centro; ⏰ Sat) Rio's newest and currently best gay dance club has a spacious dance floor, excellent DJs and go-go dancers.

tables delivering colorful cocktails. Upstairs, DJs break beats over the dance floor, occasionally accompanied by a few percussionists.

Nuth Lounge (Map p131; ☎ 3575 6850; www.nuth.com.br, in Portuguese; Av Armando Lombardi 999, Barra da Tijuca; admission men R$40-70, women R$20-30; ⏰ 9pm-4am) This club (pronounced 'Nooch') is one of the city's favorite dance spots, despite its location in Barra. Expect a friendly, well-dressed crowd grooving to DJs spinning electro-samba, house and hip-hop. There's also a newer **Nuth Club** (Map p132; Av Epitácio Pessoa 1244) in Lagoa that attracts much the same beautiful crowd.

Classical Music, Theater & Dance

Classical music lovers should try to attend a concert held during the four-month-long **Música No Museu** (www.musicanomuseu.com.br). Held from January to April each year, this event features dozens of concerts (all free) held at museums and cultural spaces around the city.

The city's most lavish setting for a performance is the beaux-arts **Theatro Municipal** (Map p138; ☎ 2332 9195; www.theatromunicipal.rj.gov.br, in Portuguese; Rua Manuel de Carvalho, Centro). You'll find a more exciting repertoire of modern dance, theater and performance art at the excellent **Espaço Sesc** (Map p134; ☎ 2547 0156; Rua Domingos Ferreira, Copacabana). In Lapa the **Sala Cecília Meireles** (Map p138; ☎ 2332 9176; www.salaceciliameireles.com.br, in Portuguese; Largo da Lapa 47, Lapa; ⏰ box office 1-6pm) is a splendid early-20th-century gem hosting orchestral concerts throughout the year.

Cinemas

One of Latin America's film centers, Rio remains remarkably open to foreign and independent films, documentaries and avant-garde cinema. The big cinematic event is the Rio International Film Festival in late September and early October (see p159). For listings and show times pick up *O Globo*, *Jornal do Brasil* newspapers or *Veja Rio* magazine. Ticket prices run R$14 to R$24. In addition to these cinemas, the major shopping centers (p180) also have cinemas.

Cineclube Laura Alvim (Map p132; ☎ 2267 1647; Av Vieira Souto 176, Ipanema) Set in Ipanema's Laura Alvim cultural center.

Cine Santa Teresa (Map p138; 2222 0203; www .cinesanta.com.br; Rua Paschoal Carlos Magno 136, Santa Teresa) Small, single-screen theater on Largo do Guimarães.

Espaço de Cinema (Map p136; ☎ 2226 1986; Rua Voluntários da Pátria 35, Botafogo) Two-screen Botafogo cinema with a café.

Estação Ipanema (Map p132; ☎ 2279 4603; Rua Visconde de Pirajá 605, Ipanema)

Odeon Petrobras (Map p138; ☎ 2240 1093; Praça Floriano 7, Cinelândia) Rio's landmark cinema is a beautiful old theater.

Roxy (Map p134; ☎ 2461 2461; Av NS de Copacabana 945, Copacabana) Copacabana's only cinema.

Spectator Sports
FOOTBALL
Maracanã Football Stadium (Map p140; ☎ 2334 1705; Av Maracanã, São Cristóvão; admission R$15-100) Brazil's Valhalla of soccer is currently receiving a major upgrade in preparation for the 2014 World Cup and the 2016 Olympics, and it remains closed until 2012. For more info see p151).

Several English-speaking tour operators organize game-day outings, including **Brazil Expedition** (☎ 9998 2907, 7894 7523; www.brazilexpedi tion.com; R$70 per person), **Be a Local** (☎ 9643 0366; www.bealocal.com; R$80 to R$90 per person) as well as independent guide **Sergio Manhães** (☎ 9210 0119; futebolnomaracana.blogspot.com, ssm10@hotmail.com; R$110 to R$120 per person).

If you go by yourself, take the metro – it's safer and generally less crowded than buses.

Rio's other football stadiums:

Estádio Olímpico João Havelange (Map p131; ☎ 2543 7272; Rua Arquias Cordeiro, Engenho de Dentro) Botafogo's home stadium, Engenhão as it's called was built for the Pan American games in 2007 and seats around 45,000. While Maracanã is closed, both Flamengo and Fluminense are likely to play home games here as well.

Estádio de São Januário (Map p131; ☎ 2580 7373; Rua General Almério de Moura 131, São Cristóvão) Vasco

da Gama's home stadium was built in 1927, and seats around 35,000.

HORSE RACING
Jockey Club Brasileiro (Map p132; ☎ 3534 9000; www .jcb.com.br, in Portuguese; Rua Jardim Botânico 1003, Gávea; 6pm-midnight Mon, 4-11pm Fri, 2-8pm Sat & Sun) One of the country's loveliest racetracks, with a great view of the mountains and Corcovado, the Joquei Clube (Jockey Club) seats 35,000 and lies on the Gávea side of the lake. Tourists are welcome in the members' area, which has a bar overlooking the track. Races are held on Monday, Friday, Saturday and Sunday. The big event is the Brazilian Grand Prix (the first Sunday in August).

SHOPPING
Rio has much in the way of shopping, from colorful markets to eye-catching Zona Sul boutiques. Some of the major strips in the city for window shopping include the following:

Av Ataúlfo de Paiva, Leblon (Map p132) Boutiques selling haute couture sprinkled among cafés, bookshops and restaurants.

Rua Visconde de Pirajá, Ipanema (Map p132) Ipanema's vibrant shopping strip.

Rua do Lavradio, Lapa (Map p138) Long rows of antique stores.

Clothing, Jewelry & Footwear
Espaço Brazilian Soul (Map p132; ☎ 2522 3641; Rua Prudente de Morais 1102, Ipanema) This two-story boutique sells designer duds (Osklen among them) in the form of board shorts, T-shirts, flip-flops and button-downs. There's more men's apparel than women's, though the dresses are worth a peek.

Forum (Map p132; ☎ 2521 7415; www.forum.com.br; Rua Barão da Torre 422, Ipanema; 10am-6pm Mon-Fri, 10am-2pm Sat) Much vaunted Brazilian designer Tufi Duek has set up his flagship store on a peaceful, tree-lined street. You'll find elegant, well-made pieces from his men's and women's collections.

Gilson Martins (Map p132; ☎ 2227 6178; Rua Visconde de Pirajá 462, Ipanema; 10am-8pm Mon-Fri, 10am-4pm Sat) Designer Gilson Martins turns the silhouette of Corcovado and the Brazilian flag into fashion statements in this colorful store. Glossy handbags, wallets and other accessories make good gifts.

Havaianas (Map p134; ☎ 2267 2418; Rua Xavier da Silveira 19, Copacabana; 9am-8pm Mon-Fri, 10am-6pm

Sat & Sun) At this sizeable store, the ubiquitous Brazilian rubber sandal comes in all different styles – sporting the flags of Brazil, Argentina, Portugal, England and Spain, plus snazzy designs for the ladies. There's a smaller Havaianas shop in Ipanema (Map p134; Rua Farme de Amoeda 76).

Isabela Capeto (Map p132; ☎ 2540 5232; Rua Días Ferreira 217, Leblon; ☼ 10am-8pm Mon-Fri, 10am-3pm Sat) Brazilian designer Isabela Capeto sells her beautiful (and expensive) handmade pieces for women from this stylish boutique.

Loja Fla (Map p134; ☎ 2541 4109; Ave NS de Copacabana 219, Copacabana) With more than 30 million fans worldwide, Flamengo is one of the most-watched teams in all of Brazil. This new shop sells all the Flamengo goods, including jerseys, logo-emblazoned socks and footballs, posters and other memorabilia. Prices aren't cheap (jerseys run R$70 to R$160).

Maria Oiticica (Map p132; ☎ 3202 1011; Forum de Ipanema, Rua Visconde de Pirajá 351) Using native materials found in the Amazon, Maria Oiticica has created some lovely handcrafted jewelry inspired by indigenous art. Seeds, plant fibers and tree bark are just some of the ingredients used to make bracelets, necklaces and earrings, and her work helps support struggling local communities with craft-making traditions.

Osklen (Map p132; ☎ 2227 2911; Rua Maria Quitéria 85, Ipanema; ☼ 10am-7pm Mon-Fri, 10am-2pm Sat) One of Brazil's hottest labels, Osklen has an excellent selection of men's and women's beachwear, outerwear, shirts, skirts and shoes.

The museums of H Stern and Amsterdam Sauer (see p142) have stores that sell jewelry, precious stones and other accessories.

Handicrafts & Artwork

In addition to the shops listed here, good places to browse include the handicrafts shop at the Museu do Índio (p144; featuring works made by indigenous artists) and the colorful contemporary design store at the Museu de Arte Moderna (p147).

La Vereda (Map p138; ☎ 2507 0317; Rua Almirante Alexandrino 428, Santa Teresa) Brazilian handicrafts as well as work from local artists and artisans are featured here. Several other handicraft shops are nearby.

O Sol (Map p132; ☎ 2294 5099; Rua Corcovado 213, Jardim Botânico; ☼ closed Sun) Run by a nonprofit organization, this delightful store displays the works of regional artists and sells baskets, woven rugs and Brazilian folk art in clay, wood and porcelain.

Pé de Boi (Map p136; ☎ 2285 4395; Rua Ipiranga 55, Laranjeiras; ☼ 9am-7pm Mon-Fri, 9am-1pm Sat) Rio's best handicrafts stores, Pé de Boi sells works in wood and ceramic as well as tapestries, sculptures and weavings that showcase the talent of artists from Amazonia, Minas Gerais and further afield.

Urucum Art & Design (Map p132; ☎ 2540 9990; Rua Visconde de Pirajá 605, Ipanema; ☼ noon-7pm Mon-Sat) In the same complex as the cinema Estação Ipanema, this tiny shop sells handcrafted woodwork, sculpture, pottery, vases, block prints, playful souvenirs and artwork, most of which is made by artists from Rio or Minas Gerais.

Liquors

Lidador (Map p132; ☎ 2512 1788; Av Ataúlfo de Paiva 1079, Leblon; ☼ 10am-8pm Mon-Fri, 10am-5pm Sat), one of Leblon's best wine shops, stocks Chilean,

---

FOOD MARKETS

The *feiras* (produce markets) that pop up in different locations throughout the week are the best places to shop for *jabuticaba* (grapefuit-like fruit), *acerola* (cherry-flavored fruit) and other fruits you won't find at home (not to mention delectable mangoes, papayas, passion fruit and more).

Cobal do Humaitá (Map p136; ☎ 2266 1343; Rua Voluntários da Pátria 446, Botafogo; ☼ 7am-4pm Mon-Sat) Flowers, veggies and fruits; there are also restaurants on hand for those looking for a bit more.

Cobal de Leblon (Map p133; ☎ 2239 1549; Rua Gilberto Cardoso, Leblon; ☼ 7am-4pm Mon-Sat) Smaller than Humaitá's market, it doubles as an open-air eating-drinking spot in the evening.

Copacabana Wednesday on Rua Domingos Ferreira, Thursday on Rua Belford Roxo and Rua Ronald de Carvalho, Sunday on Rua Décio Vilares.

Ipanema Monday on Rua Henrique Dumont, Tuesday on Praça General Osório and Friday on Praça NS da Paz.

Jardim Botânico Saturday on Rua Frei Leandro.

Leblon Thursday on Rua General Urquiza.

Urca Sunday on Praça Tenente Gil Guilherme.

Argentinean and even Brazilian wines as well as *cachaça* and other spirits. There's also a handy location in **Ipanema** (Map p132; Rua Vinícius de Moraes 120).

Markets

Rio's biggest market is found at the Feira Nordestina (p150) in São Cristóvão.

Av Atlântica Fair (Map p134; Av Atlântica near Rua Djalma Ulrich, Copacabana; ☽ 7pm-midnight) Paintings, drawings, jewelry, clothing and a fair bit of tourist junk make up this Copacabana market. It's on the median along Av Atlântica.

Hippie Fair (Feira de Arte de Ipanema; Map p132; Praça General Osório, Ipanema; ☽ 9am-5pm Sun) The Zona Sul's big market, the Hippie Fair has lots of artwork, jewelry, handicrafts and clothing. Stalls in the east corners of the plaza sell tasty plates of *acarajé* (croquettes, with a sauce of *vatapá* and shrimp, R$7), plus excellent desserts (R$3). Don't miss it.

Feira do Rio Antigo (Rio Antiques Fair; Map p138; Rua do Lavradio, Centro; ☽ 10am-6pm 1st Sat of month) Although the Rio Antiques Fair happens just once a month, don't miss it if you're in town. The colonial buildings become a living installation as the whole street fills with antiques and music.

Praça do Lido Market (Map p134; Praça do Lido, Copacabana; ☽ 8am-6pm Sat & Sun) Copacabana's response to Ipanema's widely popular Hippie Fair, this weekend affair features handicrafts and souvenirs, football jerseys and jewelry stands.

Music

Most places will let you listen to CDs before you buy.

Modern Sound (Map p134; ☎ 2548 5005; www .modernsound.com.br; Rua Barata Ribeiro 502, Copacabana) Rio's largest music stores stocks an impressive selection of samba, electronica, hip-hop, imports, classical and more. Live music shows are staged here most days at Allegro Bistrô Musical (p174).

Plano B (Map p138; ☎ 2507 9860; Rua Francisco Muratori 2A, Lapa) An underground favorite among local DJs, Plano B has new and used records and CDs, as well as a tattoo parlor in the back.

Arlequim (Map p138; ☎ 2220 8471; Av Primeiro de Março, Centro) Set inside the Paço Imperial, Arlequim is a pleasant place to browse for CDs, records and used books (in Portuguese) while exploring the area.

Feira de Música (Map p138; Rua Pedro Lessa, Centro; ☽ 9am-5pm Mon-Fri) During the week browse through bins of records and CDs at this open-air market in Centro.

Musicale (Map p134; ☎ 2267 9607; Av NS de Copacabana 1103C, Copacabana; ☽ 10am-7pm Mon-Fri, 10am-4pm Sat) Musicale has a small but well-curated selection of used CDs, most of which cost between R$16 and R$22. Albums run the gamut between samba, MPB and regional sounds, plus American and British rock and indie as well as world music.

Toca do Vinícius (Map p132; ☎ 2247 5227; www.toca dovinicius.com.br; Rua Vinícius de Moraes 129, Ipanema) Bossa nova's smooth sound lives on in this shop dedicated to old and new artists of the genre. Upstairs, Vinícius de Moraes fans can get a glimpse of his life's work in the small museum dedicated to him.

Shopping Malls

Rio has many large *shoppings* (shopping malls), particularly in Barra. Most open from 10am to 10pm Monday through Saturday. Some open on Sunday as well (3pm to 10pm, typically).

Barra Shopping (Map p131; Av das Américas 4666, Barra da Tijuca) Enormous! It has 500 stores, 42 restaurants and five movie screens.

Botafogo Praia Shopping (Map p136; Praia de Botafogo 400, Botafogo) Great views from top-floor restaurants.

Rio Design Center (Map p132; Av Ataúlfo de Paiva 270, Leblon) Four floors of galleries and stores, plus good restaurants on the ground and basement levels.

Rio Sul (Map p136; Rua Lauro Müller 116, Botafogo) Shops, cinemas, restaurants, crowds.

São Conrado Fashion Mall (Map p131; Estrada da Gávea 899, São Conrado) The city's most upscale boutiques and pretty cafés, too.

Shopping Leblon (Map p132; Av Afrânio de Melo Franco 290, Leblon) Rio's newest, with glitzy shops and enticing eateries.

GETTING THERE & AWAY
Air

Most flights depart from Aeroporto Galeão (off Map p131) also called Aeroporto Antônio Carlos (Tom) Jobim, 15km north of the center. Some flights to/from São Paulo and other Brazilian cities use Aeroporto Santos Dumont (Map p138), east of the city center.

Some airlines:

Azul (☎ 3296 2850; www.voeazul.com.br)

Gol (☎ 0300-115 2121; www.voegol.com.br; Aeroporto Galeão, Aeroporto Santos Dumont) All travel agents sell Gol tickets.

Ocean Air (☎ 4004 4040; www.oceanair.com.br)
TAM (☎ 4002 5700; www.tam.com.br)
Trip (☎ 0300-789 8747; www.voetrip.com.br)

The following lists sample prices on Gol and TAM, Brazil's major carriers. Prices quoted are one-way and leave from Aeroporto Galeão. Given frequent specials and volatile prices, this information is subject to change.

Destination	Airline	Cost (R$)	Frequency
Belém	Gol	300-500	7-10 daily
	TAM	406-724	7-10 daily
Fortaleza	Gol	389-529	14-20 daily
	TAM	428-582	6-12 daily
Foz do Iguaçu	Gol	349-589	6-8 daily
	TAM	329-439	5-7 daily
Manaus	Gol	529-789	6-8 daily
	TAM	471-639	5-8 daily
Recife	Gol	379-619	12-18 daily
	TAM	384-516	12-18 daily
Salvador	Gol	319-439	5-8 daily
	TAM	296-439	8-12 daily
São Paulo	Gol	219-329	8-10 daily
	TAM	208-307	8-12 daily

Bus

Buses leave from the **Rodoviária Novo Rio** (Novo Rio Bus Station; Map p140; ☎ 3213 1800; www.novorio. com.br; Av Francisco Bicalho, São Cristóvão), about 2km northwest of Centro. Several buses depart daily from here to most major destinations, but it's best to buy tickets in advance. Very few travel agencies sell bus tickets, although **Guanatur Turismo** (Map p134; ☎ 2548 3275; Rua Dias da Rocha 16A, Copacabana; www.guanaturturismo.com.br) does sell bus tickets to main domestic and international destinations. It's worth paying Gunatur's small commission to avoid a long trip to the bus station to buy advance tickets.

If you arrive in Rio by bus, it's a good idea to take a taxi to your hotel, as the bus station is in a seedy area. To arrange a cab, go to the small booth near the Riotur desk, on the 1st floor of the bus station. Average fares are R$35 to the international airport and R$30 to Copacabana or Ipanema.

In addition to destinations in the table, p182, buses leave Novo Rio every 30 minutes or so for São Paulo (R$70 to R$110, six hours) operated by **Viação 1001** (☎ 4004 5001) and **Itapemirim** (☎ 0800-723 2121).

GETTING AROUND
To/From the Airports

Rio's international airport, Aeroporto Galeão is 15km north of the city center, on Ilha do Governador. Aeroporto Santos Dumont, used by some domestic flights, is by the bayside in the city center, 1km east of Cinelândia metro station.

Real Auto Bus (☎ 0800-240 850) operates buses with air-con from the international airport (outside the arrivals floor of Terminal 1 or the ground floor of Terminal 2) to Rodoviária Novo Rio, Av Rio Branco (Centro), Aeroporto Santos Dumont, southward through Glória, Flamengo and Botafogo and along the beaches of Copacabana, Ipanema and Leblon to Barra da Tijuca (and vice versa). The buses run every 30 minutes, from 5:20am to 12:10am, and will stop wherever you ask. Fares are around R$7, and it takes anywhere from 90 minutes to two hours to reach the Zona Sul from the airport depending on traffic. You can also transfer to the metro at Carioca metro station in Centro.

Heading to the airports, you can catch the Real Auto bus in front of the major hotels, along the main beaches, but you have to look alive and flag them down.

Taxis from the international airport may try to rip you off. The safest course, a radio taxi for which you pay a set fare at the airport, is also the most expensive (R$80 to Copacabana/Ipanema). A yellow-and-blue *comúm* (common) taxi should cost around R$50 to Ipanema if the meter is working.

Boat

Rio has several islands in the bay that you can visit by ferry, though you can also get fine views on the commuter ferry to Niterói. See p151 for more information.

Ilha de Paquetá (off Map p131; ☎ ferry 0800-704 4113; www.barcas-sa.com.br) The ferry takes 70 minutes and costs R$9 return, leaving every two to three hours between 5:30am and 11pm. The most useful departure times for travelers are currently 7:10am, 10:30am and 1:30pm.

Niterói (Map p131) The ferry (☎ ferry 0800-704 4113; www.barcas-sa.com.br) leaves every 20 minutes from Praça XV de Novembro in Centro (Map p138). Return tickets cost R$5.60 return.

Car

Driving in Rio can be frustrating even if you know your way around. If you do chose to

BUSES FROM RIO

Destination	Duration	Cost	Frequency	Company
International				
Buenos Aires, Argentina	46hr	R$286	daily	Pluma (☎ 0800-646 0300)
Santiago, Chile	62hr	R$330	daily	Pluma (☎ 0800-646 0300)
National				
Belém	52hr	R$418	daily	Transbrasiliana (☎ 0800-726 7001)
Belo Horizonte	7hr	R$68-126	8 daily	Util (☎ 0800-886 1000)
Brasília	17hr	R$153	daily	Util (☎ 0800-886 1000)
Cabo Frio	3hr	R$24-28	20 daily	Viação 1001 (☎ 4004 5001)
Curitiba	13hr	R$70-160	5 daily	Penha (☎ 0800-646 2122)
Florianópolis	18hr	R$178	daily	Itapemirim (☎ 0800-723 2121)
Foz do Iguaçu	23hr	R$184	2 daily	Pluma (☎ 2233 0336)
Ouro Prêto	7hr	R$72	daily	Util (☎ 0800-886 1000)
Paraty	4½hr	R$52	7-10 daily	Costa Verde (☎ 3622 3100)
Petrópolis	1½hr	R$16	10 daily	Única-Fácil (☎ 0800-886 1000)
Porto Alegre	26hr	R$200	daily	Itapemirim (☎ 0800-723 2121)
Recife	38hr	R$235	daily	São Geraldo (☎ 0800-728 0044)
Salvador	28hr	R$290	daily	Aguia Branca (☎ 0800-725 1211)
Vitória	8hr	R$75-100	6 daily	Itapemirim (☎ 0800-723 2121)

drive, it's good to know a couple of things: the first is that Cariocas don't always stop at red lights at night because of the small risk of robberies at deserted intersections. Instead they slow at red lights and proceed if no one is around. Another thing to know is that if you park your car on the street, it's common to pay the *flanelinha* (parking attendant) R$2 for looking after it. Some of them work for the city; others are 'freelance,' but regardless, it's a common practice throughout Brazil, and the service is worthwhile.

HIRE

Car-rental agencies can be found at either airport or scattered along Av Princesa Isabel in Copacabana. At the international airport, **Hertz** (☎ 0800-701 7300), **Localiza** (☎ 0800-979 2000) and **Unidas** (☎ 2295 3628) provide rentals. In Copacabana, among the many are **Hertz** (Map p134; ☎ 2275 7440; Av Princesa Isabel 500) and **Localiza** (Map p134; ☎ 2275 3340; Av Princesa Isabel 150).

For more information on hiring a car, see p722.

Public Transportation
METRO

Rio's subway system (www.metrorio.com.br) is an excellent way to get around. It's open from 5am to midnight Monday through Saturday and 7am to 11pm on Sunday and holidays. During Carnaval the metro operates nonstop from Friday morning until Tuesday at midnight.

Both lines are air-conditioned, clean, fast and safe. The main line goes from Ipanema-General Osório (a station that opened in 2009) to Saens Peña, connecting with the secondary line to Estácio (which provides service to São Cristóvão and Maracanã). More stations are planned in the coming years, with plans to integrate the rest of Ipanema and Leblon into the transport system.

A single ride ticket is called a *unitário* and it costs R$2.80. To avoid waiting in lines, you can purchase a *cartão pré-pago* (prepaid card) by paying a minimum of R$10; you can then recharge it (cash only, no change given) at kiosks inside some metro stations. If you're going somewhere outside of the metro's range (Cosme Velho or Barra for example) you can purchase a *metrô-ônibus* (metro-bus) ticket. Free subway maps are available from most ticket booths.

BUS & VAN

Rio city buses (R$2.20 to R$2.80) are fast and frequent, and because Rio is long and narrow it's easy to get the right bus and usually no big deal if you're on the wrong one. Most buses going south from the center will go to Copacabana, and vice versa. The buses are, however, often crowded, stuck in traffic, and driven by raving maniacs. They also have a bad reputation for robberies. In truth, such acts are rare and usually limited to outer-suburban areas where tourists are unlikely to travel. Do keep an eye on your belongings while riding, and don't travel by bus at night; taxis are generally a safer option.

Minibuses (Cariocas call them *'vans'*) provide a faster alternative between Av Rio Branco in Centro and the Zona Sul (along the coast) as far as Barra da Tijuca. The destination is written in the front window. The flat fare costs between R$2 and R$4.50. Call out your stop (*'para!'*) when you want to disembark.

Taxi

Rio's yellow taxis are handy for zipping around town. Metered taxis charge around R$4.35 flat rate, plus around R$1 per km – slightly more at night and on Sunday.

Radio taxis are 30% more expensive, but safer. Many of the drivers lurking around the hotels are sharks, so it's worth walking a block or so to avoid them. A few radio-taxi companies include **Coopertramo** (☎ 2209 9292), **Cootrama** (☎ 3976 9944), **Coopatur** (☎ 2573 1009) and **Transcoopass** (☎ 2590 6891).

In Rocinha and some other favelas, moto-taxis (a ride on the back of a motorcycle) are a handy way to get around, with short rides (usually from the bottom of the favela to the top or vice versa) costing R$2.

Rio de Janeiro State

Say the name Rio de Janeiro and people automatically think of the city. But there's another Rio out there, the stunningly beautiful state of Rio de Janeiro, home to some of Brazil's most alluring destinations, all within a three-hour drive of the Cidade Maravilhosa (Marvelous City).

To the east, the Costa do Sol is a land of dunes and lagoons, white sands and limpid deep-blue and jade-green waters. Saquarema delights surfers with some of Brazil's best breaks. Arraial do Cabo has paradisiacal beaches and picturesque harbors tucked between steep promontories. And Búzios, chic but casual, sparkles day and night, with lots of sunshine and nightspots.

Just north of Rio, a jagged mountain wall forms the backdrop for the imperial city of Petrópolis and the climbers' paradise of PN Serra dos Órgãos. Nearby Teresópolis and Nova Friburgo straddle an equally picturesque landscape dotted with dairies, Swiss chalets and peaks whose names hint at their fantastic shapes: Friar's Wart, Finger of God, Woman of Stone.

West along the Costa Verde lies one of Brazil's true gems, the colonial town of Paraty, whose backdrop of green forest, waterfalls and flowering trees is as dazzling as the town's colorful 18th-century architecture. Offshore, the vast traffic-free island of Ilha Grande offers over 100km of hiking trails leading to more than 100 of Brazil's most secluded beaches. To the northwest is Brazil's oldest national park, PN de Itatiaia, where stark high country plateaus and rocky spires intermingle with lush, low country jungle. Bordering the park, the towns of Visconde de Mauá and Penedo welcome visitors with rustic cabins and fresh-grilled trout.

HIGHLIGHTS

- On **Ilha Grande** (p187), surf the south shore's wild waves, or chill at the floating bar in a tranquil cove nearby

- Snorkel, swim and slide down waterfalls, then learn to cook gourmet Brazilian food in picturesque, colonial **Paraty** (p191)

- Rappel up rocky Pico das Agulhas Negras in **Parque Nacional de Itatiaia** (p201)

- Stroll at sunset, or party all night on breezy beachfront Orla Bardot in **Búzios** (p215)

- Try honey *cachaça* (high-proof sugarcane alcohol) and Alpine-style goat cheese amid spectacular mountain scenery along the **Teresópolis–Friburgo Scenic Circuit** (p207)

Parque Nacional de Itatiaia

Nova Friburgo
Teresópolis

Búzios

Paraty

Ilha Grande

■ POPULATION: 16 MILLION	■ AREA: 43,696 SQ KM

RIO DE JANEIRO STATE

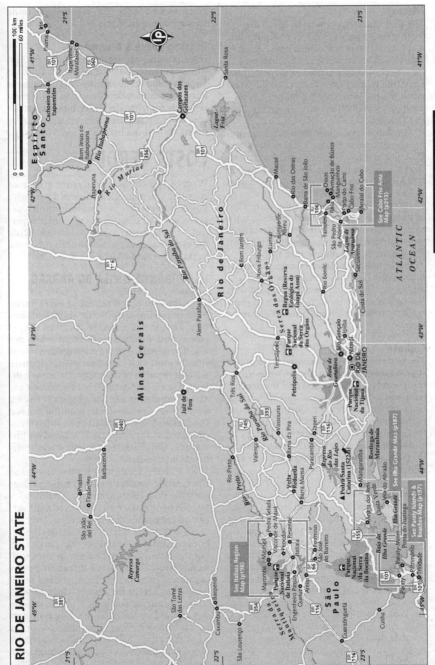

0   100 km
0   60 miles

Espírito Santo

Piúma
Itapemirim
Marataízes
BR 101
ES 060

Cachoeiro de Itapemirim
Bom Jesus co Itabapoana
Rio Itabapoana
Itaperuna
Rio Muriaé
BR 356
BR 101

Santa Rosa
Campos dos Goitacazes
Lagoa Feia
BR 101

Macaé
Rio das Ostras
Barra de São João
Oxos
Armação de Búzios
Baixa de Manguinhos
Porto do Carro
Cabo Frio
Arraial do Cabo
RJ 106

See Cabo Frio Area Map (p213)

Minas Gerais

Rio de Janeiro

Bom Jardim
Nova Friburgo
Sumaí
Casimiro de Abreu
Rio Bonito
São Pedro da Aldeia
Lagoa de Araruama
Saquarema
Costa do Sol

ATLANTIC OCEAN

BR 116

Além Paraíba
Rio Paraíba do Sul
Regua (Reserva Ecológica de Guapi Assú)
Parque Nacional da Serra dos Órgãos
Serra dos Órgãos
Teresópolis
São Gonçalo
Itaipuba
Niterói
Baía de Guanabara
RIO DE JANEIRO

Juiz de Fora
Três Rios
BR 040
BR 393
Vassouras
Barra do Piraí
Japeri
Petrópolis

Barbacena
Rio Paraíba do Sul
Valença
RJ 145

Parque Nacional da Tijuca

São João del Rei
Prados
Tiradentes
Rio Preto
Rio Preto

BR 116
Paracambi
Represa do Rio das Lajes
Seropédica
Restinga de Marambaia

See Ilha Grande Map (p187)

São Tomé das Letras
Represa Camargo

Volta Redonda
Barra Mansa
▲Pedra Santa Catarina (1522m)

Mangaratiba
Angra dos Reis
Costa Verde
Vila do Abraão
Ilha Grande
Baía da Ilha Grande

See Paraty Islands & Beaches Map (p197)

Baependi
BR 381
Caxambu
São Lourenço
BR 116

See Itatiaia Region Map (p198)

Maromba
Maringá
Pedra Selada
Visconde de Mauá
Penedo
Resende
Engenheiro Passos
Itatiaia
Parque Nacional de Itatiaia
São José do Barreiro
Queluz
Areias
Formoso
BR 66

Serra da Mantiqueira
BR 354
BR 116

São Paulo

Guaratinguetá
Cunha

Parque Nacional da Serra da Bocaina
RJ 165
BR 101

Paraty-Mirim
Ponta do Juatinga
Paraty
Patrimônio
Trindade
BR 101

21°S
22°S
23°S
22°S
23°S
45°W
44°W
43°W
42°W
41°W

History

The first European visitors to Brazil arrived by ship on January 1, 1502. For a short while it appeared that the newcomers were going to cohabit peacefully with the indigenous people, but once colonizing started in earnest in the early 16th century, everything changed. Great effort was put into enslaving indigenous people to work plantations and converting them to Christianity.

The state's development moved inland with the construction of Brazil's first major overland thoroughfare, linking coastal Paraty with the valley of the Rio Paraíba and continuing into Minas Gerais. Another important chapter in Rio's development was the establishment of coffee plantations here in the early 19th century. The crop was taken by mule train to new ports along the coast, and these roads were the main means of communication until the coming of the railways after 1855.

Modern Rio de Janeiro state is one of Brazil's economic powerhouses, where spurting oil and sunbaked tourists compete with traditional industries such as steel and shipbuilding to see which can generate the most income.

Climate

The best time to visit the coastal areas of Rio state is between May and August, when balmy trade winds cool the region and the average temperature hovers around the 30°C mark (mid-80°F). But beware: during the same period it can get downright cold (single digits Celsius) in the mountains of Petrópolis and Itatiaia. Between December and March, the rainy season, the entire state is hotter and wetter.

National Parks

For such a small state, Rio de Janeiro has an impressive array of national parks, including two of Brazil's oldest. Parque Nacional de Itatiaia (p201), established in 1937, preserves large sections of lowland Mata Atlântica (Atlantic rain forest), plus significant high-altitude habitats. Parque Nacional da Serra dos Órgãos (p207), established just north of Rio in 1939, gets its name from the remarkable organ-pipe shapes of its sheer rock walls. And little-visited Parque Nacional da Serra da Bocaina (p196) encompasses a gorgeous swath of steep coastal jungle where the intrepid hiker can discover idyllic waterfalls

and a section of the 17th-century gold route leading inland from Paraty.

Getting There & Around

International and domestic flights fly into Rio de Janeiro's Galeão and Santos Dumont airports, linking Rio state to cities throughout Brazil and the world. Rio's local bus station is a hub for virtually every bus line in the country, with fast, frequent service to nearby towns via well-maintained modern highways.

COSTA VERDE

West of Rio city is a captivating stretch of coastline where jungled hillsides dotted with flowering trees dive precipitously into a blue-green sea. The sinuous shoreline here is perfect for meandering, taking time to appreciate the ever-changing panorama of bays, islands, peaks and waterfalls.

ILHA GRANDE & VILA DO ABRAÃO

☎ 0xx24 / pop 6100

The fabulous island retreat of Ilha Grande owes its pristine condition to its unusual history. First it was a pirates' lair, then a leper colony and, finally, a penitentiary where political prisoners were held alongside some of Brazil's most violent and deranged criminals. All that remains of those days are some half-buried stone foundations, but the island's unsavory reputation kept developers at bay for a long time. Consequently, beautiful tropical beaches and virgin Atlantic rain forest (now protected as state parkland) abound on Ilha Grande, and there are still only a few settlements on the island.

Vila do Abraão, the only town of any size on Ilha Grande, was itself a sleepy fishing village until the mid-1990s, when Ilha Grande's infamous penitentiary was destroyed and tourism on the island started in earnest. Over the years, a veritable thicket of pousadas (guesthouses), restaurants and bars has popped up, but this palm-studded beachfront town with its tidy white church is still incredibly picturesque, and remains small by mainland Brazil standards. Except for Abraão's lone garbage truck, fire engine and police vehicle, cars are not allowed in town, so the only transport here is by foot or boat. The village comprises a few dirt roads, and everybody congregates down near the docks and beach at night. On weekends and during high season it can get a

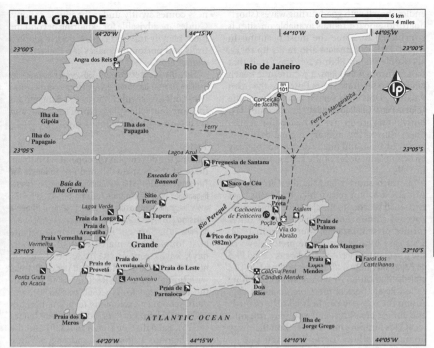

ILHA GRANDE

bit claustrophobic in Vila do Abraão, but you can easily escape the crowds by hiking a few steps out of town in any direction.

The island suffered a major tragedy in the wee hours of January 1, 2010, when a giant mudslide killed 31 New Year's Eve revelers in the community of Bananal, west of Abraão.

Orientation & Information
Ferries from the mainland (Angra dos Reis and Mangaratiba) dock at the cement pier on the west end of Abraão's beach. Private boats and most hydrofoils dock at a separate wooden pier about 150m east.

In between the two piers lies the heart of Abraão village, with its main street, the cobbled Rua da Igreja, curving to become Rua Getúlio Vargas. West of the piers is the road to Praia Preta and the ruined Lazareto prison. East of the piers, at the far end of the town beach, Ilha Grande's most popular hiking trail leads to Praia de Palmas, Praia dos Mangues and Praia Lopes Mendes.

There are no ATMs on the island, although many places accept credit cards and it's possible to change foreign cash in a pinch.

For information about the state park, a helpful scale model of the island and its trails, and displays on local history and culture, visit the **Centro de Visitante do Parque Estadual** (State Park Visitors Center; ☎ 3361 5540; Av Beira Mar s/n; ☼ 9am-5pm Tue-Sun), just west of the cement pier.

Internet service on the island tends to be extremely slow. A few hotels offer wireless connections, and there's a sprinkling of net cafés, including **Ilha Grande Turismo** (Rua da Igreja; per min R$0.20; ☼ 9:30am-midnight), with 15 computers, air-con and long hours.

Lavanderia Meros (Rua Getúlio Vargas 719; wash & dry per 3kg R$20; ☼ 8:30am-noon & 4-8:30pm) provides same-day laundry service.

Sights & Activities
Outdoor adventure options on Ilha Grande just don't quit. Posted around town are maps showing 16 different signposted trails leading through the lush forest to several of the island's 102 beaches. When visiting some beaches, it's possible to hike one way and take a boat the other. The most popular hike is the three-hour, 6.1km (each way) trek from Abraão to **Praia Lopes Mendes**. This seemingly

RIO DE JANEIRO STATE

endless beach with good surfing waves (short-board/longboard rentals available on-site) is considered by some the most beautiful in Brazil. **Praia de Parnaioca** also ranks up there, accessible via an 8km (each way) trail that passes through **Dois Rios**, a picturesque beach where two separate rivers flow into the open Atlantic. Dois Rios served as the site of the **Colônia Penal Cândido Mendes**, Ilha Grande's last functioning prison, used to hold political prisoners during the military regime that took power in 1964, and finally destroyed (literally blown up!) by order of the state government in 1994.

A much shorter jaunt is the Circuito do Abraão, a 1.7km return hike that leads past two small beaches to the claustrophobic moss-covered stone ruins of Ilha Grande's other former prison, **Lazareto**, shut down in 1954. This easy hike affords some pretty views of the distinctive parrot-shaped peak called **Pico do Papagaio** (982m) and takes you past an old **aqueduct** adjoined by a large swimming hole called **Poção**, perfect for a picnic and a dip. Along the way you can hear all sorts of birds and jungle creatures, and you may run into local kids jumping into the water on their way home from school. Beyond the aqueduct, a more challenging trail leads to **Cachoeira da Feiticeira**, a lovely 15m waterfall, before continuing to the beach at **Saco do Céu**.

Before hitting the trail, let people at your pousada know where you're going and when you'll be back, stock up on water and bug repellent and bring a flashlight, as dark-ness comes swiftly under the jungle canopy. Guides are advisable for exploring beyond the most heavily traveled routes; poorly marked trails and poisonous snakes can make things challenging.

Elite Dive Center (☎ 3361 5501; www.elitedivecenter .com.br; Travessa Buganville 1-2A) offers courses and two-tank dives with English-speaking guides in some fantastic spots. For bike, kayak and surfboard rentals, see following.

Tours

Among the dozen-plus tour operators in town, three of the best-established are **Sudoeste SW Turismo** (☎ 3361 5516; www.sudoestesw.com.br; Travessa Buganville 719A), **Ilha Grande Turismo** (IGT; ☎ 3365 6426; www.ilhagrandeturismo.com.br; Rua da Igreja) and **Phoenix Turismo** (☎ 3361 5822; www.phoenixturismo.com.br; Rua da Praia 703). Services offered include private boat tours, bike rentals (R$10/40 per hour/day), kayak rentals (R$10/30 per hour/six hours), surfboard rentals (R$40 per day), treks with bilingual guides (R$40 to R$50), round-the-island boat tours (R$60 to R$150), and daily schooner excursions to prime beaches and snorkeling spots, including Lopes Mendes (R$15), Saco do Céu (R$25 to R$30) and the twin lagoons Lagoa Azul and Lagoa Verde (R$35 to R$40).

Sleeping

Vila do Abraão is swarming with pousadas beyond those listed here. Note that prices quoted here are for high season (December to February). Prices drop by as much as 50%

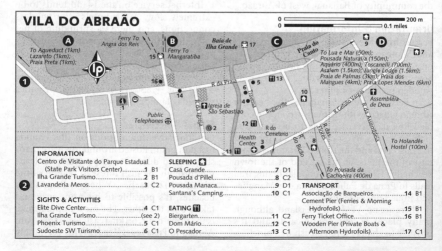

VILA DO ABRAÃO

INFORMATION	
Centro de Visitante do Parque Estadual	
(State Park Visitors Center)	1 B1
Ilha Grande Turismo	2 B1
Lavanderia Meros	3 C2

SIGHTS & ACTIVITIES	
Elite Dive Center	4 C1
Ilha Grande Turismo	(see 2)
Phoenix Turismo	5 C1
Sudoeste SW Turismo	6 C1

SLEEPING	
Casa Grande	7 D1
Pousada d'Pillel	8 C2
Pousada Manaca	9 D1
Santana's Camping	10 C1

EATING	
Biergarten	11 C2
Dom Mário	12 C2
O Pescador	13 C1

TRANSPORT	
Associação de Barqueiros	14 B1
Cement Pier (Ferries & Morning	
Hydrofoils)	15 B1
Ferry Ticket Office	16 B1
Wooden Pier (Private Boats &	
Afternoon Hydrofoils)	17 C1

between March and November. Some locals also rent out rooms, especially in high season.

BUDGET

Santana's Camping (☎ 3361 5287; www.santanascamping.com.br; Rua Santana; per person R$15) One of several campgrounds set back from the beach near Rua Getúlio Vargas, Santana's has hot showers, big shade trees and a kitchen and barbecue area for guests' use. It rents out tents for R$15 extra per night.

Aquário (☎ 3361 5405; www.aquariohostel.com; dm/d R$45/130; 🛇 🛜 🖳) The spacious sundeck overlooking the ocean, natural swimming pool and lively evening barbecues have earned this beachfront hostel/pousada a loyal following among backpackers. To get here, head 1km east along the beach from the ferry dock.

Holandês Hostel (Ilha Grande Hostel; ☎ 3361 5034; www.holandeshostel.com.br; Rua da Assembleia s/n; dm from R$45, chalet R$150) Uphill and inland from the center of town, this shady, peaceful retreat has banana trees, chirping parrots and a terrace full of hammocks. Rooms are somewhat musty but affordable. HI members save R$5 per person off rates quoted here.

MIDRANGE & TOP END

Jungle Lodge (☎ 3361 5569; www.ilhagrandeexpeditions.com; Caminho de Palmas 4; d without/with breakfast R$100/120, lodge for up to 10 people R$500; 🖳) Tucked away above town in the rain forest, this rustic, five-room guesthouse and open-air chalet is run by a wild-haired Pantanal guide and his German wife. It's an entirely different experience than sleeping in Abraão, a 1.5km hike away. The view from the outdoor shower is miraculous.

Pousada d'Pillel (☎ 3361 5075; www.ilhagrandedpillel.com.br; Rua do Bicão; r R$140-160) This friendly, family-run pousada, a few blocks from the beach, has a cool, shady garden with comfortable seating under a thatched roof out back. Additional amenities include DVD players in every room, a ping-pong table and free use of snorkeling equipment.

Pousada da Cachoeira (☎ 3361 9521; www.cachoeira.com; Rua do Bicão 50; d/tr/q with fan R$140/170/200, with air-con R$160/190/220; 🛇) It's a five-minute uphill trek from downtown Abraão, but the jungle setting, with patches of grassy lawn and trails down to a white waterfall, make the simple rooms here an appealing choice.

Casa Grande (☎ 3361 5831; www.ilhagrande.org; Rua Getúlio Vargas s/n; r R$150-170; 🛇) Up a side street

off Rua Getúlio Vargas, this tranquil hideaway has a pretty garden setting with monkeys in the trees, comfy beds, mini-fridges, good hot water, an excellent breakfast and hammocks strung along the veranda. Welcoming German-Brazilian owners Markus and Adriana speak several languages between them.

Pousada Manaca (☎ 3361 5404; www.ilhagrandemanaca.com.br; Praia do Abraão 333; r $190-230; 🛇 🛜) This French-run beachfront pousada invites guests to relax with TV-free rooms (many directly facing the ocean), a sauna and two pleasant patio areas. Rooms have minibars and solar hot water. Owner Gerard speaks English, French, Spanish, German and Portuguese.

Pousada Naturalia (☎ 3361 9583; www.pousadanaturalia.net; Praia do Abraão 149; r R$230; 🛇 🛜) Built among giant boulders on a hillside just inland from the beach, Naturalia offers 12 spacious rooms, all with pretty ocean views and most with solar hot water. Book ahead.

Asalem (☎ 3361 5602; www.asalem.com.br; Praia da Crena s/n; s/d/tr R$294/350/406; s/d/tr ste R$450/550/650; 🛇 🖳 🛜) Despite its remote, immersed-in-nature atmosphere, Asalem is only a few minutes from Abraão by boat, or a 25-minute walk via a scenic beachfront trail. Owned by an internationally acclaimed photographer, it commands gorgeous views of the forest and adjoining bay from its hillside location. Pick-up and drop-off at Abraão pier, plus use of kayaks, canoes and the hotel's nice library of art books, are included in the price.

Eating

Restaurants abound along Rua da Praia, Rua da Igreja, Rua Getúlio Vargas and the small pedestrian street Travessa Buganville. Some places offer – but don't prominently advertise – a simple *prato feito* (plate of the day) of fish, rice, beans and salad for around R$15; ask around. During busy periods you'll see sweets carts being pushed about, as well as entrepreneurial islanders selling grilled seafood and caipirinhas.

Biergarten (☎ 3361 5583; Rua Getúlio Vargas 161; per 100g R$3.40; 🕑 12:30-10pm) The self-serve buffet at this informal eatery includes everything from brown rice and soy protein to sushi and other seafood, with more vegetables than you'll see at most places around town.

Lua e Mar (Praia do Canto; mains per person R$22-45; 🕑 10am-10pm Thu-Tue) Candlelit tables on the sand make a tranquil place to watch the crashing waves and scurrying crabs while you enjoy tasty seafood dishes for two.

Toscanelli (☎ 3361 5660; Enseada do Abraão; mains R$27-48; ☺ lunch & dinner) Set on a shady terrace with stone walls and sea views, this Italian-themed restaurant east of Abraão offers delectable items including seafood risotto, salmon in a ginger-orange crust and *pêra caipirinha* (a pear stewed in *cachaça*, served with lemon-mint ice cream).

O Pescador (☎ 3361 5114; Rua da Praia; mains R$29-47; ☺ 5pm-late) The cozily furnished, romantically lit Pescador is one of the island's best choices for a fancy beachfront dinner. They make a mean caipirinha, a delicious *casquinha de siri* (stuffed crab) appetizer and main dishes such as *peixe ao molho mediterrâneo* (fish with a sauce of tomatoes, capers, olives and basil).

Dom Mário (☎ 3361 5349; Travessa Buganville; mains R$36; ☺ 6-10pm Mon-Sat) Long-time local chef Mário cooks up seafood specialties like *filé de peixe ao molho de maracujá* (fish fillet with passion fruit sauce) and scrumptious desserts, including his trademark caramelized bananas.

Getting There & Away

Barcas SA (☎ 0800 704 4113; www.barcas-sa.com.br) runs daily ferries between Ilha Grande and the mainland ports of Angra dos Reis and Mangaratiba. Ferries are sometimes added during high season and the schedule can fluctuate, so confirm locally before departure. The Angra–Abraão ferry (R$6.50 Monday to Friday, R$14 Saturday and Sunday, 80 minutes) leaves Angra at 3:30pm weekdays and 1:30pm weekends, returning from Abraão at 10am daily. From Mangaratiba, east of Angra

---

INDIGENOUS NAMES

Many place names in Rio state have their origins in indigenous words, including the following:

- Geribá – a kind of coconut palm
- Guanabara – arm of the sea
- Ipanema – place that gives bad luck or place of dangerous sea
- Itatiaia – many-pointed rock
- Mangaratiba – banana orchard
- Paraty – a kind of fish
- Saquarema – lagoon without shells
- Tijuca – putrid-smelling swamp

---

along the coast, the ferry (R$6.35 weekdays, R$14 weekends, 80 minutes) leaves for Abraão at 8am daily and 10pm Friday, returning to Mangaratiba at 5:30pm daily.

Ilha Grande Turismo (IGT; ☎ 3365 6426; www.ilhagrandeturismo.com.br) runs faster and more frequent catamarans (45 minutes, R$20 each way) between Angra and Abraão, leaving Angra daily at 8am, 11am and 4pm, and returning from Abraão at 9am, 12:30pm and 5pm. Buy tickets at the IGT offices inside Angra's bus station or just behind the church in Abraão.

These regular services are supplemented by smaller tourist boats operated by the **Associação de Barqueiros** (☎ 3361 5920; Rua da Praia s/n). Depending on demand, there may be multiple daily departures between Angra and Abraão, ranging in price from R$20 to R$25. Check schedules at the Associação de Barqueiros information booth near Abraão's ferry dock or at agencies around town. At the time of research, a new service to the mainland town of Conceição do Jacaré had also just been initiated, with shorter crossing times (one hour) and lower fares (R$15).

Several companies in Abraão – including **Speed Connection** (☎ 3361 5667) and **Guaiamum Connection** (☎ 3361 5314) – offer door-to-door service between Ilha Grande and Rio de Janeiro. The R$60 combined ticket covers boat-plus-van transport to Rio's bus station, airport or anywhere in the Zona Sul (Copacabana, Ipanema, Leme etc).

ANGRA DOS REIS
☎ 0xx24 / pop 170,000

The savage beauty of Angra dos Reis's tropical, fjordlike coastline has been badly blemished by industrialization. Supertankers dock in Angra's port, a railway heads inland to the steel town of Volta Redonda, and the nearby Petrobras oil refinery and nuclear power plant stick out like sore thumbs. If you've got your own wheels, there are plenty of gorgeous beaches to explore east and west of town, but for those traveling by bus, the main reason to pass through Angra is to catch the ferry for Ilha Grande. Angra's bus station is a 20-minute walk (or a R$10 taxi ride) northeast of the boat docks.

The helpful **Centro de Informações Turísticas** (www.turisangra.com.br; main office ☎ 3367 7826; Av Ayrton Senna 580; ☺ 8am-8pm; Santa Luzia ferry terminal ☎ 3365 6421; ☺ 7am-7pm) has two branches along the waterfront between the bus station and the docks; both provide local hotel referrals and information on Ilha Grande. Along Av Júlio Maria near the docks, you can stock up on cash at Bradesco or HSBC ATMs before heading out to Ilha Grande. There's also a **post office** (Praça Lopes Irovão) nearby.

Only steps from the docks, **Fogão de Minas** (☎ 3365 4877; Rua Júlio Maria 398; per kg R$29.90; ☒ 11am-4pm) offers delicious self-serve Mineiro food.

Getting There & Around

From Angra's **bus station** (☎ 3365 2041; Largo da Lapa), Costa Verde buses leave for Rio (R$36, 2½ hours) every hour from 7am to 8:40pm daily, while Colitur buses run to Paraty (R$8.40, two hours) at least hourly from 6am to 11pm daily.

PARATY

☎ 0xx24 / pop 36,000

Set amid jutting peninsulas and secluded beaches, with a backdrop of steep, jungled mountains plunging into an island-studded bay, Paraty is one of Brazil's most appealing and exquisitely preserved historical gems.

Paraty's colonial center is remarkable not only for its centuries-old architecture, but also for its lack of automobile traffic. The irregular cobblestone streets are closed to motor vehicles, making it a delightful place to stroll about. Elegant white buildings adorned with fanciful multihued borders and latticed windows blend harmoniously with the natural beauty that envelops the town.

Dozens of pristine beaches are within a couple of hours of Paraty by boat or bus, while inland, the Parque Nacional da Serra da Bocaina provides protection for a lush remnant of Mata Atlântica. The Brazilian government has recognized Paraty as a National Historic Site since 1966.

Paraty is crowded and lively throughout the summer holidays, brimming with Brazilian and European vacationers. The town's cosmopolitan flavor is further enhanced by the large number of artists, writers and chefs, both Brazilian and foreign, who have settled here and opened shops, galleries and restaurants in recent years.

History

Paraty was inhabited by the indigenous Guaianás when Portuguese settlers first arrived here in the 16th century. With the discovery of gold in Minas Gerais at the end of the 17th century, Paraty became an obligatory stopover between Rio de Janeiro and the mines, as it was the only point where the escarpment of the Serra do Mar could be scaled.

As gold poured from the interior, Paraty became a busy, important port, and the wealthy built churches and fine houses. Paraty's glory days didn't last long. After the 1720s, a new road from Rio via the Serra dos Órgãos cut 15 days off the journey to Minas Gerais, and Paraty started to decline. In the 19th century, the local economy revived with the coffee boom, but until the mid-20th century the sea remained the only viable commercial route to Paraty. In 1954 a modern road was built through the steep Serra do Mar, passing the town of Cunha, 47km inland. Then in 1960 the coastal road from Rio, 253km away, was extended to Paraty and 330km beyond to São Paulo, ushering in a new era of tourism-based prosperity.

Orientation

Paraty is small and easy to navigate, although street names and addresses can get confusing. Some streets have more than one name, and house numbers don't always follow a predictable pattern.

Information

Bradesco (Av Roberto Silveira) ATM.
Centro de Informações Turísticas (☎ 3371 1222/1046; turismoparaty@gmail.com; Av Roberto Silveira; ☒ 9:30am-8:30pm) Helpful staff, including some English speakers.
Internet access (Av Roberto Silveira) Several places offer internet and Skype access along this street just outside the historic center.
Livraria de Paraty (☎ 3371 6042; Rua da Praia 159; ☒ 9am-9pm) Bookstore-café with some English-language titles.
Paraty Wash (☎ 3371 3027; Shopping Martins, Loja 15; wash & dry per basket R$17; ☒ 8am-9pm Mon-Sat) Same-day laundry service opposite the bus station.
Post office (cnr Rua Marechal Deodoro da Fonseca & Rua Domingo Gonçalves de Abreu)

Sights & Activities
CHURCHES

Igreja NS do Rosário e São Benedito dos Homens Pretos (Largo do Rosario; admission R$2; ☒ 9am-noon & 2-5pm Mon-Thu) was built in 1725 by and for slaves. Renovated in 1857, the church has gilded wooden altars dedicated to Our Lady

RIO DE JANEIRO STATE

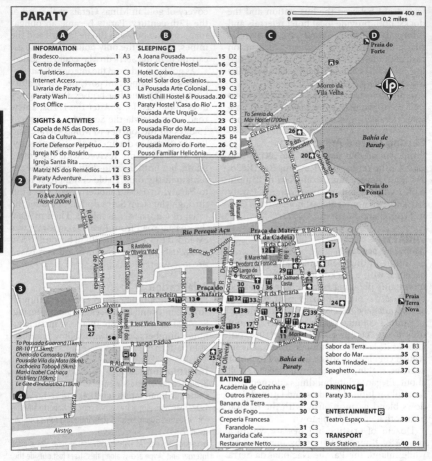

PARATY

0 ——— 400 m
0 ——— 0.2 miles

INFORMATION	
Bradesco..1	A3
Centro de Informações	
Turísticas................................2	C3
Internet Access...........................3	B3
Livraria de Paraty.......................4	C3
Paraty Wash................................5	A3
Post Office..................................6	C3

SIGHTS & ACTIVITIES	
Capela de NS das Dores............7	D3
Casa da Cultura...........................8	C3
Forte Defensor Perpétuo...........9	D1
Igreja NS do Rosário.................10	C3
Igreja Santa Rita.......................11	C3
Matriz NS dos Remédios..........12	C3
Paraty Adventure.....................13	B3
Paraty Tours.............................14	B3

SLEEPING	
A Joana Pousada.......................15	D2
Historic Centre Hostel.............16	C3
Hotel Coixino...........................17	C3
Hotel Solar dos Gerânios........18	C3
La Pousada Arte Colonial.........19	C3
Misti Chill Hostel & Pousada...20	C2
Paraty Hostel 'Casa do Rio'.....21	B3
Pousada Arte Urquijo...............22	C3
Pousada do Ouro.....................23	C3
Pousada Flor do Mar...............24	D3
Pousada Marendaz..................25	B4
Pousada Morro do Forte..........26	C2
Pouso Familiar Helicônia.........27	A3

EATING	
Academia de Cozinha e	
Outros Prazeres.....................28	C3
Banana da Terra.......................29	C3
Casa do Fogo...........................30	C3
Creperia Francesa	
Farandole...............................31	C3
Margarida Café........................32	C3
Restaurante Netto....................33	C3

Sabor da Terra.........................34	B3
Sabor do Mar...........................35	C3
Santa Trindade........................36	C3
Spaghetto................................37	C3

DRINKING	
Paraty 33..................................38	C3

ENTERTAINMENT	
Teatro Espaço...........................39	C3

TRANSPORT	
Bus Station...............................40	B4

of the Rosary, St Benedict and St John. The pineapple-like chandelier base in the roof is a symbol of prosperity.

Igreja Santa Rita dos Pardos Libertos (Rua Santa Rita) was the church for freed mulattos (persons of mixed black and European parentage). Built in 1722, it houses a tiny museum of sacred art and has some fine woodwork on the doorways and altars. At the time of writing, both the church and museum were closed for renovation.

Capela de NS das Dores (Rua Fresca; admission free; ☽ 9am-noon Mon-Fri), the church of the colonial white elite, was built in 1800 and renovated in 1901. It houses a small **art gallery** (☽ 1:30-5pm) and a fascinating cemetery in the inner courtyard.

Matriz NS dos Remédios (Praça Monsenhor Hélio Pires; admission R$2; ☽ 9am-noon & 2-5pm Fri & Sat) was built in 1787 on the site of two 17th-century churches. Inside, there is art from past and contemporary local artists. According to legend, the construction of the church was financed by pirate treasure found hidden on Praia da Trindade.

CASA DA CULTURA

In a beautiful colonial mansion, Paraty's **Casa da Cultura** (☎ 3371 2325; www.casadaculturaparaty.org.br; Rua Dona Geralda 177; admission R$8; ☽ 10am-6:30pm Wed-Mon Mar-Nov, 11am-7:30pm Wed-Mon Dec-Feb) has a fascinating permanent exhibition documenting local culture through photos and videotaped interviews with residents. The museum also displays relics from Paraty's past, with signs in English and Portuguese. There are fabulous views of town from the main gallery upstairs.

ISLANDS & BEACHES

Paraty has some 65 islands and 300 beaches in its vicinity. To visit the less accessible beaches, take an organized schooner tour; tickets average about R$30 per person (see Tours, following).

Alternatively, you can hire one of the small motorboats at the port for a private tour. Local captains know some great spots and will take you out for roughly R$50 per hour, which is a good deal if you have a large enough group.

The closest fine beaches on the coast – **Vermelha**, **Lula** and **Saco da Velha** – are all east of Paraty, roughly an hour away by boat. The best island beaches nearby are probably **Araújo** and **Sapeca**; many other islands have rocky shores and are private. The mainland beaches tend to be better; most have *barracas* (stalls) serving beer and fish and, at most, a handful of beachgoers.

Back in Paraty, walking north across the river, the first beach you'll reach is **Praia do Pontal**. A cluster of open-air restaurants lines its shore, but the water can get a bit murky. The cleaner and relatively secluded **Praia do Forte** lies a quick walk north from there. Another 2km further north is **Praia do Jabaquara**, a spacious beach with great views, shallow waters and a few small restaurants overlooking the sand.

Tours

Paraty Tours (☎ 3371 1327; www.paratytours.com.br; Av Roberto Silveira 11; ☒ 8am-9pm), located next door

---

PIRATES IN PARATY

Forte Defensor Perpétuo (admission R$2; ☒ 9am-noon & 2-5pm Wed-Sun) was built in 1703 to defend against pirate raids on the gold passing through Paraty's port, then rebuilt in 1822 upon Brazil's independence from Portugal. It's a 20-minute walk north of town. To get there, cross the bridge over the Rio Perequê Açu, then climb the Morro da Vila Velha, the hill past Praia do Pontal. The fort commands sweeping views over the bay and houses the **Centro de Artes e Tradições Populares de Paraty**, a museum and gallery that displays fishing implements and baskets, and sells local handicrafts.

---

to the tourist information office, offers hiking (R$100 to R$120, six hours), horseback riding (R$90, three hours), cycling (self-guided, R$7 per hour or R$35 per day) and diving (R$180 per day) adventures. Especially popular are five-hour schooner cruises, which cost R$30 and depart daily at 10am, 11am and noon, stopping at various beaches en route.

Paraty Adventure (☎ 3371 6135; www.paratyadventure.com; Av Roberto Silveira 80; ☒ 8am-9pm), diagonally across the street from Paraty Tours, offers similar itineraries and prices.

Festivals & Events

Carnaval here is a big street party – check out the Saturday procession of the Bloco da Lama, in which young people come in droves to cover themselves in mud and dance through the streets.

Holy Week celebrations include the beautiful **Procissão do Fogaréu**, a torchlit procession through the historic center starting just past midnight on the Thursday before Easter. The **Festa do Divino Espírito Santo** begins with colorful street decorations and processions nine days before Pentecostal Sunday (the seventh Sunday after Easter), and ends with a huge community lunch prepared by local women. **Corpus Christi** processions in June are also magnificent, with the cobblestone streets covered in carpets of colored sawdust, leaves, flowers, coffee grounds and chalk.

The **Festival Literária Internacional de Parati** (www.flip.org.br), launched in 2003, brings authors from around the world to Paraty for five days each July or August. The opening concert features big names in Brazilian music.

The Paraty region produces excellent *cachaça*, and in 1984 the town council inaugurated the annual **Festival da Pinga**. The *pinga* (another name for *cachaça*) party lasts for four days each August.

New festivals keep springing up each year. Recent additions include festivals of photography, gastronomy and street theater. See www.paraty.com.br/eventos.asp for a full list.

Sleeping

From December to February, and during festivals, hotels fill up and room prices double, so reservations are advisable. The rest of the year, finding accommodations is relatively easy. Prices quoted here are high-season rates; you can bargain for better deals during the off-season. Paraty is a favorite destination for gay and lesbian crowds and is generally gay-friendly.

BUDGET

Blue Jungle Hostel (☎ 9296 4226; www.bluejunglehostel .com; Rua Bem-Te-Vi 11; 9-bed/6-bed/4-bed dm R$22/30/35, d R$95-110, q R$140-160; 🖳 🛜 🔊) This unique hostel occupies a stone-walled 19th-century *fazenda* (farm) house on verdant grounds, 10 minutes' walk from the bus station via a pedestrian bridge. There's a guest kitchen, a big outdoor swimming pool and a hiking trail to the nearby river, where you can use the hostel's kayak to paddle to the ocean. Upstairs rooms have great mountain views.

Misti Chill Hostel & Pousada (☎ 3371 2545; www .mistichill.com; Rua Orlando Carpinelli 3; 9-bed/6-bed dm R$25/33, d/tr/q R$120/150/180; 🖳 🛜) Facing the sands of Praia do Pontal and only five minutes on foot from the colonial center, this relative newcomer offers six- and nine-bed dorms along with a couple of private rooms. The friendly reception, free wi-fi and reasonably priced bike and kayak rentals keep everyone smiling.

Sereia do Mar Hostel (☎ 3371 1930; www.sereiado mar.com; Praia da Jabaquara 33; dm R$30-35, d R$150-180; 🖳 🛜) A self-contained universe opposite Jabaquara beach, this hostel has its own restaurant, boat trips, kayak rentals and beach volleyball gear, along with private rooms and five- to 10-bed dorms. The ample chill-out spaces include bean-bag chairs, hammocks, low-lit ocean-view decks, ping-pong and pool tables and a guitar for communal twanging. Shuttle service is available for those intimidated by the 15-minute walk into town.

Historic Centre Hostel (☎ 3371 2236; www.histo riccentrehostel.com; Rua Dona Geralda 211; dm/d/tr/q R$35/140/150/160; 🎮 🛜) Conveniently located in Paraty's pedestrianized historic zone, the hostel offers a large upstairs dormitory, a guest kitchen and five smaller rooms clustered around a courtyard, including two with air-con (R$20 extra).

Paraty Hostel 'Casa do Rio' (☎ 3371 2223; www .paratyhostel.com; Rua Antônio de Oliveira Vidal 120; dm/d with HI card R$35/80, without card R$40/90; 🖳 🔊) Paraty's HI-affiliated hostel, along the river north of the bus station, has dorms plus a couple of private rooms. A riverside deck and swimming pool, hammocks, a shady sitting area, laundry facilities and free internet give it a homey feel. The hostel also organizes excursions to local beaches.

Pouso Familiar Helicônia (☎ 3371 1475; Rua José Vieira Ramos 262; s/d R$40/70) A friendly place close to the bus station, run by Joseph and Lucia, a Belgian/Brazilian couple. The pousada has five clean rooms around a central courtyard, with clothes-washing facilities and a book exchange. Joseph speaks English, German, French, Spanish and Dutch.

There are two campgrounds just north of town, across the pedestrian bridge.

MIDRANGE

Pousada Marendaz (☎ 3371 1369; www.paraty.com .br/marendaz, in Portuguese; Rua Dr Derly Ellena 9; s/d/ tr/q R$60/120/160/200; 🛜) Run by three sisters, this welcoming pousada is more of a family home than a hotel; the attractions include a big Jacuzzi tub in the bougainvillea-fringed courtyard.

Hotel Solar dos Gerânios (☎ 3371 1550; www.paraty .com.br/geranio; Praça da Matriz; s/d R$80/150; 🖳) Run by the same family for decades, this rustic place on lively Praça da Matriz is the most affordable hotel in Paraty's colonial center. Wood and ceramic sculptures, stone walls and floors, columns and beamed ceilings, and a courtyard full of plants, cats and dogs all add character. Some rooms have balconies overlooking the square.

A Joana Pousada (☎ 3371 7191; www.paraty.com.br/ ajoana; Av NS dos Remédios 9; r R$110-125; 🛜) Argentine owner Marta offers four rooms in this small home a stone's throw from Praia do Pontal. Breakfast is served on the outdoor patio, looking straight across the river at Paraty's colonial center.

Pousada Guaraná (☎ 3371 6362; www.pousada guarana.com.br; Rua 5, No 13; r from R$140; 🛜 🔊) US-Brazilian owners David and Jimena provide a warm welcome at this beautifully designed and spacious modern pousada 20 minutes' walk from the historic center. Amenities include high ceilings, a pleasant pool and lounge area and an ample breakfast with homemade bread and cake.

Pousada Vila da Mata (☎ 9999 9919; www.pousadavila damata.com.br, in Portuguese; Estrada Paraty/Cunha, 6.5km; d/tr/q R$150/200/250; 🖳 🛜 🔊) Several kilometers uphill from town along the Penha bus route, Vila da Mata features attractive, two-level rooms sleeping up to four, with kitchenettes and decks facing the jungle. There's a brand new pool, open-air lounge, library and yoga deck, and an outdoor grill and pizza oven available for guests' use.

our pick **Le Gite d'Indaiatiba** (☎ 3371 7174; www
.legitedindaiatiba.com.br; Hwy BR-101, km558; r R$150, bunga-
low R$200, loft R$400; ❄ ☜ ☒) Next to a waterfall
in a gorgeous jungle setting 18km north of
Paraty, well-traveled hosts Olivier and Valéria
rent out two *apartamentos* (rooms with a bathroom), one bungalow, and two newly refurbished 'lofts' with air-con, large bathtubs and
DVD players; all have fireplaces and verandas
offering pretty jungle views. Daytime activities
include horseback riding, jungle treks, dips in
a swimming hole beneath the waterfall, reading in the library and relaxing by the riverside
sauna and outdoor pool. The hotel's restaurant
offers superb Franco-Brazilian cuisine. Turn
inland on the unmarked dirt road at km558
on Hwy BR-101, then continue 4km, bearing
left at the fork halfway up the hill.

Pousada Flor do Mar (☎ 3371 1674; www.pousada
flordomar.com.br; Rua Fresca 257; r R$170; ❄ ⌨ ☜)
Hidden away on Paraty's beachfront, this simple little pousada has clean, spacious rooms,
a pretty front courtyard with hammocks and
couches, and one of the historic center's quietest locations.

TOP END

Pousada Morro do Forte (☎ 3371 1211; www.pousada
morrodoforte.com.br; Rua Orlando Carpinelli 21; r R$210-270;
❄ ☜ ☒) This modern pousada's incompa-
rable vistas of the town and bay are well worth
the uphill climb. Perched on the Morro do
Forte, five minutes' walk from downtown, it
has comfortable rooms with small balconies.
The owners speak English and German.

La Pousada Arte Colonial (☎ 3371 7347; www
.pousadaartecolonial.com.br; Rua da Matriz 292; r R$245-275;
❄ ☜ ☒) At this charming older house smack
in the colonial center, each unique room has
antique furnishings and plenty of character,
and many get lovely natural light. French-
speaking proprietress Nicole is a gold mine
of information on Paraty and surroundings.

Hotel Coxixo (☎ 3371 1460; www.hotelcoxixo.com.br;
Rua do Comércio 362; d/tr from R$254/360, 2-/3-/4-/5-person
ste R$340/410/480/550; ❄ ⌨ ☜ ☒) Centrally lo-
cated, this top-end hotel has cozy colonial
decor and a beautiful courtyard with pool and
bar. The spacious suites are more inviting than
the rather cramped standard rooms.

Pousada do Ouro (☎ 3371 4300; www.pousada
ouro.com.br; Rua da Praia 145; r from R$335, ste R$529;
❄ ⌨ ☜ ☒) It's easy to imagine bumping
into Mick Jagger, Sonia Braga or Tom Cruise
here, especially when you enter the lobby and

see photos of them posing in front of the pousada. The hotel has everything – bar, pool,
sauna and a gorgeous garden.

Pousada Arte Urquijo (☎ 3371 1362; www.urquijo
.com.br; Rua Dona Geralda 79; r from R$350; ☜ ☒) This
cozy little pousada is obviously a labor of love
for the artist owners. The downstairs sitting
area features plush cushions, a stylish bar and
a bubbling pool. Especially nice rooms are
Sofia, with its deck, flowering tree and ocean
view, and Xul, with its futon and floor-level
window imparting a Japanese feel.

Eating

Paraty has many pretty restaurants, but once
your feet touch the cobblestones in the picturesque historic center, prices rise.

BUDGET & MIDRANGE

Sabor da Terra (☎ 3371 2384; Av Roberto Silveira 180;
per 100g R$2.75; ☽ 11:30am-10pm) An affordable
self-serve restaurant just outside the historic
center, Sabor da Terra's tasty offerings include
shrimp and fish.

our pick **Creperia Francesa Farandole** (☎ 3371
1827; Rua Santa Rita 190; crepes R$13-22; ☽ 5pm-late
Wed-Mon) This sweet little creperie with indoor-
outdoor seating is run by Philippe, an affable Breton, and his Parisian wife Françoise.
The menu features savory and sweet crepes,
all named after characters from the Asterix
comic-book series.

Spaghetto (☎ 3371 2947; Rua da Matriz 27; mains
R$19-34; ☽ noon-11pm Tue-Sat) Candlelit tables line
the cobblestones at this Italian place serving
seafood-and-pasta specials such as *rigatoni
camarão e abobrinha* (rigatoni with shrimp
and zucchini).

Restaurante Netto (☎ 3371 6997; Rua da Lapa
402; mains for 2 from R$22; ☽ 11:30am-11pm) This
fan-cooled, no-frills eatery in the historical
center specializes in affordable fish and seafood dishes for two.

Santa Trindade (☎ 3371 1445; www.santatrindade
.com.br; Rua Dr Samuel Costa 267; fixed-price meals R$25;
☽ noon-1am) Since opening in 2009, this bar-
restaurant has become an instant hit. Its fixed-
price menu (which includes salad, main dish
and dessert) is one of the historic center's
best deals. There's live music nightly (8pm
onwards), with a R$7 cover charge.

TOP END

Casa do Fogo (☎ 9819 5111; Rua da Ferraria 390; mains
R$28-56; ☽ 6pm-midnight Mar-Nov, 1pm-1am Dec-Feb)

The name says it all here – everything's on fire! The menu focuses on seafood set ablaze with the local *cachaça*, and desserts don't escape a fiery death either.

Cheiro do Camarão (☎ 9817 2411; Hwy BR-101, km569, Corumbé; shrimp mains from R$30; ◷ 10am-5pm Tue-Sun) Escape the crowds, wiggle your toes in the sand and enjoy some of the finest shrimp around at this informal beachfront eatery 7km up the coast from Paraty.

Sabor do Mar (☎ 3371 1872; Rua Domingo Gonçalves de Abreu s/n; mains R$30-55; ◷ noon-11pm) The atmosphere's sterile but the seafood is super-fresh at this locally recommended restaurant and fish market just outside Paraty's pedestrian zone.

Margarida Café (☎ 3371 2441; Praça do Chafariz; mains R$33-55; ◷ noon-midnight) At the edge of the old town, this cavernous yet cozy café has great drinks, plus wood-fired pizzas (from R$19) and inventive meat, fish and pasta dishes. There's live MPB music (Musica Popular Brazileira, see p67) every night from 8pm, with a R$7 cover charge.

Banana da Terra (☎ 3371 1725; Rua Dr Samuel Costa 198; mains from R$60; ◷ 6pm-midnight Mon, Wed & Thu, noon-4pm & 7pm-midnight Fri-Sun) Chef Ana Bueno's creative taste combinations and artistic presentation make this one of Paraty's classiest restaurants. There's also an excellent wine list.

our pick Academia de Cozinha e Outros Prazeres (☎ 3371 6468; www.chefbrasil.com; Rua Dona Geralda 288; all-included dinner R$180) Tired of eating out? How about cooking your own gourmet dinner tonight, with the help of acclaimed local chef and cookbook author Yara Roberts? Mixing theater with haute cuisine, chef Yara stages cooking classes in Portuguese, English, French and Spanish. Guests learn about Brazilian regional cuisines, assist with the cooking (optional), then sit down to a leisurely dinner

and an evening of lively conversation. Groups are often international – residents of over 60 countries have participated to date. The price includes cocktails, wine, desserts and recipes.

Drinking & Entertainment

A slew of bars spills tables out onto the tree-shaded cobblestones of Praça da Matriz from late afternoon to the wee hours.

Paraty 33 (☎ 3371 7311; www.paraty33.com.br; Rua da Lapa 357; ◷ noon-late) With an early evening happy hour featuring MPB and bossa nova, and a late-night weekend mix of DJs and live acts, Paraty 33 is the historic center's liveliest nightspot.

Teatro Espaço (☎ 3371 1575; www.ecparaty.org. br; Rua Dona Geralda 327; admission R$40) This small playhouse presents puppetry, music and dance performances by the internationally acclaimed resident theater company, Contadores de Estórias.

Getting There & Away

The **bus station** (Rua Jango Pádua) is 500m west of the old town. Costa Verde offers frequent service to Rio de Janeiro (R$49, four hours, seven to 10 daily from 5:20am to 9pm). Colitur has buses to Angra dos Reis (R$8.40, two hours, at least hourly from 4:40am to 10:30pm) and Reunidas buses head to São Paulo (R$43, six hours, six daily between 8:30am and 11:30pm).

AROUND PARATY
Cachoeira Tobogã

In the hills 10km inland, this natural waterslide is a blast! Take a local Colitur bus to Penha (R$3, 30 minutes), and get off at the white church. Follow signs 100m downhill to an idyllic pool surrounded by jungle, with a slick rock face that makes a perfect natural

---

DETOUR: PARQUE NACIONAL DA SERRA DA BOCAINA – HIKING THE TRILHA DO OURO

The historic Trilha do Ouro (Gold Trail), which connected Paraty to the interior of Minas Gerais, has become a popular hiking route in recent years, passing through dramatic scenery in the **Parque Nacional da Serra da Bocaina**. Paraty Tours (p193) offers two-hour day hikes covering a very small fraction of the trail above Paraty, near Penha.

our pick MW Trekking (www.mwtrekking.com.br) offers a more challenging experience with the three-day, 42km Trilha do Ouro backpacking adventure. The R$492 price includes transport to the trailhead, park fees, food, simple lodging and guide. The trek starts in José do Barreiro in São Paulo state – most easily accessed by **Viação Azteca bus** (☎ 0xx24-3359 0498, R$9, 90 minutes) from Resende near Parque Nacional de Itatiaia (see p202) – and visits a number of spectacular waterfalls en route towards Mambucaba, on the coast 45 minutes northeast of Paraty.

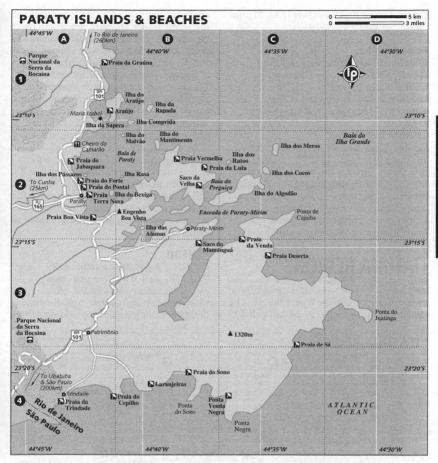

PARATY ISLANDS & BEACHES

slide (once featured in the movie *The Emerald Forest*). Tourists who value their skulls should heed the posted warnings against surfing (ie standing instead of sitting), although local teenagers have mastered the technique and it's exciting (if terrifying!) to watch. Afterwards, grab a caipirinha at Bar do Tarzan, across the swinging bridge above the falls.

Praia da Trindade

About 25km south of Paraty, Trindade occupies a long sweep of stunningly beautiful coastline. Here you can lounge or hike along four of Brazil's most dazzling beaches (Cepilho, Ranchos, Meio and Cachadaço), with surging breakers, enormous boulders, vast expanses of mountain-fringed white

sand, steep trails threading through the dense jungle, and a calm-watered natural swimming pool opposite the furthest beach, Cachadaço. The town itself has the somewhat scraggly quality of a frontier outpost that's grown up too fast (indeed, 20 years ago there was only a small fishing village here), but the sizeable cluster of pousadas, hostels, camping grounds and restaurants permits an overnight stay. Hourly Colitur buses (R$3, 40 minutes) serve Trindade from Paraty's bus station.

Praia de Paraty-Mirim

For accessibility, cost and beauty, this tranquil beach is hard to beat. Paraty-Mirim is a small town 17km southeast of Paraty, with *barracas* serving simple meals, and an 18th-century church. Colitur runs buses here (R$3, 40 minutes) from Paraty's bus station.

Praia do Sono

Praia do Sono is another stunning beach, about 35km southeast of Paraty. Catch a Colitur bus to Laranjeiras (R$3, 40 minutes) and then walk 1½ hours east to Sono. Paraty Tours (p193) has organized hikes to Sono.

Cachaça Distilleries

Paraty is renowned for its excellent *cachaça*, and many *alambiques* (distilleries) in the area offer tours. Among the best is **Maria Izabel** (☎ 9999 9908; www.mariaizabel.com.br, in Portuguese; Sítio Santo Antônio, Corumbê), 10km north of town, which often places within the top 10 or 20 in nationwide competitions. Call at least 24 hours in advance to arrange a visit.

ITATIAIA REGION

The Itatiaia region is a curious mix of Old World charm and New World jungle. The climate is Alpine temperate and the chalets are Swiss, but the vegetation is tropical and the warm smiles are pure Brazilian. There are neatly tended little farms with horses and goats, and small homes with clipped lawns and flower boxes side by side with large tracts of dense forest untouched by the machete. This is a wonderful place to tramp around green hills, ride ponies up purple mountains, splash in waterfalls and hike trails without straying too far from the comforts of civilization: a fireplace, a soft bed, a little wine and a well-grilled trout!

The region lies in the Serra da Mantiqueira's Itatiaia massif, in the northwest corner of Rio de Janeiro, and borders the states of São Paulo and Minas Gerais. This idyllic corner of Rio de Janeiro state was settled by Europeans, but it is now popular among Brazilians of all ethnic groups.

PENEDO

☎ 0xx24 / pop 40,000 / elevation 600m

Originally started as a Finnish colony in the early 20th century, Penedo has grown into a vacation resort that embraces all things non-Brazilian. In the more developed lower section

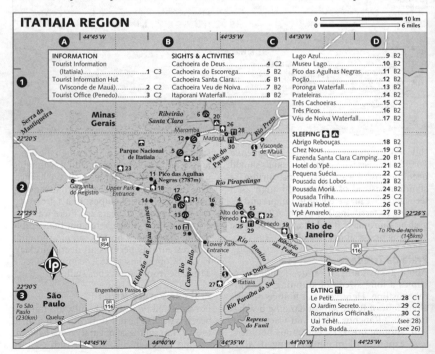

ITATIAIA REGION

INFORMATION	
Tourist Information	
(Itatiaia)................................1	C3
Tourist Information Hut	
(Visconde de Mauá)................2	C2
Tourist Office (Penedo)............3	B2

SIGHTS & ACTIVITIES	
Cachoeira de Deus....................4	C2
Cachoeira do Escorrega............5	B2
Cachoeira Santa Clara..............6	B1
Cachoeira Veu de Noiva............7	B2
Itaporani Waterfall....................8	B2

Lago Azul................................9	B2
Museu Lago............................10	B2
Pico das Agulhas Negras..........11	B2
Poção....................................12	B2
Poronga Waterfall....................13	B2
Prateleiras..............................14	B2
Três Cachoeiras......................15	C2
Três Picos..............................16	B2
Véu de Noiva Waterfall............17	B2

SLEEPING	
Abrigo Rebouças......................18	B2
Chez Nous..............................19	C2
Fazenda Santa Clara Camping...20	B1
Hotel do Ypê..........................21	B2
Pequena Suécia......................22	C2
Pousada dos Lobos..................23	B2
Pousada Moriá........................24	B2
Pousada Trilha........................25	C2
Warabi Hotel..........................26	C1
Ypê Amarelo..........................27	B3

EATING	
Le Petit..................................28	C1
O Jardim Secreto....................29	C2
Rosmarinus Officinalis.............30	C2
Uai Tchê!................................(see 28)
Zorba Budda............................(see 26)

of town, you'll find tourist traps capitalizing on the region's European heritage mixed in with authentic Old World influences. In Alto do Penedo, the upper part of town, it's easier to appreciate the luxuriant natural beauty that lies just outside the city limits. Wherever you go, you'll be sure to appreciate the emphasis on the traditional Finnish sauna, found at most hotels.

The **tourist office** (☎ 3351 1704; Av Casa das Pedras 766; ☺ 9:30am-5pm) has brochures and information in Portuguese.

Sights

Penedo's main attractions are the forest and waterfalls. Two especially worthwhile waterfalls are **Três Cachoeiras**, west of downtown Penedo along the main road just before it starts climbing to Alto do Penedo, and **Cachoeira de Deus**, about 20 minutes uphill from the bus turnaround in Alto do Penedo. Ask locally for directions, as signs are intermittent. About one hour of uphill **hiking** from the end of the asphalt in Alto do Penedo takes you into very dense forest with trails and opportunities to observe wildlife, including monkeys.

In town, you can hire horses at **From Penedo** (☎ 3351 1380; www.penedo.com/frompenedo; Rua das Palmeiras; 90min ride with guide R$45).

Sleeping & Eating

Penedo is expensive, due to the large number of weekend tourists who come up from Rio, but the accommodations and food are above average.

Pousada Trilha (☎ 3351 1349; www.trilhapousada .com, in Portuguese; Av Três Cachoeiras 3951; s/d R$80/110; ☺ ☺) Just downhill from Três Cachoeiras, this simple pousada resembles a log cabin. Rooms are small but comfy; the best have big windows overlooking the forest, with the sound of rushing water just outside.

Chez Nous (☎ 3351 1404; www.pousadacheznous .com.br, in Portuguese; Av Casa da Pedra 542; r R$80-160; ☒ ☺ ☺) This friendly French-speaking place near the town entrance gate offers rooms of varying prices around a green and peaceful central garden. The best rooms have whirlpool tubs and fireplaces; there's also a pool and sauna.

Pequena Suécia (☎ 3351 1275; www.pequenasue cia.com.br, in Portuguese; Rua Toivo Suni 33; s R$115-195, d R$195-395; ☒ ☺ ☺) A Penedo classic on the quiet (north) side of the river, this red house in the woods has provided luxurious ameni-

ties in a rustic setting for over half a century. The on-site restaurant serves Scandinavian and vegetarian food, the spa offers massage and shiatsu treatments, and the attached club features live jazz music on weekends.

Koskenkorva (☎ 3351 2532; Av Três Cachoeiras 3955; mains R$25-35; ☺ noon-4pm & 7:30-10pm) With a lovely outdoor seating area by a creek, Koskenkorva specializes in Finnish and German food. For a splurge, try Voileipäpöytä (R$65), a smorgasbord-like platter featuring smoked trout, marinated salmon, herring, trout pâté and much more. Leave room for the fruit dessert crepes.

O Jardim Secreto (☎ 3351 2516; Av Três Cachoeiras 3899; mains R$31-69; ☺ 7pm-midnight Tue-Fri, noon-midnight Sat, noon-5pm Sun) This classy, candlelit eatery, surrounded by exuberant greenery, serves a contemporary menu of fish, meat and pasta dishes.

Entertainment

There is now only a sprinkling of Finns among the assortment of Brazilian people, but they all get together for traditional Finnish *letkiss* and *jenkkas* dances at **Clube Finlândia** (☎ 3351 1374; Av das Mangueiras 2601; admission R$10; ☺ 9pm-1am Sat) every Saturday night. Finnish dancing lessons are open to the public starting at 9pm. At 10:30pm a local troupe presents a 40-minute traditional dance performance in Old World getup, then the dance floor is reopened to everyone for the rest of the night.

Getting There & Away

Cidade do Aço operates two buses daily from Rio to Penedo (R$29, 2½ hours) at 11am and 5pm. Alternatively, take one of its more frequent buses from Rio to Resende, then catch the half-hourly Resende–Penedo bus (R$2.30, 45 minutes). The bus services the 3km-long main street and continues to the end of the paved road.

VISCONDE DE MAUÁ
☎ 0xx24 / elevation 1200m
Mauá is an utterly idyllic river valley that feels like a world unto itself. Prettier and more tranquil than Penedo, it has rushing streams, tinkling goat bells, cozy chalets and country lanes graced with wildflowers. Its isolation is largely thanks to the town's limited access routes, all via rutted dirt roads over precipitous mountaintops. At the time of research, plans were underway to improve the main

road from Penedo, but until further notice, be ready for a bumpy ride!

Information

Visconde de Maná consists of three small villages a few kilometers apart along the Rio Preto. The bus stops first at Maná, the largest village, and then heads uphill to Maringá, 6km to the west (one side of Maringá is actually in Minas Gerais; Maringá addresses listed here are marked 'RJ' or 'MG' to show which side of the river they're on). Maromba is further upstream at the end of the bus route and about 2km west of Maringá. Most travelers stay in Maromba or Maringá. Maromba has the feel of a hippie hangout, while Maringá attracts a slightly more upscale crowd.

At the entrance to the village of Maná, the **tourist information hut** (☺ 10am-1pm & 2-6pm, closed Thu morning, Sun afternoon & all day Wed) has helpful photos of area accommodations and can call ahead to reserve. **Lan House** (Maringá, RJ; per hr R$2; ☺ 10am-10pm) offers broadband internet and wi-fi access.

Sights & Activities

Cachoeira Santa Clara, one of the nicest and most accessible of Maná's dozen or so waterfalls, is a 40-minute walk north of Maringá on the Ribeirão Santa Clara. Ask the locals for directions. For a bit of a hike, climb up through the bamboo groves on either side of the falls. Also worth a visit is **Cachoeira Veu de Noiva**, a very beautiful waterfall 300m off the main road just west of Maromba.

It's possible to kayak the rapids of Rio Preto, the cascading river dividing Minas Gerais from Rio state. The river also has several small beaches and natural pools. Two especially fine swimming spots are the **Poção**, a giant natural pool 1km west of Maromba and the **Cachoeira do Escorrega**, a natural water slide culminating in another gorgeous pool 2km west of Maromba.

Homo Bikers (☎ 9822 7129; homobikers@gmail.com; Alameda Gastronômica, Maringá, MG) offers paragliding, rafting and mountain-bike excursions in the surrounding mountains. It also rents high-quality mountain bikes (R$50 to R$80 per 24-hour period).

Horseback riding is also available from various private operators around town.

Sleeping

Inexpensive, bare-bones rooms (R$15 to R$25 per person) are available near the bus stops in Maná and Maromba. Ask for Antônio on Maná's main street or Moises on Maromba's central square. The valley is jam-packed with chalet-style accommodations; if places listed here are full, just ask around.

Fazenda Santa Clara Camping (☎ 3387 1508; Estrada Maringá/Maromba 1km; camping per person R$15) Occupying a grassy slope at the convergence of the Rios Preto and Santa Clara, this camping ground has a natural swimming hole, a snack bar and miniscule two-person A-frames to rent (R$45) for those without a tent. The bus stop across the river is accessible via a pedestrian bridge.

ourpick Warabi Hotel (☎ 3387 1143; www.viscondemauaturismo.com, in Portuguese; Alto Maringá, RJ; s/d midweek R$110/157, weekend R$145/210) Comfy futons, Japanese *ofuro* tubs, a goldfish pond and rock garden all contribute to the inviting atmosphere at this unique lodging just above Maringá. Best of all are the spacious riverside deck, swimming pool and on-site Japanese restaurant serving sushi (from R$16) and main dishes like tempura and sukiyaki (R$30 to R$38).

Pousada Moriá (☎ 3387 1505; www.pousadamoria .com.br, in Portuguese; Estrada da Maromba s/n; d R$160, with whirlpool tub R$230-260; ☒) This idyllic hideaway is opposite the Cachoeira do Escorrega (p200). Chalets all have electric blankets and fireplaces, and there's a sauna, outdoor pool and free DVD library. Delicious full breakfasts are served in a glass-walled cabin or out on the deck within earshot of the waterfall.

Eating

Since 1996, Maná has hosted a May culinary festival, the **Concurso Gastronômico** (www.mauagastronomico.com.br, in Portuguese), with special emphasis on the local trout and *pinhões*, giant nuts from the native *araucária* trees.

Don't miss the Alameda Gastronômica (restaurant row), a street packed with restaurants for every taste along the Rio Preto riverbank on the Minas Gerais side of Maringá. In addition to those listed here, you'll find Italian and vegetarian eateries, a German beer garden, a jazz bistro and a restaurant whose entire menu revolves around local mushrooms.

Zorba Budda (☎ 3387 1170; Alto Maringá, RJ; pizza from R$19; ☺ 8pm-1am Fri-Sun) This sweet little pumpkin-colored restaurant serves excellent pizza and is packed on weekend nights.

Uai Tchê! (☎ 3387 1364; Alameda Gastronômica, Maringá, MG; mains R$23-28; ☺ 1-8pm Wed, Thu & Sun, to

10pm Fri & Sat) This cozy hole-in-the-wall with *cachaça* bottles lining the shelves serves a mean *feijão tropeiro* (a classic concoction of rice, beans, sausage and kale) and an even meaner caipirinha to wash it down. The inspired range of artisanal sausages includes *truta* (made with local trout) and *Jamaica* (made with chicken, cinnamon, cloves, oranges and honey).

Le Petit (☎ 3387 1554; Alameda Gastronômica, Maringá, MG; mains R$23-36; ⏰ 2-11pm Thu-Sat, 1-7pm Sun-Wed) Affable owners Sapo and Miriam launched their business a generation ago as a place for locals to sip beer while waiting to use the town's lone public phone. Over 20 years later, it's still popular as much for its unhurried, convivial atmosphere as for its inspired treatments of the valley's favorite fish; try the trout in sake sauce with coconut *farofa* (sautéed manioc flour).

Rosmarinus Officinalis (☎ 3387 1550; Estrada Maringá, 4km; mains R$40-93; ⏰ 7-10pm Mon, Wed & Thu, 1-10pm Fri & Sat, 1-6pm Sun) Beautifully set amid gardens, with smoke pouring out its chimney in chilly weather and candlelight reflecting off the windows at night, this restaurant looks like a fairy-tale house, but the food is strictly gourmet. The menu of locally influenced Italian dishes, such as risotto with grilled trout, has earned it a reputation as one of Mauá's finest restaurants.

Getting There & Around

Visconde de Mauá has no bus station. Buses stop at the top of Mauá's main street and in the center of Maringá before ending their run at Maromba's town square.

Four daily Resendense buses (three on weekends) run between Resende (a transport hub just east of Itatiaia) and Maromba (R$5.75, two hours). Transfer in Resende for buses to/from Rio de Janeiro. Cidade de Aço also runs one direct bus weekly between Rio and Maromba (R$48, 4½ hours), leaving Rio at 7:30pm on Fridays and returning from Maromba at 4pm on Sundays as well as holidays.

PARQUE NACIONAL DE ITATIAIA

☎ 0xx24

Parque Nacional de Itatiaia (☎ 3352 1461; parnaitatiaia.rj.@icmbio.gov.br) is Brazil's oldest national park, and one of its most ruggedly beautiful. Its lush, dark foliage contains more than 400 species of native birds and is also home to monkeys and sloths. Divided into upper and lower sections, the park features lakes, rivers, waterfalls, alpine meadows and primary and secondary Atlantic rain forests. Don't let the tropical plants fool you; temperatures drop below freezing in June and, occasionally, the park even has a few snowy days! Bring warm clothes, even in summer.

There is a 24-hour tourist information booth in the town of Itatiaia, 1km north of the Via Dutra, the main east–west superhighway between Rio and São Paulo. The lower park entrance is 5.5km north of town.

Sights & Activities

Each section of the park (upper and lower) has its own **entrance station** (admission per person R$20; ⏰ upper entrance 7am-5pm, lower entrance 7:30am-5pm). Park headquarters and the adjacent **museum** (admission free) are 9km north of Itatiaia town, in the park's lower, tamer section. From headquarters, a simple 400m walk takes you to **Lago Azul** (Blue Lake). A few kilometers up the road, short trails lead to the **Poronga**, **Véu de Noiva** and **Itaporani waterfalls**. For a longer hike in the low country, try the five-hour, 15km return trip to **Três Picos** (1600m).

Climbing and trekking enthusiasts will want to pit themselves against the high country's more challenging peaks, cliffs and trails. The park's diminutive upper entrance station – almost two hours drive from Itatiaia town – is reached by way of a 15km extremely rugged unpaved road from a junction called Garganta do Registro, along Hwy BR-354 at the border between Rio state and Minas Gerais state.

Prominently visible as you enter the park are the dramatic pointy profiles of the **Agulhas Negras** (at 2787m, the highest peak in the area) and, a bit further on, the boulders of the **Prateleiras**. A guide is required for climbs to these peaks, or for the **Travessia Rui Braga**, a nine-hour downhill day hike that starts at the foot of Prateleiras and links the upper and lower parts of the park, allowing visitors to experience Itatiaia's alpine and Atlantic rain forest ecosystems in a single long day.

One recommended guide is the park ranger **Levy Cardozo da Silva** (☎ 8812 0006; levy.ecologico@hotmail.com). You can also contact the **Grupo Excursionista Agulhas Negras** (www.grupogean.com, in Portuguese), which organizes climbs throughout the year, or ask local pousadas to help you find a guide.

Sleeping & Eating

The fancier hotels inside the national park offer full board as noted in individual reviews. However, you'll want to bring your own food if staying in one of the area's simpler accommodations (first two listings below).

Abrigo Rebouças (☎ 3352 1461) This hikers' shelter in the high country, with a gas stove and electricity, provides basic accommodations for up to 20 people but no food or other supplies. Beyond the park entrance fee, there's no extra cost for staying here, but you should reserve as far in advance as possible; the place fills up fast!

Ypê Amarelo (☎ 3352 1232; www.pousadaypeamarelo .com.br, in Portuguese; Rua João Mauricio de Macedo Costa 352; campsite per person with/without breakfast R$35/25, r incl breakfast R$35/45; 🏊) This combination pousada/ campground just north of the Via Dutra has pleasant green grounds, hot showers, a pool, a sauna and bicycles for rent. It's a 15-minute walk west of the bus station (R$10 by taxi).

Pousada dos Lobos (☎ 0xx35-3332 2779; www.pou sadadoslobos.com.br, in Portuguese; s/d/tr with half-board R$130/200/280) High country visitors can try this pousada at 1800m, 12km off the main road and 11km from the national park's upper entrance station. Breakfast and dinner are included in the room rates, but it's wise to bring extra supplies, especially snacks and warm clothes – it gets cold up here, and it's a long, bumpy drive out!

ourpick Hotel do Ypê (☎ 3352 1453; www.hotel doype.com.br; s/d with full board from R$215/290; 🏊) About 8.5km north of the lower park entrance, this wonderful place at the end of the road is close to several hiking trails, with comfortable chalets for rent. Toucans and hummingbirds feed in abundance outside the breakfast room window, and at lunchtime there's a great outdoor barbecue served around the pool.

Getting There & Around

The village of Itatiaia is most easily reached from the nearby city of Resende (the hub for buses to/from Rio). Service between Itatiaia and Resende runs every 20 minutes on weekdays, every 40 minutes on weekends. From Itatiaia village to the park entrance, there are three daily buses (R$2 one-way, leaving the Itatiaia bus station at 6:50am, noon and 3pm; returning from the park at 8am, 1pm and 4:45pm). A taxi ride from Itatiaia village to the end of the park road costs around R$40.

NORTH OF RIO DE JANEIRO

The mountains north of Rio rise up with shapes so improbable and dramatic, they catch your attention even from a great distance. Landing at Galeão international airport or surveying the northern skyline from the top of Rio's Pão de Açúcar (Sugarloaf), your eye is automatically drawn to the intriguing sawtooth ridge on the horizon. In the 19th century, the allure of these mountains led Brazil's imperial family to set up a summer residence in Petrópolis, and inspired the country's first Swiss immigrants to choose Nova Friburgo as their New World home.

More recently, climbers from all over the world have become enamored of the vertiginous rocky faces of the Serra dos Órgãos (Organ Pipe Range). To this day, the cooler climate and recreational opportunities, along with the region's imperial and immigrant legacy, continue to attract visitors from Rio and beyond.

PETRÓPOLIS

☎ 0xx24 / pop 320,000 / elevation 809m

A lovely mountain retreat with a decidedly European flavor, Petrópolis is where the imperial court spent the summer when Rio got too muggy, and it's still a favorite weekend getaway for Cariocas (residents of Rio city). You can explore by wandering around or by riding on a horse and carriage through the squares and parks, past bridges, canals and old-fashioned street lamps.

Information

Bradesco (Rua do Imperador 268) One of many ATMs along downtown's main street.

Job Net (☎ 2231 7331; Rua 16 de Março 80; internet per hr R$3; 🕙 9am-8:30pm Mon-Fri, 11am-5pm Sat) Internet, wi-fi and Skype access.

Lavanderia Itaipava (☎ 2242 8145; Rua 16 de Março 334; per machine R$9; 🕙 8am-8pm Mon-Sat)

Post office (Rua do Imperador 350)

Tourist information (☎ 0800 024 1516; www .petropolis.rj.gov.br/fctp); main office (Praça da Liberdade; 🕙 9am-6pm Mon-Sat, 9am-5pm Sun); Centro de Cultura (Praça Visconde de Mauá 305; 🕙 9am-6pm Mon-Fri)

Trekking Petrópolis (☎ 2235 7607; m1wnk@uol .com.br) Organizes city tours, hikes, mountain-biking and bird-watching trips through nearby Mata Atlântica rain forest.

Sights & Activities

Most of the museums and other attractions are closed on Monday.

A fun way to get oriented is by taking a **horse and carriage ride**. Nineteenth-century *vitórias*, carriages of British design, make fixed-price circuits of the downtown area lasting 20 minutes (R$25) to one hour (R$50).

Petrópolis' main draw is the **Museu Imperial** (☎ 2237 8000; Rua da Imperatriz 220; admission R$8; ☾ 11am-5:30pm Tue-Sun), housed in the impeccably preserved and appointed palace of Dom Pedro II. You're given felt slippers at the entrance so you won't scuff the fine wood floors – great fun to slide around in! On display is the 1.95kg imperial crown, with its 639 diamonds and 77 pearls, as well as the ruby-encrusted, feather-shaped gold pen used to sign the *Lei Aurea*, freeing Brazil's remaining slaves in 1888.

The **Catedral São Pedro de Alcântara** (☎ 2242 4300; Rua Sao Pedro de Alcântara 60; ☾ 8am-6pm) houses the tombs of Brazil's last emperor, Dom Pedro II, his wife Dona Teresa and their daughter, Princesa Isabel. Its steeple is lit up with beautiful bluish-purple lights at night. For good city views, climb the **bell tower** (admission R$8; ☾ 11am-5pm Tue-Sat, 1-3pm Sun).

One of Petrópolis' finest mansions, the **Casa da Ipiranga** (☎ 2231 8718; casadaipiranga@yahoo.com.br; Av Ipiranga 716; admission R$6; ☾ noon-6pm Thu-Tue) is open to visitors by guided tour. Other historical buildings can be viewed from the outside only, including the **Palácio Rio Negro** (Av Koeller 255), the **Palácio da Princesa Isabel** (Av Koeller s/n) and the **Casa do Barão de Mauá** (Praça da Confluencia), across Rio Piabanha.

The **Palácio Cristal** (Alfredo Pachá) is an iron and glass structure built in France and imported in 1879 to serve as a hothouse in which to grow orchids. It now serves as a venue for evening cultural events.

West of Praça da Liberdade, the **Casa de Santos Dumont** (admission R$5; ☾ 9am-5pm Tue-Sun) was the summer home of Brazil's diminutive father of aviation and inventor of the wristwatch. The house itself is charming and there are interesting photos of Dumont's many inventions.

The **Trono de Fátima** is a 3.5m sculpture of NS de Fátima Madonna, imported from Italy. From here you have a great view of the town

RIO DE JANEIRO STATE

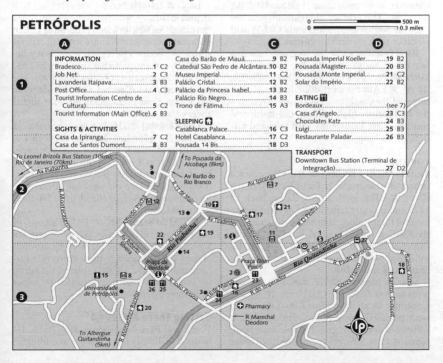

PETRÓPOLIS

0 ————— 500 m
0 ————— 0.3 miles

INFORMATION
Bradesco..............................1 C2
Job Net................................2 C3
Lavanderia Itaipava..............3 B3
Post Office...........................4 C3
Tourist Information (Centro de Cultura)...........................5 C2
Tourist Information (Main Office)..6 B3

SIGHTS & ACTIVITIES
Casa da Ipiranga...................7 C2
Casa de Santos Dumont.........8 B3

Casa do Barão de Mauá..........9 B2
Catedral São Pedro de Alcântara..10 B2
Museu Imperial....................11 C2
Palácio Cristal.....................12 B2
Palácio da Princesa Isabel.....13 B2
Palácio Rio Negro................14 B2
Trono de Fátima..................15 A3

SLEEPING
Casablanca Palace................16 B2
Hotel Casablanca.................17 C2
Pousada 14 Bis....................18 D3

Pousada Imperial Koeller.......19 B2
Pousada Magister.................20 B3
Pousada Monte Imperial........21 C2
Solar do Império..................22 B2

EATING
Bordeaux.........................(see 7)
Casa d'Angelo.....................23 C3
Chocolates Katz...................24 B3
Luigi.................................25 B3
Restaurante Paladar..............26 B3

TRANSPORT
Downtown Bus Station (Terminal de Integração)......................27 D2

To Leonel Brizola Bus Station (10km);
Rio de Janeiro (70km)
Av Piabanha

To Pousada da Alcobaça (8km)
Av Barão do Rio Branco

Av Ipiranga

R Tiradentes

R da Imperatriz

Av Tiradentes

R D'Pedro

Alfredo Pachá

Rio Piabanha

Av Koeller

Av Roberto Silva

Praça da Liberdade

R João Pessoa

R 16 de Março

Praça Dom Pedro

R do Imperador

Rio Quitandinha

R Paulo Barbosa

R Souza Franco

R Santos Dumont

Buenos Aires

Universidade de Petrópolis

To Albergue Quitandinha (5km)

R Monsenhor Bacella

Pharmacy
R Marechal Deodoro

and surrounding hills. To reach it, turn right as you leave the Casa de Santos Dumont and continue walking uphill, always taking the right fork.

Sleeping

BUDGET & MIDRANGE

Albergue Quitandinha (☎ 2247 9165; www.alberguequitandinha.com.br; Rua Uruguai 570; dm/s/d R$40/80/106; 🖾) Out of the way but affordable, this HI-affiliated hostel offers dorms and private rooms in little chalets.

Pousada 14 Bis (☎ 2231 0946; www.pousada14bis.com.br; Rua Buenos Aires 192; s/d from R$80/150; 🖾 🖭) On a quiet residential street near the downtown bus station, the restored colonial Pousada 14 Bis has handsome, well-appointed rooms with comfortable beds. The best offer lovely wood floors and balconies overlooking the peaceful street or garden out back.

Casablanca Palace (☎ 2242 0162; www.casablancahotel.com.br; Rua 16 de Março 123; s/d/tr standard R$90/105/145, deluxe R$110/130/200; 🖾) It's bland but clean, and close to the main shopping district. Deluxe rooms have minibars and wi-fi.

Pousada Magister (☎ 2242 1054; www.pousadamagister.com.br; Rua Monsenhor Bacelar 71; s/d from R$110/180; 🖾 🖾 🖭) This century-old mansion near the Casa de Santos Dumont blends Old-World elegance with modern amenities.

Hotel Casablanca (☎ 2242 6662; www.casablancahotel.com.br; Rua da Imperatriz 286; s/d/tr with fan R$160/198/270, s/d/tr/q with air-con R$200/220/290/330; 🖾 🖾 🖭) Almost next door to the Museu Imperial, the Casablanca has a range of rooms – the best feature high ceilings, old-fashioned shutters, large bathrooms with tubs and antique furnishings.

TOP END

Pousada Imperial Koeller (☎ 2243 4330; www.pousadamonteimperial.com.br; Av Koeller 99; r R$195-315; 🖳 🖾 🖭) This gabled gem, dating back to 1875 and recently refurbished, is right in the heart of things, along architecturally stunning Av Koeller. Its sister hotel Pousada Monte Imperial, in an old vine-covered house on the hillside above the Museu Imperial, shares the same rates and website.

Solar do Império (☎ 2103 3000; www.solardoimperio.com.br; Av Koeller 376; r R$318-680; 🖾 🖾 🖭) Centrally located on Praça da Liberdade, with polished wood floors, 5m ceilings, a columned entryway, grand fireplaces, a pool, sauna and spa, the meticulously restored Solar

do Império will make you feel like a member of the royal family. The attached Leopoldina restaurant (mains R$31 to R$61) is one of the city's finest.

Pousada da Alcobaça (☎ 2221 1240; www.pousadadaalcobaca.com.br; Rua Agostinho Goulão 298, Corrêas; d from R$350; 🖾 🖾 🖭) In the suburb of Corrêas, this beautiful hotel has a pool, a sauna, a tennis court and lovely gardens crossed by a small river. There's also an excellent restaurant.

Eating

Restaurante Paladar (☎ 2243 1143; Rua Barão do Amazonas 25; per 100g R$2.99; 🕙 11am-4pm Tue-Sun) Prices are higher than at your average per-kilo joint, but the atmosphere can't be beat at this classy converted mansion across from Praça da Liberdade. Watch the horse-drawn carriages clip-clop by as you enjoy classic Brazilian fare on the old-fashioned wraparound porch.

Chocolates Katz (☎ 2231 1191; Rua do Imperador 912; cake slices R$6.20, apple strudel R$6.50; 🕙 11am-8pm) This German-style coffee shop and patisserie makes excellent cappuccinos, hot cocoa and chocolate torte.

Luigi (☎ 2244 4444; Praça da Liberdade 185; pizza R$12-37, pasta R$13-23; 🕙 restaurant 11am-midnight, pizzeria 6pm-midnight Tue, Wed, Thu & Sun) A charming Italian restaurant set in an old house with tall ceilings and creaky floors. The regular menu is supplemented by an antipasto bar (per 100g R$4.69) and an all-you-can-eat buffet (R$19.90). The pizzeria next door serves a *rodízio de pizza* (all-you-can-eat pizza, R$19.90) four nights a week.

Casa d'Angelo (☎ 2242 0888; Rua do Imperador 700; mains R$13-31; 🕙 8am-1am) Opposite the obelisk at the corner of Ruas Imperador and Imperatriz, Casa d'Angelo is a Petrópolis institution for beers and reasonably priced meals. It's especially good value on weekday afternoons, when *pratos executivos* (fixed-price lunches) go for R$12.90.

our pick Bordeaux (☎ 2242 5711; Av Ipiranga 716; fixed-price lunches R$13-20, mains R$18-55; 🕙 noon-1am Mon-Sat, to 6pm Sun) On the picturesque grounds of the Casa da Ipiranga, these converted historic stables make an atmospheric backdrop for lunch or dinner accompanied by wines from their extensive cellar.

Getting There & Around

Única and Fácil buses from Rio (R$16, 1½ hours, half-hourly from 5:30am to midnight) drop you at the Leonel Brizola bus station in Bingen, 10km outside downtown Petrópolis. To reach the downtown bus station (Terminal de Integração), transfer to a local Esperança bus, number 100 (R$2.20, 30 minutes).

VASSOURAS

☎ 0xx24 / pop 34,000 / elevation 434m

Vassouras, a quiet resort 118km north of Rio, was the most important city in the Paraíba valley in the first half of the 19th century. Local coffee barons, with titles of nobility granted by the Portuguese crown, built huge *fazendas* in the surrounding hills. With the abolition of slavery in 1888 and the resulting decline in coffee production, the importance of Vassouras diminished, but several historic buildings from the boom days still survive in the pleasant town center.

The area's biggest attractions are the coffee *fazendas* several kilometers outside of town, some of them on the scale of French châteaux and with gardens to match. To visit these, you really need your own vehicle; otherwise, you'll run up some hefty cab fares or calf muscles!

For two weeks in late July, Vassouras is buzzing with more than just coffee during the annual **Festival Vale do Café** (www.festivalvaledocafe. com, in Portuguese). Daily concerts are scheduled, and some *fazendas* host dinners featuring period food and dress. In April, **Café, Cachaça & Chorinho** (www.cafecachacaechorinho.com, in Portuguese) celebrates Vassouras' triple heritage of coffee, *choro* (improvised samba) music and *cachaça* production, with concerts and tastings throughout the region.

Information

Casa de Cultura (☎ 2471 2765; Praça Barão do Campo Belo; ◷ 9am-6pm Mon-Fri, to 4pm Sat, to 2pm Sun) displays photos and distributes information brochures (in Portuguese) about nearby coffee *fazendas*.

Sights

The town's large central square, known as the **Campo Belo**, is a picturesque grassy slope dotted with palm trees and a fountain. Twin roosters crown the spires of the **Matriz NS de Conceição** church at the top of the hill.

Museu Casa da Hera (Rua Dr Fernandes Jr 160), former home of the aristocratic heiress Eufrásia Teixeira Leite, displays antique hand-carved furniture and other colonial relics. It was closed indefinitely for restoration at the time of research.

The countryside around Vassouras is teeming with old coffee *fazendas* protected by historical preservation institutes. Most are still privately owned, so prior permission is required before touring them. The most popular are the imposing **Fazenda do Secretário** (☎ 2488 0150; www.fazendadosecretario.com .br), **Mulungú Vermelho** (☎ 9829 3628; www.fazenda mulunguvermelho.com, in Portuguese), **Santa Eufrásia** (☎ 9994 9494), **Cachoeira do Mato Dentro** (☎ 9992 7350) and **Cachoeira Grande** (☎ 2471 1264; www.fazen dacachoeiragrande.com.br, in Portuguese). The Casa de Cultura has detailed information and can help arrange visits.

Sleeping & Eating

Mara Palace (☎ 2471 1993; www.marapalace.com.br; Rua Chanceler Raul Fernandes 121; s/d R$135/165; 🅿 🛜 🏊) A centrally located three-star with pools and a sauna. Rooms in the main building are preferable to the musty ones in the concrete annex out back.

Restaurante Salão Brasil (☎ 2471 8901; Rua Barão de Capivari 60; per kg R$16.90; ◷ 11am-3:30pm) Right on the main square, this self-serve is popular for its delicious home cooking, tasty desserts and the kind of high-quality *cafezinho* (after-lunch espresso) you'd expect in Vassouras.

For fine dining and a good wine list, try **Hipólito** (☎ 2471 2805; Rua Barão de Tinguá 33; mains R$25-30; ◷ dinner Tue-Fri, lunch & dinner Sat, lunch Sun), in a grand 19th-century mansion just off the main square.

Getting There & Around

From the **bus station** (☎ 2471 1055; Praça Juiz Machado Jr), **Viação Normandy** (www.normandy.com.br) runs six daily buses to Rio (R$29, 2½ hours), and **Viação Progresso** (www.viacaoprogresso.com.br) runs one daily at 3:45pm to Resende (R$23, 2¼ hours).

To get to the *fazendas*, you'll need your own wheels or a taxi.

TERESÓPOLIS

☎ 0xx21 / pop 160,000 / elevation 871m

Do as Empress Maria Tereza used to do and escape from the steamy summer heat of Rio to the cool mountain retreat of Teresópolis, the highest city in the state, nestled in the strange, organ-pipe rock formations of the Serra dos Órgãos. The gorgeous winding road from Rio to Teresópolis climbs steeply through a padded green jungle, with bald peaks towering dramatically overhead the entire way.

The Quebra Frascos, the royal family of the Second Empire, once resided here. Today the city's principal attraction is the surrounding landscape and its natural treasures. Teresópolis is not merely for alpinists: it's a center for sports lovers of all varieties. There are facilities for volleyball, motocross and equestrian activities – many of Brazil's finest thoroughbreds are raised here – not to mention football (soccer; see p206).

Information

Cyber Office Internet (☎ 2743 9460; Praça Santa Tereza; internet per hr R$3; ⏰ 10:30am-9:30pm Mon-Sat, 11am-5pm Sun) Upstairs in the New Fashion shopping center.

HSBC (Av Delfim Moreira 746) One of several ATMs near the main square.

Post office (Av Lúcio Almirante Meira)

Tourist office (☎ 2742 5561; www.teresopolis.rj.gov. br, in Portuguese; Praça Olímpica; ⏰ 9am-6pm Mon-Sat, to 5pm Sun) In the town center.

Sights & Activities

The area's main attraction is Parque Nacional da Serra dos Órgãos (p207). The **Dedo de Deus**

(God's Finger) is the town symbol, a dramatic rock spire visible from all over town. **Colina dos Mirantes**, in the southern suburb of Fazendinha, is an especially good place to view the city and its mountain backdrop. On clear days you can see as far as Rio's Pão de Açúcar and the Baía de Guanabara.

Many more attractions lie outside town along the road to Nova Friburgo (see the boxed text, p207).

Teresópolis bears the distinction of being the training base of Brazil's World Cup squad. Check with the tourist office to see if the Brazilian national team is in town during your visit. If so, you can watch players training at the **Confederação Brasileira de Futebol (CBF)** in the Comary neighborhood in the south of town.

Sleeping

Albergue Recanto do Lord (☎ 2742 5586; www.teresopo lishostel.com.br, Rua Luiza Pereira Soares 109; dm/d HI member R$25/65, nonmember R$32/80; 🖳 🛜) Designed to look like an orange castle, this hostel commands amazing views of the Dedo de Deus and other nearby peaks from its hillside perch north of downtown. The friendly owners can provide a wealth of information about the surrounding area.

Várzea Palace Hotel (☎ 2742 0878; www.varzea palacehotel.com.br; Rua Prefeito Sebastião Teixeira 41; s/d R$65/95; s/d ste R$70/110) This striking if crumbling hotel, right off the main square, has been a Teresópolis institution since 1916. There are still plenty of atmospheric touches, including ornamental tiles, parquet wood floors, spacious rooms and high ceilings. The nicer suites have terraces.

Hotel Philipp (☎ 2742 2970; www.hotelphilipp.com .br; Rua Durval Fonseca 1333; s/d/tr/q R$85/120/150/180; 🖳) Straight uphill 1km west of the bus station, the Philipp feels a bit like a German mountain lodge, with a fireplace, pool and nice views of the surrounding mountains from the glass-walled breakfast room.

Hotel Rosa dos Ventos (☎ 2644 9900; www.hotel rosadosventos.com.br; Estrada Tere-Fri 22.6km; r incl breakfast from R$444, with full board from R$516; 🖳 🛜 🍽) This luxurious Alpine-style resort belongs to the international Relais & Châteaux chain. Way up in the mountains, it has its own lake and network of hiking trails. Magnificent views abound from the many terraces and on-site restaurants. It's 22km out of town along the road to Nova Friburgo.

TERESÓPOLIS

0 — 300 m
0 — 0.2 miles

Av Presidente Roosevelt

To Petrópolis (55km)

To Mulher de Pedra (12km); Cremerie Geneve (16km); Cachoeira das Frades (21.5km); Rosa dos Ventos (22.5km); Churrascaria Linguiça do Padre (33km); Queijaria Suíça (49km); Apiário Amigos da Terra (51km); Jardin do Nêgo (55km); Nova Friburgo (70km)

R dos Aristas

R Manoel J Lebrão

Praça Olímpica

Av Delfim Moreira

R Luiz Sangossa Santos

R Duval Fonseca

Av Almirante Lúcio Meira

Pharmacy

Igreja Matriz de Santa Tereza

Av Delfim Moreira

R Plácido Sebastião Teixeira

To Alto (2.3km); Parque Nacional da Serra dos Órgãos (3.2km); Confederação Brasileira de Futebol (4km); Rio de Janeiro (93km)

Av Tenente Luiz Meireles

Av Feliciano Sodré

R Colombia

To Colina dos Mirantes (2km)

Hotel Philipp	6	A2
Várzea Palace Hotel	7	B2

INFORMATION		
Cyber Office Internet	1	B2
HSBC	2	B1
Post Office	3	A2
Tourist Office	4	B1

SLEEPING		
Albergue Recanto do Lord	5	B1

EATING		
Cheiro de Mato	8	B2
Cheiro de Mato	9	B2
La Prestineria Borges	10	B1
Paraiso da Serra	11	A2
Taberna Alpina	12	B2

TRANSPORT		
Bus Station	13	A2

THE TERESÓPOLIS–FRIBURGO SCENIC CIRCUIT

Where can you find an Alpine goat-cheese dairy, a wacked-out sculpture garden, a beekeeper who makes his own honey *cachaça*, beautiful peaks and waterfalls, and some of Brazil's spiffiest hotels? They're all on the **Circuito Turístico Tere-Fri** (www.terefri.com.br), a 68km highway connecting the towns of Teresópolis and Nova Friburgo. Points of interest are indicated on a handy map available throughout the region.

Starting from Teresópolis, highlights include the **Mulher de Pedra** (Woman of Stone) viewpoint at 12km, where a distant mountain really does look like a reclining woman; the **Cremerie Geneve** at 16km, where you can pet baby goats, buy local cheese, stroll the gardens or indulge in a fine French meal; the **Cachoeira dos Frades** turnoff at 21.5km, where an unpaved side road leads through an idyllic valley to a waterfall with a swimming hole; Hotel Rosa dos Ventos (see p206) at 22.6km, one of many opulent hotels along the route; the **Queijaria Suiça** at 49km, where a Swiss cheese factory sits adjacent to an excellent museum tracing two centuries of Swiss culture in the Friburgo area; the **Apiário Amigos da Terra** at 51km, where you can learn about bees in the bee museum and drink local honey *cachaça* while the kids play in a honeycomb-shaped play structure; and **Jardim do Nêgo** at 55km, where a local sculptor has created a bizarre landscape of moss-covered human and animal forms. It's easiest to drive the route in your own car, although local buses travel through here and will let you off wherever you like.

RIO DE JANEIRO STATE

Eating

La Prestineria Borges (☎ 2643 2652; Av Almirante Lúcio Meira 992; snacks from R$2; ☺ 7am-10pm) This newly opened café delights with exceptional baked goods, both savory and sweet; it also serves coffee, juices and – at dinnertime – all-you-can-eat soup for R$9.50.

Cheiro de Mato (☎ 2742 1899; Av Delfim Moreira 140; per 100g R$2.19; ☺ 11am-3pm Mon-Sat) This is a good place to come for self-serve health food, including brown rice, a large salad buffet and other vegetarian options. Its second branch, just off the main square in the Teresópolis Shopping Center, is open Sundays and evenings as well.

Taberna Alpina (☎ 2742 0123; Rua Duque de Caxias 131; mains R$13-39; ☺ 8am-10:30pm Tue-Sun) The Taberna's cozy interior room, sporting wooden benches with heart-shaped cutouts, is reminiscent of the Alps. So is the menu, featuring German mustard, brown bread, goulash, and smoked pork with sauerkraut.

Paraiso da Serra (☎ 2643 2526; Rua Carmela Dutra 441; all-you-can-eat lunch buffet R$24.95, dinner mains R$27-40; ☺ 11:30am-midnight Tue-Sat, to 4pm Sun & Mon) The food is superb at this newly opened downtown branch of one of the region's most traditional mountain eateries. The lunchtime buffet includes delicious Mineiro cuisine (rice, beans, pork and kale-heavy fare from the neighboring state of Minas Gerais) along with salads, dessert and coffee. Try a R$9.95 pitcher of *suco de abacaxi e hortelã* (pineapple-mint juice).

ourpick **Churrascaria Linguiça do Padre** (☎ 2641 0065; Estrada Tere-Fri km33; meals from R$25; ☺ 11am-3pm Mon-Sat) If you're touring the Tere-Fri highway (see the boxed text, above), don't miss this local favorite beside a rushing river. The menu ranges from R$4 *linguiça* (spicy Portuguese sausage) sandwiches to substantial country meals featuring trout, rabbit or goat. Save room for strawberries with whipped cream (R$6) for dessert.

Getting There & Away

The **bus station** (Rua Primeiro de Maio) is south of the main square. **Viação Teresópolis** (www.viacaoteresopolis.com.br) runs buses to Rio (R$22, 1½ hours, half-hourly from 5am to 10pm), Petrópolis (R$13, 1½ hours, six daily between 6am and 7pm) and Nova Friburgo (R$11, two hours, five daily between 7am and 7pm).

PARQUE NACIONAL DA SERRA DOS ÓRGÃOS

Created in 1939, this national park covers 118 sq km of mountainous terrain between Teresópolis and Petrópolis. The park's most distinctive features are the strangely shaped peaks of **Pedra do Sino** (2263m), **Pedra do Açu** (2230m), **Agulha do Diabo** (2020m), **Nariz do Frade** (1919m), **Dedo de Deus** (1651m), **Pedra da Ermitage** (1485m) and **Dedo de Nossa Senhora** (1320m). With so many peaks, it's no wonder that this is the mountain climbing, rock climbing and trekking center of Brazil. The region has extensive trails, the most famous

---

DETOUR: A BIRDWATCHER'S PARADISE IN RIO'S BACK YARD

our pick **Guapi Assu Bird Lodge** (☎ 21 2745 3998; www.guapiassubirdlodge.com; s/d with full board R$200/360; ❌ ☐ ☑), only 80km from Rio's Galeão airport, is part of the non-profit **Regua nature reserve** (Reserva Ecológica de Guapi Assu; www.regua.co.uk), a 50-sq-km tract at the foot of the Serra dos Órgãos where Nicholas and Raquel Locke have dedicated their lives to restoring native ecosystems. Serious birders, or anyone who wants a genuine taste of Brazil's remarkable biodiversity, should head here. Volunteers from around the world are engaged in an ambitious reforestation project, while school kids from the local community are invited to use the reserve as a hands-on environmental education laboratory.

The comfy rooms have solar hot water, meals are served family-style around a big table and the library of nature books makes for great browsing, caipirinha in hand, after a long day of bird-watching. The man-made pond ecosystem next to the lodge draws in a stupendous array of birds, as well as families of capybaras. A network of trails surrounding the lodge offers opportunities to enter into deeper forest and visit other attractions, including a lovely waterfall. For details on reaching the lodge by bus, car or van shuttle, see the lodge's website.

---

of which is the 42km, three-day traverse over the mountains from Petrópolis to Teresópolis. Unfortunately, most of the trails are unmarked and off the available maps. Hiring a guide, however, is easy. Inquire at the **national park entrance** (☎ 0xx21-2152 1100; parnaso@icmbio.gov. br; admission R$20; ☸ 8am-5pm) or with Trekking Petrópolis (see p202). The best time for walks is from May to October (the drier months).

The main entrance to the national park is at the south edge of the town of Teresópolis, off Hwy BR-116 from Rio, about 4km from the center. Walking trails, waterfalls, natural swimming pools and tended lawns and gardens make this a very pretty place for a picnic.

From the main entrance, the road extends into the park as far as Barragem Beija Flor. There are several good walks from near here. The highlight is the **Trilha Pedra do Sino** – a strenuous round-trip of about eight hours from the end of the park road (R$30 trail fee). The trail passes Cachoeira Veu da Noiva, the vegetation changes from rain forest to grassland, and the reward is a panoramic view stretching all the way to Rio de Janeiro and the Baía de Guanabara. For a shorter walk, head up to the **Mirante Alexandre Oliveira** (1100m), from where there is a good view of Teresópolis – it's about a one-hour round-trip from the park road.

There is another, secondary entrance down in the southeast corner of the national park, off the road from Rio. It also has an information center, walking trails and waterfalls.

Getting There & Away

To get to the park's main entrance from the city center of Teresópolis, take the hourly 'Soberbo'

bus (R$2.30). Alternatively, take the more frequent 'Alto' bus and get off at the Praçinha do Alto, from which it's a 10-minute walk south to the park's main entrance. A taxi ride from town to the park entrance costs about R$20.

NOVA FRIBURGO

☎ 0xx22 / pop 180,000 / elevation 846m

In 1818, newly crowned Portuguese King Dom João VI started recruiting immigrants from Switzerland and Germany to help settle his vast Brazilian territory. The first 30 families to arrive, from the Swiss canton of Friburg, immediately set out to create a perfect little village reminiscent of their home country in the mountains north of Rio. Traces of Swiss and German heritage remain in modern Friburgo, in the local architecture, the town's passion for floral decoration and the fair-haired, blue-eyed features of some residents. Nowadays the local economy revolves around the lingerie industry, while tourism revolves around the region's resplendent natural attractions: waterfalls, woods, trails, sunny mountain mornings and cool evenings.

Information

Banco do Brasil (Praça Dermeval B Moreira 10) One of several ATMs downtown.

Post office Opposite Praça Getúlio Vargas.

Sniper Lan Games (Rua Portugal 17; internet per hr R$3; ☸ 11am-9pm Mon-Fri, 2-8pm Sat & Sun) Internet access.

Tourist office (☎ 2543 6307/8; www.pmnf.rj.gov .br/turismo_index.php, in Portuguese; Praça Dermeval B Moreira 10; ☸ 8am-8pm Tue-Sat, 9am-5pm Sun & Mon) Has maps and a complete list of hotels.

Sights & Activities

Most of the sights are a few kilometers out of town. Survey the surrounding area from **Morro da Cruz** (1800m). The chairlift to Morro da Cruz runs on weekends and holidays from 9am to 6pm. Its station is in the center of town at Praça do Teleférico. **Pico da Caledônia** (2310m) offers fantastic views and launching sites for hang gliders. It's a 6km uphill hike, but the view is worth it.

Ten kilometers to the north of town, you can hike (trail fee R$6) to **Pedra do Cão Sentado**, a rock formation resembling a sitting dog that serves as Friburgo's town symbol, or visit the mountain town of **Bom Jardim** (23km northeast on Hwy RJ-116). To the southeast, **Lumiar** (34km from Nova Friburgo) is a popu-lar destination for Brazilian ecotourists, with cheap pousadas, waterfalls, walking trails, a new hostel (see p209) and white-water adventures centered on the Encontro dos Rios, the tumultuous confluence of three local rivers. Guided adventure tours of the area are available through the Alê Friburgo Hostel or **Lumiar Aventura** (☎ 8131 6768; www.lumiaraventura .com, in Portuguese).

Sleeping

Alê Friburgo Hostel (☎ 2522 0540; www.friburgohos tel.com; Rua Ernesto Bizzotto Filho 2; dm/s/d R$30/50/80; 🖳 🛜 🛋) This hostel, 2km straight uphill from Friburgo's town square, compensates for its remote location with friendly staff and great amenities, including a pool, sauna and

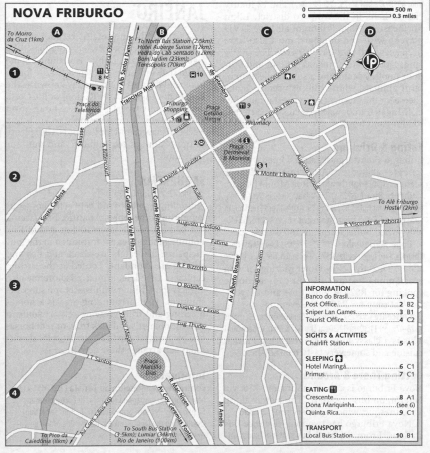

NOVA FRIBURGO

INFORMATION
Banco do Brasil...............................1 C2
Post Office.......................................2 B2
Sniper Lan Games...........................3 B1
Tourist Office..................................4 C2

SIGHTS & ACTIVITIES
Chairlift Station...............................5 A1

SLEEPING
Hotel Maringá.................................6 C1
Primus...7 C1

EATING
Crescente..8 A1
Dona Mariquinha.....................(see 6)
Quinta Rica......................................9 C1

TRANSPORT
Local Bus Station..........................10 B1

shuttle service from downtown. The owners also operate a sister hostel in the pretty forested valley of Lumiar, less than an hour away, where they offer bike rentals and excursions to nearby waterfalls.

Hotel Maringá (☎ 2522 2309; Rua Monsenhor Miranda 110; s/d/tr with shared bathroom R$45/85/105, s/d/tr/q with bathroom R$60/120/150/180) There are simple *quartos* (rooms with shared bathroom) and more expensive *apartamentos*, but both choices are clean and nicely decorated.

Primus (☎ 2523 2898; www.hotelprimus.com.br; Rua Adolfo Lautz 128; s/d/tr R$70/110/160, d/tr chalet with air-con R$150/210; 🅿 🛜 🛉) Up on a very steep hill a few blocks from the center, this hotel has a pool, pet peacocks and great views.

Hotel Auberge Suisse (☎ 2541 1270; www.auberge suisse.com.br; Rua 10 de Outubro, Amparo; s/d/tr/q chalets from R$187/288/473/525; 🅿 🛜 🛉) The 12 luxury chalets here, in the Amparo district, 12km northeast of Nova Friburgo, all have DVD players, wi-fi and minibars; most also have fireplaces, and four have air-con. The pretty landscaped grounds include indoor and outdoor pools, a sauna and a small collection of farm animals, whose milk is used to make cheese for the excellent on-site restaurant specializing in traditional Swiss cuisine: raclettes, fondues and trout.

Eating & Drinking

Friburgo's central grassy strip is lined with eateries for all budgets. A raucous youthful bar scene erupts nightly along Rua Monte Libano.

Quinta Rica (☎ 2523 3304; Praça Getúlio Vargas 104; all-you-can-eat buffet R$22; 🕒 10:30am-11pm Sun-Thu, to midnight Fri & Sat) This restaurant serves a remarkably varied buffet featuring 160 dishes.

Dona Mariquinha (☎ 2522 2309; Rua Monsenhor Miranda 110; lunch buffet R$26; 🕒 lunch Tue-Sun, dinner Mon-Fri) Directly below Hotel Maringá, Dona Mariquinha features all-you-can-eat home cooking for R$26 at lunchtime and all-you-can-eat soup for R$7 in the evening.

Crescente (☎ 2523 4616; Rua General Osório 21; mains R$28-47; 🕒 11:30am-11:30pm Thu-Sat & Mon, to 5pm Sun) This is a classy little place featuring French cuisine and some very tasty trout dishes.

Getting There & Around

Nova Friburgo is a short jaunt from Rio, via Niterói, on bus line 1001. The ride is along a picturesque, winding, misty jungle road.

Nova Friburgo has two long-distance bus stations. From the **north bus station** (Rodoviária Norte; Praça Feliciano Costa), 2.5km north of the center, **Viação Teresópolis** (☎ 2522 2708) has buses to Teresópolis (R$11, two hours, five daily) and Petrópolis (R$23, four hours, three daily at 7am, 3pm and 5pm). From the **south bus station** (Rodoviária Sul; Ponte da Saudade), 4km south of the center, **Viação 1001** (☎ 2522 0400) has hourly buses to Rio (R$24, two hours) plus one direct bus to Cabo Frio on Saturday at 6:30am (R$34).

Local buses connect both long-distance terminals to the central, local bus station just north of Praça Getúlio Vargas. Local buses also go to just about all the tourist attractions. Ask for details at the tourist office.

EAST OF RIO DE JANEIRO

East of Rio, the mountains recede and the coastal strip becomes flatter, punctuated by lagoons and dazzling white sand dunes. Some of Rio state's most beautiful beaches are found here, and the area is alternately known as the Região dos Lagos (Lakes Region) or the Costa do Sol (Sunny Coast). Only two hours from Rio by car, the area has rapidly grown into a weekend playground for Cariocas, with plenty of opportunities for nightlife and outdoor recreation.

SAQUAREMA
🕿 0xx22 / pop 70,000

Straddling a spit of sand between a gorgeous lagoon and the open Atlantic, Saquarema is a laid-back little town 100km east of Rio. Polluting industries are forbidden in the municipality; the waters are clean, and fish and shrimp are abundant. Touted as the surfing capital of Brazil, its unmarred shoreline also attracts sportfishing enthusiasts and sun worshippers. The surrounding area is a horse-breeding and fruit-growing center; you can visit the orchards and pick fruit, or rent horses or a jeep and take to the hills. Most local pousadas can arrange these activities.

Information

Centro de Atendimento ao Turista (☎ 2651 2123; http://turismo.saquarema.rj.gov.br, in Portuguese; Av Saquarema; 🕒 9am-5pm Mon-Fri, to 3pm Sat & Sun) Overlooking the lagoon, on the Itaúna side of the downtown bridge.

Lakes Shopping This tiny mall between downtown and Praia Itaúna has a Bradesco ATM downstairs and an internet place upstairs.

Post office (Praça Oscar de Macedo Soares) Close to the bus stop.

Sights & Activities

The stunning white church of **NS de Nazaré** (1837), perched on the hill near the entrance to the lagoon, is the town's focal point. From this strategic spot you can survey the long, empty beaches, the lagoon and the mountains beyond. The mass held here on September 7 and 8 attracts around 150,000 pilgrims, second only to the Nazaré celebrations of Belém.

About 3km east of town is **Praia Itaúna**, Saquarema's most beautiful beach and one of the best surf spots in Brazil. If you've ever wanted to learn to surf, what better place then Saquarema? **Surf Camp Saquarema** (☎ 2651 8651; www.surfcampsaquarema.com.br; Praia da Vila) has friendly instructors, all certified by the Confederação Brasileira de Surfe.

Saquarema plays host to national and international **surfing competitions** each year, generally between May and October.

Sleeping

Prices quoted here are for high season. Discounts of up to 30% apply in low season. The nicest places are out at Praia Itaúna, which is R$2.20 by bus (or a bit more by taxi) from the city center.

Itaúna Hostel (☎ 2653 8652; www.itaunahostel.com .br; Rua das Garoupas 100; dm/d/ste per person R$42/50/80; 🖳) A few blocks back from Itaúna beach, this small, homey hostel offers spacious two- and five-bed dorms downstairs, two private rooms upstairs and an air-conditioned suite in the main house. Perks include hammocks and free use of bicycles.

Pousada Canto da Vila (☎ 2651 1563; www.pousada cantodavila.com.br; Av Salgado Filho 52; d with fan R$112, with air-con R$144; ❄ 🛜 🌊) This friendly beachfront place, just downhill from Saquarema's historic church, features bright, airy rooms, many with great views of surfers riding the waves.

Pousada do Suíço (☎ 2651 7842; www.pousadado suico.com; Rua das Pitangas 580; r R$120-150; ❄ 🖳 🛜) Sean and Neyse, the multilingual Brazilian-American couple who run this place, are committed surfers and just plain nice people. The pleasant palm-filled courtyard and location a couple of blocks from Itaúna beach draw visitors from around the globe. Bike and board

rentals are available for R$20 per day, and discounts are offered for longer stays.

Maasai Hotel Beach & Resort (☎ 2651 1092; www .maasai.com.br; Travessa Itaúna 17; garden-view/ocean-view d R$180/270, ste R$330; ❄ 🖳 🛜 🌊) If you're looking for cushier digs, this place is a no-brainer! Maasai has a stunning beachfront location, comfy sitting rooms, a sauna and swimming pool and a pretty bar-restaurant overlooking the water.

Eating

Itaúna Café (☎ 2651 1114; cnr Av Oceânica & Rua das Garças; sandwiches & salads R$7-9; 🕘 9am-midnight; 🛜) Wi-fi, Lavazza espresso, cheesecake, Argentine-style empanadas, tasty sandwiches and salads, and Saturday *feijoada* (Brazil's famous bean-and-meat stew and national dish, R$14) make this new café across from Itaúna beach the perfect low-key, low-budget hangout.

Garota da Itaúna (☎ 2651 2156; Av Oceânica 165; mains R$20-40; 🕘 11am-11pm Sun Thu, to 1am Fri & Sat) The Garota's many attractions include a fabulous beachfront terrace and a wide variety of seafood specials. Enjoy the views but hang on to your beers – the wind can be vicious. It also rents simple rooms (single/double R$50/80).

Forno à Lenha (☎ 2651 4088; Rua dos Mariscos 511; pizza from R$23; 🕘 noon-midnight Thu-Sun, 6pm-midnight Mon-Wed) A few blocks back from Itaúna beach, this place has a cozy back room with a wood-burning oven, plus a front patio area where you can enjoy pizza and grilled meats.

Getting There & Away

The 1001 bus company buses leave Rio for Saquarema every other hour between 6:30am and 8:30pm, returning to Rio between 7:50am and 7:50pm (R$17, two hours).

Salineira/Montes Brancos (www.salineira.com.br) bus route 113 runs direct from Saquarema to Cabo Frio four times daily between 6:30am and 10:40pm (R$4.50, one hour). Alternatively, take a local Rio Lagos bus (R$2.20, hourly) to Bacaxá, where more frequent buses to Cabo Frio leave throughout the day. The bus stop in Saquarema is on the ocean side of the bridge, one block from the main square in the town center.

ARRAIAL DO CABO

☎ 0xx22 / pop 27,000

Arraial do Cabo, 45km east of Saquarema, is surrounded by gleaming white sand dunes and offers all the beauty of Búzios with half the fuss. Arraial is home to a working fishing port, Porto do Forno, which lends it a welcoming working-class demeanor. Funny little lighthouse statues at intersections around town also add a touch of charm. Some of the best beaches – pristine swaths of gorgeous sand and bright-green waters – are within an easy 15-minute stroll of the downtown bus station, while others are just a short boat ride away. Arraial is a renowned diving destination, and it's also a good place to observe humpback whales (*Megaptera novaeangliae*), whose migration routes pass directly offshore.

Information

The **tourist office** (☎ 2622 1949; admturismo@arraial .rj.gov.br; ☉ 8am-5pm) at the town's formal entry portico 3km from the center has English- and Spanish-speaking staff, and provides a helpful map.

Just around the corner from the bus station, you'll find a **multi-bank ATM**, plus internet access at **Cyber Arena Virtual** (Praça da Bandeira 3; per hr R$2; ☉ 9:30am-11pm). Av Getúlio Vargas is home to the **post office** (Av Getúlio Vargas 19) and several more internet places.

Sights & Activities

Arraial's prime attractions lie along the shoreline. **Praia dos Anjos** has beautiful turquoise water but a little too much boat traffic for comfortable swimming. Just above the beach, look for the plaque commemorating Amerigo Vespucci's landing here in 1503. Vespucci left 24 men behind to start a settlement, making Arraial one of the first European toeholds in the Americas.

Favorite beaches within a short walking distance of town are **Prainha** to the north of town; **Praia do Forno** (accessed by a 1km walking trail from Praia dos Anjos) to the northeast; and the vast **Praia Grande** to the west, where wilder surf rules in off the open Atlantic.

There are several other stunning beaches along the mountainous peninsula just south of town. For near-aerial views, and the best sunset in the area, climb up to **Pontal do Atalaia**, a popular viewpoint at the top of the peninsula that also makes an excellent spot for **whale-watching** in July and August.

Ilha de Cabo Frio is accessed by boat from Praia dos Anjos. **Praia do Farol** on the protected side of the island is a gorgeous beach with fine white sand. From here there is a 2½-hour walk to the lighthouse. The **Gruta Azul**

(Blue Cavern), on the southwestern side of the island, is another beautiful spot. Be alert, though: the entrance to the underwater cavern is submerged at high tide.

Tour operators who organize dives in these waters abound – the tourist office keeps a complete list. Dependable agencies include **PL Divers** (☎ 2622 1033; www.pldivers.com.br, in Portuguese; Rua Nilo Peçanha 57), **Sandmar** (☎ 2622 5703; www.sand mar.com.br, in Portuguese; Rua Epitácio Pessoa 21), and **Ocean Sub** (☎ 2622 4642; www.oceansub.com.br, in Portuguese; Av Luiz Corrêa 3).

Sleeping

Prices quoted here are for the high season. Discounts of up to 40% are common in the low season.

Marina dos Anjos Hostel (☎ 2622 4060; www.marina dosanjos.com.br; Rua Bernardo Lens 145; dm/d with HI card R$40/120, without card R$45/135) Located one block back from Praia dos Anjos, this hostel is a wonderful base from which to explore the area. The helpful staff rents bicycles, canoes, snorkels, surfboards and diving equipment and organizes dune-buggy tours to surrounding beaches. The central courtyard, with hammocks and pillows for lounging, is the venue for spontaneous evening barbecues and jam sessions.

Hotel Pousada Caminho do Sol (☎ 2622 2029; www .caminhodosol.com.br; Rua do Sol 50; s/d from R$140/155; 🛜 🐾) Right on Praia Grande, this pretty resort hotel with a pool and beautiful views is a big hit with visiting Brazilians looking for a romantic weekend.

Capitão n'Areia Pousada (☎ 2622 2720; www.capitao pousada.com, in Portuguese; Rua Santa Cruz 7; r R$165-225, ste R$355; 🅿 🛜 🐾) All decked out in white walls and nautical decor, this classy place in the heart of Marina dos Anjos has a sundeck, a sauna, a very shallow pool, a gym and spacious rooms overlooking the boats in the harbor below.

Pousada Pilar (☎ 2622 1992; www.pousadapilar .com.br; Rua Aprígio Martins 27; d/tr/q from R$220/280/365; 🅿 🛜 🐾) Furnished with antiques and art pieces from around the world, this new eight-room boutique hotel is a green oasis in the middle of town. All rooms (including two with wheelchair access) have safes, minibars and verandas overlooking the lush central garden and brilliant blue circular pool with sundeck.

Eating

ourpick Bacalhau do Tuga (☎ 2622 1108; Praia dos Anjos; mains R$18-29; ☉ 6pm-midnight Wed-Fri, 1pm-midnight Sat & Sun) Since opening in 2009, the 'Tuga' (Portuguese guy) has been drawing throngs of people to this beachfront hole-in-the-wall, mixing classic Portuguese codfish recipes with local specialties such as *peixe grelhado com molho de manga* (grilled fish with mango sauce).

Água na Boca (☎ 2622 1106; Praça da Bandeira 1; per kg R$31; ⏲ 11:30am-5pm) A stone's throw from the bus station, this recommended self-serve includes plenty of seafood in its daily offerings.

Saint Tropez (☎ 2622 1222; Praça Daniel Barreto 2; pizzas R$19-30, mains R$33-55; ⏲ 6pm-midnight Mon-Tue, noon-midnight Wed-Sun) Just a block up from Praia dos Anjos, Saint Tropez is another good spot for fresh fish.

Getting There & Away
The Arraial do Cabo **bus station** (Praça da Bandeira) is situated in the town center. Direct buses operated by the **1001 bus company** (☎ 2622 1488) run from Rio to Arraial every two hours from 5:15am to 9pm, returning with the same frequency between 3:40am and 7:20pm (R$31, three hours).

An alternative is to catch a municipal bus to Cabo Frio (R$3.35), then transfer to one of the half-hourly Rio-bound buses leaving from the Cabo Frio bus station.

CABO FRIO
☎ 0xx22 / pop 190,000
Built up around sand dunes and beaches, with plenty of fresh breezes, Cabo Frio's naturally gorgeous settings have been stunted by the salt and tourism industries that dominate in the area. If you are able to overlook the encroaching overdevelopment, Cabo Frio remains a relaxed beach town, ready to greet newcomers with a smile. Every weekend, and throughout the summer holidays, it attracts scores of visitors – the bars are invariably filled with happy-go-lucky Brazilians whooping it up, and the merrymaking spirit is clearly Cabo Frio's strongest attraction.

Orientation
The town of Cabo Frio is at the end of the long sweeping beach that extends northward from Arraial do Cabo. Cabo Frio lies to the west of the Canal do Itajuru, which links the Lagoa de Araruama to the Atlantic Ocean. Near the bridge is the town's focal point – a hill with a small white chapel. The town center is east of here, and the bus station is to the west (about

2km from the center) near the end of Av Júlia Kubitschek. This road runs almost parallel to the Praia do Forte, named after the fort at its eastern end.

Information
CyberTel (☎ 2649 7575; Praça Porto Rocha 81; per hr R$3; ⏲ 9am-9pm Mon-Sat) Internet access.
HSBC (Av Assunção 793) One of several ATMs on this downtown thoroughfare.
Post office (Largo de Santo Antônio 55)
Tourist office (☎ 2647 1689; turismo@cabofrio.rj.gov.br; Av do Contorno 200; ⏲ 8:30am-6pm) Directly across from Praia do Forte; English spoken.

Sights & Activities
Forte São Mateus (admission free; ⏲ 10am-5pm Tue-Sun), a stronghold against pirates, was built between 1616 and 1620 to protect the lucrative brazilwood trade. You will find the fort at the eastern end of Praia do Forte.

There are three sand-dune spots in and about Cabo Frio. The duncs of **Praia do Peró**, a super beach for surfing and surf casting, are 6km north in the direction of Búzios, near Ogivas and after Praia Brava and Praia das

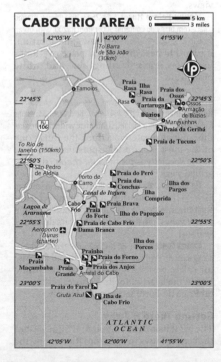

CABO FRIO AREA

0   5 km
0   3 miles

To Barra de São João (30km)

To Rio de Janeiro (150km)

42°05'W   42°00'W   41°55'W

Tamoios

Praia Rasa   Ilha Rasa
Rasa   Praia da Tartaruga
Praia dos Ossos   22°45'S
Ossos
Búzios   Armação de Búzios
Manguinhos
Praia da Geribá
Praia de Tucuns

22°45'S

RJ-106

São Pedro de Aldeia   22°50'S

Porto do Carro
Praia do Peró
Praia das Conchas
Canal do Itajuru
Ilha Comprida
Ilha dos Pargos

Lagoa de Araruama
Cabo Frio
Praia Brava
Praia do Forte
Ilha do Papagaio
Praia de Cabo Frio

Aeroporto Dunas (charter)
Dama Branca

22°55'S

Ilha dos Porcos

Prainha
Praia do Forno
Praia dos Anjos
Arraial do Cabo
Praia Grande
Praia Maçambaba

23°00'S

Praia do Farol
Gruta Azul
Ilha de Cabo Frio

ATLANTIC OCEAN

42°05'W   42°00'W   41°55'W

23°00'S

Conchas. The **Dama Branca** (White Lady) sand dunes are on the road to Arraial do Cabo. The **Pontal** dunes of Praia do Forte town beach stretch from the fort to Miranda hill. Robberies can pose a danger at the dunes, so get advice from locals before heading out.

Sleeping

Camping Club do Brasil (☎ 2644 1226; www.camping clube.com.br; Estrada dos Passageiros 700; campsite per person R$27, plus R$6 per tent) At this favorite camping site just north of town, you get to choose: sling a hammock between scrubby pines or pitch a tent.

Hotel Atlântico (☎ 2643 0996; www.hotelatlantico.tur .br, in Portuguese; Rua José Bonifácio 302; s/d/tr R$68/99/140; ⊠ 🛜) One of the most popular budget hotels in town, Atlântico has large rooms at bargain prices.

Pousada Boulevard (☎ 2643 1456; www.pousada boulevard.com, in Portuguese; Rua Marechal Floriano 237; r from R$180; ⊠ 🛜 🛢) Perfectly placed in Cabo Frio's canalside restaurant district, this new pousada in a historic building offers high-end amenities like satellite TV, a sauna and a plunge pool. The best five rooms have canal views.

Malibu Palace Hotel (☎ 2643 1955; www.malibu palace.com.br; Av do Contorno 900; r from R$200, with ocean view R$273; ⊠ 🛜 🛢) For views and location, it's hard to beat this central place overlooking Cabo Frio's dazzling blue and white beachfront.

Eating

Restaurante do Zé (☎ 2643 4277; Blvd Canal 33; mains R$14-24; ⏱ 11am-midnight) The sidewalk tables at this animated eatery overlook the canal, one of the most picturesque spots in town. The house specialty is *picanha na chapa* (sizzling grilled steak).

Tia Maluca (☎ 2647 4158; Blvd Canal 109; mains from R$17; ⏱ 11am-midnight) Just across the street from Restaurante do Zé, Tia Maluca has the same pretty views, plus good prices for its delicious seafood.

Branca Confeitaria (☎ 2645 5885; Praça Porto Rocha 15; per kg R$30.90; ⏱ 11am-5pm) A traditional favorite for cakes, pastries and self-serve lunchtime fare in the heart of town. Its sister restaurant on Praia do Forte serves pizza nightly.

Getting There & Away

The **bus station** (Av Júlia Kubitschek) is 2km west of the center. Buses to and from Rio, run by the

1001 bus company (☎ 2643 3778; www.autoviacao1001. com.br, in Portuguese), leave at least hourly between 3am and midnight (R$30, 2¾ hours).

To Arraial do Cabo, catch **Salineira** (☎ 2643 8144) bus 402 from the bus stop just to the left as you leave the bus station (R$3.35, 30 minutes). For Búzios, catch Salineiras bus 423, 425 or 428 from the stop across the road (R$3.35, 45 minutes).

BÚZIOS

☎ 0xx22 / pop 29,000

Beautiful Búzios sits on a jutting peninsula scalloped by 17 beaches. A simple fishing village until the early '60s, when it was 'discovered' by Brigitte Bardot and her Brazilian boyfriend, it's now one of Brazil's most animated seaside resorts, littered with boutiques, fine restaurants, villas, bars and posh pousadas. The Mediterranean touch introduced by the Portuguese has not been lost – indeed, the narrow cobblestone streets and picturesque waterfront add to Búzios' appeal, and contribute to its image as Brazil's St Tropez.

Orientation

Búzios is not a single town but rather three settlements on the peninsula – Ossos, Manguinhos and Armação de Búzios – and one on the mainland called Rasa. Ossos (Bones), at the northern tip of the peninsula, is the oldest and most attractive. It has a pretty harbor and yacht club, plus a few hotels and bars. Manguinhos, on the isthmus, is the most commercial. Armação, in between, has the most tourist amenities; it's here that you'll find Rua das Pedras, the hub of Búzios' nightlife. Northwest along the coast is Rasa, where Brazil's rich and powerful relax.

Information

Bradesco (Av José Bento Ribeiro Dantas 254) One of several downtown ATMs.

Canto da Tartaruga (☎ 2623 0104; Beco da Renata; ⏱ 2-11:30pm) Well-stocked bookstore just off Rua das Pedras, with a few shelves of English, Spanish and German titles.

Centro Médico Búzios (☎ 2633 0200, after hr 9943 7878; Rua César Augusto São Luiz 100; ⏱ 7:30am-7pm Mon-Fri, 10am-2pm Sat) Private clinic in downtown Armação; accepts international traveler's insurance.

ClickNet (☎ 2623 7395; Rua César Augusto São Luiz 254; per hr R$4; ⏱ 24hr Dec-Feb, 9am-1am Mar-Nov) Air-conditioned, with good prices and the best of Armação's several downtown internet places.

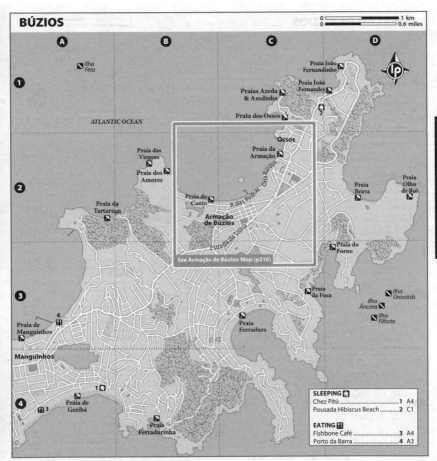

BÚZIOS

SLEEPING
Chez Pitú 1 A4
Pousada Hibiscus Beach 2 C1

EATING
Fishbone Café 3 A4
Porto da Barra 4 A3

Laveaki (☎ 9215 3823; Rua Arnaldo Bertholdo 100; per basket self-service/full service R$26/32; ⏰ 10am-8pm Mon-Sat) Wash your own laundry, or staff will do it for R$6 extra.

Multi-bank ATM (Praça Santos Dumont) Convenient but charges a hefty service fee.

Secretaria de Turismo (www.buziosturismo.com); town entrance portal (☎ 2633 6200; Av José Bento Ribeiro Dantas; ⏰ 8am-8pm); Armação (☎ 2623 2099; Travessa dos Pescadores s/n; ⏰ 8am-8pm Mon-Fri, 9am-10pm Sat & Sun) City maps and hotel information are available in both offices.

Sights & Activities

The biggest draws in Búzios are the natural setting plus the dizzying array of opportunities for relaxation, nightlife, shopping and ocean sports.

Cobblestoned **Rua das Pedras** is Búzios' main venue for shopping, dining and evening entertainment, overflowing with revelers on weekend nights. Its eastward continuation, **Orla Bardot**, is a delightful winding oceanfront promenade linking the two oldest and most picturesque sections of town (Armação and Ossos). As you walk along the beachfront, you'll notice several **statues** by sculptor Christina Motta, including representations of Brigitte Bardot and former Brazilian president Juscelino Kubitschek, plus some remarkably realistic-looking fishermen hauling in their nets.

To the north of Búzios, Rio das Ostras boasts one of Brazil's best jazz and blues fests (see p28).

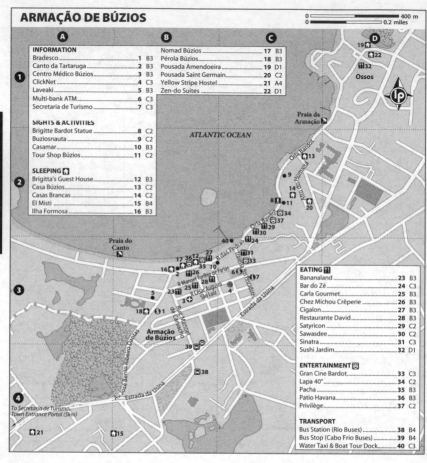

ARMAÇÃO DE BÚZIOS

INFORMATION		
Bradesco	1	B3
Canto da Tartaruga	2	B3
Centro Médico Búzios	3	B3
ClickNet	4	B3
Laveaki	5	B3
Multi-bank ATM	6	C3
Secretaria de Turismo	7	C3

SIGHTS & ACTIVITIES		
Brigitte Bardot Statue	8	C2
Buziosnauta	9	C2
Casamar	10	B3
Tour Shop Búzios	11	C2

SLEEPING		
Brigitta's Guest House	12	B3
Casa Búzios	13	C2
Casas Brancas	14	C2
El Misti	15	B4
Ilha Formosa	16	B3

Nomad Búzios	17	B3
Pérola Búzios	18	B3
Pousada Amendoeira	19	D1
Pousada Saint Germain	20	C2
Yellow Stripe Hostel	21	A4
Zen-do Suites	22	D1

EATING		
Bananaland	23	B3
Bar do Zé	24	C3
Carla Gourmet	25	B3
Chez Michou Crêperie	26	B3
Cigalon	27	B3
Restaurante David	28	B3
Satyricon	29	B3
Sawasdee	30	C2
Sinatra	31	C3
Sushi Jardim	32	D1

ENTERTAINMENT		
Gran Cine Bardot	33	C3
Lapa 40°	34	C2
Pacha	35	B3
Patio Havana	36	B3
Privilège	37	C2

TRANSPORT		
Bus Station (Rio Buses)	38	B4
Bus Stop (Cabo Frio Buses)	39	B4
Water Taxi & Boat Tour Dock	40	C3

ATLANTIC OCEAN

BEACHES

There are some fine **swimming**, **diving** and **snorkeling** sites near Búzios. In general, the southern beaches are trickier to get to, but they're prettier and have better surf. The northern beaches are more sheltered and closer to the towns.

Going counterclockwise from south of Manguinhos, the first beaches are **Geribá** and **Ferradurinha** (Little Horseshoe). These are beautiful beaches with good surf, but the Búzios Beach Club has built condos here. Next on the coast is **Ferradura**, which is large enough for windsurfing, followed by **Praia da Foca** and **Praia do Forno**, which have colder water than the other beaches. **Praia Olho de Boi** (Bull's Eye) is the area's only nude beach. It's reached by a little trail from the long, clean beach of **Praia Brava**.

Both **João Fernandinho** and **João Fernandes** are good for snorkeling, as are **Azedinha** and **Azeda**, reached by a short trail from Ossos. **Praia dos Ossos**, **Praia da Armação**, **Praia do Canto** and **Praia dos Amores** are pretty, but a bit public and not so nice for lounging on. **Praia das Virgens** and **Praia da Tartaruga** are quiet and pretty. **Praia de Manguinhos** is another town beach further west.

Offshore, the islands of **Âncora**, **Gravatás**, **Filhote** and **Feia** are especially good diving destinations.

Tours

Several operators offer tours to local beaches and islands. If you'd rather explore at your own pace, Búzios' *taxis marítimos* (water taxis) are an attractive alternative, charging R$5 to R$10 per person to individual beaches around the peninsula (rates are posted on a board at Armação's main pier).

Tour Shop Búzios (☎ 2623 4733; www.tourshop.com .br; Orla Bardot 550; tours from R$50) runs the Búzios Trolley, an open-sided bus that visits 12 of the peninsula's beaches daily. It also operates rafting tours and trips by glass-bottomed catamaran.

Buziosnauta's (☎ 2623 9005; www.buziosnauta .com.br; Orla Bardot 712; tours from R$35) boats depart Armação daily at 9:30am and 12:30pm for a 2½-hour boat circuit including 12 beaches and two islands, with stops for swimming and snorkeling at Praia João Fernandes, Ilha Feia and Praia da Tartaruga. It also has a dive center. **Casamar** (☎ 9817 6234; www.casamar.com.br; Rua das Pedras 242; 2-tank dives from R$110) offers day and night excursions for experienced divers, plus a full range of courses.

Sleeping

Búzios caters to couples, so things can get pricey for solo travelers. In general, rooms to rent are cheaper than pousadas. Rates quoted here are for the high season: December through March, plus July.

BUDGET

El Misti (☎ 2623 2383; www.elmistibuzios.com; Rua J, No 7, Ferradura; dm R$36-45, d/tr R$155/209; 🖭 🖳 🛜 🖳) This new hostel/pousada on a residential street halfway between Ferradura beach and downtown Armação is pleasant, if a bit out of the way. Entered via a hillside garden with pool and banana trees, the accommodations include fan-cooled dorms and air-conditioned private rooms. A free taxi transfer from the bus stop is available with a minimum two-night stay.

our pick **Yellow Stripe Hostel** (☎ 2623 3174; www .hostel-buzios-yellow.com; Rua da Mandrágora 13; dm R$38-47, d with fan/air-con R$100/110; 🖭 🖳 🛜 🖳) Friendly and well-run, this Canadian-Brazilian hostel offers segregated and mixed dorms and a lovely pool in a renovated old house. There are dozens of perks, including free bodyboards, discounts at local clubs and restaurants, cable TV, a book exchange and individual reading lights. It's a 15-minute walk from Rua das Pedras, or five from the main bus stop.

Nomad Búzios (☎ 2620 8085; www.nomadbuzios .com.br; Rua das Pedras 25; dm R$44-54, tw/d/tr from R$135/180/180; 🖭 🖳 🛜) The prime Rua das Pedras location is the biggest selling point at this new hostel in an air-conditioned seaside motor court. The four- to 10-bed dorms are nothing special, but the beachfront terrace and easy access to nightlife are unbeatable. There are also private rooms, some with ocean views.

MIDRANGE

Brigitta's Guest House (☎ 2623 6157; www.brigittas .com.br; Rua das Pedras 131; r R$140-160) Brigitta's privileged location between Rua das Pedras and the Armação waterfront is just one of many reasons to stay here. There are only four rooms, two with doors opening directly onto the beach. The staff speaks nine languages, and the restaurant downstairs serves an appealing mix of international food. Street noise is the only downside.

Ilha Formosa (☎ 2623 2759; www.buziosilhaformosa .com.br; Rua Maria Joaquina 26; d with fan R$150, with air-con & ocean view R$250; 🖭 🛜) A few steps from the cobblestones of Rua das Pedras, Ilha Formosa has clean, simply furnished rooms, the best of which have excellent ocean views.

Pousada Amendoeira (☎ 2623 2613; www.amen doeira.net; Rua João Fernandes 1449, Ossos; s/d R$150/180; 🖭 🛜) The rooms at this simple pousada are decorated in various cheerful shades of blue, and the affable owner adds to the generally bright atmosphere.

Zen-do Suites (☎ 2623 1542; zendobuzios@mar.com.br; Rua João Fernandes 60; r R$160-190; 🖭 🖳) This sweet little guesthouse only has three rooms. The upstairs unit is especially bright and cheery, with a balcony overlooking the spacious backyard. The friendly staff speak multiple languages.

Germain (☎ 2623 1044; www.saintgermain-buzios.com .br; Alto do Humaitá 5; r from R$200; 🖭 🛜 🖳) Although there's no ocean view, this Brazilian-US-run guesthouse receives high marks for its friendly welcome, bright spacious rooms, prime location (100m to Orla Bardot, 400m to Rua das Pedras) and tasty breakfasts featuring homemade bread. Discounts are offered for cash payment or midweek stays.

TOP END

Pousada Hibiscus Beach (☎ 2623 6221; www.hibiscus beach.com.br; House 22, Block C, Rua 1, João Fernandes; d/tr/q R$250/320/425; 🖳 🛜 🖳) The comfortable private chalets at this newly renovated British-owned guesthouse cascade down the grassy hillside to a pleasant outdoor swimming pool. It's also just a short walk from beautiful João Fernandes beach.

Casa Búzios (☎ 2623 7002; respinger.jimdo.com, in French; Alto do Humaitá 1; r R$250-420; 🅿 🛜 🅿) Just off Orla Bardot, in a sweet hillside garden setting, this French-run pousada offers five spacious and unique suites in a house with high ceilings, pretty shutters and old tile floors. The poolside front patio affords picturesque views of boats bobbing in the harbor below.

Chez Pitú (☎ 2623 6460; www.chezpitu.com.br; Aldeia de Geribá 10; r from R$445, with ocean view from R$520; 🅿 🛜 🅿) Right on the beach in Geribá, this place has an artsy feel, decorated with sculptures, mosaic designs and brightly painted French doors. There are two pools (one with a small bar), and lounge chairs on a wooden deck with tantalizing views of the ocean a few feet away. The nicest rooms are upstairs, with small verandas where you can watch the best sunset in Búzios.

Pérola Búzios (☎ 2620 8507; www.thepearl.com.br; Av José Bento Ribeiro Dantas 222; r from R$498; 🅿 🖥 🛜 🅿) This is the most central of Búzios' trendy new luxury hotels, only two blocks from Rua das Pedras, but far enough removed to guarantee you a good night's sleep. The electric-blue pool, seductively surrounded by curtained lounging beds, is fun and inviting day or night. The whole place is artistically decorated, although for the price, it's disappointing that none of the rooms have ocean views.

Casas Brancas (☎ 2623 1458; www.casasbrancas.com.br; Alto do Humaitá 10; r R$525, with ocean view from R$629; 🅿 🖥 🛜 🅿) If you've just won the lottery or are here for your honeymoon, head straight for Casas Brancas, the best of several top-end places on Alto do Humaitá hill in Armação. The ocean views from the upstairs terrace are stupendous, and the world-class spa, swimming pool and restaurant are nice enough to keep you here all day. Despite the exclusive price tag, Casas Brancas has a rather low-key, friendly attitude.

Eating

Most of the better restaurants are in or near Armação. For good seafood at more affordable prices, check out the little thatched-roof places on Brava, Ferradura and João Fernandes beaches.

Three kilometers west of town at Manguinhos, the trendy new food complex **Porto da Barra** (www.portodabarrabuzios.com.br) is also worth a look, featuring 13 bars and restaurants spread out along a tree-fringed waterfront boardwalk.

BUDGET & MIDRANGE

Carla Gourmet (☎ 2623 0302; Rua Manoel Turíbio de Farias 152; per 100g R$2.99; 🕙 noon-midnight) Not as chichi as Búzios' other per-kilo places, Carla's focuses on traditional specialties – including fresh grilled fish – at a reasonable price.

Bananaland (☎ 2623 2666; Rua Manoel Turíbio de Farias 50; per 100g R$4.50; 🕙 11:30am-10:30pm) One of several deluxe self-serve eateries on this street, Bananaland has something for everyone. The range of choices is simply astounding.

Chez Michou Crêperie (☎ 2623 6137; Rua das Pedras 90; crepes R$10-22; 🕙 noon-late) Crowds flock here not only for the incredible sweet and savory crepes, but also for the outdoor bar serving delicious *pinha coladas* (piña coladas) and the nightly DJ mixes (from 9pm).

Sushi Jardim (☎ 2623 6898; Praça dos Ossos 1358; sushi rolls R$10-25; mains R$30-50; 🕙 6pm-midnight Tue-Sun) Set in a cozy candlelit sculpture garden, this place serves a full range of Japanese delicacies, from sushi rolls to tempura, and from yakisoba to sukiyaki.

Restaurante David (☎ 2623 2981; Rua Manoel Turíbio de Farias 260; mains R$18-35; 🕙 noon-11:30pm) Still going strong after nearly 40 years, David's serves high-quality seafood at little wooden tables with checkered tablecloths in the heart of town.

our pick **Fishbone Café** (☎ 2623 7348; Av Gravatás 1196, Praia de Geribá; sandwiches R$19, salads R$20-35, mains R$45; 🕙 11am-6pm) At this trendy beach club on Praia de Geribá, the menu features everything from sandwiches to salads to seafood, but plenty of people come here just to drink and catch some rays on the waterfront outdoor deck.

TOP END

Cigalon (☎ 2623 0932; Rua das Pedras 199; mains R$30-56; 🕙 6pm-midnight) This fabulous French restaurant is right on the waterfront along Rua das Pedras. Candlelight dancing off the water and crisp white tablecloths set the elegant mood.

Sinatra (☎ 7811 3189; Travessa dos Pescadores 88; mains R$35-45; 🕙 7pm-late Dec-Apr) Excellent fusion cuisine is the name of the game at this fancy eatery with black tablecloths and white lights twined around palm trunks. The Argentine chef, whose other culinary ventures include stints in Ibiza, Spain and Arraial d'Ajuda, cooks up fabulous specials such as *risotto de* *camarão, manga e capim limão* (tiger prawns risotto with mango and lemongrass).

Satyricon (☎ 2623 2691; Orla Bardot 500; pizzas from R$37, mains from R$56; ◷ 5pm-late) Best known for its superb seafood – from avocado-and-shrimp-stuffed fish carpaccio to a let-out-all-the-stops mixed grill called *fantasia di mare* – Satyricon's wide-ranging Mediterranean menu also includes pizza, pasta and risottos.

Bar do Zé (☎ 2623 4986; Orla Bardot 382; mains from R$42; ◷ dinner daily, lunch Sat & Sun) Always packed, this classy restaurant with an open-air deck facing Orla Bardot is famous for its steak and seafood.

Sawasdee (☎ 2623 4644; Orla Bardot 422; mains from R$47; ◷ dinner Thu-Tue) Expensive but excellent, Sawasdee specializes in Thai cuisine showcasing the area's fresh seafood. The *kaipilychia* (lychee caipirinhas) are quite tasty.

Entertainment

Action on Rua das Pedras really gets going after midnight.

Patio Havana (☎ 2623 2169; www.patiohavana.com.br; Rua das Pedras 101; ◷ 6pm-late Thu-Sun) This place is worth checking out if you're a fan of jazz, samba, salsa or bossa nova. Fabulous musicians from all over Brazil (and the world) regularly pop in.

Privilège (☎ 2623 0150; www.privilegenet.com.br; Orla Bardot 510; ◷ 11pm-late Thu-Sat) For house music

among the A-list crowd, head to this sleek nightclub with two dance floors and four bars.

Lapa 40° (☎ 3970 1338; http://lapa40graus.com.br; Orla Bardot 552; ◷ 9pm-late Wed-Sat) Combining pool tables on the 2nd floor, with DJs and live music (samba, *forró*, Latin and pop) on the main floor, this recent transplant from Rio draws a large, diverse crowd.

Pacha (☎ 2633 0592; www.pachabuzios.com; Rua das Pedras 151; ◷ 11pm late) Another new addition to the Búzios club scene, Pacha brings in top-name DJs from around the world nightly in summer and Saturdays throughout the year.

Gran Cine Bardot (☎ 2623 1298; Travessa dos Pescadores 88; admission R$18) Shows movies on weekend nights, including some in English with Portuguese subtitles.

Getting There & Around

The Búzios **bus station** (Estrada da Usina 444) is a simple bus stop with no building attached, five blocks south of the Armação waterfront.

Viação 1001 (☎ 2623 2050) runs buses between Rio and Búzios (R$34, three hours) eight times daily from 6am to 8pm.

Municipal buses between Búzios and Cabo Frio (R$3.35, 45 minutes) make regular stops along Av José Bento Ribeiro Dantas and Estrada da Usina, including one directly opposite the Rio-bound bus stop.

Espírito Santo

One of the best reasons to come to Espírito Santo is that so few other tourists will be joining you. Often completely ignored by foreigners due to its lack of high-profile attractions, the state nonetheless has several hidden treasures. It's an enjoyable place to mingle with Brazilians without the hype and higher prices of neighboring Rio and Bahia states.

In the north of the state is the idyllic little hideaway of Itaúnas, a tiny beach town literally buried in the sand dunes. Its attractions include the tranquil beauty of its natural setting and the frenzied nightlife that unfolds every summer when it converts itself overnight into the *forró* (popular music of the Northeast) capital of Brazil.

South along the coast, the beaches are more developed for family-style tourism, making them very popular with visitors from the neighboring state of Minas Gerais. Here you'll find low-key beach resorts interspersed with fishing villages, plenty of good restaurants and the happy summertime buzz of Brazilian social life.

Inland, Espírito Santo's mountains form an exquisite patchwork of jungled greenery and domed rocky outcroppings, the most dramatic of which is Pedra Azul, a bare mountain crag preserved in a state park less than 100km west of Vitória.

Even without all these scenic attractions, it would be worth visiting Espírito Santo just to eat. Fabulous local seafood specialties such as *moqueca* (stew) and *torta capixaba* (seafood pie) are famous throughout Brazil.

HIGHLIGHTS

- See the sun rise over the dunes after dancing all night to *forró* (popular music of the Northeast) in **Itaúnas** (p223)

- Enjoy **moqueca capixaba** (p223), Espírito Santo's tantalizingly tasty seafood stew, up and down the coast from Vitória to Ubu

- Hold on to that rope as you scale the steep granite face of **Pedra Azul** (p231)

- Watch a baby turtle make its way to the sea in **Parque Estadual de Itaúnas** (p222)

- Eat strudel and sip hot chocolate by the fire in the German-style mountain town of **Domingos Martins** (p230)

Parque Estadual de Itaúnas

Itaúnas ★

Domingos Martins ★

Pedra Azul ★   ★ Vitória

Ubu ★

- POPULATION: 3.5 MILLION
- AREA: 46,078 SQ KM

ESPÍRITO SANTO

History

Colonized in the 16th century, Espírito Santo became an armed region to prevent gold from being smuggled out of Minas Gerais state. Coffee plantations, the prime source of income up until the 1960s, have since been superseded by mining and shipping. The capital city, Vitória, serves as headquarters to Garoto, Brazil's famous (and delicious) chocolate, as well as several chemical and agribusiness concerns.

Climate

Not quite as searingly hot as equatorial Bahia, Espírito Santo can nonetheless get quite uncomfortable in the summer months, especially along the damp, low-lying seaboard. In the mountainous interior, daytime temperatures are pleasantly warm year-round, but can drop surprisingly close to 0°C (32°F) on winter nights. Rains are common, especially in the north, but rarely last long.

State Parks

Espírito Santo has several lovely state parks. Near the border with Bahia, the vast dune- and lagoon-scape of Parque Estadual de Itaúnas includes many kilometers of undeveloped beaches where turtles come ashore to lay their eggs. In the western mountains near Minas Gerais, the dramatic soaring granite outcrop of Pedra Azul forms the centerpiece of Parque Estadual da Pedra Azul. South of Vitória, the coastal lagoons and *restinga* (zone of low trees and shrubs that thrive in sandy, nutrient-poor soil) of Parque Estadual Paulo César Vinha demonstrate the potential for habitat preservation even at the edge of a major urban area.

Getting There & Around

Vitória is the biggest city in Espírito Santo and as such boasts a domestic and international airport. Air service is offered to major cities throughout Brazil. A well-run bus service connects Vitória to Rio, São Paulo and several cities in neighboring Minas Gerais and Bahia. Regular buses also run up and down Espírito Santo's coastline.

THE COAST

Sandwiched between superstar neighbors Rio de Janeiro and Bahia, Espírito Santo's beaches frequently get lost in the shuffle. But there are plenty of pretty places to lay your towel along this coast, from Itaúnas' wild expanses of sand up north to the gentler, family-friendly coves of the south. Smack in the middle, Vitória, the state's capital and largest city, makes a good place to break your journey.

ITAÚNAS

☎ 0xx27 / pop 2500

Surrounded by a majestic state reserve and encroaching sand dunes, 270km north of Vitória near the Bahia border, Itaúnas masquerades as a sleepy fishing village most of the year. However, from New Year's Eve through Carnaval, and again in July, it's a party-mad town filled with young students who come for the lively *forró* dance parties as much as for the beautiful surroundings.

Itaúnas is one of those rare places that manages to retain a delightful 'end of the road' feel despite the intermittent barrage of tourists. In recent years, the number of pousadas (guesthouses) has increased from just a handful to over two dozen, yet locals and outsiders still seem to mix with ease. Many visitors fall under the town's easygoing spell and end up staying longer than they expected.

Sand dunes once engulfed the original village of Itaúnas, which was set about 1km closer to the ocean than it is now – nowadays the old church tower is buried in sand, indicated only by a small sign. From atop the dunes you have a great view of the Atlantic Ocean and the neighboring Parque Estadual de Itaúnas, with its gorgeous mangrove forest and wetlands.

Orientation & Information

Things are made somewhat confusing by the lack of posted street names in Itaúnas, but a pair of handy maps, on the main square and near the bridge to the dunes, can help you get oriented. Buses stop just a few yards from the village square, and most stores, restaurants and pousadas are concentrated nearby. The main road leading into town loops around the square and back out again. A few other roads feed off the square but don't go far. The beach is 1km from town, across the bridge over the Rio Itaúnas.

There are no banks in Itaúnas.

Sights & Activities

The 36.7-sq-km **Parque Estadual de Itaúnas** extends for 25km along the coast and has impressive 20m- to 30m-high sand dunes. The wilderness here is home to monkeys, sloths and *jaguatiricas* (wildcats). The park is also a base for the Tamar Project (see the boxed text, p464). From September to March you can accompany local biologists to the beach to observe sea turtles. November and December are the best months to see the females coming onshore to lay eggs, while January and February mark the peak of the hatching season.

The Itaúnas **park office** (☎ 3762 5196; pei@iema .es.gov.br; ☼ 8:30am-5pm) is in the village next to the bridge over the Rio Itaúnas. It has a souvenir shop, as well as informative displays about the local flora, fauna and culture. There's a trail map posted on the wall, but at the time of writing no such map was available for public distribution.

By far the most popular hike is the 1km **dunes trail** to the nearby beach. From town, simply cross the bridge over the Rio Itaúnas and follow the dirt road until the dunes slope down to meet it, then start climbing. At the crest of the first dune, you'll already have a panoramic view of the ocean, with several beachside *barracas* (stalls) visible straight

ahead, and a sign indicating the ruins of the old *igreja* (church) off to the right.

More ambitious hikers can follow the beach 8km north to **Riacho Doce**, a small river that forms the border between Espírito Santo and Bahia. You'll know you've arrived when you see the handpainted sign on the other side *'Sorria – voce está na Bahia!'* (Smile – you're in Bahia!) Here you'll find **Pousada do Celsão** (☎ 9951 9834; r with fan/air-con R$70/80; ✷), whose attached restaurant serves tasty home-cooked meals. (Just beware the intrepid pet parrot – he'll try to climb in the hammock with you!) For the return trip, retrace your steps down the beach (best done at low tide), or hitch a ride with one of the pickup trucks or school buses that occasionally drive the 16km road back to town.

The **Casinha de Aventuras** (☎ 3762 5081; www .casinhadeaventuras.com.br; Av Bento Daher; ☼ 9am-6:30pm daily Jan & Jul, 9am-1pm Tue-Sun Feb-Jun & Aug-Dec), near the bus stop in the center of town, arranges kayaking trips along the Rio Itaúnas, horseback and dune-buggy excursions, bike rentals and more.

Festivals & Events

For 10 days in late July, Itaúnas hosts the **Festival Nacional de Forró**. Big-name performers pour in from all over Brazil, and there's music and dancing all day and night. **Reveillon** (New Year's Eve) is an even bigger scene, drawing up to 10,000 visitors annually. Itaúnas also hosts the fledgling **International Capoeira Festival** (www.acapoeira.com.br, in Portuguese) in late August.

Sleeping

Pousada & Camping A Nave (☎ 3762 5102, 9988 8484; www.anave.tur.br; Rua Ítalo Vasconcelos; camp site per person R$15-20, s/d R$95/120; ▯) Rustic rooms with carved wooden doors abound at this attractive pousada, which is a labor of love for its sculptor/owner, Júlio. The round, open-sided thatched bar is a great place for a few late-night drinks. The attached camping ground, overlooking a mangrove forest and sand dunes, is also attractive.

Pousada Ponta de Areia (☎ 3762 5295, 9713 3170; Rua Manoel Joaquim Junior; s/d R$35/70) A delightfully simple and welcoming pousada, run by the gracious and well-traveled Bixão.

Pousada Vila Sossego (☎ 3762 5193; itaunasvila sossego@ig.com.br; Rua Paulino Guanandy; s/d R$56/80) In a breezy location on a side street, Vila Sossego has a couple of rooms (numbers 7 and 10) with great views of dunes and the river.

Pousada Tartarugas (☎ 3762 5119; www.pousada tartarugas.com.br; Rua Maria Ortiz Barcelos 181; s/d R$75/150; 🔣 🅿) With a lovely garden setting and an appealing pool tucked around back, this family-run place has been in business for nearly two decades. All rooms have air-conditioning and minibars.

Pousada Zimbaue (☎ 3762 5023; www.quiaitaunas .com.br/zimbaue.html; Rua Teófilo Cabral da Silva 6; s/d/tr with fan R$100/120/160, with air-con R$110/140/180; 🔣 🖳) This cheerful pousada just off the main square has clean white sheets, free bicycles for guests' use, a spacious common area with DVD player and internet access, a kids' play area and an attached café.

Pousada das Araras (☎ 3762 5273; www.pousadadas araras.tur.br; Rua Manoel Joaquim Junior; r R$110-140; 🔣 🅿) This place straddles both sides of the street next door to Ponta de Areia. It's got a fabulous swimming pool, and a nice courtyard garden.

Pousada dos Corais (☎ 3762 5200; www.pousadados corais.com.br; Rua Maria Ortiz Barcelos 154; d/tr R$140/160; 🔣 🖳 🅿) If you're suffering from the heat, try this friendly pousada with its air-con rooms, comfortable sitting areas and pool.

Casa da Praia (☎ 3762 5106; www.casadapraiaitaunas .com.br; Rua Prof Deolinda Lage; r R$150; 🔣) This is one of Itaúnas' loveliest pousadas, on a backstreet with a deck overlooking the river. The owners take great pride in keeping the grounds and rooms spotless.

Eating

There are plenty of inexpensive eateries around Itaúnas. Especially appealing are the half dozen *barracas* out at the beach, serving seafood and beer with ocean views. Note that hours are seasonal and prone to change.

McDunas (☎ 3762 5248; Av Bento Daher; snacks from R$5; 🕒 11am-midnight) Until the corporate lawyers from McDonald's come knocking, McDunas will continue to display its subtle modification of the golden arches logo. A convenient spot for burgers, juices and other quick snacks.

Dona Tereza (☎ 3762 5031; Rua Demerval Leite da Silva; mains R$12-25; 🕒 11am-midnight, to 8pm low season) A highly recommended family-run restaurant with a breezy outdoor terrace. The *prato feito* (plate of the day, listed simply as 'pf' on the menu) is a great deal, including fish, rice and beans for only R$12. From the central square, go one block towards the river.

Dona Pedrolina (☎ 3762 5296; Rua Linoria Lisboa Vasconcelos; mains from R$15; 🕒 11:30am-late, to 8pm low season) Another excellent family-run place just around the corner from Dona Tereza's. Simple meals of fish, rice, beans and salad are very affordable, or you can splurge on *moqueca de camarão* (shrimp stew) – which still feeds three people for under R$100.

Restaurante Sapucaia (☎ 8143 9345; Rua Maria Ortiz Barcelos; mains R$23-42; 🕒 6-11pm Wed-Sat) Chef Itamar has built his reputation on inventive seafood and pasta dishes such as *ravioli de camarão e banana* (ravioli stuffed with shrimp, ricotta and bananas); don't miss the house specialty – home-smoked fish carpaccio.

Entertainment

During high season the pounding beats of *forró* and *axé* (an Afro-Brazilian pop style incorporating samba, rock, soul and other influences) spill from every open window

---

BRAZIL'S BEST MOQUECA

The state of Espírito Santo is renowned throughout Brazil for the quality of its seafood. Topping the list of local culinary specialties is *moqueca capixaba,* a savory stew made from fish, shellfish, tomatoes, peppers and cilantro cooked in a *panela de barro* (earthenware casserole dish). Espírito Santo's *moqueca capixaba* is similar to the *moqueca baiana* so popular in neighboring Bahia, except that it's made without coconut milk.

Wherever you travel in the state, you'll see signs advertising *a melhor moqueca do Brasil* (Brazil's best *moqueca*). But who really makes the best *moqueca*? Visitors to the Vitória region have a golden opportunity to taste-test for themselves. Several award-winning restaurants can be found in a relatively small geographic area here. Three leading contenders are Pirão (p226) in Vitória, which has won *Veja* magazine's 'Best Moqueca in Espírito Santo' prize; Cantinho do Curuca (p228) in Meaípe, which has taken *Quatro Rodas'* 'Best Moqueca in Brazil' honors several years in a row; and Moqueca do Garcia (p230) in Ubu, which hasn't won any awards lately, but whose nearly 50 years in business and constant lunchtime crowds speak for themselves.

ESPÍRITO SANTO

and doorway in Itaúnas. Things don't really start swinging till after midnight, and the party lasts till dawn. Ask locals to point you toward Buraco do Tatu, Bar Forró and Forró do Coco, festive little shacks that get packed full of dancers. **Bar da Ana** (☎ 3762 5261; Rua Prof Deolinda Lage; ☯ 6pm-late) is a year-round backstreet hangout where locals go for drinks, occasional live music and unconventional snacks like shrimp-and-pumpkin cannelloni.

Getting There & Away

Itaúnas is not exactly a major transport hub. The closest place you can make connections for long-distance buses is in Conceição da Barra, 23km south. Aguia Branca runs buses from Vitória to Conceição (*convencional/executivo* R$39/47, five hours) at 6:40am, 11:40am and 4pm, returning from Conceição to Vitória at 6:20am, 2pm and 6pm.

From Conceição a local bus goes to Itaúnas (R$5.60, 40 minutes) at 7am, 12:30pm and 3:30pm daily, returning to Conceição at 8am, 1:30pm and 4:30pm. There are extra buses in summer, and on Monday and Friday throughout the year. If you get stuck overnight in Conceição, there are several pousadas to choose from.

To head north into Bahia, first catch a bus from Conceição out to São Mateus on the main highway (R$6.10, one hour), leaving Conceição at 3:10pm and 6pm. There you can catch two buses daily to Porto Seguro, at 6:15pm (R$49.60) and 12:15am (R$71).

VITÓRIA

☎ 0xx27 / pop 320,000

Vitória doesn't have much to show from its colonial past and, despite having a lush backdrop of mountains rushing down to meet sandy beaches that's vaguely reminiscent of Rio, it remains first and foremost a modern industrial city. Export coffee and timber pass through Vitória's harbor, and the port at nearby Tubarão is the outlet for millions of tons of iron ore. But that doesn't mean Vitória is devoid of charm. The beaches east of the center are pleasant, the locals (known as Capixabas) are warm and friendly, and the city has a flourishing economy, which means many bars, universities, nightclubs, restaurants and hotels.

Orientation

The remnants of old Vitória, built on an island just off the coast, are connected to the mainland via a series of bridges. The city's best beaches are Canto and Camburí to the north, and the renowned Praia da Costa to the south, in the sister city of Vila Velha. The teeming, modern **bus station** (☎ 3222 3366) is located just west of the old town center. Trains coming from Belo Horizonte (see p241) arrive at **Estação Ferroviária Pedro Nolasco** (☎ 3226 4169), 1km west of the bus station.

Information

ATMs for several banks are clustered together inside the bus station.

Bradesco (Av Jerônimo Monteiro 400) Downtown ATM.

Main post office (Av Jerônimo Monteiro 310)

Net.Point Lan House (☎ 3222 2933; Av República; per hr R$2.50; ☯ 9am-9pm Mon-Sat, 1-9pm Sun) Internet and Skype access across from Parque Moscoso.

Tourist information (☎ 3224 6074; www.descubrao espiritosanto.es.gov.br) airport (☯ 6:30am-10pm); bus station (☯ 8am-9pm Mon-Fri, 8am-noon Sat) In the airport arrivals area, or opposite track 6 at the bus station.

Sights

CITY CENTER

Downtown Vitória's grandest historic building, the yellow **Anchieta Palace** (☎ 3321 3578; www .palacioanchieta.es.gov.br, in Portuguese; Praça João Clímaco) is a former Jesuit college and church that now serves as the seat of state government. Following extensive restoration work, it was reopened to the public in 2009. **Tours** (admission free; ☯ 10am-5pm Wed-Sat, 10am-4pm Sun) allow you to see the 16th-century foundations of the original Jesuit church, an assortment of tiles, pottery and other artifacts discovered during renovation, and the tomb of Padre José de Anchieta (1534–97), an early missionary who cofounded São Paulo and was hailed as the 'Apostle of Brazil.' On Sundays, with advance notice, you can also visit the grandest rooms in the palace (used for government functions during the week).

Close by is the **Catedral Metropolitana** (Praça Dom Luiz Scortegagna; ☯ 9am-5pm Tue-Sun), with its neo-Gothic exterior and interesting stained-glass windows.

Teatro Carlos Gomes (Praça Costa Pereira) is a replica of La Scala in Milan. It stages national-caliber theater and dance productions at very reasonable prices. Check with the tourist office to see what's currently playing.

Capixabas like to walk and relax in the leafy **Parque Moscoso** (Av Cleto Nunes), just west of the city center.

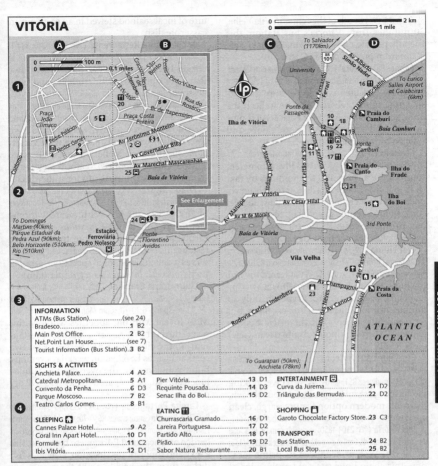

VITÓRIA

VILA VELHA

Across the river and south of Vitória sits Vila Velha, the first place in Espírito Santo to be colonized. A must-see is the **Convento da Penha** (www.franciscanos.org.br/penha; 8am-4:45pm), atop the densely forested Morro da Penha. The panoramic city views are magnificent and the chapel (founded in 1558) isn't too bad either. It's a major pilgrimage destination – around Easter expect massive crowds paying homage to NS da Penha, some climbing the hill on their knees.

BEACHES

Praia do Camburí, a 5km stretch of beach, is punctuated by kiosks, restaurants, nightspots and midrange hotels. Don't swim near the bridge – it's polluted.

Praia da Costa in Vila Velha is the city's nicest beach. It has fewer hotels and restaurants than Camburí, but you can swim and bodysurf. Keep a close eye on the horizon – huge supertankers often pop up with surprising speed!

Sleeping

Staying out at the beach is a much more attractive option than downtown, which is deserted after nightfall. Vitória receives a lot of midweek business travelers; on weekends many hotels drop their rates, except during peak holiday periods like Carnaval and Semana Santa. Decent budget options in this city are scarce.

Requinte Pousada (3349 9456; www.pousadasvila velha.com.br/requinte; Av Hugo Musso 45; r with fan/air-con

ESPÍRITO SANTO

R$75/95; 🗙 🛜) South of the center in Vila Velha, 30 minutes from Vitória's bus station, this friendly pousada has clean, small rooms only 200m from pretty Praia da Costa.

Cannes Palace Hotel (☎ 3232 7200; www.hotelcannes.com.br; Av Jerônimo Monteiro 111; s/d R$79/99; 🗙 🖳 🛜) Not quite as decrepit as it looks from the outside, this aging high-rise is close to both the bus station and the Anchieta Palace. All rooms have air-con and patterned wood floors, and nine come with in-room wi-fi.

Formule 1 (☎ 3205 6155; www.formule1.com.br; Av NS da Penha 1993; r R$89; 🗙 🖳) Five kilometers south of the airport and five minutes by taxi (R$8 to R$10) from Praia do Canto, this newly opened budget chain hotel offers dependable, cookie-cutter rooms sleeping up to three people. Breakfast costs R$7 extra and internet access is R$7/12 per hour/day.

Pier Vitória (☎ 3434 0000; www.piervitoriahotel.com.br; Av Dante Michelini 321; s/d weekend rate from R$109/129, midweek from R$179/229; 🗙 🖳 🛜) Geared toward business travelers, the Pier Vitória is conveniently located on Camburí beach, only 10 minutes from the airport. It's an excellent deal on weekends, when even the priciest room (suite 602 with whirlpool tub and ocean view) costs R$219.

Coral Inn Apart Hotel (☎ 3334 0155; www.coralinnaparthotel.com.br; Av Saturnino Rangel Mauro 230; s/d weekend R$124/134, midweek R$154/164; 🗙 🛜) Overlooking the harbor just inland from Camburí beach, this boxy modern option features large, clean apartments with kitchenettes and balconies.

Ibis Vitória (☎ 2104 4850; www.ibis.com.br; Rua João da Cruz 385, Praia do Canto; r weekend/midweek R$125/155; 🗙 🖳 🛜) Well priced given its prime location, this chain hotel sits right at the edge of the Triângulo das Bermudas, Vitória's nightlife hub, and is only a few blocks from Praia do Canto. Breakfast costs R$11 extra per person, and internet access costs R$7/12 per hour/day.

Senac Ilha do Boi (☎ 3345 0111; www.hotelilhadoboi.com.br; Rua Bráulio Macedo 417; s/d from R$335/380, s/d ste from R$620/750; 🗙 🖳 🛜 📺) For a real night of luxury, this is an excellent choice. It's located on top of a hill with fabulous views of the surrounding bay. The service is impeccable and the amenities delightful, including a tennis court, solarium, piano bar, pools and saunas.

Eating

Make sure you try the regional specialty known as *moqueca capixaba*, a savory mixture of local seafood stewed in an earthenware casserole dish.

Sabor Natura Restaurante (☎ 3322 0249; Rua 13 de Maio 85; per kg R$16.90; ⏱ 11am-2:30pm Mon-Fri) A veggie-friendly self-serve place downtown that's very popular with students and businesspeople alike.

Partido Alto (☎ 3227 4086; Rua Joaquim Lírio 865, Praia do Canto; mains from R$18; ⏱ 11am-11pm) A godsend for solo travelers, penny-pinchers and light eaters, this lively eatery serves a wide variety of *moquequinhas* (smaller portions of Espírito Santo's classic *moqueca* seafood stew), and there's also a shrimp risotto for under R$20.

Pirão (☎ 3227 1165; Rua Joaquim Lírio 753, Praia do Canto; mains from R$35; ⏱ 11:30am-4pm & 6:30-11pm Mon-Fri, 11:30am-5pm Sat & Sun) With award-winning *moquecas* and *tortas capixabas*, Pirão has earned a reputation as one of the city's best restaurants over the past 25 years. On Friday it serves a delicious regional specialty – grouper prepared with *banana da terra* (plantain).

Churrascaria Gramado (☎ 3225 1311; Av Rosendo Serapião Souza 43; all-you-can-eat per person R$35-60; ⏱ 11am-3pm & 6:30-10:30pm Mon-Sat, 11am-4pm Sun) Meat lovers with big appetites will love this place, the best *churrascaria* (barbecue restaurant) in the city. Unlimited barbecue for two costs as little as R$69.90 on weekday evenings, but if you come for the over-the-top Sunday lunch spread, be prepared to pay R$59.90 per person.

Lareira Portuguesa (☎ 3345 0331; Av Saturnino de Brito 260, Praia do Canto; mains R$50-70; ⏱ 11:30am-3pm & 7pm-midnight Mon-Sat, 11:30am-4:30pm Sun) A gorgeous garden and beautiful Portuguese tiles make this a sexy and sophisticated location. Delicious fish dishes form the backbone of the menu, but you'll also find Old World classics like roasted goat, plus plenty of Portuguese desserts.

Drinking & Entertainment

Capixabas like the nightlife – check out the Triângulo das Bermudas, a neighborhood packed with bars, eateries and nightclubs centered on the intersection of Ruas Joaquim Lírio and João da Cruz. Hip crowds also gather at Curva da Jurema, populated by shacks that serve snacks and food into the wee hours.

Shopping

At **Garoto chocolate factory store** (☎ 3320 1502; Praça Meyerfreund 1, Vila Velha; ⏱ 9am-6pm Mon-Fri, 8:30am-2pm Sat) the best chocolate in Brazil is really

GREEN DETOURS IN ESPÍRITO SANTO

Espírito Santo offers a handful of off-the-beaten-track attractions for nature lovers. All are easily accessible by car as day trips from Vitória, or can be combined into a longer itinerary progressing north towards Bahia.

Closest to Vitória, 82km northwest in the pretty mountain town of Santa Teresa, is the **Museu de Biológica Professor Mello Leitão** (☎ 0xx27-3259 1182; www.melloleitao.iphan.gov.br; admission R$2; ☽ 8am-5pm Tue-Sun). The museum celebrates the work of local ecologist Augusto Ruschi (1915–86), who conducted pioneering studies on the region's remarkable variety of hummingbirds and orchids and was a strong early proponent of environmental protection in Brazil. The verdant grounds are a peaceful oasis, and offer a chance to observe many local plant and hummingbird species.

Less than 100km further north, reached by a 23km dirt road from the city of Linhares, is the **Reserva Biológica de Comboios** (☎ 0xx27-3274 1209; www.tamar.org.br/cv_es_comboios.php), the Espírito Santo headquarters for the turtle conservation organization Tamar (see the boxed text, p464). Here you can observe giant sea turtles in the reserve's aquarium, or continue north 7km to visit the beach community of Regência, where residents earn their living from a combination of fishing and turtle conservation work.

Continuing 30km north from Linhares towards the Bahia border, the **Reserva Natural Vale** (☎ 0xx27-3371 9702; www.vale.com/reserva_natural_vale) is a privately protected 218-sq-km expanse of Atlantic rain forest whose tremendous biological diversity has earned it a place on Unesco's World Heritage list. Visitors can stay overnight at the reserve's simple but comfortable **lodge** (s/d with full board from R$168/219; ☒ ☒) and explore the surrounding network of trails.

fresh. It's off Rodovia Carlos Lindenberg in Vila Velha – take bus 500 from the city center. Hour-long **factory tours** (☎ 3320 1709; admission R$10) are available Monday afternoons, Friday mornings and all day Tuesday through Thursday.

Getting There & Away

Buses leave Vitória for Belo Horizonte in Minas Gerais state (*convencional/executivo* R$71/85, eight hours, 11 daily from 8:40am to 10:30pm), Ouro Prêto (R$61, seven hours, direct bus at 9pm), Porto Seguro (*convencional/executivo* R$79/113, 11 hours, twice daily at 2pm and 9pm), Rio (R$71 to R$111, eight hours, seven daily from 8:20am to 10:50pm) and Salvador (R$227, 19 hours, daily sleeper bus at 5pm).

There's also one daily train from Vitória to Belo Horizonte (see p241).

Eurico Salles airport (☎ 3235 6300) is 10km northeast of the city center, in Goiabeiras. Flights leave regularly for Belo Horizonte, Rio, São Paulo and other Brazilian cities.

Getting Around

Between the airport and the city center, take local bus 212 marked '*aeroporto/rodoviária*' (R$2.15). Taxis from the airport cost around R$20 to Praia do Canto or R$30 to the city center.

Local buses (R$2.15) run from the various stops outside the bus station; the route is written on the side of each bus. For the center, catch any bus that goes along Av Vitória and get off after you pass the yellow Anchieta Palace on your left. For Praia do Camburí, catch any bus that goes along Av Dante Michelini. For Praia do Canto and Triângulo das Bermudas, take any bus that goes along Av Saturnino de Brito. To Vila Velha and Praia da Costa catch the all-yellow Transcol bus 500 or any bus marked Praia da Costa.

GUARAPARI

☎ 0xx27 / pop 105,000

There are some lovely beaches just waiting to be enjoyed about an hour south of Vitória. This stretch of coast is usually passed over by foreigners, but Guarapari is a favored resort destination for Brazilians and, as such, retains a relaxed, fun and family-friendly atmosphere. There are 23 beaches in the municipality, each with an attractive mountain backdrop.

Orientation & Information

The center is 500m south of the bus station, across the bridge; the beach is 200m further on. The **tourist office** (☎ 3262 8759; www.guarapari .es.gov.br/turismo, in Portuguese; Rua Paulo de Águiar 68) has maps and information in Portuguese. There are several banks with ATMs along Rua

ESPÍRITO SANTO

Joaquim da Silva Lima in the center. Internet places are clustered in the center and along Praia do Morro.

Sights

The best beach is **Praia do Morro**, north of the city (be aware that its so-called 'healing' black monazitic sand is, in fact, said to be radioactive!). Also consider **Praia dos Namorados** (small but surrounded by rocks creating beautiful pools), **Praias Castanheiras** and **Areia Preta** (more radioactive sand but crystal-clear waters), **Praia do Meio**, aka Siribeira (great rock pools with gorgeous snorkeling), **Praia Enseada Azul** (a long stretch with lots of natural beauty) and **Praia dos Padres** (accessible only by trail from Enseada Azul, and has stunning green waters). At the far southern end of town is **Meaípe**, another good place to spend the night.

Sleeping

Camping Club do Brasil (☎ 3262 1325; Praia de Setiba; camping per person/tent R$27/7) This camping spot a few kilometers north of town is just a stone's throw from lovely Setiba beach.

Hotel Guara Pousada (☎ 3262 5210; www.guaratur .com.br/hotel.php, in Portuguese; Av Antonio Guimarães, Quadra 40; s/d/tr/q with fan from R$70/90/112/140, with air-con R$105/130/163/203) This former hostel has basic *apartamentos* (rooms with private bathrooms) on large, walled grounds not far from the bus station and the beach.

Pousada Enseada Verde (☎ 3272 1376; www.enseada verde.com.br; Rua Duarte Mattos 27; d/tr/q R$99/129/159; ✗ ⓢ ⓦ) A great option down the coast in Meaípe, Pousada Enseada Verde has rooms with minibars, hammocks and balconies, a stone's throw from the waterfront.

Hotel Atlântico (☎ 3361 1551; www.hotelatlantico guarapari.com.br; Av Edisio Cirne 332; d/tr from R$135/169, ocean-view ste d/tr/q from R$190/238/285; ✗ ▯ ⓢ ⓦ) Just across from Praia dos Namorados in the heart of Guarapari, this well-equipped hotel offers comfy rooms with panoramic terraces, plus perks including a sauna, poolside bar and beach umbrellas.

Porto do Sol Guarapari (☎ 3161 7100; www.hotel portodosol.com.br; Av Beira Mar 1; s/d from R$205/255; ✗ ▯ ⓢ ⓦ) Porto do Sol, surrounded by water on three sides, has an unbeatable location between downtown and Praia do Morro. All rooms have panoramic ocean views, with wi-fi, DVD and whirlpool tubs in the deluxe suites. Sea turtles sometimes come up onto the rocks directly below the rooms.

Eating

Up and down all the beaches, but particularly on Praia do Morro, you'll find dozens of *barracas* selling inexpensive fresh seafood and regional dishes.

Pilão (☎ 3361 6035; Av Maria de Lourdes C Dantas 141; per kg R$23.90; ⓢ 11am-late) Two blocks back from Praia do Morro, this self-serve has an excellent per-kilo lunch buffet. Hearty wood-fired Brazilian classics share the menu with seafood specialties such as *moqueca* and shrimp lasagna.

Restaurante João de Barro (☎ 3262 8825; Rua Getúlio Vargas 226; per kg R$24.90; ⓢ 11am-3pm) Atmospherically decked out with bright murals, shelves of *cachaça* (sugarcane alcohol) bottles, and an old wood stove, this high-ceilinged downtown self-serve specializes in fine *comida mineira* (the cuisine of Minas Gerais).

Peixada do Irmão (☎ 3261 0636; Rua Jacinto de Almeida 72; mains R$25-50; ⓢ 11am-10pm Tue-Sun, 11am-3pm Mon) Near the tourist office, this restaurant has a bilingual menu and an excellent reputation for seafood dishes.

our pick Cantinho do Curuca (☎ 3272 2000; Av Santana 96, Meaípe; mains for 2 R$45-145; ⓢ 11am-10pm) The *moqueca* at this beachfront eatery in Meaípe has been voted the best in Brazil multiple times. Everything from fish to squid and shrimp to bananas finds its way into the dozens of clay pots bubbling away in the cavernous kitchen. Early arrivals can grab one of the limited front tables facing the water.

Getting There & Away

From Guarapari's **bus station** (Rua João Gomes de Jesus 50), **Planeta** (☎ 3362 9613) has services to/from Vitória roughly hourly from 7:30am to 9:30pm (R$8, 1¼ hours). Half-hourly buses continue south to Ubu (R$2.20, 30 minutes), Anchieta (R$3, 40 minutes) and Iriri (R$3.80, one hour).

PARQUE ESTADUAL PAULO CÉSAR VINHA

Ten kilometers north of Guarapari lies this 15-sq-km **state park** (☎ 3242 3665; Hwy ES-060, km37.5; ⓢ 8am-5pm), part of Brazil's Atlantic Rain Forest Biosphere Reserve. The park shelters a variety of habitats, including dunes, lagoons and coastal *restinga*. The park's lone trail leads 2.5km from park headquarters to **Lagoa de Caraís**, a tranquil lagoon teeming with bird life just inland from the beach. **Viação Alvorada** (☎ 3261 0414) runs frequent buses from Guarapari to the park (R$1.60, 20 minutes).

THE GOITACÁ WARRIORS

Early European explorers reported encounters with the fearsome, long-haired, tall, robust and formidable Goitacá warriors, coastal dwellers of the Rio state–Espírito Santo border region. The tribe had long resisted invasions by rival Tupi nations and, despite the technological advantage of guns, the Europeans found the Goitacá almost impossible to capture. The Goitacá were excellent runners and swimmers, and seemed by all reports to be equally at home on land and in the water. When chased, they were so fast through the waters and jungle that nobody could catch them on foot, on horseback or by boat.

According to legend, a Goitacá could run after a wild deer and capture it with his arms, and could catch a shark using only a piece of wood. (This was accomplished by forcing a stick inside the shark's mouth to stop the jaws from closing, and pulling its guts out by hand until it died.) The Goitacá nation (around 12,000 people), never defeated in battle, was exterminated at the end of the 18th century by an epidemic of smallpox – a disease deliberately introduced by the Portuguese for that very purpose.

ANCHIETA
☎ 0xx28 / pop 20,000

South of Vitória, Anchieta is one of the oldest settlements in Espírito Santo and, as the name would suggest, contains many relics dedicated to the work of famed 16th-century Jesuit priest José de Anchieta. The beaches aren't as attractive as those leading to Guarapari (20km to the north) or to neighboring Iriri and Ubu (to the south and north respectively), but this small port town does have its own relaxed appeal – the quiet, rhythmic life of a fishing village is still very much apparent, especially at Praia dos Castelhanos just north of town.

Sights
You'll have no problem locating the **Santuário Nacional Padre Anchieta**, which dominates the town from its impressive hillside location. A 250-year-old chestnut tree spreads gracefully in front of this striking white church with its bold blue shutters and doors. The complex includes the **Museu Padre Anchieta** (admission R$2; ☉ 8am-noon & 2-5pm Tue-Sun), highlighting the evangelical work of the Jesuit priest José de Anchieta among *índios* (indigenous peoples). The church walls, built by local *índios* and Padre Anchieta, are original. The museum contains relics uncovered during restoration. If you'd rather get your history at the seashore, then stroll to the end of Anchieta beach. Just before the road goes over a small, white, wooden bridge you'll find a **statue** of José de Anchieta giving blessings to a Goitacá warrior (see the boxed text, above).

Festivals & Events
Devoted followers of Padre Anchieta participate in an annual pilgrimage commemorating his missionary work along the Espírito Santo coast. The popular 100km **Steps of Anchieta** walk along the beach from Vitória to Anchieta takes place in June (exact dates vary each year) and lasts four days. Contact the state tourism office in Vitória (p224) for specifics.

Sleeping & Eating
Anchieta doesn't provide many tourist services, and the best downtown hotel closed years ago, so you're better off staying in nearby Iriri or Ubu, or at **Pousada João de Barro** (☎ 3536 1851; www.pousadajoaodebarroes.com.br; r R$80-120), a cheery place just inland from pretty Praia dos Castelhanos, 2km north of Anchieta.

Anchieta has several *lanchonetes* (snack bars) near the bus stop.

Getting There & Away
Buses to Guarapari (R$3, 40 minutes) run every half hour or so between 5:15am and 9:30pm. To Vitória (R$14, two hours) they run 12 times daily (every one to two hours between 6am and 8:40pm). The **bus station** (☎ 3536 1147; Av Carlos Lindenberg 183) is opposite the waterfront on the main road through town.

AROUND ANCHIETA
Praia da Guanabara Turtle Research Station
Four kilometers north of Anchieta, the Tamar Project (see the boxed text, p464) operates the **Praia da Guanabara Turtle Research Station** (☎ 3536 3547; ☉ 9am-6pm daily Dec-Mar, by arrangement Apr-Nov). Here you'll find a 2km stretch of protected beach where turtles come onshore to lay their eggs every summer, plus an interesting museum of marine turtle exhibits.

ESPÍRITO SANTO

To get here, take any northbound Planeta or Sudeste bus from Anchieta. Ask to be let off at Praia da Guanabara and follow the signs 300m downhill to the beach.

Iriri
☎ 0xx28

This agreeable coastal getaway features a pretty beach tucked into a sheltered cove flanked by rocky ledges on either side. Iriri is very popular with Mineiros, who come in droves during the summer months and turn the tiny town into an upbeat, family-focused resort. Carnaval here is especially popular.

SLEEPING & EATING
Hotel Maringá (☎ 3534 1252; www.portaldehosped agem.com.br/hotelmaringa; Av Dom Helvecio 665; s/d with fan R$60/120, d with air-con R$140; 🅿 🛜) Bland but friendly, the centrally located Maringá, one block back from the beach, is one of Iriri's more affordable choices. There's a self-serve restaurant attached.

our pick Recanto da Pedra (☎ 3534 1599; www.re cantodapedra.com.br; Av Beira Mar 16; s/d R$85/150; 🅿 🛜) Hands down the best value in town, Recanto da Pedra is picturesquely sited on rocks at the northern end of Iriri beach. Many rooms have terraces with bird's-eye views of the gracefully curving shoreline. The attached restaurant serves excellent food – it's fun to lounge here and watch swimmers popping up out of the water for a quick drink at the bar.

Hotel Pontal das Rochas (☎ 3534 1369; www.pontal dasrochas.com.br; Av Beira Mar s/n; d without/with ocean view from R$270/325; 🅿 🖥 🛜 🍴) On the same point as Recanto da Pedra, this first-rate hotel offers fabulous amenities, including a panoramic restaurant, and a sauna and pool built into the rocks overlooking the water.

Restaurante do Português (☎ 3534 1222; Rua Alpoim 558; mains from R$18; ⏱ 11am-9pm) Generous portions of tasty local seafood are served at this unpretentious eatery decorated with pretty blue-and-white tiles half a block from the beach.

Ubu
☎ 0xx28

A sleepy little seaside town 9km north of Anchieta, Ubu has a picturesque waterfront with a cliff at one end and a pretty mermaid statue marking the beach's midpoint. It's also home to one of Espírito Santo's best restaurants.

Just uphill from the beach, the Swiss-run **Pousada Aba Ubu** (☎ 3536 5067; www.abaubu.com .br; Rua Manoel Miranda Garcia; d R$140-260, tr R$165-275; 🅿 🛜 🍴) has a pool, a sauna, a tennis court and nice rooms around a garden. Pricier units include air-conditioning and wi-fi.

Down by the waterfront, celebrating nearly half a century in business, **Moqueca do Garcia** (☎ 3536 5050; Av Magno Ribeiro Muqui 17; mains for 2 R$54-154; ⏱ 10am-5pm, to midnight Dec 27-Carnaval) lives up to its proud reputation as Ubu's best place for top-notch Capixaba cuisine. Don't miss it!

INLAND

The landscapes get more dramatic, the Old World influences more pronounced and the temperatures cooler as you leave Espírito Santo's coast for the mountainous interior. High season here is May to August, when Brazilians flock inland for a rare taste of winter comforts like chilly nights, fondue and a blazing fire.

DOMINGOS MARTINS
☎ 0xx27 / pop 32,000 / elevation 542m

Tucked into the highlands of the Serra Capixaba, this pretty little German-style town – also referred to as Campinho by locals – makes a good base for exploring the nearby forests, streams and mountains.

Sights
Tourist information is available at **Casa da Cultura** (☎ 3268 2550; www.domingosmartins.es.gov .br; Av Presidente Vargas 531; admission free; ⏱ 8am-5pm Tue-Fri, 8am-noon & 1-5pm Sat & Sun), opposite the first bus stop in town. Ask for Joel Velten, who speaks excellent English and can offer a wealth of advice about the town and the surrounding area. The museum upstairs features photos, documents and household objects dating from 1847, when Pomeranians first settled this colony. Further along the same road you'll find the town's main square, a pretty gathering spot with benches, trees and an old Lutheran church.

Flora lovers should head out to the **Instituto Reserva Kautsky** (☎ 3268 2300; www.institutokautsky .org.br; ⏱ by arrangement), established by dedicated botanist Roberto Kautsky, who has cultivated more than 100 species of orchids at his home at the southern end of town and on his mountainside reserve. Visits to the reserve can be arranged by contacting Cristine Feitosa at assessoria.ik@gmail.com.

Festivals & Events

In the second half of July, the **Festival Internacional de Inverno** (www.festivaldeinverno.es.gov.br) is an annual 10-day gathering of Brazilian and international musicians who offer daily classes and nightly concerts on Domingos Martins' main square.

Sleeping & Eating

Hotel e Restaurante Imperador (☎ 3268 1115; hotelimperador@gmail.com; Av Senador Jefferson de Aguiar 275; s/d midweek R$43/75, weekend R$75/135; ☎ ☎) Directly opposite the Lutheran church on the main square, the Imperador is an older hotel with traditional German architecture, a pool and sauna, and quirky vestiges of charm. Unfortunately some of the plumbing is also ancient – do a sniff test before choosing your room.

Pousada Germânia (☎ 3268 2046; pousadagermania.blogspot.com; Rua de Lazer 204; r R$100) This sweet little private home looks like it was lifted straight out of the Alps. You'll find it tucked just off the main pedestrian thoroughfare.

Sabor Café Expresso (☎ 3268 3263; Rua de Lazer 54; coffee & strudel R$6, fixed-price meals R$9; ☎ 9:30am-10pm) Homemade strudel, cake, and hot chocolate with whipped cream are the specialties at this lively sidewalk café in the heart of the pedestrian zone. Inexpensive meals are also served.

Choperia Fritz Frida (☎ 3268 1808; Av Presidente Vargas 782; mains from R$18; ☎ 5-10pm Wed-Mon) This half-timbered building with outdoor seating opposite the main square serves pizza, beer and old German favorites.

Getting There & Away

Ten buses daily Monday to Saturday and eight on Sunday make the 42km trip (R$9, one hour) from Vitória to Domingos Martins' **bus station** (☎ 3268 1243; Rua Bernardino Monteiro). Upon request, any bus between Vitória and Belo Horizonte will also stop on the main highway just outside the town entrance gate, where you can call a **taxi** (☎ 9928 3893) for the 3km, R$10 ride to the town square.

AROUND DOMINGOS MARTINS
Parque Estadual da Pedra Azul

Vitória–Belo Horizonte buses stop at the best reason to come inland: the 500m Pedra Azul, 50km west of Domingos Martins down Hwy BR-262. The dramatic rock, tinted by a bluish moss, forms the centerpiece of the **state park** (☎ 3248 1156; admission free; ☎ 8am-5:30pm). Rangers escort hikers to the rock's nine **natural pools**, a

moderately difficult hike affording magnificent views of Pedra Azul and the surrounding forest and farmland. Bring a swimsuit and sturdy shoes – there's a short section where ropes are used to scale a steep rock face. The round trip takes three hours and must be booked in advance on weekdays; departures are scheduled at 9am and 1:30pm on weekends, or by arrangement during the week. Independent climbing and camping are not permitted in the park.

Fjordland Cavalgada Ecológica (☎ 3248 0054; cavalgadapedraazul.com.br; 20-min/100-min trail rides R$20/50) leads horseback excursions around the foot of Pedra Azul, on beautiful Fjorde horses from Norway.

SLEEPING & EATING

The area is dotted with fancy resort hotels, many offering full board.

Pousada Peterle (☎ 3248 1171; www.pousadapeterle.com.br, in Portuguese; Hwy BR-262, km88; s/d with breakfast & dinner from R$155/170; ☎ ☎) Two kilometers below the park entrance, Pousada Peterle has attractive log cabins with fireplaces and balconies. On weekends, prices rise and a two-night minimum stay is often required.

Pousada Pedra Azul (☎ 3334 2420; www.pousadapedraazul.com.br; Rota do Lagarto, km1.5; d with meals from R$402; ☎ ☎) Set in lovely gardens only 500m from park headquarters, this high-end pousada is one of the region's oldest. The main brick-and-wood building with Alpine-style balconies and pagoda-like roofs was designed by Brazilian architect Zanine. Amenities include a pool, sauna, tennis courts, lake and waterfall. Guest rooms are spacious, with high ceilings, big tubs and armchairs.

our pick Valsugana (☎ 3248 1126; off Hwy BR-262, km89.5; mains R$24-40; ☎ lunch Sat & Sun, dinner Sat year-round, plus dinner Fri Apr-Sep) Hearty Italian fare and spectacular views of Pedra Azul make this one of the area's nicest restaurants. The inventive recipes feature fresh local produce and the wine list is excellent.

GETTING THERE & AWAY

Aguia Branca buses pass within 2km of the park entrance. In Vitória, buy a ticket for Fazenda do Estado (R$17, two hours, 11 daily from 5am to 10:30pm), and ask to be let off at km88. The km88 bus stop is directly opposite Peterle's pousada and restaurant. From here, it's a 2km uphill walk to the park entrance along a lovely winding cobblestone road, Rota do Lagarto.

ESPÍRITO SANTO

Minas Gerais

Geographically close to Rio de Janeiro and São Paulo, but with a culture entirely its own, Minas Gerais (Minas) is easy to reach and hard to leave. The people are among Brazil's friendliest, the food is great, the natural setting is spectacular and there's more beautiful historical architecture per square kilometer here than in any other place in Brazil.

In the early 18th century, colonial towns such as Ouro Prêto, Mariana and Diamantina sprang up along the gold road linking Minas to the coast. Built on Minas' mineral wealth, they soon developed a cultural and architectural wealth all their own. Minas was the birthplace of Tiradentes, leader of Brazil's first great independence movement, and Aleijadinho, the country's finest baroque artist. Built in the 1890s as Brazil's first planned city, Belo Horizonte's ongoing openness to innovation is evidenced by Oscar Niemeyer's audacious 1940s building designs and today's burgeoning arts scene.

Although Minas's natural wonders don't get much press, the state is home to some magnificent scenery and wildlife. In 2005 the Serra do Espinhaço, a rocky spine running the length of the state, was recognized for its remarkable biodiversity as Brazil's newest Unesco Biosphere Reserve. Parks throughout Minas provide critical habitat for endangered species such as the northern *muriqui* (woolly spider monkey). Lacking beaches, Mineiros (residents of Minas Gerais) compensate with fabulous food and drink. Minas cheese and *cachaça* (a sugarcane alcohol) are considered the best in Brazil. Meals are often cooked on the *fogão à lenha* – a traditional wood-burning stove – and local hospitality is as abundant as the food.

MINAS GERAIS

HIGHLIGHTS

- Wander the picturesque cobblestone streets and marvel at the baroque architectural wonders of **Ouro Prêto** (p244)
- Take a ride on a historic **Maria-Fumaça** (p257) steam train from Tiradentes
- Climb Brazil's third-tallest mountain, 2892m Pico da Bandeira in **Parque Nacional de Caparaó** (p271)
- Wait by starlight for the maned wolves to appear at the old monastery at **Parque Natural do Caraça** (p267)
- Check out the 16 galleries of contemporary art at **Centro de Arte Contemporânea Inhotim** (p241), near Brumadinho

Parque Natural do Caraça

Ouro Prêto ★
Brumadinho ★

Parque Nacional de Caparaó

★ Tiradentes

■ POPULATION: 20 MILLION   ■ AREA: 586,528 SQ KM

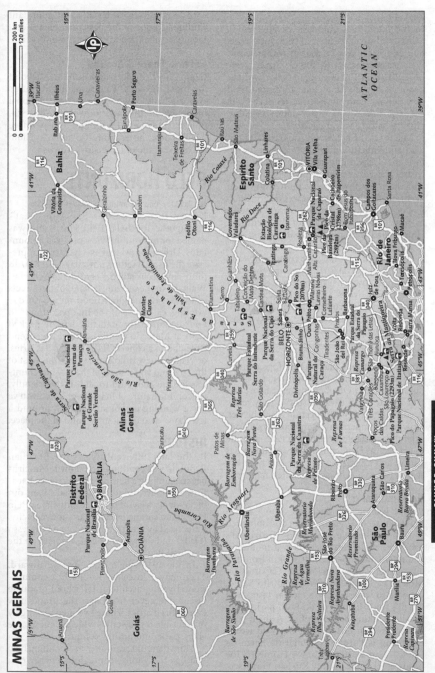

MINAS GERAIS

History

In the late 1600s gold was discovered in Minas. It didn't take long for the word to get out, and Brazilians flocked to Minas, while Portuguese flocked to Brazil. Slaves were brought from Bahia's sugar fields and the savannas of Angola, as few whites did their own mining. Until the last quarter of the 18th century, the slaves of Minas Gerais were digging up half the world's gold.

Minas set the gold-rush standard – crazy, wild and violent – more than 100 years before the Californian and Australian gold rushes. Disease and famine were rampant, and the mine towns were known for their licentiousness. Minas's gold was siphoned off to Portugal; among the few lasting benefits to Brazil was the creation of the beautiful, church-clad mining cities that dot the hills of Minas Gerais.

As Minas enters the 21st century, the old Estrada Real (Royal Rd) connecting the colonial mining towns has become one of Brazil's prime tourist draws. The government has invested heavily in promoting the route, inviting visitors to rediscover the country's past through a modern lens.

Climate

Minas is a moody place. Drab fogs drift in and out amid almost daily showers (of short duration) from October through February. During the day it's warm, so you only really need an umbrella for protection from the wet. However, temperatures can cool down considerably at night, especially in high-altitude towns such as Diamantina and São Thomé das Letras, and during the July to September dry season, when a light jacket is often required.

National Parks

Parque Nacional da Serra do Cipó – forming the heart of Unesco's Serra do Espinhaço Biosphere Reserve – is Belo Horizonte's backyard wilderness area. Its vast mountain and river landscapes lie just 100km from the city center. Parque Nacional de Caparaó, on Minas's eastern border with Espírito Santo, is home to waterfalls, spectacular vistas and Brazil's third-highest peak. Both parks offer excellent hiking opportunities. A third park not covered in this chapter but well worth exploring is Parque Nacional da Serra da Canastra in western Minas. Home to the headwaters of the mighty Rio São Francisco,

with magnificent waterfalls and abundant wildlife, it's one of the best examples of cerrado (savanna) habitat anywhere in Brazil.

Getting There & Around

Capital city Belo Horizonte is the arrival point for most travelers. Pampulha and Confins airports handle domestic and international flights, while the large downtown bus station serves as a hub for ground transport (see p240). Direct buses from Rio and São Paulo also serve some of the historic towns.

BELO HORIZONTE

☎ 0xx31 / pop 2.5 million / elevation 858m

Known to the locals as Bay-Agah (that's Portuguese for BH), Belo Horizonte was named for its beautiful view of nearby mountains. Urban sprawl makes it harder to appreciate the natural setting nowadays, but Brazil's third-largest city still has considerable charms. Walk down the buzzing cosmopolitan streets of the Savassi neighborhood on a Saturday evening, eat at one of the fine restaurants in Lourdes, stroll through the densely packed stalls at Mercado Central, attend a weekend street fair or a concert at the Palácio das Artes, or visit the new Inhotim art museum west of the city, and you'll see that the city has countless dimensions. Add to all this the friendly, welcoming nature of Belo's people and you've got a winning combination. Stick around a few days – you might grow fond of the place.

HISTORY

In the late 19th century, as the Brazilian Republic was coming into its own, Mineiros began planning a new capital to replace hard-to-reach Ouro Prêto, which had fallen out of favor as a symbol of colonialism. Belo Horizonte sprang up as an art-nouveau city, influenced by the spirit of Ordem e Progresso (Order and Progress), the new slogan on the Brazilian flag.

In the 1940s, Belo expanded northward. Then-mayor Juscelino Kubitschek commissioned young architectural-school graduate Oscar Niemeyer to design the brand-new Pampulha district. These two men are largely responsible for the city's wide avenues, large lakes, parks and jutting skylines.

More than 100 years after its founding, Belo still has the young, contagious energy of a

CENTRAL BELO HORIZONTE

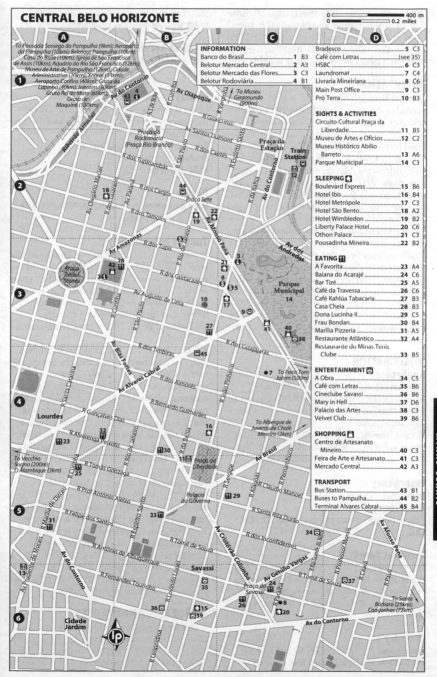

INFORMATION
Banco do Brasil...................................**1** B3
Belotur Mercado Central...................**2** A3
Belotur Mercado das Flores...........**3** C3
Belotur Rodoviária..............................**4** B1
Bradesco...**5** C3
Café com Letras...........................(see 35)
HSBC..**6** C3
Laundromat..**7** C4
Livraria Mineiriana..............................**8** C6
Main Post Office...................................**9** C3
Pró Terra..**10** B3

SIGHTS & ACTIVITIES
Circuito Cultural Praça da
  Liberdade..**11** B5
Museu de Artes e Ofícios...............**12** C2
Museu Histórico Abílio
  Barreto...**13** A6
Parque Municipal..............................**14** C3

SLEEPING
Boulevard Express.............................**15** B6
Hotel Ibis..**16** B4
Hotel Metrópole.................................**17** C3
Hotel São Bento..................................**18** A2
Hotel Wimbledon...............................**19** B2
Liberty Palace Hotel..........................**20** C6
Othon Palace.......................................**21** C3
Pousadinha Mineira...........................**22** B2

EATING
A Favorita...**23** A4
Baiana do Acarajé..............................**24** C6
Bar Tizé...**25** A5
Café da Travessa.................................**26** C6
Café Kahlúa Tabacaria.......................**27** B3
Casa Cheia..**28** B3
Dona Lucinha II...................................**29** C5
Frau Bondan..**30** B4
Marilia Pizzeria...................................**31** A5
Restaurante Atlântico........................**32** A4
Restaurante do Minas Tenis
  Clube...**33** B5

ENTERTAINMENT
A Obra...**34** C5
Café com Letras..................................**35** B6
Cineclube Savassi...............................**36** B6
Mary in Hell...**37** D6
Palácio das Artes.................................**38** C3
Velvet Club...**39** B6

SHOPPING
Centro de Artesanato
  Mineiro...**40** C3
Feira de Arte e Artesanato...............**41** C3
Mercado Central.................................**42** A3

TRANSPORT
Bus Station...**43** B1
Buses to Pampulha.............................**44** B2
Terminal Alvares Cabral.....................**45** B4

MINAS GERAIS

community reinventing itself, with a whole slew of new buildings and museums inaugurated in 2010 alone (see the boxed text, p237). Belo is also riding high as it anticipates its status as a host city for the 2014 World Cup.

ORIENTATION

Central Belo Horizonte has a grid of large avenidas (avenues) and another smaller grid superimposed at a 45-degree angle. The boundaries of the original planned city are defined by the ring road called Av do Contorno. It's a hilly town, so trips are sometimes less straightforward than they appear on the map. The main drag is Av Afonso Pena, which runs diagonally from northwest to southeast, starting at the bus station at the northern end of downtown and running past leafy green Parque Municipal. From northwest to southeast, there are three pivotal praças (squares): bustling Praça Sete, just southeast of the bus station; serene Praça da Liberdade, heart of the government-turned-museum district called Funcionarios; and trendy Praça da Savassi, the center of Belo nightlife and café society.

Outside of downtown, Pampulha is the neighborhood with most cultural attractions and tourist amenities.

INFORMATION

Bookstores

Café com Letras (☎ 3225 9973; Rua Antônio de Albuquerque 781; ❦ noon-midnight Mon-Thu, to 1am Fri & Sat, 6-11pm Sun) Bookstore-café deeply rooted in Belo's music and arts scene.

Livraria Mineiriana (☎ 3223 8092; www.mineiriana .com.br, in Portuguese; Rua Paraíba 1419; ❦ 9am-10pm Mon-Fri, to 6pm Sat) Excellent bookstore in Savassi.

Emergency

Ambulance (☎ 192)
Fire department (☎ 193)
Police (☎ 190) For nonurgent matters, call ☎ 3330 5200.

Internet Access

Internet places abound throughout the city.
Pró Terra (☎ 3785 3775; Shop 12, Av Augusto de Lima 134; per hr R$2; ❦ 8am-11pm Mon-Fri, 9am-10pm Sat, 2-8pm Sun) Centrally located, with fast connections and Skype.

Laundry

Laundromat (☎ 3224 5383; Rua dos Timbiras 1264; ❦ 8am-7pm Mon-Fri, to 2pm Sat) Wash it yourself

(R$9.25 per machine), or let them do it (R$26.75 per basket, wash and dry). Quick turnaround.

Medical Services

For nonurgent health matters call ☎ 3222 3322.

Money

Several banks with ATMs are clustered downtown between Praça Sete and Parque Municipal.
Banco do Brasil (Rua Rio de Janeiro 750)
Bradesco (Rua da Bahia 951)
HSBC (Rua da Bahia 932)

Post

Main post office (Av Afonso Pena 1270) There's another branch at the bus station.

Tourist Information

If you read a little Portuguese, check out the weekly listings in the Espetáculo section of the *Estado de Minas* newspaper. Another great source of local information is the Roteiro Cultural supplement of the *Jornal Pampulha* newspaper, published every Saturday.
Alô Turismo (☎ 156; ❦ 8am-10pm) Belotur's tourist-inquiry hotline.
Belotur (☎ 3277 9731; belotur@pbh.gov.br) Belo Horizonte's municipal tourist bureau is among the best in Brazil. Its several offices distribute the free *Guia Turístico*, an exceptionally helpful trilingual (English, Spanish, Portuguese) guide cataloging the city's restaurants, museums, cultural events and other tourist attractions, with instructions on how to get there using local buses. The *Guia Turístico* also includes a city map, airline and bus company information, and everything else you wanted to know about Belo but didn't know how to ask. Locations around the city include Belotur Confins airport (☎ 3689 2557; ❦ 8am-6pm) at the main airport exit, outside baggage claim; Belotur Mercado Central (☎ 3274 9434; ❦ 9am-4pm Mon-Sat, 8am-1pm Sun) on the ground floor of Belo's famous indoor market; Belotur Mercado das Flores (☎ 3277 7666; Av Afonso Pena 1055; ❦ 8:30am-6:30pm Mon-Fri, 8am-3pm Sat & Sun) at the flower market on the edge of Parque Municipal; Belotur Pampulha (☎ 3277 9987; Av Otacílio Negrão de Lima 855; ❦ 8am-5pm Tue-Sun) in the northern suburb of Pampulha; and Belotur Rodoviária (☎ 3277 6907; Praça Rio Branco; ❦ 8am-6pm) inside the bus station.

DANGERS & ANNOYANCES

There are more-dangerous places in the world than Belo Horizonte, but as in any big city, you should remain alert for petty theft, especially near the bus station.

MINAS GERAIS

SIGHTS

One of Belo's most appealing spots is **Parque Municipal**, an enormous sea of tropical greenery with artificial lakes and winding pathways, just 10 minutes southeast of the bus station, along Av Afonso Pena. It's especially fun on Sunday, when everyone's out strolling and socializing.

The free **Museu Histórico Abílio Barreto** (☎ 3277 8861; Av Prudente de Morais 202, Cidade Jardim; ☯ 10am-5pm Tue-Sun, to 9pm Thu), southwest of Savassi, features a renovated colonial farmhouse, the solitary remnant of Curral del Rey, the rural village destroyed in the 1890s to make room for Belo. There are some fascinating historical photos and other bric-a-brac.

The new **Museu de Artes e Ofícios** (☎ 3248 8600; www.mao.com.br; Praça Rui Barbosa; admission R$4, free Sat; ☯ noon-7pm Tue-Fri, 11am-5pm Sat & Sun), in Belo's historic train station, houses a wide-ranging collection of objects used in the daily lives of Mineiros past and present. There are interpretive cards in English adjacent to each exhibit.

The **Museu Giramundo** (☎ 3446 0686; www.giramundo.org; Rua Varginha 245, Floresta; admission R$6, under 12yr, over 60yr & student R$3; ☯ 9am-noon & 1-5pm Tue-Fri) has a fanciful display of 400 marionettes, from performances by the internationally acclaimed, Belo-based Teatro Giramundo.

Fans of modernist architect Oscar Niemeyer won't want to miss his creations dotted around a huge artificial lake in the Pampulha district, north of downtown. The **Igreja de São Francisco de Assis** (☎ 3427 1644; Av Otacílio Negrão de Lima s/n; admission R$2; ☯ 9am-5pm Tue-Sat, noon-5pm Sun) is an architectural delight and the paintings by Portinari are beautiful.

The **Museu de Arte de Pampulha** (☎ 3277 7946; Av Otacílio Negrão de Lima 16585; admission free; ☯ 9am-7pm Tue-Sun), with its cute garden designed by landscape architect Roberto Burle Marx, is also worth a look. It was designed as a casino and shows the obvious modernist influence of Le Corbusier. The **Casa do Baile** (☎ 3277 7443; Av Otacílio Negrão de Lima 751; admission free; ☯ 9am-7pm Tue-Sun), a former dance hall, now holds all types of temporary art exhibits. Its lovely on-site café is a great place to take a break.

Also in Pampulha is the brand-new **Aquário do Rio São Francisco** (☎ 3277 7100; Av Otacílio Negrão de Lima 8000; admission incl entrance to adjacent zoo R$9; ☯ 9am-4pm Tue-Sun), Brazil's largest freshwater aquarium. Opened in March 2010, it showcases the endemic fishes of Brazil's 2830km-long São Francisco river.

SLEEPING

Budget

Pousadinha Mineira (☎ 3423 4105; www.pousadinhamineira.com.br; Rua Espírito Santo 604; dm R$20) Large and institutional, but very conveniently located between the bus station and Parque Municipal, this hostel sleeps up to 200 people in 20-bed dorms. Separate fees are charged for towels, lockers and other extras.

Albergue de Juventude Chalé Mineiro (☎ 3467 1576; www.chalemineirohostel.com.br; Rua Santa Luzia 288; dm HI member/nonmember R$20/25, s with/without bathroom

---

OUT WITH THE GOVERNMENT, IN WITH THE MUSEUMS

Belo Horizonte is undergoing a major facelift as this book goes to print. It's the culmination of an ambitious plan to move Belo's government buildings away from their age-old midtown home, Praça da Liberdade, and into the Cidade Administrativa, a purpose-built, self-contained 'city' 20km north of downtown on the MG-010 highway leading to Confins airport. The futuristic complex – which officially opened for business on March 4, 2010 – includes five buildings that will provide office space for 16,000 people, all designed by centenarian architect Oscar Niemeyer. Most eye-catching is the Palácio Tiradentes, a gargantuan swinging edifice whose midsection is suspended by over 1000 steel cables.

The government's relocation has left a lot of vacant real estate in downtown Belo. Happily, a wave of new museums is taking up the slack. Already open as of mid-2010 were the five-story science museum **Espaço TIM** (☎ 3272 9584; www.circuitoculturalliberdade.mg.gov.br, in Portuguese; ☯ 11am-4pm Tue-Sun; admission free), complete with planetarium on the top floor, and the **Museu das Minas e do Metal** (☎ 9103 7608; www.mmm.org.br, in Portuguese; ☯ noon-6pm Tue-Sun; admission free), which traces the economic, cultural and social history of mining in the region. By year's end a third museum – the **Museu do Homem Brasileiro** – should be joining them. When complete, the six-museum complex – known as the Circuito Cultural Praça da Liberdade – will also include an art museum, a cultural center, a café and more.

R$50/35, d R$70/60; ⊠ ⊜ ⊛) The dorm rooms at this hostel 2km east of downtown are decent, despite the sometimes grumpy staff. Take bus 9801 from near the bus station. The central pool is a nice touch in an otherwise no-frills experience. Breakfast is not included, and internet costs extra.

Midrange & Top End

Hotel São Bento (☎ 3271 3399; www.hotelsaobento.com .br; Rua dos Guaranis 438; s/d/tr with fan from R$66/94/126, s/d/tr/q with air-con R$92/121/156/190; ⊠ ⊜) This hotel a few blocks south of the bus station is one of downtown's best-value places, provided you can avoid the claustrophobic interior rooms with windows facing the hallway.

Hotel Metrópole (☎ 3273 1544; www.hotelmetro polebh.com.br; Rua da Bahia 1023; s/d/tr with fan R$116/ 155/213, s/d with air-con R$145/194; ⊠ ⊜) A quick walk from the Parque Municipal, this faded art-deco building has comfortable rooms and a friendly staff. To avoid the street noise out front, request a room with a veranda facing quieter Rua Goiás. All rooms come with minibar and free wi-fi; the newer ones also have remodeled bathrooms, flat-screen TVs and air-con.

Pousada Sossego da Pampulha (☎ 3439 3250; www.sossegodapampulha.com.br; Av José Dias Bicalho 1258, Pampulha; s/d/tr/q with fan R$130/160/205/250, with aircon R$150/184/225/275; ⊠ ⊜ ⊛) This pousada (guesthouse) is friendly, clean, well run and convenient for people arriving by plane at Pampulha airport. Amenities include a small pool and rooftop terrace with views of Belo Horizonte and the mountains. From the airport, a taxi costs R$10, or take bus 5401 (R$2.30).

Hotel Wimbledon (☎ 3222 6160; www.wimbledon .com.br; Av Afonso Pena 772; s/d R$138/158, ste R$244/292; ⊠ ⊠ ⊜ ⊛) While the general atmosphere at this downtown hotel is welcoming, with wood floors and carpeted hallways, most rooms are extremely cramped, as is the miniscule pool on the 12th floor. The best standard rooms, at the front of the hotel, have small terraces. Suites come with saunas and whirlpool tubs.

Boulevard Express (☎ 3269 7300; www.boulevard expresshotel.com; Rua Sergipe 1415, Savassi; s/d weekend R$145/165, midweek R$165/195; ⊠ ⊠ ⊜) In the heart of Savassi, the dining and drinking center of Belo's nightlife, this hotel stands out as a great midpriced choice. Some of the large, comfortable rooms are wheelchair-accessible and many are smoke-free.

Hotel Ibis (☎ 2111 1500; www.ibis.com.br; Rua João Pinheiro 602, Lourdes; r R$149; ⊠ ⊠ ⊜) Midway between downtown and Savassi, and just steps from leafy Praça da Liberdade, this convenient chain hotel has comfortable if predictable rooms in an ugly high-rise behind a pretty town house. The optional breakfast (R$11) and internet (per hour/day R$7/12) cost extra.

Othon Palace (☎ 2126 0000; www.othon.com .br; Av Afonso Pena 1050; standard/deluxe r R$190/260; ⊠ ⊠ ⊜ ⊛) The four-star Othon's many advantages include great downtown location, multilingual staff, spacious rooms and spectacular views from the upper floors across the Parque Municipal. Don't miss the rooftop bar and pool, one of the best in the city, and feel free to bargain – suites are sometimes offered for the price of a standard room.

Liberty Palace Hotel (☎ 2121 0900; www.liberty palace.com.br; Rua Paraíba 1465, Savassi; s/d from R$275/302; ⊠ ⊠ ⊜ ⊛) With its marble floors, columns and chandeliers, the Liberty's lobby hints at the luxury that awaits upstairs. Savassi's toniest hotel has spacious rooms and big comfy beds, plus a pool, sauna, gym and an excellent restaurant.

EATING

Belo Horizonte is teeming with good food for every budget. Downtown is the best place for cheap eats, while further south, the Savassi and Lourdes neighborhoods constitute the epicenter of the city's fine dining scene. The lion's share of the city's non-Mineiro restaurants specialize in Italian food, although you can also find a world of other flavors if you look around.

If you're visiting in mid-April to mid-May, check out the **Comida di Buteco festival** (www .comidadibuteco.com.br), in which dozens of neighborhood bars compete to see who makes the best bar food.

Budget

Dozens of *lanchonetes* (snack bars), *por-kilo* restaurants (self-serve restaurants that sell food by weight) and fast-food places are clustered between Praça Sete and Praça da Liberdade.

Café Kahlúa Tabacaria (☎ 3222 5887; Rua dos Guajajaras 416; sandwiches R$5-7, coffee drinks R$3-7; ⊗ 8am-9:30pm Mon-Fri, 10am-9pm Sat) There's more brewing here than java. A young, artistic clientele pops in all day for sandwiches, and a wide selection of teas and fine tobaccos is also available.

QUICK BITES

Frau Bondan (☎ 3337 8198; Rua Espírito Santo 1909, Lourdes; 9:30am-6pm Mon-Fri. to 1pm Sat) Drawing upon recipes from her Swiss-German grandmother, Paula Bondan runs this sweet little boutique stacked to the rafters with homemade cookies, gourmet chocolates and other delicacies.

Midrange

Casa Cheia (☎ 3274 9585; Shop 167, Mercado Central; daily specials R$13-16; 9:30am-6pm Mon-Sat, to 1pm Sun) The name means 'full house,' and if you visit on a weekend you'll understand why. People line up by the dozens for a table at this long-established Mercado Central eatery, where a bevy of women cooks up traditional favorites on a giant stove. *Pratos do dia* (daily specials) include a Saturday *feijoada* (a bean-and-meat stew served with rice; the Brazilian national dish) for only R$14.50 – not to be missed!

Café da Travessa (☎ 3223 8070; Rua Pernambuco 1286, Savassi; light meals R$15-22; 11am-11pm Mon-Fri, 9am-6pm Sat) For budget dining with a touch of Savassi flair, try this sidewalk café just off Praça da Savassi. It's a great place to enjoy local street life. Sandwiches, salads and pasta are all delicious, and there's frequent live music. On weekdays, there's also a per-kilo lunch buffet (per kg R$29.90).

Baiana do Acarajé (☎ 3264 5804; Rua Antônio de Albuquerque 473, Savassi; acarajé R$10-17, mains for 2 from R$50; 6pm-midnight Tue & Wed, noon-midnight Thu-Sun) A little slice of Bahia just off Praça da Savassi, this bright, lively and informal bar-restaurant specializes in tasty and affordable *acarajé* (shrimp-stuffed brown bean fritters) served alongside pricier and more substantial dishes like *moqueca* (Bahian seafood stew).

Restaurante do Minas Tenis Clube (☎ 3516 1310; Rua da Bahia 2244, Lourdes; all-you-can-eat buffet lunches weekday/weekend R$15/28; 11:30am-11pm Mon-Sat, to 7pm Sun) For atmosphere and price combined, it's hard to beat the midweek buffet at Belo's tennis club. Gorge to your heart's content in the spacious, parquet-floored dining room overlooking the pool and giant waterslides out back.

Bar Tizé (☎ 3337 4374; Rua Curitiba 2205, Lourdes; snacks R$4-15, mains R$19-38; 5pm-1am Mon-Fri, noon-1am Sat & Sun) Since 1967, this strategically located corner bar with tables spilling onto

a long island of sidewalk has been drawing crowds with ice-cold buckets of beer and award-winning *comida di buteco* (bar food; see p238).

Top End

Belo Horizonte has a plethora of standout restaurants, many in Savassi and Lourdes.

Marília Pizzeria (☎ 3275 2027; Rua Marília de Dirceu 189, Lourdes; pizzas from R$26; 6pm-midnight Sun-Wed, to 1am Thu-Sat) Marília's has a trendy, youthful vibe and is routinely voted among the best pizzerias in Belo Horizonte.

our pick **Xapuri** (☎ 3496 6198; Rua Mandacaru 260, Pampulha; mains per person R$35-50; noon-11pm Tue-Thu, to 2am Fri & Sat, to 6pm Sun) This local institution features fabulous Mineiro food served at picnic tables under a thatched roof, with hammocks close at hand for premeal children's entertainment or postmeal relaxation. The traditional wood stove blazes up front, while colorful Mineiro desserts are attractively displayed in two long cases.

A Favorita (☎ 3275 2352; Rua Santa Catarina 1235, Lourdes; meals R$39-79; noon-1am Mon-Sat, to midnight Sun) Everything's superb at this classy restaurant featuring grilled meat, decadent desserts and homemade pasta dishes such as tagliatelle with shrimp, asparagus and Sicilian lemon cream.

Restaurante Atlântico (☎ 3275 3384; Rua São Paulo 1984, Lourdes; mains from R$39; 6pm-midnight Mon-Thu, noon-1am Fri & Sat, noon-6pm Sun) Wonderful smoky aromas fill the air and the open-air corner location conjures up the lively sidewalk dining atmosphere of a Parisian brasserie. Opt for the simplicity of the impeccably grilled fish, or splurge on *paella valenciana*, feeding two for R$149.

Dona Lucinha II (☎ 3261 5930; Rua Sergipe 811, Funcionarios; all-you-can-eat buffets R$41; noon-3pm & 7pm-11pm Mon-Sat, noon-5pm Sun) The sumptuous buffet here features 50 traditional Mineiro dishes daily. It's fairly touristy, and prices have climbed thanks to the owner's publication of a best-selling cookbook, but the food is still outstanding.

Vecchio Sogno (☎ 3292 5251; Rua Martim de Carvalho 75; mains R$41-79; noon-12:30am Mon-Fri, 6pm-2am Sat, noon-6pm Sun) Repeatedly voted Belo's best Italian restaurant (not just its best Italian one), Vecchio Sogno is worth the splurge. Mains range from duck and wild rice risotto to shrimp flambéed in grappa. Reserve ahead.

MINAS GERAIS

ENTERTAINMENT

Belo is a cosmopolitan town with a vibrant arts scene and plenty of nightlife.

The **Palácio das Artes** (☎ 3236 7400; www.palacio dasartes.com.br; Av Afonso Pena 1537), an arts complex with multiple performance spaces and galleries near the southern end of Parque Municipal, is the hub of Belo's theater, dance, and music-concert scene. Current shows are listed in the Art and Culture section of Belotur's free guide (see p236).

The city's world-class dance and theater companies, **Grupo Corpo** (www.grupocorpo.com.br) and **Grupo Galpão** (www.grupogalpao.com.br), are often on tour but sometimes perform at home. Their websites show current tour details. Also inquire at any Belotur office (see p236).

If you can, catch a performance by **Grupo Uakti** (www.uakti.com.br, in Portuguese), a fascinating local music group that invents its own unconventional instruments and creates some truly remarkable sounds.

Late-night club- and pub-based nightlife gravitates toward Savassi.

our pick **Café com Letras** (☎ 3225 9973; www.cafe comletras.com.br; Rua Antônio de Albuquerque 781; ☾ noon-midnight Mon-Thu, to 1am Fri & Sat, 6-11pm Sun) With live music on weekends, DJs on weeknights, and a bohemian buzz between sets, this is a fun place to kick back, have a drink, browse the shelves and enjoy the free internet. The café also sponsors jazz performances at the annual Savassi Festival (www.savassifestival. com.br/jazzy) and publishes the monthly arts rag *Letras*.

O Alambique (☎ 3296 7188; http://alambique.com.br; Av Raja Gabaglia 3200, Estoril; ☾ 7pm-late Mon-Sat) The decor, the music, the drinks and the food all conspire to make this one of Belo's most entertaining nightspots. There's an old waterwheel, tables made from barrels with stone tops, 70 different *cachaça*-based drinks, and *forró* (popular music of the Northeast)and *sertanejo* music to keep things lively all night long.

Savassi is full of trendy dance clubs, including **A Obra** (www.aobra.com.br; Rua Rio Grande do Norte 1168), which hosts live rock, blues and indie shows, as well as **Velvet Club** (www.velvetclub.com .br, in Portuguese; Rua Sergipe 1493) and **Mary in Hell** (www.maryinhell.com.br, in Portuguese; Rua Tomé de Souza 470), where DJs spin electronica, rock and pop from midnight till dawn.

Cineclube Savassi (☎ 3227 6648; www.usinadecinema .com.br, in Portuguese; Rua Levindo Lopes 358, Savassi; admis-

sion R$14) is a great little art-house cinema that shows an eclectic, international mix of movies on three screens nightly.

SHOPPING

The most vibrant shopping streets are clustered around Praça Savassi. Locals also favor the many high-rise shopping centers downtown and the wonderful street markets.

Feira de Arte e Artesanato (Av Afonso Pena; ☾ 6am-noon Sun, often to 3pm) One of Belo's major community events, this Sunday street fair attracts massive crowds searching for clothing, jewelry, street food and more. Located between Rua da Bahia and Rua das Guajajaras, and bordered by the soothing greenery of the Parque Municipal, it's a fun place to wander and enjoy a slice of city life, even if you're not in a shopping mood.

Feira Tom Jobim (Av Bernardo Monteiro; ☾ 10am-6pm Sat) This thriving Saturday fair just east of Parque Municipal, between Av Brasil and Rua dos Otoni, features a mix of antique dealers and stalls hawking Brazilian and international street food.

Centro de Artesanato Mineiro (☎ 3272 9516; Av Afonso Pena 1537; ☾ 9am-7:45pm Mon-Fri, to 1:45pm Sat, 8am-12:45pm Sun) Inside the Palácio das Artes at the edge of Parque Municipal, this government store specializes in Mineiro crafts. The selection is good, although prices are not as cheap as in the colonial towns.

Mercado Central (cnr Rua Curitiba & Rua dos Goitacazes; ☾ 7am-6pm Mon-Sat, to 1pm Sun) You'll find everything from parrots to perfume at this indoor market, a true Belo Horizonte institution. Sample the delicious local produce, socialize with locals at one of the bars or just roam the aisles aimlessly.

GETTING THERE & AROUND
Air

Belo Horizonte has two airports. Most planes use the international **Aeroporto Confins** (airline code CNF; 40km north). The **Aeroporto da Pampulha** (airline code PLU; 10km north) is much more convenient but only has domestic flights.

Flights from the two airports serve most locations in Brazil. A full list of airline offices, with phone numbers, appears in the front of the free Belotur guide (see p236).

Bus

Belo's **bus station** (☎ 3271 8933/3000) is near the northern end of downtown on Praça da

Rodoviária. The free Belotur guide lists bus-company phone numbers in the front pages.

Destinations include Brasília (União and Itapemirim bus lines, *convencional*/sleeper bus R$92/99, 11 to 12 hours, five daily); Diamantina (Pássaro Verde, R$63, five hours, six daily from 6:30am to midnight); Foz do Iguaçu (Gontijo and Pluma, R$240, 25 hours, daily at 8am); Ouro Prêto (Pássaro Verde, R$22, two hours, hourly from 6am to 8pm); Rio de Janeiro (Cometa and Útil, *convencional*/*executivo* (express) R$66/94, 6½ hours, 11 daily from 8am to midnight); Salvador (Gontijo and São Geraldo, R$193, 23 hours, daily at 6pm or 7pm); São João del Rei (Sandra, R$39, 3½ hours, six daily from 6am to 7pm); São Paulo (Cometa, *convencional*/ *executivo* R$80/92, eight hours, 12 daily from 9am to 11:45pm); and Vitória (São Geraldo, União and Itapemirim, R$77, nine hours, 11 daily from 8:15am to 10:45pm).

LOCAL BUSES

Belo Horizonte's local buses are color-coded. Blue buses (R$2.30) go up and down main avenues in the city center, green express buses (R$2.30) only stop at select points, red-and-beige buses (R$2.95 and up, depending on distance) connect outlying suburbs to downtown, and yellow buses (R$1.65) have circular routes through the city.

AIRPORT BUSES

Expresso Unir (☎ 3224 1002; www.expressounir.com .br) runs frequent, comfortable Conexão Aeroporto buses between downtown and Belo's two airports (Pampulha and Confins). The conventional bus (R$7.70 to either airport) leaves Belo's bus station every 15 to 45 minutes throughout the day. First/last departures from the bus station are at 4:15am/11:30pm, from Confins 5:15am/1:15am.

Unir also runs an *executivo* bus (R$17.65) to the airport from the **Terminal Alvares Cabral** (Av Alvares Cabral 387), just southwest of Parque Municipal, every 25 to 40 minutes. First/ last departures from downtown are at 3:45am/10:10pm, from Confins 5am/1:30am. Travel time is approximately 30 minutes to Pampulha airport, 50 minutes to Confins.

Train

Companhia Vale do Rio Doce (☎ 0800 285 7000; www .vale.com/vale_scripts/trem_passageiros/efvm/trem.asp, in Portuguese) operates a daily train to Vitória in Espírito Santo state (*econômica*/*executive* class R$49/75, 13 hours), departing at 7:30am from the train station at Praça da Estação, just north of Parque Municipal. It returns at 7am.

AROUND BELO HORIZONTE
Centro de Arte Contemporânea Inhotim

our pick Centro de Arte Contemporânea Inhotim (☎ 3227 0001; www.inhotim.org.br; adult R$16, student & over 60yr R$8; 🕑 9:30am-4:30pm Wed-Fri, to 5:30pm Sat & Sun), greater Belo's new tourist attraction, is an impressive, sprawling complex of gardens dotted with 16 modern art galleries and numerous outdoor sculptures, 50km west of the city, near the town of Brumadinho. Much of the international artwork on display is monumental in size. The gardens, which were opened to the public in October 2006 and are expanding constantly, boast 1600 different species of plants (including 200 types of palm alone), peacocks and lakes with swans. You can wander at will, or attend daily scheduled programs led by guides trained in visual arts and natural science. The on-site restaurant and café are both excellent.

On Saturdays and Sundays Saritur runs direct buses (R$13, 90 minutes) from Belo Horizonte to Inhotim at 9am, returning at 4pm. Alternatively, take one of Saritur's three daily buses from Belo Horizonte to Brumadinho (R$14, 80 minutes), where you can catch a taxi to the museum (R$12 to R$15).

Caves

Three fascinating caves are within two hours of downtown Belo and make great day jaunts.

Gruta de Maquiné (☎ 3715 1310; gmaquine@uai .com.br; adult/child R$12/6; 🕑 8am-5pm) is the largest, most famous and crowded of the caves. Maquiné's seven huge chambers are well lit for guided tours. **Setelagoano** (☎ 3073 7575) runs buses there (R$29, 2¼ hours, leaving Belo Horizonte daily at 8:30am, plus 12:15pm on Sundays, returning at 4:20pm daily, plus 2:45pm on Sundays).

Gruta Rei do Mato (☎ 3773 0888; adult/child R$10/5; 🕑 8am-5pm) is the most interesting of the three caves. Near Sete Lagoas, north of Belo, it has prehistoric paintings and petroglyphs. From Belo Horizonte, take any Sete Lagoas–bound bus running along Hwy BR-040 (R$15, 80

MINAS GERAIS

minutes, hourly from 7am to 11pm) and ask the driver to drop you at the cave entrance.

The highlight at **Gruta da Lapinha** (☎ 3689 8422; adult/child R$10/5; ☽ 8:30am-4:30pm) is the Véu de Noiva, a crystal formation in the shape of a bride's veil. At the time of research the cave was closed, with plans to reopen (possibly with modified hours and prices) in December 2010. Phone for the latest info. **Atual** (☎ 3271 8793) runs frequent buses to Lagoa Santa (R$5.05, 70 minutes); from there, bus 306 continues to the cave (R$3, 35 minutes, every 40 minutes from 7am).

COLONIAL TOWNS

The *cidades históricas* (historic colonial towns) are Minas's standout attraction. Collectively, they constitute one of Brazil's most alluring and accessible tourist circuits. All the towns covered here bear marks of their common Portuguese ancestry – cobblestone streets, baroque bell towers, winding alleys decked in flowers – but each has unique charms. The colonial remnants of Congonhas and Sabará have been almost entirely eclipsed by modern development, yet each still contains artistic masterpieces that warrant a day trip. Mariana's colonial center has fared better, preserved as perfectly as a pearl inside the surrounding 21st-century oyster. São João del Rei is a unique hybrid, peppered with enough 18th-century churches and bridges to hold their own and provide an interesting contrast to the encroaching high-rises and urban bustle. Tiradentes, Serro and Diamantina – thanks to their relative isolation, gorgeous settings and unadulterated architectural integrity – are perfect places to experience rural Minas' 'lost in time' quality. Ouro Prêto stands alone as the largest and best-preserved colonial center in Minas, having benefited from over 70 years of conservation efforts, dating back to 1933, when the Brazilian government declared it a national monument.

OURO PRÊTO

☎ 0xx31 / pop 69,000 / elevation 1179m

Of all the exquisite colonial towns scattered around Minas Gerais, Ouro Prêto is the jewel in the crown. Significant historically as a center of gold mining and government, and as the stage for Brazil's first independence movement, the city remains vital in modern times as a center for education and the arts, and as one of Brazil's three most visited tourist destinations.

Built at the feet of the Serra do Espinhaço, Ouro Prêto's colonial center is larger and has steeper topography than any other historical town in Minas. The narrow, crooked streets of the upper and lower towns tangle together and in places are too rough and precipitous for vehicles. Navigating the vertiginous cobblestone slopes on foot can be exhausting, but the views of 23 churches spread out across the hilly panorama are spectacular. The city is a showcase of outstanding Mineiro art and architecture, including some of Aleijadinho's finest works (see p252 for more information on Aleijadinho).

History

Legend has it that a mulatto (a person of mixed white and black ancestry) servant in an early *bandeirante* (a group of roaming adventurers who spent the 17th and 18th centuries exploring Brazil's interior, searching for gold and Indians to enslave) expedition pocketed a few grains of an odd black metal he found while drinking from a small river near the current site of Ouro Prêto (Portuguese for 'black gold'). It turned out to be gold, and within a few years, the local deposits were discovered to be the largest in the New World.

Gold fever spread fast. In 1711, Vila Rica de Ouro Prêto, the predecessor of the present town, was founded, and in 1721 it became the capital of Minas Gerais. The finest goods from India and England were made available to the simple mining town. The gold bought the services of baroque artisans, who turned the city into an architectural gem. At the height of the gold boom in the mid-18th century, there were 110,000 people (mainly slaves) in Ouro Prêto, compared with 50,000 in New York and about 20,000 in Rio de Janeiro.

In theory, all gold was brought to *casas de intendências* (weighing stations) to be turned into bars, and a *quinto do ouro* (royal fifth) was set aside for the Portuguese crown. Tax shirkers were cast into dungeons or exiled to Africa.

The greed of the Portuguese led to sedition by the inhabitants of Vila Rica. As the boom tapered off, the miners found it increasingly difficult to pay ever-larger gold taxes. In 1789, poets Claudio da Costa, Tomás Antônio Gonzaga, Joaquim José da Silva Xavier (nicknamed Tiradentes, meaning 'Tooth Puller,'

OURO PRÊTO

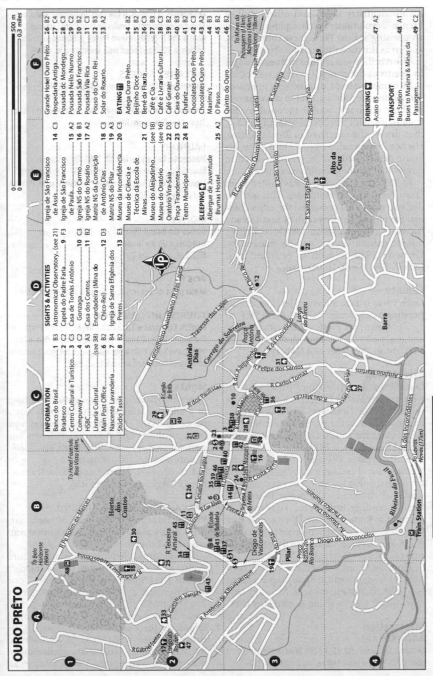

500 m
0.3 miles

INFORMATION
Banco do Brasil 1 B3
Bradesco 2 C3
Centro Cultural e Turístico 3 C2
Compuway 4 C2
HSBC 5 A3
Livraria Cultural .... (see 38)
Main Post Office 6 B2
Nascente Lavanderia 7 B4
Studio Tassis 8 B2

SIGHTS & ACTIVITIES
Astronomical Observatory ...(see 21)
Capela do Padre Faria 9 F3
Casa de Tomás Antônio
  Gonzaga 10 C3
Casa dos Contos 11 B2
Encardadeira (Mina do
  Chico-Rei) 12 B2
Igreja de Santa Efigênia dos
  Pretos 13 E3
Igreja de São Francisco
  de Assis 14 C3
Igreja de São Francisco
  de Paula 15 A2
Igreja NS do Carmo 16 B3
Igreja NS do Rosário 17 A2
Matriz NS da Conceição
  de Antônio Dias 18 C3
Matriz NS do Pilar 19 A3
Museu da Inconfidência 20 C3
Museu de Ciência e
  Técnica da Escola de
  Minas 21 C2
Museu do Aleijadinho ......(see 18)
Museu do Oratório 22 D3
Oratório Vira-Saia 23 C2
Praça Tiradentes 24 B3
Teatro Municipal 25 A2

SLEEPING ᐃ
Albergue de Juventude
  Brumas Hostel 26 B2
Grande Hotel Ouro Prêto 27 C4
Hospedaria Antiga 28 C3
Pousada dc Mondego 29 C2
Pousada Nello Nunno 30 B2
Pousada São Francisco 31 C3
Pousada Vila Rica 32 B3
Pouso do Chico Rei 33 A2

EATING ᐂ
Adega Ouro Prêto 34 B2
Beijinho Doce 35 B2
Bené da Flauta 36 C3
Café e Cia 37 B3
Café e Livraria Cultural 38 C3
Café Gerae 39 B2
Casa do Ouvidor 40 B3
Chafariz 41 C2
Chocolates Ouro Prêto 42 C3
Chocolates Ouro Prêto 43 C2
Maximu's 44 B3
O Passo 45 B2
Quinto do Ouro 46 B2

DRINKING ᐁ
Acaso 85 .... 47 A2

TRANSPORT
Bus Station 48 A1
Buses to Mariana & Minas da
  Passagem 49 C2

MINAS GERAIS

for his dentistry skills) and others, full of French-Revolutionary philosophies, hatched an uprising against Portuguese colonization known as the Inconfidência Mineira.

The rebellion was crushed in its early stages by agents of the crown. Gonzaga was exiled to Mozambique and Costa did time in prison. Tiradentes, the only man not to deny his role in the conspiracy, was abandoned by his friends, jailed for three years without defense, then drawn and quartered in Rio de Janeiro. His head was paraded around Ouro Prêto, his house demolished and its grounds salted to ensure that nothing would grow there.

In 1897 the state capital was shifted from Ouro Prêto to Belo Horizonte. This was the decisive move that preserved the city's colonial flavor. The ensuing century saw a steady increase in appreciation for Ouro Prêto's unique cultural legacy, notably marked by Unesco's 1980 decision to enshrine it as Brazil's first World Heritage site.

Climate

Ouro Prêto is 1km above sea level, and temperatures vary from 2°C to 28°C (36°F to 82°F). Winters are pretty cold. It can be rainy and foggy all year round, with showers most frequent in December and January.

Orientation

Ouro Prêto is divided into parishes, each with its own Matriz (mother church). If you stand in Praça Tiradentes facing the Museu da Inconfidência, the parish of Pilar is to the right (west), the parishes of Antônio Dias and Santa Efigênia to the left (east).

Most streets in town have two names: the official one and another used by locals because the official one is too long. For example, Rua Conde de Bobadela, the major thoroughfare descending from Praça Tiradentes, is commonly known as Rua Direita, and Rua Conselheiro Quintiliano, the road to Mariana, is also Rua das Lajes. Adding to the confusion, street names are rarely posted.

The hillside just below the bus station can feel a bit seedy at night, despite the presence of two police stations in the area. As in any city, remain alert when walking around after dark.

Information

BOOKSTORES

Livraria Cultural (☎ 3551 3239; Rua Cláudio Manoel 15) Below the tourist office; has a couple of local guidebooks in English. If you read Portuguese, check out *Tesouros, Fantasmas e Lendas de Ouro Prêto* (Treasures, Ghosts and Legends of Ouro Prêto), published in its 2nd edition in 2010 and filled with fascinating local lore.

INTERNET ACCESS

Compuway (Praça Tiradentes s/n; per hr R$4; ⏰ 8am-9pm Mon-Fri, to 6pm Sat)
Stúdio Tassis (Rua São José 119A; per hr R$3; ⏰ 10am-10pm Mon-Sat, noon-10pm Sun)

LAUNDRY

Nascente Lavanderia (☎ 3551 5070; Rua dos Inconfidêntes 5; wash & dry per kilo R$7; ⏰ 8am-5pm Mon-Fri, to noon Sat) Down near the train station. Pick-up and delivery R$4.50 extra.

MONEY

Banco do Brasil (Rua São José 189)
Bradesco (Praça Tiradentes)
HSBC (Rua São José 201)

POST

Main post office (cnr Rua Direita & Rua Coronel Alves)

TOURIST INFORMATION

Centro Cultural e Turístico (☎ 3559 3269; Praça Tiradentes 4; ⏰ 8:15am-7pm) Offers information in English, Spanish and French, including a leaflet listing museum and church hours and a rough town map.

Sights

There are virtually no 20th-century buildings to defile this stunning colonial town. For a panoramic view of the churches and rooftops, head northeast out of Praça Tiradentes and walk for five minutes along Rua Conselheiro Quintiliano towards Mariana.

Except where otherwise noted, local attractions charge admission of R$6.

PRAÇA TIRADENTES & AROUND

Praça Tiradentes is the heart of town, surrounded by some of Ouro Prêto's finest museums and churches.

If you only visit one church in Ouro Prêto, make sure it's **Igreja de São Francisco de Assis** (⏰ 8:30-11:50am & 1:30-5pm Tue-Sun), one block downhill from Praça Tiradentes. After *The Prophets* in Congonhas (see p252), Aleijadinho's masterpiece, this is the most important piece of Brazilian colonial art. Its entire exterior was carved by Aleijadinho himself, from the soapstone medallion to the cannon waterspouts to the Franciscan two-bar cross. The interior was painted by Aleijadinho's long-term partner, Manuel da Costa Ataíde.

The **Museu da Inconfidência** (🕙 noon-5:30pm Tue-Sun), formerly the old municipal headquarters and jail, is an attractive building built between 1784 and 1854, on the south side of Praça Tiradentes. The museum contains the tomb of Tiradentes, documents of the Inconfidência Mineira, torture instruments and important works by Ataíde and Aleijadinho.

A stone's throw away, the **Igreja NS do Carmo** (🕙 8:30-10:30am & 1-4:45pm Tue-Sun) was a group effort by the area's most important artists. Built between 1766 and 1772, it features a facade by Aleijadinho.

The **Museu do Oratório** (admission R$2; 🕙 9:30am-5:30pm) is in a triple-level colonial house adjacent to the Igreja NS do Carmo. Its fabulous collection of oratories includes several in the uniquely beautiful Minas style, harmoniously integrating soapstone and painted wood.

The **Museu de Ciência e Técnica da Escola de Minas** (admission R$5; 🕙 noon-5pm Tue-Sun), in the old governor's palace north of Praça Tiradentes, features dazzling gemstones from around the world. There's also an **astronomical observatory** (🕙 8-10pm Sat & Sun).

Two blocks downhill is the **Casa dos Contos** (🕙 10am-6pm Tue-Sat, to 4pm Sun, 2-6pm Mon), the 18th-century treasury building that doubled as a prison for members of the Inconfidência. The renovated mansion now houses displays on the history of gold – and money in general – in Brazil.

PILAR PARISH
On the southwest side of town, the **Matriz NS do Pilar** (🕙 9-10:45am & noon-4:45pm Tue-Sun) is the second-most-opulent church in Brazil (after Salvador's São Francisco). It has 434kg of gold

and silver and is one of Brazil's finest showcases of artwork. Note the wild-bird chandelier holders, the scrolled church doors and the hair on Jesus (the real stuff, donated by a penitent worshipper).

ANTÔNIO DIAS PARISH
Matriz NS da Conceição de Antônio Dias (🕙 8:30-11:45am & 1:30-5pm Tue-Sat, noon-5pm Sun) was designed by Aleijadinho's father, Manuel Francisco Lisboa, and built between 1727 and 1770. Note the eagle with downturned head and the Virgin Mary surrounded by cherubs: both stand atop images of the moon, symbolizing the Christians' domination of the Moors. Aleijadinho is buried by the altar of Boa Morte.

The **Museu do Aleijadinho** in the adjoining sacristy displays beautiful works by Aleijadinho and other 18th-century masters.

Nearby is the abandoned mine, Encardadeira or **Mina do Chico-Rei** (Rua Dom Silvério 108; admission R$10; 🕙 8am-5pm). There's little to see as you stoop through the low passageways, but it's the perfect place to meditate on the fascinating story of Chico-Rei (see below).

SANTA EFIGÊNIA PARISH
The **Igreja de Santa Efigênia dos Pretos** (🕙 8:30am-4:30pm Tue-Sun), built between 1742 and 1749 by and for the black slave community, sits atop a steep hill east of town. Santa Efigênia, patron saint of the church, was the queen of Nubia, and the featured saints – Santo Antônio do Nolo and São Benedito – are black. The slaves prayed to these images that they wouldn't be crushed in the mines. Despite its relative lack of gold ornamentation, the church is very rich in artwork. The altar is by Aleijadinho's master, Francisco Javier do Briton, and the exterior image of NS do Rosário is by Aleijadinho

---

CHICO-REI
Brazil's first abolitionist was Chico-Rei, an African tribal king. In the early 1700s, amid the frenzy of the gold rush, an entire tribe, king and all, was captured in Africa, sent to Brazil and sold to a mine owner in Ouro Prêto.

The king, Chico-Rei, worked as the foreman of the slave miners. Working Sundays and holidays, he finally bought his freedom from the slave master, then freed his son Osmar. Together, father and son liberated the entire tribe.

This collective then bought the fabulously wealthy Encardadeira gold mine, and Chico-Rei assumed his royal functions once again, holding court in Vila Rica and celebrating African holidays in traditional costume. News of this reached the Portuguese king, who immediately prohibited slaves from purchasing their freedom. Chico-Rei is now a folk hero among Brazilian blacks.

himself. The church was financed by gold extracted from Chico-Rei's mine. Slaves contributed to the church coffers by washing their gold-flaked hair in baptismal fonts, or smuggling gold powder under fingernails and inside tooth cavities.

Ouro Prêto's oldest chapel, built between 1701 and 1704, is the **Capela do Padre Faria** (☽ 8:30am-4:30pm Tue-Sun) at the far eastern edge of town. Named after one of the original *bandeirantes*, Padre Faria, this chapel is set behind a triple-branched papal cross (1756) representing the temporal, spiritual and material powers of the Pope. Because of poor documentation, the artists here are anonymous.

OTHER SIGHTS

Opened in 2008, the lovely **Horto dos Contos** is a verdant public park snaking downhill along a creek from the bus station to the Pilar church, passing en route under the bridge adjacent to Casa dos Contos. It's a tranquil spot with pretty views, great for a picnic lunch or simply a break from the crowds and the cobblestones.

In the early 18th century, local residents built numerous **oratories** (glass-encased niches containing images of saints) on street corners around town, to keep evil spirits at bay. Of the few that remain, there's one on Rua dos Paulistas, another on Rua Antônio Dias, and the most famous of all, the **Oratório Vira-Saia**, at the corner of Ladeira de Santa Efigênia and Rua Barão do Ouro Branco.

Launched in 2005, Ouro Prêto's *Museu Aberto/Cidade Viva* program invites you to keep your eyes open at every turn, treating the entire city as an open-air museum. Informative **historical plaques** have been placed on 150 houses around town to heighten visitors' curiosity and expand their knowledge of the city's treasures.

Now the seat of the municipal government, **Casa de Tomás Antônio Gonzaga** (Rua do Ouvidor 9) is where Gonzaga and the other Inconfidêntes conspired to put an end to Portuguese rule in Brazil.

Built in 1769, the recently renovated **Teatro Municipal** (Rua Brigadeiro Musqueira; admission R$2; ☽ noon-5:30pm) is the oldest theater in Minas Gerais, open for visits during the day and occasional live performances at night.

Tours

Official **guided city tours** (4-/8hr tour for up to 10 people R$87/170 in Portuguese, R$120/240 in English, French or

Spanish) are available at the tourist office (see p244). Note that prices quoted here are from the official table; you may be able to negotiate better rates with individual guides. The office can also help organize treks and horseback rides into the surrounding hills.

Festivals & Events

Semana Santa (Holy Week) processions in Ouro Prêto are quite a spectacle (see p247).

The Congado is to Minas what Candomblé is to Bahia and Quimbanda (also known as Macumba) is to Rio: the local expression of Afro-Christian syncretism. The major **Congado celebrations** are for NS do Rosário (October 23 to 25, at the Capela do Padre Faria), for the New Year and for May 13 (the anniversary of abolition).

You'd also be wise to reserve accommodations in July, when a month-long annual **winter festival** is held.

A decade old and still going strong, the **Festival Tudo é Jazz** (www.tudoejazz.com.br, in Portuguese) brings in jazz performers from Brazil and beyond for five days every September. Other noteworthy cultural events are the film festival **CineOP** (www.cineop.com.br) in mid-June, and the literary festival **Forum das Letras** (www.forumdasletras.ufop.br) in October/November.

Ouro Prêto reclaims the symbolic role of state capital once a year, on **Tiradentes Day**, April 21.

Sleeping

BUDGET

Pousada São Francisco (☎ 3551 3456; www.pousadasaofranciscodepaula.com.br; Rua Padre José Marcos Penna 202; dm/s/d/tr R$30/50/70/105; ☐ ☎) Set on a leafy hillside full of chirping birds, this hostel-like pousada has great views, a friendly multilingual staff and a guest kitchen. The two private upstairs rooms (R$20 to R$30 extra) are nicest. From the bus station, walk five minutes downhill toward Igreja de São Francisco de Paula and follow the signs. If you pass the church you've missed the turn. Late-night arrivals should phone from the bus station for an escort – it's close, but despite the newly installed lighting it can still be difficult to find.

Albergue de Juventude Brumas Hostel (☎ 3551 2944; www.brumashostel.com.br; Ladeira São Francisco de Paula 68; dm/s/d HI members R$30/50/80, nonmembers R$35/60/90; ☐ ☎) Just a few meters downhill from Pousada São Francisco, this HI-affiliated hostel also has clean four- and six-bed dorms,

MINAS GERAIS

SEMANA SANTA IN OURO PRÊTO

Semana Santa (Holy Week) is celebrated all over Brazil, but Ouro Prêto's festivities are especially dazzling. For four days the town becomes a giant stage, starting with Thursday night's ceremonial washing of feet and the deposition of Christ from a giant cross in front of Igreja de São Francisco on Good Friday.

The most wonderful event is saved for the wee hours preceding Easter Sunday. Around midnight Saturday, locals begin opening bags of colored sawdust on street corners all over town, unleashing an all-night public art project in which 3km of Ouro Prêto's cobblestone streets are covered with fanciful designs, a giant carpet marking the route for the following morning's Easter processions. Until the early 1960s, Ouro Prêto observed the old Portuguese tradition of decorating Easter-parade routes with flowers and leaves. More recently, colored scraps of leather, sand, coffee grounds and sawdust have become the media of choice for these *tapetes coloridos* (colored carpets).

Tourists are welcome to participate in laying out the designs, but be prepared for a late night. Things really don't get going until well after midnight. Music and general merrymaking erupt unpredictably all night long, and a few stragglers stick around till dawn to put finishing touches on Praça Tiradentes, the last spot cleared of vehicle traffic. If you prefer your beauty rest, go to bed early Saturday evening, then wake up at 5am Sunday to see the magic that's unfolded while you slept. It's like awakening to a Technicolor snowfall!

The designs – some religious, some profane – change every year and only last a few short hours. Within moments of the procession's passing, the public-works crew is out in force with brooms and shovels to clean the streets, until next year.

---

great views and a friendly, multilingual staff. Amenities include a guest kitchen and TV room with fireplace.

Pousada Vila Rica (☎ 3551 4729; pousada@antiga .com.br; Rua Felipe dos Santos 165; s/d R$45/90) The beds are a bit tatty, there's no internet and it's a trek uphill to the center of town, but if a simple room is all you need, the 250-year-old Vila Rica still retains some historical charm, with high ceilings, pretty wood floors and a facade covered in blue and white azulejos (Portuguese tiles).

MIDRANGE

Pousada Nello Nuno (☎ 3551 3375; www.pousadanello nuno.com.br; Rua Camilo de Brito 59; s/d/tr R$80/115/140) In a quiet location just northeast of Praça Tiradentes, this family-run pousada has clean and airy *apartamentos* with lots of artwork around a cute flagstoned courtyard. French and English spoken.

Hospedaria Antiga (☎ 3551 2203; www.antiga .com.br; Rua Xavier da Veiga 1; s/d/tr R$80/130/140; 🛜) Warped colonial floors, a small garden and a stunning medieval-style breakfast room are among the pluses at this friendly 18th-century guesthouse. Downstairs rooms are bigger and brighter.

ourpick Pouso do Chico Rei (☎ 3551 1274; www .pousodochicorei.com.br; Rua Brigadeiro Musqueira 90; s/d/tr without bathroom from R$88/140/190, s/d/tr/q with bathroom R$150/178/230/300; 🖥 🛜) Far and away the best midrange option in Ouro Prêto, Chico Rei occupies a beautifully preserved 18th-century mansion in the heart of town and has a long tradition of receiving famous guests (see the photos in the lobby). Each room is unique, and most have antique furniture and fabulous views. The two least-expensive rooms share a bathroom. Owners speak French and some English. Well worth booking ahead.

TOP END

Grande Hotel Ouro Prêto (☎ 3551 1488; www.grandehotel ouropreto.com.br, in Portuguese; Rua Senador Rocha Lagoa 164; s/d/tr R$187/214/268, s/d/tr ste from R$214/273/346; 🖥 🛜 🏊) Oscar Niemeyer's Grande Hotel is not as nice to look *at* as it is to look *from*. Very central, with a pool and bar area overlooking the town, it's the only modernist structure for miles and is something of an eyesore. The two-level suites offer views and are better value than the bland, rather cramped standard rooms.

Hotel Fazenda Boa Vista (☎ 3551 3423; www.hotel fazboavistaouropreto.com.br, in Portuguese; Bairro Campo Grande; d/q R$220/270; 🛜 🏊) If you've got your own wheels, consider this country mansion high in the hills, about 10 minutes outside of town. The grand main house is decorated with antiques and rustic implements of rural life, there's an outdoor pool with magnificent views of the surrounding mountains, the homemade food is excellent and the rural tranquility makes a nice break from Ouro Prêto's bustle.

Solar do Rosario (☎ 3551 5040; www.hotelsolardo rosario.com.br; Rua Getúlio Vargas 270; d R$320, ste from R$640; ❄ ▢ 🛜 ⛳) With an enviable position facing the Rosário church, this four-star is the finest new hotel to open in Ouro Prêto in recent years. The newly renovated mansion has ample rooms in the original 18th-century building, luxurious suites in the colonial-style modern annex and amenities that just won't quit spread over pretty terraced grounds out back, including indoor and outdoor pools, a sauna and more.

Pousada do Mondego (☎ 3551 2040; www.mondego .com.br, in Portuguese; Largo de Coimbra 38; r R$451, ste from R$594; ▢ 🛜) This classy inn – in an 18th-century colonial mansion with period furnishings, fine artwork and close-up views of Igreja de São Francisco de Assis – belongs to the exclusive international network Hotels de Charme. Downsides are the minuscule windows in the standard rooms tucked under the eaves, and late-night party noise from the adjacent *repúblicas* (student lodgings).

Eating
BUDGET
Many of Ouro Prêto's eateries are clustered along lively Rua Direita and Rua São José.

Café e Cia (☎ 3551 6515; Rua São José 185; per kg R$24.90; ❄ 11am-4pm) An old favorite with an airy back seating area overlooking the creek. The self-service lunch focuses on Mineiro fare.

Maximu's (☎ 9914 1209; Rua Direita 151; per kg R$27.90; ❄ 11am-4pm) One of the best *por-kilo* places, with an upstairs dining area.

Adega Ouro Prêto (☎ 3551 4171; Rua Teixeira Amaral 24; all-you-can-eat lunches R$15, pizzas R$17-26; ❄ 11:30am-3pm daily, plus 7pm-midnight Wed-Sat) The cavelike Adega is a great deal at lunchtime and also serves reasonable pizza four nights a week.

Quinto do Ouro (☎ 3552 2633; Rua Direita 76; per kg R$31.90; ❄ 11am-3pm Tue-Sun) Prices are higher here than at other *por-kilo* restaurants, but the quality and variety of the Mineiro food, including meat grilled to order, is superb.

Quick Eats
Ouro Prêto's endless labyrinth of hills, cobblestone streets, museums and churches can wear you out in a hurry. Recharging your batteries is easy, thanks to the city's many snack spots.

Chocolates Ouro Preto (☎ 3551 7330; Praça Tiradentes 114; snacks from R$4; ❄ 9am-7pm Sun-Thu, to 10pm Fri & Sat) Best known for its hot chocolate and other sinful indulgences, this newly opened branch of Ouro Prêto's hometown chocolate factory also serves sandwiches, soups and other savory snacks for under R$10. The original branch at Rua Getúlio Vargas 72 keeps the same hours and prices.

Café e Livraria Cultural (☎ 3551 3239; Rua Cláudio Manoel 15; snacks R$4.50-8.50; ❄ 9am-7pm) Tucked away just below the tourist office, this little café with exposed stone walls has simple food, fancy coffee drinks and a clean, relaxed feel. A good place to pore over the map and get your bearings.

Beijinho Doce (☎ 3551 2774; Rua Direita 134; cake slices from R$4; ❄ 11:30am-10pm) A half-block downhill from Praça Tiradentes, this coffee shop and bakery is perfect for a sweet or savory snack between museums.

MIDRANGE & TOP END
our pick **O Passo** (☎ 3552 5089; Rua São José 56; mains R$22-40; ❄ noon-midnight) In a lovely 18th-century building, this restaurant has intimate candlelit rooms with marbled walls; outside, the relaxed terrace overlooking the Casa de Contos is ideal for an after-dinner drink. Everything's superb – pizza, pasta, salads and the wine list! On Tuesday nights, don't miss the *rodizio de pizzas* (all-you-can-eat pizza, R$21.90).

Café Geraes (☎ 3551 5097; Rua Direita 122; mains R$26-36; ❄ 11am-11pm) Well-heeled students and artists favor this trendy spot to sip wine, talk shop and linger over creatively prepared salads, pasta, salmon and steak dishes. On weekdays, try the *prato executivo* lunch – main dish, salad, dessert, juice and coffee for only R$20.

Chafariz (☎ 3551 2828; Rua São José 167; all-you-can-eat buffet lunches R$30; ❄ 11:30am-4pm) Eclectically decorated with old photos, religious art, Brazilian flags and antiques, Chafariz is a local institution serving one of the tastiest (if priciest) buffets anywhere in Minas. The menu showcases traditional local favorites such as *lombo com feijão tropeiro* (beans mixed with manioc flour, crunchy pork rind, sausage, eggs, garlic and onions), followed by Minas cheese and *goiabada* (guava paste) for dessert. The formally dressed waiters will also ply you with shots of *cachaça*, coffee and *jabuticaba* liqueur, all included in the price.

Casa do Ouvidor (☎ 3551 2141; Rua Direita 42; mains R$17-43; ☺ 11am-3pm & 7-10pm) Just downhill from Praça Tiradentes, Ouvidor has garnered numerous awards for its *comida mineira* (typical cuisine of Minas Gerais) main meals. The ancient upstairs dining room is especially appealing at night, when low lighting enhances its rustic charm. Definitely come with an empty stomach – portions are immense.

Bené da Flauta (☎ 3551 1036; Rua São Francisco de Assis 32; mains R$21-43; ☺ noon-11pm) Directly below Igreja de São Francisco, this place occupies two levels of a gorgeous colonial *sobrado* (mansion). The open, airy atmosphere, the views and the wine list nicely complement the menu of trout, steak, pasta and Mineiro specialties, all presented with flair.

Drinking

At night and on weekends, students assemble in Praça Tiradentes and crowd the bars along nearby Rua Direita.

Acaso 85 (☎ 3551 2397; Largo do Rosário 85; ☺ 6:30pm-late) This atmospheric split-level bar with stone walls and high ceilings attracts a late-night crowd. There's live music and a large selection of whiskey and other drinks.

Getting There & Away

BUS

Long-distance buses leave from Ouro Prêto's main **bus station** (☎ 3559 3252; Rua Padre Rolim 661) at the northwest end of town. During peak periods, buy tickets a day in advance. **Pássaro Verde** (☎ 3551 1081) provides service to Belo Horizonte (R$21, two hours, hourly from 6am to 8pm) and Brasília (R$117, 12 hours, 7:30pm daily); **Útil** (☎ 3551 3166) goes to Rio de Janeiro (*convencional/executivo/semi-leito* R$68/96/107, 6½ hours, daily at 10pm and 10:30pm), São Paulo (R$105, 12 hours, 7am and 7:30pm daily) and São João del Rei (R$44, four hours, daily at 7am and 7:30pm); and **Vale do Ouro** (☎ 3551 5679) goes to Santa Bárbara (R$21, 2½ hours, 7:25am and 1:45pm daily).

To get to Mariana or Minas de Passagem, catch a local Transcotta bus (R$2.65, every 20 minutes from 6am to 11pm) from the local bus stop just northeast of Praça Tiradentes.

TRAIN

A renovated historic tourist train runs on weekends between Ouro Prêto and Mariana (one hour, one-way/round-trip R$18/30), leaving Ouro Prêto's **train station** (☎ 3551 7705; www.tremdavale.org; Praça Cesário Alvim 102) at 10am Friday to Sunday, returning at 2pm from Mariana. On holiday weekends, additional departures are added from Ouro Prêto at 3:30pm and from Mariana at 8:30am. The 18km journey is pretty but slow, snaking along a river gorge the whole way. Best views are from the right side leaving Ouro Prêto, and the left side leaving Mariana.

Getting Around

Viação Turin runs a small bus (R$1.70) between the bus station and Capela do Padre Faria on the eastern side of town, making various stops along the way.

AROUND OURO PRÊTO
Minas da Passagem

This old **gold mine** (☎ 3557 5000; www.minasda passagem.com.br; adult/child R$24/20; ☺ 9am-5pm Mon & Tue, to 5:30pm Wed-Sun) is a kick, starting with the descent underground in a rickety antique cable car.

The mandatory guided tour, in English or French upon request, covers the mine's history and local gold-extraction methods. Opened in 1719, the mine was worked by black slaves, many of whom died dynamiting into the rock. There's a shrine to dead miners at the bottom, plus a shallow, crystal-clear 2km-wide subterranean lake, where you can swim if you can handle the 16°C to 18°C (61°F to 65°F) water temperature.

The mine is between Ouro Prêto and Mariana. Take any local bus running between the two (R$2.65) and ask the driver to let you off at Minas de Passagem.

MARIANA

☎ 0xx31 / pop 55,000 / elevation 712m

Lovely Mariana, founded in 1711, is graced with fine colonial architecture and two of Minas' prettiest squares. Since it's only 14km from Ouro Prêto, Mariana can be used as a base to explore both cities. Its compact historical center is easier to navigate than Ouro Prêto's, not only because of its smaller size, but also because the hills are less steep. The ground floors of many historic mansions have been transformed into stores, boutiques and artists workshops where you're invited to wander at will.

Information

Bradesco (Av Salvador Furtado) One of two banks with ATMs, one block below the cathedral square.

MINAS GERAIS

Mundo Virtual Lan House (☎ 3557 3307; Praça da Sé 52; per hr R$2.50; ☯ 8am-10pm Mon-Sat, 9am-9pm Sun) Reasonably fast internet, plus Skype.

Post office (Rua Padre Gonçalves Lopes) Just below the cathedral.

Tourist information (☎ 3557 1158; agturbmariana mg@hotmail.com; Praça Tancredo Neves; ☯ 8am-5pm) Just outside the historic center, in the square where buses from Ouro Prêto stop. Offers city information and tours.

Sights

All the sights are close together. Two blocks uphill from the tourist-information office and the Ouro Prêto bus stop, Praça Minas Gerais boasts one of the state's nicest arrangements of public buildings on a single square. **Igreja São Francisco de Assis** (☯ 9am-5pm) is the final resting place of the painter Ataíde – Aleijadinho's partner – and 94 other lucky souls. **Igreja NS do Carmo** (☯ 9am-4pm) was severely damaged by fire in 1999 but has now been reopened.

One block downhill from Praça Minas Gerais, leafy **Praça Gomes Freire** is a gorgeous place to sit and watch the world go by, with a pond, a gazebo and park benches shaded by grand old trees.

Doubling back downhill, the **Museu Arquidiocesano de Arte Sacra** (☎ 3557 2581; Rua Frei Durão 49; admission R$5; ☯ 8:30am-noon & 1:30-5pm Tue-Fri, 8:30am-2pm Sat & Sun) has sculptures by Aleijadinho, paintings by Ataíde, and other religious objects. **Catedral Basílica da Sé** (Praça Cláudio Manuel; ☯ 8am-6pm Tue-Sun), with its fantastic German organ dating from 1701, holds **organ concerts** (admission R$15; ☯ 11:30am Fri, 12:15pm Sun).

While walking through the old part of town, you'll come across artists at work in their studios. Especially interesting is the **Catin Nardi Puppet Theater** (☎ 3557 3927, 8850 7660; Rua Do Seminário 290; ☯ 10am-6pm), where you can see new puppets under construction, plus old ones that have appeared on Brazilian national TV miniseries.

To witness some modern-day **gold mining**, head for the *garimpo* (mining camp), just across Mariana's last bridge at Carmo Creek, a short walk from town. Look upstream and you'll see people digging and panning.

Sleeping

Hotel Central (☎ 3557 1630; Rua Frei Durão 8; s/d/tr without bathroom R$40/60/75, s/d/tr/q with bathroom R$50/70/90/110) The drab Hotel Central's only selling point is the low price for its attractive location opposite leafy Praça Gomes Freire.

Pousada Solar dos Correa (☎ 3557 2080; www .pousadasolardoscorrea.com.br; Rua Direita 124; s/d/tr/q R$80/140/180/220; ☜) Close to the Ouro Prêto train and bus stops, Pousada Solar features nice airy apartments in an 18th-century colonial mansion.

Hotel Providência (☎ 3557 1444; www.hotelprovidencia.com.br; Rua Dom Silvério 233; s/d/tr/q R$80/150/215/265; ☐ ☜ ☝) Guestrooms in this 1849 building are airy and inviting, with clean white sheets, lovely high ceilings and internet connections. It shares a semi-Olympic-size swimming pool with the Catholic school next door.

Pouso da Typographia (☎ 3557 1577; Praça Gomes Freire 220; s/d/tr R$100/150/200; ☜) This hotel is worth a look just to see the antique printing presses in the foyer. The wonderful central location on Mariana's prettiest square can't be beat, although front rooms get noisy on the weekends.

Eating

Vagão Café (Estação Ferroviária; sandwiches R$9; ☯ 9am-5pm) A fun place for a snack, this little café is housed in a train car at Mariana's train station.

Gaveteiros (☎ 3557 2273; Praça da Sé 26; per kg R$19.90; ☯ 10am-3pm) Centrally located Gaveteiros offers self-serve Mineiro food on the downhill side of the cathedral square.

Lua Cheia (☎ 3557 3232; Rua Dom Viçoso 58; per kg R$22.90; ☯ 11am-3pm daily & 7pm-midnight Wed-Sat) Mariana's best *por-kilo* place, just a few steps from lovely Praça Gomes Freire.

O Rancho (☎ 3558 1060; Praça Gomes Freire 108; all-you-can-eat buffets R$16, pizzas R$18-34; ☯ 11am-3pm & 6pm-midnight Tue-Sun) Cozy and welcoming, O Rancho specializes in hearty Mineiro fare, with soups always bubbling on the wood-fired stove; there's also pizza for those needing a break from rice and beans.

Drinking

Offering a wide selection of drinks and homemade snacks, **Bar Scotch & Art** (Praça Minas Gerais 57; snacks from R$5; ☯ 6:30pm-2am Tue-Sun) has cozy indoor seating plus a slate terrace overlooking lovely Praça Minas Gerais.

Getting There & Away

There are regular Transcotta buses between Ouro Prêto and Mariana (R$2.65, 30 minutes, at least twice hourly from 6am to 11pm). In Mariana, the bus stop is across from the tourist information office on Praça Tancredo Neves.

Mariana's long-distance bus station, Rodoviária dos Inconfidêntes, is located about 2km outside of town. Destinations served include Belo Horizonte (R$25, 2½ hours, several daily), Brasília (R$117, 12 hours, daily at 6:50pm) and São Paulo (R$108, 11 hours, daily at 7pm). The Transcotta bus from Ouro Prêto also stops here en route to downtown Mariana.

Mariana's picturesque peach and white colored train station is just two blocks away from the local bus stop for buses to Ouro Prêto. Trains leave Mariana for Ouro Prêto at 2pm Friday to Sunday, with an additional 8:30am departure added on holidays. There's a café, museum and kids playground to keep everyone happy while you wait.

LAVRAS NOVAS
☎ 0xx31 / pop 1000 / elevation 1510m

Lavras Novas, named for the new gold strikes discovered here in 1704, sits on a high plateau 17km from Ouro Prêto. Surrounded by wide-open mountain scenery, its cobblestone main street runs between colorful single-story houses to the town's focal point, the **Igreja NS dos Prazeres**. Lavras has seen a rapid influx of tourism over the past decade, and on busy weekends it sometimes feels like outsiders outnumber the locals. For a better understanding of the town's history and a taste of its traditional off-the-beaten-path tranquility, it pays to visit Lavras Novas midweek and stay a while.

Activities
Several companies around town offer guided hikes and horseback-riding tours to local attractions, including the waterfalls **Três Pingos** and **Namorados**. An alternative resource for independent hikers is the free trail map distributed at pousada Palavras Novas (p251).

Sleeping & Eating
Pousadas empty out during the week, but reservations are advisable on weekends and holidays.

Taberna Casa Antiga e Chalés Galo do Campo (☎ 9957 8189; www.lavrasnovas.com.br/galodocampo; Rua Alto do Campo 213; d midweek R$140-210, weekend R$180-230) Nestled among trees at the edge of town are these cute chalets with views of horse pastures and mountains; the cozy bar-restaurant next door (mains R$18 to R$40) has a fireplace, live music and a varied menu.

Palavras Novas (☎ 3554 2025; www.pousadapalav rasnovas.com.br, in Portuguese; Rua NS dos Prazeres 1110; d midweek/weekend from R$150/195, chalet with whirlpool tub midweek/weekend R$280/340; ☒) With fireplaces, afternoon tea, whirlpool tubs, in-room DVD players, a sauna, spa and heated pool, nice mountain views and live music on weekends, Palavras Novas caters to a luxury-minded crowd. The pousada leads group hikes every weekend.

Getting There & Away
Local buses to Lavras Novas (R$4.40, one hour) leave from in front of the Ouro Prêto train station (not the bus station). There are three departures in each direction Tuesday through Friday, four on Monday, and one each on Saturday and Sunday. Of the 17km to Lavras Novas, 9km is unpaved; it's scenic, despite the bumps!

SABARÁ
☎ 0xx31 / pop 130,000 / elevation 705m

Sabará, 25km southeast of Belo Horizonte, is filled with houses, mansions, churches, statues, fountains and sacred art, all dating from the town's 18th-century glory days when it was Minas's first major gold-mining center and one of the world's wealthiest cities. In the boom years, when the Rio das Velhas was 15 times wider, boats would sail all the way up the Rio São Francisco from Bahia. Sabará produced more gold in one week than the rest of Brazil produced in a year.

Nowadays Sabará is a poor town dominated by a Belgian metalworks. Since it's only 30 minutes by bus from Belo, it makes an easy and interesting day trip. Don't bother visiting on a Monday – all sites are closed.

There's an information booth at the entrance to town, but major attractions are easy to find, since there are signposts at Praça Santa Rita telling where everything is.

Sights
Most of the churches, museums and other colonial attractions charge admission fees of R$1 or R$2.

A testament to the wealth of bygone days, Sabará's elegant opera house, **O Teatro Imperial** (Rua Dom Pedro II; ☒ 8am-noon & 1-5pm Tue-Sun), was built in 1770. It had crystal lamps and three tiers of carved bamboo seats.

Housed in an old gold foundry (1730), the **Museu do Ouro** (☎ 3671 1848; Rua da Intendência;

admission US$1; ☺ noon-5pm Tue-Sun) houses art and artifacts of Sabará's glory years.

The triple-naved **Matriz de NS de Conceição** (Praça Getúlio Vargas; ☺ 9am-noon & 2-5pm, closed Mon), finished in 1720, is a fascinating blend of Asian arts and Portuguese baroque, with gold leaf, red Chinese scrolls and pagodas on the sanctuary door panels.

A riot of gold, red and blue, the diminutive **Igreja de NS do Ó** (Largo NS do Ó; ☺ 9am-noon & 2-5pm Tue-Sun) is one of Minas's little gems. Dedicated to the Virgin Mary in her role as protector of pregnant women and those praying for fertility, it also features many oriental details.

The half-built **Igreja de NS do Rosário dos Pretos** (Praça Melo Viana; ☺ 8-11am & 1-5pm) – started and financed by slaves but never finished – now stands as a memorial to the abolition of slavery in 1888.

Aleijadinho was instrumental in the decoration of the **Igreja NS do Carmo** (Rua de Carmo; ☺ 9-11:30am, closed Mon). His touch is everywhere, especially in the faces of São Simão and São João da Cruz.

Getting There & Away

The Cisne company runs buses to Sabará (R$3, 30 minutes, every 15 minutes from 5am to 11pm) from the local section behind Belo's main bus station. Return buses leave the bus stop on Av Victor Fantini in Sabará; you can also catch one on the road out of town.

CONGONHAS

☎ 0xx31 / pop 49,000 / elevation 871m

This small industrial town has been saved from complete obscurity by the beautiful, brooding presence of Aleijadinho's extraordinary *The Prophets* at the Basílica do Bom Jesus de Matosinhos. The dramatic statues almost seem to be performing a balletic dance and it's a wondrous experience to be able to walk freely among them. They are Aleijadinho's masterpiece and Brazil's most famed work of art. It's worth taking the trouble to get to Congonhas just to see them.

Congonhas is 72km south of Belo Horizonte, 3km off Hwy BR-040. The city grew up with the search for gold in the nearby Rio Maranhão, and the economy today is dominated by iron mining in the surrounding countryside.

Sights

Already an old man, sick and crippled, Aleijadinho sculpted *The Prophets* between 1800 and 1805. Symmetrically placed in front of the **Basílica do Bom Jesus de Matosinhos**, each of the 12 Old Testament figures was carved from one or two blocks of soapstone. Each carries a

---

ALEIJADINHO

Antônio Francisco Lisboa (1738–1814), known worldwide today as Aleijadinho (Little Cripple), was the son of a Portuguese architect and a black slave. His nickname was given to him sometime in the 1770s, when the artist began to suffer from a terrible, debilitating disease. It might have been syphilis or possibly leprosy – either way, he lost his fingers and toes and the use of his lower legs.

Undaunted, Aleijadinho strapped hammers and chisels to his arms and continued working, advancing the art in his country from the excesses of the baroque to a finer, more graceful form known as Barroco Mineiro.

Mineiros have reason to be proud of Aleijadinho – he is a figure of international prominence in the history of art. He studied European baroque and rococo traditions through pictures, but went on to develop his own unique style, using only native materials such as soapstone and wood. Aleijadinho's angels have his stylistic signature: wavy hair, wide-open eyes and big, round cheeks.

For many years Manuel da Costa Ataíde, from nearby Mariana, successfully collaborated with Aleijadinho on many churches. Aleijadinho would sculpt the exterior and a few interior pieces, and Ataíde would paint the interior panels. With his secretly concocted vegetable dyes, Ataíde fleshed out many of Aleijadinho's creations.

Aleijadinho was buried in Ouro Prêto's Matriz NS da Conceição de Antônio Dias, within 50 paces of his birth site. He was named patron of Brazilian arts by federal decree in 1973. *The Prophets* in Congonhas, the Igreja de São Francisco de Assis and the facade of the Igreja de NS do Carmo, both in Ouro Prêto, were all carved by Aleijadinho, as were innumerable relics in Mariana, Sabará, Tiradentes and São João del Rei. The best places to see Aleijadinho's work are Congonhas, Ouro Prêto, Sabará and São João del Rei.

Latin message: some are hopeful prophecies, others warn of the end of the world.

Much has been written about these sculptures – their dynamic quality, the sense of movement (much like a Hindu dance or a ballet), how they complement each other and how their arrangement prevents them from being seen in isolation. The poet Carlos Drummond de Andrade wrote that the dramatic faces and gestures are 'magnificent, terrible, grave and tender' and commented on 'the way the statues, of human size, appear to be larger than life as they look down upon the viewer with the sky behind them.'

Before working on *The Prophets*, Aleijadinho carved (or supervised his assistants in carving) the wooden statues that were placed in the six little **chapels** below. The chapels themselves – also of Aleijadinho's design – and their placement on the sloping site are superb. The way the light falls on the pale sculpted domes against the dark mountain backdrop is truly beautiful.

Each chapel depicts a scene from Christ's Passion, and several portray Jesus with a red mark on his neck. While little is known of Aleijadinho's politics, some local historians interpret this to mean that Aleijadinho intended to draw parallels between the martyred Christ and slain independence fighter Tiradentes. Aleijadinho's sculptures of Roman soldiers lend support to this theory – they all have two left feet and sport ankle boots, a shoe style favored by the colonizing Portuguese.

Festivals & Events

Held from September 7 to 14, the **Jubileu do Senhor Bom Jesus do Matosinhos** is one of Minas's great religious festivals. Every year approximately 600,000 pilgrims arrive at the church to make promises, do penance, receive blessings, and give and receive alms. **Holy Week** processions in Congonhas are also famous, especially the dramatizations on Good Friday.

Sleeping & Eating

It's possible to catch an early bus into Congonhas and another one out that same afternoon. Since there's little to see beyond Aleijadinho's artwork, most people don't spend the night. One pleasure of staying over is the opportunity to see the statues in the early-morning light, when they're especially beautiful.

Conveniently situated right across the street from Aleijadinho's masterpieces, the **Colonial**

Hotel (☎ 3731 1834; Praça da Basílica 76; r R$85-105; 🖘) still wears faded remnants of its former glory in the huge hallways and immensely high ceilings. Most rooms are spacious and the bathrooms surprisingly modern. The restaurant downstairs, **Cova do Daniel** (☎ 3731 1834; Praça da Basílica 76; mains for 2 R$40; 🕙 11am-11pm) makes a convenient lunch option for day-trippers.

Getting There & Away

Congonhas is on the direct bus route between Belo Horizonte and São João del Rei, so these two towns make the best starting points for a day trip. Viação Sandra serves this route several times daily (R$19, 90 minutes from Belo Horizonte; R$22, two hours from São João).

Getting Around

The bus station is on Av Júlia Kubitschek, across town from the sites of interest. From here buses leave every half-hour to 40 minutes for the 15-minute ride up the hill to the basilica and *The Prophets*. For the best approach and first view of the statues, get off just after the bus passes the church (as it heads downhill). The same bus returns you to the bus station, or you can have the Colonial Hotel staff call you a taxi (R$10).

SÃO JOÃO DEL REI

☎ 0xx32 / pop 86,000 / elevation 898m

São João del Rei affords a unique look at a *cidade historica* that didn't suffer a great decline when the gold boom ended in the 1800s. Present-day São João has the unselfconscious urban vitality of a modern city, which can come as a welcome contrast to the preserved-in-amber quality of neighboring Tiradentes or some of the other more studiously conserved historical towns. Downtown there are plenty of high-rises and other trappings of 21st-century Brazil, yet around every corner lurk unexpected colonial surprises. The historic city center, which is protected by Brazil's Landmarks Commission, features two good museums, several of the country's finest churches and some gorgeous old mansions – one of which belonged to the late and still-popular never-quite-president Tancredo Neves. Floodlights illuminate the churches every night, adding to the city's aesthetic appeal.

Orientation

São João sits between mountain ridges, near the southern end of the Serra do Espinhaço.

SÃO JOÃO DEL REI

MINAS GERAIS

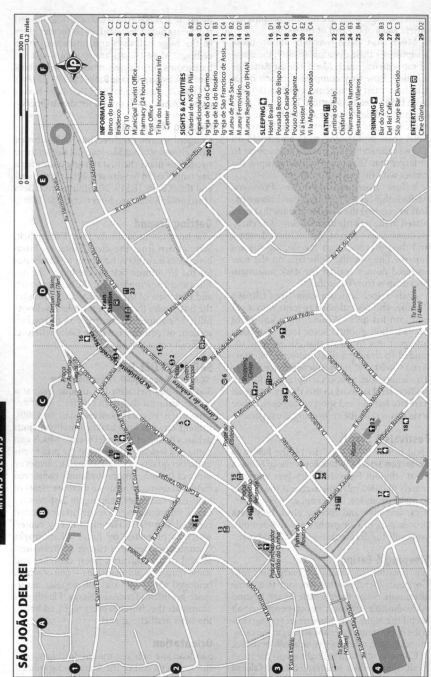

INFORMATION	
Banco do Brasil	1 C2
Bradesco	2 C2
City 10	3 C2
Municipal Tourist Office	4 C1
Pharmacy (24 hours)	5 C2
Post Office	6 C2
Trilha dos Inconfidentes Info Center	7 C2

SIGHTS & ACTIVITIES	
Catedral de NS do Pilar	8 B2
Expedicionário	9 D3
Igreja de NS do Carmo	10 C1
Igreja de NS do Rosário	11 B3
Igreja de São Francisco de Assis	12 C4
Museu de Arte Sacra	13 B2
Museu Ferroviário	14 D2
Museu Regional do IPHAN	15 B3

SLEEPING	
Hotel Brasil	16 D1
Pousada Beco do Bispo	17 B4
Pousada Casarão	18 C4
Pouso Aconchegante	19 C1
Via Hostel	20 E2
Vi la Magnolia Pousada	21 C4

EATING	
Cantina do Italo	22 C3
Chafariz	23 D2
Churrascaria Ramon	24 B3
Restaurante Villeiros	25 B4

DRINKING	
Bar do Zotti	26 B3
Del Rei Cafe	27 C3
São Jorge Bar Divertido	28 C3

ENTERTAINMENT	
Cine Gloria	29 D2

The city is bisected by the Córrego do Lenheiro – really just a glorified creek in a concrete channel. Two lovely 18th-century stone bridges serve as convenient landmarks in the colonial center. The train station is just east of downtown, while the bus station is an additional 15-minute walk to the northeast.

Information

Banco do Brasil (Av Hermilio Alves 234)

Bradesco (Av Hermilio Alves 200)

City 10 (Av Andrade Reis 120; ⏱ 7:30am-6:30pm Mon-Sat; per hr R$3) Centrally located internet place.

Municipal tourist office (☎ 3379 2952; Av Presidente Tancredo Neves s/n; ⏱ 8am-5pm) Underneath the bandstand across the river from the train station.

Post office (Av Tiradentes 500)

Trilha dos Inconfidentes info center (☎ 3372 8011; Rua Marechal Bittencourt 15; ⏱ 9am-5pm Mon-Fri) Info on excursions in the surrounding area.

Sights

Opening times vary widely, as noted below. Monday is not a good day to visit, since most attractions are closed.

IGREJA DE SÃO FRANCISCO DE ASSIS

This 1774 baroque **church** (Rua Padre José Maria Xavier; admission R$2; ⏱ 8am-5:30pm Tue-Sat, 8am-2:30pm Sun, to 4pm Mon) is exquisite. It's on the south side of the river and faces an elegant lyre-shaped plaza filled with towering palms. Inside the church are two **Aleijadinho sculptures**: the figures of São João Evangelista and São Gonçalo do Amarante in the second altar to the left. The facade, with sculptures of the Immaculate Virgin and angels executed by Francisco de Lima Cerqueira based on Aleijadinho's design, is one of the finest in Minas.

Politician Tancredo Neves is buried in the church graveyard. He was the first elected president after the 1960s-to-'80s period of military dictatorship in Brazil, though he died before he could take office. His grave is something of a pilgrimage site for Brazilians. Follow the arrows painted on the pavement behind the church.

During the 9:15am Mass on Sunday, the local Ribeiro Bastos women's orchestra and choir perform sacred baroque music.

OTHER CHURCHES & CATHEDRALS

The simple **Igreja de NS do Rosário** (⏱ 9:30-10:30am) was built in 1719 to honor the patron saint who was protector of the slaves.

Begun in 1721, the **Catedral de NS do Pilar** (⏱ 6-10:30am & 1-8pm Tue-Sun) has exuberant gold altars and fine Portuguese tiles. On Wednesday, Thursday and Friday the Lira Sanjoanense, or Coalhada (all-white) orchestra and choir, accompany the 7pm Mass.

The 18th-century **Igreja de NS do Carmo** (Rua Getúlio Vargas; ⏱ 8-noon & 3-7pm), dominating a lovely triangular praça (plaza), was designed by Aleijadinho, who also did the frontispiece and the sculpture around the door. In the second sacristy is a famous unfinished sculpture of Christ.

MUSEUMS

The **Museu Regional do IPHAN** (☎ 3371 7663; Praça Severiano Resende s/n; admission R$1, free Sun; ⏱ 12:30-5:30pm Tue-Sun) is one of the best in Minas Gerais. It is full of antique furniture and sacred art, and is housed in a colonial mansion that was built around 1859.

In a building that served as the public jail between 1737 and 1850, the **Museu de Arte Sacra** (☎ 3371 7005; Praça Embaixador Gastão da Cunha 8; ⏱ noon-5pm Tue-Sun) reopened after a 12-year renovation in March 2010. It has a small but impressive collection of art from the city's churches.

Festivals & Events

Someone's always celebrating something in São João. There are literally dozens of festivals, both religious and secular – stop by the tourist office for a full calendar.

Locals boast, credibly, that their **Carnaval** is the best in Minas Gerais, and **Semana Santa** is also quite colorful. The **Semana da Inconfidência**, from April 15 to 21, celebrates Brazil's first independence movement, culminating in a horseback procession between São João and Tiradentes.

Sleeping

Be sure to book ahead in December, when the town is filled with students sitting for exams, and during holidays such as Carnaval and Easter.

BUDGET

If saving money is your primary concern, São João offers more options than Tiradentes.

Pouso Aconchegante (☎ 3371 2637; Rua Marechal Bittencourt 61; s/d R$20/40) This place offers 10 very simple rooms, all with shared bathroom, in a family home full of colorful kitsch near the Carmo church.

Hotel Brasil (☎ 3371 2804; Av Presidente Tancredo Neves 395; s/d without bathroom R$30/60, with bathroom R$40/80) A funky, rambling 19th-century relic with high-ceilinged but slightly shabby rooms, some facing the river; it's straight across the pedestrian bridge from the train station. Prices don't include breakfast.

Vila Hostel (☎ 3371 9263; www.vilahostel.com; Av 8 de Dezembro 272; dm/d HI member R$30/72, nonmember R$38/84; 🖥 🛜) A 10-minute walk above the train station and city center, this pleasant new HI hostel features four- to six-bed dorms, a couple of doubles, a small guest kitchen, a comfortable front lounge and laundry facilities (R$5 per load). Free bus station pick-up is available with advance notice.

MIDRANGE & TOP END

Pousada Casarão (☎ 3371 7447; www.pousadacasarao.com, in Portuguese; Rua Ribeiro Bastos 94; s/d/tr R$90/150/180; 🗙 🛜 🗟) In an elegant old mansion behind the Igreja de São Francisco, the Pousada Casarão tastefully blends old with new; many rooms are decorated with antiques, yet all have modern bathrooms. The French doors in the breakfast room overlook the pool. Wi-fi is available only in the reception and pool area.

Villa Magnolia Pousada (☎ 3373 5065; www.pousadavillamagnolia.com.br; Rua Ribeiro Bastos 2; s/d/tr R$138/165/206, deluxe s/d/tr/q ste R$235/266/319/368; 🗙 🖥 🛜 🗟) Another delightful refuge just across from Igreja de São Francisco, this stylishly renovated 19th-century mansion features pure cotton bedding, oversized towels, spacious rooms, a large pool, shade trees and elegant common areas filled with art books.

Pousada Beco do Bispo (☎ 3371 8844; www.becodobispo.com.br; Beco do Bispo 93; s/d/tr R$125/190/250; 🗙 🛜 🗟) Tucked down a peaceful dead-end street a block from Igreja de São Francisco, this pousada has cheerful, cozy rooms and a pool with palm trees.

Eating

Restaurante Villeiros (☎ 3372 1034; Rua Padre José Maria Xavier 132; per kg midweek R$23.90, weekend R$29.90; 🕒 11am-3pm) A fabulous self-serve place with great variety near the Igreja de São Francisco, Villeiros is very popular with locals and has a cheerful patio out back.

Chafariz (☎ 3371 8955; Rua Quintino Bocáiuva 100; per kg R$23.90; 🕒 11am-3pm) Just behind the train station, Chafariz is another popular self-serve option – it seems half the town is in there for lunch on any given day.

Churrascaria Ramon (☎ 3371 3540; Praça Severiano Resende 52; mains for 2 R$22-54; 🕒 10am-10pm) Ramon prides itself on perfectly cooked meats and all the traditional Mineiro favorites. For a bargain, try the *prato feito* (meat, beans, rice, salad and potato salad) for R$9.50.

Cantina do Italo (☎ 3371 8239; Rua Ministro Gabriel Passos 315; pizzas R$23-29, mains R$23-47; 🕒 noon-midnight Wed-Mon) One of the city's oldest Italian restaurants, Italo serves a full range of pizza, pasta and other classics in its upstairs dining room next door to São João's downtown shopping center.

Drinking & Entertainment

Most of the city's nightlife is on the south side along Av Tiradentes.

Bar do Zotti (Av Tiradentes 801; 🕒 6pm-late) A cozy little place resembling a rustic cabin transplanted into the big city. Lots of people pack in here every night for delicious nibbles, drinks and dancing.

Del Rei Cafe (☎ 3371 1368; Av Tiradentes 553; 🕒 9pm-late) This busy corner bar, with numerous sidewalk tables, is great for people-watching. Locals congregate here daily for early-evening beers and late-night snacks.

São Jorge Bar Divertido (☎ 3371 2582; www.saojorgebardivertido.com.br; Av Balbino da Cunha 18; 🕒 11pm-5am) Very popular with the 20- to 30-year-old crowd, who come to dance and flirt the night away to live rock, samba and more.

Cine Gloria (Av Tiradentes 390) This old theater screens multiple films nightly, including many in English with Portuguese subtitles.

Getting There & Away

AIR

Trip Airlines (www.voetrip.com.br) offers non-stop flights from São João del Rei to Rio's Santos Dumont airport and Belo Horizonte's Pampulha. São João's airport is just north of downtown.

BUS

The **São João bus station** (☎ 3373 4700; Rua Cristóvão Colombo) is about 1.5km northeast of town.

Paraibuna runs direct buses to Rio at 8am and 2pm Monday to Friday (R$62, 5½ hours), stopping en route in Petrópolis (R$55, 4½ hours); there are extra departures on weekends. Sandra goes via Congonhas (R$22, two hours) to Belo Horizonte (R$39, 3½ hours, six daily from 6am to 7pm, with extra buses on Sunday); other destinations include São Paulo

---

SMOKING MARY

Sure, there are buses that will get you back and forth between São João del Rei and Tiradentes, but how can they compare with a trip on a 19th-century steam train in pristine condition? Jump aboard as this little engine hisses and belches its way through the winding valley of the Serra de São José, which gradually gets rockier and bleaker as you approach Tiradentes. The trail goes through one of the oldest areas of gold mining in Minas and you'll see the remnants of 18th-century mine workings all around. Keep a sharp eye out for modern *garimpeiros* (gold panners) still hoping to strike it rich.

Built in the 1880s as the textile industry began to take hold in São João, the Maria-Fumaça (Smoking Mary to locals) was one of the first rail lines in Brazil. More history is available at the **Museu Ferroviário** (admission R$2; ☺ 9-11am & 1-5pm Wed-Sun) inside São João's **train station** (☎ 3371 8485; Av Hermílio Alves). Trains depart São João at 10am and 3pm on Friday, Saturday, Sunday and holidays, returning from Tiradentes at 1pm and 5pm (R$18/30 one-way/round-trip). When leaving São João the best views are on the left side. If you need more time in Tiradentes than the train schedule allows, you can always bus back (there are regular connections between the two cities).

A similar historic train travels between Mariana and Ouro Prêto, with imaginative museums and train-car restaurants greeting visitors at either end of the line. See details under Getting There & Away (p249).

(Gardénia and Vale do Ouro, R$72, 7½ hours, six daily from 9:10am to 11:50pm); Caxambu (Sandra, R$38, 3½ hours, one daily at 3pm);, Ouro Prêto (Útil, R$47, four hours, twice daily at 2:45am and 7:30pm); and Mariana (Útil, R$51, 4½ hours, daily at 2:45am) – for the early-morning bus, buy tickets the day before).

For buses between São João and Tiradentes, see Getting There & Away under Tiradentes (p261).

TRAIN

The wonderful Maria-Fumaça tourist train runs on weekends between São João del Rei and Tiradentes (see the boxed text, above).

Getting Around

Local Presidente buses (gray with red letters) run between the bus station and the center (R$1.80, 10 minutes). Exiting the bus station, you'll find the local stop to your left and across the street (in front of the Drogaria Americana).

Alternatively, you have two taxi options: traditional taxis (R$10) or the cool and totally cheap **motorbike taxi** (☎ 3371 6389; R$3). For these, look for the orange Cooperativo Moto Taxi sign to your left as you exit the bus station. Drivers carry a helmet for the passenger. Use it!

Returning from the center to the bus station, you can catch a local bus in front of the train station.

TIRADENTES

☎ 0xx32 / pop 7000 / elevation 927m

Perhaps nowhere else in Minas do colonial charm and picturesque natural setting blend so perfectly as in Tiradentes. Quaint historic houses, fringed by exuberant wildflowers, stand out against a backdrop of pretty blue mountains with wonderful hiking trails. If you can, visit midweek, when the town's abundant attractions are most easily appreciated. On weekends, the swarms of visitors who come to gawk at Tiradentes's antique stores and boutiques can make the place feel a bit like a theme park, and the sudden increase in horse-drawn carriages creates some strong aromas!

History

Originally called Arraial da Ponta do Morro (Hamlet on a Hilltop), Tiradentes was renamed to honor the martyred hero of the Inconfidência (see p242), who was born at a nearby farm. In recent years, the town, which sits at the center of a triangle formed by Brazil's three largest cities, has become a magnet for artists and other urban escapees. Today the historic center is home to only a couple dozen original Tiradentes families, intermingled with new arrivals from around the world.

Orientation & Information

Tiradentes' center is a compact and picturesque cluster of cobbled streets and flowery gardens. The town's colonial buildings run

MINAS GERAIS

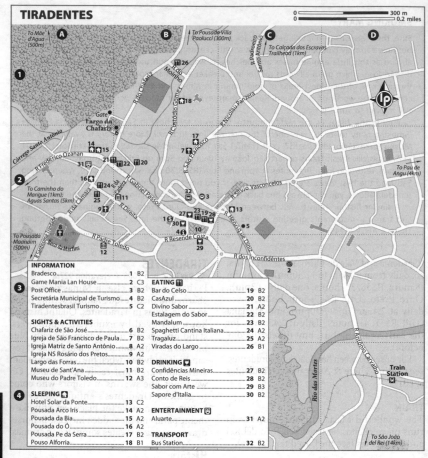

TIRADENTES

0   300 m
0   0.2 miles

up a hillside from the main square, Largo das Forras, culminating in the beautiful Igreja Matriz de Santo Antônio. From the terrace in front of the church there's a stunning view of the terracotta-tiled colonial houses, the green valley and the towering wall of stone formed by the Serra de São José. For another picture-postcard view of town, climb the hill just above the bus station to the grassy square in front of Igreja de São Francisco de Paula.

The **Secretária Municipal de Turismo** (☎ 3355 1212; www.tiradentes.mg.gov.br; Rua Resende Costa 71; ☽ 9am-5pm), in the three-story building on the main square, provides maps, plus information on hotels and guided tours.

For internet access, try **Game Mania Lan House** (☎ 3355 2002; Rua dos Inconfidentes 340A; per hr R$2.40; ☽ 9am-10:30pm Mon-Fri, to 8:30pm Sat, noon-10:30pm Sun).

There's a Bradesco bank with an ATM one block northwest of the main square.

Sights

At the time of research, Tiradentes' old town jail was being renovated to house the new **Museu de Sant'Ana**, a museum featuring 270 images of St Ann in wood, stone and terracotta from the 17th century to the present. Conceived by the creator of Ouro Prêto's Museu do Oratório (p245), it's expected to open in mid-2011.

IGREJA MATRIZ DE SANTO ANTÔNIO

Named for the town's patron saint, this **church** (admission R$3; ☽ 9am-5pm) is one of Brazil's most

MINAS GERAIS

beautiful, and among the last designed by Aleijadinho. Leandro Gonçalves Chaves made the famous sundial out front in 1785.

The all-gold interior is rich in Old Testament symbolism. The polychrome organ was built in Portugal and brought to Tiradentes by donkey in 1798. Also striking are the seven golden phoenixes (symbols of Christ's resurrection), suspending candle-holders from long braided chains.

IGREJA NS ROSÁRIO DOS PRETOS

This beautiful stone **church** (Praça Padre Lourival, Rua Direita; admission R$2; ⊙ 9am-5pm Tue-Sun), with its many images of black saints, was built in 1708, by and for slaves. Since they had no free time during daylight hours, construction took place at night – note the nocturnal symbolism in the ceiling paintings of an eight-pointed black star and a half-moon.

MUSEU DO PADRE TOLEDO

This **museum** (Rua Padre Toledo 190) is dedicated to another hero of the Inconfidência, Padre Toledo, who lived in this 18-room house where the Inconfidêntes first met. It features regional antiques and documents from the 18th century. Closed for renovation at the time of research, it was scheduled to reopen in April 2011; ask at the tourist office for prices and opening hours.

CHAFARIZ DE SÃO JOSÉ

Constructed in 1749 by the town council, this beautiful **fountain** (Rua do Chafariz) north of Córrego Santo Antônio has three sections: one for drinking, one for washing clothes and one for watering horses. The water comes from a nearby spring, Mãe d'Agua, via an old stone pipeline.

SERRA DE SÃO JOSÉ

At the foot of these mountains there's a 1km-wide stretch of protected Atlantic rain forest, with several nice **hiking trails**.

The most popular and simple leads to **Mãe d'Agua**, the spring that feeds t he Chafariz de São José fountain. From the fountain square, cross through a gate (theoretically open from 9am to 4pm, but hours vary at the whim of the elderly gatekeeper) and follow the trail north for 15 minutes along the stone viaduct into the jungle. It's a magical spot, with sun-dappled glens, and monkeys cavorting in the tall trees.

A Calçada dos Escravos is a three-hour round-trip that climbs through open fields to a windswept saddle with gorgeous views of the *serra*. Also known as Calçada do Carteiro, it includes a section of the old stone-paved road built by slaves between Ouro Prêto and Rio de Janeiro. Finding the trailhead can be tricky: head northeast on Rua Nicolau Panzera past Igreja de São Francisco de Paula and con-tinue on this road, turning neither right nor left at the first few intersections. Shortly after the road changes its name to Rua Padroeiro Santo Antônio, you'll pass Pousada Recanto dos Encantos on your right and come to a fork in the road. Take the right (gently uphill) fork and continue straight another 1km or so; after you pass house No 878 (left side), cross through a gate and look for a signpost indi-cating the Calçada dos Escravos. Fork left on the rickety bridge over the stream, then start climbing towards the saddle.

Caminho do Mangue is a walk that heads up the *serra* from the west side of town to Aguas Santas and takes about two hours. There you'll find a mineral-water swimming pool and a very good Portuguese-owned *churrascaria* (restaurant featuring barbecued meat).

You can link the latter two trails by con-tinuing along the ridgeline, a six-hour loop.

Trails are not clearly marked, and locals advise against carrying valuables or trekking alone on the Caminho do Mangue. For up-to-date English-language information on trail safety, independent hiking opportuni-ties and local guides, try Bia at Pousada da Bia or John Parsons at the Hotel Solar da Ponte. **Tiradentesbrasil Turismo** (☎ 3355 2477; www.tiraden tesbrasil.com; Rua Henrique Diniz 119; tours R$35-65) also organizes group hikes ranging in length from 2½ to 5½ hours.

Festivals & Events

Tiradentes is popular as a center for national events. Two of the biggest and longest estab-lished are the **Mostra de Cinema** (second half of January) and the **Festival Internacional de Cultura e Gastronomia** (second half of August), respectively bringing international films and world-class chefs to Tiradentes. In late June, classic-motorcycle buffs pack the streets, cel-ebrating the **Tiradentes Bike Fest** with beer, food, blues and rock and roll.

Sleeping

Tiradentes caters to a well-heeled crowd and couples looking for romance. Budget-minded and/or solo travelers can save money by renting rooms in private homes or visiting midweek, when pousadas grant discounts of 10% to 30%.

MIDRANGE & TOP END

our pick Pousada da Bia (☎ 3355 1173; www.pousada dabia.com.br; Rua Frederico Ozanan 330; s/d/tr midweek R$60/90/120, weekend R$80/100/150; 🛜 🖨) Simple but delightfully friendly, thanks to the efforts of the French- and English-speaking owner. Bia is a professional art restorer and an excellent resource for cultural goings-on in the area. The sunny breakfast house, fragrant herb garden and pool area all enhance the welcoming atmosphere.

Pousada Arco Iris (☎ 3355 1167; www.arcoiristiraden tesmg.com.br; Rua Frederico Ozanan 340; s/d R$50/95; 🖨) If Pousada da Bia is full, this place next door has similar prices and amenities. Rooms out back are brighter and more spacious than those in the main house.

Pousada Pe da Serra (☎ 3355 1107; www.pedaserra .com.br, in Portuguese; Rua Nicolau Panzera 51; s/d weekday R$90/130, weekend R$130/160; 🖨 🛜) This family-run, friendly little place sits on a ridge just above the bus station. The nine small but spotless rooms have panoramic views – the location makes up for the otherwise simple decor. Guests have free rein in the garden and sitting rooms.

Pousada do Ó (☎ 3355 1699; www.pousadadoo.com .br; Rua do Chafariz 25; s/d/tr from R$90/140/190; 🛜) This lovely 18th-century house enjoys a privileged location two blocks below the church in the heart of colonial Tiradentes. The original pousada, featuring seven snug rooms around a pretty garden, has recently expanded to include four larger rooms in the building above. Rooms 7 and 11 are the best of the bunch.

Pousada Maanaim (☎ 3355 1406; www.pousada maanaim.com, in Portuguese; Rua Santíssima Trindade 420; r R$120-200) If you like peaceful surroundings, don't require a pool or internet, and don't mind a short trek out of town, this pousada 500m behind Tiradentes's Matriz church is a good bet. The rooms surround a vast garden, and most are palatial, with 3.5m-high ceilings, large windows and gorgeous mountain views. One suite features a fireplace.

Pouso Alforria (☎ 3355 1536; www.pousoalforria.com .br, in Portuguese; Rua Custódio Gomes 286; s/d R$160/230; 🖳 🛜 🖨) This classy, secluded pousada, tucked up a flagstoned driveway five minutes' walk north of the center, features eight rooms in modern style, a reading room full of art books and some nice views of the Serra de São José. English and French are spoken.

Pousada Villa Paolucci (☎ 3355 1350; www.villa paolucci.com.br; Rua do Chafariz; r from R$398; 🛜 🖨) This sprawling mid-18th-century *fazenda* (ranch) just outside town has a palm-lined drive, a pond, tennis courts and outdoor pavilions. Rooms are immense, with fireplaces, solar hot water and antique furniture. The chef here is renowned for his *leitão à pururuca* (roast suckling pig), which he shows off at Tiradentes' summer culinary festival and also prepares for hotel guests and the general public every weekend (R$110 per person).

Hotel Solar da Ponte (☎ 3355 1255; www.solar daponte.com.br; Praça das Mercês; s/d/tr from R$344/430/516; 🔲 🛜 🖨) This magnificent re-creation of a colonial mansion is one of Brazil's finest hotels, with first-rate food and service across the board. The rooms have fresh flowers, beautiful antiques, and comfortable chairs and beds. There's a reading room, complete with fireplace, and complimentary afternoon tea is served in the garden.

Eating
BUDGET

Mandalum (☎ 3355 2176; Largo das Forras 88; snacks & sandwiches R$4-18; 🕒 9am-late Wed-Mon) The high-quality fast food at Mandalum includes everything from Lebanese sandwiches to banana splits, and from milkshakes to caipirinhas.

Divino Sabor (☎ 3355 1708; Rua Ministro Gabriel Passos 300; per kg R$26.90; 🕒 11:30am-3pm Tue-Sun) Very popular with locals for its self-serve offerings, including grilled meats and the normal range of Mineiro specialties.

MIDRANGE & TOP END

CasAzul (☎ 3355 1868; Rua da Cadeira s/n; snacks & light meals R$15-27; 🕒 7-10pm Wed-Fri, 1-4pm & 8pm-midnight Sat, 1-4pm Sun) Crepes, salads, and homemade chicken enchiladas share the menu with a good drinks list at this trendy Latin-themed bistro with vividly painted walls, rustic furniture and artsy lighting.

Pau de Angu (☎ 9948 1692; Estrada Real Tiradentes-Bichinho, Km 3; mains per person R$19-27; 🕒 11:30am-5pm Wed-Mon) In a peaceful country setting between Tiradentes and the artsy community of Bichinho, this is a great spot for homemade *linguiça* (garlicky pork sausage), hot sauces and all things Mineiro. Portions are huge and meant to be divided among two to five people.

Bar do Celso (☎ 3355 1193; Largo das Forras 80A; mains per person R$21; 🕒 11:30am-9pm Wed-Mon) On the main square, this is another locally run Mineiro restaurant with reasonable prices. Folks with less voracious appetites will appreciate the R$16 *prato mini*, a smaller plate designed for one person.

Estalagem do Sabor (☎ 3355 1144; Rua Ministro Gabriel Passos 280; mains per person R$25-38; ⊙ 11am-4pm & 7-9:30pm Mon-Fri, 11am-10pm Sat, to 4pm Sun) One of Tiradentes' finest restaurants, Estalagem specializes in meat and *comida mineira* supplemented by a good wine list.

Spaghetti Cantina Italiana (☎ 3355 1611; Rua Direita 7; mains R$25-42; ⊙ 1-11pm) Gaily decorated with red chairs, festooned with multicolored streamers and reverberating with accordion music every night, this eatery specializes in artisanal pasta, sauces and other recipes reflecting the Perrella family's southern Italian heritage.

Viradas do Largo (☎ 3355 1111; Rua do Moinho 11; mains per person R$30-38; ⊙ noon-10pm Wed-Mon) This place is among Tiradentes' best restaurants for traditional Mineiro cuisine. Crowds pack into it on weekends, spilling over into the pleasant outdoor patio and garden area.

Tragaluz (☎ 3355 1424; Rua Direita 52; mains R$40-56; ⊙ 7pm-late Wed-Mon) This restaurant prides itself on innovative home cooking served with artistic flair. Desserts here are especially divine; try the *goiabada frita Tragaluz*, guava paste mixed with cashews, fried and served on a bed of *catupiry* cheese with guava ice cream.

Drinking & Entertainment

Confidências Mineiras (☎ 3355 2770; Rua Ministro Gabriel Passos 26; ⊙ 6:30-11pm Tue-Fri, noon-11pm Sat, noon-8pm Sun) Cozy and candlelit, this is one of Tiradentes' newest nocturnal draws. Where else can you compare notes on over 500 brands of artesanal *cachaça*, most of them locally distilled in Minas Gerais?

our pick Aluarte (☎ 8814 5910; Largo do Ó 1; pizzas R$19-24, fondues for 2/4 people R$50/65; ⊙ 8:30pm-late Thu-Sun) This alluring and romantic cavelike nightspot is whimsically lit with perforated metal lamps decked with colored streamers. Lounge on the cushions with your paramour while eating fondue, or duck out back to the herbal hot tub under the trees (by reservation only, R$100 per couple for 1½ hours, including tea, fruit, water and candles). On slow nights, Pedro may invite you into the kitchen to chat while he cooks you pizza on top of the wood stove. On holiday weekends, there's live music.

Three popular bars, Conto de Reis, Sabor com Arte and Sapore d'Italia – all with outdoor seating and occasional live music – vie nightly for visitors' attention on Largo das Forras.

Getting There & Away

Tiradentes is 30 minutes by bus from São João del Rei. Two companies, Presidente and Vale do Ouro, run regular buses (R$2.50) between the two cities. Thanks to this friendly rivalry, you'll never wait longer than 45 minutes for a bus during daylight hours. After 7pm, only Vale do Ouro operates, and departures are less frequent – 7:20pm, 8:45pm and 10:25pm from São João; 7:20pm, 8:20pm, 9:20pm and 11pm from Tiradentes.

It's possible to catch a bus directly from Tiradentes to Rio if you plan ahead. The morning Pariabuna bus originating in São João del Rei (8am Monday to Friday, 6am Saturday, 10am Sunday) will pick passengers up in front of the Tiradentes train station (not the bus station), but you must buy your ticket in São João and indicate that you're boarding in Tiradentes. Coming from Rio, you can do the same thing in reverse – take Paraibuna's 6am bus Monday through Friday and let the driver know you want to disembark in Tiradentes.

Tiradentes' bus station is just north of the main square, across the stream. The train station is about 700m southeast of the main square.

DIAMANTINA

☎ 0xx38 / pop 47,000 / elevation 1113m

Isolated but fabulous, Diamantina is one of Brazil's prettiest and least-visited colonial towns. Surrounded by desolate mountains, it was the most remote mining town in Minas and the starting point for the Caminho dos Escravos, the old road to the coast built with the sweat, blood and tears of thousands of African slaves. Diamantina's fine mansions and winding streets haven't changed much in the last 200 years. Designated a Unesco World Heritage site in 1999, this *cidade histórica* is also the birthplace of Juscelino Kubitschek, former Brazilian president and founder of Brasília.

Orientation & Information

As with most Mineiro cities, Diamantina is built on precipitous slopes. The bus station sits high on a bluff, so the 500m descent

DIAMANTINA

```
0                    300 m
0                    0.2 mile
```

INFORMATION
Banco do Brasil...............................1 C3
Bradesco...2 C2
Compuway...3 C3
Conexão Lan House..........................4 C3
Livraria Café Espaço B.....................5 C3
Municipal Tourist Office................6 C3
Post Office...7 D3

SIGHTS & ACTIVITIES
Casa da Chica da Silva......................8 C4
Casa de Juscelino Kubitschek.........9 B3
Igreja de NS do Carmo 10 D3
Igreja de NS do Rosário dos
　Pretos...11 D4
Igreja de São Francisco de Assis..12 C2
Mercado Municipal.........................13 D2
Museu do Diamante........................14 C3

SLEEPING
Hotel JK...15 B4
Hotel Tijuco.....................................16 B2
Pousada Capistrana.........................17 D3
Pousada dos Cristais......................18 C4
Pousada Estalagem.........................19 C4
Relíquias do Tempo........................20 C2

EATING
Al Árabe..21 D3
Apocalipse Restaurante.................22 C3
Cantinha do Marinho......................23 C3
Churrascaria Casarão.....................24 C3
Recanto do Antônio........................25 C3

TRANSPORT
Bus Station.......................................26 B4

into town can be tough on the knees, and the return climb is a true workout. There are occasional city buses along this route, but taxis (R$10) are the easiest option. The central square is Praça Conselheiro Mota, dominated by **Santo Antônio** cathedral – both colloquially known as Sé.

Two conveniently located ATMs are at **Banco do Brasil** (Praça da Sé), behind the cathedral, and **Bradesco** (Praça Barão do Guaicuí), just below the Mercado Municipal.

Internet and Skype services are available downtown at **Conexão Lan House** (cnr Rua Augusto Nelson & Rua Silvério Lessa; per hr R$2; 10am-9:30pm Mon-Sat, 1-8pm Sun) and **Compuway** (3531 9600; Beco Modesto de Almeida 80; per hr R$2.50; 8am 10pm Mon-Thu, to 9pm Fri, to 3pm Sat).

The bookstore-café **Livraria Café Espaço B** (3531 6005; Beco da Tecla 31; snacks from R$8, mains R$20-28; 9am-midnight Mon-Thu, to 2am Fri & Sat, to 1pm Sun) is a relaxing spot to mingle with Diamantina's bohemian set. You can browse books (including English-language ones), linger over wine, snacks, salads, pasta, trout or fondue, and enjoy occasional live music on weekends.

Staff at the **municipal tourist office** (3531 8060; catdiamantinaturismo@yahoo.com.br; Praça JK; 9am-6pm Mon-Sat, to 2pm Sun) will give you a guide in Portuguese that includes a map.

The post office is on Rua do Bonfim.

Sights
Casa de Juscelino Kubitschek (3531 3607; admission R$2; Rua São Francisco 241; 8am-5pm Tue-Sat, to 1pm

Sun), childhood home of the former president, reflects his simple upbringing as the grandson of poor Czech immigrants. Kubitschek himself believed that his early life in Diamantina influenced him greatly. There are some good photos of JK along the staircase in Hotel Tijuco (see p264).

Between Praça JK and the cathedral is the house of Padre Rolim, one of the Inconfidêntes. It's now the **Museu do Diamante** (☎ 3531 1382; admission R$1; ☺ noon-5:30pm Tue-Sat, 9am-noon Sun), exhibiting religious art, old photos, furniture, weapons, and other relics of the diamond days.

The fine colonial mansion known as **Casa da Chica da Silva** (☎ 3531 2491; Praça Lobo de Mesquita 266; admission free; ☺ noon-5pm Tue-Sat, 8am-1pm Sun) was the home of diamond contractor João Fernandes de Oliveira and his longtime partner, the former slave Chica da Silva. Here it's possible to get a feeling for the lifestyle of the extravagant mulata.

Consisting of two houses located on opposite sides of the street connected by an enclosed, vivid-blue 2nd-story passageway, **Casa da Glória** (☎ 3531 1394; Rua da Glória 298; admission R$1; ☺ 8am-6pm) was originally the residence of the diamond supervisors and the palace of Diamantina's first bishop. Currently housing Diamantina's Institute of Geology, the building has plenty of historical character, but there's not much to see here other than a ragtag collection of old photos, mineral specimens and a couple of 19th-century German maps.

Diamantina's **churches** (admission to each R$2) are open variable hours throughout the year; check with the tourist office for the current schedule.

Igreja de NS do Carmo – adorned with rich, golden carvings, and with a gilded organ made in Diamantina – is the town's most opulent church. Constructed between 1760 and 1765, its tower was built at the rear – lest the bells awaken Chica da Silva.

The oldest church in town is the **Igreja de NS do Rosário dos Pretos**, dating from 1731. It's downhill on Largo do Rosário.

The **Mercado Municipal** (Municipal Market), built by the army in 1835, is in Praça Barão Guaicuí. The building's wooden arches inspired Niemeyer's design for the presidential palace in Brasília. On Saturday mornings it has a food and craft market and on Friday evenings there's live music.

A couple of kilometers outside of town, there's a 20km section of the **Caminho dos Escravos** – the stone-paved road, built by slaves, that linked Diamantina with Paraty and Rio de Janeiro. While it's theoretically possible to explore this road solo from Diamantina (follow the signs starting just north of the Mercado Municipal), it's more advisable to go with a guide, as the sections closest to Diamantina have been the scene of assaults; the tourist office can provide a list of guides and their phone numbers.

There are numerous other interesting excursions near Diamantina, including the **Gruta do Salitre**, a quartzite cave 9km south near the village of Curralinho. Also worthwhile is the 14km drive north to the picturesque historical town of **Biribiri**, via a scenic dirt road through Biribiri State Park; keep your eyes peeled near Km 7 for the multilevel **Cachoeira da Sentinela** on your right, a pretty waterfall with pools for swimming, along with some red-hued cliff paintings depicting deer and other animals.

Festivals & Events

Diamantina has recently revived an old tradition of evening serenades known as the **Vesperata**. These evening concerts are only scheduled on certain Saturdays between late March and October, so you need to plan ahead. At 8pm on Vesperata night, dozens of local musicians parade into the small triangular praça at the north end of Rua da Quitanda, disappear into various doorways, then re-emerge on the illuminated balconies of the surrounding mansions. A conductor standing in midsquare leads the performance. For the best seats in the house, pay for a table in front of Da Terra Point Bar or Café Baiuca, which face each other across the square. Alternatively, watch for free from anywhere on the surrounding sidewalks. For a full list of this year's dates, contact the Diamantina tourist office.

On Sundays throughout the year, locals throng the Beco da Tecla, a pedestrianized street between the cathedral and the market square, for **Café no Beco**, a weekly event where locals sell baked goods, play live music and offer free coffee and tea to passers-by.

Sleeping

Hotel JK (☎ 3531 8715; hotel_jk@yahoo.com.br; Largo Dom João 135; s/d without bathroom R$25/40, with bathroom $35/60; 🖳) This bare-bones hotel is directly across from the bus station, saving you a long uphill trek when you leave town. Internet access is available in the lobby, and rooms are clean, if a bit noisy.

Pousada Estalagem (☎ 3531 1629; estalagem.dtna@ gmail.com; Rua das Mercês 203; s R$35-55, d R$70-110; 🖳 🛜) A couple of blocks downhill (steeply) from the bus station, this friendly family-run pousada has nine rooms of varying size and price, plus a patio with grand views of Diamantina's rooftops and the surrounding mountains. Rooms 6 and 7 upstairs are nicest.

Pousada Capistrana (☎ 3531 6560; www.pousadacap istrana.com.br; Rua Campos Carvalho 35; s R$40-60, d R$80-120; 🛜) Rooms here are a bit cramped, but the location smack in the middle of Diamantina's historic district is hard to beat. Parking is available.

Pousada dos Cristais (☎ 3531 2897; www.pousada doscristais.com.br, in Portuguese; Rua Jogo do Bola 53; s/d/tr from R$60/90/130; 🛜 🖳) In a lovely 18th-century mansion with a swimming pool and stunning views of the surrounding countryside, this pousada offers plenty of bang for your buck. The adjacent modern wing has rooms with wi-fi, hammocks and private verandas, in a garden setting, for R$10 more.

Hotel Tijuco (☎ 3531 1022; www.hoteltijuco.com .br; Rua Macau do Meio 211; s/d midweek from R$70/125, weekend R$125/160) The modernist Tijuco is a Niemeyer creation with spacious, airy rooms and efficient chain-hotel-style service. It's worth paying R$10 extra for a veranda with panoramic views.

Relíquias do Tempo (☎ 3531 1627; www.pousada reliquiasdotempo.com.br; Rua Macau de Baixo 104; s/d/tr/q R$116/154/204/242; 🛜) Take a trip back in time at this gorgeous historical house with fantastic views, antique furniture and local artwork. Afternoon tea in the rustic dining room is a real treat. Ask to see the chapel in the back.

Eating & Drinking

Churrascaria Casarão (☎ 3531 2877; Praça Barão do Guaicuí 77; per 100g R$2.49, all-you-can-eat R$29.90; 🕙 6pm-late Tue-Fri, 11am-late Sat, 11am-4pm Sun) Grab a spot on the back patio and enjoy Casarão's ample per-kilo buffet, including items from the outdoor grill. Big eaters will enjoy the weekend *rodízio*, where itinerant waiters bring meat by your table until you beg for mercy.

Apocalipse Restaurante (☎ 3531 3242; Praça Barão do Guaicuí 78; per 100g R$3.19; 🕙 11am-3:30pm) Apocalipse serves an excellent international

per-kilo lunch in an upstairs room affording views of the municipal market.

Recanto do Antônio (☎ 3531 1147; Beco da Tecla 39; mains R$16-30; 🕙 11am-3pm & 6pm-midnight Tue-Thu, to 2am Fri & Sat, to 11pm Sun) With stone walls and wood beams, this cozy and convivial nightspot features live music on weekends (R$5 extra), and its *sanduíche de filé* (R$9) is one of the tastiest bar snacks around.

Al Árabe (☎ 3531 2281; Praça Dr Prado 124; mains per person R$19-33; 🕙 lunch & dinner Mon-Sat) From simple snacks (starting at R$4) to more elaborate dishes for two, Al Árabe's Lebanese-Brazilian chef offers an enticing lineup of Middle Eastern specialties, including many vegetarian options.

Cantinha do Marinho (☎ 3531 1686; Rua Direita 113; mains per person R$22-55; 🕙 11am-2:30pm daily, 7-10:30pm Mon-Sat) The specialty here is *bacalhau* (imported codfish – check out the Norwegian box proudly posted on the wall); for dessert, try the *doce de limão*, a sweet lemony concoction made from an old family recipe.

O Garimpo (☎ 3531 1044; Av da Saudade 265; mains from R$32; 🕙 6-10pm Mon-Fri, noon-10pm Sat & Sun) Famous for its regional dishes, Garimpo's house specialty is *bambá do garimpo*, a high-calorie concoction dating back to the diamond-mining days, featuring pork chops, beans, rice, finely chopped kale and *angu* (corn porridge). There's also a weekend all-you-can-eat buffet for R$33.

Getting There & Away

Pássaro Verde runs seven daily buses from Diamantina to Belo Horizonte (R$61, five hours, from midnight to 6pm). To the neighboring historical town of Serro, there are two buses daily (R$19, 2½ hours).

Trip Airlines (www.voetrip.com.br) recently initiated weekend flights from Belo Horizonte (Pampulha) to Diamantina's small airport, 7km west of town.

SERRO

☎ 0xx38 / pop 22,000 / elevation 781m

Founded in 1714, the charming colonial town of Serro snakes down a hillside in beautiful rural country south of Diamantina. While quite popular with Brazilians, this region remains little visited by foreigners and therefore retains a tranquil and traditional Mineiro air. Its cheese is considered the best in Minas.

Heading north from Serro towards Diamantina, the tranquil high-altitude hamlets of Milho Verde and São Gonçalo do Rio das Pedras (less than 35km away but two hours by bus along a steep, rutted dirt road) also make lovely stopovers. The entire region offers fabulous hiking opportunities.

Information
The **Centro de Informações Turísticas** (☎ 3541 2754; www.serro.tur.br; ☼ 8am-7pm) hands out a useful map of Serro's old mansions and churches and also provides information about São Gonçalo and Milho Verde.

Sights
The most striking building in town is the graceful, single-steepled **Capela de Santa Rita** (☼ 9am-1pm Mon-Sat), straight uphill from the main square via a steep series of steps. Three other 18th-century churches keep regular hours and are worth a visit: the **Igreja de NS do Carmo** (☼ 9am-5pm), the **Igreja do Bom Jesus do Matozinhos** (☼ 1-5pm Mon-Sat) and the **Capela de NS do Rosario** (☼ 1-5pm Mon-Sat). Admission to each costs R$2.

Just downhill from town, the **Chácara do Barão do Serro** (☼ 1-5pm Mon-Fri) is a lovely old mansion affording a glimpse of 19th-century baronial life in Serro.

Festivals & Events
In early July, Serro hosts one of Minas's oldest festivals, the **Festa de NS do Rosário**, dating back to 1728. Townspeople representing Brazil's three traditional social groups parade through the streets in colorful attire: *caboclos* (literally 'copper-colored'; the mixed descendants of indigenous peoples and Portuguese) beat out rhythms on bows and arrows, holding mock confrontations with sword- and guitar-wielding *marujos* (Europeans), while *catopês* (Africans) speak an ancient dialect and beat on instruments symbolizing empty plates.

Sleeping & Eating
Pousada Riques Matriz (☎ 3541 1770; Rua Alferes Luiz Pinto 82; s without bathroom R$20, s/d with bathroom R$25/50) Rooms in this historic house near Serro's Praça Matriz are quite basic, but the price is right.

Refugio dos Cinco Amigos (☎ 3541 6037; www.pousadarefugio5amigos.com.br; Largo Félix Antônio 160; r per person R$30) A charmingly rustic Swiss-run pousada next to the church green in São Gonçalo, 35km northwest of Serro.

Restaurante Itacolomi (☎ 3541 1227; Praça João Pinheiro 20; per kg lunch R$14.50, pizzas from R$25; ☼ lunch & dinner) The best of the many *por-kilo* restaurants in Serro, with an airy upstairs dining room overlooking the main square.

Getting There & Away
The bus station is one block downhill from the historical center. Destinations include Belo Horizonte (R$69, six hours, three daily), Conceição do Mato Dentro (R$16, two hours, three daily) and Diamantina (R$19, 2½ hours, two daily).

CENTRAL PARKS
Some of Minas Gerais's finest natural treasures are right in Belo Horizonte's backyard. Dazzling waterfalls, good hiking and a captivating monastery in the mountains are all within easy driving distance, whenever you're ready for a break from urban excitement.

PARQUE NACIONAL DA SERRA DO CIPÓ
☎ 0xx31
Parque Nacional da Serra do Cipó, 100km northeast of Belo Horizonte, is one of the most beautiful parks in Minas. Most of the park's vegetation is cerrado and grassy highlands, straddling the Serra do Espinhaço that divides the water basins of the São Francisco and Doce rivers. At lower elevations there are waterfalls and lush, ferny river valleys containing a number of unique orchids. Fauna here includes maned wolves, tamarin monkeys, banded anteaters, jaguars, bats and the small, brightly colored *sapo de pijama* (pyjama frog).

The park is vast, and the most popular trails involve multiday traverses of the *serra* (mountain range). Information and trail maps are available at **park headquarters** (☎ 3718 7237; parnacipo@ligbr.com.br; admission R$6), a few kilometers southeast of the town of Cardeal Mota. Two especially worthwhile day hikes are the 16km round-trip from headquarters to a 70m waterfall called **Cachoeira da Farofa**, and the 24km round-trip to the 80m-deep gorge called **Cânion das Bandeirinhas**.

Three recommended local tour operators offering hiking, rafting, horseback-riding and/ or mountain-bike excursions to the park are

Bela Geraes Turismo (☎ 3718 7394; www.belageraes
.com.br), **Cipoeiro Expediciones** (☎ 9611 8878; www
.cipoeiro.com.br) and **Tropa Serrana** (☎ 9983 2356;
http://tropa.serrana.zip.net).

Sleeping & Eating
Hotel Cipó Veraneio (☎ 3718 7000; www.cipovera
neiohotel.com.br; Hwy MG-10, Km 95; s/d/tr/q incl meals
R$298/373/570/596; ⛏ ☎ ⛽) The most conven-
ient place to stay if you're arriving by bus and
want easy access to park headquarters, Cipó
Veraneio is right on the road but has great
facilities, including an acclaimed restaurant
and a pool.

Camping in the park is not permitted, but
there are two campsites near the Véu de Noiva
waterfall, on the main road 5km north of the
park headquarters turnoff: **Grande Pedreira**
(☎ 3291 0734, 3718 7007; http://pousadagrandepedreira
.com.br, in Portuguese; campsite per person R$15) sits on a
grassy slope with nice (but distant) views of the
waterfall; **Veu da Noiva** (☎ 3274 2749; veudanoiva@
acmmg.org; campsite per person R$25; ☎ ⛽) has a
freshwater swimming pool, snack bar and
direct access to the waterfall via a 200m footpath. Buses will drop you there upon request.

Getting There & Away
Serro and Saritur run buses to the park from
Belo Horizonte (R$23, two hours, several daily
from 6am to 4pm). For park headquarters, get
off at the Hotel Cipó Veraneio, then walk or
hitch 3km east down the signposted dirt road
on your right, just past the hotel but before
the Rio Cipó bridge.

For camping, continue 5km further north
through the town of Cardeal Mota.

CACHOEIRA TABULEIRO
North of Parque Nacional da Serra do Cipó,
but still within Unesco's Serra do Espinhaço
Biosphere Reserve, is one of Minas's most
spectacular natural treasures: the 273m
Tabuleiro waterfall. It's the third-highest waterfall in Brazil and can most easily be reached
from the small town of Tabuleiro, approximately 180km north of Belo Horizonte.

Five kilometers east of the falls, the **Tabuleiro
Eco Hostel** (☎ 3231 7065, 9638 9641; www.tabuleiroeco
hostel.com.br; Rua Joaquim Costinha 1B, Vila do Tabuleiro;
campsite/dm/s/d HI member R$10/15/40/50, nonmember
R$12/20/50/60; ☎) offers grassy terraces for
camping, plus dorms and private rooms in
a series of colorful buildings running down
the hillside. Breakfast costs R$5 extra, and

soups (R$5) and fixed-price lunches (R$10)
are available when there's enough demand.
There are also some simple restaurants in
town. The hostel owners organize climbing
excursions plus hikes and horseback rides to
nearby cliff paintings, waterfalls, canyons and
swimming holes.

To get from the hostel to the falls, proceed west through downtown Tabuleiro approximately 3km to **Parque Estadual Serra do
Intendente** (admission R$5). From the entrance
station, a well-marked 2km-long trail descends steeply to the river, then peters out,
requiring you to boulder-hop the rest of the
way upstream. The views of the waterfall are
spectacular the whole way. During the dry
season you can swim in the natural pool at
the foot of the falls.

Getting There & Away
Take a Viação Serro bus from Belo Horizonte
to Conceição do Mato Dentro (R$37, four
hours, six daily from 6am to 4pm). The
trick is getting from Conceição to Tabuleiro;
local buses only leave at 3pm on Monday,
Wednesday and Friday, and at 2pm on
Saturday, returning from Tabuleiro at 8am
the same days (R$3, one hour). Buses from
Conceição back to Belo Horizonte run six
times daily between 7am and 6:15pm (4:30pm
on Sunday).

More convenient are the transfers offered
(with advance notice) by the Tabuleiro hostel:
for up to four people the trip to Tabuleiro
costs R$50 from Conceição do Mato Dentro,
R$240 from Belo Horizonte's Confins airport
or R$260 from downtown Belo Horizonte. A
one-way taxi from Conceição to Tabuleiro
costs R$60.

PARQUE NATURAL DO CARAÇA
☎ 0xx31 / elevation 1297m
Near the town of Santa Bárbara, 105km east
of Belo Horizonte, the Parque Natural do
Caraça is a blissful spot. Isolated from the
rest of the world by a mountain ridge, the park
encompasses 110 sq km of transition zone
between the Mata Atlântica (Atlantic rain
forest) and cerrado ecosystems. The park's
centerpiece, nestled in a bowl-shaped valley,
is a former monastery and boarding school
attended by several Brazilian presidents. Now
converted to a pousada, it's still owned and
run by the Catholic congregation who use
the neo-Gothic church for services. The sur-

MINAS GERAIS

THE MANED WOLVES OF CARAÇA

The maned wolf – *lobo guará* in Portuguese – is South America's largest wild canine, living happily in the protected cerrado (savanna) environment of the Parque Natural do Caraça. A few years back, one of Caraça's priests had the idea of befriending the wolves, St Francis style. After two years of patient work gradually tempting them toward the church with offerings of food, he gained the wolves' trust. Nowadays the feeding has become a nightly spectacle, open to the public.

There's no guarantee that you'll see the wolves, but the ritual itself is pure magic. After dinner in the monastery's old stone refectory, people drift out to the patio. The ceremonial plate of scraps for the wolves is placed on the flagstones just past sunset, while popcorn, herb tea, and *cachaça* are provided for the humans. Then the waiting begins. Whether or not the wolves come hardly matters: the pleasure of so many people sitting in one place, trading conversation or looking at the stars, is meaningful in itself.

And then…the patter of feet, a sudden hush rippling through the assembled crowd, the scamper up the steps, the wild eyes of this beautiful creature come to steal a quick meal and then vanish again into the night.

If you see it, it will stick with you for life. If not, you'll find yourself scheming a way to return.

---

rounding countryside includes several mountains – including **Pico do Sol** (at 2070m, the highest point in the Serra do Espinhaço) – as well as creeks forming waterfalls and natural swimming pools. The hillsides are lined with easily accessible hiking trails, all marked on a useful map provided at the park entrance. Most, including the four-hour round-trip to the gorgeous **Cascatona waterfall**, can be undertaken solo. Other, more treacherous trails (indicated in red) require you to hike with a local guide (see www.santuariodocaraca.com.br/turismo/guias.php for a list of guides and their contact info).

Sleeping & Eating

our pick **Pousada Santuário do Caraça** (☎ 3837 2698; www.santuariodocaraca.com.br, in Portuguese; pousadado caraca@hotmail.com; s/d/tr quarto R$70/105/152, s/d/tr/q apartamento from R$105/146/218/264; 🛜) Rooms here range from simple *quartos* (rooms with shared bathroom) off the garden courtyard to swank double *apartamentos* (rooms with bathroom). All rates include three meals, and advance reservations are required. The kitchen serves awesome Mineiro cuisine featuring local produce. In the mornings you can fry your own eggs on the wood-fired stove. The big highlight of staying here is the nightly feeding of the wolves (see boxed text, above). Visit midweek if you can, as it's easier to see the wolves and appreciate Caraça's isolation and tranquility without the crowds of weekend escapees from Belo. During less crowded periods meals are served in the more intimate downstairs dining room.

Getting There & Away

Pássaro Verde operates nine buses daily between Belo Horizonte and Santa Bárbara, the town nearest the park (R$25, 2½ hours, from 6am to 8:30pm). The once-daily Belo–Vitória train (see p241) also makes a stop near the park, in Dois Irmãos (regular/*executivo* R$10/19, leaving Belo Horizonte at 7:30am and arriving at Dois Irmãos at 9am).

From Santa Bárbara or Dois Irmãos, the 30-minute taxi ride to Caraça will cost around R$50. Note that the park gate is only open from 7am to 5pm (or to 9pm for pousada guests).

SOUTHERN MINAS

Such unexpected surprises lurk in this corner of Brazil! Tucked away in the green hills near Minas' southern border with Rio de Janeiro and São Paulo states, you'll find spa towns whose curative waters have been garnering international acclaim since the 19th century, peaceful little valleys just beginning to draw the attention of Brazilian and international ecotourists, and even a hilltop village allegedly favored by extraterrestrials. For anyone who has overdosed on baroque architecture or burned themselves to a crisp at the beach, this quiet corner of Minas is the perfect remedy.

CAXAMBU

☎ 0xx35 / pop 21,400 / elevation 895m

The most venerable of several mineral spa towns in southern Minas – collectively known as the Circuito das Águas – Caxambu is a tranquil resort for the middle class and the elderly, who come to escape the heat of Rio and the madness of Carnaval. Some couples have been escaping here for 30 years or more.

History

Long before Perrier hit Manhattan singles bars, Caxambu water was being celebrated on the international water circuit. Springs were first tapped here in 1870 and medical practitioners were quick to realize the waters' curative properties. Caxambu water took the gold medal in the 1903 Victor Emmanuel III Exposition in Rome, and again in the St Louis International Fair of 1904, and has also attracted other awards.

Caxambu's turn-of-the-century glory is still reflected in its old hotels, and the famous waters continue to be sold throughout Brazil, by the public-private partnership Copasa Águas Minerais de Minas.

Information

Bradesco (Rua Dr Viotti 659)

Espaço Info (Rua Dr Viotti 625; per hr R$2; ☉ 9am-10pm Mon-Sat, 2-10pm Sun) Internet and wireless access.

Post office (Av Camilo Soares) Just east of Parque das Águas.

Secretaria de Turismo (☎ 3341 5701; www.prefeit uramunicipaldecaxambu.blogspot.com, in Portuguese; Praça 16 de Setembro 24; ☉ 8am-6pm Mon-Fri) Helpful office hidden away in the Prefeitura (town hall), one block from the Parque das Águas.

Sights

The **Parque das Águas** (admission R$3, separate fees for attractions inside R$3-12; ☉ 8am-6pm) is a rheumatic's Disneyland; people come to take the waters, smell the sulfur, compare liver spots, watch the geyser spout, rest in the shade by the canal and walk in the lovely gardens. There's a spring-fed outdoor **swimming pool** where you can do laps, plus the ornate **Balneário Hidroterápico**, dating from 1912, where you can soak in a hot bath, take a shower or relax in a sauna.

The park has 12 founts, each housed in its own architectural folly, and each with different properties. Liver problems? Drink from the Dona Leopoldina **magnesium fountain**. Skin disorders? Take the **sulfur baths** of Tereza Cristina. VD? The **Duque de Saxe fountain**

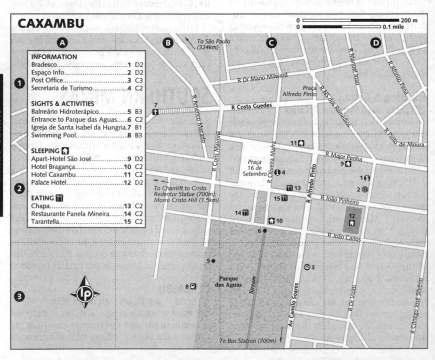

0 ——— 200 m
0 ——— 0.1 mile

To São Paulo (324km)

R Dr Mano Milward

Praça Alfredo Pinto

R Costa Guedes

R Manoel João

R Afonso Pena

R dos Remédios

R Pinto de Moura

R Cons Mavrink

R Américo Macedo

R Major Penha

Praça 16 de Setembro

P Oliveira Mafra

R Alfredo Pinto

R João Pinheiro

To Chairlift to Cristo Redentor Statue (700m); Morro Cristo Hill (1.5km)

R João Carlos

Parque das Águas

Stream

Av Camilo Soares

R Dr Viotti

R Chagas José Silvério

To Bus Station (700m)

MINAS GERAIS

helps calm the bacteria that cause syphilis. Itchy trigger finger? Hit the **rifle range**. And there's much more, from kidney-stone cures to stomach-ailment alleviators to the chairlift climbing 800m to the image of Jesus (Cristo Redentor) atop the **Morro Cristo hill**.

Caxambu gained notoriety when Princesa Isabel (daughter of Brazil's last emperor, Dom Pedro II) visited in 1868. Having tried various treatments for infertility, she finally managed to conceive after taking the miraculous waters of Caxambu. In thanks she built the **Igreja de Santa Isabel da Hungria** on Rua Princesa Isabela.

Sleeping

If you're in Caxambu outside peak holiday times you can get some good deals. The fancier hotels include meals, and many have spas and offer massages.

Apart-Hotel São José (☎ 3341 3133; www.aptsaojose .hpgvip.ig.com.br; Rua Major Penha 264; s/d R$50/80; 🐕 🖭) Quite a lot of amenities are offered at this budget location – including a pool and a gorgeous sauna.

Hotel Bragança (☎ 3341 3366; www.hotelbraganca .com.br; Rua Antônio Miguel Arnaut 34; s/d incl breakfast R$50/105, incl all meals R$90/150) A stone's throw from the Parque das Aguas, the Bragança's slightly faded 19th-century furniture and high ceilings are pleasantly reminiscent of Caxambu's glory days.

Palace Hotel (☎ 3341 3341; www.palacehotel.com.br; Rua Dr Viotti 567; s/d incl meals R$90/130; 🐕 🖭) This colonial establishment is a spectacular deal. The pool out back has a waterslide, and the card-playing rooms downstairs exude 19th-century charm.

Hotel Caxambu (☎ 3341 3300; www.hotelcaxambu .com.br; Rua Major Penha 145; s/d incl breakfast R$140/150, incl all meals R$200/250; 🐾 🐕 🖭) The Hotel Caxambu's historic facade hides a slew of modern amenities. There's a pool and a good restaurant, and it's located right in the center of town.

Eating

Locally produced honey, homemade fruit liqueurs and preserves are sold all over Caxambu.

Chapa (☎ 3341 2600; Rua João Pinheiro 323; per kg R$17.90; 🕙 lunch & dinner) In addition to Caxambu's most affordable per-kilo lunch, Chapa offers an all-you-can-eat evening buffet for R$10.

Restaurante Panela Mineira (☎ 3341 2511; Shop 18-19, Rua Caetano Furquim; per kg R$19.90; 🕙 11:30am-3pm) Half a block from the Parque das Aguas, Panela Mineira serves good Mineiro food by the kilo.

Tarantella (☎ 3341 2161; Rua João Pinheiro 326; mains R$26-48; 🕙 6pm-late) In addition to its classic Italian fare, this cozy restaurant with red-checked tablecloths specializes in smoked trout.

Getting There & Away

The **bus station** is about 1km south of the center on Praça Cônego José de Castilho Moreira.

Destinations include Belo Horizonte (Gardénia, R$65, six hours, 8:10am daily and 10:40pm Sunday to Friday), São Thomé das Letras (Coutinho, R$16, 2¼ hours, 2:15pm, in good weather only) and São Paulo (Cometa, R$46, seven hours, four daily from 8am to midnight). For Rio de Janeiro (R$60, five hours) and Resende (R$27, two hours), gateway to Parque Nacional de Itatiaia, Cidade de Aço runs a daily *executivo* bus at 8am, plus midnight service Sunday to Friday.

AIURUOCA & THE VALE DO MATUTU

☎ 0xx35 / pop 7000 / elevation 989m

About an hour east of Caxambu is the Vale do Matutu, a lush green valley flanked by waterfalls and mountains. Most prominent among the surrounding peaks is the 2293m Pico do Papagaio, which forms the centerpiece of the Parque Estadual da Serra do Papagaio. There's some great hiking in the region, and pousadas have been sprouting like mushrooms in recent years, but thanks to careful planning the surge of development has managed to respect both the land and local residents. Access to the valley is via a rough dirt road running 20km south from the small town of Aiuruoca. You could easily linger here for a few days, relaxing into the rhythms of nature, reading a good book, hiking and swimming.

Information & Sights

At the far end of the valley is the attractive century-old **Casarão do Matutu**, the headquarters of AMA-Matutu, a community organization dedicated to sustainable tourism. If somebody's home, they can provide information about the valley and nearby hiking opportunities. Recommended destinations include **Cachoeira do Fundo**, a nearby waterfall, or the valley's standout attraction, **Pico do Papagaio**.

MINAS GERAIS

If you're doing any serious off-road exploration, it's advisable to go with a guide. Local outfitters offering hikes and horseback excursions include **Portal Matutu Ecoturismo** (www .portalmatutu.com.br) and **MMA Ecoturismo** (www.ajuru .com.br).

Sleeping & Eating

There are hotels throughout the valley, most of which serve meals.

Pousada Dois Irmãos (☎ 3344 1373; Rua Coronel Oswaldo 204, Aiuruoca; s/d R$40/80) This simple hotel is the best option if you arrive in Aiuruoca at night and just need a place to lay your head.

Mandala das Águas (☎ 9948 5650; www.mandala dasaguas.com.br; Vale do Matutu, Km 15; s/d/tr with half-board weekday R$100/180/210, weekend R$110/200/270; ☎) Near the valley's far end, the delightfully tranquil Mandala features spacious rooms, verandas with hammocks, panoramic views of Pico do Papagaio and a raging river below. The American-Brazilian owners use produce from their garden in the hearty homemade meals.

Pousada Pé da Mata (☎ 3344 1421; www.pousada pedamata.com.br; Estrada Aiuruoca/Matutu, Km 12; r/chalet with full board R$160/190) Near a waterfall at the foot of Pico do Papagaio, this lovely pousada has sweeping views over the valley. Meals are cooked on a traditional *fogão à lenha*.

our pick **Kiko & Kika** (☎ 9927 4853; Estrada Aiuruoca/ Alagoa, Km 1.8; mains R$22-41; ☎ lunch daily, dinner Thu-Sat) For fine dining in a rural setting, try this sweet little restaurant just 2km south of Aiuruoca. Run by a couple with roots in France and Switzerland, it specializes in trout – both fresh and smoked – along with earthy touches such as wooden utensils and fresh herbed lemonade.

Getting There & Away

Aiuruoca's bus stop is on the central Praça Côn José Castilho. Viação Sandra operates one daily bus (R$11.60, one hour) from Caxambu to Aiuruoca at 6:20pm, plus a 10am departure on weekdays only. Buses return to Caxambu at 5:20am, 10am and 11:15am on weekdays, 5:20am and 10am Saturday and 6:20am Sunday.

To reach the more remote pousadas in the Vale do Matutu, you'll need your own car (beware the rough road) or a **taxi** (☎ 9964 1601, 3344 1601; one-way/round-trip R$80/150). Once settled in the valley, walking is the most pleasant way to get around.

SÃO THOMÉ DAS LETRAS

☎ 0xx35 / pop 7000 / elevation 1291m

If you're into mysticism or superstition, or just looking for a cheap, fun and idyllic place to relax, consider a detour to the quaint village of São Thomé das Letras, north of Caxambu and southwest of São João del Rei. High on a plateau, with a bird's-eye view of the surrounding farmland, São Thomé feels like a world apart. Perhaps this accounts for its reputation among Brazilian mystics as one of the seven sacred cities of the world. The town's name refers to the puzzling inscriptions on some of the many caverns in the region, and stories of flying saucers and visiting extraterrestrials abound. More down-to-earth attractions include the nearby mountains, caves and waterfalls, as well as the town's buildings, made from beautiful slabs of quartzite.

During the third or fourth weekend in August the three-day **Festa de Agosto** draws lots of pilgrims with live music and other festivities.

Information

São Thomé's **tourist information office** (☎ 3237 1276; turismo@saotomedasletras.mg.gov.br, Rua José Cristiano Alves 4; ☎ 9am-noon & 2-5pm Mon-Fri, 9am-5pm Sat & Sun) is just off the main square, Praça da Matriz. It provides a brochure in Portuguese with a rudimentary map of town and can point you to surrounding natural attractions.

Sights

There are two nice churches in town: **Igreja Matriz de São Thomé** (1785), on beautiful, leafy Praça da Matriz, and the raw-stone **Igreja de Pedra**, downhill towards the bus station.

Next to the Matriz church is the **Gruta de São Thomé**, a small cave containing a shrine to São Thomé, as well as some strange inscriptions. Other nearby caves with inscriptions include **Carimbado** (3km) and **Chico Taquara** (3.5km).

There's a **lookout** 500m uphill from town, with great views at sunset and sunrise.

The popular waterfalls for excursions are **Euboise** (3km), **Prefeitura** (7km) and **Véu de Noiva** (12km).

Sleeping & Eating

Pousada Serra Branca (☎ 3237 1200; www.pousadaser rabranca.com.br, in Portuguese; Rua Capitão João de Deus 7; s/d from R$30/60; ☎) One block uphill from the Gruta de São Thomé, this pousada offers bargain-priced *apartamentos* plus a sauna and a pool.

Pousada Reino dos Magos (☎ 3237 1300; www .reinodosmagos.com.br; Rua Gabriel Luiz Alves 47; s/d/tr/q R$50/77/100/132; ▢) Despite an unpromising exterior, the friendly Pousada Reino provides clean, fan-cooled rooms, including some triples and quads.

Pousada Arco Iris (☎ 3237 1212; www.pousarcoiris .com.br; Rua João Batista Neves 19; s/d from R$80/100; ▢ 🛜 ▢) Very centrally located, in an old stone building, Pousada Arco Iris is the prettiest of São Thomé's budget pousadas. It also has a pool and sauna.

Restaurante da Sinhá (☎ 3237 1348; Rua Capitão Pedro José Martins 31; per kg R$20.90; 🕑 11am-3:30pm Sun-Fri, to 10pm Sat) This family-run self-service place cooks delicious Mineiro food over the wood fire. There's pleasant outdoor seating in the courtyard of the old stone house.

Ser Creativo (☎ 3237 1266; Praça Getúlio Vargas 18; pizzas from R$12; 🕑 6-10pm) An atmospheric evening hangout with a turntable playing scratchy vintage disks, this stone-walled, stone-tabled pizzeria near the top of town wins rave reviews for its extensive menu of wood-fired pizzas.

Restaurante das Magas (☎ 3237 1326; Rua Camilo Rios 2; mains for 2 from R$46; 🕑 11:30am-5pm & 7-11pm Thu-Tue) A friendly spot for a sit-down meal, in a 180-year-old stone house. It specializes in Mineiro food, but also serves pizza.

Getting There & Away

São Thomé's bus station is at Praça Barão de Alfenas, 1km north of the center.

Coutinho runs one direct bus between Caxambu and São Thomé along a rugged but scenic dirt road, in good weather only (R$15.45, 2¼ hours, leaving Caxambu at 2:15pm, returning from São Thomé at 9:15am). Alternatively, Trectur buses (R$8.85, one hour, six daily) connect São Thomé and the nearby town of Três Corações, where you can make onward connections to São Paulo (R$50.85, five hours) or Belo Horizonte (R$61.50, five hours).

EASTERN PARKS

Unforgettable natural experiences reward the intrepid few who make it to this remote corner of Minas. These little-visited parks make nice stopovers for anyone traveling between Belo Horizonte and Vitória in Espírito Santo state.

PARQUE NACIONAL DE CAPARAÓ
☎ 0xx32

This 250-sq-km national park contains southern Brazil's highest mountains, including **Cristal** (2798m), **Calçado** (2766m) and the third-highest peak in the country, **Pico da Bandeira** (2892m). Popular with climbers and hikers from all over Brazil, it affords panoramic views of the Caparaó Valley that divides Minas Gerais and Espírito Santo. The wide open, rocky highlands that predominate here are complemented by a few lush remnants of Mata Atlântica at lower elevations.

The **park entrance** (admission R$10; 🕑 7am-10pm) is 2km straight uphill from the nearest town, Alto do Caparaó. Between November and January there's lots of rain. The best time for clear weather is between June and August – although these are the coldest months. Bring warm clothes!

The classic hike to the summit of Pico da Bandeira can be made without climbing gear or a guide, as the trail is gradual and well marked. It costs about R$60 for a taxi from town to the trailhead at Tronqueira campsite, 8km up a steep dirt road from the park entrance. Cars are prohibited beyond Tronqueira. From here, a gradual 9km climb leads to the summit. Most people go straight up and back to Alto do Caparaó the same day, but with your own tent, you can cross over to the Espírito Santo side of the park, camp overnight, and retrace your steps the following day. The drop-off from Pico da Bandeira on the Espírito Santo side is steeper than on the Minas side, making for some very dramatic views, and there are three waterfalls with idyllic swimming holes – **Farofa**, **Aurélio** and **Sete Pilões** near the last campground, Macieira.

Sleeping & Eating

There are two official campsites on the Minas Gerais side of the park: Tronqueira and Terreirão, 4.5km beyond, which marks the halfway point of the 9km hiking trail from Tronqueira to the summit. On the Espírito Santo side of the park there are two additional campsites: at Casa Queimada, 4.5km down from the summit by trail; and Macieira, 4.5km further by dirt road. Bring all food and supplies with you, and reserve sites in advance by calling **IBAMA** (☎ 3747 2555; per site R$6). All sites have flush toilets and cold showers.

MINAS GERAIS

AN ENDANGERED PRIMATE'S LAST STAND

The *muriqui* (woolly spider monkey), largest primate of the New World, is a stunning creature. Adult males stand roughly 1.5m tall, and their movements and physical presence can be startlingly humanlike. The *muriqui*'s photogenic qualities have made it a poster child for wildlife preservation in Brazil, but actually seeing one in the wild can be challenging. At the time of writing, there were only about 2500 animals left in the world – including only 500 of the rarer northern *muriqui* – down from an estimated 400,000 at the time of Portuguese colonization.

Three factors explain the *muriquis*' drastic drop in numbers: destruction of their native Mata Atlântica (Atlantic rain forest) habitat, their own docile nature (their Tupi name means 'easygoing folks') and the slow pace of their reproductive cycle. Female *muriquis* generally give birth to a single baby after a gestation period of eight months, and newborns stay with their mothers for up to three years, during which time no new mating occurs. *Muriquis* are slow-moving and less combative than most other primates – indeed, they spend most of their time eating, playing and hugging each other! – so they've historically been easy targets for hunters.

Brazil still has a couple of preserved patches of Mata Atlântica where *muriquis* thrive: the Estação Biológica de Caratinga in Minas Gerais (p272), and the Parque Estadual Carlos Botelho in São Paulo state. The former is the easiest place to spot them. Whether or not you visit the preserve, you can donate money to *muriqui* preservation efforts through **Preserve Muriqui** (www .preservemuriqui.org.br/ing/abraco.htm) or **Conservation International** (www.conservation.org).

Pousada Querência Hostel (☎ 3747 2566; www .picodabandeiratur.tur.br; turismoquerencia@uol.com.br; Av Pico da Bandeira 1061; dm/r per person HI member R$25/35) Despite its inconvenient location at the bottom of town, this HI-affiliated hostel has good facilities, including a guest kitchen. It organizes rafting trips and predawn excursions to see sunrise atop Pico da Bandeira. Querência's owners can also drive you to the smaller Rio Claro Hostel, in an ecological reserve 14km away, with hydro power supplied by a waterfall, and lodging for up to 10 people (R$300 per night regardless of group size).

Pousada Vale Verde (☎ 3747 2529; Praça da Matriz; s/d R$30/60) This place offers simple rooms, right near the bus stop on the main square. Meals are available at the restaurant next door.

Pousada do Bezerra (☎ 3747 2628; www.pousada dobezerra.com.br; Av Pico da Bandeira; s/d/tr/q incl breakfast R$79/129/179/229, incl all meals R$99/189/259/329; 🖥 🛜 🛋) The lodging option closest to the park entrance, Bezerra serves delicious trout at its attached restaurant. Full or half-board is available, and there's a sauna.

Getting There & Away

To reach Caparaó by bus from Belo Horizonte or Vitória (Espírito Santo), head first to the tiny town of Manhumirim, 25km outside the park. Pássaro Verde operates buses from Belo to Manhumirim (R$73, six hours, three daily at 7am, 7:30pm and 11:45pm, returning to Belo at 7am, 6pm and midnight). From

Vitória, take Aguia Branca's daily 6:30pm bus direct to Manhumirim (R$32, 4½ hours), or its 7:50am bus from Vitória to Manhuaçu (R$33, 4½ hours), where a Rio Doce bus connects to Manhumirim (R$4.40, 45 minutes, frequent departures between 6:15am and 9:45pm).

Rio Doce runs eight daily buses from Manhumirim to Alto Caparaó (R$4.10, 45 minutes, from 6:30am to 8pm, returning 6:25am to 9:10pm). Alternatively, it's a half-hour taxi ride (R$40). Manhumirim's **Palace Hotel** (☎ 33 3341 2255; Av Lauro Silva 656; s/d without bathroom R$36/55, with bathroom from R$45/70; ❌ 🖥 🛜), diagonally across from the bus station, is perfectly adequate if you're stuck here overnight.

ESTAÇÃO BIOLÓGICA DE CARATINGA
☎ 0xx33

This remote and little-visited nature preserve has played a critical role in rescuing the northern *muriqui* (see the boxed text, above) from extinction. In 1944 there were only eight *muriquis* on record here, when local coffee farmer Feliciano Abdalla committed himself to preserving a large chunk of the native Atlantic rain forest on his property. Forty years later, the protected status of these lands became official with the establishment of the Estação Biológica de Caratinga, and in the quarter-century since, research and preservation efforts have led to greater understanding of the *muriqui* and an impressive resurgence of its numbers. Today there are approximately 270 northern *muriquis* living within the Estação Biológica, representing more than half the world's population. Seeing the primates in their natural habitat is an amazing experience, and visitors have a better-than-average chance of a sighting, thanks to the expert skills of local guides. To arrange a day visit (R$90, including guide), write or call the **park office** (☎ 3322 2540; preservemuriqui@hotmail.com).

Sleeping

Ipanema, the town closest to the park, is your best bet for an overnight stay. Two good sleeping options are **Hotel Samurai** (☎ 3314 1240; Av 7 de Setembro 297; s/d with fan R$40/65, with air-con R$70/100; ✖ 🛜) and **Hotel Italia** (☎ 3314 1793; www.italia palace.com; Av 7 de Setembro 383; s/d with fan R$45/90, with air-con & minibar R$97/140; ✖ 🛜).

Getting There & Away

From Belo Horizonte, Pássaro Verde and Presidente run buses to Ipanema (R$83, nine hours, two daily) and Caratinga (R$64, six hours, five daily), the towns nearest the park. São Geraldo also runs a direct service from Vitória (Espírito Santo) to Caratinga (R$43, six hours, daily at 10:40pm).

From either Caratinga or Ipanema, take a Rio Doce bus (R$13, two hours from Caratinga; R$6, one hour from Ipanema) and ask to be let off at the Estação Biológica. From the bus stop, it's a 2km walk up a dirt road to park headquarters. With prior notice, **Antônio Bragança** (☎ 9962 5434; antonio_braganca@ hotmail.com), the research station's field director, can sometimes provide a ride from Ipanema to the park.

São Paulo State

It is hard to speak of São Paulo state without using superlatives. The region is home to Brazil's largest industrial output, its largest (and most ethnically diverse) population, the richest of its rich, its biggest stock exchange, its busiest port, its finest museums, its worst traffic and its vastest slums. Paulistas, as residents of São Paulo state are known, take pride in their ascendancy, sometimes irking residents of other states in the process, particularly their tetchy neighbors in Rio. But that, to a good Paulista, only proves the point. Everyone's just envious, you see.

With Rio's economic star in eclipse in recent decades (the 2016 Olympics and discovery of oil may change that) and Brasília limited to governmental functions, the sprawling city of São Paulo in many ways serves as the country's de facto capital – commercially, financially, industrially and culturally. If you're doing business in Brazil, this is where you're likely to end up. But there has also been an explosion of interest among sophisticated travelers who are catching wind of the city's extraordinary restaurants, art scene and nightlife.

Still, there are good reasons to escape the clutches of the state's main city. Just beyond the jungle-draped coastal mountains lie some of southern Brazil's finest beaches. The mountainous stretch of coast around Ubatuba is particularly winning. Inland, the area around Campos do Jordão delivers the stunning vistas – and chilly air – of the Serra da Mantiqueira, whose green peaks reach more than 2500m. Further afield, Iporanga sits amid one of the least disturbed areas of Brazilian Atlantic Forest, while the nearby state park boasts hundreds of cataloged caves, making it Brazil's Capital das Grutas (Cave Capital).

HIGHLIGHTS

- Gape at the sheer size of São Paulo city from the art-deco heights of the **Banespa building** (p283)

- Stalk the rich at their preferred eateries and watering holes in São Paulo city's leafy **Jardins district** (p297)

- Determine which of **São Paulo city's legendary nightclubs** (p299) best cater to your unique nightlife needs

- Seek out wild, deserted beaches where mountains meet sea just north of **Ubatuba** (p304)

- Hike amid the green peaks of the **Serra da Mantiqueira** (p313), known as 'Brazil's Switzerland'

Serra da Mantiqueira ★

São Paulo ★   ★ Ubatuba

| ■ TELEPHONE CODE: 11 | ■ POPULATION: 41.4 MILLION | ■ AREA: 248,800 SQ KM |

SÃO PAULO STATE

SÃO PAULO STATE

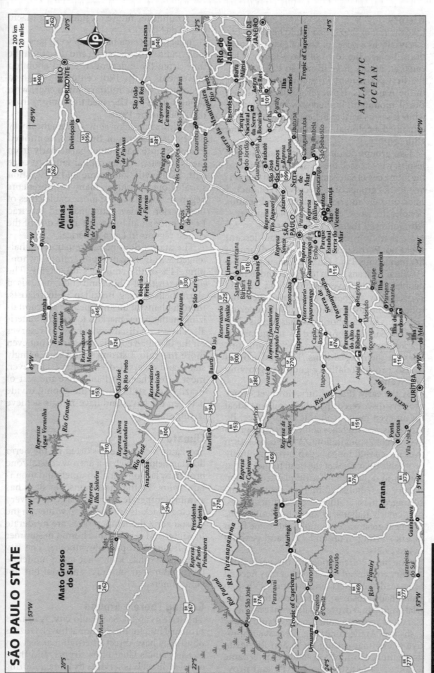

History

Like the rest of Brazil, São Paulo began its life essentially as a series of coastal sugar plantations. In fact, the town of São Vicente – located an hour's drive from São Paulo – was the first permanent Portuguese settlement in the Americas. However, unlike northeast Brazil, mountains limited growing areas and, while it seems hard to believe now, the region remained a colonial backwater well into the 18th century.

Two groups dominated early Paulista life: Jesuits, who crossed the coastal range to found the future city of São Paulo in 1554, and the *bandeirantes* – groups of pioneers who conducted raids into the interior, enslaving indigenous peoples to work the coastal plantations – who followed them. The interior was so remote that even people of European descent spoke not Portuguese but a simplified form of the indigenous Tupi-Guarani language.

When Africans began to replace indigenous peoples on the slave plantations in the late 17th century, the *bandeirantes* tried their fortune hunting for gold, eventually discovering rich veins in neighboring Minas Gerais. The town of São Paulo profited as an important market for *bandeirantes* to stock up on supplies for their expeditions. The land around it also proved relatively good for growing sugarcane.

By the early 19th century, however, sugar growers discovered that their soil was ideal for an even more profitable crop: coffee. By the 1850s vast stretches of the state were given over to coffee plantations. A rail connection over the coastal range began carrying hugely profitable quantities of the bean to the port at Santos, and then on to world markets. When slavery was abolished in 1888, growers encouraged mass immigration of Europeans, particularly Italians, to work the plantations. The next great wave of immigrants came from Japan, starting in around 1910 and peaking in the 1930s.

Crashing coffee prices in the early 20th century convinced investors that they needed to spread their bets, and by the 1950s São Paulo had transformed itself into the industrial engine that drove the national economy. Cars had replaced coffee as São Paulo's new cash crop. At the same time, the vast automotive plants that sprung up in São Bernardo do Campo, south of São Paulo city, became a hotbed of leftist union activity and proving grounds for future president Luíz Inácio (Lula) da Silva.

In fact, the trade unionists were part of a long tradition of liberalism and dissent in the state, from the independence and abolition movements of the 19th century through to opposition to the military junta that, with support from the US, ruled the country from the 1960s to the 1980s.

While immigration slowed dramatically by the 1980s, millions of Brazilians continued to stream into São Paulo, particularly from the Northeast. As the capital failed to cope with its growth, and crime and congestion spiraled out of control, many entrepreneurs began to migrate to the more stable cities of the interior. Today, Campinas and Ribeirão Preto, once small towns, sit amid one of the richest regions in Latin America.

The state's dominance remains unchallenged within Brazil, representing a whopping 34% of the country's total GDP. The mega-growth of China and India has raised alarm bells among Brazilian industrialists, though plenty of businesspeople are capitalizing on these new markets to sell raw materials. The recent discovery of huge oil reserves off the Brazilian coast is also sure to put even more fire into a strong – and increasingly stable and diversified – economy. However, most agree that São Paulo, like the rest of Brazil, must still address the gaping divide between the haves and have-nots to achieve lasting stability.

Climate

São Paulo's coastline is skirted by the Serra do Mar, below which is a narrow coastal zone broken by lagoons, tidal channels and mountain spurs. In the mountains the state has a mild, temperate climate that can be very bracing – jackets are needed in winter. In the coastal zone the temperatures are moderate in winter and very hot and humid in summer with frequent tropical downpours. The city of São Paulo has somewhat more moderate temperatures in summer, and cool but not cold winters.

Getting There & Around

The state's capital, São Paulo city, is Brazil's principal hub for international travel. Dozens of airlines have direct international services to São Paulo's Guarulhos airport, and there are also direct bus services from neighboring countries. The city is also a major center for domestic air travel, with affordable airfares available to cities around Brazil. The state's highway system is among the best in South America, making driving a good option, though São Paulo city itself can be maddening because of poor signage and horrendous traffic. Alternatively, there are also frequent and good long-distance bus services, within the state and to other parts of Brazil.

SÃO PAULO CITY

☎ 0xx11 / pop 11 million / elevation 760m

São Paulo is enormous, intimidating and, at first glance at least, no great beauty – a difficult city for the traveler to master and one that, initially, may not seem worth the sweat. Even the most partisan Paulistano – resident of São Paulo city – will rail about the smog, the traffic, the crumbling sidewalks and the gaping divide between poor and rich. But in the same breath they'll tell you they'd never live anywhere else.

Let them guide you to their favorite haunts, and the reason for this will begin to unfold. Maybe they will introduce you to the city's innumerable art-house cinemas and experimental theaters. If they're gourmands, you'll focus on the smart bistros and jewels of ethnic cuisine. If they're partiers, double up on espresso before embarking on a tour of raucous underground bars and the 24/7 clubbing scene. Whatever manmade pleasure you might covet, Sampa – as the city is known – probably has it in spades.

This fertile cultural life is supported by Brazil's biggest and best-educated middle class and further enriched by literally hundreds of distinct ethnic groups – including the largest community of people of Japanese descent outside Japan. It also has the largest openly gay community in Latin America. Sheer numbers helps too. An estimated 20 million people live in greater São Paulo, making it the third-largest metropolis on earth. Its relentless, round-the-clock pulse – a close cousin of London's or New York's – can prove taxing. Then again, it may just deliver the charge you need to discover one of the world's great cities.

Sampa has always been much more interested in making its fortune than preserving its past, and public spaces are largely neglected in favor of private oases. Beyond a handful of good museums and an increasingly well-preserved historic centre, there are relatively few sights per se. By way of compensation, higher-end restaurateurs, shop owners and impresarios tend to turn their establishments into delightful little worlds unto themselves that are, for better or worse, sealed off to the city's nuisances.

The city occupies a high plateau, making it chilly in the Brazilian winter, and very warm, but rarely stifling hot, in summer. Unfortunately, São Paulo's millions of cars, and its position in a flat basin ringed by mountains, can make smog a serious problem, especially on dry, sunny days. Frequent gray, drizzly weather can be oppressive at times but does keep temperatures moderate and the air relatively clean.

São Paulo will be a host city for the 2014 FIFA World Cup.

HISTORY

The history of the city of São Paulo largely mirrors that of the history of the state. For the first three centuries after the arrival of Jesuits here in 1554, the city grew only gradually as a posting station for fortune hunters heading for the interior, as well as growers from nearby sugar plantations.

Upon Brazil's independence in 1822, São Paulo was declared a state capital, a decision that in turn led to the founding of the College of Law – arguably Brazil's first public institution of higher learning. An increasingly important political and intellectual center, the city was soon leading the fight both to end slavery and to found the republic.

The city's fortunes began to rise in the late 19th century when the region's planters began replacing sugar with the world's new, favorite cash crop: coffee. Some of the coffee barons' mansions still line Av Paulista today. The millions of descendants of immigrants who came to work those plantations – especially Italians and Japanese – are another legacy of the coffee boom.

When coffee prices plummeted at the beginning of the 20th century, there was enough capital left over to transform the city into an industrial powerhouse. Factory jobs attracted a new wave of immigrants from around the world, and the city's population practically doubled every decade between 1920 and 1980. In the 1980s, foreign immigration slowed, but laborers streamed in from the

SÃO PAULO STATE

SÃO PAULO

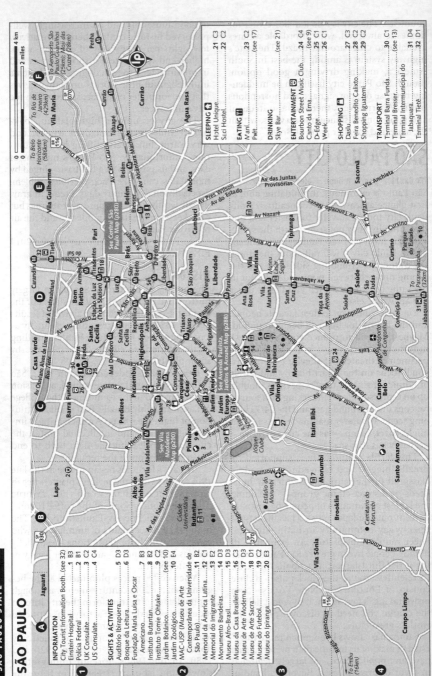

INFORMATION
City Tourist Information Booth....	(see 32)
Einstein Hospital...................	1 B3
Polícia Federal....................	2 B1
UK Consulate.......................	3 C2
US Consulate.......................	4 C4

SIGHTS & ACTIVITIES
Auditório Ibirapuera................	5 D3
Bosque da Leitura..................	6 D3
Fundação Maria Luísa e Oscar	
Americano.........................	7 B3
Instituto Butantan.................	8 B2
Instituto Tomie Ohtake..............	9 C2
Jardim Botânico....................	(see 10)
Jardim Zoológico...................	10 E4
MAC-USP (Museu de Arte	
Contemporânea da Universidade de	
São Paulo).......................	11 B2
Memorial da América Latina.........	12 C1
Memorial do Imigrante..............	13 E2
Monumento Bandeiras................	14 D3
Museu Afro-Brasil..................	15 D3
Museu da Casa Brasileira...........	16 C3
Museu de Arte Moderna..............	17 D3
Museu de Arte Sacra................	18 D1
Museu do Futebol...................	19 C2
Museu do Ipiranga..................	20 E3

SLEEPING
Hotel Unique.......................	21 C3
Sesc Hostel........................	22 C2

EATING
A'rani.............................	23 C2
Piet..............................	(see 17)

DRINKING
Skye Bar..........................	(see 21)

ENTERTAINMENT
Bourbon Street Music Club..........	24 C4
Canto da Ema.......................	(see 9)
D-Edge............................	25 C1
Week.............................	26 C1

SHOPPING
Daslu.............................	27 C3
Feira Benedito Calixto..............	28 C3
Shopping Iguatemi..................	29 C2

TRANSPORT
Terminal Barra Funda................	30 C1
Terminal Bresser...................	(see 13)
Terminal Intermunicipal do	
Jabaquara........................	31 D4
Terminal Tietê.....................	32 D1

drought-stricken Northeast. Many found work building the city's new skyscrapers. Unfortunately, growth far outpaced investment in the city's infrastructure. Today's serious traffic congestion and poorly urbanized slums are the visible result.

In recent years, São Paulo's explosive population growth has slowed, though it is now firmly established as Brazil's banking, industrial and cultural capital. As such it is enjoying the lion's share of Brazil's current economic boom. The city is making strides toward modernizing its infrastructure, including significant expansions of its metro, suburban train and highway systems. It has also finally begun to protect its historic center as well as to improve the condition of its public spaces. Traffic, crime and pollution still flummox city leaders and remain serious problems. But the dynamism of its culture and economy is still attracting the best and brightest from all over Brazil and beyond.

ORIENTATION

Because it grew at dizzying speeds and without a master plan, São Paulo has no single grid of streets but rather a hodgepodge of grids in more or less concentric circles that radiate out from the historic center. This, together with a dearth of easily identifiable landmarks, means it's easy to get hopelessly lost.

There is some good news. First, most places of interest are clustered between the historic center and Av Paulista, an area that can easily be navigated by foot – if you have a good map. Second, a safe, efficient metro also connects most central sites as well as a number of further-flung neighborhoods.

Sitting atop a low ridge and lined with skyscrapers, Av Paulista is the city's main drag, dividing its largely working-class Centro from tonier neighborhoods to the south. At its western end, Av Paulista is crossed by the corridor made up of Av Rebouças and Rua da Consolação, which roughly divides the city's eastern and western halves.

To the north of Av Paulista lies what is generally called Centro, including Praça da República and around; the traditionally Italian Bela Vista area (also known as Bixiga); Luz, a newly refurbished cultural hub; the traditionally Japanese Liberdade; and the old commercial and historic core around Praça da Sé and its cathedral, including Triângulo and Anhangabaú.

Extending for about 10 blocks south of Paulista is the leafy neighborhood known as Jardins (the neighborhood's official name is Jardim Paulista), which has a lion's share of the city's tony restaurants and boutiques. Further south is the leafy, low-rise and exclusively residential area known as Jardim Europa and also the slightly less exclusive Jardim America. Southeast of Jardim Europa is sprawling Parque do Ibirapuera, while to the west lie the upscale neighborhoods of Pinheiros and Vila Madalena. South of Jardim Europa lie the upmarket bastions of Vila Olímpia and Itaím Bibi, both of which are increasingly important business centers.

The city's international airport is located 30km east of the city center and has good connections by airport bus as well as taxi. The city's domestic airport is about 8km south of the city center and easily reached by taxi or city bus. Four intercity bus stations are spread around the city, though all are at or very near a stop of the city's excellent metro. For more information on getting around the city, see p303.

Maps

The *Guia São Paulo* by Quatro Rodas is probably the best guide for navigating the city, with street maps, hotel and restaurant listings and bus lines. It has the clearest presentation of any street directory. Pick one up at any kiosk around town for about R$30.

Tourist offices also offer a free, user-friendly map covering all of the city's most relevant neighborhoods.

INFORMATION
Bookstores

Livraria Cultura (Map p288; ☎ 3170 4033; Av Paulista 2073; ☽ 9am-10pm Mon-Sat, noon-8pm Sun) Spread out over three stores on the ground floor of the Conjunto Nacional building, this is hands-down the city's best bookstore. There is a large selection of both English-language books and travel guides, plus a pleasant café.

Livraria da Vila (Map p288; ☎ 3062 1063; Alameda Lorena 1731; ☽ 10am-11pm Mon-Sat, 11am-8pm Sun) A gem of contemporary architecture as well as a fine bookstore.

Emergency

Deatur Tourist Police (Map p280; ☎ 3257 4475; Rua Consolação 247) A special police force just for tourists, with English-speaking officers.

CENTRAL SÃO PAULO

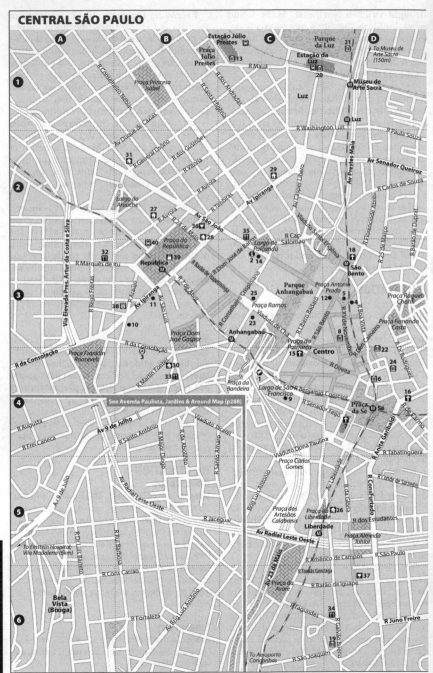

SÃO PAULO STATE

INFORMATION
Canada Consulate	1 C4
City Tourist Information Booth	2 C3
Deatur Tourist Police	3 B4
Post Office	(see 23)

SIGHTS & ACTIVITIES
Banespa	4 D3
Bovespa	5 D3
Caixa Cultural	6 D4
Catedral da Sé	7 D4
Centro Cultural Banco do Brasil	8 D3
College of Law	9 C4
Edifício Copan	10 B3
Edifício Itália	11 B3
Edifício Martinelli	12 D3
Estação Júlio Prestes	13 C1
Galeria do Rock	14 C3
Igreja de Santo Antônio	15 C4
Igreja de São Francisco de Assis	(see 9)
Igreja do Carmo	16 D4
Mercado Municipal	17 E2
Mosteiro São Bento	18 D3
Museu da Imigração Japonesa	19 D6
Museu da Língua Portuguesa	20 C1
Pinacoteca do Estado	21 D1
Páteo do Colégio	22 D4
Shopping Light	23 C3
Solar da Marquesa	24 D4
Theatro Municipal	25 C3

SLEEPING
Akasaka	26 D5
Hotel Itamarati	27 B2
Hotel Marabá	28 B2
Normandie Design Hotel	29 C2
Novotel Jaraguá São Paulo	30 B4
São Paulo Hostel Downtown	31 B2

EATING
ABC Bailão	32 A3
Estadão	33 B4
Lamen Asaka	34 D6
Ponto Chic	35 C2
Terraço Itália	(see 11)

DRINKING
Bar Brahma	36 B2
Café Floresta	(see 10)
Choperia Liberdade	37 D6

ENTERTAINMENT
Love Story	38 B3
Sala São Paulo	(see 13)
Theatro Municipal	(see 25)

SHOPPING
Feira da República	39 B3

TRANSPORT
Bus to Airports	40 B3

Internet Access
Cyber (Map p288; Rua Augusta 2346, Jardins; per hr R$5; 8:30am-10:30pm Mon-Sat, 10am-10pm Sun) Comfortable, air-conditioned and conveniently located, with fast connections.

Medical Services
Einstein Hospital (3747 1301/0405; Av Albert Einstein 627, Morumbi) Located on a southwestern corner of the city in Morumbi, Einstein is one of the best in Latin America.

Sírio-Libânes Hospital (Map p288; 3155 0200; Rua Dona Adma Jafet 91) Another recommended hospital in Bela Vista, near Av Paulista.

Money
Except on weekends, changing money at banks and exchange offices is easy. ATMs are widely available throughout the city. Note that most are closed from 10pm to 6am for security reasons. Many travel agencies and exchange offices around the city offer good rates, but avoid the smaller ones downtown – some are illegal and may rip you off.

Post
Post office Shopping Light (Map p280; Rua Xavier de Toledo; 10am-6pm Mon-Fri); Av Paulista (Map p288; Alameda Santos 2224; 9am-5pm Mon-Fri)

Tourist Information
Designed for both travelers and Anglophone expats, www.gringoes.com has lots of information in English covering restaurants to nightclubs, plus a free weekly newsletter about goings-on about town. Pick up a *Guia da Folha* at any newsstand for reviews of the city's dining, entertainment and nightlife options (also available at www1.folha.uol.com.br/guia, in Portuguese). The weekly magazine *Veja São Paulo* also has listings.

City tourist information booths (6224 0400; www.cidadedesaopaulo.com) all have good city maps, as well as helpful walking maps for individual neighborhoods. They also offer a monthly events listing guide, as well as a guide specifically for the gay and lesbian community. English is spoken. Locations include the following:

Aeroporto São Paulo/Guarulhos (6am-10pm) Kiosks in Terminals 1 and 2 at the international airport.

Avenida Paulista (Map p288; Av Paulista 1853; 8am-8pm)

Avenida São João (Map p280; Av São João 473; 9am-6pm)

Terminal Tietê bus station (Map p278; ☉ 6am-10pm) In the city's main intercity bus station.

Visas

Polícia Federal (Map p278; ☎ 3616 2166; Rua Hugo Dantola 95, Lapa; ☉ 8am-4:30pm Mon-Fri) For visa extensions, head to this office about 4km west of the Barra Funda metro.

DANGERS & ANNOYANCES

While crime levels remain high in São Paulo, the worst is largely limited to the city's periphery. During the day, you can walk most places in central São Paulo, though always exercise normal precautions. After dark, you can still walk around Av Paulista, Jardins and Rua Augusta, as well as the more chic neighborhoods of the Zona Sul (Vila Madalena, Pinheiros and Vila Olímpia), but avoid empty side streets and carry as few valuables as possible. Centro and Praça da República require more vigilance, and walking should be avoided after dark where possible – grab a taxi instead.

If you're driving, be aware that carjackings and red-light robberies can occur anywhere in the city. It's now legal (and recommended) to just slow down at red lights at night. If there's no traffic, continue without stopping. The subway is generally safe, although you should keep your eyes open; on buses, look out for pickpockets, and at night consider taxis over public transportation.

SIGHTS
Praça da Sé & Around

The old heart of the city, Praça da Sé (literally, 'Cathedral Square') has seen better days but still draws animated crowds, from street hawkers and nose-down business types to – unfortunately – more than its fair share of pickpockets and homeless people. Crowning the square is the domed **Catedral da Sé** (Map p280; ☉ 8am-5pm), a huge neo-Byzantine concoction that, for better or worse, replaced the original 18th-century structure in the 1920s. Still, its lush interior is worth a gander. On the other side of Praça da Sé stands the more modest but also more authentic **Igreja do Carmo** (Map p280), which dates to the 1630s and still preserves its original high altar. At the time of writing it was closed indefinitely for major restorations.

About 700m north of the cathedral, **Rua 25 de Março** is the traditional preserve of the city's Lebanese merchants and remains a lively, crowded wholesale shopping district where you can find remarkable deals on a variety of goods, from clothing to electronics.

CAIXA CULTURAL

This **cultural center** (Map p280; ☎ 3321 4400; www .caixacultural.com.br, in Portuguese; Praça da Sé 111; admission free; ☉ 9am-9pm Tue-Sun), sponsored by Brazil's state-owned Caixa Economica bank, occupies a grand, neoclassical-style building with an imperious facade of black marble. Temporary exhibits of major Brazilian artists are shown on the first two floors, and the executive office suite on the 6th floor has been turned into an oddly fascinating museum of the bank's history.

IGREJA DE SÃO FRANCISCO DE ASSIS

Built in the 17th and 18th centuries, this **church** (Map p280; Largo de São Francisco) just west of the cathedral is one of the best-preserved colonial structures in the city (note that there are actually two churches adjacent to each other, each with the same name; the church to the right also dates to the 17th century but is less architecturally important). The church, a classic example of Portuguese baroque, was closed for a major restoration at the time of research. Next to it is the prestigious **College of Law** (Map p280). Founded in 1827, it is considered to be Brazil's oldest institution of higher learning, though the current building dates to the early 20th century. The college is not open to the public.

MERCADO MUNICIPAL

This covered **market** (Map p280; www.mercadomunicipal .com.br, in Portuguese; Rua da Cantareira 306; ☉ 6am-6pm Mon-Sat, to 4pm Sun) is a belle époque confection of stained glass and a series of vast domes. Inside is a delightful market specializing in fresh produce and dried goods. It's also a great place to sample a couple of classic Sampa delights: mortadella sandwiches and *pasteis*, pockets of dough stuffed with meat, cheese or fish and then fried. Many Sundays there is live music, but note that approximately one Sunday per month, the market closes for maintenance. Unfortunately, there is no regular schedule for these closings.

SOLAR DA MARQUESA

Down a narrow side street near the cathedral stands the city's last surviving 18th-century residence, Solar da Marquesa (Map p280). A simple but delightful villa that was once home to a lover of Emperor Dom Pedro I, it now houses a modest museum devoted to the history of the city, though at the time of writing, it was closed indefinitely for major repairs.

PÁTEO DO COLÉGIO

Just up the street from Solar da Marquesa lies a **mission** (Map p280; ☎ 3105 6899; www.pateodocolegio .com.br, in Portuguese; Praça Páteo do Colégio; adult/student R$5/2.50; ⏲ 9am-4:45pm Tue-Fri, to 4:30pm Sat-Sun) that occupies the exact spot where São Paulo was founded in 1554 by Jesuit brothers José de Anchieta and Manoel da Nóbrega. The current structure is actually a 1950s replica of the monastery that once stood here, although inside it does possess a nice little collection of original relics from the city's first days, as well as an interesting set of drawings that chart the city's growth over the last five centuries. The museum's café also makes for a tranquil pit stop. The square in front includes a memorial column commemorating the founding of the city, and there is a series of beautiful early 20th-century government buildings arrayed around the square.

Triângulo & Anhangabaú

Just north of Praça da Sé lies the Triângulo, a triangle bounded roughly by Praça da Sé, Mosteiro São Bento and the Prefeitura (city hall). It has narrow, pedestrian-only streets and towering office buildings that in the late 19th and early 20th centuries served as the city's commercial heart. Even if Av Paulista and Vila Olímpia now attract the big money, the Triângulo still does a brisk trade, thanks largely to the presence of **Bovespa** (Map p280; ☎ 3233 2000; www.bovespa.com.br; Rua XV (15) de Novembro 275; admission free; ⏲ 10am-6pm Mon-Fri), Latin America's largest stock exchange. There is no longer a live trading floor to visit, but the beautiful main lobby serves as a de facto museum, with small but often excellent temporary exhibits of Brazilian art.

Just west of Bovespa rises the 35-story **Edifício Martinelli** (Map p280; Rua São Bento 405). São Paulo's first skyscraper, the soaring 1929 Beaux Arts structure seems to have been imported wholesale from turn-of-the-century Manhattan. The building doesn't accept visitors.

At the northern edge of the Triângulo, you'll find the austere but impressive **Mosteiro São Bento** (Map p280; ☎ 3328 8794; www.mosteiro.org .br, in Portuguese; admission free; ⏲ 6am-6pm Mon-Wed &

Fri, 2-6pm Thu, 6am-noon & 4-6pm Sat & Sun), which is among the city's oldest and most important churches, though its neo-Gothic facade dates only to the early 20th century. Step inside the church to witness its impressive stained glass. Mass at 10am on Sundays generally includes Gregorian chanting.

On the small Praça do Patriarca at the southwestern entrance to Triângulo, the more modest, better-preserved **Igreja de Santo Antônio** (Map p280; admission free; ⏲ 6am-6pm Mon-Fri, to noon & 4-6pm Sat & Sun) retains many of its original 18th-century contours.

Heading west from Praça do Patriarca, you'll cross the 1892 **Viaduto de Chá**, which crosses the Vale do Anhangabaú, along with the **Viaduto Santa Efigênia** a little to the north and dating from the same era. Both of these elaborate cast-iron bridges were long synonymous with São Paulo's cultural and economic ascendancy. In the Tupi-Guarani language, Anhangabaú means Demon's Valley, and indigenous peoples believed evil spirits dwelled there. The area can still be dicey after dark. Across Viaduto de Chá lies **Shopping Light** (Map p280; ☎ 3154 2299; Viaduto de Chá; ⏲ 9am-9pm Mon-Fri, 10am-7pm Sat), a modern, midrange mall with a decent food court on the 5th floor.

CENTRO CULTURAL BANCO DO BRASIL

Housed in an extraordinarily and lovingly restored Beaux Arts building, this **cultural center** (Map p280; ☎ 3113 3651; www.bb.com.br/cultura, in Portuguese; Rua Álvares Penteado 112; admission free; ⏲ 10am-8pm Tue-Sun) holds innovative exhibitions of contemporary art as well as excellent film series and theater performances.

BANESPA

For one of Sampa's best panoramas, head to the top of this **skyscraper** (Map p280; Rua João Brícola 24; ⏲ 10am-3pm Mon-Fri), Brazil's version of the Empire State Building, completed in 1939. Ride free to the observation deck on the top floor for views of the city. Note, you will need some form of ID to sign in. You will also have to wait in two lines, first to sign in and then to wait for an elevator to the top. Note that if lines are long, you will only get about 10 minutes at the top.

THEATRO MUNICIPAL

São Paulo's most splendid construction, this **theater** (Map p280; ☎ 3397 0300; www.teatromunicipal .sp.gov.br, in Portuguese; Praça Ramos de Azevedo) was begun in 1903 in the style of Paris' Palais Garnier. Its heavily ornamented facade seems to combine every architectural style imaginable, from baroque to art nouveau, and its interior is clad in gold and marble. The theater hosts the city's top classical music, opera and ballet performances. At the time of writing, it was undergoing a major, multiyear restoration, with no fixed date for reopening.

Praça da República & Around

Just a few blocks northwest of Anhangabaú lies Praça da República, an always-lively square that turns into an open-air market on Saturdays and Sundays, specializing in crafts, paintings, coins and gemstones. The area north of the square has become a center popular with the gay community (see p300), while to the south lies a dense nest of business hotels, huge office buildings and, especially along **Avenida São Luís**, what were once some of the city's most prestigious apartment buildings.

For Caetano Veloso fans, a visit to the corner of **Avenida Ipiranga** and **Avenida São João**, which features in his beloved song 'Sampa,' is mandatory. There are no sights to speak of, but the bustling intersection does do a good job of summing up the city.

EDIFÍCIO ITÁLIA

With 46 stories, this **skyscraper** (Map p280; Av Ipiranga 344) just south of the Praça da República, and near Av São Luís, is the tallest in the city center. Its top-floor restaurant, **Terraço Italia** (☎ 2189 2929; www.terracoitalia.com.br; ☽ noon–11pm), offers some of the best views of São Paulo, though meal prices are high and the food only passable. Strictly speaking, you're supposed to be a customer to go there; if you're not, act like one. Alternately, head to the bar just for a (pricey) drink.

EDIFÍCIO COPAN

Shorter but architecturally more remarkable, the nearby **Edifício Copan** (Map p280; Av Ipiranga 200) was designed by modernist master Oscar Niemeyer. The building's serpentine facade and narrow *brises soleil* (permanent sunshades) have become a symbol of the city. You can visit its snaking, sloping ground-floor shopping arcade, but the upper floors are made up of private apartments and thus off limits. Note that the leftist architect designed the building to bring together all classes by

including sprawling apartments for the rich as well as tiny studios for the working poor – a real rarity in class-conscious São Paulo.

GALERIA DO ROCK

Even if you're not in the market for a skateboard or a new tattoo, this seven-floor **shopping center** (Map p280; Av São João 439; ☽ 10am-8pm Mon-Fri, to 5pm Sat) is an anthropologically fascinating gathering point for São Paulo's underground communities, from punks to goths to metal heads. Hundreds of shops hawk everything from CDs and concert T-shirts to black capes and extreme piercing.

Luz

Located in a tough area just north of the city center, the Luz neighborhood has become an unlikely cultural hub thanks to major restoration of a series of grand turn-of-the-century buildings around the **Parque da Luz**. The park has also undergone a careful restoration, with spreading, tropical trees, discreetly placed modern sculpture and a generous police presence.

Across the street from the park sits **Estação da Luz** (Map p280; Praça da Luz), a classic late-Victorian train station constructed with materials entirely shipped in from Britain and completed in 1901. It too has been returned to something close to its original splendor. It services São Paulo's extensive suburban lines, with a long tunnel linking it to the Luz metro station.

PINACOTECA DO ESTADO

This elegant neoclassical **museum** (Map p280; State Art Museum; ☎ 3324 1000; www.pinacoteca.org.br; Praça da Luz 2; adult/student incl admission to Estação Pinacoteca R$6/3; ☽ 10am-6pm Tue-Sun) houses an excellent collection of Brazilian – and especially Paulista – art from the 19th century to present, including works by big names such as Portinari and Di Cavalcanti. Extensive renovations have made it a pleasant place to while away a rainy afternoon, and there is an attractive café that spills out into the adjacent Parque da Luz.

MUSEU DA LÍNGUA PORTUGUESA

Half of Estação da Luz has been given over to this **museum** (Map p280; ☎ 3326 0775; www.poiesis.org.br/mlp; Praça da Luz; adult/student R$6/3; ☽ 10am-6pm, last admission 5pm), with fascinating permanent exhibits documenting the rise of the Brazilian language as distinct from European

Portuguese, as well as creative temporary installations celebrating Brazilian literature. Note, though, that all accompanying signs are in Portuguese only.

ESTAÇÃO JÚLIO PRESTES

A short walk west of Estação da Luz is this far larger and grander **train station** (Map p280; Largo General Osório 66) in turn-of-the-century Beaux Arts style, though only completed in the 1930s. One wing houses the **Estação Pinacoteca** (☎ 3324 1000; www.pinacoteca.org.br; adult/student incl admission to Pinacoteca do Estado R$6/3; ☼ 10am-6pm Tue-Sun), an annex of the Pinacoteca do Estado, which hosts two floors of large and often very good temporary exhibitions, mostly of Brazilian art. The permanent collection of modernist Brazilian art is also excellent. The ground floor houses the **Memorial da Liberdade** (admission free; ☼ 10am-5pm Tue-Sun), a simple but powerful exhibit occupying cells used to imprison and torture political dissidents during Brazil's military dictatorship of the 1960s and '70s. Also in the Estação Júlio Prestes complex is the world-renowned **Sala São Paulo** (☎ 3367 9500; www.salasaopaulo.art.br, in Portuguese), a classical-music venue that cleverly occupies the station's principal waiting room. Part of the station is still a stop on the suburban train system.

MUSEU DE ARTE SACRA

The best of its kind in Brazil, this **museum** (Museum of Sacred Art; Map p278; ☎ 3326 1373; www.museu artesacra.org.br; Av Tiradentes 676; adult/student R$6/3; ☼ 11am-7pm, last admission 6:30pm Tue-Sun) includes

---

BRAZIL'S MELTING POT

Brazil's unparalleled racial and ethnic diversity means there is no such thing as a typical Brazilian face. That's why Brazilian passports are highly sought after on the black market. Many faces could pass for being Brazilian.

It is especially hard to say someone is a typical Paulistano. The city has been multiracial from its foundation in the 16th century, bringing together Portuguese, African and indigenous peoples. Since then, wave after wave of immigration has given the city a truly global face. Italian and Spanish immigrants poured into the country to pick coffee after Brazil emancipated slaves in 1888, and today their descendants number about five and three million respectively. These were followed by Japanese immigrants, and today São Paulo has more Japanese descendants (about 1.5 million) than anywhere else outside of Japan. Likewise, São Paulo has more Lebanese descendants (850,000) than anywhere outside Lebanon. Sampa is also home to Brazil's largest Jewish community, with some 130,000 members. There are one million people of German stock and, as well, sizable Chinese, Armenian, Lithuanian, Greek, Syrian, Korean, Polish and Hungarian communities.

For a deeper understanding of the history of immigration to São Paulo, head to the **Memorial do Imigrante** (Map p278; ☎ 6693 0917; www.memorialdoimigrante.sp.gov.br, in Portuguese; Rua Visconde de Paraiba 1316; adult/student R$4/2; ☼ 10am-5pm Tue-Sun) in the eastern suburb of Moóca. Built in 1887, it was called the **Hospedaria dos Imigrantes**, and functioned as a holding place – not always friendly – for immigrant labor before they shipped out for their first jobs in Brazil, mostly on large plantations.

The dorm rooms are immense, and one can still see the huge sliding rails that were used to bring in truckloads of people and luggage, fresh from the dock. To the millions of immigrants who came to São Paulo hoping for a better life, it must have seemed more of a prison than a hostel. Although designed to hold up to 4000 people, records show that as many as 10,000 individuals were housed there at one time. Translators explained the work contracts the immigrants were signing – many of which proved punishingly unfair. There were guards and wardens to make sure people didn't slip away – not everyone who got off the boat wanted to break their back picking coffee. Of course, a guarantee of work was the only way out of the *hospedaria*.

The museum itself has a permanent collection of period furnishings, some old documents and photographs, and often hosts visiting exhibitions that explore the nature of emigration and national identity.

To get to the memorial take the metro to Bresser. It's a five-minute walk from there, or on weekends you can take the little tram that shuttles visitors back and forth.

works by renowned 18th-century sculptor Antônio Aleijadinho, along with some 200 other ecclesiastical works from the 17th to 20th centuries. The museum is housed in the 18th-century Luz monastery, which is one of São Paulo's best-preserved buildings of the period and also a fine example of Portuguese colonial architecture. A new annex houses an amazingly large and elaborate Neapolitan manger scene, plus a collection of other manger scenes from around the world.

Liberdade

São Paulo is home to the largest population of Japanese descendants outside Japan, and the Liberdade neighborhood – a short walk south of Praça da Sé – has long been the traditional center of this community. Though most new Asian immigrants these days come from China and Korea, the gritty neighborhood is still lined with traditional Japanese shops and eateries.

Praça da Liberdade is the neighborhood's main square and also the location of its metro stop. It hosts an open-air market on Sundays. A short walk south on Rua Galvão Bueno takes you past many Asian shops and restaurants as well as some rather neglected Japanese-style gardens.

MUSEU DA IMIGRAÇÃO JAPONESA

This modest but fascinating **museum** (Museum of Japanese Immigration; Map p280; ☎ 3209 5465; Rua São Joaquim 381; adult/student R$5/2.50; ☑ 1:30-5:30pm Tue-Sun), on the 7th floor of a Liberdade office building, documents the arrival and integration of the Japanese community. Photos, period objects and a full-scale reconstruction of a typical immigrant's farm lodging tell a poignant story, from the arrival in Santos of the first 781 settlers aboard the *Kasato-Maru* in 1908 through to today. Signage is in Japanese and Portuguese only.

Higienópolis, Pacaembu & Barra Funda

Northwest of Av Paulista lies the leafy neighborhood of Higienópolis, one of the most traditional of the city's upscale neighborhoods and a good spot for a stroll. Praça Buenos Aires, a tree-filled, European-style square, serves as the neighborhood's lungs and playground. As you continue northwest, you pass through Pacaembu, a low-rise neighborhood of ramblingly luxurious homes reminiscent of upscale Los Angeles. Finally, you reach Barra

Funda, a more workaday neighborhood that at night comes alive with some of the city's trendiest nightclubs.

MUSEU DO FUTEBOL

Tucked under the bleachers of a colorfully art-deco Pacaembu Stadium, the city's newest **museum** (Museum of Soccer; Map p278; ☎ 3664 3848; www.museudofutebol.org.br; Praça Charles Miller s/n; adult/student R$6/3; ☑ 10am-6pm, last admission 5pm Tue-Sun) is devoted to Brazil's greatest passion – football (soccer). Its multimedia displays over two floors manage to evoke the thrill of watching a championship game, even for nonfans. Most signage is in Portuguese only.

MEMORIAL DA AMÉRICA LATINA

Another Niemeyer creation, the **Memorial da América Latina** (Map p278; ☎ 3823 4600; www.memorial.sp.gov.br, in Portuguese; Av Auro Soares de Moura Andrade 664; admission free; ☑ 9am-6pm Tue-Sun) is like a mini-Brasília, with a series of glass-and-cement structures in a beautiful if unsettling variety of shapes and sizes. While it looks uninviting at first glance, the sprawling complex has undergone renovations to make it more welcoming – and interesting – to visitors. The Salão dos Atos is a ceremonial space where you can see Cândido Portinari's enormous painting *Tiradentes*. The perfectly round Galeria Marta Traba de Arte Latino-Americano displays contemporary art from around Latin America. And the Pavilhão de Criatividade displays a diverse collection of Latin American arts and crafts.

Avenida Paulista, Jardins & Around

Once the domain of coffee barons and their sprawling manses, Av Paulista (often known simply as 'Paulista') began to go 'Manhattan' in the 1950s and today is lined with towering modernist office buildings. Though few of these buildings have much architectural merit, the sum of the parts is impressive. It's also a lively area both day and night, packed with restaurants, shops, theaters and cafés. Just off Paulista across from the Museu de Arte de São Paulo (MASP; see p288) lies **Parque Siqueira Campos** (☑ 6am-6pm), a beautifully designed and maintained park that re-creates the Atlantic rain forest that was leveled to build São Paulo. It's a remarkably tranquil refuge just off the city's busiest street.

North of Paulista, **Rua Augusta** is São Paulo's traditional red-light district, and at night the traffic slows to a crawl as johns troll the sidewalks from their cars. However, the area is quickly being taken over by a combination of gay, fashion-forward and alternative crowds (often all three), and its bars and nightclubs are packed after 10pm with the young, high-minded and multiply pierced.

On the southern slope of Paulista lies Jardins, the city's leafiest and most chic central neighborhood. This is where you will find some of the city's most over-the-top shopping, especially along Alameda Lorena and, above all, **Rua Oscar Freire**, with its showstopping series of boutiques and super-refined eateries.

MUSEU DE ARTE DE SÃO PAULO (MASP)

Sampa's pride, this **museum** (Map p288; ☎ 3251 5644; www.masp.art.br, in Portuguese; Av Paulista 1578; adult/student R$15/7; ☼ 11am-6pm Tue-Sun, last admission 5pm, to 8pm Thu, last admission 7pm) possesses Latin America's most comprehensive collection of Western art. Hovering above a concrete plaza that turns into an antiques fair on Sundays (see p302), the museum, designed by architect Lina Bo Bardi and completed in 1968, is considered a classic of modernism by many and an abomination by a vocal few. The collection, though, is unimpeachable, and ranges from Goya to El Greco to Manet. The impressionist collection is particularly impressive. There are also a few great Brazilian paintings, including three fine works by Cândido Portinari. The museum hosts temporary exhibits, and there is a bright, pleasant cafeteria on the lower level which hosts a very good buffet lunch for around R$30.

Regrettably, the museum seems rather neglected by its guardians, with public areas looking shabby in places. More shocking was the theft in 2007 of paintings by Portinari and Picasso, which revealed that a museum with a billion-dollar collection lacked motion detectors or cameras with infrared capabilities. Fortunately, the two paintings were eventually recovered, though the identity of the thieves was never revealed.

CASA DAS ROSAS

Housed in a classic mansion in the style of the coffee barons, this **cultural center** (Map p288; ☎ 3285 6986; www.casadasrosas-sp.org.br, in Portuguese; Av Paulista 37; admission free; ☼ 10am-10pm Tue-Sat, to 6pm Sun) was originally built in 1928 by Ramos de Azevedo, the 'starchitect' of his era. The house, which hosts occasional art exhibits and concerts, is a reminder of what Av Paulista was like before it went vertical.

Parque do Ibirapuera

The biggest green space in central São Paulo, Parque do Ibirapuera makes a fine escape from the city's seemingly infinite stretches of concrete. In addition, the leafy 2-sq-km park serves as a thriving center of the city's cultural life, with a series of museums, performance spaces and the grounds for São Paulo's renowned **Bienal** (see below).

Inaugurated in 1954 to commemorate the city's 400th anniversary, the park was designed by renowned landscape architect Roberto Burle Marx. A series of landmark buildings in the park are the work of modernist master Oscar Niemeyer; most of them are linked by a long and distinctively serpentine covered walkway. At the north entrance stands Victor Brecheret's huge **Monumento Bandeiras** (Map p278), erected in 1953 in memory of the city's early pioneers. A meandering duck pond takes up much of the western half of the park, and around it is arranged a series of shaded walks, including the **Bosque da Leitura** (Map p278) – a woodsy section that on Sundays turns into an open-air library where you can check out books for the afternoon.

SÃO PAULO BIENAL

Modeled on the Venice Biennale, the **Bienal de São Paulo** (www.fbsp.org.br; Parque do Ibirapuera), founded in 1951, has grown into one of the world's most important arts events. Many of the participants are working artists who have been nominated by their home country. In addition, a guest curator chooses a theme and invites his or her own favorites. At its best, the Bienal offers the world a chance to view mind-bending contemporary art. Certainly it cannot fail to be impressive for its sheer size and diversity.

The event is held during even-numbered years, generally from October to December, in a sprawling pavilion designed by modernist master Oscar Niemeyer in the leafy Parque do Ibirapuera (see above). In recent years, admission has been free, though this is subject to funding.

AVENDA PAULISTA, JARDINS & AROUND

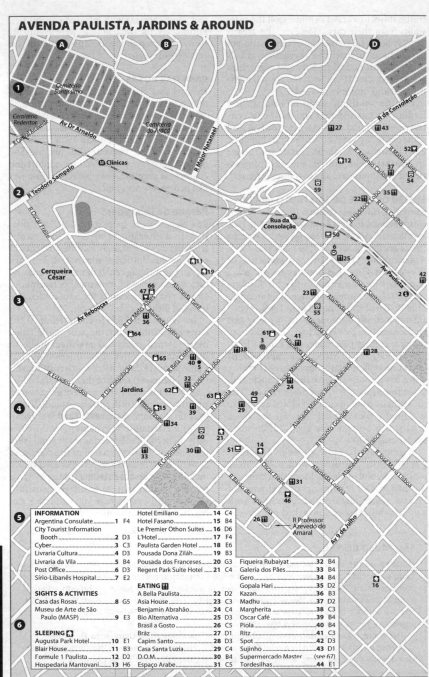

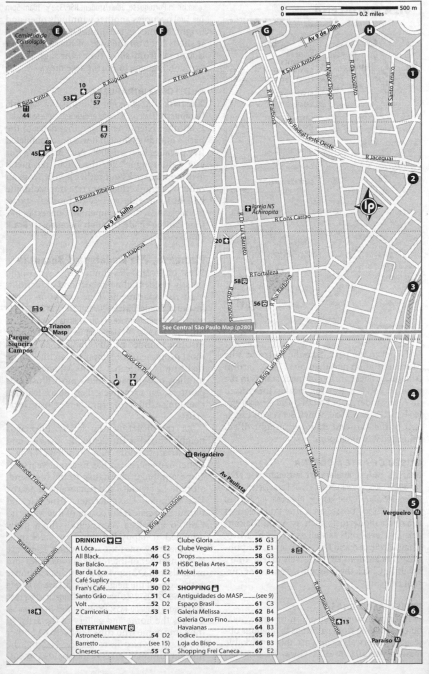

DRINKING
A Lôca **45** E2
All Black **46** C5
Bar Balcão **47** B3
Bar da Lôca **48** E2
Café Suplicy **49** C4
Fran's Café **50** D2
Santo Grão **51** C4
Volt **52** D2
Z Carniceria **53** E1

ENTERTAINMENT
Astronete **54** D2
Barretto .... (see 15)
Cinesesc **55** C3

Clube Gloria **56** G3
Clube Vegas **57** E1
Drops **58** G3
HSBC Belas Artes **59** C2
Mokai **60** B4

SHOPPING
Antiguidades do MASP ..... (see 9)
Espaço Brasil **61** C3
Galeria Melissa **62** B4
Galeria Ouro Fino **63** B4
Havaianas **64** B3
Iodice **65** B4
Loja do Bispo **66** B3
Shopping Frei Caneca **67** E2

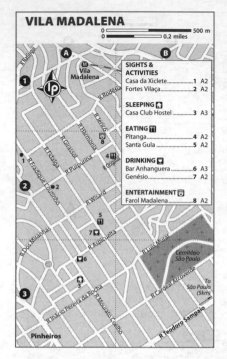

VILA MADALENA

0 _____ 500 m
0 _____ 0.2 miles

SIGHTS & ACTIVITIES
Casa da Xiclete.................1 A2
Fortes Vilaça.....................2 A2

SLEEPING 🛏
Casa Club Hostel..............3 A3

EATING 🍴
Pitanga.............................4 A2
Santa Gula.......................5 A2

DRINKING 🍷
Bar Anhanguera...............6 A3
Genésio............................7 A2

ENTERTAINMENT 🎭
Farol Madalena................8 A2

To get to the park, take the metro to Vila Mariana station and then bus 775-A 'Jardim Aldagiza.' There are lots of snack stands in the park, or you can get a full meal in the Museu de Arte Moderna, at **Prêt** (Map p278; ☾ noon-4pm Tue-Fri, 12:30-5pm Sat-Sun), which serves an excellent buffet (around R$35) in a light-filled, minimalist dining room.

MUSEU DE ARTE MODERNA
Brazil's oldest **modern art museum** (Map p278; ☎ 5085 1300; www.mam.org.br, in Portuguese; adult/student R$5.50/2.75, free Sun; ☾ 10am-6pm Tue-Sun, last admission 5:30pm) possesses a fine collection of Brazilian modernists such as Anita Malfatti and Di Cavalcanti as well as works by Miró, Chagall, Picasso and Dufy. However, the public spaces are devoted exclusively to temporary exhibits. Check the museum's website for current offerings.

MUSEU AFRO-BRASIL
With a permanent collection of some 5000 objects ranging from paintings to religious objects to historical documents, this remarkable **museum** (Map p278; ☎ 5579 8542; www.museuafrobrasil

.com.br, in Portuguese; adult/student R$6/3; ☾ 10am-5pm Tue-Sun) occupies another winningly open and bright Niemeyer pavilion. Opened in 2004, it sheds light on the lives of Brazil's African diaspora, from slave times through to the present. Signage in Portuguese only.

AUDITÓRIO IBIRAPUERA
The park's most recent addition, the **Auditório Ibirapuera** (Map p278; www.auditorioibirapuera.com.br) is another Niemeyer design that dates to the park's founding, though it was only completed five decades later, in 2005. Nicknamed 'a língua' ('the tongue') for the bright-red metal awning that sticks out rather lewdly from an otherwise bunkerlike concrete trapezoid, the hall hosts a wide variety of musical styles, from classical to experimental. Concert bookings can be made through **Ticketmaster Brasil** (☎ 2846 6000).

Pinheiros, Vila Madalena & Butantan
West of Jardins lies Pinheiros, a sprawling, mostly residential neighborhood of identikit high-rise apartments. One exception is the **Instituto Tomie Ohtake** (Map p278; ☎ 2245 1900; www.institutotomieohtake.org.br; Av Brigadeiro Faria Lima 201; admission free; ☾ 11am-8pm Tue-Sun), a cultural institute founded by Ruy Ohtake, São Paulo's most prominent contemporary architect. The institute is dedicated to his Japanese-born mother, one of Sao Paulo's most illustrious painters. An attractive gallery space features changing exhibits of prominent, mostly local artists.

At the heart of the larger Pinheiros neighborhood is the distinctly low-rise and pedestrian-friendly Vila Madalena. Long a Bohemian enclave, it has in recent years become a popular alternative to the high-end, attitude-heavy clubs and restaurants of nearby Vila Olímpia. The epicenter of the bar and restaurant scene is the corner of Rua Mourato Coelho and Rua Aspicuelta, which grow crowded at happy hour and, on weekends, stay that way until the wee hours. There are also a number of interesting shops, cafés and art galleries. Occupying a ramshackle house at the edge of the neighborhood, **Casa da Xiclete** (Map p290; ☎ 2579 9007; http://casadaxiclet.multiply.com; Rua Fradique Coutinho 1855; ☾ 2-8pm Wed-Fri, to 6pm Sat & Sun) is the home and gallery of the artist of the same name who runs a collective of other artists, many also in residence. Nearby, the more traditional **Fortes Vilaça** (Map p290; ☎ 3032

7066; www.fortesvilaca.com.br; Rua Fradique Coutinho 1500; ⏰ 10am-7pm Tue-Fri, to 5pm Sat) displays some of the city's most illustrious contemporary artists in a sprawling, cement-lined space.

The center of the Vila Madalena action sits about a 15-minute walk from the Vila Madalena metro station to the center of the action.

West of Pinheiros across Rio Pinheiros lies the Cidade Universitária, home of the prestigious University of São Paulo. The quiet, tree-lined streets make for pleasant strolling.

INSTITUTO BUTANTAN
Highly respected for its groundbreaking bio-medical research, this **institute** (Map p278; ☎ 3726 7222; www.butantan.gov.br; Av Vital Brazil 1500, Cidade Universitária; admission adult/student R$6/2.50; ⏰ 9am-4:30pm Tue-Sun) is best known as a venom farm. Researchers milk a total of tens of thousands of snakes of their poison, which is used to make antidotes to snake and spider bites, as well as in research for other medicines. Located in the leafy Cidade Universitária, the small museum displays snakes in dozens of shapes and sizes. At the time of writing a devastating fire had destroyed almost half a million preserved specimens, though no live animals. Check ahead to ensure that the museum is operating normally.

MUSEU DE ARTE CONTEMPORÂNEA DA UNIVERSIDADE DE SÃO PAULO (MAC-USP)
Set amid the verdant University of São Paulo campus, this fine **museum** (Map p278; ☎ 3091 3039; www.mac.usp.br; Rua da Praça do Relógio 160, Cidade Universitária; admission free; ⏰ 10am-6pm Tue-Fri, to 4pm Sat & Sun) possesses what is arguable the country's best collection of Brazilian art since 1960, plus a smattering of works by international masters from Max Ernst to Robert Rauschenberg.

South & East of Jardins
Extra wide Av Brigadeiro Faria Lima (called just 'Faria Lima') marks the southwestern edge of the Jardins neighborhoods. Faria Lima is also the main corridor connecting Pinheiros with the ritzy, though mostly un-inviting, neighborhoods of Morumbi, Vila Olímpia, Itaím Bibi and Moema. All of these areas are composed largely of congested streets, forbidding luxury high-rises and glittering complexes that house the majority of the city's most-profitable businesses,

from banking to technology. That said, there are plenty of fine restaurants, nightclubs and shopping opportunities that diehards may want to seek out.

Occupying an extravagant Palladian-style villa built by a local tycoon and his wife in the 1940s, the small but charming **Museu da Casa Brasileira** (Map p278; ☎ 3032 3727; www.mcb.sp.gov.br; Av Brigadeiro Faria Lima 2705; adult/student R$4/2; ⏰ 10am-6pm Tue-Sun) has a hodgepodge collection of Brazilian and European furnishings from the 17th to 20th centuries. The museum's café-restaurant is its best feature, with good food and lovely outdoor seating.

Home of the couple who developed the leafy, upscale suburb of Morumbi, **Fundação Maria Luisa e Oscar Americano** (Map p278; ☎ 3742 0077; www.fundacaooscaramericano.org.br; Av Morumbi 4077, Morumbi; adult/student R$10/5; ⏰ 10am-5:30pm Tue-Sun) makes a fine retreat as much for its gardens as for its collection of painting, sculpture and objets d'art from the 18th to 20th centuries. The 1950s house turned museum is a small masterpiece of Brazilian modernism, and there's also a lovely **café** (⏰ 11am-5:30pm Tue-Sun) that serves traditional high tea for R$50.

PARQUE DO ESTADO
In the southern suburb of Cursino, **Parque do Estado** is far from the action but worth seeking out if you find yourself craving greenery in cement-heavy Sampa. Its northern tip is given over to the **Jardim Botânico** (Map p278; ☎ 5073 6300; adult/student R$3/1; ⏰ 9am-5pm Tue-Sun), a well-tended botanical garden that includes a promenade of imperial palms, an orchid farm, picturesque ponds, a stand of brazilwood trees and a herb garden where you are encouraged to smell the aromatic flowers and leaves. An open-air café offers snacks, plus a simple but fresh and well-prepared per-kilo buffet lunch (R$25 per kg).

A short distance away lies the **Jardim Zoológico** (Map p278; ☎ 5073 0811; www.zoologico.sp.gov .br; adult/student/child under 12yr R$15/7.50/4.50; ⏰ 9am-5pm Tue-Sun, last admission 4:30pm), Brazil's largest zoo. It's home to some 3000 animal species and is spread out over some 900 hectares, much of which is old-growth Mata Atlântica (Atlantic rain forest). As well as exhibiting caged animals, the zoo offers the Zoo Safari for an additional R$13; this is a 45-minute ride through large, fenced areas where animals are allowed to roam with relative freedom. Note that the zoo does not accept credit cards.

The best way to get to the park is by metro to the São Judas station, where you can catch bus 4742 'Jardim Climax.'

MUSEU DO IPIRANGA

Set amid Versailles-like gardens in the eastern suburb of Ipiranga, this **museum** (Map p278; ☎ 2065 8000; www.mp.usp.br; Parque de Independência; adult/student R$4/2; ☒ 9am-4:45pm Tue-Sun) began its life as a memorial to Brazil's independence from Portugal. According to legend, Dom Pedro declared independence on the shores of a nearby stream. The gardens and palace are the real treat here, as are the fine vistas that its hilltop position affords. The collection, documenting the independence movement as well as Brazilian history, is of more modest interest. Signage in Portuguese only.

WALKING TOUR

If you really want to get a feel for the historic parts of São Paulo, follow this meandering 3.5km stroll that brings you past all the best-known landmarks and sights of Sampa. Note that this walk is safe enough during weekdays, though do stay attentive to your envi-ronment. Avoid doing it at night, weekends and holidays.

Start at **Praça da República (1)**, near the metro stop with the same name. Look for the big yellow edifice known as the **Caetano de Campos building (2)** – it used to be a high school but is now the headquarters of the State Department of Education. On weekends this plaza is the venue for the Feira da República (see p302), which has a huge variety of crafts, paintings, coins and stones.

Head down Av Ipiranga and then turn left onto Av São Luís to get a look at what's still one of the tallest buildings in town – the 46-story **Edifício Itália (3**; p284).

Continuing down Av São Luís (there are lots of travel agencies and money exchange bureaus on this street), check out the rather squat, grey building at the end of the small

> **WALK FACTS**
> **Start/Finish** Praça da República
> **Distance** 3.5km
> **Duration** 2-3 hours

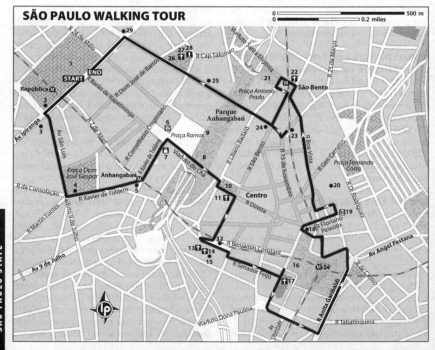

SÃO PAULO WALKING TOUR

park on the left. It looks like a prison, but it's the **Mario de Andrade Municipal Library (4)**, housing the largest book collection in the city.

Turning left onto Rua Xavier de Toledo, keeping the library on your left, follow the road downhill toward the Anhangabaú metro station a few blocks away. Keep a sharp lookout – it's easy to miss in the hustle and bustle. To the right of the station and down a few steps into a park is **Ladeira da Memória** (Memory Hill; **5**), where the Chafariz dos Piques fountain used to supply the city and cattle dealers with water. Now it's the site of the Piramide dos Piques, an obelisk-like structure pointing at the sky.

Continue down Rua Xavier de Toledo until the **Theatro Municipal** (**6**; p283) appears – this baroque building, with its art-nouveau features, is the pride of the city. Across the street from the theater is **Shopping Light** (**7**; p283), which occupies a rather grand building once belonging to the Light English Company. Opposite the theater, on the right, is the **Viaduto de Chá (8)**, a metal bridge built in 1892 and named after an old tea plantation that used to be in the area. Pedestrian traffic became too heavy for the old bridge and a new one was inaugurated in 1938.

Crossing the bridge, look out over the **Parque Anhangabaú (9)** on the left. In the Tupi-Guarani language, Anhangabaú means Demon's Valley, because indigenous peoples believed bad spirits once dwelled there. At the other side of the bridge, enter **Praça do Patriarca (10)** straight ahead. Here you'll find the **Igreja de Santo Antônio** (**11**; p283), the central church of the settlement of São Paulo at the start of the 17th century, and rebuilt in the 18th century.

Some 20 paces beyond that is Rua São Bento, a pedestrian street loaded with shops. Turn right onto Rua São Bento and eventually you'll step into the **Largo de São Francisco (12)**, a triangular plaza that is home to twin churches, both known as **Igreja de São Francisco de Assis (13, 14**; p282) and the city's well-respected **College of Law (15**; p282). The churches contain 18th-century paintings and are well worth a look when they are reopened. In front of the law school is one of Brazil's most controversial works of art – a statue by Swiss artist William Zadig that depicts a Frenchman kissing an indigenous woman. If you can read a little Portuguese, the statue's history is well documented by a plaque on its base.

Just beyond the statue is Rua Senador Feijó, leading to the famous **Praça da Sé (16**; p282). Soak up the joyous atmosphere in the square, but watch your pockets. Step inside the **Catedral da Sé (17**; p282), which reportedly can hold up to 8000 people.

As you exit the cathedral, head down the plaza and continue toward the **Caixa Economica Federal (18)**, home to the city's coffers and also a great cultural center (Caixa Cultural; see p282) that features Brazilian artists. Turning right onto Rua Floriano Peixoto, walk to the end (it's a dead-end street) and feast your eyes upon the pinkish-colored **Solar da Marquesa (19**; p282). Follow the street around to the left and **Praça Páteo do Colégio (20**; p283), the actual site where São Paulo was founded in 1554, will appear on your right. The adjacent square is surrounded by an array of other important civil buildings, most dating to the early 20th century, plus a monumental column commemorating the founding of the city.

Directly in front of this plaza is Rua Boa Vista. Following it away from Praça da Sé brings you into the heart of the city's financial district. At the end of Boa Vista, you'll find **Largo de São Bento (21)**, the square that launched thousands of *bandeirante* expeditions. Now it is home to the **Mosteiro São Bento (22**; p283), a monastery and basilica built in an eclectic style and still putting on Gregorian-chant concerts.

Leaving the square, walk up Rua São Bento, a pedestrian street, until reaching Av São João. Turn left at Av São João and another quick left at the next street, where on the right stands the art-deco **Banespa building (23**; p283). Head to the top floor for a sweeping view of São Paulo. Backtrack to Rua São Bento and then keep heading straight down Av São João. On the left just past São Bento stands **Edifício Martinelli (24**; p283). You are now crossing the Vale do Anhangabaú that you saw earlier from the Viaduto do Chá. Ahead is the **Prédio dos Correios (25)**, the largest post office in the country. It's currently being restored and will soon be a cultural center and postal museum.

To finish this tour, go up Av São João as far as **Largo de Paiçandú (26)**, where you'll find **NS do Rosário dos Homens Pretos (27)**, a church that was built in 1906 by black Brazilians on a site where sacred African religious rites were formerly performed. Behind this pretty church, which is painted an unusual yellow-orange tone, is the magnificent **Monumento á Mãe Preta**

(Monument to the Black Mother; **28**). This heart-wrenching statue depicts an African slave woman suckling a white child, and the poem underneath gives voice to her lament for her own children who must go hungry.

To wrap up a long day, continue forward and you will end up at the intersection of Av São João and Av Ipiranga, a **corner (29)** that is considered the most famous in all of São Paulo and was immortalized in Caetano Veloso's beautiful ode to the city, 'Sampa.' Turn left and you will be back where you started, in the Praça da República.

COURSES

One of the most respected language schools for Portuguese courses is **Polyglot** (☎ 3744 4397; www.polyglot.com.br; Av Eng Luiz Carlos Berrini, 96, Brooklyn). **CEL-LEP** (www.cellep.com) specializes in English and Spanish but also offers Portuguese at locations throughout the city.

SÃO PAULO FOR CHILDREN

São Paulo's sprawling **Parque do Ibirapuera** (p287) makes a great place for kids to run off their excess energy. Those without a fear of snakes will be fascinated by **Instituto Butantan** (p291).

The large and very good zoo, the **Jardim Zoológico** (p291), is a definite kid-pleaser.

FESTIVALS & EVENTS

The city's two biggest events are the **Bienal de São Paulo** (p287) and the **Gay Pride events** (see below).

Also worth checking out:

Carnaval (February &/or March) The celebrations don't approach those of Rio, but there are parties throughout the city (see p84).

Virada Cultural (one Saturday in late April or early May) A nonstop, 24-hour party of cultural, especially musical, events around the city.

São Paulo International Art Fair (late May or early June) This national and international art fair is one of the world's largest.

Festa de NS Achiropita (every weekend in August) A series of street fairs in Bixiga celebrating the city's Italian heritage.

São Paulo Restaurant Week (late August and early September) More than 100 restaurants offer special menus and promotional prices.

Mostra Internacional de Cinema (October) The country's largest film festival, with screenings throughout the city.

Reveillon (31 December) Av Paulista turns into a big outdoor party to ring in the new year.

SLEEPING

Ironically, travelers will find that the biggest discounts are given in São Paulo during the vacation months of December, January and February, when prices elsewhere in Brazil skyrocket. Weekend discounts of up to 30% or more are common at large business hotels. Competition can be fierce for clients, so it is always worth trying to bargain.

Many hotels listed here cater for travelers with disabilities.

Praça da República & Around

São Paulo Hostel Downtown (Map p280; ☎ 3333 0844; www.hostelsp.com.br; Rua Barão de Campinas 94; dm/s/d R$33/66/80; 🛜) This good if rather basic H1 hostel is hidden inside a downtown office building about a 10-minute walk from the República metro stop. Perks include 24-hour reception, free wi-fi, shared kitchen, and self-service laundry. Nonmembers of HI pay about 20% more. Exercise caution at all times in the surrounding areas, especially at night.

Hotel Itamarati (Map p280; ☎ 3474 4133; www .hotelitamarati.com.br; Av Dr Vieira de Carvalho 150; s/d R$89/113; P 🔀 🖳) Friendly but threadbare,

---

PRIDE, SAMPA-STYLE

In 1997, São Paulo's first Gay Pride parade drew a meager 3000 people. In less than a decade, it has grown into the world's largest Pride event, attracting nearly three million. That growth is a testament to the profound change in cultural attitudes toward homosexuality in Brazil, but also Sampa's long tradition of tolerance. Indeed, most of the crowd are *simpatizantes* – gay-friendly straights. Rio is often touted as Brazil's gay mecca, yet you almost never see overt displays of affection in the streets. In São Paulo, PDA (public display of affection) is becoming commonplace, at least in certain neighborhoods (p300).

During Pride week, the city's gay and lesbian venues are packed to the gills in the lead-up to the big parade, which traditionally takes place on a Sunday, usually in mid-June. There are also political meetings, street fairs, concerts and other special events.

this budget option occupies a fine, old building just a short walk from Praça da República. Rooms at the front are brighter but noisier. Some have fans only, which saves you about R$15 per night.

Normandie Design Hotel (Map p280; ☎ 3311 9855; www.normandiedesign.com.br; Av Ipiranga 1187; s/d R$140/170; P ⊠ 🖳) Inspired by the work of Philippe Starck, this hotel manages to be at once fashion-forward and reasonably priced. The stark and striking lobby raises expectations that the rooms can't quite deliver. Still, they're perfectly adequate for the price – and rigorously black and white.

Hotel Marabá (Map p280; ☎ 2137 9500; www.hotelmaraba.com.br; Av Ipiranga 757; s/d R$180/210; P ⊠ 🖳) This new sleeping place in a refurbished office building just off Praça da República provides remarkable style and comfort for the price, from quality bedding to chic lighting fixtures. Each room has an attractive sitting area, and there is a nice top-floor terrace and gym.

Novotel Jaraguá São Paulo (Map p280; ☎ 2802 7000; www.accorhotels.com; Rua Martins Fontes 71; s/d R$300/350; P ⊠ 🖳) The Accor chain has refurbished the old Hotel Jaraguá, which had long been central São Paulo's most chic hotel. Digs are large, plush and cheerfully done up in saturated hues. Rooms above the 20th floor have breathtaking city views.

Liberdade

Akasaka (Map p280; ☎ 3207 1500; www.akasakahotel.com.br; Praça da Liberdade 149; s/d R$89/99) Conveniently located across from the metro, this budget option offers good value with simple, no-frills but clean rooms. Breakfast is available for R$10.

Around Avenida Paulista

Pousada dos Franceses (Map p287; ☎ 3262 4026; www.pousadadosfranceses.com.br; Rua dos Franceses 100; dm R$35, s/d from R$60/88; 🖳 🛜) On a quiet, almost suburban street, yet just a short walk to Av Paulista, this hostel offers decent communal digs, bright and pleasant common areas, and private rooms of varying sizes and comfort. Perks include a large, free breakfast, wi-fi (R$5 per day), shared kitchen and 24-hour reception.

Formule 1 Paulista (Map p287; ☎ 3123 7755; www.accorhotels.com.br; Rua da Consolação 2303; r from R$95; ⊠ 🖳) Large and rather soulless but with a great location and price, this chain hotel is worth considering. Rooms are spartan and rather dormitory-like but perfectly adequate.

Hospedaria Mantovani (Map p287; ☎ 3889 8624; www.residenzamantovani.com.br; Rua Desembargador Eliseu Guilherme 269; s/d/tr R$85/105/119) In what looks like an Italian farmhouse on steroids, this neatly kept inn offers rooms of various sizes and shapes, all spotless and attractive, if simple. Reserve in advance.

Paulista Garden Hotel (Map p287; ☎ 3885 1362; www.paulistagardenhotel.com.br; Alameda Lorena 21; s/d/tr R$99/117/152; P ⊠) It may be on a busy intersection, but this friendly place is popular with foreign travelers for its largish and good-value, if uninspiring, rooms.

Augusta Park Hotel (Map p287; ☎ 3124 4400; www.augustapark.com.br; Rua Augusta 922; s/d R$130/155; P ⊠ 🖳 🐾) Set amid the action of Rua Augusta, the Augusta Park offers respectable if slightly dated rooms and convenient location. Rooms aren't luxurious but are perfectly comfortable, all with separate sitting room and small kitchen. Rooms on higher floors have winning views; rooms at the back of the hotel are quieter.

L'Hotel (Map p287; ☎ 2183 0500; www.lhotel.com.br; Alameda Campinas 266; d from R$700; P ⊠ 🖳 🐾) Possibly São Paulo's coziest high-end hotel and certainly among its poshest, this boutique sleep just off Paulista offers deluxe digs, impeccable service and rather traditional continental decor.

Jardins
MIDRANGE & TOP END

our pick **Pousada Dona Ziláh** (Map p287; ☎ 3062 1444; www.zilah.com; Alameda Franca 1621; s/d R$148/184; P ⊠ 🖳) A rare find, this lovely, briskly run pousada (guesthouse) occupies a Spanish-style villa in the heart of Jardins. Rooms, arranged around a courtyard, are small and simple but also tasteful and well-maintained. Attractive common areas promote sociability among a largely international clientele. A new restaurant serves sophisticated, Brazilian fusion cuisine at relatively reasonable prices. Rooms with air-con cost an extra R$10.

Blair House (Map p287; ☎ 3083 5988; Alameda Franca 1645; www.blairhouse.com.br; s/d from R$148/172; ⊠) The little studio apartments here are rather basic but comfortable – and very well situated near the action in Jardins. Angle for the brighter, corner (odd-numbered) rooms.

Le Premier Othon Suites (Map p287; ☎ 3887 1599; www.othon.com.br; Rua Guarará 511; s/d from R$177/191; P ⊠ 🖳 🐾) The ministudio apartments are standard-issue business affairs but definitely good value for Jardins, with good beds and tasteful if not latest-issue decorations. Rooms on higher floors boast good city views.

Regent Park Suite Hotel (Map p287; ☎ 3065 5555; www.regent.com.br; Rua Oscar Freire 533; s/d R$265/320; P 🅿 💻 🏊) A tony location plus fully equipped, one-bedroom apartments that are both plush and mutedly stylish. Ask for a room on a high floor for views over the Jardins district.

Hotel Emiliano (Map p287; ☎ 3068 4399; www .emiliano.com.br; Rua Oscar Freire 384; d from R$870; P 🅿 💻 🏊) Sleek, bright and minimalist, Emiliano is more brash than the Fasano but every bit as luxurious, with high-thread-count sheets, impeccable service and a sun-drenched rooftop pool.

Hotel Fasano (Map p287; ☎ 3896 4000; www .fasano.com.br; Rua Vittorio Fasano 88; d from R$1150; P 🅿 💻 🏊) This small but ultrarefined hotel seems to have been plucked straight from Milan, with muted gray marble set off with exquisite 1930s-era antiques in rooms and common areas, and a reserve and formality rare in Brazil. The Zen-like rooftop pool area alone is worth the price of admission. Many rooms have fine views.

South & West of Jardins

Saci Hostel (Map p278; ☎ 3862 5792; www.sacihostel.com; Rua Veríssimo Glória 86; dm from R$35, d R$90; 💻 🏊) A short walk from the Sumaré metro station, this new hostel is one of the most conveniently located in the city and also the first in São Paulo with its own swimming pool. Digs are snug but decent.

Casa Club Hostel (Map p290; ☎ 3798 0051; www .casaclub.com.br; Rua Mourata Coelho 973; dm from R$35; 💻) While the dorm-only facilities are cramped and pack in as many as 16 beds, this is Sao Paulo's most sociable hostel, thanks to its courtyard bar that is open to the general public. It is clean, well run and well located for Vila Madalena's nightlife and arts scene.

Hotel Unique (Map p278; ☎ 3055 4710; www.hotel unique.com.br; Av Brigadeiro Luis Antônio 4700; d from R$975; P 🅿 💻 🏊) Designed by Ruy Ohtake, the shiplike Unique is certainly the city's most architecturally ambitious hotel as well as one of its most luxurious. Rooms, with their portal-like windows, are elegantly minimalist, and the rooftop bar and pool offer some of the city's very best views.

EATING

São Paulo's dining scene is as vast as the city itself – and guaranteed to please all comers. For the frugal, there are the ubiquitous *lanchonetes* – corner bars offering beer to the thirsty and, for the hungry, full meals for under R$12. Plus, literally hundreds of ethnic groups each have their offerings, from Lebanese to Uruguayan cuisine.

Paulistanos love to dine out, and do so late. Although restaurants open by 7pm, most don't fill up until 9pm or so on weekdays, and later on weekends, when many kitchens take orders to 1am or later. There are also lots of very good 24-hour options for late-night munchies.

Anhangabaú, Triângulo, Praça da República & Liberdade

Estadão (Map p280; Viaduto 9 de Julho 193; hot sandwiches R$6-12; 🕐 24hr) Famous for its *pernil* (pork loin) sandwiches served on crusty French bread, this no-frills stand-up joint is justifiably popular with both taxi drivers and the late-night revelers they ferry about.

Ponto Chic (Map p280; ☎ 3222 6528; Largo Paissandu 27; sandwiches from R$12, mains from R$25; 🕐 11am-midnight) A São Paulo tradition, Ponto Chic is famous for its efficient, bow-tied staff and the extravagant R$12 *bauru* – a sandwich of beef, tomato, pickle and melted cheeses on French bread.

Lamen Asaka (Map p280; ☎ 3277 9682; Rua Galvão Bueno 466; mains around R$12; 🕐 lunch & dinner Tue-Sun, closed mid-Dec–mid-Jan) One of the best cheap eats in São Paulo, this Liberdade classic specializes in homemade Japanese ramen – thin noodles served in a rich broth with thinly sliced meat and veggies. The gleaming, open kitchen is staffed by descendants of Japanese immigrants to Brazil.

Around Avenida Paulista
BUDGET

Madhu (Map p287; ☎ 3262 5535; Rua Augusta 1422; meals incl drink R$12-19; 🕐 noon-10pm Mon-Fri, 1-11:30pm Sat) Brazil's first Indian fast-food joint, this simple-with-a-dash-of-style spot serves up good curry and naan amid the bustle of Rua Augusta.

Gopala Hari (Map p287; ☎ 3283 1292; Rua Antônio Carlos 429; 3-course meals R$18; 🕐 lunch Mon-Thu, lunch & dinner Fri-Sat) Cheap and elegant with delicious food, this Indian vegetarian lunch place offers two set menus daily, including soup, main and dessert. Simple food but prepared and served with care.

Asia House (Map p287; ☎ 3064 0493; Rua Augusta 1918; per kg R$33; ☿ lunch Mon-Sat) For good, fair-priced and lightning-quick sushi, this per-kilo buffet restaurant just off Av Paulista is a great option. As well as sushi and sashimi there are classic Japanese and Chinese dishes, from tempura to Kung Pao chicken.

MIDRANGE & TOP END

Bella Paulista (Map p287; ☎ 3214 3347; Rua Haddock Lobo 354; ☿ 24hr) This very agreeable, upscale bakery is especially popular with both gay and straight Paulistanos for its gourmet sandwiches (around R$18) and salads served around the clock. Expect lines in the wee hours as clubs start to close.

Bio Alternativa (Map p287; ☎ 3898 2971; Alameda Santos 2214; buffet lunches around R$25; ☿ lunch Mon-Fri) Just a block off Av Paulista lies this vegetarian oasis, which offers a buffet lunch with up to half a dozen hot dishes – some vegan and all made with carefully selected, largely organic ingredients.

Sujinho (Map p287; ☎ 3231 5207; Rua da Consolação 2078; mains around R$30; ☿ 11:30am-3am Sun-Thu, to 5am Fri & Sat) This no-nonsense steak house is a local favorite for its combination of fine, reasonably priced grilled meats, old-fashioned service and late hours. It has another dining room just across the street.

Spot (Map p287; ☎ 3283 0946; Alameda Ministro Rocha Azevedo 72; mains R$30-40; ☿ lunch & dinner) Sheathed in stainless steel, Spot looks like a US diner but with much better chow. The menu is simple, with classic but well-prepared pastas and grilled meats. The crowd, by contrast, is self-consciously sophisticated, attracting artists, performers and journalists.

Bráz (Map p287; ☎ 3214 3337; Rua Sergipe 406, Higienópolis; individual pizzas from R$35; ☿ 6:30pm-12:30am, to 1:30am Fri-Sat) Cooking up what many consider to be Sampa's best pizza in wood ovens, this rather upscale but always animated spot is worth the 10- to 15- minute walk from Av Paulista.

Tordesilhas (Map p287; ☎ 3107 7444; Rua Bela Cintra 465; mains R$35-65; ☿ lunch & dinner Tue-Sat, lunch Sun) Behind a thick tangle of plants inside a golden-yellow colonial mansion, chef Mara Salles creates some of the very best contemporary Brazilian cuisine in the city, including perfectly grilled Amazonian fish and sun-cured beef with hearts of palm.

Jardins

Jardins is your place to splurge; it offers an incredibly dense collection of Brazil's most illustrious restaurants, plus some surprisingly reasonable choices to boot.

BUDGET & MIDRANGE

Benjamin Abrahão (Map p287; ☎ 3061 4004; Rua José Maria Lisboa 1397; sandwiches R$9-18; ☿ 6am-9:30pm) Widely considered the city's best bakery, this Paulista institution also serves sandwiches as well as hot dishes (around R$25) amid a spotlessly white-and-tan interior. From cakes to foccaccia, the baked goods are superior.

Galeria dos Pães (Map p287; ☎ 3064 5900; Rua Estados Unidos 1645; sandwiches R$10-18; ☿ 24hr) This gourmet grocery store also has a great deli where the beautiful people of Jardins come to hash out their social lives over an excellent selection of gourmet sandwiches and fresh juices. There's also a buffet breakfast during the week (R$14), brunch at weekends (R$18) and a daily buffet of soups and baked goods (R$20; 6pm to 5am).

Margherita (Map p287; ☎ 2714 3000; Alameda Tietê 255; 2-person pizzas R$30-45; ☿ 6:30pm-1am) Classic thin-crust Italian pizza is cooked up in wood ovens and served in an attractive dining room that draws the young, and young-looking, of the Jardins neighborhood. Expect a line on weekends, especially Sundays.

Kazan (Map p287; ☎ 3068 9665; Rua Dr Melo Alves 343; buffet lunches/dinners R$29/39; ☿ lunch & dinner Mon-Sat) A bright, pleasant Japanese restaurant in the heart of Jardins, Kazan offers good sushi at great prices. The buffet includes soup, tempura, teriyaki and dessert, as well as all the sushi you can eat.

Espaço Arabe (Map p287; ☎ 3081 1824; Rua Oscar Freire 168; mains R$20-30; ☿ 11am-11pm) This light-filled, modernist space serves up dependably good and distinctly nongreasy versions of Arab classics, from shish kebab to falafel. The four-course lunch special (R$26) makes for a good deal.

Piola (Map p287; ☎ 3064 6570; Alameda Lorena 1765; individual pizzas R$22-39; ☿ 6pm-1am) Serving fine, thin-crust wood-oven pizza in a colorful, relaxed, chic dining room, Piola attracts a youngish and hip crowd. Expect a line Sunday evenings.

Ritz (Map p287; ☎ 3062 5830; Alameda Franca 1088; burgers around R$25; ☿ lunch & dinner) Often frequented by a gay clientele, this nouvelle take on an old-fashioned French bistro serves up classic recipes such as quiches and grilled fish with hollandaise sauce, though it's best loved for its juicy burgers.

TOP END

Oscar Café (Map p287; ☎ 3063 5209; Rua Oscar Freire 727; mains around R$35; ☾ 9:30am-10pm Mon-Sat, to 8pm Sun) A Jardins classic, this restaurant-café is a world unto itself, with natural-wood decor, a pretty waterfall, excellent coffee and baked goods, and creative Brazilian-fusion mains.

Capim Santo (Map p287; ☎ 3068 8486; Alameda Ministro Rocha Azevedo 471; mains R$35-70; ☾ lunch & dinner Tue-Sun) Young chef Morena Leite turns out excellent Bahian dishes, with an emphasis on fresh seafood, served in a relaxed, plant-filled indoor-outdoor space. The weekday buffet (R$36) is an affordable way into this high-end spot.

Figueira Rubaiyat (Map p287; ☎ 3087 1399; Rua Haddock Lobo 1738; mains R$40-80; ☾ lunch & dinner) Sprawling and luxurious like the ancient fig tree that graces its outdoor terrace, this top-of-the-line grill-restaurant serves up perhaps Sampa's best meat, plus other delicacies from fresh oysters to foie gras with figs.

our pick **Brasil a Gosto** (Map p287; ☎ 3086 3565; Rua Professor Azevedo do Amaral 70; mains from R$45; ☾ lunch & dinner Tue-Sat, lunch Sun) At once cozy and modern, this Jardins institution has won kudos for its innovative takes on classic Brazilian dishes and ingredients, from *carne de sol* (tasty, salted meat, grilled and served with beans, rice and vegetables) to Amazonian fruits such as the berry-like *açaí*.

our pick **Maní** (Map p278; ☎ 3085 4148; Rua Joaquim Antunes 210; mains R$45-65; ☾ lunch & dinner Tue-Sun) One of the most exciting recent additions to the Sampa dining scene, this rustic-chic restaurant is run impeccably by a Brazilian-Spanish couple. The inventive menu includes the remarkable starter of an extremely slow-cooked egg in a foamy sauce – amazing.

Gero (Map p287; ☎ 3064 0005; Rua Haddock Lobo 1629; mains R$55-85; ☾ lunch & dinner Mon-Sat, lunch Sun) Part of the Fasano family of high-end restaurants, Gero occupies a beautifully minimalist, brick-lined dining room that attracts a lively, fashion-conscious crowd with its brilliantly executed Italian fare, like polenta with squid in its own ink, and homemade pasta with a *ragu* of sausage and radicchio.

D.O.M. (Map p287; ☎ 3088 0761; Rua Barão de Copamena 549; mains R$60-85; ☾ lunch & dinner Mon-Fri, dinner Sat) Foie gras with a crust of wild rice?

Gnocchi with oxtail sauce? Duck breast with banana? This small and deceptively casual Italo-French restaurant serves up some of the finest food in Sampa, which is saying a lot. Reservations recommended.

Vila Madalena

Pitanga (Map p290; ☎ 3816 2914; Rua Original 162; buffets R$27; ☾ lunch) Behind a screen of vines lies a colonial minivilla that has been transformed into a quaint and airy restaurant. A creative daily lunch buffet ranges from vegetarian lasagna and pasta with filet mignon to spicy anchovy stew. Note that prices rise R$5 to R$10 at weekends.

Santa Gula (Map p290; ☎ 3812 7815; Rua Fidalga 340; mains R$30-55; ☾ dinner Mon, lunch & dinner Tue-Sat, lunch Sun) This remarkable restaurant at the end of a leafy court serves up creative Brazilian-fusion dishes such as shrimp with apricots, and cashew-encrusted salmon. It doubles as a showcase of Brazilian crafts, so you can literally take home the table you ate on.

Groceries

Self-caterers can stock up at **Supermercado Master** (Map p287; Rua Frei Caneca 569), on the ground floor of the Shopping Frei Caneca mall, or for more-gourmet fair try **Casa Santa Luzia** (Map p287; Alameda Lorena 1471, Jardins; ☾ 8am-8:45pm Mon-Sat).

For good-quality deli items, baked goods and gourmet groceries 24 hours a day, head to Galeria dos Pães (p297) in Jardins or the smaller Bela Paulista (p297) just off Av Paulista.

DRINKING

Sampa's raucous and varied nightlife is an easy rival of that in London and New York. Whether you prefer chirpy cafés or after-hour raves, live metal or flow-in electronica, São Paulo has what you're looking for. For general information on English bars and nightclubs, head to the entertainment section of www.gringoes .com. You can also check out the Portuguese-language *Guia da Folha*, which has a website (http://guia.folha.com.br, in Portuguese) as well as a supplement in the Friday edition of *Folha de São Paulo* newspaper.

Cafés

Coffee in São Paulo is generally excellent by Brazilian standards, thanks largely to the city's Italian heritage. The cafés listed here serve some of Brazil's best beans – mountain-grown arabicas, mostly from Minas Gerais.

Café Floresta (Map p280; Av Ipiranga 200; ☾ 7am-midnight) With its antique murals, excellent brew and location on the ground floor of Niemeyer's Edifício Copan building near Praça da República, this stand-up-only café is a favorite of traditionalists.

Santo Grão (Map p287; ☎ 3082 9969; Rua Oscar Freire 413; ☾ 10am-1pm Mon, 9am-1am Tue-Sat, to midnight Sun) The cappuccinos here are, quite simply, as good as those in Italy. Beans are toasted in back while the little terrace reverberates with caffeine-fueled conversation.

Café Suplicy (Map p287; ☎ 3061 0195; Alameda Lorena 1430; ☾ 7:30am-midnight Mon-Fri, 9am-midnight Sat & Sun) Santo Grão's rival is smaller, with a refined industrial-chic feel and also outrageously good coffee and pastries.

Bars

In São Paulo you are never more than a few yards from a lively drinking establishment. The young and alternative need just wander up and down Rua Augusta north of Av Paulista and choose from dozens of places, from dead simple to trashy chic. After 9pm, all types grow highly animated. Vila Madalena is the new hot spot for more mainstream types, with dozens of bars, most with outdoor terraces and often with live music, clustered around the intersection of Rua Mourato Coelho and Rua Aspicuelta. For more button-down fun, try the bars at high-flying hotels such as Fasano (p296) and Emiliano (p296) in Jardins.

CENTRO

Bar Brahma (Map p280; ☎ 3333 0855; Av São João 677, República; ☾ 11am-2:30am Mon-Sat, to midnight Sun) A Sampa classic near Praça da República with a well-preserved wood-paneled interior, Brahma remains a popular after-work hangout for professionals, and offers up live music (sometimes with cover charge) most nights after 9pm.

Choperia Liberdade (Map p280; ☎ 3207 8783; Rua da Glória 523, Liberdade; ☾ 7pm-4am) For karaoke the old-fashioned way, head to this kitsch classic, which is decked out in Christmas lights and plug-in paintings. There is a R$10 cover charge from Thursday to Saturday.

RUA AUGUSTA & JARDINS

Bar da Lôca (Map p287; cnr Rua Frei Caneca & Rua Peixoto Gomide; ☾ 8am-4am) Presided over by Saddam, beloved for his kind attention as well as his myriad gold chains, this simple place attracts a mixed gay-alternative-punk crowd until very late. Located just off the Rua Augusta corridor.

Bar Balcão (Map p287; ☎ 3063 6091; Rua Dr Melo Alves 150; ☾ 6pm-1am) With good wine, excellent light meals and a simple but elegant design built around a cleverly serpentine bar, this Jardins delight is especially popular with well-heeled designers and artists.

All Black (Map p287; ☎ 3088 7990; Rua Oscar Freire 163, Jardins; ☾ 6pm-2am Mon-Thu, to 4am Sat & Sun) For your dose of Guinness, fish, chips and Irish good cheer check out Sampa's best approximation of a Dublin pub, with live music most nights (cover R$10 to R$20).

Z Carniceria (Map p287; ☎ 2936 0934; Rua Augusta 934; ☾ 7am-2am Tue-Sun) Underground goes upscale at this latest-greatest offering on Rua Augusta. The theme is raw meat, from door handles fashioned from butchers cleavers to the cow skulls on the wall.

Skye (Map p278; ☎ 3055 4702; Av Brigadeiro Luis Antônio 4700; ☾ noon-1am) Dress up at least a little for the rooftop bar on the top floor of the Hotel Unique, whose sleek design and unparalleled views make it the perfect place for a sundown cocktail.

Volt (Map p287; ☎ 2936 4041; Rua Haddock Lobo 40; ☾ 7:30pm-12:30am Mon-Wed, to 1:30am Thu-Sat) Owner Facundo Guerra has decked out this trendy joint with the neon signs that used to light up the houses of ill repute on Rua Augusta. Today the signs attract the young and well heeled like moths.

VILA MADALENA

Genésio (Map p290; ☎ 3812 6252; Rua Fidalga 265; ☾ 5pm-4am Mon-Thu, noon-5am Fri-Sat, noon-2:30am Sun) Bow-tied waiters ferry draft beers and espressos as well as homemade pizzas and pastas to an eclectic crowd ranging from poets to the party-hearty at this perennial favorite of Vila Madalena night owls.

Bar Anhanguera (Map p290; ☎ 3031 2888; Rua Aspicuelta 595; ☾ 6pm-1am Tue-Fri, 3pm-2am Sat, 1pm-midnight Sun) This big, breezy beer joint sits in the middle of the Vila Madalena action and specializes in high-quality microbrew beers from all over Brazil, to be savored along with the big-screen sports.

ENTERTAINMENT
Nightclubs

Discos don't open until midnight, don't really get going until after 1am, and keep pumping until 5am or later. Then there are the

GAY & LESBIAN SÃO PAULO

Latin America's largest and most visible gay community supports a dizzying array of options, day and night. There are not only gay bars and discos but also restaurants, cafés, even a shopping center – **Shopping Frei Caneca** (Map p287; Rua Frei Caneca 569; 10am-10pm Mon-Sat, 2-8pm Sun), known as 'Shopping Gay Caneca,' has a largely gay clientele. And **São Paulo Pride** (p294), usually celebrated in mid-June, is by most estimates the largest gay gathering in the world. São Paulo is also the only city in Brazil where same-sex public displays of affection are a fairly common sight, at least in certain 'safe' neighborhoods. These include the area just north of Praça da República, which tends to be more working class; Rua Frei Caneca just north of Av Paulista, which attracts an alternative crowd; and Rua da Consolaçao in Jardins, largely the domain of Sampa's upscale gay guys and gals.

In addition to the places listed below, don't miss **Bella Paulista** (p297), the 24-hour restaurant where everyone ends up after the clubs close; **Bar da Lôca** (p299), where alternative types go when they can't afford entrance at the nearby A Lôca nightclub; and the largely gay **D-Edge** (p300).

Other gay and lesbian venues:

ABC Bailão (Map p280; ☎ 3333 3537; Rua Marquês de Itu 182; 11pm-late Thu-Sat) The Bailão is definitely *'brega'* (tacky), but that's the point. Basically just one big dance floor, it features everything from Whitney Houston to *forró* – the music of the Northeast, where many of the patrons were born. The crowd is refreshingly multiracial and multigenerational.

A Lôca (Map p287; ☎ 3159 8889; www.aloca.com.br, in Portuguese; Rua Frei Caneca 916; midnight-late Wed-Sun) Still the reigning queen of trashy chic, this sprawling club is the point of reference for Sampa's *alternativos* – gay, straight, male, female and various combinations thereof. Music varies from punk to electronica to classic disco.

Farol Madalena (Map p290; ☎ 3032 6470; www.farolmadalena.com.br, in Portuguese; Rua Jericó 179, Vila Madalena; 7pm-2am Tue-Sat, 4pm-midnight Sun) One of the city's top lesbian clubs, this smallish place packs in the young ladies for dinner (mains R$20 to R$30) as well as both live music and DJs as the evening progresses.

Fran's Café (Map p287; ☎ Rua Haddock Lobo 586, Jardins; 10am-midnight) Fight the local boys for an outdoor table at this cozy and very gay branch of a classic Sampa café.

Week (Map p278; ☎ 3872 9966; www.theweek.com.br, in Portuguese; Rua Guaicurus 324, Lapa) Both luxurious and cavernous, this club is the place to go if you like sweaty, shirtless, gym-hardened bodies. With two dance floors, three lounges, six bars, state-of-the-art light and sound, and an outdoor pool, it is like a big gay world unto itself.

---

after-hours places... Partying isn't always cheap: cover charges can range from R$15 to R$50 (or even $100 or more for the fanciest). Keep the card they give you on the way in – bartenders record your drinks on it, then you pay on the way out.

Clube Gloria (Map p287; ☎ 3097 9966; www.clube gloria.com.br, in Portuguese; Rua 13 de Maio 830, Bela Vista; 11:30pm-late Thu-Sat) A church remade into a temple to house and electro music, Glória is inspired by '80s-style European discos and attracts an upscale-alternative crowd.

Love Story (Map p280; ☎ 3231 3101; Rua Araújo 232, República; 1am-late Mon-Sat) Sampa's classic after-hours nightclub, Love Story attracts a rare combination of bourgeois kids, bohemians, celebrities and off-duty sex workers to its huge dance floor. Prices can be steep.

Clube Vegas (Map p287; ☎ 3231 3705; Rua Augusta 765; midnight-late Tue-Sun) Hidden in a basement in a seedy area just north of Av Paulista, neon-lit Vegas delivers a varied program, with music styles spanning jazz to rock to electronica, and attracting an eclectic, mixed crowd of die-hard night owls, both gay and straight.

Drops (Map p287; ☎ 2503 4486; Rua dos Ingleses 182, Bela Vista; 8pm-1am Wed-Sat) You feel like you're at a private house party in this elaborate little villa in a residential neighborhood. Bartenders specialize in cocktails concocted with fresh fruit, and the little dance floor features music ranging from indie rock and hip-hop to '80s hits.

D-Edge (Map p278; ☎ 3666 9022; Alameda Olga 170, Barra Funda; 11pm-late Mon & Wed-Sat) With one of the city's most remarkable sound systems and a roster of world-famous DJs, this mixed gay-straight club is a 'don't miss' for fans of electronica.

Canto da Ema (Map p278; ☎ 3813 4708; Av Brigadeiro Faria Lima 364, Pinheiros) For a break from São Paulo's upmarket danceterias, this relaxed, intimate club specializes in *forró universitário*, a

SÃO PAULO STATE

more approachable version of the high-octane dance music from Brazil's Northeast.

Mokai (Map p287; ☎ 3061 3084; Rua Augusta 2805, Jardins; ☯ 11pm-late Wed-Sat) Top-rack electronica and images of Marie Antoinette let you know you're in the newest upscale-decadent night-spot, where the outrageous cover charge (up-wards of R$100) seems only to attract more of the city's beautiful people.

Astronete (Map p287; ☎ 3151 4568; Rua Matias Aires 183; ☯ 9pm-5am Wed-Sat) Near Rua Augusta and occupying an old colonial house dressed up to look vaguely like a pub, this new favorite of Sampa's *alternativos* gets past the clichés with a clever mix of soul, funk, and indie rock.

Live Music

Bourbon Street Music Club (Map p278; ☎ 5095 6100; Rua dos Chanés 127; cover around R$30; ☯ 9pm-3am Tue-Sun) The top spot for live jazz and blues in Sampa, Bourbon Street has hosted the likes of BB King and Ray Charles.

Baretto (Map p287; ☎ 3896 4000; Rua Vittorio Fasano 88) Hands down one of the best places to see live music in the world, this bar inside the Hotel Fasano (p296) recalls prewar Milan and attracts top jazz and popular Brazilian musi-cians who normally only play large venues. Keep in mind that entrance fees match the glamor levels.

Cinemas

Virtually every big shopping center has a mul-tiplex, mostly offering standard Hollywood fare. For high art, check out the film series at the Centro Cultural Banco do Brasil (p283). Most films, especially higher-quality films, are subtitled rather than dubbed.

Also worthwhile:

Cinesesc (Map p287; ☎ 3087 0500; Rua Augusta 2075) Features excellent retrospectives.

HSBC Belas Artes (Map p287; ☎ 3258 4092; Rua da Consolação 2423) Six screens showing new, high-quality foreign and domestic films.

Classical, Ballet & Opera

Theatro Municipal (Map p280; ☎ 3223 3022; www .teatromunicipal.sp.gov.br, in Portuguese; Praça Ramos de Azevedo) Operas, classical ballets and sym-phonic music are held in São Paulo's most ornate theater (p283). At the time of writing, the theater was closed for a major restora-tion. Check website for a progress report and alternate venues.

Sala São Paulo (Map p280; ☎ 3367 9500; www.salasao paulo.art.br, in Portuguese; Praça Júlio Prestes) Excellent classical-music venue, renowned for its fine acoustics, in refurbished train station Estação Júlio Prestes (see p285).

SHOPPING

For remarkable bargains head to Rua 25 de Março, just north of the historic center, where wholesalers sell a dizzying variety of deeply discounted goods from around the world. For high fashion and high-end home furnishings, wander Rua Oscar Freire and surrounding streets in the Jardins district. Not fancy enough for you? There is always Daslu (see below).

Clothing & Shoes

Havaianas (Map p287; Rua Oscar Freire 1116, Jardins; ☯ 10am-8pm Mon-Sat, noon 6pm Sun) You will find flip-flops in every imaginable design and hue – and at quite reasonable prices – at the

---

DASLU WILL DAZZLE YOU

Don't plan on walking to **Daslu** (Map p278; ☎ 3841 4000; Av Chedid Jafet 131, Vila Olímpia; ☯ 10am-8pm Mon-Sat, to 10pm Tue). It's against the rules to arrive on foot at São Paulo's most over-the-top shopping emporium. A taxi is one option, though a much chicer option is to arrive by chopper at the rooftop heliport (see the boxed text, p303). The store itself looks like an all-white Roman villa on steroids, and over its three floors you can find every top designer, from Gucci to Tumi. Servants in black-and-white uniforms dole out free espresso, biscotti and sparkling water at bars spread throughout the store. Still hungry? There's a tearoom, a sushi bar and a more formal dining room. Daslu even has its own harem – a sprawling series of lounges and changing rooms where mirrors are ubiquitous and men are forbidden to set foot.

Despite the glittering facade, Daslu has known its share of shame. Just after the store opened in its current location in 2005, the owner Eliana Tranchesi was arrested for flagrant and massive tax fraud. She never had to serve a prison sentence, but the store did end up paying a fine of more than US$100 million.

SÃO PAULO STATE

new flagship store of Brazil's favorite beach footwear.

Galeria Melissa (Map p287; Rua Oscar Freire 827, Jardins; ☾ 10am-8pm Mon-Fri, to 6pm Sat) This temple to high-end footwear is worth checking out for its bold design – but don't expect bargains. Melissa first made its name for inexpensive but stylish plastic shoes that appealed to all social classes – unusual for Brazil.

Galeria Ouro Fino (Map p287; Rua Augusta 2690; ☾ 11am-8pm Mon-Sat) From hip-high boots to camouflage club gear, this old-fashioned, three-story mall has been turned into ground zero for *alternativo* shoppers.

Iodice (Map p287; ☎ 6445 2945; Rua Oscar Freire 940; ☾ 10am-8pm Mon-Sat, noon-6pm Sun) One of São Paulo's top homegrown brands for both men and women, Iodice prides itself on top-quality materials and creative elegance. This shop has both casual wares at relatively accessible prices as well as a high-end line with prices to match.

Markets

There are several markets worth checking out.

Feira da República (Map p280; Praça da República; ☾ 9am-5pm Sat & Sun) This open-air market specializes in handicrafts and painting.

Antiguidades do MASP (Map p287; Av Paulista 1578; ☾ 10am-5pm Sun) An antiques fair that's good for browsing, but bargains are limited.

Feira Benedito Calixto (Map p278; Praça Benedito Calixto, Pinheiros; ☾ 9am-7pm Sat) Open-air market for handicrafts and antiques, plus food stalls and live music.

Malls

Shopping Iguatemi (Map p278; Av Brigadeiro Faria Lima 2232; ☾ 10am-10pm Mon-Sat, 2-8pm Sun) Sampa's favorite high-end hulk of a mall, Shopping Iguatemi has all the top Brazilian brands, from Osklen to Ellus.

Shopping Frei Caneca (Map p287; Rua Frei Caneca 569; ☾ 10am-10pm Mon-Sat, 2-8pm Sun) Relatively modest in size, Shopping Frei Caneca is nevertheless fully equipped with food court, cinema and good midrange shops.

Souvenirs

Loja do Bispo (Map p287; Rua Dr Melo Alves 278, Jardins; ☾ 11am-8pm Mon-Fri, to 6pm Sat) This colorful, high-concept store is crammed with objets d'art, avant-garde art books, furnishings and more.

Espaço Brasil (Map p287; Alameda Franca 1167, Jardins; ☾ 10am-7pm Mon-Fri, to 3pm Sat) Spread over three stories, this light-filled store is practically a museum of Brazilian arts and crafts, ranging from carvings and paintings to soaps and linens.

GETTING THERE & AWAY
Air

From São Paulo's airports there are flights to just about every airport in Brazil and to many of the world's major cities. São Paulo is also the Brazilian hub for most international airlines, and thus the first stop for many travelers. The international airport is **Aeroporto São Paulo/Guarulhos** (off Map p278; airport code GRU; ☎ 2445 2945), which is 30km east of the center. Most domestic flights leave from **Aeroporto de Congonhas** (Map p278; airport code CGH; ☎ 5090 9000), 14km south of the center, though as traffic grows, more domestic flights are also leaving from Guarulhos.

Most of the major airlines have offices on Av São Luís, near Praça da República, or along Av Paulista.

Bus

São Paulo has four different bus stations, all accessible by metro. Each terminal tends to specialize in a certain set of destinations, but there are no hard-and-fast rules, unfortunately. If you need to check which terminal services your destination, consult www.socicam.com.br (in Portuguese) or, in São Paulo, call ☎ 3235 0322.

The main bus station, **Terminal Tietê** (Map p278; ☎ 3866 1100; Tietê metro station), located north of the historic center, is really easy to reach thanks to a metro stop inside the station itself. It is an enormous building but it's generally safe and well organized. Buses leave for destinations throughout Brazil and also for international destinations. Bus tickets are sold on the upper floor of the station. The hard part can be finding which bus company is headed in your direction. If you can't find a company serving your destination, ask at the information desk in the middle of the main concourse.

Prices listed are for buses with air-con. Expect to pay about 20% to 30% less to travel without air-con, and about 50% more for a *leito* (overnight sleeper).

International destinations include Buenos Aires in Argentina (from R$245, 36 hours), Montevideo in Uruguay (R$180, 30 hours) and Santiago in Chile (R$390, 54 hours).

Domestic buses leave from Terminal Tietê for Belo Horizonte (R$85, eight hours), Brasília (R$140, 14 hours), Cuiabá (R$120, 13 hours), Curitiba (R$80, six hours), Florianópolis (R$130, 12 hours), Foz do Iguaçu (R$140, 15 hours), Rio (R$80, six hours) and Ubatuba (R$45, four hours).

Buses to Santos, Guarujá and São Vicente leave about every half-hour from a separate bus station – the Terminal Intermunicipal do Jabaquara (Map p278), which is at the end of the southern metro line (metro Jabaquara). There is also Terminal Bresser, near the Memorial do Imigrante (Map p278) in the east-zone district of Brás, with services to the south of Minas Gerais state, and Terminal Barra Funda in the west zone, near the Memorial da América Latina (Map p278), for destinations in São Paulo state and Paraná, including Iguape and Cananéia.

GETTING AROUND
To/From the Airport

A taxi between Aeroporto de Congonhas and the city center costs R$30 to R$40 and takes around 30 to 45 minutes, depending on traffic. For buses to the center, walk out of the terminal and then to your right, where you'll see a busy street with a pedestrian overpass. Head to the overpass but don't cross; you should see a crowd of people waiting for the buses along the street. Local buses 875A and 875M run all the way to Av Paulista. Alternatively, you can take a taxi to the São Judas metro stop (R$15 to R$18) and take the metro from there to the center.

Aeroporto São Paulo/Guarulhos, São Paulo's international airport, is 30km northeast of the city center. There are **'Airport Service'** buses (☎ 6221 0244) to Praça da República, Terminal Tietê bus station, Congonhas airport and high-end hotels in Jardins and the city center. Buses leave approximately every half-hour from 6am to 11pm, with less frequent service from 11pm to 6am. All trips cost R$31 and leave from the stop just in front of the arrivals terminal. Taxis from the international airport charge a set fee depending on your destination. Fares to the city center are around R$90.

Bus

City buses, which are run by the city agency **SPTrans** (☎ toll-free 156; www.sptrans.com.br, in Portuguese), cost R$2.70, and most lines run from around 6am to 1pm. They can be slow going, crowded and prone to pickpockets. Fortunately, there is now a series of *corredores* – special, bus-only lanes that help speed up travel times. The city tourist-information booths are excellent sources of information about buses (see p281).

Public Transportation

A combination of metro and walking is the easiest way to see the city. São Paulo's efficient **metro** (www.metro.sp.gov.br/ingles/index.asp; 1-way ticket R$2.65; ☼ 5am-midnight) is one of the best in the world, with clean, modern stations – many of which are decorated with huge murals by local artists.

Taxi

Taxis are plentiful, though because of long distances and traffic they can be expensive. For example, a ride from Jardins to the historic center should cost around R$20. All taxis should be metered – if your driver doesn't

---

CLASS AIRFARE

Why has a helicopter been swaddled in cashmere and hung in the main hall of Daslu (p301), São Paulo's most exclusive shopping emporium? The answer is simple: a private chopper is the ultimate Paulistano status symbol. The city's elite took to the skies in a big way during the 1990s, rebelling against congested roads and kidnappers targeting wealthy residents. Today São Paulo is said to have more helicopter traffic than any other city, with some 300 heliports versus a mere 60 in New York City.

The problem, however, is that only the super-rich can afford their own bird. What are the merely 'very rich' to do? In a fit of class solidarity, they have founded helicopter 'collectives,' enabling members to share the cost of purchase and maintenance of the choppers, and also pilot hire. After an initial outlay of about US$70,000, members need only pony up as little as US$50,000 a year – a bargain when you consider it's a mere 10 times the typical annual salary of a domestic worker.

turn the meter on, be sure to mention it. If the driver still doesn't, ask to be let out. If you need to call a taxi, try **Ligue Táxi** (☎ 2101 3030) or **Coopertax** (☎ 2095 6000).

AROUND SÃO PAULO

PARANAPIACABA

☎ 0xx11 / pop 4000

Founded by the British-owned São Paulo Railway Company, the town of Paranapiacaba may sit amid the Atlantic rain forest of the Serra do Mar, about 40km southeast of São Paulo, but it still retains distinctly English traits, right down to a rough replica of Big Ben. The Brits made the town their headquarters as they laid the tracks that by 1867 would carry São Paulo's coffee to the port at Santos – a remarkable feat given the sheer mountainsides and rapid elevation drops. The British retained control of the railway up until 1947.

Because of its remoteness, the town has been remarkably well preserved, with a neat grid of streets populated by English-style buildings of wood and brick. The home of the railway's chief engineer, a classically Victorian wood construction known as 'Castelinho,' has been converted into the **Museu do Castelo** (Rua Caminho do Mendes; admission free; ☺ 9am-4pm Tue-Sun), a small museum with period furnishings and fine views.

Paranapiacaba also makes a good base for day hikes into the **Parque Estadual Serra do Mar**, with its dense forest that harbors a remarkable profusion of bromeliads and orchids. Trails are not marked, however, so it's best to seek out a licensed guide at the **Associação dos Monitores** (☎ 4439 0155), located near the old train station.

The best way to arrive in Paranapiacaba is by train. Take the Linha D train from São Paulo's Estação Luz to the Rio Grande da Serra station (R$4.50, one hour). From here, there is an hourly bus (R$2.70, 15 minutes) to nearby Paranapiacaba.

EMBU

☎ 0xx11 / pop 250,000

Founded in 1554, Embu spent most of its life as a quiet colonial village until, in the 20th century, it was swallowed up by São Paulo, whose center sits about 30km to the west. Yet Embu has managed to retain much of its colonial core, thanks largely to the hippies,

artists and intellectuals who made the town their refuge from São Paulo's concrete jungle, starting in the 1970s. Today the town makes a popular Sunday retreat for Paulistanos, when local artisans offer their wares at the outdoor **feira** (market; Largo dos Jesuitas; ☺ 9am-6pm Sun). The area around the *feira* is full of antique and craft shops that make good browsing on other days of the week.

There is a **tourist office** (☎ 4704 6565; Largo 21 de Abril; ☺ 9am-6pm), just off the main plaza. **O Garimpo** (☎ 4704 6344; Rua da Matriz 136; mains from R$25; ☺ 11:30am-10pm) is a pleasant spot for the peckish, with a veranda, colonial dining room, and a huge menu ranging from ceviche (raw fish marinated in lime juice) to suckling pig.

From outside the Clínicas metro station, catch the 'Embu Engenho Velho' bus (R$2.80, one hour, about every 30 minutes).

PAULISTA COAST

São Paulo's coast, known in Portuguese as the Litoral Paulista, is most spectacular in its northern reaches, especially around Ubatuba, thanks to the jungle-covered peaks of the Serra do Mar that reach all the way down to the Atlantic. Closer to the capital, the scenery is tamer but the beaches remain good, even in overbuilt Guarujá. Inviting strands stretch south all the way to the border with Paraná, including the largely undeveloped Ilha Comprida, an island that shelters the colonial towns of Iguape and Cananéia.

Note that prices along the coast tend to be quite high by Brazilian standards, especially from December to March.

UBATUBA

☎ 0xx12 / pop 76,000

Draped with the rich flora of the Mata Atlântica, the peaks of the Serra do Mar provide a dramatic, emerald-green backdrop to the winding Ubatuba coastline. This region has become a preeminent resort for well-heeled Paulistanos, with its elegant beach homes and a number of stylish hotels and pousadas, especially south of the town. Heading north toward neighboring Paraty in the state of Rio de Janeiro, beaches tend to be harder to reach but also wilder and more pristine, and the little-visited Parque Nacional Serra da Bocaina (see p196) spans both São Paulo and Rio de Janeiro states.

Orientation & Information

The town center, called 'Centro,' is a relatively compact grid of streets centered on Praça 13 de Maio, which is just north of Rua Professor Thomaz Galhardo, the main road into town. A number of restaurants and inns are located about 1km south of the center along beachfront Rua Guarani in a neighborhood known as Itaguá. Outside of Centro, neighborhoods are named for the nearest beach.

Banco 24 Horas (Av Iperoig, Centro) ATM located just next to the tourist office.

Tourist office (☎ 3833 9123; Centro; ☼ 8am-5pm) Situated where Rua Professor Thomaz Galhardo hits the beach; it has useful maps of surrounding beaches.

Sights & Activities

The town itself is uninspiring except for its handsome waterfront promenade. The real trick is to get to the remote beaches and picturesque islands outside the city. The tourist office can also offer information about hikes and guided visits to the adjacent state park, with good hiking trails into the thickly forested coastal range.

BEACHES

Within the district of Ubatuba, there are some 74 beaches and 15 islands. Regular buses run along the coastal road. Some of the best beaches south of Ubatuba include **Praia Vermelha** (3km), **Enseada** (8km), **Flamengo** (12km, on the Ponta do Flamengo), **do Lázaro** (16km) and **Domingos Dias** (18km). The big, loud party scene is 6km south of Ubatuba at **Praia Grande**.

North of town, the beaches are hidden away down steep hillsides. They're harder to find, but good for boogie boarding and surfing and well worth the effort. Among the best are **Vermelha do Norte** (9km), **de Itamambuca** (15km), **Promirim** (23km) and **Ubatumirim** (33km).

BOAT TRIPS

Boat trips leave from Itaguá for Ilha Anchieta (around R$40, three to four hours). A protected nature reserve, Anchieta offers rare glimpses of fish and birds undisturbed in their natural habitats. You can also see the local Tamar Project, which protects native turtles and their eggs. These minicruises offer enviable views of the coast and its beautiful, deep-green waters. You can make reservations at the tourist office or many hotels and guesthouses. Alternately, deal directly with operators who set up tables along the promenade in front of Itaguá beach. Cruise operators also leave from the Enseada and Saco da Ribeira neighborhoods.

Sleeping

If you're without a car, the town center is the most convenient place to stay. From here you can catch local buses (R$2.50) to the beaches.

BUDGET & MIDRANGE

Camping Itamambuca (☎ 3834 3000; www.itamambuca .com.br, in Portuguese; Praia de Itamambuca; campsites per person low/high season R$40/52) This ecoresort about 15km north of town offers excellent, if pricey, facilities near one of the region's most beautiful beaches. Rustic chalets are also available (for two people low/high season R$126/178, with big discounts for longer stays).

A Pousadinha (☎ 3832 2136; www.ubatuba.com.br /pousadinha; Rua Guarani 686, Itaguá; s/d R$100/130; P ✗) This former boarding house has been totally refurbished and offers small and simple but airily stylish rooms around a narrow, lemon-yellow courtyard, making for good value on this expensive stretch of coast.

Hotel Solar das Águas Cantantes (☎ 3842 0178; www.solardasaguascantantes.com.br, in Portuguese; Estrada Saco da Ribereira 951, Lázaro; s/d R$135/170; P ✗) With quarters ranged around a lush courtyard, this grand, whitewashed colonial affair sits a short walk from the stunning (if crowded) Praia do Lázaro. The high-ceilinged rooms have an austere elegance. The hotel's restaurant (p306) is renowned for its seafood stew.

TOP END

A Casa do Sol e da Lua (☎ 3848 9412; www.acasa dosoledalua.com.br; Rua do Refúgio do Cosário 580, Praia da Fortaleza; s/d R$180/240) This cozy, welcoming, family-run place sits right on a great stretch of beach about 10km south of town. Meals are served around a communal table, and rooms are casually but tastefully decorated.

Itamambuca Eco Resort (☎ 3834 3000; www.itama mbuca.com.br, in Portuguese; Praia de Itamambuca; d from R$450; P ✗ 💻) Rooms are simple, colorful and largely built from recycled wood and bamboo. Surrounded by dense vegetation and a short walk to one of the area's most remarkable beaches, this resort is worth the splurge.

Hotel Recanto das Toninhas (☎ 3842 1410; www.toninhas.com.br; Praia das Toninhas; d from R$575; P ✗ 💻 ✉) This sprawling, all-inclusive resort, on a privileged stretch of Toninhas beach, offers a pool, tennis courts, sauna and gym. Built largely of local straw, wood and thatch, it manages to be charming despite its size.

Eating

Don't miss *azul-marinho*, a delicious local stew of fish, rice and green bananas. There are a number of cheap eateries in the town center where you can get a simple meal of fish, rice and beans for R$10 to R$15.

Ellen (☎ 3832 3040; Rua Guarani 830, Itaguá; ☾ 8am-midnight Dec-Feb, 3-9pm Thu-Tue Mar-Nov) Sample the excellent, made-from-scratch *salgados* (savory snacks, R$4) on the pleasant veranda of this local favorite.

Atmosfera Café (☎ 3832 2515; Av Leovegildo Dias Vieira 378, Itaguá; sandwiches & salads R$10-20; ☾ 3pm-11pm) The trendiest spot in town offers great views of the sea from its huge veranda, plus creative takes on classic sandwiches and salads.

Peixe com Banana (☎ 3832 1712; Rua Guarani 255, Itaguá; mains for 2 R$50-100; ☾ noon-11pm Wed-Mon) Don't be fooled by the plastic tablecloths or the touristy seafront location. This is widely considered the region's top seafood joint, famed for its excellent version of *azul-marinho*.

Hotel Solar das Águas Cantantes (☎ 3842 0178; Estrada Saco da Ribereira 951, Lázaro; mains for 2 around R$75; ☾ lunch & dinner Wed-Mon) With a rustically elegant dining room plus pleasant poolside seating, this restaurant is renowned for its milder version of Bahian *moqueca* (seafood stew). Once again, the plastic tablecloths belie the excellence of the food.

Getting There & Around

Ubatuba has two intercity bus stations. For São Paulo (R$45, four hours, eight daily), São Sebastião (R$8, 70 minutes, hourly; change in Caraguátatuba) and other destinations within the state, head to **Litorânea bus station** (Rua Maria Victória Jean 381), located at the edge of the town center, about 1.5 km from the tourist office and beach. A taxi to the center from most locations in Centro costs around R$12.

For buses to Paraty and Rio de Janeiro, head to the **São Jose bus station** (Rua Professor Thomaz Galhardo 513), on the main street a few blocks from the beach.

Local buses (R$2.50, about hourly from 7am to 8pm) head up and down the coastal highway and come at least within hiking distance of most beaches. The main stop in the center is at Rua Hans Staden 488, between the two long-distance stations.

SÃO SEBASTIÃO

☎ 0xx12 / pop 65,000

One of the only towns on the Paulista coast that has preserved a portion of its colonial charms, São Sebastião sits on a dramatic channel dividing the mainland from Ilha de São Sebastião (popularly known as 'Ilhabela'; see p307), a 15-minute ferry trip away. Prices in town are moderate by local standards, but for good reason. There are no beaches at hand, and the town is also a major oil depot, with huge tankers somewhat diminishing the natural beauty. Still, it makes a fine stopover if you're traveling to Ilhabela or along the coast.

And the windy channel is ideal for windsurfing. For information, check out the **tourist office** (☎ 3892 2620, ext 203; Av Dr Altino Arantes 174; ☾ 10am-6pm, to 10pm Sat-Sun in summer) on the waterfront in the small colonial center of town.

Sleeping

Hotel Roma (☎ 3892 1016; www.hotelroma.tur.br; Praça Major João Fernandes 174; s/d R$60/100; [P] [⬚]) In the heart of the colonial quarter, Hotel Roma has newer, no-frills rooms with air-con ranged around a plain courtyard, plus a few rooms without bathroom and with fan only (single/double R$25/35) in the main colonial-style building.

Pousada da Ana Doce (☎ 3892 1615; www.pousada anadoce.com.br; Rua Expedicionários Brasileiros 196; s/d R$100/130) With neat, cheerful little rooms arranged around a charming, plant-filled courtyard in the colonial center, this inn is the most charming in the region, especially at such reasonable rates. Book ahead.

Eating

Be sure to try the excellent locally made Rocha brand *sorvete* (ice cream) and *picolês* (popsicles), available at a myriad seafront shops. Flavors like *milho verde* (sweet corn), *côco queimado* (burnt coconut) and *banana frita* (fried banana) are unforgettable.

Tip Top (Av Dr Altino Arantes) On the waterfront just down from the ferry dock, Tip Top serves burgers and sandwiches (R$5 to R$7), plus a serviceable lunch buffet (R$24 per kg). Sidewalk seating with sea views completes the picture.

Atobá (☎ 3892 1487; Praça Major João Fernandes 218; mains R$15-25; ☻ lunch & dinner Tue-Sat, dinner Sun) In a colonial building on the town's main square, Atobá offers a high-quality buffet (R$32 per kg) at lunch and an à la carte menu of pizzas at dinner.

Getting There & Away

The **bus station** (Praça da Amizade 10), located just off the main coastal highway and a short walk from the colonial center, has service to São Paulo about every two hours (R$40, four hours, 10 daily) and Boiçucanga (R$12, one hour, six daily) and other stops along the coast to Santos. In the same station, Util offers service to Rio (R$72, seven hours, twice daily), with a stop in Paraty.

ILHABELA

☎ 0xx12 / pop 23,000 (winter), 120,000 (summer)
Rising steeply from the narrow strait that divides it from the continent, the 350-sq-km Ilhabela (Beautiful Island) earns its name from its volcanic peaks, beautiful beaches, dense tropical jungle and some 360 waterfalls. Almost 85% of the island has been turned into a park and Unesco-protected biosphere, which shelters a remarkable profusion of plant and animal life, including toucans and capuchin monkeys. A haunt of pirates in the 16th and 17th centuries, its waters are scattered with shipwrecks, many of which make for excellent diving. The island also proffers jungle hiking, windsurfing and beach-lazing.

Be aware that in the height of summer the bugs are murder, especially the little bloodsuckers known as *borrachudos*. Use plenty of insect repellent at all times. Summer is also when the island is packed with vacationing Paulistas. Also try to avoid arriving on Friday evening and/or leaving on Sunday evening, especially in summer, as traffic, the line for the ferry and spikes in accommodations prices can tarnish your experience of paradise.

Orientation & Information

The ferry arrives from the mainland in the Barra Velha neighborhood, which blends seamlessly with the town of Perequê just to the north. About 7km north lies the historic town of Vila. Good roads run along the western coast of the island; however, the south and east coasts are reachable only by boat or foot except for a rough road accessible by

4WD that reaches Praia dos Castelhanos on the west coast.

The **tourist office** (☎ 3895 7102; Av Princesa Isabel 3039, Barra Velha; ☻ 9am-6pm Mon-Fri, 10am-5pm Sat, 9am-1pm Sun) is located about 100m from the ferry terminal in Barra Velha. You can also preview your visit at www.ilhabela.org, which includes history, hiking itineraries, listings for diving and other adventure activities – and more – in English.

For those bringing a car to the island, avoid huge lines waiting for the **ferry** (☎ (13) 3358 2277; www.dersa.sp.gov.br, in Portuguese) on summer weekends by booking in advance (R$63/45 weekdays/weekends).

ATMs in Barra Velha, Perequê and Vila Ilhabela (Vila) accept international bank cards.

Sights

Vila Ilhabela, on the northwestern part of the island, has quite a few well-preserved colonial buildings, including the slave-built **Igreja NS da Ajuda** (founded 1532); the **Fazenda Engenho d'Agua** in Itaquanduba (founded 1582); and **Fazenda Santa Carmen** at Feiticeira beach. Two kilometers inland from Perequê beach (near the ferry terminal), **Cachoeira das Tocas** has various small waterfalls with accompanying deep pools and waterslides.

BEACHES

Of the sheltered beaches on the north side of the island, **Praia Jabaquara** is recommended. It can be reached by car via a dirt road. On the east side of the island, where the surf is stronger, try beautiful **Praia dos Castelhanos** (good for camping and surfing), which is backed by the steeply rising jungle. From the town of Borrifos at the southern end of the island, you can take a four-hour walk to **Praia Bonete**, a windy surf beach lying on the southern side of the island that you will share mostly with a local community of fishermen.

Activities

Maremar Aventura Turismo (☎ 3896 1418; www.mare mar.tur.br; Avenida São João 574, Perequê) in Barra Velha near the ferry organizes all kinds of outdoor activities, including schooner trips around the island (from R$45 per person), diving to offshore wrecks (full day including equipment from R$240), and horseback riding (three hours from R$70).

Sleeping

Making a reservation is a good idea on weekends – mandatory on summer weekends. Prices are high, so some travelers choose to stay in São Sebastião, where rates are more reasonable.

Camping Canto Grande (☎ 3894 1506; www.canto grande.com.br, in Portuguese; Av Riachuelo 5638, Praia Grande; campsites per person R$30; ☺) Run by the kind Enzo, this grassy, beachside campground approximately 6km south of the ferry landing offers hot-water showers, electric plug-ins, a gurgling stream, a simple restaurant, wi-fi and beach chairs and umbrellas for hire.

Bonns Ventos Hostel (☎ 3896 2725; www.bonnsven toshostel.com.br; Rua Benedito Serafim Sampaio 371, Perequê; dm/d R$50/120; P ☺ ▯ ☺) Conveniently located about 500m from the ferry stop, the island's new hostel offers well-maintained and brightly colored digs, plus a pleasant terrace with pool.

Pousada das Maritacas (☎ 3896 3839; www.pousada dasmaritacas.com.br; Av Princesa Isabel 1788, Perequê; s/d R$100/180; P ☺ ☺) Offering good value for its simple but tasteful and comfortable rooms, this motel-style place also doubles as a lush, open-air plant store. Rooms farther from the road are quieter.

Pousada Catamarã (☎ 3894 1034; www.pousadacata marabrasil.com.br; Rua José Batista dos Santos 273, Curral; d from R$180; ☺ ☺) Hidden up an inauspiciously rutted side street, this colorful and pristinely maintained inn offers very comfortable rooms, plus a small but pretty pool hidden in a lush garden. Good value.

Refúgio das Pedras (☎ 3894 1756; www.refugio daspedras.com.br, in Portuguese; Av Governador Mário Covas 11495, Ponta da Sela; d R$400) Located near the southern end of the strait facing the mainland, this quirky-but-chic guesthouse takes its name from the natural rocks that have been incorporated in both the landscaping and the rooms. Amenities include a small fitness center and Jacuzzi bath.

DPNY Beach (☎ 3894 2121; www.dpnybeach.com .br; Av José Pacheco do Nascimento 7668; d from R$550; P ☺ ▯ ☺) Set right on the sands of Praia Curral, this top-of-the-line getaway for São Paulo fashionistas includes exquisitely appointed rooms, a huge pool, a haremlike spa and Miami-style ambient music throughout. It is also home to Hippie Chic Beach Bar (p308), the island's fanciest bar-lounge, and Tróia (p308), its top restaurant.

Eating & Drinking

Note that some places tend to close early during low season when crowds are thin, so plan for a backup.

Cheiro Verde (☎ 3896 3245; Rua da Padroeira 109, Vila; meals R$15; ☺ 11:30am-6pm Mon-Thu, to 10pm Sat & Sun) The best place in Vila for a generous *prato feito* (plate of the day) with grilled meat or fish, plus rice, beans and salad, this simply but clean and airy place attracts tourists and locals alike. The fresh juices are excellent and good value.

Casa Verde (Rua Luíz Ameixeiro 65, Perequê; meals R$15; ☺ 11:30am-5pm Mon-Thu, to 10pm Sat-Sun) From the same owner as Cheiro Verde (p308) and offering the same menu, Casa Verde adds free parking, air-conditioning and a discreetly colorful interior, adding up to the best deal on the Paulista coast.

Max Paladar (☎ 3896 3700; Av São João 243, Perequê; per kg R$32) Under a vast thatched roof, this pleasant open-air restaurant offers a good-value buffet with fresh veggies and salads, plus hot meat and pasta dishes.

O Borrachudo (☎ 3896 1499; Rua Dr Carvalho 20, Vila; sandwiches R$10-20; ☺ noon-2am Sun-Thu, to 3pm Fri-Sat) In a colonial building right on Vila's waterfront, this relaxed café proudly serves excellent burgers of all kinds (including salmon, ostrich and tofu), as well as other gourmet sandwiches.

A Redonda (☎ 3894 9154; Av Riachuelo 6852, Curral; pizzas for 2 around R$45; ☺ dinner Thu-Tue Dec-Feb, Thu-Sun Mar-Nov) Renowned for its wood-oven pizza, this rustic-chic restaurant occupies a fuchsia-colored cottage and pleasant garden. There is a pricey but good crafts store attached.

Tróia (☎ 3894 2121; Av José Pacheco do Nascimento 7668, Curral; mains R$45-85; ☺ lunch & dinner) A sea-facing terrace, a misting system that keeps diners cool even on hot days and creative takes on Mediterranean cuisine (shrimp with sauce of orange and vanilla beans) make this the island's top-rated restaurant as well as the focal point of island society.

Hippie Chic Beach Bar (☎ Av José Pacheco do Nascimento 7668, Curral) With quietly thumping lounge music, hip-tropical decor and table service on the sand, the island's fanciest bar attracts rich Paulistas eager to show off this season's designer gear. Beers run around R$10 and cocktails start at R$20.

For self-catering, hit the **Ilha da Princesa supermarket** (Av Princesa Isabel 2467), located near the ferry in Barra Velha.

Getting There & Around

The 15 minute ferry trip between São Sebastião and Ilhabela runs every half-hour from 6am to midnight (often until much later in summer). Cars cost R$11 weekdays and R$16 on weekends, motorcycles cost R$5 weekdays and R$8 on weekends, and it's free for pedestrians. A local bus (R$2.20, every 30 minutes, 6am to midnight) runs the length of the island, including a stop at the ferry. Taxis (☎ 0800 7705 221) are usually waiting at the ferry.

A decent road runs the length of the western coast. Another unsealed road (22km) crosses the island. To get to the other side of the island requires either a 4WD, a boat or a good strong pair of hiking legs.

BOIÇUCANGA & AROUND

☎ 0xx12 / pop 5800

The laid-back surfer town of Boiçucanga makes a good base to explore the stretch of coast that runs almost due west from São Sebastião. The variety of beaches, many backed by the steeply rising Serra do Mar, is remarkable, and there's good surf at nearby Camburi and Maresias, which have also developed into major party towns.

Information

Boiçucanga has a **tourist office** (☎ 3865 4335; ⏱ 8am-6pm Mon-Fri) right off the main highway about 200m west of the town center. You can also get information from José Mauro, who runs a tourist information service called **Amart** (☎ 3465 1453, 9144 4434; Av Walkir Vergani 319) and speaks English, Spanish and Italian.

Sights & Activities

Some great beaches are strung along this stretch of coastline, all accessible by bus. Both **Maresias** (9km east of Boiçucanga), and **Camburi** (3km west) are great surf beaches. A creek and a small island divide Camburi – the western end is bigger, rougher and good for surfing, and the eastern end is calmer and good for swimming. **Juqueí** (15km west) offers calm waters, making it popular with families. There is a series of deserted islands nearby. Ask at the tourist office to organize passage. Expect to pay R$20 to R$30 per person.

Sleeping

Camping Porongaba (☎ 3865 1384; www.porongaba .com.br; Travessa dos Periquitos 99, Boiçucanga; campsites per person R$20) This camping ground has a pool, snack bar and pleasant grounds. From the bus station in Boiçucanga, head up Estrada do Cascalho about 2km and cross a wooden bridge. The camping ground is 50m on the left.

Hostel Camburi (☎ 3865 1561; Rua Tijucas 2300, Camburi; www.ajcamburi.com.br; dm/r from R$25/75; 💻 🏊) Though a bit pricey, this hostel is the best budget option in Camburi; it has clean, basic rooms with fans, and a swimming pool amid green grounds. It's about 2.5km from Camburi Sertão bus stop.

Pousada Boiçucanga (☎ 3865 2668; pousadaboicu canga@yahoo.com.br; Av Walkir Vergani 522, Boiçucanga; r R$100) The cheapest pousada in town offers clean, basic rooms that feature tile floors, well-used furnishings and ceiling fans, set around a potentially noisy courtyard.

Pousada das Praias (☎ 3865 1474; www.pousada daspraias.com.br; Rua Piau 70, Camburi; d R$180) Handsomely rustic apartments, most of which are built with local wood, make this higher-end option well worth seeking out. It's located just off the main road near the eastern end of the beach.

Pousada Portal do Cacau (☎ 3865 1611; www .portaldocacau.com.br; Rua Tijucas 895, Camburi; s/d R$220; 🏊) You get good value at this rather plush miniresort, which has a sauna, tennis courts, a pool and massage studio. The rooms are comfortable, if undistinguished, and there are walks from the pousada to several nearby waterfalls.

Pousada DiMari (☎ 3865 4711; www.dimari.com.br; Av Walkir Vergani 833, Boiçucanga; d R$440; 🏊) Tranquil, airy rooms with sea views, colorful high-end decor and a lovely beachfront garden with pool. DiMari is the classiest choice in the town of Boiçucanga.

Eating

There are some bargain restaurants (meals from R$10) in Boiçucanga's new US-style mall in the center of town. Restaurants also line the beachfront in Maresias.

Big Pão (⏱ 6am-midnight) This old-fashioned bakery café, located at the bend in the highway in the center of Boiçucanga, serves sandwiches and grill food (mains around R$5).

Restaurante Caravela (☎ 3865 1541; Rua Itabira 21, Boiçucanga; mains for 2-3 around R$70; ⏱ noon-10pm Wed-Mon) Head here for delicious *caldeiradas* and *moquecas* (both a kind of fish stew) served on an attractive outdoor terrace.

Getting There & Around

The intercity bus station in Boiçucanga has services to São Paulo (R$30, four hours, eight daily), Guarujá (R$19, two hours, six daily) and São Sebastião (R$10, one hour, six daily). Intercity buses usually stop at smaller towns such as Camburi and Maresias. There is also a local bus service (R$2.50) connecting Boiçucanga with Maresias, Camburi and other nearby coastal towns.

GUARUJÁ

☎ 0xx13 / pop 285,000

With its fine beaches along the stretch of coast closest to São Paulo, once-glamorous Guarujá has suffered from overdevelopment. Still, if you can't get farther afield, it makes a good getaway from the 'other' big city – even if concrete towers line the beaches, which get packed with weekend day-trippers. A recent cleanup of waters and sands has renewed interest in a town that was the extreme of chic back in the '70s. Surfers should note that there are good waves along **Praia do Tombo**.

Information

The helpful **tourist information office** (☎ 3344 4600; Rua Marechal Deodoro da Fonesca 723; ⏲ 10am-6pm) sits on the beach at the end of the main road into town.

Sleeping & Eating

Accommodations, restaurants and bars line the waterfront area.

Hotel Rio (☎ 3355 9281; www.hotelrio.com.br; Rua Rio de Janeiro 131; s/d R$110/150) The old-fashioned, whitewashed Hotel Rio is more charming outside than in, but its clean, basic rooms are good value and are situated less than 100m from the beach.

Pousada Canto do Forte (☎ 3354 2860; www .cantodoforte.com.br; Rua Horácio Guedes Barreiro 133; s/d R$120/175; ❁ 🖳 🐾) Simple, clean rooms with fridge and tiled floors are a good deal at this well-run option at the end of Praia do Tombo. Reservations are recommended in summer and at weekends.

Combinati (☎ 3386 9005; Rua Mário Ribeira 600; mains from R$20; ⏲ lunch & dinner Wed-Mon) Good, midrange Italian food a short walk from the tourist office.

Getting There & Around

Guarujá is on a large island separated from the mainland by the Canal de Bertioga. The bus station (☎ 3386 2325) is at the edge of town on Via Santos Dumont. From there, cross the street and catch local bus 1, 15 or 41 (R$2.10) to the beach. Buses leave every half-hour for São Paulo, cost R$18, and take between 75 minutes and two hours, depending on traffic.

IGUAPE & AROUND

☎ 0xx13 / pop 28,000

Founded by the Portuguese in 1538 to defend Brazil from the Spanish, Iguape is one of the oldest towns in Brazil and one of the few along São Paulo's coast to retain its colonial contours. A new federal initiative is helping restore the old city center, which had long been neglected. While beaches are a bit of a hoof, the town makes a tranquil base from which to explore the region.

Information

There is a **tourist information booth** (☎ 3841 3358; Largo da Basílica 71; ⏲ 8-11:30am & 1:30-5:30pm) on the town's main square.

Sights

The town's colonial charms are clustered around the whitewashed main plaza, **Largo da Basílica**, and the 18th-century **basilica** (⏲ 8am-8pm). About 1.5km on the road to Barra do Ribeira is a turnoff to the **Mirante do Morro da Espia**, a lookout with a good view of the port and region.

Iguape looks across a narrow strait to **Ilha Comprida**, a long, skinny island (86km by 3km) that shelters Iguape from the open ocean. The island is covered with a combination of mangrove and Atlantic rain forest, and has an uninterrupted beach that stretches the entire Atlantic-facing length of the island. A toll bridge now connects Iguape with the island.

Sleeping & Eating

There are a number of inexpensive pizzerias and other eateries on Largo da Basílica.

Silvi Hotel (☎ 3841 1421; www.silvihotel.com.br; Rua Ana Cândida Sandoval Trigo 515; s/d without air-con R$50/70, with air-con R$70/90; ❁) Humble but decent yellow-and-green, motel-style sleep, with clean and largish, if plain, rooms. Downstairs, there is a decent restaurant with a reasonably priced buffet and a more expensive à la carte menu.

Pousada Casa Grande (☎ 3841 1920; Rua Major Rebello 768; s/d R$80/110) The exterior of this 19th-century colonial mansion remains intact, but the smallish, high-ceilinged rooms have been thoroughly, if simply, refurbished. There is a pleasant veranda and small but verdant garden. Rooms have fans only.

Pousada Solar Colonial (☎ 3841 1591; Praça da Basílica 30; s/d R$80/110) Occupying a handsome colonial building right on the town's main square, this inn offers simple but clean, refurbished rooms, plus breakfast in a bright room with French windows onto the main square. Rooms have fans only.

Panela Velha (☎ 3841 1869; Rua 15 de Novembro 190; mains for 2 from $60; ☺ lunch & dinner) Considered the best option in town, this trim and spotless little place specializes in simple but expertly prepared local seafood. Walls are hung with a combination of nautical images and Roman Catholic kitsch.

Getting There & Around

There is a direct bus service from Iguape to São Paulo (R$35, four hours, about four daily) and Cananéia (R$18, two hours, about two daily). Local buses cross the bridge to Ilha Comprida. If you have a 4WD, it is possible to drive along the long, flat beach on Ilha Comprida and take the ferry across to Cananéia (R$7.90 per vehicle, passengers free), though you must time your trip for low tide.

CANANÉIA

☎ 0xx13 / pop 14,000

Smaller and prettier than neighboring Iguape, Cananéia has an even longer lineage. Founded in 1531, it's considered one of the oldest European settlements in Brazil, and while the bulk of the old town was built in the 19th century, parts of the **Igreja São Batista** (Praça Martim Afonso de Souza; ☺ irregular) date to the 16th century. After generations of decay, Cananéia is taking renewed pride in its historic center, and many buildings are being restored and painted in an array of bright colors.

Beaches

The beaches of **Ilha Comprida** are only a 10-minute ferry ride (R$7.90 per vehicle, at least once an hour from 6am to 11pm). Passengers on foot ride free.

The highlight of the region is **Ilha do Cardoso**, an ecological reserve of gorgeous natural pools, waterfalls and untouched beaches, which has only 400 residents and no cars. Along the waterfront near the ferry to Ilha Comprida, a number of private operators offer

boat service to the island. Prices vary, but for a round-trip and a stay of at least a three hours, expect to pay around R$20 per person (four-person minimum).

Sleeping & Eating

Hotels are often booked up during peak holiday season (January and February) and on weekends all summer long.

Hotel Intermares (☎ 9715 3963; www.hotelinter mares.com.br; Av Intermares 100; s/d R$60/80) The only decent option at the beach on Ilha Comprida, the kind Dona Irene and her beloved parrot offer small but simple, clean rooms with fans and little bathrooms. Rooms have fans only.

Hotel Marazul (☎ 3851 1407; www.hotelmarazul.com .br; Av Luís Wilson Barbosa 408; s/d R$120/160; P ☺ ☺) With a waterfront pool and terrace as well as rather simple but colorful guestrooms, this brick pousada is as upscale as Cananéia gets. Cash only.

Restaurante Naguissa do Silêncio (Av Luís Wilson Barbosa 401; mains R$25-45; ☺ lunch & dinner) For locally caught fish and oysters prepared and served with care, head to this simple but well-run restaurant about 1km northeast of the historic center.

Kurt Kaffe (☎ 3851 1262; Av Beira Mar 71; mains R$20-35; ☺ 4-11pm Mon, Tue & Thu, noon-midnight Fri-Sun) A café, French-inflected restaurant and antique store, this charming waterfront place attracts travelers and local bohemians alike with its live music, fresh oysters (for which Cananéia is renowned), booze and garden seating under the shade of a cashew tree.

Getting There & Around

Intersul offers three daily buses between Cananéia and São Paulo (R$42, five hours).

The ferry terminal to Ilha Comprida is down from the main plaza. The 10-minute ferry ride is free for foot passengers (vehicles cost R$7.90), with boats leaving at least hourly from 6am to 11pm.

INLAND

IPORANGA

☎ 0xx15 / pop 5000

Nestled in the Vale do Ribeira in the hills near the São Paulo–Paraná border, Iporanga was founded in 1576 after gold was discovered here. Today, the surrounding region remains one of the least-disturbed stretches of the Brazilian Atlantic Forest and is of international importance for its biodiversity. It also makes a good base for visiting the Parque Estadual do Alto do Ribeira (PETAR). This 360-sq-km state park, with its 280 cataloged caves, is known as Brazil's Capital das Grutas (Cave Capital).

Information

Some of the staff at the town's **tourist office** (☎ 3556 1420; Praça Honório Correia; ⏰ 8am-5pm Mon-Fri) speak English. For information as well as camping and caving reservations, contact **PETAR** (☎ 3552 1875; www.petaronline.com.br). The trustworthy **Ecocave** (☎ 3556 1574; www.ecocave .com.br) organizes expeditions to the caves, as well as hiking, rappelling and inner-tubing along the local river.

Caves

PETAR's **Núcleos de Visitação** (☎ 3552 1875) are well-set-up visitors centers with information on cave trips, guides (all in Portuguese) and camping grounds.

There are four Núcleos: Núcleo Santana (18km northwest of town) has good facilities for visitors and campers, five caves and a 3.5km-long trek to a beautiful waterfall;

Núcleo Ouro Grosso (13km northwest of town) has basic accommodations for groups and offers cooking facilities, two caves and a walking trail; Núcleo Casa de Pedra (9km by road plus 3km by walking trail, northwest from town) is the base for visiting the Casa de Pedra, famous for its 215m-high entrance and pristine Atlantic forest; and Núcleo Caboclos (centrally located in the park, 86km by road from town) has good camping facilities, basic visitors' lodgings and several caves.

Sleeping & Eating

Accommodations are mostly clustered in the Bairro da Serra, near the entrance to the park about 13km from the town center. Most places offer full-board options.

Pousada Iporanga (☎ 3556 1132; www.pousadaipo ranga.com.br; Rua Celso Descio 7; s/d R$40/70) Just at the entrance of the town of Iporanga, this clean, well-run option offers digs that are simpler than its somewhat grand exterior indicates. Rooms with fan and bathroom are ranged around a bright courtyard.

Pousada Quiririm (☎ 3556 1273; www.pousadado quiririm.com.br, in Portuguese; Bairro da Serra; d incl breakfast & dinner from R$110) Run with taste and loving

---

TUDO BEM, Y'ALL?

When the South lost the American Civil War in 1865, Brazil's emperor Dom Pedro II saw dollar signs. Offering cheap land to planters in exchange for the state-of-the-art techniques for growing cotton that they would bring with them, he lured as many as 10,000 Southerners to his country.

Most of the new immigrants settled in central São Paulo state, where they found growing conditions remarkably similar to those of the southern US. They planted pecans, peaches, corn and cotton just as they had in their native soil. They also made a concerted effort to stay aloof from Brazilian culture, venerating the Confederate flag and preserving their language and many of their customs. However, they did have to forgo one luxury: slavery, the institution they had fought so hard to defend. Research indicates that only a few former Confederates actually owned slaves in Brazil.

In the neighboring towns of **Americana** and **Santa Bárbara d'Oeste**, both about 100km northwest of São Paulo, you can still hear descendants of the confederados speaking English with a distinctly Southern lilt. And every year, the Fraternity of American Descendants – the community's main social institution – holds a picnic, complete with fried chicken, biscuits and peach pie.

The Cemitério do Campo, located in a sea of sugarcane fields about 12km from Santa Bárbara d'Oeste, is the confederados' spiritual epicenter. Founded in the 1870s when Catholic authorities refused burial to the Protestant immigrants, its gravestones are inscribed with names such as Braxton and Bloxom, Sharpley and Shippey, Meriwether and Maxwell.

To explore São Paulo's Confederate heritage, head to Santa Bárbara d'Oeste's **Museu da Imigração** (☎ 0xx19-3455 5082; Praça 9 de Julho; admission free; ⏰ 8-11:30am & 1-5pm Tue-Fri, 8-11:30am & 1-2:30pm Sat), whose collections include letters, photographs and household objects. The city has direct services to and from São Paulo's Tietê bus station (R$20, two hours). Ask at the museum about arranging transportation to the Cemitério do Campo, which can be difficult to find, even for local drivers.

care by Dona Marizete, this little oasis offers a variety of simple but spick-and-span rooms (all with private bathroom, although some of the bathrooms are separate from the room itself) that are set around a lovely, bird-filled garden.

Pousada das Cavernas (☎ 3814 9153; www.pousadadascavernas.com.br, in Portuguese; d without/with air-con incl breakfast & dinner R$115/170; P ✗ ☐) One of the most attractive options around, this inn in the Bairro da Serra area offers wide verandas, colonial-style construction and simple but well-kept rooms, some with views over a pretty valley.

Churrascaria do Abel (Rua Barão de Jundiaí 88; meals R$12) You can't go wrong at this friendly, family-run place, which offers generous portions of classic Brazilian home-cooked meals, including grilled meats, rice, beans and salad.

Getting There & Away
From São Paulo's Barra Funda bus station, Intersul buses head to Eldorado (R$44, five hours, four daily). From Eldorado, catch a Moreira bus to Iporanga (R$8, one hour 30 minutes, three daily). Alternatively, from São Paulo's Barra Funda bus station, Transpen offers service to Apiaí (R$44, five hours, three daily), where you can catch a local bus to Iporanga via Barrio da Serra (R$4, one hour 45 minutes, three daily). Note that in both cases, service drops off on Saturday, and even more on Sunday. Plan to travel early in the day at weekends.

CAMPOS DO JORDÃO
☎ 0xx12 / pop 47,000 / elevation 1628m
Nestled in the green peaks of the Serra da Mantiqueira, 180km northeast of São Paulo, Campos do Jordão is at once a kitsch and rather plain confection. Still, it makes a comfortable base from which to explore the nearby peaks, which are home to some of the last remaining virgin *araucária* (Paraná pine) forests and proffer spectacular views of the Paraíba valley. There is also a renowned winter classical-music festival in July.

Be aware that the town is a hugely popular winter weekend getaway for Paulistas who enjoy the novelty of wearing woolens. Traffic and prices spike accordingly.

Orientation & Information
Campos is made up of three main districts: Abernéssia (the oldest), Jaguaribe (where the bus station is located) and Capivari, the center. The three districts are connected by a tram (R$2.50).

The **tourist office** (☎ 3664 3525; ☟ 8am-8pm) is at the gateway to the valley, on the main road into town about 2km before Abernéssia, and offers a helpful map.

Sights & Activities
The **Horto Florestal state park** (admission per vehicle R$5; ☟ 8am-5pm), 14km east from Capivari, is home to the largest *araucária* reserve in the state and offers fine walks of varying levels of difficulty. The **reception desk** (☎ 3663 3762), near the trout farm, can supply you with maps.

Close to Capivari is a **teleférico** (chairlift; R$10; ☟ 1-5pm Fri, 9am-5:30pm Sat & Sun) that takes you to the top of the **Morro do Elefante**, which has a good view of the town.

The **Palácio Boa Vista** (☎ 3662 1122; Av Dr Ademar de Barros 3001; admission R$5; ☟ 10am-noon & 2-4pm Wed-Sun), 3.5km north of Abernéssia, is the state governor's sprawling, English-style, antiques-filled summer residence.

The 19km **electric train ride** (☎ 3663 1531; 2½hr round-trip R$40) from Campos do Jordão to Santo Antônio do Pinhal is one of Brazil's best. There are five trains daily on weekends, but only two daily on weekdays. The train leaves from Campos (from the Capivari terminal at the end of Av Emílio Ribas). For the best views, sit on the right-hand side when leaving Campos.

For those who want to explore the area by bike, you can rent wheels at **Pedal Shop** (☎ 3663 8346; Av José Manoel Gonçalves 108, Capivari) and **Desafius** (☎ 3664 6096; Av Frei Orestes Girardi 3159, Capivari). **Altus** (☎ 3663 4122; Av Roberto Simonsen 1724, Vila Inglesa; www.altus.tur.br) organizes groups for hiking, rock-climbing, mountain biking and other outdoor adventure activities.

Sleeping
July is peak tourist period in Campos, when the town receives up to a million tourists. Many places require a minimum one-week stay at this time. You can expect steep discounts on weekdays and outside winter months.

Campos do Jordão Hostel (☎ 3662 2341; www.camposdojordaohostel.com.br; Rua Pereira Barreto 22; dm/d R$50/120) In a grand old building from the early 20th century, this is one of Brazil's more pleasant hostels. The recently renovated rooms are airy, with high ceilings.

Duas Quedas Park Hotel (☎ 3662 2492; www.duas quedas.com.br; Rua Leonor Przirembel 255; 4-person chalets R$210) With rustic but comfortable, well-kept (though slightly musty) chalets arranged around a pretty garden complete with water-fall, this is one of the town's most charming options.

Grande Hotel Campos do Jordão (☎ 3260 6000; www.grandehotelsenac.com.br; Av Frei Orestes Girardi; d incl full board from R$900; ✘ ☐ ☎) Set in its own pri-vate forest, this sumptuous, European-style resort is run by a prestigious hotel school. It has lovely grounds, pool and tennis courts, plus views of the surrounding countryside from many rooms.

Eating & Drinking

Bia Kaffe (☎ 3663 1507; Rua Isola Orsi 33; mains from R$24; ☺ noon-midnight Fri & Sat, to 8:30pm Sun) This cozy haunt in Capivari serves quality coffee, cakes and other sweets, as well as grilled sausage, goulash and trout. Recommended.

Harry Pisek (☎ 3663 4030; Av Pedro Paulo 857; mains from R$35; ☺ 10am-5pm Sun-Fri, to 11pm Sat) Chef Pisek studied the art of sausage-making in Germany and is celebrated for his homemade production, which he serves up in his cozy restaurant, complete with Teutonic decor, on the road to Horto Florestal.

Getting There & Away

The **bus station** (☎ 3262 1996; Av Dr Januário Miraglia) is close to Supermercado Roma, between Jaguaribe and Capivari. Buses travel to São Paulo (R$28, 2½ hours, about six daily) and to Rio de Janeiro (R$49, five hours, two daily).

GRUTA DOS CRIOULOS

The **Gruta dos Crioulos** (Creoles' Cave) was used as a hideout by slaves escaping from the surrounding farms. It's 7km from Jaguaribe on the road to Pedra do Baú, a 1950m-high mountain peak that consists of a huge, rectan-gular granite block. To get to the top of Pedra do Baú you have to walk 2km north and climb 600 steps carved into the rock. It's about 25km from Campos do Jordão.

Paraná

Since seceding from São Paolo state in 1853, Paraná has been endlessly compared with its larger neighbor to the north. Indeed, Paraná shares with São Paolo a slew of superlatives, rating among Brazil's highest standards of living, most productive economies and best educated populations.

Paraná's enviable position near the top of these lists is due to many factors. But one is undoubtedly its history of small family farms as opposed to the plantation economy that dominated in northern Brazil, resulting in a relatively equitable, democratic social order. Add to that a thoughtful approach to economic development and a progressive stance on social issues, and you have the pleasant, prosperous place to live that Paraná is today. With its efficient public transportation, innovative architecture and outstanding urban parks, the capital, Curitiba, exemplifies the state's successes.

The state boasts many geological and ecological wonders. Ilha do Mel and Parque Nacional do Superagüi include large swaths of unspoiled rain forest and pristine coastline. Sunbathers and surfers sigh for these beaches, among the least developed and most idyllic in southern Brazil. From the coast, the stunning Serra do Mar stretches up to a high inland plane.

And straddling Brazil's border with Argentina is perhaps Paraná's most amazing asset. The power and the splendor of Iguaçu Falls have always earned the awe and admiration of travelers, from indigenous tribes to Jesuit missionaries to modern-day tourists.

HIGHLIGHTS

- Hear the roar and feel the spray from the **Garganta do Diablo** (p332), the mother of all waterfalls, at Iguaçu Falls

- Dance the fandango (folk dance) in the remote village of **Barra do Superagüi** (p328), in Parque Nacional do Superagüi

- Watch the sunset from **Farol das Conchas** (p325), the lighthouse on Ilha do Mel

- Marvel at the ancient 'stone city' of **Vila Velha** (p322)

- Appreciate art and eye-popping architecture at the **Museu Oscar Niemeyer** (p318) in Curitiba

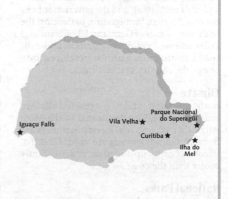

Iguaçu Falls ★   Vila Velha ★   Parque Nacional do Superagüi ★

Curitiba ★

Ilha do Mel ★

■ POPULATION: 10.7 MILLION | ■ AREA: 199,300 SQ KM

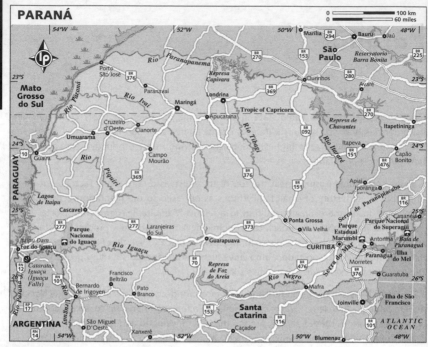

History

Like much of southern Brazil, Paraná was neglected by the Portuguese colonists; even a brief gold rush in the 17th century withered when bigger finds were discovered in Minas Gerais. When Paraná seceded from São Paulo in 1853, the economy was based on cattle and *erva maté* (tea), and the government encouraged Italian immigration to develop the economy. Waves of Germans, Ukrainians and Poles followed. With immigration and railroad construction, Curitiba developed into one of the country's richest cities.

Climate

Both the coast and the Iguaçu Falls are semitropical regions dominated by the Mata Atlântica (Atlantic rain forest). Summers are hot and humid; winters are mild. Curitiba, which lies on an upland plain, is significantly cooler than the coast.

National Parks

Parque Nacional do Superagüi (p328) is part of a huge, 4700-sq-km reserve of the Mata Atlântica, including a few largely uninhabited islands and miles of mangrove swamps. The famous falls are surrounded by the 1550-sq-km Parque Nacional do Iguaçu (p332).

Getting There & Around

Curitiba is the state's transportation hub, with bus and air services to every major city in Brazil. A passenger train links Curitiba with the coastal town of Paranaguá. Foz do Iguaçu also has a small international airport and direct bus service to São Paulo, Rio de Janeiro and every big city in the South.

CURITIBA

☎ 0xx41 / pop 1.85 million

Curitiba is not particularly sophisticated nor 'sexy,' but its residents enjoy a quality of life unparalleled in other parts of the country. With the help of a vibrant local economy, the modern city has managed to preserve historic buildings and green space.

In the 1970s and '80s, the city launched progressive incentives to get people out of their cars, lowering bus prices and improving service. The strategy worked: today it's easier to get around Curitiba than any other

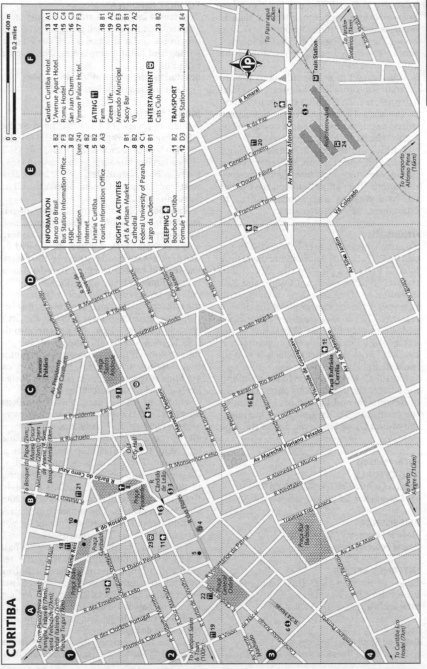

CURITIBA

large city in Brazil. The city has also taken innovative approaches to urban ills such as homelessness, pollution and poverty. To help bridge the technological divide, free internet access is provided at locations around the city.

It is pleasant to promenade along the pedestrian streets or circle the city on the Linha Turisma, visiting Curitiba's many parks and monuments. The large university population injects a youthful energy and a vibrant music scene, which gets going after dark.

Curitiba will be one of several host cities for the 2014 FIFA World Cup. Well prepared for the huge sporting event with plenty of accommodations, there's little doubt that its citizens will be using their international spotlight to boast their city's best attributes.

Orientation

Curitiba's historic center is bounded in the east by Praça Santos Andrade and the nearby Passeio Público, a pleasant city park, and in the west by Praça General Osório and Rua 24 Horas, an all-night indoor shopping strip that was slated for renovation at the time of research. The two ends are joined by the lively, pedestrian-only Rua das Flores. Just to the north of Rua das Flores the city's colonial heart is Largo da Ordem, which is also its nightlife hub.

Curitiba's long-distance bus station and the adjacent train station are about 2km east of downtown, and the airport lies 18km to the southeast. The largest parks, including the Museu Oscar Niemeyer, are on the edge of town.

Information
BOOKSTORES
Livraria Curitiba (☎ 3330 5002; Rua das Flores 78; ☒ 8am-6pm Mon-Sat) Has some foreign-language titles.

EMERGENCY
Medical emergency (☎ 192)
Polícia Federal (☎ 3360 7674)

INTERNET ACCESS
Loads of internet cafés (LAN houses) are found along Rua das Flores.
Internet (Rua das Flores 18; ☒ 10am-10pm)

MONEY
Banco do Brasil (Praça Tiradentes 410)
HSBC (cnr Rua das Flores & Av Marechal Floriano Peixoto)

TOURIST INFORMATION
The **tourist information office** (www.viaje.curitiba .pr.gov.br, in Portuguese) is well stocked with glossy brochures and maps and is well staffed with willing and helpful employees, who speak a little English.
Bus station information office (☎ 3352 8000; ☒ 7am-midnight Mon-Sat, 7am-7pm Sun)

Sights & Activities
For an overview of Curitiba, head to the 109m-high **Torre Panorâmica** (☎ 3339 7613; Rua Prof Lycio Grein de Castro Vellozo 191; adult/child R$4/2; ☒ 9am-7pm Tue-Sun), offering 360-degree views from its observation deck. Walk about 2km west from Largo da Ordem, or take the Linha Turismo (p322).

The focal point of Curitiba's downtown is **Rua das Flores**, a 500m pedestrian mall ideal for shopping and strolling. At its eastern end sits **Praça Santos Andrade**, dominated by the neoclassical headquarters of the **Federal University of Paraná**. North of Rua das Flores is **Praça Tiradentes**, site of the founding of the city. Today its most prominent landmark is the **cathedral** on the northeast corner. Just beyond the cathedral is **Largo da Ordem**, the city's old colonial heart. Here, the pedestrian-only cobblestone streets are lined with beautifully restored buildings, many of which now house trendy art galleries, pubs and cafés. On Sunday morning, Praça Garibaldi hosts a lively **art and artisan market** (☒ 9am-2pm).

North of the center, the **Museu Oscar Niemeyer** (☎ 3350 4400; www.museuoscarniemeyer .org.br, in Portuguese; Rua Marechal Hermes 999; admission R$4; ☒ 10am-6pm Tue-Sun) was designed by and named for the architect responsible for much of Brasília. The exotic, eye-shaped building is painted with whimsical dancing figures in bold colors. Rotating exhibits highlight Brazilian and international artists of the 20th and 21st centuries. The museum is a brisk 30-minute walk from the city center, or you can take the Linha Turismo (p322).

The Linha Turismo takes passengers past a series of monuments honoring the region's immigrant communities, including the Italian neighborhood known as Santa Felicidade with its **Portal Italiano**; the German memorial **Bosque Alemão**; the Ukrainian memorial in **Parque Tingui**; and the Polish memorial **Bosque do Papa**.

In the far south of the city, the **Jardim Botânico** (☎ 3264 1800; Rua Eng Ostoja Roguski; ☒ 6am-

BRAZIL'S ECOLOGICAL CAPITAL *Regis St Louis*

Although it's not the most exciting destination for visitors, Curitiba has long garnered praise for being one of the world's best models of urban planning. Over the past four decades, the capital of Paraná has developed an excellent (and much studied) public-transit system, created effective recycling initiatives and transformed urban spaces into parks, all the while promoting environmentally sustainable design long before it was fashionable.

Curitiba would probably resemble any other Brazilian city if it weren't for the bold initiatives of its three-term mayor, Jaime Lerner. Back in the 1960s, urban developers, influenced by Oscar Niemeyer and his followers, were planning to remodel the city around the automobile – tearing down buildings and widening boulevards – just as civil engineers were doing in the USA. In Curitiba, a group of young architects and urban planners fought bitterly against the idea, proposing radical zoning and transportation ideas that would save the city from the wrecking ball. Lerner, an architect, who became mayor in 1971, put those ideas into action – and came up with a few brilliant ones of his own.

One of his first daring moves was transforming a six-block length of the downtown into a pedestrian zone. Since local merchants blocked the implementation, Lerner used guerilla tactics. On a Friday evening, under secrecy, he brought in a crew, who laid walkways, installed lights and planters, and completed the task in 72 hours – before anyone could stop the project. With a huge boost in pedestrian traffic, merchants soon asked for an extension of the automobile-free zone. Some drivers, however, were less pleased and when Lerner heard that a group was planning to drive along the road, he was prepared. He gathered several hundred children along the street, where they sat, painting pictures. This cemented the success of the pedestrian district and cast Lerner as a can-do mayor.

Public transit was another big challenge. Since the city couldn't afford to build an underground system, it took the efficiencies of the underground and adapted them to the surface. It created five express-bus avenues, increased frequencies (arriving every 30 seconds at peak time) and built tubular boarding platforms, complete with fare clerks and turnstiles to allow faster boarding and exiting. It also had Volvo make double-accordion, 270-passenger buses. Today, the system transports over two million passengers daily and provides a speedy way around the city.

Lerner spearheaded some highly imaginative methods for dealing with the city's garbage. He encouraged everyone to recycle (perhaps as much as one-third of garbage was being separated for recycling) and got poorer citizens in on the city's clean-up act. Since the streets in some favelas (slums) are too narrow for garbage trucks, people cart out their own trash – 2kg of garbage is exchanged for 0.5kg of vegetables.

He has also planted trees on an enormous scale (more than one million in the last 30 years) and set aside wetlands and parks (many with lakes to catch runoff in flood-prone areas), even transforming a waste dump into a botanical garden. Despite its explosive population growth, Curitiba increased its green areas from 0.5 sq meter per person to more than 50 sq meters. The ecology also extends to business, as Curitiba decided in the 1970s to admit only nonpolluting companies to its municipality, which it houses in an industrial district surrounded by large areas of green space.

Despite Curitiba's many successes, the obstacles are growing. The city faces a flood of new, poor immigrants, attracted in part by the city's livability, plus more drivers packing the roads, and declining recycling rates (particularly alarming since the city's only landfill will likely be full by 2010). Perhaps the once-visionary city needs a Lerner for the 21st century – although modifying human behavior is likely the only way Curitiba can avoid going the way of other urban behemoths.

9pm Dec-Mar, 6am-8pm Apr-Nov) is a vast, flower-filled expanse, studded with sculpture and criss-crossed by walking paths. The centerpiece glass and metallic greenhouse is more interesting as a decorative showpiece than as a botanical wonder.

Tours

Tours of the surrounding countryside and Mata Atlântica can be arranged from Curitiba for about R$75 to $100 per day. Consider using the Linha Turismo as an urban tour (see p322).

Hotspot Safari & Tours (☎ 3022 0070; www.safari tour.com.br; Rua Carlos de Carvalho 603; ⏱ 9am-1pm Tue-Sat) Owner Christophe has three decades of experience in tourism and conservation and works with dedicated biologists to save the Paraná antwren and red-faced parrot. He runs excellent one-day and multiday tours exploring the coastal forest around Curitiba and comes highly recommended. English, French, Portuguese and German spoken.

Sleeping
BUDGET
Roma Hostel (☎ 3224 2117; www.curitibaecohostel.com .br; Rua Barão de Rio Branco 805; dm HI member/nonmember R$25/35, d R$62/77; 🖳 ☎) The rooms and dorms in this HI hostel, right off Praça Eufrásio Corrêia, are a bit dark but have high ceilings and are set around a neocolonial-style courtyard. The vibe here isn't nearly as fun as at the other HI hostel in town (Curitiba Eco Hostel; see below), but it's much more central. Breakfast goes for $9, and towels rent for R$3.50.

Formule 1 (☎ 3218 3838; www.accorhotels.com.br; Rua Mariano Torres 927; r from R$75; 🌀 🖳 ☎) In the stark white lobby at Formule 1, staff check in guests with all the efficiency and charm of a race-car crew. Every one of the 263 rooms is brightly lit and spotlessly clean. You know exactly what you're getting at this Accor hotel: comfortable accommodations at an unbeatable price, two blocks from the bus station. Breakfast is R$5, and wi-fi costs R$10 daily.

MIDRANGE & TOP END
Curitiba Eco Hostel (☎ 3029 1693; www.curitibaeco hostel.com.br, in Portuguese; Rua Luiz Tramontin 1693; dm HI member/nonmember R$70/80, d R$90/100, tr R$110/130; 🖳 🐾) On the edge of town and surrounded by forest, this hostel is a bit swankier than your usual youth hostel. The spacious rooms have bright-orange walls, tile floors and access to a fabulous outdoor deck. Catch the 'Tramontina' bus from Praça Rui Barbosa.

Garden Curitiba Hotel (☎ 3222 2524; Rua Ébana Pereira 405; s/d/tr R$87/112/132; 🖳) Nothing fancy happens at this cozy little hostelry, but it is one of the more pleasant places to stay. Thanks to its small size and homey decor, the Garden Curitiba offers an air of small-town intimacy otherwise lacking in this big city – and you'll be welcomed with a complimentary caipirinha!

Vernon Palace Hotel (☎ 3362 1222; www.vernonho tel.com.br, in Portuguese; Av Presidente Afonso Camargo 455; s/d R$96/126; 🌀 🖳 ☎ 🐾) The most luxurious

option near the bus station, this marble-heavy hotel attracts a business crowd. It wins no extra points for personality, but it does offer the level of comfort and service of an international hotel.

L'Avenue Apart Hotel (☎ 3222 5525; www.lavenue aparthotel.com.br, in Portuguese; Rua XV de Novembro 526, Rua das Flores; s/d R$130/155; 🌀 🖳) One of the few places to stay on Rua das Flores, this tasteful but not too trendy hotel has 63 suites, all with kitchenettes and sitting areas.

our pick **San Juan Charm** (☎ 3219 9900; www.san juanhoteis.com.br, in Portuguese; Rua Barao do Rio Branco 354; r R$140; 🌀 🖳 ☎) Behind a beautiful neoclassical facade, this hospice is charming indeed. Renovated in 2002, the hotel retains much of its original architectural detail, but does not skimp on modern amenities. Stained-wood floors, painted moldings and black-and-white photos give the 24 rooms an aura of understated elegance.

Bourbon Curitiba (☎ 3221 4600; www.bourbon.com .br; Rua Cândido Lopes 102; s/d R$240/280; 🌀 🖳 ☎ 🐾) Curitiba's swankiest sleeping place, this four-star chain hotel is decked out to cater to business travelers and discerning tourists.

Eating & Drinking
Rua das Flores, between Rua Westfalen and Rua Alameda Dr Muricy, has a collection of cheap fast-food restaurants with sidewalk seating.

Mercado Municipal (cnr Rua General Carneiro & Av 7 de Setembro; ⏱ 8am-6pm Mon-Sat) Just across from the bus station, the market has food stalls on the lower level.

Saccy Bar (☎ 3222 9922; Rua Mateus Leme 12; meals R$10-18; ⏱ 10am-1am) This red colonial house has a crowded bar downstairs and a loftlike 2nd floor, both ideal to drink beer and munch on pub grub. Live music on weekend nights.

Farm (☎ 3019 9376; Av Jaime Reis 40; meals R$12-15) This rustic place features large portions of Brazilian fare and a variety of pizzas. The food is tasty, but the real draw is the deck overlooking Praça Garibaldi.

Green Life (☎ 3223 8490; Rua Carlos de Carvalho 271; per kg R$18 Mon-Fri, R$22 Sat & Sun; ⏱ 11am-3pm) Most of the ingredients at this all-organic vegetarian restaurant come from the owners' farm. The menu changes daily according to what's fresh and what's in season.

Yü (☎ 3232 3500; Praça General Osório 485; per kg R$23; ⏱ 11:30am-3pm Mon-Sat) In a stylish brick-and-glass building, the big buffet features Asian fare, including sushi and sashimi, salads and hot Chinese and Japanese main dishes.

our pick **Famiglia Fadanelli** (☎ 3372 1616; Av Manoel Ribas 5667; meals R$23-40) Everyone in Curitiba knows this Italian restaurant in Santa Felicidade. It's best known for its Italian classics such as veal Parmigianino with homemade pasta, but the mile-long antipasto bar, featured most weekends, is a crowd-pleaser as well.

Entertainment

On warm nights, revelers spill out of pubs and cafés onto the streets around Largo da Ordem.

Cats Club (☎ 3224 5912; Rua Alameda Dr Muricy 949; cover R$15-30; ⏱ 11:30pm-5am Fri-Sun) It's a lovely pink colonial mansion with a smoky, underground club inside. DJs spin house music and the dance floor fills up with the young and the restless.

Opera de Arame (☎ 3355 6071; Rua João Gava; ⏱ 8am-10pm Tue-Sun) Constructed from wire with a glass roof, this theater is among Curitiba's most unusual and enigmatic land-marks. It is surrounded by the stone quarry park, which contains an outdoor stage hosting national acts throughout the year.

Getting There & Away

AIR

From Curitiba's **Alfonso Pena airport** (☎ 3381 1153) direct flights go to São Paulo (45 minutes, from R$150), Rio de Janeiro (one hour, from R$175), Foz do Iguaçu (40 minutes), Florianópolis (40 minutes), Porto Alegre (one hour) and Brasília (two hours).

BUS & TRAIN

The long-distance **bus and train stations** (☎ 3320 3121) form a single complex called the *rodoferroviária*, which is about 2km from downtown. Within Paraná, Viação Graciosa goes to Paranaguá (R$16, 1½ hours, hourly), while Sulamericana goes overnight to Foz do Iguaçu (R$100 to R$130, 10 hours). Catarinense runs hourly buses to Joinville (R$17, two hours) and Florianópolis (R$37 to R$65, five hours). Longer-distance buses

---

ALL ABOARD!

In Curitiba, with hardly a ripple on the horizon, it's hard to believe that a few dozen kilometers to the west lie sharp, jungle-covered peaks with sweeping views down to the Baía de Paranaguá and the ocean beyond. That's because Curitiba sits above the mountains on the Planalto (high plains). As the plains break apart and give way to the sea, they form the stunning Serra do Mar.

Although beautiful to behold, the landscape was a drag on the city's economy. It took two days to transport products from Curitiba to the port of Antonina, only 75km east. Finally, a railway was inaugurated in 1885, connecting Curitiba to the sea. Engineers managed to build 67 bridges and viaducts, dig 13 tunnels through granite mountainsides, and lay track along dizzyingly steep heights.

Today, the train is known as the **Serra Verde Express** (☎ 3323 4007; www.serraverdeexpress.com .br; Estação Ferroviária), and between Curitiba and Morretes it offers sublime views of threatening mountain canyons, tropical green lowlands and the vast, blue Atlantic. As you descend, watch as the climate and environment change – the weather becoming hotter and muggier, the vegetation lusher and greener. The segment between Morretes and Paranaguá is less scenic and the train inches along at an excruciating pace.

The *litorina* (tourist train) departs from Curitiba at 9:15am on Saturday and Sunday only, and goes only as far as Morretes (R$270, three hours). The *litorina* offers passengers panoramic windows, air-conditioning, snack service and a 10-minute stop for the stunning views at Santuário do Cadeado.

The less-luxurious *trem* (regular train) leaves daily at 8:15am, stopping in Marumbi (two hours later) and Morretes (three hours), and returning to Curitiba in the afternoon. It goes all the way to Paranaguá (four hours) only on Saturday and Sunday. Three classes are available: *executivo* (adult/child R$96/49), *turístico* (adult/child R$66/45) and *econômico* (R$39). The return ticket is about 30% less.

Views are most spectacular from the left side of the train (right side on the return trip). Reservations are highly recommended during summer. Prices and times change frequently, so be sure to stop by the train station or check the website in advance.

include São Paulo (R$60 to R$80, six hours, 15 daily); Porto Alegre (R$79 to R$85, 11 hours, three daily); and Rio (R$120 to R$250, 13 hours, five daily).

The train between Curitiba and Paranaguá via the Serra do Mar (see the boxed text, p321) is one of the marvels of travel in Brazil.

Getting Around
TO/FROM THE AIRPORT
Alfonso Pena airport is 18km from the city. The **Aeroport Executivo** (☎ 3283 4321; www.aero portoexecutivo.com.br; R$8) runs every half-hour between the train station and the airport, looping around the city center along the way. The bus will stop in front of your hotel if it is on the route.

BUS
The **Linha Turismo** (R$20; ☺ 9am-5:30pm Tue-Sun) is a tourist bus that loops around the city, stopping at all the major tourist attractions and the parks and monuments on the outskirts of the city. A recording in Portuguese, Spanish and English provides descriptions of each destination. It starts from Praça Tiradentes every half-hour, but you can also pick it up at the bus station or any other stop. You can board up to four times. A timetable is posted at each stop.

VILA VELHA
Located in Campos Gerais, 93km west of Curitiba, Vila Velha is known as the 'stone city.' The park's centerpiece is the 23 *aretinhas* (sandstone pillars), created over millions of years. The mysterious red-earth rock formations – some taking recognizable shapes such as boots and bottles – create striking silhouettes against the blue sky and green foliage. A bus drops you near the formations, where you can choose to follow a 40-minute walking trail or another trail that takes 90 minutes around the stone structures.

Within the boundaries of the same park, visitors can witness another geological marvel: a series of *furnas* (craters) that are the result of underground erosion. A 90-minute bus tour stops first at the Lagoa Dourada, a lovely lagoon that attracts ample birdlife. The next stop features two yawning craters that reach depths of 54m.

From Curitiba, catch a Princesa dos Campos bus to Vila Velha (R$14, 1½ hours, three daily); the prevailing wisdom is that

you should take the earliest bus at 7:45am to arrive early enough to see the whole park. Stop first at the **park center** (☎ 0xx42-3228 1138; rock formations R$7, craters R$5; ☺ 8:30am-5:30pm Wed-Mon), where you can watch an introductory video and buy tickets for the various tours. There's also a snack bar.

MORRETES
☎ 0xx41 / pop 17,000
Founded in 1721 on the banks of the Rio Nhundiaquara, this tranquil colonial town rests on an emerald-green plain at the foot of the Serra do Mar. The loveliest colonial buildings are clustered around Praça Lamenha Lins and along Rua das Flores, the cobblestone walkway that runs along the river. The **tourist office** (☎ 3462 1024; Largo Dr Jose Pereira 43; ☺ 9am-6pm) occupies a white colonial house along this stretch, and the grand **Igreja Matriz** (Mother Church) anchors one end.

The region's culinary gift to the world is *barreado*, a rib-sticking meat stew cooked in a clay pot. Originally, it served to keep revelers nourished over the course of several days of Carnaval, but you can test its sustaining qualities any time of year.

Sights & Activities
Besides the quaint colonial center, the biggest attraction in Morretes is the **Parque Estadual Marumbi** (☎ 3462 1155), a paradise for rock climbers and nature-lovers. It contains a network of old pioneer trails that were the only connections between the coast and the highland in the 17th and 18th centuries. The **Graciosa Foot Trail** passes close to the Estrada da Graciosa, while the **Itupava Colonial Trail** is a four-hour excursion that ends in the village of Porto de Cima, about 5km from Morretes. Views from both are stunning. Take the Serra Verde Express from Curitiba (see the boxed text, p321) to Marumbi station.

You don't need a guide to enjoy the trails, which are well signposted from the train station and within the park, but it can be fun. English-speaking Mauricio at **Ecobikers** (☎ 3462-4145; www.morretes.com.br/ecobikers, in Portuguese; Reta do Porto, Km 2) rents bikes and leads guided rides for about R$45 to R$60 per bike/person.

The Rio Nhundiaquara is navigable by inner tube, which you can rent at the **Pousada Itupava** (☎ 3462 1925; www.itupava.com.br, in Portuguese; per day R$10), in the village of Porto de Cima.

Sleeping & Eating

Hotel Nhundiaquara (☎ 3462 1228; www.nundiaquara .com.br, in Portuguese; Rua General Carreiro 13; per person with/without bathroom R$70/35) This old-fashioned place on the riverfront offers plain, wood-paneled rooms with high ceilings and tiny bathrooms. The on-site restaurant is famous for its *barreado* (R$22), served on the breezy colonial-style terrace overlooking a lovely bend in the Rio Nhundiaquara.

ourpick Pousada do Oasis (☎ 3426 1888; Estradas das Prainhas, Porto de Cima; r from R$195) Sweet, spacious chalets surrounded by forest and flowering bushes make a great base for exploring the Itupava Colonial Trail. There's a good restaurant (meals from R$18) at the Oasis, and prices drop about 40% midweek.

Estação Graciosa (☎ 3462 2009; Rua Cons Sinimbú 271; meals R$20; ☽ 11am-11pm Wed-Mon) Opposite the train station, Estação Graciosa occupies a blue clapboard house, decorated with folk art and mismatched furniture. A spacious porch overlooks the garden, where lemon trees bloom – an ideal setting to indulge in the local specialties.

Most of the restaurants are along Largo Dr José Pereira on the riverfront, including **Restaurante Casarão** (☎ 3462 1314; Largo Dr José Pereira 25; meals R$20-30; ☽ 11:30am-4:30pm Wed-Mon), an up-market place with a balcony on the river.

Getting There & Away

The Morretes train station is on a pretty square in the center of town. Trains to Curitiba depart daily at 3pm (see the boxed text, p321).

The bus station is about 1km from the center of town. Viação Graciosa buses runs from Antonina (R$3.50, 30 minutes) to Paranaguá (R$3.50, one hour) via Morretes every hour; and to Curitiba (R$10, one hour, four daily).

ANTONINA

☎ 0xx41 / pop 18,000

Once an important colonial port, Antonina has slipped into charming irrelevance. Fortunately, its economic decline has preserved its colonial center, which fronts the beautiful Baía de Paranaguá. The pace is languid – except during Carnaval, which is one of the region's best. Walk along the tree-lined waterfront then uphill toward Praça Coronel Macedo, a pretty square lined with stately homes built with shipping fortunes.

Viação Graciosa buses go from Antonina (R$3.50, 30 minutes) to Paranaguá (R$3.50, 1½ hours) via Morretes every hour; and to Curitiba (R$15, one hour, four daily). Trains no longer stop here.

Sleeping & Eating

Hotel Monte Castelo (☎ 3432 1163; Praça Coronel Macedo 46; r per person with/without bathroom R$30/20) A friendly budget option on the main square. An inviting entry leads to clean rooms with wood floors and sea-green walls.

Atlante Pousada (☎ 3432 1256; www.atlante.com .br, in Portuguese; Praça Coronel Macedo 266; s/d R$95/120; ☒ ▣ ▣) This restored 19th-century mansion is Antonina's top-end option. A fresh peach-colored paint job and breezy balconies bedeck the outside. The rooms do not quite live up to the lavish exterior, but they are comfortable.

Restaurante Le Bistrô (☎ 3432 3393; Travessa 7 de Setembro 01; meals R$20-25; ☽ 11:30am-3pm & 6:30-11:30pm Wed-Sun) Just below the church, this popular restaurant offers bay views and a seafaring theme in its glass-enclosed dining room. As the decor implies, seafood is on the menu. Save room for the specialty dessert, banana flambé.

Restaurante Buganvil's (☎ 3432 1434; Praça Coronel Macedo 10; meals R$28-35; ☽ 11:30am-3:30pm Tue-Sun & 7-10pm Fri & Sat) You can't miss this pretty pink colonial building, serving European cuisine. Bold colors and whimsical light fixtures add a modern touch, and the namesake bougainvillea is not lacking.

PARANAGUÁ

☎ 0xx41 / pop 140,000

This colorful old port, sitting serenely on the banks of the Rio Itiberê, has an appealing atmosphere of tropical decadence. Commercially important since the late 18th century, the city has some impressive churches and other public buildings, many of which are being carefully restored. Paranaguá remains an important port for corn, soy, cotton and vegetable oils; for travelers, it serves primarily as a point of departure to Ilha do Mel.

Information

Banco do Brasil (Hugo Simas) ATMs.
Tourist office Waterfront (☎ 3425 4542; Rua General Carneiro 258; ☽ 8am-6pm); Train station (☽ noon-4pm)

Sights

Housed in an 18th-century Jesuit college, the **Museu de Arqueologia e Etnologia** (Archeology &

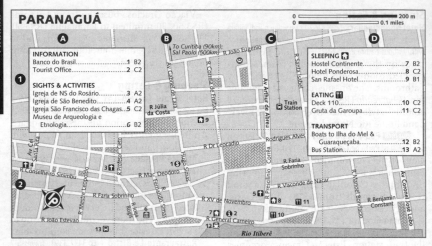

Ethnology Museum; ☎ 3422 8844; Rua XV de Novembro 575; admission R$4; ☒ 9:30am-noon & 1-6pm Tue-Sat, noon-5pm Sun) displays indigenous artifacts, primitive and folk art, and old tools and machines.

The city's colonial churches are simple but striking. The oldest is **Igreja de NS do Rosário** (Rua Marechal Deodoro), parts of which date to 1578. Several churches were constructed during the 18th century, including **Igreja São Francisco das Chagas** (Rua XV Novembro) and **Igreja de São Benedito** (Rua Conselheiro Sinimbu), built specifically for the town's slaves.

Sleeping & Eating

Hostel Continente (☎ 3423 3224; www.hostelconti nente.com.br, in Portuguese; Rua General Carneiro 300; dm HI member/nonmember R$25/30, r per person R$40/45, d R$60/65; ▯ ☎) This HI hostel is across from the tourist port, so you can enjoy your breakfast while watching the boats come in. Rooms are well lit and colorfully decorated. Facilities include laundry and communal kitchen.

ourpick Hotel Ponderosa (☎ 3423 2464; Rua Prescilinio Corrêa 68; s/d R$55/70, d with view R$80; ☒) Occupying a restored colonial building on a prominent corner, the Ponderosa evokes a grand past, with its high ceilings and wide-plank wood floors. The rooms facing the port are particularly pleasing, with lots of light and lovely views of the waterfront.

San Rafael Hotel (☎ 3432 2123; www.sanrafaelhotel .com.br; Rua Júlia da Costa 185; s/d/tr from R$165/195/220; ☒ ☎) The sleek modern facade and tinted glass doors front a contemporary tile lobby,

appropriately chilled. The rooms are slightly less sophisticated, but no less cush.

Gruta da Garoupa (☎ 3423 3896; Rua XV de Novembro 120; per kg R$18) This popular 'fast grill' has something for everyone, with a daily-changing buffet of seafood, grilled meats, pasta and sushi.

Deck 110 (☎ 3425 2927; Rua General Carneiro 110; meals R$20-25; ☒ 11:30am-midnight Tue-Sun) Sip champagne or munch on a savory appetizer on the classy outdoor deck; or slip into the swanky interior for a cocktail from the dark-wood bar. The menu features an impressive wine list and lots of fresh seafood.

Getting There & Away

Six or seven boats to Ilha do Mel leave throughout the day (one-way/round-trip R$18/36), with stops at both Nova Brasília (1½ hours) and Encantadas (two hours). Boats also go to Guaraqueçaba (R$90, two hours, two daily), an access point for Parque Nacional do Superagüi.

From the **bus station** (☎ 3420 2925) on the waterfront, Viação Graciosa goes to Curitiba (R$16, 1½ hours, hourly), Antonina (R$3.55, 1½ hours, hourly) and Morretes (R$3, one hour, hourly). The Serra Verde Express goes all the way to Paranaguá only on Sunday; see the boxed text, p321 for details.

ILHA DO MEL
☎ 0xx41 / pop 1200

This hourglass-shaped island at the mouth of the Baía de Paranaguá is the most pristine and picturesque beach resort in all of southern

Brazil. The island's tranquility and lack of development are thanks in part to its isolation. Accessible only by boat, Ilha do Mel is traversed by sandy paths and has not a single car. The fatter, northern half of the island is an ecological preserve, closed to inland exploration. The hillier southern portion is the locale of three small villages: Nova Brasília and Praia do Farol near the isthmus; and Encantadas at the far southern tip. They can be rowdy during the summer holidays, when young crowds descend on the island. But for the most part, Ilha do Mel, or 'honey island,' is the territory of surfers, campers, beachcombers and other escapists in search of simplicity and serenity.

Orientation

Most of the hotels are clustered in the village of Nova Brasília, which occupies the isthmus linking the two ends of the island, and Praia do Farol, the beach that stretches east from here. The landmark lighthouse sits atop a *morro* (hill) on its easternmost point. Another, smaller settlement, Encantadas, at the southern end of the island, is the closest point to the mainland. A 6km trail on the east coast links the two towns, traversing a series of undeveloped beaches including Praia da Fora, Praia do Miguel and Praia Grande.

Information

There is no reliable place on the island to get cash, so plan ahead. You'll find tourist-information offices at the docks in both Nova Brasília and Encantadas.

Encantadas tourist information office (☎ 3426 9091; ☺ 8am-7pm)

Ilha do Mel Online (☎ 3426 8065; www.ilhadomelon line.com; internet per hr R$9; ☺ 9am-9pm) This charming blue house is on the path between Nova Brasília and Farol das Conchas. Offers internet access, rooms for rent and information about the island.

Nova Brasília tourist information office (☎ 3426 8005; ☺ 8am-7pm)

Sights

The picturesque **Fortaleza de NS dos Prazeres** (Fort of Our Lady of the Pleasures), which dates to the 1760s, is a 3km hike from Nova Brasília via Praia da Fortaleza. Inspect the deserted fortress before climbing up to the lookout for an incredible vista of the bay.

The **Farol das Conchas** (Conchas Lighthouse), built in 1872 on orders from Dom Pedro II, stands picturesquely atop a hill at the island's most easterly point. From here you have panoramic views of the island, the bay and the Serra do Mar. It's a popular spot to watch the sun drop below the horizon.

Legend has it that the small caves at the island's southern tip, known as the **Grutas das Encantadas**, are inhabited by beautiful mermaids who enchant all who come near. Signs clearly mark the way to the caves from Encantadas and Praia da Fora.

Activities
SURFING & SWIMMING

Ilha do Mel has no shortage of beaches. Those facing the bay enjoy warm waters gently lapping at the white sand, while those facing the ocean boast the big surf. But almost all of them are unspoiled, marked only be windswept dunes, forested hills and rocky outposts. **Praia da Fora** and **Praia Grande** are a 20-minute walk (2km) from Nova Brasília and a 40-minute walk (4km) from Encantadas. According to local surfers, in winter these beaches have the best waves in Paraná.

The **Praia do Farol** is the long stretch of sand between the Nova Brasília dock and the Farol das Conchas. It is backed by the swampy, grassy protected area of the *retinga*, which also preserves the natural beauty of the beach. Surfers congregate at the base of the hill and ride the legendary **Ondas das Paralelas**.

Stop in at the Grajagan Surf Resort (p327) on Praia Grande to inquire about renting a *prancha* (surfboard) or taking a lesson.

If you didn't bring your surfboard, you might prefer the calmer, warmer waters of the beaches that face the shallow bay. In the north, **Praia da Fortaleza**, often nearly deserted, allows you to bathe in the shadow of the 18th-century Portuguese fort. The best beach near the settlement of Encantadas is **Praia da Fora**, which has big waves and a few stalls selling *cervejas* (beers) and *sucos* (fruit juices).

BOATING

In the harbors of Nova Brasília and Encantadas, you can hire a boat to explore the nearby islands, including Ilha do Superagüi, Ilha das Palmas and Ilha das Peças.

Pousada das Meninas (☎ 3426 8023; Praia do Farol) The owners (see p327) organize day trips to any of the islands.

Sea Calm Passeios & Pescaria (☎ 3426 9073; seacalm@bol.com.br; ☺ 10am) Biologists Ana and David run these five-hour excursions departing from Encantadas and making a complete tour of the island.

PARANÁ

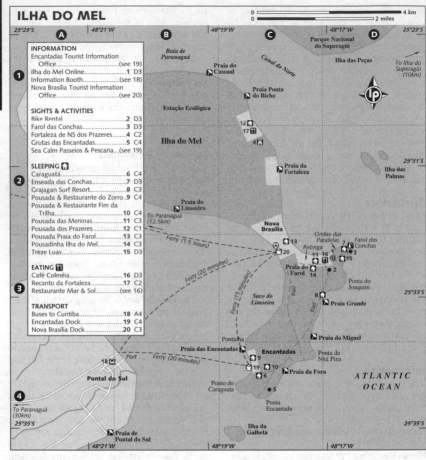

ILHA DO MEL

INFORMATION
Encantadas Tourist Information
   Office........................(see 19)
Ilha do Mel Online......................1 D3
Information Booth....................(see 18)
Nova Brasília Tourist Information
   Office........................(see 20)

SIGHTS & ACTIVITIES
Bike Rental...............................2 D3
Farol das Conchas.....................3 D3
Fortaleza de NS dos Prazeres.......4 C2
Grutas das Encantadas...............5 C4
Sea Calm Passeios & Pescaria...(see 19)

SLEEPING
Caraguatá.................................6 C4
Enseada das Conchas.................7 D3
Grajagan Surf Resort..................8 C3
Pousada & Restaurante do Zorro..9 C4
Pousada & Restaurante Fim da
   Trilha..................................10 C4
Pousada das Meninas................11 C3
Pousada dos Prazeres................12 C1
Pousada Praia do Farol..............13 C3
Pousadinha Ilha do Mel.............14 C3
Treze Luas...............................15 D3

EATING
Café Colméia...........................16 D3
Recanto da Fortaleza.................17 C2
Restaurante Mar & Sol............(see 16)

TRANSPORT
Buses to Curitiba......................18 A4
Encantadas Dock......................19 C4
Nova Brasília Dock....................20 C3

CYCLING

Biking is a great way to beat the heat and land on the sand faster. Rent a single-gear beach cruiser from **Eduardo** (☎ 3426 8076) near Farol de Conchas for R$5 per hour.

Sleeping & Eating

Book ahead for holidays and any summer weekend. Prices listed here are for high season. Expect discounts of 20% to 50% between April and November.

NOVA BRASÍLIA & PRAIA DO FAROL

Pousadinha Ilha do Mel (☎ 3426 8026; www.pousadinha .com.br, in Portuguese; d R$90-120, without bathroom R$70) This island favorite has a new annex of chic rooms built from local hardwoods and outfit-

ted with hammocks and solar-heated water. The whole place is a bit cramped, although comfortable. The Pousadinha has a popular restaurant serving pastas and seafood (mains R$18 to R$32) that nonguests like to frequent as well.

Treze Luas (☎ 3426 8067; www.pousadatrezeluas.com .br; d with/without veranda R$150/180; ⚡) This place is surprisingly slick for Ilha do Mel. Brightened by whimsical artwork and bold-colored linens, all the rooms have shiny stained-wood walls and cool tile floors, and some have private verandas. The common area is decked out with modern furniture and a flat-screen TV, while a porch overlooks the palm-fringed garden.

Pousada Praia do Farol (☎ 3426 8014; www.praia dofarol.com.br; d/tr/q R$180/260/330, without bathroom

R$120/160/210; 🏊) Set on the isthmus, this hotel boasts access to both Praia de Brasília and Praia do Farol. Rooms are small and dark, but the pousada (guesthouse) has plenty of comfy common areas, including a beachside deck that is well hung with hammocks.

Pousada das Meninas (☎ 3426 8023; www.pousada dasmeninas.com.br; d with/without bathroom R$200/150, chalets R$250; 🏊) Built from driftwood and re cycled material, this pousada offers the charm of a guesthouse and the friendliness of family. Hung with hammocks and decorated with nature's bounty, the simple but tasteful rooms are set around a cozy garden.

Enseada das Conchas (☎ 3426 8040; www.pousada enseada.com.br; s/d/tr R$135/220/290) This lovely pousada is as 'upscale' as this island goes. Four spacious guestrooms are painted in striking colors and decorated according to themes, such as 'Sunlight' and 'Sea Blue.' A wide deck is shaded by a thatch roof and scattered with lounge chairs. It is steps from the lighthouse and the island's best surf beach.

Restaurante Mar & Sol (☎ 3426 8021; meals R$23-45) Serves simple but tasty seafood dishes, including a tasty crab *moqueca* (Bahian fish stew cooked in a clay pot with *dendê* oil, coconut milk and spicy peppers). Wash it down with an ice-cold *cerveja*. For something lighter (snacks R$3 to R$10), go next door to Café Colméia (☎ 3426 8029). Follow the path to Farol das Conchas.

PRAIA GRANDE & PRAIA DA FORA

Grajagan Surf Resort (☎ 3426 8043; www.grajagan.com .br; ste with/without sea view R$490/290; 🏊 🛜) This pousada caters to surfers who like their creature comforts, including a huge breakfast buffet and a lively beach bar. The rooms with ocean views are easily the most luxurious on the island: each has a private veranda and hammock facing the sea. Ask the owner Rogério about renting boards (R$18 per hour) or taking lessons.

ENCANTADAS

Encantadas is quieter and more family oriented than Nova Brasília. The walk from Nova Brasília to Encantadas is about 4.5km and is exposed to bright sun.

Pousada & Restaurante do Zorro (☎ 3426 9052; www.hostelzorro.com.br; dm/d/tr HI member R$35/90/110, nonmember R$40/100/150; 💻 🏊) This friendly HI hostel has a great vibe, thanks to its beachfront location, helpful English-speaking staff and happy guests lounging out front. Look for

a fun recreation room, communal kitchen, and comfy clean rooms, fully equipped with fridges and TVs.

OUR PICK Pousada & Restaurante Fim da Trilha (☎ 3426 9017; www.fimdatrilha.com.br; d/tr R$180/240; 🏊 🛜) Off the trail to the Grutas das Encantadas, an enticing winding path leads to this tropical paradise. The spacious terrace is overflowing with blooming foliage and gurgling fountains. Here, you'll find one of the island's best restaurants (meals R$30 to R$50), specializing in spicy paella. In the back, the six spacious and modern guestrooms are fully equipped and tastefully decorated.

Caraguatá (☎ 3426 9097; www.caraguata-ilhadomel .com.br, in Portuguese & Spanish; d from R$230; 🏊 🛜) Just a few steps from the pier, Caraguatá's pretty chalets are adorned with flower boxes and greenery. Rooms vary in size but they all have stained-wood ceilings, whitewashed walls and crisp linens.

FORTALEZA

Fewer and farther between, accommodations around Fortaleza are effective for escaping the summer crowds. However, it's a good one-hour, 3km hike from the Nova Brasília pier. Otherwise, catch a boat taxi (about R$40).

Pousada dos Prazeres (☎ 3243 9649; www.pousa dadosprazeres.com.br, in Portuguese; s/d R$70/140) This friendly place has bright-yellow cabins with basic rooms and swinging hammocks, catering to guests in search of peace and quiet and not much more. The beachside café will sate your appetite with big plates of fresh seafood. Walk 200m past the fort.

Recanto da Fortaleza (☎ 3275 4455; www.pousadare cantodafortaleza.com.br, in Portuguese; meals R$10-12) This breezy deck is an ideal place to indulge in a seafood feast or quench your thirst with a cold one after a day on the beach. Out back are a few simple rooms (per person R$40) for rent.

Getting There & Away

See p324 for information on boats to Paranaguá island.

See p324 for information on boats to Paranaguá island.

TO/FROM PONTAL DO SUL

Viação Graciosa runs buses from Curitiba (R$20, two hours, 10 daily) that bypass Paranaguá and head straight to the pier in Pontal do Sul, which is closer to the island and offers more frequent service.

Boats depart to both Nova Brasília (20 minutes) and Encantadas (15 minutes) every half-hour from 8am to 8pm (one-way/round-trip R$13/26). Schedules vary, so check at the **information booth** (☎ 3455 1144) at the port in Pontal do Sul.

Getting Around

The ferries that run to/from Paranaguá stop in both Nova Brasília and Encantadas, so you can get a lift from one village to the other (R$6, 20 minutes, six daily).

PARQUE NACIONAL DO SUPERAGÜI
☎ 0xx41

Composed of the Superagüi and Peças islands, this national park in the Baía de Paranaguá is covered by mangroves and salt marshes, which support an amazing variety of bird and plant life. The national park is part of the 4700 sq km of Atlantic forest reserves in Paraná and São Paulo states that were given Unesco World Heritage status in 1999.

The park is famous for its array of orchids. Hummingbirds and toucans live here, not to mention the roseate spoonbill and the stunning Brazilian tanager. Every evening at sunset, hundreds – sometimes thousands – of red-tailed parrots return to roost in the canopy on **Papagaio Island**. Dolphins are often sighted in the waters between Ilha do Superagüi and Ilha do Mel. Other mammals are more elusive, but include agoutis, pacas, deer, howler monkeys and pumas. The park is also home to the endangered black-faced lion tamarin, though it is rarely sighted.

The national park is not open to visitors, although boats are allowed to motor around the islands. Boat trips depart from Ilha do Mel and the tiny fishing village of **Barra do Superagüi**, one of the few settlements within the confines of the protected area. It's worth spending a day in the village to get a taste of life in a place still relatively untouched by tourism. If you're lucky, you might catch a fandango, a local folk music and dance tradition that is dying out in other places, but thriving here.

From Barra do Superagüi, one trail leads through the rain forest and across the island. An hour's walk brings you to **Praia Deserta**, a 38km strip of sand and sea with no development and no people.

Sleeping & Eating

Pousada Superagüi (☎ 3482 7149; www.pousadasuper agui.com.br; Superagüi; r per person R$35) In this sweet blue clapboard cottage with yellow trim, rooms are simple and bathrooms are shared, but the place is lovingly decorated with local artwork. Owners Dalton and Olga eagerly share their encyclopedic knowledge of the area; they also provide transportation and offer boat tours of the islands.

The best restaurants in town both overlook the bay, serving fresh seafood and cold beer: **Restaurante Golfinos** (☎ 9959 8852; meals R$15; ☽ 11am-11pm) and **Restaurante Crepúsculo** (☎ 9959 6709; meals R$15; ☽ noon-2pm & 6-8pm). It's best to order your lunch in advance.

Getting There & Away

No regular transportation goes to Ilha do Superagüi. On weekends and holidays, boats run from Paranaguá (one hour) and Guaraqueçaba (45 minutes), but the schedule is erratic. You may have to negotiate a ride with the fishermen at the docks, or schedule a pick-up with the folks at Pousada Superagüi (p328). Expect to pay about R$30 on a boat that is already making the journey. Otherwise, you will likely pay upwards of R$150 to hire a boat for up to five people. To make transportation arrangements in advance, contact the following:

Claudinei Juruna (☎ 3424 0780; Paranaguá) Offers fishing trips and transport on his boat *Anjo Elchadag*.

Dalton (☎ 8406 0579; Superagüi) Proprietor of Pousada Superagüi (p328).

IGUAÇU FALLS & AROUND
☎ 0xx45 / pop 330,000

Rising in the coastal mountains of Paraná and Santa Catarina, the Rio Iguaçu snakes west for 600km, picking up a few dozen tributaries along the way. It widens majestically and sweeps around a magnificent forest stage, before plunging and crashing in the tiered cascades known as Iguaçu Falls. A total of 275 individual falls occupy an area more than 3km wide and 80m high, which makes them wider than Victoria, higher than Niagara and more beautiful than either.

Thousands of years before they were 'discovered' by Europeans, the falls were a holy burial place for the Tupi-Guarani and Paraguas tribes. Spaniard Don Alvar Nuñes happened upon the falls in 1541, dubbing them 'Saltos de Santa María.' But this name didn't stick and the Tupi-Guarani name, Iguaçu (Great Waters), did. In 1986 Unesco declared the region a World Heritage site.

PARANÁ

The falls are unequally shared between Brazil and Argentina, with Argentina claiming the majority. On either side, a national park surrounds the waterfalls and offers extra opportunities for adventure. It's impossible to say which side of the border is the more rewarding: the Parque Nacional do Iguaçu in Brazil offers a more panoramic view of the totality of the 275 falls, while the Parque Nacional Iguazú in Argentina provides an up-close and personal experience. Both are absolutely thrilling. Plan to spend a full day in either park.

Foz do Iguaçu & Around

The Brazilian city of Foz do Iguaçu went through a period of frenzied growth dur-ing the 18 years that Itaipu Dam was under construction, when the population increased more than fivefold. It was an edgy place then, but it has since settled down. That said, mug-gings have been reported on the bridge from Ciudad del Este (Paraguay) and on the road from the youth hostels near the airport. So take precautions and watch your back.

ORIENTATION

Av Brasil is the town's main street, running north to south. The long-distance bus sta-tion is located 4.5km to the northeast, but the local bus station – just north of Av República Argentina – serves the airport (15km south-east) and Parque Nacional do Iguaçu (17km southeast).

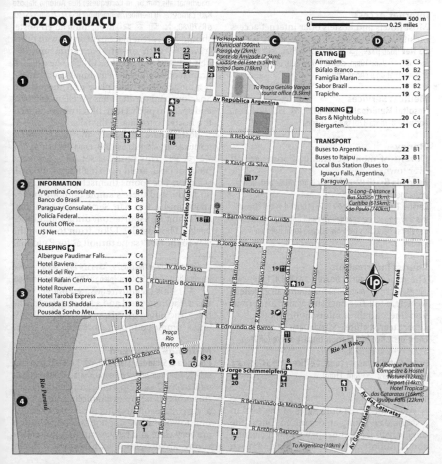

FOZ DO IGUAÇU

0 ——————— 500 m
0 ——————— 0.25 miles

To Hospital Municipal (500m); Paraguay (2km); Ponte da Amizade (2.5km); Ciudade del Este (5.5km); Itaipu Dam (18km)

To Praça Getúlio Vargas tourist office (3.5km)

EATING 🍴
Armazém....................................15 C3
Búfalo Branco............................16 B2
Famiglia Maran..........................17 C2
Sabor Brazil...............................18 B2
Trapiche.....................................19 C3

DRINKING 🍷
Bars & Nightclubs......................20 C4
Biergarten..................................21 C4

TRANSPORT
Buses to Argentina.....................22 B1
Buses to Itaipu...........................23 B1
Local Bus Station (Buses to Iguaçu Falls, Argentina, Paraguay)..................................24 B1

To Long-Distance Bus Station (3km); Curitiba (615km); São Paulo (740km)

INFORMATION
Argentina Consulate.....................1 B4
Banco do Brasil............................2 B4
Paraguay Consulate......................3 C3
Polícia Federal.............................4 B4
Tourist Office...............................5 B4
US Net...6 B2

SLEEPING 🛏
Albergue Paudimar Falls..............7 C4
Hotel Baviera...............................8 C4
Hotel del Rey...............................9 B1
Hotel Rafain Centro...................10 C3
Hotel Rouver..............................11 D4
Hotel Tarobá Express.................12 B1
Pousada El Shaddai....................13 B2
Pousada Sonho Meu..................14 B1

To Albergue Pudimar Campestre & Hostel Nature (12km); Airport (14km); Hotel Tropical das Cataratas (16km); Iguaçu Falls (22km)

To Argentina (10km)

Just south of town, the junction of the Paraná and Iguaçu rivers forms the tripartite Paraguay–Brazil–Argentina border (marked by obelisks). The Ponte Presidente Tancredo Neves crosses the Rio Iguaçu about 6km from the center of town, connecting Brazil with the Argentine town of Puerto Iguazú. Just north of the center, the Ponte da Amizade spans the Rio Paraná, crossing to the shabby Paraguayan town of Ciudad del Este.

INFORMATION
Emergency
Bombeiros (☎ 193) Handles fires and medical emergencies.
Polícia Federal (Map p329; ☎ 3523 1828; Av Jorge Schimmelpfeng)

Internet Access
Most hotels and hostels offer internet access on site.
US Net (Map p329; ☎ 3523 2289; Av Brasil 549; per hr R$4.50; ☯ 9am-10pm, closed 1-6pm Sun) Internet access and international phone calls.

Medical Services
Hospital Municipal (off Map p329; ☎ 3521 1951; Rua Adoniran Barbosa 370) Open 24hours.

Money
Dozens of money-exchange houses are all over town.
Banco do Brasil (Map p329; Av Brasil) ATMs and money exchange.
Caribe Turismo (☎ 3529 7173) Located in the airport, this travel agency exchanges Visa and American Express traveler's checks. It's the only place in town open on Sunday.

Tourist Information
The region's **tourist board** (☎ 0800 451 516; www .iguassu.tur.br; ☯ 7am-11pm) maintains an excellent website, a toll-free English-speaking information line, and three information booths:
Airport tourist office (☯ noon-1am)
Long-distance bus station tourist office (off Map p329; ☯ 6:30am-6:30pm)
Praça Getúlio Vargas tourist office (Map p329; Praça Getúlio Vargas; ☯ 7am-11pm)

TOURS
If you want to see both sides of the falls in a single day, taking an organized tour is the only way to make it happen without rushing about. Almost all the hotels in Foz do Iguaçu offer tours to Argentina for about R$75. Both parks have some organized adventures, including rafting, rappelling, kayaking, cycling and guided nature walks.
Macuco Ecoaventura (☎ 3529 9626; www.macuco ecoaventura.com.br; Brazil) For rafting, rappelling and other activities.
Iguazu Jungle Explorer (☎ 0xx54-3757 421 600; www.iguazujunglexplorer.com; Argentina) Offices are in the Sheraton Hotel inside the park.

SLEEPING
Don't be shy about trying to negotiate a lower price if the hotel is not full.

Budget
Albergue Paudimar Falls (Map p329; ☎ 3028 5503; www .paudimarfalls.com.br, in Portuguese; Rua Antônio Raposo 820; campsites HI member/nonmember R$17/17; dm $25/30; d R$70/80; ☒ ☐ ☏ ☒) Everything an HI hostel should be: a great place to meet up with other travelers, with on-site recreation options, helpful staff and good facilities. The original branch of this hostel – Paudimar Campestre – is a bigger, resort-like place near the airport. Spacious and green, it has excellent facilities and space to pitch a tent; the city bus connects the hostel to town and the falls.

Hostel Natura (off Map p329; ☎ 9116 0979; www.hos telnatura.com; Alameda Buri 333; campsites/dm R$25/40; ☒ ☏ ☒) This hostel is set on a gorgeous piece of land, amid two small lakes and lush scenery. The rooms themselves are pleasant and tidy, and there's ample outdoor lounge space and a fun bar. Service is top-notch, including transportation, dinner and other perks. The hostel is 12km from town on the way to the falls (same turnoff as for Paudimar Falls).

Hotel Rouver (Map p329; ☎ 3574 2916; www.hotelrou ver.com.br; Av Jorge Schimmelpfeng 872; d incl breakfast R$60; ☏ ☒) This recently renovated budget hotel has a boutiquey feel and a lot on offer for the price, including free airport pickup, cable TV and a simple continental breakfast.

Midrange & Top End
Pousada El Shaddai (Map p329; ☎ 3025 4493; www.pou sadaelshaddai.com.br; Rua Rebouças; s without bathroom R$25, s/d R$60/86; ☐ ☒) On a quiet residential street, this pousada occupies a rambling old house – a rare case of architectural preservation in a town of high-rise hotels. Budget rooms are very plain and rather cramped. But pricier rooms are delightful, with hardwood floors,

shuttered windows and glue-chip glass. Common areas include a clean kitchen and a sweet terrace.

our pick **Pousada Sonho Meu** (Map p329; ☎ 3573 5764; www.pousadasonhomeufoz.com; Rua Men de Sá 267; s/d R$68/101; ✗ 🖵 🛜 🌐) Sonho Meu – or 'My Dream' – feels like home away from home. Rooms are simple and sweet, with pastel-colored walls, bamboo furniture and ceiling fans. Stands out for its small size and family friendly atmosphere.

Hotel Baviera (Map p329; ☎ 3523 5995; Av Jorge Schimmelpfeng 697; s/d/tr/q R$91/115/149/195; ✗ 🛜) The faux-German facade may be kitschy, but at least this place has a bit of style. The German theme extends to the interior, which is clean, orderly and efficiently run. Appropriately, it's across the street from the popular Biergarten (see following) and the price includes a huge Bavarian-style breakfast.

Hotel del Rey (Map p329; ☎ 3523 2027; www.hoteldel reyfoz.com.br; Rua Taroba 1020; s/d/tr/q R$105/131/161/194; ✗ 🖵 🛜 🌐) The Hotel del Rey has refurbished its rooms and raised its prices, making this place a solid midrange choice. The rooms are rather utilitarian – think 'white' as a decorating theme – but they are spacious, clean and comfortable.

Hotel Tarobá Express (Map p329; ☎ 2102 7700; www.hoteltaroba.com.br; Rua Tarobá 1048; s/d/tr/q R$110/165/185/220; ✗ 🖵 🛜 🌐) This certified three-star hotel is a bustling place. Between the travel agency, gift shop and restaurant (dinner costs about R$24), and guests frequenting the busy reception area, the atmosphere is energetic and enthusiastic. The rooms are simple, but absolutely spotless, and fully equipped.

Hotel Rafain Centro (Map p329; ☎ 3521 3500; www.rafaincentro.com.br; Rua Marechal Deodoro 984; s/d/tr R$180/220/275; ✗ 🖵 🛜 🌐) This straightforward hotel does not quite justify its four-star rating. But the semiswanky place offers affordable prices for a high level of comfort and service – especially during slow periods, when prices are negotiable.

Hotel das Cataratas (Map p332; ☎ 2102 7000; www.hoteldascataratas.com; d R$500-630; ✗ 🖵 🛜 🌐) Nowhere on either side of the falls is as delightful, delicious and deluxe as the das Cataratas. The grand pink colonial edifice is located within the confines of Parque Nacional do Iguaçu, not far from the falls. So yes, you might enjoy a million-dollar view from your window.

EATING

Sabor Brasil (Map p329; ☎ 3028 7778; Av Brasil 638; meals R$8-10; 🕐 11am-10pm Mon-Sat, 3-10pm Sun) Sandwiches and ice cream are the specialties at this tiny café. Baguettes stuffed with meats and cheeses make for a hearty lunch – perfect for a picnic.

Famiglia Maran (Map p329; ☎ 3027 1212; Rua Almirante Barroso 1968; meals R$10-15; 🕐 24hr) This bakery and cafeteria has something for everyone. Sandwiches, pastas and filling hot dishes will sate your hunger, as will the irresistible soup buffet (R$7, from 6pm to 5:30am). You can enjoy the sidewalk seating during pleasant weather.

Armazém (Map p329; ☎ 3572 7422; Rua Edmundo de Barros 446; mains R$20; 🕐 6pm-2am) Seat yourself on the shady terrace at this attractive, colonial-style house – a lovely setting in which to enjoy gourmet Brazilian food and a nice selection of wines.

Búfalo Branco (Map p329; ☎ 3523 9744; Rua Rebouças 530; buffets R$25) The best *churrascaria* (restaurant featuring barbecued meat) in town is known for its succulent meat and fine service. Arrive hungry to take full advantage of the endless *rodízio* (smorgasbord) of grilled beef and pork.

Trapiche (Map p329; ☎ 3527 3951; Rua Marechal Deodoro de Fonseca 1087; mains R$30-65) The *moqueca* and other outstanding seafood stews here are big enough to sate at least a couple of big appetites, and the highest priced items include lobster and oysters (that have come a long way from the sea but are delicious nevertheless).

DRINKING & ENTERTAINMENT

Nightlife is hopping along Av Jorge Schimmelpfeng, where you will find breezy beer gardens for early evening and hot-to-trot nightclubs that stay open late. A good place to start is **Biergarten** (Map p329; cnr Av Jorge Schimmelpfeng & Rua Marechal Deodoro da Fonseca; 🕐 11am-4am).

GETTING THERE & AWAY
Air

Daily flights go from the **international airport** (☎ 3523 4244) to Asunción in Paraguay (one hour), Buenos Aires in Argentina (two hours), Rio (two hours), São Paulo (one hour) and Curitiba (40 minutes). Sit on the left hand side of the plane for good views of the falls.

Bus

The **long-distance bus station** (off ap p329; ☎ 3522 3336) is 4.5km from the center of town. Destinations include Curitiba (R$110 to R$130, *leito* –overnight sleeper – R$120, 10 hours), Florianópolis (R$160 to R$180, *leito* R$226, 14 hours), São Paulo (R$165, *leito* R$225, 16 hours) and Rio de Janeiro (R$199, *leito* R$280, 22 hours). For service to Buenos Aires (20 hours), head to Puerto Iguazú, Argentina; for Asunción (five hours), head to Ciudad del Este.

Getting to Argentina & Paraguay

To enter Paraguay, US citizens and other nationalities need a visa. Most nationalities can enter Argentina without a visa, but always confirm before crossing the border. Obtaining a visa takes about 24 hours.

Argentina consulate (Map p329; ☎ 3574 2969; 26 Travessa Eduardo Ramón Bianchi; ☑ 10am-2pm Mon-Fri)

Paraguay consulate (Map p329; ☎ 3523 2898; Rua Marechal Deodoro da Fonseca 901; ☑ 8:30am-4:30pm Mon-Fri)

To enter Ciudad del Este, Paraguay, walking across the bridge is inadvisable because of robberies, so take a bus or taxi. At the immigration posts, be sure to request your exit and entry stamps, as it may not happen automatically. From the border post, catch the next bus to Ciudad del Este (buses don't wait for travelers to complete their proceedings) or grab a taxi.

To enter Puerto Iguazú, Argentina, again, you'll have to request your exit and entry stamps if you are staying for longer than a day. Local bus drivers stop at the immigration facilities. Both borders are open 24 hours, but bus service ends at around 7pm.

GETTING AROUND

To/From the Airport

To reach the airport, 15km southeast of the center, catch a bus marked 'Aeroporto/P Nacional' (R$3, 40 minutes) from any stop along Av Juscelino Kubitschek. Buses run approximately every 20 minutes, and every hour after 7pm. A taxi from the center costs around R$40.

To/From the Bus Station

From outside the bus station, catch any 'Centro' bus to town (R$2). A taxi costs around R$10.

To/From the Falls

For the Brazilian side of the falls, catch the 'Aeroporto/P Nacional' bus (R$3) to the park entrance. You can catch it in the local bus terminal, or at stops along Av Juscelino Kubitschek and Av Jorge Schimmelpfeng.

To get to the Argentina side, catch a Puerto Iguazú bus (R$6, every 20 minutes) from the bus stop behind the local bus station or from any stop along Av Juscelino Kubitschek. In Puerto Iguazú, transfer to a 'Cataratas' bus to the falls (A$9, hourly).

Parque Nacional do Iguaçu (Brazil)

You can't miss the shiny entrance to the **Parque Nacional do Iguaçu** (Map p332; ☎ 3521 4400; www.cataratasdoiguacu.com.br; adult/child R$37/6; ☑ 9am-6pm Oct-Mar, 9am-5pm Apr-Sep), which houses bathrooms, ATMs, lockers, souvenir shops and vast parking facilities. Once you buy your ticket, you will be directed to board a free double-decker bus.

To visit the falls, take the bus to the third stop, site of Hotel das Cataratas (see p331). Here you can pick up the **Trilha das Cataratas**, or 'Waterfall Trail.' This 1200m trail follows the shore of the Iguaçu river, providing innumerable photo ops along the way. It terminates at the **Garganta do Diablo**, the most spectacular part of the falls. A manmade walkway allows you to go out to the middle of the river so you are seemingly surrounded by the force of rushing water. Expect to be dazzled – and doused.

From here, take the panoramic elevator to get a view of the falls from above. At the top, a

short walk along the road leads to **Porto Canoas** station, where you will find a nice restaurant with an excellent lunch buffet (R$28) and a food court with less expensive options. Both have seating on a pleasant outdoor terrace overlooking the flats of the river.

Remember, it's always wet at the falls, and water attracts sunlight. Pack raingear *and* sunblock. Bug repellent is a must on the walking trails. Also note that lighting for photography is best in the morning on the Brazilian side.

Boat Trips

While admiring the falls from above, you will surely spot fearless adventurers experiencing the falls from below. Such boating excursions are offered on both sides of the falls, but the Brazilian version is more elaborate (and more expensive). Get off the double-decker bus at the second stop for **Macuco Safari de Barco** (☎ 3574 4244; www.macucosafari.com.br; per person R$150; ☺ 8am 5pm).

The excursion starts with a 3km ride through the jungle, with an English-speaking guide pointing out the park's flora and fauna. The second phase is a short hike (600m) to a small waterfall called Salto de Macuco, where you can take a dip. Finally, climb aboard a Zodiac for a 4km journey over flat water and rapids, and under the falls known as the Three Musketeers. You *will* get soaked. The boat ride is 30 minutes, but the whole excursion takes about two hours.

Macuco Safari also offers a more sedate, 3½-hour boat trip along the flats above the falls.

Hiking

Parque Nacional do Iguaçu covers 550 sq km of rain forest, most of which is inaccessible to anybody but the wildlife. You can explore a few hiking trails in the company of a guide provided by the park. (English-speaking guides are available.) The **Trilha Poço Preto** (per person R$135) is a 9km trail that starts near the entrance (get off the bus at the first stop), and leads to the Lagoa do Poço Preto, a small lagoon that attracts birdlife. A quick boat ride and an optional paddle in a kayak complete the well-choreographed outing. The return trip is via the **Trilha das Bananeiras**, but you can get a lift.

Hiking is more rewarding in the morning, when weather is cooler and birds and animals

are more active. Look for butterflies, parrots, parakeets, woodpeckers, hummingbirds, toucans, lizards and spiders. Other more elusive creatures include monkeys, deer, sloths, anteaters, raccoons, jaguars, tapirs, caimans, armadillos and of course coatis. Countless varieties of orchids, lianas and vines are on display. Mosquitoes are plentiful – don't forget your insect repellent.

Adventure Activities

For more excitement, stop off at the **Campos de Deafios** (☎ 3529 6040; www.campodedesafios.com.br, in Portuguese) for rock climbing, rappelling and white-water rafting. Prices vary depending on activities. The entrance is at the third bus stop, opposite Hotel das Cataratas (see p331).

Parque Nacional Iguazú (Argentina)

The **Parque Nacional Iguazú** (Map p332; ☎ 0xx54-3757 491 469; www.iguazuargentina.com; adult/child AR$85/45; ☺ 8am-6:30pm, to 5:30pm Sep-Mar) is 18km from Puerto Iguazú, the town on the Argentine side of the border.

From the entrance, follow the **Sendero Verde**, a short trail through the jungle that offers a chance to spot butterflies, birds and coatis. You can also opt to ride the free Tren Ecológico de la Selva (Green Jungle Train, every 30 minutes). In any case, your first destination is Estación Cataratas. Two walking trails depart from this point, offering incredibly varied perspectives of the waterfalls.

Start with the short **Circuito Superior**, or Upper Circuit, which is the least spectacular, but builds anticipation. The **Circuito Inferior**, or Lower Circuit, is a 1.5km loop offering views of the falls from below. From here you can take a free boat (every 15 minutes) to **Isla San Martín**, which has trails and more close-up views.

Saving the best for last, **Garganta do Diablo** will be your final destination. Take the train to Estación Garganta del Diablo. Here, the catwalk begins at a quiet point upstream from the falls, passing a number of tranquil islands. At the Garganta, the serene river suddenly turns violent, as 13,000 cu meters of water per second plunge 90m in 14 falls around a horseshoe-shaped canyon. It's a hypnotizing, multisensory experience – hearing the falls roaring in your ears, feeling the mist on your face and seeing huge rainbow arcs stretching across the rush. Watch for the swifts, which drop like rocks into the misty

PARANÁ

I'LL BE DAMMED!

For some, it's a wonder of the modern world. For others, it's a manmade disaster. But there's no doubt that Itaipu Dam has permanently changed the face of southern Brazil and massively contributed to the rapid industrial development of the country.

First, the startling statistics. The dam's structures stretch for almost 9km and reach a height of more than 200m. The concrete used in its construction would be sufficient to build a two-lane highway from Moscow to Lisbon. At the height of construction, crews worked at a blinding pace, equivalent to building a 20-story office building every hour. No wonder it cost US$18 billion.

So was it worth it? Its generating capacity is 14,000 megawatts of clean energy – enough to supply 22% of Brazil's electricity needs and 90% of Paraguay's. To produce an equivalent amount in oil-burning thermoelectric plants, you'd need 434,000 barrels of oil per day. That's a lot of carbon dioxide emissions.

At the same time, critics of the dam estimate that 700 sq km of forest has been lost or compromised. Several species of plant life have been driven into extinction. Many native Guarani and Tupi settlements were destroyed, as were the impressive Sete Quedas waterfalls.

For its part, the Itaipu Binacional – a joint Brazilian–Paraguayan agency that administers the dam – has been sensitive to such criticisms. Innovative programs have relocated animals displaced by flooding, reforested the land along the reservoir's banks and compensated communities affected by the construction.

Another complaint came from the Paraguyans, who have claimed since the 1980s that the deal struck with Brazil by Paraguyan dictator Alfredo Stroessner forced Paraguay to sell its unused electricity to Brazil at artificially low rates. While São Paulo state's industrial growth exploded, Paraguay was left without enough revenue to build adequate electricity transmission lines between the falls and its capital.

In July 2009, Brazilian President Lula da Silva and Paraguayan President Fernando Lugo finally renegotiated the bilateral agreement concerning the dam, allowing Paraguay to sell its unused power openly on the Brazilian market and tripling its revenue.

---

abyss, catch insects in midair, shoot back up and dart to perch on the cliffs behind the falls.

For lunch, you will find snack bars at Dos Hermanas (at the Circuito Inferior). Near the entrance is a more upscale restaurant, La Selva, with a buffet serving typical Argentine food.

On the Argentine side of the falls, the light is best for photographs in the late afternoon. If you get your ticket stamped when you exit the park, you can return the following day for half-price.

Boating

Many claim that the way to truly experience the falls is to feel their wrath raining down on you. Boats from both sides of the border take adventurous passengers under the falls, but it is significantly less expensive on the Argentinean side.

Iguazu Jungle Explorer (☎ 0xx54-3757 421 696; www.iguazujunglexplorer.com) offers two versions of this adventure. The **Gran Aventura** (A$150) is a one-hour excursion that includes an 8km

ride through the jungle on the back of a jeep and a 6km ride down the Iguazú river. The trip culminates in an up-close-and-personal tour of Salto San Martin and Garganta del Diablo. This excursion departs hourly from the visitors center near the entrance.

If your primary interest is the so-called 'waterfall baptism,' you can opt for the abbreviated **Aventura Nautica** (A$90). The 12-minute trip departs from the dock opposite Isla San Martín (every 20 minutes), giving passengers a quick tour of the canyon and a sousing shower. Protective bags are provided for cameras and other gear; anything not contained therein – including you – will get wet.

Buy tickets at the park entrance or at the Iguazu Jungle Explorer office near Estación Cataratas.

Hiking

To explore the rain forest in the national park, stop at the **Interpretation Center** (☎ 0xx54-3757 491 469) near the entrance and inquire about the **Sendero Macuco**. This 7km trail is a rare opportunity to explore the park independently. Six interpretive stations explain the flora, including bamboo, palmitos and pioneer plants. The white-bearded manakin and toco toucan live in these parts, as does a troupe of brown capuchin monkeys. The trail's end point is the **Arrechea Waterfall**, a 20m cascade that has gouged out a lovely natural pool below.

Early morning is the best time for hiking. Departure before 4pm (3pm in winter) is required.

PARQUE DAS AVES

This 5-hectare **bird park** (Map p332; ☎ 3529 8282; www.parquedasaves.com.br; admission R$23; ☉ 8:30am-5:30pm), located 300m from the entrance to Parque Nacional do Iguaçu, is home to 800-plus species of birds, including red ibis, bare-throated bellbird, and flamingos galore. They live in 8m-high aviaries that are constructed right in the forest. Other exhibits are devoted to snakes, butterflies and other species.

ITAIPU DAM

On the Paraná river 14km north of Foz, the **Itaipu Dam** (☎ 3520 6999; www.turismoitaipu.com.br, in Portuguese) is the largest hydroelectric power plant *on the planet*.

The numbers are impressive. The dam is 8km long and 65 stories high. The plant provides 22% of the electric energy consumed in Brazil, and more than 90% of the energy consumed in Paraguay. Even more extraordinary is the massive size of the construction that spans the river, the palpable power of the water rushing out of the spillway, and the endless array of power lines emanating from the plant.

Construction of the dam was controversial (see the boxed text, p334), and Itaipu's public relations team is eager to publicize its immensity and accomplishments, if not its downsides. So expect a barrage of propaganda when you take the **tour** (tour R$19; ☉ hourly 8am-4pm). A short film is followed by a visit to the central observation deck, providing a panoramic view of the complex. All information is in Portuguese and English. For a more technical tour, inquire about the **special circuit** (☎ 3520 6667; tour R$50; ☉ 8am, 8:30am, 10am, 10:30am, 1:30pm, 2pm, 3:30pm, 4pm). This in-depth, two-hour tour is fascinating for anyone with engineering tendencies.

The last option to visit the dam is the hokey **sound-and-light show** (tickets R$12; ☉ 8pm Fri & Sat Mar-Nov, 9pm Fri & Sat Dec-Feb).

If you are wondering how construction of the dam affected the area's flora and fauna, check out the **Ecomuseu** (admission R$8; ☉ 8:30-11:30am & 2-5:30pm Tue-Sat, 2-5:30pm Sun).

To get to the Itaipu Dam, catch a Conjunto C bus from any stop along Av Juscelino Kubitschek (R$3, every 20 minutes). The trip takes about 30 minutes.

CIUDAD DEL ESTE (PARAGUAY)

Across the Ponte da Amizade lies this Paraguayan city – dynamic but dingy, animated but impoverished. Here, you can play baccarat at the casinos or shop for duty-free imported goods: you might find some good deals but imitations are ubiquitous. Walking over the bridge is not safe, so catch a bus from the local bus terminal in Foz do Iguaçu (R$3, every 10 minutes) from 6am to 7:30pm.

Santa Catarina

Life's a beach. Certainly that's true in sunny Santa Catarina, which boasts 560km of spectacular coastline. If you like your beach deserted, there is a spot of sand for you in the south of Ilha de Santa Catarina. If you prefer a party scene, head further north on that same island. Crave the life aquatic? You'll find excellent snorkeling and diving at Praia Bombinhas. If you're all about big surf, take your pick from any number of beaches south of Florianópolis.

While beaches might be the main draw, this southern state has more than just sun and sand. Running parallel to the coast, the Serra Geral offers cool temperatures and stunning mountain scenery, promising rewarding hiking and horseback riding.

The inland regions are also where Santa Catarina exhibits the profound influence of its German ancestry, most evident during Oktoberfest, Blumenau's huge festival for folk dancing, accordion playing and beer drinking. But the Alpine architecture and fresh-brewed beer are here to enjoy year-round.

Like the other southern states, Santa Catarina enjoys some of Brazil's highest standards of living. The state's prosperity means that its infrastructure is sound and the people are welcoming. Keep in mind that, on the coast, crowds and prices go up with the temperature. Visit outside of January and February to avoid the craziness and costliness of summer in Santa Catarina.

HIGHLIGHTS

- Catch a wave at **Praia da Joaquina** (p344) and you're sittin' on top of the world
- Snorkel in the crystalline waters off **Ilha do Campeche** (p345)
- Sample brews straight from the barrel at the **Cervejaria & Fábrica Eisenbahn** (p350) in Blumenau
- Swim and snorkel from the docks of the floating restaurants in **Caixa d'Aço** (p354) near Porto Belo
- Dress for chilly weather exploration along the verdant trails of **Parque Nacional de São Joaquim** (p357), where you just might see snow

- POPULATION: 6.1 MILLION
- AREA: 95,400 SQ KM

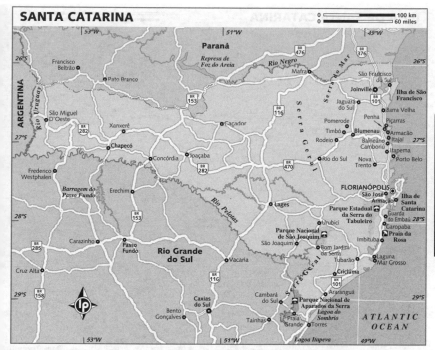

SANTA CATARINA

History
In the 1820s, a newly independent Brazil realized the strategic importance of this region on the frontier between the Spanish and Portuguese Americas. The emperor invited German-speaking immigrants to develop the land and serve as a buffer against Spanish insurgency. The German immigrants – and Italians who followed – never adopted the plantation culture of the Northeast. Instead, the economy was based on small, family-owned farms, a legacy that lives on in the region's egalitarian politics and equitable distribution of income.

Climate
The coastal lowlands of Santa Catarina enjoy a semitropical climate, with hot, humid summers and mild winters. The central highlands are drier in summer and colder in winter. At the Serra Geral's highest elevations, snow is surprisingly common.

Getting There & Around
Florianópolis is the state's transportation hub, with direct bus and air services to every

major city in Brazil. Joinville also has direct air services to São Paulo, with connections to other major cities. Most destinations within Santa Catarina are accessible from Florianópolis by bus service, which is extensive and dependable.

ILHA DE SANTA CATARINA

Ilha de Santa Catarina has a vibrant and varied coastline, from the calm, crowded bays of the north, to the wild, cliff-hugging beaches of the south. But it's not just the beaches that make this island so enchanting. A forest of protected pines protects the east coast, while the dunes near Praia da Joaquina create a lunar landscape. The spine of mountains, luxuriant with the Mata Atlântica (Atlantic rain forest), drops precipitously down to the lovely Lagoa da Conceição. The gateway to the island is Florianópolis, political capital of Santa Catarina and cultural capital of southern Brazil.

The north of the island borders on being overdeveloped, and the shores of Lagoa da

SANTA CATARINA

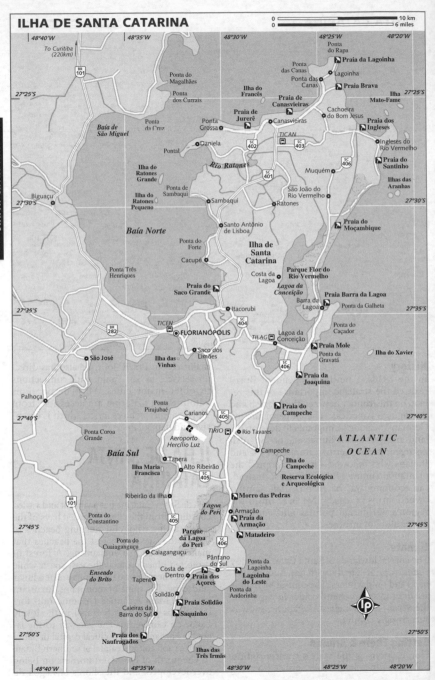

ILHA DE SANTA CATARINA

| 0 | 10 km |
| 0 | 6 miles |

To Curitiba
(220km)

BR 101

48°40'W
48°35'W
48°30'W
48°25'W
48°20'W

27°25'S

Ponta do
Magalhães

Ponta
dos Currais

Ilha do
Francês

Ponta
do Rapa

Praia da Lagoinha

Lagoinha

Ponta
das Canas
Ponta das
Canas

Praia Brava

Ilha
Mato-Fame

27°25'S

Baía de
São Miguel

Ponta
da Cruz

Praia de
Jurerê

Praia de
Canasvieiras

Ponta
Grossa

Canasvieiras

Cachoeira
do Bom Jesus

Praia dos
Ingleses

Daniela

SC 402

TICAN

SC 403

Ingleses do
Rio Vermelho

Pontal

Rio Ratones

SC 401

Muquém

SC 406

Praia do
Santinho

Ilha do
Ratones
Grande

Ponta de
Sambaqui

São João do
Rio Vermelho

Ilhas das
Aranhas

Biguaçu

Ilha do
Ratones
Pequeno

Sambaqui

Ratones

27°30'S

Baía Norte

Santo Antônio
de Lisboa

Ilha de
Santa
Catarina

Praia do
Moçambique

27°30'S

Ponta do
Forte

Cacupé

Costa da
Lagoa

Parque Flor do
Rio Vermelho

Ponta Três
Henriques

Praia do
Saco Grande

Lagoa da
Conceição

Praia Barra da Lagoa

Barra da
Lagoa

Ponta da Galheta

27°35'S

Itacorubi

SC 404

TICEN

FLORIANÓPOLIS

TILAG

Lagoa da
Conceição

Ponta do
Caçador

Ilha do Xavier

BR 282

São José

Saco dos
Limões

SC 406

Praia Mole

Ponta da
Gravatá

Ilha das
Vinhas

Praia da
Joaquina

Palhoça

Ponta
Pirajubaé

Carianos

SC 405

Praia do
Campeche

27°40'S

Ponta Coroa
Grande

Aeroporto
Hercílio Luz

TIRIO

Rio Távares

ATLANTIC
OCEAN

27°40'S

Baía Sul

Tapera

Ilha Maria
Francisca

Alto Ribeirão

SC 405

Campeche

Ilha do
Campeche

Reserva Ecológica
e Arqueológica

BR 101

Ribeirão da Ilha

SC 405

Lagoa
do Peri

Morro das Pedras

Armação

Praia da
Armação

Ponta do
Constantino

Parque
da Lagoa
do Peri

SC 406

Matadeiro

27°45'S

Ponta do
Cuaiaganguçu

Caiaganguçu

Pântano
do Sul

Ponta da
Lagoinha

Lagoinha
do Leste

27°45'S

Enseado
do Brito

Tapera

Costa de
Dentro

Praia dos
Açores

Ponta da
Andorinha

Solidão

Praia Solidão

Caieiras da
Barra do Sul

Saquinho

Praia dos
Naufragados

27°50'S

Ilhas das
Três Irmãs

27°50'S

48°40'W
48°35'W
48°30'W
48°25'W
48°20'W

Conceição are crowded with restaurants, hotels and pubs. The best beaches lie along the east coast, especially for surfers. In general, further south means less developed.

Plan on big crowds and high prices (listed here) between Christmas and early March. Prices can fall 20% to 40% outside peak times.

FLORIANÓPOLIS

☎ 0xx48 / pop 408,000

There are two sides to Florianópolis (Floripa). On the mainland, the industrial zone occupies the districts of Estreito and Coqueiros. Across the bay, the island holds the historic center and the chic district of Beira-Mar Norte. Two picturesque bridges link these halves. The old suspension bridge, the Ponte Hercílio Luz, is no longer open to traffic, but it still lights the night sky, acting as the defining feature of Floripa's spectacular skyline.

Florianópolis is a convenient transportation hub, with all of the island's 42 beaches within an hour's drive. While in the center, travelers can explore the colonial, cobblestone streets that fan out from palm-lined Praça XV de Novembro, or take a sunset stroll along the embankment in Beira-Mar Norte.

Orientation

The city's major sights, hotels and restaurants are just east of the long-distance and local bus stations. The upscale Beira-Mar Norte neighborhood sits on the bay 2km north of the center.

Information

BOOKSTORES

Livraria Catarinense (Rua Felipe Schmidt 60; ☒ 10am-8pm Mon-Sat) Sells some foreign-language titles.

EMERGENCY

Bombeiros (☎ 193) Fire and medical emergencies.
Polícia Federal (☎ 194)

INTERNET ACCESS

LAN House (☎ 3028 0477; Beiramar Shopping; per hr R$4; ☒ 10am-10pm Mon-Sat, 2-8pm Sun)
Moncho (☎ 2106 2775; Rua Tiradentes 181; per hr R$4; ☒ 9am-10pm Mon-Fri, 11am-8pm Sat)

MONEY

Change your cash at one of the money-exchange houses on Rua Felipe Schmidt.
Banco do Brasil (Praça XV de Novembro 20) For traveler's checks and ATMs.

TOURIST INFORMATION

Florianópolis and Ilha da Santa Catarina maps are available from the friendly staff here:
Tourist information (☎ 3248 0002; long-distance bus station; ☒ 8am-10pm)

Sights

The center of town is the inviting **Praça XV de Novembro**, with its shady walks and 100-year-old fig tree. On one side sits the **Museu Histórico de Santa Catarina** (☎ 3221 3504; Praça XV de Novembro 227; admission R$3; ☒ 10am-6pm Tue-Fri, 10am-4pm Sat & Sun), formerly the colonial governor's palace. The building, boasting ornate parquetry floors and outrageous 19th-century ceilings, houses indigenous and colonial artifacts and hosts interesting temporary exhibitions.

You'll hear the hourly ringing of bells in the **Catedral Metropolitana**, which sits grandly at the high end of the square. The best-preserved colonial church, **Igreja de NS do Rosário**, sits picturesquely atop the steps at Rua Trajano.

At the other end of the square, the busy promenade **Rua Felipe Schmidt** is fine for people-watching and window-shopping. Or continue down to the waterfront to the well-preserved **Alfândega** (Customs House) and **Mercado Municipal** (Municipal Market).

North of the center, **Av Beira Mar Norte** runs along the coast of the Baía Norte. The waterfront promenade attracts runners, bikers and walkers, enjoying the breeze off the bay and a sweeping view across to the mainland.

Tours

Floripa By Bus (☎ 3239 8966; www.floripabybus.com .br, in Portuguese; Av Madre Benvenuta 687; adult/child R$15/30) A double-decker, open-air bus takes passengers on day tours of the island. The office is 6km out of town, so call to reserve a seat and get picked up at the bus station.
Scuna Sul (☎ 3225 1806; www.scunasul.com.br, in Portuguese; tours R$28-45) Boat tours of the bay stop at some pretty 18th-century Portuguese forts.

Sleeping

Florianópolis suffers from a lack of budget sleeping options, although prices drop dramatically outside high season, making many midrange places more affordable.

Floripa Hostel – Centro (☎ 3225 3781; www.flori pahostel.com.br, in Portuguese; Rua Duarte Schutel 227; dm HI member/student/regular R$30/36/39, d HI member/regular R$70/75; ☒ ☒) On a residential street, halfway between the city center and Beira-Mar Norte,

SANTA CATARINA

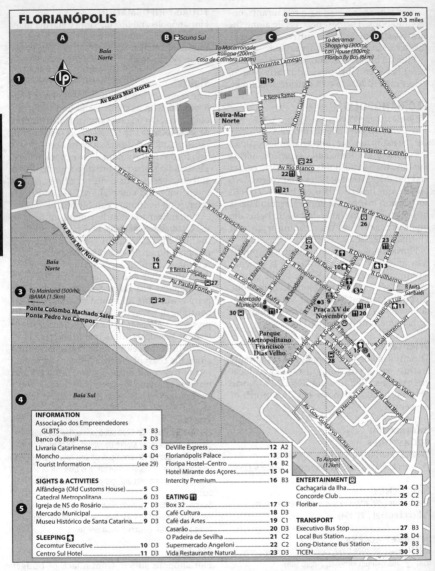

FLORIANÓPOLIS

INFORMATION

Associação dos Empreendedores GLBTS	1 B3
Banco do Brasil	2 D3
Livraria Catarinense	3 C3
Moncho	4 D4
Tourist Information	(see 29)

SIGHTS & ACTIVITIES

Alfândega (Old Customs House)	5 C3
Catedral Metropolitana	6 D3
Igreja de NS do Rosário	7 D3
Mercado Municipal	8 C3
Museu Histórico de Santa Catarina	9 D3

SLEEPING

Cecomtur Executive	10 D3
Centro Sul Hotel	11 D3
DeVille Express	12 A2
Florianópolis Palace	13 D3
Floripa Hostel–Centro	14 B2
Hotel Mirante dos Açores	15 D4
Intercity Premium	16 B3

EATING

Box 32	17 C3
Café Cultura	18 D3
Café das Artes	19 C1
Casarão	20 D3
O Padeira de Sevilha	21 C2
Supermercado Angeloni	22 C2
Vida Restaurante Natural	23 D3

ENTERTAINMENT

Cachaçaria da Ilha	24 C3
Concorde Club	25 C2
Floribar	26 D2

TRANSPORT

Executivo Bus Stop	27 B3
Local Bus Station	28 D4
Long-Distance Bus Station	29 B3
TICEN	30 C3

this orderly HI hostel is an easy walk from either. Kitchen and shared bathroom facilities are spotless. Sturdy wooden bunk beds are lined up in the gender-segregated dorms.

Hotel Mirante dos Açores (☎ 3879 7130; www.hotel mirantedosacores.com.br, in Portuguese; Rua Tiradentes 167; s/d R$85/105; 🅿 🖳 🛜) Located on a quiet cobblestone street, a blue-arched entry leads into a lobby streaming with sunlight and painted in vibrant colors. Murals adorn the guestrooms, which have wood furniture and institutional carpeting.

Centro Sul Hotel (☎ 3222 9110; www.centrosulho tel.com.br, in Portuguese; Av Hercílio Luz 652; s/d R$88/120; 🅿 🛜) CSH – as it is called – is a comfortable, kitschy midrange option. Everything is a bit worn with age, but the rooms are clean and priced well, even in high season.

ourpick Cecomtur Executive (☎ 2107 8800; www .cecomturhotel.com.br, in Portuguese; Rua Arcipreste Paiva 107; r from R$105; 🅿 🛜 ♿) This efficient business hotel isn't fancy, but it's got everything you need: modern, spotless, spacious rooms; congenial, English-speaking service and a few perks besides. It's our pick for great value.

Florianópolis Palace (☎ 2106 9633; www.floph.com .br; Rua Artista Bittencourt 14; s/d R$137/144; 🅿 🖥 🛜 ♿) The fanciest hotel in the historic center also goes by the goofy nickname 'the floph.' Both parking and a sprawling breakfast buffet are included in the price, and rooms on the upper floors offer panoramic views of the city.

Intercity Premium (☎ 3027 2200; www.inter cityhoteis.com.br; Av Paolo Fontes 1210; s/d R$168/200; 🅿 🖥 🛜 ♿) This classy, accommodating high-rise hotel is convenient to the bus station. The lobby sparkles with white marble, while plush couches are scattered with pillows. Guestrooms are fully equipped and tastefully decorated, and some enjoy impressive views of the bay and mainland.

DeVille Express (☎ 3225 6002; www.deville.com.br; Rua Felipe Schmidt 1320; s/d R$177/202; 🅿 🖥 🛜 ♿) This all-suite hotel offers the trappings of luxury at midrange prices – great value. Higher-priced rooms have balconies, from which to enjoy some of Floripa's loveliest views.

Eating & Drinking

Florianópolis has a little bit of everything, from safe bets for vegetarians to big plates of meat and seafood.

O Padeira de Sevilha (☎ 3025 3402; Rua Esteves Júnior 2144; breads & cakes R$3-10; 🕑 6:50am-8:30pm Mon-Fri, 7am-2pm Sat) 'The Breadmaker of Seville' is considered one of the top 30 bakeries in all of Brazil, owing to its scrumptious artisanal loaves and tempting sweets served at a giant community table.

Café das Artes (☎ 3322 0690; Rua Esteves Júnior 734; sandwiches R$5-10; 🕑 11:30am-11pm Mon-Sat, 4-11pm Sun) An artsy, upscale café in Beira-Mar Norte, this cozy option offers good coffee and baked goods as well as salads and sandwiches.

Casa de Coimbra (☎ 3222 9017; Av Beira Mar Norte 2568; meals R$10-15; 🕑 11:30am-midnight Tue-Sat) Heavy wood doors open up to a cool, country casa, right in the heart of the city. The rustic interior, filled with folk art, is a perfect atmosphere to enjoy hearty, home-cooked Brazilian fare.

Vida Restaurante Natural (☎ 3223 4507; Rua Visconde de Ouro Preto 298; meals R$10-18; 🕑 11am-3:30pm Mon-Fri) This all-vegetarian joint offers an appetizing buffet in a handsome, colonial-style home.

Café Cultura (☎ 3364 3223; Praça XV de Novembro 352; meals R$15-25; 🕑 8am-8pm Mon-Sat; 🖥 🛜) This modern café in a renovated neocolonial building has healthy breakfasts, lunches and dinners, as well as wonderfully unhealthy desserts.

Macarronada Italiana (☎ 3223 2666; Av Beira Mar Norte; meals R$20-30; 🕑 11am-1am) The vast dining room and terrace are often crowded with families, feasting on pasta, pizza, seafood and grilled meats. The Italian fare is delicious, and wine flows freely.

ourpick Box 32 (☎ 3224 5588; Mercado Municipal; meals R$25-30; 🕑 10am-10pm Mon-Sat, to 5pm Sun) This historic bar and restaurant in the Mercado Municipal claims to be 'the most democratic box in Brazil.' Local celebrities come during happy hour for frothy beer and fresh seafood.

For self-catering beach picnics, head to **Supermercado Angeloni** (cnr Av Rio Branco & Rua Esteves Júnior; 🕑 8am-9pm).

Entertainment

While many people flock to Lagoa for its nightlife, Floripa center has a few hot spots too.

Cachaçaria da Ilha (☎ 3224 0551; Av Osmar Cunha 164; 🕑 5pm-2:30am Mon-Fri, 8pm-4am Sat) This sophisticated bar is famous for its *cachaça* (high-proof sugarcane alcohol), but also has a fine

---

GAY FLOR-EE

Floripa is becoming Brazil's second gay capital. Its Pride celebration, **Parada da Diversidade** (www.diversidadefloripa.org.br), has grown into one of Brazil's biggest, attracting 100,000 people in 2009. The city also hosts GLBT-centered 'Gay Pop' events during Carnaval. Gay and lesbian travelers from around the world descend on Florianópolis, which is safer and more affordable than Rio.

Popular hangouts include Concorde Club (p342), Floribar (p342) and Praia Mole (p344). For more information, including the useful *Guia GLBTS*, visit the **Associação dos Empreendedores GLBTS** (☎ 4009 2595; www .aeglbts.org.br; Rua Henrique Valgas 112).

selection of draft beers. Live music makes it a popular happy-hour spot.

Floribar (☎ 3322 2550; Rua Dorval Melchíades de Souza 638; ☾ 6pm-2am Thu-Sun) A cool bilevel lounge, where Floripa's most beautiful people sip fancy cocktails and groove to house music.

Concorde Club (☎ 3222 1981; Av Rio Branco 729; cover R$15-25) Two dance floors pulse to a heavy bass, while swirling bodies lose themselves in the flashing lights. Three bars ensure that dancers do not get dehydrated.

Getting There & Away

AIR

Direct flights go to São Paulo (one hour), Porto Alegre (one hour), Rio de Janeiro (1½ hours) and Curitiba (40 minutes), with connections to most other cities.

The **airport** (☎ 3226 0229) is 12km south of the city (R$25 by taxi). Red local buses marked 'Corredor Sudoeste' run to the airport (R$2, 45 minutes) every 15 minutes from the local bus station on Rua Antônio Luz.

BUS

From the **long-distance bus station** (☎ 3212 3100), buses link Florianópolis with every major city in southern Brazil. Destinations include Blumenau (R$29, three hours, hourly); Joinville (R$35, 2½ hours, hourly); Porto Alegre (R$62 to R$92, 6½ hours); Curitiba (R$38 to R$65, four hours, hourly); São Paulo (R$88 to R$203, 12 hours); Rio de Janeiro (R$161, 18 hours); and Foz do Iguaçu (R$130, *leito* – overnight sleeper – R$226, 14 hours). International destinations include Buenos Aires, Argentina (24 hours) and Montevideo, Uruguay (20 hours).

Getting Around

The city is the transportation hub for the rest of the island, all within a one-hour drive.

BUS

The island of Santa Catarina has a remarkably efficient bus service (R$2.80). Buses leave from the TICEN station, adjacent to the long-distance bus station, for nearby destinations and other bus stations around the island. Your fare is good for connections required to reach more-distant locations. For south-island destinations, transfer at the TIRIO terminal (Map p338) at Rio Tavares; most north-island beaches and villages can be reached by transferring from TICAN (Map p338) near

Canasvieiras; for Lagoa da Conceição and most eastern beaches, head for the TILAG (Map p338) terminal at Lagoa.

Additional yellow microbuses called *executivos* (R$5 to R$8) follow the same routes; their advantages include air-con, fewer stops, direct routes to the beaches and room for surfboards.

CAR

Consider renting a car for easier exploration of the island's beaches. Beware that prices are generally high (from R$99 per day) and traffic can be deadly on weekends.

Localiza (☎ 3333 5367; www.localiza.com, in Portuguese) A reliable South American chain with counters at the airport and bus station.

NORTH ISLAND

From Praia de Jurerê to Praia dos Ingleses, the north of the island is designed for mass tourism: calm, family-friendly waters; newly widened roads that provide easy access to the international airport; and lots of anonymous hotels and restaurants.

Santo Antônio de Lisboa

On the west coast, Santo Antônio de Lisboa is among the oldest communities on the island. An old-fashioned fishing-village atmosphere is complemented by cobblestone streets and Azorean architecture. The most prominent edifice is the **Igreja da NS da Necessidade**, dating from 1750. Many other 18th-century colonial buildings now house restaurants and art galleries. Stop by the delightful **Casa Açoriana** (☎ 3235 1262; Rua Cônego Serpa 30) to peruse island arts and enjoy some sweets in the courtyard café.

Santo Antônio's seaside setting and fishing heritage guarantee that you can enjoy delicious seafood. Try **Bar & Restaurante Açores** (☎ 3235 1377; Rua Cônego Serpa 20; meals R$20-35) or **Sobrado** (☎ 3334 2403; Rua XV de Novembro 123; meals R$20-40), both in historic houses.

Canasvieiras

Canasvieiras is not the most atmospheric place on the island, but it has easy access to **Praia de Jurerê** and **Praia de Canasvieiras**. Both beaches offer options for windsurfing, fishing and jet-skiing. Nightlife in town is hopping, as crowds of young people flock to local bars and clubs. Outside the season, however, it's sleepy, and many hotels are closed altogether.

Open only in summer, **Floripa Hostel – Canasvieiras** (☎ 3266 2036; Rua Dr João de Oliveira 517; dm HI member/student/regular R$27/30/34, d HI member/regular R$65/70; 🖳) subscribes to all the hostel norms: friendly, English-speaking reception; bunk beds and lockers; shared bathrooms, kitchen and TV room. It's two blocks from the beach.

The 'apart-hotel' **Lacabana** (☎ 3266 0400; www.lacabana.com.br, in Portuguese; Av das Nações 525; d/q R$120/160; ✿) is no beauty, but it is practical, offering comfortable but small rooms with kitchenettes. About 150m from the beach, it's a decent option for families who require the convenience of Canasvieiras.

Praia da Lagoinha & Praia Brava

The northeastern tip of the island is a slender peninsula, accessed by slow-moving roads that wind around the hills to the beach. These towns are ritzier than their neighbors, though the beaches are still overbuilt. **Praia da Lagoinha** is a crescent-shaped patch of sand, surrounded on three sides by rocky cliffs that keep the water calm. Further south, **Praia Brava** has wilder waves that attract a steady stream of surfers. Adventure-seekers can try **paragliding** (OVNI Parapente; ☎ 9985 8393; www.ovniparapente.com.br, in Portuguese; per person R$165) for an unusual and exhilarating perspective on the peninsula.

Santa Catarina's Italian heritage is lovingly showcased in the design and decor at the luxurious **Villabella Villaggio** (☎ 3284 2017; www.villabellavillaggio.com.br; Av Epitácio Bittencourt 470, Praia Brava; d from R$180, chalets R$285; ✿ 🖳 📶 🐾). Every guestroom has an expansive view toward either Praia da Lagoinha or Praia Brava.

The pink **Pousada da Vigia** (☎ 3284 1789; www.pousadadavigia.com.br; Rua Côn Walmor Castro 291, Lagoinha; d with garden/ocean view R$275/340; ✿ 🖳 📶 🐾) overlooks Praia da Lagoinha – and what a view! With only 10 guestrooms, scattered around lovely gardens, service is attentive and reaches to the beach, which is accessible by a 200m footpath.

Praia dos Ingleses & Praia do Santinho

Once among the island's finest beaches, **Praia dos Ingleses** has suffered from its popularity. It's now crowded with high-rise hotels and overpriced restaurants.

Further south, **Praia do Santinho** is quieter, thanks to the protected area of dunes behind it. Santinho is the north island's best surfing beach, acclaimed for its consistent waves

and uncrowded conditions. **Floripa Surf Camp** (☎ 9615 6282; Av Madre Maria Vilac 100; rental per hr R$25) offers equipment rental, classes and multiday camps.

Readers have written us to rave about **Pousada do Atobá'** (☎ 3269 4436; www.pousadadoatoba .com.br; Servidão do Ipê; ste/chalet R$150/180), about 2km north of the main access road to Praia do Santinho. The airy, bright rooms look onto a well-kept garden, and if a seven-minute walk to the beach is too far, you can hang by the pool. The English-speaking family that runs the place takes exceptionally good care of guests.

Surfers may appreciate the expertise of the owner at **Costão Flat** (☎ 3369 3476; http://costaoflat .com/; Rua do Jornalista 76; d R$160-180; 🖳), who is a surf photographer and guru of the local waves. The rooms are spacious, and the apartments all have full kitchens and balconies.

EAST COAST

Facing the open ocean, the east coast boasts the island's cleanest waters, longest beaches and most challenging surf.

Barra da Lagoa & Around

In the north, **Praia do Moçambique** merges with **Praia Barra da Lagoa** to form a stunning, 14km strand. The beach is hidden from the road by a thriving pine forest. Surfing is sweet all along here: Praia Barra da Lagoa has gentle swells and shallow waters that are good for beginners, while the long stretch of Moçambique has more-challenging peaks.

Praia do Moçambique is protected, so the only construction is around the town of Barra da Lagoa. Restaurants, bars and pousadas (guesthouses) are plentiful.

At **Pousada 32** (☎ 3232 4232; www.pousada32.com .br, in Portuguese; Rua Angelina Joaquin dos Santos 300; s/d/q with kitchen R$75/120/180; 📶), the colorful rooms have ceiling fans and balconies, making this a decent option if you must stay in town. The '32' refers to the number of meters to the beach.

The congenial owner of **Pousada Rio Vermelho** (☎ 3296 1337; São João de Rio Vermelho; d R$125-190; ✿ 🐾), Carlota, claims that her pousada is the oldest on the island, dating back to around 1980, but its age does not show. The spacious grounds and chic chalets are clean and contemporary. The grounds cover almost 0.5 sq km, extending from the road to Praia do Moçambique.

Praia Mole

Praia Mole is famous for its world-class waves and internationally heralded party scene, especially among the gay and lesbian community. The beach is absolutely beautiful, as are most of the bodies sunning and surfing. It does get crowded, but that's part of the appeal.

To take full advantage of the surf, sign up with **Nexus Surf Experience** (www.nexussurf.com; Rodovia Jornalista Manoel de Menezes 2031/29), which also leads 'après-surf' nightlife tours to introduce newcomers to Brazil's steamiest party scene.

SLEEPING

Bangalôs da Mole (☎ 3232 0723; www.bangalosdamole.com.br, in Portuguese; Rodovia Jornalista Manoel de Menezes 1007; d R$150-200, bungalows R$120-200; 🅿 🛜) Directly across from the beach, this place has spacious suites and bilevel bungalows, all with cool tile floors and high ceilings. Higher-priced units have kitchens and sea views.

Parque Flor Essência (☎ 3232 3903; www.parquessencia.com.br; Rodovia Jornalista Manoel de Menezes 631; d from R$220; 🅿 🖥 🛜) Nestled into a hill, 10 charming cottages each offer a fabulous panorama of the lagoon and mountains beyond. If you can pull yourself away, you are 150m from the waves of Praia Mole.

Praia da Joaquina

About 3km south of Praia Mole, the huge white dunes of 'Joaca' are visible for miles. These massive sandy mounds have inspired a new sport: sand surfing. Rent a sand board and haul it up to the top of the dune, from where it is a fast, dirty ride down.

Good old-fashioned surfing is still the number-one activity at Praia da Joaquina, which boasts long, fast, powerful waves that are up to 3m high. Stop in at the surf shop **Swell** (☎ 3232 0366; Estrada Geral da Joaquina 834; 🕙 9am-9pm) for more information and lots of gear.

There's a handful of places to stay along the road to Joaquina, including the simple **Cris Hotel** (☎ 3232 5104; www.crishotel.com; Estrada Geral da Joaquina 1; s/d/tr/q R$99/120/155/190; 🅿), which wins points for its prime location on the beach.

Lagoa da Conceição

For spectacular scenery, exhilarating water sports or all-night parties, Lagoa da Conceição is a popular alternative to the beaches. Forested hills form a fabulous backdrop for the pretty lagoon. The town of Lagoa, often packed with tourists, sits on a sandbar that divides the two halves of the lagoon.

Get off the beaten track by hiking along the lagoon's undeveloped west coast. From the center of town, it is 6km to the tiny village of **Costa da Lagoa**, which is otherwise accessible only by boat (see p344).

The aptly named **Internet** (☎ 3232 1882; per hr R$4.50) is at the turnoff to Praia da Joaquina.

For more information on Lagoa, see www.lagoavirtual.com.

ACTIVITIES

The lagoon is ideal for windsurfing, kayaking and boating:

Passeio de Escuna (☎ 3232 5083; per person R$5) Boats depart from the dock at the north end of Rua das Rendeiras.

Toscani Náutica (☎ 9912 8392; per hr R$8) One of many places along the southern shore to rent kayaks.

SLEEPING

Loads of pousadas are along the southern shore of the lake. Drive over the bridge and continue east on Rua das Rendeiras.

Floripa Hostel – Barra da Lagoa (☎ 3232 4491; www.floripahostel.com.br, in Portuguese; Rua Inelzyr Bauer Bertoli s/n; dm HI member/student/regular R$39/45/48, d HI member/regular R$110/130; 🖥 🛜) This new hostel just 150m from the beach is a welcome addition to the high-priced Lagoa options. The usual HI standards are in place, and you'll also find free parking and more spaciousness than its sister hostel in Floripa.

Tucano House (☎ 3207 8287; www.tucanohouse.com; Rua das Araras 229; dm R$40, d with/without bathroom R$110/90; 🖥 🛜 🅿) The Tucano is a wildly popular hostel – recently rated the second-best hostel in South American by the *Guardian* – and a great place for fellow travelers to meet. Rooms open up to a huge balcony hung with hammocks, and you'll find a swingin' bar filled nightly with revelers.

Pousada Ilha da Magia (☎ 3232 5038; www.pousadailhadamagia.com.br; Av Santiago 23; s/d R$145/164; 🅿 🛜) Right across from the lagoon, these cute, colorful cottages come in a variety of styles, from Alpine to A-frame.

EATING & DRINKING

Lagoa is the center for nightlife on the island.

John Bull Pub (☎ 3232 8535; Rua das Rendeiras 1046; meals R$20; 🕙 9am-4am Tue-Sun Dec-Mar, Thu-Sun Apr-Nov) Live music and lovely views over the lagoon make this English pub a popular spot for a drink.

Barracuda (☎ 3232 5301; Rua das Rendeiras; meals R$30-40; ☩ noon-midnight Tue-Sat, noon-6pm Sun) This place has a huge, airy dining room, often packed with patrons feasting on fresh seafood. It's known for its *bacalhau* (cod).

Confraria das Artes (☎ 3232 2298; Rua João da Costa 31; ☩ 8pm-5am Tue Sun) It's hard to get hipper than this – if you can get in. Internationally famous DJs spin beats in a lavishly remodeled colonial-style house.

SOUTH ISLAND

With white-sand beaches and mountains that drop into the sea, the South is the most pristine and picturesque part of the island. But south-island residents are engaged in the inevitable struggle between developers and preservers: the former see the potential for more tourists and big bucks; the latter fear that their piece of paradise will soon resemble the north. The balance is delicate and ever shifting.

For now, these towns retain their idyllic appeal. The beaches are less crowded (the hottest surf spots excepted) – and the atmosphere is more laid-back – than other island destinations.

At the southern tip, **Praia dos Naufragados** is accessible only by hiking 4km on a flat, shady trail from the village of Caieiras da Barra do Sul. Your reward is a picturesque lighthouse and a fantastic vista of the islands in the vicinity.

Ribeirão da Ilha

More than any other town, the tiny village of Ribeirão da Ilha has preserved its Azorean heritage, evident in its cobblestone streets and colorful tile-roof houses. The main square centers on the lovely **Igreja NS da Lapa do Ribeirão**, which dates to 1806. Locals gather in the waterside park to play chess and watch the sun set behind the mainland mountain range.

Given the village's location overlooking the tidal flats, it is no surprise that the local specialty is oysters – as plump, juicy and fresh as you'll find anywhere. Sit on the dock at **Ostradamus** (☎ 3337 5711; Rod Baldicero Filomeno 7640; meals R$30-50) and slurp a dozen or two.

Campeche

Campeche is a bohemian outpost, home to artists, massage therapists and other free thinkers, seeking to escape the crowds of the city and the tourist hot spots.

The 5km **Praia do Campeche** is protected, so the beach is completely undeveloped. Desolate dunes and pounding surf – stretching for miles in either direction – guarantee solitude for swimmers and sunbathers. At the southern end of the beach, catch a boat (R$15 round-trip) to **Ilha do Campeche**, an ecological reserve with opportunities for hiking and snorkeling.

Pau de Canela Pousada (☎ 3338 3584; www.pousadapaudecanela.com.br, in Portuguese; Rua Pau de Canela 606, Rio Tavares; d R$150-180; ☒ ☒) looks out of place on this run-down, residential road, 1km from the beach. The eight guestrooms are simple but luxurious, fitted with Jacuzzi tubs, and decorated with shiny wooden floors and sophisticated artwork. It's one of the few places around with a fireplace.

The owner of **Pousada Natur Campeche** (☎ 3237 4011; www.naturcampeche.com.br; Servidão Família Nunes 59; s/d R$230/287, ste from R$290; ☒ ☐ ☒) has traveled the world, bringing back treasures to decorate this pousada. The exotic rooms are arranged around a green garden, just 100m from Praia do Campeche. One common area features a rare item on the island – a fireplace.

Armação

This little town dates to the 18th century, when it served as a whaling center. The impressive **Igreja Santa Ana** still stands from these days. While whaling is no longer practiced, the fishing industry still thrives here.

Armação provides access to three beaches, all excellent surfing spots. North of town, **Morro das Pedras** is popular for its consistent right, but you'll probably have to fight for a chance to ride it. Further south, **Praia da Armação** is a surfer's delight, especially at the north end of the beach. For a little adventure, follow a winding trail along the rocky coastline to the gorgeous **Matadeiro**, a near-deserted beach surrounded by lush greenery.

Inland from Armação, the **Lagoa do Peri** is a pretty lake surrounded by parkland. Lesser known and less visited than Conceição, it offers wonderful opportunities for swimming and hiking. The jumping-off point for the lake is about 1km south of Praia de Armação on the main road approaching the town – you can't miss the large park entrance.

Follow the rough dirt road 300m from the beach, through the iron gate, and enter

Pousada Alemdomar (☎ 3237 5600; www.alemdomar .com.br; Rua Lagoa do Peri 403; s/d R$140/200), a little plot of new-age paradise. Six simple guestrooms evoke tranquility and harmony with nature. Behind the main house, guests can follow a woodsy trail all the way to Lagoa do Peri.

'An overdose of health' is how **Nutri Lanches** (☎ 3237 5182; Rua Thomaz dos Santos 4615; meals R$8-15; ☽ 10am-9pm) lauds its all-organic sandwiches, salads and pastries. The lunchtime buffet is an incredible array of healthy, homemade goodness.

Pântano do Sul

Fishermen of Azorean descent still inhabit the village of Pântano do Sul, so its beach is dotted with fishing boats and seafood shacks. Ringed by mountains, the protected cove contains calm, cool waters that are ideal for sunning and swimming.

From here, you can catch a lift from a local fisherman or hike about 1½ hours to the deserted beach of **Lagoinha do Leste**. The hike is hot, so leave early and bring plenty of water. Lagoinha do Leste offers some of the island's most consistent and powerful waves, so don't be surprised when surfers run past you on the trail.

Set 30m from the beach and surrounded by forest, **Pousada do Pescador** (☎ 3237 7122; www .pousadadopescador.com.br, in Portuguese; Rua Manoel Vidal 257; s/d/tr R$100/120/140; ☒) has simple, sweet one- and two-room chalets. The rustic seafood shack **Arante** (☎ 3237 7022; meals R$15-30) has become an island institution, its walls covered with poetry and artwork that patrons have doodled on over the years.

Costa de Dentro & Around

This is the end of the road, and it feels like it. These tiny towns are home to a handful of places to stay and eat, but they are left largely to their fishing and farming residents. Costa de Dentro has access to the lovely, calm waters of the **Praia dos Açores** – making this a good escape from the surfing scene – or continue all the way to **Praia Solidão** or **Saquinho**.

Just before the paved road turns into a packed dirt path, 500m from the beach, you'll find **Albergue do Pirata** (☎ 3389 2727; www .albergueDopirata.com.br; Rua Rosália Ferreira 4973, Costa de Dentro; dm/d per person R$35/50; ☒ ☐), a simple hostel with shared bathrooms. Perks include English-speaking owners, fans, and a lively outdoor restaurant and bar.

Vila dos Escargôs (☎ 3389 2301; www.viladosescargos .com.br, in Portuguese; Rua Maurício Rosar 10, Praia dos Açores; s/d/tr R$175/195/218; ☒ ☐ ☒), a stucco hotel, is far enough from the beach so as not to impede the natural landscape of the dunes, but close enough to allow ocean views from its upper floors. Spacious, comfortable rooms are all adorned with tile mosaics depicting the creatures of the sea.

About 1.5km past Costa de Dentro, **Pousada Sítio dos Tucanos** (☎ 3237 5084; www.pousadasitiodos tucanos.com; s/d R$140/240; ☐) sits in the midst of jungly wilderness on the southern edge of the Parque da Lagoa do Peri. Rustic rooms have balconies overlooking a gurgling mountain stream.

THE MAINLAND

North and south of Florianópolis, fine sand and big surf attract beachcombers, sunbathers and surfers. Inland, the Serra Geral runs parallel to the coast, protecting some of southern Brazil's most remote destinations. This is where Santa Catarina's German and Italian heritage endures most tenaciously.

JOINVILLE

☎ 0xx47 / pop 500,000

While Joinville does not have the historic center (or the beer festival) of Blumenau, it does have decidedly German roots. They are evident in the city's nouveau-Alpine architecture and in the well-manicured parks. The economy thrives on metallurgy, plastics and information technology, but this industrial activity is tucked neatly away from the eyes of visitors. The result is a big city with the good manners of a small town. Joinville's citizens are proud of their prosperous, orderly home and welcome visitors with warm hospitality.

Information

Banco do Brasil (cnr Rua Luiz Neimeyer & Rua do Principe) Money exchange and Visa ATMs.
Information posts Long-distance bus station (☽ 8am-noon & 2-6pm); Shopping Mueller (cnr Rua Pedro Lobo & Rua Senador Felipe Schmidt; ☽ 10am-6pm Mon-Fri, 8am-6pm Sat & Sun)

Sights

In an elegant palace dating from 1870, the **Museu Nacional da Imigração e Colonização** (National Museum of Immigration & Colonization; ☎ 3433 3736; www

.museunacional.com.br; Rua Rio Branco 229; admission R$5; 9am-5pm Tue-Fri, 11am-5pm Sat & Sun) documents the history of immigration to Santa Catarina. The impressive stand of palms along **Alameda das Palmeiras** will lead you there.

Art-lovers might prefer the **Museu de Arte de Joinville** (☎ 3433 4677; Rua 15 de Novembro 1400; admission free; 9am-5pm Wed-Fri, 11am-5pm Sat & Sun), with rotating exhibits by local and national artists.

To get a vista of Joinville and the Baía da Babitonga, head to the Morro do Boa Vista, about 10km east of the center. The 250m-high **Mirante** (Rua Saguaçu) is a tall tower with a circular staircase and a 360-degree panorama.

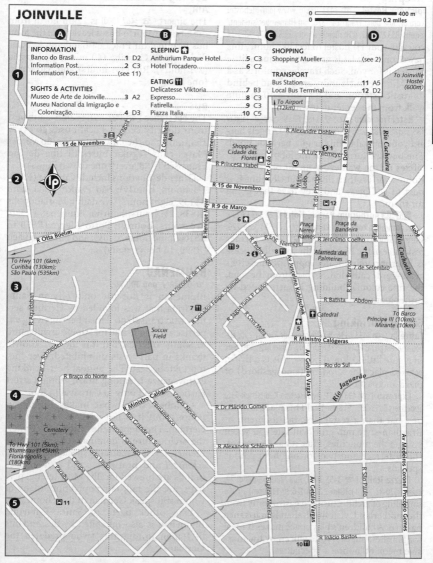

JOINVILLE

0 — 400 m
0 — 0.2 miles

SANTA CATARINA

INFORMATION	
Banco do Brasil	1 D2
Information Post	2 C3
Information Post	(see 11)

SIGHTS & ACTIVITIES	
Museu de Arte de Joinville	3 A2
Museu Nacional da Imigração e Colonização	4 D3

SLEEPING 🏠	
Anthurium Parque Hotel	5 C3
Hotel Trocadero	6 C2

EATING 🍴	
Delicatesse Viktoria	7 B3
Expresso	8 C3
Fatirella	9 C3
Piazza Italia	10 C5

SHOPPING	
Shopping Mueller	(see 2)

TRANSPORT	
Bus Station	11 A5
Local Bus Terminal	12 D2

To Joinville Hostel (600m)

R Alexandre Dohler

R 15 de Novembro

Shopping Cidade das Flores

R Luiz Niemeyer

R Princesa Isabel

R 15 de Novembro

R 9 de Março

To Airport (12km)

To Hwy 101 (6km); Curitiba (130km); São Paulo (535km)

Praça Nereu Ramos

Praça da Bandeira

R Jerônimo Coelho

R Eng Niemeyer

Alameda das Palmeiras

7 de Setembro

R Batista

Abdom

To Barco Príncipe III (10km); Mirante (10km)

R Cruz Matha

Catedral

Soccer Field

R Ministro Calógeras

Rio do Sul

Rio Jaguarão

R Braço do Norte

R Ministro Calógeras

R Dr Plácido Gomes

Cemetery

To Hwy 101 (5km); Blumenau (145km); Florianópolis (180km)

R Alexandre Schlemm

Eugênio Moreira

R São Paulo

R Inácio Bastos

SANTA CATARINA

Boat Trips

Cruise ship **Barco Príncipe III** (☎ 3455 4444; adult/child R$70/35; ☻ tours 10am; ☺) offers tours around the Baía da Babitonga, ending at São Francisco do Sul (see p352). It departs from the Espinheiros neighborhood, 10km from the center.

Sleeping

Joinville Hostel (☎ 3433 9886; www.joinvillehostel .com.br; Rua Dona Francisca 1376; dm HI member/student/ regular R$32/38/42, d HI member/regular R$70/77; ☐) If you like your HI hostel to feel like home, this newer one with large green spaces and a little garden is for you. Such traveler comforts as a DVD library and laundry are on hand behind its rustic exterior, and it's only a 10-minute walk from the center of town.

Hotel Trocadero (☎ 3422 1469; Rua Visconde de Taunay 185; s/d R$65/80, with air-con R$80/95; ☒) Angels herald your arrival in this bright, baroque hotel. The pewlike furniture in the lobby and crucifixes on the wall evoke an air of devotion. Rooms are less than divine, but cleanliness is next to godliness, and they have that going for them.

ourpick Anthurium Parque Hotel (☎ 3433 6299; www.anthurium.com.br, in Portuguese; Rua São José 226; s/d/tr R$110/145/130; ☒ ☐ ☎ ☺) This former residence of the Bishop of the Joinville diocese is appropriately located opposite the city's avant-garde cathedral. Set back from the road, the fine colonial building is surrounded by lush, blooming gardens.

Eating & Drinking

Fatirella (☎ 3433 8136; Rua Visconde de Taunay 299; all-you-can-eat pizzas R$12; ☻ lunch daily, dinner Mon-Sat) Set in a cute little colonial house, this is a lively, relaxed place for a *rodízio* (smorgasbord) of pizza and pasta.

Expresso (☎ 433 9451; Av Juscelino Kubitschek 536; appetizers R$15-25; ☻ 5pm-1am) This place is more of a bar than a restaurant, but its menu of Brazilian-style pub grub will sate you when you get the munchies. Plus, it has a pleasant, shady terrace and two-for-one happy-hour specials.

Piazza Italia (☎ 3455 3991; Rua Anita Garibaldi 79; meals R$20-35; ☻ 11:30am-2:30pm & 6:30-11:30pm) For a sampling of architecture and gastronomy from the motherland, visit this Italian Renaissance palazzo. A children's play space makes it ideal for families, but everyone will enjoy the massive menu of 'nonna's' specialties.

ourpick Delicatesse Viktoria (☎ 422 0570; Rua Senador Felipe Schmidt 400; afternoon buffets per person R$22; ☻ 9am-8pm Mon-Sat) The lovely, light-filled porch has lace tablecloths and wicker furniture. Come in the morning for coffee and freshly baked sweets, or wait for the afternoon *café colonial*, replete with sweets and savories.

Getting There & Around

AIR

The **airport** (☎ 3467 1000) is 12km north from the city; Aeroporto buses leave from the local bus terminal on Praça da Bandeira. Regular flights go to Curitiba (40 minutes), Brasília (2½ hours), Rio (1½ hours) and São Paulo (one hour).

BUS

The **bus station** (☎ 3433 2991) is 2km southwest from the city center. Local buses go every 15 minutes to the city center. Viacão Verdes Mares runs regular buses to Ilha de São Francisco (R$8, every one to two hours).

Other destinations include Curitiba (R$23, 2½ hours, hourly); São Paulo (R$80, *leito* R$139, eight hours, five daily); Florianópolis (R$38, 2½ hours, hourly); Blumenau (R$20, two hours, hourly); Porto Alegre (R$79 to R$160, nine hours, daily); and Foz do Iguaçu (R$90, 16 hours, daily).

BLUMENAU

☎ 0xx47 / pop 300,000

Blumenau is not the only city in Santa Catarina that was founded by German settlers who transplanted their beer-brewing expertise and their taste for Alpine architecture to South America. But it is the best known, thanks in part to its uninhibited, over-the-top Oktoberfest. The annual beer-drinking extravaganza is among Brazil's largest street parties, second only to Carnaval in Rio.

Oktoberfest is what makes Blumenau famous, but it is not what makes the city German. Throughout the historic city center, the architecture is dominated by Germanic themes. Local restaurants specialize in *jägerschnitzel* and bratwurst, and several beer brands are brewed locally. Most telling, perhaps, are the tall, fair population, many of whom still speak German in their homes.

Like other parts of Santa Catarina, Blumenau is also inhabited by descendants of Italian immigrants (who predated the Germans).

Information

Banco do Brasil (cnr Rua XV de Novembro & Rua Amadeu da Luz) Money exchange and ATMs.

Centro de Atendimento ao Turista (CAT; ☎ 3322 6933; www.blumenau.com.br; Rua XV de Novembro; ☯ 8am-9pm Mon-Fri) Information about the Vale Europeu. German-speaking staff.

Shopping Neumarkt (☎ 3326 5566; Rua 7 de Setembro; per hr R$4.50) Internet access, near Rua Padre Jacobs.

Sights

Learn about Blumenau's beginnings at the **Museu de Família Colonial** (☎ 3322 1676; Alameda Duque de Caxias 78; admission R$3; ☯ 9am-5pm Tue-Fri, 10am-4pm Sat & Sun), a group of houses that were occupied by the city's founder, Herman Bruno Otto Blumenau, in the 1850s. His daughter's cat cemetery – where lies interred Pepito, Mirko, Bum, Putzi, Schnurr and other beloved feline companions – is a nice spot of contemplation in the rambling backyard garden. Around the corner, the **Mausoléu Dr Blumenau** (☎ 3226 6990; Rua XV de Novembro 161; admission free; ☯ 9am-5pm Tue-Fri, 9am-noon & 2-4:30pm Sat, 9am-noon Sun) is the final resting place of Dr Blumenau

himself. Lutheran churches loom over town; the most beautiful is **Igreja do Espírito Santo**, a gem from 1858 that still stands east of the center.

If you are more interested in gastronomy than history, visit the **Museu da Cerveja** (Praça Hercilio Luz) and its inviting Biergarten.

Rua XV Novembro is home to the city's best examples of Germanic architecture, including the **Castelinho Tavan** department store, a replica of the city hall of Michelstadt, Germany, and is supposedly the second-most photographed attraction in Brazil, after Foz de Iguaçu. Nearby, the modern **Igreja Matriz do São Paolo** is named for the only Brazilian saint (who, incidentally, was born in Italy).

Festivals & Events

Blumenau's major festivals are held at Vila Germânica, a huge convention hall modeled after an Alpine villa.

Oktoberfest (☎ 3326 6901; www.oktoberfestblume nau.com.br, in Portuguese; admission per day R$5-10) A festive parade kicks off 17 days of folk music, dancing and beer drinking. This is the 'biggest German party in the Americas.'

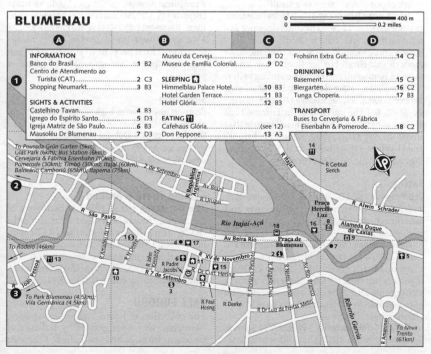

BLUMENAU

0 — 400 m
0 — 0.2 miles

INFORMATION		Museu da Cerveja........................8 D2	Frohsinn Extra Gut......................14 C2
Banco do Brasil..............................1 B2		Museu de Família Colonial...........9 D2	
Centro de Atendimento ao			**DRINKING**
Turista (CAT)..............................2 C3		**SLEEPING**	Basement.....................................15 C3
Shopping Neumarkt.......................3 B3		Himmelblau Palace Hotel............10 B3	Biergarten...................................16 C2
		Hotel Garden Terrace..................11 B3	Tunga Choperia...........................17 B3
SIGHTS & ACTIVITIES		Hotel Glória................................12 B3	
Castelinho Tavan...........................4 B3			**TRANSPORT**
Igrego do Espírito Santo...............5 D3		**EATING**	Buses to Cerverjaria & Fábrica
Igreja Matriz de São Paulo.............6 B3		Cafehaus Glória.......................(see 12)	Eisenbahn & Pomerode............18 C2
Mausoléu Dr Blumenau..................7 D3		Don Peppone..............................13 A3	

Sommerfest The celebration of beer and German traditions continues in January and February. See the Oktoberfest website for details.

Fest Itália (☎ 3323 4043; www.festitalia.com.br, in Portuguese) Not to be left out, the Italians celebrate a week of pasta, wine and music in mid-July.

Sleeping

Book accommodations well in advance if you plan to be in Blumenau during Oktoberfest.

Pousada Grün Garten (☎ 3339 6529; www.grun garten.com.br; Rua São Paulo 2457; dm R$34, s/d without bathroom R$35/55, d/tw/tr R$95/105/120) This clean, attractive HI hostel is 6km from the center in the suburb of Itoupava Seca. Laundry facilities and a restaurant are on-site. Take bus 10 toward Fonte Aterro/Via Rua São Paulo. Discounted rates for HI members.

our pick Hotel Glória (☎ 3326 1988; www.hotelgloria .com.br; Rua 7 de Setembro 954; s without bathroom R$50, s/d/tr from R$70/100/130; 🅿 💻 🛜) With its wood-paneled entrance and a traditional German *kaffeehaus* (coffeehouse) attached, this hotel offers comfortable rooms and an Old-World flair. The Glória's cheapest rooms with shared bathrooms are not advertised, so you'll have to ask about them – they're a steal!

Hotel Garden Terrace (☎ 3326 3544; Rua Padre Jacobs 45; s/d R$95/125/160; 🅿 🛜) The hotel does not exactly earn the four stars it claims, but it does boast a prime location just across from the city's modern cathedral. Higher floors have lovely views of Blumenau and the surrounding valley.

Himmelblau Palace Hotel (☎ 3036 5800; www .himmelblau.com.br; Rua 7 de Setembro 1415; s/d R$135/155; 🅿 💻 🛜 🏊) The interiors of the Himmelblau are more attractive than the brick facade that fronts the city's main drag. Rooms are brightened by light yellow walls, fresh white moldings and simple, modern furniture.

Eating

Don Peppone (☎ 3322 8682; Rua 7 de Setembro 2013; meals R$15-25) When you tire of sausages and sauerkraut, stop by this pizzeria to sample Blumenau's 'other' ethnic cuisine.

Park Blumenau (☎ 3326 5000; Rua Alberto Stein 215; meals R$20-35) This typical *biergarten* is one of many on the fringes of Vila Germânica. Even if you are not here for Oktoberfest, it's worth visiting this Disneylike complex to celebrate your German heritage, or at least your love of German beer. *Ein Prosit!*

our pick Cafehaus Glória (☎ 3322 6944; Rua 7 de Setembro 954; buffets R$22) This old-world coffeehouse is famous for its *café colonial*, an afternoon buffet (3pm to 8pm) that features cakes, pastries and sandwiches. Lunchtime (11am to 2pm Monday to Saturday) means a more traditional Brazilian buffet, while evening brings out the soup buffet (6pm to 10pm Monday to Friday).

Frohsinn Extra Gut (☎ 3326 6050; Rua Gertrud Sierich; meals R$30-45) Perched atop Morro do Aipim, this fancy restaurant offers lovely views of Blumenau. Excellent selection of European fare.

Drinking

our pick Cervejaria & Fábrica Eisenbahn (☎ 3330 7371; www.eisenbahn.com.br; Rua Bahia 5181; 🕑 4pm-midnight Tue-Thu, 4pm-2am Fri, 10am-2pm Sat) Take a tour of the brewery or just sample the goods in the taproom. Bratwurst and sandwiches (from R$18) are great paired with house beers. Tours (R$5) are offered on the hour from 2pm to 7:30pm. To get there, grab the bus marked 'Passo Mansu' on Av Beira Rio and ask to get off at Eisenbahn.

For cheap pizza, *chope* (draft beer) and live music, visit the draft houses near the Rua República Argentina bridge, such as **Tunga Choperia** (☎ 3322 2549; Rua XV de Novembro 1020; 10am-10pm). **Basement** (☎ 3340 0534; Rua Paul Hering 35; Tue & Wed 6pm-midnight, Thu-Sat 6pm-1am) offers a large selection of local beers in an authentic English pub atmosphere (accompanied by gourmet pub fare).

Shopping

Blumenau produces high-quality crystal and glassware.

Glas Park (☎ 3327 1261; Rua Rudolf Roedel 147; 🕑 9am-5pm Mon-Fri, 9am-1pm Sat) An on-site museum shows the history of the industry and the art, and demonstrations are given.

Getting There & Around

The **bus station** (☎ 3323 2155) is 6km west of the center. Hourly buses go to Florianópolis (R$26, three hours), Joinville (R$20, two hours) and Curitiba (R$26, four hours).

To get into the center of town, take bus 10 marked Fonte (R$2.30) from the far side of Av 2 de Setembro, or take a taxi for R$15.

VALE EUROPU

The collection of towns and villages around Blumenau that were settled by Italian and German immigrants is called the Vale

Europeu. Their descendants still preserve their European culture today, and during the 17 days of Oktoberfest, many towns host their own unique ethnic festivals. All year long, the area offers bucolic vistas dotted by traditional German *enxiamel* houses, characterized by high-pitched roofs and open brick facades.

The helpful website www.valeeuropeu .com.br, and the comprehensive booklet *Vale Europeu*, which can be picked up at the tourist office in Blumenau, both cover excellent biking and hiking opportunities in the valley.

Pomerode

For a profound insight into the region's Germanic roots, head about 30km north of Blumenau to **Pomerode**, where an estimated 70% of the population still speaks German (see the boxed text, p351). The Festa Pomerana celebrates its northern German heritage every January, and the **Museo Pomerano** (☎ 3387 0408; Rua Harmann Weege 111; admission R$2; ⏲ 10-11:30am & 1-5pm Mon-Fri, 10am-4pm Sat & Sun) explores the town's history in loving detail. The **Cervejaria Schornstein** (☎ 3387 6655; www.schornstein.com.br; Rua Hermann Weege 60; ⏲ 6-11pm Wed-Fri, noon-6pm Sat & Sun), which ferments pilsners, pale ale, Weiss and bock, is a must if you're on the trail of artisanal beer.

A pleasant place to lay your head in Pomerode is **Pousada Bergblick** (☎ 3387 0952; Rua Georg Zeplin 120; s/d R$112/178, s/d with balcony & Jacuzzi R$158/238; ✖), which has simply gigantic rooms with mountain views and an Alpine feel to them. Pomerode is home to the region's most renowned German restaurant, **Wunderwald** (☎ 3395 1700; Rua Ricardo Bahr 200), set in a 19th-century house. To reach Pomerode, take a local buses from Av Beira Rio in Blumenau.

Timbó

Easily one of the most attractive villages in the region, Timbó is brimming with verdant gardens and is considered by the UN to be one of the best places to live in Brazil. The heritage here is both German and Italian and can be explored at the **Museu do Imigrante** (☎ 3382 9458; Av Getúlio Vargas 211; admission R$2; ⏲ 8:20-11:30am & 1:30-5:30pm Tue-Sun). The microbrewery **Borck Choperia** (☎ 3382 0587; www.borck.com.br, in Portuguese; Rua Pomeranos 1963; ⏲ 2-6pm Tue-Fri), producing pilsner and malt beer, has tours and a tasting room.

The sprawling **Hotel Timbó Park** (☎ 3281 0700; www.timbopark.com.br; Rua Blumenau 141; s/d R$92/125) has a resort feel, although the individual balconies in each room offer more intimacy.

SPRECHEN SIE DEUTSCH?

The first German immigrants arrived in the 1820s at the behest of Dom Pedro I. The southern part of the newly independent Brazil was still disputed by Argentina and Uruguay, and the emperor wanted to populate the region with loyal followers. Successive waves of immigrants arrived in the 1850s and the 1890s, then again around the two world wars. Contrary to popular imagination, most Germans who arrived in the 1940s were political and economic refugees, rather than Nazi leaders on the run.

For a century, German was the dominant language in many parts of southern Brazil. German speakers came from different regions of Germany and spoke different dialects, so they faced their own linguistic Babel. They often resorted to a kind of Creole, which incorporated Portuguese and local Indian languages. Italians facing a similar problem relied on 'Taliã,' an amalgamation of dialects based mainly on those of the Veneto region.

The 20th century took a toll on the German language in Brazil. The world wars led to the suppression of German in public institutions like schools and government. Industrialization and increasing economic integration brought the region into closer contact with Portuguese speakers. Finally, the arrival of radio and TV, dominated by national networks, reinforced the use of Portuguese, especially among the young.

In the town of Pomerode, a confluence of forces has ensured the preservation of the German language. Only in the last generation have decent roads linked Pomerode to Blumenau, so the town remained physically isolated from its neighbors. In addition, nearly all of its original settlers spoke the same dialect (Pomeranian), so there was no need to resort to Portuguese as a lingua franca. And the settlers were Lutheran, so German remained their language of worship. These days, a growing movement is preserving Brazil's bilingual communities.

SANTA CATARINA

our pick Choperia & Restaurante Thapyoka
(☎ 3382 0198; www.thapyoka.com.br; in Portuguese; mains R$30-50; �ّ 11am-2pm, 5pm-late), housed in a renovated factory, is a bar and eatery with an extensive menu of meats and pastas and a stellar view of the river and bridge.

Catarinense has one early-morning bus daily from Blumenau to Timbó (R$6, 45 minutes).

Nova Trento

The region's Italian heritage is alive and well in small towns like **Nova Trento** (61km south of Blumenau), which celebrates local gastronomy in the Grape Festival in January and boasts the important pilgrimage site **Santuário Santa Paulina**, an imposing modern church with a dramatic slalom-like sloping ceiling. Some 40,000 pilgrims and tourists visit this church *per month*. The **Museu da Cultura Italiana** (☎ 3267 0028; Rua Geral Morro da Crz s/n; �ّ 8:30am-5pm) offers a glimpse of Italian ways imported from the old country.

our pick Pousada Portal do Vígolo (☎ 3267 1871; Rua Luiz Busnardo 504; s/d R$178/228), just 3.5km from the Santuário Santa Paulina, is in a quiet spot and has great service. The 12 rooms have medicinal plant themes, solar-heated water and a cozy carpeted feel like home. **Pizzeria di Iggo e Ivete** (☎ 3267 1024; Ros SC 411; pizzas R$14-35; ☁ 2-11pm) serves local wine and authentic pizza from its wood-fired oven.

Santa Terezinha has an early-morning bus from Blumenau to Nova Trento (R$6, 1½ hours).

NORTH OF FLORIANÓPOLIS

Varied and inviting, the beaches along the coast north of Florianópolis are both its blessing and its curse. The blessing is the crystalline waters and fine sand, not to mention the endless days of sun. The curse is the highrise hotels and condominiums that are more prominent than the forested hillsides and rocky outposts.

Balneário Camboriú, known as the Copacabana of the South, is renowned for its swinging nightclubs and crowded oceanfront boulevard. The twin towns of Penha and Armação feel more like fishing villages than holiday resorts, even though they boast some breathtaking beachfront. And the peninsula around Porto Belo is home to boisterous beach towns as well as great diving, snorkeling and surf spots.

Ilha do São Francisco
☎ 0xx47 / pop 40,000

The lovely city of **São Francisco do Sul**, 45km east of Joinville, is Brazil's third oldest, founded in 1504 by the French (only Bahia and São Vicente are older). A century later, the Portuguese arrived, in hopes of exploiting the city's strategic position at the mouth of Baía da Babitonga.

The historical center is on the Patrimônio Histórico (National Heritage list), for its decadent, colonial feel. The bus from Joinville lets you off about 2km from the historic center, which lies on the island's west coast. Walk down Rua Fernandes Dias to the waterfront **Rua Babitonga**, which is lined with colonial houses, seafood restaurants and the beautifully restored **Mercado Público**.

The city acts as a gateway to the rest of the Ilha do São Francisco, a popular destination for sun-worshippers and surfers. The closest beaches are 12km to 15km from São Francisco do Sul, but they are all served by local bus.

At the southern end of the island, both **Prainha** and **Praia Grande** are ocean beaches exposed to a lot of swell. Closer to the city, **Praia da Ubatuba** and **Praia de Enseada** are safe for swimming, but they're developed and get very crowded on weekends. Some of the more secluded beaches are **Praia Itaguaçu** and **Praia do Forte** on the island's northern tip.

SLEEPING & EATING

In the city center, the sweetest spots overlook Baía Babitonga, including the lovely colonial **Kontiki Hotel** (☎ 3444 2232; www.hotelkontiki.com.br; in Portuguese; Rua Babitonga 211; s R$67-97, d R$118-154; ☒ ☲), and the larger and more luxurious **Zibamba Hotel** (☎ 3444 2020; Rua Ferndes Dias 27; s/d R$140/185, s/d/tr with sea view R$173/235/298; ☒ ☲).

Portela (☎ 3444 1579; Rua Babitonga 84; meals R$20-35) is a bustling seafood restaurant situated on a pier that juts out into the bay.

Penha & Armação
☎ 0xx47 / pop 22,000

These two villages are side by side along the north shore of a peninsula that juts out into the ocean, 110km north of Florianópolis. The crescent-shaped beach wraps around a bay dotted with colorful fishing boats. This beach – called **Praia do Quilombo**, **Praia da Armação** or **Praia da Fortaleza**, depending exactly where you are standing – is calm, clean and quiet. The idyllic village atmosphere changes slightly on summer weekends, however, when the main beachfront turns into one big *festa* (party).

To escape the crowds, head to **Praia Grande** (5km) at the peninsula's eastern tip, or **Praia Vermelha** (9km), south of Armação village. The latter requires a taxing drive over a rocky, red-earth *morro* (hill), which gives way to fine pink sand and iridescent blue waters.

For better or for worse, the landscape of this peninsula is changing rapidly, especially with the expansion of **Beto Carrero World** (☎ 3261 2354; www.betocarrero.com.br; Rua Inácio Francisco de Souza 1597; adult/child/senior R$88/62/44; ☺ 10am-6pm daily Nov-Feb & Jul, Thu-Sun Mar-Jun & Aug-Oct), a massive theme park.

The **tourist information office** (☎ 3345 3428; www.penha.sc.gov.br, in Portuguese), located at the turnoff from Hwy SC-414, has information about local hotels and restaurants.

Escuna Vónica (☎ 9981 2709; tickets R$22; ☺ tours 9am, 11am, 3pm & 5pm) takes a tour of the bay, departing from the village of Sul Piçarras.

SLEEPING & EATING

A few hotels and restaurants are clustered around the town center on the beach. Two options are **Hotel Itapocoroí** (☎ 3345 5015; Rua Maria da Costa 62; d with/without sea view R$112/95; ☒) and **Costamar Hotel** (☎ 3345 6861; www.costamarhotel.com, in Portuguese; Av Elizabeth Kondor Reis 556; d R$95), both well located near the dock.

Sample the local cuisine, influenced by the flavors of the Azores, at the excellent **Peixe na Telha** (☎ 3398 0079; Rua Maria Emília da Costa 92; meals R$30), which enjoys lovely waterside seating.

GETTING THERE & AWAY

Three buses a day come to Penha from Blumenau (R$29; three hours) and one from Joinville (R$43, four hours). Otherwise, a local Circular or Navagantes bus to Penha and Armação leaves from the bus terminal at Piçarras (6km north).

Balneário Camboriú
☎ 0xx47 / pop102,000

Balneário Camboriú is considered a poor man's Rio, and it has a giant Christ statue, beautiful beaches, and a hopping nightlife – for a fraction of Copacabana prices – to prove it. The summer population swells to nearly a million, as Argentines, Paraguayans and Brazilians flood in to enjoy one of Brazil's hottest party scenes. Camboriú is known for being as gay-friendly as Rio, and also for its

teleférico (cable car) connecting a large central *morro* with not one, but two beaches – apparently the only one of its kind in the world. Families like Camboriú for its kid-friendly attractions and proximity to Beto Carrero World (p353).

Tourist information is offered freely at the **bus station** (☎ 3367 2901).

SIGHTS & ACTIVITIES

The 33m **Cristo Luz statue** (☎ 3367 4042; Rua Indonésia 800) holds a sombrero from which a spotlight illuminates the city at night, sometimes in streaming colors. During summer live music is often staged from 7pm.

Don't miss the **cable car**, connecting Praia de Laranjaeiras and Praia Central with Morro de Aguada, where you can also enjoy 500m of walking trails inside a 6-hectare **nature preserve**.

Kids will dig an alternative descent, taking the Youhooo! **roller coaster** (☎ 3404 7600; www .youhooo.com.br, in Portuguese; Av Atlântica 6006; R$15), which plunges 700m at 60km per hour. A large **'pirate ship'** (☎ 3367 3258; Av Normando Tedesco, Barra Sul 6020; adult/child R$22/free; ☺ hourly 9am-6pm Dec-Apr) plies surrounding waters, including the pretty Ilha das Cabras.

Praia Laranjeiras, the busiest and closest beach to town, and six beaches extending south along the Costa Brava have crystal-line waters and views of forested hills in the background. Four kilometers north, on the road to Itajaí, **Praia dos Amores** has good surf conditions, as does **Praia Atalaia** in Itajaí, 10km north of Camboriú.

SLEEPING & EATING

Discounts range up to 50% outside of the packed summer months.

Camboriú Hostel – Rezende (☎ 8833 0304; Rua 3100, 780; dm HI member/nonmember R$31/39, d R$68/78; ☐ ☎) In the middle of the beach and nightlife action, this hostel fills up fast in high season. It's a rare youth hostel with balconies in the dorms and private rooms, so enjoy the view!

Hotel Ibis Navegantes (☎ 3249 6800; Av Vereador Abrahão 587; r from R$98) This midrange Accor hotel in central Itajaí has clean, big rooms.

Hotel D'Sintra (☎ 2104 4080; Av Atlântica 1040, s/d R$189/269; ☒ ☎ ☒) Located right in front of the action of Praia Central, D'Sintra has a gorgeous rooftop pool and creature comforts befitting its price.

SANTA CATARINA

O Pharol (☎ 3367 3800; Av Atlântica; buffets R$17; ⏲ 11am-11pm) This local favorite has an over-flowing seafood buffet, and, according to some, the city's best *feijoada* (a bean-and-meat stew served with rice).

ourpick Restaurante Bom Sol (☎ 3667 4208; Rua 1021, 72; mains R$20-30; ⏲ 3pm-10pm) Specializes in Bahian-style seafood stews, with which many residents seem to be having a love affair.

DRINKING & ENTERTAINMENT

Don't miss the evening concerts at the Cristo Luz (p353).

Cult Club (33679435; Av Normando Tedesco, Barra Sul) The place of the moment for dancing and being seen into the wee hours.

Chaplin Bar (3366 1227; Av Atlântica 2200; ⏲ 4pm-late) and **Cachaçaria Uai** (☎ 3367 478; Av Atlântica 2440; ⏲ 11am-1am Tue-Sun) are great bets on the main drag for beer and *cachaça*, respectively.

GETTING THERE & AWAY

Twelve buses a day go to Bombinhas, stopping in Porto Belo. Hourly buses go to Florianópolis, Joinville and Blumenau.

Porto Belo & Around

☎ 0xx47 / pop 14,000

A small peninsula fans out from Porto Belo about 60km north of Florianópolis. Here, clear, emerald-green waters offer some of the best diving in southern Brazil.

Porto Belo is a fishing village, so the town beach is dominated by a big dock and boats moored in the bay. The principal swimming beaches are **Praia Bombinhas** (9km from Porto Belo) and the adjacent **Praia Bombas** (3km). These sandy stretches are also lined with small-scale hotels and seafood restaurants. The crowd includes bikini-clad bathers and sand-covered kids – all lounging under colorful umbrellas and cooling off amid the welcoming waves.

Experienced surfers should check out **Praia do Mariscal**, which faces the open sea; while beach bums in search of seclusion should head to **Praia Canto Grande**. The sparkling blue waters of **Caixa d'Aço** are protected by the rocky outpost that makes a tail off the tip of the peninsula. There's no beach, but you can hire a boat taxi to go to the **floating restaurants**, which invite swimming, snorkeling and sunbathing off their docks.

At the western end of Porto Belo, the **tourist office** (☎ 3369 5638; www.portobelo.com.br, in Portuguese) has information about the whole peninsula.

SIGHTS

Located 900m off the coast, **Ilha de Porto Belo** (☎ 3369 4146; www.ilhadeportobelo.com.br; admission R$5; ⏲ 9am-5:30pm daily Dec-Feb, Sat & Sun only Mar & Sep-Nov) is a nature reserve and *ecomuseu* (ecomuseum). A well-marked hiking trail leads to scenic overlooks and a sandy beach. Snorkeling spots dot the coastline. Get a lift from a boat taxi (R$8) in Praça dos Pescadores in Porto Belo or at Bombinhas pier.

Back on the mainland, another educational opportunity is at the **Instituto Kat Schürmann** (☎ 3369 3690; www.schurmann.com.br; Av Vereador Manoel José dos Santos 220, Bombinhas; admission R$10; ⏲ 2-8pm daily Dec-Feb, Sat only Mar-Nov). The Schürmann family are local celebrities, known for their worldwide travels and their research on marine biology. The visitors center in Bombinhas has a 400m ecological trail, exhibits and films about the family's expeditions.

DIVING

The **Reserva Biológica do Avoredo** consists of three islands surrounded by coral reefs and fish, dolphins, stingrays and turtles. Day-long diving and snorkeling tours leave from the Bombinhas pier (baptism/discovery/certification/open-water R$165/200/700/885; 9am to 4pm). Both schools have English-speaking instructors:

HyBrasil Mergulho (☎ 3369 2545; www.hybrazil .com.br, in Portuguese; Av Vereador Manoel José dos Santos 205)

Submarine (☎ 3369 2473; www.submarinescuba.com. br, in Portuguese; Rua Ver Manoel José dos Santos 1353)

SLEEPING & EATING

Both Porto Belo and Bombinhas are packed with places to stay. Expect discounts of up to 50% if you arrive outside of the busy summer months.

Pousada Sonho Meu (☎ 3369 4624; www.pousa dasonhomeu.com, in Portuguese; Rua São Luiz 500, Porto Belo; r per person R$87; ⏹ ⏵ ⏾) Chalets are surrounded by greenery, with trails for those who wish to explore. The wide veranda offers views of the ocean in the distance.

ourpick Pousada Ganesh (☎ 3369 0018; www .pousadaganesh.com.br; Rua Salema 231, Bombinhas; s/d R$87/115; ⏹ ⏵) With tranquil gardens accented by statues of its namesake Hindu god, the Ganesh offers affordable rooms in otherwise pricey Bombinhas and only about 200m from the beach. The on-site sushi bar is fresh and delicious.

GETTING THERE & AWAY

You need to get a bus to Balneário Camboriú, from where 12 buses a day travel to Bombinhas (R$8, 45 minutes), stopping in Porto Belo (R5, 30 minutes) on the way.

SOUTH OF FLORIANÓPOLIS

The waves have put this stretch of coastline on the map. Long gone are the quiet fishing villages and near-deserted beaches that once dotted the coast south of Florianópolis. While the local population is still largely descended from Azorean fishermen, you'll be hard pressed to find them amid the suntanned surfers and bikini-clad beauties. The beaches that don't have big surf – and there are a few – are given over to fun-seeking families who show up every summer for their fix of sun and sand.

The coast south of Florianópolis is not as built up as that north of the city: your sun will not be blocked by the overgrowth of a concrete jungle. But most of the beaches are littered with smaller-scale hotels, campgrounds, beach bars, seafood shacks and all the business that caters to holidaymakers – during summer months you are unlikely to find a secluded spot. But that, again, may be part of the fun.

Guarda do Embaú

☎ 0xx48

Famous for its excellent left that breaks at the mouth of the river, Guarda do Embaú often makes the list of Brazil's best surfing beaches. The place has a laid-back, hippie vibe – an excellent destination for wave riders, backpackers and other bohemian types.

For information on Guarda, see www.guardadoembau.com. **Sun Hostel da Guarda** (☎ 3283 2316; fernando@garopaba.com.br; Estrada Geral 713; d/tr/q R$55/80/90, chalets d/tr/q R$95/105/130; 🛠) is a colorful and laid-back surfers' hostel by the waves.

our pick **Pousada Margah** (☎ 3283 2252; www .pousadamargah.com, in Portuguese; s/d R$160/220; 🛠), a newer and well-priced hostel, offers a Buddhist vibe in its gardens and lovingly decorated rooms. Also near the beach.

Three daily Paulotur buses stop in Guarda en route to/from Pinheira and Garopaba. Some buses between Florianópolis and Garopaba also stop in Guarda.

Praia do Rosa

☎ 0xx48 / pop 900

Santa Catarina's swankiest seaside town, Praia do Rosa, is about 15km south of Garopaba.

Rosa has two things going for it: a set of stunning, nearly pristine beaches and a sophisticated, ecoconscious population. Not to mention the many opportunities for surfing.

In winter, the bay becomes a breeding ground for southern right whales, and mothers and calves can be seen from the beach (see p356).

SLEEPING & EATING

The highest road in town, Caminho do Rei, is home to accommodations options with sweeping views.

Albergue do Rosa (☎ 3355 6614; r per person R$55; 🖳) Head here for cheap digs in the middle of town. Rooms are tiny and bathrooms are shared.

La Roca (☎ 3355 6471; Caminho do Rei; d R$120) Built into rocky hillside, this Bedrock-style place has cool stone walls and shiny wood floors that evoke an ecostylish atmosphere. The shared balcony offers ocean views from the upper floors, while the lower floors are engulfed in greenery.

Fazenda Verde do Rosa (☎ 3355 7272; www.fazen daverdedorosa.com.br, in Portuguese; chalets R$300-500; 🏕 🖳 📶 🐾) Spread across a stunning bluff above the beach, this place has colorful chalets that sleep four to six people, all with kitchen facilities and private terraces. Facilities include guided hikes, surf lessons and horseback riding (open to the public). The hotel also has three excellent restaurants – French, seafood and pizza – all with breezy decks and fabulous ocean views.

GETTING THERE & AWAY

Local buses run to Garopaba (R$2, every two hours), from where you can continue on to Florianópolis; or to Imbituba (R$2, five daily), for Porto Alegre.

Laguna

☎ 0xx48 / pop 52,000

About 110km south of Florianópolis, Laguna has a quaint colonial center. Over the hill, the beach at **Mar Grosso** is less enticing. For more elbow room, head to the terrific beaches around **Farol da Santa Marta**, 18km south of town.

The old town dates to 1676. While wandering its cobblestone streets and squares, peek in the **Museu Anita Garibaldi** (Praça Anita Garibaldi; admission R$3; ⏰ 8am-6pm), which honors the Brazilian wife of the Italian leader. Nearby, the **Casa**

SANTA CATARINA

THE WHALES ARE ALL RIGHT

Every winter, between June and October, hundreds of southern right whales return to the Santa Catarina coast. These massive mammals can be 18m long and can weigh more than 60 tons. They come north from the frigid waters of Antarctica, in search of a warmer, calmer place to spawn. When the calves are born, they are usually 3m or 4m long, already weighing as much as five tons.

The right whales were on the brink of extinction in the 1970s. Their huge size and slow speeds made them prime targets for commercial fishermen. The primary goal of the **Instituto Baleia Franca** (IBF; ☎ 3255 2922; www.baleiafranca.org.br, in Portuguese), in Praia do Rosa, is to monitor and protect these amazing creatures. The organization contributed to the creation of the Right Whale Environmental Protection Area off the Santa Catarina coast in 2001; now the population is estimated at 7000 and growing rapidly.

The whales and their calves frolic in the waters very close to shore, and are often visible from the beach. Take your binoculars and go to high ground and you may spot their mammoth forms breaching or batting their fins. For a closer encounter, take a whale-watching tour with **Turismo Vida Sol e Mar** (☎ 3355 6111; www.vidasolemar.com.br, in Portuguese; tours per person R$90 Mon-Fri, R$140 Sat & Sun; ☽ tours 8am & 11am). The tours from Garopaba last for 90 minutes or more, depending on the location of the whales. Each boat has an IBF scientist on board, but whale sightings are not guaranteed. It's best to allow a couple of days for this outing, as it also depends on weather conditions.

Several daily buses leave Florianopolis for Laguna (R$19, two hours), stopping in Garopaba along the way. From Praia do Rosa, buses (R$2, 20 minutes) depart for Garopaba every other hour.

de Anita Garibaldi (Praça Vidal Ramos; admission R$3; ☽ 8am-6pm) is where she grew up.

The main drag in Mar Grosso is Av Senador Gallotti, which runs parallel to the beach. Here you'll find the **tourist office** (☎ 3646 0533; www .laguna.sc.gov.br, in Portuguese) and a slew of hotels and restaurants.

TOURS

Associação de Guias (☎ 9977 6352) Leads tours to the Farol Santa Marta and to some archaeological sites in the area.

Scuna Garibaldi (☎ 9129 8761; tours per person R$25; ☽ 10am, 3pm & 6pm) This two-hour boat ride departs from the historic center.

SLEEPING & EATING

Many hotels in Mar Grosso are only open on weekends from March to November.

Hotel Recanto (☎ 3644 0902; Rua Engenho Colombo Salles 108; r per person R$32) No-frills rooms near the bus station.

Atlântico Sul Hotel (☎ 3647 1166; www.atlanticosul laguna.com.br; Av Senador Gallotti 360; s/d/tr from R$75/105/130; ☒ ☲) Parading as a big-time beach resort but really just a basic hotel with a pool, the Atlântica is still a good deal just 30m from the beach.

In the old town, the per-kilo **Restaurante Praç de Anita** (Praça República Juliana; per kg R$14; ☽ 11am-3pm Mon-Sat) serves excellent, Azorean-influenced food in an airy colonial house. Mar Grosso has several old-style seafood restaurants, including **Arrastão** (☎ 3647 0418; Av Senador Gallotti 629; meals R$20-25).

GETTING THERE & AROUND

The long-distance **bus station** (☎ 3646 0119) is on the edge of the old town. From here you can catch a local bus to Mar Grosso or to Farol da Santa Marta. Long-distance destinations include Porto Alegre (R$65, six hours) and Torres (R$37, four hours, two daily) in Rio Grande do Sul; and Florianópolis (R$19, two hours, five daily) and Imbituba (R$5, one hour, eight daily) in Santa Catarina.

SERRA GERAL

Santa Catarina is better known for its beaches than its mountains, but this gorgeous mountain range – located about 250km west of Florianópolis – should not be overlooked. With peaks up to 1800m, this is the coolest part of Brazil, often accumulating snow during the winter months. The mountains and canyons offer opportunities for hiking, horseback riding and otherwise getting off the beaten track.

São Joaquim
☎ 0xx49 / 25,100

High in the mountains of the Serra do Rio do Rastro (an offshoot of the Serra Geral),

São Joaquim is about 290km southwest of Florianópolis. This little town in the Rio Canoas valley is famous for its apple orchards, many of which were planted by the local Japanese population. São Joaquim's other claim to fame is its snowfall: come in early July for the annual **Festival de Inverno**.

The most affordable sleeping option is **Nevada Hotel** (☎ 3233 0259; Rua Manoel Joaquim Pinto 190; r R$80). For a bit of rustic luxury, try **Villa da Montanha** (☎ 3278 4132; www.villadamontanha.com; d R$180), 10km from the center, with hiking trails and horseback riding.

Buses go to Florianópolis (R$22, 5½ hours) daily.

Bom Jardim da Serra

☎ 0xx49 / pop 4400

Founded in the 1870s by *gaúchos* (cowboys), the 'capital of the water' does indeed boast many lakes and waterfalls. About 45km south of São Joaquim, it also serves as the start of the hair-raising and spectacular winding road known as the **Estrada da Serra do Rio Rastro**, which switchbacks through high-mountain scenery toward the **Parque Nacional de São Joaquim**. The park boasts a breathtaking landscape of grassy highlands, thick *araucária* (Paraná pine) forests and Santa Catarina's highest peak, **Morro da Igreja** (1822m). The park lacks infrastructure, but hiking trails leading to panoramic lookouts and freefalling water-falls. Find information about camping in the park at the **tourist information center** (☎ 3232 0735) in Bom Jardim.

A wonderful, if pricey, place to stay within the park is the **Rio do Rastro Eco Resort** (☎ 9112 0073/0074; www.riodorastro.com.br; SC-438, Km 130; d from R$200), which has supremely comfortable cha-lets with rustic touches.

SANTA CATARINA

Rio Grande do Sul

Brazil's southernmost state is covered largely by pampas, the grassy plains that supported centuries of cattle-herding. Much of this land is now actually used to cultivate soybean crops, but the cowboy culture endures.

So it is that residents of Rio Grande do Sul call themselves *gaúchos*, after the independent-minded ranchers and cattle herders that settled the state. In the countryside, it is not unusual to see old-timers sporting wide-brimmed hats and other traditional dress. Grilled meat, or *churrasco*, is still the state's favorite food, and everywhere, everywhere, locals suck down *chimarrão*, the distinctive tea made from the maté plant. Such traditions remain, even in the cosmopolitan capital of Porto Alegre.

There is more to lure visitors to the state. In its northeastern corner, the earth opens up in an amazing geological display, giving way to the spectacular Serra Gaúcha. These mountains offer unlimited opportunities for hiking and other adventures, from the forest-covered canyons of the national parks near Cambará do Sul to the cascaded river valleys around Canela.

In the Vale dos Vinhedos, Italian-descended vintners are producing wines that rival the best vintages from Chile and Argentina. Inspired by the mountain scenery and influenced by their German and Italian heritage, towns like Gramado cast themselves as Brazilian alpine villages, selling fancy chocolates and publicizing their annual snowfall. In so many ways, Rio Grande do Sul defies notions of typical Brazil, which only makes this southern state more alluring.

HIGHLIGHTS

- Bargain for trash and treasures at the Sunday morning flea market at **Parque Farroupilha** (p362) in Porto Alegre
- Sample the crisp whites and earthy reds from the **Vale dos Vinhedos** (p365), near Bento Gonçalves
- Feel free to yodel in **Gramado** (p366), a Swiss mountain village literally flowing with fondue and other Swiss treats
- Hike the Trilha do Mirante and peer over the edge of the **Cânion da Fortaleza** (p370) in the Parque Nacional da Serra Geral
- Uncover the mystery of the Jesuit mission at **São Miguel das Missões** (p372)

São Miguel das Missões ★

Parque Nacional da Serra Geral ★

Bento Gonçalves ★ ★ Gramado

Porto Alegre ★

- POPULATION: 10.8 MILLION
- AREA: 281,800 SQ KM

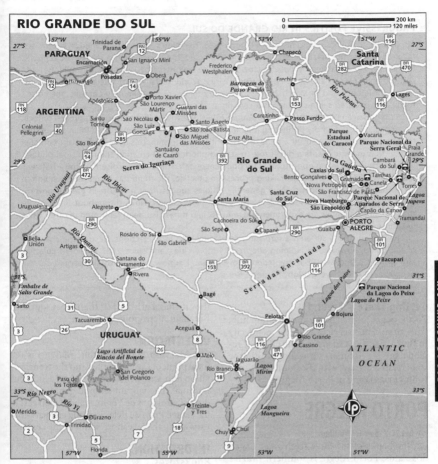

RIO GRANDE DO SUL

History

Living on land long disputed by the Spanish and Portuguese, the people of Rio Grande do Sul used the conflict to create an identity distinct from the rest of Brazil. The region even declared its independence during the ill-fated Guerra dos Farrapos, a decade-long civil war ending in 1845. A wave of immigrants, mostly German, Italian and Swiss, began arriving in the late 19th century, reinforcing the region's cultural differences.

Climate

The Brazilian state sitting furthest from the equator, Rio Grande do Sul has the most temperate climate in Brazil, with hot summers and cool winters. The mountains of the Serra Gaúcha north of Porto Alegre even see occasional snow. That said, the climate is subtropical in the coastal lowlands, with hot, humid summers.

National Parks

Parque Nacional de Aparados da Serra occupies 102.5 sq km on the border between Rio Grande do Sul and Santa Catarina states. North and south of Aparados da Serra, the parkland was extended in 1992 with the creation of the Parque Nacional da Serra Geral. These parks preserve some of the country's last *araucária* forests, as well as a series of stunning canyons that offer fine opportunities for hiking, horseback riding and rock climbing.

RIO GRANDE DO SUL

PROGRESSIVE POLITICS IN RIO GRANDE DO SUL

Rio Grande do Sul has a long history of contrariness. The state's *farroupilhas* (political extremists) revolted against the Brazilian emperor in the 1830s and 1840s, declaring a short-lived republic. In the late 1970s, strikes by *gaúcho* (cowboy) trade unions helped weaken the military junta ruling the country. In 2001, the city hosted the first World Social Forum (like a World Economic Forum for lefties). And in March 2004, in a country that is overwhelmingly Catholic, the state's high court declared same-sex unions a civil right.

In progressive political circles, Porto Alegre is best known for its innovative approach to local politics called Participatory Budgeting (PB). In 1989 the Workers' Party instituted PB in an attempt to improve democratic institutions and to create citizen ownership. This radical reform is a complex system that gives residents a direct role in setting priorities and creating the municipal budget.

In principle, PB creates opportunities for poor, uneducated or otherwise disenfranchised citizens to get involved in the decision-making process. In practice, the trend has increased spending in lower-income neighborhoods. More generally, studies suggest that it results in greater government transparency and increased levels of public participation. Now, throughout Brazil, more than 180 municipalities are experimenting with PB, and it has also been replicated in other cities in Latin America and Europe.

The Workers' Party suffered a surprising defeat in 2004's local elections. Despite the changing of the guard, however, PB is being adopted by more cities, and since 2007 President Lula has also worked to increase PB in the federal government. For now, budgets by the people, for the people, appear to have a bright future in Brazil.

Getting There & Around

Porto Alegre is the state's transportation hub, with air and bus services to every major city in Brazil. Excellent roads and the efficient regional bus service makes traveling within the state relatively easy, with most long-distance routes originating in Porto Alegre.

PORTO ALEGRE

☎ 0xx51 / pop 1.44 million

On the banks of the huge freshwater Lagoa dos Patos, Porto Alegre is southern Brazil's most important port city and a key player in Mercosul (South American free-trade agreement). It is also, thanks to its well-educated and forward-thinking population, one of the most sophisticated cities in Brazil.

The downtown area has benefited from a thoughtful approach to development, including the creation of transportation hubs and the preservation of much of the grand, neoclassical architecture. A long tradition of progressive politics has helped nurture vibrant arts and alternative music scenes, and the well-organized gay and lesbian community has won the right to register domestic partnerships.

Unfortunately, crime levels in the city have risen in recent years and the downtown area can be dangerous after dark. During the day,

the city has a grittier feel than most southern Brazilian metropolises.

ORIENTATION

The Mercado Público (Public Market) is the focal point of the city center and the transportation hub, with a metro station and a local bus terminal. The vibrant shopping and nightlife district, Moinhos de Vento, is about 3km east of the center. Praia de Belas is a long city park that runs along the lakeshore south of the center.

INFORMATION
Bookstores

SBS (☎ 3228 1260; Rua Caldas Júnior; ☼ 9am-6pm Mon-Fri, 9am-1pm Sat) Small selection of English-language classics.

Emergency

Bombeiros (☎ 193) Handles fire emergencies.
Medical emergencies (☎ 192)
Polícia Federal (☎ 194)

Internet Access

ERA Virtual (☎ 3061 7333; Rua dos Andradas 1001; per hr R$4.20; ☼ 9am-9pm Mon-Sat) One of several internet cafés inside the Rua da Praia Shopping Center.

Money

Aerotur (☎ 3228 8144; Rua dos Andradas 1137) Exchanges traveler's checks and cash.

Banco do Brasil (Av Uruguaí 185) Offers cash exchange and ATMs.
Citibank (Rua 7 de Setembro 722)

Tourist Information
Airport tourist office (☎ 3358 2000; www.portoale gre.rs.gov.br; ☾ 7:30am-midnight)
Mercado Público Tourist Office (☾ 9am-8pm Mon-Sat) Inside the main entrance of the Mercado Público.

SIGHTS
Praça 15 de Novembro, site of the 1869 **Mercado Público**, is the centerpiece of the city. The old building bustles during daytime hours, when vendors sell fresh produce, meats and seafood, as well as the all-important *erva maté* for *chimarrão* (see the boxed text, p364).

A pedestrian promenade runs into Praça da Alfândega, the leafy square that is home to the **Museu de Arte do Rio Grande do Sul** (MARGS; ☎ 3227 2311; www.margs.rs.gov.br; Praça da Alfândega; admission free; ☾ 10am-7pm Tue-Sun). The neoclassical building is an impressive venue for regional artists. On the ground floor, the inviting Bistrot de MARGS takes advantage of the leafy setting, which is a lovely spot for lunch.

Three blocks south, the picturesque Praça da Matriz is dominated by the early-20th-century, neoclassical **Catedral Metropolitana**. On the northern side, you'll find the elegant mid-19th-century edifice of the **Teatro São Pedro** and the sculpted facade of the **Biblioteca Público** (☾ 9am-1pm & 2:30-5pm Mon-Wed, Fri & Sat, till 8pm Thu). Nearby is the **Museu Histórico Júlo**

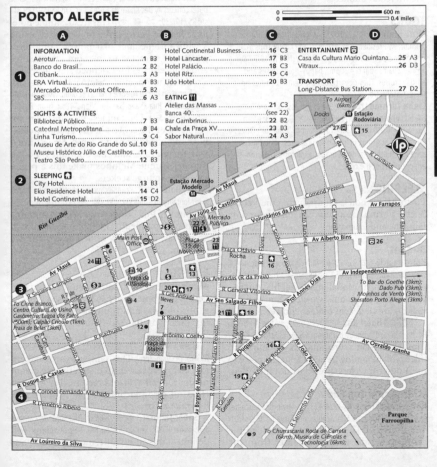

PORTO ALEGRE

0 ——————— 600 m
0 ——————— 0.4 miles

RIO GRANDE DO SUL

INFORMATION	
Aerotur	1 B3
Banco do Brasil	2 B2
Citibank	3 A3
ERA Virtual	4 B3
Mercado Público Tourist Office	5 B2
SBS	6 A3

SIGHTS & ACTIVITIES	
Biblioteca Público	7 B3
Catedral Metropolitana	8 B4
Linha Turismo	9 C4
Museu de Arte do Rio Grande do Sul	10 B3
Museu Histórico Júlio de Castilhos	11 B4
Teatro São Pedro	12 B3

SLEEPING	
City Hotel	13 B3
Eko Residence Hotel	14 C4
Hotel Continental	15 D2

Hotel Continental Business	16 C3
Hotel Lancaster	17 B3
Hotel Palácio	18 C3
Hotel Ritz	19 C4
Lido Hotel	20 B3

EATING	
Atelier das Massas	21 C3
Banca 40	(see 22)
Bar Gambrinus	22 B2
Chale da Praça XV	23 D3
Sabor Natural	24 A3

ENTERTAINMENT	
Casa da Cultura Mario Quintana	25 A3
Vitraux	26 D3

TRANSPORT	
Long-Distance Bus Station	27 D2

de Castilhos (☎ 3221 3959; Rua Duque de Caxias 1231; admission free; ☺ 10am-7pm Tue-Fri, 1:30-5pm Sat & Sun), displaying *gaúcho* artifacts in a typical 19th-century home.

About 1km southeast of the cathedral lies **Parque Farroupilha**, the city's largest park and home to a sprawling flea market on Sunday morning.

Also southeast of the center, the **Museu de Ciências e Tecnologia** (MCT; ☎ 3320 3597; www.pucrs .br/mct; Av Ipiranga 6681; adult/child/student R$13/9.50/9.50, planetarium R$2; ☺ 9am-5pm Tue-Sun) is the huge, impressive science museum of the Pontifícia Universidade Católica. Exhibits cover everything from astronomy to physics to biology, with plenty of opportunities for hands-on experimentation. Take bus 343 or 353 from the Mercado Público.

TOURS

Cisne Branco (☎ 3224 5222; www.barcocisnebranco .com.br; Av Presidente João Goulart 551) River trips include one-hour cruises down the river (adult/child R$15/7.50; ☺ 10:30am, 3pm & 4:30pm), happy-hour cruises and all-day cruises. They depart from the Centro Cultural do Usino Gasômetro.

Linha Turismo (☎ 3212 3464; Travessa do Carmo 84; bus upper/lower level R$15/10; ☺ 9am & 3:30pm Tue-Sun, 10:30am & 1:30pm Tue-Sun to 'zona sul') Offers 90-minute bus tours of local historical sites, including a *zona sul* (southern zone) tour that explores the southeast-ern periphery of the city.

SLEEPING

Porto Alegre hotels fill up during the World Social Forum, annually scheduled for late January, and Carnaval.

Budget

Hotel Palácio (☎ 3225 3467; Rua Vigário José Inácio 644; s/d without bathroom R$33/52, s/d R$54/69) The spacious rooms in institutional green feel like dorms. Fortunately the rooms are clean and well lit, making this a decent budget choice.

our pick Hotel Ritz (☎ 3225 0693; Av Des André da Rocha 225; s/d without bathroom R$36/48, s/d R$42/62) Tiny, clean rooms surround a sweet courtyard filled with blooming trees – a fantastic place to meet other travelers. Breakfast not included.

Midrange & Top End

Hotel Lancaster (☎ 3224 4737; www.hotel-lancaster -poa.com.br; Travessa Eng Acelino de Carvalho 67; s/d/tr R$75/120/170; ☒ 🖳) Yellow shutters adorn the art-deco facade, which you enter from the

pedestrian passageway. Inside, the quarters are cozy, clean and cramped.

Lido Hotel (☎ 3228 9111; www.lidohotel.com.br; Rua General Andrade Neves 150; s/d R$90/124; ☒ 🖳) The lobby is slick, but the clean and basic rooms look out over unpicturesque alleys. Weekend rates are discounted about 30%, which makes the rooms much more attractive indeed.

Hotel Continental Business (☎ 3027 1600; www .hotelcontinentalbusiness.com.br; Praça Otávio Rocha 49; r weekend/weekday R$90/120; ☒ 🖳) Short on charm but long on comfort, this towering hotel offers reasonable rooms and professional service. As per the name, it caters mainly to business travelers. Its sister property, Hotel Continental, near the bus station has slightly higher rates.

Eko Residence Hotel (☎ 3225 8644; www.residence hotel.com.br; Av Des André da Rocha 131; s/d R$159/179, ste s/d R$219/239; ☒ 🖳 📶 🖳) This fresh, simple hotel near Parque Farroupilha powers itself using a wind turbine and solar power. Long-term guests are attracted to in-room kitchenettes and reduced rates for extended stays as well as a solid environmental sustainability program.

Sheraton Porto Alegre (☎ 2121 6000; www.sheraton -poa.com.br; Rua Olavo Barreto Viana 18; r from R$300; ☒ 🖳 📶 🖳) The fanciest digs in town are 3km east of the center, in the upscale neighborhood of Moinhos de Vento. Streets lined with quaint cafés and chic boutiques and the popular Parque Moinhos make this a prime locale for splurge seekers.

City Hotel (☎ 3212 5488; www.cityhotel.com.br; Rua Dr José Montaury 20; s/dR$332/400; ☒ 📶) In the heart of downtown, this Beaux Arts classic maintains a sense of grandeur. The lobby is swanky in an old-fashioned way, while guestrooms are modern.

EATING

Many of the entertainment venues along Rua Fernando Gomes (see p363) are also excellent eating options, and you will find ample dining variety on the 2nd floor of the Mercado Público (p361).

Banca 40 (☎ 3226 3533; Mercado Público; ice cream R$3-6; ☺ 9am-7pm) This family-owned bakery and creamery serves up distinctive ice cream made from 50-year-old recipes. Try a scoop (R$3) of *coco* (coconut) or an exotic flavor like *milho* (corn).

Sabor Natural (☎ 3028 0539; Rua Siqueira Campos 890; buffet R$10; ☺ lunch Mon-Fri) Vegetarians will delight at this all-organic, meat-free, all-you-can-eat buffet that caters to the downtown lunch crowd. Enjoy limitless soups, salads and other animal-friendly fare.

Bar Gambrinus (☎ 3226 6914; Mercado Público; meals R$25-35; ☺ lunch daily, dinner Mon-Fri) This Portuguese restaurant in the Mercado Público is popular for its old-world aura and extremely fresh seafood.

Churrascaria Roda de Carreta (☎ 3336 0817; Av Ipiranga 5300; buffet R$30; ☺ lunch & dinner) This *churrascaria* (restaurant featuring meat) located near the Shopping Bourbon Ipiranga was founded by the local Center of Gaúcho Tradition (CTG) to celebrate *gaúcho* customs, from food and drink to song and dance. The huge buffet features 17 kinds of grilled meats and countless other hot and cold dishes.

Galpão Crioulo (☎ 3226 8194; Parque Maurício Sirotsky Sobrinho; buffet R$30; ☺ lunch & dinner) Considered one of the city's best *churrascaria* for its extensive all-you-can-eat buffet and well-stocked wine cellar. The designated Mestre do Chimarrão (Chimarrão Master) means that this is an excellent place to sample that local specialty (see the boxed text, p364).

our pick **Atelier das Massas** (☎ 3225 8888; Rua Riachuelo 1482; meals R$30-40; ☺ 11am-11pm Mon-Sat) An artistic flair shines bright at this downtown joint, where the walls are crammed with original artwork and funky photographs. The menu is no less creative, with an irresistible antipasti buffet and delectable homemade pastas.

Chale da Praça XV (☎ 3225 2667; Praça 15 de Novembro; meals R$30-40; ☺ noon-midnight) Housed in a pleasant, Victorian-style garden house and surrounded by a sprawling terrace, this Porto Alegre institution buzzes with activity starting at happy hour, around 6pm.

ENTERTAINMENT

Pick up a copy of *Jornal do Nuances* for nightlife listings.

Casa da Cultura Mario Quintana (☎ 3221 7147; www.ccmq.rs.gov.br; Rua dos Andradas 736) The cultural center in this pink baroque building has a cinema and two busy cafés. The 7th-floor Café Concerto Majestic is a lovely place to listen to live music and watch the sunset over Lagoa dos Patos.

Centro Cultural do Usino Gasômetro (☎ 3212 5979; Av Presidente João Goulart 551; admission free) On the banks of the Lagoa dos Patos, this former factory now houses art cinemas, temporary art exhibitions and a pleasant café.

Other bars and clubs are concentrated around Av Goethe and Rua Fernando Gomes (known as 'The Walk of Fame') in Moinhos de Vento. Check out **Dado Pub** (☎ 3395 1468; Rua Fernando Gomes 80) or **Bar do Goethe** (☎ 3222 2043; Rua 24 de Outubro 112).

Porto Alegre has an active gay and lesbian social scene, with hot spots such as the dance club **Vitraux** (☎ 3221 7799; Rua Conceição 492; ☺ from 11pm Fri & Sat, from 10pm Sun).

GETTING THERE & AWAY
Air

Porto Alegre's modern **Aeroporto Internacional Salgado Filho** (☎ 3358 2000) is located 6km from downtown. Take a taxi (R$30, 15 minutes) or ride the metro (R$2, 30 minutes).

Direct flights go to São Paulo (one hour), Rio de Janeiro (1½ hours), Florianópolis (one hour), Curitiba (one hour), Brasília (2½ hours), Montevideo and Buenos Aires.

Bus

The busy **long-distance bus station** (☎ 3210 0101; www.rodoviaria-poa.com.br), on Largo Vespiano Júlio Veppo, is accessible by metro; alternatively, a taxi downtown costs R$10.

Destinations within Rio Grande do Sul include Torres (R$30 to R$38, three hours, six daily), Gramado (R$25, two hours, seven daily), Canela (R$24, 2½ hours, seven daily), Pelotas (R$38, three hours, eight daily), Cambará do Sul (R$26, six hours, one daily) via São Francisco de Paula, and Santo Ângelo (R$83, *leito* – overnight sleeper – R$108, seven hours, eight daily). One overnight *semidireto* (semidirect) bus goes to Chuí on the Uruguayan border (R$73 to R$85, seven hours); otherwise you can connect in Pelotas.

Buses travel interstate to Florianópolis (R$65 to R$90, 6½ hours), Curitiba (R$79 to R$85, 11 hours, three daily) and Rio de Janeiro city (R$208, 25 hours, twice daily). International destinations include Montevideo (12 hours), Buenos Aires (18 hours) and Santiago (36 hours).

GETTING AROUND

Porto Alegre has a clean and efficient one-line metro that connects downtown with both the long-distance bus station and the airport. Once you are downtown, virtually all the city's main attractions are within a 15-minute walk of the metro's final stop, just behind the Mercado Público.

SERRA GAÚCHA

North of Porto Alegre, the flat coastal land disappears, as the roads climb into the mountains of the Serra Gaúcha. This scenic stretch – particularly beautiful between Nova Petrópolis and Gramado – is characterized by forested hillsides and unexpected rocky cliffs, often sparkling with waterfalls.

The region was first settled by Germans (beginning in 1824) and later by Italians (starting in the 1870s), and this heritage is still a source of pride and fascination. Although the mountains don't reach much more than 1000m, Gramado and Canela resemble Swiss villages in their architecture and atmosphere. In Bento Gonçalves and the nearby Vale dos Vinhedos, fountains flow with vino, as descendants of Italian immigrants foster a burgeoning wine industry.

Many visitors come to the Serra Gaúcha in winter (June to August) in hopes of catching sight of snow; higher altitudes get a couple of inches a year. In spring the hills are blanketed with wildflowers, while thousands of hydrangeas bloom well into summer. Hiking is excellent year-round, particularly in the Parque Nacional de Aparados da Serra.

BENTO GONÇALVES

☎ 0xx54 / pop 107,000

Considering the region's Italian heritage and its dry, mountainous landscape, it makes sense that Rio Grande do Sul would be a center for wine production. The center

for this burgeoning wine industry is Bento Gonçalves, 124km north of Porto Alegre. It is a large, loud city that does not offer much besides convenient access to the region's vineyards.

Every year in January and February, the city hosts **Fenavinho** (www.fenavinhobrasil.com.br) to celebrate and promote the wine industry.

Orientation & Information

The main drag in Bento is Rua Marechal Deodoro, where you will find a few hotels and the **tourist information office** (☎ 3453 6699; www.bentogoncalves.rs.gov.br; Rua Marechal Deodoro 70; ☺ 9am-6pm Mon-Sat).

Sights & Activities

The entrance to Bento Gonçalves is marked by the **Pórtico da Pipa**, a gigantic wine barrel that straddles the street. This is also the gateway to the Vale dos Vinhedos, the celebrated wine region that stretches 5km to the west (see p365).

The only winery in the city center is the **Vinícola Aurora** (☎ 3455 2000; www.vinicolaaurora.com.br; Rua Olavo Bilac 500; tours & tastings free; ☺ 8:15am-5:15pm Mon-Sat, 8:30-11:30am Sun), located one block north of the train station. From the Aurora vineyards on the outskirts of town, the grape juice flows to this production facility via an underground pipe network.

Twice a week, the steam engine **Maria Fumaça** (☎ 3455 2788; www.mfumaca.com.br; adult/child R$40/free; ☺ 9am & 2pm Thu & Sat Feb-Jun & Aug-Nov, daily Dec, Jan & Jul) chugs along the track between Bento Gonçalves and the small towns

---

CHEERS TO CHIMARRÃO

Rio Grande do Sul is among Brazil's most modern and most sophisticated states. Yet even the most *moderno gaúcho* (modern cowboy) reaches for a gourd when he needs a lift.

It was the indigenous Guarani who taught Spanish settlers the pleasures of *chimarrão* (tea from the maté plant) and how to sip it not from a cup but through a *bomba* (straw) stuck into a hollowed-out *cuia* (gourd). Also known as *erva maté*, this tealike beverage is made from the leaves of the maté tree, which is native to the pampas (grassy plains) that extend from Argentina and Uruguay through southern Brazil.

The original *gaúchos*, the men who tended the region's vast cattle herds, quickly became addicted to maté's pleasurable effects, which are at once energizing and calming. They even grew to love its bittersweet taste, perhaps because it reflected the lives they led on the empty plains. Even the act of sucking at the straw seems to satisfy an ancient yearning. *Chimarrão* is an acquired taste and a serious addiction.

These days, this ancient tradition is getting a boost from scientists and pseudoscientists alike, who make claims about maté's health benefits, from lower blood pressure to increased intelligence. Hard results are yet to come. However, you might make your own study by sampling *chimarrão* at Galpão Crioulo (p363).

of Garibaldi and Carlos Barbosa. At each stop, passengers are herded onto the platforms to partake of cheap wine. Riding the old steam engine has a certain appeal, but the trip is otherwise overrated.

Tours

Caminhos de Pedra (☎ 3454 5702; www.caminhosdepedra.org.br; per person R$30) visits fascinating architectural relics from the 19th century.

Vale das Vinhas (☎ 3451 4216; www.valedasvinhastur.com.br; Rua Barão do Rio Branco 245; per person R$30) runs a three-hour tour that visits four facilities in the Vale dos Vinhedos. It's located in the lobby of Hotel Vinocap (see p365).

Sleeping & Eating

The most appealing option is to stay at one of the rural hotels in the Vale dos Vinhedos. If you are dependent on public transportation, however, it is more convenient to stay in Bento.

Pousada da Pipa (☎ 3453 3157; mapellis@terra.com.br; Travessa Silva Paes 415; s/d R$45/60; 🖳) This sweet yellow house is near the Pórtico da Pipa. Simple, sunlit rooms with wood floors and ruffled linens offer excellent value, although the location is inconvenient for those relying on public transport.

Hotel Vinocap (☎ 3455 7100; www.vinocap.com.br; Rua Barão do Rio Branco 245; s/d R$90/125; 🖳 🖳) It's not the most beautiful building in Bento, but it might be the most central. The 126 rooms are pretty plain but perfectly comfortable, and you can upgrade to a newly renovated 'luxury' room (singles/doubles R$120/150) if you desire.

ourpick Villa dei Fiori (☎ 3453 7866; www.villadeifiori.com.br; Rua Herdiros Refatti 185; r R$150-179) You might not expect to discover an Italian villa so close to the bus station, but here it is. The old stone structure and the lovely garden setting make this the most charming place to stay in the city proper.

Canta Maria (☎ 3453 1099; meals R$40-50; 🕑 lunch daily, dinner Mon-Sat) The city's most vaunted restaurant is located near the Pórtico da Pipa. A buffet of soups, salads and pastas is accompanied by a *rodízio* (smorgasbord) of grilled meats, fish and lamb. If you're in need of transportation, call the restaurant and staff will pick you up from anywhere in town or the vicinity.

There is a decent food court in the Shopping Bento Gonçalves, on Rua Marechal Deodoro.

Getting There & Around

The **long-distance bus station** (☎ 3452 1311) is about 1km north of the center, at the corner of Rua Osvaldo Aranha and Rua Gen Gomes Carneiro. Buses travel hourly to Porto Alegre (R$7, 2½ hours) and Caxias do Sul (R$10, one hour), where you can connect to Canela, Gramado or Cambará do Sul. One daily bus goes to Santo Ângelo (R$75, seven hours).

See p366 for details on transportation to Vale dos Vinhedos.

VALE DOS VINHEDOS

When connoisseurs contemplate world-class wine production, Brazil isn't usually the first country that comes to mind. Discerning palates, however, are starting to rave about the outstanding vintages of southern Brazil. The award-winning cabernets and chardonnays fermented in the **Vale dos Vinhedos** (Valley of Vineyards; ☎ 3451 9601; www.valedosvinhedos.com.br) are the result of generations of hard work and innovation – particularly by Italian families that immigrated to the region starting in the 1870s – as well as excellent soil and growing conditions.

Today the valley produces more than 10 million bottles per year and welcomes hundreds of thousands of visitors to more than 30 wineries, rural inns, and restaurants along the Estrada do Vinho and Via Trento, a picturesque loop that stretches west of Bento Gonçalves. Most of the bigger and more acclaimed wineries offer tours and tastings. Wine, tempting champagnes, chocolates and handicrafts are always for sale.

RIO GRANDE DO SUL

DO-IT-YOURSELF BIKE TOUR OF WINE COUNTRY

The Vale dos Vinhedos offers great cycling conditions: gentle hills, excellent roads with wide shoulders, and courteous drivers slowly taking in the gorgeous scenery. The loop itself is approximately 25km, making for a relatively short and easily navigated circuit, and pit stops where you can stock up on water and snacks are plentiful. For now, there is nowhere to rent bikes in Bento Gonçalves, but if you have your own, you won't be the only biker on the road. Don't forget your helmet and a backpack for stocking up on wine and cheese after a day's ride.

The tourist information office in Bento Gonçalves (see p364) has maps and information about wineries. The best way to visit the wineries is on a tour (p365), which allows you to take in the beautiful countryside – and drink wine – without the worry of driving.

Wineries

These are just a few of the dozens of wine production facilities along the loop, many of which have excellent restaurants on-site. You may pay extra for a tasting – called a 'bonus' – although this amount is deductible from any purchases you make.

At **Vinícola Miolo** (☎ 3451 1994; www.miolo.com.br; Estrada do Vinho km21; bonus R$5-15; ☷ 8am-6pm Mon-Sat, 9am-5pm Sun) champagnes are notable, as well cabernet sauvignon and merlot. The huge complex spreads out from a man-made lake and tours are run every half-hour.

The small **Cave de Amadeu** (☎ 3455 7461; www.amadeu.com.br; Linha Jansen s/n; bonus R$10; ☷ 10am-5pm Sat & Sun) winery, in the Pinto Bandeiras sector of the valley, garners international awards for its sparkling varieties.

Vallontono Vinhos (☎ 3459 1005; www.vallontono.com.br; Estrada do Vinho Km 16; bonus R$5; ☷ 9am-5pm Mon-Fri, 10am-5pm Sat & Sun) is known for its cabernet sauvignon, merlot and chardonnay; the winery itself is beautiful.

Sleeping & Eating

Rural inns in the valley are expensive but unforgettable – and worth the splurge! Prices listed are for the weekend; they drop approximately 20% during the week.

Pousada Villa Valduga (☎ 2105 3154; www.casavalduga.com.br; Linha Leopoldina s/n; s/d R$260/310; ☒ ▢ ☎ ⚱) This winery also runs a charming rustic inn with bright and comfortable rooms. Its restaurant, Luis V, serves fresh and refined Italian and French dishes paired with its own cabernets and chardonnays.

our pick **Pousada Borghetto Sant'Anna** (☎ 3453 2355; www.borghettosantanna.com.br; Linha Leopoldina 868; ste R$290-310, cottages R$360-410; ☒ ▢ ☎) About 4km from Bento, perched above the Vale dos Vinhedos, this cluster of romantic stone houses gives a fantastic view of the valley below. Reminiscent of Tuscany, the lodgings mix rustic charm with sumptuous comfort.

Giordani Café da Colônia (☎ 3453 6884; Linha Leopoldina s/n; buffet without wine R$22; ☷ 8am-8pm) This colonial café has a scrumptious and wide range of sweet and savory lunch items such

as cakes and coffee – is paired well with wine offerings from the valley.

Getting There & Away

There is no public transportation to the Vale dos Vinhedos. If you don't have your own vehicle, sign on for one of the reasonably priced tours (see p367).

GRAMADO

☎ 0xx54 / pop 34,000

This tony mountain resort bills itself as 'naturally European,' and it does indeed feel like a Swiss mountain village. Boutiques sell avant-garde glassworks and gourmet chocolate, while local restaurants specialize in fondue. Hotels are decked out like Swiss chalets. At times the insistence on Alpine themes crosses over into kitsch, but the overall affect is pleasant.

In August, Gramado hosts **Festival de Gramado** (www.festivaldegramado.com.br), Brazil's most prestigious film festival.

Information

Banco do Brasil (cnr Rua Garibaldi & Rua Augusto Zatti) Has an ATM and money exchange.

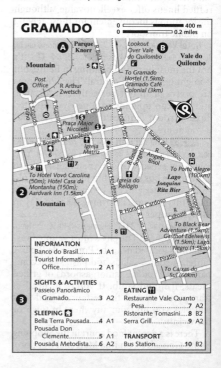

GRAMADO

0   400 m
0   0.2 miles

Tourist information office (☎ 3286 1475; www.por talgramado.com.br; Praça Major Nicoletti; ⊗ 9am-7pm)

Sights

About 1.5km southeast of the center, **Lago Negro** is an attractive, man-made lake surrounded by hydrangeas and crowded with swan boats. Closer to the center, **Parque Knorr** offers inspiring views of the Vale do Quilombo, a beautiful valley that stretches along the road between Gramado and Canela.

Tours

Black Bear Adventure (☎ 9939 7191; www.blackbear adventure.com.br; Rua Bruno Ernest Riegel 713) Organizes white-water rafting, rappelling down waterfalls and hiking in the Cânion do Itaimbezinho (p370) and Cânion da Fortaleza (p370). The office is near Lago Negro.

Passeio Panorâmico Gramado (☎ 3286 9324; www .jardineiradashortensias.com.br; Av das Hortênsias 1710; tour per person R$10; ⊗ 10am, noon, 2pm & 4pm) This 90-minute bus tour gives an overview of the town's history, architecture and nature highlights.

Sleeping

Prices listed are for weekends in summer (December to February). Rates rise significantly over Christmas and during the film festival.

Gramado Hostel (☎ 3295 1020; www.gramadohostel .com.br; Av das Hortênsias 3880; dm HI member/nonmember R$35/45; d HI member/nonmember R$45/55; ⊡ ⊜) A mere 1.5km from the Gramado center, this hostel has 65 beds in both gender-segregated dorms and private rooms. The hostel is friendly, inviting and conveniently located on the bus line to Canela.

Pousada Metodista (☎ 3286 2299; www.gramadosite .com.br/pousadametodista; Av Borges de Medeiros 2889; s/d R$65/90) Sleep in the hallowed halls behind the Methodist church. Six small rooms have bathroom, plain walls and linoleum floors; larger dorms usually cater to church groups, go figure. There's no smoking.

Hotel Vovó Carolina (☎ 3286 2433; www.vovocaro lina.com.br; Av Borges de Medeiros 3129; s/d from R$126/154; ⊡) Right in the center, this hotel has small, carpeted rooms and no-nonsense service. Don't confuse it with the Pousada Vovó Carolina, which is a much larger place 5km south of the center.

our pick **Pousada Don Clemente** (☎ 3286 5433; Rua Bela Vista 41; s/d R$165/210; ⊡) Perched halfway up the steep road to Parque Knorr, this personal and homey B&B has frilly and spacious rooms

and a pleasant backyard patio available for guests' use.

Bella Terra Pousada (☎ 3286 3333; www.pousada bellaterra.com.br; Av Borges de Medeiros 2870; s/d/ste R$175/250/335; ⊡ ⊜) This building sits back from the road, which means it does not suffer from street noise. Indeed, the place is a center of peace and tranquility; large, light-filled rooms have big box-spring beds and marble bathrooms.

Hotel Casa da Montanha (☎ 3286 2544; www .hotelcasadamontanha.com.br; Av Borges de Medeiros 3166; r weekday/weekend from R$185/265; ☒ ⊡ ⊜ ⊠) Resembling a rustic chalet on the outside, this hotel is sumptuous and luxurious on the inside. Guestrooms have fancy, old-fashioned flair. Other on-site amenities include a rich, dark-wood library, a slick spa and a gourmet restaurant specializing in fresh trout and wild game.

Aardvark Inn (☎ 3286 0806; www.aardvarkinn.com.br; Rua Pedro Candiago 305; s/d R$250/300; ⊡ ⊜) Situated in a lovely residential district, this curiously named, small-scale inn is accented with refurbished wood, and most rooms have a private garden entrance. Sit by the fire or play with the giant chessboard in the backyard.

Eating

Gramado has no shortage of Italian, German and Swiss cuisine, reflecting the ethnic makeup of the region's original settlers. Freshwater trout is a local specialty.

Restaurante Vale Quanto Pesa (☎ 3286 3457; Rua São Pedro 401; meals R$15-18; ⊗ lunch & dinner Tue-Sun) A massive buffet at midday and a pizza *rodízio* by night guarantee to sate your appetite. The buffet features over 50 dishes, and the *rodízio* offers almost as many types of pizza pie.

Serra Grill (☎ 3036 1012; Rua São Pedro; buffet R$18; ⊗ 11am-3pm) People line up around the corner to get at this higher-quality buffet, which features grilled meats and standards like *feijoada* (beans and rice).

Gramado Café Colonial (☎ 3282 2317; Estrada Canela-Gramado; per person R$22; ⊗ lunch & dinner) This amazing *café colonial* (buffet) features more than 80 dishes, ranging from fresh salads and cold cuts to freshly baked bread to tasty *salgados* (snacks) – fried polenta being a specialty – to sweet pastries and desserts. Pay one price and you can sample them all. It lies midway between Canela and Gramado.

our pick **Ristorante Tomasini** (☎ 3286 4311; Av das Hortênsias 1189; meals R$30-40; ⊗ lunch & dinner) In a

RIO GRANDE DO SUL

warm, firelit dining room, Tomasini serves up tasty pasta dishes, grilled meats and seafood from its à la carte menu. Or try the excellent *seqüência de fondues*, which includes meat cooked on a hot rock, as well as cheese and chocolate fondue.

Gasthof Edelweiss (☎ 3286 1861; Rua da Carriérie 1119; meals R$30-50; ☒ lunch & dinner) Situated picturesquely just across from Lago Negro, this homey restaurant serves up the town's best German cuisine.

Getting There & Around

The town is small enough to get everywhere by foot. Frequent buses go to Porto Alegre (R$26, two hours, seven daily). Buses for Canela leave the main bus station every 10 to 20 minutes (R$1.80, 20 minutes).

CANELA

☎ 0xx54 41,100

While lacking Gramado's sophistication, Canela has a small-town charm of its own. Centered on a leafy green square, the village center is anchored at one end by the impressive Gothic Catedral de Pedra (stone cathedral). The streets are lined with shops and cafés. Although Canela is not as chic as Gramado, it offers cheaper accommodations and more convenient access to the state parks, which are popular hiking spots.

Information

Banco do Brasil (Praça João Corrêa) Money exchange and Visa ATMs.

Posto Telefônico (☎ 3303 1107; Av Julio de Castilhos 319) Internet access (per hour R$4.50) and call center.

Tourist information (☎ 3282 2200; www.canelaturismo.com.br; Praça João Corrêa)

War Zone Lan House (Av Osvaldo Aranha 333; per hr R$4; ☒ 10am-10pm) Internet access and computer games.

Sights & Activities

The major attraction of **Parque Estadual do Caracol** (☎ 3278 3035; admission R$10; ☒ 8:30am-5:30pm), 9km from Canela, is the spectacular Cascata do Caracol, a 130m free-falling waterfall. It's particularly attractive in the morning sun, when the water sparkles as it cascades over the granite lip. If you're feeling fit, you can walk to the base of the waterfall down (and back up) the 900-plus steps.

About 3km from Caracol, the **Parque Floresta Encantada de Canela** (☎ 3504 1405; www.canelatelefe ico.com.br; adult/child R$5/free; ☒ 9am-5pm, closed Thu) offers another perspective from across the canyon. A *teleférico* (chairlift) travels 830m up and down the mountainside, providing 20 minutes' worth of fabulous views of the canyon, the waterfall and Gramado in the distance. You can get off at either end and hike back to the entrance.

A 6km hike from Caracol brings you to **Parque da Ferradura** (☎ 9969 6785; admission R$8; ☒ 9am-5:30pm), named for the 420m horseshoe-shaped canyon formed by the Rio Santa Cruz. Well-marked trails take you to three lookouts. Also along the road to the park you'll come across **Castelinho**, the oldest house in the area.

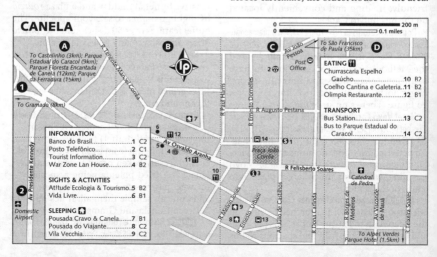

CANELA

0   200 m
0   0.1 miles

To Castelinho (3km); Parque
Estadual do Caracol (9km);
Parque Floresta Encantada
de Canela (12km); Parque
da Ferradura (15km)

To Gramado (8km)

To São Francisco
de Paula (35km)

Post Office

INFORMATION
Banco do Brasil...............1 C2
Posto Telefônico...............2 C1
Tourist Information............3 C2
War Zone Lan House............4 B2

SIGHTS & ACTIVITIES
Atitude Ecologia & Tourismo.5 B2
Vida Livre.....................6 B1

SLEEPING
Pousada Cravo & Canela.......7 B1
Pousada do Viajante..........8 C2
Vila Vecchia...................9 C2

EATING
Churrascaria Espelho
  Gaúcho......................10 B2
Coelho Cantina e Galeteria..11 B2
Olimpia Restaurante..........12 B1

TRANSPORT
Bus Station...................13 C2
Bus to Parque Estadual do
  Caracol.....................14 C2

Domestic Airport

Praça João Corrêa

R Felisberto Soares

Catedral de Pedra

To Alpes Verdes
Parque Hotel (1.5km)

This pioneer German home was built without the luxury of metal nails.

Tours

The following companies offer tours of adventure activities such as trekking, rappelling, rafting and cycling.

At!tude Ecologia & Tourismo (☎ 3282 6305; Shop 16, Av Osvaldo Aranha 391; trips per person R$80; ◷ 8:30am-noon & 2-5:30pm) Twice-daily trips visit Caracol, Ferradura and Castelinho, as well as Lago Negro in Gramado.

Vida Livre (☎ 3286 7326; www.vidalivreturismo.com.br; Room 302, Rua Madre Verônica 30; trips per person from R$50; ◷ 8:30am & 2pm) The standard four-hour trip visits all the local parks.

Sleeping

Prices listed here are for the high summer season (December to March).

Pousada do Viajante (☎ 3282 2017; www.pousadadoviajante.com.br; Rua Ernesto Urbani 1; s/d without bathroom from R$30/40; 🖳) 'Sleep good and cheap.' So promises this HI-affiliated hostel. And it lives up to its motto, with clean, quiet, single and double rooms, all with shared facilities. Discounts for HI members; breakfast costs R$6.

Vila Vecchia (☎ 3282 4220; Rua Melvin Jones 137; s/d R$72/105) This sweet Swiss-style chalet is trimmed with flower boxes and shutters. Inside, the rooms are simple and cheap. A wood-burning stove warms the common area.

Alpes Verdes Parque Hotel (☎ 3282 1162; www.alpesverdes.com.br; Rua Gilda T Bolognese 1001; s/d/tr R$135/175/195; 🖳 🞨) In a lovely green setting about 1.5km from town, this hotel features private chalets with excellent views of the Vale do Quilombo. Hospitable hosts are happy to ferry you back and forth to town.

Pousada Cravo & Canela (☎ 3282 1120; www.pousadacravoecanela.com.br; Rua Tenente Manoel Corrêa 144; r R$305-340; 🞨 🖳 🛜 🞨) Once the home of the German governor of the region, this plush pousada retains a sense of history. Many architectural details have been preserved, including the tile fireplace in the dining room and the original owner's collection of cuckoo clocks.

Eating

Olimpia Restaurante (☎ 3282 3888; Av Osvaldo Aranha 456; buffet R$12.50; ◷ lunch & dinner) This per-kilo restaurant is packed by noon, and for good reason. The well-stocked buffet is fresh and filling, and includes grilled meats, fresh vegetables and salads.

Coelho Cantina e Galeteria (☎ 3282 4224; Av Osvaldo Aranha 287; buffet R$15, ◷ lunch & dinner) The noon-time meal at Coelho is like a buffet, but they bring it to you. Save room for dessert, as you have your choice of 15 options!

Churrascaria Espelho Gaúcho (☎ 3282 4348; just off Av Osvaldo Aranha; meals R$15-20; ◷ lunch & dinner) A decent *churrascaria* with an all-the-meat-you-can-eat option.

Getting There & Around

Buses for Gramado leave the main bus station every 10 to 20 minutes (R$1.80, 20 minutes). Buses go to São Francisco de Paula (R$6, one hour), where you can connect to Cambará do Sul (R$10, two hours); and to Caxias do Sul (R$10, seven daily), where you can connect to Bento Gonçalves (R$5, hourly). Buses go frequently to Porto Alegre (R$25, 2½ hours, seven daily).

Two buses a day go to Parque do Caracol (R$1.50, 20 minutes), departing from Praça João Corrêa at 8:15am and noon and returning at 12:30pm and 6pm.

CAMBARÁ DO SUL

☎ 0xx54 / pop 7200

Located 186km northeast of Porto Alegre, this town serves as a base for both Parque Nacional de Aparados da Serra and Parque Nacional da Serra Geral, the national parks that are somewhat capriciously described as the 'Brazilian Grand Canyon.'

Cambará do Sul is a dusty little town centered on a disproportionately large church. At an altitude of 1000m, Cambará receives more snowfall than any other destination in Rio Grande do Sul, making it a popular destination during winter months (May to October, when prices are higher).

Cattle ranching has been the livelihood of this town, which retains an authentic *gaúcho* aura. But the economy is gradually giving way to ecotourism, as locals and visitors discover the area's nearby natural wonders. Cambará do Sul claims to be the 'capital of honey,' and you can sample this local sweet all over town.

Information

Cyber Serra (Rua Padre João Pazza 802; per hr R$4; ◷ 9am-11pm Mon-Sat, 5-10pm Sun) Internet access.

Tourist information office (☎ 3251 1320; www.cambaraonline.com.br; Rua 15 de Março) Across from the town's main church.

RIO GRANDE DO SUL

Sights & Activities

The magnificent **Parque Nacional de Aparados da Serra** (☎ 3251 1262; admission R$3; ☒ 9am-4pm Wed-Sun), 18km from the town of Cambará do Sul, stretches across the state line into Santa Catarina. Here, the vast, uninspired pasture-lands give way to a series of stunning canyons, where the earth opens up and drops to depths of 720m.

The park preserves one of the country's last *araucária* forests, which has earned it its protected status. But the main attraction is the **Cânion do Itaimbezinho**, a narrow, 5800m-long canyon with sheer parallel escarpments, ranging from 600m to 720m. Two waterfalls drop into this incision in the earth, which was formed by the Rio Perdiz' rush to the sea.

Three trails wind through the park. **Trilha do Vértice** runs for 2km to an observation point for the canyon and the Cascata do Andorinhas. **Trilha Cotovelo** is a 3km trail (2½ hours round-trip) passing by the Véu de Noiva waterfall, with wonderful vistas of the canyon.

For a completely different perspective, **Trilha do Rio do Boi** follows the base of the canyon for 7km, from the Posto Rio do Boi entrance. This last route is most easily accessed from the town of Praia Grande in Santa Catarina. A professional guide (see p370) is recommended for the challenging, loose, rocky trail. During rainy season it is closed because of the danger of flooding.

The adjacent **Parque Nacional da Serra Geral** (admission free), 23km from Cambará do Sul, contains two more canyons that rival Itaimbezinho. The **Cânion da Fortaleza** is an 8km stretch of escarpment with 900m drops. A gently inclining **Trilha do Mirante** leads about 7km to the edge of the canyon, yielding incredible views of the Cachoeira do Tigre Preto water-fall. The **Pedra do Segredo** is a tower of rocks that balances precariously on this precipice.

The **Cânion Malacara** is formed by the river of the same name; the **Trilha Piscina do Malacara** leads to a natural pool with cool, crystal waters and wonderful views.

About 18km west of Cambará do Sul, the 4km Trilha da Cachoeira leads to a small but spectacular waterfall, the **Cachoeira dos Venâncios** (admission R$3), which offers an opportunity for a cooling dip.

Tours

Local companies provide transportation and guides for the canyons (at a cost of R$35 per person for Itaimbezinho or Fortaleza). Meanwhile, a guided trek on the Trilha do Rio do Boi is about R$100. Horseback riding and mountain-climbing expeditions are also available.

Canyon Turismo (☎ 3251 1027; www.canyonturismo .com.br; Av Getúlio Vargas 1098)

Nativa Ecoturismo (☎ 3251 1013; Av Getúlio Vargas 1282)

Sleeping

Cambará has many economical, family-run inns, while higher-end options are outside of town. Camping in the parks is strictly pro-hibited, but the tourist-information office can help you locate municipal camp grounds.

Prices quoted here are for the high season (May to October). In other seasons, expect a discount of 25% or more.

Pousada Paraíso (☎ 3251 1352; www.paraisopousada .com.br; Rua Antonio Raupp 678; r per person R$40) Set on the edge of the village, this two-story home can house 40 guests in its fresh, simple rooms. It's the best deal in town.

Pousada Itaimbeleza (☎ 3251 1367; www.itaim bezinho.tur.br; Rua Dona Úrsula 648; s/d from R$50/100) Cute, comfy chalets are clustered around a garden bursting with birds and flowers. The accommodating owner, Loreni, is ever willing to assist with arrangements for trips to the canyons.

our pick **Pousada Corucacas** (☎ 3251 1123; www.coru cacas.com; per person r R$90) About 1km from town on the road to Ouro Verde, this working farm has rustic rooms and a big-sky setting. Endless opportunities for horseback riding and hiking are just out the back door, and a fireplace heats up the common room in the evening. Price includes both breakfast and dinner.

Estalagem da Colina (☎ 3251 1746; Av Getúlio Vargas 80; d R$170-190, q R$300; 🖳) On the edge of Cambará, this place boasts 10 stylish wooden chalets built from recycled materials. In the main lodge, guests can congregate around the fire or enjoy an excellent dinner.

Refúgio Ecológico Pedra Afiada (☎ 0xx48-3532 1059; www.pedraafiada.com.br; s R$310, d R$550-700) Splendidly located within the Cânion Malacara, this isolated inn boasts a gorgeous stone fireplace for chilly nights and a fabulous rooftop deck for clear days. Hiking, horseback riding, rafting and rappelling are all at your doorstep. Even if you don't stay here, you can explore the extensive trails on the 32-hectare reserve for R$5.

RIO GRANDE DO SUL

Parador Casa da Montanha (☎ 3286 2544; www .paradorcasadamontanha.com.br; r from R$435) Midway between Cambará and Itaimbezinho, the Parador is the poshest place in the region. Surrounded by pine forests and waterfalls, lodging is in heated, elevated tents that somehow combine luxury and rusticity. Prices include half-pension and local tours, and rates drop about 40% during the week.

Eating

Dining options in Cambará are limited.

Cafe Expresso Mata Bicho (☎ 3251 1203; Rua 20 de Setembro 90; meals R$12-15; ☑ 8am-8pm Mon-Sat) Heading out on the trail? Stop by here for a sandwich, a piece of fruit, a granola bar and a juice – packed to go.

Restaurante Bom Paladar (☎ 3251 1280; Rua João Francisco Ritter 842; meals R$20; ☑ 5-10pm Tue-Sat) Has a homey wood interior and offers filling food.

O Casarão (☎ 3251 1711; Rua João Francisco Ritter 969; meals R$20; ☑ 3-10pm Tue-Sun) This is a slightly upscale option with organic produce, homemade pastas and local wines.

Galpão Costaneira (☎ 3251 1005; Rua Dona Úrsula 1069; meals R$20-30; ☑ 11am-11pm Wed-Sat) If the *gaúcho* atmosphere has got you in the mood for *churrascaria*, try this option with live music on weekends.

Getting There & Around

Two daily buses go to São Francisco de Paula (R$18, two hours), with connections to Porto Alegre or Canela and Gramado. One daily bus goes to Caxias do Sul, where you can connect to Bento Gonçalves.

If you are coming from the north, a direct bus runs to Torres three times a week. Otherwise, you can connect in Tainhas.

The parks are not serviced by public buses. You can take a taxi from Cambará to the parks (R$80 to R$100, one way). Local tour companies (see p370) are a reasonable alternative, especially if they can hook you up with a small group. Contact them as far in advance as possible.

ROTA MISSÕES

Soon after the discovery of the New World, the Portuguese and Spanish kings authorized Catholic orders to create missions to convert the natives. The Jesuits were the most successful order, establishing a series of missions across Paraguay, Bolivia, Brazil and Argentina. At its height in the 1720s, this prosperous 'nation' claimed 30 mission villages inhabited by more than 150,000 Guarani people (see the boxed text, p373).

Today, all 30 missions are in ruins. Together, they form the Rota Missões, or 'Missions Route,' a network of pilgrimage sites for the faithful and the curious. Seven are in Brazil (in the northwestern part of Rio Grande do Sul), eight are in southern Paraguay and 15 are in northeastern Argentina. For an excellent overview of the Brazilian missions see the website of the **Rota Missões** (www.rotamissoes .com.br, in Portuguese).

SANTO ÂNGELO

☎ 0xx55 / pop 75,400

This small, pleasant city is the regional transportation hub and jumping-off point for exploring the Brazilian missions. The impressive cathedral, on **Praça da Catedral**, is a contemporary replica of the church at São Miguel das Missões (p372). A few blocks north, the **Monumento ao Índio** remembers Sepé Tiaraju, the leader of the indigenous resistance during the Guarani War.

Orientation & Information

Av Brasil is the main commercial street that runs east–west through the center of town. The Praça da Catedral is four blocks south along Rua Marques do Herval.

Maps of the city are available at the hotels listed under Sleeping & Eating (p372).

Banco do Brasil (cnr Av Brasil & Rua Marques do Herval) Money exchange and ATMs.

Suprema Internet (☎ 3313 2016; Rua Marques do Herval 1448; per hr R$4.50; ☑ 10am-10pm)

Tours

Without your own vehicle, it is difficult to visit all of the missions independently. An organized tour offers a reasonable alternative, but try to contact the companies below well in advance.

Caminho das Missões (☎ 3312 9632) Leads walking and biking tours of the missions, ranging from three to 14 days.

Golden Travel (☎ 3314 2773; Rua Marques do Herval 1446) The traditional three-day circuit (R$425) includes São João Batista (p372), São Miguel das Missões (p372) and the Santuário de Caaró (p372) and the agency can also make arrangements to visit international missions.

Sleeping & Eating

Turis Hotel Santo Ângelo (☎ 3313 5255; www.santo angeloturishotel.com.br; Rua Antônio Manoel 726; s/d R$55/70, s/d with air-con R$87/110; ⊠) Rooms vary widely, but none of them are going to win any design awards. Nonetheless, it's a decent budget option, just one block west of the Praça da Catedral.

Hotel Maerkli (☎ 3313 2127; Av Brasil 1000; s/d R$137/165; ⊠ ☎) A more upscale option, this hotel caters to business travelers and tourist groups, who appreciate the attentive service and well-appointed rooms. It's on the main drag, one block west of Praça Leônidas Ribas.

Quick (☎ 3313 4488; cnr Av Brasil & Rua Marques do Herval; meals R$12-20) Featuring a hearty lunchtime buffet and an extensive late-night menu, this is the best of several options located along this stretch between Av Brasil and the main square.

Getting There & Around

The **bus station** (☎ 3313 2618) is 1km west of the center. One daily bus goes to Bento Gonçalves (R$78, seven hours) and one overnight bus goes to Foz do Iguaçu (R$118; 12 hours) in Paraná. Buses run frequently between Santo Ângelo and Porto Alegre (R$83, *leito* R$108, seven hours, eight daily).

Four times a day, buses go to São Miguel das Missões (R$10, one hour). Renting a car from **Sulmive** (☎ 3312 1000; Rua Marechal Floriano 747) is a good option for visiting the Brazilian missions, but it is difficult to take a rental car over the border to visit international missions.

SÃO MIGUEL DAS MISSÕES
☎ 0xx55 / pop 3000

The best preserved and most moving of the Brazilian missions is **São Miguel Arcanjo** (adult/ child R$5/2.50; ⏰ 9am-noon & 2-6pm Mar-Sep, to 8pm Oct-Feb), located in the village of São Miguel das Missões, 53km southwest of Santo Ângelo. The elegant church, designed by an Italian architect who was also a Jesuit friar, earned Unesco World Heritage status in 1984. It is surrounded by mystical ruins of the Jesuit settlement, which evokes 'paradise lost' (see the boxed text, p373).

The archaeological site also includes the excellent little **Museu das Missões**. Designed by Lúcio Costa of Brasília fame, the museum contains an impressive collection of religious artifacts that were rescued from the ruins. A few Guarani families hang around selling handicrafts. A spectacular, if campy, **sound-and-light show** (adult/child R$5/2.50; ⏰ 9pm Aug-Feb, 8pm Mar-Apr, 7pm May-Jul) illustrates the history of the missions.

Orientation & Information

The mission is about 500m west of the bus station, and the small commercial center lies in between. The **tourist office** (☎ 3381 1294) is near the entrance of the mission.

Sleeping & Eating

The last bus to Santo Ângelo leaves before the sound-and-light show, so it's worth spending the night. A couple of casual restaurants are clustered around the bus station.

ourpick Pousada das Missões (☎ 3381 1202; www.pousadatematica.com.br; Rua São Nicalau 601; dm HI member/nonmember R$42/52; s/d/tr/q R$65/106/144/168; ⊠ ▯ ☎ ▣) Student groups utilize the dorm-style accommodation at this HI hostel, but more discerning travelers will be comfortable in the private rooms, each labeled with a Guarani name and accompanying explanation. It is located just behind the archaeological site; follow signs from the entrance. You can get a fan and TV for R$15 more. There's also a good restaurant.

Wilson Park Hotel (☎ 3381 2000; www.wilson parkhotel.com.br; Rua São Miguel 664; s/d/tr R$100/145/190; ⊠ ▯ ▣) Boasting mission-style architecture, stylish rooms and an international restaurant, this fancy resort is not exactly catering to pilgrims. Excellent facilities include tennis courts, a football field and a swimming pool.

Getting There & Away

From the **bus station** (☎ 3381 1226) in Missões, four daily buses go to Santo Ângelo (R$8, one hour).

OTHER BRAZILIAN SITES
São João Batista

Midway between Santo Ângelo and São Miguel, little remains from the mission at **São João Batista** (☎ 3329 1170; admission free; ⏰ 9am-noon & 2-6pm Mar-Sep, to 8pm Oct-Feb). With a little imagination, it is possible to make out the structures of the church, the cemetery and the school.

Caaró

About 20km west of São Miguel, the **Santuário de Caaró** (☎ 3505 7427; ⏰ 8:30-11:30am & 1:30-6pm Mon-Fri) is the place where the region's spiritual history is most alive. A modest monument honors three priests who were killed

RIO GRANDE DO SUL

by *bandeirantes* in 1626. One of the victims, Roque González, has been canonized. This site attracts a stream of pilgrims, especially in November, around the anniversary of St Roque's martyrdom.

São Lourenço Mártir

In 1690, a group from the Argentine reduction of Santa Maria founded **São Lourenço Mártir** (☎ 3352 2699; admission free; ⏱ 9am-noon & 2-6pm Mar-Sep, to 8pm Oct-Feb). It is located about 18km west of the turn-off to São Miguel, 9km north off the road to São Luiz Gonzaga (BR-285). The church, cemetery and school are still discernable and there is a small exhibit of findings from excavations. The most impressive find – the grand image of São Lourenço that once graced the church – is now held at the Museu das Missões (p372) in São Miguel.

São Nicolau

About 120km west of Santo Ângelo, this mission was an artistic center, producing painting, ceramics and wood sculpture. Today, all that remains at the **archaeological site** (☎ 3363 1441; ⏱ 8-11:30am & 1:30-5pm Mon-Fri, 1:30-5pm Sat & Sun) is the Jesuits' stone cellar. The **Museu Municipal** (☎ 3356 1247; Rua João Fagundes 131; admission free; ⏱ 9-11:30am & 1:30-4:45pm Mon-Fri) contains an interesting exhibit on Jesuit-Guarani culture.

If you make it here, you can spend the night at **Pousada dos Jesuítas** (☎ 3363 1101; Cel Mamed de Souza 1046; d R$80), 50m from the mission site.

ARGENTINE & PARAGUAYAN MISSIONS

Posadas is the best base for exploring the Argentine missions, the highlight of which is San Ignacio Miní (60km northeast), not to be

---

PARADISE LOST

In 1608, the governor of the Spanish province of Paraguay ordered the local Jesuit leader, Fray Diego de Torres, to convert the local Tupi and Guarani people. The Jesuits established missions across a vast region that encompassed much of southern Brazil, as well as portions of southern Paraguay and northern Argentina.

Unlike their brethren elsewhere in the New World, the Jesuits made a concerted effort to convert the indigenous people without destroying their culture or language. The missions became centers of culture and intellect, as well as religion. The arts flourished, combining elements of European and Guarani music and painting. Scholars created a written form of the Tupi-Guarani language and, beginning in 1704, published several works, using one of South America's earliest printing presses. The missions produced sophisticated sculpture, metallurgy, ceramics and musical instruments. In an age of monarchies and institutionalized slavery, the missions were an island of idealism, where wealth was divided equitably; and religion, intellect and arts were cultivated in tandem.

From the beginning, the missions faced threats from the outside world. In the 1620s they were harassed by Portuguese *bandeirantes*, bands of Paulistas who raided the interior in search of gold and *índios* (indigenous people) to enslave. Thousands of *índios* were captured, and the 13 missions of Guayra (present-day Paraná) were eventually abandoned. Beginning in the 1630s, the Jesuits consolidated their position in 30 sites across the northwest corner of present-day Rio Grande do Sul, as well as in Argentina and Paraguay. These sites, now in ruins, constitute the contemporary Rota Missões (Missions Route).

To a large part, it was the success of the missions that brought about their downfall. The independent-minded Jesuits became an embarrassment to Rome, and to the Spanish and Portuguese kings. In 1750 the Treaty of Madrid dictated that the sites be handed over to Portuguese rule, which would not protect the natives from enslavement. The Guarani were commanded to evacuate in 1754, but they refused to abandon their settlements and thus incited the Guarani War. In 1756 a combined Spanish-Portuguese army attacked the missions, killing more than 1500 Guaranis and selling many more into slavery, thus decimating the Guarani population. It was a tragic, bloody end to an amazing social experiment.

The missions were lauded by great thinkers from Voltaire to Montesquieu as a real incarnation of Christian utopia and destroyed by the very forces that created it. Robert De Niro and Jeremy Irons relive this story in the 1986 film *The Mission*, a moving, fictional account of these events (see also p69).

confused with San Ignacio Guazú, which is in Paraguay. Use either Encarnación or Posadas (just across the border) as a base for visiting the missions of Paraguay, where the most important site is the red stone ruins of Trinidad de Parana, 50km northeast of Encarnación.

The most direct route to the Argentine and Paraguayan missions is via the border town of Porto Xavier, 145km northwest of Santo Ângelo. From here it's possible to cross the Rio Uruguai by barge to the Argentine town of Santo Tomé.

LITORAL GAÚCHO

On paper, it sounds amazing: a 500km strip of Brazilian coastline that forms one seemingly endless beach, stretching from Torres on the Santa Catarina border, all the way to Chuí at the Uruguayan border. Unfortunately, the reality is less enticing. The water tends to be murky and the beaches are undistinguished, with little geographical variation.

TORRES
☎ 0xx51 / pop 34,000

On the border with Santa Catarina, Torres is the exception to the state's uninviting coastline. The town, 205km north of Porto Alegre, has attractive (if crowded) beaches punctuated by basalt rock formations. In winter, Antarctic currents bring cold, hard winds to the coast; the crowds disappear, and most hotels shut down from May to November.

Every year in April, Torres hosts a **hot-air balloon festival** (www.festivaldebalonismo.com.br), a spectacular sight.

Orientation
Av Barão do Rio Branco runs west from the beach at Prainha. Praia Grande stretches north from here, while Praia da Cal is to the south. The bus station is on the west side of the violin-shaped Lagoa do Violoão on Av José Bonifácio.

Information
Banco do Brasil (Av Barão do Rio Branco 236) For money exchange or ATMs.
Loja de Conveniência (Av Barão do Rio Branco 217; internet per hr R$3) One of many internet cafés along the main streets.
Tourist information office (☎ 3626 1937; www.torres.tur.br; cnr Avs Barão do Rio Branco & Silva Jardim) Publishes a useful city map.

Sights & Activities
Praia Grande, the town's main beach, is quite calm, but surfers can head 2km south to **Praia da Cal** for decent waves. Nearby, an 18m-high lighthouse sits atop the **Morro do Farol**, an excellent vantage point to view the city.

Further south, the gardens of **Parque Guarita** provide a gorgeous natural setting for cultural events and other recreation. The nearby beach of the same name is considered the most beautiful in Torres.

Tours
Passeios Náuticos (☎ 3626 2933; per person R$22) offers boat trips to Ilha dos Lobos, an ecological reserve that is home to a colony of sea lions between March and November. From the end of Av Silva Jardim, walk along the Rio Mampituba to Ponte Pênsil.

Sleeping
Prices listed are for summer (December to February) – expect discounts of 20% to 40% between March and November and a 25% hike during the hot-air-balloon festival.

Hotel Costa Azul (☎ 3664 3291; Av José Bonifácio 382; s/d R$30/60; ✹) This small, friendly place is an excellent option near the bus station. Rooms are slightly cramped, but they are clean, carpeted and fresh-smelling.

Pousada da Prainha (☎ 3626 2454; www.pousadadaprainha.com.br; Rua Alferes Feirreira Porto 138; s/d/tr R$75/100/160; ✹) This attractive, colonial-style hotel is a block from the quiet beach at Prainha.

Pousada La Barca (☎ 3664 2925; www.pousadalabarca.com.br; Av Beira Mar 1020; s/d R$100/180, s/d/tr with sea views R$285/320/355; ✹ ▢ ⁀ ▦) Sleek and sophisticated, this contemporary pousada is an upscale option on the beach. Rooms are equipped with ceiling fans and big balconies for maximum sea-breeze action.

Solar Inn (☎ 3626 3731; Av Beira Mar 1713; r R$180-250; ✹ ⁀ ▦) For its excellent beachfront location and welcoming small size (18 rooms), you can't beat this new inn on Prainha beach. Less luxurious – but more convivial – than the hulking Dunas Hotel next door.

Eating
Pizzaria Nápole (☎ 3664 2657; Av Benjamin Constant 163; meals R$12-25; ◷ dinner) With 40 types of pizza, you're bound to find something you like. It's one block south of Av Barão do Rio Branco.

Doce Art (☎ 3664 5591; Av Silva Jardim 295; meals R$15-25; ◷ 9am-3pm Mon-Sat) Come here for hot coffee, fresh juice and tasty pastries in the morning, or sandwiches and pastas at lunchtime. Outdoor seating overlooks Praça XV.

Restaurante A Prainha (☎ 3626 4566; Rua Joaquim Porto 151; meals R$15-25; ☺ 11am-9pm) Two blocks from the beach of the same name, this casual restaurant serves seafood and typical Brazilian platters on its pleasant, shady porch.

Getting There & Around

The town is small and all conveniences are accessible by foot, including the **bus station** (☎ 3664 1787). Destinations include Porto Alegre (R$30 to R$38, three hours, six daily) and Florianópolis (R$56, five hours, five daily). A direct bus goes to Cambará do Sul three times a week; otherwise, you can connect in Tainhas.

RIO GRANDE

☎ 0xx53 / pop 200,000

Located at the mouth of Lagoa dos Patos, Rio Grande was founded in 1737 to guard the disputed southern border of the Portuguese empire. The region's oldest city, it blossomed during the 19th century, when its port became a vital link in the profitable beef trade. Rio Grande has a charming historic center that is home to some interesting colonial and neoclassical buildings. The excellent **Museu Oceanográfico** (☎ 3232 9107; Rua Capitão Heitor Perdigão 10; admission free; ☺ 9-11:30am & 2-6pm Tue-Sun) is one of the best in Latin America.

Sleeping & Eating

our pick **Paris Hotel** (☎ 3231 3866; www.hotelvillamoura .com.br; R Marechal Floriano 112; s/d R$80/100) The oldest in Rio Grande do Sul, this hotel built in 1826 exhibits a bygone grandeur in its high ceilings, antique furnishings and leafy courtyard. At this price, it would be silly not to sleep in an antique bed and lounge in a 19th-century patio that once hosted Dom Pedro II.

Atlântico Rio Grande (☎ 3231 3833; www.hotelisat lantico.com.br; Rua Duque de Caixas 53; s/d from R$99/109; ☒ ☐ ☜) It will only catch your eye if you appreciate 1960s chic, but it has lovely views of the waterfront and adjacent park.

Hotels in Rio Grande have cafés and restaurants emphasizing steaks. Vegetarians can get by on pastas and salads.

Getting There & Away

From the **bus station** (☎ 3232 8444), buses connect Rio Grande with all major cities in south-

ern Brazil, including Chuí (R$39 to R$46, 3½ hours, two daily) on the Uruguayan border. However, Pelotas (R$10, one hour, every 30 minutes) is the major transportation hub.

CHUÍ

☎ 0xx53 / pop 5500

Located 245km south of Rio Grande, this border town is both Brazilian and Uruguayan (Chuí and Chuy, respectively). The main drag acts as the border: on the northern (Brazilian) side it is Av Uruguaí, while on the southern (Uruguayan) side it is Av Brasil. Tourists can wander freely on both sides of the town; Portuguese and Spanish are spoken interchangeably.

The Uruguayan side is home to many duty-free shops and casinos, so Chuy attracts its fair share of smugglers and gamblers. Unless these are your games, you may not wish to stick around longer than necessary.

Information

Both Brazil and Uruguay maintain consulates here. It takes about 24 hours to get a visa for either country, so plan accordingly.
Brazilian consulate (☎ 3265 1011; Rua Tito Fernandez 147)
Uruguayan consulate (☎ 3265 1151; Rua Venezuela 311)

Most establishments accept Brazilian and Uruguayan currency as well as US dollars. There is a **Banco do Brasil** (cnr Rua Venezuela & Rua Chile) two blocks from the Brazilian bus station. Money-exchange offices sit at the corner of Avs General Artigas and Brasil.

Sleeping & Eating

If you're stuck in Chuí, you can stay at the **Rivero Hotel** (☎ 3265 1271; Calle Colombia 163; s/d R$20/40) on the Brazilian side or **Nuevo Hotel Plaza** (☎ 598-474 2309; www.hotelplaza.chuynet.com; Plaça de Chuy; s/d R$20/40; ☒) in Uruguay. A semi-upscale option is **Bertelli Chuí Hotel** (☎ 3265 1266; r R$110; ☒ ☐ ☒), about 2km north of town on BR-471. Good *churrascarias* line the Uruguayan side of Av Brasil.

Getting There & Away

GETTING TO/FROM URUGUAY

The Brazilian border post is on Av Argentina, several kilometers north of town. You do not need a visa or entry or exit stamp to visit the town; however, if you are continuing into

Uruguay, you will need to tell the driver to stop at the border post for an exit stamp.

In Uruguay, the border post is 2.5km south of town. The bus will stop again for the Uruguayan officials to check your Brazilian exit stamp and Uruguayan visa (if you need one). Stop here for an exit stamp if you are entering Brazil. If you are on a *leito,* the bus crew will handle formalities on both sides of the border for you.

BUS

The Brazilian bus station is located on Rua Venezuela about three blocks from Av Brasil. Buses go to Pelotas (R$45, four hours, six daily), Rio Grande (R$46, four hours, two daily), and Porto Alegre (R$73 to R$85, seven hours). You can buy tickets to Montevideo (five hours) and other Uruguayan destinations from the bus agencies along Calle Leonardo Oliveira on the Uruguayan side.

Brasília

Brazil's futuristic capital is an attempt to create a workable, modern utopia. It's the result of a long-harnessed Brazilian dream of an inland capital, carved out of nowhere in the 1950s in a spectacular feat of urban planning, architectural design and political prophecy.

The purpose-built city and its surrounding area, known as the Distrito Federal (DF), occupies part of the Brazilian central plateau – the Planalto – with rolling hills and a large artificial lake, Paranoá. Wide-open, spectacular cerulean skies characterize the whole area, a picturesque backdrop to Brasília's clean-lined design and marvelous architecture.

For a nation often tipped as the country of the future, Brasília is its revolutionary testament to that end, a living museum lauded the world over for everything from its avant-garde grid of perfectly planned streets to its uberorganized residential apartment and commercial blocks (though the city is not without its detractors). As Brazil's seat of government, it's a city of bureaucrats and government workers, all of whom relish the national capital as a '60s version of a third-millennium city. It remains the only city in the world constructed in the 20th century to achieve World Cultural Heritage designation by Unesco.

Just over 50 years since its inauguration, Brasília is affluent, well manicured and lively. If you're interested in modern architecture, you'll easily spend a few days visiting the city's impressive buildings and monuments, each day fueled by some of Brazil's top restaurants and vibrant *vida nocturna*.

HIGHLIGHTS

- Step inside the ethereal **Santuário Dom Bosco** (p384) and watch your 'seen one church, seen them all' attitude adjusted on the spot
- Cleanse your soul or just take a walk on the weird side at the **Templo da Boa Vontade** (p383)
- Watch the sun set over the monuments from the **TV Tower** (p382)
- Dance to the sensual rhythms of samba at **Arena Futebol Clube** (p387)
- Cruise Brasília's futuristic architecture at night when the **Praça dos Trés Poderes** (p382) takes on an otherworldly glow

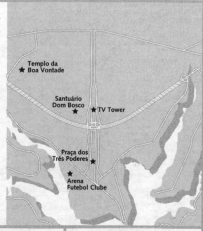

- TELEPHONE CODE: 061 ■ POPULATION: 2.6 MILLION ■ AREA: 5802 SQ KM

BRASÍLIA

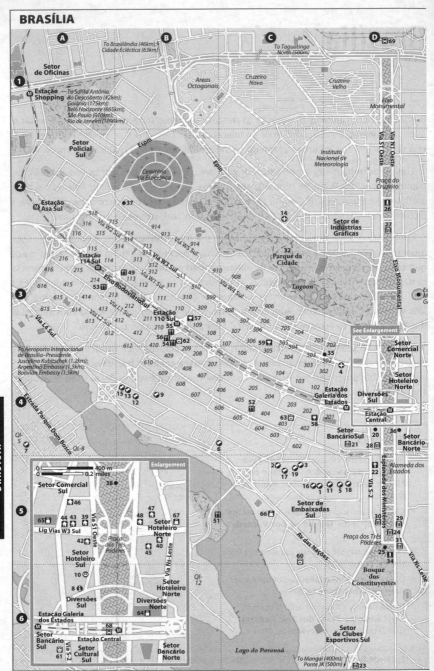

BRASÍLIA

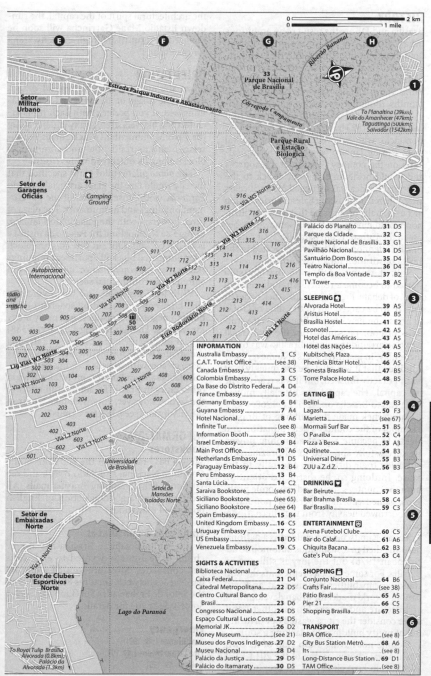

BRASÍLIA (side tab)

Scale: 0 — 2 km / 0 — 1 mile

To Planaltina (39km);
Vale do Amanhecer (47km);
Taguatinga (500km);
Salvador (1542km)

To Royal Tulip Brasília
Alvorada (0.8km);
Palácio da
Alvorada (1.3km)

Map labels:
Setor Militar Urbano
Setor de Garagens Oficiais
Autódromo Internacional
Estádio Mané Garrincha
Setor de Embaixadas Norte
Setor de Clubes Esportivos Norte
Universidade de Brasília
Setor de Mansões Isoladas Norte
Lago do Paranoá
Parque Nacional de Brasília
Parque Rural e Estação Biológica
Camping Ground
Estrada Parque Industria e Abastecimento
Córrego do Campoamento
Ribeirão Bananal
Via WS Norte
Via W3 Norte
Via W2 Norte
Via W4 Norte
Via W1 Norte
Eixo Rodoviário Norte
Via L1 Norte
Via L4 Norte
Via L2 Norte
Via L3 Norte
Lig Vias W3 Norte

INFORMATION
Australia Embassy	1 C5
C.A.T. Tourist Office	(see 38)
Canada Embassy	2 C5
Colombia Embassy	3 C5
Da Base do Distrito Federal	4 D4
France Embassy	5 D5
Germany Embassy	6 B4
Guyana Embassy	7 A4
Hotel Nacional	8 A6
Infinite Tur	(see 8)
Information Booth	(see 38)
Israel Embassy	9 B4
Main Post Office	10 A6
Netherlands Embassy	11 D5
Paraguay Embassy	12 B4
Peru Embassy	13 B4
Santa Lúcia	14 C2
Saraiva Bookstore	(see 67)
Siciliano Bookstore	(see 65)
Siciliano Bookstore	(see 64)
Spain Embassy	15 B4
United Kingdom Embassy	16 C5
Uruguay Embassy	17 C5
US Embassy	18 D5
Venezuela Embassy	19 C5

SIGHTS & ACTIVITIES
Biblioteca Nacional	20 D4
Caixa Federal	21 D4
Catedral Metropolitana	22 D5
Centro Cultural Banco do Brasil	23 D6
Congresso Nacional	24 D5
Espaço Cultural Lucio Costa	25 D5
Memorial JK	26 D2
Money Museum	(see 21)
Museu dos Povos Indigenas	27 D2
Museu Nacional	28 D4
Palácio da Justiça	29 D5
Palácio do Itamaraty	30 D5
Palácio do Planalto	31 D5
Parque da Cidade	32 C3
Parque Nacional de Brasília	33 G1
Pavilhão Nacional	34 D5
Santuário Dom Bosco	35 D4
Teatro Nacional	36 D4
Templo da Boa Vontade	37 B2
TV Tower	38 A5

SLEEPING
Alvorada Hotel	39 A5
Aristus Hotel	40 B5
Brasília Hostel	41 E2
Econotel	42 A5
Hotel das Américas	43 A5
Hotel das Nações	44 A5
Kubitschek Plaza	45 B5
Phenicia Bittar Hotel	46 A5
Sonesta Brasília	47 B5
Torre Palace Hotel	48 B5

EATING
Belini	49 B3
Lagash	50 F3
Marietta	(see 67)
Mormaii Surf Bar	51 B5
O Paraíba	52 C4
Pizza à Bessa	53 A3
Quitinete	54 B3
Universal Diner	55 B3
ZUU a.Z.d.Z.	56 B3

DRINKING
Bar Beirute	57 B3
Bar Brahma Brasília	58 C4
Bar Brasília	59 C3

ENTERTAINMENT
Arena Futebol Clube	60 C5
Bar do Calaf	61 A6
Chiquita Bacana	62 B3
Gate's Pub	63 C4

SHOPPING
Conjunto Nacional	64 B6
Crafts Fair	(see 38)
Pátio Brasil	65 A5
Pier 21	66 C5
Shopping Brasília	67 B5

TRANSPORT
BRA Office	(see 8)
City Bus Station Metrô	68 A6
Its	(see 8)
Long-Distance Bus Station	69 D1
TAM Office	(see 8)

HISTORY

Brasília and DF are the result of an ambitious urban project, which was set in motion by bold President Juscelino Kubitschek, and orchestrated by architect Oscar Niemeyer, urban planner Lúcio Costa and landscape architect Burle Marx. The new city was built in just 41 months, though it was a long time coming.

The concept of an inland capital was first conceived in 1823 by Brazilian statesman José Bonifácio, who believed moving the capital from Rio de Janeiro was central to capitalizing on the country's vast inland resources and would bring an economic shock to the interior. His idea was shrugged off until years later, when Dom Bosco, a Salesian priest living in Turin, Italy, prophesied that a new civilization would emerge in Brazil, somewhere between the 15th and 20th parallels. That caught Brazil's attention and land was allocated in the 1891 constitution for a new capital.

Still, it wasn't until 1955 that Brasília started to become a reality. After almost 150 years of debate, President Kubitschek ordered the DF to be carved out of the state of Goiás to house the new capital, Brasília. With millions of poor peasants from the Northeast working around the clock, Brasília was built, incredibly, in just three years (Niemeyer later admitted that it was all done too quickly) – it wasn't exactly finished, but it was ready to be the capital. The capital was officially moved from Rio to Brasília on April 21, 1960.

Kubitschek made the building of Brasília a symbol of the country's determination and ability to become a great economic power. He successfully appealed to all Brazilians to put aside their differences and rally to the cause. In doing so, he distracted attention from the country's social and economic problems, gained enormous personal popularity and borrowed heavily from the international banks.

Today, Kubitschek is heralded as a national hero (he died in a suspicious automobile accident in 1976) but the jury is still out on Brasília. For some, the city represents the outstanding capabilities of this great and vast nation, a world model for urban development, architecture and society. On the other hand, some consider the city a wasted opportunity, full of pretty buildings but lacking a soul.

Despite not having a top club of its own, Brasília was chosen as one of the 2014 FIFA World Cup host cities and, in keeping with the architectural spirit of the capital, the rundown Estádio Mané Garrincha will soon be replaced by a futuristic, high-capacity arena for the event.

ORIENTATION

From the air, Brasília's millennial design evokes the image of an airplane (or a hummingbird, if you prefer), with each of its architectural marvels strategically laid out along the Eixo Monumental (which forms the fuselage), and its residential and commercial blocks along its outspread wings (asas).

The plano piloto (pilot plan) specified that the city would face the giant artificial Lago do Paranoá. In the fuselage are all the government buildings and monuments. The plaza of three powers – with the Palácio do Planalto, Congresso Nacional and the Palácio da Justiça – is in the cockpit. Out on the asas are block after numbered block of apartment buildings (known as superquadras or quadras), each with its own commercial sector.

With long distances and harrowing six-lane highways connected by spaghetti junctions to negotiate, Brasília is not really a city for walkers. Though renting a car (see p388) is trial by fire, the city however is a driving dreamland whose big picture becomes all the more clearer with wheels. Driving here is incalculably safer and more comfortable than in other cities in Brazil. To get the full effect of the layout, however, you must take a tour of the city by air (see p384 for details).

INFORMATION

Bookstores

Saraiva has branches on the 2nd floor of the Conjunto Nacional and Pátio Brasil, and the 1st floor of the Shopping Brasília malls. All locations have a good selection of English books and magazines.

Embassies & Consulates

As the national capital, Brasília has a large chunk of real estate devoted to embassies and consulates. Most are located along Av das Nações between Quadras 801 and 809 in the Setor de Embaixadas Sul (Embassy Sector South). See p703 for details.

Emergency

Ambulance (☎ 192)
Fire department (☎ 193)
Police (☎ 190)

Internet Access

There is at least one internet café in both Pátio Brasil (2nd floor) and Shopping Brasília malls (ground floor), as well as at the airport.

Medical Services

Da Base do Distrito Federal (☎ 3325 5050; SMHS 101)
Santa Lúcia (☎ 3445 0000; SHLS, Quadra 716, Conjunto C)

Money

There are banks with moneychanging facilities in the Setor Bancário Sul (SBS; Banking Sector South) and Setor Bancário Norte (SBN; Banking Sector North). Both sectors are close to the city bus station. All the major malls and the airport have a variety of ATMs, most with Cirrus/MasterCard/Visa networking. Travel agencies will change cash dollars and often give better rates.

Post

Main post office (SHS Quadra 2, Bloco B; ⊗ 9am-5pm Mon-Fri) There are also branches in the arrivals hall of the airport and at the main malls.

Tourist Information

For a list of attractions, simply pick up a brochure from the front desk of any large hotel or travel agency. Though there is a scattering of information offices in the hotel district and a small booth at the TV Tower, they are either rarely open of bereft of material.

CAT tourist office (airport; ⊗ 8am-10pm) Don't leave the airport without stopping here. Most of the staff speak English and they offer a wealth of information.

Travel Agencies

Any number of travel agencies in the Hotel Nacional complex and at the airport can help you book flights and rent cars.

Infinite Tur (☎ 3321 0559; Hotel Nacional, SHS Quadra 1; ⊗ 8:30am-7pm Mon-Sat) One of the most reliable agencies that works with the major airlines.

SIGHTS
Praça do Cruzeiro

The tomb of JK (President Juscelino Kubitschek) lies underneath eerily beautiful stained glass by French artist Marianne Peretti

---

ADDRESSES FOR THE LOGICAL MIND

Brasília's addresses are as futuristic as its architecture – a series of numbers and letters that look baffling at first but are easy to decipher once you know what all the acronyms mean.

For example, the address for Pensão da Zenilda is SQS 704, Bloco Q, Casa 29. That means it's in Super Quadra South 704, *bloco* (building) Q, *casa* (house) 29. The first digit in the address (7) shows the position east or west of the Eixo Rodoviário (the main north–south arterial road) – odd numbers to the west and even to the east, increasing as they move away from the center. The last two digits (04) show the distance north or south of the Eixo Monumental. So Pensão da Zenilda is four blocks to the south of the Eixo Monumental and four blocks east of the Eixo Rodoviário (1, 3, 5, 7). The higher the number of the Super Quadra, the further it is from the center.

Get to know these acronyms:

Asa Norte/Asa Sul The two 'wings' of the city, connected by main roads, *eixo rodoviários*. The N (Norte) or S (Sul) after an acronym indicates on which side of the Eixo Monumental it's located.

SBN/SBS (Setor Bancário Norte/Sul) The banking areas either side of the Eixo Monumental.

SCEN/SCES (Setor de Clubes Esportivos Norte/Sul) The main recreational zone on the shores of Lago do Paranoá.

SCLN/SCLS (Setor Comércio Local Norte/Sul) The main shopping blocks between the *superquadras*.

SCN/SCS (Setor Comercial Norte/Sul) The commercial office block areas next to the main shopping centers.

SDN/SDS (Setor de Diversões Norte/Sul) The main *conjuntos* (shopping centers) either side of the Eixo Monumental.

SEN/SES (Setor de Embaixadas Norte/Sul) The embassy sectors.

SHIN/SHIS (Setor de Habitações Individuaís Norte/Sul) The residential areas around the lake. SHIN is reached on the Eixo Norte. SHIS is accessed via the bridges off Av das Nações.

SHN/SHS (Setor Hoteleiro Norte/Sul) The hotel sectors each side of the Eixo Monumental.

SMHN/SMHS (Setor Médico Hospitalar Norte/Sul) The hospital sectors each side of the Eixo Monumental, next to the SCN and SCS, respectively.

SQN/SQS (Super Quadras Norte/Sul) The individual *superquadras* in the main residential wings of the *plano piloto*.

If all of this seems too logical, make sure you write down the address, as all these *superquadras* start to look the same after a very short while.

SEVEN WONDERS OF BRASÍLIA?

In 2008, and to mark its coronation as the American Capital of Culture, the city authorities launched a municipal vote to pick the Sete Maravilhas do Brasília (Seven Wonders of Brasília). With almost 65,000 votes cast, this is what they came up with:

Catedral Metropolitana 9017 votes
Congresso Nacional 7113 votes
Palácio da Alvorada 6915 votes
Palácio do Planalto 6821 votes
Templo da Boa Vontade 6693 votes
Santuário Dom Bosco 5904 votes
Ponte JK 4117 votes

inside the **Memorial JK** (☎ 3226 7860; admission R$4; 9am-6pm Tue-Sun). The museum houses JK's 3000-book-strong personal library as well as a pictorial history of Brasília. Don't miss his 1973 Ford Galaxie just outside the back door.

Opposite, in a Niemeyer building inspired by the circular form of the indigenous Yanomani hut, is the **Museu dos Povos Indígenas** (☎ 3344 1155; admission free; 9am-6pm Mon-Fri, 10am-6pm Sat & Sun), a small but colorful display of indigenous artifacts put together by anthropologists Darcy and Berta Ribeiro and Eduardo Galvão. A sandy central courtyard is still used for tribal rituals.

TV Tower

The 75m-high **observation deck** (admission free; 8am-8pm) of the TV Tower gives a decent overview of the city, but it's still not quite tall enough to really get a sense of the city's airplane design. Take the left-hand lift to the viewpoint. The right-hand lift leads to the **Tower Gem Center** (admission R$3; 8am-8pm), a sparkly collection of rough and cut trinkets, most with unpronounceable names. That's not a *favela* (slum) at its base; it's a handicraft market.

Catedral Metropolitana

With its 16 curved columns and its wavy stained-glass interior, the **Catedral Metropolitana** (☎ 3224 4073; Esplanada dos Ministérios, Asa Sul; admission free; 8am-6pm) is heavenly viewing. At the entrance are the haunting *Four Disciples* statues carved by Ceschiatti, who also made the aluminum angels hanging inside. Readers who bemoaned the number of broken stained-glass panels will be glad to hear that they were

undergoing a thorough repair at the time of writing.

Complexo Cultural da República

As Niemeyer's original plans for Brasília continue to come to fruition, new attractions are popping up just west of Catedral Metropolitana. The first to open, inaugurated in late 2006 with a tribute to Niemeyer, was the **Museu Nacional** (☎ 3325 5220; admission free; 9am-6:30pm Tue-Sun). Another spherical half-dome by the architect, the inside features a discreet mezzanine mostly held up by columns suspended from the roof. A signature curved ramp juts out from its base and runs around the outside like a ring of Saturn.

The massive exterior of the new working national library, the **Biblioteca Nacional** (☎ 3325 6257; 9am-9pm Mon-Fri, to 6pm Sat & Sun), is long finished, but they still haven't loaded all the books. Free guided tours of the structure are available every half hour. Across the Eixo Monumental you can see the **Teatro Nacional**, its appearance somewhere between a waterslide and a skateboard ramp.

Praça dos Trés Poderes

Down in the cockpit, you'll find the most interesting buildings surrounding the **Praça dos Trés Poderes**. It's a synthesis of the ideas of architects Niemeyer and Costa, combining various monuments, museums and federal buildings. The space includes striking sculptures, including Bruno Giorgi's *Os Candangos*, Alfredo Ceschiatti's *A Justiça* and Niemeyer's *O Pombal* (which looks like a clothes peg). If you're lucky enough to visit on the first Sunday of the month, the military pulls out all stops for the ceremonial changing of Brasília's tallest and largest flag, a 286-sq-meter banner on the **Pavilhão Nacional** flagpole. Conceived by Sergio Bernardes, it consists of 24 separate flagpoles welded together, each one symbolising a Brazilian state.

It's worth visiting the praça during the day and again at night for two very different experiences. After dark, surreal lighting casts an eerie glow across the futuristic buildings, as though they are being lit up by the landing lights of an alien spacecraft. Robberies have been reported here at night though, so have a taxi wait for you while you visit. Note that admission to the buildings is by guided tour only (every half hour) and you will not be allowed to enter if you are wearing shorts or sandals.

Palácio do Itamaraty (Palace of Arches; ☎ 3411 8051; admission free; ⏰ 2-4:30pm Mon-Fri, 10-11:30am & 1-3:30pm Sat & Sun) is home to the Foreign Ministry and one of the most impressive buildings – a series of arches towering over a reflecting pool and floating gardens landscaped by Burle Marx. Outside, the Bruno Giorgi sculpture *Meteor* consists of five marble blocks, each representing a continent. Call in advance to schedule your tour of the interior. Opposite, across the Eixo Monumental, water cascades between the exterior arches of the **Palácio da Justiça** (Department of Justice) into a limpid koi pond. Unfortunately the interior is now closed to the public.

Featuring the photogenic 'dishes' and twin towers, the congress building, **Congresso Nacional** (Parliament; admission free; ⏰ 9am-5pm), is one of the more interesting buildings on the inside as well. In addition to the color-coded chambers of the Senate (blue) and House of Representatives (green) – so '60s gauche –

there is an architecturally interesting 'Tunnel of Time' and an exhibit of antique Senate benches and microphones from 1867. The convex dome on the roof of the House of Representatives is supposed to signify that membership is open to all ideologies.

Down a concealed flight of steps on the praça itself is the **Espaço Cultural Lucio Costa** (☎ 3325 6244; admission free; ⏰ 9am-6pm). Inside you will find a 170 sq meter scale map of the *Plano Piloto* plus images of the city during its construction and early occupation. There is even a map of the city in braille.

On the north side of the praça, the president's office, the **Palácio do Planalto** (Presidential Palace) is another Niemeyer design. From the curved lines of the exterior to the lustrous columns and sweeping curved ramp inside, it's one of the best examples of architectural modernism in the world. Visits were suspended at the time of writing due to major restoration work.

BRASÍLIA – CAPITAL OF THE THIRD MILLENNIUM

In 1883 an Italian priest, John Bosco, prophesied that a new civilization would arise between parallels 15 and 20, and that its capital would be built between parallels 15 and 16, on the edge of an artificial lake. Many consider Brasília to be that city, and a number of cults have sprung up in the area. If you tire of Brasília's architectural monuments, a visit to one of the cults may be part of your destiny.

About 45km east of Brasília, near the satellite city of Planaltina, you'll find the **Vale do Amanhecer** (Valley of the Dawn; ☎ 3388 0537; ⏰ 10am-midnight), founded in 1959 by a clairvoyant, Tia Neiva. The valley is actually a small town where you can see (or take part in) Egyptian, Greek, Aztec, Indian, Gypsy, Inca, Trojan and Afro-Brazilian rituals. The mediums in the town believe that a new civilization will come during the third millennium. The town's main temple was inspired by spiritual advice received by Tia Neiva. In the center is an enormous Star of David, which forms a lake, pierced by an arrow. Get there by bus 617 from the center of Brasília.

About 63km west of Brasília, near the town of Santo Antônio do Descoberto (Goiás), is the **Cidade Ecléctica** (Eclectic City; ☎ 3626 1391; ⏰ 8am-6pm). Founded in 1956 by Yokanam, who was once an airline pilot, the group's aim is to unify all religions on the planet through fraternity and equality. You're welcome to attend its ceremonies, but there are strict dress regulations. Women cannot wear long pants (skirts only) and men cannot wear shorts. If you're not dressed suitably, you'll be given a special tunic to wear.

The **Templo da Boa Vontade** (Temple of Goodwill; ☎ 3245 1070; www.boavontade.com; SGAS, Quadra 915, Lotes 75/76; ⏰ 24hr) was created by the Legion of Goodwill in 1989 as a symbol of universal solidarity. It incorporates seven pyramids, joined to form a cone that is topped with the biggest raw crystal you will ever see (it weighs in at 21kg). To view it, you must take off your shoes and walk along the spiraling inner circle via the black path. You must return on the white path (do not screw this up). It's all a bit dizzying. There is also an interesting Egyptian room for meditation (R$2) that will make you feel like King Tut (of course, they take all of this very seriously, so let's keep these jokes between us). Get there on bus 105 or 107 from the city bus station.

Some people also believe that in certain regions around Brasília extraterrestrial contacts are more likely – at Km 69 on Hwy BR-351, for instance, or on the plateau in the smaller city of Brasilândia. Believe it, or not!

Santuário Dom Bosco

Even more impressive than the cathedral, **Santuário Dom Bosco** (Dom Bosco's Shrine; ☎ 3223 6542; Via W3 Sul; admission free; ☑ 7am-7pm) is made of 80 concrete columns that support 7500 pieces of illuminated Murano glass symbolizing a starry sky, and which cast a blue submarine glow over the pews. The central chandelier weighs 2.5 tonnes and adds an amazing 435 light bulbs' worth of energy to the monthly electricity bill.

Setor Bancário Sul

In the lobby of the **Caixa Federal** (SBS Q4 Lote 3; admission free; ☑ 9am-9pm Mon-Fri) is a small museum of financial bits and pieces, ranging from old lottery tickets through to wooden safes. The exhibits themselves are of only passing interest, but the gorgeous stained-glass murals, each one representing a Brazilian state, make it worth the visit.

Numismatists will also be interested in a visit to the **money museum** (admission free; ☑ 10am-5:30pm Tue-Fri, 2-6pm Sat & Sun) in the Banco Central do Brasil opposite. Cash from around the world is on show, as well as a complete set of Brazilian currency, including a 1,000,000 Cruzeiro note. You'll need to show your passport to get in – they take no chances.

Setor de Clubes Esportivos (SCE)

Brasília's most important contemporary museum, **Centro Cultural Banco do Brasil** (☎ 3310 7087; SCES, Trecho 2, Conjunto 22; admission to exhibitions free; ☑ 9am-9pm Tue-Sun) is in a giant building in the South Sports Club Sector. It houses fascinating exhibitions in two galleries, an indie cinema, a café and a bookstore. The monthly cultural program is posted online at twitter.com/CCBB_DF (in Portuguese). There is a free bus every 90 minutes (from 11am to 11pm) that runs along the Eixo Monumental (look for the painted bus that says CCBB). From behind the Centro Cultural you can see the triple-arched **Ponte JK** that crosses the Lago do Paranoá, a design presumably inspired by the Loch Ness monster.

In the Setor de Clubes Esportivos Norte (SCEN) is the official presidential residence, the **Palácio da Alvorada**. A Niemeyer building, it was the first edifice in the city to be inaugurated in 1958, predating the inauguration of the city itself by two years. The name translates as 'Palace of the Dawn' in reference to JK's description of Brasília as 'a new dawn

in Brazilian history'. No visits are allowed but you can take photos from the gate, marshaled by a dapper Dragões da Independência (Dragons of the Independence) guard, from a special regiment of soldiers who date back to the War of Independence.

National Parks

In the northern reaches of the city limits, the 30-sq-km **Parque Nacional de Brasília** (☎ 3465 2013; admission R$3; ☑ 8am-4pm) is a good place to relax. It has natural swimming pools and is home to a number of threatened animals, including deer, anteaters, giant armadillos and maned wolves. The park is very popular on weekends and there's a visitors' center where you can get information. Bus 128.1 from the city bus station goes past the front gate.

A good park not far from the city center is the **Parque da Cidade** (Eixo Monumental, Asa Sul; admission free; ☑ 5am-midnight), where you'll find a swimming pool with artificial waves, and kiosks to grab a snack.

TOURS

The quickest and most exhilarating way to make sense of Brasília's confusingly sensible layout is a breathtaking 10-minute helicopter flight with **Esat Aerotaxi** (☎ 9981 1917). Departures are from the airport, and trips cost R$500 with a three-person maximum.

If that sounds too hairy, you can do a hop-on-hop-off bus tour with **Brasilia City Tour** (☎ 9304 2610; www.brasiliacitytour.com, in Portuguese; tickets R$20; ☑ 10am-5pm Tue-Sun), or combine a ride on local buses from the city bus station (104 or 108 are the best) with some long walks to see the bulk of Brasília's attractions.

For multilingual tours, **Billy Deeter** (☎ 8112 3434; billyvango@yahoo.com), who was born in the USA but has lived in Brasília since he was a child, organizes group and/or private customized tours starting at R$100, which include some off-the-beaten-track points of interest.

SLEEPING

Bank on spending a little more on accommodation in Brasília than elsewhere, with even the 'budget' options charging prices that would be considered 'midrange' elsewhere. Characterless high-rise, chain hotels are the norm, most being crammed into the central Sector Hoteleiro and subject to ubiquitous traffic noise. Those in the SHN (Setor Hoteleiro Norte) are more conveniently located for the shopping centers, but those in the SHS (Setor Hoteleiro Sul) are better value. Most hotels offer substantial discounts throughout the year when business is slow, so it's worth shopping around for the best deal.

A municipal blitz on unlicensed accommodation means that many of the budget accommodations around Via W3 Sul have been forcibly closed. Some remain open, albeit clandestinely, with all signs of habitation packed away during the day and taken out again at night. Be aware that hygiene and safety are not necessarily among their top priorities. Only licensed establishments are listed here.

Midrange

Brasília Hostel (☎ 3343 0531; www.brasiliahostel.com .br, in Portuguese; SRPN Quadra 2, Lote 2; s/d R$52/100; 🖥) This 20-room hostel has big, open breezeways, spanking-clean rooms and individual lockers in dorms of six beds each (there are a few doubles as well). It's located just west of Asa Norte in Brasília's designated camping sector.

Econotel (☎ 3204 7337; SHS Quadra 3, Bloco I; s/d R$90/135; 🖥) The closest thing to a budget hotel in the SHS, though the rooms are newer, fresher and better equipped than the majority of the other stagnant options in a higher range. No need to splash the extra cash on the 'luxury' rooms either; the standard rooms are just as good.

Hotel das Naçoes (☎ 3322 8050; www.hoteldasnacoes .com.br, in Portuguese; SHS Quadra 4, Bloco I; s/d R$99/132; 🖥🖥) Comfortable rooms with hardwood floors and a generous minibar. A cheap option at the time of writing, but with many of the rooms undergoing improvements don't be surprised if the price gets improved too, and not in your favor. The Rander Restaurant on-site specializes in exotic dishes such as frog, caiman and peccary.

Hotel das Américas (☎ 3034 3355; www.hoteldas americas.com.br, in Portuguese; SHS Quadra 4, Bloco B; s/d R$120/190; 🖥🖥🖥) Modern, friendly and businesslike, the retro rooms have king-size beds and are an odd mix of '80s style and 21st-century technology. One of the better value options in the area, though metal grates on the windows spoil your view of the highway.

Phenicia Bittar Hotel (☎ 3704 6000; www.hoteisbit tar.com.br; SHS Quadra 5, Bloco J; s/d R$135/165; 🖥🖥) Third-floor nonsmoking rooms with ceramic floors are the nicest and brightest in this large hotel.

Aristus Hotel (☎ 3328 8675; www.aristushotel.com .br, in Portuguese; SHN Quadra 2, Bloco O; s/d R$150/190; 🖥) If you spend any time in Brasília you'll eventually get sick of elevators. The Aristus is comfortably squat with only two floors, so you won't need one. Rooms are fine, if a little dingy.

Torre Palace Hotel (☎ 3961 5555; www.torrepalace .com.br; SHN Quadra 4, Bloco A; s/d R$160/190; 🖥🖥) It has spick-and-span air-conditioned rooms, which are functional but not exactly brimming over with character. Compensation comes in the form of not one but two buffet restaurants, one Japanese, the other Arabic-Mediterranean.

Top End

Sonesta Brasília (☎ 3424 2500; www.sonesta.com/ brasilia; SHN Quadra 5, Bloco B; s/d R$165/209; 🖥🖥🖥) One of Brasília's newer hotels, it's naturally in better shape than the majority. Rooms decked out in warm colors like olive green and tangerine are a soothing change of pace from the ivory-toned dominance of Brasília's cityscape.

Alvorada Hotel (☎ 2195 1122; www.alvoradahotel .com.br, in Portuguese; SHS Quadra 4, Bloco A; s/d R$180/230; 🖥🖥) Alvorada is fair value, with clean and compact (some would say small!) standard rooms. Breakfast is great and there are fine views from the restaurant.

our pick Kubitschek Plaza (☎ 3329 3333; www .plazabrasilia.com.br/kubitschek.html; SHN Quadra 2, Bloco E; s/d R$260/320; 🖥🖥🖥) The halls and lobby of this classic choice feature wonderful art by local artists and famous photographs of Juscelino Kubitschek's administration. Rooms on the upper floors have not long seen a makeover, including gorgeous hardwood floors and earth-toned pinstriped headboards.

Royal Tulip Brasília Alvorada (☎ 3424 7000; www .royaltulipbrasiliaalvorada.com; SHTN Trecho 1, Conjunto 1B, Bloco C; s/d R$320/370; 🖥🖥🖥) The capital's most stylish hotel is a horseshoe-shaped complex overlooking Lago do Paranoá, right next door to the president's residence. Famed architect Ruy Ohtake designed a futuristic, open lobby with wavy hallways that climb up towards a wiry, Zeppelinesque ceiling. It's a haven for celebs, models and, of course, architects. The website offers a variety of special deals.

EATING

Brazilians may say that Brasília is boring, but foodies flock here with abandon – the capital has one of the highest concentrations of starred restaurants in the country and eating here is definitely a highlight. The best selections are around SCLS 209/210, 409/410 and 411/412, which forms a sort of 'gourmet triangle' (it is also home to the city's most lively nightlife). Another good selection of restaurants is clustered in SCLS 405. Here you'll find Tex-Mex, Portuguese, German, Thai, Japanese, Chinese and vegetarian eateries.

Elsewhere, Brazilians in need of sustenance head to the shopping malls. With buildings so spread out and few street stalls, finding somewhere to eat out of the heat during the day can drive one to drink, except it's hard to find that as well. Not surprisingly, three centrally located oases – Shopping Brasília, Pátio Brasil and Conjunto Nacional – all have small cafés and food courts with enough variety to cater to most tastes.

Budget

Belini (☎ 3345 0777; SCLS Quadra 113, Bloco D, Loja 36; sandwiches R$5-11; ☿ noon-3pm & 7-11:30pm Tue-Sat, noon-4pm Sun) Though housed inside a very expensive-looking Italian mansion, this high-end food emporium-cum-restaurant offers reasonably priced sandwiches at the counter of its small coffee shop (anything on ciabatta should sort you out).

O Paraíba (☎ 3244 2221; SCLS Quadra 405, Bloco B, Loja 6; dishes R$8.50-15.50; ☿ noon-3pm & 4-11pm Mon-Thu, 11am-3pm & 4pm-midnight Fri-Sun) Indigenous art lines the walls at this upscale *tapiocaria* where quesadilla-like dishes are made from tapioca, a specialty of the Northeast. Try the signature dish, *queijo coalho* (cured white cheese) and *carne de sol* (salted and grilled meat with beans, rice and vegetables) served with homemade butter from the countryside.

Marietta (☎ 3327 3892; www.marietta.com.br, in Portuguese; Shopping Brasília; sandwiches R$8.90-9.80; ☿ 10am-11pm) This sandwich shop turns out the capital's best: a triangular triple-decker of arugula, buffalo mozzarella and sun-dried tomatoes. It has prize-winning juices and killer salads as well.

Midrange

Quitinete (☎ 3242 0506; SCLS Quadra 209, Bloco B, Loja 22; desserts R$5-7, sandwiches R$14-26; ☿ 7am-2am) This chic deli-restaurant-bakery serves exquisite desserts (try the *tartellete de limão*; lemon tart) and the best coffee in the city (roasted in-house). Delivery available.

Mormaii Surf Bar (☎ 3248 1265; SHIS Quadra do Lago 10, Bloco E, Lote 8; sandwiches R$15-25; ☿ 10am-2am) Locals park themselves on the outdoor lakeside patio every afternoon for tasty sandwiches and the house specialty, *açaí na tigela*, a refreshing sorbetlike meal of blended palmberries, guaraná syrup, bananas and honey. On weekends, the waterfront location (located in the Pontão) attracts a roaring nightlife crowd as well.

Pizza à Bessa (☎ 3345 5252; www.pizzaabessa.com.br, in Portuguese; SCLS Quadra 214, Bloco C, Loja 14; pizza rodízio R$16.90; ☿ 6pm-midnight) The *rodízio* (all-you-can-eat) option here is implausibly cheap and the best way to try some inventive ingredients like pureed pumpkin, broccoli, and an outrageous dessert pizza with a huge scoop of ice cream. The *queijo coalho* and *rapadura* (dried sugarcane juice) pizza is a masterpiece.

Mangai (☎ 3225 0186; SCES Trecho 2, Loja 41; per kilo R$25; ☿ noon-10pm) Newly awarded its culinary stars, this Bahian per-kilo offers a host of creative dishes served up by Natal chef João Pessoa at a startlingly low price. Try the *sovaco-de-cobra*, a kind of beef jerky with green corn. It's down by the Ponte JK.

Top End

Lagash (☎ 3273 0098; SCLN Quadra 308, Bloco B, Loja 11/17; dishes R$25-45; ☿ noon-4pm & 7pm-midnight Mon-Sat, noon-6pm Sun) A mix of Moroccan, Lebanese and Syrian cuisine earns this sparsely decorated restaurant top Middle Eastern food in town year after year. Anything with lamb is delightful.

our pick Universal Diner (☎ 3443 2089; SCLS Quadra 210, Bloco B, Loja 30; dishes R$47-64; ☿ noon-3pm & 7pm-midnight Mon-Thu, noon-3pm & 7pm-1:30am Fri, noon-4pm & 7pm-1:30am Sat, noon-4pm Sun) A junkyard-chic aesthetic greets patrons at this eclectic rock eatery (it's overflowing with funky bric-a-brac and antique knick-knacks), another of the city's Brazilicious culinary gems. Mouth-watering tenderloin *au poivre* is the way to go, served up on vinyl LP placemats.

ZUU a.Z.d.Z (☎ 3244 1039; SCLS Quadra 210, Bloco C, Loja 38; dishes R$56-190; ☿ noon-3pm & 8pm-midnight Mon-Fri, 8pm-midnight Sat) The city's hottest contemporary table honors the slow food tradition in an exotic atmosphere that highlights fresh produce from Amazonas and Pará. Chef Mara Alcamim, who trained in New York and Italy, is Brasília's *chef du moment*. Her grilled shrimp in apricot chutney, served alongside Brie risotto, is cause for genuflecting.

DRINKING

Bar Brasília (☎ 3443 4323; SCLS Quadra 506, Bloco A, Loja 15A; ☽ 5pm-2am Mon-Thu, 11:30am-2am Fri & Sat, 11:30am-midnight Sun) In the same vein as the classic bars from Rio and São Paulo, complete with a hardwood bar relocated from a pharmacy in 1928, and antique tiled floors. It's great for draft beer, but note that staff will keep bringing you beer whether you ask them to or not. Don't be afraid to tell them to stop. You can buy dishes (R$20 to R$35) here.

Bar Beirute (☎ 3244 1717; SCLS Quadra 109, Bloco A, Lojas 2/4; ☽ 11am-2am) This Brasília institution has a massive outdoor patio packed with an edgier crowd than most spots. It's a GLS point – the clever Brazilian acronym for gays, lesbians and sympathetics – but it's really a free-for-all. There's no better spot for a cold Antarctica – except maybe the South Pole! You can get Middle Eastern food here as well (dishes R$5 to R$24).

Bar Brahma Brasília (☎ 3224 9313; www.barbrahmasp.com/brasilia, in Portuguese; SCLS Quadra 201, Bloco C, Loja 33; ☽ 11am-late) The capital's newest hot spot in the former location of the historic Bar Monumental. As Brahma's plan for world domination of the beer market chugs along nicely, Bar Brahma Brasília is the first step towards a nationwide chain of bars promoting the brand. Live music most nights; check the website for upcoming events.

ENTERTAINMENT

If you're after live music, check the listings in the 'Caderno C' section of the daily *Correio Brasiliense* newspaper or the free monthly booklet *Brasiliagenda*. If you read Portuguese, www.candango.com.br is a great online source of cultural and social events in the city.

our pick Arena Futebol Clube (☎ 3224 9401; SCES, Trecho 3, Lote 1; cover R$10-15; ☽ 10pm-late Thu-Sat, 7pm-midnight Sun) It's well worth the taxi fare to the Setor de Clubes Esportivos Sul, southwest of Praça dos Trés Poderes, for this live-music mecca that takes over the football (soccer) club on weekends. Daughters of ministers and politicos sweat out to hip-shaking *forró* (popular Northeastern music), samba and samba-funk. The best we've seen outside Rio.

Bar do Calaf (☎ 3325 7408; SBS Quadra 2, Bloco S, Loja 51/57; cover R$10-15; ☽ 10pm-late) Though technically a Spanish restaurant, the food is an afterthought to the wildly mixed crowd, all of whom rate the excellent live samba, *pa-*

gode (popular samba) and *choro* (improvised samba) over the paella. Monday is the biggest draw for samba-funk. Located in the Ed Empire Center office complex.

Gate's Pub (☎ 3225 4576; SCLS Quadra 403, Bloco B, Loja 34; cover R$15-20; ☽ 9pm-3am Tue-Sun) Gate's claims to be the longest-established bar in the city. Most nights there's live music with a rock, reggae and funk flavor, then dance music until closing.

Chiquita Bacana (☎ 3242 1212; SCLS Quadra 209, Bloco A, Loja 37; ☽ 5:30pm-2am Mon, noon-2am Tue-Sun) The *patricinhas* and *mauricinhos* – as Brazil's beautiful people are affectionately called – spill out onto Quadra 210 at this trendy open-air *chopperia* (beer hall) complete with whacky-hatted waiters. A daily happy hour from 5pm to 8pm nets an excellent *chope* for R$2.59.

SHOPPING

The crafts fair at the base of the TV Tower is a good place to pick up leather goods, ceramics and art objects.

You should be able to satisfy your other shopping needs in one of Brasília's shopping malls:

Conjunto Nacional (Asa Norte SCN) Brasília's first mall, right across from the bus station. Contains a post office, pharmacies, restaurants and a supermarket.

Pátio Brasil (Asa Sul, W3 SCS) The nicest of the capital's centrally located malls. More modern than the Conjunto Nacional, with a better restaurant selection.

Pier 21 (Setor de Clubes Esportivos Sul) Has the largest concentration of restaurants, bars and nightclubs but very few actual stores. Very popular with the young and well-off.

Shopping Brasília (Asa Norte SCN Quadra 5) All amenities, including cinemas and restaurants in a weird building that looks like half a soda can (from some angles at least!).

GETTING THERE & AWAY

As the capital, Brasília has a large daily influx of sightseers and lobbyists. The international airport connects with all major Brazilian cities. Most visitors fly in, but those who choose to go overland will cover some long distances.

Air

Many domestic flights make stopovers in Brasília, so it's easy to catch a plane to almost anywhere in Brazil. Flights to Rio are 1½ hours; to São Paulo, one hour and 20 minutes.

The easiest way to book a flight is through the travel agencies in the Hotel Nacional

---

BRASÍLIA OR BUST?

Brasília celebrated its 50th anniversary in 2010, but the question remains: does it work? Well, it depends on who you ask. Brasília tends to be very polemic. Brasiliense, as locals are referred to, regard the capital as a well-organized Brazilian utopia: roads are well maintained, grass is green, vehicles actually stop for pedestrians in crosswalks (hold your hand out where you see a yellow hand symbol painted on the tarmac and watch the traffic miraculously stop) and there are no favelas (slums) in the city. Large trucks are forbidden from entering the city limits, keeping pollution in check, and there is a height limit to signs and billboards, ensuring the city's big, open skies remain unobstructed (see the oddly short golden-arches sign at McDonald's – you can nearly reach up and touch it). For Brazil, it's an impressive standard of living.

On the other hand, most folks in the rest of the country see the city as a soulless bore, a sterile metropolis full of bureaucratic nonsense. Dig a little deeper and you'll find holes in the city's perfect plan, mostly concerning traffic. If a bus breaks down or there's an accident, it can be snarled for hours. With very few exit points on the city's roadways, a missed turn can be disastrous. Conclusion – Brasília is a lot like Los Angeles – residents love it while others love to hate it.

---

complex, but if you prefer to contact the airlines directly these are the main domestic carriers:

BRA (☎ 3364 9122; www.voebra.com.br)
GOL (☎ 3364 9274; www.voegol.com.br)
TAM (☎ 3364 9102; www.tam.com.br)

Bus

The decaying **long-distance bus station** (rodoferroviária; ☎ 3364 9037), due west of the city center, will be replaced by an even more inconveniently located building in the next few years. Though the current location is also a train station, no passenger services actually run. Prices noted here are for the more-expensive *executivo* services. Bus destinations include Goiânia (R$41, three hours), Rio (R$220, 17 hours), São Paulo (R$150, 14 hours) and Salvador (R$170, 22 hours). There are also buses to Cuiabá (R$135, 20 hours) and Porto Velho (R$312, 42 hours). Buses run north along Hwy BR-153 to Belém (R$243, 35 hours, three daily), but the road around the Tocantins border can be impassable during the rainy season.

Closer to home, buses go to Pirenópolis (R$20, three hours, hourly) and Alto Paraíso (R$32, 3½ hours, two daily) for access to the Parque Nacional da Chapada dos Veadeiros. From the central (city) bus station Empresa São Antônios runs three daily services to Alto Paraíso (R$29, 4½ hours) at 7am, 11am and 3:15pm, with the 11am service continuing on to São Jorge (R$35, 5½ hours).

GETTING AROUND

Aeroporto Internacional de Brasília–President Juscelino Kubitschek international airport (☎ 3364 9037) is 12km south of the center. To get to the airport from the city, take a 102 or 102.1 bus (R$2, 40 minutes) from the city bus station. Coming from the airport you catch either bus at the bus stop to your right as you exit the airport arrivals hall. A taxi to/from the airport from the center costs R$35 to R$40.

To get from the city bus station to the long-distance bus and train station, take local bus 131 (R$2), or a taxi will cost about R$20.

Inaugurated in 2001, **Metrô DF** (one-way ticket R$3; ☉ 6am-8pm Mon-Fri) is only really useful for access to restaurants and bars in the Asa Sul. It runs from the city bus station to the huge suburb of Taguatinga and Samambaia, with a predictably named station every two blocks from the central station, 102 Sul, 104 Sul, etc. Last service is at 11:30pm.

The first phase of the groundbreaking Brastram light rail network was due to open in late 2010, making Brasília the first South American city with a modern tramway. With completion scheduled to be in time for FIFA World Cup matches in 2014, it will eventually cover 23km of tracks, with the aim to decrease pollution and traffic congestion by 30%.

Its (☎ 3223 0161; www.itsrentacar.com.br; Hotel Nacional, SHS Quadra 1; ☉ 8am-8pm Mon-Fri) rents cars for as little as R$20 per day with a kilometer cap.

Goiás

Goiás is Brazil's 'road less traveled,' though not for good reason: fiery red sunsets over endless skies and lush, rolling hills pouring into fertile valleys set the stage for this sparsely populated state's unparalleled postcard-perfect views. While oftentimes almost criminally overlooked by tourists, Goiás is home to one of the country's most important and beautiful landscapes, the breathtaking savanna-like cerrado, which is the backdrop to the unspoiled splendor of the state's flawlessly preserved national parks and sleepy colonial towns.

Sweeping across Brazil's central high plains, the endangered cerrado, characterized by dense forests and gentle, sloping plateaus, is a worldwide biodiversity hot spot. In recent years, Goiás became the center of a campaign aimed to protect this important biome, all too much of which was plowed under at a rapid rate over the years to make way for immense soy plantations. Agriculture is big business here, but soy has lost steam in recent years after too many eager beavers jumped on the bandwagon. Eventually, the banks pulled the plug on easy loans. These days, the biodiesel and ethanol industries are paying the bills.

With its vast distances and excellent regional food, it's easy to get lost in Goiás for a few weeks. It's not as hectic as Rio or the Northeast, the people and towns are more prosperous, and the raw beauty of the cerrado is spectacular (see the boxed text, p399). Major attractions include the picturesque colonial villages of Cidade de Goiás and Pirenópolis, the therapeutic hot springs at Caldas Novas, and the rivers, waterfalls and forest trails of Parque Nacional da Chapada dos Veadeiros.

HIGHLIGHTS

- Soak up the alternative atmosphere in colonially cool **Pirenópolis** (p394)
- Lazily wander the cobblestone streets of **Cidade de Goiás** (p392) in a sugar-induced coma
- Trek through the unique high-cerrado flora in **Parque Nacional da Chapada dos Veadeiros** (p399)
- Rock-hop the naturally formed lunar-scape at **Vale da Lua** (p400), near Chapada dos Veadeiros
- Cure your ills or, if you don't have any, just splash about in the hot springs at **Caldas Novas** (p398)

- POPULATION: 5.6 MILLION
- AREA: 340,100 SQ KM

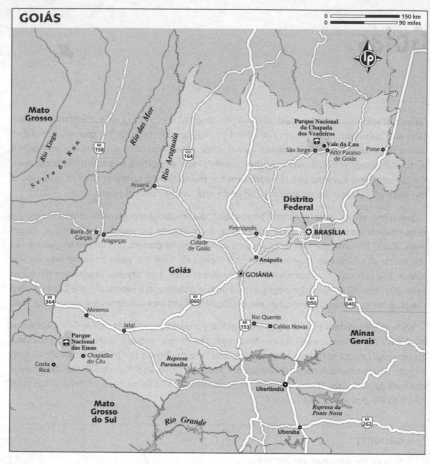

GOIÁS

0 — 150 km
0 — 90 miles

History

On the heels of the gold discoveries in Minas Gerais, *bandeirantes* (groups of roaming adventurers who explored the interior) pushed further inland in search of more precious metals and, as always, indigenous slaves. In 1682 a *bandeira*, headed by the old Paulista Bartolomeu Bueno da Silva, visited the region. The indigenous Goyaz people gave him the nickname *anhanguera* (old devil) when, after burning some *cachaça* (sugarcane alcohol) – which the Goyaz believed to be water – on a plate, he threatened to set fire to all the rivers if they didn't show him where their gold mines were. Three years later, having been given up for dead, the old devil returned to São Paulo with a few survivors, and with gold and indigenous slaves from Goiás.

In 1722 da Silva's son, who had been on the first trip, organized another *bandeira*. The gold rush was on, but with everything imported from so far away, prices in Goiás were high. Many suffered and died, particularly the slaves. The gold rush ended quickly.

Goiás achieved official statehood in 1889. Things were relatively quiet until the mid-1950s, when the Brazilian dream of an inland capital was realized and a portion of Goiás was carved out to build Brasília. Shortly thereafter, Goiás thrived. Under the wing of a colossal soy and sugar boom, the state flourished, and many farmers were made into millionaires nearly overnight. That has settled somewhat in recent years, although the state remains an agricultural hotbed.

In 1989, due to the vastness of its borders, Goiás once again forfeited some of its land, when the northern half of the state split off to become the separate state of Tocantins. Today, Goiás remains one of Brazil's most prosperous and comfortable states.

Climate

Most of Goiás lies within the Brazilian highlands, which have a tropical climate. Between October and March it's hot and humid. April to September it's hot and dusty. That said, don't be surprised if you get bogged down during the dry season or eat dust in the wet season. The temperature averages 20°C (68°F) year-round. In the south the state occupies the major part of the central plateau, at an altitude of between 750m and 900m above sea level, so temperatures tend to be cooler.

National Parks

In the mountainous area north of Brasília, the impressive Parque Nacional da Chapada dos Veadeiros (p399) is a 650-sq-km national park filled with waterfalls and canyons. Scenery is spectacular and wildlife viewing is excellent.

Getting There & Around

The gateway to Goiás is Brasília, with daily flights to all major Brazilian cities. It's also possible to travel overland via some long bus rides; from the coast via scenic Minas Gerais or from the Pantanal portals of Cuiabá and Campo Grande.

Goiás offers many attractions and is a popular stopover for travelers crossing the interior of the country. Regular bus services connect all the major towns and cities. Road conditions are generally good and renting a car is a viable option.

GOIÂNIA

☎ 0xx62 / pop 1.2 million

The capital of Goiás, Goiânia is the state's other planned city, predating Brasília by almost 30 years. Planned by urbanist Armando de Godói and founded in 1933, it's a pleasant combination of parks, leafy avenues and high-rise buildings laid out around circular streets. There is not much to see here, but it is a major transport nexus and if you are touring the state you'll inevitably find yourself passing through more than once.

Information

Goiânia is clean, relatively safe and efficiently organized. If you're traveling on to the national parks or colonial towns, it is wise to get money here.

Atan tourism agency (☎ 8146 3993; Crystal Plaza Hotel; ⏰ 8am-7pm Mon-Fri, to noon Sat) A central travel agency that can arrange everything in Goiás and beyond. Ask for Wanira. She juggles English, French and Italian like a jester.

Banco do Brasil (☎ 3216 5600; Av Goiás 980; ⏰ 10am-4pm Mon-Fri) The main branch.

Hospital Geral de Goiânia (INAMPS; ☎ 3221 6000; Av Anhanguera 4379)

Post office (☎ 3226 2110; Praça Cívica 11; ⏰ 9am-5pm Mon-Fri)

Yes Internet Café (Av Tocantins 488, Setor Central; per hr R$2; ⏰ 8am-10pm Mon-Fri, 8am-9pm Sat) Internet access.

Sights & Activities

Goiânia isn't exactly a tourist mecca, but there are a few things to see before heading off to other attractions in the state. Smack downtown near the Praça Cívica, the lush **Bosque dos Buritis** makes a nice spot to relax for a bit; it's home to fountains, lakes and palms full of chattery parakeets. You can see more parrots at the **Jardim Zoológico** (☎ 3254 1189; admission R$2; ⏰ 9am-7pm Tue-Fri), six blocks west at the end of Rua 2, as well as other regional wildlife.

The weekend markets – **Feira da Lua** (Praça Tamandaré), a few blocks west of the Praça Cívica and held on Saturday afternoon, and **Feira do Sol** (Praça do Sol), 7km from downtown held on Sunday afternoon – are both great ways to spend a weekend afternoon.

Sleeping & Eating

Ask for discounts at all city hotels if they seem quiet. The midrange and top-end hotels in particular drop as much as 50% off their prices when business is slow. There is some great regional food to try as well as some thriving nightlife.

Rodohotel (☎ 3224 2664; Rua 44 554; s/d R$70/90; ✗) Next to the bus station, this almost-cheapie will do for an overnight stay before catching an early bus.

Goiânia Palace (☎ 3224 4874; www.goianiapalace .com, in Portuguese; Av Anhanguera 5195, Setor Central; s/d R$94/160; ✗) Brick-and-wood *apartamentos* (rooms with private bathrooms) with new wardrobes and full-length mirrors. English is spoken.

Crystal Plaza Hotel (☎ 3267 4500; www.crystal plazahotel.com.br, in Portuguese; Rua 85 30, Setor Sul; s/d R$160/190; ☒ ☐) Standard rooms at this centrally located hotel just off Praça Cívica are double the size of those elsewhere. There is a handy tourist agency on the premises.

Chão Nativo I (☎ 3233 5396; www.chaonativo1 .com.br, in Portuguese; Av República do líbano 1809, Setor Oeste; fixed-price meals R$24.90; ☒ 11:30am-3:30pm Mon-Fri, 11am-4pm Sat & Sun) Serve yourself from a bonanza of bubbling cauldrons of baffling Goiânian concoctions at this all-you-can-eat smorgasbord, repeatedly voted the city's best for local cuisine.

Piquiras (☎ 3281 4344; www.piquiras.com, in Portuguese; Rua 146 464, Setor Marista; dishes R$30-65; ☒ 5pm-late Mon-Fri, 11:30am-late Sat & Sun) A Goiânia institution serving great examples of local fare. South of downtown, the expansive outside deck is packed with the city's young and fun on weekends.

Celson & Cia (☎ 3215 3043; Rua 15 539, Setor Oeste; ☒ 4pm-3am Mon-Fri, 11am-3am Sat, 11am-5pm Sun) Goiânésians of all ilks drink in droves here, filling the 65 outdoor tables under illuminated almond trees day and night.

Getting There & Around

Aeroporto de Goiânia (☎ 3265 1500) is 6km northeast of the city center (R$20 by taxi). You can fly to Rio (R$289), São Paulo (R$279) and other major Brazilian cities.

From the huge **bus station/shopping mall** (☎ 3240 0000), buses leave for Brasília (R$30, three hours, hourly), Cuiabá (R$115, 16 hours, six daily), Caldas Novas (Empresa Estela, R$27, 2½ hours, three daily), Pirenópolis (Empresa Goiânésia, R$14.50, 2½ hours, one daily), Alto Paraíso (Empresa São José, R$61.50, seven hours, one daily) and Cidade de Goiás (Empresa Moreira, R$24, three hours, hourly).

From outside the bus station, take a Rodoviária-Centro bus to town, or grab a taxi (R$12).

CIDADE DE GOIÁS

☎ 0xx62 / pop 25,000

Straddling the Rio Vermelho and surrounded by the rugged Serra Dourada, Cidade de Goiás is a sleepy town of lamplit cobblestone streets and whitewashed colonial homes. The former state capital, once known as Vila Boa (and briefly later on as Goiás Velho), was awarded Unesco World Heritage status in 2002. Its gor-

geous baroque churches shine and the town's population swells during Semana Santa (Holy Week). Every July 25 the anniversary of the town's foundation in 1727, the state governor visits Cidade de Goiás, which becomes the state capital for three days.

Information

Banco do Brasil (Av Sebastião Fleury Curado; ☒ 11am-4pm Mon-Fri) Visa/MasterCard ATM daily until 10pm.

CAT tourist office (☎ 3371 7714; www.cidadedegoias .tur.br, in Portuguese; Rua Moretti Foggia; ☒ 8am-6pm) Can at least hand out a town map.

Ouro Tur (☎ 3371 3346; Praça do Coreto) Helpful agency arranging tours and ecotourism adventures.

Sights

Strolling through town, you quickly notice the magnificent 18th-century colonial architecture, much of which is home to narrow streets and low houses hawking the region's famous *frutas cristalizados*, sugar-coated fruit concoctions that come in a plethora of flavors. Fuel up and make your way around the town's seven churches. The most impressive is the oldest, **Igreja de Paula** (Praça Zaqueu Alves de Castro), built in 1761.

The fascinating **Museu das Bandeiras** (Praça Brasil Caiado; admission R$3; ☒ 9am-5pm Tue-Sat, to 3pm Sun) is an old jail (1766–1950) and also a former town hall that's full of interesting antiques and original furniture – the 1.5m-thick cells made of *aroeira* (pepper-tree) wood are a museum piece in themselves. Outside in the square, the **Chafariz de Cauda fountain** (1778) is perfectly preserved, save the water.

Other interesting museums are the **Museu de Arte Sacra** (admission R$3; ☒ 9am-5pm) in the old **Igreja da Boa Morte** (Praça Castelo Branco), with a good selection of 19th-century works by renowned Goiânian sculptor Viega Vale; the **Casa de Cora Carolina** (Rua Dom Cândido Penso 20; admission R$4; ☒ 9am-5pm Tue-Sat, to 3pm Sun), birthplace and home of the area's renowned poet; and the **Palácio Conde dos Arcos** (Praça Castelo Branco; admission R$3; ☒ 8am-5pm Tue-Sat, to 3pm Sun), the restored colonial governor's residence.

The **Espaço Cultural de Goiandeira do Courto** (☎ 3371 1303; Rua Joaquim Bonifácio 19; admission R$2; ☒ 9am-noon & 2-5pm Tue-Sat, 9am-1pm Sun) is well worth a visit. This amazing artist in her 90s 'paints' using 551 varieties of sparkling colored sands found in the Serra Dourada, predating pixilation by decades (and by hand, it should be noted).

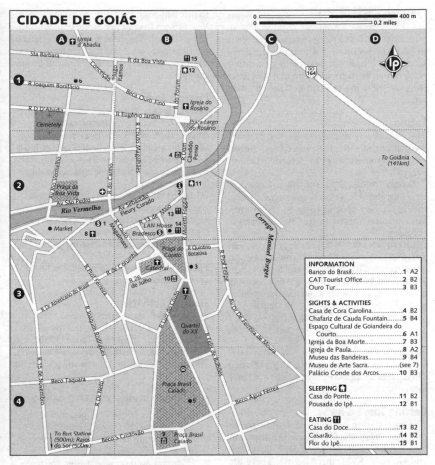

CIDADE DE GOIÁS

INFORMATION
Banco do Brasil...........................**1** A2
CAT Tourist Office......................**2** B2
Ouro Tur.....................................**3** B3

SIGHTS & ACTIVITIES
Casa de Cora Carolina................**4** B2
Chafariz de Cauda Fountain........**5** B4
Espaço Cultural de Goiandeira do
   Courto.......................................**6** A1
Igreja da Boa Morte....................**7** B3
Igreja de Paula...........................**8** A2
Museu das Bandeiras..................**9** B4
Museu de Arte Sacra...............(see **7**)
Palácio Conde dos Arcos...........**10** B3

SLEEPING
Casa do Ponte...........................**11** B2
Pousada do Ipê..........................**12** B1

EATING
Casa do Doce.............................**13** B2
Casarão.....................................**14** B2
Flor do Ipê................................**15** B1

Festivals & Events

Semana Santa Cidade de Goiás' big occasion takes place the week before Easter. The week's highlight is the Wednesday-night procession re-enacting the arrest of Christ. The streetlights are turned off and thousands of people march through the streets carrying torches, led by 40 eerie, pointy-hooded figures – the *farricocos* – whose colorful dress harks back to the days of the Inquisition. See? Those aren't klansman statues that you've been seeing around town!

Festival International de Cinema Ambiental (International Environmental Film Festival) Over five days in early June, the festival includes film and video screenings, workshops, live shows, lectures and exhibitions – all environmentally themed. It was started in 1999 in an attempt to draw worldwide attention to the town.

Sleeping

Cidade de Goiás is a popular getaway from Goiânia, so book ahead if you're arriving on a weekend. The town is packed during Semana Santa and for the International Environmental Film Festival, when prices rise.

Raios do Sol (☎ 3371 3161; Av Dario das Paivas 6; s/d without air-con R$30/55, with air-con R$40/65; ☒) Maybe not the rays of sunshine you were looking for in your life, but this new hotel next to the bus station is startlingly good value and saves you an uphill hike to the center if you arrive late.

Casa do Ponte (☎ 3371 4467; Rua Moretti Foggia s/n; s/d R$60/120; ☒ ▣) There's no accounting for taste with regards to the floral bedspreads, but this kitschy hotel is on a nice corner overlooking the Rio Vermelho.

GOIÁS

Pousada do Ipê (☎ 3371 2065; www.pousadadoipego .com.br, in Portuguese; Rua do Forum 22; s/d apt R$75/93, chalets R$84/102; ✗ ⊠) The most charming place to stay, the pousada is a tranquil property set around a lush courtyard and swimming pool. Enjoy the sugar-laden breakfast of local jams and jellies in a room just off the old-style kitchen.

Eating

The *empadão* reigns here – the tasty savory pie that's filled with meat, vegetables, cheese, olives and sometimes egg is served just about everywhere.

Casarão (☎ 8466 2603; Rua Moretti Foggia 8; dishes R$6- 10; ☽ 9am-11pm) Up a rickety wooden staircase, this is the best spot in town to try piping- hot *empadão*, served in traditional ceramic crockery.

Casa do Doce (☎ 3371 1824; Rua Moretti Foggia; sweets per kg R$20; ☽ 8am-noon & 1-5pm) If you don't mind a few bees, you'll find the colorful display of 28 crystallized fruits here too much to walk away from. Several branches are dotted around town. Eat your fill then call your dentist.

Flor do Ipê (☎ 3372 1133; Rua da Boa Vista; dishes for 2 R$20-42; ☽ noon-3pm & 6pm-midnight Tue-Sat, noon-3pm Sun) For lunch, there's a wealth of re- gional choices laid out in fiery hot clay-pots for R$22. In the evenings, the shady garden setting fills up quickly for excellent à la carte local dishes.

Getting There & Away

The bus station is 500m downhill south of Praça Brasil Caiado. There are frequent buses running between Cidade de Goiás and Goiânia (R$24, three hours). There are also buses to Barra do Garças (R$37.50, four hours), where there are regular connections to Cuiabá (Mato Grosso).

PIRENÓPOLIS

☎ 0xx62 / pop 21,000

A curious mix of art deco and Portuguese colonial architecture first strikes visitors to 'Piri,' but that's far from the only odd thing about this quirky town, on the Patrimonio Nacional (National Heritage) register since 1989. Set on striking red earth astride the Rio das Almas, it's another colonial gem with a history steeped in gold, though quite different from others in the state. An alternative move- ment took hold here in the '70s and remains today. There is a New Age, vaguely hippie vibe

to this laid-back spot and it's home to more Volkswagen Beetles per capita than any other city in Brazil. You'll be sick of waterfalls by the time you leave, but it's an excellent base from which to explore the 73 found around the area.

Information

Banco do Brasil (☎ 3331 1183; Rua Sizenando Jayme; ☽ 11am-4pm Mon-Fri) Visa/MasterCard ATM.

Brasil Central (☎ 3331 3677; www.pirenopolis.travel; Galeria Centro Histórico, Rua do Rosário; ☽ 9am-1pm & 2-6pm Tue-Fri, 9:30am-2pm Sat & Sun) A fantastic agency run by a young couple specializing in sustainable ecotour- ism and cultural tours.

CAT tourist office (☎ 3331 2633; www.pirenopolis .com.br, in Portuguese; Rua do Bonfim; ☽ 8am-6pm) Provides info on accommodations and activities in the area as well as transportation and guides.

Hospital Nossa Senhora do Rosário (☎ 3331 1592; Av Neco Mendonça 38)

X Games LAN House (Rua Sizenando Jayme; per hr R$2; ☽ 9am-midnight) Internet access.

Sights & Activities

CHURCHES & MUSEUMS

Reopened in October 2009, the town's most famous church, **Igreja NS do Carmo** (1750), with the **Museu de Arte Sacra** (Rua do Carmo; admission R$2; ☽ 11am-5pm Wed-Sun) inside it, is still undergoing

---

FESTA DO DIVINO ESPÍRITO SANTO

Pirenópolis is famous for performing the story of Festa do Divino Espírito Santo, a tradition begun in 1819 that is more popu- larly known as Cavalhadas.

Starting 50 days after Easter, for three days the town looks like a scene from the Middle Ages as it celebrates Charlemagne's victory over the Moors. A series of medieval tournaments, dances and festivities, includ- ing a mock battle between the Moors and Christians in distant Iberia, takes place. Combatants ride decorated horses, wear- ing bright costumes and bull-head masks. The Moors are defeated on the battlefield and convert to Christianity, 'proving' that heresy doesn't pay in the end.

The festival is a happy one, and more folkloric than religious. If you're in the neighborhood, make a point of seeing this stunning and curious spectacle, one of the most fascinating in Brazil.

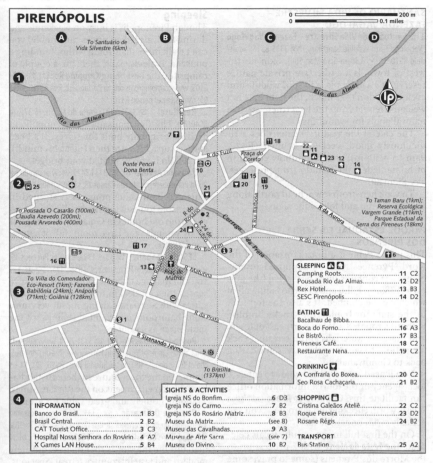

PIRENÓPOLIS

0 ——— 200 m
0 ——— 0.1 miles

To Santuário de
Vida Silvestre (6km)

Rio das Almas

Ponte Pencil
Dona Benta

Praça do
Coreto

To Taman Baru (1km);
Reserva Ecológica
Vargem Grande (11km);
Parque Estadual da
Serra dos Pireneus (18km)

To Pousada O Casarão (100m);
Claudia Azevedo (200m);
Pousada Arvoredo (400m)

To Villa do Comendador
Eco-Resort (1km); Fazenda
Babilônia (24km); Anápolis
(71km); Goiânia (128km)

To Brasília
(137km)

SLEEPING 🏕 🏠

Camping Roots	11	C2
Pousada Rio das Almas	12	D2
Rex Hotel	13	B3
SESC Pirenópolis	14	D2

EATING 🍴

Bacalhau de Bibba	15	C2
Boca do Forno	16	A3
Le Bistrô	17	B3
Pireneus Café	18	C2
Restaurante Nena	19	C2

DRINKING 🍸

A Confraría do Boxea	20	C2
Seo Rosa Cachaçaria	21	B2

SHOPPING 🛍

Cristina Galeãos Ateliê	22	C2
Roque Pereira	23	D2
Rosane Régis	24	B2

TRANSPORT

Bus Station	25	A2

SIGHTS & ACTIVITIES

Igreja NS do Bonfim	6	D3
Igreja NS do Carmo	7	B2
Igreja NS do Rosário Matriz	8	B3
Museu da Matriz	(see 8)	
Museu das Cavalhadas	9	A3
Museu de Arte Sacra	(see 7)	
Museu do Divino	10	B2

INFORMATION

Banco do Brasil	1	B3
Brasil Central	2	B2
CAT Tourist Office	3	C3
Hospital Nossa Senhora do Rosário	4	A2
X Games LAN House	5	B4

restoration. You can see the restorer at work on the 2nd floor.

Full of charisma, the Portuguese-built **Igreja NS do Bonfim** (1750) is a simple, rectangular adobe church with wooden floors and ceiling, flanked by two lateral chapels. The gilded turquoise altar and wooden pulpit are worth a look but the church is open only at times of worship.

The town's oldest church, the 1732 **Igreja NS do Rosário Matriz** (Praça de Matriz; admission R$2; 7-11am & 1-5pm Wed-Sun, 7-11am Mon) is open again after being tragically gutted by fire in 2002 (arson is suspected). Inside, the **Museu da Matriz** explains the history and ongoing renovation. The new altar was restored and brought in from the former slave church (a

necessary house of worship since slaves were banned from this one).

Two interesting museums are devoted to the Festo do Divino Espírito Santo (see the boxed text, p394). The glitzy new municipal **Museu do Divino** (☎ 3331 1460; Rua Bernardo Sayão; admission R$4; 11am-5pm Wed-Sun) exhibits the masks and costumes used during the festival. These masks were made by local craftsmen using methods passed down from generation to generation.

The privately owned **Museu das Cavalhadas** (☎ 3331 1166; Rua Direita 39; admission R$2; 10am-5pm) is cluttered with bright and colorful artifacts brought to life in a guided tour from the owner. The sign says to ring the doorbell if the museum appears to be closed.

GOIÁS

SANTUÁRIO DE VIDA SILVESTRE – FAZENDA VAGAFOGO

The **Santuário de Vida Silvestre – Fazenda Vagafogo** (Vagafogo Farm Wildlife Sanctuary; ☎ 3335 8515; adult/child R$10/5; ☯ 8:30am-5pm Mon-Sun), 6km northwest of town, is a 44-hectare private nature reserve. It's a great place to spot wildlife and even if you don't see much, the light hike is a welcome retreat from the heat (there are two natural pools for swimming).

The café at the visitors' center does a ridiculously good weekend brunch (R$22; 9am to 4:30pm), with a rainbow coalition of homemade wild cerrado fruit preserves. Try them all.

To walk here from town, head north along Rua do Carmo and follow the signs.

PARQUE ESTADUAL DA SERRA DOS PIRENEUS

This park's name is a Brazilianization of the word 'Pyrenees' (for its supposed resemblance). It contains three peaks, Pai (the tallest at 1385m), Filho and Espírito Santo, all of which can be climbed. It's also the top spot in the state for bouldering (rock climbing without a rope). It's 18km northeast of town, and there are waterfalls and interesting rock formations to see along the way, some dating back to Gondwanaland.

You'll need an accredited guide to enter. A local agency or the tourist information office can facilitate this. **Cachoeira do Abade** (admission R$10) is worth checking out en route as you can actually swim under the falls.

On the first full moon in July, locals celebrate the **Festa do Morro** with a procession to the Morro dos Pireneus (some to pray, some to play), where there is a small chapel on Pai. The festival is a modern tradition, more New Age than religious, and serious partying ensues.

RESERVA ECOLÓGICA VARGEM GRANDE

This 360-hectare **park** (☎ 3331 3166; admission R$15; ☯ 9am-5pm) on private land contains two impressive waterfalls – **Cachoeira Santa Maria** and **Cachoeira do Lázaro**. There are small river beaches and natural pools for swimming. If you're here for waterfalls, these two plus **Abade** are the ones to see.

The reserve is 11km east of town on the road to Serra dos Pireneus. You don't need a guide to enter, but unless you have a car, you'll need a ride from one.

Sleeping

Though Pirenópolis is busy on weekends and during festivals (when prices can double) you can't walk more than 100m without finding a pousada. If all else fails, there are a couple of campsites, the best being **Camping Roots** (☎ 3331 2105; www.campingroots.org, in Portuguese; Rua dos Pireneus 95; campsite per person R$10).

Rex Hotel (☎ 3331 1121; Praça de Matriz 15 37; s/d R$40/70) The first pousada in Pirenópolis in a house originally built for slaves. It's been spruced up a bit since then (just a bit mind!), but it'll do if you've busted your budget.

Pousada Arvoredo (☎ 3331 3479; www.arvoredo.tur.br, in Portuguese; Av Abercio Ramos 15; s/d R$50/80; ☒ ☒) This excellent-value pousada is steeped in sustainable tourism (all the bricks were recycled from old homes in Goiânia) and features lovely verandas and large rooms full of natural handicrafts.

SESC Pirenópolis (☎ 3331 1333; Rua dos Pireneus 45; www.sescgo.com.br, in Portuguese; s/d R$84/135; ☒ ☒) If you can manage to book rooms 1 to 3, you've scored the best deal in town: well-appointed suites with a separate living room, very nice stone bathroom, and vaulted ceilings for the same price as a double.

Pousada Rio das Almas (☎ 3331 2744; www.pousadariodasalmas.pirenopolis.tur.br, in Portuguese; Rua dos Pireneus; chalet for 2 people R$150, additional beds R$30; ☒) Go country in the town centre in these rustic chalets set in green gardens on the Rio das Almas. Tranquil, homely and great value for groups.

Pousada O Casarão (☎ 3331 2662; www.ocasarao.pirenopolis.tur.br, in Portuguese; Rua Direita 79; s/d R$170/185; ☒ ☒) The building is late 19th-century colonial, but the interior is that of an exquisitely modern and tasteful country retreat. Spacious, stately and cheap at the price.

Taman Baru (☎ 3331 3880; www.tamanbaru.com.br, in Portuguese; Estrada dos Pireneus km2; s/d apt R$205/240, bungalows R$390; ☒ ☒ ☒) A romantic retreat with the occasional Balinese touch set inside a forest, located just east of town. The colorful bungalows and gorgeous infinity pool both offer outstanding views across the cerrado.

Villa do Comendador Eco-Resort (☎ 3331 2424; www.villadocomendador.com.br, in Portuguese; GO 431 Km 1; r R$250; ☒ ☒ ☒) Opened in 2007 and situated 1km outside town, this is the first pousada in Pirenópolis to be sanctioned by national environmental watch groups as truly eco. It offers pools, playgrounds, horseback riding, volleyball and outstanding cerrado views. A haven for kids!

CAFÉ COLONIAL: THE FOOD OF THE TROPEIROS

After the *bandeirantes* swept Goiás clean of its gold, the *tropeiros* (the famed muleteers of Brazil) followed in their path, conquering the region and bringing slaves from Brazil's coast. Food was scarce en route, so the *tropeiros* adapted various foods from Afro-Brazilian, Portuguese and indigenous cultures to allow for the lengthy journey without refrigeration.

This long-lost subculture of Brazilian cuisine has been resurrected at **Fazenda Babilônia** (☎ 3331 1226; GO 431A, Km 24; ✆ 8am-5pm Sat & Sun), an 1800 sugar plantation and *fazenda* (farm) on the Patrimonial Nacional (National Heritage) register since 1965. Every weekend, this restored *fazenda*, 24km southwest of Pirenópolis, breaks out the historical gastronomy for a fascinating breakfast called Café Colonial. Hearty meats, cheeses and pastries highlight the near-endless options. *Carne de porco* (a succulent pork dish stored in its own fat for conservation), *mané pelado* (a sweet cake of grated manioc, eggs, cheese and coconut milk) and *matula galinha* (chicken with saffron, eggs, aromatic peppers and toasted corn wrapped in a corn husk) highlight an absolutely thrilling banquet that includes some 28 dishes that you're likely to have never seen before. The whole thing costs just R$25, including a fascinating tour of the *fazenda* itself.

Eating & Drinking

Rua do Rosário, aka Rua do Lazer, is the main restaurant-café strip and turns into a pedestrianized free-for-all of outdoor tables and lively city dwellers on weekends. Cheaper buffet-type restaurants are mainly along Rua da Aurora. Most restaurants close on Monday, and some only open on weekends.

Pireneus Café (☎ 3331 3047; Rua dos Pireneus 41; sandwiches R$4-9; ✆ 10am-10pm Mon-Wed, to 2am Thu-Sat, to 11pm Sun) A sophisticated spot overlooking Praça do Coreto for life-changing grilled focaccia sandwiches and first-rate coffee.

Restaurante Nena (☎ 3331 1470; Rua da Aurora 4; buffet R$19; ✆ noon-4pm Fri-Sun) One of the nicer buffets you'll come across, with great regional food and a varied selection of salads. Get in early before the offerings are picked thin.

Boca do Forno (☎ 3331 1790; Travessa Santa Cruz s/n; pizza R$19-34; ✆ 6pm-midnight Tue-Sun) The owner of this cozy pizzeria is from Brazil's pizza capital, São Paulo. If that means nothing to you, it will once you try the pizza. Wednesday's pizza *rodízio* (all you can eat; R$12) is a real treat.

Le Bistrô (☎ 3331 2150; www.lebistropirenopolis.com; Rua Direita 5; meals R$25-70; ✆ noon-2pm Mon-Fri, 8pm-midnight Thu-Sat) Colorful and proudly Goiánense in its decor, award-winning chef Márcia Pinchemel serves up a fantastic *surubim ao sabor do cerrado* (surubi fish with a taste of the cerrado). Widely considered by locals to be the best restaurant in town.

Bacalhau da Bibba (☎ 3331 2103; Rua do Rosário 42; dishes for 2 people R$25-100; ✆ 11am-midnight Thu-Sun) Oh my cod! A restaurant that serves nothing but *bacalhau*! That's not the only thing that's slightly surreal about this place either. It doubles as an antiques shop!

Seo Rosa Cachaçaria (☎ 3331 2046; Rua do Rosário 17; cachaça R$3-5; ✆ from 5pm Sun-Thu, from 11am Fri & Sat) More than 150 different *cachaças* to choose from.

A Confraría do Boxea (☎ 3331 1518; Rua do Rosário 38; beer R$3-22; ✆ from 5pm Tue-Sun) If beer is your poison then you could spend a few nights working through the 35 different types on the menu.

Shopping

Ruas Aurora and Rosário and Rui Barbosa are lined with places selling commercialized handicrafts from the region – everything from silver and ceramic pots to colorful cloths and statues of slaves. If you are looking for something more unique, then it's worth visiting the artist workshops on the Circuito de Criação (pick up a leaflet from the CAT office).

Among the more interesting workshops are those of **Roque Pereira** (☎ 3331 1084; Rua dos Pireneus 77), with his ecological furniture made from fallen trees, and the adobe pottery in **Cristina Galeãos Ateliê´s** studio (☎ 3331 1084; Rua dos Pireneus 67). Intent on proving that all that glitters is not gold, **Rosane Régis** (☎ 3331 3148; Rua 24 de Outubro) has been working silver from the region for a quarter of a century. If fashion is more your scene, visit **Claudia Azevedo** (☎ 3331 1328; Rua Direita 58) and peruse her creative dyed fabrics.

Getting There & Away

The bus station is 300m northwest of Igreja Matriz. There are buses to Brasilia (R$21, three hours, 165km, seven daily), one to Goiânia (R$14.50, three hours, 128km), leaving at 9:15am, and Anápolis (R$5, 1½ hours, five daily), where you can also catch a connection to Goiânia. Getting around town is easily done on foot or by moto-taxi.

CALDAS NOVAS
☎ 0xx64 / pop 68,000

Suffering from high blood pressure after Brasília? Poor digestion after your visit to a truck-stop café in Minas? Exhausted after your extended Carnaval in Salvador? Then Caldas Novas, with more than 30 curative hot springs, may be just the place for you. Now an upmarket resort, the town's population swells to around 200,000 during holidays.

Information
Banco do Brasil (☎ 3453 1186; Rua Capitan João Crisostómo 325) Visa/MasterCard ATM.
CAT tourist office (☎ 3454 3564; Praça Mestre Orlando; ☯ 8am-6pm) Located on the main square, it can help with accommodations and hot-springs info. There is another small office at the bus station.
Post office (☎ 3455 4107; Rua Capitan João Crisostómo 361)

Hot Springs
Nearly everyone in Caldas Novas has a thermal pool to cure what ails ya, but not all of them are open to the public. Besides the hotels and pousadas, there are a few good options in and around the city for day-use only. Working your way from the city center out, **SESC Caldas Novas** (☯ 8am-8pm Mon-Sun) is the most conveniently located and favorably priced. The 11 thermal pools in the SESC complex are well

---

DETOUR: RIO QUENTE

The aquatic playground of **Rio Quente**, 22km from Caldas Novas, is home to the world's only thermal-water river and enough water-themed entertainment to ensure you'd rather drown by the time it's all over. **Hot Park** (☎ 3453 7757; adult/child R$42/26; ☯ 9:30am-5pm, closed Thu) is the epicenter of the fun, a sort of waterlogged Disney for bronzed Brazilian beauties. Its 22,000 sq meters of slippery amusement, including a R$2.5 million mega half-pipe imported from Canada, is the only one of its kind in Latin America.

---

maintained and within walking distance of Praça Matriz. A little further out is **di Roma Acqua Park** (☯ 7am-5pm Mon-Sun; see di Roma Thermas Hotel), an all-out aquatic extravaganza featuring the world's first thermal wave pool, waterslides, lazy river, restaurants and numerous therapeutic waters.

Sleeping & Eating
During holidays and long weekends the town is packed, so reservations are advisable. Rooms in all categories tend to be nearly identical – pick based on hot-springs action – and expect to break your budget in high season.

SESC Caldas Novas (☎ 3455 9400; www.sescgo.com.br, in Portuguese; Av Ministro Elias Bufáiçal 600; s/d R$84/135; ☐ ☐) A large recreation area with 11 thermal pools. One of the best deals in town.

Hotel Roma (☎ 3453 1335; www.diroma.com.br, in Portuguese; Praça Mestre Orlando 368; r R$180; ☒ ☐) The six thermal pools, whirlpool and massive sauna skew a bit toward *On Golden Pond*, but the location on the main square is hard to beat. The bedside condoms next to the New Testament present an interesting dilemma!

Hotel Parque das Primaveras (☎ 3453 1355; www.hpprimaveras.com.br; Rua do Balneário 1; s/d R$250/290; ☒ ☐ ☐) Feisty macaws roam the jungly grounds at this lush pousada, the top digs in town. The four thermal pools feel more private than others.

di Roma Thermas Hotel (☎ 3453 9393; www.diroma.com.br, in Portuguese; Av Santo Amaro 1800; r R$320; ☒ ☐ ☐) A recently renovated megaresort a few kilometers out of town, di Roma has nine thermal pools and lots of action for kids (including a zip line!).

Picanha Na Brasa (☎ 3453 8023; Rua José Luiz Pereira & Pedro Branco de Souza 241; rodízio R$17.90; ☯ 11am-midnight) This popular *rodízio*-style *churrascaria* (all-you-can-eat barbecue restaurant) is one of the cheapest and tastiest you'll find.

Paneteria Famigli Amoroso (☎ 3453 5702; Rua Antônio Coelho de Godoy 37; pizzas R$19.50-28; ☯ 7-11pm Sun-Thu, to midnight Fri & Sat) This small bakery boasts 91 varieties of pizza cooked in a wood-fired oven.

Getting There & Away
The bus station is at the end of Rua Antônio Coelho de Godoy. Regular buses run to Brasília (R$49.50, six hours, two daily) and Goiânia (R$23.50, three hours, hourly), as well as to Rio de Janeiro (R$164) and São Paulo (R$115).

UNIQUE CERRADO

Calling cerrado 'the South American Savanna' is to oversimplify an extremely complex and varied ecosystem. True, it may look like bushy grassland for part of the year, but visit at the right time of year and it is converted into an immense flower garden of breathtaking scale and beauty. Nor is it strictly even grassland, in fact in some areas it is a type of forest. Confused? Let us explain!

Cerrado can be classified into four distinct types, each of which mesh together to form a mosaic of savanna-like habitat. *Cerradão* is dry cerrado forest, either in solid blocks or in small forest islands; *campo limpo* (clean field) consists entirely of grass; *cerrado sensu strictu* is composed of low bushy vegetation with no grass at all; and *campo sujo* (dirty field) is a mix of all the other types into one. The different types are quite easily distinguishable to the naked eye even to non-specialists, but when you consider that the plant species that make up each of these broad classifications may differ dramatically from one area to the next, you begin to get an idea of the immense biodiversity that the cerrado harbors. In fact, of the 10,000 or more species of plants found in the cerrado, 44% are found nowhere else in the world.

But it's not just the plants that make the cerrado so important for conservation. Besides providing a home for some of Brazil's most spectacular and threatened mammal species such as the maned wolf, giant armadillo, pampas deer and giant anteater, it also protects a number of highly threatened and localized birds, such as the white-winged nightjar, dwarf tinamou, lesser nothura and the gorgeous yellow-billed blue finch, all of which depend on this unique habitat for their continued survival.

Sadly that struggle for survival is getting harder with every passing year. Since the 1970s, vast tracts of native cerrado vegetation have been converted to soybean, rice, corn, wheat and cattle production – only 20% of the original vegetation is left. The rate of habitat loss makes it one of the world's fastest disappearing eco-regions, and the destruction shows no sign of abating.

Though the natural vegetation of most of Goiás state is cerrado, PN Chapada das Guiamaraes and PN da Chapada dos Veadeiros showcase the cerrado in dramatically beautiful surroundings, with picturesque cerrado habitat framed against a stunning backdrop of rocky mountainsides and craggy cliffs.

PARQUE NACIONAL DA CHAPADA DOS VEADEIROS

This spectacular national park in the highest area of the Central West showcases the unique landscape and flora of high-altitude cerrado across 650 sq km of pristine beauty.

With high waterfalls, raging canyons, natural swimming pools and oasis-like stands of wine palms, the park is a popular destination for ecotourists. In fact, the whole area is beautiful, with its big skies, exotic flora and dramatic hills rising up like waves breaking across the plains.

The sublime landscape, much of it based on quartz crystal and multihued sandstone, has also attracted New Agers who have established alternative communities and a burgeoning '*esoturismo*' industry in the area. It is also noticeably well maintained – you won't find a Skol beer can within miles.

Travelers visiting the park base themselves in one of two nearby towns: **Alto Paraíso de Goiás** (p400), 38km from the park; or tiny **São Jorge** (p401), 2km from the entrance. The best time to visit the park is between April and October, before the rivers flood during the rainy season and access becomes very slippery. You'll need two days to see the main attractions.

Sights & Activities

All visitors to the **park** (☎ 3455 1114; admission R$3; ⏱ 8am-6pm Tue-Sun) must be accompanied by an accredited guide. Private guides can be organized at the visitors' center, through the local guide association, ACV-CV, or at hotels in Alto Paraíso or São Jorge. Guides usually cost R$80 (Portuguese) or R$100 (English) per day, plus R$100 (up to four passengers) if you need transport to/from Alto Paraíso.

The guides run half-day tours to the park's three main attractions – *canions* (canyons) and *cariocas* (rocks), which are usually combined as they transverse the same trail in the park; and *cachoeiras* (waterfalls). The tours are included in the price of the guide and can be divided by up to 10 people.

The **canions-cariocas tour** weaves along the Rio Preto, which runs through the middle of the park. The river has cut two large canyons (imaginatively named Canyon I and Canyon

II) through sandstone, with sheer, 20m-high walls on either side. It's a spectacular sight. There are natural platforms for diving into the cold water at the bottom of the rushing river. Canyon I is usually flooded from September to May and inaccessible. The **cariocas** (named for two girls from Rio who went missing here in the '80s) picks up at the end of the river valley on the trail from Canyon II and leads to interesting rock formations and a huge cascading waterfall.

The more difficult (and rewarding) **cachoeiras tour** takes in Salto do Rio Preto I and II, two spectacular waterfalls (80m and 120m, respectively) that cascade to the ground just 30m apart. The falls are set in a picturesque valley at the end of a trail that weaves through a classic cerrado landscape of meadows and gallery forests. There is a small lake for swimming under II, where the sun creates a dazzling celestial effect under the water. Take loads of water and sunscreen; it's about a 6km ascent all the way back and the sun can be brutal.

VALE DA LUA

A unique sight in the Chapada dos Veadeiros area is the **Vale da Lua** (Valley of the Moon; admission R$5; 7am-5:30pm). Over millions of years, the rushing waters of the Rio São Miguel have sculpted rock formations and craters with a striking resemblance to a lunar landscape. Small *kalango* lizards dart across the ethereal metaconglomerate of quartz, sand and clay as shades of silver, gray, white and occasional patches of red (from rose quartz) reflect off the rocks. The chilly emerald waters add to the otherworldly atmosphere.

Vale da Lua is outside the national park, so you don't need a guide, but the area is subject to flash flooding during the rainy season (it takes all of three minutes for a flood of biblical proportions to rise), so check with locals before you head off. Walk out on the road to Alto Paraíso and take the first unmarked trail on the right – from there it's a 4km hike (there is no sign, as some guides remove them to enslave you to their services). If you miss this, it will be an 11km jaunt on the main road. Take sunscreen and water with you.

ALTO PARAÍSO DE GOIÁS

0xx61 / pop 7000

Crystals, dreadlocks and dirty feet are ubiquitous in Alto Paraíso, 38km from the park. It is one of Brazil's kookiest towns, but besides unleashing your inner hippy, crystal shopping or planning your trip to Chapada dos Veadeiros, there is not much else to do here.

Information

Banco do Brasil (Av Ari Valadão Filho 690; 10am-3pm Mon-Fri) Visa/MasterCard ATM.

CAT tourist office (3446 1159; www.altoparaiso. go.gov.br, in Portuguese; Av Ari Valadão Filho s/n; 8am-6pm) On the main street, 200m from the bus station. Helpful, but light on printed material.

Tours

Though most travelers stay in the village of São Jorge, it is in fact easier (if more expensive) to arrange visits to Chapada dos Veadeiros in Alto Paraíso.

Ecorotas (3446 1820; www.ecorotas.com.br; Rua das Nascentes 129; 8am-7pm Mon-Fri, 9am-2pm Sat & Sun) Organises a variety of eco-minded tours in the park area, including guided bird-watching tours.

Travessia Ecoturismo (3446 1595; www.travessia .tur.br; Av Ari Valadão Filho 979; 8am-7pm Mon-Fri, 9am-2pm Sat & Sun) An excellent eco-agency on the main road in Alto Paraíso that can arrange everything in Chapada, including more-adventurous canyoning and rappelling trips, transportation and English-speaking guides.

Sleeping & Eating

Alto Paraíso has a wide range of accommodations, with several good options to rest and refuel here. Prices rise by 30% or more at weekends and in high season.

Pousada Veadeiros (3446 1820; www.pousada veadeiros.com.br, in Portuguese; Rua das Nascentes 129; s/d R$48/68;) Cool kitschy little cabins not far from the bus station, each named after a native bird and decorated in its colors (you'll need a bit of imagination to associate the bird with some of them!). Take your first right after CAT. If you pass a building that looks like King Arthur's castle then you are nearly there.

Pousada Camelot Inn (3446 1449; www.pou sadacamelot.com.br, in Portuguese; GO 118 Km168; r/ste R$143/273;) Continuing the medieval theme, this replica castle is one you can actually stay in. In fact, it is more of a resort with 20-hectares of gardens, themed suites, a sauna, outdoor pools and even a helipad! Try the Merlin Suite and see if it works its magic on you. It's at the entrance to town.

Oca Lila (3446 1006; Av João Bernardes Rabelo 449; lunch per kilo R$28, meals R$12-25; noon-midnight, closed Tue) The all-natural vegetarian lunch-per-kilo place is highly recommended. Oca Lila turns à la carte for dinner (with excellent pizza) and there's a bit of *vida nocturna* in the evenings.

Getting There & Away

From Goiânia there's an 8:30pm bus daily to Alto Paraíso (R$53.50, six hours), with two daily buses doing the reverse leg on Monday, Wednesday and Friday. There are four buses a day from Brasília (R$29, 4½ hours), with the 11am departure continuing on to São Jorge (from Alto Paraíso R$6.50, one hour, at 3:30pm), but it can be pretty flexible in its arrival time so it pays to get there early.

SÃO JORGE

☎ 0xx61 / pop 1200

With sandy streets and a laidback vibe, the former crystal-mining hamlet of São Jorge (2km from the national park entrance) has the feel of a beach town despite its inland location. Though logistically Alto Paraíso is more convenient for arranging trips to Parque Nacional da Chapada dos Veadeiros, many travelers prefer to stay in São Jorge because it is prettier, closer to the park and has more of a village atmosphere.

Information

CAT tourist office (☺ 8am-6pm) There is a small tourist desk at the bus station at the entrance to town that can help you find a guide.

Phyto Cerrado (☎ 3453 1113) On the main street, offers massages from R$60 per hour.

Sleeping & Eating

Quality pousadas are plentiful and usually very fairly priced, though prices rise con-siderably at weekends. Camping starts from around R$12 per person, with shady Camping Taiva at the entrance to town about the best of several similar options.

Pousada Flor do Cerrado (☎ 3455 1138; www.pousa daflordocerrado.com.br, in Portuguese; s/d R$55/75) Small, cozy and the best of the cheaper options in town, with all wood furniture, earthy decora-tion and hammocks for lounging in the shade. You could be forgiven for feeling like you are robbing the owners at this price!

Pousada Bambu Brasil (☎ 3455 1004; www.bambu brasil.com.br, in Portuguese; r R$120; ✿ ▯ ▣ ▣) Great value for couples, this charming pousada with hand-painted furniture and poolside ham-mocks is a stylish place to relax.

our pick Baguá Pousada (☎ 3455 1046; www.bagua pousada.com.br; bungalows R$350; ✿ ▯) Massive (82 sq meters!), breathtakingly classy bungalows at this designer eco-pousada have raised the bar on sophistication in Goiás, while safari-chic lounge furnishings in the common area should suit Brazil's fashion *cognoscenti*. It's closest to the park's entrance as well.

Lua de São Jorge (☎ 3455 1054; pizzas R$22-46; ☺ from 6pm Thu-Sun) Intensely researched con-clusion: the best of the numerous wood-fired pizzerias in town.

Getting There & Away

São Jorge has a tiny bus station at the entrance to town, but it doesn't really need one. There is an 11am bus daily from Brasília to São Jorge (R$35, 5½ hours) via Alto Paraíso. The bus returns at 9am daily, leaving from the main street. Private transport to and from Alto Paraíso costs around R$100.

Mato Grosso & Mato Grosso do Sul

Mato Grosso was once Brazil's wild, wild West, where explorers, indigenous hunters, animal poachers, gold seekers and naturalists collided under miraculous sunsets and marvelous moons. Today, the massive area, split into the two separate states of Mato Grosso and Mato Grosso do Sul in the late 1970s, is still a wonderfully feral region that is home to some of Brazil's most spectacular wildlife and incredible scenery. It is a prime destination for ecotourists and anglers, the majority of whom come to visit the star attraction of the region, the Pantanal, an enormous floodplain that extends its watery tentacles across both states.

Though the Amazon has the glamor, it is the Pantanal that shines as Brazil's top destination for wildlife-viewing and bird-watching. It makes up one of the most important and fragile ecosystems on the planet and is home to an impressive concentration of animals. Jaguars, caimans, anacondas, giant otters and capybaras are here in great numbers, as are seemingly endless collections of extraordinary birds, including macaws, toucans and jabiru storks.

Cuiabá, Corumbá and Campo Grande are all gateways to this celebrated wetland, but the region's offerings certainly don't stop there. There's the far-north town of Alta Floresta, where the cerrado morphs into the Amazon in a vast, fervently preserved forest full of copious bird species and picturesque waterways; and the Serra do Bodoquena surrounding Bonito, where high waterfalls, deep canyons, caves and crystal-clear rivers present world-class ecotourism opportunities. Between the two is the stunning Parque Nacional da Chapada dos Guimarães, an imposing tableland with some of the most commanding views in Brazil.

HIGHLIGHTS

- Gawk at incredible wildlife while driving the 145km **Transpantaneira 'highway'** (p419) in the northern Pantanal
- Watch the sunset over dramatic landscapes in **Parque Nacional da Chapada dos Guimarães** (p409)
- Spot one-third of Brazil's bird species on safari in **Alta Floresta** (p412) in the southern Amazon rain forest
- Snorkel with exotic fish in the crystal-clear water world surrounding **Bonito** (p428)
- Savor genuine Pantaneira cuisine at authentic ranches in the southern Pantanal, such as **Fazenda Santa Sophia** (p420)

- POPULATION: 5.2 MILLION
- AREA: 1,260,200 SQ KM

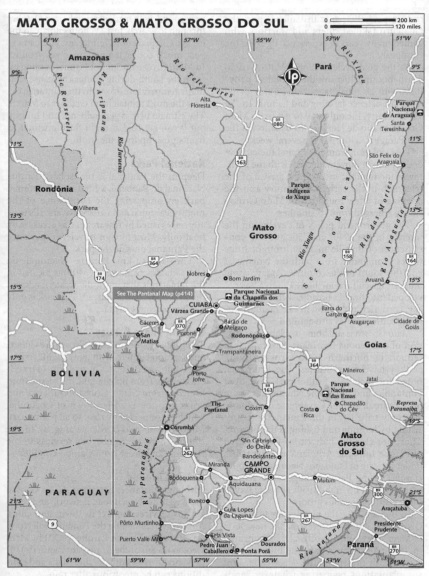

MATO GROSSO & MATO GROSSO DO SUL

History

According to the Treaty of Tordesillas, the state of Mato Grosso belonged to Spain. For years its exploration was limited to occasional expeditions by adventurers and Jesuit missionaries.

With the discovery of gold in the early 18th century, the region was invaded by thousands of fortune hunters. To reach Cuiabá, they had to cross the lands of several groups of indigenous people, many of whom were formidable warriors. They included the Caiapó (who even attacked the settlement at Goiás), the Bororo of the Pantanal, the Parecis (who were enslaved to mine gold), the Paiaguá (who defeated several large Portuguese flotillas and caused periodic panic in Cuiabá) and the Guaicuru (skilled riders and warriors who gained many years of experience fighting the Europeans).

As the gold cycle declined, Mato Grosso again became just another isolated province, with its inhabitants eking out a living from subsistence farming and fishing. In the 19th century, the only way to get from Mato Grosso to Rio de Janeiro was by ship via the Rio Paraguai, a journey of several weeks.

This isolation from the capital fueled several separatist movements but, with the coming of the republic in 1889, the arrival of the telegraph in the early 20th century and the opening of a few rough roads, Mato Grosso slowly emerged from its slumber.

The government policy of developing the interior in the 1940s and '50s and the construction of Brasília in 1960 brought huge waves of migrants from both the Northeast and the South of the country. Today, using modern agricultural methods, the area has developed into Brazil's breadbasket, cultivating soy, corn, rice and cotton in vast plantations. Huge cattle ranches also abound.

Mato Grosso is still home to a large population of indigenous Brazilians. Several tribes remain in northern Mato Grosso, living as they have for centuries. The Erikbatsa, noted for their fine featherwork, live near Fontanilles and Juima; the Nhambikuraa are near Padroal; and the Cayabi live near Juara. The only tribe left in the Pantanal still subsisting by hunting and fishing is the Bororo. There are also the indigenous Cinta Larga of Parque Indígena Aripuanã and the tribes under the care of Fundação Nacional do Indio (Funai) in the Parque Indígena do Xingu, which was set up in the 1950s as a safe haven for several indigenous groups.

In the late '70s, the massive area of Mato Grosso was cut in half, creating the new state of Mato Grosso do Sul, officially inaugurated in 1979. Agriculture pays the bills in both states, with massive cattle, sugarcane, and soy plantations peppering whatever landscape isn't protected by national parks and the *reserva particular patrimônio natural* (national private heritage reserve).

Climate

Given its geographic diversity, the climate varies considerably throughout Mato Grosso. In the north, Cuiabá remains hot and humid year-round, with marked rainfall from October through to March. Just 1½ hours north, in the higher Chapada dos Guimarães, you can expect much cooler temperatures year-round. In Mato Grosso do Sul, cold fronts coming up from the south during winter can cause dramatic temperature drops. In the Pantanal, expect the most rainfall from October to March. The climate here is generally hot and humid, but it can get cold at night during winter as fronts push up from the south.

National Parks

Deep in the Pantanal is the isolated Parque Nacional do Pantanal, a 1380-sq-km national park encompassing the confluence of the mighty Paraguai and Cuiabá Rivers. It's usually only visited by researchers, as access is by boat only. Most foreign travelers experience the Pantanal outside the park.

The 330-sq-km Parque Nacional da Chapada dos Guimarães (p409) is located in the tablelands that mark the western edge of the Brazilian central plateau. The park is only 1½ hours from Cuiabá.

Getting There & Away

The gateway cities to Mato Grosso are Cuiabá and Campo Grande, with daily flights to Rio, São Paulo and Brasília. The majority of travelers coming from Bolivia take the scenic train journey from Santa Cruz to Quijarro and cross into the Brazilian town of Corumbá, which is connected by road to all points east. Mato Grosso also borders Paraguay to the south. There are regular bus services to the Paraguayan border from Campo Grande.

Getting Around

Although distances are great, Mato Grosso has a well-developed road network, and regular bus services connect its towns and cities. Most travelers visiting the Pantanal will travel on either the Estrada Parque (p420) in Mato Grosso do Sul or the Transpantaneira (p419) in Mato Grosso. Both are dirt roads and conditions can be precarious after rain.

MATO GROSSO

Mato Grosso means 'thick forest.' Part of the highland plain that runs through Brazil's interior, it's a dusty land of rolling hills, endless plantations, abundant savannas and some of the best fishing rivers in the world. Three of Brazil's major ecosystems – Pantanal, Amazon and cerrado – thrive within its borders.

CUIABÁ
☎ 0xx65 / pop 550,000

Cuiabá is a frontier boomtown basking in the relentless Mato Grosso sun. The town's name is an indigenous Bororo word meaning 'arrow-fishing,' though it was first gold and later agriculture that led to the city becoming one of the fastest-growing capitals in Brazil over the last 30 years. The population explosion has tailed off in recent times, but Cuiabá is still a lively place and a good starting point for excursions to the Pantanal and Chapada dos Guimarães. Cuiabá will be a host city for the 2014 FIFA World Cup.

History
In 1719 a Paulista, Pascoal Moreira Cabral, was hunting indigenous groups along the Rio Cuiabá when he found gold. A gold rush followed, but many of those seeking gold never reached the new settlement at Cuiabá. Traveling more than 3000km from São Paulo by river took five months; along the way, gold seekers found little food, many mosquitoes, dangerous rapids, lengthy portages, disease and incredible heat.

With the end of the gold boom and the decay of the mines, Cuiabá would have disappeared, except that the soil along the Rio Cuiabá allowed subsistence agriculture, while the river itself provided fish.

By 1835 the town was the capital of Mato Grosso but, apart from a brief resurgence as a staging point for the war against Paraguay in the 1860s, it remained a backwater. Today, thanks mostly to the construction of Brasília and a massive agri-economy, Cuiabá has finally been propelled into the modern world.

Orientation
The city is actually two sister cities separated by the Rio Cuiabá: Old Cuiabá and Várzea Grande (where the airport is located). The center of the city is approximately 2.5km north of the river.

Information
EMERGENCY
Ambulance (☎ 192)
Fire department (☎ 193)
Police (☎ 190)

INTERNET ACCESS
Onix LAN House (Map p407; ☎ 3624 1127; Rua Pedro Celestino 8; per hr R$2.50; ☺ 7am-8pm Mon-Sat) The entrance is through Mistura Cuiabana.

MEDICAL SERVICES
Hospital Regional (☎ 3624 5284; Rua 13 de Junho 2101)

MONEY
There are ATMs (open until 10pm) outside the airport for Visa/MasterCard withdrawals.
Banco do Brasil (Map p407; Av Getúlio Vargas 915; ☺ 11am-4pm Mon-Fri) Visa/MasterCard ATMs and money exchange.
HSBC (Map p407; Av Getúlio Vargas 346; ☺ 9am-5pm Mon-Fri) Visa/MasterCard ATM.

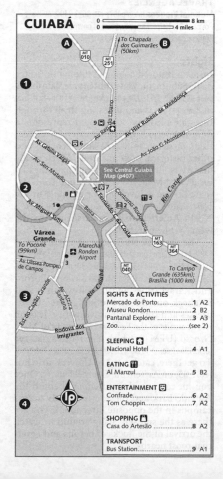

CUIABÁ

SIGHTS & ACTIVITIES
Mercado do Porto..................1 A2
Museu Rondon......................2 B2
Pantanal Explorer 3 A3
Zoo..................................(see 2)

SLEEPING
Nacional Hotel 4 A1

EATING
Al Manzul.............................5 B2

ENTERTAINMENT
Confrade..............................6 A2
Tom Choppin........................7 A2

SHOPPING
Casa do Artesão 8 A2

TRANSPORT
Bus Station............................9 A1

POST
Post office (Map p407; Praça da República 101; 9am-5pm Mon-Fri, 8am-noon Sat)

TOURIST INFORMATION
CAT tourist office (Map p407; Praça Rachid Jaudy; 8am-6pm Mon-Fri) This tourist office is frequently and inexplicably closed, but there is a small tourist-information booth in the arrivals hall of the airport and at the bus station. The cartoonish city map is unfortunately pretty useless.

Sedtur (Map p407; 3613 9300; Rua Voluntários da Pátria 118; 8am-8pm Mon-Fri) An alternative source of information in the city center is the office of the secretary of tourism, which has some helpful maps and brochures in Portuguese.

TRAVEL AGENCIES
Mundial Viagens (Map p407; 3623 3499; Av Isaac Póvoas 586) Helpful agency, west of downtown, for domestic and international flights.

Sights
Inside a restored colonial building on Praça da República, the **Museu Histórico de Mato Grosso** (Map p407; 3613 9234; admission free; 8am-8pm Tue-Fri, 8am-3pm Sat) is an interesting stroll through the state's history. Each room represents a different period and houses extensive collections of silver, military paraphernalia, and other historical odds and ends. Much of the history is illustrated in vibrant paintings by local artist Moacyr Freitas, though some artistic license is involved, for example in the *Destrução do Quilombo do Piolho*, where a North American bald eagle soars over the weary yet bemused slaves.

The small **Museu Rondon** (Map p405; 3615 8489; Av Fernando Correia da Costa; admission free; 1:30-5:30pm Mon, 7:30-11:30am & 1:30-5:30pm Tue-Sat, 9am-5:30pm Sun) has exhibits on the Xavante, Bororo and Karajá tribes and is well worth a visit to check out the ornate indigenous headdresses and some vicious weaponry. It is on the grounds of the Federal University of Mato Grosso (UFMT), which also has a small **zoo** (admission free; 7:30-11:30am & 1:30-5:30pm Tue-Sun). To get there, catch a 103 Jd Universitário bus (R$1.85) on Av Tenente Coronel Duarte. Once you hit campus, the museum is behind the Aquatic Park and the zoo is directly across campus in the opposite direction. If you are there as the sun sets, hang around to watch the arrival of the flocks of herons and egrets that roost nearby.

Probably the city's oddest museum is the **Museu Morro da Caixa D´Agua Velha** (off Map p407; Rua Comandante Costa; admission R$2, free Thu; 9am-noon & 2-6pm Tue-Fri, 10am-noon & 1-5pm Sat & Sun), which brings together a variety of frankly weird water-themed trinkets, from old tubes to shower heads. Far more interesting than the display is the construction itself, the city's former water tank dating from 1882 and built in the style of a Roman aqueduct. A short walk away, an obelisk marks the **Centro Geodésico da America do Sul** (off Map p407; Rua Barão de Melgaço), one of the exact centers of the continent according to the locals. There is of course only one real exact centre of South America, but inhabitants of Chapada dos Guimarães claim that it actually resides there. If you care enough to find out who is right, check Google Earth!

Close to the municipal aquarium, the **Mercado do Porto** (Map p405; 6am-6pm Mon-Sat, to noon Sun) houses the fish market, with a variety of species, as well as a vegetable and spice market. It's a good place to check out what the region's fish look like before they arrive at your table.

Tours
For details about excursions from Cuiabá into the Pantanal, see p417.

Festivals
The **Festa de São Benedito** takes place during the first week of July at the Igreja NS do Rosário and the Capela de São Benedito. The holiday has a more Umbanda than Catholic flavor; it's celebrated with colorful, traditional dances and regional foods such as *bolos de queijo* (cheese balls) and *bolos de arroz* (rice balls).

Sleeping
Price reductions are common during the week and out of season (November to May).

Pousada Ecoverde (Map p407; 3624 1386; www .ecoverdetours.com.br; Rua Pedro Celestino 391; s/d R$25/40) If you are looking for a place with character, this rustic pousada in a 100-year old colonial house has bags of it. Owner and local wildlife expert Joel Souza of Ecoverde Tours (p417) is one of the founders of ecotourism in the area and his homely hotel is full of antique radios and books on the Pantanal. There's also a small courtyard and garden, plus washing machine and kitchen for guest use.

Hotel Ramos (Map p407; 3624 7472; www.hotelramos.com.br; Rua Campo Grande 487; s/d R$25/50;) Big,

CENTRAL CUIABÁ

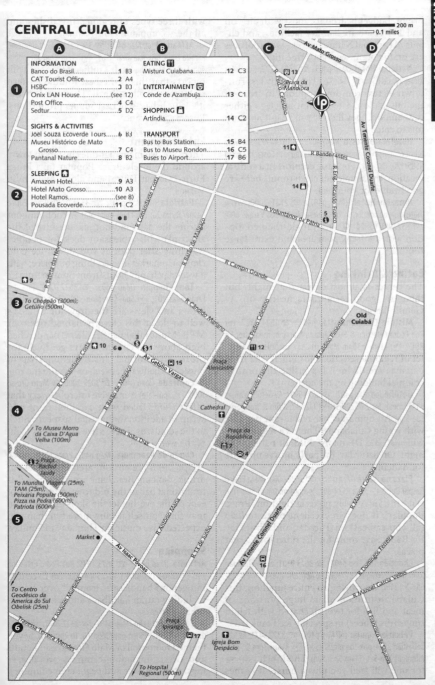

INFORMATION
Banco do Brasil.............................**1** B3
CAT Tourist Office.......................**2** A4
HSBC..**3** D3
Onix LAN House.....................(see **12**)
Post Office...................................**4** C4
Sedtur...**5** D2

SIGHTS & ACTIVITIES
Joël Souza Ecoverde Tours.......**6** B3
Museu Histórico de Mato
    Grosso.......................................**7** C4
Pantanal Nature.........................**8** B2

SLEEPING
Amazon Hotel..............................**9** A3
Hotel Mato Grosso..................**10** A3
Hotel Ramos........................(see **8**)
Pousada Ecoverde....................**11** C2

EATING
Mistura Cuiabana.....................**12** C3

ENTERTAINMENT
Conde de Azambuja..................**13** C1

SHOPPING
Artíndia.......................................**14** C2

TRANSPORT
Bus to Bus Station...................**15** B4
Bus to Museu Rondon..............**16** C5
Buses to Airport.......................**17** B6

bright, budget bedrooms, most with air-con and TV. There are laundry facilities, and clients of Pantanal Nature (p417) – whose offices are on the premises – get a free night.

Nacional Hotel (Map p405; ☎ 3621 3277; Rua Jules Rimet 22; s/d R$45/90; ✂ ▯) The slightly less rundown of two run-down options in front of the bus station. There is not much to either of them, but they'll do if you've got an early bus to catch.

Hotel Mato Grosso (Map p407; ☎ 3614 7777; www.ho telmt.com.br, in Portuguese; Rua Comandante Costa 2522; s/d R$85/120; ✂ ▯) For basic comfort in a central location, the simple but clean rooms here are good value for your real.

Amazon Hotel (Map p407; ☎ 2121 2000; www .hotelamazon.com.br, in Portuguese; Av Getúlio Vargas 600; s/d R$279/370; ✂ ▯ ▭) Jungle-themed option with a kitschy pool area and extra-large rooms.

Eating & Drinking

The center is almost deserted at night, but there are good restaurants nearby on Av Getúlio Vargas.

Mistura Cuiabana (Map p407; ☎ 3624 1127; cnr Rua Pedro Celestino & Rua Cândido Mariano; meals per kg R$17; ✆ 11am-2:30pm Mon-Fri) An excellent buffet of regional selections for lunch (the fried bananas are divine). It's inside the orange colonial building on the corner.

Getúlio (off Map p407; ☎ 3624 9992; Av Getúlio Vargas 1147; meals for 2 R$22-55; ✆ 11am-2:30pm & from 5pm Tue-Sun) An upmarket bar-restaurant popular with young Cuiabános. There's a respectable wine list, and DJs on the outdoor patio every night. On Saturday, the party moves upstairs for dancing.

Pizza na Pedra (Map p407; ☎ 3622 0060; Praça Eurico Gaspar Dutra 45; pizza R$34-89; ✆ 6pm-midnight Sun-Thu, to 1am Fri & Sat) A lively pizzeria right on 'Praça Popular'. It does an excellent pizza *rodízio* (all you can eat) on Tuesday and Thursday for R$28. Save room for the ridiculous sweet pizzas.

Choppão (off Map p407; ☎ 3623 9101; www.choppao .com.br, in Portuguese; Praça 8 de Abril s/n; meals for 2 R$35-65; ✆ 24hr) Occupying an entire junction, this Cuiabá institution offers huge portions of meat and fish for two, all chased with frigid *chope* (draft beer) in specially iced tankards.

Peixaria Popular (off Map p407; ☎ 3322 5471; Av São Sebastião 2324; prix-fixe meals R$44; ✆ 11am-3pm & 7pm-midnight Tue Sat, 11am-5pm Sun) The lunch course for one will feed you plus a horse. It comes

with three types of regional fish dishes and all the accompaniments. A must.

Al Manzul (off Map p405; ☎ 3663 2237; Av Arquimedes Pereira Lima; prix-fixe meal R$89; ✆ 11am-3pm Sat, noon-4pm Sun, 7-11pm Thu-Sat) It's difficult to argue with reports that this is the best Middle Eastern restaurant in all of Brazil. There's no menu: it's a 30-dish feast of Last Supper proportions. Reserve in advance.

Entertainment

There are two main nightlife clusters in town, around the lovely Praça Popular (aka Praça Eurico Gaspar Dutra) and along Av Getúlio Vargas.

Patriota (off Map p407; ☎ 3324 0740; Praça Eurico Gaspar Dutra 20; ✆ 11am-midnight) A cool hangout during the day (and not just because of the air-con!) with a pleasant deck for people-watching after dark as you sip an ice-cold *chope*. Upmarket in everything but price, with a weekday happy hour (from 5pm to 9pm).

Tom Choppin (Map p405; ☎ 3627 7227; Rua das Laranjeiras 701; ✆ 5pm-late Mon-Sat) Outstanding brews and views are the draw for Cuiabá's well-to-do at this cleverly named open-air MPB (Música Popular Brasileira) bar perched high above the city. Mondays get lively for *choro*, an informal, instrumental style of music. It's halfway between *centro* and the zoo.

Confrade (Map p405; ☎ 3027 2000; Av Mato Grosso 1000; ✆ 5pm-late) A massive microbrewery that offers *chope* laced with caramel, mint and syrup in addition to the usual suspects. Stick to the standards. There's live MPB every night of the week.

Conde de Azambuja (Map p407; Praça da Mandioca; ✆ 7pm-late) If pretensions aren't your bag but drunk, dancing Brazilians are, then give this traditional bar in the old town a try. It's not easy on the eye, but let the Skols flow and you may find yourself having more fun than you expected. Live music on Thursday to Sunday.

Shopping

Artíndia (Map p407; ☎ 3623 1675; Rua Pedro Celestino s/n; ✆ 8:30-11:30am & 1:30-5:30pm Mon-Fri) Excellent indigenous handicrafts from all over Brazil, including rattan handbags and a healthy arsenal of spears.

Casa do Artesão (Map p405; ☎ 3322 2047; cnr Rua 13 de Junho 315; ✆ 9am-6pm Mon-Fri, to 2pm Sat) Seven themed rooms full of Mato Grosso handicrafts and sweets, including ceramics, woodcarvings, straw baskets and *pequi* créme liquor.

Getting There & Away

There are flights between Cuiabá and many airports in Brazil (with the notable omission of Corumbá in Mato Grosso do Sul) by **Gol** (☎ 3614 2500), **TAM** (☎ 3624 0055), **Azul** (☎ 0800 884 4040) and **Avianca Brasil** (☎ 0800 286 6543). The latter and **Trip** (☎ 3682 2555) fly to Alta Floresta.

Frequent buses make the trip to Poconé (R$15.85, 2½ hours, six daily); the first leaves at 6am. There are two buses daily to Barão de Melgaço (R$24.85, 2½ hours). For Chapada dos Guimarães (R$11, one hour) there are buses every hour from 7am; take an early bus if you're doing a day trip.

Buses go to Cáceres (R$42, four hours, seven daily), with connections to Santa Cruz in Bolivia. Porto Velho (R$99, 24 hours, two daily) is a long ride. There are buses to Goiânia (R$134, 15 hours, six daily) and Brasília (R$143, 15 hours, five daily). Most of the buses to Campo Grande (R$80.50, 11 hours, four daily) stop at Coxim (R$62, seven hours). To Alta Floresta (R$145, 13½ hours, four daily), the first bus leaves at 6am, but to arrive early in the morning the 4pm departure suits you best.

Getting Around

Marechal Rondon airport (☎ 3614 2500) is in Várzea Grande, 7km from Cuiabá. To catch the local bus to town, turn left as you leave the airport and walk to the Las Velas Hotel. On the left side of the hotel, catch a bus labeled Shopping Pantanal and get off at Av Getúlio Vargas and Av Tenente Coronel Duarte. Praça da República is 200m northwest on Av Getúlio Vargas. A taxi costs R$30.

Cuiabá's **bus station** (Map p405; ☎ 3621 3629) is 3km north of the center on the highway toward Chapada dos Guimarães. From inside the bus station, you can get a Centro bus to Praça Alencastro (R$2.30). More frequent buses marked 'Centro' leave from outside the bus station and can drop you along Av Isaac Póvoas; get off in front of the CAT office. A taxi from inside the bus station costs R$12, or mototaxis run the trip for R$9. Bus 7 runs between the airport and the bus station.

All the car-rental places have branches in the center and in or near the airport. There are often promotional rates, so shop around. **Referência** (☎ 3682 6689) and **Localiza** (☎ 3624 7979) are a couple of reliable companies. The best car for the Pantanal is the Volkswagen Gol, but in the wet season (November to March) you'll need a 4x4 and off-road driving experi-

ence. A rental car with unlimited kilometers will cost around R$120 a day.

CHAPADA DOS GUIMARÃES

☎ 0xx65 / pop 18,000

After the Pantanal, the Parque Nacional da Chapada dos Guimarães is Mato Grosso's leading attraction. As little known as it is spectacular, the park is on a rocky plateau 64km northeast of Cuiabá and 800m higher, offering a cool change from the state capital. The region is reminiscent of the American Southwest and surprisingly different from the typical Mato Grosso terrain. The town of the same name is a convenient base for exploring the park and surrounding areas and is home to one of the lushest central squares in Brazil.

The area surrounding the park has numerous attractions. On the way from Cuiabá to Chapada town, you pass **Rio dos Peixes**, **Rio Mutaca** and **Rio Claro**, which are popular weekend bathing spots for Cuiabános; and three commanding valleys, **Vale do Salgadeira**, **Vale do Paciência** and **Vale do Rio Claro**. The sheer 80m drop called **Portão do Inferno** (Hell's Gate) is also unforgettable – it was formerly the town 'prison' in the early 1900s (use your imagination). In **Salgadeira**, 14km outside of Cuiabá, you can take a waterfall shower or grab a beer at one of the four restaurants that sit under the imposing cliffs. The whole thing is one drawn-out Kodak moment.

Information

If you're driving, drop by the official tourist office, **CAT** (☎ 3301 2045; Rua Penn Gomes s/n; ⏰ 7am-6pm Mon-Sat, 8am-noon & 2-5pm Sun), where a cartoonish map is available. You'll need it!
Bradesco (Rua Fernando Corréia da Costa 868) The only ATM in town accepting foreign cards.
Post office (Rua Fernando Corréia da Costa 848) Next door to Bradesco, a block from the main square.

Parque Nacional da Chapada dos Guimarães

Only receiving national park status in 1989, the outstanding Parque Nacional da Chapada dos Guimarães remains a tad under the radar in the context of Brazil's most impressive national parks. Let us pray for status quo. As its offerings are as spectacular as anything in Brazil, you usually won't have to share them with anyone. Amen.

The two exceptional sights inside the park are the Véu de Noiva falls and the Cidade de

Pedra. There is a **visitors center** (☎ 3301 1133; admission free; ⏰ 8am-5pm) at the park entrance, but note that access to the attractions is controlled to avoid congestion. Try to visit during the week when it is quietest.

The impressive **Véu de Noiva** (Bridal Veil), an 86m free-falling waterfall, provides the park's ubiquitous postcard moment. It is around 15km west of the town of Chapada dos Guimarães. You can get off the bus from Cuiabá and walk from the road, spend a couple of hours there, then flag down the next bus coming through to Chapada town. Start walking downhill over the bluff, slightly to your right. A small trail leads to a magical **lookout**, perched on top of rocks with the canyon below. This is one of Chapada's most dazzling spots.

From there, most visitors join the **Caminho das Águas**, a 6km hike that takes in seven swimmable waterfalls throughout the park. But it's **Cidade de Pedra** (Stone City) that provides Guimarães' most transcendent moment. Jagged sandstone rock formations reminiscent of stone temples jut up into the sky from the tops of enormous cliffs that drop down into the vast green valley below. The best time to visit is sunset, when fiery red light illuminates the whole area in a monumental display of color and light. It's 20km north of Chapada town along the road to Água Fria. The turnoff to Água Fria is 6km west of Chapada town on Hwy MT-251. Note that at the time of writing the Cidade de Pedra was temporarily closed to visitors pending a review of safety procedures.

Mirante

The Mirante (Lookout) is the unofficial geographic center of South America. It's a tad underwhelming, with nothing marking the occasion beyond a blank concrete slab that looks more like a manhole cover than a major geographical designator. That said, the views are miraculous; off to your right you can see the Cuiabá skyline, and beyond that, the flatlands that eventually become the Pantanal. It's outside the national park, 8km from town. Take the last road in Chapada on your right and go 8km; you'll see a dirt road. The rim of the canyon is a couple of hundred meters away.

Tours

Chapada Explorer(☎ 3301 1290; www.chapadaexplorer .com.br; Praça Dom Wunibaldo 57, Chapada dos Guimarães;

⏰ 8-11:30am & 1:30-6:30pm Mon-Fri, 8-11:30am Sat & Sun) is an excellent agency run by a couple of young locals who have grown up around ecotourism. They are actively involved in teaching the benefits of low-impact tourism to locals. It runs excursions to all of the area's attractions in groups up to a maximum of 10. Bring your own food; the price does not include admission costs, which range from R$2 to R$17.60.

Sleeping & Eating

There is camping with good facilities at Salgadeira, just before the climb into the Chapada park. Chapada town has plenty of accommodations.

Pousada Bom Jardim (☎ 3301 2668; Praça Dom Wunibaldo 461; s/d R$60/80) There's no reason to spring for air-con at this cheapie right in the main square – the fans are high-octane. A favorite with backpackers.

Turismo Hotel (☎ 3301 1176; www.hotelturismo .com.br, in Portuguese; Rua Fernando Corrêa da Costa 1065; s/d R$163/217; 🅿 🛉) A spotless place run by a German family. The traditional breakfast spread is encased in glass – no flies!

Pousada do Parque Eco Lodge (☎ 3391 1346; www.pousadadoparque.com.br; Estrada do Parque Ecológico Km 52; s/d R$210/235; 🅿 💻 🛉) This high-end ecochoice borders 150 hectares of newly preserved park land and is the closest accommodations to the park's entrance (4.5km). All the wood used in the construction of this pousada came from recycled sources and the roofs are made of recycled milk cartons. Book in advance.

Solar do Inglês (☎ 3301 1389; www.solardoingles .com.br, in Portuguese; Rua Cipriano Curvo 142; s/d R$240/330; 🅿 💻 🛉) This quaint pousada owned by an English former Jaguar hunter is full of Victorian charm and European antiques. The afternoon tea is one of Brazil's most authentic. No children.

Felipe (☎ 3301 1793; Rua Cipriano Curvo 596; meals per kg R$18; ⏰ noon-11pm) Fill your boots without emptying your pockets at this per-kilo extravaganza just off the main square.

Da Mata Bistro (☎ 3301 3483; Estrada do Mirante km1, dishes R$18-32; ⏰ 8pm-2am Fri, 5pm-2am Sat, 11am-5pm Sun) A romantic bistro with stupendous views from the same owners as nearby Morro dos Ventos (also good). It's high-class contemporary Brazilian cuisine 4km east of town along Hwy MT-251 in the direction of Campo Verde. The homemade pasta buffet on Sunday is worth telling your grandchildren about.

DETOUR: BOM JARDIM & LAGOA AZUL

If you can't make it to Bonito (p428) then you can get a similar experience by making a detour to the attractions in the area around **Bom Jardim** (www.rotasdasaguas.tur.br), 150km north of Cuiabá. The number one attraction here is **Recanto Ecológico Lagoa Azul**, 8km from town, where you can snorkel (R$65) in the 'Reino Encantado' (Enchanted Kingdom) and float leisurely along the 'Rio Triste' (Sad River). A natural aquarium reminiscent of Rio da Prata in Bonito, the difference here is that you will likely have the place to yourself. Nearby are some hidden caves (the guide will show you the way) complete with roosting bats and weird rock formations.

There is one bus a day from Cuiabá to Bom Jardim at 2:30pm (R$35, five hours) with the return leaving at 5am. The town itself has a number of small hotels and a natural swimming pool to while away the hottest hour of the day. Just a 15-minute walk outside of town (ask for directions, it's easy to find!) is **Lagoa das Araras**, where several species of colorful macaws come noisily to roost each night.

Restaurante Cachoeirinha (☎ 9216 3497; MT-251 km51; meals for 2 R$45-97; ☼ 8am-6pm) An outstanding restaurant on private parkland under the nose of two beautiful waterfalls. The pricy *pintado na telha* (pintado grilled on tiles; R$52) is unforgettable. Of the R$10 admission price, R$5 goes toward your check. Highly recommended.

Getting There & Away

Buses leave Cuiabá's bus station for Chapada town (R$11, 1¼ hours) hourly from 5:45am to 7:30pm. In the other direction, the first bus leaves Chapada town at 6:30am and the last at 7:30pm. The miraculous views are out the right-side window from Cuiabá.

CÁCERES

☎ 0xx65 / pop 87,000

Boats and bikes get top billing in sweltering Cáceres, a quiet little town that hugs the banks of the impressive Rio Paraguai. Anglers flock here for the rich fishing waters in the area, especially during September, when it attracts 150,000 visitors for the world's biggest fishing competition (see the boxed text, p412). The main attractions here are the *barco-hotels*, floating accommodations for anglers that set off along the Rio Paraguai for days at a time. When not on the water, locals love to be on two wheels, and the town has a progressive amount of bike lanes for Brazil. It's also an access point for a few Pantanal lodges and Bolivia. Note that fishing for dourado has been temporarily prohibited until 2013.

Information

Banks (Praça Barão do Rio Branco) All the major banks have ATMs here.

Federal Police (☎ 3211 6300; Av Getúlio Vargas 2125; ☼ 8am-6pm) If you're traveling on to Corixio on the Bolivian border, get a Brazilian exit stamp from here. It is 4km from town, close to the *prefeitura* (city hall).

Hospital São Luis (☎ 3223 1000; Av 7 de Setembro) For yellow-fever vaccinations.

Orion LAN House (Praça Barão do Rio Branco 27; per hr R$2.50; ☼ 10am-midnight) Internet access.

Post office (Av 7 de Setembro; ☼ 9am-5pm Mon-Fri)

Sematur (☎ 3223 3455; Rua Riachuelo 1; ☼ 7am-8pm Mon-Fri) For help hiring boats and arranging accommodations in the Pantanal, this local tourist office is currently the be all and end all, though there is talk of a new CAT office opening at the entrance to town. Head to the river and follow the road to the right as far as it goes.

Sleeping & Eating

All the action in Cáceres happens around the riverfront and nearby Praça Barão do Rio Branco, where there are many restaurants and bars.

Gasparin Hotel (☎ 3223 4328; www.hotelgasparin .com.br, in Portuguese; Rua 13 de Junho 650; s/d R$30/60; ✷) It's run-down and a little depressing, but what do you expect so close to the bus station?

Hotel Porto Bello (☎ 3224 1937; Av São Luís 1888; s/d R$55/85; ✷ 🖳) Too bad the nicest digs in town sit 5km from the city center and doesn't offer a pool. But it's otherwise the most colorful and comfortable option.

La Barca Hotel (☎ 3223 5047; Rua General Osório s/n; s/d R$60/108; ✷ 🖳 🐾) A good option 2km from the center, with rooms around a large courtyard and a wonderful pool. The singles are good value.

Riviera Pantanal Hotel (☎ 3223 1177; Rua General Osório 540; s/d R$120/160; ✷ 🖳) Tries hard to achieve a chain-hotel style of service, rendering it functional, but a little uptight. That

CATCH OF THE DAY

Every September, 150,000 people, most of them toting fishing poles, descend on Cáceres for the **Festival Internacional de Pesca**, recognized by the *Guinness Book of World Records* as the world's largest fishing fête. Since 1979 the waters of the Rio Paraguai have been inundated by feverish fisherman from some 15 countries, all out to nab (and release) the largest pintado, dourado and pacu fish they can get their hooks on. Winners take home R$30,000 cars or boat motors. There are dance troupes by the river and local children – some 1500 strong – are taught the ecobenefits of catch-and-release fishing.

said, it has all the facilities you might expect from a chain hotel at a fraction of the cost.

Restaurant Hispano (☎ 3223 1486; Praça Barão do Rio Branco 64; meals per kg R$20; 11am-4pm) A solid per-kilo option on the main square with river views. The homemade potato chips are nice.

Kaskata Restaurante Flutuante (☎ 3223 2916; Beira-Rio; meals for 2 R$30-60; 9:30am-11pm) The best floating restaurant in town. Regional fish is the specialty here, but if you're looking to try *jacaré* (caiman), it is served three ways.

Betto's (☎ 3223 1048; Rua 15 de Noviembre 1; meals for 2 R$36-58; 10:30am-midnight) A lively outdoor spot by the river with a ridiculously diverse menu, including *jacaré*. Tell them to make it snappy!

Getting There & Away

The little bus station is 10 blocks north of the riverfront, though the bus from Cuiabá stops first at the big station just outside the city center in Vale do Araguaia, which is confusingly called the 'Terminal Rodoviario de Cáceres'. Frequent buses make the journey between Cuiabá and Cáceres (R$42, four hours, seven daily). There are also bus services to Porto Velho (R$140, two daily). You will be asked to show your passport to buy bus tickets. Regular minibuses run to the border town of Corixio from where there is onward transport to the Bolivian town of San Matías.

ALTA FLORESTA

☎ 0xx66 / pop 51,000

Technically, Alta Floresta, 873km from Cuiabá in the extreme north of Mato Grosso, sits at the interface of the northern cerrado and the southern Amazon rain-forest biomes. Its landscapes, however, are all Amazon. The area around Cristalino Private Natural Heritage Preserve is considered one of Amazonia's best for spotting rare birds and mammals, including the endangered white-nosed bearded saki monkey, lowland tapir, giant otter, three-toed sloth and five species of macaw.

Alta Floresta is the end of the road: beyond it to the north is the vast expanse of the jungle, with the exception of a brief reappearance of cerrado in the northern neighbor state of Pará. The town itself has no attractions and has grown rapidly as an agricultural and logging center since its foundation in the early 1970s.

Tours

If you are short on time or money and can't spend the night at the Cristalino Jungle Lodge (the only way to see the abundant wildlife here unless you are on a fishing trip), **Floresta Tours** (☎ 3521 7100; www.florestatour.com.br; 8am-5pm Mon-Fri, to noon Sat) offers day trips into the Cristalino Private Natural Heritage Preserve for around R$200 per person. The trip takes nine hours and includes transfers, guides, excursions and lunch at the lodge. The agency is located at the Floresta Amazônica Hotel. Advance reservations are required.

Sleeping & Eating

Many visitors to the area are naturalists on expensive package tours to isolated jungle lodges, but independent travelers will find a few good accommodations in town.

Lisboa Palace (☎ 3521 2876; www.hotellisboa.com.br; Av Jaime Verissimo de Campos 251; s/d R$75/100;) The sizable rooms here are clean and modern, though the beds are a tad hard. A suitable alternative if Floresta Amazônica is booked out.

Floresta Amazônica Hotel (☎ 3512 7100; www.fah .com.br; Av Perimetral Oeste 2001; s/d R$80/100;) Not your average business hotel, set in jungly surroundings 5km from *centro*. It's in need of a touch-up, but the rooms with balconies around a lovely garden are pleasant, as is that wonderful pool. It's affiliated with the Cristalino Jungle Lodge.

Cristalino Jungle Lodge (☎ 3521 1396; www.cristalinolodge.com.br; s/d packages per person from R$500/400) On the banks of the Rio Cristalino (39km north of Alta Floresta) in an area rich in Amazon flora and fauna, the lodge offers a 50m-high observation tower and 20km of good bird-watching trails (it is considered one of the top 50 spots in the world for birding). The new VIP bungalows ooze creature-comfort luxe. Rates include transfers, all meals, guides, excursions and insurance.

Café Mostarda (☎ 3521 3103; Av Ariosto da Riva 3493; meals per kg R$22; ☽ 6am-6pm Mon-Fri, to 2pm Sat) An exceptionally well-to-do per-kilo place with excellent regional food.

Getting There & Away

From Cuiabá there are frequent buses to Alta Floresta (R$145, 13½ hours, four daily). **Trip** (☎ 0xx65-3682 2555) flies from Cuiabá to Alta Floresta (R$395, two hours) at 11.55am and 8:30pm. **Avianca Brasil** (☎ 0800 286 6543) also runs the route.

POCONÉ
☎ 0xx65 / pop 32,000

The main entry point to the Pantanal for travelers heading south from Cuiabá, Poconé marks the beginning of the Transpantaneira 'highway.' Poconé still has a sleepy, frontier feel (as one local put it, 'In Poconé, even the restaurants close for lunch!'). The locals, many of whom are descended from the original tribe in the area, the Beripoconeses, have a strong sense of tradition.

In May, Poconé celebrates the week-long **Semana do Fazendeiro e do Cavalo Pantaneiro** with a cattle fair and rodeos.

Information

Banco do Brasil (Praça da Matriz) Has a Visa/MasterCard ATM but don't bet your life on it working.
CAT Office (Praça Menino Jésus; ☽ 7am-noon & 2-5pm Mon-Fri, 8am-noon Sat & Sun)
Dibtop LAN House (Praça da Matriz; per hr R$1.50; ☽ 8am-11pm) Internet access.
Hospital (☎ 3345 1963; Rua Dom Aquino 406)
Police (☎ 3345 1456)
Post office (Rua Coronel Salvador Marques 335)

Tours

The only agency in town that caters to serious fishers, **Transpantanal** (☎ 3345 2343; www .transpantanal.com.br, in Portuguese; Av Aníbal de Toledo 1895; ☽ 7:30am-6pm Mon-Fri, to noon Sat) offers seven-day fishing packages along the rivers Cuiabá, São Lourenço, Piquiri and Paraguai for R$2500 per person (minimum 12).

Sleeping, Eating & Drinking

The best places to stay, especially if you're trying to organize a lift down the Trans-

pantaneira, are a couple of kilometers out of town near the beginning of the road.

Hotel Santa Cruz (☎ 3345 2634; Rodovia Transpantaneira 450; per person R$25) The least attractive option but will do if the others are full.

Pousada Pantaneira (☎ 3345 3357; Transpantaneira Km 0; s/d R$40/60; ✗ ▢) With remodeled bathrooms, this simple pousada and churrascaria (barbecue restaurant) sits at the beginning of the Transpantaneira – a good base for organising a relaiable ride down the highway.

Hotel Skala (☎ 3345 1407; Praça Bem Rondon 64; s/d R$50/75; ✗ ▢) The best option in the center, with spacious if slightly dark rooms and the most sophisticated restaurant in town, Tradição, right next door.

Tropeiro Grill (☎ 8403 5401; Praça da Matriz; meals R$12-15) Great open-faced picanha (steak) sandwiches are the specialty here, but anything with meat is good. It's a simple little spot on the main square.

Atellier do Luizão (☎ 3345 2733; Rua Generoso Ponce 1101) A little bar in a huge craft shop of souvenirs and decorations all made on the premises. Unsurprisingly, most feature Pantanal wildlife designs.

Getting There & Away

Buses to/from Cuiabá first stop at the Poconé bus station about 10 blocks from the center of town, then continue on to Praça da Matriz; behind the Matriz church is the road that leads to the beginning of the Transpantaneira.

There are buses from Cuiabá to Poconé (R$15.85, two hours, every three hours) from 6am to 7pm, and six in the opposite direction from 6am to 7:30pm. Alternatively, taxis leaving from the **Ponto de Taxi** (☎ 3345 1441) at Praça da Matriz will drop you at your final destination in Cuiabá for a mere R$30 per person if full.

THE PANTANAL

The Amazon may attract more fame and glory, but the Pantanal is a better place to see wildlife. The dense foliage of the Amazon makes it difficult to observe the animals, but in the open spaces of the Pantanal, wildlife is much easier to see. If you like to see animals in their natural environment, the Pantanal should not be missed.

Located in the center of South America, the world's largest wetland is 20 times the

MATO GROSSO & MATO
GROSSO DO SUL

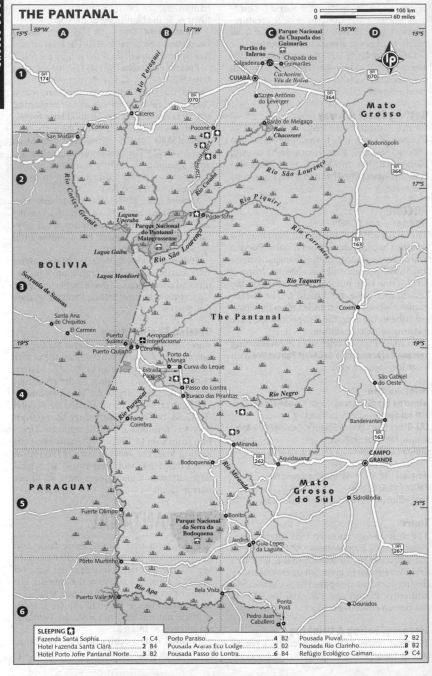

THE PANTANAL

| | | 0 | | 100 km |
| | | 0 | | 60 miles |

size of the famed Everglades in Florida – some 210,000 sq km. Something less than 100,000 sq km of this is in Bolivia and Paraguay; the rest is in Brazil, split between the states of Mato Grosso and Mato Grosso do Sul.

The Pantanal has few people and no towns. Distances are so great and ground transport so poor that people get around in small airplanes and motorboats; 4WD travel is restricted by the seasons. The only road that runs deep into the Pantanal is the Transpantaneira. This raised dirt road sectioned by about 125 small wooden bridges ends 145km south of Poconé, at Porto Jofre. Two-thirds of the intended route from Poconé to Corumbá (at the border with Bolivia) is incomplete for lack of funds and, more importantly, for ecological concerns.

The Parque Nacional do Pantanal Mato-grossense occupies 1350 sq km in the south-west of Mato Grosso, but most of the Pantanal is privately owned. Cooperation between eco-tourism and the landowners in the region (mostly cattle ranchers) has contributed to the sustainable conservation of the environment. By providing ranchers with an income that encourages their coexistence with the wildlife it covers the shortfall created by the seasonal flooding of the area, which would otherwise be covered by more intensive (and hence more destructive) ranching efforts. The national park and three smaller private nature reserves nearby were given Unesco World Heritage listing in 2000.

GEOGRAPHY & CLIMATE

Although *pantano* means 'swamp' in both Spanish and Portuguese, the Pantanal is not a swamp but, rather, a vast alluvial plain. In geological terms, it is a sedimentary basin of quaternary origin, the drying remains of an ancient inland sea called the Xaraés, which began to dry out, along with the Amazon Sea, 65 million years ago.

First sea, then immense lake and now a seasonally flooded plain, the Pantanal – 2000km upstream from the Atlantic Ocean yet just 100m to 200m above sea level – is bounded by higher lands: the mountains of the Serra de Maracaju to the east, the Serra da Bodoquena to the south and the Serra dos Parecis and Serra do São Geronimo to the north. From these highlands the rains flow into the Pantanal, forming the Rio Paraguai and its tributaries (which flow south and then east, draining into the Atlantic Ocean).

During the wet season (November to March), the rivers flood their banks, inundating much of the low-lying Pantanal and creating *cordilheiras* (vegetation islands above the high-water level), where the animals cluster together. The waters reach their high mark – up to 3m – in January or February, then start to recede in March. This seasonal flooding has made systematic farming impossible and has severely limited human incursions into the area. However, it does provide an enormously rich feeding ground for wildlife.

The floodwaters replenish the soil's nutrients, which would otherwise be very poor, due to the excessive drainage. The waters teem with fish, and the ponds provide protective niches for many animals and plants. Enormous flocks of wading birds gather in rookeries several square kilometers in area.

Later in the dry season, the water recedes, the lagoons and marshes dry out and fresh grasses emerge on the savanna (the Pantanal's vegetation includes savanna, forest and meadows, which blend together, often with no clear divisions). The hawks and caimans (*jacaré*) compete for fish in the remaining ponds. As the ponds shrink and dry up, the caimans crawl around for water, sweating it out until the rains return.

PLANNING
When to Go

Go whenever you can, but if possible go during the dry season (April to September). The best time to watch birds is from July to September, when the waters have receded and the bright-green grasses pop up from the muck. Temperatures are not hot by day and cool by night, with occasional short bursts of rain.

Flooding, incessant rains and heat make travel difficult during the wet season (November to March), though this time is not without its special rewards – this is when the cattle and wildlife of the Pantanal clump together on the *cordilheiras*. However, the islands are covered with dense vegetation that can make spotting wildlife difficult. The heaviest rains fall in February and March. Roads become impassable and travel is a logistical nightmare. Every decade or so, the flooding is disastrous, killing both humans and animals.

From June to August, the driest months, the chances of spotting jaguars rise dramatically. The heat peaks in November and December, when temperatures higher than 40°C (104°F)

CHOOSING A GUIDE IN THE PANTANAL

Pantanal tourism is big business and in the past some companies have been guilty of employing underhand tactics in the race to hook in clients. Though measures have finally been taken to clamp down on the worst offenders, it is still worth bearing a few suggestions in mind to have a safe and enjoyable trip.

- Resist making a snap decision, especially if you've just climbed off an overnight bus.
- Do not make your decision based on cost. Cheaper very rarely means better.
- Speak to other travelers. What was their experience like? Note that where Campo Grande is concerned many internet travel blogs have been flooded with a host of false reports posted by rival tour companies. Get your advice straight from the horse's mouth.
- Compare your options, but remember that the owner or salesperson is not always your guide, and it's the guide you're going to be with in the wilderness for three to five days. Ask to meet your guide if possible.
- Don't hand over your cash to any go-betweens.
- If you are even remotely concerned about sustainable tourism, do not use operators and lodges that harm this fragile environment. That means no picking up the animals for photographs or any touching them whatsoever.
- If time is a problem and money isn't, or if you'd just like a quality guide, contact **Focus Tours** (www.focustours.com) in the USA. Focus Tours specializes in nature tours and is active in trying to preserve the Pantanal.
- Budget tours focus squarely on the spectacular and easy-to-see species. If you are a serious wildlife-watcher you should be prepared to pay more for a private guide.

are common, roads turn to breakfast cereal, and the mosquitoes are out in force. Many hotels close at this time.

Fishing is best during the first part of the dry season (April to May), when the flooded rivers settle back into their channels, but locals have been known to lasso 80kg fish throughout the dry season. This is some of the best fishing in the world. There are about 20 species of piranha, as well as the tasty dourado, a feisty fellow (known locally as the river tiger) that reaches upwards of 9kg and preys on hapless fellow fish. Other excellent catches include pacu, suribim, bagre, giripoca, piraputanga, piapara, cachara, pirancajuva and pintado, to name but a few.

Although hunting is not allowed, fishing – with the required permits – is encouraged between about February and October. It is, however, prohibited during the *piracema* (breeding season) from November to the end of January, though the time frame varies year to year. Banco do Brasil branches in Cuiabá, Campo Grande and Coxim issue permits (from shore/boat R$24/60) valid for three months for fishing in the Pantanal. National fishing permits valid for one year are also available from **Ibama offices** (☎ in Cuiabá 0xx65-3644 1200, Campo Grande 0xx67-3317 2952, Corumbá 0xx67-3231 6096, Coxim 0xx67-3291 2310).

What to Bring

You can't buy much in the Pantanal, so come prepared. The dry season is also the cooler season. Bring attire suitable for hot days, coolish nights, rain and mosquitoes. Leave behind red (it scares animals), yellow (mosquitoes love it) and black clothing (it's too hot and mosquitoes love it, too). You'll need sunscreen, sunglasses, a hat, lightweight clothes, sneakers or boots, light rain gear and something warmer for the evening. Mosquito relief means long pants and long-sleeved shirts, vitamin B12 and insect repellent.

Bring binoculars, a towel and a strong flashlight. Don't forget your camera and, if you're serious about photography, a tripod and a long lens (300mm is about right for wildlife).

Health

There is no malaria in the Pantanal, but a dengue-fever outbreak in Mato Grosso do Sul in 2008 has the government taking preventative measures. It shouldn't be a problem for travelers, but if you're concerned, consult a travel-health expert for the latest information before you leave home. For more on these and other traveler's health concerns, see p725, or check out Lonely Planet's *Healthy Travel – Central & South America* by Isabelle Young.

There are medical services available in Cuiabá, Corumbá and Campo Grande.

TOURS

The principal access towns are Cuiabá in the north and Campo Grande in the south, with Corumbá on the Bolivian border more of a sideshow these days. You can arrange guided tours (or head off on your own) from any of these three towns. Tours from Cuiabá tend to be slightly more expensive, but more professional with smaller groups and better-trained guides than those from either Campo Grande or Corumbá. They also go deeper into the Pantanal. For tips on choosing a guide, see the boxed text, p416.

Cuiabá

From Cuiabá (p405), the capital of Mato Grosso, small tour operators arrange safaris along the Transpantaneira that include transportation, ranch accommodations on farms and guides. Guides are English-speaking and well-trained on the whole, and smaller groups increase your chances of seeing the shier animals. Fortunately, while there is healthy competition between tour operators in Cuiabá, it's not as intense as in Mato Grosso do Sul and typically operators share the same Pantanal camps.

Tours here are well organized and quite comfortable, starting from around R$180 per day – if you are serious about seeing animals they are worth the extra money. Some companies also offer a 'jaguar trek' for around R$400 per day, with an excellent chance of seeing this magnificent feline in the Porto Jofre area from June to October.

Joel Souza Ecoverde Tours (Map p407; ☎ 0xx65-3624 1386; www.ecoverdetours.com.br; Av Getúlio Vargas 155; ☺ 8am-6pm Mon-Sat) Top-notch company with 25 years of service and experienced guides. Working with local pousadas towards an ecofriendly approach, Joel Souza and his son Lauro can guide you in English, German, French, Portuguese or Spanish. You can also contact him at Pousada Ecoverde (p406).

Pantanal Explorer (Map p405; ☎ 0xx65-3682 2800; www.pantanalexplorer.com.br; Av Governador Ponce de Arruda 670, Várzea Grande) Owner Andre Von Thuronyi has been working with sustainable tourism in the area for 30 years and fights harmful government interference in the Pantanal with ferocity. He is actively involved in saving the hyacinth macaw and giant otter. Affiliated with Pousada Araras Eco Lodge.

Pantanal Nature (☎ 0xx65-3322 0203; www.pantanalnature.com.br; Rua Campo Grande 487) A new agency run by Ailton Lara that has quickly built up a sterling reputation for its professional tours and expert guides. It also runs a Jaguar Camp near Porto Jofre with excellent success

---

PANTANAL CUISINE

Pantaneiros – the local Pantanal folks – make good use of regional ingredients in preparing their delicacies. You'll find lots of restaurants offering regional specialties on your travels in the area – stop in and try some.

In the northern Pantanal, the cuisine is decidedly fishy. Pacu, dourado and pintado are the most consumed fish, and they come *frito* (fried), *grelhado* (grilled), *assado* (baked) or *defumado* (smoked). Both dourado and pacu have lots of small bones, but they separate easily when baked slowly. Pacu is often baked and served with an *escabeche* sauce consisting of onions, tomatoes and peppers. Another favorite fish is pintado, excellent when spiced with rough salt and pepper and grilled. One specialty is *peixe à urucum*, where the chosen fish is served topped with spices, condensed milk, coconut milk and melted mozzarella. Piranha soup is another exotic favorite, considered an aphrodisiac by the Pantaneiros.

On farms and in southern Pantanal, the dishes are more strongly influenced by the cattle and grains produced in the area. Specialties include *carne seca com abobora* (sun-dried beef with pumpkin) and *paçoca-de-pilã* (sun-dried beef with manioc flour), the latter eaten with bananas and unsalted rice. There's also *arroz de carreteiro* (rice with sun-dried beef served with fried manioc and banana) and *galinha caipira* – chicken served with white rice and *pequi*, a small yellow fruit of the cerrado. Don't bite into the *pequi* – its seed contains lots of spines! Pantanal desserts are sweet and tasty. Some popular ones are *furrundu* – a mixture of papaya trunk (not the fruit), sugarcane juice and coconut – and ice cream made from *bocaiúva*, another local fruit.

rates in seeing the animal in the dry season. The company has an office in Hotel Ramos (p406).

Campo Grande

Campo Grande (p421) has really cleaned up its act in recent years, with the opening of a new bus station on the outskirts of town that will hopefully make the mobbing and bullying of disembarking tourists a thing of the past. Local government also finally responded to the barrage of complaints it had been receiving from visitors by closing down the lodges that didn't comply with ecological legislation and tightening the screws on dodgy operators. Some problems still persist, but it's a big step in the right direction. The cheapest tours are rough-and-tumble affairs and groups are often large, but with prices starting at around R$100 per day it is an economical way to see the Pantanal and its wildlife.

Luiz Paivo Filho (☎ 0xx67-3042 4659) If you can't make your mind up about which agency to travel with, freelance guide Luiz comes highly recommended. Sure you'll pay a bit more for his personalized service, but Luiz's knowledge and fluent English will ensure a memorable trip.

Pantanal Discovery (Map p422; ☎ 0xx67-3383 9791; www.gilspantanaldiscovery.com.br; Rua Mercurio 42) Now associated with Fazenda Santa Clara, this is one of the most experienced agencies in Campo Grande. If buying a package it's worth paying a little extra for private accommodation in the *fazenda* rather than using the camp.

Pantanal Viagens & Turismo (Map p422; ☎ 0xx67-3321 3143; www.pantanalviagens.com.br; Rua Joaquim Nabuco 200, Loje 9 in the old bus station) A nice agency working mainly with Pousada Passo do Lontra that has worked hard to maintain its excellent reputation.

Corumbá

Nearly all of the tour companies once in Corumbá (p424) have decamped to Campo Grande or at least have offices there.

Canaã Viagens e Turismo (off Map p425; ☎ 0xx67-3231 2208; www.pantanalcanaa.com; Rua Colombo 245) is a recommended agency specializing in high-end fishing tours up the Rio Paraguai. It offers trips in two different *barco-hotels* and travels as far up the river as 300km. Minitours of three days and two nights leave twice a week and start at R$1000 per person, including all meals, fishing, guides and transfers.

SLEEPING

Pantanal accommodations are divided into three types: pousadas include all meals and range from simple to top-end; *fazendas* are ranch-style hotels that usually have horses and often boats for use; and *pesqueiros* cater for anglers and usually have boats and fishing gear for rent. Typical rental costs would be R$30 per person per hour for boat excursions and R$30 to R$45 for a couple of hours on horseback. If you have doubts about roughing it on the budget tours, it is probably better to spend a bit more money for basic comforts – a bed, running water and some hope of avoiding a million mosquito bites.

If you travel independently, rates will usually include modest lodgings, three meals and at least one excursion per day. Drinks – even soda and water – are extra. Transportation is almost never included in the room rates and can take a sizable chunk out of your budget. From Cuiabá, transfers in and out, via whatever combination of 4WD, boat, horseback and plane is necessary depending on the season, can run between R$250 to R$500 one-way. For this reason, it is almost always cheaper – not to mention logistically less stressful – to go in under the services of a tour operator. Transportation in and out is then included and they often have access to more remote lodges.

Mato Grosso

For accommodations in Cuiabá, see p406.

ALONG THE TRANSPANTANEIRA

Accommodations along the Transpantaneira are plentiful and offer a good variety of choices, from rustic to high end.

Porto Paraiso (☎ 0xx65-3345 2271; www.portalparaiso.com.br; Transpantaneira Km 17; camping R$25, s/d per person with full board R$150/250; ⌗ ▢ ▨) An excellent budget option on a small working buffalo and cattle farm near the beginning of the Transpantaneira. There are excellent camping facilities around the luxe pool area and some great bird-watching in the surroundings.

Pousada Rio Clarinho (☎ 0xx65-9959 2985; Transpantaneira Km 40; s/d R$120/240) An avian symphony is your wake-up call at this rustic *fazenda* right on the Rio Clarinho (there's a small river platform for swimming). With an extensive area of forest, there are more than 260 species of birds on the property, as well as capybaras and giant otters. The food is authentic Pantanal. Rates include all excursions.

Pousada Piuval (☎ 0xx65-3345 3479; Transpantaneira Km 10; www.pousadapiuval.com.br, in Portuguese; s/d with full board R$220/280; ❌ 🖥 🍴) It's a trade-off at the first pousada along the Transpantaneira: it's more commercial (feeding caimans) but also more comfortable. It sits on 70 sq km and is popular with Germans and bird-watchers. The pool is wonderful, as are sunset boat rides. It offers horseback riding, trekking and night safaris as well.

Pousada Araras Eco Lodge (☎ 0xx65-3682 2800; www.araraslodge.com.br; Transpantaneira Km 32; s/d R$250/330; ❌ 🖥 🍴) This pioneering lodge offers the most comfort and luxury along the Transpantaneira. Rooms have lovely artisanal bedspreads and all feature nice patios with hammocks separated by bamboo curtains.

There is a treetop tower for bird-watching (hyacinth macaws are always around) and an extensive bird list is available at check-in. Much of the food comes from its own farm. There is a cheaper, more rustic lodge, Passo da Ema, 4km into the property, which specializes in horseback riding.

PORTO JOFRE

Porto Jofre is where the Transpantaneira meets its end, at the Rio Cuiabá. It's a one-hotel town – in fact, it's not even a town; it's just a hotel.

Hotel Porto Jofre Pantanal Norte (☎ 0xx65-3637 1593; Transpantaneira Km145; www.portojofre.com.br; s/d

---

DRIVING THE TRANSPANTANEIRA

In 1973 the government decided to push a road through the Pantanal from Cuiabá to Corumbá. After they had arrived at Porto Jofre, 145km from Poconé, they then made the wise choice of stopping and questioning the wisdom of putting a road through an area that was underwater for six months a year. The result, or remnant, is the Transpantaneira, a raised dirt road that extends deep into the Pantanal. Wildlife is plentiful along the roadside and you'll typically see *jacarés* (caimans), capybaras and lots of birds. Once you get off the Transpantaneira and onto some of the farms, the impressive display of wildlife becomes even more varied. There are several places to stay along the Transpantaneira, with all offering horseback riding, walking and boating expeditions (see p418).

If you are driving from Cuiabá, head out around 4am to reach the Transpantaneira by sunrise, when the animals come to life. Though the road officially starts in Poconé, most folks mark the wooden sign and guard station 17km south of the city as the beginning of the Transpantaneira. Don't forget to fill up your fuel tank in Poconé, though technically you should be able to make it to Porto Jofre and back on one tank. There is a gas station at Hotel Porto Jofre for client use only but you'll pay twice the going rate.

Heading south, it won't take long for a caiman or a macaw to cross your path as you navigate around 125 little wooden bridges and meter-wide potholes. Notice the interesting carved statue of São Francisco, Protector of Ecology, around Km 18. He was installed by a priest in Poconé a few years back. Barara is a small bar at Km 32, where you can stop for a beer and *galinhada* (boneless chicken and rice) or fried fish. You can also purchase a ticket here to go to the top of the lookout tower next door at **Pousada Araras Eco Lodge** (per person R$15), a real treat if you can't afford to empty your savings account for a night at the lodge.

At Km 65 you leave the electricity grid – everything for the next 40km is run on solar energy or generators. After Km 105, the landscape changes, with denser vegetation and an altogether wilder feel. You are now in jaguar country, where deep Pantanal begins. Even if you don't spot a jaguar, you are rewarded for your intrepid efforts once you hit the beautiful wide-open spaces of Campo do Jofre, just north of Porto Jofre. Here the wildlife is so plentiful, you'll zap your camera batteries in a few kilometers.

Weekdays are better for driving, as there's less traffic kicking up dust. At the end of the road, check out the gigantic water lilies you always see in photos from the Amazon: there are hundreds in the pond at the back of Hotel Porto Jofre, out on the small wooden pier beyond the swimming pool.

In Cuiabá there are car-rental agencies just outside the airport grounds, and they're often cheaper than the agencies inside the airport. In the dry season, and providing it hasn't recently rained, a Fiat Uno or VW Gol is all you need to drive the Transpantaneira. Don't even think about it at other times of the year.

R$329/556; 🕒 Mar-Oct; ⊠ 💻 🐾) is the only hotel at the end of the road, catering mostly to serious fishermen on expensive packages. There's an airstrip, a marina (3.6m, 115HP boats rent for R$1100 per day for up to four people) and a nice restaurant.

Mato Grosso do Sul

Southern gateways to the Pantanal are the cities of Corumbá, Campo Grande, Aquidauana and Miranda. Most backpackers head to Campo Grande (see p423) or Corumbá (see p426). Aquidauana and Miranda are popular with Brazilian anglers and more high-end travelers.

All the budget tour operators working in Mato Grosso do Sul offer similar packages at camps along Estrada Parque, a 117km stretch of dirt road through the region known as Nhecolândia. Estrada Parque is actually closer to Corumbá than to Campo Grande, but unless you're traveling to or from Bolivia, there's no real need to travel all the way to Corumbá to join a tour. Most of the Corumbá agencies also have offices in Campo Grande, a travel hub and more convenient for onward travel to other parts of Brazil. If you are visiting Bonito, go to the Pantanal first as the tours end in Buraco das Piranhas, much closer to Bonito than Campo Grande.

People pressure finally led to the local government clamping down on unlicensed pousadas and camps in the southern Pantanal in 2009. Many of these had failed to meet even the basic ecological requirements for operation in a protected area. Though this had a knock-on effect for the local tourist industry, the overall impact for the environment and the tourists that come to see it is likely to be positive in the longer term. Only licensed establishments are listed here. All listings that follow are shown on the Pantanal map (p414).

AROUND AQUIDAUANA

There are several excellent, high-end hotel-*fazendas* in this area.

our pick **Fazenda Santa Sophia** (☎ 0xx67-9648 9352; www.fazendasantasophia.com.br; s/d incl meals & excursions R$550/950; 🕒 May-Oct) A beautifully appointed 3400-sq-km cattle and horse ranch owned by fourth-generation Pantaneira Beatriz Rondon. It caters to high-end horse enthusiasts from around the world. Guests are welcomed as family, and the food, especially the *pudim de queijo* (cheese pudding), is miraculous. Access is by plane only.

Refúgio Ecológico Caiman (☎ 0xx11-3706 1800; www.caiman.com.br; s/d incl meals & 3 excursions R$900/950; ⊠ 💻 🐾) This 520-sq-km, ecopioneering *fazenda* 36km north of Miranda is like a private Pantanal for a privileged few. There are three lodges: Sede, the main lodge, is the most luxurious; Cordilheiro, the most remote and rustic with a great lookout tower; and Baiazinha, a little more playful, with the best pool deck and position for spotting jaguars. There are an estimated 40 jaguars and 300 macaws on the property. Multilingual guides who live on the *fazenda* lead tours. Prices include meals and numerous activities, from canoeing to horseback riding; there is a three-night minimum in high season.

ESTRADA PARQUE

Estrada Parque runs off the main Campo Grande–Corumbá road (Hwy BR-262) at Buraco das Piranhas, 72km from Corumbá and 324km from Campo Grande. The first stretch of Estrada Parque penetrates 47km into the Pantanal, before it doglegs back toward Corumbá. At Porto da Manga, a barge ferries vehicles over the Rio Paraguai (R$20) before Estrada Parque rejoins Hwy BR-262 at Lampião Aceso, about 12km from Corumbá.

To get to the Estrada Parque you can take the Campo Grande–Corumbá bus and arrange for your lodge to pick you up (for a small fee) by the Posto Florestal guard station at the Buraco das Piranhas intersection. At Passo do Lontra, 7km from Buraco das Piranhas, you cross Rio Miranda. There are lots of accommodations from here to Curva do Leque.

Hotel Fazenda Santa Clara (☎ 0xx67-3384 0583; www.pantanalsantaclara.com.br; camping per person incl meals R$60, apt per person incl meals R$150) A new elevated camping area along the Rio Abobral is an excellent choice for the more intrepid, while the comfortable lodge is the best value in the south. For a few more reais, book a three-day package here and get all the same benefits with triple the comfort.

Pousada Passo do Lontra (☎ 0xx67-3231 9494; www.pousadapassodolontra.com.br, in Portuguese; s/d apt incl meals R$165/187, s/d chalets incl meals R$300/340; ⊠) A comfortable place with large *apartamentos* (rooms with private bathroom) and riverside chalets. Safaris along Rio Miranda are the focus.

GETTING THERE & AWAY

From Cuiabá, the capital of Mato Grosso, there are three gateways to the Pantanal – Cáceres, Barão de Melgaço and Poconé, the latter being the one most used by tour companies.

Campo Grande, the capital of Mato Grosso do Sul, is a transportation hub, while Corumbá is best accessed by bus from Campo Grande. The route to Corumbá from Campo Grande runs via Aquidauana and Miranda, part of the route being covered by the Pantanal Express Train (p424). For transportation details, see the relevant city and town sections.

There are direct flights to Cuiabá and Campo Grande from Brasília and connecting flights from Rio and São Paulo. TAM is the only major Brazilian airline connecting other capitals, including Campo Grande and São Paulo, to Corumbá.

GETTING AROUND

Only a few roads reach into the periphery of the Pantanal; they are frequently closed by rain, and reconstructed yearly. Since the lodges are the only places to sleep, drink and eat, and public transportation is very limited, independent travel is difficult here. Unless you have extensive off-road experience, hiring a car is an option in the dry season only. Only the Transpantaneira in Mato Grosso and Estrada Parque in Mato Grosso do Sul go deep into the region. Save yourself the stress and stick to a tour operator or arrange transport in advance through a lodge.

MATO GROSSO DO SUL

Mato Grosso do Sul was created in 1979 when the military government decided it would be the best way to administer and develop such a large region (cynics claimed it was to provide more high-paying bureaucratic jobs for cronies). But even before the split, the area had a different economic and social makeup from the northern Mato Grosso.

In the late 19th century, many migrants from the south and southeast of Brazil arrived in the area, so the south has a greater number of smaller farms and a much more intensive agriculture when compared to the large farms and ranches in the north. All this is thanks to the rich, red earth, known as *terra rocha*.

The wealth created by the *terra rocha* has helped develop the state's modern agricultural sector. The main crop is soy, but there's also lots of corn, rice, cotton production and cattle farms. Mato Grosso do Sul also contains two-thirds of the Pantanal and the Serra da Bocaina, two wonderful natural areas that are popular with both Brazilian and foreign travelers.

CAMPO GRANDE

☎ 0xx67 / pop 760,000

Known as the Cidade Morena not for its beautiful women but rather its red earth, Campo Grande is the capital of Mato Grosso do Sul, a modern city that has become a major gateway to the Pantanal. Manganese, rice, soy and cattle are the traditional sources of its wealth, while education (there are four universities in the city), commerce and tourism are growing industries. Campo Grande lies 716km south of Cuiabá and 403km southeast of Corumbá. There's not much to see in the city itself, but it's a lively place, especially at night.

Founded around 1875 as the village of Santo Antônio de Campo Grande, Campo Grande really began to grow when the railway came through in 1914. By decree of military president Ernesto Giesel, the city became the capital of Mato Grosso do Sul in 1977 when the new state splintered off from Mato Grosso.

Orientation

The downtown area of Campo Grande is compact and easily navigated on foot. Av Afonso Pena, the main boulevard, runs east–west. Going west, it becomes Av Duque de Caxias and then Hwy BR-262 before passing the airport (7km) and heading on to Corumbá. To the east, it runs past the Shopping Campo Grande and the Parque das Nações Indígenas. The center of the city is a grid, with the main commercial area concentrated around Afonso Pena and cross streets Av Calógeras and Rua 14 de Julho.

Information

EMERGENCY
Ambulance (☎ 192)
Fire department (☎ 193)
Police (☎ 190)

INTERNET ACCESS
Matrix Cyber Café (☎ 3029 6706; Av Calógeras 2069; per hr R$2.50; ☯ 7:30am-10pm Mon-Sat)

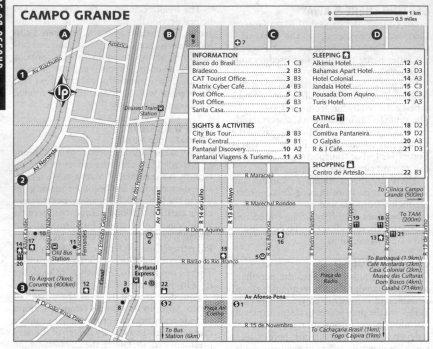

CAMPO GRANDE

INFORMATION
Banco do Brasil.................................1 C3
Bradesco...2 B3
CAT Tourist Office...........................3 B3
Matrix Cyber Café...........................4 B3
Post Office..5 C3
Post Office..6 B3
Santa Casa...7 C1

SIGHTS & ACTIVITIES
City Bus Tour.....................................8 B3
Feira Central......................................9 B1
Pantanal Discovery.........................10 A2
Pantanal Viagens & Turismo......11 A3

SLEEPING
Alkimia Hotel...................................12 A3
Bahamas Apart Hotel....................13 D3
Hotel Colonial..................................14 A3
Jandaia Hotel...................................15 C3
Pousada Dom Aquino....................16 C3
Turis Hotel..17 A3

EATING
Ceará...18 D2
Comitiva Pantaneira.....................19 D2
O Galpão...20 A3
R & J Café...21 D3

SHOPPING
Centro de Artesão.........................22 B3

MEDICAL SERVICES
Clínica Campo Grande (☎ 3323 9000; Rua Marechal Rondon 1703)
Santa Casa (☎ 3322 4000; Rua 13 de Mayo s/n)

MONEY
Banco do Brasil (Av Afonso Pena 2202; ◷ 11am-4pm Mon-Fri) Visa/MasterCard ATM and money exchange.
Bradesco (Av Afonso Pena 1828; ◷ 11am-4pm Mon-Fri) Visa/MasterCard ATM.

POST
Post office (cnr Av Calógeras & Rua Dom Aquino; ◷ 8am-5pm Mon-Fri, 8am-noon Sat)
Post office (cnr Rua Barão do Rio Branco & Rua Rui Barbosa)

TOURIST INFORMATION
In a big mustard-colored colonial building, the Morada dos Bais, the **CAT tourist office** (☎ 3314 9968; Av Afonso Pena; ◷ 8am-6pm Tue-Sat, 9am-noon Sun) is the best in the region and home to a museum dedicated to local miniature artist Lidia Bais. Friendly staff (most are tourism students) offer an excellent city map and an extensive database with informa-tion about hotels and attractions through-out the state. There are smaller tourist office branches at the bus station (☎ 3314 2350), airport (☎ 3314 3116) and the Feira Central (☎ 3314 3872).

Sights
The **Museu das Culturas Dom Bosco** (Parque das Nações Indígenas; adult/child R$5/2.50; ◷ 8am-6pm Tue-Sun) has undergone a R$2 million relocation to a new building designed by Italian archi-tect Massimo Chiappetta a few kilometers from its old city-center location. The new space, a 3400-sq-meter expansion houses an excellent collection of over 10,000 in-sects. There is a beautiful new exhibit of indigenous Bororo headdresses and other artifacts from the indigenous Moro, Karajá and Xavante groups.

A great market worth a stroll is the **Feira Central** (☎ 3324 8129; cnr Av Calógeras & Rua 14 de Juhlo; ◷ 5pm-late Wed, Fri & Sat, 10am-late Sun), a massive open-air food and shopping court lined with Japanese *sobá*-noodle joints (p423) and other food and merchandise stalls. It's packed with revelers on weekends.

Tours

A **City Bus Tour** (☎ 3321 0800; www.campograndecvb
.com.br, in Portuguese; Av Aníbal de Toledo 1895; tickets R$12;
☽ Tue-Sun) visits 42 sites of local interest and
departs regularly from in front of the CAT
office. For information on tours into the
Pantanal, see p417.

Sleeping

The area immediately around the old bus station is seedy, with no shortage of small-time
crooks and prostitutes.

Turis Hotel (☎ 3382 2461; Rua Allan Kardec 200; s/d
R$55/88; ✸ ▣) Modern and minimalist, this
excellent option is entirely too trendy for its
location.

Alkimia Hotel (☎ 3324 2621; Av Afonso Pena 1413;
s/d apt R$60/80; ✸ ▣) A newish option just two
blocks from the old bus station in a slightly
safer area. Rooms are spotless and the bathrooms are large. Discounts for cash.

Hotel Colonial (☎ 3382 6061; Rua Allan Kardec 211;
s/d apt without air-con R$56/80, with air-con R$68/100;
✸ ▣) Pokey rooms are compensated for
by a monster breakfast and pool access at its
more upmarket sister Hotel Internacional
next door.

Pousada Dom Aquino (☎ 3382 3303; pousada_dom_
aquino@hotmail.com; Rua Dom Aquino 1806; s/d apt R$69/98;
✸ ▣) A wonderful, relaxed pousada that is
an oasis in the city and walking distance from
nearly everything. The staff is very friendly
and there's even international cable TV. Book
ahead.

Jandaía Hotel (☎ 3316 7700; www.jandaia.com.br;
Rua Barão do Rio Branco 1271; s/d R$172/220; ✸ ▣ ☎)
An upscale business hotel with plush rooms,
marble floors and two decent restaurants.
English is spoken.

our pick **Bahamas Apart Hotel** (☎ 3303 9393; www.
bahamasaparthotel.com.br, in Portuguese; Rua José Antônio

1117; s/d apt R$174/226; ✸ ▣ ☎) Sleek high-rise
hotel with massive two-story *apartamentos*
with kitchenette, living and dining areas and
a small patio. By far the most luxury in town
for the money.

Eating & Drinking

There is a distinctly Paraguayan influence on
some of the culinary curiosities here. *Sopa
Paraguaia,* a savory cake made with eggs,
corn, milk, cheese and onions, is popular,
as is *tereré,* a cold and refreshing maté tea.
Finding somewhere to eat on a Sunday night
can be tough, as most places close!

R & J Café (☎ 3025 6020; www.buffetromeueju
lieta.com.br, in Portuguese; Rua Dom Aquino 2350; meals
R$8.90-12.90) A swanky bistro that inexplicably
charges corner-café prices for inventive, top-
drawer, lunchtime meals. There is a fantastic
variety of desserts on offer, too.

O Galpão (☎ 3382 6108; Rua Allan Kardec; meals
R$12.90) If you like the all-you-can-eat experi-
ence but don't have a wallet as big as your
stomach, then give this central cheapie a go.
It has the added bonus of being open on a
Sunday, too.

Fogo Caipira (☎ 3324 1641; Rua José Antônio 145;
dishes R$22-70; ☽ 11am-2pm & 7-11pm Thu-Fri, 11am-
midnight Sat, 11am-4pm Sun) The best dishes at this
regional institution require an advance order,
such as the *galinhada* (chicken stew, six hours)
or *pacu recheado* (a tasty fish stuffed with
manioc and spices, three hours). It's pricey,
but as the only restaurant in the city with
culinary stars, it's worth it.

Comitiva Pantaneira (☎ 3383 8799; www.comitiva
pantaneira.com.br, in Portuguese; Rua Dom Aquino 2221; meals
per kg R$28.90; ☽ 11am-2pm Mon-Fri, to 3pm Sat & Sun) A
massive per-kilo swarming with locals digging into seriously good Pantaneira cowboy
cuisine.

CAMPO SOBÁ

What's with the fascination with Japanese *sobá* noodles in Campo Grande? Well, there's an explanation. This Japanese delicacy was integrated into the culinary hierarchy here along with an
influx of Japanese immigrants from Okinawa in the early 1900s – Campo Grande now boasts
the third-highest Japanese population in Brazil (behind São Paulo and Paraná) – and eating
sobá here is just about as popular as a Globo soap opera. The Okinawan version of the dish uses
flour noodles instead of buckwheat and is served in a hot broth with pork and various other
accompaniments. In Campo Grande, the Brazilianization of the dish includes options with filet
mignon in place of pork and alongside *carne de sol* (salted beef) inside tapioca pancakes. The
best place to try *sobá* is the Feira Central (p422), which is lined with *sobárias*. Slurp away…it's
a nice antidote to rice and beans.

Ceará (☎ 3321 3927; Rua Dom Aquino 2249; meals for 2 R$31-42; ☺ 11:30am-2:30pm & 6:30-11pm Tue-Fri, 11am-3pm & 6:30-11pm Sat, 11am-3pm Sun) One of the city's best *peixarias* (fish restaurants). The pintado in a tomato stew with banana *mandioca* (cassava) incites tears of culinary joy.

Entertainment

Campo Grande's nightlife knows no evening off, especially around the 3900 block of Av Afonso Pena, east of downtown where there is a cluster of happening bars.

Barbaquá (☎ 3321 8576; Av Afonso Pena 3900; ☺ 6pm-late Mon-Sat) A beautiful candlelit bar in a restored house, full of local art. The intimate space attracts an artistic crowd, which comes for the live jazz and MPB nightly and upscale *tereré*.

Cachaçaria Brasil (☎ 3313 6731; www.cachacaria brasilms.com.br, in Portuguese; Rua José Antônio 194; ☺ 5pm-2am Mon-Sat) Samba, over 100 kinds of *cachaça* (sugarcane alcohol) and live *futebol* make this Campo Grande's new in place for a crowd of all ages. With a bamboo beach-bar atmosphere, gigantic menu of food and drink, pool tables and live music every night, there is a little bit of something for everybody here.

Casa Colonial (☎ 3383 1633; www.casacolonial.com .br, in Portuguese; Av Afonso Pena 3997; ☺ 6:30pm-midnight Mon-Sat, 1-3pm Sun) The walk-in wine cellar is the first thing that catches your eye when you enter this sophisticated bar, which oozes medieval romance.

Café Mostarda (☎ 3301 9990; www.cafemostarda .com.br, in Portuguese; Av Afonso Pena 3952; ☺ 6pm-late Wed-Mon) The rich and beautiful practically trip over themselves onto Av Afonso Pena at this trendy outdoor café with live music nightly.

Shopping

Centro de Artesão (☎ 3383 2633; Av Calógeras 2050; ☺ 8am-6pm Mon-Fri, to noon Sat) sells colorful indigenous ceramics, wooden crafts, sacred art and locally brewed liquor.

Getting There & Around

AIR

Daily connections link Campo Grande to São Paulo (R$400), Cuiabá (R$327), Corumbá (R$205), Rio (R$498), Brasília (R$444) and Porto Velho (R$674). For additional information call **TAM** (☎ 3312 9500), **Gol** (☎ 3368 6128) or **Trip** (☎ 3368 6136).

Aeroporto Internacional de Campo Grande (☎ 3368 6000; Av Duque de Caixas) is 7km from town;

to get there, take the Indubrasil bus from the bus station (R$2.10, every 30 minutes). To get a bus to the center from the airport, walk out of the airport to the bus stop on the main road. A taxi costs R$22.

BUS

Campo Grande's plush new **bus station** (☎ 3026 6789; Av Gury Marques 1215) is 6km outside the centre on the road to São Paulo. Local buses 061, 085, 087, 162, 165 and 189 run from here to the centre, or a taxi will cost you R$20. There are frequent buses to Corumbá (R$72, six hours, 11 daily), but only one is direct. Nondirect buses to Corumbá stop in Miranda and Aquidauana, and can drop you at the intersection with Estrada Parque.

Regular buses make the trip to Cuiabá (R$84.20, 10 hours, nine daily) and there are buses to Bonito (R$53, five hours, seven daily) and Ponta Porã (R$45, four hours, hourly) on the Paraguayan border. Further afield there are regular buses to São Paulo (R$150, 15 hours, five daily), Rio de Janeiro (R$226, 23 hours, four daily), Brasília (R$180, 16 hours, two daily) and Foz do Iguaçu (R$97, 14 hours, six daily).

TRAIN

The **Pantanal Express Train** (☎ 3888 3488; www.pan tanalexpress.com, in Portuguese; cnr Av dos Ferroviarios & Av Afonso Pena) runs between Campo Grande and Miranda (R$77, 11 hours) via Aquidauana (R$61, five hours). It departs Campo Grande at 7:30am on Saturday mornings and returns from Miranda at 8:30am on Sundays, with a lengthy lunch stop at Aquidauana en route. It's a scenic, if not particularly quick, way of making the journey.

CORUMBÁ

☎ 0xx67 / pop 99,000

'Corumbaly' old Corumbá is a port city close to the Bolivian border and the southernmost gateway to the Pantanal. Also known as Cidade Branca (White City), it is 403km northwest of Campo Grande by road. The city sits atop a steep hill overlooking the Rio Paraguai; on the far side of the river, a huge expanse of the Pantanal stretches out on the horizon.

Founded in 1776 by Captain Luis de Albuquerque, by 1840 it had become the biggest river port in the world and boasted a dozen foreign consulates. The impressive buildings along the waterfront reflect the wealth that passed through the town in the 19th century. However, with the coming of the railway, Corumbá lost its importance as a port and went into decline.

These days, despite spending most of the year as a sleepy backwater, the city is home to the regions biggest **carnaval** (www.carnavalde corumba.com.br) during a long weekend in mid-February. The tradition was imported here by naval officers, many from Rio, who found themselves stationed here and felt the need to liven things up.

Orientation & Information

The city is divided into two parts: the upper city contains most of the commerce, and the lower city takes in the port. The streets are laid out in a grid pattern and are easy to navigate.

EMERGENCY

Federal Police (☎ 3231 5848; Praça da República 51; ❤ 8-11:30am & 1:30-5:30pm Mon-Fri) There's also an office at the bus station for migration purposes.

IMMIGRATION

At present all Brazilian border formalities (including entry and exit stamps) must be completed at the **Federal Police office** (☎ 3231 0173; ❤ 8am-noon & 2-4pm Mon-Fri, 2-5pm Sat & Sun) at the long-distance bus station. Bolivian entry/exit formalities can all be completed at the border post. You won't be allowed to enter Bolivia without a current yellow fever vaccination certificate, so organize one well in advance.

Moneychangers at the border accept cash only and will change both reais and dollars.

INTERNET ACCESS

It's surprisingly hard to get online, with most places closing at 6pm.

M@b Cyber (Rua Antônio Maria Coelho; per hr R$2.50; ❤ 8am-9pm Mon-Sat)

MEDICAL SERVICES

Hospital Sociedade Beneficência Corumbaense (☎ 3231 2441; Rua 15 de Novembro 854)

MONEY

It seems shady business, but some shopkeepers on Rua 13 de Junho change reais, dollars, euros and Bolivianos.

Banco do Brasil (Rua 13 de Junho 914) Usual high commissions for cash and traveler's checks.

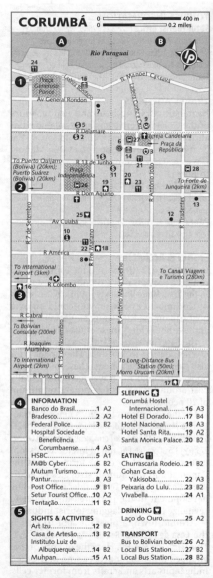

CORUMBÁ

INFORMATION	
Banco do Brasil.............1	A2
Bradesco.....................2	A2
Federal Police...............3	B2
Hospital Sociedade	
Beneficência	
Corumbaense...............4	A3
HSBC...........................5	A1
M@b Cyber....................6	B2
Mutum Turismo..............7	A1
Pantur.........................8	A3
Post Office....................9	B1
Setur Tourist Office........10	A2
Tentação....................11	B2

SIGHTS & ACTIVITIES	
Art Izu........................12	B2
Casa de Artesão...........13	B2
Instituto Luiz de	
Albuquerque.............14	B2
Muhpan.......................15	A1

SLEEPING	
Corumbá Hostel	
Internacional.............16	A3
Hotel El Dorado...........17	B4
Hotel Nacional............18	A3
Hotel Santa Rita..........19	A2
Santa Monica Palace....20	B2

EATING	
Churrascaria Rodeio......21	B2
Gohan Casa do	
Yakisoba.................22	A3
Peixaria do Lulu...........23	B2
Vivabella....................24	A1

DRINKING	
Laço do Ouro...............25	A2

TRANSPORT	
Bus to Bolivian border...26	A2
Local Bus Station..........27	B2
Local Bus Station..........28	B2

Bradesco (Rua Delamare 1067) Visa/MasterCard ATM.
HSBC (Rua Delamare 1068) Visa/MasterCard ATM.
Tentação (☎ 3232 4267; Rua 13 de Junho 883; ❤ 8am-6pm Mon-Sat) Money exchange.

POST

Post office (Rua Delamare 708; ❤ 8:30am-5pm Mon-Fri, 8-11:30am Sat)

TOURIST INFORMATION

Setur tourist office (☎ 3231 2886; www.corumba
.com.br, in Portuguese; Rua 15 de Novembro 659B;
⏲ 7:30am-1:30pm Mon-Fri) The office of the secretary of
tourism is in a nice colonial house, but is light on material.
There's also a small branch at the airport.

TRAVEL AGENCIES

Pantanal tours and boat and fishing tours
of the Corumbá environs are available from
all travel agencies or by consultation in the
boat offices along the port road Rua Manoel
Cassava. They also organize some day trips
to Bolivia.

Mutum Turismo (☎ 3231 1818; www.mutumturismo
.com.br; Rua Frei Mariano 17; ⏲ 8am-6pm Mon-Fri, to
1pm Sat)

Pantur (☎ 3231 2000; Rua Frei Mariano 1038; ⏲ 8am-
6pm Mon-Fri, to noon Sat)

Sights & Activities

Corumbá's star attraction is the Pantanal; you
can get a preview of it from the highest point
in the area, **Morro Urucum** (1100m), 20km south
of Corumbá. Otherwise, you could enjoy a
boat trip on the Rio Paraguai. Between three
and five hours long, these cruises usually take
in the **Base Fluvial de Ladário**, Brazil's first river
arsenal, dating from 1872. The longer trips
also stop for a little fishing. These tours can be
booked through any travel agent and usually
cost around R$65, but require a minimum
of 20 people.

On the waterfront the city's newest attraction is **Muhpan** (Museu de História do Pantanal; ☎ 3232
0303; www.muhpan.org.br, in Portuguese; Rua Manoel Cassava
275; ⏲ 1-5:30pm Tue-Fri), full of interactive exhibits that tell the story of the formation of the
Pantanal and the human struggles faced by
its settlers. It is part of considerable ongoing
development in the port area that hopes to
revitalize the city's flagging tourist industry.

Around town, a pleasant spot to visit is
the **Casa de Artesão** (Rua Dom Aquino 405; ⏲ 8:30-
11am & 1:30-5pm Mon-Fri). Here the old prison has
swapped inmates for artists, who hawk their
indigenous arts and crafts from former cells.
Art Izu (Rua Cuiabá 558; ⏲ 7-11am & 1-5pm Mon-Fri) is
home to one of Corumbá's premier artists.
You can't miss it – the giant bird sculptures
and bronze statue of São Francisco in the
front yard are stunning and the crazy paving
in front is, well, crazy. The **Instituto Luiz de
Albuquerque** (☎ 231 5757; Praça da República; ⏲ 8am-
noon & 2-5:30pm Mon-Fri) houses the Museu do

Pantanal, which contains a reasonably interesting collection of indigenous artifacts, local
modern art and a library.

Forte de Junqueira (☎ 3231 5828; Rua Cáceres 425;
⏲ 9:30-11am & 2-4:30pm) is the only intact fort left
near the city. It's a tiny hexagonal fort with
50cm-thick walls, though the real attraction
is the excellent view of the Rio Paraguai and
the Pantanal in the distance. To get there, go
east along Rua Dom Aquino and turn left at
the athletics ground. Once you hit the waterfront, continue east for another 10 minutes.
The entrance is an unmarked door to the left
of the main gate.

The Christ statue that overlooks the bus
station on the hillside is the **Cristo Rei do
Pantanal**.

Canaã Viagens e Turismo offers fishing
tours; see p418 for details.

Sleeping

There are some cheap hotels close to the long-
distance bus station if you're just spending a
night in Corumbá. Otherwise, there are better
places closer to the waterfront and the restaurants and bars in the center of town.

Corumbá Hostel Internacional (☎ 3231 1005; www
.corumbahostel.com.br; Rua Colombo 1419; dm without/with
air-con R$30/33, s R$35/40, d R$65/75; ⏹ ▯ ▯) HI-
affiliated hostel on a quiet residential street
seven blocks from the river. Rooms are clean
and spacious and the bathrooms are above
and beyond. Breakfast isn't up to much, but
it's served on better-than-average porcelain.

Hotel Santa Rita (☎ 3231 5453; Rua Dom Aquino
860; s/d R$55/90; ⏹ ▯) Cheapish central option
with everything you are likely to need without being the sort of place that memories are
made of.

Hotel El Dorado (☎ 3231 6677; www.hotel-eldorado
.net; Rua Porto Carreiro 554; s/d R$90/118; ⏹) A good
option just off the corner of the bus station.
The best value in town, all said and done.

Santa Monica Palace (☎ 3234 3000; www.hsanta
monica.com.br, in Portuguese; Rua Antônio Maria Coelho 345;
s/d R$105/125; ⏹ ▯ ▯) A favorite with tour
groups, it's an aging building in the center of
town. A recent makeover didn't quite stretch
to replacing the telephones and minibars.
They are like museum pieces!

Hotel Nacional (☎ 3234 6000; www.hnacional.com.br,
in Portuguese; Rua América 936; s/d R$126/168; ⏹ ▯ ▯)
The rooms here are a bit nicer than the institutionalized hallways suggest. It's the top
option in town.

Eating & Drinking

Gohan Casa do Yakisoba (☎ 3232 1040; Rua Frei Mariano 730; dishes for 2 R$20-45; ☷ 6pm-midnight Tue-Sun) Nuts about noodles? Then give this place a whirl, locally renowned for its homemade noodles. There is a delivery option if you are too lazy to actually go and look for your food.

Vivabella (☎ 3231 9464; Rua Arthur Mangabeira 1; meals for 2 R$24-40; ☷ 5pm-late Mon-Sat) Vivabella is perched precariously on a hillside over the Rio Paraguai. Beautiful sunsets over the Pantanal and Bolivia beyond are the main attraction on the outdoor deck at this small Italian restaurant and bar.

Churrascaria Rodeio (☎ 3231 6477; Rua 13 de Junho 760; meals per kg Mon-Fri R$28, Sat & Sun R$35; ☷ 11am-4:30pm & 7-11pm) A fairly standard *rodízio*, but the owner is very proud of her 60 salads.

Laço do Ouro (☎ 3231 7371; Rua Frei Mariano 556; meals for 2 R$28-52; ☷ 10am-2am) Corumbaense flock to this lively bar-restaurant to beat the heat: extralarge *garrafas* of beer line the outdoor tables, which fill up fast on the weekends.

Peixaria do Lulu (☎ 3232 7855; Rua Dom Aquino 738; meals for 2 R$35-45; ☷ 10:30am-3pm & 6:30-10pm Mon-Sat, 10:30am-3pm Sun) Lulu is the fried-fish king in Corumbá. Don't let the humble appearance fool you – Peixaria do Lulu offers superb regional fish dishes. It's a friendly, family-run place.

Getting There & Away

Corumbá is a transit point for travel to/from Bolivia and, with considerably more difficulty, Paraguay.

AIR

Corumbá **international airport** (☎ 3231 3322) is 3km west of the town center. **TAM** (☎ 3232 2280) is currently the only airline serving Corumbá. There are regular flights to Campo Grande (R$205), São Paulo (R$504), Brasília (R$610) and connections to other major cities.

BUS

From the **long-distance bus station** (☎ 3231 2033; Rua Porto Carreiro), buses run to Campo Grande (R$70, 6½ hours, nine daily) and to Bonito (R$57, seven hours, one daily at 2pm). A taxi to the center from here costs R$15, a moto-taxi around R$4.

TO/FROM BOLIVIA

If you're heading from the city to the border, catch the Fronteira bus on Praça Independência or Rua Dom Aquino (R$2, every 30 minutes). If you're in a hurry, grab a moto-taxi for R$7. Taxis cost around R$20.

There isn't much to the Bolivian border town of Puerto Quijarro, but if you wish to stay here, there is a great new HI hostel, **Tamengo** (☎ 591 3978 3356; Calle Costa Rica 57). Taxis navigate the 4km between the border and Quijarro station (trains travel to Santa Cruz in Bolivia from there) for around R$10.

Getting Around

From the bus stop, located outside the long-distance bus station, the Cristo Redentor bus (R$2) runs to the **local bus terminal** (Rua 13 de Junho). From here you can catch the Popular Nova bus to the airport (R$1.70, every 50 minutes). Taxis usually cost R$15 for the same trip – make sure the taxi has a meter or establish a price before you get in, as some drivers like to play gringo rip-off.

COXIM

☎ 0xx67 / pop 33,000

Coxim is a small town about halfway between Cuiabá and Campo Grande, on the eastern border of the Pantanal. The town's main draw is the visual spectacle of the Piracema, when fish migrate up the Rios Taquari and Coxim, leaping through rapids to spawn. The Piracema takes place from November to late February; fishing is not allowed during this period, but if you're traveling through it's worth stopping off to have a look. The fishing is best from August to October, but due to migratory changes, it isn't what it used to be.

The town itself is divided into the riverfront, a little older but still where most of the action is, and the more upscale Av Virginia Ferreira, which climbs up and away from the riverfront and is home to high-priced real estate and trendier boutiques and restaurants. Coxim is also an entry point to the Pantanal, but it has limited infrastructure for wildlife-spotting tours, with most operators catering exclusively to fishing tours.

Information

Before you throw a line, you'll need to legalize your rod. Permits valid for three months cost R$60 if you want to fish from a boat, or R$24 from the banks. Pick one up at Banco do Brasil or ask your hotel to obtain one for you.
Banco do Brasil (Rua Antônio de Alberqueque 248; ☷ 10am-3pm Mon-Fri)

Bradesco (Rua Filinto Müller 885; ☺ 11am-4pm Mon-Fri) Visa/MasterCard ATM.

Directoria de Turismo e Meio Ambiente (☎ 3291 1143; cnr Rua Filinto Müller & Rua Antônio de Alberqueque) Inside Casa de Artesão.

Hospital (☎ 3291 1398; Av Virginia Ferreira 361) This hospital will soon be replaced by the new regional hospital on Rua Gasper Coelho.

Peixe Viva (☎ 3291 1798; Rua Getúlio Vargas 350; ☺ 6am-6pm) In the center, this is the place to rent boats and fishing rods and buy bait. It can also provide information on fishing in the area.

Post office (Rua Antônio João 111; ☺ 8:30am-5pm Mon-Fri, 8-11:30am Sat)

Seven LAN House (Rua Delmira Bandeira 400; internet per hr R$2; ☺ 8am-10pm Mon-Sat, 10am-10pm Sun)

Sleeping & Eating

Hotel Rio (☎ 3291 1295; Rua Filinto Müller 651; s/d apt without air-con R$25/50, with air-con R$40/80; ❄) White floors, walls, bedclothes and ceilings in this great-value riverfront option, so try to avoid getting anything dirty! Breakfast is served on a very pleasant patio practically spilling into the river.

Hotel Coxim (☎ 3291 1480; BR-163 Km 726; s/d R$55/100; ❄ ▯ ▧) About 4km from town on the road to Campo Grande, the Hotel Coxim is the flashiest in town, though that's not saying much. There's a poolside pizzeria, and it is well equipped for fishing tours.

Santa Ana Turismo Hotel (☎ 3291 1602; Rua Miranda Reis s/n; s/d R$80/105; ❄ ▧) It's hard to tell if it's the Stone Age or the future, but this concrete jungle of a hotel on the riverfront at least has a great pool. Ask to see your room first, as some of the cabins are pokey and might make you feel like you are in hospital.

Cabana do Osmar (☎ 3291 3902; Av Coronel Pedro Severo 37; meals R$16; ☺ 7am-10pm) The best of the riverside fish restaurants, run by Osmar, a fishing guide known all over Brazil. The shady riverside patio is also nice for a few cold Skols.

Getting There & Around

Pretty much every bus passing through Coxim is headed to either Cuiabá (R$59, eight hours) or Campo Grande (R$40, four hours), with approximately hourly departures to each. The bus station is quite a distance from the riverfront. It'll cost you R$15 in a taxi, or a mototaxi will take you for R$4.

The hotels along the river have small outboard boats for hire; daily rates start at about R$150.

BONITO & AROUND

☎ 0xx67 / pop 18,000

Bonito is *the* ecotourism model for Brazil. This small aquatic playground in the southwestern corner of Mato Grosso do Sul has few attractions of its own, but the natural resources of the surrounding area are spectacular, and local authorities have taken the high road in their regulation and maintenance. There are caves with lakes and amazing stalactite formations, beautiful waterfalls and incredibly clear rivers surrounded by lush forest where it's possible for divers to swim eyeball to eyeball with hundreds of fish.

Since Bonito exploded on the ecotourism map in the early 1990s, the number of visitors has risen dramatically every year, leading to the creation of the 76-sq-km Serra da Bodoquena national park in 2000. Though some of the attractions are within the park boundaries, the vast majority of the protected area is off-limits to visitors.

Orientation & Information

Bonito is a one-street show. Rua Coronel Pilad Rebuá is a 3km stretch that's home to bars, restaurants, tourism agencies and souvenir shops.

INTERNET ACCESS

Most hotels have internet access.

Discovery LAN House (Rua Pedro Alvares Cabral; per hr R$2; ☺ 8am-11pm)

MEDICAL SERVICES

Hospital (☎ 3255 3455; Rua Pedro Apóstolo 201)

MONEY

Banco do Brasil (Rua Luiz da Costa Leite 2279; ☺ 9am-2pm) Visa/MasterCard ATM.

Bradesco (Rua Coronel Pilad Rebuá 1942) Visa/MasterCard ATM.

POST

Post office (Rua Coronel Pilad Rebuá 1759; ☺ 8-11:30am & 1-5pm Mon-Fri)

TOURIST INFORMATION

Comtur (☎ 3255 2160; www.bonitoweb.com.br; Rua Coronel Pilad Rebuá 1250; ☺ 8am-5pm Mon-Fri) The office of the secretary of tourism is some way from the center.

TRAVEL AGENCIES

All agencies in Bonito are strictly regulated and all prices are fixed – so there's no use

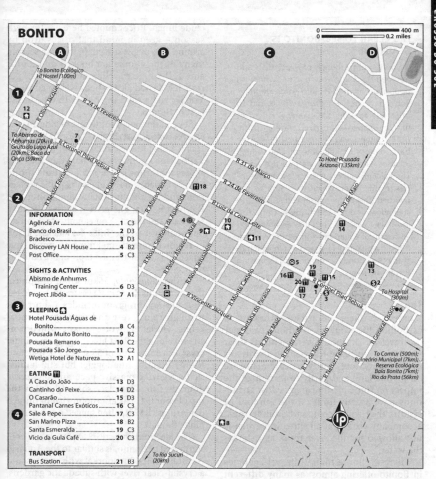

BONITO

0   400 m
0   0.2 miles

To Bonito Ecológico HI Hostel (100m)

To Abismo de Anhumas (20km); Gruta do Lago Azul (20km); Baía do Onça (59km)

To Hotel Pousada Arizona (1.35km)

To Hospital (300m)

To Comtur (500m); Balneário Municipal (7km); Reserva Ecológica Baía Bonita (7km); Rio da Prata (56km)

To Rio Sucuri (20km)

shopping around. Some, however, are more helpful than others. Regardless, most hotels can organize your tours for you at no extra cost.

Agência Ar (☎ 3255 1008; www.agenciaar.com.br; Rua Coronel Pilad Rebuá 1184; ⏰ 24hr) A more commercial all-purpose agency, handy if for no other reason than that it's open 24 hours.

Sights & Activities

There are numerous attractions and activities in the area these days, but only a few are exceptional. See Tours, following, for information on visiting sites that where taking a tour is mandatory. The only natural attraction in and around Bonito that doesn't need a guide or tour is the **Balneário Municipal** (admission R$15;

⏰ 8am-6pm), a natural swimming pool on the Rio Formoso with clear water and lots of fish, 7km southeast of town. You can spend the whole day here mingling with locals and have lunch at the kiosks. Macaws also make regular appearances. Grab a moto-taxi to get there (R$7 one way).

There is at least one activity in Bonito that has nothing to do with water at all. **Project Jibóia** (☎ 8419 0313; www.projetojiboia.com .br, in Portuguese; Rua Nestor Fernandes 610; admission R$20; ⏰ 7pm) represents a one-man crusade to change the world's opinion of snakes. Visiting here represents an entertaining hour or so, complete with boa constrictors that you nearly swap spit with by the end of the night.

IT'S CLEAR TO SEE: BONITO IS BEAUTIFUL

If you bought a bunch of exotic fish and dumped them into your uncle's swimming pool, then jumped in with some goggles, you'd have an idea of what Bonito has to offer. But how did this happy accident of nature happen? The river waters spring from subterranean sources in a limestone base, almost entirely free of clay, which releases calcium carbonate into the water. The calcium carbonate calcifies all impurities in the water, which then sink to the riverbed (this is the reason you're asked to stay afloat and not touch the bottom during river tours). The result is an area filled with natural aquariums surrounded by lush forest – a beautiful environment in which to study the abundant number of fascinating fish in the rivers.

Tours

If only everywhere in Brazil was as organized as Bonito, life would be a whole lot easier for travelers. The local government has strict regulations in place for visiting the area's natural attractions, partly because many are on private land and partly to minimize the impact on some pristine areas. Most attractions have a daily limit on the number of visitors they will accept, and a guide must accompany visitors at all sites. Sunscreen is not allowed for the river tours as it taints the water.

There are more than 30 travel agencies in Bonito offering almost as many different tours, though in truth it is easier to organize your trips through your hotel. Only guides from local travel agencies are authorized, so you're obliged to book tours through them. Not all the guides speak English, and it will cost an additional R$50 to R$80 to guarantee one; otherwise, it's potluck. Transport is never included, so the costs add up faster here than in other parts of Brazil, but service is typically excellent.

Bonito's incredibly clear waters are the main attraction, but there are plenty of other adventurous diversions, including rappelling (abseiling) down to and diving in underground lakes, and some challenging *arvorismo* (treetop rope courses and sightseeing). Many of the best tours take a full day and will in-clude lunch. Prices quoted here are for high season – keep in mind that prices drop by around 25% in low season. In the high season, many of these tours are booked up months ahead. If you're traveling during a peak period, it is a good idea to book well in advance. You'll need a solid three days to take in the best of Bonito.

Seven kilometers southeast of Bonito, the **Reserva Ecológica Baía Bonita** (3hr tour R$125; 6am-7pm) is home to the Aquário Natural and the Trilha dos Animais. The half-day tour includes snorkeling in a beautiful natural spring with 30 varieties of fish and subaquatic vegetation, and then a short 900m flotation in the Rio Baía Bonita. The price includes wetsuits, snorkels and lunch. You can also tack on an optional visit to the **Trilha dos Animais**, a zoo of regional animals including an impressive anaconda, a well-trained tapir and a cute little ocelot.

Within a *fazenda*, 56km south of Bonito, the marvelous **Rio da Prata** (5hr tour incl lunch R$140; 6:30am-2pm) program includes a short trek through rain forest and some great snorkeling. The latter involves a 3km swim downstream along the Rio Olha d'Agua, amazingly crystal clear and full of 55 species of fish; and Rio da Prata, a little foggier but still fantastic for viewing massive pacu and big, scary dourado fish. This place should be near the top of your list. The afternoon visit to Buraco das Araras (R$25), often tagged on, is forgettable, though.

The **Rio Sucuri** (2hr tour R$79; 8am-3pm), 20km southwest of Bonito, is similar to the Aquário Natural – a 1500m snorkel with springs and a crystal-clear river with subaquatic gardens, surrounded by lush forest – but it's further out in the wild and is better for vegetation than for fish.

A bargain attraction is the **Gruta do Lago Azul** (admission R$36; 6am-2pm), a large cave with a luminous underground lake and stalactite formations 20km west of Bonito. It's often the postcard view of Bonito, and is worth seeing, but it's only truly miraculous in late December and early January, when the sun shines in at just the right angle.

The **Boca da Onça Ecotour** (www.bocadaonca.br; trekking incl lunch R$110; 9:30am-6pm), 59km northwest of Bonito, is a nicely manicured 4km trail through the forest to a series of 11 waterfalls, a few of which you can take a chilly dip in. It all culminates with the 156m Boca da Onça waterfall, an impressive cascading waterfall that takes the state's highest honors. It's an 880-step climb back to the *fazenda*, where there is an excellent lunch and hang time by a fantastic natural river-water pool, full of local fish.

Abismo de Anhumas (www.abismoanhumas.com.br; rappelling R$330, scuba diving R$530; ☺ 7am-5pm), 20km west of Bonito, is like a journey to Middle Earth. It's a 72m abyss culminating in an underground lake, home to incredible stalactite formations. The tour involves rappelling down to the bottom and snorkeling in the lake (visibility is 30m). You can also opt for diving if you have a basic certificate. The whole thing is otherworldly – Bonito's most unforgettable attraction by a landslide, but it's limited to 18 visitors per day. The **rappelling training center** (Rua General Osório) is in town and you must successfully complete your training before 6pm on the day before your visit.

Sleeping

A proliferation of new accommodations has sprung up in Bonito in recent times and it is no longer as difficult to find a room in high season as it used to be. That said, you should definitely book ahead to get the hotel you want at peak times. Out of season, higher-end options may slash their prices by as much as 50%.

our pick **Bonito Ecological HI Hostel** (☎ 3255 1462; www.ajbonito.com.br; Rua Lúcio Borralho 716; dm R$38, apt with/without air-con R$90/70; ✗ ▣ ▣) Undoubtedly one of Brazil's top HI hostels, this well-oiled backpacker paradise has a virtual monopoly on the budget end of the Bonito market. Hammocks, pools, kitchen, laundry, bikes for hire, multilingual staff – there is nothing they haven't thought of. Dorm rooms come with private bathrooms, and the private rooms just around the corner from the main hostel are hotel standard. There is also a booking office in the bus station at Campo Grande.

Pousada São Jorge (☎ 3255 4046; www.pousadasaojorge.com.br, in Portuguese; Rua Coronel Pilad Rebuá 1605; s/d R$40/70; ✗ ▣) There's decent English spoken and a nice breakfast at this good-value budget option, run by an extremely friendly couple. Some rooms are a little dark.

Pousada Muito Bonito (☎ 3255 1645; www.muitobonito.com.br; Rua Coronel Pilad Rebuá 1444; s/d R$50/80; ✗) Owner Mario Doblack speaks five languages and offers very well-appointed budget

rooms around a small courtyard. He is also a mine of information on the area.

Pousada Remanso (☎ 3255 1137; www.pousadaremanso.com.br, in Portuguese; Rua Coronel Pilad Rebuá 1515; s/d R$89/135; ✗ ▣) A good-value midrange option right in the heart of town, with leather hammocks, nicely maintained landscaping and a small pool.

Hotel Pousada Águas de Bonito (☎ 3255 2330; www.aguasdebonito.com.br; Rua 29 de Maio 1679; s/d R$137/197; ✗ ▣ ▣) This pousada offers a little more character than others in town. Rooms are modern and spacious and the ones on the second level have pleasant patios.

Hotel Pousada Arizona (☎ 255 1040; http://hotelpousadaarizona.com.br, in Portuguese; Rua das Águas Marinhas 680; s/d R$137/199; ✗ ▣ ▣) Colorful brick-and-wood bungalows surround the best pool (and poolside bar) in town at this 16-room retreat 2km from the main drag.

Wetiga Hotel de Natureza (☎ 3255 1699; www.wetigahotel.com.br; Rua Coronel Pilad Rebuá 679; s/d R$755/800; ✗ ▣ ▣) The remarkable wood-and-stone architecture is more interesting than the rather simple rooms, which all overlook a nice courtyard and pool. Ask for a reduction during the off season.

Eating & Drinking

Vicio da Gula Café (☎ 3255 2041; Rua Coronel Pilad Rebuá 1852; sandwiches R$7; ☺ noon-2am) Popular corner spot for great burgers, fries and *açaí na tigela* (a berrylike fruit, in a bowl).

Sale & Pepe (☎ 3255 1822; Rua 29 de Maio 971; meals for 2 R$15-31; ☺ 6pm-2am) Has a decent selection of Chinese and Japanese dishes with a Pantaneiro slant, such as yakisoba *jacaré*.

San Marino Pizza (☎ 3282 2656; Rua Luiz da Costa Leite 1543; pizzas R$16-24; ☺ 6pm-midnight, closed Tue) The four-cheese pizza from this outlet of the Campo Grande pizzeria of the same name is the best in town.

O Casarão (☎ 3255 1970; Rua Coronel Pilad Rebuá 1835; rodízio R$16.90, with fish R$35.90; ☺ 11am-3pm & 6-11:30pm) Bouncing buffet joint on the main drag. It's worth paying the extra for the fish *rodízio*.

Cantinho do Peixe (☎ 3255 3381; Rua 31 de Março 1918; meals R$20-52; ☺ 11am-3pm & 6-11pm Mon-Sat) Pintado (a type of catfish), fresh from Rio Miranda, ends up on plates 15 different ways at this simple but tasty spot just off the main drag. Try the *pintado á urucum*, a lasagna-like dish of pintado smothered in a tomato, condensed milk and mozzarella sauce.

Santa Esmeralda (☎ 3255 1943; Rua Coronel Pilad Rebuá 1831; meals for 2 R$25-42; ◷ 11am-2:30pm & 6pm-midnight) Pastas (R$14 to R$18) with your choice of sauce, and excellent barbecue meat served on lengthy *espetinhos* (skewers).

our pick A Casa do João (☎ 3255 1212; www.casa dojoao.com.br, in Portuguese; Rua Nelson Felicio; meals for 2 R$37, for 3 R$40, for 4 R$47; ◷ 6pm-late Sun-Thu, 5pm-late Fri & Sat) The new top spot in town for fish dishes, being especially famous for its traíra (a predatory fish) which comes in a range of sizes depending on your appetite. All the furniture here is made from recycled wood from fallen trees in the local area.

Pantanal Carnes Exóticos (☎ 3255 2763; Rua Coronel Pilad Rebuá 1808; meals for 2 R$40-60; ◷ 11am-2pm & 6-10:30pm) Got a craving for capybara with bacon? What about peccary with pineapple? Make a beeline for Pantanal Carnes Exóticos. It's pricey but you'll find dishes here that you don't get in your local café. Don't worry, the meat is farmed, not wild.

Getting There & Away

Cruzeiro do Sul is the only bus company that serves Bonito. There are buses to Bonito from Campo Grande (R$53, five hours, seven daily) and six in the opposite direction beginning at 5:30am. There is one bus to Corumbá (R$57, seven hours, 6am). For Foz do Iguaçu it is easier to head back to Campo Grande and catch a direct bus from there. Heading south involves at least three separate changes of bus, and they don't always synchronize well. For Ponta Porã and the border crossing to Paraguay, you need to switch buses in Jardim (R$10, one hour), and catch the daily onward service (R$40, four hours, 3:30pm).

Getting Around

Unfortunately, many of Bonito's attractions are a fair hike from town, and there's no public transport. To make matters worse, tours booked with travel agencies in Bonito don't include transport, though those booked at hotels generally do. If you find yourself looking for transport, try the local shuttle service, **Vanzella** (☎ 3255 3005), which will take you to any excursion provided there is a minimum of four people. The costs are R$100 for half-day tours and R$200 for a full day.

If you are part of a group, it might end up being more economical to hire a taxi for the full day (R$120, the same as renting a car, but without the gas bill) from any Ponto de Táxi.

Lastly, there are your friendly neighborhood mototaxis: to the Rio Sucuri (38km round-trip) and Gruta do Lago Azul (38km round-trip) and back to town costs around R$36; to Rio da Prata (100km round-trip) costs R$70; and to Boca da Onça (120km round-trip) R$75. The drivers will wait around for the duration of the tour. No matter which form of transportation you choose to take, remember to keep an eye on the landscape. It's not uncommon to see some impressive wildlife along the way, including deer, rheas and even an occasional anteater.

PONTA PORÃ

☎ 0xx67 / pop 76,000

It's a strange feeling to cross a street and change countries, but you can do just that in Ponta Porã, a bustling little border town divided from the Paraguayan town of Pedro Juan Caballero by Av Internacional. The beer changes from Skol to Pilsen and prices on electronics are slashed – other than that, it's hard to even notice there is a border here (Portunhol vernacular is rampant). Though it prospered as a center for the *yerba maté* trade in the late 19th century, it now caters to Brazilians by the truckload, who flock to the Paraguayan shopping centers. It's a get-in, get-out town – if you spend more than one night here, it had better be due to hospitalization.

Information

Banco Continental (cnr Calles Mariscal Estigarribia & Mariscal López, Pedro Juan Caballero) Visa/MasterCard ATM for Paraguayan guaranis.

Banco do Brasil (Av Brasil 2623) Visa/MasterCard ATM.

Bradesco (Av Brasil 2765) Visa/MasterCard ATM.

Centro Digital (☎ 3431 2446; Rua 7 de Setembro 223; per hr R$2; ◷ 8am-9pm Mon-Fri, to 5pm Sat, 2-9pm Sun) Internet access.

Federal Police (☎ 3431 1428; Av Presidente Vargas; ◷ 9am-noon & 1-4pm Mon-Fri) Near the Paraguayan consulate. This is where you get Brazilian exit/entry stamps; this involves a bit of legwork, so if you're in a hurry, grab a cab and ring the bell if it is closed.

Norte Cambios (cnr Calles Mariscal López & Curupayty, Pedro Juan Caballero) Changes cash at a reasonable rate.

Paraguayan immigration office (☎ 3431 6312; Av Dr Francis; ◷ 7am-noon & 1:30-9pm Mon-Fri, 8am-noon & 1:30-9pm Sat, 7-9pm Sun) For Paraguayan entry/exit stamps. The office is about 2km east of the local bus terminal. It's a large, yellow building next to Goodyear.

Post office (Av Brasil 2861)

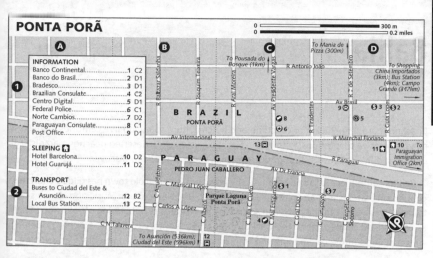

PONTA PORÃ

INFORMATION
Banco Continental...............1	C2
Banco do Brasil....................2	D1
Bradesco...............................3	D1
Brazilian Consulate...............4	C2
Centro Digital......................5	D1
Federal Police.......................6	C1
Norte Cambios......................7	D2
Paraguayan Consulate...........8	C1
Post Office............................9	D1

SLEEPING
Hotel Barcelona..................10	D2
Hotel Guarujá.....................11	D2

TRANSPORT
Buses to Ciudad del Este & Asunción.........................12	B2
Local Bus Station................13	C2

Sleeping & Eating

This area is not suburban Rio by any means, but drug trafficking is widespread and altercations along the border are not uncommon. Travelers are generally left alone, but it's a good idea to use extra caution, especially at night.

Hotel Guarujá (☎ 3431 9515; Rua Guia Lopes 63; s/d apt without air-con R$35/60, with air-con R$45/70; ✷) A bit tatty but still a good budget option with large *apartamentos*.

Pousada do Bosque (☎ 3431 1181; www.hotelpousada dobosque.com.br, in Portuguese; Av Presidente Vargas 1151; s/d apt R$70/150; ✷ ☑) A little forested oasis just outside the center on the ritzy side of town. It's too nice for Ponta Porã, truth be told.

Hotel Barcelona (☎ 3431 8494; Av Guia Lopes 50; s/d R$98/135; ✷ ☑) The nicest digs in the center, with big rooms (aged furniture free of charge) and a nice pool.

Mania de Pizza (☎ 3431 2620; Rua Tiradentes 754; pizza R$20-35; ☺ 6pm-midnight) No fewer than 55 different toppings to choose from, with some interesting combinations such as *Coreana* and *Stroganoff*, as well as a raft of dessert pizzas for those with a sweet tooth. Delivery option available.

Shopping

To see what all the fuss is about, **Shopping China Importados** (☎ 0xx36-74343; Ruta V c/Callejón Internacional, Pedro Juan Caballero; ☺ 8:30am-7pm Mon-Sat, 9am-2pm Sun) is a good place to start. This megastore has...well, *everything* and is teeming with wide-eyed Brazilians throwing down real after real for massive discounts on everything from Johnny Walker to Canon.

Getting There & Around

From the **bus station** (☎ 3431 4145), about 4km from the center of Ponta Porã, frequent buses go to Campo Grande (R$45, four hours, 11 daily). There are also buses to Corumbá (R$120, 13½ hours) and São Paulo (R$245, 25 hours, two daily). For Bonito, you must first travel to Jardim (R$40, four hours, 6am) and then on to Bonito (R$10, one hour, seven daily). If you are arriving from Bonito, get off outside the Hotel Internacional on the main street, as it is considerably more central than the bus station and will shave R$20 off your taxi fare. Alternatively, a local bus (R$2.20) runs between the main bus station and the more central local bus station every 45 minutes until 10pm.

For Foz do Iguaçu, take a bus from the bus station on Calle Alberdi in Pedro Juan Caballero (on the Paraguayan side) to Ciudad del Este (70,000 guaraní, eight hours, two daily). Cuidad del Este (Paraguay) is just across the border from the Brazilian town of Foz do Iguaçu. You don't need a Paraguayan visa to transit through Paraguay on your way to Foz do Iguaçu but you do need an entry stamp. From the same bus station in Pedro Juan Caballero, there are also buses to Asunción, the capital of Paraguay (70,000 guaraní, six hours, 12 daily) and Concepción (25,000 guaraní, four hours, 10 daily). Choose your company carefully, some are much better than others and there isn't much difference in price. La Santaniana is recommended to Asunción.

Bahia

BAHIA

Boasting more than 900km of coastline and a rich culture spanning five centuries, Bahia is a state of massive proportions. With World Heritage–listed sites, deserted beaches, paradisaical islands and lively festivals throughout the year, there is much to discover.

Bahia's centerpiece is Salvador, where the jewel-box colonial old town has gilded churches, cobblestone streets and an incredibly vibrant Afro-Brazilian culture. Music and dance seem to be everywhere, with the powerful sounds of drum corps reverberating off old stone walls as capoeiristas battle against the backdrop of a 16th-century cathedral. Catching open-air concerts, Candomblé ceremonies and impromptu fests are ways to celebrate an evening.

Nearby scenic colonial towns such as Cachoeira have picturesque river settings and a long tradition of wood carving. Just short journeys north and south lead to pretty coastal spots such as the car-free island of Morro de São Paulo or lovely Praia do Forte.

In the south, the idyllic villages of Arraial d'Ajuda and Trancoso perch on hillsides near vast stretches of white-sand beaches. A fun, diverse crowd gathers at outdoor restaurants and bars, and there's a charming assortment of guesthouses. More off-the-beaten-track locales include the sleepy fishing village of Caraíva, the rustic island of Barra Grande, and Parque Nacional Marinho de Abrolhos, which is great for diving and whale-watching. Inland, the peaceful town of Lençóis, once a center for diamond-mining, lies amid breathtaking scenery, with waterfalls and rushing rivers setting the stage for hiking and exploring.

HIGHLIGHTS

- Follow the sounds of the pounding rhythms in **Salvador** (p437), Latin America's inspiring Afro-Brazilian capital
- Hike across dramatic plateaus and swim in fresh waterfalls in the magnificent **Parque Nacional da Chapada Diamantina** (p496)
- Island-hop by speedboat across lovely **Morro de São Paulo** (p467) and traditional **Boipeba** (p470)
- Linger at outdoor restaurants, take long coastal walks and join the beach fests at **Arraial d'Ajuda** (p484)
- Watch tiny sea turtles hatch outside of **Praia do Forte** (p463)

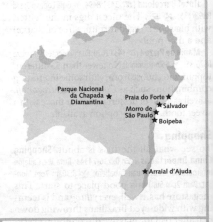

Parque Nacional da Chapada Diamantina ★ Praia do Forte ★
Morro de ★ ★Salvador
São Paulo ★Boipeba

★ Arraial d'Ajuda

- POPULATION: 13.5 MILLION
- AREA: 567,300 SQ KM

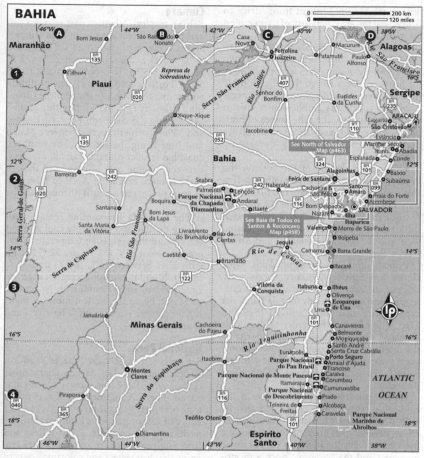

BAHIA

BAHIA

History

Prior to the Portuguese arrival, the region known today as Bahia had a wide variety of ethnic groups scattered inland and along the coast, speaking dozens of languages. Many of the tribes were wiped out by the Portuguese, though some – like the Pataxó (see the boxed text, p489) – are still around today. The indigenous tribes practiced some form of agriculture, raising manioc, sweet potatoes and maize, and practiced hunting and fishing, while gathering fruits from the forests. Little else is known of the area's native population, who, for the most part, would disappear following the European arrival.

Portuguese sailors first made landfall near Porto Seguro in 1500, but it wasn't until one

year later – All Saints' Day (November 1), according to legend – that Italian navigator Amerigo Vespucci sailed into Salvador's bay and named it Baía de Todos os Santos. Two generations later, in 1549, Tomé de Souza returned under orders by the Portuguese crown to found Brazil's first capital, Salvador da Bahia.

To fuel this new country, the colonists grew sugarcane and later tobacco in the fertile *recôncavo* (region named after the concave shape of the bay) that surrounds the Baía de Todos os Santos. The Portuguese enslaved the indigenous people to work these fields, and when they proved insufficient, they brought over Africans in staggering numbers. From 1550 to 1850, at least 3.6

million slaves were brought from Africa to Brazil, and the great majority of them ended up in the northeast.

In such numbers, the slaves managed to maintain much of their African culture. When their own religious practices were prohibited, for instance, slaves moved their Candomblé *terreiros* (venues) underground and syncretized their gods with Catholic saints. African food and music enriched the homes of both blacks and whites, and the African culture deeply influenced the newly developing Brazilian culture.

Throughout the life of the colony, the Portuguese utilized a harsh plantation system that would keep African slaves tied to the land until their emancipation in 1888. In addition to sugar and tobacco, the Portuguese created cattle ranches, which spread inland, radiating west into the *sertão* (backlands) and Minas Gerais, then northwest into Piauí.

Primary products were shipped out, while slaves and European luxury goods were shipped in. Bahia was colonial Brazil's economic heartland, with Salvador da Bahia the capital of colonial Brazil between 1549 and 1763. The city was the center of the sugar industry, which sustained the prosperity of the country until the collapse in international sugar prices in the 1820s. During the gold and coffee booms in the south, Salvador continued its decline.

Industrialization in Bahia began in the mid-19th century and continued slowly, with developments in banking and industry, as new rail lines brought goods from the interior to Salvador's large port. Factories appeared and the economy, once a monoculture of the sugarcane industry, diversified. The most important event of the late 19th century was the emancipation of slaves, which brought freedom for many of Bahia's inhabitants.

In the 20th century, oil discoveries in the 1940s helped bring Bahia out of economic stagnation and contributed to the state's continued modernization. Today, Salvador remains an important port, exporting soy, fruits, cocoa, petrochemicals and sugarcane – which is once again achieving prominence for its role as a highly efficient biofuel. In recent decades, tourism has emerged as an important industry and, with the influx of cash, the state has invested in much-needed infrastructure and public-health projects.

Climate

Bahia's tropical Atlantic coast remains hot and humid all year long, with high temperatures averaging between 26°C (79°F) and 30°C (86°F) and lows between 22°C (72°F) and 24°C (75°F). The southern coast (from about Porto Seguro south) is cooler during winter months, with low temperatures dropping as low as 17°C (63°F). Monthly rainfall averages on the coast run between 100mm and 350mm, with the period between March and June being the wettest. The southern coast has smaller monthly rainfall averages, between 100mm and 170mm, and though there is more rain from April to July, rain is seen pretty consistently throughout the year.

The Chapada Diamantina remains hot during the day and pleasantly cool at night throughout the year. High temperatures average between 27°C (81°F) and 32°C (90°F), with lows between 16°C (61°F) and 20°C (68°F). Monthly rainfall averages range between 50mm and 170mm, with November to March being the wettest months, making for greener scenery and fuller rivers and waterfalls.

National Parks

Set well west of Salvador, the 1520-sq-km Parque Nacional da Chapada Diamantina (p496) is by far Bahia's most spectacular national park. A well-developed network of tour providers and guides offers treks and a range of adventure sports in and around the park, with its waterfalls, green valleys and towering peaks. Divers and snorkelers will enjoy the clear waters and colorful variety of coral and marine life in the Parque Nacional Marinho de Abrolhos (p491). The 913-sq-km marine park includes an archipelago and expanses of coral reef off the very south of the Bahian coast. Also in southern Bahia, coastal Parque Nacional de Monte Pascoal (p488) offers limited hiking and excellent views from its peak, and is overseen by the indigenous Pataxó tribe.

Getting There & Away

Bahia's primary airport (see p456) is located in its capital, Salvador, though Porto Seguro also has frequent and inexpensive flights.

Hwy BR-101 skirts the Bahian coastline but remains between 50km and 75km inland. It is the main thoroughfare through the state and the chosen route of most long-distance buses. There are good coastal highways only between Canavieiras and Itacaré and from Salvador north to the border with Sergipe.

Getting Around

Transportation is a snap in Bahia: there's always some way to get where you want to go. Aside from buses, Kombi vans and *bestas* (vans that run a specific route and will stop anywhere to drop off or pick up passengers) are common in rural areas, as are collective taxis.

SALVADOR

☎ 0xx71 / pop 3 million

Salvador da Bahia has an energy and unadorned beauty that few cities can match. Once the magnificent capital of Portugal's great New World colony, Salvador is the country's Afro-Brazilian jewel. Its brilliantly hued center is a living museum of 17th- and 18th-century architecture and gold-laden churches. More importantly, Salvador is the nexus of an incredible arts movement. Wild festivals happen frequently, with drum corps pounding out powerful rhythms against the backdrop of colonial buildings almost daily. At night, capoeira (see the boxed text, p455) circles form on plazas and open spaces, while the scent of *acarajé* (bean and shrimp fritters) and other African delights fills the evening air. Elsewhere in town, a different spirit flows through the crowd as religious followers celebrate and reconnect with African gods at mystical Candomblé ceremonies. In fact, there's no other place in the world where descendants of African slaves have preserved their heritage as well as in Salvador – from music and religion to food, dance and martial arts traditions.

Aside from the many attractions within Salvador, gorgeous coastline lies right outside the city – a suitable introduction to the tropical splendor of Bahia.

Chosen as one of Brazil's 12 host cities for the 2014 FIFA World Cup, Salvador is bracing for a major influx of visitors. Preparations have been slow to start, though. At the time of writing, the beginning stages of construction were underway for an overhaul of the old Fonte Nova Stadium and city officials were discussing plans for improving the congested public transportation system.

HISTORY

In 1549, Tomé de Souza landed on Praia Porto da Barra under Portuguese royal orders to found Brazil's first capital, bringing city plans, a statue, 400 soldiers and 400 settlers, including priests and prostitutes. He founded the city in a defensive location: on a cliff top facing the sea. After the first year a city of mud and straw had been erected, and by 1550 the surrounding walls were in place to protect against attacks from hostile *índios* (indigenous people). Salvador da Bahia remained Brazil's most important city for the next three centuries.

During its early years, the city depended upon the export of sugarcane and later tobacco from the fertile *recôncavo* region at the northern end of Baía de Todos os Santos. Later, cattle ranching was introduced, which, coupled with gold and diamonds from the Bahian interior, provided Salvador with immense wealth, as is visible in the city's opulent baroque architecture.

African slaves were first brought to Salvador in the mid-1500s, and in 1587 historian Gabriel Soares tallied an estimated 12,000 whites, 8000 converted *índios* and 4000 black slaves. The number of blacks eventually increased to constitute half of the city's population, and uprisings of blacks threatened Salvador's stability several times.

After Lisbon, Salvador was the secondmost important city in the Portuguese empire. It was the glory of colonial Brazil, famed for its many gold-filled churches, beautiful mansions and numerous festivals. It was also renowned as early as the 17th century for its bawdy public life, sensuality and decadence – so much so that its bay won the nickname Baía de Todos os Santos e de Quase Todos os Pecados (Bay of All Saints and of Nearly All Sins)!

Salvador remained Brazil's seat of colonial government until 1763 when, with the decline of the sugarcane industry, the capital was moved to Rio.

In 1798, the city was the stage for the Conjuração dos Alfaiates (Conspiracy of the Tailors) – the beginning of a wave of battles between Portuguese loyalists and those wanting independence. It was only on July 2, 1823, with the defeat of Portuguese troops in Cabrito and Pirajá, that the city found peace. At that time, Salvador numbered 45,000 inhabitants and was the commercial center of a vast territory.

BAHIA

BAHIA

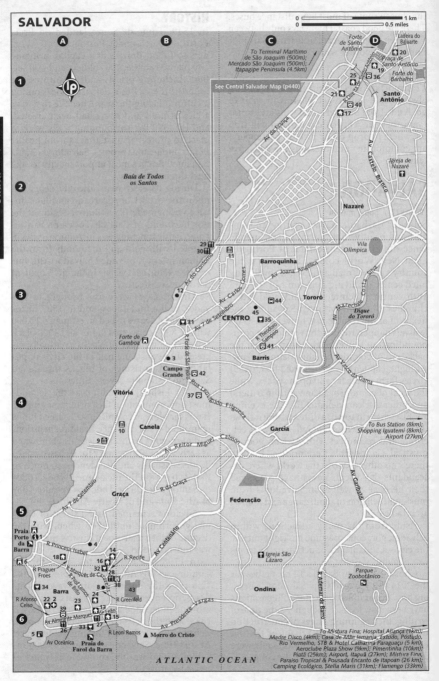

SALVADOR

0 _____ 1 km
0 _____ 0.5 miles

See Central Salvador Map (p440)

To Terminal Marítimo
de São Joaquim (500m);
Mercado São Joaquim (500m);
Itapagipe Peninsula (4.5km)

Forte
de Santo
Antônio

Ladeira do
Baluarte

Praça de
Santo Antônio

Forte do
Barbalho

Santo
Antônio

Baía de Todos
os Santos

Igreja de
Nazaré

Nazaré

Vila
Olímpica

Barroquinha

Av Joana Angélica

Tororó

Dique
do Tororó

CENTRO

Barris

Forte de
Gamboa

Campo
Grande

Vitória

Rua Leonidio Filgueira

Canela

Av Reitor Miguel Calmón

Garcia

Graça

R da Graça

Federação

Av Carlos Gomes

Praia
Porto
da
Barra

R Princesa Isabel

R Recife

Igreja São
Lázaro

Parque
Zoobotânico

R Praguer
Froes

Barra

R Afonso
Celso

Av Almirante Marques de Leão

Ondina

R Greenfeld

R Leoni Ramos

Morro do Cristo

Praia do
Farol da Barra

Av Oceánica

Av Presidente Vargas

To Mistura Fina; Hospital Aliança (1km);
Madre Disco (4km); Casa de Mãe Iemanja; Exstudo; Postudo;
Rio Vermelho; STB & Hotel Catharina Paraguaçu (5km);
Aeroclube Plaza Show (9km); Pimentinha (10km);
Piatã (25km); Airport; Itapuã (27km); Mistura Fina,
Paraiso Tropical & Pousada Encanto de Itapoan (26 km);
Camping Ecológico, Stella Maris (31km); Flamengo (33km)

To Bus Station (8km);
Shopping Iguatemi (8km);
Airport (27km)

ATLANTIC OCEAN

For most of the 19th and 20th centuries the city stagnated as the agricultural economy foundered on its disorganized labor and production. Today, Salvador is Brazil's third-largest city, and it has only begun moving forward in the last few decades. New industries such as petroleum, chemicals and tourism have brought wealth to the city's coffers, but the rapidly increasing population is still faced with major economic and social problems.

ORIENTATION

Salvador sits at the southern tip of a V-shaped peninsula at the mouth of the Baía de Todos os Santos. The city can be difficult to navigate as there are many one-way, no-left-turn streets that wind through Salvador's hills and valleys. The center of the city is on the bay side of the peninsula and is divided by a steep bluff into two parts: Cidade Alta (Upper City) and Cidade Baixa (Lower City).

The heart of historic Cidade Alta is the Pelourinho (or Pelô), which is also the heart of Salvador's tourism and nightlife. This roughly refers to the area from Praça da Sé to Largo do Pelourinho.

From Praça Castro Alves, Av 7 de Setembro runs through the Centro to the wide Praça Campo Grande, then continues southwest through the well-to-do Vitória neighborhood, and down to the mouth of the bay. Here, at the tip of the peninsula, is the affluent Barra district, with its lighthouse, forts and popular beach.

A main thoroughfare, which constantly changes names (one being Av Presidente Vargas), snakes east from Barra along the Atlantic coast. It passes through middle-class coastal suburbs such as Rio Vermelho, and a chain of beaches all the way to Itapuã.

Cidade Baixa contains the Comércio (the city's commercial and financial center), the ferry terminals and port. North, the land curves around the bay to create the Itapagipe Peninsula, including the Bonfim and Boa Viagem neighborhoods. The suburbs along the bay are poor, and the level of poverty generally increases with the distance from the center.

Maps

Tourist information offices give out free basic maps, but for a more in-depth map, look for Guia Cartoplam's *O Melhor de Salvador* (R$15), sold alongside similar options in newsstands about town.

INFORMATION
Bookstores

Berinjela (Map p440; ☎ 3322 0247; Travessa da Ajuda 1, Cidade Alta; 🖳) Sells used foreign-language books, CDs and LPs; the café serves vegetarian food.

Sebo Brandão (Map p440; ☎ 3243 5383; Rua Rui Barbosa 15B, Cidade Alta) Sells and trades used foreign-language books.

Emergency

Deltur (Map p440; ☎ 3322 7155; Cruzeiro de São Francisco 14, Pelourinho; 🕑 24hr) Any crime involving a tourist must be handled by the city's tourist police. A few speak English or French.

Pronto Socorro (First Aid; ☎ 192)

BAHIA

INFORMATION		
Bahiatursa	1	A5
Bahiatursa	(see 43)	
Hospital Espanhol	2	A6

SIGHTS & ACTIVITIES		
Associação Cultural Brasil-Estados Unidos	3	B4
Diálogo	4	A5
Farol da Barra	(see 5)	
Forte de Santo Antônio da Barra	5	A6
Forte Santa Maria	6	A5
Forte São Diogo	7	A5
Idioma Escola de Português	8	A6
Museu Carlos Costa Pinto	9	A4
Museu de Arte da Bahia	10	B4
Museu de Arte Moderna	(see 12)	
Museu de Arte Sacra da Bahia	11	C3
Solar do Unhão	12	B3

SLEEPING 🛏		
Âmbar Pousada	13	A6
Barra Guest Hostel	14	A5
Che Logarto	15	A6
La Villa Françaíse	16	A5
Nega Maluca	17	D1
Pousada Azul	18	A5
Pousada das Flores	19	D1
Pousada do Baluarte	20	D1
Pousada do Boqueirão	21	D1
Pousada Noa Noa	22	A6
Pousada O Ninho	23	A6
Villa Romana	24	A6
Villa Santo Antônio	25	D1

EATING 🍴		
Cabana de Cely	26	A6
Caranguejo de Sergipe	27	A6
Ramma	28	A6
Restaurant Solar do Unhão	(see 12)	
Soho	29	B3
Trapiche Adelaide	30	B3

DRINKING 🍷		
Bahia Café	31	B3
Bar da Ponta	(see 30)	
Bar do Chico	32	A6
Barravento	33	A6
Pereira	34	A6
Quixabeira	35	C3

ENTERTAINMENT 🎭		
Alphorria	36	D1
Beco dos Artistas	37	B4
Bohemia Music Bar	38	B6
Off Club	39	A6
Olivier	40	D1
Queens Club	41	C3
Teatro Castro Alves	42	B4

SHOPPING		
Shopping Barra	43	B6

TRANSPORT		
Lapa	44	C3
Ticket Center	45	C3

BAHIA

CENTRAL SALVADOR

A   **B**   **C**   **D**

INFORMATION
BahiaCafe.com...............................1 D4
Bahiatursa.....................................2 E4
Bahiatursa...............................(see 64)
Banco do Brasil.............................3 E4
Berinjela.......................................4 C5
Bradesco.......................................5 D4
Café Conosco................................6 E4
Central Post Office........................7 C3
Deltur...8 E1
Emtursa..9 C4
Grupo Gay da Bahia....................10 F4
Post Office..................................11 E4
Post Office..................................12 D4
Sebo Brandão.............................13 C5
Toursbahia..................................14 E4

SIGHTS & ACTIVITIES
Associação Brasileira de
  Capoeira Angola.....................15 F3
Câmara Municipal.......................16 D4
Catedral Basílica.........................17 D4
Diáspora Art Center.....................18 E4
Elevador Lacerda.....................(see 66)
Escadas do Carmo.......................19 F2
Escola de Dança..........................20 E4
Faculdade de Medicina
  Building..................................21 E3
Federação Baiana do Culto
  Afro-Brasileiro........................22 E3
Fundação Casa de Jorge
  Amado....................................23 E3
Fundação Mestre Bimba..............24 F3
Igreja da Ordem Terceira de
  São Francisco..........................25 E4
Igreja da Ordem Terceira do
  Carmo....................................26 F2
Igreja do Santíssimo
  Sacramento do Passo...............27 F2
Igreja e Convento São
  Francisco.................................28 E4
Igreja NS do Rosário dos
  Pretos.....................................29 F3
Mercado Modelo.....................(see 64)
Mestre Lua..................................30 F4
Mestre Souza.........................(see 59)
Museu Afro-Brasileiro..............(see 21)
Museu da Cidade.........................31 F3
Museu da Misericórdia................32 D4
Museu de Arqueologia e
  Etnologia.............................(see 21)
Palácio Rio Branco.......................33 C4
Plano Inclinado Gonçalves......(see 67)
Senac.....................................(see 60)

SLEEPING
Albergue da Juventude do
  Pelô..34 E2
Albergue das Laranjeiras..............35 F4
Casa do Amarelindo.....................36 E3
Hostel Cobreu..............................37 F2
Hostel Galeria 13.........................38 E4
Hostel Solar dos Romanos............39 E3
Hotel Villa Bahia.........................40 E4
Pestana Convento do Carmo........41 F2
Pousada da Praça Hotel................42 C6
Pousada Terra Nossa....................43 E3
Studio do Carmo.........................44 F2

EATING
A Cubana.....................................45 C4
A Cubana.....................................46 E3
Cafélier.......................................47 F1
Jardim das Delicias.......................48 F4
Mamabahia..................................49 E3
Maria Mata Mouro.......................50 E4
O Coliseu.....................................51 E4

Panorámico..................................52 E4
Ristorante La Figa.........................53 F5
Senac.....................................(see 60)

DRINKING
Café Alquimia..............................54 F2
Camafeu......................................55 B4
Cantina da Lua.............................56 E4
Casa do Amarelindo Bar..........(see 36)
Odoyá..57 E4

ENTERTAINMENT
Sankofa.......................................58 E4
Teatro Miguel Santana.................59 F3
Teatro SESC-Senac.......................60 F3

Docks

R da Polônia

Av Frederico Pontes

R da Argentina

R Fran Gonçalves

Praça da
Inglaterra

R Miguel Calmon

R Cons Dantas

R Cons Lafaiete

R da Grécia

Comércio

R Portugal

R Santos Dumont

R Lopes Cardoso

Ladeira da Misericórdia

67

Baía de
Todas os
Santos

Praça
da Sé

32

17

1

Igreja da
Misericórdia

R 3 de Maio

R da Misericórdia

45

12

**Cidade Baixa
(Lower City)**

Small Boat
Anchorage

Ladeira da Montanha

65

66

19

5

Praça Municipal
(Praça Tomé de
Souza)

33

R José Gonçalves

R Saldanha da Gama

16

R Chile

68

Ladeira da Praça

Lad da Praça

R do Tesouro

4

Igreja NS
da Conceição

Av da França

R da Ajuda

Praça dos
Veteranos

R Padre Vieira

**Cidade Alta
(Upper City)**

Ladeira da Palma

R Ruy Barbosa

13

Ladeira Pau da Bandeira

R Dom Marcio Cota

42

R Lama

R do Castanheda

R 24 de Maio

Ladeira da Barroquinha

Av Carlos Gomes

Av 7 de Setembro

R DJ JJ Seabra

To Centro (50m); Vitória (2km);
Barra (4km); Coastal Suburbs

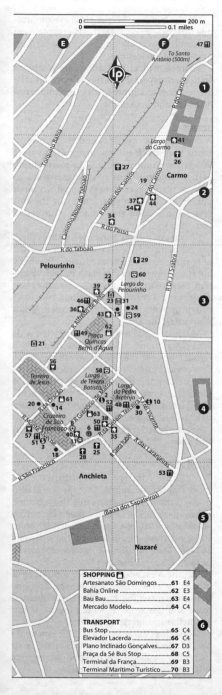

BAHIA

Internet Access
BahiaCafe.com (Map p440; Praça da Sé 20, Pelourinho; per hr R$4; 10am-midnight) Sandwiches, salads and drinks are also available at this centrally located café.
Café Conosco (Map p440; Rua da Ordem Terceira 4, Pelourinho; per hr R$3)

Left Luggage
Airport (3204 1150; per 24hr R$5-8; 24hr)
Bus station (3460 8300; per 24hr R$3; 24hr)

Medical Services
Hospital Espanhol (Map p438; 3421 8000; www .hospitalespanhol.com.br; Av 7 de Setembro 4161, Barra)

Money
Banco do Brasil (Map p440; Cruzeiro de São Francisco 11, Pelourinho) Also in the airport and scattered around Barra.
Bradesco (Map p440; Rua da Misericórdia, Cidade Alta) Also with international ATMs in the Pelourinho, Barra, the bus station and the airport.
Toursbahia (Map p440; 3320 3280; www.toursba hia.com.br; Cruzeiro de São Francisco 4, Pelourinho) One of Salvador's two official moneychangers changes cash or traveler's checks. Nearby impostors do the same thing.

Post
Central post office (Map p440; Praça da Inglaterra, Comércio)
Post office Cruzeiro de São Francisco (Map p440; Cruzeiro de São Francisco, Pelourinho); Rua 3 de Maio (Map p440; Rua 3 de Maio, Pelourinho)

Tourist Information
Bahiatursa (www.bahiatursa.ba.gov.br, in Portuguese) airport (3204 1244; 7:30am-11pm); bus station (3450 3871; Av Antônio Carlos Magalhães, 4362 - Iguatemi); Mercado Modelo (Map p440; 3241 0242; Mercado Modelo, Praça Cayru); Pelourinho (Map p440; 3321 2463; Rua Francisco Muniz Barreto 12, Pelour- inho; 8:30am-9pm Mon-Thu, 8:30am-10pm Fri-Sun); Porto da Barra (Map p438; 3264 5440; Instituto Mauá, Av 7 de Setembro, Porto da Barra); Shopping Barra (Map p438; 3264 4566; SAC) The multilingual state tourism authority is friendly if not terribly organized; the young staff attending the tourist desks are known for not getting things right at times. The Pelourinho office, which has a noticeboard listing what's happening around town, is your best bet.
Disque Bahia Turismo (Dial Tourism Bahia; 3103 3103) Round-the-clock tourist information or help (in English).
Emtursa (Map p440; 3321 3127; www.emtursa.sal vador.ba.gov.br, in Portuguese; Elevador Lacerda, Cidade

Alta) The city's tourism office can be helpful; as with Bahiatursa, these agents slip up sometimes, so it's best to reconfirm any important information they give you.

Grupo Gay da Bahia (Map p440; ☎ 3322 2552; www .ggb.org.br, in Portuguese; Rua Frei Vicente 24, Pelourinho) A cultural center for gays, lesbians and transgenders.

Travel Agencies

Dozens of travel agencies are scattered around Barra and the Pelourinho.

STB (☎ 3334 7566; www.stb.com.br; Rua Fonte do Boi 12, Rio Vermelho) Finds student discounts on international flights.

DANGERS & ANNOYANCES

The city has a reputation for theft and muggings, and pickpocketing is common on buses and in crowded places where tourists are easily singled out. Paranoia is counterproductive, but be aware of the dangers and minimize the risks. The following small sacrifices could assure a trouble-free visit (for more tips, see p702).

When visiting Salvador: dress down; wear cheap jewelry and watches, if any at all; take only enough money with you for your outing; carry only a photocopy of your passport; and be roughly orientated before you set out. If you must carry a bank card, take only one – and use ATMs inside banks instead of free-standing machines that are more susceptible to hackers. Leave expensive electronics locked up in your hotel or hostel; if you're carrying a camera, keep it concealed as much as possible. Don't hesitate to use taxis after dusk or in areas where you feel apprehensive, though taking buses in the evening is not necessarily unsafe.

In the center, tourist police maintain a visible presence, particularly in the Pelourinho. However, it is best not to rely solely on their protection, and you may find them apathetic should something occur.

Crime in the Pelô increases during the high season (especially around Carnaval) and on crowded Tuesday nights. Avoid empty areas. Not carrying a bag (and therefore little money and no valuables) at night will make you less of a target.

The Pelourinho shifts quickly into sketchy areas, so avoid wandering off the beaten path. Cidade Baixa is deserted and unsafe at night and on weekends, and the *ladeiras* (steep roads) that connect it to Cidade Alta should never be taken on foot.

On the beaches, keep a close eye on juvenile thieves – or *capitães d'areia* (captains of the sand) – who are quick to make off with unguarded possessions.

Women will attract annoying attention from men, especially in the Pelourinho. The best tactic is to simply ignore the comments, *psssu*-ing and beckoning.

Scams

A common way for bars and their customers to keep track of how many drinks were ordered without dispute is to place empty bottles underneath or next to the table. To prevent your server from getting it wrong or pulling one over on you, make sure the area under and around your table is clear before you open your tab.

Be wary of motley bands of hotshots playing capoeira on the Terreiro de Jesus. Not only can you see better capoeira elsewhere, but if you even bat an eyelash in their direction, they will come scurrying across the plaza demanding a contribution. When you don't cough up, you will likely be accused of not supporting the arts.

Meandering vendors, especially the kids with the ribbons, will offer you things as a *regalo* (present; they often say 'presente,' as Spanish and English speakers understand this term). But as the street-weary say, nothing in life is free. Once you accept a free 'present,' you'll likely have to buy something in order to be free of your new vendor buddy.

See the boxed text, p443, for another prevalent scam.

SIGHTS

The Cidade Alta is packed with the city's most impressive sights, though you'll also find worthwhile museums in Vitória, scenic lighthouses in Barra and other fascinating attractions scattered about the city. If you're short on time, climb aboard the open-air **Salvador Bus** (☎ 3356 6425; www.salvadorbus .br; tickets R$30; ☼ 8:30am-6pm Mon-Sat) at Farol da Barra, the Mercado Modelo or a number of other downtown destinations; the hop-on-hop-off sightseeing bus offers multilingual tours and has stops as wide-ranging as Rio Vermelho and Igreja do Bonfim.

Toursbahia (Map p440; ☎ 3320 3280; www.toursba hia.com.br; Cruzeiro de São Francisco 4, Pelourinho) is an extremely professional multilingual agency offering local and national tours.

Cidade Alta

The centerpiece of the Cidade Alta is the **Pelourinho** (Map p440), a Unesco-declared World Heritage site of colorful colonial buildings and magnificent churches. The area has undergone major restoration work – which remains ongoing – since 1993 thanks to Unesco funding. Admittedly, the Pelô has lost a lot of its character in the process, but to say that it is now safer and better preserved is an understatement.

As you wander the narrow streets, tripping over cobblestones and gazing up at the city's oldest architecture, you'll realize that the Pelô is not just for tourists. Cultural centers and schools of music, dance and capoeira pack these pastel-colored 17th- and 18th-century buildings.

IGREJA E CONVENTO SÃO FRANCISCO

One of Brazil's most magnificent churches, the baroque **Igreja e Convento São Francisco** (Map p440; Cruzeiro de São Francisco; admission R$3; ☿ 8:30am-5:30pm Mon-Sat, 1-5pm Sun) is crammed with displays of wealth and splendor. An 80kg silver chandelier dangles over ornate wood carvings smothered in gold leaf, and the convent courtyard is paneled with hand-painted *azulejos* (Portuguese tiles). The complex was finished in 1723.

Forced to build their masters' church and yet prohibited from practicing their own religion, African slave artisans responded

---

HELPING HAND OR AIDING THE PROBLEM?

In the Pelourinho, everyone and their mother will ask you for something, even if it's just a sip of your water. You will be shown unfilled prescriptions, broken limbs, infants and empty bellies. Street kids may lead you to the store to buy them powdered milk. It is of course up to you whether you believe their stories, but it should be remembered that the use of drugs such as crack and solvents is high in this impoverished community. Everything from a can of milk, a sandwich, your wrapped-up dinner leftovers and, obviously, cash is capable of being traded for drugs. The best way to help someone out, if you can swing it, is to buy him food and start a short chat while he eats it.

---

through their work: the faces of the cherubs are distorted, some angels are endowed with huge sex organs, while others appear pregnant. Most of these creative touches were chastely covered by 20th-century sacristans.

The polychrome figure of São Pedro da Alcântara by Manoel Inácio da Costa shows a figure suffering from tuberculosis – just like the artist himself. One side of the saint's face is more ashen than the other, so he appears to become more ill as you walk past him. José Joaquim da Rocha painted the entry hall's ceiling using perspective technique, a novelty during the baroque period.

TERREIRO DE JESUS

A colorful intersection of vendors, tourists, capoeiristas and colorful locals, the **Terreiro de Jesus** (Map p440; Praça 15 de Novembro) is a historic site of religious celebrations, and is ringed by four churches, as well as the 19th-century **Faculdade de Medicina Building**. The plaza feeds into the **Cruzeiro de São Francisco**, named for the cross in the square's center.

MUSEU AFRO-BRASILEIRO

Holding one of Bahia's most important collections, the **Museu Afro-Brasileiro** (Map p440; ☎ 3321 2013; www.ceao.ufba.br/mafro, in Portuguese; Faculdade de Medicina Bldg, Terreiro de Jesus; admission R$5; ☿ 9am-6pm Mon-Fri, 10am-5pm Sat & Sun) exhibits wood carvings, baskets, pottery and other artwork and crafts linking Brazilian and African artistic traditions. The highlight of the museum is a room lined with 27 huge, breathtaking carved wooden panels by Argentine-born Carybé, who is perhaps Salvador's most renowned 20th-century fine artist. The panels are stylized depictions of *orixás* (deities of the Afro-Brazilian religions), inlaid with shells and metals. There's also a worthwhile exhibit of photography, sacred objects and ceremonial apparel demonstrating the African roots of Brazilian Candomblé (see the boxed text, p454).

IGREJA DA ORDEM TERCEIRA DO CARMO

The original **Igreja da Ordem Terceira do Carmo** (Map p440; Largo do Carmo; admission R$2; ☿ 8am-noon & 2-5pm Mon-Fri), founded in 1636, burnt to the ground; the present crumbling neoclassical structure dates from 1828. The nave has a French organ and a baroque altar with a scandalous statue of Nossa Senhora do Carmo. Church historians claim the statue was modeled in the likeness

BAHIA

CHURCH SECRETS

A little-known fact is that the churches in the historic center are connected by a network of underground tunnels that feed to the port and the Forte de Santo Antônio. Supposedly they were constructed for defensive purposes, but one can't help but wonder what else they were used for. (Romantic encounters? Illegal slave trade? Contraband smuggling?)

---

of Isabel II, the daughter of Garcia d'Ávila (of Praia do Forte fame), the largest landholder in the Northeast. The artist, known as O Cabra (Half-Caste), was a slave with no artistic training, who was supposedly besotted with Isabel II. The Christ-child cradled in the statue's arms has black features – could this be what O Cabra imagined their love child would look like? O Cabra took eight years to finish the life-size image of Christ (1630), with blood made from 2000 rubies. It's on display in the church's small museum.

CATEDRAL BASÍLICA
The **Catedral Basílica** (Map p440; Terreiro de Jesus; admission R$2; 9-11am & 2-5pm Mon-Sat, 10am-noon Sun) dates from 1672 and is a marvelous example of Jesuit architecture. The interior is elegant and simple, with marble-covered walls and pillars that emphasize verticality. The sacristy has a beautiful carved jacaranda archway and a painted dome and floor.

LARGO DO PELOURINHO
The steep **Largo do Pelourinho** (Map p440; Praça José de Alencar) is a wide square that was once the site of the *pelourinho* (whipping post), where slaves were auctioned (historians disagree about whether slaves were publicly tortured here).

MUSEU DA CIDADE
Rather like the city itself, **Museu da Cidade** (Map p440; Largo do Pelourinho; admission R$3; 9am-6pm Mon & Wed-Fri, 1-5pm Sat, 9am-1pm Sun) contains an eclectic assortment of the old and the modern, the sacred and the profane. Exhibits include Candomblé *orixá* costumes, the personal effects of the poet Castro Alves (author of *Návio Negreiro*, or Slave Ship, and one of the first public figures to protest slavery), and traditional rag dolls enacting quotidian colonial life, as well as paintings and sculptures.

IGREJA NS DO ROSÁRIO DOS PRETOS
The king of Portugal gave the Irmanidade dos Homens Pretos (Brotherhood of Black Men) the land for the periwinkle-blue **Igreja NS do Rosário dos Pretos** (Map p440; Largo do Pelourinho; admission by donation; 9am-6pm Mon-Fri, 9am-2pm Sat & Sun) in 1704. Building in their free time, it took these slaves and freed slaves almost 100 years to complete it. The rococo facade includes design elements pertaining to Candomblé (ask a guide to point them out) and tiled towers with an indigenous flavor.

FUNDAÇÃO CASA DE JORGE AMADO
If you read Portuguese, pay a visit to the **Fundação Casa de Jorge Amado** (Map p440; 3321 0070; www.jorgeamado.org.br; Largo do Pelourinho; admission free; 9am-6pm Mon-Sat) and learn about the life of Brazil's best-known international novelist (see the boxed text, p477). A wall of Amado's book covers in every major language demonstrates his widespread popularity.

PRAÇA DA SÉ
The slick, L-shaped **Praça da Sé** has cool fountains and the fenced-off ruins of the foundations of its namesake church. A motley assortment of street performers congregates here, attracting crowds of locals and tourists alike. At the far end of the plaza, the 1874 funicular railway **Plano Inclinado Gonçalves** (Map p440; fare R$0.15; 7am-7pm Mon-Fri, 7am-1pm Sat) rolls 30-passenger cars between Cidade Alta and Cidade Baixa on terrifyingly steep tracks.

ELEVADOR LACERDA
The beautifully restored, art-deco **Elevador Lacerda** (Map p440; 3322 7049; fare R$0.15; 24hr) connects the Cidade Alta with Comércio, via four elevators traveling 72m in about 20 seconds. The Jesuits installed the first manual rope-and-pulley elevator around 1610 to transport goods and passengers from the port to the settlement. In 1868 an iron structure with clanking steam elevators was inaugurated, replaced by an electric system in 1928. Facing the elevator are the impressive arches of the **Câmara Municipal**, the 17th-century city hall, which occasionally puts on cultural exhibitions.

PRAÇA MUNICIPAL & PALÁCIO RIO BRANCO
Once the political seat of colonial Brazil, the **Praça Municipal** (Praça Tomé de Souza; Map p440) is now a lively place to people-watch

while enjoying a cool breeze. There are fine panoramic views over the bay – and free viewing telescopes for getting in close.

Overlooking the plaza, the impressive **Palácio Rio Branco** (Map p440; ☎ 3322 7255; admission free; ☻ 2-7pm Mon, 9am-5pm Tue-Sat) was reconstructed in 1919 after being partially ruined in a bombing and subsequent fire. The original 1549 structure housed the offices of Tomé de Souza, Brazil's first governor general.

IGREJA DA ORDEM TERCEIRA DE SÃO FRANCISCO

Displeased with the inclusion of a Mason symbol – an eagle – in the facade of the **Igreja da Ordem Terceira de São Francisco** (Map p440; Rua São Francisco; admission R$3; ☻ 8am-5pm), church fathers ordered the whole thing covered over in the late 18th century. It wasn't seen until a workman installing wiring in the 1930s serendipitously discovered the beautiful, baroque sandstone facade (the only one of its kind in Brazil).

MUSEU DE ARQUEOLOGIA E ETNOLOGIA

Below the Museu Afro-Brasileiro, the **Museu de Arqueologia e Etnologia** (Archaeology & Ethnology Museum; Map p440; ☎ 3321 3971; Faculdade de Medicina Bldg, Terreiro de Jesus; admission R$5; ☻ 10am-5pm) exhibits indigenous Brazilian pottery, bows and arrows, masks and feather headpieces. Also tucked between the building's arching stone foundations is 19th-century glass and porcelain found during the excavations for the metro.

MUSEU DE ARTE SACRA DA BAHIA

Housed in a tranquil 17th-century cloister, the **Museu de Arte Sacra da Bahia** (Map p438; ☎ 3243 6511; Rua do Sodré 276; admission R$5; ☻ 11:30am-5:30pm Mon-Fri) has high stone walls, a shady courtyard and bay views. Displayed in the former monks' quarters (of the Carmelitas Descalços, or Barefoot Carmelites, order) is a collection of 17th- and 18th-century sacred art, including carvings from the demolished Igreja da Sé.

MUSEU DA MISERICÓRDIA

The **Museu da Misericórdia** (Map p440; ☎ 3322 7355; www.scmba.com.br, in Portuguese; Rua da Misericórdia 6; admission R$5; ☻ 10am-5pm Mon-Sat, 1-5pm Sun) is housed in yet another marvelous 17th-century edifice, this one serving as Brazil's first hospital. Visits here include a guided tour (in Portuguese) that allows a glimpse of fine period furnishings, portraits and assorted finery dating back four centuries. You'll also see the attached Igreja da Misericórdia, with its *azulejos* and a sacristy featuring impressive 18th-century woodwork.

LADEIRA DO CARMO

Leading away from the Pelourinho, the steep Ladeira do Carmo provides access to the **Escadas do Carmo** (Map p440), a wide set of steps that were the setting of *O Pagador de Promessas* (1962). This was the first Brazilian film to win a Cannes film festival award. They lead to the eternally 'closed for renovation' **Igreja do Santíssimo Sacramento do Passo** (1737).

Cidade Baixa

Interspersed between the Comércio's modern skyscrapers is some fantastic 19th-century architecture in various stages of decay.

MERCADO MODELO

The original 1861 Customs House was partially destroyed in a fire in 1986. After reconstruction, it was transformed into a tourist market, the **Mercado Modelo** (Map p440; Praça Cayru). When shipments of new slaves arrived into port, they were stored in the watery depths of this building while awaiting auction. Night guards report all sorts of phantasmic activity after closing hours. Live music and free capoeira demonstrations often occur out back – be sure to ask the price before snapping photos of the capoeiristas. There's a touristy but fun café-restaurant, Camafeu (p453), on the upper level; the terrace, looking over the bay, is ideal for a shopping break.

SOLAR DO UNHÃO

The **Solar do Unhão** (Map p438; Av do Contorno) is a wonderfully preserved 18th-century complex that served as a transfer point for sugar shipments. Legends say it is haunted by the ghosts of murdered slaves. Today, this dark place houses the **Museu de Arte Moderna** (☎ 3329 0660; www.mam.ba.gov.br, in Portuguese; admission free; ☻ 2-7pm Tue-Fri, 2-10pm Sat), with a changing display of avant-garde exhibits (and erratic opening times). A fine restaurant staging a popular evening folklore show (and Saturday evening concert) occupies the former store house. The hillside sculpture garden, with bay views, is stunning at sunset. Take a taxi – the place is off bus routes and the desolate walk is known for tourist muggings.

Vitória

This leafy suburb has several worthwhile museums on its main boulevard; it's an easy stop between Barra and the Pelourinho.

MUSEU CARLOS COSTA PINTO

In a lovely two-story mansion, the **Museu Carlos Costa Pinto** (Map p438; ☎ 3336 6081; www.museucosta pinto.com.br; Av 7 de Setembro 2490; admission R$5; ⏱ 2:30-7pm Wed-Mon) houses one of Salvador's best collections of decorative art. Nicely lit displays highlight the unique works of talented artisans working in gold, crystal, porcelain and silver. Beautifully carved coral jewelry, tortoiseshell fans and elaborate *balangandans* (ethnic waist chains with attached charms) are among the highlights. Don't miss the chocolate mousse at the charming outdoor café.

MUSEU DE ARTE DA BAHIA

Set in an attractive neocolonial edifice, the **Museu de Arte da Bahia** (Map p438; ☎ 3336 9450; www .funceb.ba.gov.br/mab; Av 7 de Setembro 2340; admission R$5; ⏱ 2-7pm Tue-Fri, 2:30-6:30pm Sat & Sun) showcases works from Bahian artists, with paintings by José Teófilo de Jesus (1758–1817) among others. There's also an assortment of furniture and other antiques from the 18th and 19th centuries, as well as sacred art pieces.

North of the Center

To reach these sights north of the center, take a taxi or a Ribeira or Bomfim bus from the base of the Elevador Lacerda.

The die-hard market fan will enjoy **Mercado São Joaquim** (off Map p438; ⏱ 6am-6pm Mon-Sat, 6am-2pm Sun), a small city of sketchy waterfront stalls about 2km north of the Elevador Lacerda. Puddles of green slime, a meat neighborhood capable of converting the unprepared into a devout vegetarian, and bar stalls where rough hands grip glasses of rougher *cachaça* (sugarcane alcohol) let you know this is the real thing.

ITAPAGIPE PENINSULA

Jutting into the bay, a few kilometers north of Comércio, the Itapagipe Peninsula (off Map p438) is a much-visited destination for the 18th-century **Igreja NS do Bonfim** (☎ 3316 2196; www.senhordobonfim.org.br; admission free; ⏱ 8am-noon & 2-5:30pm Tue-Sun). If you wonder where Pelourinho vendors get all their *fitas* (colored ribbons), look no further. As is printed on them, *fitas* are a souvenir of the Igreja NS do Bonfim and have come to symbolize Bahia itself. (If you sign on, and tie a *fita* around your wrist, you are making a commitment that lasts for months. With each of the three knots a wish is made, which come true by the time the *fita* falls off. Cutting it off is inviting doom.)

Bonfim's fame derives from its power to effect miraculous cures, which has transformed it from a rather ordinary church into a popular shrine. In the Sala dos Milagres (Room of Miracles) on the right side of the church, devotees leave photos, letters and ex-votos: wooden and wax replicas of body parts left by those in need of curing (see the boxed text, p506).

Due to Candomblistas' syncretization of Jesus Christ (Nosso Senhor do Bonfim) with Oxalá, their highest deity, Bonfim is their most important church. Huge services are held hourly from 6am to 9am and at 5pm and 6pm on Fridays, Oxalá's day of the week. The 6am mass (on the first Friday of the month) attracts the most followers – wearing white is essential.

Barra

Barra's busy waterfront has three jutting points of land, occupied by the colonial forts of **Forte São Diogo** (Map p438), **Forte Santa Maria** (Map p438) and the most impressive of the bunch, **Forte de Santo Antônio da Barra** (Map p438; ☎ 3264 3296; admission R$6; ⏱ 9am-7pm Tue-Sun). Built in 1698, Bahia's oldest fort is more commonly called the Farol da Barra for the lighthouse (South America's oldest) within its walls. In addition to having superb views, the fort houses an excellent nautical **museum**, with relics and displays from the days of Portuguese seafaring (and lots of interesting information in English.) As you catch the sunset here – from the grassy ledge behind the fort or from the museum's gorgeous terrace café – realize that Salvador's peninsula is the only location in Brazil where the sun appears to set over the ocean.

Beaches

Praia Porto da Barra (Map p438) is rather like the Pelourinho: small, picturesque, usually crowded, loaded with vendors selling everything imaginable, and roughly half those present are foreigners. The bay's waters are clear and calm, and the people-watching is fantastic. To the left of the lighthouse, **Praia do Farol da Barra** (Map p438) has a beach break popular with surfers. Barra's waterfront is

BAHIA

lined with bars and restaurants and is well lit at night, but it gets a bit sleazy in the later hours.

Smaller crowds and an unpolluted Atlantic are about 40 minutes' bus travel east from the center (or more with traffic), but it's worth it. Calm seas lap on flat white sands with *barracas* (stalls) and swaying palms at popular city beaches **Piatã** (25km) and **Itapuã** (27km). As you reach the beaches of **Stella Maris** (31km) and **Flamengo** (33km), the waves get progressively stronger, *barracas* begin to space out, and sand dunes and more greenery create a more natural setting. Catch an Itapuã, Aeroporto or Praia do Flamengo bus, making sure it goes up the coast (*via orla*) and as far as you are going.

COURSES
Capoeira, Dance & Percussion
Individual class prices range from R$10 to R$20, with discounts for longer commitments. The following are in the Pelourinho:

Associação Brasileira de Capoeira Angola (Map p440; ☎ 3387 4972; Rua Gregório de Mattos 38)

Diáspora Art Center (Map p440; ☎ 3323 0016; 3rd fl, Cruzeiro de São Francisco 21) Classes in traditional and contemporary Afro-Brazilian dance, capoeira and percussion.

Escola de Dança (Map p440; ☎ 3322 5350; Rua da Oração 1) Traditional and contemporary Afro-Brazilian dance, capoeira and percussion.

Fundação Mestre Bimba (Map p440; ☎ 3322 5082; Rua Gregório de Mattos 51) A school run by the son of the founder of Capoeira Regional, Mestre Bimba.

Mestre Lua (Map p440; ☎ 3488 3600; Rua Frei Vicente 19) To set up a percussion class, pass by this shop of instruments handmade by the *mestre* (master) himself.

Mestre Souza (Map p440; ☎ 3321 9783) Afro-Brazilian drumming classes; inquire at Teatro Miguel Santana.

Cooking
Senac (Map p440; ☎ 3224 4550; www.senac.br/cursos/rest-escola.html, in Portuguese; Largo do Pelourinho 13-19) Cooking classes for tourists can be arranged at this culinary school. There's also a slick museum here dedicated to Bahian gastronomy and a first-class lunch buffet put on by the cooking school (see p451).

Language
The following schools offer group and private classes, and can set you up with a host family. A minimum one-week commitment is common. Contact the schools for the latest prices.

Associação Cultural Brasil-Estados Unidos (Map p438; ☎ 0800 284 2828; www.acbeubahia.org.br; Av 7 de Setembro, Vitória)

CAPOEIRA
Capoeira was developed by Afro-Brazilian slaves in Brazil about 400 years ago as a means of maintaining a ready self-defense against their masters. It is said to have originated from a ritualistic African dance. Capoeira was prohibited by slave owners and banished from the *senzalas* (slave barracks), forcing slaves to practice clandestinely in the forest. Later, in an attempt to disguise this act of defiance from the authorities, capoeira was developed into a kind of acrobatic dance. The clapping of hands and striking of the *berimbau,* a one-string musical instrument that looks like a fishing rod, originally served to alert fighters to the approach of the boss and subsequently became incorporated into the dance to maintain the rhythm.

As recently as the 1920s, capoeira was still prohibited and Salvador's police chief sent out cavalry squads to ban it from the streets. In the 1930s, Mestre Bimba established his academy and changed the emphasis of capoeira from its original function as a tool of insurrection to a form of artistic expression that has become an institution in Bahia.

Today, there are two schools of capoeira: the slow and low Capoeira de Angola, led by Mestre Pastinha, and the more aggressive Capoeira Regional, initiated by Mestre Bimba. The former school believes capoeira came from Angola; the latter maintains it was born in the plantations of Cachoeira and other cities of the *recôncavo* region (region named after the concave shape of the bay).

Capoeira combines the forms of the fight, the game and the dance. The movements are always fluid and circular, the fighters always playful and respectful as they exchange mock blows. Capoeira is typically practiced by two fighters at a time inside a *roda* (circle) of spectators/fighters who clap and sing. In addition to the *berimbau,* other instruments such as the *pandeiro* (tambourine), *agogô* (bell) and *atabaque* (drum) provide musical accompaniment. Capoeira gains more followers by the year, both nationally and abroad. Throughout Brazil – particularly Bahia – you will see people practicing their moves on the beach and street *rodas* popping up in touristy areas.

Diálogo (Map p438; ☎ 3264 0053; www.dialogo-brazil study.com; Rua Dr João Pondé 240, Barra) Singing, dance, cooking and capoeira classes are also offered.

Idioma Escola de Português (Map p438; ☎ 3267 7012; www.portugueseinbrazil.com; 1st fl, Rua Greenfield 46, Barra) Also features courses in capoeira and Bahian cooking.

FESTIVALS & EVENTS

Salvador delights in its wild festivals, which have links to both Catholicism and Candomblé. Although Carnaval (see the boxed text, below) steals the show, there are numerous festivals, particularly in January and February. Check with Bahiatursa (p441) for dates.

Processão do Senhor Bom Jesus dos Navegantes (January 1) A maritime procession transports the image of Bom Jesus from Igreja NS da Conceição in Cidade Baixa north along the bay to Igreja de NS da Boa Viagem. A festival ensues on Praia da Boa Viagem.

Festa da Lapinha (January 6) On the Dia de Reis, a procession of the reis magos (wise men) statues travels to a crèche in the Igreja da Lapinha.

Lavagem do Bonfim (2nd Thursday in January) In the morning, a procession of baianas (women dressed as Bahian 'aunts') in ritual dress carrying buckets of flowers walks 6km from Igreja NS da Conceição in Cidade Baixa to Igreja NS do Bonfim. Here they perform a ritual lavagem (washing) of the church steps overseen by Catholic priests together with mães de santo (Candomblé priestesses). Then the Filhos de Gandhi (an Afro-Brazilian percussion group) and trios elétricos (trucks loaded with speakers) take the scene for a rowdy street party lasting into the night. This is Salvador's largest festival outside of Carnaval.

Festa de São Lázaro (last Sunday in January) A procession, ritual cleansing of the Igreja São Lázaro (end of Rua Professor Aristides Novis, São Lázaro) and festival honors the saint's Candomblé orixá counterpart Omolú (the god of plague and disease).

Festa de Iemanjá (February 2) Groups from local terreiros and other devotees of the orixá Iemanjá, goddess of the sea and fertility, descend on Praia Rio Vermelho in the morning, where ceremonies are held to bless offerings of flowers, cakes, effigies, cans of beer and bottles of perfume. The ensuing street festival packs with people and some of Salvador's best bands and lasts into the night. This is probably Candomblé's most important festival.

Lavagem da Igreja de Itapuã (15 days before Carnaval) The actual church washing is a mini version of

---

SALVADOR'S CARNAVAL

Salvador's Carnaval is the second largest in Brazil, attracting upwards of two million revelers. The focus is on nationally famous city bands playing axé and pagode (Bahia's pop music) atop creeping trios elétricos (long trucks loaded with huge speakers). Between them march a few blocos afros (groups with powerful drum corps promoting Afro-Brazilian culture) and afoxés (groups tied to Candomblé traditions). A trio elétrico or a drum corps, together with its followers grouped in a roped-off area around it, form a bloco. People pay up to R$500 for the abadá (outfit) for their favorite band, mostly for prestige and the safety of those ropes. Choosing to fazer pipoca (be popcorn) in the street is still a fine way to spend Carnaval, as you'll see a variety of music and be spared the hassle involved with picking up the abadá.

Crowds clearing (in order to escape a fight) pose the greatest threat during Carnaval, so be aware of your surroundings. A large police presence helps to keep violence to a minimum. On the Barra–Rio Vermelho circuit, avoid the section where the coastal road narrows near the Morro do Cristo – the tension heats up there. Hands will be all over you, searching your pockets and groping the ladies.

To have a trouble-free Carnaval, take note of the following:

- Carry only a small amount of money and stash it in your shoe.
- Stash a photocopy of your passport somewhere private.
- Leave any jewelry, watches or nice-looking sunglasses in your hotel.
- Don't challenge pickpockets – the ensuing fight isn't worth it.
- Form small groups.
- Women should not walk alone or wear skirts (hands will be up them in no time).
- Avoid deserted places, especially narrow alleyways.

For more information see p80 and visit www.portaldocarnaval.ba.gov.br (in Portuguese).

Bonfim's, but the street party in Itapuã is loaded with *trios elétricos* and is equally raucous.

Festa de São João (June 23-24) Pyrotechnics and street parties spring up all over town and *genipapo* (local fruit) liqueur flows like water.

Festa Santa Bárbara (December 4-6) Rio Vermelho's Mercado do Peixe is probably the best place to catch this Candomblé festival celebrating markets.

Festa de NS da Conceição (December 8) Candomblistas honor the saint's *orixá* alter ego, Iemanjá, with a procession and ceremonies in Cidade Baixa.

Passagem do Ano Novo (December 31) New Year's Eve is celebrated with all the zest of Carnaval, especially on the beaches.

SLEEPING

Staying in Cidade Alta means being close to the action, but the beach suburbs are mellower (and just a short bus or taxi ride away from the Pelourinho). Santo Antônio is a peaceful neighborhood with classy pousadas in renovated old buildings, just a short walk from the Pelourinho. Reservations during Carnaval are essential.

Pelourinho
BUDGET
Hostel Solar dos Romanos (Map p440; ☎ 3321 6812; www.hostelsolardosromanos.com; Rua Portas do Carmo 14; dm from R$25, d with fan from R$65) This clean and affordable hostel boasts an unusual combination: both a location in the heart of the Pelourinho and bay views (from some rooms.) Doubles are simple with private bathrooms; perks include a book exchange and tour desk.

Albergue da Juventude do Pelô (Map p440; ☎ 3242 8061; www.alberguedopelo.com.br; Rua do Passo 5; dm R$30; 🅿) A popular option among Salvador's many hostels, the Albergue da Juventude do Pelô has basic rooms (with six to 12 beds in each) and a small but comfy lounge.

Pousada Terra Nossa (Map p440; ☎ 3321 5267; www.pousadaterranossa.com, in Portuguese; Rua Leovigildo de Carvalho 3; dm/d from R$30/70; 🅿) This cozy pousada offers private rooms and dorm-style accommodations; both have high ceilings and exposed brick walls that remind you that you're on one of the city's most historic blocks. A bit noisy at night, but the atmosphere is warm.

Pousada da Praça Hotel (Map p440; ☎ 3321 0642; www.pousadadapracahotel.com.br; Rua Rui Barbosa 5; dm R$27, s/d without bathroom R$38/65, with bathroom R$45/77; 🅿) A few blocks south of the cobblestones, this well-liked budget hotel has attractive two-tone wood floors and tidy fan-cooled

rooms that open onto the street. The quiet back porch is a fine place to unwind.

MIDRANGE & TOP END
our pick Hostel Galeria 13 (Map p440; ☎ 3266 5609; www.hostelgaleria13.com; Rua da Ordem Terceira 23; dm/d R$30/80; 🅿 🛜) This brand-new hostel, located in an old colonial house complete with a swimming pool, Moroccan-style lounge, and tapas bar is already a huge success with backpackers. The owner is a native English speaker and the location can't be beat.

Albergue das Laranjeiras (Map p440; ☎ 3321 1366; www.laranjeirashostel.com.br; cnr Rua das Laranjeiras & Rua da Ordem Terceira; dm R$38, d with/without bathroom R$140/106; 🅿 🛜) This attractive, well-organized HI hostel is set in a restored colonial building in the heart of the action. Dorm rooms have staggered beds like hanging trays, while private rooms are artfully designed (though small). There's an inviting café on the 1st floor.

our pick Casa do Amarelindo (Map p440; ☎ 3266 8550; www.casadoamarelindo.com; Rua das Portas do Carmo 6; d R$345-575; 🅿 🅿) This charming, new-on-the-scene boutique hotel is truly a gem: 10 impeccable guest rooms are equipped with first-class bedding, rainfall showers and huge windows. There's an adorably petite rooftop swimming pool and a delightful breakfast served anywhere you like.

Hotel Villa Bahia (Map p440; ☎ 3322 4271; www.lavillabahia.com; Largo do Cruzeiro de São Francisco 16; d R$380-520; 🅿 🅿) In a lovely colonial building near the Igreja São Francisco, this boutique hotel has 17 rooms with wood floors, shuttered windows and antique furnishings (solid armoires, chandeliers). There's an excellent restaurant on the 1st floor.

Carmo & Santo Antônio
BUDGET
our pick Hostel Cobreu (Map p440; ☎ 3117 1401; www.hostelcobreu.com; Ladeira do Carmo 22; dm/d/tr R$26/65/90; 🅿 🛜) Colorful and cool, Cobreu offers tidy dorms and rooms with powerful showers, a small DVD theatre, balconies overlooking the quaint Ladeira do Carmo, and interiors done by a well-known local graffiti artist. The candlelit Café Alquimia downstairs regularly hosts musicians and serves tasty vegetarian cuisine.

Nega Maluca (Map p438; ☎ 3242 9249; www.negamaluca.com; Rua dos Marchantes 15; dm with fan R$26, d with/without bathroom R$80/70; 🅿 🛜) This small expat-run guesthouse gets mixed reviews, but generally it's well-liked for the warm welcome and complimentary extras from coffee to a guest phone to laundry soap – staff will even let you use the showers or internet after you've checked out.

MIDRANGE & TOP END

Pousada do Baluarte (Map p438; ☎ 3327 0367; www .pousadabaluarte.com; Ladeira do Baluarte 13; s/d R$120/170; ☒) Run by a friendly French-Brazilian couple, Baluarte feels more like a B&B, with just six rooms amid a welcoming, homelike ambience. All the rooms feature two-toned wood floors, and are hung with the marvelous block prints of local artist Nilo.

Pousada do Boqueirão (Map p438; ☎ 3241 2262; www.pousadaboqueirao.com.br; Rua Direita de Santo Antônio 48; s/d without bathroom from R$150/180, s/d ste from R$200/230) Two early-20th-century houses have been joined together to form this elegant pousada, tastefully decorated with antiques and artwork. Spacious common rooms back onto a porch with a fantastic bay view, where a lovely breakfast is served.

Pousada das Flores (Map p438; ☎ 3243 1836; www .pflores.com.br; Rua Direita de Santo Antônio 442; d/ste from R$200/250; ☒ ☏) In a charming 18th-century home, Pousada das Flores has a mix of attractive spacious rooms with vaulted ceilings and wide-plank wooden floors. Upper-floor rooms have verandas with potted plants and idyllic views over the neighborhood.

Villa Santo Antônio (Map p438; ☎ 3326 1270; www .hotel-santoantonio.com; Rua Direita de Santo Antônio 130; d/ ste from R$210/305; ☒) Among a growing crop of well-dressed guesthouses in Santo Antônio, this one offers value for money. Its stylish rooms have polished wood floors and are decorated with original artwork and other thoughtful touches.

Studio do Carmo (Map p440; ☎ 3326 2426; www .studiodocarmo.com; Ladeira do Carmo 17; d R$240-290; ☒) Above an art gallery, this guesthouse offers just four rooms – each beautifully set with polished wood floors, big windows, artwork and fresh flowers. All have small kitchen units, and a delightful breakfast is brought to your door.

Pestana Convento do Carmo (Map p440; ☎ 3327 8400; www.pestana.com; Rua do Carmo 1; d/ste from R$600/675; ☒ ☏ ▣) Set in a restored 17th-century convent, this magnificent hotel has elegantly furnished rooms with old-world details and modern comforts, and even more impressive common areas. There's a

stone chapel and arched walkways around the cloister.

Barra & Coastal Suburbs

Of all the beachside suburbs, happening Barra attracts the majority of visitors due to its proximity to the Pelourinho (roughly 5km). During Carnaval, the further from the waterfront between the Farol da Barra and Praia de Ondina, the quieter it should be.

BUDGET

Camping Ecológico (off Map p438; ☎ 3374 0102; Alameda da Praia, Stella Maris; per person R$12) Flat, shady campsites near Praia de Catussaba with hot showers and a restaurant serving breakfast.

Che Logarto (Map p438; ☎ 3235 2404; www.chela garto.com; Av Oceanica 84B, Barra; dm from R$30, d from R$70; ☒ ☏) Occupying a coveted spot of real estate just across the street from the beach, this spacious new branch of the Che Logarto hostel chain is a great place to meet other travelers. Drinks are free-flowing on the wide terrace at sunset.

MIDRANGE & TOP END

Barra Guest Hostel (Map p438; ☎ 8774 6667; www .barraguesthouse.com; Rua Recife 234, Barra; dm/d from R$35/130; ☒ ☏) Around the corner from various lively bars and restaurants, this welcoming hostel is run by a cool British-Brazilian couple. Perks include a large communal kitchen, tidy dorms, free-flowing caipirinhas at night (the first is free), weekly barbecues and surfboard rentals. A minimum two-night stay is required.

our pick La Villa Françáise (Map p438; ☎ 3245 6008; www.lavilafrancaise.com; Rua Recife 222, Barra; dm R$40; s/d/ tr from R$70/100/120; ☒ ☏) Readers rave about the peaceful atmosphere, tasty breakfast and kind owners at this cozy French-influenced guesthouse. The kitchen is open for guest use and the shared spaces are inviting.

Âmbar Pousada (Map p438; ☎ 3264 6956; www.am barpousada.com.br; Rua Afonso Celso 485, Barra; dm R$42, d with fan R$122; ☏) A favorite among travelers, this lovely pousada has a relaxed atmosphere and a welcoming vibe. Private rooms are small, but there's ample outdoor lounge space with hammocks. Dorms have eight beds.

Pousada Azul (Map p438; ☎ 3264 9798; www.pou sadaazul.com.br; Rua Praguer Froes 102, Barra; s/d R$98/136; ☒) Azul is a sweet, safe, well-cared-for pousada close to the beach and bus stops. Spacious, comfortable rooms are sparsely furnished with polished wood floors and gleaming white bathrooms.

ourpick Pousada O Ninho (Map p438; ☎ 3264 6952; www.pousadaoninho.com.br; Rua Afonso Celso 371, Barra; s/d R$110/140; 🅿 🛜) This easygoing pousada, just two blocks from the beach, has a variety of tidy rooms with bathrooms. The atmosphere is quiet but friendly.

Villa Romana (Map p438; ☎ 3264 6748; www.villaromana.com.br; Rua Prof Lemos de Brito 14, Barra; s/d R$135/186; 🅿 🍴) Set on a hill in a quiet part of Barra, Villa Romana has polished wood floors and an inviting lobby/sitting room laden with antiques. The rooms are pleasant, but much simpler; some have sea views.

Pousada Noa Noa (Map p438; ☎ 3264 1148; www.pousadanoanoa.com; Av 7 de Setembro 4295, Barra; d R$150; 🅿 🛜) This small, welcoming guesthouse offers 15 nicely decorated rooms (four have views) and attractive common areas making good use of its oceanside location.

Pousada Encanto de Itapoan (off Map p438; ☎ 3285 3505; www.encantodeitapoan.com.br; Rua Nova Canaã 48, Farol de Itapuã; s/d R$198/231; 🅿 🛜 🍴) A beach-lovers' retreat outside the busy city center, this guesthouse has small, pleasantly set rooms, each with sliding glass doors opening onto a balcony facing a vine- and orchid-covered wall.

Hotel Catharina Paraguaçu (off Map p438; ☎ 3334 0089; www.hotelcatharinaparaguacu.com.br; Rua João Gomes 128, Rio Vermelho; s/d from R$207/228; 🅿) A colonial-modern mix, this charming hotel is decorated with beautiful tiles and antiques. Both the rooms and the gardens, complete with reflecting pool and sculptures, are lovely.

EATING

Dining out is a delight in Salvador, where most restaurants have wonderful ambience and live music. Typical Bahian cuisine has a heavy African influence and features ingredients like coconut cream, tomato, seafood, bell pepper and spices of ginger, hot peppers and coriander. Lately, restaurant quality has decreased somewhat in the Pelourinho, though it's still worth going for the atmosphere. Foodies may find better-value meals in Barra.

Pelourinho

The Pelourinho is packed with restaurants; some feel uncomfortably touristy while others are wonderfully charming. It's worth wandering up Rua do Carmo and out the Rua Direita de Santo Antônio for a mix of bohemian and bourgeois.

A Cubana Pelourinho (Map p440; ☎ 3321 6162; Rua Alfredo de Brito 12, Pelourinho); Praça Municipal (Map p440; ☎ 3322 7000; Praça Municipal) One of Salvador's oldest and best ice-cream shops (cones R$6 to R$12).

Mamabahia (Map p440; ☎ 3322 4397; cnr Rua Frei Vicente & Rua Alfredo de Brito; mains R$15-40) This conveniently located *churrascaria* (barbecued-meat house) and restaurant is an excellent place for a lunch break while sightseeing. You'll likely be lured in by someone passing out 'free caipirinha' tickets.

Panorámico (Map p440; ☎ 3322 2013; Rua das Laranjeiras 18; per kg R$20) Popular for its filling lunch buffet, Panorámico is hidden on the 2nd floor of an old, characterful building.

O Coliseu (Map p440; ☎ 3321 5585; www.ocoliseu.com.br; Cruzeiro de São Francisco 9; per kg R$22; 🕑 lunch) Look for a costumed *baiana* (Bahian aunt) handing out tickets in the doorway to find this vegetarian-friendly restaurant on an upper floor. Most of the dishes are regional. Ask about the folkloric show, starting at 9pm on weeknights in summer.

Ristorante La Figa (Map p440; ☎ 3322 0066; www.ristorantelafiga.com; Rua das Laranjeiras 17; mains R$22-40) This well-loved Italian restaurant turns out traditional pastas enhanced with Bahia's fabulously fresh seafood. The setting is casual but elegant.

ourpick Jardim das Delícias (Map p440; ☎ 3321 1449; Rua João de Deus 12; mains R$25-45) This stylish yet pleasantly old-fashioned eatery started receiving accolades from the international press as soon as it opened. The flower-bedecked central courtyard is a dreamy place to sample a traditional *moqueca* (a spicy stew of coconut milk, pepper, and seafood or meat) or to just relax with a fruity cocktail while musicians serenade the small crowd.

Senac (Map p440; ☎ 3224 3440; www.ba.senac.br, in Portuguese; Largo do Pelourinho 13-19; buffet R$32) With the best buffet in town, the cooking school Senac spreads a tempting array of Bahian dishes. Sample some 40 regional dishes plus desserts. There's also a small self-service restaurant (*por-kilo*; per kilo R$20) open for lunch Monday to Friday and an attached gastronomic museum.

Maria Mata Mouro (Map p440; ☎ 3321 3929; www.mariamatamouro.com.br; Rua da Ordem Terceira; mains for 2 R$40-80) The cozy garden patio or classically set dining room are fine settings to enjoy one of Pelô's top menus. You'll find Bahian classics and unique dishes like lamb in tamarind sauce and rich paella.

Carmo

Cafélier (Map p440; ☎ 3241 5095; www.cafelier.com.br; Rua do Carmo 50; snacks R$2-8; ⏰ 2-9pm Mon & Wed-Sat) Hidden behind a small storefront of antiques, this quaint hideaway café has strong coffee, rich desserts and other snacks, and bay views.

Cidade Baixa

In the Comércio, cheap *lanchonetes* (snack bars) and self-service restaurants abound. For something more memorable, head south along the bay, where there are several excellent restaurants.

Restaurant Solar do Unhão (Map p438; ☎ 3321 5551; Av do Contorno 8; mains for 2 R$48-74; ⏰ show summer 8:30pm) The Solar do Unhão is set in an 18th-century *senzala* (slave quarters) that was part of the larger surrounding sugar mill. Grab a table on the breezy back dock and order fresh seafood; the restaurant also hosts an impressive nightly folkloric show in summer. Take a taxi.

Soho (Map p438; ☎ 3322 4554; www.sohorestaurante .com.br, in Portuguese; Av do Contorno 1010; dinner for 2 R$50-80; ⏰ lunch Tue-Sun, dinner daily; ✸) This stylish Japanese restaurant has an impressive bay view and spreads succulent plates of sashimi and sushi, along with other traditional Japanese fare.

Trapiche Adelaide (Map p438; ☎ 3326 2211; www .trapicheadelaide.com.br, in Portuguese; Av do Contorno s/n; mains R$50-80) One of Salvador's finest restaurants serves creative and delectable cuisine in a lovely setting overlooking the bay. Top-notch service, fine views and unique flavors (octopus carpaccio, lamb chops, sesame-crusted tuna with wasabi) mean you'll be dining among Salvador's A-list crowd.

Barra & Coastal Suburbs

Some of the restaurants in the coastal suburbs have superb tropical ambience – dining with sea views.

Cabana de Cely (Map p438; ☎ 3264 0250; www .cabanadacely.com.br, in Portuguese; Av Almirante Marques de Leão 183, Barra; mains R$15-35) You'll have to battle for a sidewalk table at this popular casual restaurant where local couples and families come for cold beer and fresh fish. Do as the Bahians do with a pot of piping-hot *lambreta* (clams) or a pile of fresh garlic shrimp.

Ramma (Map p438; ☎ 3264 0044; Rua Lord Cochrane 76, Barra; per kg R$22; ⏰ lunch Sun-Fri; ✸) Specializing in freshly prepared organic food (including vegetarian options), Ramma is a good place for a healthy lunch.

our pick Caranguejo de Sergipe (Map p438; ☎ 3248 3331; www.caranguejodesergipe.com.br, in Portuguese; Av Oceânica s/n, Barra; mains R$22-45) Another local favorite, this always-packed eatery is known for fresh crabs and platters of grilled seafood and vegetables. Don't miss the expertly prepared *maracujá* (passion fruit) caipirinha – perhaps the most delicious drink on the beach.

Mistura Fina (off Map p438; ☎ 3375 2623; Rua Prof Souza Brito 41, Itapuã; mains R$25-50; ✸) The ambience is airy and bright at this fantastic seafood restaurant with outdoor seating.

Paraíso Tropical (off Map p438; ☎ 3384 7464; Rua Edgar Loureiro 98B, Cabula; mains R$30-55) One of Salvador's top restaurants, Paraíso Tropical serves beautifully prepared Bahian cuisine with a twist. Expect long waits on weekends.

DRINKING

The Pelourinho is Salvador's nightlife capital and is filled with bars offering outside tables on the cobbled streets. In Barra, outdoor ambience and live music are found along Av Almirante Marques de Leão and the waterfront around the Farol da Barra; Rua Recife and the Morro do Cristo also have some popular bars. Bohemian Rio Vermelho has by far the hottest nightlife scene along the Atlantic shore and a reputation for drawing all types. Its Largo de Santana and Largo de Mariquita are lined with outdoor restaurants and bars that fill up nightly.

Pelourinho & Carmo

Many restaurants and cafés spill out onto the side streets of the Pelourinho at night as live musicians play and a mix of tourists and locals kick back at sidewalk tables to hear live music.

our pick Café Alquimia (Map p440; ☎ 3326 4079; Ladeira do Carmo 22, Carmo) Located on the quaint cobblestoned hill leading up to Largo do Carmo (on the ground level of Hostel Cobreu), this bluesy café-bar is a happening spot for young travelers, musicians and artistic types. Arabic finger foods are on the menu alongside inexpensive cocktails and cold beer.

Casa do Amarelindo Bar (Map p440; ☎ 3266 8550; Rua das Portas do Carmo 6, Pelourinho) The chic tropical-style bar at the lovely Casa do Amarelindo hotel (see p495) is the ideal spot for a nightcap; better still is the panoramic terrace where a skilled bartender shows up after dark to mix classic cocktails.

Odoyá (Map p440; ☎ 3242 5218; Cruzeiro de São Francisco, Pelourinho) You'll have to deal with an endless stream of panhandlers sitting at these outdoor tables, but the views at night – several gorgeously illuminated churches surround you – are memorable as you relax with a caipirinha or two.

Cantina da Lua (Map p440; ☎ 3241 7383; Terreiro de Jesus, Pelourinho) This outdoor patio bar and restaurant is prime people-watching territory, given its setting in the heart of the Pelourinho. Live music nightly ranges from vocals to salsa.

Cidade Baixa

Bahia Café (Map p438; ☎ 3329 0944 www.bahiacafe.com. br, in Portuguese; Mirante dos Aflitos) Located just south of the Pelô, this slightly upscale bar has an eclectic environment, great food and a choice of three dozen cocktails to enjoy with those great bay views.

Bar da Ponta (Map p438; ☎ 3326 2211; Av do Contorno) This small, stylish bar is set on the end of a pier perched over the bay, making it a draw around sunset. Expect a well-dressed crowd and pricey cocktails as well as excellent *petiscos* (bar bites).

Quixabeira (Map p438; ☎ 3328 3286; Travessa dos Barris 30, Barris) A mixed crowd frequents this gay-friendly bar to enjoy drinks and small bites in a charming old house; there's often live music on the pleasant back patio.

Camafeu (Map p440; ☎ 3242 9751; Mercado Modelo, Praça Cayru) Food is available at this casual spot on the upper terrace of the Mercado Modelo (p445) but most shoppers just stop here for coffee or cold beer with great views over the bay.

Barra & Coastal Suburbs

Pereira (Map p438; ☎ 3264 6464; Av 7 de Setembro 3959, Barra; ☾ lunch Thu-Sun & 6pm-late) On Barra's seaside road, Pereira is a stylish indoor and outdoor bar with a Japanese restaurant and a wine bar attached. Excellent *chope* (draft beer) is on tap.

Bar do Chico (Map p438; ☎ 3267 4386; Rua Recife 86, Barra) In an area of lively bars, this spot attracts a fun, festive crowd. There are other indoor-outdoor spots next door – lots of young people come to Rua Recife for informal bar-hopping.

our pick **Barravento** (Map p438; ☎ 3247 2577; Av Oceânica, Barra) Barra's only waterfront bar and restaurant is a choice spot for a sundowner.

Póstudo (off Map p438; ☎ 3334 0484; Rua João Gomes 87, Rio Vermelho; ☾ noon-3pm & 6pm-last customer Mon-Sat) This perpetually cool bar and restaurant

has an ocean view and is known for its flavorful fare.

Extudo (off Map p438; ☎ 3334 0671; www.extudo. com, in Portuguese; Travessa Lydio de Mesquita 4, Rio Vermelho; ☒) Frequented by those dialed in on Salvador's arts scene, it has dishes appropriately named after famous cinematic and literary works. Choose between a tranquil enclosed space or a rowdier open-air patio.

ENTERTAINMENT

Bars and clubs tend to come and go quickly in Salvador, so ask around to see what's hot at the moment. Good sources of information are the Friday editions of *A Tarde* and *Correio da Bahia*.

The Pelourinho explodes with people and action on Tuesday nights, which are called Terça da Bencão (Blessing Tuesday).

Live Music

Salvador is the pulsing center of an incredible music scene, where a blend of African and Brazilian traditions has produced mind-blowing forms of percussion that Salvadorenhos mix into their reggae, pop and rock, *pagode* and *axé*. The city has also produced unique styles such as *afoxé* and samba reggae. Since hardly a bar or restaurant in the city lacks live music at least one night of the week, catching some of Salvador's talented artists shouldn't be hard.

GAY & LESBIAN VENUES

Salvador's gay nightlife scene may be subdued compared to those of other Brazilian capitals, but these off-the-beaten-path venues are worth seeking out.

Art mavens and a young, gay-friendly crowd flock to **Beco dos Artistas** (Map p438; Av Cerqueira Lima, Garcia), a small alley with several bars (and a dance club). Enter next to Pizzaria Giovanni on Rua Leovigildo Filgueira.

Queens Club (Map p438; ☎ 3328 6220; Rua Theodoro Sampaio 160, Barris; ☾ 10pm-6am Fri & Sat) is one of the biggest, best places to dance. Expect throbbing electronic beats, go-go boys and a dark room.

Off Club (Map p438; ☎ 3267 6215; www.off club.com.br; Rua Dias D'Ávila 33, Barra; ☾ 10pm-6am Thu-Sun) is another great spot for dancing. This place brings in a mixed and assorted crowd of drag queens, gays, lesbians, straights, go-go boys and more.

BAHIA

BAHIA

A NIGHT AMONG THE GODS *Regis St Louis*

The wild and little-understood Candomblé religion is deeply rooted in Bahian culture and connects countless Afro-Brazilians to a long line of West African ancestry. Ceremonies, held frequently throughout the year, take place in spacious, richly decorated halls called *terreiros*, and they can last for hours.

The celebrants are mostly women who arrive dressed in lace and hooped skirts. Drummers – all male – pound out powerful rhythms behind a gauzy curtain, and the dance begins. Around and around they go, with light steps at first, graceful hand motions accompanied by twirling skirts. The dancers, chanting in Yoruba, glide in a counterclockwise circle, which represents the rolling back of the centuries, as they reach out to their ancestors. A festive, celebratory atmosphere prevails, with the *mãe de santo* or *pai de santo* (literally saint's mother or father – the Candomblé priests) and attendants watching over everyone from the center.

As the evening progresses, the music picks up, the dance becomes more heated, and over the drumming one can hear the chiming of bells – a haunting sound to conjure the spirits. The second phase of the ceremony is all about the dancers and the *orixás* (Candomblé deities) – and the possession of one by the other.

Each Candomblista has an *orixá*, and if a person has the gift (which not all have), he or she can become a medium for the spirit – going into a trance or becoming filled with frenetic energy. One's *orixá* can be male or female, regardless of one's own sex. Usually, when the spirit arrives, those dancing take on the attributes of that spirit.

One steamy evening, we visited the Casa Brava, one of Salvador's oldest *terreiros*, and watched as a man shook and writhed – and even shrieked – as the spirit of Iansã, goddess of wind, entered him. As he shuttled about the room, another woman felt the presence of Changó. She stood in the center of the room for much of the evening as silent as a stone until the song dedicated to Changó was played and her energy was suddenly released. Other dancers showed the powerful strides of Ogun, god of war, or the predatory movements of Oxossi, god of hunters, while others simply danced madly about, occasionally letting out a loud cry.

Although it's discouraged, sometimes spectators go into trances, swooning and possibly collapsing as the ceremony continues. Others are just grateful to feel the energy from the celebrants. When those in the trance come by, they sometimes interact with spectators, exchanging hugs and caresses, in hopes of passing on the god's powerful energy from one to another.

The last part of the ceremony features elaborate costumes. The dancers leave the floor and return dressed as *orixás*, and the dancing resumes long into the night.

Those interested in attending a ceremony should contact the **Federação Baiana do Culto Afro-Brasileiro** (Map p440; ☎ 3321 1548; Rua Portas do Carmo 39, Pelourinho; ☼ 9am-noon & 2-5pm Mon-Fri), which can provide schedules and addresses for some *terreiros*. A good list of *terreiros* can also be found at www.bahia-online.net/Candomble.htm. Pelourinho travel agencies can arrange group visits. If you go without a guide, make sure there will be taxis for the return trip. Wear clean, light-colored clothes (no shorts).

For more on Candomblé, read the vivid tale *Tent of Miracles* by Jorge Amado, a Baiano and Candomblé initiate himself (Changó was his *orixá*).

During the high season, there are almost nightly concerts in the inner courtyards of the Pelourinho, with cover charges ranging from free to R$35. Take a stroll by the following places and find out what's on for the evening: Largo de Tereza Batista, Largo do Pedro Arcanjo and Praça Quincas Berro d'Água (usually free). There are also occasional concerts on the Terreiro de Jesus. You can also frequently hear drum corps, which rehearse by walking through the Pelourinho,

blocking traffic and gathering a following as they go.

Traditional groups (characterized by strong Afro drum corps) to be on the lookout for include Ilê Aiyê (the first exclusively black Carnaval group), the all-female Dida, Muzenza and Male Debalê. More pop and with strong percussion sections are worldfamous Olodum – a Tuesday-night Pelourinho institution – Araketu and Timbalada, brainchild of master composer and musician

Carlinhos Brown. The queens of Salvador pop music – Margareth Menezes, Ivete Sangalo and Daniela Mercury – also often 'rehearse' publicly.

If you aren't going to experience Carnaval in Salvador, don't worry: the two months leading up to it are the next best thing. *Ensaios* showcase secret big-name guests; and clubs around the city put on special balls.

For the biggest acts, keep your eye on Salvador's finest venue, the **Teatro Castro Alves** (Map p438; ☎ 3535 0600; www.tca.ba.gov.br, in Portuguese; Campo Grande). Its Concha Acústica (amphitheater) has weekly concerts throughout summer.

Alphorria (Map p438; ☎ 3242 0053; Rua Direita de Santo Antônio 97, Santo Antônio; ☺ 6:30pm-last customer) This bar in Santo Antônio packs a diverse crowd and even more eclectic sounds. Live bands play *forró* (popular music of the Northeast), rock, Afro pop and even salsa.

Sankofa (Map p440; ☎ 3321 7236; www.sankofabrasil. com; Rua Frei Vicente 7, Pelourinho) This centrally located bar in the Pelourinho hosts live salsa, samba, and DJs who mix everything from reggae to Congolese rumba.

Casa de Mãe Iemanja (off Map p438; ☎ 3334 3041; Rua Guedes Cabral 81, Rio Vermelho; ☺ 2pm-2am Fri-Sun) Named after the Yoruba goddess of the sea (the Festa de Iemanja happens nearby), this Rio Vermelho bistro/cultural center is a great space to hear live music. It's on the coastal road, just up from Largo de Santana.

Olivier (Map p438; ☎ 3241 3829; Rua Direita de Santo Antônio 61, Santo Antônio) This attractive restaurant has a cozy backyard setting where you can catch live jazz and bossa nova several nights of the week.

Bohemia Music Bar (Map p438; ☎ 3332 5774; Rua Belo Horizonte 177, Barra; admission R$5-15) This Barra favorite sees live pop and rock bands playing throughout the week.

Pimentinha (off Map p438; ☎ 3230 1725; Rua Dom Eugênio Sales 11, Boca do Rio; admission R$20; ☺ 9pm-3am Mon) On Monday nights, Pimentinha is the place to head. Decorated with LPs, mannequins, old umbrellas and other found materials, it hosts spirited bands (often playing MPB or Música Popular Brasileira) and a diverse crowd.

Folkloric Shows

Seeing a folkloric show in the Pelourinho shouldn't be missed (just be sure to reconfirm dates and times – if you save it for your last night in Salvador, you could be disappointed by a sudden cancellation). The shows include Afro-Brazilian dance, the dances of the *orixás*, *maculêlê* (stick dance) and capoeira, to live percussion and vocals.

The most astounding professional show is put on by the world-renowned Balé Folclórico da Bahia at **Teatro Miguel Santana** (Map p440; ☎ 3322 1962; www.balefolcloricodabahia.com.br; Rua Gregório de Matos 49; admission R$20; ☺ 8pm Mon & Wed-Sat). The Grupo de Danças Folclóricas SESC also puts on a lively show at **Teatro SESC-Senac** (Map p440; ☎ 3324 4529; www.sesc-ba.com.br/teatro.htm, in Portuguese; Largo do Pelourinho 19; admission R$15; ☺ 8pm Thu-Sat), as does Restaurant Solar do Unhão (p452).

Capoeira

Most capoeira schools in the Pelourinho charge a few reais for watching a class (often called a 'show') and for taking pictures. Just remember that you are helping to support the studio. See p447 for a list of studios.

Nightclubs

Madre Disco (off Map p438; ☎ 3346 0012; Av Otávio Mangabeira 2471, Jardim dos Namorados, Pituba; cover R$20; ☺ 11pm-last customer Thu-Sat) A large, terminally hip dance club (previously known as Fashion Club) with nights ranging from salsa to electronic music. Minimum age for women is 21; for men, 18.

The young and wealthy head for **Aeroclube Plaza Show** (off Map p438; Av Otávio Mangabeira, Boca do Rio), an outdoor entertainment complex with a few bars, dance clubs and free live *forró* nights. Inside, **Rock in Rio** (☎ 3461 0300; ☺ 10pm-last customer Tue-Sun) is a 1700-sq-meter dance club with eight bars that gets packed on weekends. Also in Aeroclube, **Café Cancun** (☎ 3461 0603; ☺ 9pm-last customer Tue-Sat) has a Mexican theme to its food and decor, and makes for a fun night of dancing and some tequila drinking.

SHOPPING

Mercado Modelo (Map p440; ☎ 3243 6543; Praça Cayru) This two-story, enclosed tourist market has dozens of stalls selling local handicrafts. More of the same can be purchased in Pelourinho shops.

Artesanato São Domingos (Map p440; ☎ 3322 6979; Terreiro de Jesus, Pelourinho) Adjoining the Igreja São Domingos, this small shop sells lovely Bahian lacework dresses, tablecloths, blouses and the like.

BAHIA

Bahia Online (Map p440; ☎ 3321 0536; Rua João de Deus 22, Pelourinho; ⏰ 10am-10pm Mon-Sat) This Pelourinho music store has a great selection of Bahian artists as well as samba, electronica and MPB CDs.

Bau Bau (Map p440; ☎ 3323 0008; Rua Gregório de Matos 37, Pelourinho) One of a growing crop of colorful boutiques.

GETTING THERE & AWAY
Air
Aeroporto Deputado Luis Eduardo do Magalhães (code SSA; ☎ 3204 1010; São Cristóvão) is serviced by **Gol** (☎ 3204 1603; airport), **TAM** (☎ 3365 2324; airport), **Varig** (☎ 3204 1050) and **Webjet** (☎ 0800 723 1234; airport). There are daily flights to any Brazilian destination, but multiple stops are common. One-way fares from Salvador to São Paulo start at around R$240, to Rio R$319, to Recife R$190 and to Fortaleza R$200.

TAP (Air Portugal; ☎ 3204 1531; airport) connects Salvador with Europe. Flights to other international destinations go via São Paulo or Rio.

Boat
Boats to points on Baía de Todos os Santos leave from the **Terminal Marítimo Turístico** (Map p440), behind the Mercado Modelo, and the **Terminal Marítimo de São Joaquim** (off Map p438; ☎ 3633 1248; Av Oscar Pontes, Água de Menino). See p458 for more information.

Boats heading for Morro de São Paulo also leave from the Terminal Marítimo Turístico. A handful of companies run *lanchas rapidas* (speedboats) and two run catamarans (both R$75, two hours). The number of daily departures varies according to demand.

Bus
Most Salvador buses coming from the south go around the Baía de Todos os Santos, but alternatively you can disembark at Bom Despacho on the Ilha de Itaparica and catch a boat across the bay. Some bus companies sell their tickets at convenient locations throughout the city, usually at shopping malls. Ask Emtursa or Bahiatursa (see p441) for more information.

Ticket Center (Map p438; ☎ 3329 5433; Rua Portão da Piedade, Piedade), facing Shopping Piedade, sells tickets for a variety of bus companies – there's also a branch at Shopping Iguatemi. Travel agencies around town also sell bus tickets, but most tack on service charges (usually R$10 to R$15 per ticket).

GETTING AROUND
To/From the Airport
The airport is located about 30km east of the center. A taxi to the center will cost you around R$75 in a metered taxi, or R$98 for a taxi paid in advance at the airport. There are also air-conditioned minibuses (R$8) that head to the center, marked 'Praça da Sé/Aeroporto.' City buses leave from a depot behind the parking garage.

Buses to the airport depart regularly from the so called Praça da Sé bus stop (Map p440), a block southeast of Praça Municipal. Supposedly they leave every 30 minutes, but the schedule is rather flexible, so leave plenty of time. The bus goes down Av 7 de Setembro to Barra, and continues along the coast before heading inland to the airport. In light traffic, the ride takes about an hour; with traffic allow 1¾ hours.

A municipal Aeroporto bus follows the same route to the airport, but gets very crowded and isn't recommended if you're carrying a bag.

To/From the Bus Station
Salvador's **bus station** (☎ 460 8300) is 8km east of the city center. A taxi to Cidade Alta or Barra runs R$24 to R$32. Air-con minibuses (R$6) marked 'Praça da Sé' go to the center from in front of Shopping Iguatemi, just across the footbridge out front. For Barra, catch the Barra 1 bus in front of the bus station. Any bus that goes to Shopping Iguatemi will get you to the bus station.

Public Transportation
Linking Cidade Alta and Cidade Baixa are the **Elevador Lacerda** (Map p440; ☎ 3322 7049; R$0.15; ⏰ 24hr) and the **Plano Inclinado Gonçalves** (funicular railway; Map p440; R$0.15; ⏰ 7am-7pm Mon-Fri, 7am-1pm Sat).

Public buses crisscross the city; note that passengers board the bus through the rear door (and pay the attendant seated there), then disembark from the front door of the bus (near the driver).

There are two main city bus terminals in the center that can serve as destinations or transfer points: Terminal da França (Map p440) in the Comércio and Lapa (Map p438), behind Shopping Lapa and Shopping Piedade.

If heading north to the Igreja NS do Bonfim, catch a bus from the stop at the base of the Elevador Lacerda.

BUSES FROM SALVADOR

Destination	Duration	Cost	Frequency	Company
Aracaju	4-6hr	R$50-78	8-14 daily	Bomfim (☎ 3460 0000)
Belo Horizonte	24hr	R$190	daily	São Geraldo (☎ 3450 4488)
Ilhéus	7hr	R$75-118	3 daily	Águia Branca (☎ 4004 1010)
João Pessoa	14hr	R$133	3 weekly	Bomfim (☎ 3460 0000)
Lençóis	6-7hr	R$50	3 daily	Real Expresso (☎ 3450 2991)
Maceió	9-11hr	R$85-105	2-3 daily	Bomfim (☎ 3460 0000)
Natal	21hr	R$159-182	2 daily	São Geraldo (☎ 3450 4488)
Penedo	9hr	R$70	daily	Bomfim (☎ 3460 0000)
Porto Seguro	12hr	R$136	daily	Águia Branca (☎ 4004 1010)
Recife	12hr	R$127-165	daily	Itapemirim (☎ 3450 5644) & Penha (☎ 0800 646 2122)
Rio de Janeiro	25-28hr	R$250-290	daily	Águia Branca (☎ 4004 1010) & Itapemirim (☎ 3450 5644)
São Paulo	33hr	R$266	3 daily	São Geraldo (☎ 3450 4488)
Vitória	19hr	R$225	daily	Águia Branca (☎ 4004 1010)

BAHIA

Taxis can be taken at meter price (legal) or negotiated.

BAÍA DE TODOS OS SANTOS

The Baía de Todos os Santos is Brazil's largest bay, and was at one time among the hemisphere's most important. The 56 islands contained in the 1000-sq-km bay have lush vegetation and architectural remnants of their historic past.

ILHA DE ITAPARICA
☎ 0xx71 / pop 21,000

Itaparica has long been an escape for the residents of Salvador, and its shores are lined with vacation homes. The beaches are unimpressive compared with those on Salvador's northern coast, and Club Med has privatized the best one, but many travelers enjoy taking a day trip to the likable island town of Mar Grande (9km south of Bom Despacho), with bars, restaurants and a relaxed atmosphere.

Sights & Activities

Guarding the northern tip of the island, the **Forte de São Lourenço** (1711) was built by Dutch invaders and figured prominently in Bahia's battle for independence in 1823. Nearby, the city of Itaparica has a few historic constructions, including the **Solar Tenente Botas** (Lieutenant Botas Manor; Praça Tenente Botas; admission by donation), the **Igreja Matriz do Santíssimo Sacramento** (Rua Luís Gama), built in 1715, and the **Fonte da Bica** (mineral-water fountain), from 1842. In the center of the island, a huge tree wraps its roots around the ruins of the **Igreja Baiacu** and grows right out of them.

BEACHES

Praia Ponta da Areia (2km north of Bom Despacho) is a thin strip of sand with clear, shallow water and *barracas* serving good seafood. **Praia da Penha** (10km south of Bom Despacho) is a nice beach with excellent views of Salvador. **Praia Barra Grande** (7km further south) is Itaparica's finest public beach. It has clear water and weekend homes, and lies in front of its namesake village. Bahians, who love a beach with lots of people on it, consider **Praia Cacha Pregos** (20km further south) the island's best.

Sleeping & Eating

Plenty of casual restaurants and pousadas are clustered near the ferry dock; a number of fine accommodations are also found just north and south of Mar Grande.

  Camping Praia de Berlinque (☎ 3638 2435; per person R$10) Shaded campsites are spread around

BAÍA DE TODOS OS SANTOS & RECÔNCAVO

an enticing area just a few steps from the beach. Services are minimal, so bring food and essentials with you. It's located 30km south of Bom Despacho.

Zimbo Tropical (☎ 3638 1148; www.zimbo-tropical .com; Aratuba; s/d with fan from R$60/100) Sweet bungalows are spread through a gorgeously lush garden a short walk from the beach. The laid-back owners offer group meals (R$25) and excursions to local sights, and can make tiny monkeys magically emerge from the trees. A taxi from Bom Despacho or Mar Grande is about R$30.

Pousada Arco-Íris (☎ 3633 1130; www.parcoiris.na -web.net, in Portuguese; Estrada da Gamboa 102; d with fan R$90-110; 🏊) Arco-Íris is set on the unmanicured grounds of an old mango ranch. A variety of rooms are available in the antique-laden main house, and cabins overlook the yard.

Pousada Grande Mar (☎ 3633 2210; www.pousada grandemar.com.br, in Portuguese; Rua Praça Anísio Nelson de Brito 38; d with fan from R$100) This basic pousada, located near the ferry station in the center of the action in Mar Grande, looks like a colorful beach motel. Rooms are clean and cool, but the place is loud on summer nights.

Manga Rosa (☎ 3633 1130; Estrada da Gamboa 102; mains R$25-32) Attached to the Arco-Íris, this restaurant serves large portions of acclaimed Bahian and international cuisine and its tropical ambience is a great setting for a meal.

Restaurante Philippe (☎ 3633 1060; Praça São Bento 113; mains R$32-48) Near the dock in Mar Grande, the well-respected Restaurante Philippe serves a rich variety of Brazilian and European fare in an oceanfront setting.

Getting There & Away
BOAT
Schedules change with the seasons, so verify departure times.

Passenger ferries (R$3.30, 40 minutes, every 30 minutes from 7am to 6:50pm) leave from Salvador's Terminal Marítimo Turístico for Mar Grande's **terminal** (☎ 3633 1248), and return from 6:30am to 7:30pm. Buy your return ticket ahead of time on summer days.

A car ferry (per person/car R$7/27, one hour, hourly from 5am to 11:30pm) and a catamaran (R$7, 30 minutes, seven daily) run between Salvador's Terminal Marítimo de São Joaquim and Bom Despacho. Expect a long wait to drive onto the ferry on weekends, especially in summer.

BUS
Frequent buses leave from Bom Despacho's **bus/ferry terminal** (☎ 3319 2890) for Valença (R$16, two hours, five daily).

Getting Around
Kombis leave from the boat terminals in both Bom Despacho and Mar Grande and run a circuit around the island until about 8pm. Some unscrupulous drivers overcharge tourists, so remember that no fare should be over R$10. Rental bicycles are widely available (R$20 per day).

OTHER ISLANDS
The lesser Baía de Todos os Santos islands include **Ilha Bom Jesus dos Passos**, which has traditional fishing boats and artisans; **Ilha dos Frades** (named after two monks who were killed and cannibalized there by local *índios*), which has attractive waterfalls and palm trees; and **Ilha da Maré**, with the quiet beaches of **Itamoabo** and **Bacia das Neves** and the 17th-century **Igreja de NS das Neves**.

Tour companies in Salvador offer boat tours of the bay to either Ilha da Maré, or Ilha dos Frades and Ilha de Itaparica, from Salvador's Terminal Marítimo Turístico. Alternatively, boats to Ilha da Maré (R$5, 20 minutes, every 40 minutes from 8am to 5:30pm) leave from São Tomé de Paripe's **terminal** (☎ 3307 1447), 25km north of the city. To get there, take the Base Naval/São Tomé bus to the end of the line (ask at tourist information about the best place to catch the bus). For Ilha dos Frades, take an Oxalá bus from Salvador's main bus station to Madre de Deus (70km northwest of the city) and catch a boat for Paramana (R$3).

RECÔNCAVO

A region of green, fertile lands surrounding the Baía de Todos os Santos, the *recôncavo* brought riches to Salvador (and the Portuguese crown) with its sugar and tobacco crops. The profits reaped off these lands also spurred the growth of once-rich towns like Cachoeira, which is resplendent with colonial architecture and history. For more of an adventure, hire a boat across Baía de Todos os Santos to Maragojipe, a sweet colonial village, and then catch a bus on to Cachoeira and São Félix.

CACHOEIRA & SÃO FÉLIX
☎ 0xx75 / pop 50,000
Cachoeira, affectionately known as the jewel of the *recôncavo*, is a sleepy place, full of colorful, mostly preserved colonial architecture uncompromised by the presence of modern buildings. The town sits below a series of hills, strung along the banks of the Rio Paraguaçu in a face-off with its twin, São Félix. A steady trickle of tourism flows through the area, attracted by Brazil's best tobacco, its reputation as a renowned center of Candomblé and a strong wood-sculpting tradition. If you get an early start, Cachoeira and São Félix make a great day trip from Salvador.

History
Diego Álvares, the father of Cachocira's founders, was the sole survivor of a ship bound for the West Indies that was wrecked in 1510 on a reef near Salvador. This Portuguese Robinson Crusoe was saved by the indigenous Tupinambá of Rio Vermelho, who dubbed the strange white sea creature Caramuru, or 'Fish-Man.' Álvares lived 20 years with the *índios* and married Catarina do Paraguaçu, the daughter of the most powerful Tupinambá chief. Their sons João Gaspar Aderno Álvares and Rodrigues Martins Álvares killed off the local indigenous people, set up the first sugarcane *fazendas* (ranches) and founded Cachoeira.

By the 18th century, tobacco from Cachoeira was considered the world's finest, sought by rulers in China and Africa. The 'holy herb' also became popular in Brazil, taken as snuff, smoked in a pipe or chewed.

Early in the 19th century, Cachoeira achieved fame as a center for military operations in Bahia to oust the Portuguese rulers, and was the first place to recognize Dom Pedro I as the independent ruler of Brazil. Since then, not much has happened in this sleepy town.

Information
There is a helpful **tourist office** (☎ 3425 1123; Rua Ana Nery 4; ☉ 8am-noon & 1-5pm Mon-Fri, 1-4pm Sat & Sun) in Cachoeira, as well as a Bradesco bank and a post office, both overlooking Praça Dr Milton. São Félix also has a bank.

BAHIA

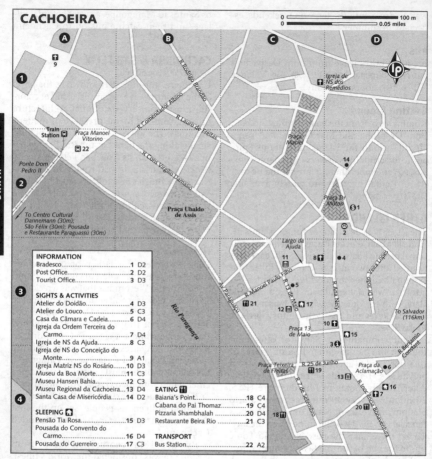

CACHOEIRA

Sights & Activities

At some sights here, especially at churches, theft has been a problem, so you may want to pre-arrange a visit through the tourist office. When visiting São Félix, watch your footing while crossing the narrow and dilapidated bridge (built by the British in 1885).

CHURCHES & HISTORIC BUILDINGS

The **Igreja da Ordem Terceira do Carmo** (Praça da Aclamação, Cachoeira; admission R$2; ⏰ 2-5pm Tue-Sat, 9am-noon Sun) has a gilded baroque altar, paneled ceilings and *azulejos*, and dates from 1702. A side gallery contains several polychrome Christs, imported from the Portuguese colony in Macau, and dripping with bovine blood mixed with Chinese herbs and sparkling rubies.

The **Igreja Matriz NS do Rosário** (Rua Ana Nery, Cachoeira) dates between 1693 and 1754. It has beautiful *azulejos* and a ceiling painted by Teófilo de Jesus. On the 2nd floor, the Museu das Alfaias contains remnants from the abandoned 17th-century Convento de São Francisco do Paraguaçu. The church is usually open mornings, but try knocking if it's closed.

Cachoeira's oldest church is the tiny **Igreja de NS da Ajuda** (Largo da Ajuda, Cachoeira), built in 1595 when the town was known as Arraial d'Ajuda.

The climb to the 18th-century **Igreja de NS do Conceição do Monte** is rewarded only by views as it is closed to visitors.

At the **Casa da Câmara e Cadeia** (Prefecture & Jail; Praça da Aclamação, Cachoeira), organized criminals ran the show upstairs and disorganized criminals were kept behind bars downstairs. The building dates to 1698 and served as the seat of the Bahian government in 1822. The old marble pillory was removed from out front after abolition.

The municipality's oldest hospital, the **Santa Casa de Misericórdia** (Praça Dr Milton, Cachoeira; ☾ 2-5pm Mon-Fri) has a pretty chapel (1734) with a painted ceiling, gardens and an ossuary.

MUSEUMS & CULTURAL CENTERS

The **Museu Hansen Bahia** (☎ 3425 1453; Rua 13 de Maio, Cachoeira; admission free; ☾ 9am-5pm Tue-Fri, 9am-2pm Sat & Sun) occupies the birthplace and former home of Brazilian heroine Ana Nery, who organized the nursing corps during the Paraguay War. Today, it houses the work of German-Brazilian artist Hansen Bahia. Among his powerful block prints and paintings on the theme of human suffering, depicting primarily prostitutes and Christ, is a series of illustrations of Castro Alves' poem *Návio Negreiro* (Slave Ship).

For a small donation, members of the exclusively female Boa Morte (Good Death) religious society will lead you around their barren one-room **Museu da Boa Morte** (Rua 13 de Maio, Cachoeira; admission by donation; ☾ 10am-6pm). There are some good photos here and usually society members sit around in their whites, smoking pipes and trading gossip. The society began as a sisterhood of slaves that assured dead slaves a proper burial and bought old slaves their freedom, while on the side they passed on information regarding slave uprisings and carefully disguised Candomblé events.

Housed in an 18th-century colonial mansion, the humble **Museu Regional da Cachoeira** (Praça da Aclamação, Cachoeira; admission R$2; ☾ 8am-noon & 2-5pm Mon-Fri, 8am-noon Sat) displays colonial furnishings and priestly vestments.

In São Félix, the riverfront **Centro Cultural Dannemann** (☎ 3425 2208; www.centroculturaldan nemann.com.br; Av Salvador Pinto 29; admission free; ☾ 8am-noon & 1-4:30pm Tue-Sat, gallery only 1-4pm Sun) has modern art displayed throughout a converted warehouse. In a large room in the rear of the building, heavy with the rich smell of tobacco, women dressed in white with flowered head wraps sit at antique wooden tables rolling *charutos* (cigars), as has been done here since 1873. Dannemann cigars are considered Brazil's finest.

WOOD CARVING

Cachoeira has maintained a tradition of wood carving with a heavy African flavor. Stop in on the *ateliers* (studios) of two of the best sculptors in town, **Doidão** (Rua Ana Nery) and **Louco** (Rua 13 de Maio), to get a sense of the local style; they operate roughly from 10am to 4pm Monday to Friday.

CANDOMBLÉ

Cachoeira is one of Candomblé's strongest and perhaps purest spiritual and religious centers. The *terreiros* are in small homes and shacks in the hills, where long ceremonies are usually held on Friday and Saturday nights. You can try contacting the tourist office for information about local guides who takes visitors to ceremonies (around R$50 per person).

Tours

For boat trips along the river, contact the owner of **Restaurante Beira Rio** (☎ 3425 5050; beirariotour@uol.com.br; Rua Manoel Paulo Filho 19, Cachoeira; per person R$15-60), who offers trips to Maragogipe, riverside convents and other nearby destinations.

Festivals & Events

Festa de São João (June 22-24) The largest popular festival of Bahia's interior, celebrated with folklore, music, dancing and a generous amount of food and drink.

Festa da NS da Boa Morte (Friday, Saturday & Sunday closest to August 15) Organized by the Boa Morte sisterhood; slave descendants pay tribute to their liberation with dance and prayer in a mix of Candomblé and Catholicism.

NS do Rosário (2nd half of October) Includes games, music and food.

NS da Ajuda (1st half of November) Features a ritual *lavagem* (washing) of the church and a street festival.

Santa Bárbara (Iansã; December 4) A Candomblé ceremony held in São Félix.

Sleeping & Eating

Accommodation prices double during festivals.

Pensão Tia Rosa (☎ 3425 1792; Rua Ana Nery 12, Cachoeira; s/d R$35/60) Tia Rosa is a friendly born-and-bred Cachoeiran who rents rustic rooms in her home. The best room is upstairs, with a view of the neighboring rooftops. She can also help arrange outings to Candomblé ceremonies.

Pousada do Guerreiro (☎ 3425 1104; Rua 13 de Maio 14, Cachoeira; s/d from R$40/70) This simple guesthouse has fan-cooled rooms with wood floors;

BAHIA

the best are rather spacious, and one room has a small balcony.

Pousada e Restaurante Paraguassú (☎ 3438 3386; Av Salvador Pinto 1, São Félix; s/d from R$60/75; ✷) Located on the riverfront in São Félix, Paraguassú has clean, cozy rooms surrounding a small garden. The restaurant serves good typical food and pizza with riverside seating.

Pousada do Convento do Carmo (☎ 3425 1716; Praça da Aclamação, Cachoeira; s/d R$115/130; ✷ ✷) The 18th-century convent attached to the Igreja da Ordem Terceira do Carmo has been converted into a comfortable pousada, with no loss of atmosphere. Rooms are spacious, with tall ceilings and heavy wood floors.

Pizzaria Shambhalah (☎ 3425 5318; Rua Inocência Bonaventura, Cachoeira; mains R$10-24; ✷ dinner) This small cozy pizzeria has brick walls, a varied menu and nicely lit tables with views onto the plaza.

Cabana do Pai Thomaz (☎ 3425 1288; Rua 25 de Junho 12, Cachoeira; mains R$15-22) Pai Thomaz serves good Bahian food and is filled with carved wooden panels and furniture.

Restaurante Beira Rio (☎ 3425 5050; Rua Manoel Paulo Filho 19, Cachoeira; mains R$16-32) This laid-back spot serves tasty seafood and Bahian fare with bench tables and artisan-produced decor. There are decent wines, outdoor river-facing tables and inexpensive lunch plates.

Baiana's Point (☎ 3425 4967; Rua Virgílio Reis, Cachoeira; mains R$27-38; ✷ dinner) Perched over the river, this place makes a great setting for an early evening drink; fine Bahian fare is available.

Getting There & Away

The Cachoeira bus station is located at the base of the bridge in Praça Manoel Vitorino. Numerous daily buses operated by **Transporte Santana e São Paulo** (☎ 3450 4951) run from Salvador to São Félix (R$16, two hours, from 5:30am to 7pm). Hourly buses to Salvador from Cachoeira can be caught in either town from 4:30am to 6:30pm. You can also continue on to Feira de Santana (R$8, 1½ hours, 12 daily) to make further connections. For Valença, take one of the two daily buses going from São Félix to Santo Antônio (R$10) and connect from there.

SANTO AMARO
☎ 0xx75 / pop 58,000

Santo Amaro is a friendly colonial sugar town that sees very few tourists and has an unpretentious charm. It is most well known for being the hometown of the brother-sister pair Caetano Veloso and Maria Betânia, two of Brazil's most popular singers (who often put in an appearance during Carnaval). The center bustles with people, especially around the small outdoor market. Paper production has replaced sugar as the major industry, visible in the invasion of bamboo on the hillsides where sugarcane once flourished, and a large paper mill outside of town.

The decrepit sugar-baron mansions along the old commercial street, Rua General Câmara, and the numerous churches are reminders of Santo Amaro's prosperous days. The ornate **Matriz de NS da Purificação** (1668) is the largest church, with *azulejos* and a painted ceiling. Unfortunately, a gang of thieves stole most of the church's holy images and exported them to France.

The **Lavagem da Purificação** (January 23 to February 2) is celebrated by a procession and ritual washing of the church steps by *baianas* in traditional dress, before bands and *trios elétricos* take over the streets.

Some of the good nighttime local music is played at the sterile **Hotel Lôbo** (☎ 3241 1721; Rua Conselheiro Paranhos 52; s/d from R$45/65; ✷), which has modern, tiled rooms.

Buses leave Salvador for Santo Amaro (R$12, one hour 10 minutes) almost every 30 minutes from 5:30am to 9:30pm. Most continue on to Cachoeira/São Félix (R$8, 50 minutes).

NORTH OF SALVADOR

Bahia's northern coast is not as startling as its southern, but the beaches here are still lovely, boasting tall bluffs with rustling palms and white sands (that grow finer the further north you go), which front a mix of calm inlets and wild surfable breaks. Keep in mind that when Salvadorenhos want a day at the beach, they naturally head for Bahia's northern coast. As a result, the sands close to the city get packed on weekends. To escape the crowds, head further north where there are many kilometers of deserted pristine shoreline.

The Estrada do Coco (Coconut Hwy) runs as far north as Praia do Forte, where the Linha Verde (Green Line) picks up, continuing all the way to the Sergipe border. You may feel that you are going against the grain

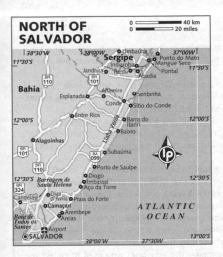

NORTH OF SALVADOR

if you are trying to access this coast heading north to south. Grassy medians in the highways require buses to pass town entrances and then double back, so few do. Instead, they drop passengers on the highway, leaving you to walk or pick up other transportation into the small towns and fishing communities along this stretch of coast. Traveling from south to north is a much smoother process.

AREMBEPE

☎ 0xx71 / pop 6200

Arembepe is practically synonymous with the **aldeia hippy**, a hippie village that Mick Jagger and Janis Joplin got rolling in the 1960s. Unfortunately, pollution from the giant chemical plant to the south and an abundance of weekend homes detract from the beauty of the rocky coast. If you're looking for a quick escape from Salvador, there are prettier beaches and more charming coastal villages. For a taste of a simpler life, however, the *aldeia*, inhabited by artists and artisans who sell their wares to visitors, is a curious place to explore. To get there, take a left at the roundabout when arriving in town, and follow the signs. You can also reach the *aldeia* by walking north from Arembepe along the beach (3km).

In town, the **Pousada Arembepe** (☎ 3624 2222; www.pousadaarembepe.tur.br; 1a Travessa da Glória 1; d with/ without breakfast R$100/80; 🅿 🛜 🖳) is a friendly place with bright, well-equipped rooms and a swimming pool. On the road to the *aldeia*

hippy, the **Hostel Bahia Albergue Pousada** (☎ 3624 1031; www.aldeiadearembepe.com.br; d with lake/ocean view R$110/132; 🖳) has an excellent location perched on a small grassy dune overlooking the beach. Quarters consist of freestanding concrete cabins, some with sea views.

From Salvador, catch an Arembepe bus from Terminal da França (just outside the Mercado Modelo), or a Monte Gordo bus from Lapa (both R$7, 1¼ hours). Arembepe is 2km off the highway. Frequent buses continue on to Praia do Forte.

PRAIA DO FORTE

☎ 0xx71

Beloved by tourists, upmarket Praia do Forte is an attractive and somewhat ecologically sensitive beach village overflowing with stylish restaurants and shops. The main drag, Alameda do Sol, is a pedestrian walkway that leads to an adorably tiny church, a sea-turtle reserve and fantastic, palm-lined beaches with sparkling white sands that fill up on weekends. Surrounding the village are castle ruins, a lagoon for canoeing and the Sapiranga forest reserve, which has hiking and biking trails and a zip-line. If you can, time your visit for the full moon and walk along the beach past the resort at sunset, when the sun turns the waters of the Rio Timeantube red as the moon rises over the sea.

Orientation & Information

Buses stop at the northern end of the pedestrian thoroughfare, Alameda do Sol (also called Av ACM). Opposite the bus stop, **Bahiatursa** (☎ 3117 3000; Av de Farol s/n; 🕑 8am-12:30pm & 3:30-6pm Tue-Sun) distributes maps and brochures and gives the lowdown on Praia do Forte. A number of travel agencies around town can also provide general information on excursions and activities. A few doors down from Bahiatursa, along Alameda do Sol, there's a HSBC ATM. You'll also find an ATM inside the **Albergue Praia do Forte** (Rua da Aurora 3).

Sights

The extremely worthwhile **Tamar Project station** (☎ 3676 0321; admission R$12; 🕑 9am-5:30pm) is located on the beach next to the church and lighthouse. See the boxed text, p464, for a description of the station and details on this national project designed to protect endangered sea turtles.

BAHIA

THE SEA TURTLES OF TAMAR

Tamar, an abbreviation for sea turtles (TArtaruga MARinha), is a highly successful nonprofit organization (Fundação Pró Tamar; www.tamar.org.br, in Portuguese) dedicated to saving five species of sea turtles in Brazil.

At the Praia do Forte station you can see several small exhibiting pools with marine turtles of various sizes and species, as well as urchins, eels and other sea life. If you visit during the turtles' nesting season (September to March) you will see the hatcheries functioning.

Tamar researchers protect around 550 nests a year along 50km of coast close to Praia do Forte. The moist, leathery, ping-pong-size eggs are buried in the sand when laid and either left on the beach or brought to the hatcheries for incubation. When they hatch, the baby turtles are immediately released into the sea.

Tamar has another 18 stations along the coast and two stations on oceanic islands, in all protecting some 1000km of coastline. Tamar estimates that under its protection some 600,000 baby turtles hatch per year. Of these only about 600 will reach adulthood. The Comboios station (Espírito Santo state, north of Vitória and near Linhares) protects the loggerhead and leatherback turtles. The Fernando de Noronha station protects green and hawksbill turtles. Praia do Forte station protects loggerhead, hawksbill, olive ridley and green turtles. Of the 60km of beach under Tamar's jurisdiction in Bahia, 13km are patrolled by the scientists alone; the remainder is protected by a cooperative effort in which fishermen – the very ones who used to collect the eggs for food – are contracted to collect eggs for the scientists.

The **Castelo do Garcia d'Ávila** (☎ 9985 3371; www.fgd .org.br, in Portuguese; admission R$6; ☼ 8:30am-6pm), dating from 1552, was the first great Portuguese edifice in Brazil. Today, it's an impressive ruin with great views. Desperate to colonize as a way to control his new territory, the king of Portugal had set about granting lands to merchants, soldiers and aristocrats. For no apparent reason, a poor, 12-cow farmer named Garcia d'Ávila was endowed with a tract of land that extended inland all the way to the state of Maranhão, with Praia do Forte as its seat. Overnight he became the largest landholder in the Northeast. For the site of his home, Garcia chose an aquamarine ocean-view plot studded with palm trees. It's a 7km walk along the only road out of town – there is a sign indicating where to turn – or you can take a taxi or moto-taxi.

A turn-off from the road to the castle leads down a dirt track to the **Reserva da Sapiranga** (☎ 9623 5412; www.fgd.org.br/ecoturismo/index.html, in Portuguese; admission R$6; guided hikes R$5-15; ☼ 8am-5pm), where local student guides take visitors along trails skirting through 600 hectares of secondary Atlantic rain forest. Hikes range from 30 minutes to five hours, with one of the more popular hikes leading down to the Rio Pojuca (bring your swimsuit).

Tours

Worthwhile tours in the area include hiking and bird-watching treks, canopy tours, kayaking and whale-watching (in season). A handful of professional outfitters such as **Portomar** (☎ 3676 0101; www.portomar.com.br; Rua da Aurora 1; ☼ 9am-7pm) handle these trips and run popular excursions at low tide to nearby *piscinas naturais* (natural pools), where you can snorkel or scuba dive around colorful coral reef.

Sleeping

Praia do Forte has an abundance of attractive midrange guesthouses, with fewer budget options (Rua da Aurora, parallel to Alameda do Sol, has a handful of more affordable pousadas).

Camping da Sapiranga (☎ 9976 9450; www.camping reservadasapiranga.cjb.net, in Portuguese; per person R$20) One of several campsites 3km outside of town, Sapiranga has shady grass and sand sites, with a kitchen available (R$3 extra). It's on a signed turn-off from the road to Castelo do Garcia d'Ávila.

Albergue Praia do Forte (☎ 3676 1094; www.al bergue.com.br; Rua da Aurora 3; dm/d with fan R$40/130, d with air-con R$160; 🖳 🛜) The popular HI hostel has six-bed, tile-floor dorm rooms, which face onto a grassy courtyard. There's a kitchen, and bikes and surfboards are available for hire.

Pousada Balanço do Mar (☎ 3676 1059; www .pousadabalancodomar.com.br; Rua da Aurora 25; s/d with fan R$90/110, with air-con R$100/160; 🖳) This tidy guesthouse has seven cozy, simply furnished rooms, the best with small verandas and hammocks.

Montreux Pousada (☎ 3676 1494; www.praiadoforte pousada.com.br, in Portuguese; Rua da Aurora 22; d with fan/air-con R$130/160; ❄) One of Forte's better deals, Montreux is a friendly Swiss Brazilian–run guesthouse with clean, pleasant rooms with balconies.

Pousada dos Artistas (☎ 3676 1147; www.pousada dosartistas.tur.br; Praça dos Artistas; s/d R$160/200; ❄) This is a friendly pousada – run by a dancer and a painter-sculptor, as the name suggests – where lovely rooms look out on a lush, tropical garden.

Pousada Ogum Marinho (☎ 3676 1165; www.ogum marinho.com.br; Alameda do Sol; d from R$220; ❄) One block from the beach, Ogum Marinho has attractive rooms with stone-slab floors, comfortable furnishings and private decks strung with hammocks.

Praia do Forte Eco Resort (☎ 3676 4000; www .ecoresort.com.br; Av do Farol; s/d with dinner from R$550/690; ❄ 🖥 🏊) It's all luxury at this excellent resort, where walkways wind through groomed gardens to the beach out front and the food is fabulous. Rooms all have verandas and the spa offers a wide range of treatments. Although there's nothing particularly 'eco' about the design, the hotel does contribute to social and educational programs.

Eating

Countless eateries – offering everything from sushi and bagels to Mexican food – line the town's pedestrian walkways. Around the central plaza, casual cafés offer Bahian staples and outdoor seating; at sunset, the atmosphere is lively and cold beer flows freely.

Vila Gourmet (☎ 3676 1088; www.sobradodavila .com.br; Alameda do Sol; mains for 2 R$25-75; ❄ breakfast, lunch & dinner) This stylish tropical-style eatery (connected to the centrally located Pousada Sobrado da Vila) serves regional cuisine that's a cut above the rest – thanks to organic vegetables and eggs sourced from a private farm.

Restaurante do Castelo (☎ 3329 3939; mains R$28-52) Located at the Castelo do Garcia d'Ávila, this elegant, breezy restaurant serves a small selection of seafood, grilled steak and Brazilian favorites to marvelous views.

Sabor da Vila (☎ 3676 1777; Alameda do Sol; mains for 2 R$35-65) One of the top Bahian restaurants in town, Sabor da Vila serves excellent *moquecas*, *picanha* (tender seirloin steak), grilled fish and other mouthwatering dishes.

our pick **Souza Bar** (☎ 9987 8638; Tamar Project station; snacks R$10, mains for 2 R$40-70) Inside the Tamar Project station complex, this laid-back bar-restaurant enjoys a dramatic setting along the rocky coastline – sit too close to the cliffs and you'll be splashed by big waves as you feast on fresh clams and caipirinhas.

Getting There & Around

Praia do Forte is 3km off the highway. **Linha Verde** (☎ 3460 3636) has regular departures to Praia do Forte from Salvador's bus station (R$7 to R$9, 1¾ hours, 14 daily between 5am and 6pm). Buses return every 30 minutes between 7am and 6:30pm. **Catuense** (☎ 3450 4004) has one to three daily buses to Praia do Forte from Salvador's bus station.

Bicycles are available for hire at **Ciclo Forte** (☎ 3676 0309; Alameda do Sol; per hr/day R$7/50; ❄ 7am-5pm Mon-Sat, 7am-noon Sun).

PRAIA DO FORTE TO SÍTIO DO CONDE

Imbassaí is a rustic beach town 16km north of Praia do Forte. A tall sand dune and the peaceful Rio Barroso, which runs parallel to the beach, separate the village from a fine beach with choppy, rough surf. Most guesthouses in town are midrange and top-end options, though **Imbassaí Eco Hostel Lujimba** (☎ 3677 1056; www.imbassaihostel.com.br; dm/d from R$31/80) offers good value for its pleasant wood-floor rooms in a rustic, thatched-roof guesthouse amid greenery. Hammocks, fruit trees and excursions add to the allure.

A few kilometers north of Imbassaí lies the more rustic town of **Diogo**, which sees fewer visitors and retains the charm of village life. It's located along a river, about a 1km walk to the beach. **Too Cool Na Bahia** (☎ 9952 2190; www .toocoolnabahia.com; d from R$100) has eight colorfully designed chalets with verandas overlooking the lush surroundings. The friendly owner can arrange kitesurfing, kayaking, horseback riding and other activities. For a delicious meal stop in **Sombra da Mangueira** (☎ 9943 2745; Rua do Diogo; mains R$22-35; ❄ 10am-5pm), which serves excellent *moquecas* and other Bahian fare in a charming setting beneath a large *mangueira* (mango tree).

Another 6km north is the immense **Costa do Sauípe** tourist resort complex, with luxury hotels, a golf course, an equestrian center and a windsurfing lake, but no good natural beach. A further 6km north lies **Porto de Sauípe**, a working-class fishing village with a few midrange

BAHIA

pousadas and a pretty stretch of beach that gets wild a few kilometers from town.

To reach any of the places listed above, take the **Linha Verde** (☎ 3460 3636) bus from Salvador's bus station (almost hourly between 5am and 6pm) and alert the driver to your destination.

SÍTIO DO CONDE & BARRA DO ITARIRI
☎ 0xx75

Wet lowlands full of cattle surround this quiet, working-class beach retreat. While there's little to the town itself – just a few main streets and a sleepy central plaza – Sítio has a lovely beach with pounding surf (located 1km from the plaza). North or south along the coast quickly leads to a deserted shore with churning seas and flat sands backed by bluffs topped with coconut trees.

Overlooking the beach, **Pousada Praiamar** (☎ 3449 1150; www.praiamarpousada.com.br, in Portuguese; s/d from R$65/95;) has comfortable rooms surrounding a sandy, palm-studded yard, a sea-facing porch with hammocks, and a constant breeze. Next door, **Pousada Talismã** (☎ 3449 1252; s/d with fan R$50/70) offers more rustic accommodation but the same great view (and a lovely restaurant).

Between the main plaza and the ocean, the flowery **Pousada Laia** (☎ 3449 1254; s/d from R$60/90) has well-kept, good-value rooms and great home cooking. **Zecas & Zecas** (☎ 3449 1298; Praça Arsênio Mendes 51; mains for 2 R$24-36), on the main square, is a colorful seafood restaurant serving the town's best *moqueca*.

Direct transportation to Sítio do Conde is infrequent. You will most likely travel through Conde on the Linha Verde. From Salvador, São Luís has buses to Conde (R$25, 3½ hours, nine daily) from 6am to 5pm. Buses and more-frequent *topiques* (vans) make the 8km trip on to Sítio until about 5:30pm (R$2), or you can get a taxi (R$18).

Heading north, buses go through a picturesque coconut-palm forest to **Seribinha** (16km north), a small fishing community with a pretty riverside setting and good beach. From here, boats cross the Rio Itapicuru, from where it's a 30-minute walk to **Cavalo Russo**, a tea-colored lake with a sand dune sliding into it.

Down a rough dirt road, some 13km from Sítio do Conde, lies the pretty beach of **Barra do Itariri** (known as Barra), with a wide, white sand bar that curves into the bank of the idyllic Rio Itariri. Outside of Sundays and

Carnaval, Barra is pretty much deserted. To get there take one of three daily São Luís buses from Sítio do Conde (R$2, 30 minutes). The last bus back leaves at 2pm.

MANGUE SECO
☎ 0xx75 / pop 920

Mangue Seco is a tiny, beautifully rustic riverfront village at the tip of a peninsula formed by the Rio Real, which delineates the Bahia/Sergipe border. The town itself is just a scattering of simple dwellings along sandy paths, a tiny church and plaza, a modern lighthouse (yielding lovely views for intrepid climbers) and a few friendly guesthouses and restaurants. The town ends at the edge of an enormous expanse of tall white sand dunes, beyond which the wide flat sands of the Bahian coast stretch to the south. Mangue Seco's remote location causes most visitors to come on guided day tours, preventing rapid growth and leaving nights decidedly quiet. Guesthouses can arrange dune-buggy trips through the sand dunes (around R$50 for up to four people). It's about a 1.5km walk to the ocean (or a R$12 dune-buggy ride), which has a handful of simple *barracas* strung with hammocks.

Sleeping & Eating
Pousada Grão de Areia (☎ 3445 9064; www.praiademan gueseco.com.br; s/d with fan R$45/60, with air-con R$80/110;) In the village (stay to the right when exiting the dock), this is a simple, economical option with clean, light-colored rooms.

Pousada Suruby (☎ 3445 9061; www.pousadasuruby .com.br, in Portuguese; d with fan R$80) Suruby has a row of simple, fan-cooled rooms lined with hammocks that overlook a small front yard and the river beyond. The breezy restaurant serves seafood (mains R$27 to R$40). To get to this riverfront pousada, exit the dock and follow the riverfront to the left (toward the beach).

Pousada O Forte (☎ 3445 9039; www.pousadaoforte .com; s/d with fan R$80/100, with air-con from R$120/140;) Located 300m from the village center on the riverfront (past Suruby) and on the way to the beach, this ecofriendly French Brazilian–owned pousada is in an isolated spot overlooking the river. Note that high tides swallow the riverbank 'road' to the village center, leaving you to either wait, wade or take a lengthy detour through the sand dunes.

Fantasias do Agreste (☎ 3445 9070; www.pousada fantasiasdoagreste.com, in Portuguese; d with fan R$150) In the center of the village, Fantasias do Agreste is the most comfortable guesthouse in town, with modern, colorfully painted rooms, big windows (no view) and terra-cotta tile floors. The restaurant is worth a stop even if you're not staying here.

Mangue Seco's culinary specialty is *aratu*, a tiny red shellfish sometimes prepared in *moquecas*. In addition to restaurants at the pousadas Suruby, O Forte and Fantasias do Agreste, visitors can sample seafood at **Restaurant Frutas do Mar** (☎ 3445 9049; mains R$18-35), a pleasant outdoor spot located on the riverbank.

To satisfy sweet cravings, stop by local favorite **Recanto de Dona Sula** (☎ 3445 9008; snacks R$6-15), where homemade candies, ice creams and liqueurs are made from local fruits. The café next door opens in the evenings and serves sandwiches, pizzas and light meals. Both charming and environmentally conscious (recycling is a priority here), Dona Sula's is located next to the church.

Getting There & Around

The easiest access to Mangue Seco is through Pontal, though boats also leave from Ponto do Mato; both are in Sergipe. Since there are few direct buses to Pontal, you'll have to route through either Indiaroba or Estância. From Salvador, Linha Verde has one daily bus to Indiaroba (R$36, five hours). **Bomfim** (www.bomfim.com.br) buses go four times daily to Estância (R$40 to R$64, four to five hours). From Aracaju, Rota Sul has one daily bus to Pontal (R$12, 2½ hours) as well as three daily departures to Indiaroba (R$10, 2¼ hours). Upon arriving in Indiaroba you can hire a taxi for around R$40 to Pontal.

Alternatively, frequent minibuses/vans heading to Pontal leave from in front of Estância's hospital. If coming from the north, ask to be let off at the *posto de gasolina* (gas station) before Estância's bus station and walk one block up into town to the hospital. A taxi from Estância to Pontal costs about R$55.

From Pontal, speedboats charge R$30 for up to six people. Slow boats (R$3) leave when they have 15 people together, which could take hours on quiet days.

Vans leave Pontal (R$6, 90 minutes, hourly from 5:30am to 8:30am Monday to Saturday) and Ponto do Mato (R$6, two hours, hourly until 6pm) for Estância.

SOUTH OF SALVADOR

MORRO DE SÃO PAULO
☎ 0xx75

As postcard-pretty as any Mediterranean island village, Morro de São Paulo has long been a favorite weekend getaway for travelers and Salvador locals alike. Though Morro is overtly touristy, many visitors don't care, since it's also a fabulous tropical paradise with sandy lanes, calm waters and a candlelit nightlife scene. Remotely perched at the northern tip of the Ilha de Tinharé, Morro's appeal stems from its relaxed pace – no cars are allowed on the island – and unique geography: three jungle-topped hills on a point at the meeting of the mangrove-lined Canal de Taperoá and a clear, shallow Atlantic. At the dock, wheelbarrow valets wait to help you transport your luggage past countless restaurants and boutiques to the pousada of your choice (be sure to negotiate the price beforehand). During the high season the village booms, dozens of vendors mix fresh-fruit caipirinhas on the sand, and lighthearted dancing and music enliven the beaches every night.

Orientation

Unless arriving by charter flight, all visitors to the island disembark on the northern tip of the island (every visitor pays a R$10 tourist tax here). Uphill lies the main square (Praça Aureliano Lima) in the Vila, with an information office and a few restaurants. To reach the beaches, take a left at the square; this passes along the main street, Rua Caminho da Praia, and is lined with restaurants and shops. Continue downhill to access the shores, reaching Primeira Praia (First Beach), then Segunda Praia, and so on. Heading right from the main plaza, you'll go through an archway down Rua da Fonte and pass the spring-fed fountain that was once the village's freshwater source. Pousadas are scattered about the island, with the cheapest being in the Vila area.

Information

There are a few ATMs on the island: two in the Vila and another on Segunda Praia. It's wise, however, to bring necessary funds with you from the mainland, especially during high season when hundreds of tourists deplete the ATMs' cash supply. Many establishments also accept credit cards. Internet cafés are plentiful (R$4 to R$6 per hour).

At the top of the hill up from the dock, **Centro de Informações ao Turista** (☎ 3652 1083; www .morrosp.com.br; Praça Aureliano Lima s/n) sells boat and domestic airline tickets, organizes excursions and distributes maps. Travel agencies scattered around town and on the beaches, like **Zulu Turismo** (☎ 3652 1358; www.morrodesaopauloba hiabrasil.com; Rua da Mangaba 98), provide similar services.

Sights & Activities
The town's icon is a 17th-century carved-stone **fortress gate**, which welcomes each arrival from its position above the dock. Around the corner at the point are the **fort ruins** (1630). Catching the rare sight of the sun setting over the river and mangroves from the fort is a visitor ritual. The **lighthouse** (1835) above the fort affords a fantastic view over Morro's beaches and has a **zip-line** descending to Primeira Praia.

The waters of Morro's four conveniently named main beaches are mostly calm, shallow and warm, and their sands are narrow and swallowed by the high tides. Tiny **Primeira Praia** is lined with pousadas, occasionally hosts lively football matches on the sand, and has a decent surf break. Deep **Segunda Praia** (500m) is the 'action' beach with pousadas, restaurants, nightclubs and a sea of tables and chairs. Pousadas and anchored boats dominate one end of **Terceira Praia** (1km). Once you pass a pair of restaurants, **Quarta Praia** (2km) is a long, lovely stretch of sand graced by tall, swaying palms. For even more isolated peace, continue on at low tide to **Praia do Encanto** (5km) or further down the island to **Garapuá**, which has one pousada.

At low tide, take a walk to **Gamboa**, the next village on the river side of the island. The coast between the villages is filled with nooks to hide in and rocks to climb on. To start, head down Rua da Fonte Grande and head right at the crossroads. You can catch the ferry back.

Tours
A boat trip around the island (R$65), with stops at the Garapuá and Moreré offshore reefs and the villages of Boipeba (p470) and historical Cairu, is obligatory. You'll fly over waves in a 10-person speedboat past gorgeous beach and mangrove scenery, swim, snorkel and stop at a floating oyster restaurant outside Caravelas. Jeep trips to Boipeba are also possible (R$60). Also worthwhile is a hike to the small Fonte do Ceu waterfall, passing through the neighboring village of Gamboa, with an opportunity to do a bit of body painting from a cliff of colored clays (R$30). Horseback rides can also be arranged (R$25 per hour). All these tours can be booked through the many local agencies.

Sleeping
Reservations for Morro's 100 or so pousadas are required for all major holidays, especially Carnaval and *resaca* (five days of post-Carnaval hangover). Be forewarned that staying on Segunda Praia during summer means sleeping to the nightclubs' pounding beats.

VILA
Hostel Morro de São Paulo (☎ 3652 1521; www.hostel domorro.com.br; Rua da Fonte Grande; dm/d from R$48/120; ⊠) This pleasant HI hostel has fine rooms with big shuttered windows, a little garden, hammocks and a guest kitchen. To get here, take the first left after passing through the archway leading to the spring.

Pousada Ninho da Águia (☎ 3652 1201; Rua Caminho do Farol 8; d with fan/air-con R$70/90; ⊠) On the hill above the dock, the tranquilly set Ninho da Águia is indeed at eagle's-nest heights. It's a friendly, family-run affair with tidy, simple rooms (upstairs rooms have great views).

Pousada Caravelas (☎ 3652 1350; www.morrosao paulo.com/caravelas; Rua da Fonte Grande; s/d/tr R$90/100/ 135; ⊠) This small, simple pousada, just around the corner from the historic fountain, is run by a delightful Argentinean couple. A first-rate breakfast is served on your balcony – it's a rare pleasure to enjoy coffee and home-made pastries while watching hummingbirds flitting through the lush courtyard.

Pousada Gaucho (☎ 3652 1243; www.pousadagau cho.com.br, in Portuguese; Rua Caminho da Praia 74; d with fan/air-con R$100/135; ⊠) This tidy, family-run place has fine, cheap rooms that can be a little noisy. Pricier, better rooms are on the upper floors and are run by a separate pousada of the same name.

Pousada Colibri (☎ 3652 1056; www.pousada-colibri .com; d R$125-185; ⊠) In a marvelous hilltop position, the lushly landscaped Colibri has round cabins and well-finished two-room suites with verandas and hammocks. Two hectares of surrounding jungle assure beauty and quiet. To reach Colibri, take the path to the spring, then turn right up a quiet forested lane.

O Casarão (☎ 3652 1022; www.pousadaocasarao .com; Praça Aureliano Lima 190; d/bungalow from R$180/287;

⊠ ⊠) Reigning over the wide, main plaza, this renovated colonial mansion has lovely rooms with classical furnishings and large windows. Eclectically furnished chalets in back overlook a small garden.

BEACHES

Pousada e Camping Oxum (☎ 3652 1048; Segunda Praia; campsite/d R$20/70) One of several campsites near the beaches, Oxum has a small backyard of equal parts grass and sand, with some shade. The rooms are boxy wooden cabins without charm.

Morro Hostel Albergue (☎ 3652 1701; www.morro hostel.com.br, in Portuguese; Rua Beco do Elefante 3; camping per person R$20, dm/d from R$25/60; ⊠ ⊠) Located 100m from Primeira Praia, this budget-friendly hostel offers basic dorms as well as private rooms and a camping area. There's a community kitchen and restaurant on-site, too.

Pousada Aradhia (☎ 3652 1341; www.pousadaara dhia.net; Terceira Praia; d R$95; ⊠ ⊠) Popular with young travelers, Aradhia offers fair value for its worn, basic rooms. Hammocks and a pool sweeten the deal. Aradhia lies on a narrow lane, just off Terceira Praia.

Morro Praia Hotel (☎ 3652 1244; www.morropraia hotel.com.br, in Portuguese; Terceira Praia; d R$140-200; ⊠) Decent value among beachfront hotels, Morro Praia has small, simple rooms with colorful murals and decent windows, some opening onto the sea.

Pousada Paraíso do Morro (☎ 3652 1121; www.parai sodomorro.com.br; Terceira Praia; d with/without sea view R$230/160; ⊠) This charming guesthouse is all about peace and tranquility: colorful, stylish rooms overlooking the sea or a small garden in back; guests receive a free yoga class.

Pousada Ilha do Sol (☎ 8871 1295; www.pousada ilhadosol.com, in Portuguese; Rua da Prainha, Primeira Praia; d R$180-200; ⊠) At the base of the steep road leading to the ocean, this well-established guesthouse is good value for its open, two-room suites catching the ocean breeze, and porches for people-watching.

Eating

Casual dining options abound on the island. Sample *pasteles* (empanada-like pastries stuffed with meat and other savory fillings), freshly squeezed juices and a variety of other Bahian snacks at the food stands along the beaches and the plaza. At night, Segunda Praia is alive with restaurants competing for your

business – don't miss the chance to dine or have a drink with the sand between your toes.

Tia Lita (☎ 3652 1532; www.pousadatialita.com.br; Rua da Prainha, Terceira Praia; mains R$8-10) This inexpensive, popular restaurant serves home-cooked grilled fish, chicken or beef. It's down a narrow lane, just off the beach.

Café das Artes (☎ 3652 1057; Praça Aureliano Lima; mains R$12-25) This pretty café doubles as an art space; the patio overlooking the square is a plum spot for a light lunch or a little night music.

Ponto de Encontro Arte & Culinária (☎ 3652 1165; Rua Caminho da Praia; mains R$15-35) Filled with vibrant paintings, sculpture and tilework, this inspired eatery serves eclectic dishes, including vegetarian options – try the baked stuffed eggplant or the chocolate-covered pears.

Sabor da Terra (☎ 3652 1490; www.pousadaperolado morro.com.br; Rua Caminho da Biquinha 10; mains R$18-40) Excellent seafood is prepared simply or with Bahian spice. Fish *moqueca* and *casquinha de siri* (shredded crab meat) are excellent. The attached pousada rents pleasant rooms (doubles R$150).

Pizza & Restaurante Bianco e Nero (☎ 3652 1097; Rua Caminho da Praia; mains R$18-45; ☾ dinner) This fashionable Italian pizzeria and eatery is hugely popular for its fresh seafood pastas and oven-fired pizzas served on a large terrace overlooking the main pedestrian thoroughfare.

Chez Max (☎ 3652 1754; Terceira Praia; mains R$22-46) Overlooking Terceira Praia, Chez Max is an idyllic retreat where you can dine on a grassy lawn facing the sea. Sizzling grilled dishes, seafood and plenty of Bahian cuisine fill out the menu.

Drinking

Don't miss dexterous vendors along Rua Caminho da Praia and on Segunda Praia mixing delicious caipirinhas – made with a wide range of fresh fruits, many of which you've probably never heard of. Outdoor bars are scattered along Segunda Praia. Current favorites are Music Bar 87, with its live music nightly (usually a bossa nova guitarist), and the reggae-infused Jamaica Bar. Pick up fliers for current dance parties (admission R$10 to R$30) at shops along Rua Caminho da Praia.

Getting There & Away

A handful of operators run catamarans (R$75, two hours, three to four daily) and *lanchas rapidas* (speedboats; R$75, two hours, daily) between Morro and the Terminal Marítimo Turístico in Salvador. The ride can be rough – come with Dramamine if you're especially prone to seasickness. For reservations, call **Biotur** (☎ 3641 3327; www.biotur.com.br), **Farol do Morro** (☎ 3652 1083; www.faroldomorrotour.com) or **IlhaBela** (☎ in Salvador 0xx71-9195 6744; www.ilhabela tm.com.br).

If coming from the south, passenger ferries travel upriver to Morro from Valença (R$6 to R$7, 1½ hours, hourly from 7am to 5pm), stopping first in Gamboa. At low tide, passengers are bussed to Atracadoro, then transferred to a waiting ferry. *Lanchas rapidas* (R$12 to R$15, 40 minutes) leave whenever they have a full load.

Three daily flights go between Salvador and Morro (R$225 to R$235, 20 minutes). Contact **Aerostar** (☎ in Salvador 0xx71-3377 4406; www.aerostar .com.br), **Addey Taxi Aéreo** (☎ in Salvador 0xx71-3204 1393; www.addey.com.br) or a travel agency.

BOIPEBA
☎ 0xx75 / pop 4900

South of the Ilha da Tinharé, across the narrow Rio do Inferno, sits the Ilha de Boipeba. The village of Boipeba, on the northeastern tip of the island, is quiet, rustic and said to be what Morro de São Paulo was 20 years ago. The island's coastline is pristine, with more than 20km of beautiful, deserted beaches, including **Ponta de Castelhanos**, known for its diving.

Sleeping & Eating

Restaurants serving great seafood line the beach where the river meets the sea. Rounding the point, a string of top-end pousadas face Praia Boca da Barra.

Pousada 7 (☎ 3653 6135; www.pousada7.com.br; Praça Santo Antônio; d from R$110; 🕸) In the village center, overlooking the main plaza–football pitch, this friendly place has small attractive rooms with stone-slab floors and hammocks outside the door. A restaurant serves up tasty seafood for dinner daily.

Pousada Pérola do Atlântico (☎ 3653 6096; www .ilhaboipeba.org.br/peroladoatlantico.html; s/d with fan from R$120/170) On the beach, this welcoming guesthouse has lush gardens with winding pathways leading to pretty wooden cabins spread about the tranquil setting.

Pousada Vila Sereia (☎ 3653 6045; www.ilhaboipeba .org.br/en/vilasereia.html; d with fan R$250-350) Brightly

painted, thatched-roof cabins sit raised on stilts throughout a beachfront garden at this inviting pousada. The owners can arrange private transportation from Salvador or Ilhéus.

Getting There & Away

From Valença, passenger ferries for Boipeba (R$15, four hours) leave daily Monday to Saturday (currently at noon). Faster boats also make the trip daily (R$35, one hour). Two daily buses (11am and 2pm) leave Valença for Torrinhas, where passengers are transferred to a ferry for Boipeba (R$12 to R$18, bus and ferry 2½ hours). Ferries stop first at the historic town of Cairu, a recommended stopover if you can catch a later boat on to Boipeba.

From Morro de São Paulo, a boat leaves for Boipeba at 9:30am and then leaves Boipeba for the return journey to Morro at 2pm (both R$75, 2½ hours). Alternatively, you can negotiate a jeep ride (around R$60) with a travel agency in Morro de São Paulo, and then the ferry across the river.

VALENÇA
☎ 0xx75 / pop 90,000

Valença is a colonial fishing town on the banks of the Rio Una, historically the site of Portuguese struggles with both indigenous tribes and the Dutch. For most it is simply the gateway to Morro de São Paulo, but it has its own little-known secrets. Local shipbuilders maintain 15th-century techniques to such a degree that the town was chosen to produce a replica of the Spanish galleon *La Niña* for the American epic film *1492* (1992) about Christopher Columbus' journey.

To see the building of *saveiro* fishing boats in action, wander to the far end of the port where the smell of sap and sawdust, old fish and sea salt mingles with the wonderful odor of nutmeg drying in the sun. For a good walk and a beautiful view, follow the river's left bank upstream toward the **Igreja NS de Amparo** (1757) on the hill.

Orientation

From the port, walk straight uphill to reach the pedestrian center of town. If you keep going straight up along this main street, named Rua Governador Gonçalves, you will eventually reach the bus station (which is located 1km from the port). The Praça da Independencia is one block west of Rua Governador Gonçalves.

Information

All of the following are within a short walk of the port.

Banco do Brasil (Rua Governador Gonçalves 10)

Bradesco (Rua Governador Gonçalves 178)

Lys.com (Praça Admar Briga Guimarães; per hr R$3; ☼ 8am-10pm) Internet access near the port.

Tourist office (☎ 3641 0553; www.valenca.tur.br, in Portuguese; Rua Comandante Madureira 10; ☼ 8am-noon & 2-5pm Mon-Fri, 8am-noon Sat) Facing the port (go to the left), this office is mildly helpful.

Festivals & Events

During Carnaval and at Christmas, people dressed as cowhands accompany Catarina the *baiana* throughout the city while chanting and playing tambourines in the celebration of **Boi Estrela**. **Carnaval** and **Micareta** (held 15 days after the end of Lent) are lively, with *trios elétricos* blasting *axé* music. A weeklong festival in honor of **NS do Amparo**, the patron saint of workers, climaxes on November 8. On New Year's Eve, **Zambiapumba** is celebrated by musical groups running through the streets playing improvised instruments.

Sleeping

Hotel Valença (☎ 3641 3807; Rua Dr Heitor Guedes De Melo 15; s/d from R$40/60; ☒) A few blocks off Praça da República, Hotel Valença is a good value for its clean, basic rooms.

Hotel Guaibim (☎ 3641 4114; Praça da Independencia 74; s/d with fan R$50/70, with air-con from R$65/85; ☒) Up from the port area, this nice, simple hotel has friendly staff and clean rooms with tile floors.

Onda Azul Hotel (☎ 3641 4964; Rua Conselheiro Ferraz 5; s/d from R$70/110; ☒) One block from the Praça da Independencia, Onda Azul is a sprightlier option, with stone-slab floors and pleasant furnishings.

Hotel Portal Rio Una (☎ 3641 5050; www.portalhoteis.tur.br, in Portuguese; Rua Maestro Barrinha; d from R$235; ☒ ☎ ☒) This large, attractive hotel has Valença's finest restaurant and its best rooms, each with verandas overlooking the river. It's 1km from the river (on the opposite side of the port).

Eating & Drinking

Casual outdoor bars/snack stands are scattered along the riverfront near the bridge.

Mega Chic (☎ 3641 4704; Av Maçônica 11; per kg R$18; ☼ lunch) Across the bridge from the town center, Mega Chic spreads a decent self-service buffet and offers an à la carte menu of pastas, sandwiches and cocktails.

Sabor do Sol (Rua Governador Gonçalves 113; mains R$15-25; ☼ lunch) This low-key *churrascaria* and *por-kilo* restaurant is a popular lunch spot. It's on the pedestrian walkway.

Getting There & Away

Valença's tiny airport, served only by small air-taxi companies, is 15km from the center.

There are daily boat services to Boipeba, Gamboa and Morro de São Paulo from the port in the center.

The **bus station** (☎ 3641 4894) is a 1km hike from the port (or a R$10 taxi ride). Águia Branca buses go to Porto Seguro (R$63, nine hours, one daily), Ilhéus via Itabuna (R$31, five hours, two daily) and Camamu (R$11, 1½ hours, two daily). Other bus companies follow similar routes – you'll find at least two more daily departures to Ilhéus and several more to Camamu. Inquire at the bus station for more information. For Salvador, take a bus to Bom Despacho (R$16, two hours, hourly from 5am to 11:45pm) on the Ilha de Itaparica, and then a ferry (see p458) across the bay.

CAMAMU

☎ 0xx73 / pop 33,000

On the mainland, shielded from the open ocean by the Peninsula de Maraú, Camamu is primarily the jumping-off point for Barra Grande. The town is the port of call for the many tiny fishing villages in the region and overlooks a maze of mangrove-filled islets and narrow channels. *Saveiro* fishing boats are built and repaired right outside the port. The beautiful **Açaraí Waterfalls** are 5km away by local bus or taxi (R$55 round trip).

The **Pousada Green House** (☎ 3255 2178; Rua Djalma Dutra 61; s/d with fan from R$40/60), where the buses stop, is friendly, family-run and great value. Up a steep road from the port, the **Hotel Rio Açaraí** (☎ 3255 2315; www.hotelrioacarai.com.br, in Portuguese; Praça Dr Francisco Xavier Borges; s/d from R$80/100; ☒ ☒) is a rather bland modern hotel, but it boasts a fine setting overlooking the river. Several pleasant riverside cafés lie just past the boat dock.

There is no real bus station here; buses stop near the port. **Águia Branca** (☎ 3255 1823; www.aguiabranca.com.br) and **São Geraldo** (☎ 3255 2508; www.saogeraldo.com.br) have adjoining offices, and run buses to Ilhéus (R$22, three hours, three daily), Bom Despacho (R$24 to R$27,

BAHIA

BAHIA

3½ hours, four daily) and Ubaitaba (R$10, 1¼ hours, three daily), where connections south can be found.

BARRA GRANDE
☎ 0xx73

Deliciously off the beaten path, Barra Grande is a remote, tranquil fishing village at the northern tip of the Peninsula de Maraú. It has the same charm and tree-shaded magic that originally attracted bohemian types to similar sand-street villages further south, but it hasn't yet experienced a tourism boom. With a fair number of pousadas and restaurants, Barra Grande makes a great base for checking out the rest of the peninsula. Much of the village closes in winter.

Separating the peninsula from the mainland is the island-riddled Baía de Camamu, Brazil's third-largest bay. One long, dirt road (often impassable after rain) heads down the peninsula, providing access to stunning beaches with crystal-clear water, such as **Praia Taipús de Fora** (7km, rated among Brazil's top beaches), and a handful of very small fishing villages. Pricey excursions to **Lagoa Azul**, viewpoints, bay islands and down the Rio Maraú are offered by local providers.

Other lovely destinations are accessible on foot. At the base of the village lies the 2km-long **Barra Grande beach**, where the calm waters are fine for swimming. A short walk along the beach leads to the **Ponta da Mutá**, the northeast point of the peninsula, with a lighthouse marking the bay's entrance. Around the rocky point, you access a long stretch of coast, with **Praia da Bombaça** the next notable beach (3.5km from Barra Grande) before reaching Praia Taipús de Fora (located 3.5km further).

Information
Get funds before going to Barra Grande, as there are no banks.

Sleeping & Eating
Cantinho da Ivete (☎ 8105 7579; campsite per person R$8, d without bathroom R$35) On the beach path, Ivete offers campsites on a shaded lawn; shabby wooden cabins are also available.

Maria de Firmino (☎ 3258 6482; s/d R$60/100;) The first pousada as you leave the pier, Maria de Firmino has spacious, somewhat worn rooms.

Pousada Canto do Sol (☎ 3258 6018; Rua José Melo Pirajá; d R$80-90;) Near the main plaza, this is

a good budget choice for its small, spotless rooms. Hammocks and greenery are part of the setting.

Ponta do Mutá (☎ 3258 6028; www.pousadapontado muta.com.br; Rua do Anjo; s/d without view R$157/217, with sea view R$197/257;) This welcoming guesthouse has 10 simple, pleasantly decorated rooms, each with a veranda and hammock, and many with sea views. Bicycles and kayaks are available for rental. It's on the beach, left from the dock.

Pousada Porto da Barra (☎ 3258 6349; www.pou sadaportodabarra.com.br, in Portuguese; Av Beira Mar 13; d from R$160;) On the beach, this mustard-yellow, two-story pousada offers clean, simple rooms with tile floors and hammocks strung outside the doors; the beach is steps away.

Pousada Barrabella (☎ 3258 6285; www.pousada barrabella.com.br; Rua Vasco Neto s/n; s/d/ste from R$165/179/232;) This pretty pousada, decorated with furnishings made by local craftsmen, offers tranquil rooms with sea or bay views, a good restaurant, and an appealing swimming pool with a cocktail bar that overlooks the ocean.

Café Latino (☎ 3258 6188; Rua Dr Chiriquinho 19; mains R$15-25; dinner Wed-Mon) On a street leading off the main plaza, this charming bistro and photo gallery serves tasty grilled dishes, pastas and desserts alongside wine and refreshing cocktails.

Churrasquinho do Zelitinho (☎ 8111 1536; Praça das Mangueiras; mains for 2 R$25-38) In the main plaza, this steak restaurant serves good grilled meats.

A Tapera (☎ 3258 6119; Rua Dr Lili; mains for 2 R$30-50; 3-8pm) Just off the plaza, this traditional Bahian restaurant serves seafood, including amazing squid *moqueca*.

Bar e Restaurante Taparão (☎ 3258 6006; Rua Vasco Neto; mains for 2 R$32-55) This waterfront eatery specializes in fresh clams and lobsters, not to mention fresh fruit caipirinhas. It's a calm place to sit at sunset.

Getting There & Around
Passenger ferries (R$6, 1¼ hours, five to six daily from 7:30am to 5:30pm) and *lanchas* (R$25, 30 minutes, four daily) depart for Barra Grande from Camamu. Heading to or from Itacaré, you will need to negotiate a ride with a tour provider (around R$75 per person).

Four-wheel-drive *jardineiras* (R$6 to R$8) park off the main path in town, and leave for the beaches as soon as they have a full load.

ITACARÉ

☎ 0xx73 / pop 27,000

At its heart, Itacaré is a quiet, colonial fishing town, long sought out by hippies and surfers mesmerized by wide stretches of virgin Atlantic rain forest, picturesque beaches and reliable surf breaks. In recent years, the paving of the road into town has led to a tourism boom, with dozens of pousadas and restaurants now packing the streets. In spite of this, the mellow, youthful vibe prevails, surf culture reigns supreme, and many establishments in the area are committed to environmentally friendly practices (look for the Carbon Free Tourism sign proudly posted around town).

Orientation

Itacaré lies at the mouth of Rio de Contas, where the river meets the sea. A short walk east of the working-class neighborhoods around the fishing port leads to the area known as Pituba, which is essentially one long street, Rua Pedro Longo, lined with pousadas, restaurants and shops. Follow this road east out of town to access Itacaré's prettiest beaches. North of the Pituba strip is known as Condomínio Conchas do Mar, and has higher-end restaurants and pousadas in a more verdant setting. The neighborhood ends at the small beach of Praia da Concha.

Information

There are several exchange offices near Praça dos Cachorros as well as a **Banco do Brasil ATM** (Rua João de Deus 150) just off the main strip. Internet cafés are plentiful, costing around R$6 per hour. Visit www.itacare.com.br for an overview.

Dangers & Annoyances

There has been a rash of muggings at and around Itacaré's beaches, so take little money and nothing of value. Avoid the trails through the forests past late afternoon.

Activities

The coast south of Itacaré is characterized by rough surf (which is better for surfing than for swimming) and cove beaches separated by hills covered with rain forest. Some beaches, such as idyllic **Prainha** (reachable by trail from Praia do Ribeira), are private and charge entrance fees. **Praia da Concha** is an ordinary city beach. **Resende**, **Tiririca** and **Ribeira** beaches

lie within 1.5km south of town and are frequented by surfers. Highly recommended are the paradisiacal **Engenhoca**, **Havaizinho** and **Itacarezinho** beaches, located 12km south of town.

Many travel agencies and seemingly every hotel offer canoe trips upriver, rafting, mountain biking, rappelling and excursions on foot or horseback to local sights. The principal excursion is up the Peninsula de Maraú, with stops at **Lagoa Azul** and **Praia Taipús de Fora** (R$65). A word of advice: maximize your comfort by assuring that the vehicle's seats face forward.

Several reliable agencies offering these adventures include the multilingual **Brazil Trip Tour** (☎ 8157 5155; www.braziltriptour.com; Rua Pedro Longo 245). Specializing in English-speaking surf lessons and ecological tours, it also arranges volunteer work in the community (English teachers are especially welcome, see p714) and 10- to 14-day 'Cruz the Coast' tours between Rio and Salvador.

Surfboard rental and surf lessons are also arranged through outfitters around town. Board rentals start around R$20 per day and three-day classes for R$200. For a more structured weeklong surfing experience, including classes and accommodation, look into surf camps like **Easy Drop** (☎ 3251 3065; www.easydrop .com; Rua João Coutinho 140).

For a do-it-yourself excursion and a swim, catch a bus leaving town and hop off at the **Cachoeira Tijuipe** (admission R$5), a wide waterfall of tea-colored water on private, forested land.

Sleeping

The majority of guesthouses are scattered along Rua Pedro Longo. For a quieter, more idyllic stay that's still close to the action, look for guesthouses in Condomínio Conchas do Mar.

Pousada Navio Albergue Camping POP (☎ 3251 2305; Praia da Concha; www.pousadanavio.com.br, in Portuguese; camping per person R$15; dm/d with fan from R$30/80) Yes, the name is a mouthful, but with good reason – this friendly backpacker's haven offers a little of everything. Shady campsites, close to the beach, include access to decent showers, a laundry area and a café-bar; there are also fan-cooled rooms sleeping up to four.

Buddys Pousada & Guesthouse (☎ 8137 3456; www.buddysitacare.com; Caminho das Praias; dm/d with fan R$35/90) Friendly, economical and centrally located, Buddys is run by a pair of jovial Irish

BAHIA

guys who fire up the barbecue for guests, offer cold beer on arrival and are happy to help arrange surf lessons. See Brazil Trip Tour (p473) for information on their tours between Salvador and Rio.

Itacaré Hostel (☎ 3251 3037; www.itacarehostel.com .br; Rua Lodônia Almeida 120; dm/d from R$40/120; ▢ ▣) In the heart of the action, this HI hostel has small, tidy rooms fronted by hammocks and a narrow courtyard with a pool.

Albergue O Pharol (☎ 3251 2527; www.albergueopha rol.com.br; Praça Santos Dumont 7; dm/d with fan R$42/110, d with air-con from R$140, ste R$250; ▣ ▢) A favorite among backpackers, this low-key hostel has tidy rooms, some with private verandas. There's a shared kitchen, a guest laundry area, and a lovely two-suite apartment with a full kitchen upstairs that's big enough for a family. No breakfast.

Pousada Estrela (☎ 3251 2006; www.pousadaestrela .com.br; Rua Pedro Longo 34; s R$50-70, d R$60-100; ▣) One of Itacaré's better deals, Estrela has a range of fine rooms, some quite spacious with big windows. There are hammocks and a garden in back.

Casa Zazá (☎ 3251 3022; www.casazaza.com; Condomínio Conchas do Mar; s/d R$100/130; ▣ ▢) Run by a welcoming Dutch owner, Casa Zazá has a warm, homelike feel with nicely furnished rooms, some with small balconies. There's a tree-shaded backyard and plenty of relaxing lounge space.

Pousada Maresia (☎ 3251 2338; www.maresiapou sada.com.br; Caminho das Praias; d R$150-160; ▣) Simple but nicely painted rooms and a lush garden courtyard are part of the charm of this fairly priced guesthouse that's focused on sustainable tourism and community involvement.

Pousada Nainas (☎ 3251 2683; www.nainas.com .br; Praia da Concha; d from R$160; ▣) Set around a pretty garden, Pousada Nainas has uniquely designed rooms with romantic canopied beds and vibrantly colored decor. All have private verandas strung with hammocks for soaking up the tropical vibe.

our pick **Pousada Ilha Verde** (☎ 3251 2056; www .ilhaverde.com.br; Rua Ataíde Setúbal 234; s/d from R$180/220; ▣ ▢) In a lush setting, Ilha Verde has seven handsome, uniquely decorated rooms and one family bungalow. There's a Jacuzzi, a pool and abundant outdoor lounge space for luxuriating in the greenery.

Burundanga (☎ 3251 2543; www.burundanga.com .br; Condomínio Conchas do Mar; d from R$265; ▣ ▢) This boutique hotel has beautifully furnished rooms, hung with local artwork and uniquely decorated with tropical woods and textures. Common to all rooms are private wooden decks overlooking the greenery.

Sage Point (☎ 3251 2030; www.pousadasagepoint .com.br; d with fan from R$329) Perched on a hill overlooking Praia Tiririca are beautiful wooden chalets with ocean views. With rustic-chic decor and sweeping verandas, the place looks straight out of the pages of a magazine – worthy of a splurge.

Eating & Drinking

A browse up and down Itacaré's main strip, Rua Lodônia Almeida (which turns into Rua Pedro Longo), is the best way to discover what's on offer.

Gelato Gula (☎ 3251 3483; Rua Pedro Longo 388; scoops R$6; ☙ noon-10pm) This popular ice-cream shop serves creamy rich *sorvete* (ice cream) made with Brazilian fruits.

Habitat Café (☎ 3251 2480; Praia da Concha; sandwiches R$10-15; ☙ 4-11pm) A casual grassy spot one block from the beach, this outdoor café serves addictive sandwiches (including burgers and soy burgers), juices and salads.

Meio Natural (☎ 3251 3422; Rua Pedro Longo 378; mains R$12-20) Specializing in garden salads and healthy sandwiches, this easygoing eatery has a few outdoor tables and reasonable prices. It uses some organic produce and all-natural ingredients.

Restaurante Mar e Mel (☎ 3251 2358; www.maremel .com.br; Praia da Concha; mains R$18-35; ☙ 7pm-midnight) This is the place to hear (and dance to) live *forró*. There's a spacious wooden deck in front and abundant seafood and drink choices.

Boca do Forno (☎ 3251 2174; Rua Lodônia Almeida 108; pizzas R$18-35; ☙ dinner) This place serves pizzas everyone raves about in a beautiful flower-bedecked outdoor setting. Live music some nights.

our pick **Casarão Amarelo** (☎ 3251 3133; Av Castro Alves; mains R$22-38; ☙ dinner) A short walk away from Pituba on Praia da Coroa, this old-fashioned yellow house welcomes a sophisticated clientele with fine seafood pastas and good wine. Linger over your meal in the small courtyard or soak up the historic atmosphere in the beautifully restored dining room.

Estrela do Mar (☎ 3251 2230; www.aldeiadomar.com; Praia da Concha; mains R$25-42) Overlooking Concha beach, the elegant Estrela do Mar serves expertly prepared seafood, as well as pastas, salads and crepes. It has huge windows for taking in the sea and picturesque outdoor seating.

Mistura Fina (☎ 3251 2289; Rua Pedro Longo 265; mains for 2 R$50-60; ☻ dinner) Serves a wide variety of appealing dishes, from fish *moqueca* and sea-food risottos to *yakisoba* and pizza.

Canoa Bar e Restaurante (☎ 3251 2721; www.canoaitacare.com; Av Castro Alves 284) This mellow new waterfront bar wears many hats: there's a brief and budget-friendly menu offering fresh shrimp, pastas and chocolate cake, there's a lively bar with a caipirinha happy hour (8pm to 10pm Tuesday to Friday), and there are free film screenings every Monday and Wednesday at 8pm.

Getting There & Around

Itacaré's **bus station** (☎ 3288 2019) is just out of the center, but it's a bit of a hike from many of the pousadas. To get to Itacaré, you will most likely need to connect through Itabuna or Ilhéus. **Rota** (☎ 3251 2181) has frequent buses to Ilhéus (R$10.50, 1½ hours, from 5:15am to 7:30pm) and Itabuna (R$13.50, 2½ hours, from 6am to 7:30pm). Several daily buses go to Porto Seguro (R$48 to R$55, eight hours).

A ferry carries cars and passengers across the river to the Peninsula de Maraú (R$10). Several agencies in town hire cars.

ILHÉUS

☎ 0xx73 / pop 220,000

Bright, early-20th-century architecture and oddly angled streets lend a vibrant and rather playful air to slightly rough-around-the-edges Ilhéus. The town's fame comes from its history as a prosperous cocoa port, as well as being the hometown of Jorge Amado (Brazil's best-known novelist). He used it as the setting for one of his best novels, *Gabriela, Cravo e Canela* ('Gabriela, Clove and Cinnamon'). When you combine all this with Ilhéus' attractive city geography, its affable people and the nearby Atlantic rain-forest reserves, you can argue it's worth a quick stopover.

History

Ilhéus was a sleepy place until cacao was introduced into the region from Belém in 1881. With the sugar plantations in the doldrums, impoverished agricultural workers and freed or escaped slaves flocked from all over the Northeast to the hills surrounding Ilhéus to participate in the new boom: cacao, known as the *ouro branco* (white gold) of Brazil.

Sudden, lawless and violent, the scramble to plant cacao displayed all the characteristics of a gold rush. When the dust settled, the land and power belonged to a few ruthless *coroneis* (so-called 'colonels') and their hired guns. The landless were left to work, and usually live, on the *fazendas*, where they were subjected to a harsh and paternalistic labor system. This history is graphically told by Amado, who grew up on a cacao plantation, in his book *Terras do Sem Fim* (published in English as *The Violent Land*).

In the early 1990s, the *vassoura de bruxa* (witch's broom) disease left cacao trees shriveled and unable to bear fruit, hurting the area's economy dramatically. Though the disease persists to this day, you can still see cacao *fazendas* and rural workers like those Amado described throughout the lush, tropical hills.

Orientation

The city center is located on a beach-lined point that reaches into the mouth of the Rio Cachoeira, and is sandwiched between two hills. On the southern side of the S-curving river mouth is the modern neighborhood of Pontal – catch a taxi over the bridge to reach it.

Information

There are ATMs next to the cathedral.
Banco do Brasil (Rua Marquês de Paranaguá 112)
Post office (Rua Marquês de Paranaguá)
Reality Internet (Rua Dom Eduardo; per hr R$5) Speedy internet access.
Tourist information (☎ 3634 1977; www.ilheusdabahia.com.br; Praça Dom Eduardo)

Sights & Activities

The best thing to do in Ilhéus is explore the old streets. The center has several old, gargoyled buildings such as the **Prefeitura** (Praça Seabra) and pedestrian-only thoroughfares (Rua Marquês de Paranaguá and Rua Oliveira) where you can wander or stop for a snack.

The **Casa de Jorge Amado** (Rua Jorge Amado 21; www.jorgeamado.org.br; admission R$2; ☻ 9am-noon & 2-6pm Mon-Fri, 9am-1pm Sat, 3-5pm Sun), where the great writer lived with his parents while working on his first novel, has been restored and turned into a lovely and informative museum honoring Amado's life. Not many writers can boast this sort of recognition while still alive, but he became a national treasure well before his death in 2001. While many of Amado's novels are set in the region, the book most closely associated with his hometown is *Gabriela,*

BAHIA

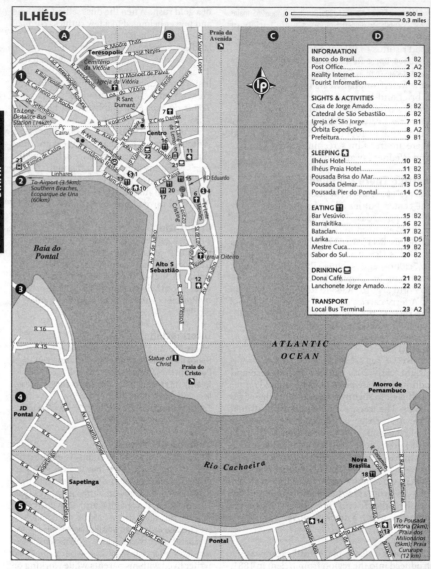

ILHÉUS

INFORMATION	
Banco do Brasil	1 B2
Post Office	2 A2
Reality Internet	3 B2
Tourist Information	4 B2

SIGHTS & ACTIVITIES	
Casa de Jorge Amado	5 B2
Catedral de São Sebastião	6 B2
Igreja de São Jorge	7 B1
Órbita Expedições	8 A2
Prefeitura	9 B1

SLEEPING	
Ilhéus Hotel	10 B2
Ilhéus Praia Hotel	11 B2
Pousada Brisa do Mar	12 B3
Pousada Delmar	13 D5
Pousada Pier do Pontal	14 C5

EATING	
Bar Vesúvio	15 B2
Barrakitika	16 B2
Bataclan	17 B2
Larika	18 D5
Mestre Cuca	19 B2
Sabor do Sul	20 B2

DRINKING	
Dona Café	21 B2
Lanchonete Jorge Amado	22 B2

TRANSPORT	
Local Bus Terminal	23 A2

Cravo e Canela. For more on Amado, see the boxed text, p477.

The **Catedral de São Sebastião** (Praça Dom Eduardo) is the city's icon – construction began in 1931 – and is a unique, eclectic mix of architectural styles. For an unforgettable view of the fairy-tale-like spires, walk out onto the beach at sunset and look back at the cathedral silhouet-ted against the clouds. The **Igreja de São Jorge** (Praça Rui Barbosa; admission by donation; ☒ Tue-Sun) is the city's oldest church, dating from 1534, and houses a small sacred-art museum.

BEACHES

City beaches aren't the cleanest (though that doesn't stop local surfers from taking to the waves). Your best bet is to head south, but even then you'll find that the area's beaches are best for a *futebol* game (broad and flat), and it takes kilometers for the water to lose the muddy color of the river outflow. **Praia dos Milionários** (7km) has some *barracas* and is popular with locals, as is the prettier **Praia Cururupe** (12km), where a small river curves into the sea.

Tours

Trips to a tree-sloth recuperation center, a chocolate factory and Primavera Fazenda, where you'll be taken through the process of cacao production, can all be arranged through local travel agencies. Tours are also given of Lagoa Encantada, a state-protected area of Atlantic rain forest with waterfalls and wildlife; Rio do Engenho, an estate with Bahia's first sugarcane mill; and the Capela de Santana (1537), Brazil's third-oldest church. For information on the Ecoparque de Una tour, see the boxed text, p479.

Órbita Expedições (☎ 3634 7700; www.orbitaex pedicoes.com.br; Rua Marquês de Paranaguá 270) is an adventure outfit that offers a wide range of tours, including rafting, canoeing, hiking and cycling trips.

Festivals & Events

As any Amado fan would guess, Ilhéus has highly spirited festivals. The best are the **Gincana da Pesca** in early January, **Festa de São Sebastião** (much samba and capoeira) from January 11 to 20, **Festa de São Jorge** (featuring Candomblé) on April 23 and **Festa das Águas** (Candomblé) in December. **Carnaval** has a full complement of *trios elétricos*.

Sleeping

Ilhéus' best hotels are located south of the city along the road to Olivença, making them convenient only for those traveling by car. Accommodations in the center are generally a bit run down, while Pontal has more modern options.

Pousada Brisa do Mar (☎ 3231 2644; Av 2 de Julho 138, Alto São Sebastião; s/d R$50/60; 🗷) This pleasant modern pousada really does have a sea breeze *(brisa do mar)* and a privileged view over the river. The walk to the center at night, though short, is dark and desolate. Take a taxi.

Pousada Delmar (☎ 3632 8435; mamorim@cepec.gov .br; Rua Castro Alves 322, Pontal; d from R$70; 🗷 🛜) This is a popular modern hotel, with an open-air breakfast patio. It's nicely set on the Pontal.

Ilhéus Hotel (☎ 3634 4242; www.ilheushotel.com.br; Rua Eustáquio Bastos 144, Centro; s/d from R$70/80; 🗷) This multistoried 1930s hotel has a fading grandeur and a vintage elevator that was hand-cranked until electrified in 1950. The place is quiet now; rooms are fairly comfortable and some have views over the bay.

Ilhéus Praia Hotel (☎ 2101 2533; www.ilheuspraia .com.br; Praça Dom Eduardo, Centro; s/d with fan R$100/130, with air-con R$180/220; 🗷 🛜 🖳) This high-rise

---

BAHIA'S FAVORITE SON

Nobody is more responsible for bringing Bahian culture to the rest of the world than Jorge Amado, Brazil's most famous romanticist author. Amado's tales have been translated into 49 languages and read the world over.

Born in 1912, Jorge spent his youth in Ilhéus, the scene of many of his later novels. After secondary studies in Salvador, Amado studied law in Rio, but instead of going into practice he decided to become a writer. He surprised critics and the public by publishing his first novel, *O País do Carnaval*, when he was only 19 years old.

An avowed communist, Amado participated in the rebel literary movement of the time, launching two romances set in the cacao zone around Ilhéus: *Cacau* and *Suor*. The first novel was banned by the fascist-leaning Vargas government, which only increased Amado's popularity. Sent to prison several times for his beliefs, Amado was elected a federal deputy for the Brazilian communist party (PCB) in 1945, but he lost his seat after a disagreement with the party several years later. He left Brazil and lived for more than five years in Europe and Asia, finally breaking ties with the communist party after the crimes of Stalin were revealed to the world.

With *Gabriela, Cravo e Canela* ('Gabriela, Clove and Cinnamon'), published in 1958, he entered a new writing phase, marked by a picturesque style that intimately described the colorful escapades of his Bahian heroes and heroines.

Amado died in Salvador in August 2001, just short of his 89th birthday.

hotel is fraying around the edges, but service is good and many rooms have fine views of the cathedral across the plaza.

Pousada Pier do Pontal (☎ 3221 4000; www.pierdopontal.com.br; Av Lomanto Jr 1650, Pontal; d from R$200; ☒ ☒) In a peaceful location across the river, this guesthouse has colorfully decorated rooms, some with sea-fronting verandas, and a Japanese restaurant.

Pousada Vitória (☎ 3632 4997; www.pousadavitoria.com.br; Sítio São Paulo, Praia do Sul; d from R$215; ☒) Overlooking the pretty Praia do Sul, this attractive guesthouse resembles a Swiss chalet. Rooms are comfortably furnished, the best with verandas overlooking the sea.

Eating & Drinking

For inexpensive snacks, sandwiches and cold drinks during daylight hours, try the stands along the pedestrian streets downtown. At night, visit the vendors selling tapioca and other treats across from the cathedral on the waterfront.

Barrakítika (☎ 3231 8300; Praça Antônio Muniz 39; per kg R$13) This casual hangout has outdoor tables and an inexpensive lunch buffet. There's live music on weekend evenings.

Sabor do Sul (☎ 3231 3281; Rua Colonel Paiva 53; mains R$15-35; ☽ 6-11pm Tue-Sun) Dozens of different varieties of calzone and pizza, including one topped with fresh shrimp, are on offer at this downtown pizzeria that's popular with locals.

Mestre Cuca (☎ 3634 1092; 2nd fl, Rua Eustáquio Bastos 126; per kg R$19; ☽ lunch) This popular spot spreads an excellent self-service lunch, and the airy dining room has partial sea views.

our pick **Bataclan** (☎ 3634 0088; Av 2 de Julho; mains R$20-35; ☽ dinner) Once a cabaret frequented by cocoa tycoons (and one of the settings for Amado's *Gabriela*) the Bataclan was restored to its original brilliance in 2004. Now the colonial building serves as a restaurant, lounge and cultural center staging frequent concerts and art exhibitions. Stop by at night for Bahian cuisine or cocktails.

our pick **Bar Vesúvio** (☎ 3634 2164; Praça Dom Eduardo; mains R$21-35) This landmark bar and restaurant attracts both Amado fans (two of his protagonists met here) and those interested in *moquecas* and cold beer served at the outdoor tables facing the cathedral, which is beautifully illuminated at night.

In Pontal, major traffic turns south off the road along the bay, creating a quiet area near the end of the point with great views back

to the center. Nearby are a few restaurants, including **Larika** (Av Getúlio Vargas; sandwiches R$7; ☽ 6pm-1am), a stand serving sandwiches and fresh fruit juices at bayside tables.

There are several cute and casual cafés in Ilhéus; try **Dona Café** (Praça Dom Eduardo), the pretty coffee stand on the main square across from the cathedral, or have a morning coffee on the tiny patio of the literary-themed **Lanchonete Jorge Amado** (Praça Seabra), just across from the Prefeitura.

Getting There & Away

AIR
TAM (☎ 3234 5259; airport) and **Gol** (☎ 0800 280 0465) can fly or connect you to anywhere in Brazil from Ilhéus' **Aeroporto Jorge Amado** (code IOS; ☎ 3231 7629).

BUS
The **long-distance bus station** (☎ 3634 4121) is about 15km from the center. Buses go to Valença (R$31, five hours, two daily), Porto Seguro (R$42, six hours, four daily) and Vitória (R$108 to R$155, 13 hours, two daily) among other destinations.

Buses to Salvador (R$75 to R$118, seven hours, three daily) make a long sweep around the Baía de Todos os Santos, recommended if you are stopping in the *recôncavo* on the way. Otherwise, catch a bus to Bom Despacho on the Ilha de Itaparica, and then a ferry into Salvador. For ferry information, see p458.

More frequent connections can be made in Itabuna, located 30km inland. Local buses to Itabuna leave from the local bus terminal in the town center and also from outside the long-distance bus station (R$5, 40 minutes) every 15 minutes from 5:30am to midnight.

Getting Around

The airport is in Pontal, 3.5km from the center. Taxis cost R$12.

From the center, Teotónio Vilela, Circular and Santo Brinto buses pass the bus station. Taxis cost R$18 to R$25.

OLIVENÇA
☎ 0xx73

Olivença is a small, charming beach town 16km south of Ilhéus. Sights include a spa, where the baths are believed to have healing powers, and a nearby indigenous village. The grassy town shore has beautiful cove beaches with rock formations and flat sand, powerful waves

ECOPARQUE DE UNA

The **Ecoparque de Una** (☎ 3633 1121; www.ecoparque.org.br, in Portuguese; admission R$15; ⏰ 8am-5pm Tue-Sun) is a lush Atlantic rain-forest reserve 60km south of Ilhéus. Here, guides lead visitors on a 2km trail, including four suspended tree-canopy walkways. The tour lasts two hours and ends with a cool pond dip.

Taking refuge in the park are rare species such as the golden-headed lion tamarin (*Leontopithecus chrysomelas*). These unusual monkeys have the look and proud gaze of miniature lions: a blazing yellow, orange and brown striped coat, a golden mane and a long, scruffy tail. If you're lucky you'll also see *tatus* (armadillos), *pacas* (agoutis), capybaras and *veados* (deer), all native to the area.

Visits can be arranged through a travel agency or you can make a direct appointment – but you'll need to call at least one day in advance. If you go on your own, the bus to Canavieiras drops you at the park gate, where a park jeep picks you up.

and a restaurant or two. Deserted beaches with calmer water stretch south of Olivença.

There are great waves just north of town at **Batuba** and **Backdoor**, Brazil's third-best surf break. The multilingual Marcio of **Pokoloco Surf Shop** (☎ 3269 1493) rents long and short boards (per day R$20) and gives surf lessons (from R$100).

The artfully decorated **Pousada Fazenda Tororomba Hostel** (☎ 8125 0293; www.fazendatororomba.com.br, in Portuguese; Rua Eduardo Magalhães; dm/s/d with fan from R$37/50/80, d chalet from R$160; 🖳) is a HI option spread over a large grassy property with big trees and a pond. A house with a living room and full kitchen has several collective rooms. There are also comfortably set doubles and rustic chalets, some with outdoor spa baths. **Camping Estância das Fontes** (☎ 3269 1480; per person R$10), 15km south of Ilhéus, is close to the beach and has hot showers.

City buses leave every 30 minutes from the Ilhéus bus station (passing the city bus terminal) for Olivença (30 minutes) from 6am to 11pm. The bus travels close to the beaches, so you can hop off when you see one you like. Private transfer can also be arranged through Ilhéus travel agencies (around R$60 for up to four people).

PORTO SEGURO

☎ 0xx73 / pop 120,000

The state's second-most-visited destination (if not the second most-beautiful – not by a long shot), Porto Seguro swarms with Brazilian and Argentinian package tourists who come from all across the country for partying and beach action. Not surprisingly, there's well-developed infrastructure here, with dozens of hotels and colorful buildings (none over two stories) that lean toward a colonial aesthetic.

This is, after all, the region where Portuguese sailors first landed in the New World, and you can see relics from those early settlement days. Aside from history, Porto Seguro is really only for inveterate nightlife seekers: during the day, the streets are quiet and things look rundown, like the whole city is experiencing a hangover the morning after the party. Most travelers linger in town only long enough to change money and catch the ferry toward Arraial d'Ajuda. If you're staying in mellow Arraial, you can always pop back over to Porto Seguro on the ferry in the evening to enjoy the night-time action and a few caipirinhas.

History

Pedro Cabral's landing 16km north of Porto Seguro (Safe Port) at Coroa Vermelha is officially considered the first Portuguese landfall in Brazil. The sailors didn't stay long, just long enough to stock up on supplies. Three years later Gonçalvo Coelho's expedition arrived and planted a marker in what is now Porto Seguro's Cidade Histórica (Historic City). Jesuits on the same expedition built a church, now in ruins, in Outeiro da Glória. In 1526, a naval outpost, convent and chapel (Igreja NS da Misericórdia) were built in the present-day Cidade Histórica.

The Tupininquin, not the Pataxó, were the indigenous tribe around the site of Porto Seguro when the Portuguese landed. They were rapidly conquered and enslaved by the colonists, but the Aimoré, Pataxó, Cataxó and other inland tribes resisted Portuguese colonization and constantly threatened Porto Seguro. Military outposts were built along the coast in Belmonte, Vila Viçosa, Prado and Alcobaça to defend against both European attacks by sea and *indio* attacks by land.

BAHIA

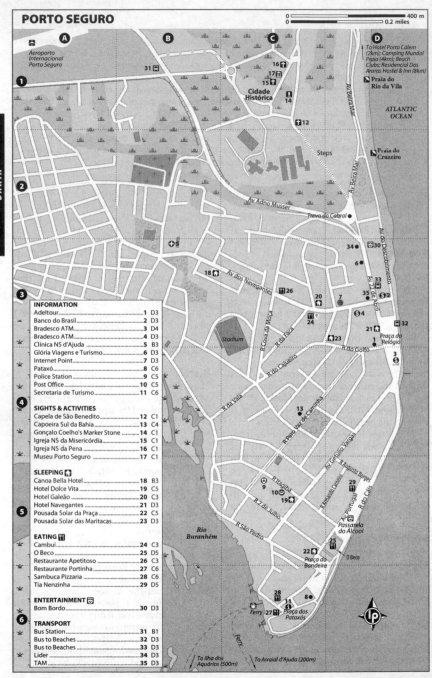

PORTO SEGURO

INFORMATION	
Adeltour	**1** D3
Banco do Brasil	**2** D3
Bradesco ATM	**3** D4
Bradesco ATM	**4** D3
Clínica NS d'Ajuda	**5** B3
Glória Viagens e Turismo	**6** D3
Internet Point	**7** D3
Pataxó	**8** C6
Police Station	**9** C5
Post Office	**10** C5
Secretaria de Turismo	**11** C6

SIGHTS & ACTIVITIES	
Capela de São Benedito	**12** C1
Capoeira Sul da Bahia	**13** C4
Gonçalo Coelho's Marker Stone	**14** C1
Igreja NS da Misericórdia	**15** C1
Igreja NS da Pena	**16** C1
Museu Porto Seguro	**17** C1

SLEEPING	
Canoa Bella Hotel	**18** B3
Hotel Dolce Vita	**19** C5
Hotel Galeão	**20** C3
Hotel Navegantes	**21** D3
Pousada Solar da Praça	**22** C5
Pousada Solar das Maritacas	**23** D3

EATING	
Cambuí	**24** C3
O Beco	**25** D5
Restaurante Apetitoso	**26** C3
Restaurante Portinha	**27** C6
Sambuca Pizzaria	**28** C6
Tia Nenzinha	**29** D5

ENTERTAINMENT	
Bom Bordo	**30** D3

TRANSPORT	
Bus Station	**31** B1
Bus to Beaches	**32** D3
Bus to Beaches	**33** D3
Lider	**34** D3
TAM	**35** D3

The *índios* managed to take Porto Seguro twice and, according to colonial documents, reduced Porto Seguro to rubble in 1612 (thus undermining the city's claims to have 16th-century buildings).

Information

Adeltour (☎ 3288 1888; www.adeltour.com.br, in Portuguese; Shopping Avenida, Av 22 de Abril 100) For national and international air travel. Changes cash and traveler's checks. Also in the airport.

Banco do Brasil (Av 22 de Abril)

Bradesco ATM (Praça do Relógio) Also on Av dos Navegantes.

Clínica NS d'Ajuda (☎ 3288 1307; Av dos Navegantes 640) Medical service.

Internet Point (☎ 3268 4191; Av dos Navegantes 90; per hr R$5) Internet access; also changes US dollars and euros.

Pataxó (☎ 3288 1256; www.pataxoturismo.com.br; Praça dos Pataxós; ☾ 9am-6pm Mon-Sat) This tourism outfit and handicrafts shop provides information.

Police station (Rua Itagibá s/n)

Post office (Rua Itagibá 85)

Secretaria de Turismo (☎ 3288 3708; www.portose gurotur.com.br, in Portuguese; Av Portugal 350)

Dangers & Annoyances

It's best to take a taxi or the bus on Av Beira Mar at night as muggings are all too common.

Sights & Activities

BEACHES

North of town is one long bay dotted with *barracas* and clubs with invisible divisions creating **Praia Curuípe** (3km), **Praia Itacimirim** (4km), **Praia Mundaí** (6km) and **Praia de Taperapua** (7km). The sands are white and fluffy, backed by green vegetation and lapped by a tranquil sea. **Tôa Tôa** (Praia de Taperapuã), **Axé Moi** (Praia Mundaí) and **Barramares** (Praia de Taperapuã) are the biggest beach clubs and all have MCs and dancers leading crowds through popular dances. The best advice is to get off the bus at Tôa Tôa and walk north until you find your spot.

CIDADE HISTÓRICA

Motivation is required to climb the stairs to the Cidade Histórica. Rewards include a sweeping view, colorful old buildings and free and humorous capoeira demonstrations given on the roof behind the churches (hourly in high season). Housed in the former Câmara Municipal (Town Council), the **Museu Porto Seguro** (☎ 3288 5182; admission R$3; ☾ 9am-5pm) contains exhibits on Brazil's early settlement, with rooms dedicated to exploration and colonial life; even more interesting are the museum's exhibits on indigenous life, including films covering important rites and celebrations.

Opposite the museum is **Gonçalo Coelho's marker stone**, now encased in glass and ringed with a fence. Other reminders of the past are the **Igreja NS da Misericórdia** (1526), which houses the **Museu de Arte Sacra** (admission by donation), with a collection of chalices, crucifixes and other religious pieces. Other old stone churches to peer inside include the **Igreja NS da Pena** (1772) and the **Capela de São Benedito**, dating from the 16th century.

Warning: the area is beautifully illuminated at night, and definitely worth a look, but the steps are not safe after dark. Take a bus or taxi.

Courses

The friendly **Capoeira Sul da Bahia** (☎ 3268 2247; www.capoeirasuldabahia.com.br; Rua Benedito Claudio 98; per class R$12) welcomes visitors to watch or take a class at its academy.

Tours

Local travel agencies offer schooner tours to Praia do Espelho (R$50) as well as trips to Trancoso (R$60), Caraíva (R$100) and the Parque Nacional de Monte Pascoal (R$50). Trips are also offered to Recife de Fora and Coroa Alta (R$50) offshore reefs, which are fantastic locales for snorkeling with a wide variety of bright tropical fish. Unfortunately, since visitors are encouraged to walk over coral reefs in order to enter internal pools, we don't officially recommend it. Travel agencies are scattered along Av 22 de Abril – excursion prices often vary from those listed here, so ask around before booking a trip.

Glória Viagens e Turismo (☎ 3288 4230; www.glo riaviagenseturismo.com.br; Av 22 de Abril 288) offers a range of tours.

Festivals & Events

Porto Seguro's **Carnaval** is Bahia's most famous after Salvador's. It is relatively small and safe, consisting of a few *trios elétricos* cruising the main drag blasting *axé* music, and lasts until the Saturday after Ash Wednesday, an additional four days longer than in other places.

On April 19 to 22 the discovery of Brazil is commemorated with an outdoor mass and *indio* celebrations on Av do Descobrimento.

This seems a rather baffling celebration since indigenous groups lived here before the 'discoverers' and fared poorly after their arrival. The **Festa de São Benedito** is celebrated in the Cidade Histórica on December 25 to 27. Children blacken their faces and perform African dances, such as *congo da alma*, *ole* or *lalá*, to the percussion of drums, *cuica* and *xeque-xeque* (gourd-like instruments).

Sleeping

Porto Seguro overflows with hotels but receives a surprisingly high number of visitors on package tours, meaning decent low-cost rooms are difficult to find during high season. Alternatively, you could catch the ferry to Arraial d'Ajuda and stay in a nicer hotel for the same price – transportation between the two towns is quick and easy, but Arraial's accommodations options are superior.

Camping Mundaí Praia (☎ 3679 2287; www.camp ingmundai.com.br, in Portuguese; per person from R$15; 🍴) Opposite the beach, 4km north of town, this place has shaded campsites and abundant facilities; it's packed in summer.

OUR PICK **Residencial das Araras Hostel & Inn** (☎ 3679 1054; Village 1, Taperapuan; dm R$60; 🍴 🛜 🍴) This friendly hostel, north of the center near a pleasant stretch of sand, offers dorm-style accommodations and common areas including a swimming pool, a grassy yard with hammocks, and a bar and barbecue. A taxi here costs about R$30 (buses go, too); ask your taxi driver to call the hostel for directions if necessary.

Pousada Solar da Praça (☎ 3288 2585; www.pousada solardapraca.com, in Portuguese; Rua Assis Chateaubriand 75; s/d from R$60/95; 🍴) This clean, friendly guesthouse has a range of small tidy rooms; the best have balconies with partial sea views. Noisy at night.

Hotel Galeão (☎ 3288 2122; www.galeaohotel.com .br, in Portuguese; Av dos Navegantes 300; s/d from R$65/100; 🍴 🍴) This tidy guesthouse has trim, inexpensive rooms with tiny balconies.

Hotel Dolce Vita (☎ 3288 1058; Rua Itagibá 67; s/d from R$70/90; 🍴 🍴) A peaceful option several blocks from all the action, Dolce Vita – like many area hotels – has aging rooms surrounding a pool.

Canoa Bella Hotel (☎ 3288 1510; www.canoabella .com.br, in Portuguese; Av dos Navegantes 555; d/tr from R$110/145; 🍴 🍴) There's a bit of charm to the Canoa Bella, with exposed-beam ceilings, mosaics and a cascade of bougainvillea surrounding the pool.

Pousada Solar das Maritacas (☎ 3288 2082; Rua dos Periquitos 50; d from R$120; 🍴 🍴) Maritacas has homey touches in its clean, pleasant rooms, with tall windows that face a pretty garden of flowering vines.

Hotel Navegantes (☎ 3288 2390; www.portonet.com .br/navegantes, in Portuguese; Av 22 de Abril 212; d from R$150; 🍴 🛜) Judging by its location in the middle of the action, you'd think this midrange hotel would be loud and chaotic, but two levels of tranquil guest rooms are located deep inside the building down a leafy walkway.

Hotel Porto Cálem (☎ 3268 8400; www.portocalem .com.br, in Portuguese; s/d from R$210/220, d with ocean view R$250; 🍴 🍴) Located 2km north of town, the modern Cálem has spacious rooms looking out towards the ocean or over the large pool.

Eating

Though Porto is not known for its restaurants, it can't be said that it lacks selection. Most restaurants are found along the Passarela do Álcool. **Cambuí** (Av dos Navegantes 222; 🕙 8am-10pm Mon-Sat, 8am-1pm Sun) is large, convenient supermarket.

Restaurante Apetitoso (☎ 3288 1537; Av dos Navegantes 404; per kg R$18) This self-service restaurant has a good selection and is always packed.

OUR PICK **Restaurante Portinha** (☎ 3288 2743; www.portinha.com.br; Rua Saldanha Marinho 32; per kg R$20) One of the classiest per-kilo eateries around, Portinha puts out a mouthwatering buffet of gourmet dishes, from pasta with sun-dried tomatoes and basil to fresh fish fillets. Both the leafy patio tables and the stylish rustic interior offer plenty of atmosphere.

Tia Nenzinha (☎ 3288 1846; Passarela do Álcool 170; mains for 2 R$34-60) A classic for over 30 years, Tia Nenzinha serves a fine assortment of Bahian dishes.

O Beco (cnr Beco & Rua do Cáis; 🕙 dinner Tue-Sun) This quaint little open-air galleria, just around the corner from the Passarela do Álcool, is lined with small bistros and cafés where you'll find everything from sushi to crepes. The elegant Portuguese bakery here, A Torre, is particularly delightful.

Sambuca Pizzaria (☎ 3288 2366; Praça dos Pataxós 216; mains R$22-28; 🕙 dinner) Porto's best pizza is served in a nicely decorated dining room removed from Passarela do Álcool's madness.

Entertainment

At night, the Passarela do Álcool (Alcohol Walkway) has craft stalls and street performers, with live music spilling onto the plazas. Look for fresh-fruit cocktail stands making *capeta* (guaraná, cocoa powder, cinnamon, sweetened condensed milk and vodka) – just the thing to bring a bang to the evening.

Young partiers selling club and party tickets (R$20 to R$40) around the Passarela will let you know what's happening that night. The major beach clubs all put on weekly nighttime *luaus* (parties); the one at **Barramares** (☎ 3679 2980; www.barramares.com.br, in Portuguese; Av Beira Mar Km 6, Praia de Taperapuã) is the most stunning. It's about 6km north of town, and several other good nightspots are on the way, including **Tôa Tôa** (☎ 3679 1555; www.portaltoatoa.com.br, in Portuguese; Av Beira Mar km 5, Praia de Taperapuã).

Across the river, **Ilha dos Aquários** (☎ 3268 2828; www.ilhadosaquarios.com.br, in Portuguese; Ilha Pacuío) is traditionally a good party, probably because of the novelty of the aquariums and its river-island setting (reachable by boats from the port on party nights).

Up the coast, Transilvânia and Alcatraz are clubs decorated like their namesakes. Each of these enormous venues has separate areas for *axé*, *forró*, samba or MPB and electronic music. If the party is up the coast, there are usually round-trip courtesy buses leaving from the *trevo do Cabral* (traffic circle at the entrance of town). For further information about these *luaus* and clubs, call **Porto Night** (☎ 3268 2828; www.portonight.com.br, in Portuguese).

In town, **Bom Bordo** (☎ 3288 4113; www.bom bordobar.com.br, in Portuguese; Av 22 de Abril 151) can be fun when it fills up with people swinging to *axé* and *forró*.

Getting There & Away

AIR
Gol (☎ 3268 4460; airport), **Avianca** (☎ 4004 4040; airport) and **TAM** (☎ 3288 3399; Av 22 de Abril 245) can connect you anywhere in Brazil from **Aeroporto Internacional Porto Seguro** (code BPS; ☎ 3288 1880), about 2km northwest of town. There are no buses to the airport. Taxis run R$15 to R$20.

BUS
The turnoff for Porto Seguro from Hwy BR-101 is at Eunápolis. The **bus station** (☎ 3288 1914) is 1.5km outside town on the road to Eunápolis. Additional buses run during high season.

São Geraldo (☎ 3288 1198) goes to São Paulo (R$195 to R$258, 26 hours, two daily), Rio (R$195 to R$210, 19 hours, one daily) and

Belo Horizonte (R$134 to R$176, 18 hours, two daily), and its tickets can be purchased through travel agencies in the center. **Águia Branca** (☎ 3288 1039) goes to Vitória (R$82 to R$118, 10 hours, two daily), Valença (R$70, nine hours, one daily), Bom Despacho (R$85, 12 hours, one daily) and Salvador (R$136, 11 hours, one daily).

Rota Sul (☎ 3288 3065) goes to Ilhéus (R$42, six hours, four daily and shares the Itabuna (R$35, five hours, eight daily) route with Águia Branca. **Brasileiro** (☎ 3288 3065) goes to Itamaraju (R$23, three hours, six daily) for access to Corumbau, and Teixeira de Freitas (R$30, five hours, six daily) for access to Caravelas.

For more frequent connections, three companies run buses to Eunápolis (R$10, one hour, every 30 minutes from 5:30am to 10pm).

Getting Around

From Porto Seguro, take the Riacho Doce, Alto do Mundaí, Campinho–Barramares or Cabrália buses to the beach. On the return trip, hop off at the traffic circle if your bus is heading up to the bus station. Taxis and mototaxis are widely available throughout the city. For car and buggy rental, try **Lider** (☎ 3288 1505; www.alugueldecarrosportoseguro.com; Av 22 de Abril 397; per day from R$100), which also has a branch at the airport.

NORTH OF PORTO SEGURO

The beaches maintain the same look from Porto Seguro north: long, gently curving bays of powdery sands and gentle seas backed by flowering vines. A good paved road runs along the coast, so it is much more developed than the southern coast.

Coroa Vermelha, a village 13km north of Porto Seguro, has a beach lined with *barracas* and reefs, and several pousadas. A walkway bordered by Pataxó craft stands selling bow-and-arrow packs and smooth wooden bowls leads to a monument to the discovery of Brazil. Just off the walkway is the **Museu do Índio** (admission R$1; ☖ 8:30am-5pm), displaying color photos and traditional objects.

Much more attractive, but still not worth staying overnight in, is **Santa Cruz Cabrália**, 23km north of Porto Seguro. Climb up the bluff to visit the **Igreja NS da Imaculada Conceição**, a small church built by Jesuits in 1630, and for a rewarding view over terra-cotta roofs, colorful lobster boats and the Rio João de Tiba. Departing with the morning low tide (usually around 9am to 10am), schooners cruise upriver and then out to **Coroa Alta coral platform** (R$20). Santa Cruz Cabrália buses (R$10, 40 minutes, hourly from 6am to 7pm) leave from Porto Seguro's bus station and pass through the center.

To continue north, a ferry (pedestrian/car R$2/10, every 30 minutes from 6am to 8pm, hourly from 8pm to midnight, every two hours from midnight to 8am) crosses the river. It's 2.5km further along to **Santo André**, a tiny fishing village with a lovely, tree-shaded magic similar to Arraial d'Ajuda's. There are four pousadas ranging from super simple to a deluxe luxury resort, and a pair of bohemian restaurants and bars. **Victor Hugo** (☎ 3671 4064; www.pousadavictorhugo.com.br; s/d from R$120/140; 🛏) has elegantly simple chalets with decor from the owner's travels, a beachfront garden area and a gay-pride flag in the lobby. Surfers will be interested to know that **Mogiquiçaba** (22km north) has waves.

SOUTH OF PORTO SEGURO

South of Porto Seguro is a series of touristy villages, each with their own unique charms. The comforts of civilization decrease with each kilometer traveled south. The coast from Arraial d'Ajuda to Trancoso is a long stretch of pristine beaches backed by colored cliffs. From Trancoso to south of Corumbau, the beaches remain just as attractive, though the cliffs begin to flatten out.

Arraial d'Ajuda
☎ 0xx73 / pop 12,000

Atop a bluff overlooking an enchanting stretch of coastline, Arraial d'Ajuda is a peaceful tourist village with indisputable appeal. Its narrow paved roads and dusty lanes wind beneath large, shady trees, with lovely pousadas and open-air restaurants hidden among the greenery. Solid, brightly painted facades surround its plazas, and the air remains tinged with the scent of tropical vegetation. In the past, Arraial was the playground of the wealthy, which isn't far removed from the upmarket tourists the town tends to attract: the place is an extremely popular vacation spot for well-off Argentineans. More recently, however, a new wave of international backpackers and nouveau hippies have brought a little diversity to the idyllic surroundings.

INFORMATION
A few places on Broadway (spelled Bróduei by locals) and the Praça São Brás exchange US dollars and euros and offer internet access for around R$6 per hour. Withdraw cash at the **Banco do Brasil ATM** (Rua do Mucugê 333) and other ATMs scattered around town. For a map and tourist information, stop by the kiosk near the top of Rua do Mucugê.

SIGHTS & ACTIVITIES
Billed as the largest water park in Latin America, **Eco Parque** (☎ 3575 8600; www.arraialeco parque.com.br; Praia d'Ajuda; adult/child R$60/30) has long, twisting waterslides, a wave pool and a slow 'river' you can float down on rafts. There's also a *tiroleza* (zip-line), kayaks for rent and heaps of other activities. Big-name bands from Salvador play here for summer concerts.

Praia Mucugê is Arraial's main tourist beach and is crowded with *barracas* and blasted by music. As you continue south, **Praia do Parracho** is also built up, but with beach clubs and a few condominium complexes. Both of these beaches are sheltered by offshore reefs. Around the point, beautiful **Praia Pitinga** has red striped sandstone cliffs, pretty, calm waters and a few *barracas*. South of Pitinga, **Praia da Lagoa Azul** and **Praia Taípe** are backed by tall cliffs, and face stronger waves.

COURSES
Newcomers are warmly received at **Capoeira Sul da Bahia** (☎ 3575 2981; www.capoeirasuldabahia.com.br, in Portuguese; Rua da Capoeira 57; per class R$15), which also offers *lambada*, samba and Afro-Brazilian dance classes.

TOURS
Arco-Íris Turismo (☎ 3575 1672; Rua do Mucugê 199) organizes schooner and van trips to Caraíva, Praias Espelho and Curuípe (both south of Trancoso, from R$92), Trancoso and the offshore reefs Recife de Fora and Coroa Alta (R$52). It also occasionally runs three-day catamaran trips to the Parque Nacional Marinho de Abrolhos (p491).

SLEEPING
The road from the ferry dock to the center is lined with places to stay (some of them quite chic) but most find the center to be more convenient. However, if you're more interested in the beach than the village, or if you plan to come and go on the ferry between Porto

Seguro and Arraial, you'll like these laid-back pousadas and their relative peace and quiet. Frequent buses and vans carry travelers between the dock and the town.

Pousada Alto Mar (☎ 3575 1935; www.pousadaalto mar.net, in Portuguese; Rua Bela Vista 114; dm/d with fan from R$25/50; 🖳) Pousada Alto Mar remains a travelers' favorite for the good mix of youthful international guests that arrive. Rooms are basic, with fans and mosquito nets.

Arraial d'Ajuda Hostel (☎ 3575 1192; www.arraialda judahostel.com.br; Rua Campo 94; dm/d/tr R$35/120/180; 🌐 🛜 🛋) This colorful HI hostel offers well-equipped private rooms as well as dorm-style accommodations in a funky Greco Bahian-style building with a courtyard swimming pool. Travelers like the communal outdoor kitchen and the location near the beach.

our pick **Vila do Beco** (☎ 3575 1230; www.viladobeco .com.br; Beco do Jegue 173; d with fan from R$110, with air-con from R$140; 🌐 🛋) This tranquil property spreads toward the edge of the bluff – white buildings are spread through lush grounds, ending at a pool with jaw-dropping ocean views. Many guest rooms, outfitted with rustic wood furnishings and romantic mosquito nets, offer two levels and a terrace.

Saudosa Maloca (☎ 3575 1266; www.saudosamaloca .tur.br; Alameda das Eugênias 31; d R$120-150; 🌐 🛜 🛋) Saudosa Maloca has clean, well-kept rooms – some with verandas – overlooking a pool and grassy lawn. It's a few blocks from the main drag.

Pousada Erva Doce (☎ 3575 1113; www.ervadoce. com.br; Rua do Mucugê 200; d R$140; 🌐 🛋) Off the main strip, this peaceful guesthouse has spacious, nicely designed rooms surrounding a pool and tropical garden. There's ample outdoor lounge space with hammocks and a thatched-roof bar.

EATING
Arraial's excellent restaurants serve a wide variety of cuisine.

Beco dos Cores (Rua do Mucugê; mains R$20-45) This galleria is a big draw for its variety: you'll find great sushi, crepes, pizza and fancier fare; there's usually live music on summer weekend nights. It's also a cozy spot for cocktails on balmy summer evenings.

Soveteria Sumatra (☎ 3575 1951; Rua do Mucugê 118; ice cream R$3.50) Delicious, creamy ice cream made right here in Arraial. Rich flavors like guava or pistachio are great, but the coffee with chocolate chips is famous.

Paulinho Pescador (☎ 3575 1242; www.paulopes cador.com.br; Praça São Brás 116; mains R$6 10) The ordering couldn't be easier at this incredibly friendly, good-quality *prato feito* (plate of the day) restaurant: the menu has large photos of its appealing Bahian dishes.

A Portinha (☎ 3575 1289; www.portinha.com.br; Rua do Campo 1; per kg R$22) This upscale self-service restaurant serves a rotating menu of veggie quiches, salads, seafood stews and meats of all kinds – all kept hot over a wood fire.

Manguti (☎ 3575 2270; www.manguti.com.br; Rua do Mucugê 99; mains R$22-34; 🕑 dinner) This cute, old-fashioned house turns out tasty grilled fish fillets as well as hearty gnocchi and other classic pastas. The location is ideal if you're shopping or exploring the village at night.

Rosa dos Ventos (☎ 3575 1271; Alameda dos Flamboyants 24; mains R$25-35; 🕑 dinner Thu-Tue) One of Arraial's most delightful restaurants, Rosa dos Ventos offers an eclectic array of seafood, meats and crepes. The candlelit front patio is the ideal place to linger over a bottle of wine.

our pick **Aipim** (☎ 3575 3222; Beco do Jegue 131; mains R$28-45; 🕑 dinner) This stylish restaurant exudes tropical chic with its old-world decor, new-world music and superb grilled seafood. A first-rate locale for a romantic evening.

Boi nos Aires (☎ 3575 2554; Rua do Mucugê 200; mains R$30-35; 🕑 dinner) Steak lovers – especially those who need a break from Bahia's famous seafood – shouldn't miss this stylish Argentinian-style eatery.

La Plage Blanche (☎ 8821 0388; www.laplageblanche .com; Praia do Mucugê; mains R$30-50) Down on the beach, this open-air, French-run café is an inviting place to tuck into a gourmet seafood plate between dips in the ocean.

ENTERTAINMENT
Arraial has great nightlife throughout the summer, when beach clubs like **Magnolia** (☎ 3575 1576; Estrada da Pitinga 1770, Praia do Mucugê) host dance parties (cover R$25 to R$35). Sweaty nights spent dancing rootsy *lambada* and *forró* are an Arraial staple. Ask around for the current hot spot.

Girasol (☎ 3575 1717; Rua do Mucugê; 🕑 5pm-last customer) Here, dancers surround the pool tables on crowded nights, and pillowed window seats offer a comfortable vantage point.

Beco dos Cores (Rua do Mucugê) This shop and restaurant galleria has a few bars with a magical atmosphere and always attracts a crowd with live music from Thursday through Saturday.

BAHIA

Morocha Club (Estrada do Mucugê 290; Mon-Sat) An atmospheric place that's relaxed and lounge-like earlier in the evening but crowded with dancers late at night.

Cineteatro Fellini (Rua do Mucugê 201) Doubles as a live-music venue and a wine bar, and is perfect for an easygoing nightcap.

Doc (Shopping d'Ajuda, Rua do Mucugê; cover around R$25) This enclosed place provides a more typical dance-club environment with pounding techno.

GETTING THERE & AROUND
Two ferries travel between Porto Seguro and Arraial d'Ajuda. The passenger ferry (R$2.50 to Arraial, free return) runs every 30 minutes from 7:15am to 7:45pm. The car ferry (car R$9.50 to R$11.50) runs every 30 minutes from 7am to midnight, then hourly between 1am and 7am. From the dock, jump on a bus or Kombi van to Arraial (R$2). It's also possible to walk the 4km along the beach, but be cautious about carrying valuables or walking alone during hours when the beaches are deserted. Tourist muggings have occurred.

Bicycles and motorcycles are available for hire in the village. It's also possible to rent a car or a convertible-like buggy from an agency such as **Buggy Mania** (www.buggymania.com; Rua do Mucugê 250). Be sure to have a good map before you set out for excursions – when we last visited, our buggy broke down without warning on an unmarked dirt road.

Trancoso
0xx73 / pop 6000
Smaller in scale than Arraial, youthful Trancoso is also quite captivating. Sitting atop a grassy bluff overlooking fantastic beaches, this tiny village has a relaxed air with an assortment of pretty guesthouses, expensive boutiques and open-air bars and restaurants surrounding the grassy (and car-free) *quadrado* (square). The sight of the candlelit *quadrado* at night is magical. Rave culture still thrives in 'Trance-coso,' and it's famous for full-moon beach parties. Rich tourists fill the village in summer, but in the low season you'll find it in hibernation.

INFORMATION
Near the Praça da Independencia, there is a **Banco do Brasil ATM** (Rua Dudero 3) inside Supermercado Nogueira; you'll find more ATMs near the entrance to the *quadrado*.

Tourist information is also available here, at the office across the street from Pandoka café. Several places offer internet access for around R$6 per hour.

SLEEPING
Reservations are a must during January and major holidays.

Café Esmeralda Albergue (3668 1527; www.tranco sonatural.com; quadrado; d from R$100) The cheapest overnight on the *quadrado* is a friendly multilingual guesthouse with extremely basic, fan-cooled rooms. It's behind the café of the same name. No breakfast.

our pick **Pousada Quarto Crescente** (3668 1014; www.quartocrescente.net; Rua Principal s/n; s/d from R$110/125;) Gardens surround handsomely decorated rooms with thoughtful touches. There's also a well-stocked library, a pool and a fine breakfast spread. It's on the road into town next to the school, a short walk from the *quadrado*.

Bom Astral (3668 1270; www.bomastral.net; quadrado; d from R$140;) Decent value on the *quadrado*, Bom Astral has pleasant, simple rooms, small but well maintained. Several rooms have air-con and kitchens, but most quarters are fan-cooled only.

Pousada Jequitibá (3668 1028; www.pousada jequitibatrancoso.com.br; Rua do Bosque s/n; d from R$140;) On the grassy plaza to the right of the *quadrado*, Jequitibá has tidy rooms, opening onto a shared veranda, with crisp white canopied beds and pretty decor.

Pousada Porto Bananas (3668 1017; www.por tobananas.com.br; quadrado; d/ste from R$250/400;) Spread through a towering junglelike garden, Porto Bananas has lovely minimalist rooms with smooth cement floors and bright bathrooms (the shower faces tropical greenery – a great way to start your day).

Pousada Mundo Verde (3668 1279; www.pous adamundoverde.com.br; d from R$285;) Not far from the *quadrado* and set on a quiet bluff overlooking the ocean, stylish Mundo Verde has spacious, airy rooms painted in cheerful colors. There's a pool with a spectacular view.

Hotel da Praça (3668 2121; www.hoteldapraca .com.br; quadrado; d/ste from R$290/390;) The most fashionable hotel on the *quadrado* invites you to splurge: each beautifully designed room incorporates traditional Bahian wood, hand-painted fabrics and contemporary artwork.

EATING

In the evening, colorful glowing lanterns illuminate the restaurants around the *quadrado* – each looks prettier than the one before, so take a stroll before settling into a seat.

ourpick **Pandoka** (☎ 3668 1158; Rua 9 de Agosto 117; snacks R$3-10; ✆ 7am-10pm) A few steps from the entrance to the *quadrado*, this stylish and hugely popular bakery and café has coffee, pastries and homemade sandwiches. There's often a crowd in the evening when acoustic music performances occur.

A Portinha (☎ 3668 1054; quadrado; per kg R$22; ✆ lunch & dinner) A Trancoso favorite (with bigger branches in Arraial and Porto Seguro), A Portinha serves gourmet *por-kilo* food: quiches, seafood, salads and more.

Il Mercato (☎ 3668 2050; quadrado; mains R$25-45; ✆ dinner) With Moroccan lanterns and antiques, jewel-toned floor cushions, and gauzy curtains opening onto an airy patio, this Italian trattoria – known for rich risottos – still feels true to Trancoso's free-spirited tradition.

Japaiano (☎ 3668 2121; quadrado; mains R$45-65; ✆ dinner) At the lovely Hotel da Praça, this chic restaurant and lounge serves Japanese-Bahian fusion with surprising success. There are enticing cocktails, giving prominence to Brazil's tropical fruits, and picture-perfect garden seating.

Cantinho Doce (☎ 3668 1410; quadrado; mains for 2 R$45-70; ✆ dinner) One of several candlelit *quadrado* gems, Cantinho Doce features delectable seafood dishes, plus the famed *doces* (desserts) for which the restaurant is named.

ENTERTAINMENT

The two main night spots are on the road leading to the *quadrado*. **Loucos** (Av Principal) has hip-hop, reggae, *axé* and lambada nights, but its Friday-night *forró* is renowned with locals. **Pára-Raio** (www.pararaiotrancoso.com.br; quadrado) is an ambient restaurant with outdoor tables under massive trees and an enclosed dance space where DJs spin. During summer, some of the most happening beach parties are put on by **Tostex** (www.tostexpraia.com.br; Praia dos Nativos).

There is always live music somewhere on the *quadrado*, but if local legend Elba Ramalho is giving a show, don't miss it. Beach *barracas* such as Pé na Praia sometimes have nighttime parties with pumping trance music and psychedelic decor.

GETTING THERE & AWAY

Hourly buses connect Trancoso with Arraial d'Ajuda and the ferry dock and run from 7:15am to 8pm (R$6, 50 minutes). Many informal Kombi vans run the same route for the same price. Two buses a day travel between Trancoso and Porto Seguro (R$8, two hours). It is also possible to walk the entirely beautiful 13km along the beach from Arraial d'Ajuda, but be cautious about carrying valuables or walking alone during hours when the beaches are deserted. For further connections north or south, head for Eunápolis (R$10, 2½ hours, five daily) on Hwy BR-101.

TRANCOSO TO CARAÍVA

Rated among Brazil's top-10 beaches, **Praia do Espelho** is 27km south of Trancoso and 14km north of Caraíva. Protective offshore reefs create calm, warm, transparent waters, while reefs closer to shore create natural pools at low tide. The shore is thick with coconut palms. White and orange cliffs divide Espelho from **Praia do Curuípe**, its neighboring beach, which has a collection of top-end pousadas.

Caraíva
☎ 0xx73 / pop 5200

Time moves slowly in the remote and beautiful village of Caraíva, where cars, banks and cell-phone reception don't exist (neither did electricity before 2007). The easygoing atmosphere has long attracted hippies and those looking for a quiet pace of life. The village is strung along the eastern bank of the mangrove-lined Rio Caraíva and a long deserted beach kissed by strong waves. Noisy generators light up the dozen-or-so shops and restaurants lining the sand streets, and most importantly keep the *forró* hopping on Friday night. In the low season, the town all but shuts down.

Boat trips upriver, south to Parque Nacional de Monte Pascoal or Corumbau, and north to Praia do Espelho and Praia do Curuípe are easily organized through pousadas (around R$60 per person). Horseback riding along the beach to **Barra Velha**, the indigenous Pataxó village, is also an option if walking or boating the 6km isn't appealing. When going to the village, bring lots of water and small bills in case you'd like to purchase handicrafts.

On April 19 the village celebrates the **Festa do Índio** with traditional games and dancing.

SLEEPING & EATING

Air-con isn't available at most hotels, though essential mosquito nets are usually provided. Most budget places don't serve breakfast, either – these are fairly basic accommodations.

Camping Caraiva (☎ 0xx24-2231 4892; www.camping caraiva.com.br, in Portuguese; camping/r per person R$20/60) On the main riverside road, this place has sandy shaded campsites and a few basic but attractive cabins that are ideal for families or groups of friends.

Brilho do Mar (☎ 3668 5053; d with fan from R$90) This guesthouse has a sparkling bleached facade, matched by spotless rooms, with windows opening on two sides that allow a nice cross-breeze.

Pousada Casinhas da Bahia (☎ 9985 6826; www .casinhasdabahia.com.br; d with fan R$140-180) Tucked around behind the *forró* club, and sharing the same owner, is a grouping of breezy, comfortable rooms in a pretty garden setting.

Pousada da Terra (☎ 9985 4417; www.terracaraiva .com.br, in Portuguese; d from R$150) Terra has small, attractive bungalows and a relaxing café and communal space with hammocks and pillows.

Pousada da Lagoa (☎ 3668 5059; www.lagoacaraiva .com.br; d/bungalow R$180/210) Surrounding a small pond are seven simple but stylish cottages with small verandas slung with hammocks. Regular doubles are available, but families or groups of three or four can save money by renting the whole bungalow. The restaurant-bar is a popular nighttime hangout.

Pousada San Antonio (☎ 9962 2123; www.pousada sanantonio.com.br, in Portuguese; d with fan R$250) Overlooking the sea, San Antonio is set with freestanding cabins scattered about a grassy lawn and garden. Rooms are bright, comfortable and inviting.

Boteco do Pará (☎ 9991 9804; mains R$12-20) One of several casual eateries specializing in fresh seafood, this laid-back spot is a great place to relax by the river.

Mangue Sereno (☎ 9991 1711; mains R$32-38; ☻ dinner) This marvelous restaurant serves eclectic dishes, including pumpkin ravioli, bruschetta, curry shrimp and other seafood, in a romantic but rustic setting.

GETTING THERE & AWAY

Buses travel twice daily along a reasonable dirt road (keep an eye out for grazing buffalo) between Trancoso and Caraíva (R$12, two hours). The bus stops on the far side of the river in Caraíva, where small dugout canoes ferry passengers across to the village (R$3). Boat transportation between Caraíva and Porto Seguro may also be available in high season through **Cia do Mar** (☎ 3288 2107).

There is no road south along the coast from Caraíva. If heading for other destinations north or south, catch the daily bus to Eunápolis via Itabela, both on Hwy BR-101.

Corumbau

☎ 0xx73

Corumbau sits at the mouth of a river on a sand spit reaching into the ocean. It is barely the semblance of a hamlet, just a charming collection of buildings without electricity. The spit creates calm, blue waters for a long white-sand beach dotted with a few simple restaurants.

The very comfortable, German-run **Jocotoka Eco Resort** (☎ 3288 2291; www.jocotoka .com.br; d from R$280; ☷ ⛱) is a collection of round, thatched-roof bungalows 100m from the ocean. Included in the room price is an excellent buffet dinner served in the dining room. The resort offers activities such as snorkeling, river trips by canoe, kayak or boat, trekking in the national park, a visit to the nearby Pataxó village and whale watching (August to October).

For something simpler, try **Pousada Lourinho** (☎ 3294 5656; s/d with fan R$50/70), one of several inexpensive guesthouses offering basic concrete bungalows 200m from the beach.

One daily bus leaves Itamaraju on Hwy BR-101 for Corumbau (R$14, three hours). Otherwise, access is via beach buggy (R$30), boat (R$35) or on foot along the beach from Caraíva, 12km north.

PARQUE NACIONAL DE MONTE PASCOAL

On April 22, 1500, the Portuguese, sailing under the command of Pedro Álvares Cabral, sighted the broad, 536m-high hump of Monte Pascoal (Mt Easter), their first glimpse of the New World. The sailors called the land Terra da Vera Cruz (Land of the True Cross).

The 225-sq-km national park contains a variety of ecosystems: Atlantic rain forest, secondary forests, swamplands and shallows, mangroves, beaches and reefs. Wildlife includes several monkey species, including the endangered spider monkey, two types of sloth, anteaters, rare porcupines, capybara, deer, jaguars and numerous species of bird.

The northeastern corner of the park, below Caraíva, is home to a small number of indigenous Pataxó people, who took over control of the park in 2000. They allow visitors access to two trails while accompanied by a guide (settle fees before setting out), one of which climbs the mountain. The **visitors' center** (☎ 3294 1110) is 14km from the western (Hwy BR-101) end of the park. The coastal side is accessible by boat or on foot from Caraíva to the north and Corumbau to the south.

There are no direct buses to the park. A taxi from Itamaraju runs about R$50.

CARAVELAS

☎ 0xx73 / pop 22,000

Caravelas is a calm fishing town on the banks of the mangrove-lined Rio Caravelas. Though it has a friendly, down-home Carnaval and a pleasant enough atmosphere, the primary reason visitors come here is to visit the Parque Nacional Marinho de Abrolhos and other offshore reefs.

Information

Abrolhos Turismo (☎ 3297 1149; www.abrolhostur ismo.com.br; Praça Dr Imbassaí) Travel agency; also acts as a kind of unofficial tourist office. Runs recommended tours (diving, whale-watching and trips to Parque Nacional Monte Pascoal).

Banco do Brasil (Praça Dr Imbassaí) Has ATMs.

Sights & Activities

To get a feel for the town's thriving fishing industry, check out the **Cooperativa Mista dos Pescadores** (Rua da Cooperativa), opposite the hospital, or wander along the riverfront where the fishers return with the day's catch. The **Instituto Baleia Jubarte** (Humpback Whale Institute; ☎ 3297 1340; www.baleiajubarte.com.br; Rua do Barão do Rio Branco 26; ✆ Mon-Fri) shows videos and offers information about its projects and Abrolhos at its visitors' center.

When the locals go to the beach, most head north for **Praia Grauçá** (10km) or the more isolated **Praia Iemanjá** (20km). Both have calm water colored brown with river silt. Reachable by boat are **Praia Pontal do Sul** (across Rio Caravelas) and the island beach **Coroa da Barra** (30 minutes offshore).

Tours

Travel agencies offer snorkeling day trips (R$130) to nearby reefs and islands such as Parcel das Paredes, Sebastião Gomes and Coroa Vermelha. Since most tourists head for

---

THE PATAXÓ

Bahia's largest indigenous group, the Pataxó (pa-ta-*sho*), who number 3500, are among Brazil's many indigenous groups facing an uncertain future. Historically, the Pataxó are survivors. They were a strong tribe who held out against the Portuguese, and up until the 1800s were one of the most feared indigenous groups of the interior. Their resistance hindered frontier expansion, though by the early 19th century their power had waned.

Today, the Pataxó practice subsistence agriculture in the south of Bahia, supplemented by hunting, fishing and gathering. Similar to Amazonian indigenous groups, the Pataxó utilize local plants as their pharmacy, with the rain forests of southern Bahia providing a vital source for traditional medicine. The region boasts incredible biodiversity, with many of its plants and animals found nowhere else on earth. In all, the Pataxó use more than 90 different plant species to treat colds, asthma, fever, toothaches, rheumatism, anemia and dozens of other illnesses.

Despite the wide acceptance of the healer's powers within the community, the Pataxó are struggling to maintain their traditions. As elsewhere in indigenous communities, the youth are not actively embracing the customs of the older generation. Traditional healers *(curandeiros)*, who can be male or female, haven't passed their knowledge down to the next generation. In Barra Velha, the largest Pataxó community (numbering some 1800), all of the healers are over 60, meaning that if nothing changes, their knowledge will be lost within two decades. Today's *curandeiros* may be the final generation of traditional healers in Pataxó culture.

In addition to internal struggles, the Pataxó face severe threats from outside. As Bahia's population grows, farmers have pushed them off their lands, leading to violent skirmishes. In 2007, 15 indigenous Pataxó went to Brasília to settle the matter of their land rights. Yet whether the tribe can flourish – and successfully preserve its customs – may be a matter less for government officials to decide than for Pataxó youth, who will be instrumental in ensuring the tribe's longevity.

GREAT CREATURES OF THE SEA

One of the world's great migratory animals, the humpback whale travels up to 25,000km each year. Massive in scale, adults can reach 17m long and weigh up to 36,000kg. Although they were hunted to near-extinction by the turn of the 20th century, the population is slowly recovering following a moratorium on whale hunting in 1966. Biologists estimate that 30,000 to 60,000 now remain.

Identified by their long pectoral fins, distinct humps and knob-covered heads, the humpbacks feed only during the summer in polar waters on a diet of krill and small fish. In the winter, they migrate from the poles to tropical waters, where mating occurs. Thus, the austral winter (June to September) is the best time to observe them off the coast of Brazil, when they come in large numbers to mate and give birth.

During this time, the humpbacks fast and live off their fat reserves. Competition for females is intense, with groups of two to 20 males (called escorts) sometimes trailing a lone female. To win her over, each male competes to establish dominance – tail slapping, charging and parrying over the course of several hours.

The whale song is perhaps one of the most fascinating and least understood attributes of these mammals. Whales within an area sing the same song – or variations of the same song – while those from different regions sing entirely different songs. Performed only by males, each song lasts 10 to 20 minutes and can be repeated over several hours (some scientists have recorded whales singing continuously for over 24 hours). The songs are staggeringly complex. One research team from the Universidade Estadual de Campinas studied whales off Abrolhos in Bahia one winter and identified 24 note types, organized in five themes.

No one knows the purpose of the song, which changes from year to year, though scientists originally thought it had a role in mating (observations of males singing far from the presence of a female has thrown doubt onto this).

In Bahia, whale-watching is a growing tourist industry, with numerous places from which to embark on a seagoing observation trip. During the winter, they can often be observed outside of Salvador, while Parque Nacional Marinho de Abrolhos (p491) is among the world's best places to observe them.

Elsewhere in Brazil, other good sighting spots are Praia do Rosa (p355) in Santa Catarina state, where mother and calf pairs can come within 30m of the shore, and Arraial do Cabo (p211) in Rio state.

Those who want a deeper understanding of the great mammals can volunteer at the **Brazilian Humpback Whale Project** (www.gvi.co.uk), based in Praia do Forte. Volunteers spend much time out on the sea, collecting data and contributing to the whale's long-term conservation.

Abrolhos, these trips rarely meet the minimum number of people required (five) for departure.

Sleeping

Pousada Canto do Atobá (☎ 3297 1009; http://pousadacantodoatoba.wordpress.com; Rua da Palmeira; s/d with fan R$60/90; ☒) A few friendly dogs and cats wander through the garden of this pretty pousada just outside the entrance of town. Airy, bright rooms open onto a hammock-strung veranda.

Pousada & Spa da Ilha (☎ 3297 2218; http://netpage.estaminas.com.br/jelihovs; s/d R$90/130) Across the river, on Ilha da Caçumba, this multilingual bohemian pousada has two sweet and simple rooms with furniture built by the owners, and solar power. Nonguests are also welcome to their leisurely (and all-natural) lunch and dinner.

Hotel Marina Porto Abrolhos (☎ 3674 1060; www.marinaportoabrolhos.com.br; Rua da Baleia 333, Praia Grauçá; s/d from R$135/150; ☒ ☒) The fanciest hotel in town is located 7km from Caravelas, and has round, thatched-roof, beachfront chalets surrounding a gigantic pool. There are also tennis courts, a pool bar, gym and library.

Eating

Restaurants at Praia Grauçá serve excellent seafood.

Carenagem (☎ 3297 1280; Av das Palmeiras 10; mains R$18-30) This popular meeting spot has an extensive menu of seafood and meat dishes as well as classic cocktails.

Encontro dos Amigos (☎ 3297 1600; Av das Palmeiras 370; mains R$25-50) Another top place for fresh fish, shrimp and clams.

Getting There & Around

One daily bus goes between Porto Seguro and Caravelas (R$36, five hours). Otherwise, access to Caravelas is via Teixeira de Freitas, 74km west. The **bus station** (☎ 3297 1422) is in the center of town. Brasileiro goes to Teixeira de Freitas via Alcobaça (R$13, two hours, five daily).

Local buses do a round trip between Caravelas and the neighboring village of Barra (providing access to Praia Grauçá), leaving every 30 minutes from 6:30am until 10:30pm.

PARQUE NACIONAL MARINHO DE ABROLHOS

It is thought that the name of Brazil's first marine park comes from a sailor's warning: when approaching land, open your eyes (*abre os olhos*). Abrolhos covers an area of 913 sq km, including reefs noted for the variety of colors and a five-island archipelago that Charles Darwin, aboard the HMS *Beagle*, visited in 1832. These days the primary residents of the archipelago are migrating birds and humpback whales (June to October), which come here to rest and give birth. Only the Ilha de Santa Bárbara has a handful of buildings, including a lighthouse built in 1861.

The preservation of the islands is important to Ibama (Instituto Brasileiro do Meio Ambiente e dos Recursos Naturais Renováveis; Brazilian Institute of the Environment and Renewable Natural Resources), so visitor land access is limited to daytime hours on only the Ilha da Siriba. But you didn't come to a marine park for land; you came to snorkel and dive in crystal-clear waters, the visibility of which can reach 20m in the dry season (May to September).

Getting There & Around

Abrolhos is located 80km offshore from Caravelas, the primary gateway, where travel agencies (p489) offer one- to three-day trips to the park. Day trips run around R$260 per person, including park fees and lunch. Abrolhos Turismo also runs schooner trips lasting from two to three days, with overnight stays onboard, for R$650 to R$1000 per person, including park fees and meals. Snorkel-kit rental is R$15 per day.

From Arraial d'Ajuda, **Arco-Íris Turismo** (☎ 3575 1672; Rua do Mucugê 199) occasionally organizes three-day catamaran trips that cruise south along the Bahian coast, then on to Abrolhos.

WEST OF SALVADOR

The great attraction in Bahia's interior is the Parque Nacional da Chapada Diamantina, a verdant area of scenic plateaus, grassy valleys, waterfalls and rushing rivers. Opportunities for trekking and outdoor adventures abound.

In contrast to this verdant area, the rest of this region comprises the bizarre moonscapes of the *sertão*, a vast and parched land on which a struggling people eke out a living raising cattle and tilling the earth. When the periodic tremendous droughts sweep the land, thousands of Sertanejos (inhabitants of the *sertão*) pile their belongings on their backs and head out in search of jobs. But with the first hint of rain they return to renew their strong bond with this land.

FEIRA DE SANTANA

☎ 0xx75 / pop 590,000

Feira de Santana is the main city of Bahia's interior, and a great cattle center. There's not much to do or see here except the **Feira do Couro**, the big Monday cattle market, which is great fun, with lots of leather bargains, and the **Mercado de Arte Popular** (☼ Mon-Sat), which has folk art for sale.

Festivals & Events

Feira invented the now widespread concept of **Micareta**, an out-of-season Carnaval. In 1937 a flood caused the city's Carnaval to be celebrated late, a tradition the citizens decided to adopt and rename. In April or early

---

FOLK ART

Bahia has some of Brazil's best artisans, who usually have small shops or sell in the local market. You can buy their folk art in Salvador, but the best place to see or purchase the real stuff is in the town of origin. Feira de Santana is known for its leatherwork. Maragojipinho, Rio Real and Cachoeira produce earthenware. Caldas do Jorro, Caldas de Cipo and Itaparica specialize in straw crafts. Rio de Contas and Muritiba do metalwork. Ilha de Maré is famous for lacework. Jequié, Valença and Feira de Santana are woodworking centers. Santo Antônio de Jesus, Rio de Contas and Monte Santo manufacture goods made of leather and silver.

May thousands of spectators fill the city to see Salvador's best *trios elétricos* parade for four days along with local samba schools and folklore groups. For those who missed out on Carnaval in Salvador, this could be the next best thing.

Sleeping & Eating
There are several cheap hotels near the bus station, such as **Hotel Samburá** (☎ 3623 8511; Praça Dr Jackson Amauri 132; s/d R$40/55; ✷). Nearby **Hotel Acalanto** (☎ 3612 6700; www.hotelacalanto.com.br; Rua Torres 77; s/d R$85/130; ✷) offers sprightlier rooms and more services.

O Picuí (☎ 3221 1018; Av Maria Quitéria 2463; mains R$15-25) has good regional food. Several other bars, cafés and restaurants, many with live music and *forró* at night, are scattered around town.

Getting There & Away
At the crossroads of three major highways, Feira is a major transportation hub. The **bus station** (☎ 3623 3667) features an eye-catching mural painted by Lénio Braga in 1967. Frequent buses go to Salvador (R$15, two hours). Real Expresso buses for Lençóis originating in Salvador pass through Feira de Santana.

LENÇÓIS
☎ 0xx75 / pop 10,000
Lençóis is the prettiest of the old diamond-mining towns in the Chapada Diamantina, a mountainous wooded oasis in the dusty *sertão*. While the town itself has charming cobbled streets, brightly painted 19th-century buildings, and appealing outdoor cafés and restaurants, the surrounding areas are the real attraction. Caves, waterfalls, idyllic rivers and panoramic plateaus set the stage for some fantastic adventures, with the town of Lençóis serving as a base for treks into the surrounding Parque Nacional da Chapada Diamantina (p496) and for sights outside the park. Lençóis is also noted for Jarê, the regional variation of Candomblé. If you want to see a flip side to surf-and-sand Brazil, or have time for only one excursion into the Northeastern interior, this is it.

History
The history of Lençóis epitomizes the story of the diamond boom and subsequent bust. After earlier expeditions by *bandeirantes*

(Paulista explorers and hired guns) proved fruitless, the first diamonds were found in Chapada Velha in 1822. After large strikes in the Rio Mucujê in 1844, a motley collection of prospectors from across Brazil arrived seeking their fortunes.

Miners began searching for diamonds in alluvial deposits. They settled in makeshift tents, which, from the hills above, looked like bedsheets drying in the wind – hence the town's name: Lençóis (sheets). The tents of these diamond prospectors grew into villages: Vila Velha de Palmeiras, Andaraí, Piatã, Igatu and Lençóis. Exaggerated stories of endless riches in the Diamantina mines precipitated mass migrations, but the area proved rich in clouded industrial stones, not display-quality gems.

At the height of the diamond boom, the French – who purchased diamonds and used them to drill the Panama Canal (1881–89), St Gothard Tunnel and London Underground – built a vice-consulate in Lençóis. French fashions and *bons mots* made their way into town, but with the depletion of diamonds, the fall-off in French demand and the newly discovered South African mines, the boom went bust at the beginning of the 20th century.

Despite these developments, mining held on. Powerful and destructive water pumps were introduced in the 1980s, which increased production until they were finally banned in 1995. The few remaining miners have returned to traditional methods to extract diamonds from the riverbeds. With the establishment of the national park in 1985, the town's economy turned instead to tourism, which continues to be the major industry of Lençóis.

Information
The online portal of Guia Lençóis (www.guia lencois.com.br) is a great resource for tourist information.

Associação dos Condutores de Visitantes de Lençóis (☎ 3334 1425; Rua 10 de Novembro 22; ☷ 8am-noon & 2-8pm) Information about tour guides. Guides may also be hired through the town's various outfitters and travel agencies.

Banco do Brasil (Praça Horácio de Mattos 56) Has ATMs.

Café.com (Mercado Municipal, Rua José Florencio; per hr R$6; ☷ 4-11pm Mon-Sat) Internet access. Other internet cafés are around town.

Post office (Av 7 de Setembro)

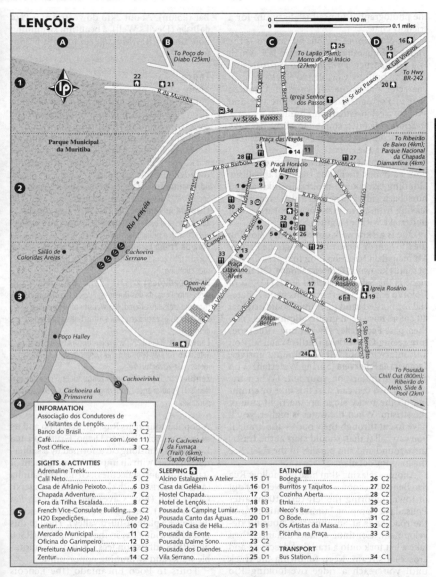

LENÇÓIS

Sights & Activities

Take a stroll by the 19th-century **French vice-consulate building** (Praça Horácio de Mattos), where diamond commerce was negotiated, and the beautiful **Prefeitura Municipal** (Praça Otaviano Alves), which displays interesting old photos of Lençóis. The **Casa de Afrânio Peixoto** (Praça do Rosário; admission free; 10am-4pm Tue-Sat) displays the works and personal effects of Lençóis' most illustrious native, in addition to yet more old town photos. Peixoto was a writer, doctor, politician and academic.

The photo gallery of **Calil Neto** (Rua da Baderna; 8am-1pm & 6-11pm Wed-Mon, 6-11pm Tue) will leave no doubts about this area's beauty. Small prints of the artist's shots are for sale, and the photographer himself is always up for a friendly chat.

One of the more curious attractions is the **Oficina do Garimpeiro** (Rua São Benedito 140), which is a reconstructed *garimpeiro* (prospector) dwelling built by Coriolando Rocha, a local character and former prospector. A guided tour in Portuguese reveals the lifestyle and skills of freelance diamond hunters.

For handicrafts, stop by the lively **Mercado Municipal** (Rua José Florencio; 🕒 8am-11pm Mon-Sat) overlooking the river.

Local agencies offer a wide range of outdoor activities, including hiking, rappelling, climbing, kayaking, mountain biking and horseback riding. There are also great hikes leaving from town that the adventurous can undertake without a guide.

One is a 3km walk out of town, following the Rio Lençóis upstream through the Parque Municipal da Muritiba. You first pass a series of rapids known as **Cachoeira Serrano**. Off to the right is the **Salão de Coloridas Areias** (Room of Colored Sands), where artisans gather material for bottled sand paintings, so its original 40 colors have been greatly diminished. You then pass **Poço Halley** (Swimming Hole), before seeing **Cachoeirinha** (Little Waterfall) on a tributary to your left. Continuing upriver, **Cachoeira da Primavera** (Spring Waterfall) is on another tributary on your left. (When the water is low, you can start this hike by climbing up the rocky slope on the right side of the stream. When the water is higher, you'll have to cut through the woods – the 'trail,' if you can call it that, should start at the traffic turnaround and run parallel to the river. See the map for details.)

Another relaxing 4km hike is to follow Rua São Benedito (known as Rua dos Negros) out of town, ignoring the left turn 100m after Pousada & Camping Lumiar. Continue until the road ends at an upmarket housing development. Continue a short distance, then take a left fork onto a trail that descends and crosses a stream. Keep following the track until you reach a ridge overlooking Rio Ribeirão. At the foot of the ridge is **Ribeirão do Meio**, a series of swimming holes with a natural waterslide (bring shorts or something to slide on). Avoid assured injury by climbing the dry rocks (not the slide's wet ones) before launching off.

For more swimming, catch the morning bus to Seabra and hop off at Mucugêzinho

Bar (25km). About 2km downstream is **Poço do Diabo** (Devil's Well), a beautiful swimming hole on the Rio Mucugêzinho with a 25m waterfall.

Tours

Many of the area's best-known sights are outside of the national park on private land. Given the lack of public transportation, the easiest way to visit them is by taking a tour through a local agency. For information on longer treks, and tours within the national park, see p497. The following are recommended Lençóis agencies:

Adrenaline Trekk (☎ 3334 1896; Rua das Pedras 112) Specializes in adventure sports and treks.

Chapada Adventure (☎ 3334 2037; www.chapada adventure.com.br; Praça Horácio de Mattos 114) A friendly agency with multilingual staff.

Fora da Trilha Escalada (☎ 3334 1326; www .foradatrilha.com.br; Rua das Pedras 202) Specializes in rock-climbing.

H20 Expedições (☎ 3334 1229; www.h20traveladven tures.com; Pousada dos Duendes, Rua do Pires) Both day trips and treks are offered; the website offers detailed descriptions of each excursion's attractions and level of difficulty.

Lentur (☎ 3334 1271; www.lentur.com.br; Av 7 de Setembro 10) Day trips and treks organized, including motorcycle adventures.

Zentur (☎ 3334 1397; www.zentur.tur.br; Praça das Nagôs 1) Popular agency offering appealing weeklong tour packages.

A popular tour visits Rio Mucugêzinho and its swimming hole Poço do Diabo, Gruta da Lapa Doce (an 850m-long cave, formed by a subterranean river, with an impressive assortment of stalagmites and stalactites), Gruta da Pratinha (a cave and river with clear, light-blue waters), Gruta Azul (Blue Cave) and Morro do Pai Inácio (an 1120m peak affording an awesome view over a plateau-filled valley). Though this makes for a long day in the car, the tour (R$60 plus R$18 admission fees) includes memorable walks and swimming opportunities.

Tours to Poço Encantado (the Lençóis poster child: a cave filled with stunningly beautiful blue water) and Poço Azul (another rainwater-filled cave you can swim in) are also offered (R$70 plus R$17 admission fees). Verify with agencies the quality of the light; after rains, the water remains murky.

If you're not interested in going on a formal tour, you should still consider going into the national park or the surrounding areas with a guide: they're affordable (a half-day trek runs R$60 for up to four people), incredibly knowledgeable about local flora and fauna, and they can find the best swimming holes – all priceless in a park with few signs or official trails.

Festivals & Events

The **Festa de Senhor dos Passos** begins on January 24 and culminates on February 2 with the Noite dos Garimpeiros (Prospectors' Night). **Lamentação das Almas** is a mystical festival held during Lent. Celebrated from June 23 to 25, the **Festa de São João** is a huge street party with traditional dancing and bonfires outside every house. The **Semana de Afrânio Peixoto** is held from December 11 to 18 and coincides with the municipality's emancipation from slavery.

Sleeping

Lençóis' best pousadas are famous for their fantastic breakfast spreads.

BUDGET

Pousada & Camping Lumiar (☎ 3334 1241; lumiar .camping@gmail.com; Praça do Rosário 70; camping per person R$15, s/d with fan R$40/80, bungalows R$160; 🐾) Lumiar has grassy campsites in an attractive, tree-filled setting, along with simple rooms in a converted colonial home (bathrooms are shared). There are also roomier bungalows with private terraces.

Pousada Daime Sono (☎ 3334 1445; www.pousada daimesono.com.br, in Portuguese; Rua das Pedras 102; dm from R$30) Right in the middle of the action, this hostel-like pousada is run by friendly English-speaking owners Patricia and Rodrigo. Kitchen access is free and treks are easily arranged here.

our pick **Pousada dos Duendes** (☎ 3334 1229; www .pousadadosduendes.com; Rua do Pires; dm R$35, s/d without bathroom R$50/75, s/d with bathroom R$65/100) A relaxed atmosphere, good budget rooms and open-air lounge space makes Duendes a backpacker institution. It serves group dinners with vegetarian options, organizes volunteer work in the community, and runs park tours, excursions on horseback and kayak trips.

Hostel Chapada (☎ 3334 1497; www.hostelchapada .com.br; Rua Boa Vista 121; dm/d with fan R$38/83; 🖥) This HI hostel attracts young travelers to its simple, fan-cooled dorm rooms (sleeping between four and six). If you're coming from Salvador, check into its five-day package (R$686 per person) that includes round-trip bus tickets

and accommodations in Lençóis plus several guided day treks in the national park.

Pousada Chill Out (☎ 3334 1024; www.pousadachil lout.com; Lot Parque do Ribeirao 313; s/d with fan R$40/60) Just outside of town near the entrance to the national park, this mellow new pousada features multilingual staff, seven suites and a stylish bar where you can order exotic cocktails while contemplating nature.

MIDRANGE

Pousada da Fonte (☎ 3334 1953; www.pousadadafonte .net, in Portuguese; Rua da Muritiba 3; s/d with fan R$55/90) With stone walls, outdoor hammocks and an open breakfast porch surrounded by lush forest, this quaint six-room pousada has the feel of a weekend mountain home.

Pousada Casa de Hélia (☎ 3334 1143; www.casade helia.com.br; Rua da Muritiba s/n; d/tr from R$70/90) Casa de Hélia has pretty, rustic rooms featuring stone-slab floors and furniture fashioned out of twisted branches. Readers complain about unfriendly service; our recent visit was fine, though the place isn't as well kept as it used to be.

Casa da Geléia (☎ 3334 1151; www.casadageleia .com.br; Rua Gal Viveiros 187; d R$100) A row of large rooms looks out onto a grassy yard and the surrounding countryside beyond. In addition to pretty rooms, the Casa da Geléia (House of Jams) is open to the public and stocks an unbelievable range of homemade jams, chutneys, liqueurs and dried fruits and vegetables.

Alcino Estalagem & Atelier (☎ 3334 1171; www .alcinoestalagem.com; Rua Tomba Surrão 139; s/d without bathroom R$105/140, s/d with bathroom R$155/210) This lovely yellow mansion has tastefully decorated rooms all designed and built by local artist Alcino. His artwork from his ceramic workshop out back is visible throughout the property.

Vila Serrano (☎ 3334 1486; www.vilaserrano.com.br; Rua Alto do Bonfim 8; s/d R$150/195) In a lush setting, the classy and environmentally conscious Vila Serrano comprises nine spacious apartments, each handsomely designed, with a veranda attached. There's a library-lounge area for meeting other travelers.

TOP END

Pousada Canto das Águas (☎ 3334 1154; www.len cois.com.br; Av Senhor dos Passos 1; d R$275-455; 🐾 🖥) At the river's edge, this attractively designed hotel has classically furnished rooms, ranging from comfortable to luxurious. The sound of the river fills the rooms, with large toads adding a countermelody to the flowing water at night.

Hotel de Lençóis (☎ 3334 1102; www.hoteldelencois .com.br; Rua Altina Alves 747; d from R$300; 🅿 🛜 🛋) This ecofriendly hotel has good-looking rooms set with hammocks overlooking greenery and a pretty pool area. There's also a gourmet restaurant and shaded paths for wandering.

Eating

Lençóis offers a range of excellent cuisine, including vegetarian choices. Many cafés will pack lunches for hikes if you prearrange it. At night, the town's atmosphere is wonderfully charming as many restaurants on Praça Horácio de Mattos and Rua das Pedras put candlelit tables out on the cobblestone walkways. For sweet treats and cheap caipirinhas, stop at the late-night stands set up inside the Mercado Municipal.

Burritos y Taquitos (☎ 3334 1083; Rua José Florencio 3; mains R$12-20; 🕒 dinner Tue-Sun) Below the pousada Parador de Santiago (double/triple rooms with fan R$95/130), this Mexican restaurant serves tasty burritos, tacos and guacamole. A back patio overlooks the river.

Neco's Bar (☎ 3334 1179; Praça Clarim Pacheco 15; meals R$16; 🕒 dinner) Rustic Neco's Bar is renowned for having the best regional food in town, but you have to place orders the day before.

Os Artistas da Massa (☎ 3334 1886; Rua da Baderna 49; mains R$16-24) Fantastically fresh pastas and other Italian dishes are served to the jazz and pop tunes you pick off the menu at this gourmet restaurant.

O Bode (☎ 3334 1600; Praça Horácio de Mattos; per kg R$18) On an open-sided terrace over the river, this pleasant, well-liked *por-kilo* restaurant spreads a small but enticing buffet that includes meats, pasta and salads.

Etnia (☎ 3334 1066; Rua da Baderna 111; mains R$18-28; 🕒 dinner) Sick of pasta and seafood yet? This cool and casual eatery serves Asian dishes from pad Thai to Indian curry.

Bodega (Rua das Pedras 121; mains R$22-35) This stylish pizzeria and Italian eatery offers prime people-watching, gourmet pies and potent cocktails.

our pick Cozinha Aberta (☎ 3334 1321; www.cozinha aberta.com.br, in Portuguese; Av Rui Barbosa 42; mains R$24-35) This gourmet bistro, specializing in slow food, serves eclectic fare from Thai noodles to Italian pastas. The setting is charming and homelike, with daily specials spelled out on chalkboards.

Picanha na Praça (☎ 3334 1080; Praça Otaviano Alves 62; mains for 2 R$28-35) Choice cuts of beef, chicken and fish are brought sizzling to your table at this well-frequented institution.

Getting There & Away
BUS
If coming from the south, the journey, though indirect, will be a lot quicker if you route through Salvador. **Real Expresso** (☎ 3334 1112) buses for Salvador (R$50, six to seven hours) leave two to three times daily. Buses stop in Feira de Santana, where connections can be made to just about anywhere.

CAR
Lençóis is 13km off Hwy BR-242, the main Salvador–Brasília route. There's a gas station 22km east of Lençóis on Hwy BR-242, in Tanquinho. The nearest station to the west is around 30km away. There's an improvised fuel station in Lençóis, which is usually open.

PARQUE NACIONAL DA CHAPADA DIAMANTINA
☎ 0xx75
Within this national park's 1520 sq km, waterfalls cascade over the Sincora Range's mountains and plateaus, dropping into rivers and streams that wind their way through grassy valleys and clean swimming holes. An endless network of trails is dotted with cactus and strawflowers in some places, and the philodendrons, velosiaceas, orchids and other bromeliads that have escaped poaching in others. Several species of monkey swing through trees where *araras* (macaws) perch. *Veados* (deer) pick their way past gaping caves, while *mocós* (native rodents) and *cutia* (agouti) scurry underfoot. Even an *onça pintada* (jaguar) or two sharpens its claws on a towering tree, but you're much more likely to cross paths with a cute *quati* (small, furry carnivore with a brown-and-yellow-ringed tail).

The region's unique natural beauty and the tranquility of its small, colonial towns have attracted a steady trickle of Brazilian and foreign travelers for several decades; some have never left. These introduced residents, moved by the degradation of the environment and depletion of the wild-animal population, spearheaded an active ecological movement in direct opposition to the extractive mentality of diamond miners and many locals. After six years of bureaucratic battles, biologist Roy Funch helped convince the government to create the Parque Nacional da Chapada Diamantina in 1985.

The park has little, if any, infrastructure for visitors. Bus service is infrequent and scarce, particularly to the remote parts of the park. However, camping or sleeping in the park's small caves is free and can be done without a permit. You'll want gear such as backpacks, sleeping bags or tents, which can easily be rented in Lençóis, and reasonably warm clothes.

Geology

According to geologists, the diamonds in Chapada Diamantina were formed millions of years ago near present-day Namibia (Bahia was contiguous with Africa before continental drift). The diamonds were mixed with pebbles, swept into the depths of the sea that covered what is now inland Brazil, and imprisoned when the seabed turned to stone. Ultimately this layer of conglomerate stone was elevated, and the forces of erosion released the trapped diamonds, which then came to rest in the riverbeds.

Day Hikes & Trips

The most popular day trip into the park is to the top of Brazil's tallest waterfall, **Cachoeira da Fumaça** (Smoke Waterfall), so named because before it has plummeted the entire 420m, the water evaporates into mist. This 6km hike requires a guide, so contact an agency in Lençóis. Alternatively, you can originate from the closest village, **Capão** (80km west of Lençóis by road), which has a number of pousadas and a few travel agencies. The nearby mystical Vale do Capão, or **Caeté-Açu**, has attracted an international community of folks interested in an alternative, back-to-the-land lifestyle.

Up the road and outside the park, **Palmeiras** (54km west of Lençóis by car) is a drowsy little town with a scenic riverside position. The streets are lined with colorful houses and a couple of cheap pousadas.

Hikers may want to take the trail along Barro Branco between Lençóis and **Morro do Pai Inácio**, an 1120m peak affording a brilliant view over a plateau-filled valley. Allow four or five hours one-way for the hike.

Just southwest of Lençóis, upstream from Ribeirão do Meio (p494), is the lovely **Cachoeira do Sossêgo** waterfall, with a deep pool at its base and rock ledges for diving. The 7km hike involves a great deal of stone-hopping along the riverbed and should not be attempted without a guide, or when rain or high water has made the lichen-covered rocks slippery.

Gruta do Lapão is probably the largest sandstone cave in South America and is just a 5km hike north of Lençóis. A guide is required as access is tricky.

'Chapada's Pantanal', or **Marimbus**, is a marshy microregion 94km south of Lençóis where you can canoe or kayak while fishing for *tucunaré* (peacock bass) and keeping a lookout for capybaras and *jacarés* (caimans). H20 Expedições and several other Lençóis agencies offer kayak tours here (from R$80; see p494).

Longer Hikes

Navigating the correct routes for these treks can be very difficult, so using a guide is strongly recommended. Treks organized with a guide can last anywhere from two to eight days, and can be custom fitted to the group. They usually involve a combination of camping and staying in local homes and pousadas.

THE BASE OF FUMAÇA

This extremely beautiful yet tiring 36km trek traverses the park from Lençóis to Capão in three days. Detours to other waterfalls are taken along the way, in addition to reaching the base of **Cachoeira da Fumaça**. An extra day can be added walking back to Lençóis or you can continue with the Grand Circuit. Be forewarned that the area around Fumaça's base gets extremely crowded at times, so you may find yourself sharing your sleeping cave with unexpected companions.

VALE DO PATÍ

Much easier than the Fumaça trek, this recommended hike starts and ends in Vale do Capão, and can last from four to six days depending on detours. You are more likely to have the trails to yourself here, and the views over the plains and Chapada's table mountains are spectacular. Stopping in at a local home for a meal or a night is a wonderful possibility. For those who don't want to carry anything, pack mules can be used.

BAHIA

BAHIA

GRAND CIRCUIT

The Grand Circuit of the park covers about 100km, best done in a counterclockwise direction. It takes about five days, but eight days are required to include side trips. Many of these sights have been described on p497.

On the first day, you hike from Lençóis via Vale do Capão to Capão. While there, you can take a side trip to the top of **Cachoeira da Fumaça**. In Capão, you can camp or stay at a pousada such as the pleasantly alternative **Pousada Candombá** (☎ 3344 1102; www.infochapada .com, in Portuguese; Rua das Mangas; d R$145).

From Capão, you can take one very long day or two comfortable ones to cross the beautiful plains region of Gerais do Vieira to the **Vale do Patí**. You can camp overnight on the plains or sleep in the Toca do Gaucho cave.

You can power on in one day to Andaraí, or take a recommended day to putter around the Vale do Patí, checking out **Cachoeirão** (a delightful waterfall) or the tiny ghost settlement of **Ruinha**, before heading out.

Once in Andaraí, side trips to **Poço Encantado** (56km from Andaraí) and the intriguing diamond-era stone ruins in **Igatu** (12km from Andaraí) are highly recommended. In Andaraí, either camp or try the comfortable, riverside **Pousada Ecológica** (☎ 3335 2176; www.pousadaecologicadeandarai.com.br, in Portuguese; d/ tr R$150/180; 🕸 🐾).

In Igatu, the charming **Hospedagem Flor de Açucena** (☎ 3335 7003; www.igatur.com; Rua Nova; campsite per person R$15, d with fan from R$90; 🐾) has wildly natural rooms built into the rocky hillside, abundant greenery and striking views, with a trail leading down to the river.

Another Igatu option is the **Pousada Pedras do Igatu** (☎ 3335 2281; Rua São Sebastião; d with fan R$145; 🖳 🐾), which has lovely views over the hillsides.

Most choose to drive from Andaraí to Lençóis as the walk is on an uninteresting dirt road passing scenery destroyed by machine mining. If you decide to walk, allow two days, camping the first night near Rio Roncador. The next day you'll pass the **Marimbus** microregion, which you could arrange to explore if you set it up ahead of time.

Tours

See p494 for a list of reputable travel agencies offering tours into the park.

Otherwise, knowledgeable guides can greatly enhance enjoyment of any trip into the park, and we recommend you take one, especially as park trails are not marked. Whether you take a guide or not, you should definitely not go alone. Be wary of guides off the street – in the past, groups led by undertrained guides have gotten lost, gone hungry and even been abandoned!

US-born **Roy Funch** (☎ 3334 1305; funchroy@ yahoo.com, Rua Pé de Ladeira 212, Lençóis) has very detailed knowledge of the region, as you can guess from all of his work in, and research on, this area. His book *A Visitor's Guide to the Chapada Diamantina Mountains* expertly demystifies the local flora, fauna, history and geology. It's available at shops in Lençóis.

Another excellent guide is British Olivia Taylor,who can be found at Pousada dos Duendes (see p495); she is familiar with the history, geography and biology of the area, as well as the trails.

Reputable pousadas in Lençóis such as Vila Serrano and Hotel de Lençóis can also recommend excellent guides. For further information about guides, contact the **Associação dos Condutores de Visitantes de Lençóis** (☎ 3334 1425; Rua 10 de Novembro 22; 🕑 8am-noon & 2-8pm) in Lençóis.

Sergipe & Alagoas

Overshadowed by big Bahia to the south, Sergipe and Alagoas are often overlooked by travelers. Those seeking off-the-beaten-path gems would do well to explore these tiny states.

Although Sergipe's provincial capital has few attractions of its own, Aracaju is a great place to arrange a scenic tour up the Rio São Francisco, which at times is unrivalled in beauty. Aracaju is also a gateway to several sleepy colonial towns, where the sound of horse and cart still clatters through the streets, and the scattering of 17th-century churches attests to the area's prominence in Brazil's early settlement days.

Even more enticing than Sergipe is the state of Alagoas, which is known by the cognoscenti for its beautiful coastline. Highlights here include bumping around quaint coastal towns planted among swaying palms and vast stretches of isolated white-sand beaches. Alagoas' laid-back capital, Maceió, overlooks emerald green water and offers fine dining and nightlife – many travelers spend evenings at beachside bars dining on local seafood specialties as the moon rises over the sea.

North and south of Maceió lie surfing beaches, tiny fishing villages and the dazzling, ever-present coastline, with a mix of rustic lodgings and lovely, high-end pousadas (guesthouses). Inland travel offers its own rewards: Penedo, along the Rio São Francisco, is a charming riverfront town with picturesque churches, hilly cobblestone streets and a welcoming atmosphere that's hard to leave behind. If you visit just one inland town in the Northeast, Penedo is an excellent choice.

HIGHLIGHTS

- Playing in the surf and sipping refreshing *agua de côco* (coconut juice) on enchanting **Praia do Gunga** (p513)
- Dancing to the addictive rhythms of *forró* music in an old-school bar in **Maceió** (p511)
- Dining on fresh seafood at a riverside restaurant in colonial **Penedo** (p516)
- Snorkeling the coral reefs and exploring the breathtaking coastline outside of **Barra de Santo Antônio** (p516)

Barra de Santo Antônio ★
Maceió ★
★ Praia do Gunga
★ Penedo

■ POPULATION: 5 MILLION | ■ AREA: 49,980 SQ KM

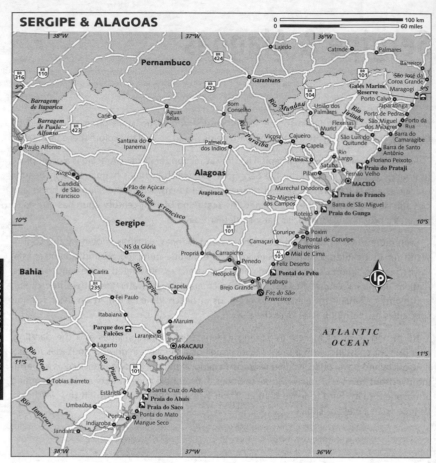

History

During the invasion by the Dutch in 1630, many slaves took advantage of the confusion and escaped to the mountains behind the coasts of northern Alagoas and southern Pernambuco. Where the Alagoan towns of Atalaia, Capela, Viçosa, União dos Palmares and Porto Calvo stand today, virgin forests with fruit and wildlife once provided for colonies of runaway slaves. Palmares, the mightiest republic of escaped slaves, led by the former African king Zumbi, covered present-day Alagoas and Pernambuco. In the 18th and 19th centuries, sugarcane and cotton brought the region prominence; today, sugarcane is still an important crop in the area, alongside oranges and cassava, though

tourism is making in-roads in Maceió. Unfortunately, the states are also known for extreme poverty in the interior and rampant corruption.

Climate

The tropical Atlantic coast of Sergipe and Alagoas remains hot and humid throughout the year. High temperatures range from 30°C (86°F) to 36°C (97°F) and low temperatures run between 20°C (68°F) and 25°C (77°F). Monthly rainfall averages run from 65mm in dry months (August to March) to 335mm in the rainy months (April to July). The interior of Sergipe is part of the semiarid drought-prone *sertão* (backlands), which receives 500mm to 800mm of rainfall a year – though it falls only during a few months of the year (March to June), if at all.

Getting There & Away
Hwy BR-101 skirts the coastline of both Sergipe and Alagoas between 25km and 50km inland. It is the main thoroughfare through the region and the chosen route of most long-distance buses. The main airports in the region are in the capital cities, Aracaju and Maceió.

Getting Around
As is the norm in the Northeast, there is always some form of transportation between where you are and where you need to go, whether by buses, Kombi vans (aka *bestas*), *taxis colectivos* (collective taxis) or moto-taxis (motorcycle taxis).

SERGIPE

Brazil's smallest state, Sergipe is a land of sugarcane fields with a coastline of swamp, mangrove and sandy shores. In addition to attractive beaches just south of Aracaju, the state capital, Sergipe, is home to the sleepy, picturesque colonial towns of São Cristóvão and Laranjeiras.

ARACAJU
☎ 0xx79 / pop 550,000
Friendly and unpretentious if not exactly beautiful, Aracaju has a slightly run-down historic center with pedestrian walkways and a leafy main square. Outlying beaches boast a seemingly endless number of restaurants and hotels to accommodate summertime crowds. Though not a major tourist draw, the area is a pleasant enough location to take care of business before continuing on to your next destination.

History
The seat of state government was moved from São Cristóvão to Aracaju in 1855, in part because of its good, deep harbor – badly needed to handle large ships transporting sugar to Europe – and because residents of the old capital were on the verge of armed revolt. Within a year, an epidemic broke out and decimated Aracaju's population, which the residents of São Cristóvão naturally saw as an omen that the new capital had a doomed future. The city received a makeover in the

early 1900s with the advent of streetcars and other urbanizing elements. In recent days, the newest addition to Aracaju is the bridge over the Rio Sergipe (completed in 2006), connecting the capital to the suburb of Barra dos Coqueiros, and bringing steady development to this quiet coastal area.

Orientation
Aracaju's Centro sits on the Rio Sergipe, guarded from the ocean by a sandy barrier island, the Ilha de Santa Luzia. To the south, past the river mouth, are the city beach neighborhoods of Coroa do Meio, Jardim Atlantico (Praia dos Artistas) and Atalaia, collectively referred to as the *orla* (waterfront). Most of the action and nightlife concentrates in these suburban neighborhoods.

Information
EMERGENCY
Police (☎ 190)

INTERNET ACCESS
Centernet (Rua João Pessoa 64, Centro; internet per hr R$4)

MEDICAL SERVICES
Hospital Governador João Alves Filho (☎ 3216 2600; Av Tancredo Neves, América)

MONEY
Banco do Brasil (Rua Geru 341, Centro)
Bradesco (cnr Rua Geru & Av Rio Branco, Centro)
HSBC Rua Estância (Rua Estância 168, Centro); Rua São Cristóvão (Rua São Cristóvão 56, Centro)

POST
Central post office (Rua Laranjeiras 229, Centro)

TOURIST INFORMATION
Emsetur (www.emsetur.se.gov.br, in Portuguese); Atalaia (Praia de Atalaia s/n); Centro (☎ 3214 8848; Rua Propriá, Centro) Also has an office in Rodoviária Nova; the helpful Centro main office of the state tourism authority distributes free maps of Aracaju.

Sights & Activities
The Tamar Project's small, interesting **Oceanário** (Aquarium; ☎ 3243 3214; Av Santos Dumont, Atalaia; adult/child/student R$8/free/4; ⏰ 9am-9pm Tue-Sun) has tanks with sea turtles, rays and eels as well as examples of specific local freshwater environments and their species. For more on Tamar, see the boxed text, p464.

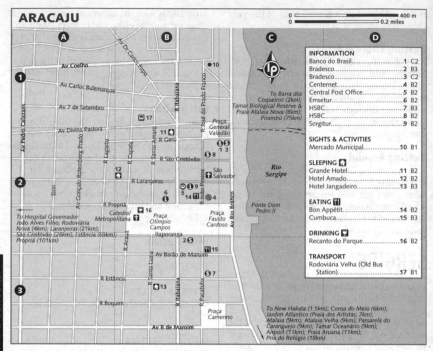

ARACAJU

INFORMATION	
Banco do Brasil........................1	C2
Bradesco...................................2	B3
Bradesco...................................3	C2
Centernet.................................4	B2
Central Post Office....................5	B2
Emsetur....................................6	B2
HSBC..7	B3
HSBC..8	B2
Sergitur....................................9	B2

SIGHTS & ACTIVITIES	
Mercado Municipal..................10	B1

SLEEPING	
Grande Hotel...........................11	B2
Hotel Amado............................12	B2
Hotel Jangadeiro.....................13	B3

EATING	
Bon Appétit..............................14	B2
Cumbuca..................................15	B3

DRINKING	
Recanto do Parque...................16	B2

TRANSPORT	
Rodoviária Velha (Old Bus Station)....................................17	B1

For a more concentrated look at this conservation and education project, go and visit its **biological reserve** (☎ 3276 1202; Pirambú; admission free; ☒ 8am-5pm), where you can see tanks of sea turtles and have a talk with the biologists. To get there, take a Pirambú-bound bus, which passes in front of the Mercado Municipal in the center.

Speaking of the market, the **Mercado Municipal** (Rua José do Prado Franco, Centro; ☒ 6am-6pm Mon-Sat, to noon Sun) is one of the livelier attractions in town, with a wide range of goods sold and bartered inside the two-story building.

BEACHES

With rustling palms and a relative lack of buildings, **Praia Atalaia Nova** (6km), on the Ilha de Santa Luzia, is preferred over the city beaches of **Praia dos Artistas** (7km), **Praia Atalaia** (9km) and **Praia Aruana** (11km) to the south. These beaches are heavily developed but are popular with locals; they are also good sources of inexpensive seafood. Further south, **Praia do Refúgio** (18km) is the prettiest and most secluded beach nearby.

Tours

Local travel agencies offer a variety of day tours, including catamaran trips on the Rio São Francisco to the green waters of the canyon of **Xingó**, or to the **Foz do São Francisco**, where the river meets the sea. A tour is also a pretty good way to check out difficult-to-reach **Mangue Seco** (R$75, p466), on the border with Bahia. Exotic-bird enthusiasts will enjoy a visit to the **Parque dos Falcões** (www.parquedosfalcoes .com.br, in Portuguese), a reserve located 45km from Aracaju; contact **Ecotur** (☎ 3224 9115; www.ecotur .tur.br; tours R$65) for details.

Nozes Tur (☎ 3243 7177; www.nozestur.com.br; Av Santos Dumont 348, Atalaia) Offers a range of day tours, including catamaran departures to Foz do São Francisco (R$98 including lunch) and all-day trips to Xingó (R$110) along the Rio São Francisco.

Sergitur (☎ 3214 2525; www.sergitur.com.br, in Portuguese; Rua João Pessoa 71/75, Centro) Offers a similar assortment of day tours. It's inside the Galeria Norcon Shopping Center.

Festivals & Events

On January 1 a huge fleet of fishing boats sails along the Rio Sergipe following the image of their patron saint to celebrate **Bom Jesus dos Navegantes**. The largest festival of all is the **Festa de São João**, which runs for the entire month of June and includes live *forró* (a music and dance style of the Northeast; see the boxed text, p529) bands and *quadrilha* (a type of square dancing) presentations. The **Festa de Iemanjá** is celebrated on December 8, when followers perform ceremonies and make offerings to the sea goddess. Aracaju celebrates **Carnaval** a full two weeks before Shrove Tuesday, with street parties and other Salvador-style revelry.

Sleeping

The majority of Aracaju's hotels are on the waterfront at Praia dos Artistas and Atalaia (around 7km and 9km from the center, respectively). For a short stay, you'll find those in the center cheaper and more convenient, though lacking charm.

BUDGET & MIDRANGE

Grande Hotel (☎ 3211 1388; Rua Itabaiana 371, Centro; s/d R$45/65; ✷) The best budget option in town, Grande Hotel has sizable, aging rooms with wood floors and decent natural light.

Hotel Amado (☎ 3211 9937; www.infonet.com.br/hotelamado; Rua Laranjeiras 532, Centro; s/d R$50/90; ✷) Potted plants line the porch of this old house, adapted and expanded into a hotel, making it almost pretty. The rooms are spacious, but most lack windows.

Pousada Mirante das Águas (☎ 3255 2610; www.mirantedasaguas.com.br; Rua Delmiro Golveia 711, Coroa do Meio; s/d R$80/100; ✷ 🖥) Two blocks from the waterfront, the Pousada Mirante das Águas has quarters ranging from roomy and well-ventilated to dark and cramped.

Hotel Jangadeiro (☎ 3211 1350; www.jangadeirose.com.br, in Portuguese; Rua Santa Luzia 269, Centro; s/d from R$86/110; ✷ 🖥) The plain gray-walled Jangadeiro features an uninspiring lobby,

---

VELHO CHICO: THE RIVER OF NATIONAL UNITY

For the Nordestino, it's impossible to speak about the Rio São Francisco without a swelling of pride. There is no river like the São Francisco, which is Brazil's third most important river, after the Amazon and the Paraguay/Paraguai. Those who live along its banks speak of it as a friend – hence the affectionate nickname Velho Chico or Chicão (Chico is a diminutive for Francisco).

The location of the São Francisco gave it great prominence during the colonial history of Brazil. With its headwaters in the Serra da Canastra, 1500m high in Minas Gerais, the Rio São Francisco flows north across the greater part of the Northeast *sertão* (backlands) and completes its 3160km journey at the Atlantic Ocean after slicing through the states of Minas Gerais and Bahia, and delineating the Bahia–Pernambuco and Sergipe–Alagoas state borders.

For three centuries the São Francisco, also referred to as the 'river of national unity,' represented the only connection between the small towns at the extremes of the *sertão* and the coast. 'Discovered' in the 17th century, the river was the best of the few routes available to penetrate the semiarid Northeastern interior. Thus, the frontier grew along the margins of the river. The economy of these settlements was based on cattle, which provided desperately needed food for the gold miners in Minas Gerais in the 18th century and later fed workers in the *cacao* (cocoa) plantations throughout southern Bahia.

The history of this area is legendary in Brazil: the tough *vaqueiros* (cowboys of the Northeast) who drove the cattle; the commerce in salt (to fatten the cows); the cultivation of rice; the rise in banditry; the battles between the big landowners; and the odd developments, like Canudos (see the boxed text, p48), with its strange religious fanaticism (and later its horrific destruction).

The slow waters of the São Francisco have been so vital to Brazil because, in a region with devastating periodic droughts, the river provides one of the only guaranteed water sources. Today the river valley is irrigated to produce a huge amount of produce for local consumption and export.

Owing to its life-sustaining importance, the São Francisco has been the source of much myth-making and storytelling. The *bicho da água* (water beast), for example, is part animal and part human. It walks on the bottom of the river and snores. The crews on the riverboats placate the *bicho da água* by throwing handfuls of tobacco into the water. Nordestinos also believe that São Francisco is a gift from God to the people of the *sertão* to recompense all their suffering in the drought-plagued land.

but rooms are nicely kept with big beds and modern bathrooms.

Pousada do Sol (☎ 3226 5500; www.psol.com.br; Rua Eng Francisco Manoel de Costa 43, Atalaia; s/d from R$131/160; ❀ ☎) This well-located pousada, a stone's throw from many of Atalaia's waterfront attractions, offers simple but bright *apartamentos* (rooms with private bathrooms) as well as private cabins that are great for families.

TOP END

Tropical Praia Hotel (☎ 3255 2799; www.tropical praiahotel.com.br; Rua Renato Fonseca Oliveira 55, Atalaia; s/d R$200/220; ❀ ☎ ☒) This waterfront place has clean rooms of varying size. Overall, it's a little worn but is better value than other waterfront hotels.

Aquarios Praia Hotel (☎ 2107 5200; www.aquarios hotel.com.br; Av Santos Dumont 1378, Atalaia; d from R$250; ❀ ☎ ☒) This good-looking hotel has colorful decor, modern rooms with sea-facing balconies, and an inviting pool bar.

Mercure Aracaju del Mar (☎ 2106 9100; www .delmarhotel.com.br; Av Santos Dumont 1500, Atalaia; d from R$260; ❀ ☎ ☒) This contemporary high-rise, featuring minimalist interior design and several bars and restaurants, is a slick addition to Atalaia's waterfront.

Eating & Drinking

The best selection of restaurants and drinking spots stretches out along the waterfront in Atalaia; it's a good spot to stroll at night, when the center is empty (and unsafe for wandering).

Praça de Eventos (Av Santos Dumont, Atalaia; snacks R$4-8) This hangarlike waterfront restaurant complex is surrounded by sidewalk stands selling snacks from crepes and sandwiches to tapioca sweets.

Bon Appétit (☎ 3221 1113; Rua João Pessoa 75, Centro; per kg R$16) One of several simple per-kilo lunch spots in the center.

Cumbuca (☎ 3211 9122; cnr Av Barão de Maruim & Rua Pacatuba, Centro; per kg R$20; ☻ 7:30am-6pm Mon-Fri) This contemporary per-kilo lunch spot, serving tasty fish and vegetable dishes, is a cut above the downtown competition. In the morning, look for the takeaway coffee counter serving up strong espresso and sugar-dusted pastries.

our pick **Parati** (☎ 3227 2100; www.praiaparati.com .br; Rodovia José Saney 47, Praia do Refúgio; mains R$20-40) Aracaju's best restaurant serves excellent seafood plates, with crab and shrimp dishes

---

CRAB FEASTING

Although Aracaju is hardly a culinary capital, it does offer one particularly succulent dish: fresh, savory crabs. Just south of Atalaia, you'll find the popular Passarela do Caranguejo (Crab Lane), a row of open-sided restaurants facing the waterfront that serve the respected local dish. Look for signs advertising 'caranguejo dobrado' (two-for-one crabs).

---

earning top billing. The idyllic outdoor tables overlook one of Aracaju's prettiest beaches, about 10km down the coast from Atalaia.

O Miguel (☎ 3243 1444; www.restauranteomiguel.com .br; Av Antônio Alves 340, Atalaia Velha; mains R$22-40) A top place in town for Northeastern food, specializing in *carne de sol* (tasty, salted meat) grilled and served with beans, rice and vegetables.

New Hakata (☎ 3213 1202; www.newhakata .com.br; Av Beira Mar s/n, Treze de Julho; dinner for 2 R$80; ☻ dinner) This popular Japanese restaurant draws crowds with fresh seafood dishes, all-you-can-eat sushi and live jazz nights (Wednesdays from 7pm, R$35 to R$40). It's next to the Iate Clube (Yacht Club).

Recanto do Parque (Praça Olímpio Campos; ☻ noon-8pm Mon-Sat) A casual, open-air spot for a drink under the trees on the plaza.

Cariri (☎ 3243 1379; www.cariri-se.com.br, in Portuguese; Av Santos Dumont 530, Atalaia; ☻ 10pm-last customer) This Northeastern restaurant on the Passarela do Caranguejo features live *forró* in the traditional style of *pé de serra* (Luis Gonzaga's signature 'foothills' *forró*).

Shopping

There are several places in town good for handicraft-browsing, including the dozen shops specializing in handmade embroidery surrounding the courtyard behind the **Emsetur tourist office** (Rua Propriá, Centro). A wider selection of handicrafts can be found at the waterfront **Praça de Eventos** (Av Santos Dumont, Atalaia); look for the vendors after the sun goes down.

Getting There & Away

AIR

Either **Avianca** (☎ 4004 4040; www.avianca.com.br), **Gol** (☎ 0800-280 0465; www.voegol.com.br) or **TAM** (☎ 3212 8567; airport) can fly or connect you to other Brazilian cities from Aracaju's **airport** (code AJU; ☎ 3212 8500).

BUS

Most long-distance buses leave from the **Rodoviária Nova** (New Bus Station; ☎ 3259 2848), 4km east of the center.

Bomfim (☎ 3211 2210; www.bomfim.com.br, in Portuguese) runs eight daily buses to Salvador (R$50 to R$78, four to six hours). Bomfim buses also go to Maceió (R$43 to R$77, four to five hours, four daily) and Penedo (R$16, three hours, one daily). **Real Alagoas** (☎ 3259 2832; www.realalagoas.com.br) goes to Recife (R$68, five hours). For further access to Penedo, catch a pricier but quicker and more direct Kombi van (R$30, four daily) – just ask around to find out where the vans are currently departing from. Alternatively, you can take one of several daily buses run by **Santa Maria** (☎ 3259 3000) to Neópolis (R$11, two hours) and then a ferry from there (see p516).

Coopertalse (☎ 3259 3028; www.coopertalse.com.br, in Portuguese) and Santa Maria depart for Propriá (R$8, two hours, 10 daily) from the **Rodoviária Velha** (Old Bus Station; ☎ 3214 2578; Centro).

Getting Around

TO/FROM THE AIRPORT

Aracaju's airport is 11km south of the center. A taxi to the airport from the center will cost about R$30. From the Rodoviária Velha, take the Aeroporto city bus.

BUS & TAXI

City buses depart from a large shelter with a series of triangular roofs beside the Rodoviária Nova. For the center, catch any bus going to the Rodoviária Velha, such as Centro or Terminal Rodoviária/Desembarcador.

The Circular Cidade 02 bus (R$2.10) leaves from the Rodoviária Velha and runs down Av Rio Branco south to Atalaia, terminating at the Terminal Integração Atalaia. From there, change to a Circular Praias 01 bus to reach the southern beaches. From the beaches to the center, hop on the Santa Tereza/Bairro Industrial bus.

If you're not ready to brave the bus system, try **Disk Táxi** (☎ 3241 1342). Taxis between the center and Atalaia cost about R$25.

CAR HIRE

Most car-rental agencies are on or near Atalaia's waterfront, including **Sergiloc** (☎ 3255 2323; www.sergiloc.com.br; Av Mário Jorge Vieira 2746), with prices starting at R$95 per day for unlimited kilometers (taxes included).

LARANJEIRAS

☎ 0xx79 / pop 25,000

Nestled between three grassy, church-topped hills, Laranjeiras is the colonial gem of Sergipe. With a quiet grandeur that's somewhat reminiscent of Penedo (p514), Laranjeiras has picturesque cobblestone roads, colonial buildings topped by terracotta roofs and views over the meandering Rio Cotinguiba. The whole town seems unblemished by modern development. Churches here are simple, while the museums offer a glimpse of the region's rich cultural heritage. The surrounding countryside hides crumbling ruins of old sugar mills and estates.

First settled in 1605, Laranjeiras became the commercial center for its surrounding verdant sugar and cotton fields during the 18th and 19th centuries. At one point there were more than 60 sugar mills in and around Laranjeiras sending sugar down the Rio Cotinguiba to Aracaju for export to Europe.

Information

There is usually someone lingering inside the Trapiche building who can answer questions about local sights. Free guides paid by the city, or private guides charging around R$20, can be picked up around the bus station and Trapiche.

Sights

Facing the bus station, the **Trapiche** is an imposing 19th-century structure that historically held cargo waiting to be shipped downriver.

A few kilometers from town is a partly restored sugar mill, known simply as **Engenho** (Mill), in a lovely setting. It is privately owned and not generally open to the public, but it may be possible to arrange a visit through a guide.

CHURCHES

At the top of Alto do Bonfim (Bonfim Heights) is the picturesque 19th-century **Igreja NS do Bonfim**. Although the church is often closed, the fine views make it worth the climb. Reach it by following the street to the left of Nice's Restaurant.

Out at the Engenho Boa Sorte, 4km upriver from town, is the baroque **Igreja de Comandaroba**, constructed by Jesuits in 1734. Only a few guides have keys to it, and unfortunately the church is not well maintained, despite past restoration efforts. A 1km tunnel leads from the church to the **Gruta da Pedra**

SERGIPE & ALAGOAS

MIRACLE MAKERS

In many shrines and churches in the Northeast, visitors come face-to-face with carved wooden heads, arms, feet and other body parts, hung from ceilings or piled in baskets in a special room. A unique mixture of faith and folk art, these ex-votos are called *milagres* (miracles) and are left by supplicants seeking a cure for a specific ailment such as an injured limb or a congenital deformity. In exchange, the petitioner makes a vow (usually to a particular saint) promising to give up their wicked ways or perhaps make a long pilgrimage – which may even be performed on the knees.

The makers of these ex-votos are often self-taught artisans and their work has a primitive, almost cubist, quality. If the artisans are particularly skilled they may model their work – made of either wood or clay – on the sufferer. No one knows exactly how this custom originated, but the *milagre* probably has links to old Iberian traditions, mingled with African and indigenous customs. In some communities, there is an element of mysticism to these carved objects, as if they could absorb the ills of the sufferer.

Many churches and shrines in the *sertão* (backlands) have a *casa dos milagres* (miracle house), where such objects are displayed. During religious festivals, *milagre* artisans make the rounds, offering their services for a small fee.

Furada (a large cave built by the Jesuits to escape their persecutors and used for Mass in the early days).

MUSEUMS
The **Museu de Arte Sacra** (Museum of Sacred Art; Praça Dr Heráclito Diniz Gonçalves; admission R$2; ☺ 10am-5pm Tue-Fri, 1-5pm Sat & Sun) is located in a beautifully restored colonial house next door to the Igreja da Matriz on the main plaza. Built in 1897, the place still has its original wood floors and walls bordered with hand-painted flowers. Guided tours (in Portuguese) reveal pieces gathered from area churches. The last room includes life-size wooden statues of saintly figures, including several used in the town's religious processions. Christ beneath the cross and NS das Dores have real human hair – donated by the faithful for prayers answered. Temporary exhibits delve into the town's contemporary culture (on our last visit, an unusual photography collection showed locals performing self-flagellation during a religious celebration).

Laranjeiras is considered to be the stronghold of Afro-Brazilian culture in Sergipe. At the **Museu Afro-Brasileiro** (☎ 3281 2418; Rua José do Prado Franco 19; admission R$2; ☺ 10am-5pm Tue-Fri, 1-5pm Sat & Sun), a knowledgeable guide will explain (in Portuguese) displays on sugar production, slave torture methods, Afro-Brazilian religions and Laranjeiras' cultural traditions.

Festivals & Events
During the last week of January, Laranjeiras hosts the **Festa de Reis** (also called Encontro Cultural), a religious and folklore festival of traditional music and dance. More folklore revelry occurs during **Semana Folclórico** (Folklore Week), usually the second week of August. You can also catch colorful religious processions during **Semana Santa** (Holy Week; the week preceding Easter).

Sleeping & Eating
Pousada Vale dos Outeiros (☎ 3281 1096; Rua José do Prado Franco 124; s/d R$20/45; 🖭) The only pousada in town has rooms that are small, simple and fairly clean; some have views of the surrounding hills.

Nice's Restaurant (☎ 3281 2883; Praça da Matriz; mains R$12-20) This casual eatery on the main square serves up excellent grilled meats and seafood. Grab a table on the breezy patio.

Getting There & Away
Both Coopertalse and São Pedro buses make the 21km trip between Laranjeiras and Aracaju's Rodoviária Velha (R$2.10, 25 minutes, half-hourly) from 6am to 9:30pm. Unofficial collective taxis run the same route at the same price. If you're coming from the north on Hwy BR-101, get off at the turnoff for Laranjeiras and catch a ride or walk the 4km into town.

SÃO CRISTÓVÃO
☎ 0xx79 / pop 75,000
Atop a steep hill with expansive views over the countryside, the historic center of São Cristóvão houses a sleepy concentration of 17th- and 18th-century colonial buildings

along narrow stone roads and a few wide plazas. Founded in 1590, São Cristóvão is reputedly Brazil's fourth-oldest town and was the capital of Sergipe until 1855. There are no pousadas in São Cristóvão, but it's an easy and worthwhile day trip from Aracaju.

São Cristóvão does not lack for churches. Of particular distinction is **Igreja de Senhor dos Passos** (Praça NS dos Passos; admission free), with a ceiling painted by José Teófilo de Jesus.

Igreja e Convento de São Francisco houses the excellent **Museu de Arte Sacra** (Praça São Francisco; admission R$2; 9am-5pm Tue-Fri, 1-5pm Sat & Sun), which contains some 500 pieces dating back to the 17th century. On the opposite side of the plaza, the **Museu Histórico Sergipe** (☎ 3261 1435; Praça São Francisco; admission R$2; 1-5pm Tue-Sun) is housed in the former Palácio do Governo. It has paintings from Carybé and other Northeastern artists, a room for aficionados of the outlaw Lampião and antique furniture and other relics recalling bygone days.

During one weekend in mid-December, the town comes alive for the **Festival de Arte de São Cristóvão**, featuring popular bands and dance troupes from all over Brazil as well as theater and art exhibitions.

Restaurante O Sobrado (☎ 3261 1310; Praça da Matriz 40; mains R$12-18; 7:30am-9:30pm) serves grilled meats and other standards in an old building overlooking a grassy plaza. Next door, the **Casa de Queijada** (Praça da Matriz 36; sweets R$1; 8am-noon & 2-6pm) is a friendly place to sample *queijadas* (cheese pastries) and other local delicacies.

Frequent buses make the 28km trip between São Cristóvão and Aracaju's Rodoviária Velha (R$2.50, 45 minutes). The town is 8km off Hwy BR-101.

ALAGOAS

MACEIÓ
☎ 0xx82 / pop 940,000

One of the hot, up-and-coming destinations in the Northeast, Maceió is a navigable modern city set on some truly beautiful beachfront. It has a small but buzzing bar and restaurant scene and fairly laid-back streets; it's also the gateway to wonderfully idyllic shorelines to the north and south. On the city's beaches, vivid, emerald-hued water laps the powdery sands that are lined with palms and brightly painted *jangadas* (traditional sailboats). By night, locals follow the meandering beachside path as it weaves past thatched-roof restaurants and palm-shaded football pitches. Maceió's sights are relatively few, leaving you plenty of time to catch some rays and soak up the relaxed atmosphere.

Orientation
Maceió sits on a jagged peninsula between the Lagoa Mundaú and the ocean. The peninsula features two main points: one is the site of the city's port, and the other divides Praia de Pajuçara and Praia dos Sete Coqueiros from the more northern Praia de Ponta Verde and the long Praia de Jatiúca. The Centro is located near the oceanfront, 2km from Pajuçara and 4km from Ponta Verde.

Information
EMERGENCY
Police (☎ 190)
Pronto Socorro (First Aid; ☎ 3221 5939)

INTERNET ACCESS
Internet Cybercafé (Av Dr Antônio Gouveia 1113, Pajuçara; per hr R$3) Inside a shopping arcade.

MEDICAL SERVICES
Unimed (☎ 3215 2000; Av Dom Antônio Brandão, Farol)

MONEY
Major bank ATMs can also be found at the 24-hour Bom Preço grocery store in Pajuçara.
Banco do Brasil (Rua João Pessoa, Centro)
Bradesco ATM (Av Senador Robert Kennedy, Ponta Verde)

POST
Central post office (Rua João Pessoa, Centro)

TRAVEL AGENCIES
Aeroturismo Centro (☎ 3218 2000; Rua Barão do Penedo 61, Centro); Pajuçara (☎ 2126 6060; Av Antônio Gouveia 971, Pajuçara) Though decidedly unhelpful if you're not booking one of their excursions, these agents at least offer free maps and change travelers' checks. Also at the airport.
Jaraguá Turismo (☎ 3337 2780; www.jaraguaturismo .com; Rua Jangadeiros Alagoanos 712, Pajuçara) Handles city tours, trips up the coast and car rentals.

Sights & Activities
The **Museu Théo Brandão** (☎ 3221 2651; Av da Paz 1490, Centro; admission R$2; 9am-5pm Tue-Fri, 2-5pm Sat-Mon) is housed in a handsomely renovated colonial building on the seafront. Excellent

exhibits cover the state's history and popular culture; the most impressive displays are festival headpieces modeled after churches, which are loaded with mirrors, beads and multicolored ribbons and weigh up to 35kg. Traditional dance performances are staged some evenings.

BEACHES

Protected by an offshore coral reef, Maceió's ocean waters are calm and a deep emerald color. The most popular and beautiful of the city beaches are **Praia de Ponta Verde** (4km from the city center) and **Jatiúca** – a pair of lounge chairs and a rental umbrella will run you about R$8 for the afternoon. Be forewarned that Praia do Sobral and Praia da Avenida, close to the center, are polluted. **Praia de Pajuçara** and **Praia dos Sete Coqueiros** sometimes suffer from pollution as well.

The nicest beaches north of the city are thought to be **Garça Torta** (14km) and **Pratagi** (17km), but **Jacarecica** (9km), **Guaxuma** (12km) and **Riacho Doce** (17km) are also tropical paradises. The Riacho Doce bus runs up the coast to these northern beaches.

Tours

From Praia de Pajuçara, *jangadas* sail out 2km at low tide to natural pools formed by the reef (R$20). On a busy day, the pools fill up with people (clouding the water for those interested in snorkeling) and waiters run around serving drinks from floating bars. You can arrange trips with any boat captain – stop in early to find out when the boats are sailing or just stroll down the beach and wait for someone to approach you first.

From the nearby village of Pontal da Barra (see Shopping, p511), schooners leave at around 9am and 1pm on the Nove Ilhas (Nine Islands) tour (R$30). The trip lasts four hours and, in addition to cruising the Lagoa Mundaú, you'll stop at the outlet of the lake into the ocean. Departures are from Pontal da Barra's lakefront restaurants, such as **O Peixarão** (☎ 3325 7011) or **Alípio** (☎ 3351 9151); you can also arrange the trip through a local tour agency.

Festivals & Events

Maceió Fest, a Salvador-style, out-of-season Carnaval in the third week of November, is

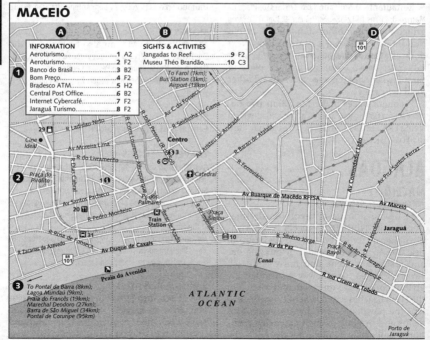

MACEIÓ

INFORMATION		SIGHTS & ACTIVITIES	
Aeroturismo	1 A2	Jangadas to Reef	9 F2
Aeroturismo	2 F2	Museu Théo Brandão	10 C3
Banco do Brasil	3 B2		
Bom Preço	4 F2		
Bradesco ATM	5 H2		
Central Post Office	6 B2		
Internet Cybercafé	7 F2		
Jaraguá Turismo	8 F2		

To Farol (1km);
Bus Station (3km);
Airport (18km)

R. Ladislau Neto

Cine Ideal

Av. Moreira Lima

R. do Livramento

Centro

R. Conte Lourenço Albuquerque

R. João Pessoa

R. Saldinha de Gama

Av. C. da Fonseca

R. Aristeu de Andrade

R. Barão de Atalaia

R. Ferroviário

Av. Comendador Leão

Av. Prof. Santos Ferraz

Praça do Pirolito

Dias Cabral

R. Santos Pacheco

Pç. dos Palmares

Catedral

Av. Buarque de Macêdo RFFSA

Av. Maceió

R. Pedro Monteiro

Train Station

Praça Sinimbu

R. Silvério Jorge

Jaraguá

R. Barão de Jaraguá

R. Prof. Santos Ferraz

R. Rosa de Fonseca

R. Zacarias de Azevedo

Av. Duque de Caxias

Av. da Paz

Praça Rayol

R. Sá e Albuquerque

Canal

R. Ind. Cícero de Toledo

To Pontal da Barra (8km);
Lagoa Mundaú (9km);
Praia do Francês (19km);
Marechal Deodoro (27km);
Barra de São Miguel (34km);
Pontal de Coruripe (95km)

Praia da Avenida

ATLANTIC OCEAN

Porto de Jaraguá

the city's largest festival. As for Carnaval, the city empties and locals head for the beaches, especially Barra de São Miguel (p513).

Sleeping

The best selection of hotels is out at the beaches, with accommodations in Pajuçara being cheaper than in other beach neighborhoods. In general, Maceió's lodging options are on the pricey side.

BUDGET & MIDRANGE

ourpick Maceió Hostel e Pousada (☎ 3231 7762; www .maceiohostel.com.br; Rua Almirante Mascarenhas 85, Pajuçara; dm/d/tr R$35/90/120; 🖭 🛜) This attractive new hostel is a great budget choice a few blocks from the beach. The place is small – shared quads don't leave much room for your backpack – but friendly and efficiently run; doubles are basic and spotless with good showers and large lockers.

Maceió Praia Albergue (☎ 3231 2246; alag@superig .com.br; Rua Abdon Arroxelas 327, Ponta Verde; dm/d R$40/99; 🖭 🛜) Travelers gripe about cramped quarters and chilly showers at this HI hostel (previously known as Alagamar Hostel); still, the place has a wide front veranda and a TV room as well as the usual amenities.

Gogó da Ema (☎ 3327 0329; www.hotelgogodaema .com.br; Rua Francisco Laranjeiras 97, Ponta Verde; s/d R$80/100; 🖭) On a quiet street near two lovely beaches, Gogó da Ema is a five-story guesthouse with bright murals along the hallways but rather bland, aging rooms.

Hotel Ibis (☎ 2121 6699; www.accorhotels.com.br; Av Dr Antônio Gouveia 277, Pajuçara; s/d R$89/119; 🖭 🛜) The Ibis is a clean but generic modern highrise hotel with decent rates (considering its beachfront location.)

Pousada Girassol (☎ 3231 4000; Rua Jangadeiros Alagoanos 535, Pajuçara; s/d R$100/120; 🖭) Girassol has clean, simply furnished rooms. Those in front are bright and breezy, but noisy. Those out back are short on natural light.

Dover Hotel (☎ 4009 5077; www.dover-hotel.com.br; Av Dr Antônio Gouveia 361, Pajuçara; d from R$128; 🖭 🛜) This basic beachfront hotel is nothing to write home about, but the value is fair – and friendly staff man the front desk at all hours, in case you're arriving in Maceió in the middle of the night.

Pousada Aquarela do Brasil (☎ 3231 0113; www .pousadaaquareladobrasil.com; Rua Des Almeida Guimaraes

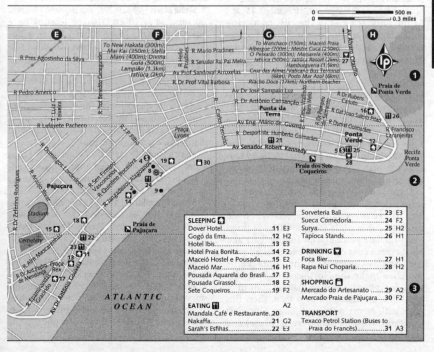

SLEEPING 🏨		
Dover Hotel.............................11	E3	
Gogó da Ema.........................12	H2	
Hotel Ibis..............................13	E3	
Hotel Praia Bonita.................14	E3	
Maceió Hostel e Pousada.....15	E3	
Maceió Mar..........................16	H1	
Pousada Aquarela do Brasil...17	E3	
Pousada Girassol..................18	E2	
Sete Coqueiros.....................19	F2	

EATING 🍴	
Mandala Café e Restaurante.20	A2
Nakaffa................................21	G2
Sarah's Esfihas.....................22	E3

Sorveteria Bali......................23	E3
Sueca Comedoria.................24	F2
Surya....................................25	H2
Tapioca Stands......................26	H1

DRINKING 🍸	
Foca Bier..............................27	H1
Rapa Nui Choparia................28	H2

SHOPPING 🛍	
Mercado do Artesanato.........29	A2
Mercado Praia de Pajuçara....30	F2

TRANSPORT	
Texaco Petrol Station (Buses to	
Praia do Francês).................31	A3

367, Pajuçara; d/tr R$140/180; 🖵) Tucked behind the Hotel Ibis just off the waterfront, this pretty pousada offers simple but (relatively) sophisticated rooms with flat-screen TVs and modern artwork. Ground-level rooms have tiny private patios.

Hotel Praia Bonita (☎ 2121 3700; www.praiaboni ta.com.br; Av Dr Antônio Gouveia 943, Pajuçara; s/d from R$140/160; 🖵 🛜 🖳) This two-story waterfront hotel has an attractive, modern design. Rooms are simple and cheery with sizable windows.

TOP END

Sete Coqueiros (☎ 3213 8583; www.hotelsetecoqueiros .com.br; Av Dr Antônio Gouveia 1335, Pajuçara; s/d from R$210/300; 🖵 🛜 🖳) The decor at this water-front hotel might be described as '70s chic – think lime-green bedspreads and faux-wood fixtures. Whether you consider the look humorous or outdated, Sete Coqueiros is bright and comfortable.

Maceió Mar (☎ 2122 8000; www.maceiomarhotel .com.br; Av Álvaro Otacílio 2991, Ponta Verde; d from R$300; 🖵 🛜 🖳) This high-rise, beachfront hotel has spacious, brightly lit rooms with floor-to-ceiling windows, all with sea views.

Jatiúca Resort (☎ 2122 2000; www.hoteljatiuca.com .br; Lagoa da Anta 220, Mangabeiras; d from R$320; 🖵 🖳) At the northern end of the city, bordering both a lagoon and the ocean, Jatiúca has expansive grounds with sports facilities and a tropical-lagoon-like pool.

Eating

Maceió offers an impressive selection of eateries, from casual to trendy, with the beachfronts of Pajuçara, Ponta Verde and Jatiúca sprinkled with snack stands and restaurants. Take a stroll before choosing – you'll find everything from casual pizzerias to classy seafood restaurants. A good culinary street is Rua Eng Paulo B Nogueira in Jatiúca.

Local seafood specialties worth trying are *sururu* (small mussels) and *maçunim* (shellfish) cooked in coconut sauce, served as main courses or in a *caldo* (soup). Other seafood treats include *peixe agulha* (needlefish) and *siri na casca com coral* (crab in its shell with roe). Stands clustered on the Ponta Verde shoreline make the Northeastern specialty *beiju de tapioca* by heating manioc flour until it solidifies, folding it like a taco, then filling it with savory or sweet fillings. The most traditional is *queijo coalho* (curd cheese) and coconut (R$4).

Sorveteria Bali (☎ 3231 8833; Av Dr Antônio Gouveia 45, Pajuçara; 1 scoop R$2.50) Grab an outdoor table and enjoy Maceió's best ice cream. Among favorites are walnut, guava and tapioca.

Hamburgueria (☎ 3235 3772; Av Álvaro Otacílio 6595, Ponta Verde; mains R$7-14) This stylish bistro has drawn a loyal following with thick, tasty sandwiches, salads and juices amid colorful, vinyl-loving ambience. Electronic music plays overhead – a counterpoint to the slow service.

Nakaffa (☎ 3235 6459; Av Silvio Carlos Luna Viana 1785, Ponta Verde; snacks R$12; ⏲ noon-midnight Mon-Sat, 10am-midnight Sun) This cool, contemporary café specializes in frothy cappuccino, light salads and sandwiches and decadent chocolate desserts.

Sarah's Esfihas (☎ 3327 8877; Rua Dr Lessa de Azevedo 59, Pajuçara; mains R$12-18; ⏲ 3-10pm) Great for a light snack, Sarah's is a popular Middle Eastern joint with outdoor tables that fill at night with young people eating *esfihas* (fluffy breads topped or filled) to order. The *quatro queijos* (four-cheese *esfiha*) is divine.

Massarela (☎ 3325 6000; Rua José Pontes Magalhães 271, Jatiúca; mains R$12-25; 🖵) This is the place to come for homemade pastas and brick-oven pizzas. Decor consisting of hanging cheese and decorative plates adds authenticity.

Stella Maris (☎ 3235 3939; Rua Eng Paulo B Nogueira 290, Jatiúca; all-you-can-eat R$14) For feasting on a budget, it's hard to beat Stella Maris, a no-nonsense *churrascaria* (barbecued-meat restaurant) bringing juicy grilled meats to your table.

Divina Gula (☎ 3235 1016; Rua Eng Paulo B Nogueira 85, Jatiúca; mains R$16-24) A Maceió institution, Divina Gula specializes in the hearty cuisine of Minas Gerais and the Northeast. The *picanha* (steak) is excellent as is the *carne de sol* with plantains, corn and zucchini.

Mestre Cuca (☎ 3327 1970; Av Deputado José Lages 453, Ponta Verde; per kg R$20) An unpretentious self-service restaurant with an excellent lunch spread of regional dishes and salads.

Sueca Comedoria (☎ 3327 0359; www.suecacome doria.com.br; Av Dr Antônio Gouveia 1103, Pajuçara; mains $20-28; ⏲ lunch daily, dinner Mon-Fri) This sleek eatery across from the beach specializes in fresh seafood and innovative regional cuisine.

Mandala Café e Restaurante (☎ 3323 7863; Rua Barão de Maceió 105, Centro; per kg R$22; ⏲ lunch Mon-Fri, music & drinks from 8pm Fri & Sat) In restaurant-starved Centro, this hip eatery, which doubles as an art space and acoustic music venue, is a traveler's oasis. Fill up your plate at the self-service lunch or come in the evening to support local arts while enjoying a cold *cerveja* (beer).

Surya (☎ 3377 0042; Rua Desportista Humberto Guimarães 882, Ponta Verde; per kg R$25) One of the city's best vegetarian restaurants, Surya provides a peaceful setting to enjoy healthy salads, sandwiches and juices.

ourpick Wanchaco (☎ 3377 6114; Rua São Francisco de Assis 93, Jatiúca; mains R$25-48; ⏱ lunch Mon-Fri, dinner Mon-Sat) This highly acclaimed Peruvian restaurant serves excellent seafood in a cozy, creatively decorated setting.

O Peixarão (☎ 3325 7011; www.opeixarao.com.br, in Portuguese; Av Dr Júlio Marques Luz 50, Jatiúca; mains for 2 R$32-40) This casual restaurant is a longtime local favorite for its filling seafood dishes. Grilled fish with shrimp sauce and *caldeirada* (Portuguese seafood stew) are top picks.

New Hakata (☎ 3325 6160; www.newhakata.com.br; Rua Eng Paulo B Nogueira 95, Jatiúca; buffet R$38) Maceió's top Japanese restaurant is a popular spot for sashimi and sushi, particularly on Tuesday's all-you-can-eat buffet night.

Drinking & Entertainment

Maceió's nightlife is scattered among the beach areas, with a few places in Jaraguá, a semi-restored colonial area located near the port. For a laid-back caipirinha with an ocean view, just pick any place along the waterfront in Ponta Verde or Pajuçara.

Mai Kai (☎ 3305 4400; www.maikaimaceio.com.br; Rua Alfredo G de Mendonça s/n, Jatiúca; cover R$10; ⏱ 9pm-last customer Thu-Sun) This Polynesian-themed bar features live pop, rock or *axé* (Bahian pop music). The crowd can be young, especially on *axé* nights.

ourpick Rapa Nui Choparia (☎ 3305 4405; Av Silvio Carlos Viana 2501; ⏱ 6pm-last customer Tue-Fri, from 11am Sat & Sun) Happy-hour specials and a stylish tropical design draw a nightly crowd to this beachfront bar. Features live music on weekends.

Lampião (☎ 3325 4376; Av Álvaro Otacílio, Jatiúca; cover R$6-10; ⏱ 9pm-last customer Tue-Sun) A mix of locals and tourists gathers at this well-known beachfront spot for dancing to Northeastern beats on the breezy shoreline.

Foca Bier (☎ 3304 3100; www.focabier.com.br; Av Álvaro Otacílio 3115, Ponta Verde; cover R$5-10; ⏱ 4pm-2am Tue-Sun) This castle-like bar and music venue hosts live Música Popular Brasileira (MPB) and *forró* bands throughout the week. Come for the outdoor seating and good happy-hour specials from 4pm to 8pm.

Shopping

The Mercado Praia de Pajuçara is an enclosed craft market on Pajuçara's waterfront that sells lacework, hammocks, baskets and ceramics. However, you'll get a better deal at the **Mercado do Artesanato** (Centro). To get there, catch a bus that stops in front of the *antigo* (old) Cine Ideal.

If you are interested in doing some shopping for Alagoas' characteristic *filé* crochetwork, head for Pontal da Barra (8km south), a fishing/crafts village beside the Lagoa Mundaú. Women weave outside the shops that line the streets, and prices are generally the lowest around. To get there, catch any bus heading south with Barra in its name.

Getting There & Away

AIR

Gol (☎ 3214 4078; airport) and **TAM** (☎ 3214 4048; airport) can fly you or connect you to anywhere in Brazil from **Aeroporto Zumbi dos Palmares** (code MCZ; ☎ 3036 5200).

BUS

The **bus station** (☎ 3221 4615) is 4km north of the city center.

Bomfim (☎ 3336 1112) buses go to Salvador on Hwy BR-101 via Entre Rios (R$85, 11 hours, daily) or along the coastal Linha Verde highway (R$105, nine hours, two or three daily). Bomfim also has four daily buses to Aracaju (five hours); choose between *convencional* (R$43) and *executivo* (R$77).

São Geraldo (☎ 3223 4560) goes to Recife (R$40 to R$65, four hours, several daily) and Natal (R$78, nine hours, daily).

For Penedo, **Real** (☎ 3356 1324) has an *expresso litoral* (coastal express; R$25, 2½ hours, two daily), *pinga litoral* (coastal drip; R$20, four hours, two daily) and numerous *bestas* (R$20, 2½ hours). These buses provide access to Barra de São Miguel and Pontal de Coruripe. For more on the *pinga*, see the boxed text, p514.

For day trips to coastal destinations (Maragogi, Praia do Francês etc) north or south of Maceió, contact the tour agency **Cícero Matuto** (☎ 9931 9060). Excursions leave daily around 8:15am and run from R$25 to R$60 per person, depending on where you're going.

Transportation for the northern coast (except Maragogi) can be caught at the bus station or at the *posto* (gas station) Mar Azul at the northern edge of town, two blocks from the Cruz das Almas/Vaticano city bus terminal.

To reach Praia do Francês and nearby points south, there are frequent minibuses departing from a **bus stop** (Ruas Dias Cabral & Zacarias de Azevedo) behind a Texaco petrol station southwest of Maceió's center.

Getting Around
TO/FROM THE AIRPORT
Maceió's airport is 20km north of the center. To reach the center, hop in one of the spiffy taxis operated by the local taxi collective (R$55) – you pay inside the airport and take your ticket to a driver waiting curbside. Buses also run between Ponta Verde and the airport (signed Aeroporto–Ponta Verde) every 45 minutes or so (R$2.15). The same bus can be picked up in Pajuçara across the street from **Pousada Girassol** (Rua Jangadeiros Alagoanos 535); again, look for a bus with 'Aeroporto' on the front.

TO/FROM THE BUS STATION
To reach the center, take the Ouro Prêto bus; for the beaches, catch the Circular 1. A taxi to the center costs R$10, and around R$17 to the beaches.

SOUTH OF MACEIÓ
This stretch of coast is characterized by small, quaint coastal villages – some with amazing beaches – surrounded by wide stretches of coconut plantations. The tourism hot spots on Alagoas' south coast are Praia do Francês and Barra de São Miguel.

Praia do Francês
☎ 0xx82
Given its proximity to Maceió (22km), Praia do Francês functions much like a remote city beach: cars and buses roll in on weekend days and completely clear out by 5pm. Everyone concentrates on one end of Francês' fine, white sands, where just-offshore reefs create calm green waters, and a string of restaurants have beer and fried shrimp. Francês, after all, is a surfer's paradise. Alagoas' best waves are at the southern end (don't despair if you're not traveling with your own equipment – both bodyboards and longboards are available for rent right on the sand). Swimmers opt for the protected reef at the beach's northern end. Walk 15 minutes in either direction to escape the crowds.

SLEEPING & EATING
Pousada Tortuga (☎ 3260 1539; www.pousadatortuga .xpg.com.br; Av dos Arrecifes 14; d with fan from R$100) Among the budget options in town, Tortuga is the best value, a bit battered but clean, calm and right on the beach.

Pousada Miroku (☎ 3260 1187; www.pousadamiroku .com.br; Rua Cavalo Marinho 16; d from R$130; ▨ ▨) A few blocks from the beach, Miroku is a tastefully decorated hotel; rooms have verandas strung with hammocks overlooking a garden.

Pousada do Aconchego (☎ 3260 1193; www.pousada aconchego.com.br; Rua Carapeba 159; d R$150; ▨ ▨) Aconchego has pleasant, well-ventilated rooms that are set around a lush garden. Hammocks, a pool and friendly service add to the charm.

Cesar's Lanches (burgers R$2-5; ☉ 10am-5pm) Worth seeking out, Cesar's cooks up fantastic burgers on the beach. Look for young locals gathering around the tiny stand.

Restaurant Chez Patrick (☎ 3260 1377; Rua Marisia 15; mains R$28-35; ☉ lunch Tue-Sat, dinner Tue-Sun) Run by a French chef, this charming bistro serves seafood casserole, risottos and other tasty fare in a lovely setting.

GETTING THERE & AWAY
From Maceió, catch a minibus (R$2.50, 35 minutes), every 15 minutes from 5am to 10:30pm, from a stop behind the Texaco petrol station (Rua Dias Cabral and Zacarias de Azevedo) southwest of Maceió's center. **Real Alagoas** (☎ 3336 6816) runs the same route for the same price, just less frequently; catch the bus at Maceió's bus station.

Marechal Deodoro
☎ 0xx82 / pop 48,000
On the banks of the tranquil Lagoa Manguaba, Marechal Deodoro is a small, peaceful town with pretty churches and a few streets of colonial architecture dating back to early settlement days. Marechal served as capital of Alagoas between 1823 and 1839 and, although there's not a lot to see, it's an easy and relaxing day trip from Maceió. The Saturday market, held until noon along the waterfront, is particularly lively. Arrive early in the morning to see fishermen working their nets out along the water.

SIGHTS
Marechal Deodoro has picturesque churches, though several of these are crumbling and not open to the public. At the top of the hill above

the lagoon, the **Igreja de NS da Conceição** (8am-1pm Mon-Sat) has a white-and-yellow facade with a modern interior. Nearer to the water, the 17th-century **Igreja e Convento São Francisco** (8am-1pm Mon-Sat) houses the **Museu de Arte Sacra** (Sacred Art Museum; 8am-1pm Mon-Sat), which was closed for renovations at the time of research.

A block from the lagoon, the **Museu Deodoro** (Rua Marechal Deodoro 92; donations accepted; 8am-5:30pm) is set inside the house where Brazil's first president was born. The exhibits give a deodorized view of Manuel Deodoro da Fonseca, emphasizing his role as a military hero and president, but omitting to mention that he achieved this position with a military putsch in 1889 and that he later proved to be a poor politician. Next door, **Artesanato NS Aparecido** (Rua Marechal Deodoro 82; 9am-6pm) sells the lace for which the town is renowned.

A few simple restaurants on the water sell plates of fried fish.

GETTING THERE & AWAY

Buses and minibuses for Marechal Deodoro (R$2.50, 35 minutes) via Praia do Francês depart frequently from a stop behind a Texaco petrol station (Rua Dias Cabral and Zacarias de Azevedo) southwest of Maceió's center. Buses, Kombi vans and collective taxis leave from Marechal's plaza for Praia do Francês (R$2.50, 15 minutes) and back to Maceió.

Barra de São Miguel
☎ 0xx82 / pop 7500

Barra de São Miguel is best known as the gateway to **Praia do Gunga**, an idyllic, white-sand beach that curves to a point at the meeting of the Rio São Miguel and the sea. The center of this small village sits on the riverbank, facing Praia do Gunga. The river mouth and local beaches are protected by a huge offshore reef, leaving the waters calm for bathing or kayaking. A daytime destination throughout the year, Barra only explodes with people during the high season and during Carnaval, when *trios elétricos* (electrically amplified bands playing atop trucks) take over the scene.

Boats for Praia do Gunga (R$25 to R$35) leave in the morning from the town's port, as well as from Praia de Barra de São Miguel.

SLEEPING

Most hotels are located 3km from the center at Praia Niquin, which is a better option for overnighting if you want to be near the beach.

Pousada Aconchego (☎ 3272 2090; Rua João Florêncio 97, Centro; d R$70;) Just a short walk to the boat dock, this modern, simple hotel offers a range of clean, sparsely furnished rooms, some of which are rather spacious.

Hotel Portal Dueleste (☎ 3272 1089; www.hotel portalduleste.com.br; Rua Edison Frazão 108, Niquin; s/d/d R$120/195/240;) Overlooking the beach, this modern hotel has tidy rooms, many with beach views.

Pousada Sete Mares (☎ 3272 1054; www.pousada setemares.net; Av Leonita Cavalcante 371, Niquin; d R$150;) Opening onto a palm-shaded pool area, the spacious rooms of Sete Mares are fairly charming, with decorative touches.

EATING

Dining options are extremely limited. Restaurants at Praia do Gunga are infamously overpriced.

Sarah's Esfiha's (☎ 3272 1637; Rua Leonita Cavalcante 403, Niquin; snacks R$3-8; 2-10pm Wed-Sun) A local favorite after a day in the sun, Sarah's serves Middle Eastern snacks and a few substantial plates.

Bar e Restaurante do Tio (Cais do São Pedro s/n, Centro; mains for 2 R$25-38) On the waterfront near the boat dock, this simple restaurant serves seafood and Brazilian standards (try the shrimp with coconut sauce).

GETTING THERE & AWAY

Buses leave Maceió hourly for the 35km trip to Barra de São Miguel from a Texaco petrol station in the southwest of town. Just ask your taxi driver to take you there.

From here, buses to Maceió (R$6, one hour) via Praia do Francês (R$4.50, 20 minutes) leave hourly until 7pm. Collective taxis run the same route for the same price, leaving from behind the church in the center. Both buses and taxis pass through Praias Niquin and Barra de São Miguel.

If you're coming from Maceió, **Cícero Matuto** (☎ 9931 9060) runs day trips, including stops in Praia do Gunga, Barra de São Miguel and Praia do Francês (R$25).

Pontal de Coruripe
☎ 0xx82

A traditional fishing village that sees few visitors, Pontal de Coruripe lies in an area of verdant coconut plantations, on the edge of a long, deserted beach with beautiful emerald waters. On the peaceful streets of town,

DRIPPING ALONG THE COAST

When traveling from Penedo to Maceió, throw in an extra two hours and opt for the *pinga litoral* (coastal drip) bus. If constant stops and deviations off the main road don't drive you crazy, you'll get a refreshing glimpse into rural life, passing tiny churches, dusty roads leading off into jungle, and rustic fishing huts, with children waving as the bus rolls by.

From Penedo, the bus travels along the river toward the coast, passing the scattered fishing community in **Piaçabuçu**, then swings in from the river and north to Pontal do Peba, where it does a U-turn on the beach. From there it passes through Feliz Deserto, which has lots of cowboys and coconuts, one pousada and plenty of seafood.

The bus turns off Hwy AL-101 a bit further north at **Miaí de Cima**, where there are no pousadas, but many locals on the beach on weekends. The next time the bus turns off the main road is into Barreiras and pretty Coruripe before continuing to Pontal de Coruripe.

Next stop is **Lagoa do Pau**, with shrimp cultivation, weekend homes and a couple of pousadas. Then it's on to Poxim, past sugarcane fields and coconut palms. Approaching Maceió, it stops at the turnoffs for Barra de São Miguel and Praia do Francês. Passing the huge estuaries of the Mundaú and Manguaba lagoons, it's not long before the bus reaches the capital. If you plan to stay at Pajuçara or beaches further north, get off the bus as soon as it turns off the coast road and before it continues into the center of Maceió.

women sit in front of their homes gossiping and weaving palm baskets, placemats and handbags, while out at the cove just opposite the lighthouse, fishermen guide their boats across the sunlit sea.

SLEEPING & EATING

our pick **Pousada da Ada** (☎ 3273 7209; www.adapousada.com; d R$100; ⌘) Travelers breathe a sigh of relief upon entering this pousada, with its shelves of books, lush, unmanicured garden, pets loafing about and a generally bohemian atmosphere. Ada speaks Italian, French, German and English and offers Portuguese lessons in her garden. Her rooms are tastefully simple and bright, and her breakfast and meals (dinner R$20, with vegetarian options) are unforgettable.

Pousada Surf Paradise (☎ 3273 7303; d/chalet with 3 meals from R$320/380; ⌘ ☎) Boasting marvelous views over the ocean, Surf Paradise comprises 15 chalets and four guest rooms spread about a grassy area above the beach. You'll find surfboards for rent and thoughtful touches like free bicycles.

Of the restaurants clustered at the lighthouse, **Peixada da Madalena** (☎ 3273 7234; mains R$15-30; ☺ lunch) cooks up the town's best seafood, alongside tasty Italian dishes.

GETTING THERE & AWAY

The *pinga litoral* bus heading for Maceió (R$10, two hours) passes through Pontal de Coruripe twice daily. You can also catch a daily bus to Penedo (R$12, 2½ hours), which leaves in the mid-afternoon. There's also more frequent collective transport (R$9 to R$15, one hour) to Maceió, with many more options out of Coruripe (9km); or you can get a ride up to the highway (1km) and catch a passing *besta*.

PENEDO

☎ 0xx82 / pop 61,000

Penedo, known as the capital of the lower São Francisco, is the colonial masterpiece of the state and is almost unaltered by tourism. Attractions include the city's many baroque churches and colonial buildings and the opportunity to travel the sometimes-jade-colored waters of the Rio São Francisco. Penedo's downtown bustles with a daily market, Saturday being the biggest day, when people from surrounding villages pour in to do their shopping. When we last visited, major restorations were in the works, so look for an extended riverfront promenade, a refurbished *Mercado Público Municipal* (central market) and several churches gleaming like they used to.

History

Since its founding, Penedo has been a commercial center, owing to its prime position on the Rio São Francisco. The town was founded sometime between 1535 and 1560 by Duarte Coelho Pereira, who descended the Rio São Francisco in pursuit of the indigenous Caetes who were responsible for killing a bishop. Penedo is claimed to be the river's first colonial settlement. It was also the scene of a fierce 17th-century battle between the Dutch and the Portuguese for control of the Northeast. In the 19th century, Penedo was one of the focal points of the abolitionist movement in Alagoas. In the 20th century, the city lost its prominence as a commercial center, which probably saved its colonial buildings from destruction.

Information

You'll find a **Bradesco bank** (Av Duque de Caixas 71) with an ATM on the riverfront. Two other ATMs are located nearby, around the central square.

Tourist office (☎ 3551 2727; Praça Barão de Penedo) Located in the Casa da Aposentadoria; staff hand out maps and offer city walking tours (for a fee and in Portuguese).

Sights & Activities

Penedo has a rich collection of 17th- and 18th-century colonial buildings, including many churches.

CHURCHES

The **Convento de São Francisco e Igreja NS dos Anjos** (Praça Rui Barbosa; admission R$2; ☑ 8–11am & 2–5pm Tue-Fri, 8–11am Sat & Sun) was under construction for nearly 100 years before its completion in 1759, and is considered the finest church in the state. Even Dom Pedro II (Brazil's second and last emperor) paid a visit. Of particular note are the richly colored ceiling, the gold rococo altar and the statue of St Francis to the left of it that was carved by Aleijadinho.

The **Igreja de NS da Corrente** (Praça 12 de Abril; ☑ 8am–6pm Tue-Sun), completed in 1765, has some fine Portuguese *azulejos* (tiles), painted in green, purple and gold – colors rarely seen in Brazil, or Portugal for that matter. The Lemos family were big benefactors of the church (their family seal is marked on the floor) and abolitionists; slaves fled to the church for protection – some were even hidden behind panels of the church walls.

The **Igreja NS do Rosário dos Pretos** (Catedral do Penedo; Praça Marechal Deodoro; ☑ 8am–6pm) was built by slaves. The **Igreja de São Gonçalo Garcia** (Av Floriano Peixoto; ☑ 8am–6pm Tue-Sun) was built at the end of the 18th century. The small **oratório** (Praça Barão de Penedo) is where the condemned spent their last night praying before being hanged.

MUSEUMS

Occupying the top floor of the house Dom Pedro II once slept in, the **Museu do Paço Imperial** (Praça 12 de Abril 9; admission R$4; ☑ 11am–5pm Tue-Sat, 8am–noon Sun) displays lamps, portraits, furniture and elegant finery from the imperial period (17th and 18th centuries); it's tiny but nicely presented. The **Casa do Penedo** (www.casadopenedo .com.br; Rua João Pessoa 126; admission R$2; ☑ 9am–noon & 2–6pm Tue-Sun) is a modest museum of relics and photographs from Penedo's history.

RIVER TRIPS

Regular ferries depart from the center for **Neópolis**, a colonial town on a hill with some interesting buildings and good crafts for sale, and **Carrapicho** (officially Santana de São Francisco; R$1, every 30 minutes), a small town noted for its ceramics.

An organized tour takes visitors to the **Foz do São Francisco** (R$25, four-person minimum), where the river meets the sea at a beach with dunes and natural pools. The most frequent departures for this trip leave 28km downriver from Piaçabuçu. Inquire at the tourist office for more information or call ☎ 3552 1226.

Festivals & Events

The **Festa do Senhor Bom Jesus dos Navegantes** is held over four days from the second Sunday of January, and features an elaborate procession of boats and a sailboat race.

Sleeping

Pousada Ribeirinha (☎ 3551 2691; Av Comendador Peixoto 49; s/d with fan R$35/50) This bare-bones option lies on the waterfront and has simple rooms (some without windows), though one room overlooks the river. No breakfast, but showers (R$2, towel provided) are available to the public.

Pousada Estylos I (☎ 3551 2429; Praça Jácome Calheiros 79; s/d with fan from R$40/60) A local family rents clean, simple *apartamentos* in its home on a colonial plaza. The rooms here are nicer than those in its sister location (Rua Dâmaso do Monte 86).

Hotel Turista (☎ 3551 2237; Rua Siqueira Campos 143; d with fan R$50) Traffic noise fills this simple hotel, and the rooms are small and bare, but it is clean and cheap.

Pousada Central (☎ 3551 2460; www.pousadacentral -al.com.br; Av Floriano Peixoto 64; s/d from R$60/90; ☒) This cheerful pousada on the main square has small, basic rooms – clean, if a little dark – and a cozy living room with wicker furniture.

Hotel São Francisco (☎ 3551 2273; www.hotelsaofrancisco.tur.br; Av Floriano Peixoto 237; s R$98-166, d R$129-212; ✹ ❄) The rooms in this 1960s-style hotel (something of an eyesore on the town's otherwise scenic skyline) have varnished wood floors and trim furniture.

Pousada Colonial (☎ 3551 2355; Praça 12 de Abril 21; d without/with view R$100/120; ✹) The rooms in this beautifully converted colonial house on the waterfront have stained wood floors, dramatic high ceilings and antique furniture.

Eating

Several supermarkets are on the main waterfront plaza near the bus stop.

Padaria São Francisco (Rua Nilo Pessanha 149; pastries R$1; ✹) Up the street from the São Francisco convent, this atmospheric bakery has a small selection of fresh baked goods.

Esquina Imperial (☎ 3551 5858; Av Floriano Peixoto 61; lunch R$10) A favorite budget spot, Esquina Imperial has a simple self-service lunch, and soups and sandwiches at night.

our pick Oratório (☎ 9961 2385; Av Beira Rio 301; mains for 2 R$23-45) Penedo's best restaurant, Oratório serves excellent plates of seafood stews and grilled fish in a pleasant outdoor river setting. When in season, the *pitu* (giant river shrimp) should not be missed.

Forte da Rocheira (☎ 3551 3273; Rua da Rocheira 2; mains for 2 R$25-45) This former Dutch fortification, perhaps better for drinks than dinner, has a splendid view out over the water.

Getting There & Away

The **bus station** (☎ 3551 2602) is on a riverfront traffic island. For Maceió, bus options are the *expresso litoral* (R$20, 2½ hours, two daily) and the *pinga litoral* (R$20, four hours, two daily). *Bestas* leaving from the same spot run a more frequent service to Maceió (R$17 to R$25, every 30 minutes). Any of these options provide access to Pontal de Coruripe, Barra de São Miguel and Praia do Francês. For more on the *pinga* see the boxed text, p514.

There is one daily bus to Salvador (R$70, nine hours) via Propriá (R$6, 1½ hours) and Aracaju (R$13, three hours). It may be more convenient to take a ferry to Neópolis (R$1.50, 15 minutes, every 30 minutes from 5:30am to 10pm), where there are more frequent buses.

Topiques (vans) also go to Aracaju, Propriá and most frequently to Piaçabuçu (R$2, 40 minutes) every 30 minutes from 6am to 6pm). Ask the *topique* drivers hanging out on the riverfront for departure times.

NORTH OF MACEIÓ

The coast up to Barra de Santo Antônio has fluffy sands, green waters and no shortage of coconut palms. From that point to Maragogi, the ocean takes on a calm, shallow and warm aspect due to the many reefs close to shore. Low tides can allow you to walk 1km out to sea. The stretch from Barra do Camaragibe to Porto de Pedras is a sweet little pocket off the highway and a great place to treat yourself. Strung along one road are tiny villages with barely the basics to support tourism, save for a few luxury pousadas. Maragogi is the seat of tourism in the area. Wherever you go, it's advisable to get cash before heading out – the only reliable bank between Maceió and Recife is in Maragogi.

Getting There & Around

There are a variety of transport options to reach northern destinations. The Real Alagoas bus to Porto de Pedras (R$18, 3½ hours, five daily) runs via Barra do Camaragibe, São Miguel dos Milagres and Porto da Rua from the bus station in Maceió. This bus, as well as minibuses, *bestas* and collective taxis traveling the same route, can be caught at the *posto* Mar Azul at the northern edge of Maceió (ask your taxi driver to take you). Travel between these little towns is extremely easy up until about 7pm.

Barra de Santo Antônio
☎ 0xx82 / pop 15,000

Barra de Santo Antônio is a mellow fishing village built along the mouth of the Rio Jirituba. Across the river, on the narrow Ilha da Croa, is a small settlement known as 'Barra II' and a collection of weekend houses. The main attraction of the area is the deserted **Praia de Carro Quebrado**, an exotic white-sand beach backed by thick palms. It is a 7km walk or beach-buggy ride (R$25 per car) from Barra II.

Praia Tabuba is a pretty, tranquil bay with a few bars and a couple of pousadas 4km south of Barra de Santo Antônio. There are reef tidal pools off the beach – ask at the bars about a ride there by *jangada*.

SLEEPING & EATING

Chalés Costa Dourada (☎ 3291 2148; luizmendonca@
nornet.com.br; s/d with fan R$100/120) Barra II has
three pousadas, and the Costa Dourada's
two-bedroom brick chalets are surprisingly
the most economical. Though they feel a little
like government housing, each one has a full
kitchen and a hammock hung on the porch.
There's no breakfast.

our pick **Pousada Arco-Íris** (☎ 3291 1250; www.ta
buba.tk; Rua 10, Praia Tabuba; d with fan/air-con R$110/135;
🔀) Arco-Íris is an attractive, high-quality
pousada surrounded by greenery, 30m from
the beach. The comfortable rooms are tastefully decorated and open onto a leafy back
veranda. The delightful restaurant (mains
R$13 to R$25, open for lunch and dinner
Tuesday to Sunday) is a good place to enjoy
fondues, pizzas, pastas, chicken curry and
other unique dishes.

GETTING THERE & AROUND

You can catch minibuses to Barra de Santo
Antônio (R$5, one hour, every 30 min-
utes) from 5am to 6:30pm at Maceió's bus
station or *posto* Mar Azul at the northern
edge of town. Collective taxis also leave from
the Mar Azul but charge extra to enter the
town.

For Maceió, catch one of the frequent buses
leaving Barra de Santo Antônio's bus station.
To head north, walk or catch a ride to the
main highway, where you can flag down a
bus, *besta* or collective taxi.

Canoes cross the river from behind the
bus station (R$2), while the car ferry (return
R$10 per car) leaves from beside the Banco
do Brasil, up the road from the bus station.

Barra do Camaragibe
☎ 0xx82

This idyllic fishing village is strung along the
road, on the edge of a small, reef-laden bay.
Jangadas make trips south to **Praia do Morro**, a
deserted beach with cliffs and clear waters.
On the main road, **Restaurante & Pousada Foz do
Camaragibe** (☎ 3258 5140; Rua São José s/n; s/d R$30/50;
🔀) has clean, simple rooms, several with tiny
windows that open onto the sea. The seafood
at the outdoor restaurant is quite good (mains
R$20 to R$30). A few doors down, the **Pousada
& Restaurante Barra Mar** (☎ 3258 5141; Rua São José
s/n; s/d R$35/65; 🔀) has a similar mix of simple
rooms and a good seafood restaurant. It's 7km
to São Miguel dos Milagres.

São Miguel dos Milagres
☎ 0xx82 / pop 7600

São Miguel dos Milagres has fine beaches
with warm, shallow seas protected by offshore
reefs. **Pousada e Restaurante do Gordo** (☎ 3295
1181; s/d with fan R$25/50), on the main road, rents
out extremely basic rooms. The restaurant in
front serves hearty, home-cooked fare (mains
R$10 to R$25). It's a five-minute walk through
coconut-palm plantations to the beach and
4km to Porto da Rua.

Porto da Rua
☎ 0xx82

Much like its neighbors, Porto da Rua is a small
and sweet village of colorful houses spread
along the road. A stretch of coconut plantation
about 2km deep separates the center from the
beach, where there are a few bars. The area's
accommodations options are fairly spread out
and set up for those traveling by car. The nicer
pousadas have no problem picking up guests
from as far away as Maceió; just call them.

SLEEPING

Pousada das Acácias (☎ 3295 1142; Av de Francisco Lima
125; d from R$100; 🔀) On the main road in Porto
da Rua, this friendly, family-run guesthouse
has simple, modern rooms, and the owners
offer hiking and biking excursions around
the area.

The following two pousadas are 1.5km
down a dirt road (look for the signs), south
of Porto da Rua.

Pousada do Caju (☎ 3295 1103; www.pousadacaju
.com; d/bungalow from R$320/440; 🔀) This estate
house with a wraparound porch achieves the
cool, urban-antique look in its lovely rooms.
It has gorgeous gardens, an inviting restaurant (mains R$28 to R$40) and is just a short
stroll to the beach. The pousada was recently
chosen by *Budget Travel* magazine as one of
'50 Totally Charming Hotels' of the world.

Pousada do Toque (☎ 3295 1127; www.pousadado
toque.com.br; d with 2 meals from R$750; 🔀 🍴) Truly
one of the top pousadas in the state, Toque
is an oceanfront property with a lushly landscaped garden and beautiful thatched-roof
bungalows (with decks and unique features
like private saunas and pools).

Porto de Pedras
☎ 0xx82 / pop 11,000

Porto de Pedras is a sweet little fishing town
and, as it is the most established on this stretch

of road, it boasts a few shops, bars and restaurants. It is located where the Rio Manguaba meets the sea, with a hilltop lighthouse offering great views.

Pousada dos Ventos (☎ 3298 1301; Rua 12 de Janeiro 12; s/d with fan from R$40/70) Near the ferry dock, this basic pousada offers a handful of clean rooms – a few with sea views. It's nothing special, but the location is convenient and the price is right.

Pousada Costa das Pedras (☎ 3298 1176; Rua Dr Fernandes Lima s/n; s/d R$120/130; 🔀) On the main road into town, this guesthouse has five rooms that are handsome but a little dark. There's also a restaurant – its outdoor tables on the grassy lawn make a charming setting for the eclectic cuisine.

Peixada da Marinete (☎ 3298 1267; Rua Seu Avelino Cunha s/n; mains R$35-55) One of the best restaurants in town, this modest family-run spot serves tasty plates of shrimp, octopus and other fresh catch.

GETTING THERE & AWAY

A pedestrian ferry (R$2, 6am to 7pm) and a car ferry (car/pedestrian R$8/free, 6am to midnight) provide access to Japaratinga. Once across the river, you'll need to catch a collectivo (R$5) the rest of the 9km into Japaratinga.

Japaratinga
☎ 0xx82 / pop 7700

Japaratinga's shallow waters are protected by coral reefs, and the beaches are backed by coconut trees and fishing huts. Under the moonlight, you can walk a couple of kilometers into the sea. The town is small but more touristy than the beach towns to its south, and it has a bustle to it.

Accommodations on the whole are overpriced, but **Pousada dos Mares** (☎ 3297 1398; www .pousadadosmares.com.br; d with fan/air-con R$60/80; 🔀) is a cute place with simple, economical rooms.

Kombi vans regularly make the 10km trip north to Maragogi (R$5).

Maragogi
☎ 0xx82 / pop 27,000

Maragogi is a small town with a waterfront strip along a white-sand beach and amazingly turquoise sea. It is probably the most visited beach in the state, due to its major draw: the sandbars and reefs that make up the **Galés marine reserve**, 6km offshore. Trips to the reserve (R$45 to R$50) are easily organized through

---

LIFE & DEATH OF THE SAND DOLLAR

Many beachgoers around Maragogi find themselves tripping over countless sand dollars that have washed up on the sand – some bleached by the sun, others covered in a moss-like covering of tiny spines. If you don't know whether the sand dollar is mineral or animal (or dead or alive, for that matter) here's a crash course: they're marine animals related to the star fish and the sea urchin.

While alive in the ocean, water passes through the porous purple sand dollar, allowing it to move, or 'swim,' while spines on its underside permit it to creep slowly along the ocean's sandy floor in search of tiny organic particles – the sand dollar's food source. The sand dollar's life span ranges from one to 15 years – what you find on the beach are just the skeletal remains.

---

the beachfront restaurants or hotels. It is a very touristy affair, with touts trying to sell you everything from fish food (unnecessary) to underwater photos, but if you grab a mask and snorkel and swim away from the crowd, the reefs are rich with sea life.

Maragogi's tourism is mostly day-use but, despite this, it has quite a few pousadas and Pernambucano weekend homes. Check out the full list of accommodation options and more tourist information (including a section in English) at www.maragogionline.com .br. The helpful travel agency **Costazul** (☎ 3296 2125; www.costazulturismo.com.br; Rua Francisco Holanda Cavalcante 6) can help book rooms and arrange excursions, too. Maragogi has a Banco do Brasil with an ATM.

On the waterfront, **Pousada Mariluz** (☎ 3296 1511; www.pousadamariluz.com.br; Rua Sen Rui Palmeira 885; s/d R$90/180, d with view R$200; 🔀) is fair value (for the area), offering small but cheerfully painted rooms, some with verandas facing the ocean. For something a bit more budget-friendly, try **Pousada Canto Das Sereias** (☎ 3296 1521; www.telelista .net; Av Sen Rui Palmeira 1118; d from R$120; 🔀) and try to snag the 3rd-floor ocean-view room with a private balcony.

One of numerous seafood restaurants on the water, **Restaurante Frutas do Mar** (☎ 3296 1403; Rua Sen Rui Palmeira 876; mains for 2 R$40-55) is particularly noted for its *caldeirada*. It has relaxing outdoor seating on the beach.

A casual, open-air dining spot, **Pizzeria Regina** (☎ 3296 1279; Av Beira Mar s/n; pizzas R$14-28; ☾ dinner) serves many varieties of pizza, as well as pasta, lasagna and desserts.

Real Alagoas runs buses to Maragogi (R$20, four hours, two daily) from Maceió's bus station and also from Recife (R$16, two hours, two daily). Taxi vans also run to Maragogi from Maceió (R$20) from a petrol station north of town (ask around for directions); the trip takes just over two hours, thanks to the race-car-style drivers who weave in and out of traffic along the coastal roads.

Pernambuco

Small Pernambuco is one of the most exciting and varied destinations in the Northeast. Among the earliest centers of Portuguese settlement in Brazil, it has had five centuries to develop rich cultural traditions melding European, African and Indigenous influences, especially in music and dance. Pernambuco gave Brazil the now universally popular *forró* but, especially in Recife and Olinda, you'll discover a whole gamut of musical styles from frenetic *frevo* to the big drum beats of *maracatu* – particularly at those cities' wild and euphoric Carnavals.

Recife, Pernambuco's capital, is one of Brazil's biggest cities, a very urban place with a rich cultural and entertainment scene and a fascinating history. By contrast its much smaller and calmer neighbor, Olinda, is a charming, historic town, full of picturesque churches, colonial colors and talented artisans.

North and south of these centers stretches a short but glorious coast with dozens of palm-fringed sandy beaches, great surfing waves and crystal-clear reef pools. Porto de Galinhas, south of Recife, has developed into one of Brazil's more popular coastal resorts; nearby Tamandaré is a mellower spot for a more relaxed beach stay.

But Pernambuco's most glittering gem sits over 500km out into the Atlantic. The archipelago of Fernando de Noronha is a tropical-island getaway to dream about, a fervently protected aquatic Eden with near-empty, postcard-perfect beaches and surrounded by warm, brilliantly clear waters with world-class diving. It is probably Brazil's most awed destination.

PERNAMBUCO

HIGHLIGHTS

- Dance in the streets of **Recife** (p526) or Unesco-betrothed **Olinda** (p534) during euphoric Carnaval
- Beach-hop Brazil's most stunning – and gloriously empty – beaches in **Fernando de Noronha** (p541)
- Lose a few days embedded in beautiful sands at **Praia dos Carneiros** (p537)
- Mingle with bronzed revelers in and around the coastal resort of **Porto de Galinhas** (p536)
- Dive or snorkel Brazil's most heavenly seas in **Parque Nacional Fernando de Noronha** (p541)

Fernando de Noronha (525km)

Olinda ★
Recife ★
Porto de Galinhas ★
Praia dos Carneiros ★

■ POPULATION: 8.9 MILLION   ■ AREA: 98,310 SQ KM

History

The history of Pernambuco centers on Recife and Olinda. Both were founded in the 1530s at the same time as sugarcane was introduced to Brazil. With the indigenous population brutally subdued, coastal Pernambuco quickly became one of Brazil's most important sugarcane producers, using the labor of African slaves. Plantation owners built their homes and churches on the hills of Olinda, the original capital of the captaincy of Pernambuco. Recife was Olinda's port.

Dutch invaders sacked Olinda in 1630 but, doubtless feeling more at home among the waterways of Recife, developed it as the capital of ambitiously named New Holland. In 1637 they shipped in Prince Maurice of Nassau to govern the colony. Maurice's enlightened freedom-of-worship policy helped keep things calm while the Dutch extended their control as far north as Maranhão. But after the prince was ordered home in 1644, uprisings against Protestant Dutch rule eventually led to their expulsion in 1654.

Olinda was rebuilt, but Recife outgrew it to become South America's biggest city in the late 17th century. Recife's merchants eclipsed the power of Olinda's sugar barons in a bloody feud called the Guerra dos Mascates in the 18th century. The city finally became Pernambuco's capital in 1837. As the sugar economy floundered in the 19th century, Brazil's balance of population and power tipped from the Northeast to the Southeast, and Pernambuco declined to backwater status. Recife remained a significant port and commercial center, however, and industries developed in the 20th century. But the city still has double the Brazilian average number of households living below the official poverty line.

In recent years tourism has become a new commodity for Pernambuco, helping to waken Olinda from its slumber and turning the fishing village of Porto de Galinhas into one of Brazil's booming beach towns.

Climate

Pernambuco is hot and dry, and has a light rainy season from December to March. Temperatures along the coast rarely dip below the high 20°Cs (low 80°Fs) and the interior is a lot hotter. Any time of the year is a good time to visit, but the temperatures are a bit more moderate and the foliage greener during the rainy season.

National Parks

Approximately 70% of the 21-island Fernando de Noronha archipelago (p539), 525km from Recife, is a national marine park, featuring crystal-clear waters and abundant marine life, from iridescent fish and hundreds of spinner dolphins to giant sea turtles. The park is tightly controlled by the Instituto Chico Mendes de Conservação da Biodiversidade (ICMBio; Chico Mendes Institute of Biodiversity Conservation) and the government of Pernambuco.

Getting There & Around

Recife's Guararapes airport receives regular scheduled flights from Lisbon, Madrid, Miami and all over Brazil, and charter flights from a few European and North American cities. Direct buses to nearly all major Brazilian cities serve Recife's large bus station.

Bus transport around Pernambuco is straightforward and easy. Buses are more frequent in the coastal areas than in the more provincial interior. Fernando de Noronha is reached via flights from Recife or Natal.

THE COAST

RECIFE

☎ 0xx81 / pop 1.5 million

Recife ('heh-*see*-fee'), capital of Pernambuco, is the Northeast's most exciting city after Salvador, with a vibrant cultural and entertainment scene, an intriguing coastal setting and a fabulous Carnaval. It's an edgy urban place of glassy high-rises, crowded commercial areas, thundering traffic and sprawling suburbs, both wealthy and poverty-stricken. It will take a little time to negotiate your way round the city and unlock its secrets. There are no must-visit beaches, but if you like your cities gutsy, gritty and proud, and can bear a whiff of putrefaction from the waterways, Recife is for you. It takes its name from the offshore *recifes* (reefs) that calm the waters of the city's ports and shoreline.

The charming and far more tranquil historic town of Olinda lies on Recife's northern edge, just 6km from the city center, and many visitors opt to stay in Olinda and visit Recife during the day, or venture in for the animated nightlife.

As a 2014 FIFA World Cup host city, Recife was planning a new stadium, subway station

PERNAMBUCO

PERNAMBUCO

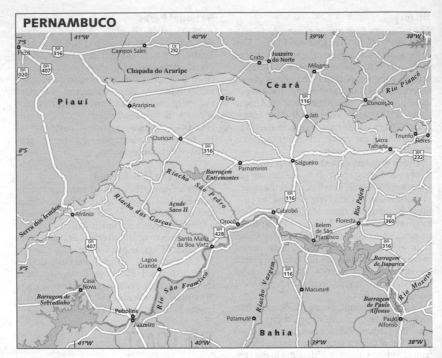

PERNAMBUCO

and passenger terminal, 700 new hotel beds and major airport improvements at the time of writing.

Orientation

Recife is sprawling and more difficult to negotiate than most cities in the Northeast. The city center, a jumble of high-rise offices, colonial churches and thronged market areas, is spread over a number of islands and peninsulas at the mouths of the Rio Capibaribe and other, lesser rivers, with a dozen bridges crisscrossing the waterways. The main districts of interest are the historic Recife Antigo on the ocean side; Santo Antônio (the governmental area) in the middle, with a bustling commercial district to its south; and Boa Vista to the west. After dark and on Sunday afternoon many streets in the center are empty.

The middle-class suburb of Boa Viagem, with the best range of accommodations and restaurants, begins 3km south of the center and extends about 5km along the coast. Recife's airport is at the south end of Boa Viagem, 2km inland; the bus station is a 17km metro ride west of the center.

Information

BOOKSTORES
Livraria Cultura (Map p524; ☎ 2102 4033; Paço Alfândega, Rua da Alfândega; ☿ 10am-10pm Mon-Sat, 2-8pm Sun) The best bookstore north of Salvador, with a huge English-language section.

EMERGENCY
Medical emergency (☎ 192)
Police Boa Viagem (Map p527; ☎ 3081 1710; cnr Av Conselheiro Aguiar & Praça Cidade do Porto, Boa Viagem); emergency (☎ 190)
Tourist police (☎ 3322 4867; ground fl, airport; ☿ 24hr)

INTERNET ACCESS
Internet cafés are hard to come by in Boa Viagem. Try Shopping Recife (Map p527).
Lan-House (Map p524; Rua do Hospício; per hr R$1.50; ☿ 8am-7pm Mon-Sat) Inexpensive little city-center spot.

INTERNET RESOURCES
Destino Pernambuco (www.destinopernambuco.com .br) Site of the Recife Convention & Visitors Bureau.
Guia Pernambuco (www.guiapernambuco.com.br)

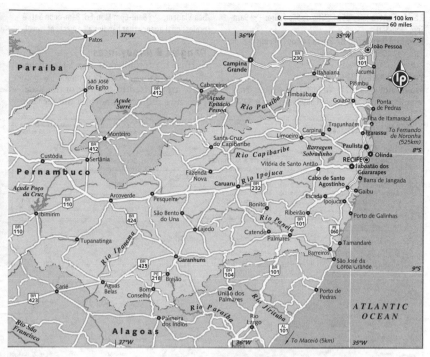

LAUNDRY

Most hotels will arrange affordable laundry services for guests.

Vivaz Lavanderia (Map p527; ☎ 3466 3755; Av Conselheiro Aguiar 2775, Boa Viagem; per 10/20 items R$25/42; ⏱ 7am-7pm Mon-Fri, 8am-5pm Sat)

MEDICAL SERVICES

Boa Viagem Medical Center (Map p527; ☎ 3343 9386; Av Visconde de Jequitinhonha 1144, Boa Viagem) Large, modern hospital with 24-hour emergency service.

Real Hospital Português (off Map p524; ☎ 3416 1122; www.rhp.com.br; Av Agamenon Magalhães 4760) Private 24-hour hospital; with a smaller 24-hour clinic on Av Conselheiro Aguiar in Boa Viagem (Map p527).

MONEY

At the airport there are plenty of ATMs as well as the exchange office **Confidence Câmbio** (☎ 3322 4222; ⏱ 24hr).

Banco do Brasil (Map p524; Av Dantas Barreto 541; ⏱ 10am-4pm Mon-Fri, ATMs 6am-10pm daily) Currency exchange and ATMs.

Bradesco (Map p524; Av Conde da Boa Vista 126; ⏱ 10am-4pm Mon-Fri, ATMs 6am-10pm daily) Currency exchange and ATMs.

Bradesco (Map p527; Av Conselheiro Aguiar 3236, Boa Viagem; ⏱ 6am-10pm) ATM; accepts foreign cards.

Hipermercado Extra (Map p527; Av Domingos Ferreira 1818, Boa Viagem; ⏱ 7am-midnight) Two ATMs that accept foreign cards, but use Banco do Brasil to avoid the R$10 fee.

HSBC (Map p527; Av Domingos Ferreira 2589, Boa Viagem)

POST

Main post office (Map p524; Av Guararapes 250, Santo Antônio; ⏱ 9am-5pm Mon-Fri)

TOURIST INFORMATION

Most Recife tourist offices (see below) have helpful, professional, English-speaking staff and can provide good city maps. **Disque Recife Turístico** (☎ 3232 3594; ☎ 24hr) is the tourist information line, in English or Portuguese.

Airport (☎ 3182 8299; ⏱ 24hr)

Boa Viagem (Map p527; ☎ 3182 8297; Praça de Boa Viagem, Boa Viagem; ⏱ 8am-8pm)

Casa da Cultura (Map p524; Rua Floriano Peixoto; ⏱ 9am-7pm Mon-Fri, 9am-6pm Sat, 9am-noon Sun) In the shopping complex.

Recife Antigo (Map p524; ☎ 3232 2942; Praça do Arsenal; ⏱ 8:30am-9pm)

Recife Centro (Map p524; Pátio de São Pedro; ☼ 9am-5pm Mon-Sat)

Terminal Integrado de Passageiros (TIP; bus station; ☎ 3452 1892; ☼ 8am-7pm)

TRAVEL AGENCIES

Asa Branca (Map p527; ☎ 3466 2244; www.asabran caturismo.com.br; Shop 11, Av Conselheiro Aguiar 3150,

Boa Viagem; ☼ 8am-6pm Mon-Fri, 8am-noon Sat) A professional agency that handles all aspects of travel.

Dangers & Annoyances

Surfing is prohibited at Boa Viagem beach due to the danger of shark attacks. Swimmers there are advised to stay out of the water at high tide and not go beyond the reef at any

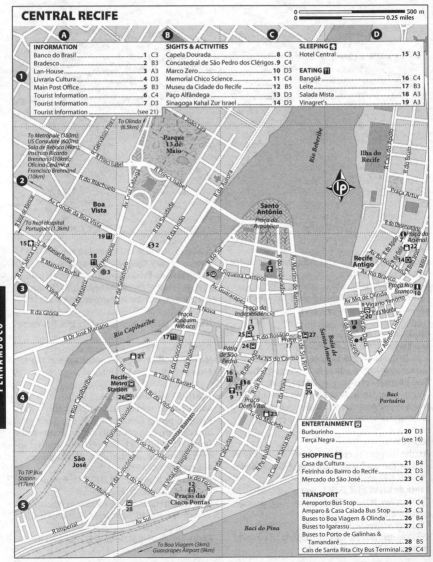

CENTRAL RECIFE

0 — 500 m
0 — 0.25 miles

INFORMATION		
Banco do Brasil	1	C3
Bradesco	2	B3
Lan-House	3	A3
Livraria Cultura	4	D3
Main Post Office	5	B3
Tourist Information	6	C4
Tourist Information	7	D3
Tourist Information	(see 21)	

SIGHTS & ACTIVITIES		
Capela Dourada	8	C3
Concatedral de São Pedro dos Clérigos	9	C4
Marco Zero	10	D3
Memorial Chico Science	11	C4
Museu da Cidade do Recife	12	B5
Paço Alfândega	13	D3
Sinagoga Kahal Zur Israel	14	D3

SLEEPING		
Hotel Central	15	A3

EATING		
Banguê	16	C4
Leite	17	B3
Salada Mista	18	A3
Vinagret's	19	A3

ENTERTAINMENT		
Burburinho	20	D3
Terça Negra	(see 16)	

SHOPPING		
Casa da Cultura	21	B4
Feirinha do Bairro do Recife	22	D3
Mercado do São José	23	C4

TRANSPORT		
Aeroporto Bus Stop	24	C4
Amparo & Casa Caiada Bus Stop	25	C3
Buses to Boa Viagem & Olinda	26	B4
Buses to Igarassu	27	C3
Buses to Porto de Galinhas & Tamandaré	28	B5
Cais de Santa Rita City Bus Terminal	29	C4

PERNAMBUCO

time. Since 1992, 19 fatal shark attacks, and more than 30 other incidents, have been recorded along a 20km stretch of coast that includes Boa Viagem.

Recife has a well-earned reputation as a dangerous city and, indeed, Pernambuco is home to the highest murder rate per capita of all Brazilian states, largely due to its capital. Local buses here are robbed shockingly often, with the perpetrators forcing drivers to drive as normal while robbing each passenger that enters. Tourists are more at risk from pickpockets and bag snatchers, so stay alert to your surroundings.

Sights

RECIFE ANTIGO

The narrow streets of Recife Antigo are a reminder that this was where the city began and the neighborhood, an Iphan (national cultural heritage) site, is well worth a stroll. The waterside **Marco Zero** (Map p524; Praça Rio Branco), a small monument on a broad square, marks the spot where the Portuguese founded Recife in 1537. Just north is **Rua Bom Jesus**, formerly known as Rua dos Judeos (Jews' St) because a number of Jewish businesses opened here during Dutch rule (1630–54).

The first synagogue in the Americas, **Sinagoga Kahal Zur Israel** (Map p524; ☎ 3224 2128; Rua Bom Jesus 197; admission R$5; 🕑 9am-6:30pm Tue-Fri, 2:30-5:30pm Sat & Sun), now a Jewish Cultural Center open to visitors, still has a bit of its original 17th-century structure and interesting murals (in Portuguese and English) depicting the role of Jews in Recife's development. This area is at its best during the colorful Sunday crafts market (see p530). On Recife Antigo's southern waterfront stands the **Paço Alfândega** (Map p524; Rua Alfâdega, 35; www.pacoalfandega.com.br; 🕑 10am-10pm Mon-Sat, noon-9pm Sun), the 19th-century customs house converted into a glitzy shopping mall – worth a pop in for a *cafezinho* (small coffee).

SANTO ANTÔNIO

Praça da República (Map p524) at the northern end of Santo Antônio has a formal park with tall trees and a pretty fountain, and is surrounded by imposing 19th-century buildings.

Just south is the **Capela Dourada** (Golden Chapel; Map p524; Rua do Imperador; admission R$2; 🕑 8-11:30am & 2-5pm Mon-Fri, 8-11:30am Sat), a church begun in 1696 that is a gem of Brazilian baroque and also houses the Museu de Arte Sacra. Further south stretches a bustling commercial area with shops and stalls lining every street, dotted with dilapidated colonial churches and fine facades. In its midst is the **Pátio de São Pedro**, a traffic-free square lined with bars, restaurants and colorfully painted 19th-century houses. The **Concatedral de São Pedro dos Clérigos** (Map p524; 🕑 9am-noon & 2-5pm Mon-Fri), an 18th-century baroque church with incredibly fine wood carvings, overlooks the Pátio.

Though the government could have and should have done so much more, the new **Memorial Chico Science** (Map p524; ☎ 3232 2426; www.recife.pe.gov.br/chicoscience; Pátio de São Pedro 21; admission free; 🕑 9am-7pm Mon-Fri) highlights the work of former Nação Zumbi singer Chico Science (see the boxed text, p526), a revered musician and founder of the *mangue beat* cultural movement who died tragically in a car accident in Recife in 1997.

The **Museu da Cidade do Recife** (Map p524; ☎ 3232 2812; Praça das Cinco Pontas; admission R$1; 🕑 9am-5pm Tue-Fri, 1-5pm Sat & Sun) is housed in the Forte das Cinco Pontas, a fort built by the Dutch in 1630. It has interesting exhibits on Recife's history and popular culture, but was closed during research with a scheduled reopening of late 2010.

OFICINA CERÂMICA FRANCISCO BRENNAND & INSTITUTO RICARDO BRENNAND

A surreal sculpture garden of bizarre sexualized earthworms, frogs and turtles covers the landscape at the unique **Oficina Cerâmica Francisco Brennand** (☎ 3271 2466; www.brennand.com.br; Várzea; admission R$6; 🕑 8am-5pm Mon-Thu, to 4pm Fri). The artist Francisco Brennand, descended from 19th-century Irish immigrants and considered Brazil's greatest ceramicist, revitalized his family's abandoned tile factory to create his own line of decorative ceramic tiles. The rest of the huge space is dedicated to a seemingly exhaustive exhibition of his peculiar sculptures, including gardens with Moorish arches and rows of contorted busts. A trip out to the Oficina Cerâmica, set amid thick Atlantic rain forest some 10km west of downtown, is a regional highlight, so set aside some time.

From Tuesday to Friday afternoons, you can combine it with a visit to the scenic **Instituto Ricardo Brennand** (☎ 2121 0352; www.institutoricardobrennand.org.br; Alameda Antônio Brennand, Várzea; admission R$5; 🕑 1-5pm Tue-Sun), Francisco's cousin's museum, 10 minutes south by taxi. This contains a massive collection of European and Brazilian art, swords, armor and historical artifacts in a fake medieval castle on lovely grounds.

The best way to reach these exhibitions is to arrange a round-trip by taxi. From Boa Viagem, with about 1½ hours at each place, this costs around R$100 to R$120. The alternative is to take a CDU/Várzea bus west along Av Conde da Boa Vista in central Recife, get off at the end of the line and then take taxis to the Oficina Cerâmica, from there to the Instituto, and back to the bus stop. A taxi round-trip from the bus stop to both sites and back should be R$60 to R$80.

Festivals & Events

The Recife **Carnaval** is one of Brazil's most colorful and folkloric festivals, and has its claims to being the best in the country. It is a participatory event with an infectious euphoria and fabulous dancing: people don't sit and watch here, they join in. It also attracts far fewer tourists than Carnaval in the cities of Salvador or Rio. Carnaval groups and spectators don elaborate costumes and dance for days to most conceivable Brazilian rhythms, but especially to Recife's very own, frenetic *frevo* (see the boxed text, p526).

Galo da Madrugada, which is claimed, probably correctly, to be the largest Carnaval *bloco* (themed singing/dancing group) in the world, brings over a million and a half people cramming onto the streets of central Recife for the official Saturday-morning Carnaval opening. Activity generally focuses around a number of *pólos* (poles) dotted about the city center. Av Guararapes is the *pólo de frevo*; the Alfândega area is for mangue beat and electronica; Marco Zero and the Pátio de São Pedro feature varied rhythms. Programs are widely available, including on the **Prefeitura website** (www.recife.pe.gov.br).

Recifolia, held in November, is a nonstop dance party and a showcase for music from the Northeast.

Carnaval in Olinda (see p534) is so close that you could participate in both on the same day, and there is a lot of crossover in the events.

Sleeping

The city center has limited accommodations. The majority of travelers head to the much

---

MUSIC OF RECIFE & OLINDA

In Recife and Olinda you'll hear plenty of the very popular, typically Northeastern country music called forró (see the boxed text, p529). There is also music from further south in Brazil such as samba and its offshoots, *pagode* and *choro*. But these two towns are also an exciting music-and-dance world of their own – home to a variety of original genres, mostly bound up with Carnaval.

Top of the list has to be *frevo*. Its name is said to come from the Portuguese *ferver* (to boil). *Frevo* (in its most common form, known as *frevo-de-rua*) is feverishly fast brass music that inspires feverishly energetic dancing. People in performing troupes dress in supercolorful shiny costumes and twirl, for some reason, mini-umbrellas. Its origins are thought to lie in a fusion of 19th-century marching-band music (polkas, quadrilles, tangos) with the movements of capoeira. *Frevo* really began to take over Recife Carnaval in the 1960s and celebrated its official 100th birthday in 2007.

Maracatu nação involves large African-style drum ensembles with dancers dressed as members of the Portuguese royal court from the baroque era – another curious juxtaposition that is said to derive from investiture ceremonies for the Reis do Congo (Kings of the Congo), leaders of the African community in times past.

Then there's *caboclinho*, in which a set of characters from kings and queens to *índios* (indigenous people) and witch doctors and the *caboclinhos* themselves (*índio*/African mixed-race characters wearing loincloths, bead and seed necklaces, and feathered headdresses) dance with much agility to pipe and percussion music.

All these combined music-and-dance styles, with clear origins in African, indigenous and European influences, play prominent parts in Carnaval in Recife and Olinda. A more recent arrival is *mangue beat*, which emerged in the 1990s among young bands who combined traditional local forms such as *maracatu* with electrified rock instruments and rhythms of rap, hip-hop and electronica. Leader of the genre was singer Chico Science (p525) with his group Nação Zumbi. Science died in a car crash in 1997 and is still much mourned: Nação Zumbi plays on.

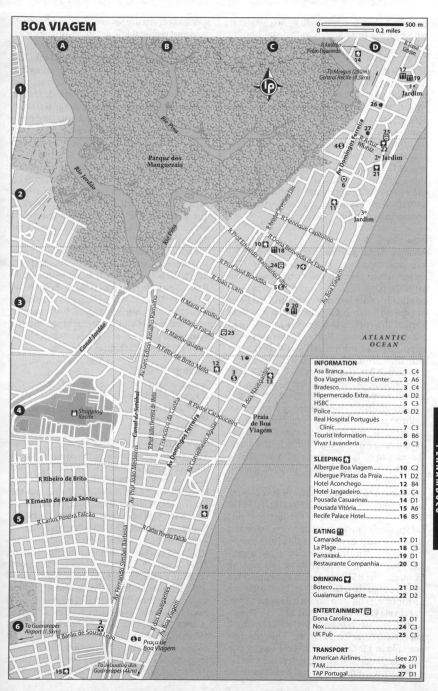

BOA VIAGEM

0 — 500 m
0 — 0.2 miles

ATLANTIC
OCEAN

Parque dos
Manguezais

Praia
de Boa
Viagem

Praia de
Boa Viagem

To Guararapes
Airport (1.5km)

To Jaboatão dos
Guararapes (4km)

To Mingus (250m);
Central Recife (4.5km)

PERNAMBUCO

INFORMATION	
Asa Branca	**1** C4
Boa Viagem Medical Center	**2** A6
Bradesco	**3** C4
Hipermercado Extra	**4** D2
HSBC	**5** C3
Police	**6** D2
Real Hospital Português	
Clinic	**7** C3
Tourist Information	**8** B6
Vivaz Lavanderia	**9** C3

SLEEPING	
Albergue Boa Viagem	**10** C2
Albergue Piratas da Praia	**11** D2
Hotel Aconchego	**12** B4
Hotel Jangadeiro	**13** C4
Pousada Casuarinas	**14** D1
Pousada Vitória	**15** A6
Recife Palace Hotel	**16** B5

EATING	
Camarada	**17** D1
La Plage	**18** C3
Parraxaxá	**19** D1
Restaurante Companhia	**20** C3

DRINKING	
Boteco	**21** D2
Guaiamum Gigante	**22** D2

ENTERTAINMENT	
Dona Carolina	**23** D1
Nox	**24** C3
UK Pub	**25** C3

TRANSPORT	
American Airlines	(see 27)
TAM	**26** D1
TAP Portugal	**27** D1

nicer and safer beach suburb of Boa Viagem, with options from hostels to five-star hotels.

CITY CENTER

Though its heyday as Recife's most glamorous hotel is well embedded in the none too recent past, the salmon-toned **Hotel Central** (Map p524; ☎ 3222 4001; www.hotelcentralrecife.com.br; Av Manoel Borba 209; dm/s/d/tr/q from R$40/55/84/144/144; ☒), built in 1927, still stands out proudly on its tree-lined street in Boa Vista. At eight storys, it was once Recife's tallest building, but the rise of Boa Viagem left it stranded long ago; these days it remains the city's oldest running hotel. With antiquated furnishings and a 1930s caged elevator, it's the best budget option in the center.

BOA VIAGEM

Albergue Piratas da Praia (Map p527; ☎ 3326 1281; www.piratasdapraia.com; Av Conselheiro Aguiar 2034; dm with/without air-con R$44/38, r with/without air-con R$130/120; ☒ ☜) You'd never know it was here, but this friendly hostel occupies the 3rd floor of Edifício Barão de Camaçari and feels a little homier than others in the area, like staying in a friend's apartment. Private rooms are cutely appointed but overpriced; you're better off here if you're looking for a dorm.

Albergue Boa Viagem (Map p527; ☎ 3326 9572; www.hostelboaviagem.com.br; Rua Aviador Severiano Lins 455; dm R$48, d with/without air-con R$110/100; ☒ ▢ ☜) The HI-affiliated choice is pretty dismissible: bathrooms are cramped, breakfast is barely continental, and staff is a little off-putting, killing some of the traditional hostel buzz. It seems to be quite popular with Brazilians, though, who perhaps prefer the small garden and murky pool.

Pousada Vitória (Map p527; ☎ 3462 6446; www.pousadavitoriarecife.com.br; Rua Capitô Zuzinha 234; s/d R$94/130; ☒ ☜) To say nothing of the fact that this cute pousada (guesthouse) has more color and character than any other in this price range, it's a mere 2km from the airport, so a perfect spot to bed down for those just passing through. The R$10 taxi fare to the airport is a steal, but hardly relevant – staff will pick you up for free if you land between 6am and 8pm.

Pousada Casuarinas (Map p527; ☎ 3325 4708; www.pousadacasuarinas.com.br; Rua Antônio Pedro Figueiredo 151; s/d/tr from R$95/129/153; ☒ ☜ ☒) This tranquil pousada in a former family home run by two friendly, English-speaking sisters is a marvelous retreat from the heat and bustle outside.

Spotless rooms are set around a shady courtyard and regional folk art spices up the decor.

Hotel Aconchego (Map p527; ☎ 3464 2989; www.hotelaconchego.com.br; Rua Félix de Brito Melo 382; s/d from R$135/165; ☒ ☜ ☒) The well-run Aconchego has immaculate rooms, substantial common areas, an affordable 24-hour poolside restaurant (and bar!) and good, multilingual service. It is popular with Brazilian tourists, and is the best-value hotel in its price range.

Hotel Jangadeiro (Map p527; ☎ 3086 5050; www.jangadeirohotel.com.br; Av Boa Viagem 3114; s/d/tr R$205/249/289; ☒ ☜ ☒) One of the few upmarket places on the beachfront, the high-rise Jangadeiro has amiable staff, tasteful rooms with good-size bathrooms, and hallways in dire need of a slab of color. All rooms have a sea view of some kind and breakfast is a winner with beautiful views.

Recife Palace Hotel (Map p527; ☎ 4009 2500; www.lucsimhoteis.com.br; Av Boa Viagem 4070; s/d from R$319/365; ☒ ☜ ☒) The mid-'80s beachfront Recife Palace, now part of the Golden Tulip hotel group, is still one of Boa Viagem's most luxurious hotels. Public areas are all black marble, polished woods and gleaming brass, and the rooms are spacious and very comfortable, all with sea views. Parking is available.

Eating

Recife has great places to eat, from the cheerful-and-bustling kind to refined establishments comparable with Rio's and São Paulo's finest.

CITY CENTER

The city center is loaded with self-serve places, most charging around R$23.90 per kilo. Two good ones are **Vinagret's** (Map p524; ☎ 3334 9616; Rua do Hospício 203; ☽ 10:30am-4pm Mon-Fri) and the nearby **Salada Mista** (Map p524; ☎ 3231 0583; Rua do Hospício 59; ☽ 10:30am-8pm Mon-Fri, 10:30am-4pm Sat).

Banguê (Map p524; ☎ 3224 5249; Pátio de São Pedro 20; mains for 2 R$16-85; ☽ 11am-1am Tue, Fri & Sat, to 10pm Mon, Wed, Thu & Sun) The restaurant lovingly detailed in Peter Robb's *A Death in Brazil* is still a good spot for a meat or seafood meal, with a great setting on Pátio de São Pedro and its unique sugar-plantation decor. Call to reserve an outdoor table front-and-center for Terça Negra.

Leite (Map p524; ☎ 3224 7977; Praça Joaquim Nabuco 147; mains R$29-65; ☽ 11:30am-4pm Sun-Fri) One of the oldest restaurants in the country, this famous traditional lunch place was opened in 1882. Though modernized these days and void of much historical air, it remains a power-lunch favorite of politicos and businesspeople. Go for the excellent Pernambuco shrimp in coconut sauce.

BOA VIAGEM

Restaurante Companhia (Map p527; ☎ 3465 9066; Rua João Cícero; mains R$4.50-22.50, lunch per kg R$27.90; 🕙 11am-midnight) A quality sidewalk restaurant with a good-value, self-service lunch, satisfying meat dishes and top *chope* (draft beer).

La Plage (Map p527; ☎ 3465 1654; Rua Prof Rui Batista 120; crepes R$9.50-16; 🕙 6-11:30pm Mon-Thu, to 1am Fri-Sat, 5-11pm Sun) At first we found it irritating that a crepe and salad place wouldn't be open for lunch, then we realized: it's too trendy for daylight! La Plage serves up great-value savory and sweet crepes and fab salads in a near-bar atmosphere. It has good vegetarian options.

Parraxaxá (Map p527; ☎ 3463 7874; Rua Baltazar Pereira 32; per kg R$30.90; 🕙 11:30am-10pm Mon-Fri, 6am-11pm Sat & Sun) Festive decor and staff in police and *cangaceiro* (outlaw) outfits spice up your meal at this fun Northeast-themed restaurant. The self-serve food is a cornucopia of tasty Northeastern dishes – *carne de sol* (salted beef), *macaxeira* (a type of cassava), *baião de dois* (a spicy rice, beans and cheese dish) and grilled meats – with good salads, too.

Mingus (off Map p527; ☎ 3465 4000; Rua do Atlântico 102; mains R$31-62; 🕙 7:30pm-midnight Mon-Thu, 8pm-2am Fri-Sat, noon-5pm Sun) An excellent spot to drop some extra reais for a stylish meal of contemporary Brazilian cuisine. From pan-roasted wild boar to fig-stuffed quail to whiting in peppermint pesto, there's something for everyone, served amid larger-than-life B&W photos of jazz greats.

our pick **Camarada** (Map p527; ☎ 3325 1786; Rua Baltazar Pereira 130; mains for 2 R$50-75; 🕙 noon-12:30am Sun-Tue, to 1am Wed-Sat) This modern restaurant does shrimp in endlessly creative ways – fondue, salads, beer-marinated, *moquecas* (stews) – but it's also wildly popular for happy hour, as patrons flood the front deck with ice cold Brahma or Stella Artois draft in hand. If you're not into crustaceans, there are a few meat and fish dishes as well.

Drinking & Entertainment

Recife is justly proud of its nightlife and the variety of music that can be found in the city. You can easily find somewhere exciting to go every night of the week. Many venues are located in Boa Viagem but there are others in Recife Antigo and elsewhere. Tourist offices hand out useful entertainment guides, and many Portuguese-language websites have good listings, including www.guiametropole .com.br, http://pe360graus.globo.com (see the 'Diversão' section) and www.pernambuco .com.

FORRÓ FOR ALL

During WWII, the officers' clubs at the US military bases in Pernambuco would have balls open to the general public under the title 'For All'. Local bands that played the accordion, triangle and a hand-held African drum, the *zabumba*, provided the music. The rhythm was a fast-paced, two-by-four dance beat originally called *baião*. Couples danced to songs with simple lyrics speaking of the hard life of the countryside, the trials and tribulations of love and the beauty of dance. 'For All' became *forró* (fo-*hoh*) in Portuguese and the name became synonymous not only with the events, but with the spirit, the dance and the music.

The first icon of *forró* was Luiz Gonzaga (1912–89). 'Gonzagão' was responsible for taking the sound of Pernambuco to the rest of the country, later becoming the musical influence for some internationally renowned Brazilian musicians. Despite his personal popularity, *forró* continued to be looked down upon by São Paulo, Rio de Janeiro and other southern cities as backwoods Northeastern music.

During the 1990s, after the international success of lambada, and inspired by the country bands of São Paulo, *forró* musicians modernized their sound. They added electric guitars, keyboards and drum sets. The music and the dance became a national craze, with *forró* events throughout Brazil. It filled a void for an upbeat music that is easily danced with a partner – it's a simple two steps to the left and two steps to the right. The music is now known around the world.

Today the disputed capital of *forró* is Caruaru (p544), whose annual São João festival claims to be the largest festival of its kind in Brasil (Paraíba's Campina Grande makes similar claims). Arrive in May and you'll find *quadrilhas* of some 4000 people. They don't stop dancing for a month!

CITY CENTER

Terça Negra (Black Tuesday; Map p524; Pátio de São Pedro; ☺ from 8pm Tue) This great free weekly night of Afro-Brazilian rhythms takes place in the picturesque Pátio de São Pedro. Come ready to dance and go home very late.

Burburinho (Map p524; ☎ 3224 5854; Rua Tomazina 106; admission R$7-15; ☺ 6pm-last customer Mon-Sat) This bar, frequented by musicians, artists and journalists, has live blues on Friday and rock on Saturday. It's nicer inside than it appears.

Metrópole (off Map p524; ☎ 3423 0123; Rua das Nínfas 125; admission after midnight R$20; ☺ 10pm-6am Thu-Sat) Recife's best gay (and GLS) club has drag shows, go-go boys, Saturday theme parties and a bar with live music.

BOA VIAGEM

Boteco (Map p527; ☎ 3325 1428; Av Boa Viagem 1660; ☺ 5pm-1am Sun-Thu, noon-2am Fri-Sat) Like most Brazilian cities, the *boteco* (Brazilian neighborhood bar) culture usually rules the nightlife and, though a chain, the obviously-named Boteco packs in the Recifenses. We're not sure what whips through faster, the ocean breezes or the waiters loaded down with *chope* and Brazilian bar munchies such as *picanha* (choice beef cuts) and savory *pesticos* (bar snacks). It's very hard to say no.

Guaiamum Gigante (Map p527; ☎ 3327 1413; Av Boa Viagem, 2a Jardim; ☺ 11:30am-1am Mon-Thu, to 2am Thu-Sat, 11:30am-11:30pm Sun) Slightly more upscale *boteco* that was under renovation during our visit, but packed nonetheless. Seafood sets this apart from its neighbor, Boteco, and its breezy outdoor patio serves as a decadent drinking den.

UK Pub (Map p527; ☎ 3466 9192; Rua Francisco da Cunha 165; admission R$8-25; ☺ 8pm-late Tue-Sun) This sophisticated lounge draws a sexy Anglophile crowd – especially on Thursday – for live pop, rock, samba rock and DJs, and proper pints (Guinness, Erdinger, Newcastle and 1664) – but you will pay dearly for the privilege.

Nox (Map p527; ☎ 3326 8836; Av Domingos Ferreira 2422; admission women/men from R$20/30; ☺ 10pm-6am Fri-Sat) Nox is the trendiest dance club in town, with a rave-like atmosphere, huge dance floor and spectacular lighting.

Dona Carolina (Map p527; ☎ 3466 2743; Av Boa Viagem 123; admission women/men R$20/30; ☺ 6pm-late Tue-Sat, 7-11pm Sun) This is the *bola da vez* (current hot spot) in Recife, a sleek, modern bar and restaurant with live MPB (Música Popular Brasileira), soul and jazz and enough hotness to melt Antarctica.

OTHER AREAS

The best down-home *forró* in town is played – and danced – at the rustic-style **Sala de Reboco** (off Map p524; ☎ 3228 7052; www.saladereboco.com.br; Rua Gregório Junior 264, Cordeiro; admission R$10-15; ☺ 10pm-4am Thu-Sat), 4km west of the center.

Shopping

Pernambuco's traditional handicrafts, such as clay figurines, wood sculptures, lace and leather goods, plus plenty of T-shirts, are found at the **Mercado do São José** (Map p524; Praça Dom Vital; ☺ 8am-5:30pm Mon-Fri, to noon Sat & Sun), and the **Casa da Cultura** (Map p524; Rua Floriano Peixoto; ☺ 9am-7pm Mon-Fri, 9am-6pm Sat, 9am-noon Sun). The latter is a creepy colonial-era prison with shops in cells where prisoners languished until 1973 (cell 106 is preserved as it was).

The **Feirinha do Bairro do Recife** (Map p524; Rua Bom Jesus; ☺ 2-10pm Sat & Sun) is an interesting street market specializing in high-class artisanry – dresses, jewelry, ceramics – that brings Recife Antigo to life on Sundays.

Getting There & Away

AIR

From Recife's **Guararapes Airport** (code REC; ☎ 3322 4188), there are direct flights to most major Brazilian cities, often on a choice of several airlines, plus Lisbon and Madrid with TAP Portugal and Miami with American Airlines. The following airlines have offices in Recife.

American Airlines airport (☎ 0300 789 7778; airport); Boa Viagem (Map p527; ☎ 3326 2640; Av Conselheiro Aguiar 1472, Boa Viagem)

Azul (☎ 3322 5080; airport)

Gol/Varig (☎ 3322 4313; airport)

Ocean Air (☎ 3322 4647; airport)

TAM airport (☎ 3322 4255; airport); Boa Viagem (Map p527; ☎ 3198 6700; Av Conselheiro Aguiar 1360, Boa Viagem)

TAP Portugal airport (☎ 0300 210 6060; airport); Boa Viagem (Map p527; ☎ 0300 210 6060; Av Conselheiro Aguiar 1472, Boa Viagem)

Trip (☎ 3464 4610; airport)

BUS

Recife's bus station is the large **Terminal Integrado de Passageiros** (TIP; ☎ 3452 1088), 17km west of the center. TIP handles all inter-state buses and many destinations within Pernambuco. You can purchase many bus tickets at outlets in town, or by calling **Disk Rodoviária** (☎ 3452 1211), a bus-ticket delivery service. You can leave luggage at the Guarda Volumes (per 12 hours R$2.80 to R$5.60).

Destinations include Caruaru (R$18 to R$23, two hours, 34 daily), Fortaleza (R$120 to R$181, 12 hours, three daily), João Pessoa (R$21 to R$28.50, two hours, 17 daily), Maceió (R$34 to R$45, four hours, nine daily), Natal (R$60.50, 4½ hours, eight daily), Rio (R$325, 38 to 42 hours, three daily), Salvador (R$127 to R$138, 15 hours, one or two daily) and São Paulo (R$321, 44 to 48 hours, two daily).

To/From Olinda

From central Recife to Olinda's main bus stop on Praça do Carmo, take a 992 Pau Amarelo or 983 Rio Doce bus from outside the Recife metro station or from Cais de Santa Rita terminal; or a Casa Caiada bus from Av Dantas Barreto; or a Rio Doce bus westbound on Av Conde da Boa Vista. From Praça do Carmo, Rio Doce/Princesa Isabel buses go to the Recife metro station; Casa Caiada buses also go to central Recife. The Amparo bus shuttles between Av Dantas Barreto in central Recife and the street below the Igreja NS do Amparo in Olinda, but only from March to December.

From Boa Viagem to Olinda take a 910 Rio Doce/Piedade bus (R$2.80). A taxi between central Recife and Olinda is around R$25.

CAR & MOTORCYCLE

These recommended car-rental agencies have airport offices.

Avis (☎ 0800 725 2847)
Budget (☎ 3464 4030)
Localiza (☎ 3341 2082)

Getting Around

Recife is spread out and the buses (R$1.85) take some circuitous, confusing routes. A few taxis will save you time and stress.

TO/FROM THE AIRPORT

Pre-paid taxis from the airport cost between R$12 to R$20 to Boa Viagem, R$27 to R$31 to the city center, R$42 to the bus station and R$37 to R$49 to Olinda (higher prices at night). During high traffic times, these can be a better option than metered taxis.

City buses marked 'Aeroporto' run to Boa Viagem and the center from a stop five minutes' walk from the airport. Once outside the terminal, walk to the right and across busy Av Mascarenhas de Moraes, then turn left onto Rua 10 de Julho between the car

showrooms and the gas station. Different Aeroporto buses go to different destinations, so check with the driver. For Olinda, you can get off on Av Conselheiro Aguiar in Boa Viagem and take a Rio Doce/Piedade bus from there to Olinda.

Going to the airport from Boa Viagem, get any Aeroporto bus on Av Domingos Ferreira; from the center, take a 033 Aeroporto bus from the Cais de Santa Rita terminal (Map p524) on Av Martins de Barros; or any Aeroporto bus from Av Dantas Barreto or Av NS do Carmo.

The Aeroporto metro station on Rua 10 de Julho opened in 2009, though it's of little help to most travelers since the line skirts by Boa Viagem. The 20-minute ride to the city center (Estação Central) costs R$1.40. Technically, you could save money to Boa Viagem one of two ways, but both require a radical devotion to cutting costs. The quickest would be to hop on the metro two stations to Shopping (R$1.40), then grab a taxi to your hotel from there; or, ride all the way into Estação Central (R$1.40), then catch a Setúbal/Príncipe bus back to Boa Viagem outside the station (R$1.85).

TO/FROM THE BUS STATION

From the TIP to all Recife and Olinda destinations, catch a metro train to the central Recife station (R$1.40, 25 minutes) and take a bus or taxi from there. Going out to the TIP, take a Camaragibe-bound metro train to the Rodoviária stop. If you arrive outside metro hours (5am to 11pm), taxis run R$36 to R$44 to Boa Viagem, R$34 to R$40 to central Recife and R$50 to Olinda.

TO/FROM BOA VIAGEM

From the center, take a Setúbal/Príncipe bus from outside Recife metro station; a 033 Aeroporto bus from Av NS do Carmo; or a 032 Setúbal/Conde da Boa Vista bus from Av Marques de Olinda (Recife Antigo)/Praça da Independência/Av Conde da Boa Vista.

In Boa Viagem, southbound buses run along Av Domingos Ferreira; northbound buses run along Av Conselheiro Aguiar. The 032 Setúbal/Conde da Boa Vista bus runs to Recife Antigo, Av Guararapes and Av Conde da Boa Vista; bus 061 Piedade/Boa Vista heads to the Cais de Santa Rita city bus terminal (Map p524) along Av Martins de Barros and Av Dantas Barreto.

PERNAMBUCO

A taxi between central Recife and Boa Viagem costs around R$15.

OLINDA

☎ 0xx81 / pop 397,000

Picturesque Olinda, set around a tree-covered hill, is the historic and artsy counterpart to the big-city hubbub of Recife. It's an artist colony full of creative types all seemingly living in a painting of themselves and brimming with galleries, artisans' workshops, museums, lovely colonial churches and music in the streets. With twisting streets of colorful old houses and gorgeous vistas over trees, church towers and red-tile roofs, this is one of the best-preserved colonial cities in Brazil – and a kaleidoscopic wonderland for photo buffs.

The historic center has some lovely pousadas and makes a much more tranquil base for exploring the area than the bigger neighbor that stands towering in the distance. Olinda was the original capital of Pernambuco, founded in 1535. Sacked and burnt with all its Catholic churches by the Calvinist Dutch in 1631, it was rebuilt but lost its ascendancy to Recife in the 18th century. Although many buildings were originally constructed in the 16th century, most of what you see today dates from a later period. The whole picturesque center was declared a Unesco World Heritage site in 1982.

Orientation

Olinda is 6km north of central Recife. The historic district, about 10% of the city, is concentrated on and around the hill and is easily visited on foot. The main bus stop is on Praça do Carmo, in the lower part of town near the coast.

Information

EMERGENCY

Tourist police (☎ 3181 3703; off Praça do Carmo; ☾ 24hr) Very helpful, English speaking.

INTERNET ACCESS

Empório do Carnaval (Rua Prudente de Morais 483; per hr R$3; ☾ 9am-7pm)

Vivo (Praça do Carmo 5C; per hr R$3; ☾ 9am-7pm Mon-Fri) The cellular-phone operator fulfills the internet niche as well.

MONEY

There are no ATMs in the old town. The nearest ATMs are Bradesco/Banco24Horas options at the **BR Mania** (Av Olinda 150; ☾ 7am-11pm Mon-Fri, 24hr Sat-Sun) gas station just west of Monsteiro São Bento; or the **HSBC** (Av Getúlio Vargas 1050, Bairro Novo; ☾ 9am-5pm Mon-Fri, ATMs 6am-10pm daily), reachable by any 974 Jardim Atlântico bus heading north from the stop next door to the post office across from Praça do Carmo.

TOURIST INFORMATION

Casa do Turista (☎ 3305 1060; Rua Prudente de Morais 472; ☾ 8am-8pm Mon-Fri, 9am-7pm Sat-Sun) The city's tourist information office has helpful staff, but little English.

Tourist Information Pernambuco (☎ 3429 0244; www.peconhecepe.com; Praça do Carmo s/n; ☾ 8am-6pm) The state tourist info office with lovely, English-speaking staff.

Dangers & Annoyances

Crime (mostly petty) exists, especially during Carnaval. To avoid false information or payment discrepancies it's best to use only accredited guides (see p534).

Sights

Olinda's sights are easy and enjoyable to visit on a walking tour, although highly random opening hours make it impossible to look in on everything in one day.

A good place to start is Praça do Carmo, overlooked by the **Igreja NS do Carmo** (1580; has been closed for three years for restoration). Up Rua de São Francisco, the **Convento de São Francisco** (☎ 3429 0517; admission R$3; ☾ 8am-noon & 2-5pm Mon-Fri) is a large structure containing the 16th-century **Igreja NS das Neves** and two later chapels, with rich baroque detailing and lovely *azulejos* (Portuguese ceramic tiles).

Climb up to **Alto da Sé** (Cathedral Heights), which affords superb views of Olinda and Recife. There are food and drink stalls here and a small **craft market** with woodcarvings, figurines and jewelry. The imposing **Igreja da Sé** (☾ 9am-5pm) was originally built in 1537. Burnt in 1631, it has been reconstructed four times since, most recently from 1974 to 1984 in a Mannerist style that attempts to re-create the original 16th-century look. Check the touching inscription in simple Portuguese on the wooden door to the left inside the entrance.

The **Museu de Arte Sacra de Pernambuco** (Rua Bispo Coutinho 726; admission R$1; ☾ 9am-5pm Mon-Fri, 1-5pm Sat & Sun) is housed in Olinda's former

Episcopal Palace, built in 1676. It was closed for restorations during our visit, but normally contains a good collection of sacred art and a photographic homage to the city. Along the street, the **Igreja da Misericórdia** (8-11am & 2-4pm), built in 1540, has fine *azulejos* and gilded carvings, but was closed for restorations during our visit.

Head down Rua Saldanha Marinho to look at the restored 1613 **Igreja NS do Amparo** (9-11:30am Sun), and then round the corner to the **Igreja NS do Rosário dos Homens Pretos de Olinda** (Largo do Bonsucesso 45; 9am-5pm), built by an African brotherhood in the 17th century. Frescoes painted by slaves were revealed here during a recent restoration.

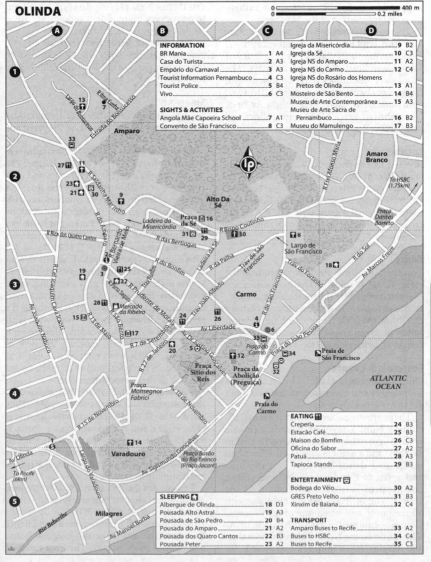

OLINDA

0 400 m / 0 0.2 miles

INFORMATION
BR Mania 1 A4
Casa do Turista 2 A3
Empório do Carnaval 3 A3
Tourist Information Pernambuco 4 C3
Tourist Police 5 B4
Vivo 6 C3

SIGHTS & ACTIVITIES
Angola Mãe Capoeira School 7 A1
Convento de São Francisco 8 C3

Igreja da Misericórdia 9 B2
Igreja da Sé 10 C3
Igreja NS do Amparo 11 A2
Igreja NS do Carmo 12 C4
Igreja NS do Rosário dos Homens
  Pretos de Olinda 13 A1
Mosteiro de São Bento 14 B4
Museu de Arte Contemporânea ...15 A3
Museu de Arte Sacra de
  Pernambuco 16 B2
Museu do Mamulengo 17 B3

EATING
Creperia 24 B3
Estacão Café 25 B3
Maison do Bomfim 26 C3
Oficina do Sabor 27 A2
Patuá 28 A3
Tapioca Stands 29 B3

ENTERTAINMENT
Bodega do Véio 30 A2
GRES Preto Velho 31 B3
Xinxim de Baiana 32 C4

TRANSPORT
Amparo Buses to Recife 33 A2
Buses to HSBC 34 C4
Buses to Recife 35 C3

SLEEPING
Albergue de Olinda 18 D3
Pousada Alto Astral 19 A3
Pousada de São Pedro 20 B4
Pousada do Amparo 21 A2
Pousada dos Quatro Cantos 22 B3
Pousada Peter 23 A2

PERNAMBUCO

The **Museu de Arte Contemporânea** (☎ 3184 3153; Rua 13 de Maio 149; admission R$5; ☼ 9am-5pm Tue-Sun) is recommended for both its permanent and temporary exhibits. It's housed in an 18th-century Inquisition jail.

The **Museu do Mamulengo** (☎ 3493 2753; Rua São Bento 344; admission R$2; ☼ 10am-5pm Tue-Sun) has a unique and surprisingly interesting collection of over 1000 pieces devoted to the traveling puppet shows called Mamulengos, an authentic popular tradition of the Northeast.

The huge **Mosteiro de São Bento** (☼ 6-11:45am & 2-6:30pm), built in 1582, has some exceptional woodcarving in its church. Brazil's first law school was housed here for 24 years. The monastery celebrates mass complete with Gregorian chants at 6am daily and 10am and 6pm Sunday. To arrive here, follow Av 10 de Novembro to Praça Monsegnor Fabrici and turn left on Rua São Bento.

Courses

If you'd like to check out a capoeira school, **Angola Mãe** (☎ 9925 1728; angolamae@hotmail.com; Rua Ilma Cunha 243; per 1½hr class R$15; ☼ classes 9am & 7pm Mon, Wed & Fri, roda 6pm Sun) teaches the slower and more traditional Angola style. The roda is the circular formation around which capoeira is performed.

Tours

Throughout Olinda you'll no doubt hear the offer 'Guia!' ('Guide!'). The best guides are those accredited by the local guides association, the Assocação de Conductores Nativos de Olinda (ACNO). They wear blue (old uniform) or green (new) shirts and an ACNO badge, and charge R$30 for a two-hour tour.

Festivals & Events

Olinda's **Carnaval** lasts a full 11 days and has a spontaneity and inclusiveness that you don't get in big-city Carnavals.

There are organized Carnaval events, including balls, a night of *maracatu* (music with a percussion-heavy Afro-Brazilian rhythm) and a night of *afoxé* (Afro-Brazilian music and dance based on the rhythms and spirit of Candomblé), but everything else happens in impromptu fashion on the streets. The official opening events – with all the pomp and ceremony of the Olympic Games – commence with the parade of As Virgens do Bairro Novo, a *bloco* of more than 400 'virgins' (men in drag), and awards for

the most beautiful, the most risqué and the biggest prude.

Fabulously costumed groups of musicians and dancers, some thousands strong, parade right through the day from early morning to evening, with spectators joining them to dance *frevo* and *maracatu* through the narrow streets. It's playful and very lewd. Five separate areas have orchestras (as the bands call themselves) playing nonstop from 8pm to 6am every night. For schedules, see www.olinda.pe.gov.br, in Portuguese.

The **Folclore Nordestino** festival, in late August, features dance, music and folklore from many parts of the Northeast. It's highly recommended.

Sleeping

Book several months ahead for accommodations during Carnaval and be prepared for massive price hikes.

Albergue de Olinda (☎ 3429 1592; www.alberguedeolinda.com.br; Rua do Sol 233; dm R$30-38, s/d from R$55/80; ☁ ▨) Olinda's excellent HI hostel isn't on a colorful street (though it faces the sea), but offers modern installations, spotless, no-frills rooms and a sizable garden with outdoor kitchen and lovely pool. Parking is available.

Pousada Peter (☎ 3439 2171; www.pousadapeter.com.br; Rua do Amparo 215; s R$55-132, d R$83-160; ▨ ▨) This German-owned pousada seems to specialize in polarizing travelers, who either loathe it (being locked in is annoying, some rooms are likened to damp dungeons, staff is indifferent, Peter is quirky) or think it's great value. Rooms 1 to 7 *are* windowless petri dishes and should be avoided, while room 9 is the size of a (ladies) shoebox. We slept in room 10, which was cramped but fine and included 26 electrical outlets to make up for the lack of them everywhere else!

Pousada Alto Astral (☎ 3439 3453; www.pousadaaltoastral.com.br; Rua 13 de Maio 305; s/d without view R$70/80, with view R$80/90; ▨ ▨) This colorful charmer is great value if you can manage to snag rooms 8, 9 or 10, which are extra spacious with stupendous views, some with outdoor decks and/or four-poster beds. The cheaper interior rooms are distinctly average.

Pousada dos Quatro Cantos (☎ 3429 0220; www.pousada4cantos.com.br; Rua Prudente de Morais 441; s/d without bathroom R$80/90, s/d from R$133/152; ▨ ☁ ▨) High ceilings, tall windows, hardwood floors and attractive art make this colonial home a delightful place to stay. There's a range of rooms at different prices. The cheapest *quarto* rooms (shared bathrooms) are basically a dorm with nicer bedding, but a steal at this price for this atmosphere, if you don't mind sharing a bathroom. English is spoken.

Pousada de São Pedro (☎ 3439 9546; www.pousadapedro.com; Rua 27 de Janeiro 95; s/d/tr R$90/140/190; ☒ ☎ ☒) Charming and friendly, the São Pedro occupies a 19th-century house full of art and antiques and has a lovely pool in the leafy garden.

our pick **Pousada do Amparo** (☎ 3439 1749; www .pousadadoamparo.com.br; Rua do Amparo 199; s/d from R$190/240; ☒ ☎ ☒) Part of Brazil's Relais & Châteaux equivalent, Roteiros de Charme, the refined Amparo occupies two 17th-century houses with lovely gardens and views back toward Recife. It's full of character and very comfortable, and will give you the full Olinda experience. Two new restaurants, the famous Porto de Galinhas/Tamandaré restaurant, Beijupirá, and Flor de Coco, have opened post-research. English, Italian and Spanish are spoken.

Eating

A variety of restaurants is tucked away among the old city's cobblestone streets. A great way to start an evening is with a beer and a tapioca snack from the **tapioca stands** (snacks R$2-6) on Praça da Sé.

Estação Café (☎ 3425 7575; Rua Prudente de Morais 441; items R$2-16; ☺ 1-9pm Tue-Thu, 2-10pm Fri-Sat, 1:30-8pm Sun) Olinda is buzzing over this artsy café, a perfect little cappuccino and macchiato pit stop or for lighter bites such as quiche, salad and sandwiches. The hand-painted tabletops are a beautiful touch. There's free *chorinho* (little choro) at 7pm on Saturday.

Creperia (☎ 3429 2935; Praça João Alfredo 168; crepes R$5-24, pizza R$19-30; ☺ 11am-11pm) A nice spot for crepes, pizza and salads, which you can enjoy on a pleasant outdoor patio under tall bamboo trees.

Maison do Bomfim (☎ 3429 1674; Rua do Bonfim 115; mains R$21-54; ☺ 8pm-midnight Mon, noon-4pm Tue, noon-4pm & 6pm-1am Wed-Sat, noon-9pm Sun) A smart, French-run place that has been around more than a decade, with nice decor and even better filet mignon, fish and prawns (there's pizza, too, but only for dinner). Service is friendly but isn't spawned from the same European gene.

Patuá (☎ 3055 0833; Rua Bernardo Vieira de Melo 79; buffet R$23, mains R$23; ☺ noon-4pm Sun-Tue, to 11pm Wed-Sat) The friendly Patuá does a very nice

regional all-you-can-eat lunch buffet (try the *bobó de camarão* – fresh shrimp in pureed manioc) in air-conditioned circumstances with actual smiling waitresses, while à la carte options are seafood-heavy.

our pick **Oficina do Sabor** (☎ 3429 3331; Rua do Amparo 335; mains for 2 R$32-82; ☺ noon-4pm & 6pm-midnight Tue-Thu, noon-1am Fri-Sat, noon-5pm Sun) Baked pumpkin stuffed with shrimp and lobster in passion fruit sauce – best single dish this author has ever had in Brazil! This is one of the Northeast's best, and worth every centavo.

Entertainment

Alto da Sé gets busy in the evening as locals and visitors buy drinks and snacks from the street vendors, watch capoeira and savor the view and the breeze.

Bodega do Véio (☎ 3429 0185; Rua do Amparo 212; ☺ 9am-11pm Mon-Sat) Part small store, part bar, Olinda's best dive serves ice-cold bottled beer and little charcuterie plates, and tries its best to manage the crowds of locals and tourists congregating on the street and the small terraces. A *choro* group plays here from 7:30pm most Thursday and Saturday evenings, with the former swelling to an all-out street party by 9pm.

GRES Preto Velho (☎ 8898 6878; Rua Bispo Coutinho 681; admission R$2-5; ☺ 10pm-late Fri, 7pm-late Sat, from 5pm Sun) This Alto da Sé bar is worth checking out late Fridays for local bands, Saturdays for live *afoxé*, and Sundays for samba school rehearsal – all soundtracks to a spectacular view.

Xinxim de Baiana (☎ 8634 3330; Praça do Carmo; ☺ 9pm-late) Dark, sweaty Xinxim really fills with a hip crowd for the live *forró* from 10pm on Wednesday. There's a R$10 cover when it hosts live *afoxé* (rare).

Shopping

Olinda is full of small shops and galleries selling a plethora of art and artisanry such as ceramics, textiles and wood and stone carvings. Much of the work is incredibly colorful and browsing these places is one of the town's great pleasures. The hub of the creative scene is Rua do Amparo, where many of the best artists and artisans have their homes, workshops and galleries.

Getting There & Away

Recife is the stepping stone to Olinda. See p531 for information on transport between Recife and Olinda.

PERNAMBUCO

BEACHES SOUTH OF RECIFE

South of the capital, the sea is calm, the waters are clear and the beaches are lined with coconut palms. The coastal Hwy PE-060 doesn't hug the ocean like the road in northern Alagoas, so you have to travel a dozen or so kilometers on an access road to see what each beach is like. Porto de Galinhas, 70km south of Recife, has mushroomed into one of the most popular beach resorts in the Northeast. Further south, the Tamandaré area is much less frenetic.

Porto de Galinhas

☎ 0xx81 / pop 10,000

Less than 20 years ago, Porto de Galinhas was just another fishing village at the end of a dirt road, with a palm-fringed beach and a few Recifenses' holiday homes. Today it is one of Brazil's booming beach destinations, with several large resort-hotels strung along Praia Muro Alto and Praia do Cupe, north of the center. The development has been vertiginous and dense crowds flock to Porto at holiday times, but pedestrianizing the few streets that make up the town center, where the odd restaurant opens right onto the beach, has preserved some village ambience. These streets are mainly lined with eateries, travel agencies and shiny little shopping galleries. Porto is a place for fun and festivity, and beautiful white-sand beaches stretch several kilometers in both directions from the town.

Porto de Galinhas (Port of Chickens) gets its name from the fact that between 1853, when Brazil outlawed the slave trade, and 1888, when it abolished slavery itself, illicit slaving ships would land here loaded with crates of chickens *(galinhas)* as cover for their human cargo. Today, sculptures of brainless-looking chickens are dotted round town as a kind of on-street tourism logo.

PERNAMBUCO

INFORMATION

You'll find pharmacies and laundries along Rua da Esperança.

Banco do Brasil (Rua Beijupirá; 🕑 24hr) Across from Tourist Information – use its international ATM (not the Banco24Horas next door) to avoid the R$10 fee.

HSBC (Rua da Esperança 94; 🕑 24hr)

Local Point (Rua da Esperança; per hr R$3; 🕑 9am-11pm Mon-Sat, 2-11pm Sun) The best internet café, near the corner of Rua Beijupirá.

Tourist Information (☎ 3552 1461; Rua Beijupirá; 🕑 9am-3pm) Across from Banco do Brasil.

ACTIVITIES

Porto's fisherfolk have mostly given up fishing and now ferry tourists out to the **piscinas naturais** (tide pools) in the coral reefs, 100m in front of the main beach. Clusters of their triangular-sailed *jangadas* (boats) on the aquamarine waters are Porto's main postcard image. Take a snorkel to scrutinize the abundant marine life in these pools. The one-hour outing costs R$10 per person and you can rent snorkel and mask from most accommodations for around R$10. Just walk onto the beach and you'll find a *jangadeiro*.

The breezes here are often good for **windsurfing** and **kitesurfing** off Pontal de Maracaípe, just south of Praia de Maracaípe, especially from June to September. **Beach-buggy rides** are popular; a three-hour trip from Muro Alto to Pontal de Maracaípe costs R$120 for up to four people. Drivers are easy to find around town.

Diving is also prevalent, but be wary: there have been reports that some operators here are none too professional or safe. Stick with the Swiss-owned **Aicá Diving** (☎ 3552 1895; www.aicadiving.com.br; Rua Beijupirá 1001; 🕑 8am-5pm). Best visibility is October to March.

SLEEPING

Pousada A Casa Branca (☎ 3552 2332; www.pousadaacasabranca.com.br; Loteamento Recanto Porto de Galinhas, Praça 18; dm with/without air-con R$42/37, s with/without air-con R$100/80, d with/without air-con R$110/100; ❄ 📶) This HI hostel is a few hundred meters back from the beach, but sits on a quiet plaza and is one of the few decent budget options. It's nice but rigid with its rules, like no air-con in the dorms between 10am and 10pm, when it's most needed!

Maleleo Bed & Breakfast (☎ 8714 3719; maleleomaracaipe@hotmail.com; Praia de Maracaípe; s/d R$130/160, chalet R$180; ❄ 💻) Great word of mouth has this cozy B&B firmly on the traveler radar. It's run by a talkative English-speaking Italian and her husband, and includes just a few cute rooms on a palm-strewn, well-manicured private home along a somewhat isolated stretch of Maracaípe. The lovely outdoor café uses organic produce where possible and breakfast includes house-made multigrain breads.

Pousada Beira Mar (☎ 3552 1052; www.pousadabeiramar.com.br; Av Beira Mar 12; r R$170-310; ❄ 📶) In a great location right on the beach in the middle of town, comfortable Beira Mar offers worthwhile discounts in the low season. It's Swiss-owned, GLS friendly, and has parking and a Nespresso machine to boot.

Pousada dos Coqueiros (☎ 3552 1294; www.pousada doscoqueiros.com.br; Praia de Maracaípe; s/d from R$196/245; 🐾 🛜 🅿) A relaxing pousada in Maracaípe, the Coqueiros is good value for its simple but attractive rooms, with hammock-strung verandas, and bar and pool in neat grassy gardens. Parking is available.

EATING
Famed for its seafood, Porto de Galinhas has several good eateries. The beach bars serve inexpensive, fresh crabs.

Café do Brasil (☎ 3552 1212; cnr Rua da Esperança & Rua Beijupirá; items R$3-18; ☺ 8:30am-2am) There's prime people-watching at this sidewalk café serving up *cafezinhos*, *cocos* (coconuts), juices and small snacks.

La Crêperie (☎ 3552 1831; Rua Beijupirá; crepes R$12-19; ☺ 1:30pm-midnight) A quiet and affordable little place with a small garden area serving soups, salads and over 45 tasty crepes.

Munganga Bistro (☎ 3552 2354; Rua Beijupirá; mains R$26-97, risotto/paella for 4 R$65-269; ☺ noon-midnight Sun-Thu, to 4am Fri-Sat) Though Rua Beijupirá is cuter and more famous, your money (a little less of it, actually) is better off at this creative, part open-air seafood restaurant serving exceptional fish (try the yummy terra mar) as well as risottos and paellas that serve four.

Peixe na Telha (☎ 3552 1323; Av Beira Mar; mains for 2 R$43-130; ☺ 10am-10pm) The excellent fish dishes at this longstanding seafooder are served in orange roof tiles (*telhas*) and staff can bring them right down to the sand. Mains are priced for two, but they'll halve it for one person for 60% of the price – puzzling gastronomic math unique to Brazil.

ENTERTAINMENT
The bars at Maracaípe get pretty lively after dark and sometimes big open-air concerts are held there. In town, go local and start off with a *caldinho* (spicy bean soup, served here also with fish, shrimp etc) and Original beer at **Caldinho de Claudio** (☎ 3552 1757; Rua da Esperança 446; ☺ 11am-midnight Tue-Thu, to 1am Fri-Sat). *Caldinhos* here cost R$2 to R$4.50.

Italians run **Luz de Limão** (☎ 3552 2025; Av Beira Mar; cocktails R$5.50-22; ☺ 6pm-late), a trendy new lounge with plush sofas, groovy tunes and Asian-inspired carpets. **Birosca** (☎ 3552 1257; Rua Beijupirá; cover R$15-50; ☺ 10pm-late Mon-Sat) packs

in sweat-soaked Pernambucanas, who groove as a collective room (a very tiny one) to *brega* ('tacky' Northeastern pop), funk and sometimes techno. DJs apear nightly.

GETTING THERE & AROUND
Cruzeiro (☎ 3476 2350; Av Dantes Barreto 1321, Recife) buses to Porto de Galinhas (R$6.20, two hours) depart about twice an hour between 5am and 7:15pm from Av Dantas Barreto, just south of Rua do Peixoto, in central Recife. Perhaps easier for those coming from Boa Viagem, however, is to catch the 191 Recife–Camala–Porto de Galinhas bus from the southwest corner of Praça Salgado Filho in front of the airport. Buses depart here every 30 minutes between 5am and 6pm daily. Coming from the south, get off your bus at Ipojuca, where buses run to Porto de Galinhas (R$2, 45 minutes) about every half-hour. Buses and Kombi vans to Maracaípe (R$2, 10 minutes) stop every 15 to 30 minutes across the road from the Recife bus stop in Porto.

Buses return to Recife from a small booth next to the police station on the main highway to Ipojuca.

Tamandaré
☎ 0xx81 / pop 19,000
Tamandaré, 30km south of Porto de Galinhas (75km by road), is a small beach town boasting a big stretch of coastline – 16km of lovely palm-fringed beaches. It's far less hyper than Galinhas, but with plenty of local tourism on weekends and holidays. Fishing boats will take you out to the tidal pools here for R$10 per person. Eight kilometers north up the beach, ultra-relaxed **Praia dos Carneiros** is the area's fashionable strand. It has wonderful, calm, shallow waters and tidal pools formed by a rocky bar stretching across the wide mouth of the Rio Formosa.

Tamandaré has plenty of places to stay. **Pousada Recanto dos Corais** (☎ 3676 2155; www.pou sadarecantodoscorais.com.br; Rua Hermes Samico 317; s/d R$100/140; 🐾) is run by a welcoming, German-speaking, southern Brazilian couple and has comfy, spotless little rooms, a good breakfast as well as parking. Upping the cutesy quotient is **Pousada Beira Mar** (☎ 3676 1567; www.pousada beiramartamandare.com; Rua Almirante Tamandaré 140; s/d R$100/190; 🐾 🛜), with bright, design-forward rooms and well-manicured lawn right on the beach. It has parking.

On the beach, the Austrian-run **Quiosque Pimenta Rosa** (☎ 9274 2163; Rua São José 17; items R$4-34) is the best of the long line of beach kiosks, serving *caldinho*, *açaí* (forest berry) and fresh fish. The Italian-owned **Pizzaria do Farol** (☎ 3676 1556; Av Dr Leopoldo Lins; pizza R$11-31; ☻ 10am-10pm) serves thin and authentic brick-oven pizza. **Restaurante Tapera do Sabor** (☎ 3676 1509; Rua São Jose; mains R$22-30; ☻ 9am-10pm) is an excellent little sand-side seafooder with makeshift daybeds and straw-strewn *palapas* (thatched huts), just back from the water.

Nightlife commences at the '60's-themed **Quiosque Submarino Amarelo** (☎ 3676 1361; Rua São Jose; ☻ 7pm-late), which hosts live music on the sand on Fridays and Saturdays from 10pm.

Praia dos Carneiros is lined with private coconut groves and, unless you're staying in one of the handful of lodgings there, beach access is only via few beach restaurant-bars, which usually have a minimum consumption for planting yourself on their stretch of paradise all day. More tranquil **Sitio da Prainha** (☎ 3676 1498; minimum consumption R$50, mains R$29-120; ☻ 9:30am-5pm) sits at the far northern end of the beach, where the Rio Ariquindá spills into the Atlantic.

A tad too much like Club Med **Bora Bora** (☎ 3676 1482; minimum consumption R$50, mains R$46-112; ☻ 9am-4pm), can get crowded with large tour groups. In between is **Bar Ariquindá** (☎ 3676 1342; mains R$26-67; ☻ 7:30am-10pm), which has no consumption restrictions. All are fine bases for a day of swimming, snorkeling, snoozing and strolling. **Bangalôs do Gameleiro** (☎ 3676 1421; www.praiadoscarneiros.com.br; r from R$250; ☷) offers 12 brick-and-tile cottages, most with kitchen, spaced among the palms. It has parking.

GETTING THERE & AWAY

Cruzeiro (☎ 3476 2350; Av Dantes Barreto 1321, Recife) runs buses to Tamandaré (R$10, three hours) at 10am and 5:40pm Monday to Saturday, and 7:30am Sunday, from central Recife, just south of Rua do Peixoto. If you're coming north up Hwy PE-060 from Alagoas, get off your bus at Barreiros, where buses and Kombi vans to Tamandaré (R$3, 40 minutes) leave about every half-hour till 8pm. The majority of tourists, especially those without cars, visit Tamandaré on a day trip from Porto de Galinhas (p536). To reach Porto on your own from Tamandaré, catch a Kombi to Rio Formoso (R$3, 30 minutes), and from there on to Ipojuca (R$5, 1½ hours), where you'll need to switch to another Kombi for Porto (R$2, 45 minutes).

Moto-taxis (R$5 each way) will take you from Tamandaré to Praia dos Carneiros.

ILHA DE ITAMARACÁ
☎ 0xx81 / pop 19,000

Less than 40km north of Olinda, Ilha de Itamaracá (separated from the mainland by a wide channel) is a pleasant weekend beach scene. During the week it's pretty calm.

Sights & Activities

The best area to head for is the southeast tip of the island. Here, **Forte Orange** (☎ 3544 1193; admission R$3; ☻ 9am-5pm Mon-Sat, 8am-5pm Sun) was built by the Dutch in 1631 and reconstructed by the Portuguese in 1654. It's an impressive citadel, with a nice view, right on the water. A short distance back along the road, the **Eco-Parque Peixe-Boi** (☎ 3544 1056; admission free; ☻ 9am-4pm Tue-Sun) exists to study and rehabilitate the endangered West Indian manatee. You can watch up to 10 manatees, some rescued from injury or captivity, in a series of tanks, and see displays and films about them.

In front of the fort is the small sand island of **Coroa do Avião**, with several *barracas* (stalls). Small boats from the beach will run you across to the island for R$7 per person, or take a boatload to the nearby reef pools and mangroves for R$35. **Adilson Marcos** (☎ 9997 5367) offers two-hour kayak excursions to the mangroves and reef pools (R$15).

Three kilometers west of Forte Orange is **Vila Velha**, a small port founded in 1540, one of the earliest Portuguese settlements in Brazil. A walking trail, the **Trilha dos Holandeses**, leads here from a chapel about 500m back up the road from the Eco-Parque Peixe-Boi.

Itamaracá island has plenty more beaches, strung out along its 15km ocean shore. The quietest and prettiest are north of the central, most built-up part of the coast around **Jaguaribe** and **Pilar**. If you don't have a vehicle you can hike 3km or 4km north along the coast from Jaguaribe to **Praia do Sossego** and palm-lined **Praia do Fortinho**; or cut most of the work by catching the semi-hourly **trenzinho** (R$1.50) to Pilar, a green train-like truck on wheels that plies the main road.

Sleeping & Eating

Pousada Refúgio do Forte (☎ 3544 1675; www .pousadarefugiodoforte.adm.br; Rua Desembargador Ângelo

Vasconcelos 91, Praia Forno da Cal; s/d/tr R$80/100/120; 🔲 🛜 🔲) About 1km back from Forte Orange, this friendly, family-run place offers clean rooms – choose your bed, hard or soft! – with hammock-strung verandas and a boatload of cows out back.

Recanto da Cigana Euzanira (☎ 3544 2971; Praia do Forte Orange 3400; mains for 2 R$35-80; 🕑 8am-6pm) The best of several beach restaurants near the fort, serving excellent seafood, meat and salads and (oddly) impressive beans. A definite don't miss.

Getting There & Away

To reach Itamaracá, take the 946 Igarassu bus (R$3.80, one hour), with departures every few minutes from Av Martins de Barros in central Recife.

At Igarassu's Terminal Integração bus station, change to one of the frequent 968 Itamaracá buses (free). A few of these go to Forte Orange; most of the others head to Jaguaribe but you can get off at the Forte Orange turn-off (the *entrada do forte*) and catch a frequent Kombi van or *colectivo* (shared taxi; R$1) for the remaining 5km.

FERNANDO DE NORONHA

☎ 0xx81 / pop 3100

While religion, science and philosophy continue to battle out what happens when we die, in Brazil, there is little discourse on the subject: Heaven plays second fiddle to the Fernando de Noronha archipelago. In the Atlantic, 525km from Recife and 350km from Natal, Noronha is often considered Brazil's most stunning destination, and its natural beauty holds its own against any tropical locale in the world. With its crystal-clear water, rich marine life and spectacular tropical landscapes, it's in a Brazilian class all by its lonesome. The country's 'Beach Bible,' *Guia Quatro Rodas Praias 2010*, awards five stars to just four beaches in the whole country – and one, two and three are right here.

Give yourself plenty of time because Noronha is addictive. The average stay is five nights. It's a wonderful place for doing things both water-based (diving, surfing, snorkeling) and on land (horseback riding,

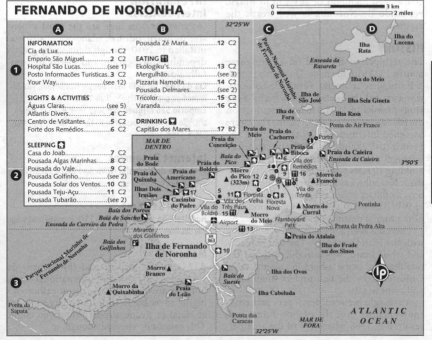

FERNANDO DE NORONHA

0 — 3 km
0 — 2 miles

INFORMATION
Cia da Lua..........................**1** C2
Emporio São Miguel...........**2** C2
Hospital São Lucas.........(see 1)
Posto Informacões Turisticas.**3** C2
Your Way.........................(see 12)

SIGHTS & ACTIVITIES
Águas Claras....................(see 5)
Atlantis Divers...................**4** C2
Centro de Visitantes..........**5** C2
Forte dos Remédios...........**6** C2

SLEEPING 🛏
Casa do Joab.....................**7** C2
Pousada Algas Marinhas......**8** C2
Pousada do Vale................**9** C2
Pousada Golfinho............(see 2)
Pousada Solar dos Ventos...**10** C3
Pousada Teju-Açu.............**11** C2
Pousada Tubarão.............(see 2)

Pousada Zé Maria............**12** C2

EATING 🍴
Ekologiku's.......................**13** C2
Mergulhão......................(see 3)
Pizzaria Namoita.............**14** C2
Pousada Delmares............(see 2)
Tricolor..........................**15** C2
Varanda..........................**16** C2

DRINKING 🍸
Capitão dos Mares............**17** B2

hiking, touring), and is Brazil's top 'eco' destination. Thanks in large part to the Fernando de Noronha Marine National Park and conservation projects based here, the marine and coastal environment is tightly regulated – locals like to joke that it's the island of 'No' – no, you can't do this, no, you can't do that etc.

With only an average of 258 to 328 plane seats per day available to Noronha depending on the season, tourism can never overwhelm the islands and it's normally no problem whatsoever to find an isolated patch of sand on a beach you've only previously dreamed of – even in high season. However, it's advisable to reserve accommodations and flights well ahead for December to February, and July and August. The week or so either side of New Year's can get booked up six months in advance. The showery season is from February to June and the islands are blessed by fresh breezes year-round. The time zone here is one hour ahead of Brasília time.

Prices are high – in fact, downright unrealistic – due to the cost of transporting goods from the mainland and, put more simply, because paradise comes at a price. But as a guaranteed highlight of any trip to Brazil, Fernando de Noronha is well worth the expense.

HISTORY

The archipelago appeared on a Portuguese map in 1502 with the name Quaresma (Lent). A Portuguese aristocrat, Fernão de Loronha, was awarded the islands by his friend King Dom Manoel in 1504. He never set foot on the islands and forgot about them. They were occupied intermittently by the English, the French (twice) and the Dutch (twice) before Portugal definitively retook them in 1737, building 10 forts to defend the islands. Since then, Noronha has been used as a penal colony, a military base (including for US troops in WWII), a US missile-tracking station, and now a tourist destination.

There has been some misguided tampering with the island's ecology. The teju, a black-and-white lizard, was introduced to eat the rats that had come ashore in colonial days. Unfortunately, the teju prefers small birds and crabs to rats.

A struggle between developers and environmentalists over the islands' future was resolved in 1988 when 75% of the archipel-

ago, including much of the main island, was declared a marine national park, to protect its natural treasures. It was included on the Unesco World Heritage List in 2002.

ORIENTATION

Fernando de Noronha has 21 islands. The largest and only inhabited island, Ilha de Fernando de Noronha, is 10km long. The population is concentrated toward its northeastern end in the village of Vila dos Remédios and the adjoining, spread-out neighborhoods of Vila do Trinta, Floresta Velha and Floresta Nova. The airport is in the middle of the island. A single paved road, the BR-363 (or Transnoronha Hwy!), runs 7km from the port near the island's northeast tip, through the populated area then to the airport and down to Baía do Sueste on the southeast coast. Unpaved side roads lead from the BR-363 to several of the island's other beaches. Morro do Pico, an extinct volcanic cone and the most spectacular of the islands' many striking rock formations, is the highest point, 323m above sea level – and more than 4300m above the ocean floor. 'No,' you cannot climb it.

INFORMATION
Internet Access

Internet services here are the most expensive in Brazil, but free island-wide wi-fi was installed in 2010, though signals vary greatly depending on location, and speeds are painfully slow.

Cia da Lua (☎ 3619 1631; Bosque Flamboyant, Vila dos Remédios; per hr R$12; ☼ 9am-11pm)

Emporio São Miguel (☎ 3619 1859; Rua São Miguel s/n, Vila dos Remédios; per hr R$12; ☼ 9am-11pm Mon-Sat, 5-11pm Sun)

Internet Resources

Fernando de Noronha (www.noronha.pe.gov.br) Has every detail imaginable.

Medical Services

Hospital São Lucas (☎ 3619 1377; Bosque Flamboyant, Vila dos Remédios)

Money

ATMs at the airport and the Centro de Visitantes (p541) accept international cards, but they are often out of order or cash, so it's highly advisable to withdraw a large amount at Natal or Recife airport before you come. This cannot be stressed enough.

> **VISITORS' TAX**
>
> The state government imposes an environmental preservation tax on visitors. The daily, exponentially rising bill costs R$38 per day to start, then rises: four days/one week/two weeks/one month costs R$153/237/631/3155. You pay by cash or credit card on arrival at the airport; or online prior to arrival (www.noronha.pe.gov.br – Brazilian bank accounts only at time of writing). If you decide to stay longer than planned, go to the airport at least one day before your original departure date and pay for your extra days – otherwise you'll pay double. Future plans include an additional tax for entering the national marine park itself – almost impossible to avoid.

Post

Post office (Vila dos Remédios; 8am-3pm Mon-Fri, to noon Sat)

Tourist Information

Posto Informacões Turisticas (Porto; 8am-5pm) Pick up a helpful map here at this tourist info booth above the port. There is also a small booth at the airport arrivals hall.

Travel Agencies

Pirata Passeios (3619 1904; www.piratanoronha .com; Pousada Aleffawi, BR-363, Vila do Boldró) Friendly Fábio 'Pirata' speaks English and Italian and is an experienced dive instructor. He specializes in trekking and island tours.

Your Way (9949 1087; www.yourway.com.br; Floresta Velha) An indispensable contact on the island, this small, 10-year ecotourism veteran is perfect for independent travelers of all budgets. Fluent English-speaker Adriana will help you find the best-value flights to the island and offers unbiased tips and bookings of accommodations, restaurants and activities that suit you best – at no additional cost.

SIGHTS

The Centro de Visitantes (visitors center), at Vila do Boldró, on the road between Vila dos Remédios and the airport, includes an open-air **turtle museum** (24hr) with displays on sea turtles by the **Tamar Project** (3619 1171; www.tamar.org.br), as well as on Noronha's spinner dolphins by **Projeto Golfinho Rotador** (www .golfinhorotador.org.br). There are also Tamar information desks and a good café.

Easily the best preserved of the island's Portuguese forts, **Forte dos Remédios** (admission free; 24hr) is well worth a visit and has great views from its hilltop above Vila dos Remédios.

ACTIVITIES
Beaches

There are 16 or 17 beaches on Noronha (depending on who you ask), all clean, postcard-ready and almost deserted. The 'five-star' **Baía do Sancho**, **Baía dos Porcos** (named after the infamous Cuban Bay of Pigs) and **Praia do Leão** are all impossibly gorgeous. However, there is a lot of competition. The sandy beaches facing the Mar de Dentro (Inner Sea) on the northwest side of the island – **Cachorro** (at Vila dos Remédios), **Conceição**, **Boldró**, **Americano**, **Quixaba** and **Cacimba do Padre** – are also good for surfing.

Inside the national park, ICMBio restricts access to some beaches in the interest of protecting marine life. Praia do Leão is closed off from 6pm to 8am from December to July, which is the turtle-nesting season. **Praia do Atalaia**, which has shallow tide pools great for snorkeling, can only be accessed by a guided hike (see p542). Vehicle access from **Baia do Sueste** was suspended at the time of research pending further review. No flippers and or sunscreen are permitted.

Baía dos Golfinhos (see Dolphin Watching, p542), is strictly off-limits to swimmers.

Boat Tours

A number of boats make enjoyable daily three-hour tours from the port, out to the Ilhas Secundárias (Secondary Islands) to the northeast, then back along the main island's northwest coast. Spinner dolphins like to swim and perform acrobatics near the boats, and a 40-minute snorkeling stop at Baía do Sancho is normally part of the trip. **Naonda** (3619 1307; www.barconaonda.com.br; Porto) is a recommended boat, charging R$85 including pick-up.

Diving

With 30m to 40m of visibility (at its very best in October), beautifully warm seas, abundant marine life and a well-preserved underwater environment, the diving around Noronha is world class. There are 230 fish species, 15 coral varieties and five types of (harmless)

PERNAMBUCO

shark. Some of the best sites include Ilha Rata, Enseada da Rasureta, Ponta da Sapata and Corveta Ipiranga (a 63m shipwreck), but each day's sites are chosen by ICMBio, not divers. There are no offshore dive sites.

There are three dive operators, two of which are committed members of Abeta, Brazil's only ecotourism and safety operator association:

Águas Claras (☎ 3619 1225; www.aguasclaras-fn.com .br; Alameda do Boldró) Friendly operation based near the Centro de Visitantes.

Atlantis Divers (☎ 3619 1371; www.atlantisdivers .br; Vila dos Remédios) French-run and very professional.

For certified divers, a two-tank dive normally costs R$316 including transfers and all equipment. Open Water courses are R$1700 and *batismo* (baptism) dives for first-timers are around R$280.

Snorkeling

There are simply hundreds of good places to snorkel on the islands, from the rocks in Baía do Sancho to the tranquil tide pool of Atalaia, or Baía do Sueste where you can swim with marine turtles at high tide (local guides on the spot will swim you to the turtles for R$25). Masks, snorkel and flippers can be rented for R$15 per day at a few stores in the village, at the harbor and at Baía do Sueste. A popular activity is snorkel-by-boat, where you are slowly pulled along behind a boat, enabling you to cover greater distances; try **Naonda** (☎ 3619 1307; www.barconaonda.com.br; Porto; 2 half-hour tows incl transfers R$75).

Dolphin Watching

From the clifftop lookout **Mirante dos Golfinhos** you can watch an average of more than 300 spinner dolphins cavorting in the Baía dos Golfinhos at approximately 5:30am. Trainee biologists provide Portuguese commentary from Monday to Saturday.

Hiking

Most trails within the national park can only be walked with a local guide. A great one runs from Vila do Trinta to Praia do Atalaia, with cliff scenery and good snorkeling along the way – three to four hours in all. Portuguese-language guides charge R$50 per person for this hike; Fábio from Pirata Passeios travel agency (p541) does it in English, Italian or Spanish for R$80.

Surfing

Cacimba do Padre is the most famous surfing beach here and it hosts surf championships during the December to March season. Waves can reach 5m in height. Other surfing beaches on the Mar de Dentro, including Boldró and Bode, are also good, and in a big swell there are some thrilling waves among the Ilhas Secundárias. Most people bring their own boards but you can rent at **Restaurante do Jacaré** (☎ 3619 1947; Vila dos Remédios; per day R$30), which also offers classes for R$50 to R$70 per hour.

SLEEPING

Noronha has around 120 pousadas, mostly in the Remédios/Trinta/Floresta area. Prices are surreal – don't expect value for money. The only true budget option is an informal scheme of local homes. Contact Your Way (p541) for more info. Otherwise, 'budget' pousadas run from R$140 to R$300 per double occupancy and prices skyrocket from there, topping out at R$2541 for the island's most expensive choice, Pousada Maravilha, one of only eight with a sea view.

Budget

Pousada Golfinho (☎ 3619 1837; www.pousadagolf inhofn.com.br; Rua São Miguel 144, Vila dos Remédios; s/d R$90/140; 🅿 🛜) This is the best value-for-money budget option in a true pousada, right in the village. No breakfast.

Pousada Tubarão (☎ 3619 1391; Rua São Miguel 361, Vila dos Remédios; s/d R$90/140; 🅿) No-frills but adequate. No breakfast.

Pousada Delmares (☎ 3619 1243; www.pousada delmares.com.br; Rua do Sol 141, Vila dos Remédios; s/d R$180/240; 🅿 🛜) Another friendly choice in an intimate family home, with spotless rooms, exposed brick and super-sized bathrooms.

Midrange & Top End

Pousada Algas Marinhas (☎ 3619 1341; www.pousadaal gasmarinhas.com.br; Alameda das Flores 514, Floresta Nova; s/d R$200/280; 🅿 🛜) In Noronha's 'upscale' neighborhood, Floresta Nova, Algas Marinhas sits at the top end of Noronha's 'budget' category, but outclasses its competition with charming rooms and extra care throughout. The owners are fiercely nonsmoking, so much so that even casual smokers are not welcome – you will be asked to leave.

our pick **Casa do Joab** (☎ 3619 1267; dricaschmidt@ gmail.com; Estrada da Conceição, Vila Italcable; s/d R$240/300; 🅿 🛜) Local workhorse Joab and his wife

Monica have slowly turned their simple beachfront home into a friendly and tasteful choice that sits steps from Conceição beach – something no other pousada can boast. Satellite TV and bathrooms add to the sweet deal. If Monica happens to whip up her famous *pudim de leite* (sweet condensed-milk flan), you won't even care about the beach.

Pousada do Vale (☎ 3619 1293; www.pousadadovale.com; Rua Pescador Sérgio Lino 18, Vila dos Remédios; s/d from R$414/684, bungalows R$684/918; 🛏 🛜 🖵) Tucked away down a lush alley off the main village, intimate Vale is one of the friendliest and service-oriented pousadas on the island. Rooms aren't as high-end as the prices suggest (though the bungalows are), but are well-appointed with design-forward touches like *mantas nordestinas* (colorful throws). All-you-can-eat pizza (Sunday) and grilled-fish nights (Thursday) keep the camaraderie level high between locals and guests.

Pousada Zé Maria (☎ 3619 1258; www.pousadazemaria.com.br; Rua Nice Cordeiro 1, Floresta Velha; s/d R$733/775, bungalows from R$1353/1573; 🛏 🛜 🖵) Luxurious Zé Maria boasts a stunning view of the Morro do Pico from its pool and is famed Brazil-wide for its over-the-top, all-you-can-eat R$120 seafood buffet spectacle on Wednesdays and Saturdays (by reservation only).

Pousada Solar dos Ventos (☎ 3619 1347; www.pousadasolardosventos.com.br; Sueste Bay; r R$986; 🛏 🛜) There's comfy wood-and-brick bungalows around extensive lawns but more importantly, the same view down to Baía do Sueste as Pousada Maravilha for R$1555 less per night!

Pousada Teju-Açu (☎ 3619 1277; www.pousadateju.com.br; Estrada da Alamoa, Boldró; s/d from R$1025/1139; 🛏 🛜 🖵) Almost underneath Morro do Pico, Pousada Teju-Açu is a well-managed (via London), fun-designed eco-pousada with a good restaurant, spacious rooms (tiny bathrooms but huge beds) and a pleasant wood-decked pool area. There's an ecological outlook (solar showers, sustainable wood) throughout. Of the island's three true (overpriced) luxury choices, it's the best bang for the buck.

EATING

There are popular pay-by-weight kilo joints in and around Flamboyant Park charging between R$30 and R$37 per kilo.

Raízes Noronha (☎ 3619 0058; BR-363, Floresta Nova; sandwiches R$4-14; 🕑 9am-midnight; 🛜) Locals and tourists people-watch from the front porch of this Mundo Verde natural-foods store that's good for *açaí* and fresh sandwiches. It's one of the best spots to pick up the island's free wi-fi signal.

Pizzaria Namoita (☎ 3619 1914; BR-363, Vila do Trinta; pizza R$28-40; 🕑 dinner Fri-Wed) São Paulo expat Mauricio Vilela does his best to recreate *pizza paulistana* on the island and does a damn fine job considering Noronha logistics. Favorites like *cearense* (spicy ground sausage with peppers, onions and mozzarella) are served in an atmospheric setting under a giant cashew tree in his front yard.

Mergulhão (☎ 3619 0215; Porto; mains R$35-68; 🕑 lunch & dinner Tue-Sun) A little haphazard but loaded with potential, this interesting newcomer makes full use of stupendous views over the port, while the Mediterranean menu with a Brazilian twist is one of Noronha's most innovative. There's proper wine and one of Brazil's most delicious and creative desserts: *banana mil folhas* (flambéed bananas on a bed of tapioca and the caramel *doce de leite*).

Varanda (☎ 3619 1546; Rua Major Costa 130, Vila do Trinta; mains R$46-149; 🕑 lunch & dinner) One of the best-value upscale choices, within walking distance of most pousadas and run by a professional chef formerly of Zé Maria fame. The *moqueca* and crunchy shrimp risotto are standouts, and the crispy *farofa* (manioc flour sautéed in butter) is a game-changer.

Tricolor (☎ 3619 1479; Alameda das Cajazeiras, Vila dos Três Paus; mains for 2 R$60-74; 🕑 12:30-4:30pm & 5-10pm Thu-Tue) A hidden native favorite; specialties include the island's most economical *moquecas* and divine octopus rice. It's run out of the home of Jorge and Edna, who also make a snappy little hot sauce.

Ekologiku's (☎ 3619 0031; Antiga Vila DPV; mains for 2 R$80-105; 🕑 7-10:30pm) A kitchen staff trained by a sassy *baiana* (Bahian woman) oversees this consistently great seafood restaurant beyond the airport. It serves up superb *moqueca capixabas* (seafood stew made with olive oil instead of palm oil) in a surprisingly tropical-cool space considering its remote location. Take a taxi (R$25) – you'll never find it in the dark (if you're at least a group of four, they'll send a free transfer).

our pick Palhoça da Colina (☎ 3619 1473; Estrada da Colina, Vila do Trinta; dinner without drinks R$80; 🕑 from 8pm) The single most memorable dining experience on the island: a feast for only 15 to 20 people per night under an atmospheric *palapa* hut with tatami mats and pillows, in the backyard of a local fisherman's home. All-you-can-eat grilled catch of the day (barracuda, tuna, *carvala* – sometimes too dry) is served on banana leaves along with great side dishes such as island arugula salad and banana *farofa*. Reservations essential.

DRINKING & ENTERTAINMENT

Almost none of Noronha's beaches offer any food/drink services (exceptions are Conceição, Cachorro and Meio) and the island on the whole is nightlife-challenged. The clifftop bar Capitão dos Mares, beside the ruined Forte de São Pedro do Boldró, is a spectacular favorite for a sunset drink.

Bar do Cachorro (Vila dos Remédios; cover R$5-10; ☺ 5pm-late) The famous 'Dog Bar' is the hub of Noronha social life, busy almost every night but really packed Thursday through Sunday. There's rhythmic *maracatu* on Monday nights, and *forró* nightly from about 11pm, sometimes live.

Feitiço Da Vila (Vila dos Remédios; ☺ 6pm-midnight Mon-Sat, from 4pm Sun) More commonly known as 'The Pizza Place,' this bar-pizzeria (skip the pizza), next to the church, is the first stop in the standard two-stop Noronha pub crawl. There's live music (reggae, MPB, *swinguiera* etc) from 10:30pm to midnight most nights of the week, but Thursday and Saturday reign. After, the crowd moves to Cachorro.

GETTING THERE & AWAY

Fernando de Noronha's **airport** (code FEN; ☎ 3619 1311) sits in the middle of the island. Most incoming flights do a loop around the island as they arrive: views are best from the left side of the plane. Both expensive fares and an average daily visitor limit of 750 people per day facilitate the island's protected status.

Trip (☎ Noronha 3619 1148) and **Gol/Varig** (☎ Noronha 3619 0424) both fly from Recife to Noronha and back daily. Trip also flies Natal–Noronha–Natal daily. Round-trip fares with Trip and Gol/Varig range from R$900 to R$2400 from Recife, slightly less from Natal. Buy your ticket as early as you can. Your Way (p541) travel agency can usually find you the best deal.

All seats on the Gol/Varig flights are available to Brazil airpass holders; Trip codeshares with TAM but only five seats are available to airpass holders. Either way, an airpass is by far the best way to economically visit the island.

GETTING AROUND

A good bus service (R$3.10) runs the length of the BR-363 between the port, Vila dos Remédios, the airport and Baía do Sueste, about every 30 to 40 minutes during daylight and early evening. You'll see bus-stop signs along the road. Hitchhiking is safe and commonplace.

Buggy taxis are sticker-shock expensive, especially after the ballsy move by the taxi association to increase prices by 30% during a recession in 2009. Rides now cost R$15 to R$25 for any distance. There's a stand by the central park in Vila dos Remédios.

A popular way to get around is to rent your own buggy. Rates are R$120 to R$180 per 24 hours, plus fuel (be aware: there is no insurance on the island for rental vehicles). They often break down, so a reliable operator is key. Contact **JMR Locadora** (☎ 3619 1267; www.jmrlocadora.com.br) or **Flor do Atlântico** (☎ 3619 1160), who will deliver the buggy to you. You can also rent motorcycles, but only if you are licensed for one back home.

INLAND

CARUARU
☎ 0xx81 / pop 298,500

Though modern and without architectural appeal, this city 137km west of Recife does have cultural riches. Caruaru is known as the capital of *forró*, and its big **Festa de São João** (late May to late June) is, among other things, claimed to be the largest *forró* festival in the country – 30 straight days of couples swaying to the accordion and triangle. It is also a huge market town and South America's biggest center for ceramic-figurine art, famous for its brightly painted little people captured in activities such as dancing and chasing chickens.

Sights
FEIRA DE CARUARU

This enormous **market** (Parque 18 de Maio; ☺ 6am-5pm) is the largest in the Northeast and has become a popular tourist attraction. It's busiest on Saturday. Among the thousands of stalls selling flowers, shoes, food, medicinal herbs, clothes and household goods is a large area devoted to handicrafts, the **Feira de Artesanato**, with leather goods, woven baskets, representations of strange beasts and mythical mon-

---

DETOUR: PAIXÃO DE CRISTO

The small town of Fazenda Nova, 50km northwest of Caruaru, is famous for its theater-city reconstruction of Jerusalem, known as Nova Jerusalém. Surrounded by a 3m-high wall with seven gateways, 70 towers and 12 granite stages, the reconstruction occupies an area equivalent to one-third of the walled city of Jerusalem in the time of Jesus.

The time to visit is during Semana Santa (Holy Week, the week before Easter; otherwise it feels like an abandoned movie set), when several hundred inhabitants of Fazenda Nova plus imported *novela* (soap opera) stars from Rio perform the *Paixão de Cristo* (Passion of Christ) play. Tickets cost R$40 to R$50.

---

sters, colorful figurines and much more. Also here is the **Feira do Troca-Troca** (Barter Market), where junk and treasure are traded without money.

If you're interested in buying some figurines and seeing the ceramic artists at work, visit Alto de Moura (see below) before buying at the Feira.

MUSEUMS

The **Museu do Forró** (☎ 3701 1533; Praça José de Vasconcellos; admission R$1; ☽ 8am-5pm Tue-Sat, 9am-1pm Sun) holds every bit of memorabilia on Luiz Gonzaga, the father of *forró* (see the boxed text, p529), that it could get its hands on – including the pajamas he died in.

Museu do Barro (☎ 3701 1533; Praça José de Vasconcellos; ☽ 8am-5pm Tue-Sat, 9am-1pm Sun), upstairs from the Museu do Forró, is the best place to see original pieces created by Mestre Vitalino (1909–63), the city's original ceramic-figurine genius, and numerous works by other accomplished local potters.

ALTO DE MOURA

The home village of Mestre Vitalino, 7km west of the city center, is a small **community of potters** (and goat-meat lovers!) that still specializes in producing *figurinhas* (figurines). Their pieces sell for anything from R$1 to R$3000. Many of the potters are descendants of Mestre Vitalino himself. Other noted artists include Manuel Eudócio, Luiz Galdino and the family of Zé Caboclo. The **Museu Casa do Mestre Vitalino** (☎ 3725 0805; Rua Mestre Vitalino; admission R$1;

☽ 8am-5pm), in the simple home of the master, contains his tools and personal effects.

Catch a taxi (R$20 to R$25) or bus 135 (R$1.60) from Rua Duque de Caixas in central Caruaru – next to Catedral Nossa Senhora das Dores – to Alto de Moura, then browse at the dozens of workshops and galleries. The quality of the figurines here is generally higher than in Caruaru.

Sleeping & Eating

Caruaru is a long day trip from Recife, but there's no real need to stay overnight. Lots of places in the center serve regional food at good prices.

Hotel Vila Rica (☎ 3722 9666; vilaricahotel@bol.com.br; Rua Dalvino Pedrosa 160; s/d R$60/95; ☒ ☜) If you do decide to stay, this hotel in the southwestern Pinheirópolis district is decent value, with clean, basic rooms and a (slow, subpar) restaurant, and is walkable from the bus station.

Bode Assado do Luciano (☎ 3722 0413; Rua Mestre Vitalino 511; mains for 2 R$25-40; ☽ 11am-4pm Tue-Fri, 10am-6pm Sat-Sun) For lunch in Alto de Moura, head for this place, the justifiably most famous of the dozens of *churrascaria* (barbecued-meat restaurants) serving the village specialty, roast goat.

Getting There & Around

Buses run at least hourly to Caruaru from Recife (R$17 to R$20, two hours). Caruaru's **bus station** (☎ 3721 2480; Hwy BR-104, km68) is 3km southwest of the center. It's easy to get a taxi, Kombi van or local bus into town.

PERNAMBUCO

Paraíba & Rio Grande do Norte

The region's highlights may not roll off the tongue with quite the same international recognition as some of the country's more idealized destinations, but the northeastern corner of Brazil, made up of the states of Paraíba and Rio Grande do Norte, is no worse for wear. Here you'll find kilometer upon kilometer of spectacular scenery, much of which is largely unexplored by intrepid globe trekkers. Glorious beaches, some of them small palm-lined bays, others 20km long and backed by huge dune fields piled up by the coastal winds, dominate this pristine stretch of coastline, but inland treasures abound as well for those willing to forgo the breezy beach-blanket Babylon.

The region's main gateways, the largely sedate cities of Natal and João Pessoa, are more well known for their quality of life than tourist draw, though both are perfectly enjoyable places for a layover on your way to the region's more stunning attractions, and the latter boasts a little-known historic side that's worth a glimpse. The hip international beach town of Praia da Pipa, a good-time 'global village' south of Natal, lures the bulk of travelers, but beaches less traveled such as São Miguel do Gostoso and Galinhos, both north of Natal, are emerging stretches of sands of equal beauty and far more tranquility.

A different type of adventure awaits those willing to venture inland. The parched interior is home to dramatic landscapes and some of Brazil's most spectacular ancient remains, from remarkably preserved rock art many millennia old to eerie, otherworldly stone formations.

Though short on major allure itself, Natal does cut loose when it comes to festival time – its famous out-of-season carnaval, Carnatal, in December, is Brazil's best.

HIGHLIGHTS

- Take in the river sunset saxophone spectacle set to Ravel's *Bolero* at **Praia do Jacaré** (p551) in João Pessoa
- Enjoy the stylish but unpretentious international scene of beautiful **Praia da Pipa** (p560)
- Send your adrenaline into the red on a spectacular dune ride by buggy in **Genipabu** (p556)
- Dig your toes into sands less traveled in **São Miguel do Gostoso** (p562)
- Unwind at the remote beach village of **Galinhos** (p563)

- POPULATION: 6.9 MILLION
- AREA: 109,240 SQ KM

PARAÍBA & RIO GRANDE DO NORTE

History

This area of Brazil was a hotly contested colonial property, with both the French and Dutch vying for control against the Portuguese. French brazilwood traders had a decent foothold in Rio Grande do Norte until the Portuguese sent a fleet from Paraíba to kick them out in 1597. Natal was lost again to the Dutch from 1633 to 1654 before being retaken by the Portuguese.

Thereafter, the states of Paraíba and Rio Grande do Norte largely languished in obscurity until the early 20th century. Paraíba made a name for itself as the home state of João Pessoa, who allied himself with Getúlio Vargas in 1929 in a bid for the vice-presidency. Judging by the sheer number of João Pessoa tributes in the state, it seems that not much has happened since.

In 1935 rioting in Natal led to the declaration of a short-lived communist government in Rio Grande do Norte. The communist movement was suppressed and before long Rio Grande do Norte's strategic location as Brazil's closest point to Africa saw it become a supply base for the US in WWII. The injection of military money spurred significant development in the region. Today, the region's fabulous beaches bring in major income from tourism, especially in Rio Grande do Norte.

Climate

Although this area is no hotter than neighboring states, Rio Grande do Norte in particular is really dry and the sun can be very strong in the almost-always-clear skies. Temperatures in both states can top 40°C (104°F) in January and February. Although the weather is nice year-round, some find it the most pleasant in the slightly cooler months of June to August.

Getting There & Away

Natal has direct and indirect flights from every major Brazilian city and Lisbon (Portugal). It has seen an increasing number of European charter flights and, once in a while, a US charter flight. João Pessoa's airport also has a few European charters, plus domestic flights.

Both state capitals, Natal and João Pessoa, are served by buses from the main Northeastern cities. Natal also has direct connections from Rio.

Getting Around

The bus network is good for travel between larger towns and more popular beach spots. Rental cars are available too. For anything more remote you should get a group together to hire a 4WD or buggy with a driver.

PARAÍBA

Sandwiched between Pernambuco and Rio Grande do Norte, the small, sunny state of Paraíba contains the easternmost point of the continent, Ponta do Seixas, where you are considerably closer to Senegal than you are to southern Brazil. The tranquil and reasonably well-developed coast is this small state's most important economic region, fueled by the farming of sugarcane and pineapples, and aided by a bit of tourism. Cattle ranching dominates the drought-affected interior, which also harbors some intriguing archaeological sites.

JOÃO PESSOA

☎ 0xx83 / pop 702,000

The coastal city of João Pessoa is the capital of Paraíba and the third-oldest city in Brazil. It claims to have more trees than any other capital city, including an Atlantic rain forest preserve, and has a reputation for being friendly and safe (some would say boring). Tourism has developed gradually here, and the city is an increasingly popular destination for Brazilian families. The historic city center has a few interesting patches and was taken under the preservation wings of Iphan (national cultural heritage) and declared a National Heritage Site in 2008; and Praia de Tambaú is particularly clean and sunny for an urban beach. It would be odd to plan a trip here solely, but 'John Person' is a very nice little spot to break up a journey.

History

Founded in 1585, the city was originally known as Vila de Felipéia de NS das Neves. It was later renamed for João Pessoa, the governor of Paraíba who formed an alliance with Getúlio Vargas to run for the presidency of Brazil in 1929. When courted by opposing political parties, João Pessoa uttered a pithy 'nego' (I refuse), which is now given prominence in all Brazilian history books and is emblazoned in bold letters on the state flag of Paraíba.

Yet João Pessoa's aspirations to the vice-presidency were short-lived. In July 1930 he was assassinated, an event that sparked a revolutionary backlash that swept Getúlio Vargas to power (with plenty of help from the military) later that year.

Orientation

The bus station is located on the western edge of the center, a little over 1km from the central Parque Solon de Lucena with its lake, which is called the Lagoa. Praia de Tambaú, 8km east of the center, is the heart of João Pessoa's tourist area. The airport is 11km west of the center.

Information

Banco do Brasil Centro (Map p549; Praça 1817 No 129; ☒ 10am-4pm Mon-Fri, ATMs 6am-10pm daily); Tambaú (Map p550; Av Senador Rui Carneiro 166; ☒ 10am-4pm Mon-Fri, ATMs 7am-10pm daily)

Deatur (Tourist Police; Map p550; ☎ 3214 8022; Av Almirante Tamandaré 100, Tambaú; ☒ 24hr)

PBTUR (☎ 0800 281 9229) bus station (Map p549; ☎ 3218 6655; bus station, Rua Francisco Londres; ☒ 8am-6pm); Tambaú (Map p550; Av Almirante Tamandaré 100, Tambaú; ☒ 8am-7pm) These state tourism offices are reasonably well informed.

Prefeitura (www.joaopessoa.pb.gov.br) City Hall internet site with some useful stuff.

Varanda do Mar (Map p550; Av João Maurício 157, Tambaú; per hr R$3; ☒ 11am-midnight Mon-Fri, from 8am Sat & Sun) Enjoy an espresso, beer or caipirinha while you check your email.

Sights & Activities

Orlando Berton (☎ 9984 8010; www.taxitourpb.com) Orlando speaks English and is the most professional and knowledgeable guide in João Pessoa. He can be contacted through Pousada do Caju (p550).

IGREJA SÃO FRANCISCO

This **church** (Map p549; ☎ 3218 4505; Praça São Francisco; admission with guided tour R$4; ☒ 9am-noon & 2-5pm), the principal tourist attraction in the center, is one of Brazil's finest. Construction was interrupted by battles with the Dutch and French, resulting in a beautiful but architecturally confused complex built over two centuries (1589–1779). The facade, the church towers and the adjoining Santo Antônio monastery display a hodgepodge of styles. Portuguese-tile walls lead up to the church's carved jacaranda doors.

CENTRAL JOÃO PESSOA

INFORMATION
Banco do Brasil...............**1** B3
PBTUR..........................(see 4)

SIGHTS & ACTIVITIES
Igreja São Francisco.........**2** C1

SLEEPING
Hotel Aurora..................**3** B3

TRANSPORT
Bus Station....................**4** A1
Buses to Airport...............**5** A2
Buses to Jacumã...............**6** A2
Buses to Tambaú...............**7** C3
Terminal de Integração...**8** A1

ESTAÇÃO CABO BRANCO

Inaugurated in 2008, the **Estação Cabo Branco** (off Map p550; ☎ 3214 8303; www.joaopessoa.pb.gov.br/estacao cabobranco; Av João Cirillo da Silva s/n, Ponta de Seixas; admission free; ☉ 9am-9pm Tue-Fri, 10am-9pm Sat & Sun) is one of the latest buildings designed by famed Brazilian architect Oscar Niemeyer. The exhibition and cultural space is well worth tacking on to a visit to the easternmost tip of the Americas in Ponta do Seixas; or for fans of Niemeyer's space-age work in general. It houses rotating art exhibits, a small planetarium and, best of all, a spectacular view over João Pessoa when the panoramic café opens.

BEACHES

Praia de Tambaú (Map p550), 8km directly east of the center, is an urban beach but an enjoyable area to spend time. Bars, restaurants, coconut palms and fig trees are strung along Av João Maurício (north) and Av Almirante Tamandaré (south). A whole series of good urban beaches stretches north along the bay.

Ilha de Areia Vermelha (off Map p550) is an island of red sand that emerges off the northern coast at low tide about half the days in each month. Boats park around the island and the party lasts until the tide comes in. You can catch a boat out there from Praia do Poço (13km north of Tambaú; off Map p550) for R$15. **Praia Cabo Branco** (off Map p550), a beautiful stretch of sand, cliffs and palms, runs south to **Ponta do Seixas** (off Map p550), the easternmost tip of the Americas, 8km from Tambaú, with calm, blue waters, a restaurant, camping ground and lighthouse at the point.

Festivals & Events

João Pessoa cuts loose in the **Folia da Rua** (Party in the Streets), the week before Carnaval proper (Saturday to Saturday), with *blocos* (drumming and dancing processions) parading through parts of the city. The city's **Paixão de Cristo** (Passion of Christ play) is second in size and fame only to the spectacle at Nova Jerusalém (see the boxed text, p545). It's staged outdoors on Praça Dom Adauto and recruits well-known actors.

Sleeping

Hotel Aurora (Map p549; ☎ 3241 3238; Praça João Pessoa 41, Centro; s/d without bathroom R$15/30, s/d R$22/42, with

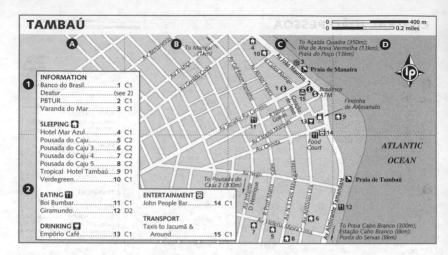

TAMBAÚ

INFORMATION	
Banco do Brasil	1 C1
Deatur	(see 2)
PBTUR	2 C1
Varanda do Mar	3 C1

SLEEPING	
Hotel Mar Azul	4 C1
Pousada do Caju	5 C2
Pousada do Caju 3	6 C2
Pousada do Caju 4	7 C2
Pousada do Caju 5	8 C2
Tropical Hotel Tambaú	9 D1
Verdegreen	10 C1

EATING	
Boi Bumbar	11 C1
Giramundo	12 D2

DRINKING	
Empório Café	13 C1

ENTERTAINMENT	
John People Bar	14 C1

TRANSPORT	
Taxis to Jacumã & Around	15 C1

fan R$25/42; 🔅) The Aurora is for true *centavo*-pinchers only, and hardened travelers at that, as the handsome square it overlooks (home to several state government buildings and a João Pessoa monument bearing his '*Nego*' dictum) is unsafe at night. Very dark hallways lead to shabby rooms that are bare-bones basic, but do the job at unheard of prices for Brazil. Parking is available.

Hotel Mar Azul (Map p550; ☎ 3226 2660; Av João Maurício 315, Manaíra; r from R$80) No frills here at this beach bum of a hotel, but the sand is across the road and the rooms are very large.

Pousada do Caju (Map p550; ☎ 2107 8700; www.pousadadocaju.com.br; Av Helena Meira Lima 269, Tambaú; s/d R$150/170; 🔅 🛜 🖭) This great-value, professionally-run chain guesthouse is two blocks from the beach and contains two swimming pools, a games area and numerous giant *caju* (cashew) trees. A modern makeover now offers rooms with comfy beds and flat-screen TVs set on lovely sandstone exposed brick – but are seriously low-light – while common areas are adorned with all sorts of cute Brazilian accoutrements. The Caju has four other branches of varying quality and prices within a few blocks.

our pick Verdegreen (Map p550; ☎ 3044 0004; www.verdegreen.com.br; Av João Maurício 255, Manaíra; s/d from R$242/280; 🔅 🛜 🖭) The city's newest hotel, on Praia de Manaíra, is the eco-conscious choice, doing its part for the environment with solar-heated showers, an organic produce garden, reforested wood, and LED lighting throughout. It's all very hip and stylish, too, decked

out in soothing greens and beiges, with sweet and helpful staff. Offers parking.

Tropical Hotel Tambaú (Map p550; ☎ 2107 1900; www.tropicalhotel.com.br; Av Almirante Tamandaré 229, Tambaú; s/d from R$264/305; 🔅 🛜 🖭) The Tropical must have looked very space-age when it was built in 1971. It's a large, circular construction surrounded by grassy banks, with rooms looking either onto large central gardens (with a lovely big pool) or out to sea. Rooms are not super-luxurious, but it's fair value for an upmarket hotel, though it feels as if you're staying at the Pentagon. Parking available.

Eating & Drinking

Açaí da Quadra (Map p550; ☎ 3247 5933; Quadra da Manaíra, Manaíra; items R$3-6; 🕑 9am-midnight) This unassuming spot is the place for an afternoon/early evening bowl of Brazilian delight: *açaí completo*: overflowing with bananas, honey, raisons and cashews.

Empório Café (Map p550; ☎ 3247 0110; Rua Coração de Jesus 201, Tambaú; sandwiches R$4.75-14.50, cocktails R$5-11; 🕑 7pm-3am) Early evening this retro-indie café/bar dishes up great value salads, sandwiches, quiches and soups – you name it, with loads of veggie options – to a beautiful crowd. As the evening wears on, it packs in more trend and beauty for cocktails and indie tunes (DJs on weekends after 11pm).

Giramundo (Map p550; ☎ 3226 2324; Av Almirante Tamandaré s/n, Tambaú; mains R$12-22; 🕑 6pm-1am Mon-Thu, to 2am Fri & Sat) Overcooked *picanha* (choice beef cuts) shouldn't stop you from having a good time at this wildly popular beach kiosk, a Swiss-Brazilian endeavor, notable not only for the usual suspects, but the out-of-place grilled bratwurst, *currywurst*, *kalbsbratwurst* and Eisenbahn microbrews – none of which are often seen north of Santa Catarina.

our pick **Mangai** (off Map p550; ☎ 3226 1615; Av General Édson Ramalho 696, Manaíra; per kg R$31.90; ☼ 11am-10pm Mon-Sat, 7am-10pm Sun) This spectacular regional buffet is worth the stop in João Pessoa alone. Nearly everything is labeled in English and there's plenty for vegetarians. Save room for the decadent caramelized cashews smothered in *doce de leite* (creamy milk-and-sugar concoction) and chocolate.

Boi Bumbar (Map p550; ☎ 3247 2847; Rua Isidro Gomes 246, Tambaú; per kg R$43; ☼ 11:30am-3pm Mon-Fri, noon-4pm Sat & Sun) Another excellent self-serve lunch place in Tambaú; good for meats and fish, and great for salads and cheeses.

Entertainment

Nightlife is centered on and around Rua Coração de Jesus in Tambaú as well as in the kiosks that line the beach, some of which offer live music. For cultural and nightlife rundowns, pick up the free *Cenário* magazine.

Praia do Jacaré (off Map p549; cover R$5; ☼ sunset) Almost every Brazilian tourist who comes to João Pessoa comes to the Rio Paraíba north of the city to hear saxophonist Jurandy play Ravel's *Bolero* at sunset, which has spawned a tourism empire along the water's edge (some come from as far away as Natal and Recife *just* for this). It sounds corny but it's definitely a spectacle worth witnessing, and quite beautiful. Four overwater bars play host (try Bombardo for the added bonus of violinist Belle Soares, who plays afterwards). Arrive by 4:30pm (4pm in winter) to get a choice seat. A round-trip taxi from Tambaú (including wait time) is R$50.

John People Bar (Map p550; ☎ 3247 1005; Av Olinda 57, Tambaú; cover R$5-10; ☼ 6pm-midnight Tue-Thu, to 3:30am Fri & Sat) This modern *boteco* (neighborhood bar) sits on prime people-watching real estate in Tambaú. There's a front patio and breezy rooftop deck overlooking the stage elevated above the bar. Live music starts at 9:30pm and varies between *forró pé-da-serra*, a slower form of *forró*, on Tuesday, MPB (Música Popular Brasileira) by a Dave Matthews-esque power trio from Wednesday to Friday and samba on Saturday. A 2500ml tube of *chope* (draft beer) here runs R$28 – *saúde*!

Getting There & Away

AIR
Presidente Castro Pinto Airport (☎ 3041 4200) has flights to Rio, São Paulo and the major cities of the Northeast and the Amazon.
Gol/Varig (☎ airport 3753 2700)
TAM (☎ airport 3232 2002)

BUS
From the **bus station** (Map p549; ☎ 3221 9611, Rua Francisco Londres) there are services to many destinations, including Fortaleza (R$95.50 to R$150.50, 10 hours, two daily), Natal (R$25.50 to R$30.50, three hours, eight daily), Recife (R$17.50 to R$24.50, two hours, 24 daily from 5am to 7pm), Salvador (R$127 to R$146, 16 hours) departing 7:30pm except Saturday, and Sousa (R$59, six hours, up to 12 daily).

Getting Around

Local buses run from the Terminal de Integração (Map p549), across the street outside the bus station. Buses 510, 511 and 513 run frequently to Tambaú (R$1.90, 25 minutes) via Parque Solon de Lucena. A taxi from the bus station to Tambaú is around R$20.

Buses to the airport marked 'Aeroporto/Auto da Boa Vista' or 'Jardim/Aeroporto' leave from Rua Cícero Meireles near the bus station every 15 minutes ($1.60) – catch them the opposite way from the airport. A taxi from the airport to Tambaú costs around R$40.

JACUMÃ & AROUND
☎ 0xx83 / pop 4500

The string of good beaches and small, spread-out villages from Jacumã to Tambaba, halfway between João Pessoa and the Pernambuco state border, make a relaxed and inexpensive stop on a journey north from Recife or south from João Pessoa. They are popular on weekends with people from the city, some of whom have holiday homes here.

Jacumã, the biggest of the villages, has a long, thin beach featuring colored sandbars and natural pools, and *forró* (popular music of the Northeast) bars by night. **Praia de Gramame**, 5km north, is postcard-ready, a gorgeous string of sand and sun where the Rio Gramame dips into the ocean. There are no overnight options here, but a few restaurants exist, facilitating an outstanding day trip.

Praia de Carapibus, 2km south of Jacumã, is also narrow, and is backed by low cliffs, with more natural pools. The broader **Praia da Tabatinga** curves south from the end of Carapibus, with a lagoon behind it after high tides. Though most folks will tell you the most beautiful beach is **Praia dos Coqueirinhos**, a 2km walk from the end of Tabatinga, with lots of coconut palms, high red cliffs, freshwater springs and a dozen *barracas* (stalls), it can get overly crowded on weekends. **Praia de Tambaba**, 6km further south, is famed as the only official nudist beach in the region. Attendants will explain the rules of the nude section: men can only enter if accompanied by a woman. The bathing suit required (what prudes!) part of Tambaba is also stunning, with a broad swath of petrified sandstone dotting the shoreline and forming natural tidal pools.

Sleeping & Eating

Pousada do Inglês (☎ 3290 1168; Rua Sebastião Ribero 100, Jacumã; dm from R$35, s/d from R$100/120; 🅿 🛜 🍴) There's better value for those seeking private rooms (try Beija-Flor a few blocks away), but this British-run option has now been adapted into a hostel and is part of HI. It's 30m from the beach (though not the most idyllic sands around here) and now offers male and female dorm rooms, HI discounts and parking.

Pousada dos Mundos (☎ 3290 1356; www.pousa dadosmundos.com.br; Rua dos Juazeiros, Tabatinga; s/d R$60/100; 🅿 🍴) Mundos offers airy rooms with river-facing hammock terraces and simple but pleasing decorations, around a nice garden with a pool (400m back from Tabatinga beach), but the fun and games ended when we found ourselves soaped up in the shower at 4am without water and management laughed it off. Parking available.

Pousada das Conchas (☎ 3290 1303; www.con chaspousada.com.br; Tabatinga; s/d from R$140/160; 🅿 🛜 🍴) Perched just above Tabatinga beach, this superb option is run by an impossibly cute and accommodating Swede, who has jazzed up this rustic-style lodge with her own brightly-designed rooms around a well-manicured courtyard garden, all with box-spring beds, verandas and hammock-chairs. Offers parking.

Recanto das Tulipas (☎ 3290 1108; Hwy PB-008, Tabatinga; mains for 2 R$36-60; ⏰ 10am-8pm Sun-Thu, to 10pm Fri & Sat) A Dutch-Brazilian team holds

---

THE TIMELESS SERTÃO

The interior of the Northeast *(sertão)* is not all drought-stricken countryside and dirt-poor towns, as its stereotype might have us believe. There's no denying it gets broiling hot and dry in the second half of the year, nor that the cattle-dominated economy makes only a few rich. But the Sertanejos (residents of the interior) are a proud people with a rich popular culture evident in their music, their festivals and their artisanship. There is also amazing natural beauty out there in the rocky backlands – and fascinating evidence of a history and prehistory stretching right back to the dinosaurs. For those tempted to adventure into the *sertão*, the ideal months are June and July, when it is at its greenest and coolest. The towns of the *sertão* are equipped with adequate hotels and pousadas and well enough served by buses. Natal-based Cariri Ecotours (p555) and Pipa-based Mandacaru Expedições (p560) specialize in tours to these areas. There are a few highlight destinations to find your way to:

■ Ingá, Paraíba – features beautiful prehistoric carvings covering a rock 23m long and nearly 4m high. It's located 46km east of Campina Grande, a city famed for its huge **Festa Junina**, a party lasting all June.

■ Lajedo da Soledade, Rio Grande do Norte – rock paintings (including the world's oldest macaw pictures), ancient ceremonial sites and ice-age animal fossils are all found here. Guided visits are run from the **Museu da Soledade** (☎ 0xx84-3333-1017; ⏰ closed Mon), 85km southwest of Mossoró, near Apodi.

■ Lajedo de Pai Mateus, Cariri, Paraíba – features a bizarre, otherworldly, rocky landscape of round boulders, granite blocks, caves and ancient petroglyphs. It's some 70km southwest of Campina Grande; several recent Brazilian films were shot here. Good lodgings are available at **Fazenda Pai Mateus** (www.paimateus.com.br).

■ Serra da Capivara, Piauí (p589) – this has the earliest evidence of humanity in the Americas and 30,000 rock paintings in a dramatic rocky landscape near São Raimundo Nonato.

down this fort, a colorful and discerning restaurant decked out to the sounds of MPB and the tulip paintings of the co-owner. Seafood is the specialty but the menu is well-rounded otherwise. Try the Jorge Amado caipirinha, a lime and passion-fruit cocktail made with cinnamon and clove-infused *cachaça* (sugarcane alcohol) from Paraty.

Getting There & Around

A car makes things easier around here. Buses run every 20 to 30 minutes to Jacumã (R$5.20, 45 minutes to 1¼ hours) from Rua Cícero Meireles near João Pessoa bus station. Those marked 'Jacumã PB-008' take a quicker route to Jacumã and also continue to Carapibus. The last bus back to João Pessoa from Jacumã is at 11:20pm. Buses direct to Tambaba (R$5.20) leave from the same stop only at 5:50am, 7:50am, 9:55pm and 3:45pm. Traveling north from Pernambuco on Hwy BR-101, ask to be dropped off at the turnoff for Conde and Jacumã, and catch a local bus from there.

A fixed-price taxi from João Pessoa to these beaches costs R$38 to R$50.

Moto-taxis from opposite the gasoline station on the main road in Jacumã will take you to the other beaches (R$7 to Tambaba).

RIO GRANDE DO NORTE

Pure air, sun, fine beaches and sand dunes symbolize this small state in the extreme Northeast of Brazil. Rio Grande do Norte has one of the most spectacular coastlines in Brazil, some 400km of beautiful beach after beautiful beach interspersed with rivers, many of them fronted by reefs with natural pools and backed by tall dunes or cliffs. The most famous dunes are the 50m-tall piles at Genipabu. The locals, known as Potiguenses, are generally friendly and welcoming. As in Paraíba, the interior of the state is drought-prone, and many former inhabitants have migrated to other parts of Brazil.

NATAL

☎ 0xx84 / pop 806,000

Natal, the capital of Rio Grande do Norte, is a clean, bright and rather bland city that has swelled as the entry point for coastal package tourism. Surrounded by impressively large sand dunes, Natal's main attractions are beaches, buggy rides and nightlife –

don't come here if you seek museums and theater.

The city's northern beaches of Praia do Meio and Praia dos Artistas are no longer the attraction they once were. These days, most visitors stay in the southern beach neighborhood of Ponta Negra, about 12km from the center. It is a striking location, overlooked by fantastic dunes, and with steady surf and some wild nightlife in the Alto de Ponta Negra area.

Natal's new R$300 million, 2014 World Cup stadium, Arena das Dunas, should be under construction by the time you read this. Ground has already been broken on a new airport, Aeroporto Internacional da Grande Natal/São Gonçalo do Amarante, 11km west of the city center.

History

An early attempt to settle the Natal area by a Portuguese contingent sailing from Recife in 1535 failed due to the hostility of the local indigenous Potiguar people and French brazilwood traders. The Portuguese didn't return until December 1597, when a fleet arrived at the mouth of the Rio Potengi with orders to build a fort to keep the French and Potiguars at bay. On January 6, 1598, the day of Os Reis Magos (Three Wise Men), the Portuguese began building the fortress, the Forte dos Reis Magos.

The following year, on December 25, 1599, a town was founded nearby and christened Natal (Portuguese for Christmas). Apart from a period of Dutch occupation (1633 to 1654), Natal remained under Portuguese control thereafter. It stayed relatively unimportant until WWII, when its strategic location close to Brazil's northeastern tip prompted Presidents Getúlio Vargas and Franklin D Roosevelt to turn the sleepy city into a supply base for Allied operations in North Africa. Thousands of US military were stationed here and the city became known as the 'Trampoline to Victory.' These days, it's known as the Cidade do Sol (Sun City), for good reason.

Orientation

The older part of Natal is on a peninsula flanked by the west by the Rio Potengi and to the east by Atlantic beaches and reefs. The Forte dos Reis Magos sits just off the peninsula's northern point. The unexciting

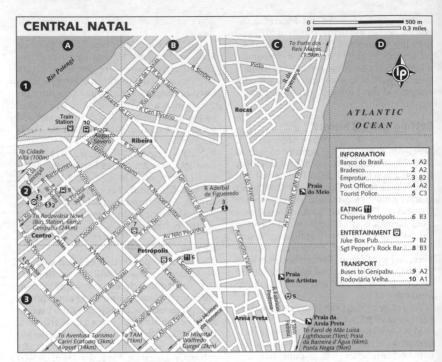

CENTRAL NATAL

INFORMATION	
Banco do Brasil................1 A2	
Bradesco..........................2 A2	
Emprotur..........................3 B2	
Post Office.........................4 A2	
Tourist Police...................5 C3	

EATING 🍴	
Choperia Petrópolis..........6 B3	

ENTERTAINMENT 🎭	
Juke Box Pub....................7 B2	
Sgt Pepper's Rock Bar.......8 B3	

TRANSPORT	
Buses to Genipabu............9 A2	
Rodoviária Velha.............10 A1	

city center, Cidade Alta, was developed around the river port, which was built in 1892. The beach neighborhood of Ponta Negra is 12km southeast of the center. Via Costeira, the coast road running north from Ponta Negra towards the Forte dos Reis Magos, is lined by resort hotels.

The bus station is 6km south of the center and 10km northwest of Ponta Negra; the airport is 15km south of the center and 8km west of Ponta Negra.

Information
EMERGENCY
Ambulance (☎ 192)
Tourist Police Praia dos Artistas (Map p554; ☎ 3202 2920; Av Presidente Café Filho, Praia dos Artistas; 🕐 8am-11pm); Praia Shopping (Map p555; ☎ 3232 7402; Praia Shopping, Central do Cidadão, Av Engenheiro Roberto Freire 8790, Ponta Negra)

INTERNET ACCESS
Click.Net (Map p555; ☎ 3219 5552; Av Praia de Ponta Negra 8956; per hr R$2; 🕐 8am-10pm Mon-Sat, noon-9pm Sun) Good, air-conditioned, high-speed facility.

INTERNET RESOURCES
Emprotur (www.brasil-natal.com.br) The government's official tourism portal, with a variety of helpful introductory information.
Natal Brazil (www.natal-brazil.com) Fairly useful tourism site.

MEDICAL SERVICES
Hospital Walfredo Gurgel (off Map p554; ☎ 3232 7530; www.walfredogurgel.rn.gov.br; Av Senador Salgado Filho, Tirol) The main public hospital, with emergency service.

MONEY
The following banks have ATMs that normally accept foreign cards.
Banco do Brasil Centro (Map p554; Av Rio Branco 510, Central; 🕐 6am-8pm); Praia Shopping (Map p555; Praia Shopping, Central do Cidadão, Av Engenheiro Roberto Freire 8790, Ponta Negra; 🕐 7am-10pm)
Bradesco (Map p554; Av Rio Branco 477, Centro; 🕐 6am-8pm)

POST
Post office (Map p554; Av Rio Branco 538, Centro; 🕐 8am-5pm Mon-Fri, to noon Sat)

TOURIST INFORMATION

Emprotur (☎ 3232 2500) Aeroporto (arrivals hall;
⏱ 8am-9pm); Centro de Turismo (Map p554; Centro
de Turismo, Rua Aderbal de Figueiredo 980, Petrópolis;
⏱ 8am-noon); Praia Shopping (Map p555; ☎ 3232 7248;
Praia Shopping, Central do Cidadão, Av Engenheiro Roberto
Freire 8790, Ponta Negra; ⏱ 10am-10pm); Rodoviária Nova
(bus station; Av Capitão Mor Gouveia 1237) Information
kiosks run by the marketing wing of Rio Grande do Norte's
state secretary of tourism.

TRAVEL AGENCIES

Aventura Turismo/Cariri Ecotours (off Map p554;
☎ 3086 3601; www.aventuraturismo.com.br; Av Prudente de Morais 4262, Lagoa Nova) This long-standing pair
is experienced in tours from Natal; Aventura does coastal
routes and Cariri handles inland trips. They also provide
travel-agency services.

Sights & Activities

FORTE DOS REIS MAGOS

Enjoy a tapioca ice cream at the **Forte dos
Reis Magos** (off Map p554; ☎ 3202 9006; admission R$3;
⏱ 8am-4:30pm) that got Natal started. The fort,
founded in 1598, is still in its original five-
point star shape and contains a chapel, a well,
cannons and soldiers' quarters. The views of
the city and the dunes across the Rio Potengi
are fantastic from this prime location on the
reef at the tip of the peninsula north of town.

BEACHES

Natal's northern beaches stretch 5km south
from the fort to Farol de Mãe Luiza lighthouse. **Praia do Meio** (Map p554), 2km south of
the Forte dos Reis Magos, is an urban beach
with reefs and a lot of people getting drunk.
Praia dos Artistas (Map p554) is another urban
spot, with good surfing waves but a little too
close to a favela (shantytown).

South of the lighthouse, the coast road Via
Costeira continues 7km south to Ponta Negra,
passing the calm **Praia da Barreira d'Água** with
its resort hotels. **Ponta Negra** (Map p555), at the
far south end of the city, is the nicest beach
in Natal – nearly 3km long and full of hotels,
pousadas, restaurants, beach bars, surfers
and sailing boats. On weekends it gets pretty
packed: the northern part of the beach, with
its pedestrian-only walkway, is less crowded.
The surf here is consistent if small: you can
rent boards from a few places along the beach
for around R$10 per hour.

At the south end of the beach is **Morro da
Careca**, a spectacularly high sand dune with

a steep face that drops straight into the sea.
Access to the dune has been closed off to
prevent further erosion and damage to the
primary Atlantic rain forest that covers it.

BUGGY RIDES

Dune-buggy excursions are offered by a host
of would-be Ayrton Senna *bugeiros* (buggy

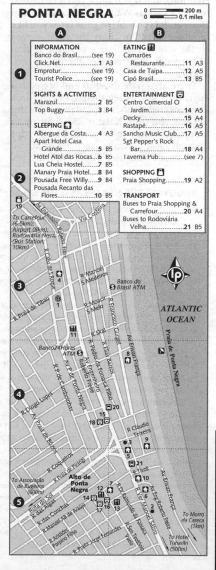

PONTA NEGRA　　　　　　　0 ⸻ 200 m
　　　　　　　　　　　　　　　0 ⸻ 0.1 miles

INFORMATION
Banco do Brasil..........(see 19)
Click.Net.....................1 A3
Emprotur................(see 19)
Tourist Police..........(see 19)

SIGHTS & ACTIVITIES
Marazul.......................2 B5
Top Buggy...................3 B4

SLEEPING
Albergue da Costa.........4 A3
Apart Hotel Casa
　Grande........................5 B5
Hotel Atol das Rocas.....6 B5
Lua Cheia Hostel..........7 B5
Manary Praia Hotel.......8 B4
Pousada Free Willy........9 B4
Pousada Recanto das
　Flores.......................10 B5

EATING
Camarões
　Restaurante...............11 A3
Casa de Taipa.............12 A5
Cipó Brasil..................13 B5

ENTERTAINMENT
Centro Comercial O
　Jardim......................14 A5
Decky.......................15 A4
Rastapé.....................16 A5
Sancho Music Club......17 A5
Sgt Pepper's Rock
　Bar..........................18 A4
Taverna Pub............(see 7)

SHOPPING
Praia Shopping...........19 A2

TRANSPORT
Buses to Praia Shopping &
　Carrefour..................20 A4
Buses to Rodoviária
　Velha.......................21 B5

ATLANTIC OCEAN

Banco do Brasil ATM

Banco24Horas ATM

drivers), mostly in Brazilian-built vehicles with brand names such as Bird, Baby, Praya or Malibuggy. To the north are the dunes of **Genipabu**, about 12km north of Natal, which are the biggest around and Natal's best and most beautiful activity by a landslide. You'll be asked if you want the trip, called *Dunas Moveis* ('Moving Dunes') *com emoção* (with emotion), and if you agree you'll be treated to thrills such as Wall of Death and Vertical Descent. It is possible to go as far as you like in either direction along the coast – even all the way to Fortaleza – covering 750km of gorgeous coastline (see the boxed text, below).

There are pirate *bugeiros* and accredited *bugeiros* – ask to see their Associação de Bugeiros credentials. A typical price for a trip to Genipabu from Natal is R$300 for up to four passengers. You can arrange buggy trips through most pousadas, agencies or, if you speak some Portuguese, directly with drivers.

Two reputable operators are **Top Buggy** (Map p555; ☎ 3082 5464; www.topbuggy.com.br; Rua Cláudio Teixeira, Ponta Negra; ◷ 7-11am & 3-6pm Mon-Fri, 7-11am Sat & Sun) and **Marazul** (Map p555; ☎ 3219 2221; www.passeiodebuggy.com.br; Rua Vereador Manoel Sátiro 1, Ponta Negra; ◷ 8am-noon & 3-8pm Mon-Sat).

You can save a little money by arranging a Genipabu excursion directly in Genipabu with the **buggy-drivers association** (APCBA; ☎ 3225 2077) in the center of town. From here, the ride costs R$180 for up to four passengers (plus a R$5 per-person entry fee). You can get a buggy all the way to Fortaleza from Genipabu.

Buses to Genipabu (R$2, 45 minutes) leave frequently from the corner of Av Rio Branco and Rua Auta de Souza in central Natal.

Festivals & Events

Natal's out-of-season Carnaval, **Carnatal** (www.carnatal.com.br), takes to the streets at the beginning of December with Salvador-style *trios elétricos* (bands playing atop huge trucks) and

---

BUGGYING THE NORTHEAST: THE GOOD, THE BAD & THE UGLY

Adventurous travelers who have time on their hands and don't mind sand in their faces or wind in their hair can make a fabulous trip of approximately 750km along the shore from Natal to Fortaleza by beach buggy. You can travel in either direction. The trip takes three to five days and you'll pass approximately 92 beaches. The average cost for the trip is R$2600 to R$3600 for up to three passengers (depending on season), including lodgings, breakfast and the driver. Make sure you go with an accredited *(credenciado)* driver. Top Buggy (p556) is a well-known Natal option. It's also possible to do the trip in Jeeps, with agencies such as Aventura Turismo (p555) in Natal, or Nordeste Off Road (p571) in Fortaleza.

The good: this stretch of coastline is one of the most beautiful and undeveloped in Brazil. There are cliffs of colored sands, rolling dunes, salt flats, reefs, palm-lined beaches, freshwater lagoons, tiny traditional fishing villages and some larger settlements popular with local weekenders. The stretch between Zumbi, some 60km north of Natal, and Galinhos, about 130km further, is particularly rugged and in parts quite isolated. Between Galinhos and Porto do Mangue you have to head inland along roads to get around the mangrove and salt swamps near the coast.

You'll spend nights in pousadas along the way, in places like São Miguel do Gostoso, Praia do Marco, Galinhos and Canoa Quebrada.

The bad: agencies in Natal won't bowl you over with hospitality and are not part of Abeta, Brazil's high-standard ecotourism association, so that is something to consider. If you opt for the buggy over a Jeep, your backside is going to take a beating and you'll be digging sand out of crevices for weeks to come. But hey, this is an adventure!

The ugly: few people in Brazil seem overly concerned about the environmental impact of beach buggies, and many stretches of beach are routinely used as highways by off-road vehicles (though Ceará planned to implement new laws in 2010 banning vehicles from certain stretches of coastline). While the impact of vehicles on dune configurations seems less than that of natural factors such as wind and rain, research in some countries, notably the USA, has indicated that living beach and dune organisms, while largely invisible to the casual passerby, can be seriously affected by the repeated passage of noisy, heavy vehicles. It's also true that dune buggies consume a liter of gasoline about every 6km (making them about twice as thirsty as normal cars) – and that they make an unholy racket!

blocos (drumming and dancing processions) sporting names such as *Jerimum* (Pumpkin) and *Burro Elétrico* (Electric Donkey). It's the wildest out-of-season Carnaval in the country and is a great substitute for anyone who can't make it to the real deal.

Sleeping

Most travelers make their way to Ponta Negra, where options for all budgets abound.

BUDGET

Albergue da Costa (Map p555; ☎ 3219 0095; www .alberguedacosta.com.br; Av Praia de Ponta Negra 8932, Ponta Negra; dm/s/d R$40/70/100; ✷ 🛜 🖳) Two Brazilian, ex-Colorado ski-bums-turned-surfers run this laid-back hostel with a more internationally-focused vibe than Lua Cheia. It has a good kitchen and hammock area, mixed and separate dorms and a few double rooms with air-con for the same price as fans (but shared bathroom). There's also a surf and kitesurfing school. English, Italian, Spanish and Portuguese are spoken.

Lua Cheia Hostel (Map p555; ☎ 3236 3696; www .luacheia.com.br; Rua Manoel AB de Araújo 500, Ponta Negra; dm with/without HI membership R$42/52, r with/without HI membership R$105/115; 🛜) In a famous castlelike building (drawbridge, turrets and all), Lua Cheia has a bizarre medieval-sorcery theme that you may dig for novelty. Facilities are good, staff are helpful, and it's located in the heart of the Alto de Ponta Negra nightlife and restaurant area (it's own pub is wildly popular). If you are looking for party fun in Natal, this is the place (free condoms at front desk, FYI).

Pousada Recanto das Flores (Map p555; ☎ 3219 4065; www.pousadarecantodasflores.com.br; Av Engenheiro Roberto Freire 3161, Ponta Negra; s/d R$60/80; ✷ 🖳) This small pousada has nicely kept rooms with bamboo furnishings and offers great discounts in the low season. Some rooms suffer traffic noise from the busy street outside. Parking is available.

MIDRANGE & TOP END

Apart Hotel Casa Grande (Map p555; ☎ 3236 3401; www.aparthotelcasagrande.com; Rua Pedro da Fonseca Filho 3050; r from R$80, apt R$120-150; ✷ 🛜 🖳) For those willing to forgo breakfast, this former longstay-turned-hotel offers exceptional rates (especially in low season) for spacious rooms and apartments with kitchenettes and sea views – three blocks from the beach.

Hotel Tubarão (off Map p555; ☎ 3641 1683; www .hoteltubarao.com.br; Rua Manoel Coringa Lemos 259, Ponta Negra; s/d R$120/155; ✷ 🛜 🖳) An attractive small-ish hotel set on the hill above Ponta Negra beach, Tubarão has a beautiful sea view, good pool and common areas and unadorned but pleasant rooms. Parking is also provided. Desk staff speak good English and are very helpful.

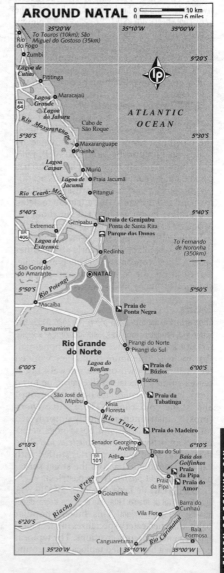

Pousada Free Willy (Map p555; ☎ 3236 2825; www .freewilly.com.br; Rua Francisco Gurgel 9292, Ponta Negra; d/tr/q R$150/170/190; ✛ 🌐 🖭) Free Willy, named for a 1990s whale movie, doesn't look that great from outside but it has clean if rather old-fashioned rooms, helpful and friendly staff and an excellent beachfront location. Parking available.

Hotel Atol das Rocas (Map p555; ☎ 3311 3900; www.atoldasrocas.com.br; Av Engenheiro Roberto Freire 3220, Ponta Negra; d/tr R$194/292; ✛ 🌐 🖭) Newly remodeled (new plasma TVs, upgraded air-con), these clean and spacious rooms all have sea views, and share a pool in attractive gardens. English is spoken, there's parking, and prices come down by about one-third in the low season.

ourpick **Manary Praia Hotel** (Map p555; ☎ 3204 2900; www.manary.com.br; Rua Francisco Gurgel 9067, Ponta Negra; s/d from R$499/555; ✛ 🌐 🖭) One of the Northeast's best pousadas is owned by hands-on Eduardo Bagnoli, one of Brazil's most famous nature photographers, who has decked out his romantic oasis with his beautiful photos as well as tasteful artisanal artifacts from around the world (the attention to detail is stunning if you get him talking about it). Mood-enhancing music is piped through the halls and more thought has been put into the new, one-room spa than nearly all the other spas in Brazil combined. Parking is available. To top it off, the restaurant – and its *peixe crocante* (crunchy fish) – is divine.

Eating

Choperia Petrópolis (Map p554; ☎ 3086 0155; Rua Seridó 511, Petrópolis; cover R$3, items R$3-20; ✹ 5:30pm-1am Mon-Sat) This corner *boteco* in bohemian Petrópolis is little more than a few wooden tables thrown down on the sidewalk but it serves yummy specialties like *pernil ao forno* (pork leg), good *caldinhos* (spicy bean soup) and stone cold *chope*. There's live *choro* (mostly instrumental, highly improvised music), samba, MPB and bossa nova catering to an artsy crowd. Its *pastelaria* (place that serves fried dough pastries stuffed with various ingredients) across the street serves decadent sweet *pastéis* (fried pastries).

ourpick **Casa de Taipa** (Map p555; ☎ 3219 5798; Rua Manoel AB de Araújo 130A, Alto de Ponta Negra; dishes R$4-19; ✹ 5pm-midnight) This hugely popular palm-thatched eatery specializes in great local tapioca and couscous creations. The tapiocas come with a lightly fried tapioca shell around

fillings ranging from vegetables and cheeses to *carne de sol* (grilled salted meat) or prawns. The mini-tapioca appetizers *(pesticos)* are a real riot.

Cipó Brasil (Map p555; ☎ 3219 5227; Rua Aristides Porpino Filho 3111, Alto de Ponta Negra; mains R$15-53; ✹ 6pm-midnight) A unanimous favorite with a jungle theme, this is a fun place for sesame-crusted pizza (the newly added *pesto* was a knockout) and crepes, both savory and sweet, and is a starting point for evenings out. Prepare for a wait list.

Camarões Restaurante (Map p555; ☎ 3209 2424; Av Engenheiro Roberto Freire 2610, Ponta Negra; mains for 2 R$48-145; ✹ lunch & dinner) Natal's most famous restaurant is a prawn-lover's palace – some 36 varieties of creative shrimp dishes are served with a few meat choices for those allergic to shellfish. *Cabugi* (sautéed with farm butter, mushrooms, capers, white wine, cilantro and tomatoes) and *potiguar* (sautéed with vegetables, *dendê* – a reddish palm oil – and creamy coconut sauce) are the most popular preparations. Dishes serve two people only.

Entertainment

The Alto de Ponta Negra neighborhood in the upper part of Ponta Negra, around Rua Manoel AB de Araújo and Rua Aristides Porpino Filho, is dense with a variety of bars, though most are almost cringingly steeped in sex tourism, a major problem in Natal. This area, especially around Centro Comercial O Jardim, is packed from Wednesday to Saturday nights. By all means go, but be aware. **Sancho Music Club** (Map p555; Rua Aristides Porpino Filho, Alto de Ponta Negra), with tapas and *chope*, and **Rastapé** (Map p555; Rua Aristides Porpino Filho 2198, Alto de Ponta Negra), famous for live *forró*, are a couple of the least slimy spots.

To see what's on, pick up the free *Solto Na Cidade* cultural guide around town.

Decky (Map p555; Av Engenheiro Roberto Freire 9100, Ponta Negra; cover R$5-10; ✹ 5pm-late Tue-Sat) Stocks Brazil's most accessible microbrews (Eisenbahn, Devassa and Baden Baden) along with live rock, blues, jazz and MPB every night from 8pm. Plop down on the massive, wind-struck patio or inside the spacious main room with air-con – it's the most popular spot in Ponta Negra and caters across several age brackets.

Sgt Pepper's Rock Bar (cover R$7-25 ✹ 10pm-2:30am Mon-Sat); Ponta Negra (Map p555; Av Engenheiro Roberto Freire 9102, Ponta Negra); Petrópolis (Map p554; Rua Potengi 541, Petrópolis) Good for food (excellent burgers) and fun, both downtown and at its newest location in Ponta Negra, this hip bar/restaurant dreamed up the Northeast caipirinha (pineapple, mint and cinnamon/clove-infused *cachaça*) and hosts a handle of resident pop, rock and blues acts. It skews slightly younger and a smidgeon more alternative than Decky in Ponta Negra, but the larger, more established Petrópolis location is brimming with coolness of all ilk.

Taverna Pub (Map p555; ☎ 3236 3696; Rua Manoel AB de Araújo 500, Ponta Negra; cover R$12-40; ☺ 10pm-late Mon-Sat) Attached to the Lua Cheia Hostel and resembling a pub inside a medieval castle, this ever-popular tavern has nightly music, from live Brazilian rhythms to '70s disco and blues. No flip-flops.

Juke Box Pub (Map p554; ☎ 3201 0108; Rua Potengi 417, Petrópolis; cover R$20-30; ☺ from midnight Tue-Sat) This new 1950s-themed hot spot in the city center hosts live bands and DJs in two environments: the corner bar (with live *pagode*; popular samba music, on Saturdays) and the much more popular nightclub above.

Getting There & Away

AIR

Natal's **Augusto Severo Airport** (☎ 3087 1270) has scheduled flights from Lisbon with TAP Portugal, charter flights from other European cities, and flights to many Brazilian cities with several airlines.

Azul (☎ airport 3087 1380)
Gol/Varig (☎ airport 0300 115 2121)
TAM airport (☎ 4002 5700); Tirol (off Map p554; ☎ 3198 1500; Av Afonso Pena 844, Tirol)
TAP Portugal (☎ airport 0300 210 6060)
Trip (☎ airport 3643 1038)
Webjet (☎ airport 3087 1333)

BUS

Long-distance buses go from the dreary **Rodoviária Nova** (New Bus Station; off Map p554; ☎ 3232 7312; Av Capitão Mor Gouveia 1237), which will soon be true to its name: a World Cup–ready facelift is planned. Destinations include Aracati (near Canoa Quebrada, R$51 to R$60, six hours, three or more daily), Belém (R$291, 38 hours, at 9:30am daily), Fortaleza (R$74 to R$140, eight hours, seven daily), João Pessoa (R$25 to R$30, 2½ hours, eight daily), Recife (R$56, four hours, nine daily), Rio de Janeiro (R$380, 44 hours, noon daily) and Salvador (R$159 to R$182, 21 hours, at 9:30am and 5pm).

Disk Passagens (☎ 3205 2428) will deliver bus tickets to you for a R$10 fee.

CAR & MOTORCYCLE

Recommended car-rental companies include the following:
Avis (☎ airport 3087 1404)
LocarAlpha (☎ airport 3087 1363)

Getting Around

TO/FROM THE AIRPORT

The 'Aeroporto' bus runs between the airport and the city center (R$2.60). For Ponta Negra, get off opposite Natal Shopping, cross the footbridge and take bus 46 or 54, which go along Av Engenheiro Roberto Freire and Rua Manoel Coringa Lemos in Ponta Negra. A taxi from the airport costs about R$45 to the city center or R$35 to Ponta Negra.

TO/FROM THE BUS STATION

For Ponta Negra (Av Engenheiro Roberto Freire), catch bus 66 from the stop opposite the Petrobras gas station next to Rodoviária Nova; a taxi is R$25 to R$30. Buses 19, 38 and 23–69 run between the Rodoviária Nova and the **Rodoviária Velha** (Map p554; Praça Augusto Severo), a local bus terminal in the city center.

BUS

From stops north of Rota do Sol on Av Engenheiro Roberto Freire in Ponta Negra, buses 46 and 54 run to the Praia Shopping mall and on to the center; buses 7, 26 and 73 head to Natal Shopping, right next door to Carrefour, from where you can catch buses on to Pipa. From stops south of Rota do Sol on Av Engenheiro Roberto Freire, 56 goes along the Via Costeira then heads inland to the Rodoviária Velha. Buses 54 and 56 go from the Rodoviária Velha to Ponta Negra.

If you're arriving in Natal by bus from the south and want to get to Ponta Negra, ask to be let off opposite Natal Shopping, cross the footbridge and catch bus 46 or 54.

City bus fares are R$2.

SOUTH OF NATAL

Like the rest of the Rio Grande do Norte coast, the stretch south of Natal has some fantastic beaches – it's difficult to find one that's not worth raving about. Praia da Pipa is famous and a great place to hang around for a few days, but there are other quieter places to be discovered, too.

Praia da Pipa

☎ 0xx84 / pop 6500

Pipa is one of Brazil's magical destinations – an idyllic combination of wide-eyed postcard beauty and firmly planted tourism infrastructure: pristine beaches backed by tall cliffs, dreamy lagoons, decent surfing, dolphin- and sea turtle–filled waters, a great selection of global restaurants and good nightlife. It rivals Jericoacoara as the Northeast's hippest beach town, but was just another small, roadless, fishing village when discovered by surfers in the 1970s. Telephones came in 1999. Now, Pipa attracts partiers from Natal, João Pessoa, Recife and beyond at holiday times and weekends and a slew of international travelers all year round.

Though Pipa's laid-back vibe still reigns and the town is one of Brazil's most prominently multicultural, the brakes need to be applied soon: traffic can snarl the main cobblestones through town even during the week, and mass tourism – notably the ridiculous CVC trolley that hauls day-trippers from beach to beach like cattle – are serious warning signs that Pipa is on its way to becoming overrun (if not already), putting its sensitive ecological treasures at serious risk. The recent inauguration of an official Tamar Project base, Brazil's sea-turtle protection project (see the boxed text, p464), is a step in the right direction.

ORIENTATION & INFORMATION

Pipa is small but it can be a little hard to get your bearings on arrival and widespread construction adds to the problem. The narrow main street, Av Baía dos Golfinhos, runs about 2km through town from west to east, parallel to the main beach and curving south at its eastern end. The main bus stop is at the west end. Small streets and lanes run down to the beach or uphill inland from Av Baía dos Golfinhos.

Pipa is extraordinarily well endowed with helpful, informative websites. **Pipa** (www.pipa .com.br) is probably the best organized and most comprehensive, but **Pipa On Line** (www.pipaonline .com.br) and **Guia da Pipa** (www.guiadapipa.com.br) are good too.

Bring plenty of cash – credit cards are not yet widely accepted and the ATMs here are often skint.

Banco do Brasil ATM (Falésia Galeria, Av Baía dos Golfinhos 369; ⏱ 8am-10pm) Located 150m east of the main bus stop. Skip beyond Banco24Horas to avoid the R$10 fee.

Bookshop (☎ 9142 9841; Rua Beija-Flor; ⏱ 4pm-midnight) A good selection of books in a variety of languages, for rent or trade.

Internet Telefone (Rua da Gameleira; per hr R$3; ⏱ 10am-midnight) Internet access.

Mandacaru Expedições (☎ 9988 5892; www.manda caruexpedicoes.com.br) This excellent ecotourism agency can arrange off-the-beaten-track adventures with a sustainable slant around Pipa and further afield, as well as more basic travel needs.

Pipatour (☎ 3246 2234; Galeria das Cores, Av Baía dos Golfinhos 767; ⏱ 9am-noon & 3-7pm) A more straightforward travel agency for general needs.

DANGERS & ANNOYANCES

An alarming drug problem has found its way to Pipa and, with it, the usual partners in crime. Waves of pousada robberies began in 2007 and a Swedish tourist was murdered while interrupting one in 2009. As a result, charter flights from Stockholm and Oslo – Pipa's bread and butter – were cancelled. Keep alert and don't leave valuables lying out in the open in your room while you are out at the beach.

SIGHTS & ACTIVITIES

The main beach, **Praia da Pipa** (Praia do Centro), about 1.5km long, has fishing boats, several bars, and rock pools at low tide. **Baía dos Golfinhos**, to its north, is where dolphins are most often seen: it's backed by cliffs and is only accessible by walking from the main beach at low tide. **Praia do Madeiro** curves northwards from the headland at the far end of Baía dos Golfinhos and has a few upmarket hotels dotted along its length. It's good for beginner surfers (lessons run R$50). **Praia do Amor**, the advanced surf beach, is round the headland at the east end of the main beach, accessed off the eastern part of Av Baía dos Golfinhos. You can rent surfboards here and in town for around R$60 per day. **Lagoa de Guaraíras**, 8km north of Pipa in Tibau do Sul, is one of Pipa's most stunning landscapes, a massive lagoon bound by dunes that's the choice spot for watching the sunset. Excellent sunset kayak excursions run through here and the mangroves for R$30.

The privately owned **Santuário Ecológico de Pipa** (☎ 9982 8044; www.ecopipa.org.br; admission R$5; ⏱ 8am-5pm), 1.5km west along the road from the main bus stop, does a valuable job of protecting at least some of the Pipa coast from development. Well-marked trails lead

> ### DETOUR: THE WORLD'S LARGEST CASHEW TREE
>
> The pretty twin beach towns of Pirangi do Sul and Pirangi do Norte, 15km south of Ponta Negra, are split by a river that weaves through palm-crested dunes on its way to the ocean. The town is home to the world's largest cashew tree: its sprawl of branches is over 500m in circumference, and it's still growing!
>
> Buses to Pirangi (R$3, one hour) leave from the side of the BR gas station on Av Cel Estevam next to the Rodoviária Nova every 30 minutes between 6am and 7:30pm.

through secondary forest to impressive look-outs over Baía dos Golfinhos and Praia do Madeiro, from which you can often see large green turtles at high tide.

SLEEPING

Pipa has dozens of pousadas and hotels, ranging from dumpy to 5-star gorgeous. In the last two years, a string of hostels have finally popped up, some more legal than others. Most accommodations offer good discounts in low season.

Sugar Cane Hostel (☎ 3246 2723; www.sugarcanehostel.com.br; Rua do Arara 19; dm/s/d R$30/35/70; 🛜 🖳) This new hostel/surf school run by a young British surfer and his Brazilian bud is the best hostel in Pipa, with the right traveler camaraderie around the tasteful grounds strewn with several hammocks and solid tunes. There are separated six-bed dorms – air-con on the way – and a guest kitchen. The 2nd-floor open-air patio makes for an excellent hang spot.

Pipa Hostel (☎ 3246 2151; www.pipahostel.com.br; Rua do Arara 105; dm from R$35; r from R$110; 🌀 🛜 🖳) More sedate than Sugar Cane, the newish HI hostel is also a good choice, with separated eight-bed dorms and tasteful private rooms (No 5 is the best), most overlooking the grassy courtyard. The sweet staff are English-speaking and there's a guest kitchen, a nice pool, parking and a flat-screen-TV lounge. Discounts for HI members.

Pousada Alto da Pipa (☎ 3246 2281; www.pousadaaltodapipa.com.br; Rua da Gameleira 555; s/d R$90/130; 🌀 🛜 🖳) This cute and colorful pousada up on the hill above the main street is perfect value for those who have outgrown hostels but still appreciate bang for the buck. The

pastel-hued rooms are small and clean, but it's their sidelining of a lush courtyard with cashew trees and small footbridges over tiny ponds that make it a special find. Parking is available.

our pick Spa Da Alma (☎ 3246 2357; www.spadaalma.net; Rua do Spa 9; s/d from R$239/266; 🌀 🛜 🖳) On sprawling grounds lush with dune vegetation at the south end of town, this great-value place boasts luxury form and function at almost midrange prices. Each bungalow offers wide bay windows and verandas with wowing views over Praia das Minas and Sibaúma – a rarity in Pipa – and are perched about the elevated property almost isolated from one another. It's stunning, very private and the price is very right. Parking available.

Toca da Coruja (☎ 3246 2226; www.tocadacoruja.com.br; Av Baía dos Golfinhos; r from R$300, deluxe chalets R$890; 🌀 🛜 🖳) One of Brazil's most charming luxury pousadas, Toca da Coruja is wrapped in an oasis of sprawling tropical gardens with monkeys, birds and two gorgeous pools. It's an eco-conscious place built with some recycled materials and rescued 19th-century farmhouse furniture, and low-energy lighting and copper ionization treatment for the pools. The exquisite large deluxe chalets, in the style of old Northeast ranch houses, have breezy wraparound verandas and outdoor spas. Parking is offered. Children under 12 not permitted.

EATING

Pipa is a wonderful place to eat out, but finding quality is more challenging than cheap.

Natural Brasil (☎ 3246 4250; Rua Dr Helío Galvão 441, Tibau do Sul; sandwiches R$6-15; �ržeн noon-10pm Thu-Tue) *Good* lunches in Pipa are few and far between, so it's worth the R$2 bus fare or tacking on a late lunch to a kayak or sunset excursion to Lagoa de Guaraíras at this wonderful and cozy spot in Tibau do Sul. It has superb sandwiches, salads and creative veggie-minded options (soy stroganoff, spinach pesto penne). Everything is good.

Garagem (☎ 3246 2154; Ladeira do Cruzeiro; mains R$7-27; ☸ 10:30am-1am Tue-Sun) 'Holy Shit' views, good tunes and excellent food to boot, Garagem got its start as a famous bar (and is still good for that) but during the day, it's the best spot in Pipa proper to drop down for a beach lunch (excellent Argentine *picanha*, fresh fish) and a Bohemia to wash it down. During full moons, there's live music at night as well.

Oba (☎ 9188 3928; Rua dos Bem-Te-Vis 32; mains R$13-20; ☽ 7pm-midnight) It's not often you'll find genuine *Japazilian* yakisoba from São Paulo at these prices, but this place is the real deal, with huge portions to boot. Heaped plates of noodles with veggies, shrimp, chicken, steak etc are the highlight, and the lychee *sakerinhas* (using sake instead of *cachaça*) add to the fun.

Tapas (☎ 9414 4675; Rua dos Bem-Te-Vis 8; dishes R$22-31.50; ☽ 6:30-11pm, closed May-Jun) Just up from the main street, Tapas is another culinary godsend here, serving large Brazilian tapas peppered with Thai, Indian, French and Italian influences in a casual and artsy space. Fresh tuna is the house specialty, but it's all tasty, especially the filet with Gorgonzola and orange sauce.

Pacífico (☎ 9982 8981; Rua dos Bem-Te-Vis 8; mains R$29-57; ☽ 7-10:30pm, closed Tue) High-end cuisine is rarely this low-end on your wallet in touristy Brazil, but the Californian owner-chef here prides himself on value along with his exceptional Nouveau California-Brazilian dishes with Asian flare, such as Thai-tinted *moquecas* (fish stews) and black and blue pepper tuna. The cognac-flambé pepper steak is a treat. Side dishes are extra but you'll still come away surprised at the bill.

ourpick Cruzeiro do Pescador (☎ 3246 2026; cnr Av Baía dos Golfinhos & Rua Concris; mains for 2 R$85-185; ☽ lunch & dinner) It looks like a typical mess of a house, but a closer look reveals a home transformed into a don't-miss culinary experience. Chef Daniel (a former copywriter) and his former gardener are gastronomic anomalies: everything down to the coffee is done with homegrown finesse and no formal training. Smoked or grilled seafood is the way to go, but call ahead as some dishes take two hours to prepare, like the *Seleção do Mar*, a slow-grilled seafood feast of Biblical proportions.

DRINKING & ENTERTAINMENT
Nightlife tends to start off at and outside Tribus and Oz bars, opposite each other on Av Baía dos Golfinhos, which is lined with lots of come-and-go options. Around midnight or later, people move on to some live music. **Calangos** (☎ 3246 2396; ☽ from midnight Fri-Sun) at the end of Av Baía dos Golfinhos, has live *forró* on Sunday and Euro-style DJs the other nights. **A Tasca** (☎ 3246 2562; Rua da Gameleira 37; ☽ 10pm-3am) offers samba on Sunday nights.

GETTING THERE & AWAY
Eight daily buses (only four on Sunday and an extra on Monday, Friday and Saturday) run to Pipa from the Rodoviária Nova in Natal (R$10, two hours). You can also catch them in front of Carrefour in Lagoa Nova and avoid the bus station altogether. Minibuses straight to Natal's airport from Pipa run four times daily except Sunday and three times return (R$15).

If you are arriving from the south, get out at Goianinha (1½ hours from João Pessoa), where minibuses run frequently to Pipa (R$3, 40 minutes) departing 5am to 11:30pm from behind the blue church, 250m off the main road.

For travelers heading south from Pipa, Pipatour (p560) can reserve bus seats from Goianinha for a R$6 fee.

NORTH OF NATAL
From Genipabu, this stretch of nearly 200km, in which the coast veers from east-facing to north-facing, is a growing playground for weekenders and day-trippers from Natal, but there are still dozens of lovely beaches. The further from Natal you go, the more isolated and empty they become. Several beaches on the east-facing coast have reef pools that are good for snorkeling at low tide. The charming villages of São Miguel do Gostoso and Galinhos have both firmly planted themselves as idyllic getaways and are well worth some time as you travel along towards Ceará.

São Miguel do Gostoso
☎ 0xx84 / pop 9200
Located 110km from Natal, 'Gostoso' is an emerging destination that has been brewing for some time now. It is an increasingly popular weekend getaway, with pousadas, restaurants and bars, but also with several nearby beaches that are gorgeous and for the most part near-empty. If you want to go somewhere undiscovered thus far by charter tourism and still be awed by the scenery, go now or forever hold your peace.

There is a Banco do Brasil ATM on the main road and a few internet places.

SIGHTS & ACTIVITIES
The main beaches in town, **Praia do Maceió**, **Praia da Xêpa** and **Praia do Cardeiro**, make up a wide and continuous stretch of relaxing sands, but the true gem is **Praia de Tourinhos**, located 8km north of town at the end of a long and

deserted gravel road. It's a beautiful semicircle bay with just a few kiosks, nothing more. It just *feels* special and you won't share it during the week. **Ponta do Santo Cristo**, at the far south end of Maceió, catches the gusts of wind and is a very popular wind- and kitesurfing spot.

SLEEPING & EATING

Pousada Casa de Taipa (☎ 3263 4227; www.pousada casadetaipa.com.br; Rua Bagre Caia Coco 99; s/d R$120/150; ✄ �🖿 ⛛) English-speaking and lovely to the core, this creative spot tucked away down a residential street 300m from the beach is made memorable by the artsy endeavors of one of the owners, who has fashioned the tables from egg and coconut shells and painted large murals in each room – little upscale *taipas* themselves – that are simply gorgeous. There is a small museum devoted to *taipa*, a rudimentary clay construction technique of the Northeast. Parking is available.

    Pousada dos Ponteiros (☎ 3263 400/; www.pousa dadosponteiros.br; Praia do Maceió; s/d from R$200/250; ✄ 🖿 ⛛) Right on Maceió beach in town, this charming spot offers near-luxury chalets accented by old B&W photos of the area. The mini-spa specializes in Ayurvedic treatments. Parking available.

    Esquina Brasil Bistro (☎ 9156 1920; Av dos Arrecifes 1976; mains R$5.50-25; ☽ dinner Thu-Tue, lunch noon-4pm Sat & Sun) Simple but adorable, this Portuguese-Brazilian run café does *tapiocas*, *açaí* and *cupuaçu* (an Amazonian fruit), light sandwiches on Indian chapatti bread and a fabulous cashew-nut pesto pasta. All the greens are organic and little touches such as ramekins of sea salt put it a cut above.

GETTING THERE & AWAY

Buses run here five times daily from Natal's Rodoviária Nova (R$13.10 to R$16.80, 2½ hours) at 6:15am, 8:40am, 10:15am, 1:40pm and 5:30pm. Some require switching buses in Touros.

Galos & Galinhos

☎ 0xx84 / pop 1000

On the tipping point of a narrow sandbar between a 'river' (it's not, really) and the sea, 160km northwest of Natal, the isolated fishing villages of Galos and Galinhos are only emerging as beach destinations. With sandy streets and warm, gentle waters, it's a great place to unwind. More famous Galinhos holds the bulk of accommodations, from which pristine

beaches and dunes stretch 2km west to a small lighthouse at the river mouth, and endlessly along the coast to the east. Next door in Galos, only 400 or so people live in even more peaceful surroundings. You can take an enjoyable four- or five-hour boat excursion (R$120 per boat, up to 12 people) along the estuary between the two villages, via mangroves, dunes and the local saltworks.

SLEEPING & EATING

Pousada Galinhos (☎ 3552 0047; www.pousadagalinhos .com.br; Rua Walfran Ribeiro 207, Galinhos; r R$100) This budget option has small but clean rooms with verandas on a quiet side street.

    our pick **Pousada Vila Galinhos** (☎ 3552 0169; www .kitesurfgalinhos.com; Rua Walfran Ribeiro 140, Galinhos; r R$190; ✄ 🖿) Packed with artistic touches and loaded with charm, this French-Portuguese-run pousada and kitesurfing school is a hippie-chic gem. Colorful rooms with romantic mosquito nets (hard to pull off) and beautiful rock murals surround a peaceful pool, and it's the only option in town with mineral water for showers. It's nearly booked solid from August to January with would-be kitesurfers on week-long courses.

    Pousada Peixe Galo (☎ 3552 2001; www.pousada peixegalo.com.br; Rua da Candelária 30, Galos; r R$210; ✄ 🖿 ⛛) Galos' only option sits in a privileged position just 5m from the water flanked by tall palm trees. Rooms with solar-heated showers are comfortable but nothing fancy and surround a nice pool; service is more professional than its competition in Galinhos. The charming lookout tower boasts wonderful views over the peninsula.

    Pousada Brésil Aventure (☎ 3552 0085; www.bresil -aventure.com; Rua Senador Dinarte Maris, 123, Galinhos; mains R$19-52; ☽ lunch & dinner) This restaurant/pousada run by a French tour company is the center of attention in Galinhos, serving the usual suspects and somewhat adventurous additions like stingray *moquecas* and a rich seafood spaghetti laced with coconut milk. Sunsets from here are worthy of writing home about.

GETTING THERE & AWAY

Access to Galos and Galinhos is not particularly easy, which is part of its charm. Access is via 4WD or buggy along the beach via São Bento do Norte, some 30km east, or by small boats along the river from Pratagi, 2km southeast (R$2 per person to Galinhos, R$25 per boat to Galos, up to four passengers). If you have a vehicle you can leave it safely parked at Pratagi for free.

Just one bus a week leaves Natal's Rodoviária Nova for Galinhos (R$22.50, 3½ hours) at 7am Sunday. It returns to Natal from Galinhos at 5:30pm. Alternatively, pirate taxis depart Galinhos daily between 5:30am and 7am for Natal (R$25) and drop you in front of Nordestão supermarket on Av Tomaz Lamdim on the northern border of Natal and São Goncalo do Amarante, 18km north of Ponta Negra.

Horse carts traverse the sands between the two villages (R$20 one way, 30 minutes).

Ceará, Piauí & Maranhão

The Northeast's three northernmost states stretch along Brazil's only north-facing coast and deep into the arid interior. While Ceará in the east is mostly caatinga (semi-arid land), the west of Maranhão is on the fringe of the Amazonian rain forest. The main draw for visitors, the beaches of Ceará, stretch either side of Fortaleza, the region's biggest city. Fortaleza itself, while not big on culture or charm, is a fun-loving beach town where you can dance to *forró* (popular music of the Northeast) and other beats. From here are arrayed hundreds of kilometers of some of the best beaches in Brazil, some supporting growing resort towns, others with at most a small, traditional fishing village. Super-relaxed Jericoacoara, with its unique location inside a dune-swept national park, is the jewel of Ceará's gorgeous coastline.

In Piauí, tranquil Parnaíba is the gateway to the large and intriguing Delta do Parnaíba. An adventurous coastal route leads west from here to the enormous expanses of high dunes and clear lagoons known as the Lençóis Maranhenses, one of Brazil's highlights. Its beauty will floor you. Further west still is the half-decayed, half-restored colonial city of São Luís, and its perfect sleepy neighbor Alcântara, two of Brazil's most picturesque colonial gems.

The region's interior, known as the *sertão*, is a land where life has never been easy for its predominantly agricultural and ranching inhabitants, who suffer periodic horrific droughts. But there is spectacular country to explore here, with the bonus of fascinating rock art and archaeological remains in the Serra da Capivara and Sete Cidades national parks.

HIGHLIGHTS

- Gawk at spectacular sunsets from towering dunes in the remote backpacker village of **Jericoacoara** (p578)

- Step back in time and admire the red ibis in the stunning colonial town of **Alcântara** (p596)

- Monkey-spot in small canoes along narrow tributaries of the wildlife-rich **Delta do Parnaíba** (p586)

- Ponder quirky rock formations and ancient graffiti in the Unesco-designated inland **Parque Nacional da Serra da Capivara** (p589)

- Dip into pristine lagoons surrounded by endless dunes in Maranhão's surreal **Lençóis Maranhenses** (p597)

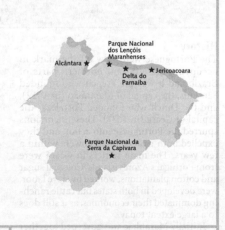

- ★ Parque Nacional dos Lençóis Maranhenses
- ★ Alcântara
- ★ Delta do Parnaíba
- ★ Jericoacoara
- ★ Parque Nacional da Serra da Capivara

- **POPULATION: 18 MILLION**   ■ **AREA: 732,340 SQ KM**

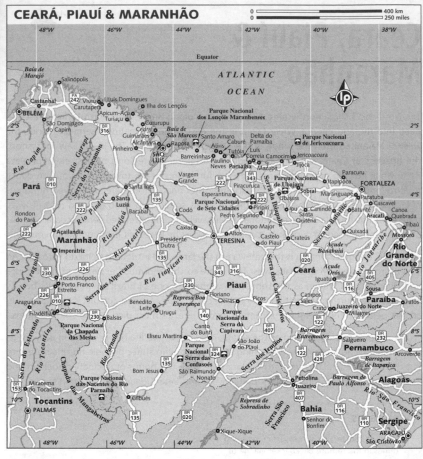

History

The Portuguese were slow off the mark in occupying these distant northern parts of Brazil, and it was the French who founded São Luís, the capital of Maranhão (in 1612), and the Dutch who founded Fortaleza, the capital of Ceará (in 1637). These incursions spurred the Portuguese into action and they expelled both rival colonial powers within a few years. The main settlers in Ceará were from Portugal's Azores islands. Colonial sugar and cotton plantations, worked by slave labor, were developed in both states but cattle ranching dominated their economies, as it still does to a large extent today.

Initially Maranhão was governed together with Pará to its west as a separate entity from the rest of Brazil, with their capital at São Luís. They were placed under the same administration as the rest of Brazil in 1774. Piauí, between Ceará and Maranhão, was first settled inland by poor cattle herders moving westwards from Ceará and north from São Paulo in the 17th and 18th centuries.

Despite resistance, the indigenous population of all three states was subdued by the 18th century. Once the wars ended, the colonists in the interior were faced with serious droughts. As many as two million people died in droughts in Ceará in the 1870s, with survivors streaming into Fortaleza. Neighboring Piauí was initially landlocked but eventually a land swap was arranged with Ceará in the 19th century so that it could enjoy the benefits of a coastline. Piauí still has the lowest population density of any Brazilian state.

The city of Fortaleza, with its commerce and tourism, is the region's economic powerhouse. Some large industrial projects have been sited near São Luís in the last couple of decades in an effort to boost its economy, but all three states are still among Brazil's poorest.

Climate

These states are warm year-round and experience a rainier season – with some tropical downpours – from about December to March in the west (Maranhão) and February to May in the east (Ceará). The interior doesn't get any coastal breezes, so it doesn't see much cold or rain. While the interior of Piauí claims to be hottest part of the country, it's slightly less broiling in June and July.

National Parks

Lençóis Maranhenses (p597), east of São Luís, is one of the highlights of the region, a vast expanse of high sand dunes only interrupted by clear pools of water.

In deep southern Piauí, **Serra da Capivara** (p589) contains 128 visitable archaeological sites and 30,000 prehistoric rock paintings in a dramatic rocky landscape. It is a Unesco World Heritage site and well worth the trip if you have time.

Nearer the coast, **Sete Cidades** (p588) contains bizarre rock formations that resemble seven cities, and hundreds more prehistoric rock paintings.

The small **Ubajara** (p583) is famous for its vast caves, reached on foot or by cable car. It also contains lush forests and impressive waterfalls.

Chapada das Mesas (p600) is a zone of impressive rocky bluffs and gorgeous waterfalls near Carolina in southern Maranhão.

Parque Nacional Nascentes do Rio Parnaíba, straddling the far south of Piauí and Maranhão as well as bits of Tocantins and Bahia states, is a superb wildlife-viewing location for those who can get there. It's famed for its beautiful hyacinth macaws and ultra-intelligent capuchin monkeys. See p588 for details.

The 63-sq-km **Jericoacoara** (p578) is an otherworldy dunescape of pristine shorelines, freshwater lagoons and an isolated village that's a mecca for travelers.

Getting There & Away

Fortaleza has an international airport with flights from Europe, the US and most Brazilian cities. São Luís and Teresina are served by domestic flights.

You can get to Fortaleza by bus from Brasília, Rio or São Paulo to the south, Natal or Recife to the east, or Belém to the west. For the longest trips, airfares can be little more expensive than buses. Teresina and São Luís receive buses from Fortaleza, Belém, Brasilia, Rio and São Paulo.

Getting Around

Buses link pretty much every town and village in this region. Road quality is steadily improving, though much of the São Luís–Belém road within Maranhão is in poor shape, and access to some coastal villages including Jericoacoara is partly unpaved. Beach buggies and 4WDs with drivers provide trips along the coasts and dunes. A hire car is useful if you plan to visit some smaller places with limited bus service, but you should research road conditions first as some less-traveled routes require 4WD. Fortaleza is the easiest place to get a rental vehicle.

CEARÁ

In a country of glorious coastlines, Ceará has one of the most glorious of all – nearly 600km of beautiful and varied beaches, from idyllic little palm-fringed bays to 20km strips washed by ocean breakers. From the busy urban beaches of Fortaleza to hip Jericoacoara and Canoa Quebrada to the smallest of fishing villages where people still sail *jangadas* (triangular-sailed fishing boats) and live in thatched-roof homes, Ceará has anything you could wish for in terms of beach ambience. Much of the coast is backed by large expanses of high, white dunes, lending a starkly elemental touch to the landscape, while the waves and winds provide some of the best conditions in the world for surfing, windsurfing and kitesurfing.

FORTALEZA

☎ 0xx85 / pop 3.3 million

Considering its isolation on the Brazilian map, Fortaleza is a surprisingly large and sprawling place. It's one of Brazil's biggest cities and an economic magnet for people from all of Ceará and beyond. It's also a magnet for tourists from Brazil and overseas, who come for the beaches and the party atmosphere. Some of the city beaches are reasonably attractive and the nightlife is definitely a lot of fun. With its international and domestic airport, Fortaleza also serves as the jumping-off point to truly spectacular beaches, rolling dunes and idyllic fishing villages up and down the Ceará coast.

Fortaleza will be making over its Castelão stadium as it prepares to be a host city for the 2014 FIFA World Cup. Elsewhere, major roadwork improvements and renovations, including a new terminal at Aeroporto Internacional Pinto Martins, are taking place.

History
According to many historians, the Spanish navigator Vicente Yáñez Pinzón landed on Praia Mucuripe on February 2, 1500, more than two months before Pedro Álvares Cabral first sighted Monte Pascoal in Bahia (the officially recognized European discovery of Brazil). The first Portuguese attempts to settle here, in the early 17th century, were short-lived, and it was the Dutch who founded what ended up as Fortaleza by building Fort Schoonenborch in 1637. When the Dutch

abandoned their Brazilian possessions in 1654, the Portuguese renamed this fort the Fortaleza de NS da Assunção (Fortress of Our Lady of the Assumption). Around it grew a village, then a town, then a city that came to be called Fortaleza.

Resistance from the indigenous population slowed Portuguese colonization of interior Ceará until the 18th century, but cattle ranchers, and later cotton growers, occupied land. It was cotton exports in the 19th century that made Fortaleza into an important town (it had previously played second fiddle to Aracati). Growing commerce and industry in Fortaleza have since attracted ever more migrants to the city, and droughts in the interior have driven people to the city. Since the early '90s tourism has joined textiles and food among the leading industries here. Under Workers' Party mayor Luizianne Lins, elected in 2004, Fortaleza has had some success in shrugging off an unwanted reputation as a capital of sex tourism.

Orientation
Fortaleza stretches 20km along the coast and up to 10km inland. Centro is the old-

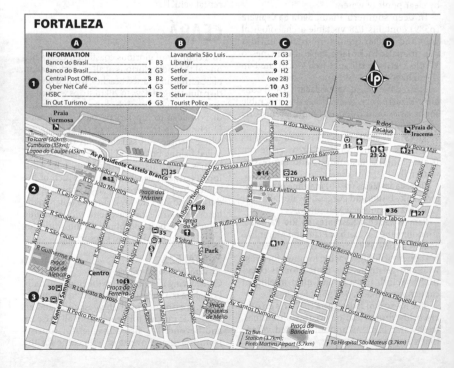

est part of town, on a slight elevation beginning 200m from the seafront, and has many busy streets full of small stores. The main areas of interest are east of Centro. First is Praia de Iracema, a tightly packed nightlife and restaurant area – with some hotels and pousadas (guesthouses), but no real beach. Then there's Meireles, the middle-class beach suburb with many of the best places to stay, 2km to 4km east of Centro. There's the port area, Mucuripe, and finally, starting some 8km east of Centro, Praia do Futuro, with the best beach, stretching 5km south along an east-facing coast.

The bus station is 4km south of Centro and the airport is 2km further south.

Information

BOOKSTORES

Fortaleza is principally a beach town and bookstores are hard to come by. The following are good for maps and guides.

Livraria Laselva (☎ 3477 1547; Aeroporto Pinto Martins) Upstairs in the airport.

Livraria Saraiva(☎ 3241 1986; Shopping Iguatemi, Av Washington Soares 85; ☒ 10am-10pm)

EMERGENCY

Ambulance (☎ 192)

Police (Polícia; ☎ 190)

Tourist Police (Delegacia de Proteção ao Turista; ☎ 3101 2488; Av Almirante Barroso 805, Praia de Iracema)

INTERNET ACCESS

Cyber Net Café (☎ 3242 5422; Av Abolição 2655, Meireles; per hr R$4; ☒ 9am-9pm Mon-Sat, from 10am Sun)

INTERNET RESOURCES

Setfor (www.fortaleza.ce.gov.br/turismo) The city tourism site, in Portuguese only but a useful reference.

Setur (www.setur.ce.gov.br) Ceará's official tourism site.

LAUNDRY

There are laundries all over town and most will pick up and deliver. Many hotels and pousadas also offer services.

Lavandaria São Luis (☎ 3242 2096; Av Abolição 2679, Meireles; 3kg minimum R$36; ☒ 8am-noon & 1-7pm Mon-Fri, 8am-noon & 1-2pm Sat) A good drop-off option. You'll find do-it-yourself next door at Lav & Lev.

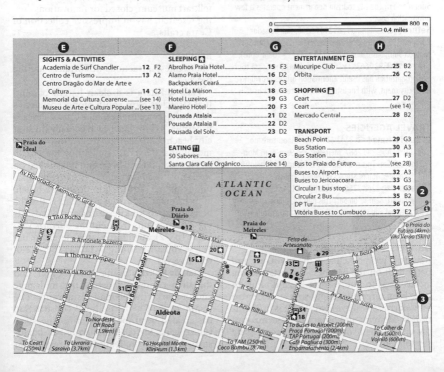

SIGHTS & ACTIVITIES	
Academia de Surf Chandler	12 F2
Centro de Turismo	13 A2
Centro Dragão do Mar de Arte e Cultura	14 C2
Memorial da Cultura Cearense	(see 14)
Museu de Arte e Cultura Popular	(see 13)

SLEEPING	
Abrolhos Praia Hotel	15 F3
Alamo Praia Hotel	16 D2
Backpackers Ceará	17 C3
Hotel La Maison	18 G3
Hotel Luzeiros	19 G3
Mareiro Hotel	20 F3
Pousada Atalaia	21 D2
Pousada Atalaia II	22 D2
Pousada del Sole	23 D2

EATING	
50 Sabores	24 G3
Santa Clara Café Orgânico	(see 14)

ENTERTAINMENT	
Mucuripe Club	25 B2
Órbita	26 C2

SHOPPING	
Ceart	27 D2
Ceart	(see 14)
Mercado Central	28 B2

TRANSPORT	
Beach Point	29 G3
Bus Station	30 A3
Bus Station	31 F3
Bus to Praia do Futuro	(see 28)
Buses to Airport	32 A3
Buses to Jericoacoara	33 G3
Circular 1 bus stop	34 G3
Circular 2 Bus	35 B2
DP Tur	36 D2
Vitória Buses to Cumbuco	37 E2

MEDICAL SERVICES

Hospital Monte Klinikum (☎ 4012 0012; www.mon teklinikum.com.br; Rua República do Líbano 747, Meireles)
Hospital São Mateus (☎ 3234 1444; www.hospital saomateus.com.br; Av Santos Dumont 5633, Papicu)
SAT Medical Services (☎ 3261 2220; www.gruposat .com.br) The area's best travel medicine specialist, with multilingual 24-hour house-call service.

MONEY

ATMs on the upper level of the airport accept international cards.
Banco do Brasil Centro (Praça Waldemar Falcao; ☾ 10am-4pm Mon-Fri, ATMs 6am-10pm daily); Meireles (Av Abolição 2311; ☾ 10am-4pm Mon-Fri, ATMs 6am-10pm daily) These branches also do currency exchange.
HSBC (Av Monsenhor Tabosa 1200, Praia de Iracema)

POST

Central post office (Rua Senador Alencar 38; ☾ 8am-5pm Mon-Fri, to noon Sat)

TOURIST INFORMATION

Setfor Centro (☎ 3105 1444; Praça da Ferreira; ☾ 8am-5pm Mon-Sat); Mucuripe (☎ 3105 2670; Av Beira Mar; ☾ 9am-9pm); Mercado Central (☎ 3105 1321; ☾ 9am-5pm Mon-Fri) The city tourism department operates a few information booths.
Setur Centro de Turismo (☎ 3101 5508; Rua Senador Pompeu 350, Centro; ☾ 8am-5pm Mon-Fri, to 4pm Sat, to noon Sun); bus station (☎ 3230 1111; ☾ 6am-8pm); airport (☎ 3392 1667; ☾ 6am-midnight) The Ceará tourism organization has useful information offices providing good city maps, with English-speaking attendants usually available.

TRAVEL AGENCIES

In Out Turismo (☎ 3242 4347; www.inoutturismo .com.br; Av Abolição 2687, Meireles; ☾ 9am-6pm Mon-Fri, to noon Sat) This small agency is friendly and helpful, and the owner, Jonas, speaks excellent English.
Libratur (☎ 3248 3355; Av Abolição 2194; ☾ 9am-6pm Mon-Fri, 8am-noon Sat) This helpful, bilingual agency is for national and international ticketing and currency exchange.

Dangers & Annoyances

Beware of pickpocketing in the city center and petty theft on the beaches. Tourists waiting at bus stops to return from Praia do Futuro have been targeted. Empty streets in Centro after dark are best avoided. There is prostitution in Meireles and especially Iracema, but the city has had some success in combating sex tourism.

Sights & Activities

CENTRO DRAGÃO DO MAR DE ARTE E CULTURA

This excellent modern **cultural center** (☎ 3488 8616; www.dragaodomar.org.br; Rua Dragão do Mar 81) includes museums, cinemas, theatres, galleries, a good café and a planetarium in an extensive complex with elevated walkways joining blocks on different streets. It blends well with the surrounding older buildings, many of which have been restored to house bars, restaurants and artisans' workshops. It's a successful social focus for the city, very popular with locals. The **Memorial da Cultura Cearense** (admission free; ☾ 9am-6:30pm Tue-Thu, 2-10pm Fri-Sun) is a museum dedicated to the popular culture of Ceará. Free capoeira lessons are given at 6pm Tuesday and Friday under the planetarium.

CENTRO DE TURISMO

The **Centro de Turismo** (☎ 3101 5508; Rua Senador Pompeu 350; ☾ 8am-6pm Mon-Sat, to noon Sun), a converted 19th-century jail, houses a lot of craft stalls, and upstairs from the tourist information office, the **Museu de Arte e Cultura Popular** (admission R$1; ☾ 8am-4pm Mon-Sat, to 11am Sun). This folk-art museum, closed for renovations during research, has an impressive collection of Ceará crafts.

BEACHES

The greatest attractions in Fortaleza are the beaches.

Praia do Futuro is a clean length of sand that stretches 5km south along Fortaleza's east-facing coast to the Clube Caça e Pesca, a fishermen's club. The beach is easily the best city beach, although far from most accommodations. *Barracas* (stalls) line the beach, serving seafood and beer, and it is packed on weekends. It doesn't start getting really nice until you are 1km to 2km down the beach, away from the industrial port. This is also the best city beach for kitesurfing and windsurfing – participants frequent the *barraca* Vira Verão (p572). Swimming is OK here, too, but unless you are a strong swimmer, beware of rough waves.

Praia do Meireles fronts Av Beira Mar, and this area contains most of the midrange and upmarket hotels and restaurants. The frantic pace of high-rise hotel construction has created what looks like a northeastern Copacabana. Meireles' numerous beach bars, shaded among the leafy trees, are popular places to hang out by day or evening. The water here is less clean than at Praia do Futuro, although that doesn't deter surfers. **Academia de Surf Chandler** (☎ 8803 4487; www .chandlersurf.com.br; surfboard rental per day/hr R$25/40; ⊗ 1-6pm Wed-Fri, 9am-6pm Sat & Sun), under a yellow awning on the beach, rents boards and gives classes for R$30 per hour.

Near the Ponte Metálica or Ponte dos Ingleses, the city's old dock built in the 1920s, **Praia de Iracema** was a source of inspiration to Luís Assunção and Milton Dias, Ceará's bohemian poets of the 1950s. Today Iracema has mainly been taken over by larger restaurants and bars catering to visiting partygoers. It also has an obvious prostitution scene. The beach itself is not worth your time.

Northwest of Fortaleza, **Icaraí** (20km from the center) and **Cumbuco** (35km from the center) are much cleaner than the city beaches and are easy day trips. Cumbuco, with its dunes, is popular for buggy rides, especially on weekends. Kitesurfing (best from July to February) is also good at Cumbuco beach and at Lagoa do Cauípe, 10km west of Cumbuco – rental and classes are available. Cumbuco has several hotels and pousadas if you want to stay over. **Vitória** (☎ 3342 1148) runs minibuses to Icaraí and Cumbuco (R$4.50 to either) from in front of Ideal Clube in Praia do Meireles at 9am, 11am, 3:50pm and 6:20pm. They run east along Av Beira Mar, then westward along Av Abolição.

Tours

Day trips to beaches along the coast to the east and west are very popular from Fortaleza. Dozens of travel agencies, hotels and pousadas will arrange these for you, and minivan and dune-buggy operators line up on Av Beira Mar near the Meireles tourist office in the early evening, looking for business for the next day. They will normally come and pick you up from your accommodations. The main destinations are Brazil's best water park, Beach Park (R$25 per person, transport only), Cumbuco (R$25), Morro Branco (R$35), Canoa Quebrada (R$40), Lagoinha (R$35) and Mundaú (R$40). The tours are easier than taking public buses and you can use them just one way if you want to stay over.

Some agencies also offer longer-distance 4WD or beach-buggy tours, along Ceará's glorious beaches wherever possible, as far afield as Jericoacoara or even Natal or the Lençóis Maranhenses. A three-day return trip to Jericoacoara costs around R$1700 to R$1950 for two people, with accommodations and outings from Jeri included; a four-day one-way jaunt to Natal is around R$2200 to R$4250 for two. These trips can be done in less time for less money. Try Hotel La Maison (p572), **Nordeste Off Road** (☎ 3246 4023; www.nord esteoffroad.com; Av Barão de Studart 2360, sala 202, Joaquim Távora), a member of Abeta or **Jeri Off Road** (p579) in Jericoacoara.

Festivals & Events

Fortal, Fortaleza's lively out-of-season Carnaval, is held during the last week of July. The **Iemanjá festival**, which celebrates the sea goddess, is held on August 15 at Praia do Futuro. The **Regata de Jangadas**, a sailing regatta with traditional northeastern *jangadas*, takes place between Praia do Meireles and Praia Mucuripe during the second half of July.

Sleeping

If you are here strictly for nightlife or on a tight budget, stay in Iracema. It's more dicey but most of the accommodations are a quick walk from Dragão do Mar, one-stop shopping for art, culture and nightlife. For beaches and relaxation, stay in Meireles (or nearby).

Despite the claims of many pousadas, there was no hostel affiliated with Hostelling International in Fortaleza at time of research.

BUDGET

Backpackers Ceará (☎ 3091 8997; www.backpackersce .com.br; Av Don Manuel 89; dm R$17, r from R$35; 🛜) The vibe is super informal at this sociable hostel with English-speaking Brazilian owners. Worse for wear but prettily decorated rooms line up on two floors alongside a scruffy lawn, and there are ample kitchen and hangout areas. Security is high, with entry codes and CCTV. The hostel is a stone's throw from the Centro Dragão do Mar.

Pousada Atalaia I (☎ 3219 0755; www.atalaiahos tel.com.br; Av Beira Mar 814, Iracema; dm/s/d R$40/90/120; ⚿ 🛜) This once belonged to Hostelling International but it is no longer affiliated. However, it remains set up like a hostel, (though the customer service was really poor while we were there) with simple but decent rooms and lots of computers for use. The original location is on a cute Iracema block, and the dorm beds are located a block away in a new annex location, Atalaia II, on Av Almirante Barroso.

Pousada del Sole (☎ 3219 3690; www.pousadadel sole.com.br; Av Almirante Barroso 966, Iracema; s/d with fan R$65/85, with air-con 75/95; ☒ ☜) Probably better value than most around here, this is another bare-bones option, but with a little color sprinkled about courtesy of the new Brazilian owner. There are options for all budgets and forgoing breakfast saves R$5.

MIDRANGE
Discounts of 25% to 35% are offered at many of these places outside the short mid-December-to-late-January high season.

Alamo Praia Hotel (☎ 3219 7979; www.alamo hotel.com.br; Av Almirante Barroso 885, Iracema; s/d/tr R$80/100/120; ☒ ☜) Charm is wearing thin here, but this hotel is only a block back from the action. There's lots of competition in the area, but this place still maintains higher prices than it should. The front desk told us it was, *'bem simple'* (very simple), which begs the question: why the higher prices?

Abrolhos Praia Hotel (☎ 3248 1217; www.abrolhos praiahotel.com.br; Av Abolição 2030, Meireles; s/d R$100/135; ☒ ☜) Busy Abrolhos, a couple of blocks back from the beach, is friendly, clean and well run, with one of the best breakfasts you'll find anywhere in the Northeast. Some English spoken.

ourpick Hotel La Maison (☎ 3242 6836; www.hotel lamaison.com.br; Av Desembargador Moreira 201, Meireles; r/tr R$120/140; ☒ ☜) The best-value midrange place in Meireles, La Maison is just a couple of blocks from the beach, with bright, spotless rooms. The attentive French owner knows the city very well, speaks English, and can point you in the right direction, no matter what your interest. His son offers buggy and 4WD trips as far as Jericoacoara and Natal. Free airport/bus station pick-ups.

TOP END
Because of the competition between Meireles' many fancy hotels, some good prices can be found.

Mareiro Hotel (☎ 3266 7235; www.mareiro.com.br; Av Beira Mar 2380, Meireles; r from R$242/314; ☒ ☜ ☒) A name change and modern makeover of rooms on the 2nd and 5th floors breathe new life into the former Olimpo Praia Hotel. Set back from the busy beachfront, it has a big pool area and lovely open-air lobby. Rooms are efficient and some feature new LCD televisions, but the hotel can get wildly hectic with events and

groups. Avoid the rear rooms overlooking noisy Av Abolição.

Hotel Luzeiros (☎ 4006 8585; www.hotelluzeiros .com.br; Av Beira Mar 2600, Meireles; s/d from R$300/385; ☒ ☜ ☒) The designer of this design hotel – Fortaleza's first – could have been a little more daring, but this sleek, Portuguese-owned option remains the discerning choice for rock stars and the artistically inclined. Clean-lined, modern spaces and rooms and probably the best breakfast in Ceará ensure it remains a mainstay with high-end clientele.

Eating
50 Sabores (☎ 3263 1714; Av Beira Mar 4690, Mucuripe; items R$5-7; ☼ 10am-midnight) Ice cream heaven, though with a terribly misleading name: there are actually 100 flavors here, including caipirinha (made with *cachaça*, a white spirit made from sugarcane – you must be 18 to purchase!), beer flavor, crispy cheese and cream corn, among loads of Brazilian fruits and more classic options. It's absolutely wonderful.

Santa Clara Café Orgânico (☎ 3219 6900; Rua Dragão do Mar 81; items R$9-12; ☼ 3-10pm Tue-Sun) Santa Clara is one of the city's hot *'Pontos de Encontros,'* which loosely translated means where hot people go to mingle. It's a wonderful little café serving organic Joe, sandwiches, wraps, waffles (despite its 3pm opening time), cheesecake, tapioca and a plethora of fancier coffee drinks. It's located on the upper level of Dragão do Mar.

Colher de Pau (☎ 3267 3773; Rua Frederico Borges 204, Varjota; mains for 2 R$15-95; ☼ 11am-midnight) This is one of the best places on a street lined with good-value, medium-range restaurants, many of them started by waiters from fancier places elsewhere in Fortaleza. It's consistently voted the best in town for regional cuisine.

Vira Verão (☎ 3262 6227; Av Zezé Diogo 3345, Praia do Futuro; mains for 2 R$21-46; ☼ 8am-6pm Fri-Wed, to 1am Thu) Praia do Futuro is lined with enormous *barracas*, some with hundreds of tables under sunshades on the sand. It's good for seafood meals and snacks – *pargo assado* (grilled red snapper) with salad is a favorite dish here. Vira Verão boasts a sea of golden-tanned goodness under coconut tree *palapas* (thatched-roof hut) on any given day, a requisite stop for surfers, windsurfers, kitesurfers and pretty much everyone else who owns a revealing swimsuit.

ourpick Coco Bambu (☎ 3242-7557; Rua Canuto de Aguiar 1317, Varjota; pizza R$25-64, per kg R$34.90;

10:30am-midnight Mon-Wed, to 1am Thu, to 2am Fri-Sun) This huge and festive eatery is one of those ridiculous Brazilian restaurants that does a whole lot of everything and – one would think – not a whole lot well. Oh no, not here. The 14-page menu covers pizza, tapioca, crêpes, sushi and regional mains (as well as *por-kilo* for lunch) but here's the rub: everything is excellent, including the clientele, which is always a bit raucous with Fortaleza's finest.

Vojniló (☎ 3267 3081; Rua Frederico Borges 409, Varjota; mains R$32-69; ✆ lunch & dinner Tue-Fri, dinner Sat, lunch Sun) With a confusing Macedonian name and under-the-radar appeal, this subtly maritime-themed restaurant won top seafood accolades in the city in 2009. The seafood spaghetti (R$59), topped with two whole *langostas* (small lobsters), and the house whole fish in caper sauce are both phenomenal.

Entertainment

Fortaleza is famed for its nightlife. Many tourists head for Iracema, which is packed with bars and clubs playing everything from *forró* (the quintessential popular music and dance of the Northeast) to techno, but has a big prostitution scene. The nearby Centro Dragão do Mar area is more popular with locals and is one of the best places to go out in the city.

For what's on culturally, grab the free monthly, *Cultura de Bolso*.

Órbita (☎ 3453 1421; Rua Dragão do Mar 207; admission R$15-30; ✆ 9pm-3am Thu-Sun) Reminiscent of a college town rock club (with way better looking people than your college or ours), the large, black-and-purple Dragão do Mar bar hosts live reggae, rock, surf and samba rock amid snooker tables and a legion of flirtatious upper-class clientele.

Mucuripe Club (☎ 3254 3020; Travessa Maranguape, 108, Centro; admission R$25-30; ✆ 10:30pm-6am) In addition to being the best and most stylish disco in the Northeast, Mucuripe is a mind-blowingly huge, modern, nontouristy venue with a dinner club and five different dance areas where you skirt between techno or *forró*, live rock and pop or jazz. If you lose a friend in here, they'll see you tomorrow.

Café Pagliuca (☎ 3224-1903; Rua Barbosa de Freitas 1035, Aldeota; admission R$5-8; ✆ lunch & dinner Mon-Sat) Fortaleza's most bohemian live venue is a sophisticated café offering jazz (Tuesday, Wednesday and Friday), tango (Thursday) and *bossa jazz* (Saturday) from 9pm. It also

does a good *feijoada* with a free caipirinha on Saturdays from noon (R$23). It skews 30-something-plus and draws artists, musicians and intellectuals.

Engarrafamento (☎ 3224 3237; Av Antonio Sales 2760, Aldeota; admission R$10-15; ✆ 5pm-3am Tue-Sun) The name means 'traffic jam,' and that's just what you'll get at the door of this fun middle-class venue for live *pagode* (popular samba music), Música Popular Brasileira (MPB), *forró* and pop/rock. It looks little more than a restaurant from the outside, but inside it's near disco-like, teeming with a cool kids knocking back buckets of cheap Skol and picking at tasty bar food. Worth the R$15 taxi fare, especially on Sundays.

Shopping

You can find handicrafts from all around Ceará in Fortaleza. Some of the finest work is in delicate lace, a tradition that came with the Portuguese. Artisans also work with *carnaúba*-palm fronds, bamboo, vines and leather.

Ceart Dragão do Mar (☎ 3101 2740; Centro Dragão do Mar; ✆ 9am-8pm Tue-Thu, 2pm-9pm Fri-Sun); Iracema (☎ 3101 2747; cnr Av Monsenhor Tabosa & Rua João Cordeiro; ✆ 9am-6pm Mon-Fri, to 5pm Sat); Aldeota (☎ 3224 7291; Av Santos Dumont 1589; ✆ 9am-6pm Mon-Fri, 8am-3pm) These beautiful state-run craft stores sell lace, ceramics, woven baskets and bags, leather goods and textiles.

Mercado Central (☎ 3454 8586; www.mercadocentralfortaleza.com.br; Av Alberto Nepomuceno 199, Centro; ✆ 8am-6:30pm Mon-Fri, to 5pm Sat, to noon Sun) Mainly geared to a tourist clientele, the three-story Central Market has good prices at more than 500 stalls selling everything from hammocks and leather bags to excellent local cashews and a huge variety of *cachaça* – some bottles have fruit salad or crabs pickled inside.

Centro de Turismo (☎ 3101 5508; Rua Senador Pompeu 350, Centro; ✆ 8am-6pm Mon-Sat, to noon Sun) The many stalls here focus on lace and embroidery and you can usually see lace-makers at work.

Getting There & Away

AIR

Pinto Martins airport (☎ 3392 1030) has daily flights to/from Miami with TAM, Atlanta with Delta, Lisbon with TAP, plus every major Brazilian destination with a variety of Brazilian airlines. There are also regular charter flights from several European cities.

Airline offices include the following (at the airport unless otherwise stated):

Azul (☎ 3392 1888)

Delta (☎ 4003 2121)

Gol/Varig (☎ 3392 1937)

Ocean Air (☎ 4004 4040)

TACV (Cabo Verde Airlines; ☎ 3392 1354)

TAM airport (☎ 3392 1193); Aldeota (☎ 3133 9222; Av Santos Dumont 2626)

TAP Portugal Aldeota (☎ 3458 1540; Sala 910, Shopping Aldeota, Av Dom Luís 500); airport (☎ 3392 1884)

Webjet (☎ 3392 1965)

BUS

From the **bus station** (☎ 3256 2100; Av Oswaldo Studart) buses run to destinations including Belém (R$212, 24 hours, 9am, 1pm and 6:30pm), Canoa Quebrada (R$17, three hours, five daily), Juazeiro do Norte (R$45 to R$87, 11 hours, nine daily), Natal (R$77 to R$90, eight hours, six daily), Parnaíba (R$71 to R$130, nine hours, four daily), Recife (R$115 to R$175, 12 hours, 8am, 7:30pm and 8pm), Rio de Janeiro (R$329, 48 hours, 12:30pm except Sunday; 8pm Monday, Wednesday, Friday and Saturday), Salvador (R$186, 22 hours, 7pm), Teresina (R$61 to R$97, 10 hours, six daily), São Luís (R$136 to R$145, 20 hours, 9am and 12:30pm) and Ubajara (R$29 to R$37, six hours, six daily). You can buy tickets in town at agencies including one run by the welcoming and fluent English-owned **DP Tur** (☎ 3219 3377; www.diskpassagens.tur .br; Av Monsenhor Tabosa 631, Loja 3, Iracema; ☒ 8am-6pm Mon-Fri, 9am-2pm Sat).

For Jericoacoara, **Redenção** (☎ 3256 2728) runs two buses daily from the **Praiano Palace Hotel** (Av Beira Mar 2800) on Meireles beach. The 8:30am and 5:30pm departures (R$48, seven hours) go every day and also pick up passengers at the airport (8am and 6pm) and bus station (10:30am and 6:30pm). In July and December (sometimes extended through March) there is an extra 9:30am departure from the Praiano (R$38). A 7:30am separate 'VIP' departure leaves from Hotel Amuarama opposite the bus station (R$50, daily). It's a good idea to buy your ticket a day ahead: one outlet is **Beach Point** (☎ 3242 2946; Náutico, Meireles). The fare includes a 23km ride in an open-sided *jardineira* (4WD bus) for the final stretch from Jijoca to Jericoacoara along sandy tracks and the beach.

Buses also make trips to the beaches northwest of Fortaleza (see p577).

CAR & MOTORCYCLE

Recommended rental agencies, with airport offices:

Avis (☎ 3477 1369)

Hertz (☎ 3477 5055)

Getting Around

TO/FROM THE AIRPORT

A taxi from the airport to Meireles, Iracema or Centro costs R$25. Bus 404 'Aeroporto' (R$1.80) runs both ways between the airport and Rua Pedro Pereira (near corner of Rua General Sampaio) in Centro throughout the day, taking about 20 minutes. Bus 27 Siqueira/Papicu/Aeroporto stops on Av Dom Luiz just east of Praça Portugal in Meireles. In Centro you can get another bus to Iracema or Meireles, but, for safety reasons, it's not advisable to change buses in Centro after late afternoon.

TO/FROM THE BUS STATION

Bus 099 Siqueira/Mucuripe/Barão de Studart (R$1.80) passes from the bus station to Av Beira Mar in Meireles and Mucuripe Monday to Saturday. On Sunday, bus 078 'Siqueira/Mucuripe' (R$1.80) runs to Iracema and Meireles. To catch them, walk left outside the bus station, turn right at the traffic signal along Av Borges de Melo, and the stop is about 200m along on the far (south) side of the street, in front of the Oi! building. For Iracema, buses 013 Aguanambi or 13 de Maio/Rodoviária from the bus station go to Iracema via Av Dom Manuel. Bus 504 Rodoviária also departs Rua Pedro Pereira (near corner of Rua General Sampaio) in Centro throughout the day.

BUS

From Centro to Iracema and Meireles take the Circular 2 bus (R$1.80) from Rua Castro e Silva or the Iguatemi-Centro bus (R$3.50) from Praça da Ferreira or the Igreja da Sé. The Circular 2 follows Av Almirante Barroso and Av Abolição. The Iguatemi-Centro goes along Av Monsenhor Tabosa and Av Abolição.

The Circular 1 bus (R$1.80) runs from Meireles (Av Abolição) to Iracema (Av Almirante Barroso), Centro Dragão do Mar and Centro (Av Alberto Nepomuceno and Rua João Moreira).

For Praia do Futuro you can take Top Bus 049 from the Mercado Central, Av Almirante Barroso or Av Abolição, or a Caça e Pesca bus from Av Beira Mar, Meireles.

BEACHES SOUTHEAST OF FORTALEZA

The coast southeast of Fortaleza, dubbed the Costa Sol Nascente (Sunrise Coast) by the publicity folk, has many fine beaches, a lot of them backed by dunes, but is increasingly developed and built up in the first 100km from Fortaleza. Hwy CE-040 runs about 10km inland, through a mostly flat, dry landscape of shrubs, stunted trees and some lakes.

CANOA QUEBRADA

☎ 0xx88 / pop 3000

Once a tiny village cut off from the world by its huge, pink sand dunes and beloved of early hippy travelers, Canoa Quebrada enjoyed a time in the Brazilian Destinations of Yore spotlight throughout the '90s and '00s. Today, it seems that tourism sucked the soul out of Canoa and it's difficult to find a Brazilian that has a single good thing to say about it. It's a casualty of the Brazilian in-crowd's build-them-up, tear-them-down mentality.

Still, beautiful Canoa possesses dozens of pousadas, plenty of restaurants and abundant nightlife. The craggy, eroding sand cliffs behind the narrow beach still lend a touch of the other-worldly feel for which Canoa was famous – and there magnificence cannot be denied. Other than the beach, the main attractions are exploring the endless beaches and dunes by buggy, kitesurfing (the season is from July to December) and sailing in *jangadas*.

Orientation & Information

The main street, known as Rua Principal or Rua Dragão do Mar, runs along the ridge of the hill from which Canoa slopes down to the beach. A pedestrianized strip of Rua Principal with most of the restaurants and bars is known as Broadway.

There's a temperamental stand-alone **Banco de Brasil ATM** (Rua Dragão do Mar) opposite the bus stop, but it's often broken down and is a clone risk. You will save yourself loads of potential hassle if you arrive flush with cash. The nearest international-friendly banks are Bradesco and Banco do Brasil in Aracati, 13km south-west. **Pousada Latin Pirates** (Rua Dragão do Mar; per hr R$3.50; ⏰ 9am-10:30pm) offers internet access.

Activities & Tours

There are lots of high dunes and secluded beaches in both directions from Canoa and it's a shame not to get out and see them. Ask staff at your pousada to recommend a buggy

driver. A one- to two-hour buggy tour of the dunes on the northern side of town costs around R$120 for up to four people. Quad-bike trips are also popular. A longer trip along the beautiful, cliff-lined coast to Ponta Grossa, 30km southeast is about R$200 round-trip (1½ hours each way). It's possible to get a buggy all the way to Natal for R$1700.

Kitesurfing is best around the mouth of the Rio Jaguaribe, 12km northwest. **Kite Surf Adventure** (☎ 8813 5891; jmdusa1@netzero.com; classes per 12hr R$800) and **Brasil Kite Flat Water** (☎ 9604 4953; www.brasilkiteflatwater.com; classes per hr R$100) are recommended schools.

Sleeping

There are lots of foreign-owned pousadas in Canoa Quebrada, and standards are generally high.

Pousada Europa (☎ 3421 7004; Rua Nataniel Pereira; s/d with fan R$35/45; 🖳 🌐) Canoa's main back-packer scene is hardly worth the hassle – we experienced an off-putting front desk, overly simplistic rooms and a common garden/pool area heading towards shambles, which make it only for those desperately low on cash. You are far better off at California or Toby for prices that just skirt budget class in high season.

our pick Pousada Califórnia (☎ 3421 7039; www.californiacanoa.com; Rua Nascer do Sol 136; s/d/tr from R$100/110/140; 🅿 🌐 🌐) This popular 28-room pousada has a variety of neat, comfortable rooms on two sides of the street, and an attractive courtyard with a sociable bar and pool. Free fruit and coffee are available all day in the new annex breakfast room and TV lounge, a chill hang spot. English-owned, Dutch-managed means it's got its act together.

Pousada do Toby (☎ 3421 7094; www.pousadadotoby.com; Rua Leandro Bezerra 143; r R$100-350; 🅿 🌐 🌐) Here since 1990, the Toby is a Canoa land-mark, with rooms ranging from modest to upscale. All are clean, cool and attractive. The rooftop pools and deck have panoramic views and the restaurant serves breakfast until 2pm (for those who have truly enjoyed the nightlife).

Pousada Azul Marinho (☎ 3421 7003; www.azul-marinho.com; Rua Leandro Bezerra; s/d R$130/160; 🅿 🌐 🌐) With just five intimate rooms, all with spectacular seaviews, this is the little high-value pousada that could. Each offers in-room hammocks, large bathrooms and some contain four-poster beds. You can take

CEARÁ, PIAUÍ & MARANHÃO

CEARÁ COAST

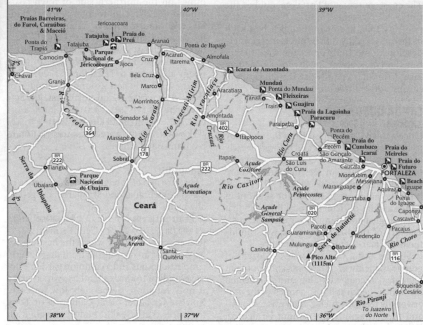

breakfast in bed, and both the pool and large veranda outside the rooms boast unimpeded Atlantic views.

Pousada Dolce Vita (☎ 3421 7213; www.canoa-quebrada.it; Rua Descida da Praia; r R$130-220; ❊ 🛜 🎦) The Dolce Vita is friendly and relaxed, with a beautiful pool set in gardens of palms, flowers and lawns. The cabins have more character than your average pousada, each being named after a Fellini film and decorated with movie memorabilia and new LCD TVs.

Eating

Cabana (☎ 3421 7018; Rua Principal; mains R$8-37; ❊ 5-11:30pm Tue-Fri, from noon Sat & Sun) Cabana has churned out consistently good international cuisine for nearly two decades, a rare feat in the Northeast indeed. Go for the filet mignon with Roquefort. The service is great, too – they actually returned to the table and asked how everything was. Pinch us; we're dreaming!

Lazy Days (☎ 8801 5996; Rua Dragão do Mar 999; mains R$11-36; ❊ 9am-5pm Fri-Wed, dinner Thu) At the eastern end of the beach, Lazy Days is the best of the beach *barracas* that rub up against Canoa's

picturesque red cliffs. It does excellent seafood and curries and a bang-up barbeque on Thursday nights only – though some say the food takes a dive sometimes. *Globo* recently filmed a popular telenovela here, so it's more popular now than ever.

Bar Evolução (☎ 3421 7291; Rua Eliziário 146; pizza R$12-22; ❊ 6pm-midnight) Great little Italian-run place serving up thin-crust pizzas with farm-fresh mozzarella in a shady open-air spot. It's especially atmospheric at night.

El Argentino (☎ 3421 7123; Rua Nascer do Sol; mains R$20-150 ❊ 6pm-midnight Mon & Wed-Fri, noon-midnight Sat & Sun) Off-Broadway (just), Argentino is the best spot for grilled meats and does a *rodízio* (all-you-can-eat; R$36).

Drinking & Entertainment

There's no need to structure your evening, just walk along Broadway and you'll find what's going on. Caverna (towards the beach end of the street, with darts and pool) is usually the center of the action.

Reggae parties start every Friday and Sunday night about 1am at Freedom *barraca* on the beach.

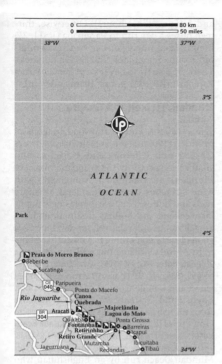

Getting There & Away

BUS

There are five daily buses to/from Fortaleza (R$15, three hours), or you can go by tour van (R$40, two hours, 3:30pm; see p571). Both leave from in front of Hotel Tropicalia near the Banco do Brasil ATM. Coming from Rio Grande do Norte, get off your bus at Aracati, 13km southwest of Canoa. From there, with any luck you can catch the São Benedito Fortaleza–Canoa bus (R$1.50, 9am, 11:30am, 1:40pm, 4:30pm or 8:20pm). Otherwise, minibuses (R$2, about every half-hour, 6am to 8pm) depart about 1km away at the Igreja Matriz in the center. Taxis charge R$25 for the quick run to Canoa.

SOUTHEAST TO RIO GRANDE DO NORTE

Road access to this stretch of coast is limited, so there are some great deserted beaches and small fishing villages. It's classic beach-buggy territory, and a great outing from Canoa Quebrada is the buggy ride along the beach to Ponta Grossa (30km).

The first town after Canoa Quebrada is **Majorlândia**, 7km southeast, a popular local

resort that gets crowded on weekends. Another 4km southeast are the distinctive, chalky-white sandstone bluffs of **Quixaba**, a fishing village famed for its prawns. From the bluffs, cut by gullies between cacti and palms, you can see back to the pink hills of Canoa Quebrada.

The beach at the next fishing village, **Lagoa do Mato**, combines dunes, cliffs and coconut palms. It's a good snorkling spot, too. Picturesque **Fontainha**, **Retirinho** and **Retiro Grande** follow at intervals of a few kilometers before you reach **Ponta Grossa**, with its curve of beach backed by colorful cliffs. Just beyond Ponta Grossa, **Redondas** is a great place to eat lobster at lower-than-usual prices – try the restaurants in Pousada Oh Linda or Pousada Beija-Flor. These places also have good rooms at around R$100 a double.

From Barreiras, 8km beyond Redondas, a paved road continues to Icapuí and on to Tibaú in Rio Grande do Norte.

BEACHES NORTHWEST OF FORTALEZA

The 'Costa Sol Poente' (Sunset Coast), northwest of Fortaleza, is strung with beautiful beaches and villages that are great for unwinding and exploring dunes, bays, lakes and rivers. The winds and waves along here provide some perfect conditions for surfing, windsurfing and kitesurfing.

Paracuru

☎ 0xx85 / pop 32,500

On a curving bay 95km northwest of Fortaleza with palms and rustic fishing boats, Paracuru is a popular weekend retreat from the city. Although it can get crowded on weekends, it's quiet the rest of the week. Paracuru also has a good Carnaval for a town of its size.

Surfing can be good here year-round, and the kitesurfing conditions from August to January are among the best in Brazil, with November and December optimal. The best kite spot is 4km east of the town center.

Twelve plus buses a day run to Paracuru from Fortaleza's bus station (R$9, two hours, 6am to 6pm).

SLEEPING & EATING

Pousada Villa Verde (☎ 3344 1181; www.pousadavilla verde.webnode.com; Rua Professora Maria Luísa Sabóia 205; s R$50-60, d R$60-70; 🖭) This friendly place has nice, clean rooms with verandas in a lovely big green garden with huge, shady trees. It's just 150m west of the church on the central square, close to the beach.

Fórmula 1 (☎ 3344 2048; Praia da Munguba; mains for 2 R$35-65; ☺ 10am-midnight) A well-known restaurant on Paracuru's central beach, Fórmula 1 serves a variety of dishes including its specialty snails, and is also a good place for cold beers battered by salty seawater at high tide. The French owner, Michel, has several good, large, colorful rooms (R$70/100 for singles/doubles) with air-con and access to a pool at his house, 2km back from the beach.

Paiol (☎ 3344 2890; Rua Ormezinda Sampaio 811; mains for 2 R$25-34; ☺ 11am-3am) Serves a range of pasta, pizza, seafood and meat in a pleasant courtyard setting.

Praia da Lagoinha
☎ 0xx85

Round the headland northwest of Paracuru (45km by road), Praia da Lagoinha has a beautiful, expansive beach with coconut palms, *jangadas* and a small, deep lagoon near the dunes. This stretch of sand is one of the best and prettiest in the state (and it has some competition). Extending 15km to the northwest, it is still not heavily developed (though large constructions have broken ground) and is a good choice for a short visit from Fortaleza.

The cliff-top **Pousada Mar à Vista** (☎ 9680 4436; www.pousadamaravista.cjb.net; Av Azevedo 78910; r with fan R$50, r with air-con R$75-100; ☒ ☐ ☒) was closed for a major facelift during research. Soon joining the stupendous views will be a new pool, rooftop lounge, beach bar (with stairway beach access) and terrace restaurant at this popular Chilean/Swedish-run budget choice.

Pousada Vivamar (☎ 3363 5046; www.vivamarhotel .com.br; Praia da Lagoinha; s/d R$120/180; ☒ ☐ ☒) offers good, clean rooms in a scenic location right on the beachfront. Its sister property 50m down the beach offers a nicer, more expensive near-resort-type atmosphere.

Marzari (☎ 3363 5078; Av Beira Mar s/n; mains for 2 R$41-84; ☺ 8am-4pm) Capitalizing on the successful formula of Fortaleza's popular *barracas*, Marzari serves excellent fish, *moquecas* (seafood stew cooked in a clay pot) and seafood risottos for lunch on privileged beachfront real estate. Though day-tour groups from Fortaleza fuel its business, it welcomes indie travelers as well and offers lockers for your stuff if you head to the water.

There are two direct buses daily to Lagoinha from Fortaleza's bus station (R$28.40, 6:30am and 3:45pm, three hours). Otherwise, thirteen buses a day run to Paraipaba (R$11, 2½ hours), from where you can switch to a minibus for the remainder (R$2.50, 15 minutes). There are also two a day (except Sunday) from Paracuru (R$5, 1½ hours; 10am and 5pm).

Mundaú, Fleixeiras & Guajiru
☎ 0xx85

The excellent, end-of-the-road beaches of Mundaú (150km from Fortaleza along Hwys CE-085 and CE-163) and Fleixeiras and Guajiru (respectively 13km and 18km east of Mundaú), are traditional fishing areas with wide stretches of beautiful sand, offshore reefs and dunes. They are increasingly popular weekend and holiday destinations from Fortaleza but still relatively undeveloped – a good place to do nothing in a postcard setting.

In Mundaú village the well-run **Estrela de Mundaú Hotel** (☎ 3351 9063; www.estrela.cc; Rua Vila Nova 50; r R$95; ☒ ☒) has some rooms with sea views and a huge tropical garden with pool. English and German are spoken. There are some more basic pousadas right on the beach. Don't miss the paella at **our pick Pousada Beach Hotel** (Rua da Praia 537, Mundaú; mains for 2 R$18-48; ☺ lunch & dinner), a *barraca* and pousada on Mundaú Beach run by an Englishman who spent 10 years in Barcelona.

Four buses daily leave Fortaleza bus station for Fleixeiras (R$16, three hours) and two for Mundaú (R$18, four hours).

ICARAÍ DE AMONTADA

On a beautiful bay at the end of a 30km dirt road (and 195km from Fortaleza), Icaraí de Amontada is beyond the reach of Fortaleza tour buses and is a top windsurfing spot (best from July to December). It's a place to completely unwind: apart from windsurfing, the arrival of the morning fish catch is the day's main event. There's a small handful of good-standard pousadas including **Pousada Les Alizés** (☎ 0xx88-3636 3006; www.lesalizes.com.br; s/d R$115/150; ☒ ☒), with nice gardens right on the beach at the eastern end of the bay. One daily bus runs here from Fortaleza bus station (R$24, 4½ hours).

JERICOACOARA
☎ 0xx88 / pop 3000

Jericoacoara, simply known as 'Jeri,' magnetizes travelers with its perfect combination of hard-to-reach location (its isolated position inside a far-flung national park at the top edge of the country is unique in Brazil), stunning coastal scenery, enjoyable activities and good-value pousadas, restaurants and nightlife. The village's six sandy streets are wedged between a broad beach, a series of grassy hills and the majestic Pôr do Sol (Sunset) dune, a towering mountain of sand that affords one of South America's most stunning sunsets. It is here each evening that Jeri's allure climaxes: a crowd swells – drinks in hand – to one of Earth's few locations where you can allegedly see the rare phenomenon known as the 'Emerald Sunset,' a last-millisecond flash of green as the sun disappears under the horizon. Bring your camera!

Jeri's magical charm is further implanted in Brazilian folklore by more cosmetic, but sensible, initiatives: power lines here are buried under the ground, preserving the natural illumination from the starry night sky. It is neutralized, however, by a main road that is entirely too commercial and hectic.

Orientation & Information

With the exception of a few holidays, Jeri is closed to unauthorized vehicles, though there is still more traffic than there should be. The main streets (of sand) run parallel to each other, towards the beach. In the middle is Rua Principal: buses from Fortaleza arrive at the central square here. To the east are Rua do Forró and Rua da Igreja; to the west (the dune side) are Rua São Francisco, Rua das Dunas and Rua Novo Jeri. You'll find the 'laundry district' clustered at the end of Rua São Francisco.

Many pousadas and restaurants will accept Visa or MasterCard.

Banco do Brasil (Jijoca; ☉ ATM 6am-5pm) This is the nearest international-friendly ATM, 23km away in Jijoca. 4WD trucks leave each morning between 7am and 8am in front of Paderia Jeripan on Rua São Francisco (R$10 one way). Or catch a buggy (R$100 return).

Cyber Cachaça (Rua Principal; internet per hr R$4; ☉ 9am-11pm Mon-Sat, 2pm-11pm Sun)

Global Connection (Rua do Forró; internet per hr R$2.50; ☉ 11am-11pm Mon-Sat, 1-11pm Sun)

Supermercado Tem de Tudo (Rua Principal; ☉ 7am-midnight) This supermarket will sometimes give cash back depending on its cash flow.

Activities

The steady winds between July and January make Jericoacoara a top destination for windsurfing and kitesurfing, and the gigan-

tic dunes mean good sandboarding. There are also nightly capoeira classes on the beach and decent waves for surfing. If you are of a calmer demeanor, you can visit the dunes and lakes outside town by buggy, sail on a *jangada*, take yoga classes or stroll to **Pedra Furada**, an arched rock 3km east of town.

BUGGY RIDES

Organize buggy rides through your pousada or agencies in town or the **Associação dos Bugueiros** (Buggy Drivers' Association; ☎ 3669 2284; www.jabjeri.com.br; central square, Rua Principal). The buggies take up to four passengers and prices are for the vehicle (with driver), so if you join with others it's cheaper. **Jeri Off Road** (☎ 3669-2268; www.jeri.tur.br; Travessa da Rua do Forró 207) is a helpful and environmentally conscious agency that also organizes buggy adventures near and far.

It's a memorable trip to the crystal-clear **Lagoa do Paraíso** and **Lagoa Azul**, inland near Jijoca. A five-hour trip costs R$220 in high season. Another good outing is to **Tatajuba**, 18km west, a fishing village with a beach at the mouth of a tidal river, and a large lagoon among the dunes behind the village. There are *barracas* beside the lagoon. One of the dunes actually overtook the old Tatajuba, which had to be moved out of the way – brick by brick. You can still see evidence of where the church used to be. A five-hour Tatajuba trip costs R$250.

CAPOEIRA

Classes (R$20, 1½ hours) are held at 8am and 4pm on the beach followed by a sunset *roda de capoeira* (open capoeira performance), which always attracts a crowd. There are also classes at 8pm Monday to Friday at **Pousada Solar da Malhada** (☎ 3669 2094; Rua da Igreja) – all welcome.

KITESURFING

The best spot in the area is Praia do Preá, 10km east of Jeri along the beach. Here **Kite Club Preá** (☎ 3669 2359; www.kiteclubprea.com), an official IKO (International Kiteboarding Organization) center, offers classes (R$380 for four hours), equipment rental (around R$150 for four hours) and guided kiting. For an outstanding English-speaking instructor, call **Marcio Hernandez** (☎ 9922 2614), who does nine-hour classes for R$750.

SURFING & SANDBOARDING

There are good waves for surfing (best from about March to May) right out in front of Jeri beach. **Roots Brasil** (☎ 9910 0778; Rua do Forró), just back from the beach, rents boards (R$20/60 per hour/day) and gives classes (R$50 per hour). It also rents sandboards (R$8 per hour).

WINDSURFING
The east-west-aligned coast here brings excellent breezes almost any time of year, but July to January is best. Jeri hosts international competitions. Abeta member **ClubeVentos** (☎ 3669 2287; www.clubventos.com; classes beginner/advanced per 1½ hr R$120/215, rentals per 3hr/1 day/2 day R$104/165/260), on Jeri beach just east of Rua do Forró, is professional and well-equipped, though there are cheaper operators. It also rents kayaks, surfboards and Stand Up Paddle boards (save 10% by booking rentals in advance on the web).

Tours
Apart from buggy day trips (p579) you can also take buggy or 4WD trips as far west as Parnaíba (p586) and the Lençóis Maranhenses (p597) – easier though more expensive than public transport. Good agencies are the pioneering **Jeri Off Road** (p579) and **Jeri Moon** (☎ 3669 2231; Rua do Travessa Smael; www.jerimoon.com). You can also organize trips from Jeri through a number of Fortaleza agencies.

Sleeping
There are dozens of pousadas and small hotels in Jericoacoara.

Hostel Jeri Brasil (☎ 3669 2263; www.jeribrasil.com.br; Rua da Matriz 305; dm from R$30, r from R$80; ☒ ☎) The new HI-affiliated option was in complete renovation disarray on our visit, but it appeared to offer simple rooms with TV, storage lockers, air-con and hot-water showers. Same-sex dorms sleep six. There is a small kitchen for guest use.

Jeri Bed & Breakfast (☎ 3669 2268; www.jeri.tur.br; Rua do Forró; s/d/tr with fan R$60/80/100) It has three adorable rooms (five more are on the way), all with hot water, in-room safes, TVs, great bathrooms and well-appointed beds with nice exposed-brick walls and hardwood floors. It's run by the English-speaking folks at Jeri Off Road. Can't be beaten for value.

Vila dos Ipês (☎ 3669 2241; www.viladosipespousada.com.br; Rua São Francisco 50; s R$100-150, d R$170-250; ☒ ☎) A charming little pousada with a palm-shaded garden a stone's throw from the beach. The colorful rooms and duplexes have

attractive wooden floors, doors and staircases, and you'll enjoy the sea view as you breakfast on bonus mini-tapiocas or crêpes on the deck. But the owner's insistence on Brazilian bank deposits from foreign tourists puts a damper on the party.

Pousada Casa do Turismo (☎ 3669 2286; www.casadoturismo.com; Rua das Dunas; r from R$150; ☒ ☎ ☒) This is a cute little purple pousada with reasonably priced, if smallish, rooms facing expansive gardens and pool area.

Pousada Jeribá (☎ 3669 2206; www.jeriba.com.br; Rua do Ibama; s/d from R$270/300, ☒ ☎ ☒) A beautiful newcomer, with tasteful, exposed-brick bungalows peppered about colorful grounds draped in lush tropicalia and bougainvillea. Spacious rooms boast gorgeous hardwood verandas with hammock chairs. The oceanfront patio and lounge is a near-perfect chillout pad with views over the dunes.

our pick **Vila Kalango** (☎ 3669 2289 www.vilakalango.com.br; Rua das Dunas 30; r from R$270, bungalows from R$460; ☒ ☎ ☒) A longtime top-end favorite, Vila Kalango's round-brick bungalows are little serene escape pods (some are elevated on stilts with driftwood staircases leading the way), with beautiful canopy beds and native wood furniture. There is a small spa, nice pool and sandy lounge area. Blossoming couples beware: bathrooms here are not all that private.

Eating
Jeri offers a great variety of excellent food for such a small place and a number of restaurants serve vegetarian dishes.

Café Brasil (☎ 3669 2272; sandwiches R$3-15; Beco do Guaxeló 65A; ☒ 1-10:30pm) In an alley between Rua Principal and Rua São Francisco, smart Café Brasil makes massive, shareable, natural sandwiches with wholegrain breads (R$10), salads, cakes, coffee, juices and smoothies. Consistently some of the best food in town.

Pizza Dellacasa (☎ 9962 3640; Rua Principal; pizza R$8.50-32; ☒ dinner) A Paulista (resident of São Paulo city) told us it was the best pizza in town. In reality, it's a far cry from *pizza paulistana*, but the frozen drinks in scrumptious flavors such as mango, tangerine and passion fruit are a tropical godsend in this heat.

Cantina Jeri (Rua do Forró; pasta R$14.50-22.50; ☒ lunch & dinner, closed Wed in low season) Excellent value spot offering a ridiculously extensive (and good) list of pastas and risottos. Dishes are meant for one, but when they show up –

placed on the table in the very pan in which they were cooked – they can easily serve two, catapulting this Italian-run midrange into the budget category.

our pick **Tamarindo** (☎ 9962 4301; Rua da Farmacia; mains R$18-56; ⏱ dinner) Far and away the most creative dining experience in Jeri, under the shadow of a giant tamarind tree. Nearly everything is cooked in the brick oven, which is the norm for the pizza, but not for exquisite gems like Brazil nut–crusted filet mignon or seasoned fish with grilled mango. From the cocktails (frozen *tangeroskas* with ginger) to the staff and service, it's a class act above anything in town.

Chocolate (☎ 9948 5536; Beco do Chocolate; mains R$22-59; ⏱ 4pm-midnight) A lovely spot with a charismatic chef-owner (Pat Gâteau), cutely nicknamed after her home-run dessert, one of Brazil's best petite gâteaux. But you'll first want to tuck into the excellent risottos here, namely the Amazonian special, with *tucupi* (a sauce extracted from wild manioc root) and *jambú* (an Amazonian herb).

Peixaria Peixe Brasileiro (☎ 9969 2173; Beco do Guaxeló; fish per kg R$30; ⏱ dinner) Some local fisherman got a bright idea: run a *peixaria* (fish shop) by day, throw some hot coals and nice tables in the sand alley by night and grill whole fresh fish for tourists. Pick your dinner – *pargo* (red snapper), *robalo* (sea bass), shrimp and/or *langosta* – right out of the fish cooler, where it arrived only hours ago. An experience!

Pimenta Verde (☎ 9916 0577; Rua São Francisco; mains for 2 R$42-46; ⏱ 2pm-11pm) This delightful little corner café with only a few tables pumps out memorable cuisine from the former chef at longtime favorite Carcará. The octopus *Provençal* (best dish in Jeri?) and the green peppercorn filet are both divine. Cute artistic touches round out the culinary happiness.

Entertainment

Everything starts – and frequently ends – at **Planeta Jeri** (Rua Principal), near the beach. Things don't get going until at least 10pm, the caipirinhas (R$5) are divine, and the music runs the gamut from hip-hop to samba. Nocturnal cocktail carts parked on the street here provide an alternative source of inebriation with concoctions such as *maracujaroska* (passion fruit and vodka).

Past midnight the late-night crowd moves on to dance at **Bar do Forró** (Rua do Forró; admission

R$5-10; ⏱ 11:59pm-late Mon, Wed, Fri & Sat) or the reggae/electronic **Mama África** (Rua Nova Jeri; admission R$5-10; ⏱ 10pm-late Tue, Thu & Sun). For something a little classier and trendier, **Tropicana** (Rua do Forró; cocktails R$7-18; ⏱ 4pm-1am) had just opened its doors when we came through. It's reminiscent of South Beach/Miami's whitewashed pool bars.

Getting There & Away

Buses to Fortaleza leave from Pousada do Norte at 8am (direct), 2:30pm and 10:30pm daily (R$38 to R$50, six to seven hours), and at 6:30pm daily with no definitive timetable in high season. You can buy tickets in advance (cash only) at their bus ticket agency office inside the pousada or at the pousada itself when nobody is in.

If you are coming to Jeri by non-4WD car, leave it parked in Jijoca, where there are parking lots for R$10 per day. The ride on to Jericoacoara – over and around sweeping dunes, lagoons and flat scrub terrain – runs R$50/150 per vehicle (buggy/4WD).

Moving on westward from Jeri, the easiest and costliest option is a tour (p580). Second easiest is to get a buggy ride about 40km along the coast to Camocim, where you can pick up a bus to Parnaíba or Sobral. The buggy will be about R$300 for up to four people. Thirdly, *lotacãos* (big, modified jeeps) leave for Camocim (R$25 to R$40; 1½ hours) every morning at 6:30am. **Carlinhos** (☎ 9932 8147) will pick you up at your pousada. Trips to Sobral (R$25; 2½ hours) go once a week at 3am on Tuesday with **Benone** (☎ 9917 5758). Sobral has bus connections to Ubajara, Teresina, Camocim, Parnaíba and beyond.

Coming to Jeri from the west, you have the same options in reverse. The 4WD *lotacão* leaves Camocim at 11:30am; and from Sobral at noon on Tuesdays. The Sobral–Jijoca minibus (R$25) departs from across the street from Sobral bus station about 10:30am (not Sunday).

CAMOCIM
☎ 0xx88 / pop 61,000

Camocim is a low-key fishing port and market town near the mouth of the Rio Coreaú in northwestern Ceará, 40km west of Jericoacoara near the Piauí border. After Jericoacoara's blissed-out traveler vibe, Camocim is a reintroduction to the rest of Brazil and, though not likely a planned stop, it's a pleasant spot to break up your journey in the shadow of beautiful river and dune scenery.

Just a short distance from town, you can sip coconuts while tanning at **Praia Barreiras**, **Praia do Farol**, **Praia Caraúbas** or **Praia de Maceió**. However, for the great majority of travelers, Camocim is just a stop on the road.

Information

Banco do Brasil (Rua José de Alencar; ☾ 10am-3pm Mon-Fri, ATM 7am-8pm daily) Exchange and ATM.

Inc-Camocim (☎ 3621 6800; www.incomingcamocim .com.br; Rua Alcindo Rocha 56; ☾ 8am-4pm Mon-Fri, 8am-noon Sat) This helpful agency can help you to maneuver through a region with little public transportation.

Sleeping & Eating

Hotel Ilha do Amor (☎ 3621 1570; www.hotelilhadoamor .com.br; Av Beira Mar 2081; s from R$85, d from R$95; 🅿 🛜 🛝) The dated interior may need a bit of renovation, but, hey, you're in Camocim. The Ilha is spacious and well-equipped, with comfortable rooms set around a pool, directly across from the picturesque waterfront.

O Fortim (Av Beira Mar; mains for 2 R$23-33; ☾ 9am-11pm) Don't judge this unfussy seafooder by its rough staff or simple appearance – the cook knows the deal. Tasty dishes at down-to-earth prices, 650m down from Hotel Ilha.

Getting There & Away

From Camocim's **bus station** (☎ 3621 0028; Praça Sinhá Trévia) buses run to Parnaíba (R$16.50, two hours, 4pm), Sobral (R$11.50 to R$15, three hours, four to five daily) and Fortaleza (R$30 to R$99, seven hours, four to five daily). One bus daily departs for Ubajara (R$10.90, three hours, 2pm) on a new road that now offers travelers a more direct route from Jericoacoara to Parque Nacional de Ubajara (p583).

A 4WD truck and/or Jeep leave the Mercado Central for Jericoacoara (R$35, 1½ to three hours) at 11am Monday to Friday. Or you can hire a beach buggy in Camocim for the ride to Jericoacoara. Prices start at R$230 but are negotiable.

SOBRAL

☎ 0xx88 / pop 182,000

Although Sobral is an industrial center of some importance with a riverside walkway along the Rio Acaraú, it's a hot, characterless place where you won't likely linger longer than to change buses.

There are buses to Camocim (R$12.50 to R$16, 2½ hours, five daily, 1:15am to 8pm), Fortaleza (R$25, four hours, 12 daily), Parnaíba (R$33 to R$85, five hours, five daily), Ubajara ($9.50 to R$12.50, two hours, six daily) and points beyond.

Minibuses to Jijoca (R$25) leave at 10:30am across the street from the bus station Monday to Saturday.

SERRA DE BATURITÉ

☎ 0xx85

The interior of Ceará is not limited to the harsh landscapes of the *sertão*. There are also ranges of hills breaking up the monotony of the sun-scorched land. The Serra de Baturité is the range closest to Fortaleza – an island of green, with coffee, bananas and flowers cultivated around the cliffs and jagged spines of the hills. The climate is tempered by rain and the evenings are cool.

The two prettiest villages on the heights of the *serra* (mountain range) are **Guaramiranga** and **Pacoti**, 99km and 92km respectively from Fortaleza and reached by roads that wind uphill between lushly vegetated slopes with flowering trees. Everywhere you turn here seems to have a fantastic view. The villages are dotted with prettily painted houses and the tropical flowers cultivated here add further splashes of color. A visit here is good for a change of temperature, beautiful scenery, and walks and horseback rides along the many trails. A paved road leads to Pico Alto (1115m), the highest point in the range, 13km from Guaramiranga. When the morning mist clears the views over the *sertão* from here are fantastic.

Sleeping & Eating

There are plenty of places to stay and eat in Guaramiranga at a range of budgets, and other lodgings dotted around the countryside. As the hills are a popular weekend retreat from Fortaleza, prices can go up from Friday to Sunday. Many hotels offer lunch and dinner.

Estância Vale das Flores (☎ 3264 6365; www.vale dasflores.com.br; Sítio São Francisco; r from R$120; 🅿 🛝) An attractive country hotel close to Pacoti, Vale das Flores offers plenty to do, with a swimming pool, a fishing lake, games and horse rental. Prices double on weekends.

Hotel Senac Guaramiranga (☎ 3321 1106; senac guaramiranga@ce.senac.br; Sítio Guaramiranga; s R$120-170, d R$150-190; 🅿 🛜 🛝) The Senac doubles as a training center for hotel staff in

Guaramiranga. It has ample rooms with wooden shutters, and in most cases verandas, in luxuriant grounds with a good pool. It's 750m from the main street, up Rua Matos Brito.

Hofbräuhaus (☎ 3328 0004; www.hofbrauhaus-brasil.com; Estrada de Aratuba; d R$125-150; ☒ ☜) The mountain chalets of Hofbräuhaus are your little bit of Deutschland in Ceará. Each of the 20 odd chalets was designed by a different Ceará architect/artist. There's hearty food and plentiful beers (first one on the house if you email them), but wi-fi runs per hour (R$5). It's about 20km from Guaramiranga, past the village of Mulungu.

Getting There & Away

Buses to Pacoti (R$8.50, three hours) and Guaramiranga (R$10.50, 3½ hours) leave Fortaleza's bus station seven times per day.

PARQUE NACIONAL DE UBAJARA
☎ 0xx88

The entrance to this **national park** (admission with guide R$4; ☒ 8am-4pm Tue-Sun) is 3km from the small town of Ubajara, 325km west of Fortaleza. The main attractions are giant caves, the cable car down to them, and walks in the surrounding forest. At 850m above sea level, the surrounding area has relatively cool temperatures that provide a welcome respite from the searing heat of the *sertão*.

Caves

Nine chambers with strange limestone formations extend more than 500m into the side of a mountain. The main formations seen inside the caves are **Pedra do Sino** (Bell Stone), **Salas da Rosa** (Rose Rooms), **Sala do Cavalo** (Horse Room) and **Sala dos Retratos** (Portrait Room). A **cable car** (per person one way R$4; ☒ 9am-2:30pm) makes the descent from the park entrance to the cave quick and easy. Last entry to the cave is at 2pm and the last cable car up is at 3pm. But if you fancy a beautiful hike take the 7km trail down to the caves via two waterfalls and a lookout point. Hikers must be accompanied by a park guide, leaving from the entrance at 8am, 9am and 10am. Wear sturdy footwear and take enough to drink. You can catch the cable car back up.

Sleeping & Eating

Sítio do Alemão (☎ 9961 4645; www.sitio-do-alemao.20fr.com; Sítio Santana; s R$35-65, d R$50-80; ☒ ▢) There are wonderful vistas over the *sertão* from this property, 4km from Ubajara and 1.5km from the park entrance. It's run by a German-Brazilian couple. Trips to the region's highlight, the beautiful Cachoeira do Frade (a series of waterfalls in a canyon 25km away) and (reluctantly due to the strain on the car) to the Parque Nacional de Sete Cidades (p588) are also offered. The rustic chalets are tucked away on lushly vegetated grounds.

Pousada Gruta (☎ 3634 1375; pousadagruta@hotmail.com; Sítio Amazonas; s/d from R$40/80) This small pousada offers basic rooms – some spiffier than others – but the difference here is with the owner's special attention to regional details: coffee roasted on premises with *rapadura* (dried sugarcane juice), served with sugar cane honey; and his dangerous invention, the *maracuchaça*, a lethal cocktail made with *cachaça* and *maracujá* (passion fruit), served in the frozen shell of the fruit.

Nevoar (☎ 3634 1312; Av Mons Gonçalo Eufrásio 171; mains for 2 R$16-70; ☒ lunch & dinner) The best restaurant in town offers good regional fish and meat dishes, a wildly varied, world-savvy wine list and better sushi than some parts of Germany (so reported at least one German tourist).

Getting There & Around

Buses leave Ubajara for Fortaleza (R$27.50 to R$35.50, six hours, six daily) via Sobral, and for Piripiri (R$15, two hours) and Teresina (R$35, six hours) at 7:30am. There are more connections from Tianguá, on Hwy BR-222 17km north of Ubajara. Frequent minibuses link Tianguá to Ubajara (R$2 to R$4); a taxi is R$30. If you are heading to Jericoacoara from here, there is one bus for Camocim (R$10.90, three hours, 9:30am), where you can most easily connect to Jeri, but you'll need to sleep one night in Camocim.

To reach the park entrance from Ubajara, either walk or take a taxi (R$12).

JUAZEIRO DO NORTE
☎ 0xx88 / pop 250,000

Juazeiro do Norte, 528km from Fortaleza in the deep south of Ceará, is a magnet for followers of Padre Cícero (1844–1934), who lived here in the early 20th century and became a controversial figure of the *sertão*. Not only was he a priest with several miracles to his credit and a great record of care for the poor, he also exercised a strong political influence.

CEARÁ, PIAUÍ & MARANHÃO

His astonishing rise to fame started when an elderly woman received the host from him at Mass and claimed that it had miraculously turned to blood. Soon he was being credited with all kinds of miracles, and thousands of his followers settled in Juazeiro. Padre Cícero and his followers were later drawn into the rivalry between different factions of the Ceará elite, with Juazeiro becoming a scene of armed conflict in the so-called Sedition of Juazeiro (1913–14). Despite the Catholic Church's unwillingness to beatify Padre Cícero, the adoration of his followers is as strong as ever. Some two million pilgrims come to Juazeiro every year.

Though the town itself is not particularly attractive, Juazeiro lies close to the main roads across the *sertão*, and the Cícero phenomenon makes it an interesting detour.

Sights
On the hill above town, the Colina do Horto, accessible either by road or along a path laid out like a cross, is the colossal **statue of Padre Cícero** (25m), built in 1969 and claimed to be the third-highest concrete statue in the world – only beaten by Cristo Redentor (in Rio) and the Statue of Liberty (New York). Nearby are a small chapel and a building filled with wooden and wax replicas of every conceivable body part – offerings that represent areas of the body supposedly cured by Padre Cícero's miraculous powers. **Padre Cícero's tomb** (Praça do Socorro) is beside the Capela NS do Perpétua Socorro.

If you are interested in *literatura de cordel*, popular pamphlet literature for the masses with woodcut illustrations and verses on topics such as biographies of famous figures, love stories, opinions and views, visit the **Gráfica de Literatura de Cordel** (☎ 9201 1143; cnr Av Castelo Branco & Rua José de Alencar; ⏰ 7:30-11:30am & 1:30-5:30pm Mon-Sat), a workshop where you can see the pamphlets being produced for sale.

Festivals & Events
The best time to witness the devotion Padre Cícero inspires is during the festivals and pilgrimages. On March 24, the **Aniversário do Padre Cícero** celebrates Padre Cícero in legend and song. The commemoration of his death takes place on July 20. The **Dia do Romeiro e Festa do Padre Cícero**, November 1, sees 200,000 worshippers processing from the city's Igreja Matriz to his tomb. The four days leading up to it are filled with *romarias* (pilgrimage processions).

Sleeping & Eating
There is no lack of accommodations, except during the main festivals.
Hotel San Felipe (☎ 3511 7904; www.sanfelipehotel .com.br; Rua Dr Floro Bartolomeu 285; s R$50-83, d R$70-110; 🅿 🛇) This centrally located hotel has comfortable rooms at a range of prices.
Panorama (☎ 3566 3150; www.panoramahotel .br; Rua Santo Agostinho 58; s/d R$141/174; 🅿 🛇 🖳) The Panorama is older than the San Filipe but nicer, with a good restaurant and bar.
Mão de Vaca (☎ 3512 2543; Rua Rui Barbosa 25; per kg R$20-40; ⏰ 11am-3pm & 6pm-11:30pm Mon-Sat) A good regional *por-kilo* meat restaurant (chicken is cheaper then beef).

Getting There & Away
From the **bus station** (☎ 571 2868; Rua Delmiro Gouvéia) there are 16 daily departures for Fortaleza (R$46 to R$85, 11 hours), and daily buses to all other major cities in the Northeast.

PIAUÍ

Piauí, one of the largest states in the Northeast, boasts several fantastic natural attractions, including the Delta do Parnaíba, the Parque Nacional de Sete Cidades and the Parque Nacional da Serra da Capivara (one of the top prehistoric sites in South America). Colonial settlement in Piauí began in the arid southern *sertão* and gradually moved north toward the coast, creating an oddly shaped territory with underdeveloped infrastructure. Today, Piauí is Brazil's poorest state.

If you're heading into the interior, the best time for festivals and bearable temperatures is July and August. The worst time, unless you want to cook yourself, is between September and December. The climate on the coast is kept cool(er) by sea breezes.

TERESINA
☎ 0xx86 / pop 802,500
Teresina, the flat and sun-baked capital of Piauí, is famed as the hottest city in Brazil. Founded in 1852, it was Brazil's first planned city. The fatal flaw? Failure to plan anything interesting. It has a lot of hospitals and, as a regional medical center, receives patients from neighboring states. However, most people who have a choice in the matter don't

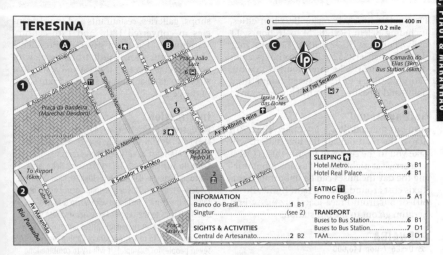

TERESINA

0 ———————— 400 m
0 ———————— 0.2 mile

INFORMATION
Banco do Brasil.....................1 B1
Singtur.................................(see 2)

SIGHTS & ACTIVITIES
Central de Artesanato............2 B2

SLEEPING
Hotel Metro..........................3 B1
Hotel Real Palace..................4 B1

EATING
Forno e Fogão.......................5 A1

TRANSPORT
Buses to Bus Station..............6 B1
Buses to Bus Station..............7 D1
TAM.....................................8 D1

make it to Teresina or, if they do, are simply in transit.

If you are keen to see a provincial Brazilian city unadulterated by tourism, this is your chance; otherwise, keep moving.

Information

Banco do Brasil (Rua Álvaro Mendes; 10am-4pm Mon Fri, ATMs 6am-10pm daily) Just one of the ATMs here accepts international cards.

Piemtur (www.piemtur.pi.gov.br) The state tourism department's website has some useful information.

Singtur (8852 9448; Central de Artesanato, Praça Dom Pedro II; 8am-2pm Mon-Sat) The local guide syndicate has a small information desk for tourist information.

Sights & Activities

The **Central de Artesanato** (3222 5772; Praça Dom Pedro II; admission free; 8am-6pm Mon-Fri, 9am-3pm Sat) has crafts from all over Piauí and is Teresina's main focus of interest for visitors. It is pleasant to browse around a broad courtyard of shops that sell small sculptures, leather articles, extremely intricate lacework, colorful hammocks, opals and soapstone from the town of Pedro Segundo. There are also liqueurs and sweet preserves made from such native plants as *genipapo* (genipap), *caju* (cashew), *buriti* (a palm-tree fruit) and *maracujá*. There's a café here as well and the courtyard is enlivened by sculptures including an interesting iron monument commemorating finds at Parque Nacional Serra da Capivara.

Sleeping & Eating

Hotel Metro (9408 0685; metro_hotel@hotmail.com; Rua 13 de Maio 85; s/d R$75/85;) Rooms are a lot more bland than the hip retro logo, but staff is friendly and breakfast sizable at this nicely central hotel with a popular lunch *por-kilo*.

Hotel Real Palace (2107 2700; www.realpalace hotel.com.br; Rua Areolino de Abreu 1217; s/d R$145/170;) This is a smooth midrange option that guarantees a comfortable stay in central Teresina and has a good restaurant.

Forno e Fogão (3222 9700; Luxor Piauí Hotel, Praça Marechal Deodoro 310; buffet R$24; noon-3pm) You'd be a fool to lunch anywhere other than this great-value, well presented regional buffet.

Camarão do Elias (3232 5025; Av Pedro Almeida 457; mains for 2 R$32-50; 5:30pm-1am Mon-Sat, 11am-4pm Sun) A 10-minute taxi ride (about R$12) east of the center, Camarão do Elias is famed for its original seafood recipes. Try the house specialty *moqueca á R Drummond,* a delicious fish stew with lime sauce, garlic and vegetables.

Getting There & Away

AIR

The **airport** (3133 6270) is on Av Centenário, 6km north of the center. Direct flights go to Fortaleza, Brasília and Rio de Janeiro City. Airline offices:

Gol/Varig (0300-115 2121; airport)

TAM (3228 8600; Rua Félix Pacheco 2008)

BUS

Teresina's **bus station** (3222 8276) is 6km southeast of the town center on Hwy BR-343.

Destinations include major Brazilian cities, including Belém (R$128, 14 to 16 hours, 11 daily), Fortaleza (R$72 to R$98, 11 hours, four daily), Parnaíba (R$52 to R$67, six hours, eight daily), Piripiri (R$26, three hours, 13 daily), São Luís (R$54 to R$94, seven hours, nine daily) and Ubajara (R$38, five hours, noon).

Getting Around

Any bus marked 'Praça João Luiz' (R$1.70), across the road outside the bus station, will take you to the center of town – this is OK if you arrive at night, when it's cooler, but during the day the buses can be unbearably hot. Taxis cost around R$20 in light traffic. Buses 601 or 602 from Praça João Luiz or Av Frei Serafim go out to the bus station.

PARNAÍBA

☎ 0xx86 / pop 146,000

Parnaíba was a major port until its river silted up (the port was moved to nearby Luís Correia) and its carnaúba-palm wax industry died when artificial waxes were invented for cosmetics and car polish – and along with it surely its charms. It's a stepping stone on the coastal route from Jericoacoara to the Lençóis Maranhenses, and the starting point for trips into the beautiful Delta do Parnaíba, but otherwise not likely to make the highlight reel itself.

Orientation

Visitors gravitate to Porto das Barcas on the Rio Igaraću waterfront, a complex of craft shops, galleries, restaurants and travel agencies in converted 18th- and 19th-century warehouses. The main street, Av Presidente Vargas, runs 1km south from here, with commercial streets to its west and residential streets to its east. The bus station is 5km south of the center.

Information

Bradesco (Av Presidente Vargas 403; ☼ 10am-3pm Mon-Fri, ATMs 6am-10pm daily) Does currency exchange and has ATMs that accept international cards.

Casa do Turismo (☎ 3321 1243; www.deltaparna iba.com; Porto das Barcas; ☼ 7:30am-9:30pm Mon-Sat, 7:30am-11am Sun) This very helpful agency offers boat tours of the delta – including with Micro & Macro – and 4WD trips to the Lençóis Maranhenses, Sete Cidades and Jericoacoara, at reasonable prices (around R$550 for a one-day trip to Jericoacoara or Caburé for up to seven people, for example). It will try to combine lone travelers with groups if you prefer. English and German are spoken.

Ecoadventure Tour (☎ 3323 9595; www.ecoadven ture.tur.br; Porto das Barcas) Offers a range of tours in the region.

Prefeitura Tourist Information (Av Pinheiro Machado; ☼ 7-11am & 4-8pm Mon-Fri, 7am-noon Sat) Has a few maps and pamphlets to hand out. Located at the bus station.

Sleeping

Residencial Pousada (☎ 3322 2931; www.residencial pousada.com.br; Rua Almirante Sampaio 375; s/d R$26/37, with air-con R$32/47; ☒ ☐) The staff can be severely

DETOUR: DELTA DO PARNAÍBA

The **Delta of the Rio Parnaíba** (sometimes called the Delta das Américas) is a 2700-sq-km expanse of islands, beaches, lagoons, channels, sand dunes and mangrove forest, teeming with wildlife. Around 65% of its area is in the state of Maranhão, but the easiest access is from Parnaíba. Tour boats leave from Porto dos Tatus, 14km north of Parnaíba. Three types of day trips lasting eight or nine hours are offered by the agencies at Porto das Barcas. The least desirable options include small-boat trips costing R$50 per person (minimum R$200) plus transfer (R$10) to and from Porto dos Tatus (food and drink not included) and the larger party boats holding 40 to 80 people. The latter go daily in high season (Christmas to Carnaval, July and August), but otherwise Saturday only. The price of R$50, plus R$10 for transfers to/from Porto dos Tatus, includes meals.

By far the best option is a new trip called – for lack of a better name – **Micro & Macro** (R$80 per person including transfers, four-person minimum), which travels to smaller tributaries by canoe (read: silence), allowing for a better chance of viewing caimans, monkeys, iguanas and, if you're lucky, highly colorful guará (red ibis) – the large party boats and their noise make this unlikely on the other trips. There's usually a beach stop at the murky-but-beautiful apocalyptic sands at Pontal das Canárias just over the Maranhão border and the option of a seafood lunch at lovely waterside restaurant. Casa do Turismo is a good agency to organize the smaller boat trips – go to any agency to book the party boat.

short on personality, but this budget spot in a neat, cottagelike building is good value, and, one block east of Av Presidente Vargas, excellently located. The rooms are large and have high ceilings.

Hotel Cívico (☎ 3322 2470; www.hotelcivico.com.br; Av Chagas Rodrigues 474; s/d R$55/80, with air-con R$75/105; ❉ ❉)) Just off the south end of Av Presidente Vargas, the well-run Cívico has pleasantly campy 1970s decor, a big buffet breakfast and an attractive pool area, and it slashes prices in the low season.

Recanto dos Pássaros (☎ 9977 4411; Ilha das Canárias; chalets R$50/100) This tranquil pousada and restaurant is the usual lunch stop (mains for two R$30 to R$46) on the excellent Micro & Macro tour – there's fabulous *moquecas*, fish with orange sauce and homemade potato chips! – but you can also nab one of four rustic but cute chalets if you want to spend a few days in the delta itself, far from less desirable Parnaíba. The pousada is on the banks of the Río Igarapé do Galego on Ilha das Canárias.

Eating

Sabor e Arte (☎ 3321 1234; Av 7 de Janeiro 121, Porto Salgado; mains R$8-45; ❉ 11am-last customer) In a new riverfront location 200m southeast of Porto das Barcas, this longtime favorite is a relaxed place with interesting original art on the walls. The dishes themselves are works of art – beautifully presented, delicious seafood and meat dishes. The owners also run the Casa do Turismo agency nearby.

Caranguejo Expresso (☎ 3323 9653; Rua Quentinha Peres 64; mains for 2 R$22-35; ❉ 11am-midnight) Locally famous for its enormous and delicious *torta de caranguejo* (crab omelette; R$35; serves three easily). Don't expect *expresso* service but do expect it to be worth the wait. Take mosquito repellent in the evening.

Getting There & Around

From the **bus station** (☎ 3323 7300; Av Pinheiro Machado) there are services to Fortaleza (R$69 to R$127, nine hours, four daily, via Camocim and/or Sobral), São Luís (R$60 to R$71, eight hours, 6am, 7am and 8pm), Teresina (R$50 to R$65, six hours, eight daily via Piripiri), and Tutóia (R$16, three hours, seven a day Monday to Saturday). You can buy tickets for these destinations (except Tutóia) at **Clip** (☎ 3322 3129; www.clipecoturismo.com.br; Av Presidente Vargas 274; ❉ 7:30am-noon & 2-6pm Mon-Fri, 7:30am-noon Sat).

Any city bus (R$1.20) outside the bus station will take you to Av Presidente Vargas. A taxi should be R$15. Going back, you can catch them on Praça Santo Antônio, three blocks west of southern Av Presidente Vargas.

TO/FROM THE LENÇÓIS MARANHENSES

The adventurous and fun direct route to the Lençóis Maranhenses (p597) involves getting to Tutóia, 65km west of Parnaíba, then via rough tracks to the town of Barreirinhas or along the beach to the tiny village of Caburé. To Tutóia, the options are bus or a chartered boat through the delta costing around R$550 for the six-hour trip (ask at the Casa do Turismo). From Tutóia, passenger trucks run to Paulino Neves and from there to Barreirinhas. You would be lucky to get through in one day but there are accommodations in Tutóia and Paulino Neves. Alternatively, Parnaíba agencies offer 4WD trips to Barreirinhas or Caburé for around R$550 per vehicle.

AROUND PARNAÍBA

Piauí's 66km coastline is the result of a land swap with Ceará in the 19th century. There are some fine beaches, many of which are fast being developed. **Lagoa do Portinho** is a lagoon surrounded by dunes about 14km east of Parnaíba on the road to Luís Correia. It's a popular spot for swimming, boating, sailing and fishing.

The busiest beaches east of Luís Correia are **Praia do Coqueiro** and **Praia Atalaia**. Coqueiro has been discovered by kitesurfers. Atalaia is very popular on weekends and is lined with bars selling drinks and seafood. **Carnaubinhas**, 15km east of Luís Correia, is another fine beach but much more tranquil. **Lagoa do Sobradinho**, 6km inland here, is renowned for its shifting sands that bury surrounding trees. **Macapá**, 43km east of Luís Correia, has a few pousadas and is a possible base for exploring the deserted beaches further east – including **Barra Grande** (considered by many to be the pick of the bunch and a budding kitesurfer destination) and, just before the border with Ceará, **Cajueiro da Praia**.

Local buses to Luís Correia leave Parnaíba's Praça Santo Antônio about hourly, but the best way to get around this coast is in your own vehicle or a taxi, or to take a tour. A taxi from Parnaíba to Praia Atalaia costs R$30 to R$40.

THE EINSTEIN MONKEYS OF PIAUÍ

In the deep, deep south of Piauí, the **Parque Nacional das Nascentes do Rio Parnaíba** (Parnaíba River Headwaters National Park), Brazil's biggest national park outside the Amazon region, was only declared in 2002. The park's beautiful landscape of red rock mesas rising from cerrado grasslands straddles neighboring Maranhão, Tocantins and Bahia states as well. It is already celebrated as the home not only to a sizable population of the endangered hyacinth macaw (a gorgeous, large, deep blue-colored bird), but also to the most technologically advanced monkeys on the planet.

Brown capuchin monkeys here, dubbed 'Einstein monkeys' by scientists, have the intelligence to select exceptionally hard igneous stones from a river bed – sometimes half their own weight – and drag them hundreds of meters to a clearing where they use them to crack open their favored diet of palm nuts by slamming them down on the nuts from above their heads. No such advanced tool use by monkeys anywhere else on the planet is known to scientists.

The monkeys, macaws and plenty more wildlife can all be seen at Hyacinth Camps, a comfortable three-site lodge in the park. Visits are available through **Tropical Nature Travel** (www .tropicalnaturetravel.com): a five-day stay costs US$1447 per person, based on double occupancy. The price includes transfers from Barreiras, some 300km south in Bahia state, which can be reached by bus or flight from Brasília.

PARQUE NACIONAL DE SETE CIDADES
☎ 0xx86

Sete Cidades is a small national park (62 sq km) with bizarre rock formations that some have claimed are *sete cidades* (seven cities) left behind by some mysterious long-departed culture (aliens, Vikings etc). The place doesn't need such fantasies to make it worth visiting, however. The rock formations are indeed fantastic – some look like giant turtle shells, others resemble a castle, an elephant, a map of Brazil or the head of emperor Dom Pedro II – but there are also superb vistas over a landscape that combines caatinga and cerrado (savanna) vegetation. There are some 1500 intriguing rock paintings between 3000 and 5000 years old, wildlife that includes marmosets, small rodents called *mocós* that like to pose for photos, tarantulas and (we're told) rattlesnakes, and two delectable natural bathing pools.

The park **entrance** (☎ 3343 1342; 🕑 8am-5pm) is 190km northeast of Teresina, 26km northeast of Piripiri and 8km north by paved road off Hwy BR-222. From the entrance it's another 5km (unpaved) to the visitors center. There was no admission fee to the park at time of writing, but there was talk of a R$6 to R$12 fee in the near future. Obligatory guides are expensive, so it's best to group up – guides are dished out for up to 10 people.

Tours cost R$60 for a three-hour tour by vehicle; or it's R$80 for a six-hour walking tour or R$60 for a three-hour circuit by bicycle (plus R$12 per hour for the bikes). Shortened tours are also available by foot

(R$50, three hours), car (R$30 to R$40, 1½ to two hours) or bike (R$40, two hours). Be sure to bring insect repellent, water, a hat and sunscreen.

Sleeping & Eating

Parque Hotel Sete Cidades (☎ 3223 3366; www.hotel setecidades.com.br; camp sites per person R$10, s/d R$65/80; ❌ 🏊) This simple hotel inside the park, next to the visitors center, has an inviting natural pool and its own restaurant. It's a great place to crash after a hot day in the park.

Califórnia Hotel (☎ 3276 1645; www.californiahotel .com.br; Rua Antenor Freitas 546, Piripiri; s/d R$35/45; ❌ 🖸) This big-value modern hotel is the place to stay in Piripiri, with well-kept rooms, wi-fi and cheap rates. It even has an English-language website. It's 700m from the bus station and two blocks off the central square.

Pizzaria Julio's (☎ 3276 1912; Praça da Bandeira 542; pizza R$16-22; 🕑 7am-2am) On the main square, Julio's has three outlets in São Paulo and one in Piripiri – odd – but the 56 pizzas here are your best bet for sustenance, with strange names like 'Scottish' – with *catupiry* cheese, which we're pretty sure isn't common in Scotland.

Getting There & Around

A taxi from Piripiri costs R$50 to or from the park, or R$80 round-trip including a two-hour driving tour of the park. A moto-taxi is R$20 and R$40 respectively. Alternatively, you can try to catch the free workers' bus at 7am in the main plaza, returning at 5pm, providing there's space available.

From **Piripiri bus station** (☎ 3276 2333) there are buses to Fortaleza (R$26 to R$89.50, seven hours, 18 daily, via Tianguá and Sobral), Parnaíba (R$26 to R$32, three hours, seven daily), São Luís (R$83.20, 11 hours, 7:30pm), Teresina (R$23 to R$33, three hours, seven daily) and Ubajara (R$16, two hours, noon).

PARQUE NACIONAL DA SERRA DA CAPIVARA

In the south of Piauí, 35km north of the small town of São Raimundo Nonato, the dramatic rocky landscape of the 1300-sq-km **Parque Nacional da Serra da Capivara** (admission R$3; ☷ 6am-6pm), a Unesco World Heritage site, contains over 30,000 rock paintings – claimed to be the greatest concentration on the planet. It has 800 archaeological sites and has yielded what's considered the oldest evidence of human presence in the Americas, at least 50,000 years ago. The dates put forward by researchers here were revolutionary in the archaeological world because they predated other 'earliest' finds by about 30,000 years, but they are now gaining increasing acceptance. The rock art is mostly 6000 to 12,000 years old and includes depictions of deer and caimans, and people dancing, hunting and having sex.

Over R$50 million has been spent on developing the park's facilities and the museum in São Raimundo, and a surprising number of visitors do find their way to these distant parts. The park has wooden walkways, disabled access to many sites, good vehicle tracks, walking trails, a visitors' center, lookout points and helpful bilingual signs.

Up to 128 sites are open to the public, organized into 14 circuits helping visitors appreciate the landscape, geology, vegetation and wildlife as well as the evidence of ancient humanity. The outstanding sites include the **Boqueirão da Pedro Furada**, where remains of cooking fires provided evidence of human presence 50,000 years ago (this site is equipped with illumination for night visits); and the **Baixão do Sítio do Meio** and **Desfiladero da Capivara**, both with wealths of rock art.

A local guide is obligatory for visiting the park, costing R$60 per day for up to 10 people. It's best to organize a guide through your accommodations in São Raimundo Nonato. Round-trip transport options, including wait times and/or touring, are moto-taxi (R$60) and taxi (R$130 to R$150). It's best to start at the modernized **Museu do Homem Americano**

(☎ 3582 1612; www.fumdham.org.br; Bairro Campestre; admission R$8; ☷ 9am-5pm Tue-Sun) on the outskirts of São Raimundo, with excellent English info on what you will see in the park. It also exhibits the oldest human skull found in the Americas, nearly 10,000 years old.

Another attraction of the area is the appealing ceramics decorated with designs from Capivara rock art, produced by the villagers of Barreirinho just outside the park.

São Raimundo Nonato has half a dozen hotels and pousadas, the best value being **Hotel Serra da Capivara** (☎ 3582 1389; hotelserradacapivarra@ firme.com.br; Santa Luzia; s/d/tr R$78/97/115; ☷ ☷ ☷), 2km north of the center on Hwy PI-140, with comfortable facilities including a restaurant serving on cute Capivara ceramics.

Four daily buses make the 509km odyssey from Teresina to São Raimundo Nonato (R$59 to R$66, 10 hours, 5am, 2:45pm, 8:15pm and 8:30pm). Buses return to Teresina at 1pm, 8pm and 8:30pm. There are also buses from Petrolina in Pernambuco, 350km east, to which you can fly from Recife, Salvador or São Paulo.

MARANHÃO

The atmosphere-laden colonial city of São Luís and its tranquil but gorgeous neighbor, Alcântara; and the wild natural beauty of the Parque Nacional dos Lençóis Maranhenses have put the Northeast's furthest-flung state firmly on the travel map. The coastal route from Jericoacoara (Ceará) to the Lençóis Maranhenses is an adventure in itself.

Although the southern and eastern areas of Maranhão are characterized by vast expanses of *babaçu* (palms) and typical *sertão* landscapes, the western and northwestern regions of the state merge into humid Amazon rain forests.

SÃO LUÍS
☎ 0xx98 / pop 997,000

The historic center of the island-city of São Luís is an enchanting neighborhood of steamy cobbled streets and pastel-colored colonial mansions, some handsomely restored, many still deep in tropical decay. It's a charming area with a unique atmosphere and one of the best concentrations of museums, galleries and craft stores in the Northeast; but unfortunately, a general sketchiness pervades much of

CEARÁ, PIAUÍ & MARANHÃO

these streets. That, coupled with the fact that this fascinating Iberian urban fabric could be the Cartagena of Brazil were it fulfilling its enormous potential (especially at night), means São Luís could leave you wishing it would get its act together.

The trip across Baía de São Marcos to Alcântara, an impressive historic town slipping regally into decay, is an added reason to put São Luís on your itinerary. São Luís is also the reggae capital of Brazil, it is home to the highly colorful and unusual Bumba Meu Boi festivities, and it has a lively beach scene.

History

São Luís is the only city in Brazil that was founded by the French. In 1612 three French ships sailed for Maranhão to try to commandeer a piece of South America. Once established at São Luís, the French used the local indigenous population, the Tupinambá, to assail tribes around the mouth of the Amazon to try to expand their foothold in the region. But the French colony could not hold off the imminent Portuguese attack, which came in 1614. Within a year, the French fled and before long the Portuguese had 'pacified' the Tupinambá.

After a brief Dutch occupation between 1641 and 1644, São Luís developed slowly as a port for the export of sugar, and later cotton. Despite relatively poor land, the plantation owners prospered and by the early 19th century São Luís was one of the wealthiest cities

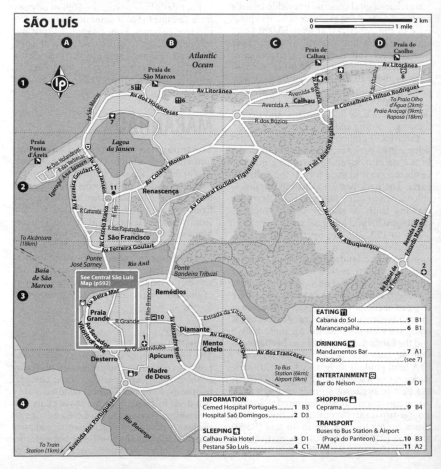

SÃO LUÍS

INFORMATION		
Cemed Hospital Português	1	B3
Hospital Saõ Domingos	2	D3
SLEEPING		
Calhau Praia Hotel	3	D1
Pestana São Luís	4	C1
EATING		
Cabana do Sol	5	B1
Marancangalha	6	B1
DRINKING		
Mandamentos Bar	7	A1
Poracaso	(see 7)	
ENTERTAINMENT		
Bar do Nelson	8	D1
SHOPPING		
Ceprama	9	B4
TRANSPORT		
Buses to Bus Station & Airport (Praça do Panteon)	10	B3
TAM	11	A2

in Brazil. All this was achieved through the labor of African slaves and today the city has the third-highest Afro-Brazilian population in the country (after Rio and Salvador).

When demand for São Luís' crops slackened later in the 19th century, the city went into a long decline, but the economy has been stimulated by several megaprojects in the past two decades. In the 1980s a big port complex was constructed at Itaqui, just west of São Luís, to export the mineral riches of the Carajás in neighboring Pará state, and Alcoa built an enormous aluminum-processing plant on the highway south of the city. A missile station was established in Alcântara, and oil was discovered in the bay. And thanks to the restoration of many of São Luís' beautiful old buildings, domestic and international tourism are now important to the city's economy.

Orientation

São Luís sits at the northwest corner of a 50km-long island, Ilha de São Luís, which is separated from the mainland only by narrow channels. The city itself is divided by the Rio Anil. South of the Anil, the Centro Histórico's street grid rambles up and down over hilly terrain, with its heart in the lower, tourism-dominated area known as Praia Grande. East of Praia Grande is the city's commercial heart; north of the Anil are the more modern suburbs, such as São Francisco, as well as the city's beaches stretched along the island's north coast.

The bus station is about 8km southeast of the center and the airport 3km further southeast.

Roteiro e Mapa Turístico São Luís (R$6), sold at many shops, pousadas and museums, is an excellent map and information guide to the historic center but be forewarned: many street names will not match the street signs – it seems each new mayor likes to re-name the streets to their liking.

Information

EMERGENCY

Ambulance (Pronto Socorro; ☎ 192; ☼ 24hr)
Tourist police mobile post (Map p592; ☎ 190; Rua da Estrela; ☼ 24hr)

INTERNET ACCESS

Neti@ando (Map p592; Rua João Vital; per hr R$2.50; ☼ 9am-9pm Mon-Sat) Air-conditioned.

INTERNET RESOURCES

Guiasaoluis (www.guiasaoluis.com.br) This site has some useful information, but only in Portuguese.
Maranhão (www.turismo.ma.gov.br) Maranhão's official bilingual tourism site has helpful descriptions, though less so in English.

MEDICAL SERVICES

These are some of the better private hospitals.
Cemed Hospital Português (Map p590; ☎ 3231 3651; Rua Passeio 365, Centro Histórico)
Hospital São Domingos (Map p590; ☎ 3216 8100; Av Jerônimo de Albuquerque 540, Bequimão)

MONEY

These bank branches do currency exchange and have ATMs accepting foreign cards.
Bradesco (Map p592; Av Dom Pedro II 120; ☼ 10am-4pm Mon-Fri, ATMs 6am-10pm daily)
Banco do Brasil Av Dom Pedro II (Map p592; Av Dom Pedro II 78; ☼ 10am-4pm Mon-Fri, ATMs 6am-8pm daily); Travessa Boa Ventura (Map p592; Travessa Boa Ventura 26; ☼ 10am-4pm Mon-Fri, ATMs 6am-10pm daily)
HSBC (Map p592; Rua do Sol 105; ☼ ATMs 6am-10pm daily)

TOURIST INFORMATION

These information offices usually have helpful, English-speaking attendants.
Airport (☎ 3244 4500; ☼ 24hr)
Bus station (☎ 3249 4500; ☼ 8am-8pm)
Central de Informações Turísticas (Map p592; ☎ 3212 6211; Praça Benedito Leite; ☼ 8am-7pm Mon-Fri, to 1pm Sat) The main information office of Setur, the city tourism department.
Tourist information (☎ 3231 4696; Rua Portugal 165; ☼ 8am-7pm Mon-Sat, 9am-2pm Sun) There's also a branch at Praia Grande.

TRAVEL AGENCIES

São Luís is full of agencies offering city tours and trips to the Lençóis Maranhenses and other destinations around Maranhão and beyond.
Giltur (Map p592; ☎ 3231 7065; www.giltur.com.br; ☼ 7:30am-6:30pm Mon-Fri, to 1pm Sat) Rua da Palma (Rua da Palma 196B); Rua Montanha Russa (Rua Montanha Russa 22) A pioneering and trustworthy agency with an ecotourism focus and reasonable prices. English-speakers are usually on hand.
Terra Nordeste (Map p592; ☎ 3221 1188; www.terra-nordeste.com; Rua Direita 295) An excellent and friendly French-run, multilingual ecotourism agency specializing in trekking, but can arrange the gamut of activities from Belém to Fortaleza.

Sights

The center of São Luís is the best-preserved colonial neighborhood in the Northeast, full of 18th- and 19th-century mansions covered in colorful 19th-century *azulejos* (decorative ceramic tiles, often blue or blue-and-white) from Portugal, France, Belgium and Germany. The tiles provided a durable means of protecting walls from São Luís' ever-present humidity and heat. The historic center has been under piecemeal restoration under Projeto Reviver (Project Revival) since the late 1980s, after many decades of neglect and decay. Many of the restored buildings house interesting museums, galleries, craft shops and restaurants, though much still needs to be restored.

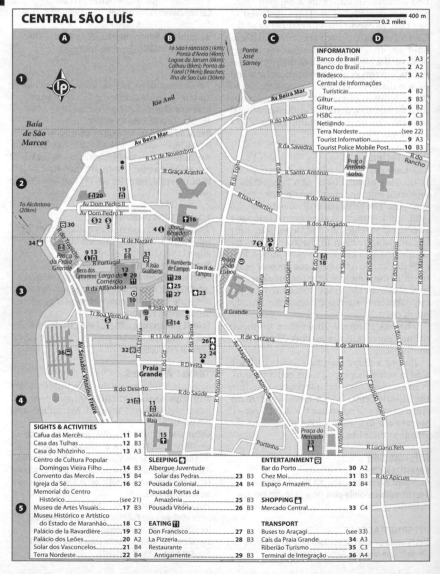

CENTRAL SÃO LUÍS

0   400 m
0   0.2 miles

CASA DO NHÔZINHO

At the eclectic and fascinating **Casa do Nhôzinho** (Map p592; ☎ 3218 9953; Rua Portugal 185; admission free; 🕑 9am-6pm Tue-Sun), you can see a collection of ingenious fish traps, a room of Maranhão *índio* (indigenous) artisanry, a great range of textiles and baskets made from cotton and the *buriti* palm, and hosts of colorful, delicate Bumba Meu Boi figurines made by the 20th-century master artisan Mestre Nhôzinho.

MUSEU DE ARTES VISUAIS

There's a fine collection of old *azulejos*, engravings and paintings at the **Visual Arts Museum** (Map p592; ☎ 3218 9938; Rua Portugal 273; admission R$2; 🕑 9am-6pm Tue-Sun).

CASA DAS TULHAS

Opposite the Museu de Artes Visuais, this 19th-century **market building** (Map p592; Largo do Comércio; 🕑 6am-8pm Mon-Fri, to 6pm Sat, to 1pm Sun) now trades in a fascinating variety of typical Maranhão crafts and foods, from dried prawns and live ducks to big bags of cashews and a bright, artificially colored purple cassava liquor called *tiquira*.

AVENIDA DOM PEDRO II

This long, handsome plaza is lined with important and historic buildings. The **Palácio dos Leões** (Map p592; ☎ 2108 9000; admission free; 🕑 2-5pm Mon, Wed & Fri) is the governor's palace, built in the 18th century on the site of the original French fort; the quick guided tour reveals a wealth of valuable antique furnishings and art, mostly French from later eras. Next door, the **Palácio de la Ravardière** (Map p592; ☎ 3212 8000) is the Prefeitura (City Hall) and dates back to 1689. A bust of São Luís' French founder, Daniel de la Touche, stands before it. The 17th-century cathedral, the **Igreja da Sé** (Map p592; 🕑 8-11:30am & 2-6pm Tue-Sun) looks along Av Dom Pedro II from its top end. Inside are ceiling frescoes decorated with *babaçu* motifs and a fine baroque altar.

CENTRO DE CULTURA POPULAR DOMINGOS VIEIRA FILHO

An impressive 19th-century mansion houses this **popular cultural center** (Map p592; ☎ 3218 9924; Rua do Giz 221; admission free; 🕑 9am-6pm Tue-Sun), with interesting exhibits on Carnaval and São Luís' Afro-Brazilian cults – especially *tambor de mina*, a local variant of Candomblé; but there's no signage so you have no idea what you're looking at.

CAFUA DAS MERCÊS

In this building that once housed a slave market (notice the absence of windows), the **Museu do Negro** (Map p592; Rua Jacinto Maia 43; admission R$2; 🕑 9am-6pm Mon-Fri) exhibits relics of slavery including a replica whipping-post, and a striking collection of wood carvings and statuettes from West Africa.

SOLAR DOS VASCONCELOS

This restored 19th-century mansion (Map p592) houses the **Memorial do Centro Histórico** (Map p592; ☎ 3231 9075; Rua da Estrela 562; admission free; 🕑 8am-6pm Mon-Fri), with models and before-and-after photos of some of the outstanding restoration works, plus a display on traditional boats of Maranhão.

MUSEU HISTÓRICO E ARTÍSTICO DO ESTADO DE MARANHÃO

In a restored 1836 mansion, the **Museu Histórico e Artístico** (Map p592; ☎ 3218 9927; Rua do Sol 302; admission R$5; 🕑 9am-5pm Tue-Sun) is set out as it might have been in days of yore, displaying all the furnishings, valuables and everyday belongings of an upper-class 19th-century family – including a private theater. It's very well-done.

BEACHES

The city's beaches are north of the center, beyond the São Francisco district. They can be busy and fun, but are far from Brazil's finest and a distinct smell pervades most of the city's water, including the *lagoa* (lake). Beware of rough surf, tides and pollution.

Praia Ponta d'Areia is the closest beach to the center (4km), and is the busiest, with bars and restaurants for beach food. It can be polluted. Two kilometers further out, **Praia de São Marcos** is frequented by younger groups and surfers.

The best local beach, **Praia de Calhau**, is broad and attractive, with hard-packed sand perfect for football (soccer) games. It is 9km from the city and popular on weekends. The large circular *barracas* along the beach cater to late-night partiers throughout the week. The calm far end of the beach is known as Praia do Caolho.

Praia Olho d'Água, 12km from São Luís, has plenty of houses and kiosks and is backed by cliffs and dunes. Another 7km further is spacious and enjoyable **Praia Araçagi**, with a

BUMBA MEU BOI

São Luís is famous for its Bumba Meu Boi – a fascinating, wild, folkloric festival. Derived from African, *índio* and Portuguese influences that mingled in colonial times, it's a rich mixture of music, dance and theater, with fantastic and colorful costumes and masks. In a Carnavalesque atmosphere, participants dance, sing, act and tell the story of the death and resurrection of the bull – with plenty of room for improvisation. It happens all over Maranhão, and in São Luís alone some 400 groups take to the streets every June. New songs, dances, costumes and poetry are created every year.

The story and its portrayal differ throughout the Northeast, but the general plot is as follows: Catrina, goddaughter of the local farm-owner, is pregnant and feels a craving to eat the tongue of the best *boi* (bull) on the farm. She cajoles her husband, Chico, into killing the beast. When the dead bull is discovered, several characters (caricatures drawn from all levels of society) track down the perpetrator of the crime. Chico is brought to trial, but the bull is resuscitated by magic incantations and tunes. A pardon is granted, and the story reaches its happy ending when Chico is reunited with Catrina.

Most groups start rehearsing at the end of Semana Santa (Easter week) in preparation for the 'baptism' of their *boi* on June 13, the feast of Santo Antônio, or June 23 (São João). Several groups perform in different places in the city every night from June 13 to 30. The more commercial performances may last only one hour, while local community celebrations can go on all night. Things get especially lively on the nights of June 23–24 and 29–30.

A smaller, but still genuine, Bumba Meu Boi festival happens at the **Convento das Mercês** (Map p592; Rua da Palma 502) on each Thursday to Sunday evening in July. In addition, many rehearsals are open to the public and some groups begin months before the traditional Easter Saturday start (check with tourist offices or your accommodations for schedules).

lighthouse, bars, restaurants and more good surfing waves.

You can reach the beaches of Ponta d'Areia, São Marcos and Calhau on bus 403 'Calhau/ Litorânea,' and Olho d'Água on bus 701, both from the Terminal de Integração on Av Senador Vitorino Freire. Fares are R$1.70. Araçagi buses go from Rua Antônio Rayol next to the Mercado Central.

Festivals & Events

São Luís has one of Brazil's richest folkloric traditions, evident in its many festivals. The city's famous festival **Bumba Meu Boi** (see above) commences in mid-June. The **Tambor de Mina** festivals, in July, are important events for followers of the Afro-Brazilian religions. **Marafolia**, the out-of-season Carnaval, is held in mid-October, and can be livelier than the main one.

Sleeping

BUDGET

Albergue de Juventude Solar das Pedras (Map p592; ☎ 3232 6694; www.ajsolardaspedras.com.br; Rua da Palma 127; dm/s/d R$25/55/70; ☞) This moody HI hostel in a restored colonial home has acceptable facilities including a sizable sitting area,

though the rooms are rather dark and poorly ventilated. Overall, it's the best backpacker option – just don't expect red carpets and welcome mats.

Pousada Vitória (Map p592; ☎ 3231 2816; pousadavitoria@hotmail.com; Rua Afonso Pena 98; s/d without bathroom R$30/50, with air-con R$70/100; ☒ ☞) Near the more expensive Pousada Colonial, the Vitória has ample rooms with improvised bathrooms, along an inner patio. It's also a family home, offering a gruff-but-disarming welcome.

MIDRANGE & TOP END

Pousada Colonial (Map p592; ☎ 3232 2834; www.clickcolonial.com.br; Rua Afonso Pena 112; s/d R$135/157; ☒ ☞) Pousada Colonial offers rooms in a lovely restored colonial mansion. Some rooms have fantastic views over the old city but others (on the first floor) have no natural light and some have mattresses as thin as sliced bread. The building is covered inside and out with unique raised *azulejos*.

our pick **Pousada Portas da Amazônia** (Map p592; ☎ 3222 9937; www.portasdaamazonia.com.br; Rua do Giz 129; s/d from R$139/189; ☒ ☞) Rambling corridors in this Italian-run restored mansion lead around two patio-gardens to attractive rooms with polished wood floors and furniture. Rooms are spacious, offer excellent mattresses and are the most charming on offer in the Centro Histórico. The excellent pizzeria (attached) doesn't hurt the appeal, either.

Calhau Praia Hotel (Map p590; ☎ 3311 1133; www .calhaupraiahotel.com.br; Av Litorânea 1, Praia do Calhau; s/d R$244/286; 🅿 🛜 🏊) This is a clean-cut, modern but small-scale friendly hotel near the division of Calhau and Caolho beaches. Though only a few rooms face the sea and upgrades such as flat-screen TVs and hi-tech air-con has pushed the prices slightly above where they should be, it's a very nice option near much of the Calhau action.

Pestana São Luís (Map p590; ☎ 2106 0505; www.pes tana.com; Av Avicênia 1, Calhau; s R$793-1340, d R$840-1389; 🅿 🛜 🏊) Don't judge a hotel by its exterior; the stylish Pestana is the most sophisticated choice in São Luís. It's a comfortable resort hotel near Calhau Beach decked out in hip earth tones surrounded by attractive gardens.

Eating

The best Maranhense food comes from the sea. Regional specialties include *casquinha de caranguejo* (stuffed crab), *caldeirada de camarão* (shrimp stew) and the city's specialty, *arroz de cuxá* (rice with shrimp, toasted sesame and the slightly bitter herb *vinagreira*). Unfortunately, compared with São Luís' other attractions, the culinary scene is rather sparse and foodies must descend on the north beaches for the best options. Many restaurants in the Centro Histórico are shut at night as well.

Restaurante Antigamente (Map p592; ☎ 3232 3964; Rua da Estrela 220; mains R$15-33, per kg R$19.90; 🕑 lunch & dinner Mon-Sat) It's a bit of a tourist trap and not as good as it used to be but this French-owned place is still a dependable lunch stop to soak up the feeling of the historic center, and a lively night option with live music shared with Le Comptoir next door (same owner).

La Pizzeria (Map p592; ☎ 3222 9937; Rua do Giz 129; pizza R$19-36, mains R$12-84; 🕑 6:30pm-midnight) Italian-run pizzeria serving excellent thin-crust pizzas…and less lovely pastas and risotto in a long, atmospheric 19th-century warehouse with historic crumbling walls. For dinner, it's the best option in the Centro Histórico.

Don Francisco (Map p592; ☎ 3221 1445; Rua do Giz 152; per kg R$22.90; 🕑 lunch & dinner) A excellent buffet that doesn't try to do every dish ever known to Maranhão, but rather a select repertoire of meals that are all wonderful. The space, full of large arches and exposed brick, is also very pleasant. It's open at night for á la carte.

our pick Maracangalha (Map p590; 3235 9305; Rua Alto Parnaiba 12, Ponta do Farol; mains for 2 R$42-155; 🕑 lunch & dinner Mon-Sat, lunch Sun) This colorful restaurant is a step above in food and service and is the spot for a blowout meal. Chef/owner Melchíades Dantas turns out creative seafood and meat dishes that match the artsy atmosphere in flair and presentation (the *caldeirada maranhense* – a seafood stew – is excellent). Staff is impeccably on point. If there's a flaw, it's either the freezing red wine or the large, noise-hugging space that can swell with kids.

Cabana do Sol (Map p590; ☎ 3235 2586; Rua João Damasceno 24A, Praia de São Marcos; mains for 2 R$51-146; 🕑 lunch & dinner) A starred restaurant since 1998, this is São Luís' other memorable spot for the Portuguese, *índio* and African-influenced *comida maranhense* (the region's traditional cuisine). It's pricey, but the irresponsibly enormous portions for two can serve four with gusto. The specialty is *carne do sol* (tasty, salted meat, grilled and served with beans, rice and vegetables – the *picanha*, steak, version is superb), but there is a wealth of chicken and seafood dishes, too.

Drinking

The sidewalk tables of Restaurante Antigamente are good for evening drinks in the heart of the old town, to the sound of live MPB Monday to Saturday.

The *barracas* along Ponta d'Areia, São Marcos and Calhau beaches are also popular drinking spots, with the added attraction of a sea breeze. On weekends, fashionable middle-class locals go to Lagoa da Jansen to listen to relaxing music and sip drinks at lakeside live music bars like **Mandamentos** (Map p590; Lagoa da Jansen) and **Poracaso** (Map p590; Lagoa da Jansen).

Entertainment

São Luís is the reggae center of Brazil, and many bars and clubs have regular reggae nights, sometimes live, other times just with DJs and vast banks of speakers. It's worth asking locals or tourist offices for recommendations – or check the entertainment listings in *Estado do Maranhão* newspaper or at **Guiasaoluis** (www.guiasaoluis.com.br). There is also a vibrant GLBT scene here.

Bar do Porto (Map p592; ☎ 3232 1115; Rua do Trapiche 49; admission R$4; 🕑 6pm-late Mon-Sat) This old standby hosts live reggae on Friday night, when the street out front becomes a party and reggae fans pack the inside.

Espaço Armazém (Map p592; ☎ 3254 1274; Rua da Estrela 401; admission R$20; ☺ 9pm-late Thu-Sat) A fashionable upper-class crowd frequents this beautiful bar, which hosts live samba, blues, jazz and reggae in a narrow, shotgun-style space under historical archways.

Chez Moi (Map p592; ☎ 3221 5877; Rua da Estrela 143; admission R$20; ☺ 10pm-late Thu-Sat) A frenetically popular club in the Centro Histórico. The downstairs operates as a disco with DJs from all over Brazil (and occasionally overseas) while the live pop, rock, samba, reggae and *pé de serra* (a slower style of *forró*) happens in the hastily thrown together dance area upstairs.

Bar do Nelson (Map p590; ☎ 3226 4191; Av Litorânea 135, Calhau; admission R$10; ☺ 8am-6pm Mon-Fri, 10pm-late Sat) With its shanty clubhouse feel, Bar do Nelson is the most famous reggae spot in town and is good for live music and dancing on Saturday nights.

Shopping

São Luís is the place for Maranhão handicrafts such as painted tiles, woodcarving, basketry, lace, ceramics and leather work. There are plenty of shops around Rua Portugal and Rua da Estrela in the historic center. The large **Ceprama** (Map p590; Centro de Comercialização de Productos Artesanais do Maranhão; Rua de São Pantaleão 1232, Madre de Deus; ☺ 9am-6pm Mon-Sat), 2km southeast of the city center, is housed in a renovated factory and functions as an exhibition hall and interesting sales outlet for handicrafts.

Getting There & Away

AIR

From the **airport** (☎ 3217 6100; Av Santos Dumont, Tirirical) there are direct flights to many Brazilian cities.

Gol/Varig airport (☎ 3217 6216)
TAM Renascença (☎ 3227 0816; Av Colares Moreira 23); airport (☎ 3217 6174)
Trip airport (☎ 3217 6175)

BOAT

Ferries for Alcântara depart from the **Cais da Praia Grande** (Map p592; ☺ 3232 0692) on Av Senador Vitorino Freire. See p597 for more details.

BUS

The **bus station** (☎ 3275 9886; Av dos Franceses, Santo Antônio) has departures to many destinations

including Barreirinhas (R$29, 4½ hours, four daily), Belém (R$95 to R$110, 12 hours, at 7pm and 7:30pm), Brasília (R$250, 30 hours, 5pm), Carolina via Balsas (R$131, 18 hours, 6:30pm), Fortaleza (R$138 to R$147, 15 to 20 hours, 8:30am and 5:30pm), Parnaíba (R$73, eight hours, 8am and 8pm) and Teresina (R$51 to R$86, seven hours, nine daily). Tickets are sold at some city center travel agencies including **Riberão Turismo** (Map p592; ☎ 3231 1621; Rua do Sol 141; ☺ 8am-6pm Mon-Fri, to noon Sat).

There have been many robberies reported on *leito* (overnight sleeper) buses between São Luís and Belém. Think twice.

Getting Around

A taxi to the Centro Histórico costs R$18 and R$30 from the bus station and airport, respectively. From the airport, bus 160 'São Cristóvão' (note: not 'Terminal São Cristóvão') runs to and from Praça do Panteon, 1km to the east of the historic city center. To catch it, walk out of the airport to the left and follow the signs.

Four lines serve the bus station from the Terminal de Integração, a city bus terminal in Praia Grande. The fastest route is bus 089 'Circular Rodoviária' but you can also catch 902 'Rodoviária-Joao Paulo', 066 'São Raimundo-Rodoviária,' or 972 'Vila São José-Rodoviária;' from Praça do Panteon, 'Rodoviária-Alemanha' and 'Rodoviária-São Francisco' buses connect with the bus station.

Bus fares are R$2.10.

ALCÂNTARA

☎ 0xx98 / pop 22,000
Across the Baía de São Marcos from São Luís is the colonial town of Alcântara. Built between the 17th and 19th centuries with slave labor, Alcântara was the preferred residence of Maranhão's rich plantation owners. In decline since the latter half of the 19th century, Alcântara today is an atmospheric amalgam of ruined, maintained and restored mansions, houses and churches set upon artistic crisscrossed cobblestones. Some experts claim that it is the most homogeneous group of 17th- and 18th-century colonial buildings in Brazil. In fact, it is better preserved than São Luís, more tranquil, and quite frankly one of the most stunning examples of historical beauty in all of Brazil. Better still is the lack of tourists, which adds to Alcântara's authentic and seductive atmosphere.

Since 1990 the Centro de Lançamento de Alcântara (CLA), the rocket-launching facility for the Brazilian space program has operated nearby. It is an odd juxtaposition: rockets alongside a slumbering colonial town.

There is a small tourist information booth inside the ferry terminal that keeps hours according to boat arrivals. Keep an eye out for *guará*, beautiful red ibises that are unusually plentiful around here and add yet another wonderful element to a trip here.

Sights

Don't miss **Praça da Matriz**, where the best-preserved **pelourinho** (whipping post) in Brazil stands beside the ruined 17th-century **Igreja de São Matias**. Around the *praça* (plaza or town square) are the interesting **Museu Histórico de Alcântara** (admission R$2; ☼ 9am-2pm) where each room has its own guardian, a source of employment for the locals; the 18th-century **Casa Histórica** (admission free; ☼ 10am-4pm Mon-Fri) with exhibits of colonial artifacts; and the **Prefeitura**, which was originally the town's 18th-century jail.

Moving along Rua Grande, with its beautiful row of two-story houses, you come to the pretty, two-towered **Igreja de NS do Carmo** (1665), recently restored, on Largo do Carmo, with the ruins of the 18th-century **1° Palácio do Imperador** (First Palace of the Emperor) beside it.

Festivals & Events

The **Festa do Divino**, on the first Sunday after Ascension Day (usually in May), is one of the most colorful annual festivals in Maranhão. It represents a fusion of African and Catholic elements and features two children dressed as emperor and empress, who are paraded through the town accompanied by musicians.

Sleeping & Eating

Alcântara is a straightforward day trip from São Luís, but an overnight stay here is the way to go and allows more time for excursions to colonies of red ibis. Both options below are about a 20-minute walk or R$10 taxi ride from the docks. Most visitors choose to eat at their pousada.

Pousada Bela Vista (☎ 3337 1569; Vila Jericó; s/d with fan R$30/60; ☒) A wonderful budget option with simple, clean rooms and an outdoor patio/restaurant full of antique knickknacks, art, a welcoming pool with stunning views across to São Luís and an inviting hammock tower that beckons lazy afternoons of doing a whole lot of nothing. It's run by one of Alcântara's most famous local guides, born and raised Danilo, who doesn't speak English but offers concise and interesting tours just the same.

Pousada dos Guarás (☎ 3337 1339; pousadados guaras@terra.com.br; Praia da Baronesa; s/d with fan R$35/60, with air-con R$65/85; ☒) Right on the beach at the east end of town, this is a very relaxing place to stay, with rustic chalets in a pretty tropical garden, and a good, open-sided restaurant-bar. You can organize a boat here to see the *guarás* themselves.

Getting There & Away

Boats to Alcântara leave from the **Cais da Praia Grande** (Map p592; ☼ 3232 0692; Av Senador Vitorino Freire) in São Luís. Two ferries leave between 6:30am and 10am and one comes back from Alcântara between 2pm and 5pm (R$12 one way, 1¼ hours). It's a good idea to buy your ticket the day before, and confirm the departure times, which vary with tides.

Full-day tours from São Luís are around R$190 per two persons.

PARQUE NACIONAL DOS LENÇÓIS MARANHENSES
☎ 0xx98

The name of this 1550-sq-km **national park** (admission free) refers to its immense expanses of dunes, which look like *lençóis* (bed sheets) strewn across the landscape and stretch 70km along the coast and up to 50km inland. Halfway between São Luís and the Piauí border, the park also includes beaches, mangroves, lagoons and some interesting fauna, especially turtles and migratory birds. The area's designation as a national park in 1981 staved off potentially ruinous land and oil speculation. It is a spectacular place, especially from March to September when rain that has filtered through the sand forms crystal-clear pools and lakes between the dunes.

The main base for visiting the park, on 4WD tours, is the small town of **Barreirinhas** on the Rio Preguiças near its southeast corner, 260km from São Luís. Other access points are Atins and Caburé, on the Preguiças near the park's northeast corner, and remote Santo Amaro on the park's western border, where the dunes come right to the edge of the village. **Atins** is a small village from which you can walk to the dunes in about an hour (a four-hour hike costs R$80 with a guide or R$30 to R$40 if you ask some local kids to lead the way). Tiny, sandy Caburé, on a sandbar between the river and an ocean beach, is a fine place to bliss out with the sun, surf and stars.

A highlight of the surrounding area is the boat trip along the tall-mangrove-lined Preguiças between Barreirinhas, Caburé and Atins. Between the last two you can call at the fishing village of Mandacaru and climb its **lighthouse** for a great panorama.

Barreirinhas has a couple of undependable cybercafés, and a branch of **Banco do Brasil** (Av Joaquim Soeiro de Carvalho; 9am-2pm Mon-Fri, ATMs 6am-10pm daily) on the main street.

Tours

Several agencies in Barreirinhas offer daily 4WD trips to Lagoa Azul and Lagoa Bonita, two of the park's biggest lakes, northwest of town. The five-hour trip to either lake costs R$50 per person in open-sided 4WD buses, or R$300 for up to four people in a Jeep. You can also take a wonderful eight-hour boat tour (R$60) down the Rio Preguiças to Caburé, Mandacaru, and Atins, at the river mouth. On a private basis for up to four people, this trip costs R$300. Both excursions are absolute don't misses.

A tour to Santo Amaro from Barreirinhas, with a visit to the nearby Lagoa da Gaivota, costs R$400 to R$500 for up to 10 people. Santo Amaro is 40km north by a sandy track off Hwy MA-402.

Recommended agencies in Barreirinhas which follow strict safety and environmental standards include **Ecodunas** (3349 0545; www.ecodunas.com.br; Rua Inácio Lins 164), **São Paulo Ecoturismo** (3349 0079; www.turismospt.com; Rua Antônio Dias 3) and **Tropical Adventure Expedições** (3349 1987; www.tropical-adventure-expedicoes.com; Rua Anacleto de Carvalho 260), but year-round, agencies pool together, so it often won't matter which you choose.

You can also take tours to the Lençóis Maranhenses from São Luís. Giltur (p591) offers some interesting options including a four-day trip with a night at Caburé for R$1046 per person (minimum two people) or, on Monday, Wednesday and Friday, R$1769 per person (minimum two people) traveling by small plane between São Luís and Barreirinhas – the aerial view of the park is fantastic. A three-day land tour staying at

Santo Amaro starts around R$672 per person (minimum two people).

São Luís–based Terra Nordeste (p591) arranges well-organized hikes right across the Lençóis from east to west (or vice versa) – the walk takes three or four days, plus a day getting there and a day getting back. English, French and Spanish are spoken.

Operatur (see p599) does half-hour flights over the park from Barreirinhas for R$180 per person (minimum four people).

You may also be offered quad-bike and 4WD tours *across* the park or *over* 'free dunes' (those *without* vegetation), but keep in mind these are not only damaging to the environment, but also illegal.

Sleeping & Eating
BARREIRINHAS

Barreirinhas has plenty of accommodations and several restaurants dotted along pedestrianized Av Beira Rio on the riverfront.

Pousada d'Areia (9961 7191; www.pousadadareia.com.br; Av Joaquim Soeiro de Cavalho 888; s R$70-80, d R$90-120;) A simple choice with nicer rooms than the common areas suggest. New, renovated rooms are bigger, with modern touches, minibars, switch-controlled air-con and reading lights.

Pousada Lins (3349 1494; pousadalins@hotmail.com; Av Joaquim Soeiro de Cavalho 550; s/d R$80/110;) A nice place to stay on the main street with a helpful staff and welcoming common area. Rooms are *'bem simples!'* but clean.

Encantes do Nordeste (3349 0691; www.encantesdonordeste.com.br; Rua Boa Vista s/n; chalets from R$150;) About 3.5km from Barreirinhas' center, this ecofriendly pousada is a little gem of comfort outside the hubbub; some upgraded chalets with biodegradable soaps, solar-heated showers and small modern touches ensure a higher-end stay. The agency within can arrange all excursions. The pousada's lovely riverside restaurant, Bambaê, is a few minutes' walk away.

Restaurante Barlavento (3349 0627; Av Beira Rio 175; mains R$21-33, pizza R$10-38; lunch & dinner) This place does well-prepared seafood priced for one or two and good pizza. The specialty *filet de peixe al molho de maracujá* (fish fillet in passion fruit sauce) is great, if a tad salty.

Restaurante Doña Maria (3349 1109; Av Beira Rio s/n; mains for 2 R$50-132.50) Out of place at the moment but what simple Barreirinhas needs more of: an upscale option serving a wonderful range of shrimp, fish and meat dishes, including seldom seen options like lamb and temperature-controlled wine. The excellent *caipirinha 'Especial'* is surely Brazil's most artistic.

CABURÉ

This tiny, beautiful and isolated sand peninsula between the Rio Preguiças and the Atlantic was built for tourism, which makes some uneasy (there was nothing here before the late 90's, and construction here has now been halted by law). The result is a few rustic pousadas and restaurants that can fuel a wonderful, get-away-from-it-all sojourn.

The best place to stay is **our pick Pousada do Paturi** (☎ 9155 7277; www.pousadadopaturi.com.br; s/d R$70/100; 🖳) on the riverside, owned by a talk-your-ear-off character named Paturi. The cabins have brick walls, tile roofs and hammocks and are set round a spotless, brick-laid courtyard. The restaurant (mains for two R$30 to R$59) is superb – the fried fish is a revelation, as much as fried fish can be, and the *camaradas* (seafood stews) are also fantastic.

ATINS

Atins is a small village spread amid dune vegetation with a sizable foreign population. More isolated parts of the park can be accessed from here – you can have many gorgeous dunes and lagoons all to yourself.

our pick Rancho do Buna (☎ 9616 9646; www.ranchodobuna.com; s/d R$90/110; 🖳) This is easily the best pousada, despite the property's chickens, guinea fowl, peacocks, ducks, dogs and cats wailing a dawn chorus from 5am. The comfortable brick chalets (built mostly from recycled materials), a fascinating common area and well-prepared food (the breakfast tapiocas are world-class) are all long on charm. The owner, Buna, can arrange an excursion to an isolated lagoon inside the park that will blow your mind. English is spoken.

Restaurante da Luzia (☎ 9132 3187; Canto de Atins; mains R$20) Get there on foot, horseback, car, boat or ox cart (ask at your pousada), but get yourself to this rustic culinary destination and pousada (R$20/40 per singles/doubles) 6km northwest from Atins proper. The venerable Luzia exquisitely prepares the simple menu, scribbled in various languages by tourists and guides. The location, isolated between the dunes and the sea, is travel memory fodder at its finest.

Getting There & Around

A good paved road, Hwy MA-402, runs east to Barreirinhas from Hwy BR-135 south of São Luís. Minibuses and non-committal shared taxis run between São Luís and Barreirinhas (R$35, four hours) with door-to-door service. You can arrange these through your accommodations at either end.

If you don't feel like getting jerked around by the shared taxis, reserve a more guaranteed option such as **BR Tur** (☎ 3236 6056), who depart São Luís at 7am, returning from Barreirinhas at 5pm daily. Buses make the same journey (R$29, 4½ hours, four daily) but start and finish at São Luís' bus station, way out of the city center. The most spectacular way to go is by small plane. **Operatur** (☎ 3217 6244; airport, São Luís; ☎ 3349 0488, Rua Brasília, Barreirinhas; www.operatur.com.br) flies for R$300 per person one way (four to six people) on Monday, Wednesday and Friday only, unless you charter the whole plane (R$2500); it also offers 30-minute flight tours for R$180 per person (minimum four people).

Approaching the Lençóis from the east, a paved road from Parnaíba in Piauí state runs as far as the small port of Tutóia. Up to seven daily buses (except Sunday) link the two towns. From Tutóia an unpaved road runs 40km west to Paulino Neves, and from there sandy tracks head 30km or so west to Barreirinhas and Caburé. Passenger trucks (4WD) normally leave Tutóia for Paulino Neves (R$10, 1½ hours) near Tutóia Palace Hotel between 8:30am and 9:30am and 3pm and 4pm Monday to Saturday, and vice versa at 4am and 1pm. Similar vehicles normally leave Paulino Neves for Barreirinhas (R$15, two hours) at 4:30am and 12:30pm from Aline Restaurant Monday to Saturday, starting back from Barreirinhas (opposite Banco do Brasil) between 8:30am and 9:30am and 3pm and 4pm. Schedules on these routes are not precise. On Sunday there may be one service in each direction. The Paulino Neves–Barreirinhas track is a very poor one passing by (and over) some superb dunescapes and isolated fishing communities.

To reach Caburé from the east without going via Barreirinhas, you need 4WD transport that can make it along the beach for the final stretch from Paulino Neves – see p587 for more information.

A public passenger boat leaves Atins for Caburé and Barreirinhas (R$8, 3½ hours) between 3pm and 5pm Monday to Saturday (depending on tides), and starts back down-river from Barreirinhas about between 9am and 10am. You can usually find other boats to take you up or down the Rio Preguiças if you don't leave it too late in the afternoon; ask at your pousada. Grabbing a seat between Barreirinhas and Caburé should be around R$60 or R$250 to charter a six-seat fast launch (1¼ hours).

PAULINO NEVES/RIO NOVO
☎ 0xx98

Due to political redistricting, this town has ended up with two names that are used interchangeably. A small fishing and farming community between Barreirinhas and Tutóia, it's a tranquil place with one main attraction: its coastal dunes, the Pequenos Lençóis. These are almost an extension of those in the national park to the west, and they're much more accessible – just a 20-minute walk from the village.

The venerated **Pousada Oásis dos Lençóis** (☎ 3487 1012; s/d with fan R$30/60, with air-con R$80; ⊠) is very comfortable and has a garden running down to the Rio Novo. Dona Mazé oozes tranquility and cooks a fabulous *moqueca* or *mariscada* (seafood stew).

TUTÓIA
☎ 0xx98 / pop 48,500

Tutóia is a relatively large yet somewhat underdeveloped town at the western end of the Delta do Parnaíba (p586). People from all over the countryside descend on Tutóia to do their shopping. The main plaza is lined with 4WD trucks that wait until they are filled with people, sacks of rice, rolls of toilet paper and plastic broom handles before departing. Trips of a few hours into the delta from here cost around R$200 to R$300 per boat.

If you'd like nothing but the best, **Pousada Jagatá** (☎ 3479 1551; www.pousadajagata.com.br; Av Beira Mar 1000; s/d R$60/120; ⊠ 🖳) is it, with simple but well-kept rooms at the mouth of the Río Parnaíba, about 1km from Praça Tremembés. Grab a moto-taxi.

THE NORTH COAST

Beyond Alcântara, the Maranhão coast is a maze of estuaries, islands and mangrove-lined channels. The region is being promoted as the **Floresta dos Guarás** (Forest of the Red Ibis) for its colonies of these colorful birds. The main town is Cururupu, with a couple of hotels and half a dozen pousadas. The **Ilha dos Lençóis** is a

large sand island with beaches, a fishing village, dunes like the Lençóis Maranhenses and a mangrove forest that is a sanctuary for red ibis. It's reached by a 3½-hour boat ride from the small fishing port of Apicum-Açu, 80km beyond Cururupu. The area has not yet been developed at all for tourism and is home to the largest community of albino people in Brazil.

Two buses a day go to Cururupu from São Luís' bus station (R$41, 11 hours, 7am and 8:30pm). For tours with a veteran, multilingual guide to the area, try **Sandwalkers** (☎ 0xx98-8864 0526; sandwalkers.ma@gmail.com), based in Atins.

IMPERATRIZ
☎ 0xx99 / pop 236,500

An expanding city 636km southwest of São Luís, Imperatriz is on the border with Tocantins state. The Belém-Brasília highway comes through here, so you might need to change buses here en route between São Luís and Tocantins or Brasília. There are six daily buses from São Luís (R$67 to R$80, 10 to 12 hours).

CAROLINA
☎ 0xx99 / pop 25,000

The town of Carolina, 242km south of Imperatriz, lies beside the Rio Tocantins and is the best base for visiting the recently designated (2006) **Parque Nacional da Chapada das Mesas**, east of town. The park's attractions are its dramatic flat-topped rocky bluffs (the *mesas*, or tables, of its name) and its many beautiful waterfalls, canyons and crystalline swimming holes.

Contact **Companhia do Cerrado** (☎ 3531 3222; www.ciadocerrado.com.br; Praça José Alcides de Carvalho 236) for 4WD day trips into the park, though be forewarned: distances are great and, due to the outlawing of open pick-up trucks on federal roads, Land Rovers are now the chosen transport and prices have risen accordingly.

One of the best routes takes in the 76m-high **Cachoeira Santa Bárbara** waterfall and the lovely **Poço Azul** and **Encanto Azul** bathing pools, for R$225 per person. A trip to the thundering, 33m-wide **Cachoeira de São Romão** and the **Cachoeira de Prata** is also R$225 per person. Outside the national park are **Pedra Caída** (admission by guided tour R$10; 🕙 10am-2pm Mon-Fri, to 4pm Sat & Sun), a dramatic combination of canyons and waterfalls 37km north of Carolina on the Estreito road; and the twin falls of **Cachoeira do Itapecuru** (admission R$5; 🕙 8am-5pm), 33km east of town on the BR-230.

Sleeping & Eating

Pousada do Lajes (☎ 3531 2499; www.pousada dolajes.com.br; Hwy BR-230 km2, Sucupira; s/d R$95/135; ⊠ ⊜ ⊠) This family-run pousada, 3km east of the center towards Riachão, has straightforward but well-kept rooms, a nice garden, and a good pool and restaurant.

Restaurante K-Funé (☎ 3531 2468; Rua José Augusto dos Santos 90; meals R$30; ☽ lunch & dinner Tue-Sun) Head here for good home-style cooking.

Getting There & Around

The most direct option from São Luís to Carolina (R$131, 18 hours) is with **JR4000** (☎ 0xx98 3243 4000) and requires a change in Balsas. You should arrive at around 7:30am from São Luís, with plenty of time to catch the 11:30am to Carolina. A faster option is flying to Imperatriz from São Luis (from R$139), then reaching Carolina via daily van service (R$35, 3½ hours, three daily).

The Amazon

THE AMAZON

Every traveler has fantasized about a trip to the Amazon. Just the name alone evokes images of dense rain forest, indigenous tribes, and abundant wildlife.

The numbers are certainly mind-boggling: the Amazon Basin is twice the size of India, and spans eight countries. At its height, the river can measure 40km across and dump 300 million liters of freshwater into the ocean per second. That's more than the next eight largest rivers combined. Yet many travelers leave the Amazon underwhelmed, having come expecting a Discovery Channel–like encounter with jaguars, anacondas, and spear-toting tribes. That simply doesn't happen – surprise, surprise – much less on the schedule or budget of most travelers.

The Amazon's quintessential experiences are more sublime than they are superlative: canoeing through a flooded forest, dozing in a hammock on a boat chugging upriver, waking up in the jungle to the call of a thousand birds or the otherworldly cry of howler monkeys.

It's only in the halogen glare of unreasonable expectations (or too short a visit) that a trip to the Amazon will feel disappointing. The river itself is massive and unrelenting, as much a living thing as the plants and animals that depend on it. Wildlife is hard to see, but that much more special when you do; the rain forest is everywhere and awesome. Indigenous tribes are extremely reclusive, but the Caboclo (mixed indigenous and European) communities that populate the riverbanks are vital and compelling.

On a river whose size is legendary, it's actually the little things that make it special. Give it some time, forget your expectations, and the Amazon cannot fail to impress.

HIGHLIGHTS

- Glide through the flooded forest at **Mamirauá Reserve** (p662), in search of the shaggy-coated uakari monkey

- Soak up night sounds and river life on **jungle tours** (p655) outside Manaus

- Rough it with rubber-tappers in **Floresta Nacional do Tapajós** (p627) outside Santarém

- Become a beach bum at **Alter do Chão** (p629), the Caribbean of the Amazon

- Ply the windy Atlantic beaches at **Ilha de Marajó** (p620) – but steer clear of the buffalos!

- POPULATION: 15.25 MILLION

- AREA: 3.85 MILLION SQ KM

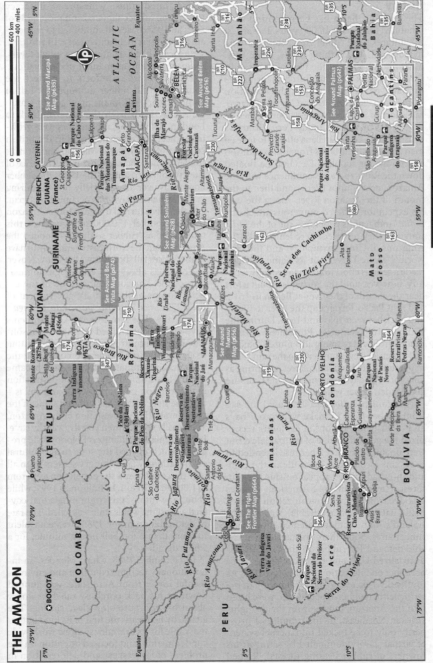

THE AMAZON

THE AMAZON

History

The Amazon Basin has been continuously inhabited for at least 10,000 years. Its earliest inhabitants were Stone Age peoples, living in hundreds of far-flung tribes, some tiny, others numbering in the tens of thousands. It was from the west that European explorers first arrived. In 1541 a Spanish expedition from Quito, Ecuador, led by Gonzalo Pizarro, ran short of supplies while exploring east of the Andes in what is today Peru. Pizarro's cousin Francisco de Orellana offered to take 60 men along with the boats from the expedition and forage for supplies. De Orellana floated down the Rio Napo to its confluence with the Amazon, near Iquitos (Peru), and then to the mouth of the Amazon River. Along the way his expedition suffered numerous attacks by *índios* (indigenous people); some of the *índio* warriors, they reported, were female, like the Amazons of Greek mythology, and thus the world's greatest river got its name. No one made a serious effort to claim this sweaty territory, however, until the Portuguese built a fort near the mouth of the river at Belém in 1616, and sent Pedro Teixeira up the river to Quito and back between 1637 and 1639. During the 17th and 18th centuries, Portuguese *bandeirantes* (groups of roaming adventurers/plunderers) penetrated ever further into the rain forest in pursuit of gold and *índio* slaves, exploring as far as present-day Rondônia, and the Guaporé and Madeira river valleys.

Amazonian *índio*s had long used the sap from rubber trees to make waterproof bags and other items. European explorers recognized the potential value of natural latex, but were unable to market it because it tended to grow soft in the heat, or brittle in the cold, and thus had limited appeal outside the rain forest. However, in 1842 American Charles Goodyear developed vulcanization (which made natural rubber durable) and in 1890 Ireland's John Dunlop patented pneumatic rubber tires. Soon there was an unquenchable demand for rubber in the recently industrialized USA and Europe, and the price of rubber on international markets soared. As profits skyrocketed, so did exploitation of the *seringueiros* (rubber-tappers) who were lured into the Amazon, mostly from the drought-stricken Northeast, by the promise of prosperity only to be locked into a cruel system of virtual slavery dominated by *seringalistas* (owners of rubber-bearing forests). Rigged scales, hired guns, widespread illiteracy among the rubber-tappers, and monopoly of sales and purchases all combined to perpetuate the workers' debt and misery. In addition, *seringueiros* had to contend with jungle fevers, *índio* attacks and all manner of deprivation.

Despite Brazilian efforts to protect the country's world rubber monopoly, a Briton named Henry Wickham managed to smuggle rubber seeds from the Amazon back to London. Before long, rubber trees were growing in neat and efficient groves in the British colonies of Ceylon and Malaya, and Brazil's rubber monopoly was punctured. The price of latex plummeted and by the 1920s the rubber boom was over. It was briefly revived during WWII, when Malaya was occupied by Japan, and the Allies turned to Brazil for its Amazon rubber. Another 150,000 *seringueiros* – this time hailed as 'rubber soldiers' – flooded the Amazon from the Northeast again, only to have rubber prices fall shortly after the war was over.

Brazil has always feared foreign domination of the Amazon region. One of the official slogans of the military government of the 1970s was '*Integrar para não entregar*' (essentially, 'Use it or lose it'). Governments have made a determined attempt to consolidate Brazilian control of Amazonia by cutting roads through the jungle and colonizing the interior. Unfortunately, those roads became the arteries from which rampant destruction of the Amazon rain forest was – and still is – fed. The state of Pará has suffered some of the most devastating deforestation in the Amazon, a fact easily visible when you fly over the state. In Rondônia, the infamous Polonoroeste program, which opened the state to agricultural colonization by land-hungry settlers from all over the country, saw the population leap from 111,000 in 1970 to 1.13 million in 1991, while about one-fifth of the virgin jungle that covered almost the whole state was felled. The rate of deforestation in the 1980s was equivalent to more than a football field a minute, for a whole decade.

In December 1988, Chico Mendes, an internationally recognized union and environmental leader from Acre state, was gunned down on his back porch by ranchers angry about his efforts to stop clear-cutting. The attack, by no means the first of its kind but remarkable for its brazenness, drew worldwide condemnation, and focused attention on the problem of lawlessness and deforestation in the Amazon. Efforts to stem the destruction grew through the 1990s; Brazil hosted the UN Earth Summit in 1992, the same year the World Wildlife Fund launched a program that, in six years, helped place 250,000 sq km of rain forest under federal protection. Yet the Amazon remained a dangerous place to advocate for environmental protection: dozens of activists have been kidnapped and killed, including, in 2005, an American nun named Dorothy Stang in Pará state.

It was also in 2005 that the Amazon suffered one of the worst droughts on record, followed, in 2009, by some of its worst-ever flooding. Neither event appeared to be related to the usual causes, such as El Niño in the case of drought, but rather arguably man-made ones such as warming trends in the North Atlantic. Yet there are no easy solutions when it comes to the Amazon: in 2010 Brazil announced it would go ahead with a controversial dam on the Rio Xingu in southern Pará. Advocates say it will provide clean power for tens of millions of people – Brazil leads the world in hydroelectric generation – while opponents (ranging from indigenous leaders to celebrities such as Sting and filmmaker James Cameron) say the energy savings are inflated, and don't justify the impact on the forest and native people living there.

Climate

The Amazon has two seasons: rainy and dry. The rainy season runs from December to June, with temperatures ranging from 23°C (73°F) to 30°C (86°F) and frequent, even daily, rains in April and May. The dry season lasts from July to November, with temperatures from 26°C (78°F) to 40°C (104°F), with less rain, though showers are still possible. As with any area as large as the Amazon, regional differences can be stark. Belém is one of the rainiest cities in the world, with no true dry season. Downpours can be expected almost daily from December to June, tapering off somewhat in October, the driest month. By contrast, Palmas, the capital of Tocantins, lies in a low river valley where the sun can be intense and uninterrupted for weeks on end, even while nearby hills are cool, even chilly. Rain-forest areas manage to pack in both extremes: heavy rains and high humidity, but surprisingly cool temperatures, especially at night or when there's rain, thanks to relatively little sunlight penetrating the canopy.

National Parks

The largest national park in the Amazon (and Brazil) is the Parque Nacional Montanhas do Tumucumaque (Tumucumaque National Park; p636), spanning nearly 40,000 sq km in the state of Amapá. Parque Nacional do Jaú (p659) is next in line, protecting around 23,000 sq km of the Jaú and Carabinani river systems, both major tributaries of the Rio Negro located northwest of Manaus. Tocantins's Parque Nacional do Araguaia is located on Ilha do Bananal, arguably the world's largest river island, while Parque Nacional do Pico Neblina, located almost a thousand kilometers up the Rio Negro in the northwest corner of Amazonas state, contains the eponymous 3014m 'Foggy Peak,' the highest point in Brazil. Still other national parks include Parque Nacional da Amazônia (p631), near Itaituba in Pará, Parque Nacional do Cabo Orange in Amapá, Parque Nacional de Pacaás Novos (p686) in central Rondônia, Parque Nacional da Serra do Divisor in western Acre, Parque Nacional da Serra da Mocidade in Roraima, and Parque Nacional Campos Amazônicos in Amazonas and Rondônia.

But national parks are just one of many designations used to protect the Amazon rain forest. *Reservas extrativistas* (Resex; extractive reserves), *reservas de desenvolvimento sustenável* (REDS; sustainable development reserves), and *florestas nacionales* (usually abbreviated FLONA; national forests) are innovative preservation designations that maximize protection while allowing sustainable use by local residents, including tourism. Mamirauá Reserve (p662), Reserva Xixuaú-Xipariná (p659), and FLONA do Tapajós (p627) are three of the better-known examples of such reserves, all with excellent ecotourism programs. Other reserves include Reserva Amaná in Amazonas state, Reserva Tapajós Arapiuns in Pará, and Reserva Extrativista Pedras Negras (p685) in the Guaporé Valley in southern Rondônia.

Of course, indigenous reserves also afford effective ecological protection by limiting access to outsiders. The largest and best known is Terra Indígena Yanomami (Yanomami Indigenous Reserve) in northern Amazonas state (see the boxed text, p672), but there are dozens more, including Parque Indígena do Tumucumaque in Pará, Reserva Indígena Waimiri Atroari straddling Roraima and

Amazonas states, and Área Indígena Vale do Rio Javari along the Brazil–Colombia border.

There is at least one notable state park – Parque Estadual do Jalapão (p642), in Tocantins – though state park status is often a precursor to national park designation. And in 2006 the state of Pará ordered a whopping 150,000 sq km of the Guiana Shield – a mostly untouched swath of tropical rain forest along the Guyana, French Guiana, and Suriname borders – to be preserved and used for the future establishment of various parks and reserves

Getting There & Away

Manaus (p644) and Belém (p606) are the major transportation hubs of the Amazon. Most travelers arrive by air – Manaus receives the bulk of international flights, including direct flights from Miami and Buenos Aires, while both cities have frequent domestic air service. Manaus has limited bus service, while Belém has buses arriving and departing from all over Brazil. Some travelers enter the Brazilian Amazon by boat from Peru or Colombia, crossing at what is known as the Triple Frontier (p664); others arrive overland from Venezuela (p674) or Guyana (p674) where there's bus service to Manaus, or from Bolivia, at the border towns of Guajará-Mirim (p681) or Brasiléia (p692). Those coming from the interior of Brazil, including Brasília or the Pantanal, can enter the Amazon via Porto Velho (p677), where they catch a plane or riverboat to Manaus, or via Palmas in the state of Tocantins (p637), connecting by bus to Belém.

Getting Around

Virtually every major town along the Amazon, Solimões, and Madeira rivers has both a port and an airstrip – but no roads in or out – so travel is limited to plane or boat. Choosing between flying and boating is really a matter of time, money and preference. Boat travel is certainly an experience, and most travelers cover at least one or two legs by water. But the distances are enormous and the boats very slow, especially going upstream. Flying gives you more time to do the fun stuff (hiking, canoeing etc) and frequent promotions can make the cost of flying surprisingly close to that of taking a boat. Bus service is available in states along the edges of the rain forest, like Pará, Tocantins, and Rondônia. Highways

conditions are improving, and there are more deluxe and direct options available, which help make the invariably long bus routes a bit less taxing.

PARÁ

Pará doesn't have the name 'Amazonas' like the state next door, so it might be easy to think it's not part of 'the Amazon' either. In fact, Pará has some terrific Amazonian destinations, and not ones you may have expected to find. You can wander deserted beaches on the islands of Algodoal and Marajó, or chill out on the white sands of Alter do Chão, a thousand kilometers from the ocean. The Rio Tapajós and national forest (Floresta Nacional (FLONA) do Tapajós) offer plenty of rain forest and riverboat options, plus a fascinating living history of rubber boom and bust. Pará has a lively modern city in Belém, and South America's oldest cave paintings just upriver in Monte Alegre.

Pará is also ground zero for Amazonian deforestation, the front lines of a pitched battle between preservationists and agro-industrialists, especially soy farmers and cattle ranchers. It's here that an American nun and environmentalist was gunned down in 2005 on the orders of a landowner she accused of illegally cutting trees. But it is also the state that, in 2007, set aside 150,000 sq km – more than twice the size of Ireland – as protected territory.

Travelers understandably see Pará as 'not deep enough' in the Amazon to warrant an extended visit. But it doesn't take long to see that Pará has plenty to offer, and those who give it a chance are rarely disappointed.

BELÉM

☎ 0xx91 / pop 1.4 million

Belém is a surprisingly rewarding city, with streets and parks shaded by mango trees, and a number of fascinating monuments and museums. The sloping central park is quiet during the week and bustling on weekends, when locals come out en masse for free performances and tasty street food. Nightlife tends toward the bohemian intellectual set: art-house theaters, small music venues, heady café-bars. From Belém you can take overnight trips to Algodoal and Ilha de Marajó, both appealing coastal destinations, and it's an important launchpad for journeys up the Rio Amazonas

(Amazon River). The Amazon is not known for its cities, and Belém can't compete with places such as São Luis or Salvador for charm or urban flair. But given time to explore, most find Belém is not nearly as rough around the edges as they expected.

History

Belém was one of the first Portuguese settlements on the Amazon River, founded in 1616. It prospered for over two centuries, relying on enslaved *índios* (and later enslaved Africans) for finding and harvesting Amazonian treasures such as cacao, indigo and animal skins, all for export to Europe. It was a fragile success, though, and an economic downturn in the early 19th century helped spark a popular uprising and bloody civil war.

The rubber boom at the turn of the century sent Belém's population rocketing, from 40,000 in 1875 to more than 100,000 in 1900. The city suddenly had electricity, telephones, streetcars and a distinctly European feel. Officials erected a few grand monuments such as the Teatro da Paz, earning the city the nickname 'the tropical Paris.'

By 1910 rubber constituted 39% of Brazil's total exports, and new ports and wharves were commissioned and built in Belém to handle the flow. Rubber eventually crashed, but the ports have remained active ever since. Today some 800,000 tons of cargo pass through Belém, mostly timber, but also soy, fish, shrimp, Brazil nuts and palm hearts.

Orientation

Belém's central park is called Praça da República, a quiet leafy spot despite the fact that several major avenues converge there. West of there, and closer to the water, is Comércio, a gritty commercial district that's not terribly pleasant or safe, especially at night. Further south is Cidade Velha (Old City), where Belém's best museums are located. East of the center is an upscale neighborhood called Nazaré, with cafés, a few hotels, and Basílica Santuario de Nazaré, Belém's most important church.

Information

BOOKSTORES
Clio (☎ 210 6369/68; airport; ☼ 24hr) Belém's best English-language selection, including guidebooks.
Livraría Newstime (☎ 3212 3298; Estação das Docas; ☼ noon-midnight Mon-Fri, 10am-midnight Sat & Sun)

EMERGENCY
Police (☎ 190)
Tourist Police (CIPTUR) Central station (☎ 3222 2602; Rua 28 de Setembro); Paratur office (☎ 3212 0948; Praça Waldemar Henrique s/n)

INTERNET ACCESS
Equilibrium (Rua Ó de Almeida; per hr R$2.50; ☼ 8:30am-9pm Mon-Fri, noon-8pm Sat)
Hilton Belém (Av Presidente Vargas 882; per min R$0.10, per hr R$6; ☼ 8am-10:30pm)
Órbitas (Av Serzedelo Correia; per hr R$3; ☼ 9:30am-9:30pm)

LAUNDRY
Many hotels do laundry for guests; or try one of the following:
Lava Na Hora (Av Serzedelo Correia;; wash, dry & fold up to 5kg R$20; ☼ 8am-6pm) Look for a narrow stairway leading to the 2nd floor. The owners live on-site, so knock if the door is closed.
Lav & Lev (☎ 3223 7247; Travessa Dr Moraes 576; ☼ 8am-6pm Mon-Sat) Self-serve R$10/12 for 7/12kg; drying R$10 per 25 minutes, drop-off R$10.

MEDICAL SERVICES
Airport health post (☼ 8am-noon & 2-6pm Mon-Fri) Provides free yellow-fever vaccinations.
Hospital Adventista de Belém (☎ 3246 8686, 0800-91 0022; Av Almirante Barroso 1758) One of the better private hospitals.

MONEY
Bradesco (Av Presidente Vargas 988; ☼ 10am-1pm & 2-4pm Mon-Fri)
Estação das Docas Has numerous cash machines in a secure setting.
HSBC (Av Presidente Vargas 670; ☼ 10am-5pm Mon-Sat)
Turvicam (☎ 3201 5465; Av Presidente Vargas 636) Busy travel agency has currency exchange in rear.

POST
Main post office (☎ 3211 3147; Av Presidente Vargas 498; ☼ 9am-5pm Mon-Fri)
Post office (☎ 3212 7093; Travessa Frutuoso Guimarães; ☼ 9am-3pm Mon-Fri)

TOURIST INFORMATION
Paratur (☎ 3212 0575; www.paraturismo.pa.gov.br; Praça Waldemar Henrique s/n; ☼ 8am-6pm Mon-Fri) Reasonably helpful state tourism agency.

TRAVEL AGENCIES
Amazon Star Turismo (☎ 3212 6244; www.amazonstar.com.br; Rua Henrique Gurjão 210) Organizes day trips

around Belém, including bird-watching and city tours (per person R$80 to R$210; see p615), plus pricey multiday packages to Ilha de Marajó (per person R$630 to R$1020). **Turvicam** (☎ 3201 5465; Av Presidente Vargas 636) Sells plane tickets.

Dangers & Annoyances

The Mercado Ver-o-Peso and the Comercio district are prime places to get pickpocketed – this shouldn't prevent you from going, but do take care. Parts of the Reduto district (between Av Assis de Vasconcelos and Av Visconde de Souza Franco) are dark and dodgy at night – definitely grab a cab when you're returning to your hotel after a night at the bars.

Sights & Activities

CENTRAL AREA
Estação das Docas

An ambitious renovation project converted three down-at-heel riverfront warehouses into a terrific commercial and gathering center. **Estação das Docas** (Av Marechal Hermes) has restaurants, artsy shops, a small theater, plus a post office and ATMs. There are also interesting displays, in Portuguese and English, about the founding of Belém and the growth and importance of the shipping trade here. The waterfront promenade is lined with attractive yellow cranes, further reminders of Belém's port-town roots, and outdoor tables with great lunchtime views. There's live music most nights, performed from a moving platform up in the rafters, slowly rolling the length of the dining area.

Teatro da Paz

One of Belém's finest buildings, the **Teatro da Paz** (☎ 3224 7355, 3212 7915; Praça da República) was built between 1869 and 1874 overlooking Praça da República. Built in neoclassical style, the architecture has all the sumptuous trappings of the rubber-boom era: columns, busts, crystal mirrors and an interior decorated in Italian theatrical style. Half-hour guided tours (R$4, free on Wednesday) are offered hourly from 9am to 1pm Tuesday to Friday, and 9am to noon on Saturday.

Mercado Ver-o-Peso

A symbol of the city, the name of this **waterfront market** (Av Castilho França) comes from colonial times, when the Portuguese would *ver o peso* (check the weight) of merchandise in order to impose taxes. The market's four-turreted

iron structure is known, aptly enough, as the Mercado do Ferro. It was brought over in parts from Britain, and assembled and inaugurated in 1901. A profile of the turrets is commonly used as a symbol of Belém.

The display of fruits and animals, not to mention the people, is fascinating. It's best to get there early, when the fishing boats are unloading at the southwest end of the market. Other shops sell medicinal plants, shoes, clothes, food and more, all at cut-rate prices. Pickpocketing is a persistent problem, so be alert when you visit (and avoid going after 5pm). Also, don't be fooled by tricksters who pose as foreigners who've been robbed and then ask you for money.

Museu do Índio do Pará

More a gallery than a museum – for now – the **Pará Índio Museum** (☎ Av Castilho França at Travessa 7 de Setembro da França) has a small but rich collection of artifacts from most of Pará's 30-plus indigenous groups. Ceremonial costumes, hunting tools, and other items are displayed in a huge converted warehouse near the historic Mercado do Ferro.

River Tours

Valeverde (☎ 3213 3388; Estação das Docas; ⏰ 9am-10pm Tue-Sun) and **Amazon Star Turismo** (☎ 3212 6244; www.amazonstar.com.br; Rua Henrique Gurjão 210) offer a variety of short tours on the river (per person R$30 to R$100), including sunrise bird-watching tours and pleasant evening cruises. Valeverde has an office and daily schedule at the pier at Estação das Docas; in most cases you can simply show up. Amazon Star requires reservations and will usually fetch you from your hotel.

CIDADE VELHA

The 'Old City' has most of the city's museums and galleries, fronting the river and four nearly adjoining plazas. The area is safe during the day, with plenty of people about, but is tucked below the Comercio neighborhood, which gets seedy at night. Take a taxi if you stay late.

Forte do Presépio

The city of Belém was founded in 1616 with the construction of the **Forte do Presépio** (Praça Frei Brandão; admission R$2, free Tue; ⏰ 10am-4pm Tue-Sun), which was intended to protect Portuguese interests upriver against incursions by the

French and Dutch. Today it houses a small but excellent museum, primarily about Pará's indigenous communities (displays in Portuguese only). There are great views of the city and Amazon River from atop the fort's thick stone walls.

Palácio Antonio Lemos & MABE

This rubber-boom palace served as city hall between 1860 and 1883, and now houses, among other things, the **Museu de Arte de Belém** (MABE; ☎ 3283 4665; Praça Dom Pedro II; admission free; ☻ 10am-4pm Tue-Fri, 10am-1pm Sat). The museum has gorgeous wood floors – cloth slippers are provided at the entrance – and a fine collection of Brazilian 20th-century paintings, including Cândido Portinari's 1957 oil *Seringal*. It has been closed for restoration for some time, but should reopen soon, better than ever.

Palácio Lauro Sodré & Museu do Estado do Pará

This grand, rambling building was once the residence of Portugal's royal representatives in Belém, and later of various governors of Pará state. One governor, Ernesto Lobo, was killed on the staircase during the Cabanagem Rebellion in 1835. Today it's the home of the **Museu do Estado do Pará** (Pará State Museum; ☎ 3225 2414; Praça Dom Pedro II; admission R$2, free Tue; ☻ 10am-4pm Tue-Sun), a mildly interesting collection on the founding and growth of Belém and Pará.

Casa das Onze Janelas

Once the home of a sugar baron, then a military hospital, the **Casa das Onze Janelas** (☎ 3219 1165; Praça Frei Brandão; adult/student R$2/1, free Tue; ☻ 10am-4pm Tue-Sun) now houses an excellent art gallery and one of Belém's finest restaurants, Boteco das Onze (see p613). The medium-sized gallery contains a mix of classical and modern artwork, plus a good photography exhibit upstairs. The café in back has a view of the mouth of the Amazon.

Museu de Arte Sacra

The **Museu de Arte Sacra** (Museum of Sacred Art; Praça Frei Brandão; adult/student R$4/2, Tue free; ☻ 10am-4pm Tue-Sun) consists of the impressive Igreja do Santo Alexandre and the adjoining Palácio Episcopal (Bishop's Palace). Santo Alexandre was Belém's first church, founded by Jesuits in the early 17th century. Impressive in size alone, the church nave also contains brilliant sculpture and detailing, virtually all done by indentured *índios* using plaster and local red cedar. The rambling Bishop's Palace has a decent collection of modern art and installation pieces, plus a café and gift shop.

Museo do Círio

From the discovery of a tiny statue of Mary in a riverbank in 1700, to idiosyncrasies of the massive procession of today, the handsome new **Círio Museum** (Rua Jóao Alfredo; adult/student R$4/2, Tue free; ☻ 10am-6pm Tue-Sun) breaks down Belém's famous religious festival, the Círio de Nazaré (p611). There's the story of how, in 1855, a rope was used to steady the statue's carriage, and has since become an integral part of the march, with the faithful jostling for a chance to pull or touch it. The rope was banned by the church for being 'unsanctified,' then brought back by public demand. It's grown along with the festival – at last measure, it was 400m long and weighed over a thousand pounds. Explanations are in Portuguese only.

Catedral da Sé

It took a while, but the restoration of Belém's **cathedral** (Praça Frei Brandão; ☻ 7am-noon & 2-7:30pm) was worth it. After years of slow, sad decline, the historic cathedral now radiates inside and out. The exterior gleams a brilliant white, while the soaring interior has polished marble floors and intricate geometric designs on the walls and ceiling, and oversized paintings of the Virgin Mary and other saints in ornate gold-encrusted frames.

EAST OF THE CENTER
Basílica Santuario de Nazaré

A bit humdrum from the outside, the **Basilica Santuario de Nazaré** (Praça Justo Chermont; admission free; ☻ 5:30am-8pm) has a truly spectacular interior, with soaring marble columns, brilliant stained-glass windows and ornate wood and tile work in every direction, even the ceiling, with faces peering straight down. The basilica is the focal point of Brazil's largest religious festival, Círio de Nazaré (see p611), which draws more than a million worshippers to Belém every October.

Museu Emílio Goeldi & Parque Zoobotánico

This excellent **museum and zoo** (☎ 3249 1233; Av Governador Magalhães Barata 376; park, aquarium & permanent exhibit each R$2; ☻ 9am-5pm Tue-Sun) contains many Amazonian animal species, from manatees and anacondas to jaguars and giant otters, plus an aviary, aquarium and excellent permanent exhibit of artifacts from ancient Amazonian peoples. It's popular with families on Sundays.

Bosque Rodrigues Alves

Though often overshadowed by the Emílio Goeldi and zoo, **Bosque Rodrigues Alves** (☎ 3249 1233; Av Almirante Borroso at Travessa Lomas Valentinas; admission R$2; ⏱ 9am-5pm Tue-Sun) is no less appealing, with well-maintained animal enclosures (including monkeys, manatees, and tropical birds) and wide, tree-shaded paths. It's especially good for families, with numerous play areas, and huge curious structures including a castle and replica grotto. From the center,

THE AMAZON

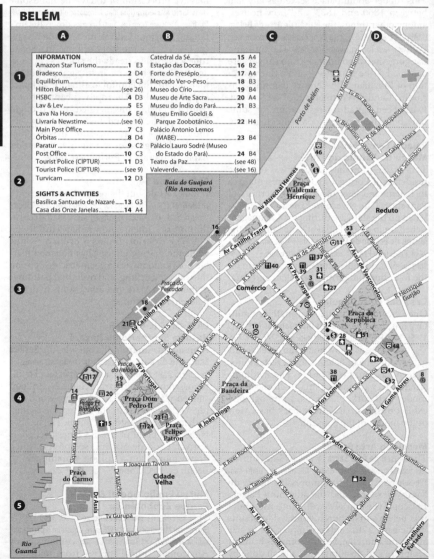

BELÉM

INFORMATION
Amazon Star Turismo.................................1 E3
Bradesco...2 D4
Equilibrium...3 C3
Hilton Belém...(see 26)
HSBC..4 D3
Lav & Lev..5 E5
Lava Na Hora...6 E4
Livraría Newstime...............................(see 16)
Main Post Office...7 C3
Órbitas..8 D4
Paratur..9 C2
Post Office...10 C3
Tourist Police (CIPTUR)...........................11 D3
Tourist Police (CIPTUR)......................(see 9)
Turvicam..12 D3

SIGHTS & ACTIVITIES
Basílica Santuario de Nazaré.................13 G3
Casa das Onze Janelas............................14 A4
Catedral da Sé...15 A4
Estação das Docas.....................................16 B2
Forte do Presépio......................................17 A4
Mercado Ver-o-Peso.................................18 B3
Museo do Círio...19 B4
Museu de Arte Sacra.................................20 A4
Museu do Índio do Pará...........................21 B3
Museu Emílio Goeldi &
  Parque Zoobotánico................................22 H4
Palácio Antonio Lemos
  (MABE)..23 B4
Palácio Lauro Sodré (Museo
  do Estado do Pará)..................................24 B4
Teatro da Paz.....................................(see 48)
Valeverde...(see 16)

take any 'Alm. Borroso' bus, and get off when you see the park's long yellow exterior wall.

Festivals & Events

Every year on the morning of the second Sunday of October, Belém explodes with the sounds of hymns, bells and fireworks. Started in 1793, the **Círio de Nazaré** is Brazil's biggest

religious festival. People from all over the country flock to Belém, and even camp in the streets, to participate in the grand event.

The diminutive image of Nossa Senhora de Nazaré (Our Lady of Nazareth) is believed to have been sculpted in Nazareth (Galilee) and to have performed miracles in medieval Portugal before getting lost in Brazil. It was

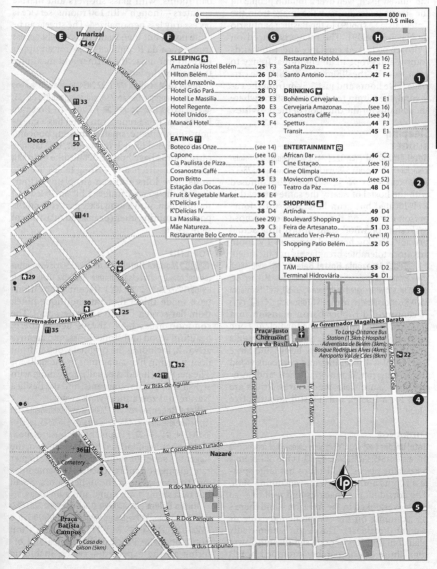

SLEEPING 🏠	
Amazônia Hostel Belém	25 F3
Hilton Belém	26 D4
Hotel Amazônia	27 D3
Hotel Grão Pará	28 D3
Hotel Le Massilia	29 E3
Hotel Regente	30 E3
Hotel Unidos	31 C3
Manacá Hotel	32 F4

EATING 🍴	
Boteco das Onze	(see 14)
Capone	(see 16)
Cia Paulista de Pizza	33 E1
Cosanostra Caffé	34 F4
Dom Britto	35 E3
Estação das Docas	(see 16)
Fruit & Vegetable Market	36 E4
K'Delícias I	37 C3
K'Delícias IV	38 D4
La Massilia	(see 29)
Mãe Natureza	39 C3
Restaurante Belo Centro	40 C3

Restaurante Hatobá	(see 16)
Santa Pizza	41 E2
Santo Antonio	42 F4

DRINKING 🍷	
Bohêmio Cervejaria	43 E1
Cervejaria Amazonas	(see 16)
Cosanostra Caffé	(see 34)
Spettus	44 F3
Transit	45 E1

ENTERTAINMENT 🎭	
African Bar	46 C2
Cine Estação	(see 16)
Cine Olimpia	47 D4
Moviecom Cinemas	(see 52)
Teatro da Paz	48 D4

SHOPPING 🛍	
Artíndia	49 D4
Boulevard Shopping	50 E2
Feira de Artesanato	51 D3
Mercado Ver-o-Peso	(see 18)
Shopping Patio Belém	52 D5

TRANSPORT	
TAM	53 D2
Terminal Hidroviária	54 D1

rediscovered in 1700 by a humble cattleman on the site of the basilica, to which it later returned of its own accord after being moved away several times.

The day before the main annual event, the little statue, having previously been taken 23km north to Icoaraci, is carried in a river procession back to the cathedral in Belém. On the Sunday itself, well over a million people fill the streets to accompany the image from the Catedral da Sé (p609) to the Basílica Santuario de Nazaré (p609). The image is placed on a flower-bedecked carriage, and thousands squirm and grope in an emotional frenzy to get a hand on the 400m rope pulling the carriage. Five hours and just 3.5km from the cathedral, the Virgin reaches the basilica, where she remains for the duration of the festivities.

Sleeping
BUDGET

Hotel Amazônia (☎ 3222 8456; hotelamazônia@globo .com; Rua Ó de Almeida 548; dm R$13, s/d with fan R$28/35, with air-con R$40/55; 🔀 💻 🛜) Not to be confused with the hostel of nearly the same name, this well-located but grim hotel has stuffy four-person dorms and tiny private rooms whose makeshift plywood walls afford little actual privacy. The kitchen and common TV room are more tolerable; breakfast is not included.

ourpick Amazônia Hostel Belém (☎ 4008 4800; www.amazoniahostel.com.br; Av Governador José Malcher 592; dm R$38, s/d with shared bathroom R$60/80, with bathroom R$70/85, HI cardholders receive R$10 discount; 🔀 💻 🛜) A century-old rubber-baron mansion in a safe area is the perfect home for Belém's one and only youth hostel. Smallish women's and men's dorms have new bunks and large lockers, plus 4m ceilings and gorgeous wood floors. Internet, common kitchen, and laundry service are welcome features. Prices are high for a hostel, but it's still an attractive place.

MIDRANGE

Hotel Unidos (☎ 3224 0660; hotel.unidos@bol.com.br; Rua Ó de Almeida 545; s/d R$65/85; 🔀 💻) One of Belém's best-value places, the Unidos has large spotless rooms and competent, welcoming staff. The corridors are spacious and well lit – so often overlooked in the Amazon – and there's no skimping on the complimentary café de manhã (breakfast). The decor is admittedly plain, but the rates here are significantly lower than those of comparably equipped hotels

around town. And just a half-block off Av Presidente Vargas, the hotel is within walking distance of most places, and close to the bus stops for everything else.

Hotel Grão Pará (☎ 3221 2121; www.hotelgraopara .com.br; Av Presidente Vargas 718; s/d R$70/90; 🔀 🛜) Another great-value option, rooms here are a bit newer than at the Unidos – especially the bathrooms, with glass showers and marble counters – though with 150 rooms, service is necessarily less personalized. The street can be quite noisy, but then again you're right across from Praça da República – ask for an upper floor to minimize the former and maximize the view of the latter.

Hotel Le Massilia (☎ 3222 2834; le_massilia@yahoo .com; Rua Henrique Gurjão 236; s/d standard R$120/135, superior R$130/150; 🔀 🛜 🍽) Close to Praça da República, this French-run hotel has a guesthouse atmosphere, small swimming pool and recommended French restaurant, La Massilia. Most rooms have homey details like beanbag chairs, hair driers and writing tables. Deluxe units have lofts and can sleep up to four, though the space can feel a bit enclosed. All rooms open onto a long leafy garden, and the pool is tempting after (or instead of!) a day of sightseeing.

TOP END

ourpick Manacá Hotel (☎ /fax 3242 5665; www.mana cahotel.com.br; Travessa Quintino Bocaiúva 1645; s/d/tr R$165/195/235; 🔀 🛜 🍽) Recent renovations have made this a first-rate boutique hotel, from flat-screen TVs to a tidy new pool. The common areas have always been superb: beautiful wood and stone floors, and creative artwork, including the original wooden front door hanging like a painting in the hallway. The neighborhood is equally appealing, with stylish shops and restaurants, and the Basílica Nazaré and zoo a short walk away.

Hotel Regente (☎ 3181 5000; www.hotelregente.com .br; Av Gov José Malcher 485; standard s/d R$167/185, superior R$190/214; 🔀 🛜 🍽) Popular with businesspeople, though well located for travelers too, the Regente's superior rooms are worth the higher rate, giving you more space, better amenities and fine views from the upper floors. Small but refreshing pool, sauna and gym areas.

Hilton Belém (☎ 4006 7000, toll free 0800 728 0888; www.hilton.com; Av Presidente Vargas 882; s R$470-790, d R$500-820; 🔀 💻 🛜 🍽) This is Belém's top hotel, opposite Praça da República and offering all the expected services, including a business center, exercise room, lobby bar and small swimming pool. And the rooms are spacious. That said, the hotel could really use updating, especially its gaudy fabrics and aging furniture.

Eating

CENTER

our pick **Estação das Docas** (Av Marechal Hermes; 🕙 lunch & dinner) One of the best places in Belém to get a meal, no matter what you're in the mood for. The complex has almost a dozen restaurants, most with indoor and outdoor seating and serving per-kilo lunches and à la carte dinners. Many stay open well past midnight on Friday and Saturday. Restaurante Hatobá (mains R$18 to R$45) serves quality Asian food including sushi, while Capone (mains R$18 to R$40) has a large selection of pasta and pizza.

Restaurante Belo Centro (☎ 241 8677; 2nd fl, Rua Santo Antônio 264; per kg $20; 🕙 lunch Mon-Fri) This friendly, airy restaurant cooks up tasty self-serve, with plenty of options for vegetarians and carnivores. It can be hard to find – look for a sandwich-board sign and narrow stairway at the back of an eyeglasses store.

Mãe Natureza (☎ 3212 8032; Rua Sen Manoel Barata 889; per kg R$27; 🕙 lunch Mon-Sat) The sterile dining room doesn't do justice to the unique vegan lunch buffet, though the air-con will have you ahh-ing even before you get to the food. Mãe Natureza – the name is Portuguese for 'Mother Nature' – uses only fresh veggies and ingredients (even raw sugar) and makes its own soy milk.

Dom Britto (Travessa Dr Moraes 21; per kg R$27; 🕙 lunch & dinner) A cool sleek interior and expertly prepared dishes make this a popular spot with professionals and guests at nearby upscale hotels. Though it's more expensive than other per-kilo places – but not by much – the mellow ambience and always-on air-conditioning can be just the respite you need in the middle of a long hot day. The Sunday spread is even fancier, and costs $35 per kg.

K'Delícias IV (Rua Carlos Gomes 237; per kg R$27, Sun R$33; 🕙 lunch) One of the few eateries open on Sunday, its extensive and smartly displayed spread makes this one of the center's best per-kilo spots, and with air-con blasting, one of the most comfortable too. The original K'Delícias I (lunch Monday to Saturday) is smaller but better located, on Rua 28 de Setembro 276 just off Av Presidente Vargas.

On weekends head to the **fruit and vegetable market** (Av Conselheiro Furtado & Travessa Dr Moraes; 🕙 6am-7m Fri-Sun) alongside Belém's cemetery for fresh produce.

OUTSIDE THE CENTER

our pick **Santo Antonio** (Travessa Quintino Bocaiúva; dishes R$8-18; 🕙 breakfast, lunch & dinner) One of Belém's best and coolest eateries, this café-bakery-restaurant has a large selection of sandwiches and hot meals, and a spacious artsy interior with tile-topped tables and bossa nova tunes. Create your own 'wich from made-today breads and tasty meats and cheese (R$8 to R$12) or order from the menu: the open-face *francesinha* sandwiches are to die for, with hot meat and melted cheese on a French roll.

Cosanostra Caffé (Travessa Benjamin Constant 1499; mains R$7-20; 🕙 noon-1am) The dim lighting and unmarked entrance lend a certain *Goodfellas* ambience, and Frank Sinatra happened to be playing when we visited, but the beefy guys at the bar are mostly businesspeople on a break. Lunch specials include a main dish, side dish and soda for R$10, or order larger plates off the menu. The bar is open late, and there's live music after 11pm (see p614).

Santa Pizza (☎ 34409 6450; Travessa Quintino Bocaiuva 945; mains R$15-40; 🕙 dinner) Sharp decor, hip music and mood lighting make Santa Pizza, between Travessa Tiradentes and Rua Boaventura da Silva, feel more like a lounge bar than a pizzeria, which was precisely the point. The outdoor tables are especially nice on warm evenings.

Cia Paulista de Pizza (☎ 3212 2200; Av Visconde de Souza Franca 559; dishes R$18-35; 🕙 10am-1am Sun-Thu, 10am-4am Fri-Sat) You wouldn't know from the dining room that this is actually a chain restaurant, as the wineglasses, tablecloths, attentive waiters and recorded jazz create a unique and classy ambience. Prices are quite affordable, and the pizza and pasta excellent.

Boteco das Onze (Casa das Onze Janelas, Praça Frei Brandão; mains R$20-55; 🕙 lunch & dinner) Part of Casa das Onze Janelas gallery (see p609), this classy joint is one of the city's best restaurant-bars for lunch, dinner and beyond. You can sit in either the dining room with modern art on the walls, or on the breezy back patio overlooking the river. Meals include *moqueca de filhote*, a tasty stew prepared with catfish, shrimp and lobster. There's live music virtually every night (cover R$6 to R$10), and plenty of good beer and drinks to choose from.

THE AMAZON

THE AMAZON

Drinking

Cervejaria Amazonas (Estação das Docas, Av Marechal Hermes; 🕑 5pm-1am) As much as Brazilians love beer, it's remarkably difficult to find a brew any darker than lemonade. This boutique brewery is an exception, with an amber and a dark (though not a true stout) among the five handcrafted beers brewed and served on the premises.

Bohêmio Cervejaria (Av Visconde de Souza Franco; 🕑 6pm-3am Mon-Fri, noon-3am Sat & Sun) Cool, laid-back bar with dark wood tables and a huge bank of beer bottles as modern art against the back wall (pray for no earthquakes). There's live music most nights – and a R$3 to R$4 cover when there is – varying from rock to pop to MPB (Música Popular Brasileira).

Spettus (Travessa Quintino Bocaiúva; 🕑 6pm-midnight) For the quintessential Brazilian pastime of sitting around a plastic table with cold beers and hot munchies, head to this popular but low-key watering hole, tucked away in a mostly residential neighborhood, between Av Gov José Malcher and Rua Boaventura da Silva.

Transit (cnr Rua 28 de Setembro & Travessa Almirante Waldenkolk; 🕑 5pm-2am Thu-Sat) Across the street from a swanky new restaurant, Transit caters to a younger and somewhat less-moneyed crowd. There's a lively open-air bar and dining area, and a stage for live music – from rock to bossa nova – Thursday to Sunday nights.

Cosanostra Caffé (Travessa Benjamin Constant 1499; 🕑 noon-1am) Already a pleasant wood-beamed lunch and dinner spot, the bar stays open late and is popular among intellectuals and professionals, with varied live instrumental music starting at 11pm nightly (8pm on Sunday).

Entertainment

Av Visconde de Souza Franco has several bars and clubs, where you can simply follow the music to find the latest hot spot. Elsewhere in the city, try the following places.

African Bar (☎ 3241 1085; cnr Av Marechal Hermes & Travessa da Piedade) Across from the state tourist office, this longtime club often stages samba groups on Saturday nights. Check the posters by the door for upcoming events.

Casa do Gilson (☎ 3272 7306; Travessa Padre Eutíquio 3172; 🕑 8pm-3am Fri, noon-3am Sat & Sun) Frequently voted as having Belém's best live music, to no one's surprise. Opened in 1987, Gilson's draws intellectuals and hipsters alike with first-rate samba, *choro* (improvised samba-like music) and other music, and terrific food and atmosphere to boot – don't miss the *patinha de carenguejo* (crab cake). It's between Ruas Nova and Tambés.

Moviecom Cinemas (www.moviecom.com.br) shows mostly Hollywood films at its top-floor location in Shopping Pátio Belém on Travessa Padre Eutíquio. **Cinépolis** (Boulevard Shopping, Av Visconde de Souza Franco) is located at another megamall, with seven screens, including one for 3D films, and supercomfy stadium seating. For art-house fare, **Cine Olimpia** (☎ 3223 1882; cnr Av Presidente Vargas & Rua Silva Santos) and **Cine Estação** (☎ 3212 552; Estação das Docas) are the most convenient to the center. The former hosts international film festivals, while the latter shows Brazilian and international art films on weekends.

Teatro da Paz holds a variety of theatrical events, from plays to symphonies to international dance performances. Most events have same-day tickets available; info and tickets are available just inside the main doors.

Shopping

Feira de Artesanato (Praça da República; 🕑 Fri-Sun) A large crafts fair that has the city's biggest range of attractive artwork, and a lot of it is homemade. It's especially busy on Sundays.

Mercado Ver-o-Peso (Av Castilho França) This and the surrounding area is probably the most interesting place to shop, whether for pants or piranha or anything in between. There are no set hours, but there is something interesting to see from 5:30am to 8:30pm every day. However, you should be especially wary of pickpockets and assailants in the early and late hours.

Artíndia (☎ 223 6248; Av Presidente Vargas 762; 🕑 9am-5pm Mon-Fri) Sells authentic and inexpensive *índio* crafts at its main shop, at the end of an arcade, in the center of town, and from a kiosk (open from noon to midnight) in Estação das Docas.

Shopping Pátio Belém (Travessa Padre Eutíquio) The former 'Iguatemi Shopping' has a new name and much more highbrow orientation, with upscale shops, from jewelry to electronics to designer clothing, spread over four floors.

Boulevard Shopping (Av Viconde de Souza Franco 776) Belém's latest, biggest mall is a modern cement, steel and glass structure, brilliantly lit at night, and boasting top-tier clothing, electronics and department stores as well as a cinema complex.

Getting There & Away

AIR

Belém's **Aeroporto Val de Cães** is a hub for international, domestic and regional flights.

Air Caraibes (☎ 3224 0000; www.aircaraibes.com)

Air France (☎ 4003 9955, 0800 888 9955; www.airfrance.com)

Gol (☎ 3210 6312, 0300 115 2121; www.voegol.com.br)

Surinam Airways (☎ 3210 6436; www.slm.nl)

TAM (☎ 3212 2166; www.tam.com.br; Av Assis de Vasconcelos 265)

TAP (☎ 0300 210 6060; www.flytap.com)

TRIP (☎ 3003 8747, 0300 789 8747; www.voetrip.com.br)

BOAT

All long-distance boats leave Belém from the **Terminal Hidroviária** (Av Marechal Hermes). Purchase tickets from the booths inside the terminal, or contact **Amazon Star Turismo** (☎ 3212 6244; www.amazonstar.com.br; Rua Henrique Gurjão 210), whose multilingual attendants can book boat tickets, including over the phone or internet, for no extra cost – a great service if you don't speak Portuguese or want to make arrangements well in advance (recommended in high season). See the boxed text, below, for tips on riverboat travel.

BUSES OF THE WATERWAYS

Rivers are roads in Amazonia, and riverboat trips are a uniquely Amazonian experience: the slow pace, sleeping in hammocks, watching the river and forest and local life glide by. But they can also be tedious, with day after day of the same food, same scenery, same ear-splitting music and drunken banter on the top deck.

For most people two or three days is enough to get the experience, but not tire of it. Instead of taking one of the marathon five- or six-day trips (such as Belém to Manaus, or Manaus to Tabatinga), consider stopping off halfway, doing some fun stuff, and then either continuing or even flying the rest. In many cases, boat and plane tickets cost the same.

■ You'll need a hammock (R$15 to R$40) and some rope to hang it. A sheet or sleep sack is nice if the temperature dips.

■ Your gear probably won't get wet, but play it safe by keeping it in a large plastic bag, tied at the top. This also helps keep prying fingers out of any side-pockets.

■ Get to the boat six to eight hours early to secure a good hammock spot. By departure time, the hammock areas will be jammed – you may end up with fellow passengers swinging above or beneath you!

■ Most boats have three decks. The top deck is for hanging out, while the middle and lower ones are for hammocks. The middle deck is definitely better, since the engine is on the first. Try to get a spot away from the toilets (in case they smell) and the buffet area (crowded and noisy during mealtimes). A porter may offer to help you pick a spot and tie up your hammock, a service that's well worth the R$2 to R$3 tip that's expected. A few boats have air-con or women-only hammock areas – ask when you buy your ticket.

■ Theft isn't rampant, but you should take common-sense precautions, like locking your zippers and knotting all drawstrings. Don't leave valuables unattended and be especially alert when the boat stops in port. Be friendly with the passengers around you, as they can keep an eye on your gear. The captain may stow your bag in a secure area on request, though it may be hard to access midtrip.

■ Most boats have a few *camarotes* (cabins with two to four bunks and a fan) and suites, with air-con and bathrooms. The advantage is you sleep in a bed instead of a hammock, can lock up your gear, and usually get better food. The disadvantage is you miss out on the comradeship (and bragging rights) that come from sleeping in a hammock alongside everyone else. If you book a cabin or suite, avoid those on the top deck, where there's blasting music.

■ Buffet-style meals may or may not be included in the fare. Either way, consider skipping them – you really don't want the runs during a boat trip. Instead, order made-to-order burgers and sandwiches at the kitchen on the upper deck, and pack food that travels well, such as apples, nuts or energy bars.

■ Bring a couple liters of water and extra toilet paper.

THE AMAZON

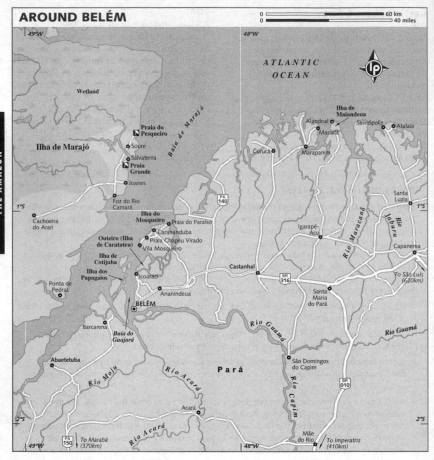

AROUND BELÉM

Marques Pinto Navigação (☎ 3272 3847) and ENART (☎ 3224 1225) offer boat service to and from Manaus, and most points along the way. At last check, boats to Manaus left Wednesday and Friday evenings, with stops at Monte Alegre (hammock/cabin R$150/200, two days), Santarém (R$160/250, 2½ days), Óbidos (R$180/260, three days), Parintins (R$210/300, four days), and Manaus (R$250/350, five days). Keep in mind that cabins fit two people for the listed price; some boats have an air-conditioned hammock area and/or suites.

Arapari Navigação (☎ 3241 4977) and Rodofluvial BANAV (☎ 3269 4494) alternate service to Ilha de Marajó, with daily ferries from Belém to Foz do Rio Camará, better known as Camará,

(R$13.50, three hours) twice daily from Monday to Saturday, once on Sunday.

São Francisco de Paula (☎ 3242 2070) has service to Macapá (hammock/cabin R$110/150, 24 hours, departures on Wednesday and Saturday) with return trips Tuesday and Friday.

BUS

Belém's long-distance bus station is 3km east of the town centre. Major destinations may be served by several lines, while *leito* and *semi-leito* (overnight sleeper) seats are available on some longer routes. Note that there have been a number of accounts of roadside robberies of buses coming to and from São Luis. If possible, flying is recommended.

Beira-Dão (☎ 3226 1162) Runs buses to Vila Mosqueiro (R$5, 1½ hours, departures every 60 minutes 6am to 11pm, to 10pm Saturday, to 9pm Sunday).

Itaperim (☎ 3226 3382) Serves Fortaleza (R$209, 24 hours, once daily), Salvador (R$283, 33 hours, three departures weekly) and Rio de Janeiro (R$426, 53 hours, four departures weekly).

Rápido Excelsior (☎ 3249 6365) Has service to Marudá (R$17, 3½ hours, four departures daily, five on Friday and Saturday, including 6am and 9am).

Sinprovan (☎ 3226 5872) Also has van service to Marudá (R$15, 3½ hours, direct at 5:45 and 8am, otherwise transfer in Canstanhal).

Transbrasilia (☎ 3226 1942) Serves dozens of cities, near and far, including São Luis (R$111, 10 hours, one departure daily), Rio de Janeiro (R$399, 50 hours, four departures weekly) and Paraíso do Tocantins (R$133, 17 hours, three times daily).

Getting Around

Aeroporto Val de Cães is 8km north of the center on Av Júlio César. The 'Pratinha – Pres Vargas' bus (638) runs between the airport and Av Presidente Vargas (R$2, 40 minutes); the 'E Marex' bus also goes there, but you may have to change buses at the depot (no charge). Arriving by plane, turn left as you leave the terminal; buses stop at the traffic circle about 50m past the end of the terminal. A taxi between the airport and center is a fixed R$35 when booked inside the terminal; you can catch one for less at the bus stop (R$20 to R$25), though they pass somewhat infrequently.

The long-distance bus station is on the corner of Av Almirante Barroso and Av Governador José Malcher, 3km east of the city center. Going into town, catch almost any westbound bus on Av Governador José Malcher or cross to the far side of Av Almirante Barroso and catch any bus saying 'Aero Club' or 'P Vargas' – both can drop you at Praça de República. Going out to the bus station, take any 'Guama – P Vargas' bus (316) from Av Presidente Vargas.

ILHA DO MOSQUEIRO

☎ 0xx91 / pop 27,000

Thousands of Belemenses (Belém residents) beat the heat by flocking to Mosqueiro's 18 freshwater beaches. The area gets crowded on weekends between July and October.

Orientation

The island's main town, Vila Mosqueiro, is on the southwest tip of the island. Av Beira Mar, the main drag, starts in town at Praia Farol and runs northward along the shore past Praia Chapéu Virado, Praia do Murubira, Praia Marahú and Praia do Paraíso. The other main road is Av 16 de Novembro, which intersects with Av Beira Mar between Praia Farol and Praia Chapéu Virado, at a small plaza and church.

Sights & Activities

The best beaches are **Praia do Farol** (in town) and **Praia do Paraíso** and the more remote **Baía do Sol** in the north. Stingrays may be present – shuffle your feet when entering the water to scare them off.

Mosqueiro's traditional **folklore festival**, in June, features plenty of Amazonian *carimbó* music and *Boi-Bumbá* performances, from the popular regional celebration. The **Círio de NS do Ó** is celebrated on the second Sunday of December. Like Belém's Círio (see p611), this is a beautiful and joyous event, well worth seeing if you're in the area.

Sleeping & Eating

Hotel Farol (☎ 3771 1219; Praia do Farol; r with air-con R$120-130, with fan R$110; ☒) In a converted lighthouse overlooking the south end of Praia do Farol, this unique hotel is reasonable value and easy to get to even if you don't have a car. The building's circular shape makes for interestingly shaped rooms; those with a view are worth the extra R$10. Discounts available midweek.

Hotel Fazenda Paraíso (☎ hotel 3618 2022; www .hotelfazendaparaiso.com.br; Praia do Paraíso; d R$150, tr/q chalet R$180/220; ☒ ☐ ☒) More a resort than a hotel; the rooms here are large and chalets even larger, both with pleasant wood construction.

Food can be a bit hard to find, especially late at night and on weekdays. The restaurants at Hotel Farol and Hotel Fazenda Paraíso serve good, standard dishes for R$12 to R$25. There are lots of *barracas* (food stalls) in the main square and on Praia do Farol.

Getting There & Around

Buses from Belém (R$4, 1½ hours) pass Praia Murubira and Praia Chapéu Virado, then turn up Av 16 de Novembro just before Praia Farol. The actual terminal is another 4.5km away from the beach, but you can ask the driver to let you off anywhere along the line.

THE AMAZON

ALGODOAL
☎ 0xx91 / pop 1200

The small fishing village of Algodoal on Ilha de Maiandeua, 180km northeast of Belém, attracts younger Belenenses and a few foreign travelers. It's an attractive natural retreat with hard, windswept beaches and a sometimes turbulent sea.

The island's name comes from an *índio* word meaning 'uncountable riches beneath the sea.' Legend has it that an enchanted city is submerged off the island's northern tip; it emerges occasionally and is visible from Praia da Princesa, which was named for the city's royal daughter.

Orientation & Information

Algodoal village is on the island's west coast. The streets are unpaved – some dirt, others grass – and have no street signs; ask passersby for directions. A tidal channel marks the northern end of town; across it are Praia do Farol and, beyond that, Praia da Princesa. Around the island are three more small communities: Fortalezinha, Mocoóca, and Camboinha.

There is no bank or ATM in Algodoal or elsewhere on the island, and only a handful of businesses accept credit cards. Pousada Kakurí (p619) and Jardim do Éden (p619) have internet access, but the connection is spotty at best. Around the corner from Kakurí, **Farmacias Kadosh** (✆ 7:30am-8pm Mon-Thu, 7:30am-9pm Fri & Sat, 7:30am-7pm Sun) is a small pharmacy selling sunscreen, bug spray, condoms, medicines etc.

Check out www.algodoal.com for info on the island's news, history, hotels and activities.

Dangers & Annoyances

The island has several tidal channels (known as *furos*, or 'punctures,' in Portuguese) that connect inland lagoons to the ocean, and vary in size and strength according to the tide. Canoes are available day and night to ferry you across the channel separating Algodoal from Praia do Farol (R$1). A second channel, Furo Velho, is just over halfway between Algodoal and Fortalezinha (walking clockwise). It's larger and deeper than the others and should *never* be crossed on foot, even at low tide. If there's no one to ferry you across, turn back.

Sights & Activities

Across the channel from town is **Praia do Farol**, a broad attractive beach that's good (and convenient) for swimming and sunbathing. Continuing clockwise along the shore, a rocky outcrop called Ponta do Boiador marks the beginning of **Praia da Princesa**. This is the island's best beach, stretching 8km, with rough surf and backed by dunes, palms and the occasional structure or rocky outcrop. At dusk,

---

SURF THE POROROCA!

Every month or so, when alignment of the sun and moon makes tides their strongest, powerful waves can form at the mouth of certain rivers and barrel upstream with tremendous force. The phenomenon – which occurs when the tide briefly overpowers the force of the river – is technically a 'tidal bore' but in Brazil is better known as the *pororoca*, an indigenous word for 'mighty noise.' And no wonder: the waves can reach 4m high and speeds of 30km per hour, and can rip full-sized trees off the bank with their force.

All of which is music to the ears of extreme surfers (and wave-surfing kayakers) in search of the mythic 'endless wave.' The record for the longest ride is 37 minutes, covering nearly 13km. Surfers generally report the *pororoca* to be stronger than a like-sized ocean wave, and it constantly changes size and speed according to the river's contours. What's more, the water is loaded with debris that's been swept off the shore and river bottom, including tree trunks and abandoned canoes. (At least the caimans tend to stay away.)

The National Pororoca Surfing Championship has been held at the town of São Domingos do Capim, 120km east of Belém on the Rio Guamá, since 1999. (A related competition is held on the Rio Araguari in Amapá.) The event usually takes place in March, on the full moon nearest the spring equinox, when the *pororoca* is strongest. The bash draws top-ranked surfers and includes street fairs, cultural performances, even a Miss Pororoca competition. A paved road makes getting there easier, though there still is no direct service; from Belém, go to Castanhal and transfer. Alternatively, Amazon Star Turismo (p615), a travel agency in Belém, organizes *pororoca* packages.

ask a waiting boatman if he'll paddle up the channel (R$10 to R$15 for half-hour) between town and Praia do Farol; it's a great time and place to see the bright-red *guará* (scarlet ibis), plus kingfishers, egrets and more.

You can also hike or canoe to an inland lake called **Lago da Princesa**, or even clear across the island to the small community of **Fortalezinha**. Most hotels can arrange for local boatmen or fishermen to take you, often returning by boat along the shoreline. Start by inquiring at Jardim do Éden, Pousada Marhesias, or Pousada Ponta do Boiador, which seem to have the most experience with such excursions; prices range from R$50 to $150 per person.

Sleeping

It can be hard to find a room during high season, especially at Carnaval, Semana Santa (Holy Week), the month of July and all holiday weekends. Otherwise, there are many more beds than bods to fill them.

Pousada da Chilena (☎ 3744 1128; jgapmaga@hot mail.com; dm with hammock R$15, camping per person R$15, r R$30) The eponymous 'Chilena' doesn't live here full-time, meaning the pousada (guesthouse) is often closed during off-peak periods, but it's a delightful place all the same, with simple boho-style rooms and well-tended hammock and camping areas. Breakfast can be purchased for R$5 to R$10.

Pousada Kakurí (☎ 3854 1156, 8157 9619; hammock without breakfast R$15, s/d without bathroom R$30/40, with bathroom R$40/55) The second little pig evidently oversaw the construction of this hotel, the largest stick house you may ever see. Accommodations are very basic – you can literally peek through the walls – but the laid-back atmosphere keeps it popular with backpackers and young Brazilians. The hammock area is in another building, two blocks away.

Pousada Bela Mar (☎ 3854 1128, www.belamar.hpg vip.com.br; s/d without bathroom R$25/50, with bathroom & fan R$40/65, with air-con & minibar R$55/85; ☒) A clean, reliable choice, this is the first hotel you reach from the boat drop-off. Fifteen tidy rooms are arranged around a pretty central garden, all with high ceilings and attractive decor. An ample breakfast spread is served in the hotel's spacious restaurant.

ourpick Pousada Marhesias (☎ 3854 1129, 9112 3461; www.marhesias-algodoal.com; Rua Bertoldo Costa 47; s R$50-60, d R$84-120; ☒ ☏) Four spacious guestrooms face a quiet rear courtyard. All

have air-con, firm comfortable beds, bathroom with hot water, satellite TV, and a small patio for hanging a hammock; a large leafy garden and sitting area are planned for the adjoining lot. The restaurant here is well recommended, with a great selection of jazz (and even the occasional live performance). Located at the far end of town.

Estrela Sol Hotel (☎ 3854 1107; www.estrelasol.algo doal.com.br; r with fan R$50, with air-con R$60-80; ☒ ☏) Rooms here are plain but clean, and surround a large leafy garden. The swimming pool is a lovely idea, though keeping it full and clean is a challenge the staff isn't always up to.

Pousada Ponta do Boiador (☎ 3279 0060; www .boiador.com; r with fan R$70-80; ☒ ☏) All-wood construction gives rooms here a clean, dry air, and small patios with hammocks afford great sea views. There's more of the same at the large waterfront deck, and the beach is decent during the dry season; otherwise, Praia do Farol is just across the channel. Good value.

Jardim do Éden (☎ 9623-9690; www.algodoal-amazon -tourism.com; Praia do Farol; hammock or tent per person R$25, r without bathroom R$75, d cabin R$130-150, extra person R$25) Located across the channel from town on Praia do Farol, the appealingly eclectic main house has large comfortable rooms with fan; three private cabins (one tiny and cute, the others large enough for four) are nearby. Meals are served on a 2nd-floor deck on the main house, which also has hammocks for chilling out. Room prices are steep, but it's the only true beach hotel on the island. The multilingual owner can lead or arrange tours around the island.

Eating

Virtually all the recommendable places to eat in Algodoal are at hotels, which are always open to their own guests, but in the low season may close to nonguests (or cut back to, say, just dinner). Fortunately, the town is small enough that it's not hard to find a place that's open.

Pousada Kakurí (☏ lunch & dinner; mains R$9-25) The dining area consists of a few tables set up on the porch, but that's all you need to enjoy the kitchen's tasty creations – mostly fresh fish, grilled or fried, with veggies and rice – and a couple cold beers. Usually has great music playing, to boot.

Jardim do Éden (☎ 9623-9690; www.algodoal -amazon-tourism.com; Praia do Farol; mains R$8-35; ☏ lunch & dinner) Tasty, creative meals, including plenty

THE AMAZON

of vegetarian options, are served on the hotel's 2nd-floor deck, with great sea views and breezes. Canoes are available to cross the channel day and night, so don't worry about staying late.

Pousada Marhesias (Rua Bertoldo Costa 47; mains R$8-40; ☺ lunch & dinner, bar till late) Serving a little of everything, from fish and seafood to pasta and pizza, all freshly made and served in a large 2nd floor dining area with views across the channel to Praia do Farol. You can count on hearing some great jazz over your meal – it's all they play. Live music is presented here every once in a while.

Pousada Bela Mar (☎ 3854 1128; www.belamar.hpg vip.com.br; mains R$10-25; ☺ breakfast, lunch & dinner) Yet another hotel restaurant, this one serving good no-frills Brazilian fare in a spacious indoor dining area.

Getting There & Around

Access to Algodoal is via the mainland village of Marudá. Boats leave there for Algodoal (R$5.50, 40 minutes) at 9am, 10:30am, 1:30pm and 5pm Monday to Thursday, and at 9am, 10:30am, 12:30pm, 2:30pm and 5pm Friday to Sunday. The boats typically wait for the bus from Belém to arrive before departing. Hiring someone to take you across by motorboat runs around R$70.

Arriving at Algodoal, the boat drops you at the beach, where a slew of donkey carts will vie for the chance to take you to your hotel (per person R$5). Be aware that some hotels pay commissions to drivers to bring tourists there; it's possible that 'such-and-such hotel burned down' is true, but you can still insist on seeing for yourself, usually at no extra cost.

Boats return to the mainland at 6am, 8am, 10:30am and 1:30pm Monday to Thursday, and at 6am, 8am, 10:30am, 1:30pm, 3pm and 5pm Friday to Sunday.

ILHA DE MARAJÓ

☎ 0xx91 / pop 250,000

The 50,000-sq-km Ilha de Marajó, slightly larger than Switzerland, lies at the mouths of the Amazonas and Tocantins rivers. It was the ancient home of the Marajoaras indigenous culture, notable for their large ceramic burial urns. Today, Marajó's friendly residents live in a few towns and villages and on the many *fazendas* (ranches) spread across the island. This is a world apart, where bicycles outnumber cars and water buffalo graze around

town. Legend has it the buffalo are descended from animals that swam ashore from a French ship that sank while en route from India to French Guiana. The island is well known for its buffalo cheese, buffalo steaks and buffalo-mounted police force.

Only the island's eastern shore is easily accessible to tourists, and has three small sleepy towns: Joanes is the smallest of the three, with a decent beach and small hotel (and not much else); Salvaterra has the island's best and largest beach but the town itself is a bit lacking; and Soure offers the most in terms of hotels, services and overall ambience, though the beaches are a bit harder to reach. Much of the island's interior is wetland, and is home to tens of thousands of birds, including the graceful *guará*, with its long, curved beak.

It's a good idea to bring extra cash, as credit cards are rarely accepted and the one ATM in Soure doesn't recognize all foreign cards. Also be aware that Marajó is very wet from January to June, with almost-daily rain.

Getting There & Away

Passenger ferries (R$14.50, three hours) leave Belém's main boat terminal at 6:30am and 2:30pm Monday to Saturday and 10am on Sunday, arriving at a port south of Joanes called Foz do Rio Camará, or Camará for short. They return from the same port at 6:30am and 3pm Monday to Saturday, and 3pm Sunday.

Catamaran Álamo (☎ 3249 3400) offers slightly faster service (R$25, 2½ hours, from Belém at 7:30am Monday, Tuesday, Thursday, Friday and Saturday; from Camará at 3:30pm Monday, Tuesday, Thursday, Friday and Sunday) and enclosed air-conditioned seating. In Belém, it ports at Estaçao das Docas rather than the main boat terminal.

Getting Around

Buses and minivans meet ferries arriving from Belém and at Camará, Marajó's main port. Each has a sign to its destination; simply look for the place you're going to and get on. It's R$3.50 to Joanes, Salvaterra, or the ferry port, or R$9 all the way to your hotel in Soure, including the barge across the river. (The large buses don't do hotel drop-offs, however.) When you're leaving, ask your hotel to call for the shuttle to swing by the next day.

Moto-taxis are common in all three towns, and cost R$1 to R$2 around town, R$4 to R$7 to outlying beaches and R$15 between Joanes and Salvaterra.

In Salvaterra, boats to Soure leave from the town pier (R$2, 15 minutes, 7am to 6pm) but you may have to wait a half hour or more for enough passengers to gather. Alternatively, take a cab or mototaxi to the car ferry port (R$3 to R$8) about 8km from town, where small passenger boats cross day and night, even with just one passenger (R$1.50, five minutes). If the barge happens to be leaving (hourly 6am to 6pm), you can hop on it for free.

Coming from Soure, the boats that go directly to Salvaterra – the ones you may have to wait a half hour for – leave from a dock at the end of Travessa 14, while the motorized canoes to the car ferry port leave from a dock at the end of Travessa 15.

Joanes

Head to sleepy Joanes for total isolation. It's got an appealing hotel and beach, the remains of a 17th-century Jesuit church, and hardly a soul in sight. It is thought that Spanish navigator Vicente Yáñez Pinzón landed on Joanes beach on February 26, 1500 – a couple of months before Pedro Cabral's 'discovery' of Brazil for Portugal.

There are no services in Joanes, save a **post office** (🕑 8am-noon Mon-Fri) on the main road. Shuttles from the ferry port cost R$3.50; moto-taxis are an easy way to get elsewhere around the island (R$15 to Salvaterra) or you can rent bikes from Pousada Ventania do Rio-Mar (see p621).

SLEEPING & EATING
Pousada Ventania do Rio-Mar (☎ 3646 2067, 9992 5716; www.pousadaventania.com; s/d/tr/q R$55/85/105/110) Atop a breezy headland overlooking the shore. Large rooms have whimsical decor and over-sized paintings, bathrooms (but no TV or air-con), and open onto a large patio. The beach is just steps away, and the staff can arrange a variety of excursions, including canoeing and fishing with local guides. Service has proved less reliable is recent years, but it's still a relaxing and agreeable spot. Pay in reais, dollars or euros.

Three **beach restaurants** (mains R$12-25) serve Joanes' best lunch and dinner, especially the Marajoana favorites of grilled fish and buffalo steaks. One is even open 24 hours, for those late-night munchies.

Salvaterra

Eighteen kilometers north from Joanes, Salvaterra (population 18,000) has the island's best and longest beach, the aptly named Praia Grande, a short walk outside town. Salvaterra isn't as big as Soure (p622), but is more compact, so it can feel busier. The town is building an ambitious *orla fluvial* (waterfront promenade), extending from the central plaza all the way to Praia Grande, which when completed will make for a pleasant diversion from the heat and bustle in town.

ORIENTATION & INFORMATION
The main street through town is Av Victor Engelhard, which ends at the town pier. The cross streets are numbered starting at the pier – 1a Rua, 2a Rua etc – though few people refer to them as such. Praia Grande is about 500m south of town.

Along the main drag is the **post office** (🕑 8am-noon & 2-5pm Mon-Fri) and an internet café **Cyber Marajó Online** (per hr R$3; 🕑 8am-midnight Mon-Sat, 8am-noon & 6pm-midnight Sun). **Pousada Bosque dos Aruãs** (☎ 3765 1115; per hr R$5) also has internet access, and **bike rental** (per hr/day R$2/12). **Hotel Beira Mar** (☎ 3765 1450) rents bikes (per hour/day R$2/15) and has laundry service (per item R$0.50) as well, open to guests and nonguests alike. **BANAV** (☎ 3269-4494; 🕑 8-11am only) sells ferry tickets from its office near Cyber Marajó; outside of those hours, use the booth at the port.

See p620 for info on getting from Salvaterra to Soure, and vice versa.

SIGHTS
Praia Grande is, as the name suggests, a big beach, a long wide swath of golden-brown sand about 500m south of Salvaterra proper. A slew of beach restaurants perched on tilts overlook the first section of the beach, but the far end is virtually deserted, save one large resort.

As everywhere on Ilha de Marajó, sting-rays are common and they pack a nasty sting. Always try to enter and leave the water where other people have done so, as the rays have likely been scared off. Otherwise, shuffle your feet or use a stick to poke the sand in front of you to avoid stepping on a ray.

SLEEPING & EATING
Hotel Beira Mar (☎ 3765 1400; Rua 5 at Travessa 2; s/d with fan R$30/40, with air-con R$50/60; 🗙 🛜) A short walk from the center and Praia Grande; rooms

here are of the large and plain variety, with graying tile floors, TV, and thin mattresses and linens. Bike rentals (R$2/15 per hour/day) and laundry service (R$0.50 per piece) are available.

Pousada Bosque dos Aruãs (☎ 3765 1115; s/d/tr R$60/70/80; 🍽) Set on an oceanfront lot shaded by mango trees, large wood cabins have two smallish rooms apiece, each with bathroom, hot water, air-con, and polished wood floors. The fixtures are definitely aging, but the sound of the ocean waves and mangoes thudding in the courtyard makes for a peaceful stay. Too rocky to swim in front, but Praia Grande is a 10-minute walk away. The patio restaurant is quite good.

Pousada dos Guarás (☎ 3765 1149, in Belém 4005 5656; www.pousadadosguaras.com.br; s/d R$130/150; 🍽 🖥 🏊) This upscale resort caters to package tourists from Belém, but is still decent value for independent travelers, especially considering it's right on Praia Grande. Suites here are spacious and attractively decorated, with solar-heated water, and are surrounded by large grassy grounds. There's a midsized swimming pool if you tire of the ocean.

Restaurante Umuarama (cnr Travessa 2 & Rua 6; mains R$10-25; 🕐 breakfast, lunch & dinner) Specializes in pizza but also serves up shrimp, fish and buffalo, all locally raised or caught, and served at plastic tables in an low-key open-air dining area.

Pousada Bosque dos Aruãs (mains R$15-$35; 🕐 lunch & dinner) Serves guests and nonguests alike on its small wooden patio.

There are many beach restaurants on Praia Grande, where you can fill up for R$12 to R$25.

Soure

The 'Capital of Marajó,' Soure (population 22,500) is on the far side of the Rio Paracauari and is the biggest town on the island. Most travelers assume it's less appealing than Salvaterra and Joanes, yet it's got fewer cars than Salvaterra and is less isolated than Joanes, which can be just the right balance. Something about the water buffalo grazing on the soccer field and the double-wide streets – many of them grass with just a bike track weaving down the middle – lends Soure a certain charm.

ORIENTATION & INFORMATION

The streets running parallel to the river are Ruas (with Rua 1 closest to the river). The perpendicular streets are Travessas, with Travessa 1 closest to the seashore. The main bus and passenger ferry deposits you near the corner of Rua 1 and Travessa 15; the motorized canoes leaving from the same spot will drop you one block up at Travessa 16, while the direct boats to and from Salvaterra dock a block down at Travessa 14. See Getting Around, p620, for more info on getting to and from Soure and the rest of the island.

Banco do Brasil (Rua 3; 🕐 10am-3pm Mon-Fri) Between Travessa 17 & Travessa 18; has an ATM that accepts most Plus and Cirrus cards. It's still a good idea to bring plenty of cash from Belém, however.

Cyber Gigabyte (Travessa 15 at Rua 2; per hr R$2-3; 🕐 9am-noon & 3pm-midnight Mon-Sat, 4pm-midnight Sun) Fast internet connection and long hours.

Drogaria Big Farm (🕐 7am-9pm Mon-Sat, 8am-8:30pm Sun) Pharmacy and minimart.

Post office (Rua 1; 🕐 9am-noon & 2-5pm Mon-Fri) Between Travessa 13 and Travessa 14.

A bicycle is a great way to get around Soure. A guy named **Bimba** (☎ 8268 3606; bike hire per hr/day R$1.50/7) has the island's lowest rates, operating out of his house on Rua 4 between Travessa 18 and Travessa 19 (it's the one with a stone facade, squeezed between a fruit stand and a hardware shop). You can also ask at **Pousada O Canto do Francês** (p623, half-/full day R$8/12) and **Hotel Casarão da Amazônia** (p623, per hour R$5); guests have preference, but there's no harm in asking.

BEACHES

The beaches near Soure, which have a mix of salt- and freshwater, are often covered with fantastic seeds washed down from the Amazonian forests. But beware of stingrays, which are common here and have an extremely painful sting. Stay well away from the mouth of streams (rays prefer the muddy silt) and enter and exit the water only where other people have recently done so. If the beach is deserted, use a stick to poke the sand in front of you, and shuffle your feet to kick up a cloud.

Praia do Pesqueiro is Soure's most popular beach, a broad swath of soft beige sand, backed by thatch-roofed restaurants with tables set up in the sand. Pesqueiro is further from town (about 9km) than the other beaches, but along the way you can spot buffaloes wallowing in marshes, and catch a glimpse of Marajó's lush interior. A moto-taxi runs R$8 each way, while cabs charge R$25 for up to four people.

Praia Barra Velho and Praia de Araruna are narrow beaches edged by thick mangrove stands and separated from each other by a wide tidal channel. Barra Velho has several small restaurants, while Praia de Araruna stretches virtually deserted for miles. High tide can reduce both shorelines to a thin strip of sand, but otherwise they're pleasant, and easy to reach by foot, bike, or taxi. To get there, follow Travessa 14 out of town for about 3km to a fork in the road; to the right is a walkway leading to Praia Barra Velho, while to the left and a short distance further on is a footbridge across the channel to Praia de Araruna.

TOURS
Pousada O Canto do Francês (p623) offers a variety of excursions for guests and nonguests alike. One of the most popular is a boat-and-hiking tour (per group R$140) up the tidal channel, or *furo*, separating Salvaterra and Soure. Another is a trip to Fazenda Bon Jesus (per person R$60), a semi-working ranch that has opportunities for terrific bird-watching and animal-spotting.

FESTIVALS & EVENTS
On the second Sunday in November, Soure has its own Círio de Nazaré (see p611 for details of Belém's) with a beautiful procession. Hotels can be booked up at this time.

SLEEPING & EATING
Hotel Araruna (☎ 8163 7731; Travessa 14; s/d R$40/50) Soure's best budget option, located between Ruas 7 and 8, next to the tall Cosampa water towers. Clean, simple rooms opening on a breezy outdoor corridor. Friendly owners.

our pick **Pousada O Canto do Francês** (☎ 3741 1298; Rua 6 at Travessa 8; s/d/tr R$80/90/110; ☒ ☎) An attractive foyer gives way to nine elegantly decorated suites, with whitewashed walls, fine woodwork and comfortable beds. Breakfast is served on a patio overlooking a huge private grassy yard. Well removed from the center, but the hotel rents bikes; the French owner can also arrange guided excursions.

Hotel Casarão da Amazônia (☎ 3741 2222; www .hotelcasarao.com; cnr Rua 4 & Travessa 9; s/d/tr 110/150/170; ☒ ☎ ☒) Occupying a restored 19th-century *casarão* (mansion), rooms at this newish hotel have high ceilings, flat-screen TVs, and stylish (albeit tiny) bathrooms. An annex has slightly larger rooms, with patios and hammocks, but they lack the colonial-era charm.

The hotel also has bike rentals and a clean, beckoning pool.

Restaurante Patú Anú (☎ 3741 1359; Rua 2 at Travessa 14; mains R$7-20; ☼ breakfast, lunch & dinner) A simple, reliable menu and a convenient location make this a popular eatery among locals, first-timers and repeat visitors alike. Large servings of chicken, beef, fish or shrimp, plus rice and beans.

Restaurante-Pizzeria Casarão da Amazônia (☎ 3741 2222; cnr Rua 4 & Travessa 9; mains R$20-40; ☼ lunch daily, dinner Fri-Sun) Pizzas at this hotel restaurant are fired in a traditional wood-burning oven but, alas, they're only offered Friday to Sunday in the evenings. Otherwise the menu features buffalo, shrimp, chicken and other standbys, served in an open-air dining area.

SHOPPING
Cerâmica Mbara-yo (Travessa 20) This is the modest shop of ceramicist Carlos Amaral, who combines traditional Aruã and Marajoara ceramic traditions with award-winning results. You can have a short tour of the workshop to see how the pieces are made. Numerous small, affordable pieces are for sale, and each has a particular tale or significance behind it. It's between Ruas 3 and 4.

SANTARÉM
☎ 0xx93 / pop 275,000

Santarém is a pleasant city, blessed with river breezes and a mild climate. Its location at the confluence of the creamy-brown Amazon River and the much darker Rio Tapajós means Santarém has its very own 'Meeting of the Waters,' as the two rivers flow side by ide without mixing, two bands of different-colored water clearly distinguishable from the waterfront. A stop here is a good way to break up the five-day boat trip between Belém and Manaus.

Most travelers who do stop in Santarém hop right on a bus to Alter do Chão (p629), a cool little town 35km away with white-sand river beaches and a laid-back backpacker ambience. Both towns provide easy access to the Floresta Nacional (FLONA) do Tapajós (p627), a beautiful national forest where you can hike, canoe, and stay the night with rubber-tapper families. And while Alter do Chão has good tours to FLONA (and elsewhere), Santarém is where you catch the bus to go there independently. Santarém also has a couple of good museums, a nearby private reserve, and an agreeable waterfront, all handy for a day or two's stay.

History

The Santarém region has been a center of human settlement for many thousands of years (see the boxed text, p632). In 1661, more than 20 years after Pedro Teixeira's expedition first contacted the local Tupaiu indigenous people, a Jesuit mission was established at the meeting of the Tapajós and Amazonas rivers, and officially named Santarém in 1758.

The later history of Santarém was marked by the rubber boom and bust, and a series of gold rushes that started in the 1950s. The economy today is based on rubber, soy and hardwoods, plus Brazil nuts, black pepper, mangoes, jute and fish. The discovery of gold and bauxite and the construction of the Curuá-Una hydroelectric dam, 60km southeast of Santarém, have brought some development in the last 25 years, but it is still largely isolated. A movement to form a new state of Tapajós has some popular support here, but little traction outside the region.

Information

EMERGENCY
Ambulance (☎ 192)
Police (☎ 190)

INTERNET ACCESS
Amazon's Star Cyber (☎ 3522 3648; Av Tapajós; per hr R$3; ☉ 8am-10pm Mon-Fri, 9am-10pm Sat, 10am-10pm Sun)
Centro de Copias (Av Rui Barbosa; per hr R$2.50; ☉ 8am-7pm Mon-Fri, 8am-2pm Sat)

LAUNDRY
Lavandería Storll (☎ 3523 1329; Travessa Turiano Meira 167; per kg R$11; ☉ 8am-6pm Mon-Sat) Same-day service if you drop off clothes in the morning.

MEDICAL SERVICES
Hospital Municipal (cnr Av Presidente Vargas & Av Barão do Rio Branco) Has an emergency room.

MONEY
Bradesco (Av Rui Barbosa) Reliable ATMs.
HSBC (Av Rui Barbosa) Reliable ATMs.
Ourominas (☎ 3522 7655; Travessa dos Mártires 198; ☉ 8am-6pm Mon-Fri, 8:30am-1pm Sat) Good rates for euros and US dollars; also has Western Union service.

POST
Main post office (Rua Siqueira Campos; ☉ 9am-5pm Mon-Fri)

TRAVEL AGENCIES
Gil Serique (☎ 8803 7430; www.gilserique.com; Rua Adriano Pimentel 80) A lithe groovy guy who speaks near-perfect English and leads unique personalized tours to FLONA, nearby wetlands and elsewhere, when he feels like it and is not otherwise occupied windsurfing or chilling in his decaying river-view apartment. He happens to be one of the area's top naturalists, and is a fount of historical information about his beloved Santarém.
Santarém Tur (☎ 3522 4847; www.santaremtur.com.br; Rua Adriano Pimentel 44) Plane tickets and tour packages, including city tours, day trips to Alter de Chão by boat or car, and overnight riverboat tours to FLONA. Friendly and helpful staff.

Sights
MUSEU DE SANTARÉM
Housed in a large yellow waterfront mansion, the **Museu de Santarém** (Rua do Imperador, Praça Barão de Santarém; admission by donation; ☉ 8am-5pm Mon-Fri, 8am-1pm Sat) is also known as the Centro Cultural João Fona, after the Pará artist who painted the frescoes on its interior walls. The building dates from 1867 and has been a jail, city hall and courthouse. In addition to several paintings and documents related to the city's founding, the museum features a small but excellent collection of stone pieces and pottery, including burial urns and ceremonial figurines, from the Tapajoara culture that flourished locally more than 6000 years ago.

MUSEU DICA FRAZÃO
Nonagenarian Dona Dica Frazão (b 1920) is the creator, namesake, tour guide and main advocate of the **Museu Dica Frazão** (☎ 522 1026; Rua Floriano Peixoto 281; admission free; ☉ daytime). Slight and cheerful, Dona Dica has spent more than 50 years making women's clothing and fabrics from natural fibers, including grasses and wood pulp. Pieces on display include reproductions of a dress made for a Belgian queen, a tablecloth for Pope John Paul II and costumes for the Boi-Bumbá festival at Parintins (p660).

WATERFRONT PROMENADE
The Nova Orla Fluvial promenade follows Av Tapajós over a mile from the Museu de Santarém almost as far as the Docas do Para. A nice stroll starts at Praça da Matriz, heading west, passing colorful boats before ending in

SANTARÉM

INFORMATION		SLEEPING		Restaurante O Mascote..................21 C2
Amazon's Star Cyber.....................1 B2		Barão Center Hotel.......................12 B3		Sabor Caseiro.................................22 B3
Bradesco.......................................2 B3		Brasil Grande Hotel......................13 B3		
Centro de Cópias..........................3 B3		Brisa Hotel....................................14 C2		**TRANSPORT**
Gil Serique....................................4 C2		Hotel Brasil..................................15 B2		Buses to Airport and Alter do Chão..23 B3
HSBC..5 C3		New City Hotel.............................16 C3		Buses to Maguari & Jamaraquá......24 B3
Lavaderia Storil............................6 C3		Rio Dourado Hotel........................17 A3		Buses to Pini and Tauri..................25 A3
Main Post Office...........................7 B2		Santarém Palace Hotel..................18 C3		
Ouromínas....................................8 B3				
Santarém Tur................................9 C2		**EATING**		
		Delícias Caseiras...........................19 B2		
SIGHTS & ACTIVITIES		Mais Sabor...................................20 C2		
Museu de Santarém.....................10 D3				
Museu Dica Frazão.......................11 C3				

THE AMAZON

the shadow of the massive Cargill facility, a symbol of Brazil's burgeoning soy trade. There is little shade, so bring a hat.

Festivals

The patron saint of fisherfolk, São Pedro, is honored on June 29, when boats decorated with flags and flowers sail in procession before the city.

Sleeping

BUDGET

Hotel Brasil (☎ 3523 5177; Travessa dos Mártires 30; s/d R$30/50, with air-con R$50/60; ✷) In a big old building in a bustling commercial area, this backpacker favorite has aging but comfortable rooms at bargain prices. Large shutter windows allow for plenty of light and air, though you'll have to close them when the mosquitoes come out. Rooms share a reasonably clean bathroom (cold water only), and breakfast is served in the spacious 2nd-floor dining room. Often full, so call ahead.

New City Hotel (☎ 3523 3149; Travessa Francisco Corrêa 200; s/d R$60/75) Rooms come in all shapes and sizes (as do the furnishings) in this big ram-

bling hotel with a maze of stairs and hallways – claustrophobes may start to sweat – and a peppy yellow paint job throughout. A few rooms have balconies or large windows, which help considerably; all have crisp, clean linens.

Brisa Hotel (☎ 3522 1018; brisahotel@hotmail.com; Rua Senador Lameira Bittencourt 5; s/d R$60/80; ✷) The Brisa's exterior, once a sea of green, is now a wall of yellow, though remnants of its minty past remain in the ceilings and staff uniforms. Rooms are the same as always: simple, clean, a bit claustrophobic, but overall they're decent value. Upstairs units are somewhat more charming, and therefore often full. The location is ideal, with restaurants and the waterfront promenade right in front.

MIDRANGE & TOP END

Rio Dourado Hotel (☎ 3522 4021; riodouradohotel@ yahoo.com.br; Rua Floriano Peixoto 799; s R$90-130, d R$110-155; ✷ 🛜) Upstairs rooms are well worth their higher rate, with polished floors, gleaming bathrooms, mini-split air-conditioners, even fake flowers and a proper writing table and chairs. Don't be put off by the proximity to the market area; it's busy but not overwhelmingly so, and you're near restaurants, internet cafés and the waterfront promenade.

Brasil Grande Hotel (☎ 3522 6665; Travessa 15 de Agosto 213; s/d R$75/90) You half expect Lucille Ball to be staying in the room next door here, with 1950s decor everywhere you look: the faux wood paneling, pea-green bathrooms and old-fashioned TVs with a button for each channel (all nine of them). Not that we're complaining: rooms are large, bright and come with an excellent breakfast spread, making this one of the better-value places in town.

Santarém Palace Hotel (☎ 3523 2820; stmpalace@ netsan.com.br; Av Rui Barbosa 726; s/d R$95/105; 🄐) Rooms here are quite spacious, with large windows and that eclectic Brady Bunch decor that's so common in Amazon hotels – lacquered wood figures prominently. Smoking is permitted in the common areas and most rooms, which is nice for some but a turnoff to many. Definitely ask for a top-floor room as they're newer and provide a little more distance between you and the busy street below. Side rooms have even less street noise, though somewhat smaller windows.

Barão Center Hotel (☎ 3064 9950; www.baraocenter hotel.com; Av Barão do Rio Branco; r R$180-220; 🄐 🖳 🛜) Santarém's best hotel, and the second home for businesspeople connected to the massive soy and timber river ports just outside of town. The rooms are comfortable and well equipped – wireless internet, electronic key cards, mini-splits, in-room safes – though the minimalist decor goes too far: with stark white walls and curiously few windows, you might feel a little like a lab rat. Fortunately, you can always escape to the rooftop restaurant, which has a terrific view of the city and river.

Eating

ourpick Mais Sabor (☎ 3522 0509; Av Tapajós; R$7-25; 🄐 dinner) Occupying a raised pier perched over the water, this popular open-air restaurant opposite Praça do Pescador has nice breezes and views of both rivers – the regular one and the one made up of joggers, families and teenage couples flowing down the wide promenade. The menu has mostly pizza and pasta.

Sabor Caseiro (Rua Floriano Peixoto 521; self-service per kg R$23; 🄐 lunch) With a new name and new look, this popular per-kilo joint has gone from downtrodden to upscale, but remains good value. Ample and tasty options are served in gleaming stainless-steel service, while the sturdy wooden tables and chairs and blasting

air-conditioners make Sabor Caseiro a comfy place to linger.

Delicias Caseiras (Travessa 15 de Agosto; dishes R$6-10; 🄐 lunch Mon-Sat) Budget travelers rejoice: for just R$6, you can pile as much grub on your plate as humanly and physically possible. Alas, some of the specialty items are doled out by hairnetted ladies behind the warming trays, but portions are still generous and they often include some less-common options like tongue and chicken patties. Air-con is intermittent.

Restaurante O Mascote (☎ 3523 2844; Praça do Pescador; dishes R$14-40; 🄐 lunch & dinner) The lunch buffet is tasty and good value. Fish plates are the specialty at night – try the *tucunaré ao molho de camarão* (peacock bass in shrimp sauce).

Getting There & Away

AIR

All flights go through Manaus or Belém.

Gol (☎ 3522-3386; www.voegol.com.br; at airport only)

TRIP (☎ 3523 3287/3899; www.voetrip.com.br; at airport only)

TAM (☎ 3523 9450; www.tamairlines.com; Av Mendoça Furtado 913 at Travessa Turiano Meira)

BOAT

There are two ports for passenger boats. For tips on boat travel, see the boxed text, p615.

From Docas do Pará (2.5km west of the center) you can catch a *recreo* (slow boat) to Belém (hammock R$160, double cabin $500, 48 hours, 10am Friday to Sunday), which stops at Monte Alegre (hammock R$40, five to seven hours) along the way; or to Manaus (hammock R$120, double cabin R$400, 2½ to three days, 1pm Monday to Saturday), with a stop at Parantins (hammock R$60, 25 to 30 hours). Buy your ticket a day or two in advance, especially in high season, to be sure you'll get a spot. Competing ticket booths at the port can make buying a ticket somewhat confusing, but they're all selling the same thing.

Praça Tiradentes (1km east of center on Av Tapajós) has a port with departures for less-common destinations; there are a handful of ticket booths, or look for signs on the boats themselves. There's frequent service to Macapá (hammock R$120, 36 hours, once daily), Monte Alegre (hammock R$25, six hours; take Macapá boat), and Alenquer (hammock R$15, seven hours, once daily).

There are two speedboat companies that dock their boats at or near Praça Tiradentes. **Hidroviaria Tapajos** (☎ 9184 8781) has service to Alenquer (R$25, three hours, 4pm daily) and Monte Alegre (R$30, three hours, Saturday at 4:30pm), while Lanchas Perola (no phone) has service to Itaituba (R$63, eight hours, 2pm). Once upon a time there was speedboat service to Manaus; it hasn't been available for several years now, but is certainly worth asking about.

BUS
The **bus station** (☎ 3523 4940) is 2.5km west of town. However, departures from there – primarily to Rurópolis, Itaituba, Cuiabá, and Marabá – are unreliable in the rainy season, and can be dangerous year-round due to highway robberies.

Buses to Alter do Chão (R$2.50, 45 minutes) stop on Av Rui Barbosa, Av Barão do Rio Branco, and Travessa João Otaviano roughly every hour between 5am and 6:30pm.

Getting Around
The airport is 14km west of the city center; buses (R$1.50) run to the city every hour or so between 6:15am and 6:15pm. Going to the airport, catch a bus marked 'Aeroporto' on Av Rui Barbosa just west of Av Barão do Rio Branco, between 5:30am and 5:30pm. Avoid buses marked 'Aeroporto Velho'; these go elsewhere. Taxis to and from the airport cost a whopping R$50.

If arriving by boat, 'Orla Fluvial' minibuses (R$1.50) shuttle between the city center and Docas do Pará, passing the Praça Tiradentes port every 20 to 30 minutes until 7pm. The 'Circular Esperança' bus (R$1.50) runs from the center to the Docas and then the bus station; avoid it returning from the Docas, however, as it does not go directly to the center. A taxi costs R$10 to R$15.

Moto-taxis are the best way, beyond walking, to get around town. Most trips cost R$2 to R$3.

AROUND SANTARÉM
Floresta Nacional (FLONA) do Tapajós
Behemoth *samaúma* trees, with trunks too big for even 20 people to stretch their arms around, are a highlight of this 5440-sq-km reserve on the east side of the Rio Tapajós. Within the reserve, numerous small communities live primarily by fishing and Brazil nuts,

though several now have modest ecotourism initiatives as well. Some villages are better set up than others, but no matter where you go, the experience is memorable: exploring the forest, staying with local villagers, and learning more about extractive trades that are so important to preserving the Amazon.

The side-by-side villages of **Maguarí** and **Jamaraquá** have been hosting visitors the longest, and remain the preferred choices for most visitors. Maguarí has a well-maintained trail (9km each way) that weaves past a number of impressive trees, including a cluster of *samaúmas* at the end. On the way back, you can visit families that use natural rubber to make toys, flip-flops, even stylish bags and purses.

Jamaraquá is smaller than Maguarí but is located near a lovely *igarapé* (inlet) with great canoeing when the water is high. Besides the simple pleasure of gliding silently through the trees, canoe trips are the best way to spot animals, birds, and reptiles. Jamaraquá also has a hiking trail, about 7.5km each way, with impressive trees along the way.

Other communities with ecotourism projects include Pini, Tauri, Prainha, Paraíso and Itapuama. Canoeing, fishing and even snorkeling are the highlights, partly because maintaining long hiking trails is difficult and time-consuming. For that reason, it's best to visit when the water levels are high.

Lodging and meals are with local families (though Maguarí and Jamaraquá are building simple pousadas). Let the bus driver know which town you'd like to visit, and he'll drop you at the home of the main host family there. You'll pay the *taxa comunitaria* (community tax, R$7 to R$10 per day) to the family, along with R$20 to R$35 per day for meals and a place to hang your hammock. Your hosts can help arrange outings, too, for which you'll pay the guide directly (typically R$20 to R$30 for one or two people). Be sure to bring a hammock, bottled water, toilet paper, mosquito repellent, flashlight, and cash (in small bills!); needless to say, a friendly, go-with-the-flow attitude also helps.

Authorization from IBAMA and a park fee are required for visiting FLONA do Tapajós and the villages there. If you're going to Maguarí or Jamaraquá, the bus will stop at an **IBAMA base station** along the way, where you can get permission and pay the fee. For the other villages, which are reached via a different entrance, it's best to visit the **IBAMA office in**

THE AMAZON

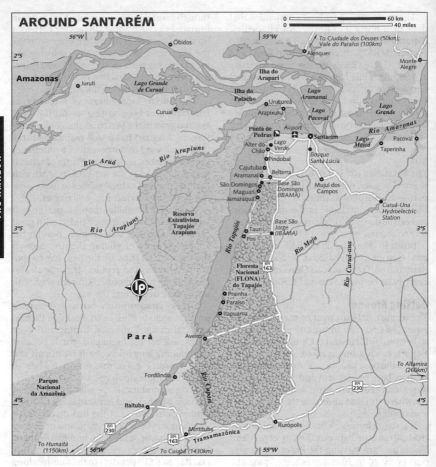

AROUND SANTARÉM

(☎ 3523 2964; Av Tapajós 2267; ☼ 8am-noon & 2-6pm Mon-Fri) beforehand.

There's bus service into FLONA do Tapajós from Santarém. Buses to Maguarí and Jamaraquá (R$7, four hours, 11am Monday to Saturday) depart from a stop on Av São Sebastião between Av Barão do Rio Branco and Travessa Silvino Pinto. Buses to villages further south, such as Nazaré, Tauri, and Pini, take a different route into the reserve, and leave from a stop located on Av Rui Barbosa between Travessa João Otaviano and Travessa Senador Lemos (R$15, six hours, noon Monday, Wednesday and Friday.) Be aware that buses returning to Santarém pass through the various FLONA villages at around 3am or 4am (ouch!).

Alternatively, agencies in Santarém and Alter do Chão offer tours to FLONA do Tapajós. Many use a riverboat to get there, and stay a night or two; you sleep on board, and take day trips with local guides. Gil Serique (p624) is a recommended private guide offering more-personalized one-day excursions.

Bosque Santa Lúcia

A privately owned patch of forest 18km south of town, **Bosque Santa Lúcia** (Santa Lucia Forest; http://bosque-santa.blogspot.com, amazonto@gmail.com) is home to over 400 different species of native plants. Guided walking tours (per person R$75, minimum two people) are an easy and excellent introduction to Amazonian flora, from ironwood and Brazil-nut trees to famously medicinal plants such as *andiroba* and guaraná, and much more. A 'Museum of Wood' has samples, cuttings and descriptions of the many types of Amazonian trees and their wood.

Santa Lúcia is owned by American Steve Alexander, who does most of the guiding himself, by advance reservation only.

Alter do Chão
☎ 0xx93 / pop 7000

Alter do Chão, 33km west of Santarém, is justly the subject of a thousand postcards. A sandbar directly in front of the town forms a picturesque white-sand island, known as Ilha do Amor (Island of Love). The island is largest and most attractive when the water is low, usually June to December. In the wet season it's greatly reduced, though still pretty.

Besides its famous beach, Alter do Chão also stands at the entrance to a huge lagoon, Lago Verde, which you can explore in rented canoes. FLONA do Tapajós and other spots on the Rio Tapajós make for good boat tours. Also accessible is the lesser-known Rio Arapiuns, whose nickname, 'the Caribbean of the Amazon,' is a forgivable exaggeration: the dry season reveals white-sand beaches and, on sunny days, transparent, even turquoise water. And don't miss Arariba (p631), one of the best indigenous art stores in the Amazon region.

ORIENTATION

Most of the streets in the center of Alter do Chão are now paved, a welcome improvement, especially in rainy season. Buses stop at the corner of Travessa Antônio A Lobato, in front of Pousada Tia Marilda and Arariba store. There's an official bus station a bit further on, but by disembarking at that corner – as most people do – you'll be within a couple blocks of just about everything, including Praça 7 de Septembro, the main square.

Alter do Chão's riverfront area has been completely refurbished, with a new *orla fluvial* that extends several hundred meters along what was once just a muddy bank. Stairs, rails and a new dock area make catching a rowboat to Ilha do Amor easier and safer, while the wide walkway and numerous benches make the riverfront a nice place for a stroll.

INFORMATION

Alter do Chão is growing year by year, but there were still no banks, ATMs or exchange offices in town at the time of research. A few hotels accept credit cards, but it's better to bring a stash of cash from Santarém.

You can use the internet at **Mãe Natureza** (☎ 3527 1264, 9125 8721; www.maenaturezaecoturismo .com.br; Praça 7 de Setembro; per hr R$5; ⏰ 8am-late) and at the hotel **Mirante de Ilha** (☎ 3527 1268; www .hotelmirantedailha.com.br; Rua Lauro Sodré 369; per hr R$5; ⏰ 9am-7pm). **Pousada Tupaiulândia** (☎ 3527 1157; Rua Pedro Teixeira 300) serves as the local post office and there are public phones in the main plaza.

DANGERS & ANNOYANCES

Stingrays are a concern in shallow areas of Ilha do Amor, Lago Verde and in the river; fortunately they're very skittish and prefer muddy areas over sandy ones, which means they're fairly uncommon in busy areas of Ilha do Amor. That said, always shuffle your feet when entering and exiting the water – this will kick up a cloud of sand in front of you and scare rays away. You can also use a long reed or stick to poke the sand in front of you.

SIGHTS & ACTIVITIES
Beaches

When the water is low, you can wade from the waterfront to **Ilha do Amor**. Otherwise, rowboats will take you across for R$2 per person. On the tip of the island closest to town, a bevy of shacks serve food and drinks year-round, and have chairs set up along the water's edge. For a little more solitude, simply walk further down the island (but be especially careful of stingrays if you do.) Another good sandy beach, **Praia do Cajuiero**, faces Rio Tapajós on the west side of the village. Beaches further afield are best reached in a car, including **Pindobal** (8km), **Cajutuba** (16km), **Aramanai** (26km) and **Ponta de Pedras** (28km). And tour operators in town offer day trips that include stopping at isolated **no-name beaches** along the main channel.

Lago Verde

This huge three-fingered lake is surrounded by forest, and has places to swim, snorkel, and spot birds and animals (including a resident family of monkeys). Tour operators offer enjoyable **boat tours** (per person R$60 to R$100, minimum two people); if you go in the afternoon, the tour usually ends at Ponta de Cururú, a good spot to see the sunset and river dolphins. Freelance boatmen on the waterfront do the same cheaper, but typically

THE BELO MONTE DAM

In February 2010 the Brazilian government gave the go-ahead for the Belo Monte Dam, a massive hydroelectric project planned for the Rio Xingu in southern Pará. The controversial dam would be the world's third largest, capable of generating 11,000 megawatts (enough to power 23 million homes) when running at full capacity. But critics say the numbers are deceiving: the dam would generate only a thousand megawatts during the region's long dry season, and overall would operate at just 40% of its capacity. Subtract from that the energy lost in the thousands of kilometers of transmission lines, and Belo Monte could well rank as the world's most inefficient power-generating dam.

Then there's the impact on the forest and the people living there: at least 12,000 people would be displaced by the project, and many thousands more when secondary dams – needed to regulate the water level in the main reservoir – are constructed upstream. Around 450 sq km of forest would be permanently flooded, while a 100km stretch of the mighty Xingu River would essentially dry up, including the part that runs alongside the Paquiçamba territory, home of the Juruna indigenous group.

The Brazilian environmental agency (IBAMA) says the current plan is an improvement on the original one, which was announced in the 1990s and promptly shelved amid international uproar. Among other things, the flooded area has been reduced by two-thirds (albeit with the construction of twin feeder canals, each 500m wide and 75km long) and contractors will be required to pony up US$800 million on resettlement and environmental protection projects. Still, two senior IBAMA officials resigned in protest and environmental groups and celebrities (such as *Avatar* director James Cameron) have already launched campaigns to block the project a second time.

don't have the same service or equipment that agencies do. Or you can rent a kayak at the waterfront and explore the lagoon on your own; just be alert to strong waves and currents.

TOURS

Alter do Chão has terrific options for exploring the river and forest. Popular day trips include snorkeling in Lago Verde, dolphin-spotting at Ponta do Cururú, exploring the animal-rich Canal do Jarí, or beach-hopping by car or boat. Multiday riverboat tours can be personalized according to your time, budget and interest, whether hiking in FLONA do Tapajós, visiting small communities on the far side of Rio Tapajós, or camping on the beach on the Arapiuns river. Day trips start at R$70 for a group of four people, while longer tours run R$130 to R$250 per person per day, with everything included.

Areia Branca Ecotour (☎ 3527 1317; www.areiabrancaecotour.com.br; Orla Fluvial; ☼ 8am-noon & 2-7pm) Located on the waterfront walkway a short distance from the plaza, this energetic new agency is run by friendly multilingual siblings from Alter do Chão.

Mãe Natureza (☎ 3527 1264; www.maenaturezaecoturismo.com.br; Praça 7 de Setembro; ☼ 9am-late) A reliable and experienced agency run by Argentinean expats Jorge Bassi and Claudio Chena.

FESTIVALS

The **Festa do Çairé** in the second week of September is the major folkloric event in western Pará. The Çairé is a standard held aloft to lead a flower-bedecked procession; its origins may go back to symbols used by early missionaries to help convert *índios*.

SLEEPING

Pousada Tia Marilda (☎ 3527 1144; Travessa Antônio A Lobato 559; s/d R$60/70; ☒) Literally steps from where everyone piles off the bus from Santarém, this simple place has decent-sized rooms and friendly owners. The decor is an honest attempt at cute…it's the thought that counts. The 2nd-floor rooms are larger and breezier, though all the units now have air-con.

Pousada Tupaiulândia (☎ 3527 1157, 9975 4928; Rua Pedro Teixeira 300; s/d $50/80; ☒) The suites here occupy two circular buildings, making for curving walls and uncommon angles. No matter, the units are spacious and clean, all with TV, minibar and air-conditioning. Decor is rather bare, but the shellacked brick interior walls make up for it. Good value.

our pick **Albergue Pousada da Floresta** (☎ 9651 7193; www.alberguepousadadafloresta.com.br; Travessa Antônio Pedrosa s/n; hammock or camping per person R$10-15, cabin R$60-90) This super-laid-back backpacker favorite has spacious hammock area, and several cozy wood cabins, all with fan, private bathroom, reasonably comfortable beds, small patio with hammock, and artsy details like stools painted with Asian or floral patterns. Guests can rent bikes and kayaks (per day R$10 to R$15), and use a small outdoor kitchen. The friendly young proprietor offers guided tours to lesser-known spots. The hostel is nestled in the trees a short walk from the center; follow the signs past Pousada Alter-do-Cháo, and turn left on the fifth side road.

Pousada do Mingote (☎ 3527 1158; www.pousada domingote.com.br; Travessa Antônio A Lobato s/n; s R$70-100, d R$90-120; ❷) Just a half-block down from the bus stop, and a half-block up from the plaza, rooms here are on the small side, but clean and comfortable, all with TV and air-con; superior rooms have mini-splits, hot water, and (in some) flat-screen TVs. Rooms are arranged on two floors, looking onto a small shady interior courtyard.

Mirante da Ilha (☎ 3527 1268; www.hotelmiranteda ilha.com.br; Rua Lauro Sodré 369; s/d R$125/145; ❷ 🖵) Only a handful of rooms at this big boxy hotel have, as the name suggests, a view of Ilha do Amor, which makes all the difference. Assuming you can snag one, the rooms are the center's best – clean and modern, with a large balcony, and friendly professional service to boot. Be sure to check out the rooftop patio, for even better views.

Beloalter Hotel (☎ 3527 1230; www.beloalter.com .br; end of Rua Pedro Teixeira; r R$184-252, 2-room ste R$480; ❷ 🛜 🖵) Alter do Chão's most upscale hotel is near Lago Verde, about 500m east of the highway down a shady dirt road. Standard rooms are spacious and modern, with ceramic floors, tasteful decor and small terraces. Split-level 'ecological' rooms have wood interiors, shutter windows and, in at least one case, a huge tree trunk angling through the room. A private beach and clean pool make this a comfortable getaway.

EATING & DRINKING
Farol da Ilha (Orla Fluvial s/n; dishes R$12-35; ❤️ dinner Fri-Sun) Back to its original name after a brief spell as 'La Oca,' this waterfront restaurant has always had first-rate fish meals to match its outstanding river and island vistas. Most dishes serve two people, and are priced accordingly. Single dishes aren't much of a value; solo travelers can order cheaper

chicken dishes or just come here for drinks and the view.

Tribal (☎ 3527 1226; Travessa Antônio A Lobato s/n; mains R$15-40; ❤️ lunch & dinner) Huge and well-prepared fish dishes serve two easily, with potato salad to spare at this popular open-air restaurant. Good grilled beef and chicken also served. Single portions available.

Mãe Natureza (☎ 3527 1264, 9125 8721; www.mae naturezaecoturismo.com.br; Praça 7 de Setembro, R$7-24) Nightly bar and pizza service, with great international music and tables set up on the street right outside the shop. Good place to meet other travelers.

SHOPPING
Arariba (☎ 3527 1251; www.araribah.com.br; cnr Travessa Antônio A Lobato & Rua Dom Macêdo Costa; ❤️ 9am-noon & 3-8pm Tue-Sun) Arguably the best indigenous art store in the Amazon, with items ranging from inexpensive necklaces to museum-quality masks and ceremonial figures. Credit cards accepted.

GETTING THERE & AWAY
Buses from Alter do Chão to Santarém (R$2.50, 45 minutes) depart hourly from 6am to 7:20pm, except on Sunday, when service ends around 6pm. Catch the bus opposite Pousada Tia Marilda. There is no bus to the airport from Alter do Chão; if you've got plenty of time, you can take the bus as far as the airport turnoff, and wait for the shuttle from Santarém to pass, usually once an hour. Otherwise, a taxi to the airport (or to Santarém or the riverboat ports) costs a painful R$60 to R$70.

PARQUE NACIONAL DA AMAZÔNIA
This large (9940 sq km) Amazonian rainforest national park lies west of the town of Itaituba (population 65,000), which is 250km southwest of Santarém. To visit, you must obtain prior permission from the **IBAMA office** (☎ 0xx93-3518 1530; Av Marechal Rondon s/n, Itaituba) and an IBAMA staff member must accompany you on your visit. It is possible to stay at rudimentary facilities at an IBAMA post inside the park, but there's no real visitor infrastructure here. Alternatively, ask at **Mãe Natureza** (☎ 3527 1264, 9125 8721; www.maenaturezaecoturismo.com.br; Praça 7 de Setembro, Alter do Chão; ❤️ 8am-late) or **Areia Branca Ecotour** (☎ 3527-1317; www.areiabrancaecotour.com.br; Orla Fluvial; ❤️ 8am-noon & 2-7pm), both in Alter de Chão, about arranging a trip there.

MONTE ALEGRE

☎ 0xx93 / pop 23,300

The sandstone hills behind Monte Alegre, about 120km downstream from Santarém, are dotted with caves and bizarre rock outcroppings. They, in turn, are adorned with dozens of rock paintings believed to be around 11,000 years old, the oldest known human creations in Amazonia and possibly Brazil (see below). Most are in red and yellow, and depict human and animal figures, plus geometric designs and handprints of the painters themselves. Some are clustered tightly together, others appear to be isolated doodling.

Tour agencies in Santarém and Alter do Chão also arrange trips to Monte Alegre; see those sections for details. To do it yourself, contact **Nelsí Sadeck** (☎ 3533 1430; nelsi@netsan.com.br; Rua do Jaquara 320), a local teacher and engineer who bears much of the credit for the conservation of the paintings, and is the go-to guide for visiting them.

Hotel Panorámica (☎ 3533 1282; s/d R$60/75; ⚙) is one of the better places in town. Rooms are plain but relatively clean, with air-con and TV.

Restaurante Panorama (Travessa Oriental 100; dishes R$7-18) is a reasonable fish restaurant.

There's once-weekly speedboat service from Santarém to Monte Alegre aboard **Hidroviaria Tapajos** (☎ 9184 8781; R$30, 3hr, 4:30pm Sat) and slow boats headed both upstream and downstream stop here most days (Santarém R$40, four to five hours; Belém R$140, 44 hours); see p626 for more info.

ALENQUER

☎ 0xx93 / pop 27,300

Across the Amazon from Santarém, the village of Alenquer was founded in the 18th century by missionaries attempting to convert the local Abaré indigenous people. Alenquer has several impressive waterfalls relatively nearby, including **Cachoeira Açu das Pedras**. The town is also the gateway to **Ciudade dos Deuses** (City of the Gods), a field of bizarre rock formations 50km north of the town. Another 50km further is the **Vale do Paraíso** (Valley of Paradise), which has a fine pousada and additional waterfalls.

Tour agencies in Santarém and Alter do Chão offer trips here, which are advisable

---

PREHISTORIC AMAZONIA

Archaeologist Anna C Roosevelt (a great-granddaughter of Theodore Roosevelt) caused a stir in her field when she reported, in 1996, that remains of an ancient settlement in the Amazon were 11,100 years old. If true, it means humans settled in the area at least a thousand years earlier than thought. The site is near the town of Monte Alegre (p632) in Pará state, and includes a plethora of intriguing rock paintings that travelers can visit with a guide or on a tour from Alter do Chão.

The Roosevelt controversy notwithstanding (nor that surrounding a site in northeast Brazil, where some archaeologists say there's evidence of human settlement dating as far back as 48,000 BC), most researchers agree that large populations of Stone Age peoples had settled the Amazon Basin by around 10,000 years ago, living in extended family groups and practicing primitive hunting and gathering. And it was around 6000 years ago that the Tapajoara people, living near present-day Santarém, carved stone representations of animals and humans, and created simple clay urns, the oldest known pottery in the Americas. At the same time, indigenous Amazonians started fishing and collecting shellfish, and mastering rudimentary agriculture.

By the last few centuries of the pre-Christian era, the Amazon was home to numerous cohesive communities, numbering in the thousands and led by chiefs. They produced good-quality pottery and cultivated maize and manioc intensively. It was in this time that the techniques of itinerate agriculture still used today were first developed, including selective burning, crop rotation, and allowing the land periodic 'rest periods' to regenerate.

On Ilha de Marajó, in the mouth of the Amazon River, early people built earth platforms called *aterros* to escape the annual floods, and buried their dead in elaborate urns. The Marajó cultures reached their most advanced stage in the Marajoara phase (AD 400–1350), when hundreds of *aterros* up to 6m high and 250m long were built around Lago Arari. Marajoara ceramics – elaborate funerary and ceremonial vases and simpler domestic ones – are the most sophisticated artifacts known from precolonial Brazil, exhibiting exuberant decoration in red, black and white. Marajoara influence reached as far as Lago de Silves, 200km east of Manaus, and the Rio Cunani in northern Amapá.

considering the lack of transportation and tourism infrastructure. Adventurous travelers can try renting motorcycles in Alenquer and making it to the waterfalls on their own; however, the road is unpaved and can be quite rutted, so only experienced motorcyclists should attempt it. Hiring a taxi is another option. **Pousada Vale do Paraíso** (per person R$30) in Vale do Paraíso has quaint, comfortable bungalows sleeping four to seven people.

From Santarém, **Hidroviaria Tapajos** (☎ 9184 8781) has daily service to Alenquer (R$25, three hours, 4pm) while slow boats leave once or twice daily from Praça Tiradentes (R$15, seven hours). Most slow boats headed to Belém stop in Alenquer as well.

AMAPÁ

Stretching from the Amazon delta to the borders of French Guiana and Suriname, Amapá has just over a half-million inhabitants, most of whom live in the capital, Macapá. The climate is equatorial and super humid, though drier from September to November. Owing to the proximity of French Guiana, many Amapaenses (residents of Amapá) speak some French.

Amapá is home to the huge – and hugely promising – Tumucumaque National Park (p636). The park is Brazil's largest, and now opening for tourism. It's an untouched swath of tropical rain forest blanketing a cluster of mountains, rich in flora and fauna.

Beyond that, however, Amapá has precious little to offer most travelers, except those looking for a land route into French Guiana.

MACAPÁ

☎ 0xx96 / pop 366,500

The state capital lies on the equator, in a strategic position on the north side of the Rio Amazonas estuary. Though not really worth a trip on its own, anyone headed to French Guiana must pass though Macapá and won't regret spending a day or two here, with its delectable sea breezes and a couple of nice sights. If you have extra time, visiting the San Antônio waterfall or forging a path to the national parks can be rewarding (though tough) before you head up to the border.

Downtown Macapá is a reasonably walkable place, though the fierce heat and general lack of shade can make for sweaty exploring. Consider taking a cab or moto-taxi between sights. For relief, Rua Beira Rio gets nice river breezes.

Information

EMERGENCY

Ambulance (☎ 192)
Police (☎ 190)

INTERNET ACCESS

Babuu Prime (cnr Gen Rondon & Av Presidente Vargas; per hr R$2; 🕒 24hr)
Virtual.com (Frota Palace Hotel, Rua Tiradentes 1104; per hr R$2; 🕒 9am-10pm Mon-Sat, noon-6pm Sun)

LAUNDRY

Lava Bem (☎ 3633 6092; Av Mendonça Furtado 815; 20 pieces R$25; 🕒 8am-6pm Mon-Fri, 8am-noon Sat) Next-day service available on request.

MONEY

Bradesco (cnr Rua Independência & Av Prof Cora de Carvalho) Reliable ATMs.
FITTA (☎ 3223 2788; airport; 🕒 9am-5pm Mon-Fri) Changes euros, US dollars and traveler's checks.
Santander (Rua Cândido Mendes) Reliable ATMs; between Av Presidente Vargas and Av Coriolano Jucá.

POST

Post office (☎ 3223 3803; Av Corialono Jucá; 🕒 9am-4pm Mon-Fri) Between Ruas São José and Cândido Mendes.

TOURIST INFORMATION

IBAMA (☎ 3214 1122/1116; Rua Hamilton Silva at Av Antônio Coelho de Carvalho; 🕒 8-11am & 2-4pm Mon-Fri) For info on national parks.
Setur (☎ 3212 5335; www.setur.ap.gov.br; Rua Independência 29; 🕒 8am-noon & 2-6pm Mon-Fri) Friendly state tourism office.

TRAVEL AGENCIES

Marco Zero Turismo (☎ 3223 1922; mztour@bno.com.br; Av Presidente Vargas 540; 🕒 8am-6:30pm Mon-Fri, 8am-1pm Sat) Sells plane tickets.
Sonave Turismo (☎ 3223 9090; Rua Padre Júlio Maria Lombaerd 48; 🕒 8am-6pm Mon-Fri, 9am-1pm Sat) Sells plane and boat tickets.

Sights

FORTALEZA DE SÃO JOSÉ DE MACAPÁ

The Portuguese built the large stone **Fortaleza de São José de Macapá** (entrance Av Henrique Galúcio; admission free; 🕒 9am-6pm) between 1764 and 1782 to defend the north side of the Amazon against French incursions from the Guianas.

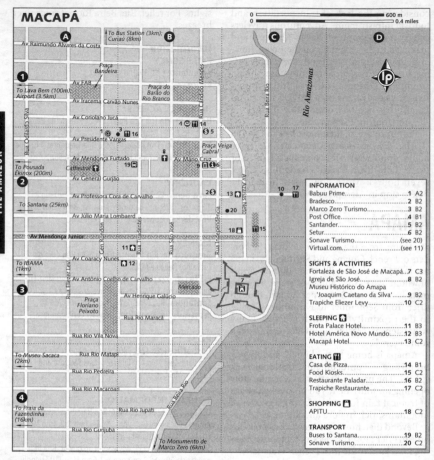

MACAPÁ

INFORMATION
Babuu Prime...1 A2
Bradesco..2 B2
Marco Zero Turismo.............................3 B2
Post Office...4 B1
Santander..5 B2
Setur..6 B2
Sonave Turismo...........................(see 20)
Virtual.com.................................(see 11)

SIGHTS & ACTIVITIES
Fortaleza de São José de Macapá..7 C3
Igreja de São José...............................8 B2
Museu Histórico do Amapa
 'Joaquim Caetano da Silva'.......9 B2
Trapiche Eliezer Levy.......................10 C2

SLEEPING
Frota Palace Hotel...........................11 B3
Hotel América Novo Mundo........12 B3
Macapá Hotel....................................13 C2

EATING
Casa de Pizza....................................14 B1
Food Kiosks.......................................15 C2
Restaurante Paladar........................16 C2
Trapiche Restaurante......................17 C2

SHOPPING
APITU..18 C2

TRANSPORT
Buses to Santana..............................19 B2
Sonave Turismo...............................20 C2

It makes for a reasonably interesting visit, with cavernous barracks and impressively thick walls, yet there's bizarrely little in the way of plaques or information.

MUSEU SACACA

About 2km west of the city center is the unique **Museu Sacaca** (Sacaca Sustainable Development Museum; ☎ 3212 5361; Av Feliciano Coelho 1509 at Rua Manoel Cudoxo Perreira; admission free; ☺ 9am-6pm Tue-Sun). The primary exhibits, arranged in a large outdoor plot, are reconstructions of various rural homes, from the thatched huts of *castanheiros* (Brazil-nut harvesters) to riverboats used by traveling merchants. Slightly corny, yes, but the Portuguese-speaking guides give interesting explanations.

There are no convenient buses here, and it's a long, hot walk. Moto-taxis (R$3) are a good option.

MUSEU HISTÓRICO DO AMAPÁ 'JOAQUIM CAETANO DA SILVA'

The new **Museu Histórico do Amapa 'Joaquim Caetano da Silva'** (Av Mario Cruz at Rua Cândido Mendes; admission free; ☺ 9am-6pm Tue-Sun), near Praça Veigal Cabral, covers various aspects and eras of Amapá's history. The most interesting displays describe archaeological work done here, including Emílio Goeldi's discovery of 14th-century clay urns in the form of seated figures, which you'll find to be widely replicated in craft stores throughout the Amazon area.

MONUMENTO DO MARCO ZERO

A large obelisk-cum-sundial, the **Monumento do Marco Zero** (Zero Line Monument; Av Equatorial at Rodovía Juscelino Kubitscheck) stands on the equator, about 6km southwest of the city center. A hemisphere-straddling sports stadium and a sambadrome (a stadium built for the express purpose of holding huge samba concerts and dances) are part of the same complex.

To get there, take a southbound 'Fortaleza' or orange 'Universidad' bus on Rua Tiradentes at Av Mendonça Furtado, behind Igreja de São José. The same bus returns to the centro. The Zerão bus also works, but takes a more roundabout route.

PRAIA DA FAZENDINHA

This is a reasonably attractive beach 16km southwest of Macapá, which has a number of beachside restaurants with good seafood. From Macapá, take a 'Fortaleza' or 'Santana – Vila Fazendinha' bus southbound from the stop on Rua Tiradentes behind Igreja de São José (R$1.85, 20 minutes).

Festivals & Events

O Marabaixo is an Afro-Brazilian celebration, with music and dance, held 40 days after Semana Santa. In mid-August, the nearby town of Curiaú hosts an exuberant Afro-Brazilian celebration called **Festa de São Joaquim**.

Sleeping

Hotel América Novo Mundo (☎ 3223 2819; Av Coaracy Nunes 333; r with/without bathroom R$60/45; ✱) Rooms and service are about as no-frills as they can get, but the price and location make this a good choice for budget travelers.

Frota Palace Hotel (☎ 2101 3999; www.hotelfrota.com.br; Rua Tiradentes 1104; s/d R$103/127; ✱ 🖘) Popular with visiting businesspeople – the airline arrival and departure times are posted in the lobby – the Frota has clean efficient rooms, with small granite and glass bathrooms, flat-screen TVs and firm beds (but old-school air-conditioners). Discounts often available on request; upstairs rooms are newest.

Macapá Hotel (☎ 3217 1350; www.macapahotel.com.br; Av Azarias Neto 17; s R$100-134, d R$120-160; ✱ 🖘 ❄) This grand old dame is showing her age, but the ample, airy construction and terrific location make it a fine choice all the same. There's a pleasant pool and constant breezes off the river – both much appreciated on hot afternoons.

ourpick Pousada Ékinox (☎ 3223 0086; www.ekinox.com.br; Rua Jovino Dinoá 1693; r R$155; ✱ 🖘) Macapá's most charming accommodations are owned and operated by a former French honorary consul and his Brazilian wife, and feature excellent mattresses, modern TV and air-con units, and artful decor. Some units share shady patios, or have hammocks hanging in upper-floor balconies. It's a moderate walk from the center.

Eating & Drinking

Food kiosks lining the waterfront, north of the fort, are popular for cheap evening snacks, served at plastic tables and customarily accompanied by a tall beer.

Restaurante Paladar (Av Presidente Vargas 456; per kg R$23; 🕑 lunch) An innocuous exterior makes it

AROUND MACAPÁ

0 — 80 km
0 — 50 miles

easy to miss this large, excellent self-service restaurant, featuring seafood and fresh-grilled meats and daily vegetarian options. Clean air-conditioned dining area and good service.

Casa de Pizza (☎ 3225 1212; Av Coriolano Jucá; mains R$12-25; ☯ dinner Mon-Sat) This big new pizza joint has a pleasant dining area with wood tables and chairs and high peaked ceiling. The food reasonably good, and you can get it delivered.

Trapiche Restaurante (Trapiche Eliezer Levy; mains R$15-35; ☯ 10am-midnight Tue-Sun, dinner only Mon) This would be just another typical restaurant if it weren't on the end of a long pier sticking into the Amazon River. Dishes are large enough for two (mostly fish with a few meat and chicken options) and come with a terrific view – during the rainy season you can watch storm clouds march up and down the river.

Shopping

APITU (Av Mendonça Jr at Rua Azarias Neto; ☯ 8am-noon & 2-6pm Mon-Sat) A small but authentic selection of art and jewelry of the Tumucumaque indigenous people who come from the mountainous borders of Amapá, Pará and Suriname. Not to be confused with the hugely (and hugely disappointing) state-run handicrafts store next door.

Getting There & Away
TO/FROM THE AIRPORT
Taxis charge R$20 from the airport into town, and R$15 in the other direction. There's no bus service that stops within a kilometer of the airport.

TO/FROM THE BUS STATION
To get to the bus station, 3km north of town, take bus 'Jardim' or bus 'Pedrinhas Novo Horizonte' on Rua São José, in front of Igreja de São José (R$1.50, 20 minutes). The same buses return.

AIR
Gol (☎ 3222 4857, 0300 115 2121; www.voegol.com.br; airport only, ☯ 9am-8pm & 11:10pm-4:50am)
TAM (☎ 3223 8100/2688; www.tamairlines.com; airport only; ☯ 11:30am-6:30pm & 10pm-4:50am Mon-Sat, 11:30am-3pm Sun)

BOAT
Sonave Turismo (☎ 3223 9090; Rua Padre Júlio M Lombaerd 48; ☯ 8am-6pm Mon-Fri, 9am-1pm Sat) sells tickets in Macapá, but the boats leave from a port in the town of Santana, 25km

southwest of Macapá. A taxi there costs around R$30. Otherwise take a southbound 'Macapá-Santana' bus from the stop on Rua Tiradentes behind Igreja de São José (R$1.85, 30 minutes).

Slow boats for Belém depart on Monday, Thursday and Friday (hammock R$140, double cabin R$450, 24 hours). There are daily departures for Santarém (hammock R$140, double cabin R$450, 48 hours) and continuing to Manaus (hammock R$260, 72 hours). See the boxed text, p615, for tips on riverboat travel.

BUS
Macapá's bus station is on the BR-156 in Barrio São Lázaro, about 3km north of the center. Rain and mud make long-distance bus travel in Amapá very rough, especially from January to June, and temporary cancellations are common year-round.

Bus service to Oiapoque and the French Guiana border (R$75, 16 to 24 hours, four departures daily) take Hwy BR-156, which is paved for the first 140km only. If service is suspended, freelancers offer *camioneta* (truck) service for R$140 to R$170.

For Cachoeira Santo Antônio, take a bus to Laranjal do Jarí (US$40, seven to 12 hours, two departures daily); dirt road the entire way.

TRAIN
An enjoyable train ride links Santana, 25km southwest of Macapá where the docks are located, and Serra do Navio (R$10, five hours), near Parque Nacional Montanhas do Tumucumaque. Departures are on Monday, Wednesday and Friday.

TUMUCUMAQUE NATIONAL PARK

Parque Nacional Montanhas do Tumucumaque (Tumucumaque National Park) is Brazil's largest national park, spanning nearly 39,000 sq km. It borders the similarly immense Parque Indígena do Tumucumaque, in Pará; together they form the largest swath of protected rain forest in the world. The parks are part of an even larger preservation zone – in concept, though only partially in law – called the Guiana Shield Zone, which spans a whopping 150,000 sq km in Brazil, the Guianas, Suriname and Venezuela, and was designated in 2006 to encourage member countries to establish national parks in the area.

Tumucumaque park is currently closed to visitors, as IBAMA has yet to establish and ratify an environmental management plan for the area. There's no telling when it'll be complete – they've been at it for five years and counting – much less a time frame for establishing trails, camping areas, guide services and other infrastructure needed for visits. The **Instituto Chico Mendes de Conservação e Biodiversidad** (ICMBio, ☎ 2101 9016) has direct oversight of the park and is the best source of information; it was located in Macapá's IBAMA office at the time of research, but was planning to relocate. Otherwise, you may be able to find guides in the small town of Serra do Navio, which is just outside the protected area but enjoys much of the same ecology.

Other protected areas in Amapá include **Ilha de Maracá**, the **Floresta Nacional do Amapá** and **Parque Nacional do Cabo Orange**. Like Tumucumaque, they are not yet open to tourism, but plans are in the works. Check with IBAMA.

OIAPOQUE
☎ 0xx96 / pop 21,000
Oiaoque is a rough-and-tumble border town at the end of Highway BR-156, with muddy streets and aggressive moneychangers. It's separated by the Rio Oiapoque from St Georges, French Guiana, which itself is about four hours (200km) southeast of Cayenne, the French Guiana capital. The town is notable for its substantial indigenous population – nearly half the city belongs to one of four local ethnic groups – but is primarily a way to cross between Brazil and French Guiana.

Oiapoque was long thought to mark the northernmost point of Brazil. The saying '*Do Oiapoque ao Chuí*' ('From Oiapoque to Chuí') is still a common phrase meaning all of Brazil. The town itself has a monument, Marco Inicial do Brazil, and a motto, *Aqui começa o Brazil* (Brazil starts here), to mark the distinction. The only problem is that it is *not* the northernmost point: Monte Caburaí, on the Venezuela border in Roraima, beats it by a good hundred kilometers! Oiapoque took the news in its stride, tweaking its claim to say the town has the northernmost coastline, which is true.

Orientation & Information
The Rio Oiapoque forms the curving northern edge of town. Av Barão do Rio Branco is the principal avenue in town, running from the Marco Inicial do Brasil on the riverfront south past Igreja NS das Graças and through the residential part of town.

The pier is a block west of Av Barão do Rio Branco. **Hospital Geral** (☎ 3521 1280; Rua Presidente Vargas & Av Veiga Cabral) is four blocks south of the pier.

The **Polícia Federal** (☎ 3521 1380; ☻ 8am-8pm) handles passport control, coming or going from Brazil.

Oiapoque has branches of Banco do Brasil and Bradesco.

Sleeping & Eating
Arizona Hotel (☎ 3521 2185; Av Coaracy Nunes 551; s/d R$40/50, incl breakfast R$50/60) A few blocks inland from the waterfront. Rooms here are basic but clean with TV, minibar and air-conditioning.

Restaurante Beija Flor (Rua Joaquim C da Silva; mains R$14-35) Near the pier; recommended for Brazilian and French food.

Getting There & Away
The bus station is on BR-156, a few hundred meters southeast of the center. The airport is further east, also off BR-156. A motorboat ride across the Rio Oiapoque to St Georges costs R$15 and takes about 20 minutes.

See Getting There & Away under Macapá (p636) for information on bus and air transportation.

TOCANTINS

The state of Tocantins was created in 1989 by hiving off what was previously the northern half of Goiás. It's in a transition zone between the Amazon rain forest to the north and the cerrado (savanna) in the southeast. This makes for plenty of outdoor opportunities, and the state is making a concerted effort to portray itself as Brazil's next ecotourism hot spot. It certainly has the potential, from easy-reach hiking and waterfalls around Taquarussú to vast protected areas like Jalapão state park and Ilha do Bananal, a Pantanal-like wetland. But progress has been slow: the fact that Palmas is 14 hours by bus from Brasília and 20 hours from Belém, and that flights remain expensive, surely has something to do with it.

PALMAS
☎ 0xx63 / pop 189,000
Less than 20 years ago, the broad valley bisected by the Rio Tocantins held just a scattering of rural *fazendas*. Starting in 1989, a

new state capital was built from scratch, and construction, state government and economic incentives brought thousands of Brazilians to this unlikely landscape, 1000km north of Brasília and 1600km south of Belém.

There is a surprising number of good outdoor options around Palmas, which are the main reason to make a trip here. The city itself is sure to strike most first-timers as sterile and shadeless, but it has a way of growing on you. It's basically a smaller, newer version of Brasília, with a handful of interesting sites and that same planned-city weirdness.

Orientation

Palmas' layout is confusing to most first-time visitors. The current system is actually a simplified version of the original one, which was scrapped because even the mailmen couldn't find the correct addresses.

Praça Girossóis is the center of town, the lake is to the west, and the hills are to the east. Palmas's two primary thoroughfares – Av Juscelino Kubitschek (known as Av JK, or 'Jota-Kah') and Av Teotônio Segurado – are the only streets with regular names. All other roads are named according to their direction and location. Main avenues start with either 'NS' (norte–sul, or north–south) or 'LO' (leste–oeste, or east–west), depending on which direction they run. Between the avenues are smaller ruas (roads), which are named according to their quadrant, like 'NO' for the northwest or 'SE' for southeast, plus a number: east–west ruas have odd numbers, north–south ruas have evens. Finally, every block is numbered, eg Quadra 101 Norte or Quadra 104 Sul, with numbers increasing as they get further from the center.

Most hotels and restaurants listed here are on the west side of Praça Girossóis, near a small commercial center called Galeria Bela Palma on Av NS-01. Buses to and from the airport, the bus station and Taquaruçú (p641) stop right in front. Palmas Shopping, a large red-painted mall with movies and restaurants, is on the south side of the plaza at Avs LO-01 and NS-01.

To really enjoy Palmas' outdoors areas, you will need to rent a car. Fortunately, driving in Palmas is a blast, with huge roundabouts at most intersections instead of streetlights.

Information

As well as those options listed below, there are cash machines located at Palmas Shopping,

a small busy mall on the south side of Praça Girossóis.

ESSENTIALS

Agência de Desenvolvimento Turístico (ADETUR; ☎ 3218 2396; ☼ 8am-noon & 2-6pm Mon-Fri) On the east side of Praça Girossóis, this is the state tourism agency, though it's more an administrative office than a public one.

Ambulance (☎ 192)

Bananal Ecotour (☎ 3028 4200; www.bananalecotour .com.br; Quadra 103 Sul, cnr Av NS-01 & Rua SO-07) Offers tours to the Ilha Bananal and Jalapão areas, and operates a well-recommended ecolodge (p642) near Taquaruçú.

Banco do Brasil (Quadra 103-Sul, cnr Av Juscelino Kubitschek & Av NS-01) Handy to the listed hotels.

Bradesco (Quadra 104 Nte, cnr Av Juscelino Kubitschek at Av NS-02) Across the plaza from Banco do Brasil; ATM.

Centro de Atendimento ao Turista (CATUR; ☎ 3218 5339/5570; Av LO-11; ☼ 8am-noon & 2-6pm Mon-Fri) The city's tourist office, inconveniently located in Parque Cesamar, in Quadra 506 Sul, between Av NS-02 and Av NS-04. It's a long (3.5km) hot walk southeast of the center; better to drive or take a mototaxi there.

Hospital Geral de Palmas (☎ 3218 7802; Quadra 201 Sul, Av LO-5) Between Av Teotônio Segurado and Av NS-01, this is the city's main public hospital; 24hr emergency room.

Hospital Oswaldo Cruz (☎ 3219 9000; Quadra 501 Sul; Av NS-01) Between Av LO-09 & Av LO-11, this recommended private hospital is in Palmas's medical district; 24hr emergency room.

HSBC (Av Juscelino Kubitschek) Reliable ATM; near Av NS-02.

MSD Inform@tica (☎ 3215 8562; Quadra 103 Nte, Rua NO-03; per hr R$2; ☼ 9am-10pm Mon-Sat, noon-10pm Sun) Fast, inexpensive internet service.

Police (☎ 190)

OTHER SERVICES

Droganita (☎ 3228 5804; ☼ 24hr) One of several pharmacies in Galeria Bela Palma.

Quality Lavanderia (☎ 3215 5060; cnr Av NS-01 at Av LO-01; wash/dry per kg R$8.50, plus ironing per kg R$14; ☼ 8am-6:30pm Mon-Fri, 9am-1pm Sat) Can do your laundry the same day if you drop it off early, and will deliver loads of 2kg or more to your hotel.

Post office (Palmas Shopping; ☼ 10am-9pm Mon-Fri, 10am-1pm Sat) There's another post office on Av JK between Rua SE-04 and Av NS-04.

Viagem & Cia (☎ 3215 2085; www.viagemecia.com.br; Quadra 104 Nte; Av NS-02) Sells plane tickets.

Sights & Activities

Most of the sights of interest are in **Praça Girossóis**, purportedly Brazil's largest municipal plaza and the second-largest in the world (after Moscow's Red Square).

PALACIO ARAGUAIA

Built on the only hill in town, the **Palacio Araguaia** (☎ 3218 1000; admission free; ☟ 8am-6pm), the state capitol, looks over the plaza and Palmas itself. The lobby is adorned with huge colorful mosaics and in one corner there's an impressive scale model of Praça Girossóis, which you can then compare to the real thing from windows on the 2nd floor.

Be aware that you may not enter the palace with shorts or tank tops, and the 2nd floor is closed on weekends.

MEMORIAL COLUNA PRESTES

Housed in a curious white, tubular structure near Palacio Araguaia, the **Memorial Coluna Prestes** (admission free; ☟ 8am-6pm Tue-Sun) tells the life story of Captain Luis Carlos Prestes, who led 1500 rebel soldiers against the military dictatorship in 1924. The march lasted three years and covered 25,000km, and is credited with helping bring democracy to Brazil, especially its long-isolated interior.

SERRA DO LAJEADO

East of town, **Serra do Lajeado** has scores of beautiful ecological attractions, especially waterfalls, swimming holes, trails and even ancient cave paintings. Its sheer cliffs also make it a popular destination for rappelling and paragliding. Unfortunately, most of the land is privately owned, and at the time of research the best and most accessible attractions were closed to visitors by the landowners. Call **CATUR** (☎ 3218 5339/5570; ☟ 8am-noon & 2-6pm Mon-Fri) for the latest info.

Sleeping

Hotel Serra Azul (☎ 3215 1505; Rua NO-03; s/d R$50/70; P ☒ ☎) Clean rooms, affordable price and convenient location make this Palmas's best budget option. Rooms are small with no frills, but face onto a sunny courtyard with a quaint dining room where breakfast is served. Close to the bus stop for those who don't have a car, and secure parking for those who do.

Carvalho's Hotel (☎ 3215 5758; www.hotelcar valhopalmas.com.br; cnr Rua SO-01, btwn Fua SO-02 & Av NS-01; s/d/tr standard R$70/85/100, deluxe R$100/12/140; ☒ ☎ ☒) Popular with businesspeople, the standard rooms here are functional if charmless, while the deluxe units are a substantial

step up in style, with flat-screen TVs, minisplit air-conditioners, and updated bathrooms. The pool is nice after a long hot day.

Eduardu's Palace Hotel (☎ 3215 9300; www.edu ardosphotel.com.br; cnr Rua NO-01 & NO-02; s/d standard R$113/150, deluxe R$150/189; ☒ ☎ ☒) Whatever you do, don't miss the rooftop pool and patio, which has a terrific view of the city and lake. Large rooms have fresh paint and modern appointments; deluxe rooms are larger, but standards have balconies. Street parking only.

Pousada dos Girassóis (☎ 3219 4500; www.pousada dosgirassois.com.br; Av NS-01; s/d deluxe R$139/149, superior r R$170; ☒ ☎ ☒) Superior rooms are definitely that, with large windows and private verandas. Rooms in both categories are rather small, but have details like a writing desk with leather chair, modern paintings and glass showers. The pool area is oddly small and uninviting. You'll find the pousada between Ruas SO-03 and SO-05.

Eating

our pick **Pizzería Paço do Pão** (☎ 3215 5665; Av Juscelino Kubitschek; mains R$18-25; ☟ dinner Wed-Mon) The pizza menu at this popular eatery between Ruas NO-02 and NO-04 runs into the dozens, with a house special that comes loaded with three types of meat, corn, heart of palm, olives and a thick layer of cheese. Outdoor seating makes it a great place for lingering over a pie and a Skol (or two).

Trattoria Toscana (☎ 3218 2795; Quadra 104 Sul, cnr Av NS-04 at Rua SE-09; mains R$16-$27; ☟ lunch Sat & Sun, dinner Mon-Sat) The gnocchi, ravioli and lasagna are all made in-house, and served in hefty portions. The spaghetti and linguini use store-bought noodles, but the sauces – salmon, *puttanesca*, and others – are excellent. For dessert, splurge on the divine *petit gateau di cioccolato* (petite chocolate cake; R$10).

Restaurante Seara (Rua NE-03; per kg R$22; ☟ lunch Mon-Sat) Between Av NS-02 & Rua NE-02, this large bustling per-kilo place is popular with workers at nearby government offices. It has two banks of prepared food and friendly service, and better still, it's open until 3pm, when every other self-service restaurant is dead and gone by 2pm.

Restaurante Cerrados (Quadra 103 Nte, Rua NO-03; per kg R$22; ☟ lunch & dinner) Opposite the Hotel Serra Azul, serving reliable and reasonably priced per-kilo fare, including freshly grilled meats sliced right onto your plate.

THE AMAZON

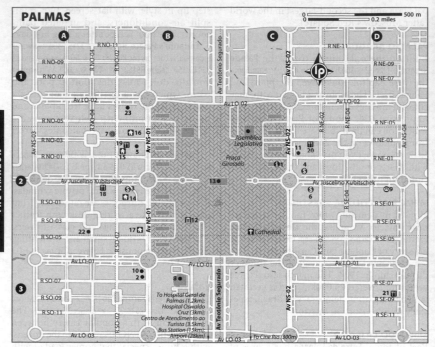

Entertainment

Cine Rio (Karavella Center Park; www.cineblue.com.br; tickets R$8-12) Palmas's one and only movie theater isn't much to rave about, with just three screens showing none-too-recent Hollywood flicks. It's located in a somewhat moribund amusement center, down a no-name street just east of Av Teotônio Segurado between Av LO-03 and Av LO-05.

Getting There & Around

AIR

GOL (☎ 3218 3738; airport only) and **TAM** (☎ 3219 3777; airport only) are the primary airlines serving Palmas. All flights go via Brasília.

The airport is located 28km south of the city center. A taxi from the airport to the hotel area costs R$40 to R$45, and the same to return. Alternatively, catch the red bus 75 at the airport curb (hourly from 7am to 7pm) to the 'Terminal,' where you can switch to bus 20 (hourly from 7:35am to 7:35pm), which passes Galeria Bela Palma in the center. Do the reverse to get back. In either direction, the first leg is R$1.70; the second leg is free.

BUS

Most long-distance buses do not enter Palmas anymore, stopping instead in the highway-side town of Paraíso do Tocantins, 15km west of Palmas; note that departures listed here are from Paraíso. To get between Paraíso and Palmas, minibuses operated by **Tocantinsense** (☎ 3228 5652) has buses every 30 to 60 minutes (R$8, 25 minutes) from 6:30am in Paraíso until 8:30pm from Paraíso (7:30pm on Saturday) and until 10:30pm from Palmas (9:45pm on Saturday); catch them at the Paraíso bus station or the bus stop in front of Galeria Bela in Palmas.

Itapemirin (☎ in Paraíso 3602 6756) has daily buses to Belém (R$120, 18 hours, 7pm daily) and São Paulo ($230, 26 hours, 5am), among others.

Transbrasiliana (☎ in Paraíso 3361 2475, in Palmas 3217 5604) has service to Belém (R$146, 18 hours, 9am and noon), Brasília (R$85 to R$100, 13 hours, 3pm, 5pm, 7:30pm and 8:30pm), São Paulo (R$187, 25 hours, 1:30am and 5am).

For Taquarussú, take bus 90 from Praça Girossóis in front of Galeria Bela Palma.

CAR
Car-rental agencies include **Avis** (☎ 3215 3336, airport 3219 3802; cnr Rua SO-03 & Rua NO-04), **Hertz** (☎ 3215 1900; Av LO-02 at Av NS-01) and **Localiza** (☎ 9978 9995, toll-free 0800 979 2020).

AROUND PALMAS
Taquarussú
This cozy town is nestled in the green Serra do Carmo hills, 30km southeast of Palmas, in an area studded with beautiful waterfalls and healthy forest. The state and local tourism boards have dedicated themselves to making Taquarussú an ecotourism mecca, with modest success. There's no local transportation, however, so you'll need a rental car from Palmas to really enjoy the area's attractions (some sites even require a 4WD during the rainy season). Weekends and holidays can be quite busy.

ORIENTATION & INFORMATION
Street signs are few and far between in Taquarussú, but it's a small town, and locals and the folks at CATUR are happy to give directions. There's a Banco do Brasil cash machine next to CATUR, and a small clinic (☏ 24hr) on the road toward Fazenda Encantada. Look for a couple of small *artesenato* (handicrafts) shops as you enter town.

Near the plaza, **Centro de Atendimento ao Turista** (CATUR; ☎ 3554 1515; Rua 20-A; ☏ 8am-noon & 2-6pm Mon-Fri, to 4pm Sat & Sun) is the best place for information about the area, and to hire a guide (per half-/full day R$20/45) to visit the falls and other sites.

ACTIVITIES
There are 80 identified waterfalls, caves and pools in the area, of which 10 to 15 are open and accessible to the public during most of the year. The tourist office encourages visitors to use guides for all the sites, though several of the most popular ones are perfectly easy to visit on your own. **Cachoeria de Roncadeira** is the tallest in the area (70m), and **Cachoiera Escorrega Macaco**, just 100m away, is nearly as tall (60m). Both tumble picturesquely down sheer rust-brown cliffs, fringed by green vegetation and moss-covered stones. Both have small pools for wading and swimming, while Roncadeira is sometimes used for rappelling (per person R$30). The falls are located 1.5km down a leafy well-marked trail; follow signs toward Hotel Fazenda Encantada and look for a large turnoff and parking area as the road ascends just out of town. **Cachoiera Taquaruçú** is a beefy cascade with a choppy swimming hole that can get crowded on hot summer weekends. (There's even a restaurant here.) Look for the large roadside parking area along the highway from Palmas, about 4.5km before reaching Taquarussú; the falls are a 150m walk from there. A R$3 per person trail fee applies if you come without a guide.

Other popular spots that are best visited with a guide include the **Cachoeira do Rappel**, on the Fazenda Encantada grounds and used for rappelling (naturally), and **Vale do Vai-Quem-Quer**, a broad valley with a series of falls and good swimming spots. Before setting out, discuss with your guide what type of falls you'd like to see, how much hiking and driving you want, and whether the car you have is adequate for all sites (some require 4WD, especially in the rainy season).

SLEEPING & EATING
You can stay in town or a nearby ecolodge. All accommodations come with free breakfast.

Pousada Lokau (☎ 3554 1238; 3a Av; r per person R$40) Part art gallery, part pousada, the Lokau

THE AMAZON

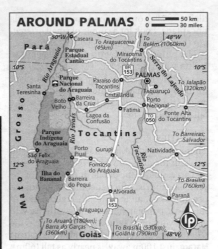

AROUND PALMAS

has five clean, comfortable rooms that open onto a pleasant garden. The heat and vegetation can make some rooms a bit musty, though high ceilings and stand-up fans help. To get here, turn left after the plaza, right just before Restaurante Mandala, and left at the roundabout. The pousada is at the next corner on your left.

Pousada Catarse (☎ 3554 1237; Rua 20, 2 blocks from CATUR; s R$45-55, d R$75-85) This place is very homey, with a common kitchen and small TV room, complete with aquarium. One room has a bathroom, while the other two share one in the hallway; all have ceiling fans and simple cozy decor. Usually open on weekends only; call ahead if you'll be visiting during the week.

Hotel Fazenda Encantada (☎ 3533 1054, 3215 5089; www.hotelfazendaencantada.com.br; 10.5km from Taquarussú; s/d incl half board R$200/280, full board R$223/332; 🛜 🖳) Taquarussú's best accommodations, the Fazenda Ecantada is a complete ecoresort, with comfortable upscale rooms and bungalows, and 9km of private trails (and several waterfalls, including one for rappelling) on the hotel's extensive property. Open on Saturday and Sunday for independent travelers, midweek for large groups only.

Restaurante Mandala (Av Belo Horizonte; 🍽 lunch daily, dinner Wed-Sun) Right around the corner from the plaza, on the road toward Fazenda Encantada. The fixed-plate lunch comes with pasta, rice, beans, salad, *farofa* (manioc flour sautéed with butter) and a choice of meat, all for R$7.

GETTING THERE & AWAY

By car, take Hwy TO-010 past the bus station and follow the signs, passing first through the town of Taquaralto.

Bus 90 passes Galeria Bela Palma on its way to and from Taquarussú (US$2, 45 minutes). Remember that you need a car to visit the falls there.

Parque Estadual do Jalapão

Jalapão state park is a unique 34,000-sq-km area in far eastern Tocantins, combining cerrado vegetation, hills, caves, crystalline rivers and springs, 40m-high sand dunes, waterfalls, freshwater bathing spots, odd rock formations, quite a range of wildlife – including anteaters, armadillos, macaws and rheas – and very few people indeed. (That changed temporarily in 2009, when a massive CBS television crew descended onto Jalapão to film *Survivor: Tocantins*.) The best season to explore Jalapão is the dry season from May to September.

Bananal Ecotour (☎ 3028 4200; www.bananalecotour .com.br; Quadra 103 Sul, Av NS-01 at Rua SO-07, Palmas) arranges wide-ranging tours of the park, including short hikes, climbing sand dunes, and swimming beneath waterfalls. You overnight in area hotels, and get about in tour vans. Prices average a hefty R$1250 to R$1500 per person for three days and two nights, including transport, hotels, food and guide services, though you really need four days or more to take it all in.

Ilha do Bananal

Ilha do Bananal is arguably the world's biggest river island – only Ilha do Marajó in Pará state is bigger, and some say Marajó doesn't qualify since part of it faces the ocean. Bananal covers 19,000 sq km, slightly less than the size of Israel, and is formed where the Rio Javaés splits from the Rio Araguaia and rejoins it 350km downstream. The island is so big it has its own rivers, stretching over 250km. Three distinct ecosystems converge here – rain forest, cerrado and wetland – and the island teems with plant and animal life; the bird-watching is especially noteworthy. Tours are available during the dry season only, from roughly June through October.

Bananal Ecotour (☎ 3028 4200; www.bananalecotour .com.br; Quadra 103 Sul, Av NS-01 at Rua SO-07) arranges three-day, two-night all-inclusive tours to Ilha do Bananal and Lagoa da Confuão, a large lake east of the island (per person R$1500 to R$2000 for groups of two to four people). The trips include mild forest walks, nighttime caiman spotting, fishing, boat trips and visits to a freshwater-turtle rescue program and (when possible) an indigenous community. The birding is great and you can count on seeing dolphins, caimans and giant river turtles. It's possible – but quite difficult – to see the island's other inhabitants, including tapirs, foxes and marhays, and jaguars.

NATIVIDADE

☎ 0xx63 / pop 9500

The pleasant little town of Natividade is 230km from Palmas in southeast Tocantins, in a valley beneath the green and wooded Serra Geral. Natividade is Tocantins's oldest town, founded in 1734. The Portuguese and their African slaves came to the Serra Geral in a minor gold rush in the 1720s, but when the gold gave out they moved down the hill and turned to cattle herding.

Sights & Activities

The cobbled streets and prettily painted, tile-roofed, 18th- and 19th-century houses of Natividade's historic center are protected as part of the national historic heritage.

Igreja NS do Rosário dos Pretos, known as the Igreja dos Escravos (Slaves' Church), was built in 1828 by slaves, who were not allowed to use the whites' church. Construction was reportedly never completed, and it remains roofless.

Museu Municipal (Praça Leopoldo de Bulhões; ☯ 8am-1pm Mon-Fri) occupies the old prison, evident by the thick walls and heavy doors. Simple exhibits tell the story of Natividade; among the artifacts is a tree trunk to which slaves were tied for whipping.

Half a kilometer from Praça Leopoldo de Bulhões – and reputedly connected to it by a tunnel – are the **Poções**, a series of small waterfalls and refreshing natural bathing pools, and beyond that the remains of **São Luiz**, the original settlement of the 1720s gold prospectors. About 4km from town are the **Cachoeiras do Paraíso**, another series of natural bathing pools, though they often dry to a trickle from June to September. Local kids can lead you to either for a small tip.

Sleeping

Hotel Serra Geral (☎ 3372 1160; 1.7km north of the center, 300m before the Trevo Norte; s/d with fan R$48/79, with air-con R$66/100, with air-con & minibar R$72/106; ☯)

Natividade's best hotel is a short distance from town, with friendly management and clean, modern rooms that open onto breezy corridors. There's also a decent restaurant in case you don't feel like going back into town to eat.

Getting There & Away

Natividade is on the best road between Palmas and Brasília (Hwy TO-050; longer but in much better condition than Hwy BR-153).

Buses or vans for Palmas (R$28, three hours) leave every one to two hours from 7am to 3pm; arrive 30 minutes early as the bus is known to leave ahead of schedule. There are also night buses to Brasília (R$70, eight hours) with connections to Lençóis, Salvador and Goiânia.

AMAZONAS

Amazonas is Brazil's largest state, spanning almost 1.6 million sq km. You could fit four Germanys within its borders with room left over for, say, Greece. It is here that the massive Solimões, Negro and Madeira rivers converge to form the Rio Amazonas, the granddaddy of them all. Life in Amazonas state is lashed inextricably to those waterways, and the thousands of smaller ones: transportation, food, water, waste removal and, of course, tourism. For travelers, Amazonas state is not the only place to visit 'the Amazon' but it's certainly the most popular, with Manaus as the main hub. Tour operators in Manaus specialize in three- to six-day excursions into the forest, or you can book a stay at one of the nearby jungle lodges. Manaus also is a jumping-off point for trips deeper into the state's vast rain forest, whether up the Rio Negro to reserves such as Parque Nacional do Jaú or Xixuaú-Xiparíná or the Rio Solimões, to Mamirauá and the 'Triple Frontier.'

History

The modern history of the Amazon begins in 1842, in the USA, when Charles Goodyear developed the vulcanization process that made natural rubber durable. Fifty years later Irishman John Dunlop invented pneumatic rubber tires, and soon there was an unquenchable demand for the milky white sap of *Hevea brasiliensis,* the Brazilian rubber tree.

Poor farmers in Brazil's drought-ridden Northeast were lured into the Amazon by the

THE AMAZON

promise of land and prosperity as *seringuei-ros* (rubber-tappers). A feudal system quickly took root, with rubber-tappers trapped in virtual serfdom by debt, illiteracy, and the trickery and brutality of rubber barons and their armed thugs. As if that weren't enough, *seringueiros* also had to contend with jungle fevers, *índio* attacks and all manner of deprivation. It was primarily on their backs that Manaus was built, a grand prosperous city rising improbably from the Amazon rain forest.

Despite Brazilian efforts to protect the country's world rubber monopoly, rubber-tree seeds were smuggled to London, and before long cultivated in massive plantations in British colonies in the South Pacific. By the 1920s, prices fell and the Amazon's great rubber boom was over. WWII brought a temporary revival, as thousands of 'rubber soldiers' were recruited to gather rubber for the Allied cause.

In the 1970s, the slogan *'Integrar para não entregar'* (essentially, 'Use it or lose it') was part of the rationale for building roads deep into the Amazon, including the infamous Transamazônica highway. Speculators and squatters poured into the rain forest, and the trees fell at prodigious rates. Satellite images of thousands of fires burning across the Amazon – slash and burn being the easiest way to clear the forest – eventually awakened the international environmental community. Ecotourism was promoted here, as elsewhere, as a new and better way to 'Use it or lose it.'

MANAUS
☎ 0xx92 / pop 2 million

Manaus is the Amazon's largest city, an incongruous pocket of urbanity in the middle of the jungle, a major port for ocean vessels that's 1500km from the ocean. The rain forest has a population density half that of Mongolia's, but the journey there invariably begins in (or passes through) this bustling city of two million souls. Don't be surprised if you feel a little out of whack.

The city itself has some genuinely rewarding sights, including a leafy zoo with as many animals out of the cages as in them, and a beach-and-museum combo that gets you out of the city center. It's a place to stock up on anything you forgot to pack, or to refill your tank with beer and internet after a week in the forest.

Manaus is also where most Amazon tour operators are based; plenty are honest professionals, but the city is also full of scammers. See p658 for tips on avoiding them, including right when you step off the plane. And remember that Manaus is not the only place to book a jungle tour! There are numerous options in cities further up- and downstream that may give more options off-the-beaten path than possible in well-worn Manaus.

Manaus will be a host city for the 2014 FIFA World Cup.

Information

EMERGENCY
Police stations are located across from the bus station on Praça da Matriz and inside the main boat terminal (Estação Hidroviária).

Ambulance (☎ 192)
State Police (☎ 190)
Tourist Police (Map p645; ☎ 3215 7125; cnr Av Lourenço da Silva Braga & Rua Lima Bacuri; ☒ 24hr)

INTERNET ACCESS
Amazon Cyber Café (Map p645; Av Getúlio Vargas; per hr R$3.50; ☒ 9:30am-11pm Mon-Thu, 9:30am-10pm Fri, 10am-9pm Sat, noon-8pm Sun)
Juliana Cyber Café (Map p645; Av Joaquim Nabuco; per hr R$2; ☒ 8am-11pm)
Selva Net (Map p645; Rua Joaquim Sarmento; per hr R$2.50; ☒ 7am-7pm Mon-Fri, 7am-6pm Sat)

LAUNDRY
In addition to listing below, most hotels offer laundry service to guests.
Lavandería Paradise (Map p645; ☎ 3633 6092; Rua Quintino Bocaiúva; per piece R$1.50-3, per kg R$10; ☒ 8am-6pm Mon-Sat)

LEFT LUGGAGE
Most hotels will store extra luggage (for free or a small fee) for guests who are taking short excursions, even if you do not plan to stay there when you return. The airport and long-distance bus station also have left-luggage service.

MEDICAL SERVICES
Hospital de Doenças Tropicais (Hospital of Tropical Illnesses; Map p645; ☎ 3238 1146; Av Pedro Teixeira 25) Specializes in tropical diseases.
Unimed (Map p645; ☎ 3633 4431; Av Japurá 241; emergency ☒ 24hr) One of the best private hospitals in the city.
Yellow-fever vaccines airport (☒ 24hr); long-distance bus station (☒ 8am-noon & 2-5pm Mon-Fri); Hospital de Doenças (☒ 9am-6pm) Yellow-fever vaccines are free,

but are not effective until 10 days after administration. A yellow-fever vaccine certificate is usually required when entering Brazil by land or water.

MONEY

Amazônia Turismo (Map p645; ☎ 3622 7206; Av Sete de Setembro 1251) Decent exchange rates for US dollars and euros, plus Amex and Visa traveler's checks. A

branch at Millennium Shopping Mall is open from 10am to 10pm.

Banco do Brasil (Map p645; Rua Guilherme Moreira 315; exchange office ☒ 9am-3pm Mon-Fri) Exchange foreign cash and traveler's checks at the exchange office on the 3rd floor.

Bradesco (Map p645; Av Eduardo Ribeiro at Rua Saldanha Marinho) Reliable ATMs.

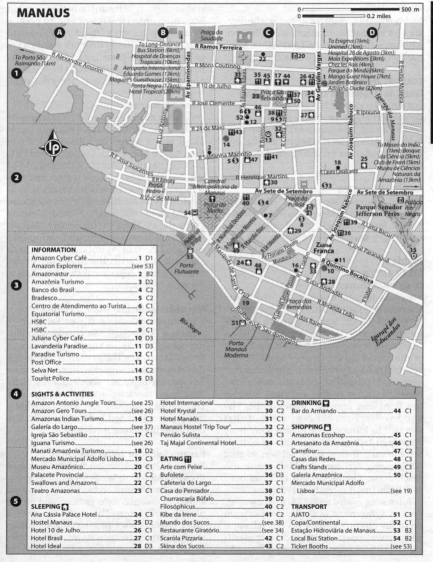

THE AMAZON

MANAUS

0 — 500 m
0 — 0.2 miles

INFORMATION	
Amazon Cyber Café	**1** D1
Amazon Explorers	(see 53)
Amazonastur	**2** B2
Amazônia Turismo	**3** D2
Banco do Brasil	**4** C2
Bradesco	**5** C2
Centro de Atendimento ao Turista	**6** C1
Equatorial Turismo	**7** C2
HSBC	**8** C2
HSBC	**9** C1
Juliana Cyber Café	**10** D3
Lavandería Paradise	**11** C1
Paradise Turismo	**12** C1
Post Office	**13** C2
Selva Net	**14** C2
Tourist Police	**15** D3

SIGHTS & ACTIVITIES	
Amazon Antonio Jungle Tours	(see 25)
Amazon Gero Tours	(see 26)
Amazonas Indian Turismo	**16** C3
Galería do Largo	(see 37)
Igreja São Sebastião	**17** C1
Iguana Turismo	(see 26)
Manati Amazônia Turismo	**18** D2
Mercado Municipal Adolfo Lisboa	**19** C3
Museu Amazônico	**20** C1
Palacete Provincial	**21** C2
Swallows and Amazons	**22** C1
Teatro Amazonas	**23** C1

SLEEPING	
Ana Cássia Palace Hotel	**24** C3
Hostel Manaus	**25** D2
Hotel 10 de Julho	**26** C1
Hotel Brasil	**27** C2
Hotel Ideal	**28** D3

Hotel Internacional	**29** C2
Hotel Krystal	**30** C2
Hotel Manaós	**31** C1
Manaus Hostel 'Trip Tour'	**32** C2
Pensão Sulista	**33** C3
Taj Majal Continental Hotel	**34** C1

EATING	
Arte com Peixe	**35** C1
Bufolete	**36** D3
Cafeteria do Largo	**37** C3
Casa do Pensador	**38** C1
Churrascaria Búfalo	**39** D2
Filosóphicus	**40** C2
Kibe da Irene	**41** C2
Mundo dos Sucos	(see 38)
Restaurante Giratório	(see 34)
Scarola Pizzaria	**42** C1
Skina dos Sucos	**43** C2

DRINKING	
Bar do Armando	**44** C1

SHOPPING	
Amazonas Ecoshop	**45** C1
Artesanato da Amazônia	**46** C1
Carrefour	**47** C2
Casas das Redes	**48** C3
Crafts Stands	**49** C1
Galeria Amazônica	**50** C1
Mercado Municipal Adolfo Lisboa	(see 19)

TRANSPORT	
AJATO	**51** C3
Copa/Continental	**52** C1
Estação Hidroviária de Manaus	**53** B3
Local Bus Station	**54** B2
Ticket Booths	(see 53)

THE AMAZON

HSBC Rua Dr Moreira 226 (Map p645; Rua Dr Moreira 226; ⏰ 9am-3pm Mon-Fri); Rua 24 de Maio (Map p645; cnr Rua 24 de Maio & Rua Costa Azevedo; ⏰ 9am-3pm Mon-Fri)

POST
Post office airport (lower level, airport; ⏰ 9:30am-12:30pm & 1:30-5pm); Rua Barroso (Map p645; Rua Barroso 220; ⏰ 8am-4pm Mon-Fri, 8am-noon Sat)

TELEPHONE
Embratel cards, available at the post office, are best for making international calls from payphones (per minute R$0.50 to R$1). Most internet cafés have Skype-ready computers.

TOURIST INFORMATION
Centro de Atendimento ao Turista (Tourist Assistance Center; Map p645; ☎ 2123 3800; www.amazona stur.am.gov.br) Amazonastur, the state tourism agency, maintains this tourist-assistance center at the corner of Av Eduardo Ribeiro and Rua José Clemente, while the administrative office is on Rua Saldanha Marinho near Rua Lobo D'Almada.

TRAVEL AGENCIES
Equatorial Turismo (Map p645; ☎ 3622 2599; Rua Quintino Bocaiúva 149; ⏰ 8am-6pm Mon-Fri, 8am-noon Sat)
Paradise Turismo (Map p645; ☎ 3633 8301; Av Eduardo Ribeiro 656; ⏰ 8am-6pm Mon-Fri, 8:30am-noon Sat)

Sights
CITY CENTER
Teatro Amazonas
Manaus's famous opera house, the **Teatro Amazonas** (Map p645; ☎ 3232 1768; Rua José Clemente; ⏰ 9am-5pm Mon-Sat), was designed in eclectic neoclassical style by engineers from Lisbon and a team of interior designers at the height of the rubber boom. Opened in 1896, this beautiful theater symbolizes the opulence that once was Manaus. The artists and most of the materials (Italian marble and glass, Scottish cast iron) were imported from Europe. The wood is Brazilian, but even some of that was sent to Europe to be carved. One truly homespun feature was the roadway outside the entrance; it is made of rubber, so that late-arriving carriages wouldn't create too much noise. The theater has been restored four times (most recently in 1990).

Interesting guided tours (R$10, 30 minutes, 9am to 4pm), often in English, are offered every day except Sunday. Concerts (classical and popular), opera, theater and dance events are held all year, with tickets ranging from R$5 to R$60. There's an excellent opera festival held here every April and May (see p649).

Igreja São Sebastião
Although it's by no means Manaus' largest or oldest church – the cement block exterior belies as much – **Igreja São Sebastião** (Map p645; Rua 10 de Julho; ⏰ 7am-8pm) has a beautifully restored interior (completed to mark the 100-year anniversary of the arrival of the Capuchin Franciscan order) that is well worth a peek. A short nave gives way to the church's opulent altar, with surprisingly dramatic paintings of saints and priests presiding over earthly battles. The handy location doesn't hurt; it's opposite the Teatro Amazonas facing the plaza.

Porto Flutuante
Officially called the Estação Hidroviária de Manaus, the **Porto Flutuante** (Floating Dock; Map p645) is where you'll disembark if you come to Manaus by boat. Inaugurated in 1902 and designed by the British, it was considered a technical marvel because it rises and falls with seasonal water levels, which can vary as much as 14m (annual high-water points are marked on the wall beside the bridge leading to the dock). There's a reasonably pleasant indoor-outdoor shopping and eating area with good views of the docks. From Praça da Matriz, look for stairs and an elevated bridge (next to a large department store) leading to the main terminal area.

Mercado Municipal Adolfo Lisboa
This imposing cast-iron city **market** (Map p645; Rua dos Barés; ⏰ 8am-5pm Mon-Sat, 6am-noon Sun) building opened in 1882, a copy in miniature of Paris's famed Les Halles market. Although the art-nouveau ironwork was imported from Europe, the place has acquired a distinctly Amazonian character. In and around the market, you can purchase just about anything, from leather hats and *índio* crafts to bizarre fruits and traditional medicines.

Parque Senador Jéfferson Péres
Known as Parque Jéfferson, this new Y-shaped **city park** (Map p645; Av Sete de Setembro) has grass, benches, and a small orchid house, plus food stands in colonial-style gazebos and ample nighttime lighting. This area was once a gritty favela (slum), and the park's creation was not without controversy, requiring scores of homes to be torn down, and hundreds of

residents relocated. A rotten smell wafting up from the creek running through the park is the main drawback.

Palacete Provincial

Once a blight on the downtown area, the newly restored **Palacete Provincial** (Map p645; Praça da Polícia; admission free; ☺ 9am-7pm Tue-Fri, 9am-8pm Fri-Sat, 4-9pm Sun) is now a handsome cultural complex. There's a decent art gallery, and the 'Image and Sound' center has a remarkable collection of films, including century-old documentaries by Portuguese filmmaker Silvino Santos, who made some of the first-ever recordings of Amazonian native people. (The police and archaeology displays are snoozers, however.) The outdoor cinema has free films every Sunday at 7pm.

Galeria do Largo

Right on Praça São Sebastião, **Galeria do Largo** (Map p645; Rua Costa Azevedo; admission free; ☺ 5 9pm Tue-Sun) has a modern-minded rotation of art exhibits, from contemporary paintings to a miniature scale model of the city. Cafeteria do Largo (p652) serves innovative snacks and drinks at tables set up on the plaza in front.

Museu Amazônico

Housed in a converted mansion a short walk from the center, the **Museu Amazônico** (Map p645; ☎ 3234 3242; www.museuamazonico.ufam.edu.br; Rua Ramos Ferreira; admission free; ☺ 8am-noon & 2-5pm Mon-Fri) has a small but excellent collection of indigenous items and artifacts from around the Amazon, many from ongoing archaeological studies in Amazonas state. Highlights include Matis and Maku hunting tools, and terrific masks and costumes used in Yanomami and Ticuna rituals. The 1st floor houses temporary art exhibits.

OUTSIDE THE CITY CENTER
Museu do Índio

Sandwiched between two churches and run by Salesian nuns, the **Museu do Índio** (off Map p645; Rua Duque de Caxias 296; admission R$5; ☺ 8:30-11:30am & 2-4:30pm Mon-Fri, 8-11:30am Sat) displays artwork, musical instruments, fishing and hunting tools and ritual objects of indigenous groups from mostly Amazonas and Pará states. The collection is large and quite good, but the displays are artless and explanations seriously lacking. You'll find similar pieces but a more modern and engaging presentation – and free admission! – at the Museu Amazônico (above).

The Museu do Índio is a kilometer down busy Av Sete de Setembro; take bus 606 from the center.

Bosque da Ciência

Occupying a 13-hectare plot of secondary forest within the city, the **Bosque da Ciência** (Forest of Science; off Map p645; ☎ 3643 3135/92; admission R$5; ☺ 9am-4pm Tue-Sun, ticket office closed noon-2pm weekdays) has aging enclosures containing animals such as manatees, giant otters and caimans, but a great many creatures roam freely about the park – in the underbrush, high in the trees, and even ambling down the paths – including monkeys, sloths, turtles, various tropical birds, pacas and anteaters.

Bosque da Ciência is located in the Petrópolis district, 5km northeast of the center. From Praça da Matriz in the center, the 810 'Especial' minibus (R$2.50) stops right outside the gates, while bus 519 (R$2) stops a half-block away. A taxi costs R$20 to R$25. Consider combining this with a visit to the (relatively) nearby Museu de Ciências Naturais da Amazônia (below).

Museu de Ciências Naturais da Amazônia

Known by many locals as the Museu Japonesa (Japanese Museum), because it is run by Japanese-Brazilians and located in a predominately Japanese-Brazilian area, the **Museu de Ciências Naturais da Amazônia** (Amazon Natural Sciences Museum; off Map p645; ☎ 3644 2799; Estrada Belém s/n; adult/child R$12; ☺ 9am-noon & 2-5pm Mon-Sat) has an extensive exhibit of stuffed fish, preserved butterflies and some unnervingly large beetles and spiders from the region, with descriptions in English, Portuguese and Japanese. A modest aquarium contains live Amazon fish, including the impressive 2m-long *pirarucú*.

Take bus 519 from Praça da Matriz; it's the same bus that passes Bosque da Ciência, so you can visit both places in a day. Follow the 'Museu' signs from the stop; it's about a kilometer (half-mile) walk. An easier option is to take the bus to the Bosque da Ciência and then cab it from there (R$15); to get back, ask the taxi driver to return (an hour ought to be enough) or ask in the museum gift shop for directions to the bus stop.

Parque do Mindú

Believe it or not, Manaus has its own endemic primate: the tiny *Sanguinus bicolor*, better known as the pied bare-faced tamarin.

THE AMAZON

The species is critically endangered, with no known groups in the open forest – they seem to have evolved to thrive only in areas of secondary growth – yet notoriously difficult to breed in captivity. The best place to observe this curious and vanishing creature is **Parque do Mindú** (off Map p645; Av Perimetral s/n; admission free; 8am-5pm Tue-Sun), a 33-hectare park in a residential area of Manaus about 6km from the center. The park has a system of eight intersecting trails, including sections of elevated walkways and an orchid house. Volunteer guides can help visitors locate the tamarins (early morning and late afternoon are best) and point out other flora and fauna along the way, from açaí palms to jacaré (caimans). This is by no means a journey into the wild – the trails are wide and the river running through the park is heavily polluted from upstream dumping – but it's a worthwhile outing nonetheless, especially if you manage to spot the resident monkeys. Sunday can be very crowded, however, when locals turn out for a buffet breakfast spread. Parque do Mindu is in the Parque Dez district; from the center, take bus 423, 433, 407 or 427 (R$1.50, 30 minutes).

Jardim Botânico Adolpho Ducke

Spanning over 100 sq km on the eastern edge of Manaus, this massive **park and protected area** (admission free; 8am-noon & 2-5pm Tue-Fri, 8am-4pm Sat & Sun) is reportedly the world's largest urban forest. Its namesake was an Italian-born botanist and entomologist who spent decades studying the Amazon rain forest, especially its complex tree systems. The park has long been used for ecological research, but the city is working hard to make it accessible to casual visitors too. There's a network of eight short trails (3km in all) and plans to build a nature museum, observation tower, and canopy-level walkway – even an aquarium – are well underway. To get there and back, take bus 448 'Ciudad de Deus' from Praça da Matriz; it's a solid 90 minutes each way, though quite interesting, winding through neighborhoods that few travelers visit.

Museu do Seringal Vila Paraíso

This **museum** (Rubber Museum; Map p656; admission R$5; 8am-4pm Wed-Sun) is a 25-minute boat ride from Ponta Negra, which is itself a 20-minute bus ride from the center. Fortunately, the trip there is part of the fun, and can be combined with a stop at Praia da Lua, Manaus' best beach. Guided tours include an opulent rubber baron's townhouse and a replica rubber-tapper shack, and walking a short trail to see how rubber trees are tapped, and the latex processed in a thatched smokehouse. It's a bit gimmicky but still interesting, and the only place in Manaus to learn about this all-important history.

Boats to the museum (R$6, 25 minutes) leave frequently from Marina Davi, just past Ponta Negra. Take bus 011, 012, or 120 (R$1.50, 20 minutes) from the center, get off at the turnaround (right in front of the Hotel Tropical) and hop onto the free 'Especial' to the marina.

Praia da Lua

Manaus's best beach (Map p656) is a short boat ride up the Rio Negro and can be coupled with a visit to the Museu do Seringal for a nice city escape. The sand is surprisingly fine and the water good for swimming, despite the tea color. Like all river beaches, Lua is biggest when the water is low (November and December) and smallest when it's high (June and July). Trees provide some shade, but the midday sun can be intense. Semipermanent eateries serve fish and beer at tables set up along the water. The big drawback: no toilets.

Catch a boat to Praia da Lua (R$2 to R$3, 10 minutes) from Marina Davi, just past Ponta Negra. Take bus 011, 012, or 120 (R$1, 20 minutes) to the turnaround and wait for the free 'Especial' bus to the marina.

Encontro das Águas

Just downriver from Manaus, the 'black' water of the Rio Negro (actually clear reddish brown) meets the 'white' water of the Rio Solimões (more a creamy tan) but the rivers resolutely refuse to mix, instead flowing side by side for several kilometers. The phenomenon, which occurs in various places along the river system but nowhere quite as dramatically as here, is known as the Encontro das Águas (Meeting of the Waters; Map p656). It's caused by differences in temperature (the Solimões is a few degrees cooler), velocity (17m per second for the Solimões compared with just 6m per second for the Negro) and the fact that the Solimões carries nearly eight times more sediment per liter than the Negro. It reportedly was the inspiration for the wavy black-and-white tilework in front of the Teatro Amazonas, and was borrowed again for Rio de Janeiro's famous beach promenade.

RECORD FLOOD

The rise and fall of the Amazon River and its tributaries, by as much as 15m in a normal year, is an ordinary part of life there, and every living thing plans accordingly: houses are built on stilts, trees have adapted to live for months underwater, and fish, dolphins, even monkeys migrate according to water levels. But in 2009, the river just kept rising, reaching levels not seen in over 50 years. More than 300,000 people were forced from their homes, and at least 39 people died – some swept right out of their houses, or while escaping in canoes loaded with household belongings. Many riverside villages were completely flooded, and even large cities such as Manaus and Santarém had whole neighborhoods under several feet of water.

Occasional super floods are part of the life cycle of the Amazon, too, but it's hard not to suspect that global climate change was partly to blame. Ice melt from the Andes has been increasing steadily, while the 2009 rainy season was unusually intense and prolonged. Ditto for the previous year – in fact, one little-mentioned factor is that the river system was already several meters higher than normal when the rains began, having never reached its normal lows during the 2008 dry season. And meteorologists noted that abnormally high atmospheric pressure helped concentrate the rainfall over northern Brazil; the Guianas, meanwhile, were unusually dry even as the Amazon was getting drenched.

You can still see signs of the 2009 floods throughout the Amazon, in the form of high-water marks on the sides of buildings and tree trunks, or bits of garbage and debris tangled high in the treetops. President Lula da Silva, touring the worst-hit areas, remarked 'We need to look more seriously into the climate situation these days.' No kidding.

That said, booking a tour just to see the Meeting of the Waters may not be time or money well spent – it's not *that* intriguing. Fortunately, getting to most lodges includes passing by the spot. Most others are happy to arrange a detour or side trip, usually for less time and effort than a full-blown tour.

If you insist, **Amazon Explorers** (Map p645; ☎ 3232 3052; www.amazonexplorers.com.br, Estação Hidroviária de Manaus, Porto Flutuante; ☼ 8am-6pm Mon-Sat, 8-9:30am Sun) offers daily trips to the Meeting of the Waters plus nearby Parque Ecológico Janauary, where you can eat, shop, admire captured animals, eat, shop, wander short nature trails, and then eat and shop.

Tours

A cadre of **registered guides** offer personalized tours of Manaus's main sights, including the port area, the fish and fruit markets, the opera house, and more – a good way to see a lot in a short time. Most are friendly and knowledgeable, some speak several languages; look for them around the northwest corner of Praça São Sebastião. Rates average R$50 per group for three to five hours; taxi or boat fare is additional.

Festivals & Events

Inaugurated in 1997, the annual **Manaus Opera Festival** brings high-quality opera deep into the rain forest at the Teatro Amazonas. The three-week gala usually takes place in late April and early May, and audience apparel ranges from tuxedos and ballroom gowns, to jeans and T-shirts that have obviously done duty in the jungle (they do draw the line at shorts, tank tops and flip-flops, however). Tickets (R$5 to R$60) are available at the Teatro Amazonas (p646) several weeks before the festival opens.

In November, the ever-more-popular **Amazon Film Festival** screens dozens of films related in some way to the Amazon, from rare Brazilian features filmed in Manaus, to foreign documentaries about destruction of the rain forest. Headliners are shown in Teatro Amazonas (p646) but you can see films every night of the week for free at a large outdoor screen set up right in the Praça São Sebastião.

The June **Festival Folclórico do Amazonas** features a wide variety of regional folklore performances, including rehearsals of the Parintins Boi-Bumbá teams. The festival culminates on June 29 with the Procissão Fluvial de São Pedro (St Peter River Procession), when hundreds of riverboats parade on the Rio Negro before Manaus to honor the patron saint of fishers.

Sleeping

Below are hotels in Manaus itself; for jungle trips and lodges outside the city, see p655.

BUDGET

Pensão Sulista (Map p645; ☎ 3234 5814; Av Joaquim Nabuco 347; dm $20, s without bathroom R$25, s/d/tr with bathroom & air-con R$40/50/75; ✖ ☎) Occupying a former hospital of all things, this tenement-style budget hotel has attractive blond and chocolate wood floors, and large rooms that open onto a sunny corridor. The charm flags considerably with the saggy beds, ancient bathrooms and walls that don't quite reach the high ceilings, but it's still decent value and (as a result) often full. The area can be dodgy at night.

our pick **Hostel Manaus** (Map p645; ☎ 3233 4545; www.hostelmanaus.com; Rua Lauro Cavalcante 231; dm with fan R$20, with air-con R$24, d with fan & without bathroom R$55, with air-con & bathroom R$65; HI discounts available; ✖ ▢ ☎) It took a while, but hostels have finally arrived in the Amazon, here as well as in Belém. This HI-registered, Australian-operated hostel has comfortable dorms and private rooms (including a women-only dorm), self-serve laundry machine, and two open-air patios ideal for nursing a beer – the one on the roof has great city views. You also get lockers, luggage storage, kitchen access and internet service, and a recommended tour operator has its main office here.

Hotel 10 de Julho (Map p645; ☎ 3232 6280; www .hoteldezdejulho.com; Rua 10 de Julho 679; s/d R$65/70, with hot water & minibar R$80/85; ✖ ☎) Rooms are pretty sterile, especially for the price – R$15 extra for hot water? – but Manaus isn't exactly awash in clean affordable digs. The location is ideal, in a safe area, with two recommended tour agencies nearby and the Teatro Amazonas a block away. Check out the interior patios with potted plants and molded Amazonian murals.

Hotel Ideal (Map p645; ☎ 3233 9423; www.hotelideal manaus.com.br; Rua dos Andradas 491; s/d with fan R$37/46, with air-con R$48/60, with air-con, TV & minibar R$60/70; ✖) A multistory block of plain but adequate rooms coated in gray and white high-gloss paint. Ask for a room with a window, or one on the top floor where at least the corridor is sunny. Be wary of freelance guides who hang around here, peddling cut-rate tours on the sidewalk. The hotel doesn't allow them in the lobby or up to the rooms, but be ready to be pounced on once you step outside the door.

Manaus Hostel 'Trip Tour' (Map p645; ☎ 3231 2139; www.manaushostel.com.br; Rua Costa Azevedo 63; dm with fan R$20, with air-con R$30, s/d with air-con R$65/90; ✖ ▢ ☎) The fact this hostel has virtually the same name as Manaus' other (and origi-nal) hostel is pretty fishy, and more than a few travelers have ended up here by mistake. Anyway, dorms are standard issue, with high ceilings, sturdy bunks and large lockers; those with air-con are worth the extra R$10, as fan-only units can get stiflingly hot. The other hostel has better breakfast, service and overall ambience, though the location of this one can't be beat, just two blocks from Praça São Sebastião.

MIDRANGE

Hotel Brasil (Map p645; ☎ 3233 6575, 2101 5000; Av Getúlio Vargas 657; s/d R$75/90, incl breakfast R$83/106; ✖) An eight-story hotel on safe, busy Av Getúlio Vargas. Rooms here are spacious enough for two beds, a table and chair, even a sofa. The old-school air-conditioners and itty-bitty bathrooms are drawbacks, but overall it's good value. The breakfast spread is ample, and buses to and from the airport and bus station stop a half-block away.

Chez les Rois (off Map p645; ☎ 3584 3549; www.chez lesrois.com.br; Conjunto Manauense Q/G 01, Barrio Vieiralves; s/d R$110/145; ✖ ▢ ☎ ⛶) Occupying an attrac-tive colonial home in a swanky neighborhood, Chez les Rois has great common areas, with beautiful wood floors, comfy sofas and chairs, and plenty of nooks and crannies to read a book or soak up the sun, plus a welcoming little pool. The rooms are rather less inspired (and some quite small) but for most guests the overall ambience, including exceptional service, is well worth a few bumped elbows. The center is a R$20 cab ride away.

Maguire's Guesthouse (Map p645; ☎ 3239 0280; www.maguirenet.com; Rua Modolva 28, Conjunto Jardim Friburgo; per person R$80-110; ✖ ▢ ☎ ⛶) With just two rooms you're sure to feel part of the family, especially since they both open right onto the home's main living area – some travelers may find the arrangement a bit too cozy, in fact. The larger deluxe room is well worth the higher rate, with a better bed and TV and a view of the guesthouse's lush rear grounds. There's a clean pool and plenty of outdoor hang-out space, and the owners can arrange all sorts of excursions; they even pro-vide guests with a mobile phone and a lift to and from the center whenever possible.

Mango Guest House (off Map p645; ☎ 3656 6033; http://mango-guesthouse.com; Rua Flávio Espirito Santo 01, Barrio Kissia II; s/d R$130/160; ✖ ▢ ☎ ⛶) The hotel grounds are the highlight here, shaded by giant mango trees and located well outside the center's hustle and bustle. The rooms are admittedly a bit cement-block sterile, but attractive hand-painted murals, printed cotton sheets and good towels do a lot to soften them up, and the pool is appealing. The center of town is a R$25 to R$30 cab ride away, which may be a drawback for travelers who want to spend time exploring Manaus.

Hotel Internacional (Map p645; ☎ 3633 7034; www .hotelinternaional.brasilcomercial.com; Rua Dr Moreira 168; s/d R$128/154; 🍴 💻 🛜) The Internacional wins no awards for decor – the rooms and lobby could teach most hospitals a thing or two about austerity – but the spotless, sizable rooms are perfectly comfortable, with high ceilings, air-con, TV and fridge. A cable internet connection is available in most rooms, and there's a computer for guests' use near reception. It's the best of several hotels in this busy, safe commercial area.

Hotel Krystal (Map p645; ☎ 3233 7535; www.krystal hotel.com.br; Rua Barroso 54; s/d/tr R$125/160/210; 🍴 🛜) The lobby could be more 1980s only if the Charlie's Angels themselves were chilling on the leather sofas; then again, the painfully slow automatic front doors would probably cramp their style. Rooms here are clean though rather dark, with bold mint-green walls, attractive wood headboards, granite-topped writing desks, pedestal sinks and tinted-glass shower doors. And you gotta dig the brown sheets with the hotel logo printed on them. If you don't mind the decor, it's a well-located and reliable option in this price range.

Ana Cássia Palace Hotel (Map p645; ☎ 3303 3637; www.hotelanacassia.com.br; Rua dos Andradas 14; s/d/tr R$120/150/185; 🍴 🛜 🍽) Definitely request a room with a view – the river, port, market and theater are all within sight from the Ana Cássia's upper floors, as well as vast stretches of green forest beyond. If none are available, you can still get that Wow-I'm-in-the-Amazon feeling from the rooftop pool and restaurant areas. Rooms here are modern and clean, despite their painfully dated decor. Some single rooms are quite tight, while doubles are more reasonably sized. The area has an appealing hustle and bustle during the day, but is not a place to stroll about at night.

TOP END

Hotel Tropical (Map p655; ☎ 2123 5000; www.tropicalma naus.com.br; Av Coronel Teixeira 1320, Ponta Negra; r US$177-425; 🍴 💻 🛜 🍽) Manaus's premier luxury hotel is a self-contained resort built in a

sprawling hacienda style that never rises more than three stories. The newest rooms (3104 to 3142) have granite bathroom counters, dark wood floors, and furniture brightened by bird-of-paradise bedspreads over the firm mattresses; definitely better than the older, '70s-style units. The hotel has a wave pool, a mini zoo, an orchid house, various sports fields (including archery) and no fewer than five bars.

Hotel Manaós (off Map p645; ☎ 3633 5744; www .hotelmanaos.com.br; Av Eduardo Ribeiro 881; s/d R$179/230; 🍴 💻 🛜) Most of the center's top-end hotels offer disappointingly unattractive rooms, and the boxy, mint-green exterior here seems to promise more of the same. Not so: rooms, albeit generic, have sharp modern touches like honey-colored wood trim and polished-stone bathroom counters. Most have large windows, including some with a view of the Teatro Amazonas.

Taj Mahal Continental Hotel (Map p645; ☎ /fax 3627 3737; www.grupotajmahal.com.br; Av Getúlio Vargas 741; s/d R$247/357, with view R$420/567; 💻 🛜 🍽) Find every excuse to spend time in the hotel's rooftop revolving restaurant – the view and food are excellent, and after enough revolutions you'll know all the waitstaff's children's names. Rooms have the expected fixings, though the hodge-podge of colors, textures and styles are definitely dated (brace yourself for the bathrooms). There is a small pool on the roof, and a travel agency, a jewelry shop and wireless internet in the lobby.

Eating

Skina dos Sucos (Map p645; cnr Av Eduardo Ribeiro & Rua 24 de Maio; sandwiches & snacks R$2-8; 🕒 7am-8pm Mon-Fri, 7am-7pm Sat) Stake out some counter space at this busy eatery, where you can order snacks and sandwiches to go along with *sucos* (fresh juices) made from Amazonian fruits, including guaraná (a tropical berry thought to have numerous medicinal properties), *cupuaçú* (sweet cousin of the cacao fruit) and *graviola* (custard apple).

Kibe da Irene (Map p645; Rua Barrosa at Rua Saldanha Marinho; snacks R$2-8) Though pretty much devoid of character, the friendly service and cheap tasty fare make this a great choice for travelers on a budget. At lunchtime, fill up on a *prato feito* for just R$5.50, or drop in anytime for fresh-made *lanches*, most R$2 apiece or less. The namesake *kibes* are a bit tough, but the rest, including breaded chicken legs and *bolinhas* (fried cheese balls) is plenty good. Look for a narrow stairway off the street.

Mundo dos Sucos (Map p645; Praça São Sebastião; mains R$4-9; ✆ breakfast, lunch & dinner Mon-Sat, 3-11pm Sun) Next door to the popular Casa do Pensador, Mundo dos Sucos is indeed a 'world of juices,' with page after page of fresh fruity creations served in plastic cups. There's a world of hot tasty sandwiches, too, with various combinations of chicken, hamburger, sausage, cheese, and egg, or, for the hopelessly indecisive, *tudo* (everything). Still widely known by its former name, 'Africa House,' which remains painted in huge letters above the door.

Cafeteria do Largo (Map p645; Praça São Sebastião; mains R$4-20; ✆ 4-10pm) This unassuming boutique eatery specializes in all-natural tapas-style appetizers, and they may well be the most creative and well-prepared edibles anywhere in Manaus. Most are distinctly Amazonian, like smoked *pirarucú* pâté with *açaí* (berry-like fruit) rolls or a miniature log cabin made of tender palm hearts. The caipirinhas are stellar, and the setting – a scattering of outdoor stainless-steel tables opposite Teatro Amazonas – is hard to beat.

ourpick Casa do Pensador (Map p645; Praça São Sebastião; mains R$13-22; ✆ 11am-11pm Mon-Fri, 4:30-11pm Sat & Sun) Simple wood tables set up on the plaza facing Teatro Amazonas make this an easy low-key place for dinner and a beer. The menu is equally low-key, mostly pizza (including a couple veggie options) and standard rice-beans-meat dishes.

Scarola Pizzaria (Map p645; ✆ 3234 8542; Rua 10 de Julho 739; mains R$10-30, per kg R$20-22; ✆ lunch & dinner) Good food, good service and good *chope* (draft beer) make for a varied clientele, from backpackers back from jungle trips to professionals pontificating on the latest opera performance. The affordable lunch spread has all the standards, including fresh grilled meats, while pizza and beer are the dinner of choice. One of the few places around that's open late, even on Sunday.

Filosóphicus (Map p645; 3rd fl, Av Sete de Setembro 752; self-service per kg R$21; ✆ lunch Mon-Fri) Vegetarians should head to this small upstairs restaurant, serving a creative, genuinely meat-free lunch buffet. A bit hard to find, and not exactly bursting with atmosphere, but worth the effort all the same.

Bufolete (Map p645; Av Joaquim Nabuco; per kg R$32; ✆ lunch Mon-Sat) If Churrascaria Búfalo is a little rich for your blood, try its smaller sister restaurant next door. The service and ambience are less refined – and the dining area rather cavelike, with low ceilings and arches – but the food is nearly as good and the prices much more palatable.

ourpick Arte com Peixe (Map p645; Rua 10 de Julho; mains R$15; ✆ lunch Mon-Sat) 'Art with Fish' may be a bit of a stretch, but the dishes here are still pretty damn good, with friendly service and an ideal location opposite Teatro Amazonas to boot. Large plates of *pirarucú* and *tambaquí* are served up grilled, fried or in a spicy *escabeche*, the house specialty.

Restaurante Giratório (Map p645; ✆ /fax 3627 3737; tajmahal@internext.com.br; Taj Mahal Continental Hotel, Av Getúlio Vargas 741; dishes R$18-45; ✆ lunch & dinner) She's starting to creak and groan a bit, but the revolving restaurant atop the Taj Majal hotel still offers unbeatable views and better-than-average meals. Snag a table just upstream from the view of Teatro Amazonas so you're sure to get at least two passes. The menu is a bit pricey, but not outrageously so; try the filet mignon or *tucanaré* in *cupuaçu* (a tart, tropical fruit) sauce.

Churrascaria Búfalo (Map p645; Av Joaquim Nabuco 628; mains R$36-45; ✆ lunch daily & dinner Mon-Sat) There's no better place in Manaus for *rodizio*, an all-you-can-eat meat extravaganza in which a cadre of tuxedoed waiters bring skewer after skewer of sizzling meat right to your table, accompanied by a full salad and pasta bar. There's no chance of leaving here hungry.

Drinking & Entertainment

There are a few quiet bars in town, but for more of a party scene, head to Ponta Negra.

Bar do Armando (Map p645; Rua 10 de Julho 593; ✆ noon-midnight Mon-Sat) Near the opera house, this is a traditional rendezvous place for Manaus's intellectual and bohemian types, but all sorts of people crowd around the outdoor tables for beers and conversation.

Ecko Lounge (off Map p645; Av Coronel Teixeira 293, Ponta Negra; ✆ 8pm-4am Wed-Sat) You can pick your pleasure here – the main dancing area pulses with techno music, while the lounge area has acoustic music and a mellower vibe. Cover is R$40 most nights; the VIP pass is a pricey R$100, but includes open bar.

Laranjinha Bar (Ponta Negra; ✆ from 9pm Mon-Sat) On the waterfront in Ponta Negra, Laranjinha is a good place to start out your night. You can order beer and burgers, and check out live music and dance shows, held most nights at the bar's large outdoor stage. A small cover charge may be added to your bill if you're there for the show.

Club de Forró (Estrada do Aleixo s/n, near Bosque de Ciência, Ponta Negra; ☽ from 11pm Thu only) A good *forró* spot, also known as the Club dos Sargentos da Aeronautica (Sergeants Aeronautical Club).

Enigma (off Map p645; ☎ 3234 7985; Rua Silva Ramos 1054; ☽ 11pm-late Thu-Sat) A mixed gay-lesbian-straight *boate* (nightclub) about 1km north of the center, with beat music and dancing.

Purão do Alemão (Ponta Negra; ☽ from 11pm Fri & Sat) and **Coração Blue** (☎ 3658 4057; Ponta Negra; ☽ from 9pm Mon-Sat) are both located on Estrada de Ponta Negra, and are lively, safe bars frequented by tourists and locals alike. Coração Blue is good for dancing, with a different theme every night, including *forró* and 'Tourist Night.'

Shopping

Galeria Amazônica (Map p645; ☎ 3233 4521; www .galeriamazonica.org.br; Rua Costa Azevedo 272) Right on Praça São Sebastião, this is Manaus's top shop for genuine-article Amazonian handiwork, including gorgeous basketwork, pottery and folk art. Prices are on the high side, but so is the quality.

Artesanato da Amazônia (Map p645; ☎ 3232 3979; Rua José Clemente 500; ☽ 9am-6:30pm Mon-Fri, 9am-3pm Sat) Once a terrific store for folk art; the good stuff here is getting buried by a growing amount of predictable kitsch. But you can still find some quality items, especially indigenous masks and handmade weapons.

Amazonas Ecoshop (Map p645; ☎ 3633 3569; www .ecoshop.com.br; Rua 10 de Julho) Smallish store with art, jewelry and other gift items. The selection is a bit lacking, but most items are made in the region and certified 'fair trade.' An in-store coffee shop has appealing coffees and pastries.

Carrefour (Map p645; Av Eduardo Ribeiro; ☽ 7:30am-9pm Mon-Sat, 7:30am-2pm Sun) The biggest and best downtown supermarket. Also a good place to buy batteries, flashlights and rain ponchos.

Numerous *casas de redes* (hammock shops; see Map p645) are clustered on Rua Rocha dos Santos and the side streets, and around Praça Tenreiro Aranha. For riverboat trips, suitable cloth hammocks start at R$15, while larger, prettier, or more durable ones go for R$45 and upwards. If you'll be sleeping in the jungle, consider getting a mosquito net (R$12 to R$25) as well.

Near Porto Manaus Moderno, the **Mercado Municipal Adolfo Lisboa** (Map p645; Rua dos Barés; ☽ 8am-5pm Mon-Sat, 6am-noon Sun) is good for inexpensive crafts and T-shirts, cheap stuffed piranhas and natural medicines.

Numerous **crafts stands** (Map p645; ☽ 9am-6pm Mon-Sat) sell mostly identical souvenir-type items in Praça Tenreiro Aranha.

Getting There & Away
AIR
The **Aeroporto Internacional Eduardo Gomes** (Map p656; ☎ 3652 1210; Av Santos Dumont 1350) is 13km north of the city center. Smaller regional airlines may use a smaller airport (known as 'Eduardinho'), about 600m east of the main one. The large modern airport terminal has a tourism office (open from 7am to 11pm), cash machines, an exchange booth, an internet café, and a clinic for yellow-fever vaccinations.

Fares fluctuate greatly – ask travel agents about promotions, especially when flying within the Amazon region. All flights from Gomes airport are subject to a R$20 departure tax; those from Eduardinho pay R$16. The tax is usually charged to your ticket at the time of purchase.

Azul (☎ 4003 1118; www.voeazul.com.br)

Copa/Continental (centro ☎ 3622 1381; www.copaair .com; Av Eduardo Ribeiro 654)

Delta (☎ 4003 2121, 0800 881 2121; www.delta.com)

Gol (☎ 3652 1593, 3652 1601; www.voegol.com.br)

LAN (☎ 0300 788 0045; www.lan.com)

TRIP (☎ 3652 1355; www.voetrip.com.br)

TAM (☎ 3652 1300, 4002 5700; www.tam.com.br)

TAP (☎ 0300 210 6060; www.flytap.com)

BOAT
Large passenger boats arrive and depart at the **Estação Hidroviária de Manaus** (Map p645; Porto Flutuante). Speedboats to Tefé, Tabatinga and Parintins use the **Porto Manaus Moderna** (Map p645; behind Mercado Municipal Adolfo Lisboa). See the boxed text, p615, for tips on riverboat travel.

Ticket booths (Map p645; ☎ 3088 5764, 3232 7062; ☽ 6am-6pm) inside the Porto Flutuante terminal sell passage on long-distance riverboats. Boats going downstream to Belém usually make stops in Itacoatiara, Parintins, Santarém and Monte Alegre. Up the Rio Solimões, boats call at Tefé, Benjamin Constant and Tabatinga. Boats to Porto Velho, along the Rio Madeira, make stops at Manicoré and Humaitá. You can buy tickets at slightly discounted prices from the men hanging around the entrance, but you may be bumped if the boat is full.

AJATO (Map p645; ☎ 3622 6047, 9984 9091; Porto Manaus Moderna; ☒ 8am-5pm Mon-Fri, 8am-noon Sat) operates comfortable speedboats upstream to Tefé (R$190, 13 hours, 7am daily except Tuesday and Sunday) and to Tabatinga and Benjamin Constant (R$420, 38 hours, Tuesday only), and downstream to Parantins (R$150, nine hours, 7am Monday and Friday). There's also service up the Rio Madeira as far as Manicoré (R$150, 14 hours, 6am Wednesday and Friday). Service to Santarém was dropped several years ago, but there are persistent rumors it will be reinstated – here's hoping. All trips include meals. Boats can fill up, so plan on buying your ticket a day or two in advance.

Slow boats going up the Rio Negro leave from Porto São Raimundo, in the Bairro São Raimundo, an unsavory district 1.5km northwest of the Porto Flutuante. A few boats a week go to Barcelos (two days) and onward to São Gabriel da Cachoeira (five to six days), typically leaving in the evening.

BUS

Manaus's **long-distance bus station** (Map p645; Rua Recife 2784) is rather small and dumpy, probably a consequence of the fact that there aren't many places you can get to by bus. It's 6km north of town, in the same direction as the airport.

Eucatur (☎ 3648 1493) has service to Boa Vista (R$100, 12 hours, 10am, 6pm, 7pm, 8pm and 11pm) with *semi-leito* service on the 6pm and 7pm departures. Take the 6pm bus if you're heading into Venezuela, with connections to Santa Elena (R$120, 16 hours from Manaus), Puerto Ordaz (R$180, 24 hours) and Puerto La Cruz (R$200, 32 hours).

Aruanã (☎ 3236 8305) has a bus service to Presidente Figueiredo (R$16.50, two hours, 6am, 10am, noon, 5pm and 9pm) and to

Itacoatiara (R$33, four hours, 6am, 7:30am, 10am, 2pm and 7pm).

CAR

Few travelers rent cars in Manaus, but if you feel the need there are several agencies at the airport that can put you behind a wheel in no time. They include **Localiza** (☎ 3652 1176), **Unidas** (☎ 3652 1327), **Avis** (☎ 3652 1579) and **Hertz** (☎ 3652 1421).

Getting Around

City buses and downtown streets get superbusy around 1pm to 2pm and 5pm to 7pm; avoid trying to move too far across the city at these times. Bus fare is R$2.25 on most routes. Taxis are plentiful, but rather expensive – from R$15 within the center, more for destination beyond that or if you get mired in traffic.

TO/FROM THE AIRPORT

Buses 306 'Aeroporto' (R$2.25) and 813 'Aeroporto-Ejecutivo' (R$3) run about every half-hour between the airport and Praça da Matriz in the center of town; the latter is air-conditioned, less crowded, and definitely worth the extra reais. At the airport, turn right out of the main doors and walk to the bus stop at the end of the terminal. In town, the most convenient stops are Praça da Matriz and on Av Getúlio Vargas near Rua José Clemente.

Taxis at the airport charge a fixed R$49 for the 20-minute ride into town. The return trip costs roughly the same, though you may be able to bargain the price down a bit.

TO/FROM THE BUS STATION

Buses 306 and 813 (the same ones you take to the airport) also pass the bus station; pick up either at Praça da Matriz or on Av Getúlio Vargas. The bus station is small and easy to miss, so be sure to tell the driver where you're

RIVERBOATS FROM MANAUS (ESTAÇÃO HIDROVIÁRIA)

Destination	Days	Time	Upper Deck	Lower Deck	Cabin (2 pax)
Belém	Wed & Fri; 11am	4 days	R$260	R$217	R$1000
Porto Velho	Tue & Fri; times vary	4 days	R$202	R$194	R$500
Santarém	Tue-Sat; 11am	36hr	R$115	R$98	R$400
Tabatinga	Wed & Sat; 11am	7 days	R$340	n/a	R$1000
Tefé	Wed & Sat; 6am	36hr	R$115	n/a	R$300

headed and keep your eyes peeled. It's the second stop after the stadium on the left.

You can catch the same buses back into town. Leaving the bus station, use the pedestrian bridge to cross Rua Recife and turn left along the busy street on the far side of the gas station there. The bus stop is 100m further along, on the far side of the street.

A taxi between the bus station and the center costs R$20 to R$25.

AROUND MANAUS
Jungle Trips
JUNGLE-TOUR OPERATORS

Most agencies have a small lodge or jungle camp where guests stay, and from which activities such as canoeing, hiking and fishing are launched. Many have amenities such as electricity and flush toilets, but not all. Prices usually include meals, lodging, transport and guides, and average R$140 to R$200 per person per day (including the time it takes to get to and from the lodge, not just the time you're actually there). Prices vary primarily by the type of accommodations: hammocks with shared toilets are the cheapest option, followed by dorms and private rooms, then riverboats and specialized tours. For the most luxury (and we use that word guardedly) check out the jungle lodges in the next section (p658). Be extremely wary of prices that seem too good to be true: there's a limit to how low an agency can go and still maintain quality and safety.

Amazon Antonio Jungle Tours (Map p645; ☎ 3234 1294, cell 9961 8314; www.antonio junglctours.com; Hostel Manaus, Rua Lauro Cavalcante 231) This well-run jungle lodge is on the Rio Urubú, 200km northeast of Manaus and, because it's black water, home to blessedly few mosquitoes. The lodge features private rooms (most with en suites), a huge hammock area overlooking the river, even an observation tower and canoes for guests to use between outings. Overnight jungle trips are not to be missed, hiking through primary forest and sleeping at makeshift camps. And unlike most lodges, you can hang out here for a few days after your tour is over, for a reduced price.

Amazon Gero Tours (Map p645; ☎ 3232 4755, cell 9983 6273; www.amazongerotours.com; Hotel 10 de Julho, Rua 10 de Julho 679) Gero Mesquita, an all-round good guy, offers a variety of tour options, most in the Lago de Juma area. He's got a large comfortable lodge, with hammocks, dorms and

private cabins (complete with bathroom and screened patio) and a team of experienced guides for hiking, canoeing, sleeping in the jungle, and more. He recently inaugurated a 'social sustainability' project, in which travelers stay with local families (or on a riverboat, or both) and help with community projects, like building schools or teacher housing; advance notice usually required.

Iguana Turismo (Map p645; ☎ 3633 6507, cell 9105 5659; www.amazonbrasil.com.br; Hotel 10 de Julho, Rua 10 de Julho 679) Run by Guyanese transplant Gerry Hardy – not to be confused with Gero, whose office is next door – Iguana has an appealing lodge at the mouth of Lago de Juma. A large dorm area has hammocks and beds, while several wood cabins have bathrooms and partial views of the river. There are a couple large decks for spotting dolphins and hanging out between excursions; daily excursions include all the usuals, including overnighting in the forest, plus visiting a local community to learn about manioc processing and other customs.

Malocas Jungle Lodge (☎ 3648 0119; www.malocas .com) Peace and quiet prevail at this simple jungle lodge, owned and operated by a friendly French-Brazilian couple, and located 80km down the winding Rio Preto da Eva. The lodge is 100% solar powered, and the motorboats are rarely used, allowing the jungle sounds to come through. Guestrooms have thin beds and walls, high ceilings and passable bathrooms, and occupy one of three large circular structures, or *malocas*; another is used for hammocks, and the third for eating and hanging out. Tours including hiking, canoeing, fishing, sleeping in the forest and swimming in the area's many small waterfalls.

Amazonas Indian Turismo (Map p645; ☎ 3232 4248; www.amazonasindianturismo.tur.br; 2nd fl, Rua dos Andradas 311) This longtime budget agency has a very rustic camp on the Rio Urubú, with hammocks, latrine toilets and no electricity. The agency specializes in long hikes in the forest, so you may spend a night or two roughing it even more, in a makeshift camp and your hammock slung between two trees. This agency is notable for being indigenous-owned and operated; most guides are Wapixano, and all speak English.

Swallows & Amazons (Map p645; ☎ 3622 1246; www.swallowsandamazonstours.com; Rua Ramos Ferreira 922) Another long-established and well-recommended tour operator, Swallows & Amazons specializes in riverboat tours, where

THE AMAZON

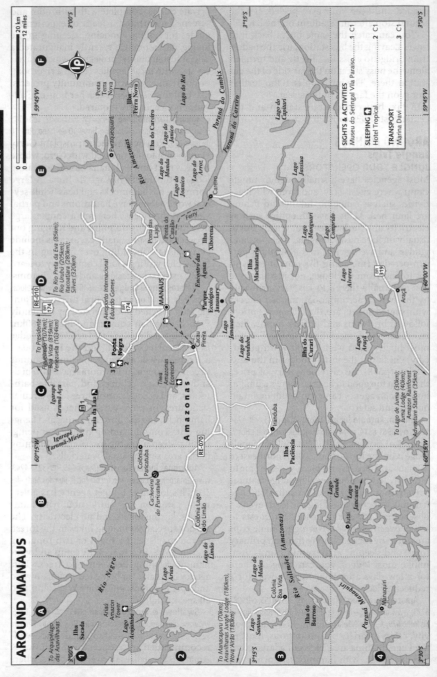

AROUND MANAUS

SIGHTS & ACTIVITIES
Museu do Seringal Vila Paraiso......1 C1

SLEEPING
Hotel Tropical...............................2 C1

TRANSPORT
Marina Davi..................................3 C1

you sleep on board – either in hammocks or in private air-conditioned cabins, depending on the boat – and visit several areas in one trip. Tours go up the Rio Negro, exploring smaller tributaries along the way, with plenty of hiking, canoeing and fishing along the way. Given enough time, you can reach as far as Anavilhanes Archipelago (a profusion of islands known for their bird-watching) or Jaú national park.

Maia Expeditions (off Map p645; ☎ 3877 9247, cell 9983 7141; www.maiaexpeditions.com; Rua Badajo 5, Parque Shangri-la Barro de Flores) This highly professional outfit specializes in boat excursions, from deluxe yachts to simple riverboats for groups of two to eight people. It also owns a well-maintained lodge in the Lago Juma area (roughly between Amazon Gero's and Iguana's) with eight small cabins, all with high thatched roof and most with bathroom. The dining room and screened hammock area are great for relaxing. Most independent travelers book trips just at the lodge – from which you take standard excursions – but combination boat-and-lodge tours are possible. The main office is not in the downtown area, however.

Amazon Tree Climbing (☎ 8195 8585; www.amazon treeclimbing.com; per person from R$200) This smartly run outfit offers one-of-a-kind tours into massive *angelín* or *samaúma* trees – an amazing Amazonian experience that's been oddly lacking until now. Day trips include just one ascent, but there's more to it than just up and down; it can take an hour to reach the top, with mid-dangle discussions of canopy ecology, and plenty of time to soak up the view, a dozen-plus stories above the ground. Itineraries range from morning outings near

THE AMAZON

JUNGLE TRIPPING

The top priority for most foreign visitors to Manaus is a jungle trip. While anything's possible, the most common trip is two to four days, including hiking in the jungle, fishing for piranha, spotting caiman at night and visiting a local village. Best of all, you'll canoe through narrow river channels and eerie flooded forests (in the high water), which are beautiful and better for spotting wildlife than the main river.

Different tour operators specialize in different things; thinking carefully about what sort of trip you want can help determine which operator is best for you. How much do you want to rough it? Do you want a bed or a hammock? What about sleeping aboard a boat? Private bathroom, shared, or pit toilet? Do you want to spend a night or two in the forest or do day trips from the lodge? How much do mosquitoes bother you? Do you prefer hiking or canoeing? There is no shame in choosing more or less comfort – you are there to enjoy yourself, after all.

There are also a few questions to ask the tour operator: does the guide speak English (or a language you understand)? How long will you spend getting there? What is the trip itinerary? How much hiking and/or canoeing will you do? Ask to see recent pictures of the accommodations and activities, and a guest comment book.

And talk to other travelers! Virtually every foreigner you see in Manaus is planning a trip or returning from one, and they are the best source of honest, up-to-date info.

A word about what you'll see: many travelers come to the Amazon expecting to see jaguars in every tree and a village of spear-toting *índios* around every river bend. This just doesn't happen, not in Manaus and not anywhere in the Amazon. On a typical trip, you are likely to see dolphins and a slew of birds, including herons, parrots and macaws. Monkeys, sloths and caimans are relatively common, but seeing them is no sure thing. Manatees, anacondas and jaguars are extremely hard to spot. Some tour operators may dissuade you from taking a trip on 'black' rivers, claiming they have fewer animals. While this is technically true, white rivers also have more mosquitoes and thicker vegetation, inhibiting even the keenest observer. The single biggest factor in seeing animals is luck. The diligence of your guide is also important: during your trip, politely insist that morning excursions leave on time, and that they last the full allotted time.

Bring sturdy shoes or boots, long-sleeved shirt and pants, mosquito repellent, a hat and sunscreen, a raincoat, flashlight, extra batteries, roll of toilet paper, daypack and a water bottle. If you don't have binoculars, ask your tour operator if you can borrow or rent a pair. For photos, high-speed film and/or flash are often necessary. Pack as light as possible: most hotels in Manaus offer secure luggage storage for whatever you don't bring along.

JUNGLE TRIP SCAMS

Manaus is teeming with scammers and touts. Most go after budget-conscience travelers, peddling cut-rate tours that turn out to be woefully uninspired: overcrowded, surly guides, caged animals, hiking through cow pastures, skipping activities etc. Worse, in 2007 a tourist drowned after the boat he was in capsized in a storm. The boat had no lifejackets, was driven by an inexperienced guide, and had been booked by an agency known for snagging tourists off the street (and which is still operating today). Some precautions worth taking include the following:

Never pay for a tour anywhere except the agency's main office in town. Touts often pretend they are with a legitimate agency but steer you to a café or airport bench to make the deal. They even make phony phone calls to convince you the main office is closed, or that you must commit right away to get the best price or the 'last seat on the boat.' These are all scams.

Firmly turn down anyone who approaches you at the airport about booking a tour. No legitimate agency fishes for tourists there, so anyone who does so is a tout. If you've reserved ahead of time and are being picked up, look for a sign with your name on it.

Do not tell touts what hotel or agency you're interested in, nor accept help locating them. They're only trying to squeeze a commission out of the owners, which of course gets passed on to you. If a persistent tout follows you into a hotel or tour office, make it clear you arrived on your own.

Confirm the agency is registered with the state tourism authority. Go to www.amazon astur.am.gov.br, select the Portuguese version (it's more up-to-date than the English one), then *Agências de Turismo*.

Above all, don't risk your life to save a little money. In the end, the reason there are so many scammers is because travelers keep booking with them. Be smart: the Amazon is not a place to cut corners.

Manaus, to all-day excursions in the Rio Preto da Eva or Presidente Figueiredo areas, to multiday trips up the Rio Negro.

Manati Amazônia Turismo (☎ 3234 2534; www .manatiamazonia.com; Rua Lauro Cavalcante 11 Rm 201) This agency doesn't have facilities of its own; instead it helps travelers select among the various options (including many of the operators and lodges listed here) and handles all the bookings.

JUNGLE LODGES

The following lodges cater to a more upscale client base; the activities are usually the same as those offered by operators in Manaus, but the lodging, food and service tend to be somewhat more refined (and the prices substantially higher).

Anavilhanas Jungle Lodge (off Map p656; ☎ 3622 8996; www.anavilhanaslodge.com; per person per day all-inclusive from R$250; 🏊) This well-run and well-liked lodge is located on a remote and lovely bend of the Rio Negro, yet is accessible by paved road. That cuts your transfer time considerably, leaving more time to do fun stuff. The cabins have electric lighting, bathrooms, even (gasp!) air-con, yet guests have direct access to pristine forest and waterways, including

the namesake and lushly forested Anavilhanas Archipelago.

Juma Lodge (off Map p656; ☎ 3232 2707; www.juma lodge.com; all-inclusive packages from 3 days/2 nights s/d jungle view US$950/1500, lake view US$1150/1800) The deluxe lakefront cabins here stand on 15m stilts, connected by wood walkways, and have huge screened windows and a private patio overlooking the lake. They can get hot in the late afternoon, but that's when you might be sipping a caipirinha in the lodge's shady deck, having just returned from a canoe trip in the forest. All cabins have bathroom, and meals are served in a spacious communal dining area.

Amazon Rainforest Adventure Station (off Map p656; ☎ 3656 6033; www.naturesafaris.com; all-inclusive packages from 4 days/3 nights per person US$799) A homey floating lodge in Lago de Juma, about 80km from Manaus. Standard rooms are comfortable but tiny, while two larger suites, each with private outdoor showers, are well worth the extra cost. (None have private toilets, however.) This used to be called Amazon Eco-Lodge, and was the area's first ecolodge.

RIO NEGRO BASIN

Trips up the Rio Negro tend to be a week or more, simply because it takes 24 to 36 hours on a boat to get most places. You'll do many of the same activities as elsewhere – hiking, canoeing, fishing – but the area is far less developed so you'll encounter fewer villages, pastures and other human footprints. That is not to say you will necessarily see more animals; as always, that depends on luck and the skill of your guide. One advantage: most of the rivers here are 'black,' meaning they are blissfully mosquito-free.

Reserva Xixuaú-Xipariná

This gorgeous but little-visited reserve covers a massive swath of pristine rain forest along the Rio Jauaperí in southern Roraima, some 500km (35 to 40 hours by boat) from Manaus. It is one of the best places in the Amazon to see giant river otters, not to mention monkeys, dolphins, wild boars and caimans. Founded by a Scottish transplant named Cris Clark (who still lives there full time) the reserve and lodge are actually owned and operated by **Asociación Amazônia** (☎ 9197 0949; www.amazonia.org), an organization of local residents.

A large new *maloca*-style lodge was due to be completed in 2011, with common dining and hammock areas. Also in the works are five smaller *malocas*, each with double beds, bathroom, and verandas. A nearby community has a public telephone and even satellite internet; Clark arranges your transport and activities, but the tours themselves are typically led by local guides. The reserve is open year-round, though April and May see extremely heavy rain.

Visits cost €100 to €120 per person per day, including transportation, with a week being the bare minimum, considering you burn up almost three days just getting there and back.

Parque Nacional do Jaú

Spanning nearly 23,000 sq km (22,720 sq km, to be exact), Jaú is Brazil's second-biggest national park, and one of the largest tracts of protected tropical rain forest in the world. It stretches west from the Rio Negro along the Jaú and Carabinani rivers, and is rich in flora and fauna. The park was designated a Unesco World Heritage listing in 2000.

There are no lodges in the park, so it's best to visit with a tour outfit that specializes in riverboat tours, such as Swallows & Amazons or Maia Expeditions, both in Manaus (see p655). Booking is essential, as the operator must obtain special permission to enter the park.

PRESIDENTE FIGUEIREDO

☎ 0xx92 / pop 26,300

Self-named the 'Terra de Cachoeiras' (Land of Waterfalls), this dusty little town is surrounded by dozens of waterfalls and caves. Just 100km north of Manaus by good highway, this is the only leisure spot easily accessible by road from the capital, and it gets obscenely packed on weekends. A midweek visit can be a nice diversion if you've got time to kill.

Sights & Activities

You need a vehicle to visit the waterfalls here. You can rent a car from Manaus, or take the

---

BLACK & WHITE

There are three types of rivers in the Amazon Basin: *negro* (black), *branco* (white) and *claro* (clear). White rivers (actually more a creamy beige) come from the Andes, and get their color from sediment eroded from those 'young' mountains. These rivers – including the Solimões and Madeira – are loaded with nutrients and can support more plants and animals along their path.

Black rivers, such as the Rio Negro and Rio Urubú, originate in northern Amazonia and flow over much older land, long swept clean of sediment. Black rivers tend to be slower and warmer than white ones (which start as snowpack in the Andes, after all) and the vegetation in them has time to rot, releasing organic acids. Those acids turn the water 'black,' actually a tealike color. The same acids kill mosquito larvae, meaning black-water areas have amazingly few mosquitoes and a low incidence of malaria and other diseases.

Clear rivers have neither the sediment nor the organic acids that would make them white or black. The massive Tapajós and Arapiuns rivers are clear, and small tributaries in predominantly white or black water areas can be clear if their course happens to allow it.

Both white and black water rivers flood seasonally, but the result is not the same, at least in name. Forest flooded with black water is referred to as *igapó*, while forest flooded with white water is called *várzea*.

bus and hire a taxi in Presidente Figueiredo, though a guided tour allows you to see and do the most; Pousada das Pedras (p660) in Presidente Figueiredo and Amazon Gero Tours (p655) in Manaus offer recommended and affordable tours to the area.

Your time and appetite for hiking will determine which waterfalls to visit; among the most impressive are **Iracema, Cachoeira da Onza, Caverna do Maroaga, Gruta Judéia, Santuario, Asaframa** and **Pedra Furada** (the most distant of the falls, at 60km from town).

About 12km from town is the town of Balbina, where the **Water Mammals Preservation Center** (☎ 3312 1202; admission free; ⏱ 8am-noon & 2-4pm Mon-Sat, 8am-noon Sun) shelters manatees and other animals.

Sleeping & Eating

All room prices listed following include breakfast.

Pousada das Pedras (☎ 3324 1296; www.pousada daspedras-am.com.br; s/d weekday R$50/70, weekend R$60/80) Operated by friendly Francisco 'Pimenta' de Mazi, this is easily the best and most convenient place to base your visit. Rooms are small but attractive with bathroom; suites are quite spacious. Meals are served in a nice garden patio. De Mazi arranges guided trips in the area, including long hikes to beautiful Neblina and Natal falls (rates depend on the type and length of tour) A taxi from the bus station is R$7, but De Mazi may pick you up if you call ahead.

Hotel Marauga (☎ 3324 1110; opposite bus station; r R$70-90; ⏺) Large but plain rooms have air-con, TV and minibar. The owner can arrange tours.

Delícias no Esteto (mains R$8-20; ⏱ 8am-10pm) Basic self-serve and menu restaurant, across from the bus station, with soups, fish and more.

Getting There & Away

Aruanã (☎ in Manaus 3236 8305) has five daily buses from Manaus to Presidente Figueiredo (R$16.50, two hours, 6am, 10am, noon, 5pm and 9pm). Buses north to Boa Vista and Venezuela pass several times per day.

PARINTINS

☎ 0xx92 / pop 107,000

The **Boi-Bumbá festival**, held here on the last Friday, Saturday and Sunday of June, is the biggest annual shindig in Amazonas. It's an Amazonian version of Bumba Meu Boi, a traditional festival of mixed African and European origins that uses music, theater and dancing to enact the kidnapping, death and resurrection of an ox – a metaphor for agricultural cycles. In Parintins the event incorporates a rivalry between two 'clans,' the Caprichoso, who dress all in blue, and Garantido, who dress in red.

Tens of thousands of people descend on Parintins for the event, for which the tiny town has a 35,000-capacity purpose-built stadium known as the *bumbódromo*. Parintins' hotels are booked months in advance, most charging around R$1500 for a five- to seven-day package for up to three people, while hundreds of riverboats from Manaus and elsewhere go especially for the festival, and passengers sleep onboard. A five-night boat trip from Manaus (transportation, hammock space and meals) costs around US$350. Private houses also rent rooms during the festival. Most travel agencies in Manaus can arrange a trip.

If you arrive any other time, the **Brito Hotel** (☎ 3533 3632; www.britohotel.com; Av Amazonas 2526; s/d R$50/70; ⏺ ⏺) and **Hotel Avenida** (☎ 3533 1279; Av Amazonas 2416; s/d R$30/45, incl breakfast R$35/50; ⏺) offer passable rooms with air-conditioning, TV and minibar.

Most riverboats between Manaus and Belém stop at Parantins, and **AJATO** (Map p645; ☎ 3622 6047, 9984 9091; Porto Manaus Moderna; ⏱ 8am-5pm Mon-Fri, 8am-noon Sat) has speedboat service there from Manaus (R$150, eight to nine hours, 7am Monday and Friday).

TRIP (☎ 0300 789 8747; www.voetrip.com.br) has daily flights to Parantins from Manaus.

TEFÉ

☎ 0xx97 / pop 65,000

Tefé is the jumping-off point to the Mamirauá reserve (p662), one of the best ecotourism experiences in the Amazon. Visits there are closely coordinated with airline schedules, so those coming and going by plane generally have little or no time to explore the town. Those travelling by boat may have a half-day or more to spare. Until recently, extra time in Tefé wasn't much to get excited about, but that's changing somewhat. A new hotel in town offers a variety of interesting tours, including to indigenous communities, and there's a handful of appealing restaurants and bars.

Orientation

Most of the listed hotels, restaurants and services are within a block or two of Tefé's two
central plazas. The main plaza – not because
it's larger, but because it has the church – is
Praça Santa Tereza, a long tapered wedge running roughly east–west, with the church on
the western end. A block north is Praça Tulio
Azevêdo, a more traditional square with trees,
benches, and newsstands. Beyond that is the
municipal market and the waterfront. Both
plazas are bordered by busy streets, down
which flows a constant stream of scooters
and moto-taxis.

Information

EMERGENCY
Ambulance (☎ 192)
Hospital São Miguel (☎ 3343 2469; Rua Marechal
Deodoro 66)
Police (☎ 190)

INTERNET ACCESS
Eganet (Rua Gétulio Vargas; per hr R$3; ☺ 8am-11pm
Mon-Sat, 2-11pm Sun) Opposite Ega's Hotel.

LAUNDRY
Lavandería do Paulo (Rua Daniel Servalho 345; per
item R$0.50-2)

MONEY
Banco do Brasil (Rua Olavo Bilac at Praça Tulio Azevêdo;
☺ 9am-2pm Mon-Fri)
Bradesco (cnr Ruas Getúlio Vargas & Daniel Servalho)

POST
Post office (Estrada Aeroporto; ☺ 8am-4pm Mon-Fri)

TOURIST OFFICES
Instituto Mamirauá (☎ 3343 4160; www.mamiraua
.org.br; Rua Brasil 197; ☺ 8am-noon & 2-6pm Mon-
Fri, 8am-noon Sat) Oversees the Mamirauá reserve and
Pousada Uacari; stop in or call for info and reservations.
English spoken.

TRAVEL AGENCIES
Guest House Multicultura (☎ 3343 6632; http://
sites.google.com/site/guesthousemulticultura; Rua 15 de
Junho 136) The multilingual owners can purchase boat
and plane tickets to and from Tefé, and even email you a
printable ticket in some cases; service fee is 15% to 20% of
the ticket price. They also offer highly informative tours to
local sights, natural areas and indigenous villages.
Motivos Viagens e Turismo (☎ 3343 5633; Rua
Benjamin Constant 382) Purchase plane tickets here.

Sights & Activities

There are a few sights and activities in Tefé if
you happen to have time to spare.

Finally, there's something to do in Tefé besides visit Mamirauá! The Dutch-Brazilian
owners of **Guest House Multicultura** (☎ 3343 6632;
http://sites.google.com/site/guesthousemulticultura; Rua
15 de Junho 136) offer highly informative tours
of the area, including visiting nearby indigenous villages (belonging to Kokama, Picuna,
Kambeba and other groups) where you'll learn
about farming, domestic life and more. Trips
can also include canoeing, hiking, fishing,
animal-spotting and more, and range from a
few hours to all day. Rates are reasonable, and
vary by itinerary.

In town, **O Seminario** (☺ 8-11:30am Mon-Fri) is
a striking structure that occupies the entire
northern side of Praça Tulio Avevêdo. Oddly
New England-ish in its design, it was once a
seminary and is now the local headquarters
of a Dutch mission with numerous congrega-
tions in the Amazon. It's not technically open
for visits, but you might finagle a tour if you
ask nicely.

Operated by the same mission, **As Misões**
(☎ 3343 3011) is a mildly interesting complex overlooking the mouth of Lago de Tefé
and the main channel of the Rio Solimões.
Founded in 1897, it has a well-kept garden,
huge decaying church, and a cemetery full
of former missionaries. The main building
was a church-run vocational school where
many of Tefé's masons, metalworkers and
other skilled tradesmen were trained. The
elfish priest, Padre Altino from the north of
Portugal, gives spirited tours to anyone who's
interested. The best time to come is Tuesday
to Friday; to get there, hire a boat from the
waterfront.

Sleeping & Eating

Hotel Patricia (☎ 3343 2541; Praça Tulio Azevêdo; s/d
R$35/60; ❄) The best of Tefé's cheap hotels is
run like a guesthouse by a friendly grandma
figure. Some rooms are bright and tolerable,
others musty and unpleasant; all have air-con
and satellite TV, but no hot water.

Guest House Multicultura (☎ 3343 6632; http://
sites.google.com/site/guesthousemulticultura; Rua 15 de
Junho 136; dm R$30, s/d R$45/65, r with lake view R$80;
❄ ☺) A great new addition to Tefé's hotel
scene, not least because the Dutch-Brazilian
owners speak English, Portuguese, Spanish,
German, Dutch, even Tagalog, and can help

arrange everything from boat reservations to tours of the area. The rooms are simple but tidy, all with hot-water bathrooms, some with excellent views of Lake Tefé. There's a small rooftop café with even better views. It's located about 15 minutes by foot from the center.

Ega's Hotel (☎ 3343 2929; egashoteltur@hotmail.com; cnr Ruas Getúlio Vargas & Daniel Servalho; s/d/tr R$50/70/90; ▣ ☎) Large clean rooms and bathrooms, and a convenient location near both parks and opposite a bank and cybercafé, make this a perfectly adequate choice. Just be sure there isn't loud music coming from inside – the hotel occasionally rents out its interior courtyard for private parties, which last into the wee hours.

Hotel Anilçe (☎ 3343 2416; Praça Santa Tereza; s/d R$60/80) A reasonable alternative to Ega's if the latter is full or hosting a party, though the rooms aren't as large nor the bathrooms as clean. The top-floor breakfast area is pleasant enough, as is the location – opposite the church and plaza.

Stylos (Rua Floriano Peixoto 190; mains R$8-35; ♥ lunch & dinner Mon-Sat) The most reliable eatery in the center, with hefty, well-prepared dishes served at outdoor tables right on the street corner. The menu includes all the standard fish, meat and chicken dishes, plus a few less-common ones, such as huge portions of *lingua na brasa* (grilled tongue).

Grão de Mostarda (mains R$12-30; ♥ lunch & dinner) Friendly new restaurant serving classic Brazilian dishes at reasonable prices.

Barzinho (Rua Olavo Bilac) Perched on a small rise above one of Tefé's main drags – with a tree growing through the floor and out the roof – this is a cool little spot to have a beer or two and listen to live music, mostly of the singer-songwriter variety.

Muralha (Rua Olavo Bilac) One of Tefé's newer watering holes, with nice river views and live music most Friday nights.

Getting There & Away

AIR

TRIP (☎ 0300 789 8747; www.voetrip.com.br) was the only airline serving Tefé at the time of research, with daily flights from Manaus and twice weekly to and from Tabatinga. Service changes frequently on this route, however, along with prices, which can range from R$299 to R$700 each way, depending when you fly.

BOAT

Slow boats to Manaus depart five to six days per week (hammock R$150, cabin R$350, 30 to 36 hours). Prices vary somewhat according to the boat, and bargaining is sometimes possible. Coming from Tabatinga, boats don't dock in Tefé but small motorboats typically meet the boat midstream to ferry passengers there. Be sure to tell the captain of the slow boat you're going on to Tefé.

AJATO (☎ 3343 5306) has comfortable speedboat service to and from Manaus; it's quicker than the regular boat but cheaper than a flight. Refer to the Manaus section for AJATO's schedule from there (p654); departures from Tefé are at 7am on Monday, Tuesday, Thursday, Friday and Saturday. Advance reservations are recommended, as the speedboats frequently fill up; contact **Guesthouse Multicultura** (☎ 3343 6632) about booking your return passage, as you usually can't do so in Manaus.

Slow boats going upstream to Tabatinga pass near Tefé on Mondays and Fridays, but do not dock there, so catching them is a bit tricky. The most common way is to simply hire a boat taxi to motor you into the middle of the river and wait for the boat to pass. Alternatively, catch a regional boat to Fonte Boa or Jutaí (R$55 to R$90, 18 to 24 hours upriver) and wait there for the Tabatinga boat (hammock R$210, three to four days).

You also can catch an AJATO speedboat from Tefé to Santo Antonio do Içá on Saturday morning (R$180, 12 hours, 7am) then hang out until Sunday, when AJATO has continuing service to Tabatinga (R$150, 13 hours, 6:30am).

Both the **Instituto Mamirauá** (☎ 3343 4160; www.mamiraua.org.br; Rua Brasil 197, Tefé) and Guesthouse Multicultura have up-to-date transport information for getting to and away Tefé, and are good places to inquire when planning your travel.

MAMIRAUÁ RESERVE

One of the Amazon's best ecotourism options, Mamirauá offers the visitor pristine rain forest, comfortable lodging, excellent guide service, and affordable prices, plus it's just 1½ hours by boat from a large town with reliable air and boat service. With so many places claiming to be eco-this and eco-that, Mamirauá is one of few places in the Amazon that really does it right.

The Reserva de Desenvolvimento Sustentável Mamirauá (Mamirauá Sustainable Development Reserve) is Brazil's last large area of *várzea* (forests seasonally flooded with sediment-rich 'white water'). It covers 12,400 sq km northwest of Tefé between the Solimões and Japurá rivers. The park's eastern edge merges with the Amanã reserve, which in turn borders Jaú national park. Together the three reserves span 57,000 sq km, making up the second-largest block of protected tropical rain forest in the world.

Mamirauá was Brazil's first sustainable development reserve (there are now 20). Its purpose is to combine nature conservation and scientific research, while promoting sustainable practices and improved opportunities for the local population. There are numerous small communities within the Mamirauá reserve; many residents work part time as tour guides, cooks and boat drivers while continuing traditional work such as fishing, planting and hunting under a mutually agreed sustainable-use plan.

The reserve is ably managed by the **Instituto Mamirauá** (☎ 3343 4160; www.mamiraua.org.br; Rua Brasil 197, Tefé; ☷ 8am-noon & 2-6pm Mon-Fri, 8am-noon Sat). Packages are coordinated with the Manaus–Tefé flight schedule, and priced according to the length of stay: US$660 per person for four days/three nights (Friday to Monday); US$760 per person for five days/four nights (Monday to Friday); and US$1090 per person for eight days/seven nights or US$1000 per person for groups of four or more (Monday to Monday, or Friday to Friday). Accommodations are in the **Pousada Uacari** (www.pousadauacari.com.br), an excellent floating lodge with spacious, comfortable bungalows, each with hot-water bathrooms, solar energy and a small patio with

hammock, plus a large common area where generous meals are served. (The lodge is now completely community run, with proceeds reinvested into community development and conservation efforts.)

Tours include food, lodging, guides, and boat transfer to and from Tefé, plus pick-up and drop-off at airport or speedboat port. Visitors to Mamirauá can be reasonably assured of seeing sloths, caimans, and dolphins, and dozens of birds, such as macaws and toucans. There are five species of monkeys, including howlers, capuchins, and the highly elusive white uakari, an endemic species that's notable for its crimson face and shaggy white coat. Manatees, anacondas and jaguars also live in the reserve but are extremely difficult to spot.

You'll also visit a local village and one of the reserve's ongoing research projects. Both can be fascinating, and you'll likely see dolphins, birds and even monkeys along the way. A new option is a night in the 'tree house,' a one-room cabin on 5m stilts a short way into the forest with great early-morning bird-watching. An English-speaking naturalist is at the main lodge at all times (and accompanies some excursions) but most guides speak Portuguese only. Binoculars can be rented (per day US$10) and are highly recommended.

High water here is in June and July, when the forest is completely flooded and you glide through the water in canoes. (This is not to be confused with rainy season, which runs from January to April). This is when monkeys and sloths are most visible, and tends to be the busiest time. In low water, roughly October and November, hiking is possible and aquatic animals, especially fish and caimans, are more concentrated.

THE AMAZON

UP RIVER, DOWN RIVER

From the time South America and Africa went their separate ways, and for 150 million years after that, the Amazon actually flowed east to west, the opposite direction it does today. That's why Amazonian stingrays are more closely related to Pacific species than Atlantic ones, and how telltale sediment from eastern South America ended up in the middle of the rain forest. It was only 15 to 20 million years ago that the Andes shot up and blocked the water's westward exit. Around the same time, a smaller ridge of land, now called the Purus Arch, rose like a spine in the middle of the continent.

East of the Purus Arch the river started draining into the Atlantic Ocean, but west of there, the water was trapped and a huge inland sea formed. Eventually the water poured over the Purus Arch, gouging a deep channel near present-day Parantins – still the narrowest and deepest part of the river – and the Amazon returned to being a river, but now flowing west to east.

THE AMAZON

THE TRIPLE FRONTIER

The Brazilian town of Tabatinga and the Colombian town of Leticia lie side by side on the eastern bank of the Amazon River, about 1100km west of Manaus, while the far bank belongs to Peru. A logical travel hub, the 'triple frontier' also happens to be a good area for taking jungle trips, particularly to remote areas up the Rio Javari (the Brazil–Peru border) and further up the Amazon in Colombia.

Most travelers stay in Leticia, which is more pleasant and better equipped than Tabatinga or the small villages on the Peruvian side.

Tabatinga

☎ 0xx97 / pop 48,000

Tabatinga is most notable as the place where the Amazon River enters Brazil; otherwise, it's a nondescript border town. Boats headed down to Manaus and up to Iquitos in Peru depart from Tabatinga's two ports, and its airport serves Brazilian and Peruvian destinations.

ORIENTATION

Tabatinga's main artery is Av da Amizade (aka Av Principal), which runs parallel to the river

THE TRIPLE FRONTIER

for 3km from Tabatinga's airport to Leticia and the international border. The most useful cross streets include Rua Marechal Rondon (250m south of the border), Rua Rui Barbosa (650m), Av Marechal Mallet (900m), Rua Santos Dumont (1.2km) and Rua Duarte Coelho (1.7km). Rua Santos Dumont leads to Porto da Feira, Tabatinga's small-boat port; you can also get there by going down Av Marechal Mallet, turning left at the end and passing the market. Porto Fluvial, where boats for Manaus dock, is at the end of Rua Duarte Coelho.

INFORMATION

Consulates

Colombia consulate (☎ 3412 2104; Rua General Sampaio 623; ⏰ 8am-2pm Mon-Fri)

Emergency

Hospital Militar (☎ 192, 3412 2403, 3412 2117; Rua Duarte Coelho at Av da Amizade)
Police (☎ 190)

Immigration

Polícia Federal (☎ 3412 2180; Av da Amizade 650; ⏰ 8am-6pm) 100m south of Rua Duarte Coelho.

Internet Access

Digital Net (☎ 3412 3505; Rua Pedro Teixera 397; per hr R$2; ⏰ 8am-noon & 1:30-9pm Mon-Fri, 9am-noon Sat, 2-6pm Sun) On the street parallel to Av Marechal Mallet, one block south.

Money

Bradesco (Av da Amizade at Av Marechal Mallet)

Post

Post office (Av da Amizade s/n; ⏰ 8am-5pm Mon-Fri) Located 300m north of the federal police station.

Travel Agencies

CNM Câmbio e Turismo (☎ 3412 3281; Av da Amizade 2017) Also exchanges money.

SLEEPING & EATING

Hotel Restaurant Te Contei? (☎ 3412 4548; Av da Amizade 1813; s/d R$50/70; 🆒) Large rooms with air-conditioning off a breezy upstairs patio and corridor. The back rooms have less street noise, and there's a popular self-serve restaurant (per kg $25) on the ground floor.

Pousada Takanás (☎ 3412 3557; Rua Oswaldo Cruz 970; s/d R$78/98; 🆒) Tabatinga's best hotel has reasonably modern rooms, with hot water, air-conditioning, TV and minibar, plus a lush central courtyard. A bit removed from the main drag, but that's not necessarily a bad thing.

Restaurante Tres Fronteiras do Amazonas (☎ 3412 2341; Rua Rui Barbosa, 200m west of Av da Amizade; mains R$9-20; ⓧ breakfast, lunch & dinner) Try the *peixe tres fronteiras*, a fish fillet with spices from Peru, Brazil and Colombia, served on a large banana leaf. Wash it down with a beer or caipirinha.

Churrascaria Tia Helena (☎ 3412 2165; Rua Marechal Mallet 12; all-you-can-eat per person R$28; ⓧ lunch) Waiters bring skewered meats directly from the grill and carve it at the table in classic *churrascaria* fashion. Decor is austere (think cement floors and fluorescent lights) but the food is good and the ambience cheerful.

GETTING THERE & AWAY
Air
The airport is 4km south of Tabatinga; coming from Leticia, catch one of the *colectivos* marked 'Comara.'

TRIP (reservations ☎ 0300 789 8747; www.airtrip.com .br) has twice-weekly flights between Tabatinga and Manaus (R$500 to R$625), always via Tefé (R$345). Some TRIP flights make additional stops at the towns of Carauari and Coari.

Boat
Slow boats to Manaus (hammock R$150; three to four days) leave from the Porto Fluvial on Wednesday, Friday, and Saturday afternoons. Arrive in the morning to stake out good hammock space, as boats can be quite crowded. See the boxed text, p615, for more tips on riverboat travel.

Speedboats operated by **AJATO** (Map p645; ☎ in Porto Manaus Moderna 3622 6047, in Tabatinga 3412 2227; ⓧ 8am-5pm Mon-Fri, 8am-noon Sat) leave Tabatinga for Manaus (R$420, 35 hours) on Friday mornings at 7am. The boats have airplane-style seating, TVs playing movies, and meal service.

To get to Tefé, take a long-distance slow boat or AJATO speedboat to Fonte Boa or Jutaí and transfer to a regional slow boat, or continue all the way to Alvarães, which is just a short taxi and motorboat ride from Tefé.

To/From Colombia
The international border is marked by nothing more than a few moneychangers on the Brazilian side and a Colombian police officer directing traffic on the other side. You are free to move between Tabatinga and Leticia as much as you like, but if you plan to travel onward, even to Amacayacu national park, you should clear immigration for both countries – DAS in Colombia, the Polícia Federal in Brazil – before leaving town. If you need it, there's a Colombian consulate in Tabatinga (p664).

To/From Peru
Transtur (☎ 3412 2945; www.portaltabatinga.com.br/ transtur.htm; Rua Marechal Mallet 248) runs high-speed passenger boats – known in Portuguese as *rápidos* – from Tabatinga and Iquitos (US$65, nine to 10 hours, two meals served). Boats depart Tabatinga's Porto da Feira on Wednesday, Friday and Sunday at 5am (boarding begins at 4am). Be sure to get a Brazilian exit stamp the day before; you'll stop at the island community of Santa Rosa, where the Polícia Internacional Peruviano (PIP) handles Peruvian border control.

If you just want to get to Santa Rosa, small motorboats go back and forth frequently from Porto de Feria (R$2, five minutes) from around 6am to 6pm.

There is a Peruvian consulate in Leticia, Colombia (p666) as well.

GETTING AROUND
For a *colectivo* (minibus) from the airport to town (R$1.50), walk to the left outside the airport terminal and down the approach road to the corner of the main road. Some continue into Leticia. Taxis and mototaxi are ubiquitous and inexpensive.

A taxi from the airport costs R$15 to hotels in Tabatinga and R$20 to those Leticia. Moto-taxis are ubiquitous and cheap (R$2 to R$5) but most cannot cross the international border.

Leticia (Colombia)
☎ 8 / pop 37,000
Leticia is a remarkably spruce little town, with brightly painted houses, pleasant outdoor eateries and well-maintained parks and streets. For travelers, it's got hotels in all price categories, regularly scheduled flights between Leticia and Bogota, and a long-standing military presence that keeps the city and surrounding region safe. It's also the starting point for trips to the Colombia's Parque Nacional Natural Amacayacu, and up the Rio Javari into Peru.

THE AMAZON

There are no border checkpoints between Tabatinga and Leticia, and you're free to pass back and forth provided you stay within either town. However, do clear immigration if you plan to go any further into Colombia or Peru, even on short-term jungle trips.

INFORMATION
Consulates
Brazil consulate (☎ 592 7530; Carrera 9 No 13-84; ☺ 8am-3pm Mon-Fri)
Peru consulate (☎ 592 3947; Calle 11 No 5-32; ☺ 8am-3pm Mon-Fri)

Emergency
Hospital San Rafael de Leticia (☎ 592 7075; Av Vásquez Cobo 13-78) Has a 24-hour emergency room and pharmacy.
Police (☎ 112; Carrera 11) Between Calles 12 and 13.

Immigration
DAS (Departamento Administrativo de Seguridad; ☎ 592 7189); centro (Calle 9 btwn Carreras 9 & 10; ☺ 8am-noon & 2:30-6pm); airport (☺ 8am-noon & 2-6pm) You have to go to the airport for entry and exit stamps.

Internet Access
Centro de Negocios (Carrera 10 No 8-96; per hr COP$1500; ☺ 7am-10pm)

Laundry
Lavandería Aseo Total (☎ 592 6051; Calle 9 No 9-85; wash & dry per pound COP$2700; ☺ 7am-9pm Mon-Sat, 8am-1pm Sun)

Money
Most businesses in Leticia accept Brazilian reais as well as Colombian pesos. At the time of research, the exchange rate was roughly COP$1000 per R$1. Banks have ATMs but no longer change traveler's checks.
Banco de Bogotá (cnr Calle 7 & Carrera 10)
BBVA Banco Ganadero (cnr Calle 7 & Carrera 10; ☺ 8-11:30am & 2-4:30pm)
Casas de cambio (several at cnr Calle 8 & Carrera 11) To exchange Colombian, Brazilian, Peruvian, US or European currency.

Tourist Information
City tourist office (Secretaría de Turismo y Fronteras; ☎ 592 7569; Calle 8 No 9-75; ☺ 8am-noon & 2pm-5pm Mon-Fri)

SIGHTS
Museo del Hombre Amazónico (☎ 592 7729; Banco de la República, Carrera 11 at Calle 9; admission free; ☺ 8:30-11:30am & 2-5pm Mon-Fri, 9am-1pm Sat) has a small collection of *índio* artifacts and implements. Located inside the Banco de la República.

Museo Uirapuru (☎ 592 7056; Galeria de Arte Indígena Uirapuru; Calle 8 No 10-35; admission free; ☺ 9am-noon & 3-7pm) is in the rear section of Leticia's largest craft shop, selling artifacts of indigenous *índio* groups. Less a museum than the personal collection of the shop owner; displays include indigenous artifacts, dried plants and woods, and preserved reptiles and animals.

At **Reserva Tanimboca** (☎ 592 7679, 310 774 5919; Km 8 Via Tarapacá; ☺ 6am-6pm) visitors can monkey around atop 35m-high trees, then slide 80m along zip-lines from one tree to another through the beautiful forest canopy (COP$60,000). Other activities include kayaking (COP$20,000) and nocturnal jungle hikes (COP$150,000). Or splurge for an overnight stay in a treehouse (single/double/triple COP$150,000/200,000/300,000).

SLEEPING
Unlike in Brazil, hotels do not commonly offer free breakfast.

Mahatu Jungle Hostel (☎ 311 539 1265; www .mahatu.com; Carrera 7 No 9-69; dm per person COP$15,000, s/d COP$25,000/30,000; ▯ ☎) An urban jungle in the heart of Leticia, this charming hostel is the new favorite in town, with simple but sparkling-clean rooms, shared bathrooms and kitchen, and free use of internet and bicycles. Owner-philosopher Gustavo Rene speaks English, Spanish, Dutch, French, and Portuguese.

Hospedaje Los Delfines (☎ 592 7388; losdelfineslet icia@hotmail.com; Carrera 11 No 12-81; s/d COP$40,000/60,000) A 10-minute walk from the center, this small, family-run guesthouse offers basic but spacious rooms around a lush courtyard. Rooms are clean, have fans and bathrooms; it's often full, so call ahead.

Hotel Yurupary (☎ 592 7983; www.hotelyuru pary.col.nu, in Spanish; Calle 8 No 7-26; s/d/tr COP$79,000/ 85,000/95,000; ▨ ☎ ▣) Recently refurbished, the large spotless rooms here have cheerfully eclectic furnishings, including armchairs, fake flowers and oversized original paintings. All have air-conditioning and hot water, and face a bright courtyard, which features a refreshing swimming pool, garden, bar and restaurant.

Hotel Anaconda (☎ 592 7119; www.hotelanaconda .com.co; Carrera 11 No 7-34; s/d per person incl breakfast COP$123,000/114,000; ▨ ▣) Located just across from Parque Orellana; the rooms are comfortable and spacious, though they have a distinctly utilitarian feel. Those on the top floor are the best value, with less street noise and nice views over the Amazon. There's also a welcoming courtyard, lobby bar and swimming pool.

Decalodge Ticuna (☎ 592 6948; www.decameron .com; Carrera 11 No 6-11; s incl breakfast & dinner COP$228,000-281,000, d per person incl breakfast & dinner COP$175,000-228,000; 🍴 🖳 🛜 🏊) Leticia's only luxury option, this international resort chain has plush, stylish cabanas that open onto a leafy courtyard and pool area, complete with fountains and night lighting. Note that these are walk-in rates; multiday packages reserved in advance are much better value.

EATING

Food in Leticia is generally good and reasonably priced. The local specialty is fish, including *gamitana* and *pirarucú*.

Restaurante El Sabor (☎ 592 4774; Calle 8 No 9-25; mains COP$6000-10,000; 🕑 6am-11pm Mon-Sat) Leticia's best budget option serves set meals, vegetarian burgers, and fruit salads, plus unlimited free fruit juice with your meal. The banana pancakes are excellent.

La Casa del Pan (☎ 592 7660; Calle 11 No 10-20; 🕑 6:30am-11pm Mon-Sat) Facing Parque Santander, this is an excellent spot for breakfast (eggs, French bread, coffee and juice for COP$3500) or an afternoon snack.

A Me K Tiar (☎ 592 6094; Carrera 9 No 8-15; mains COP$5000-13,000; 🕑 lunch & dinner) Serving good

THE AMAZON

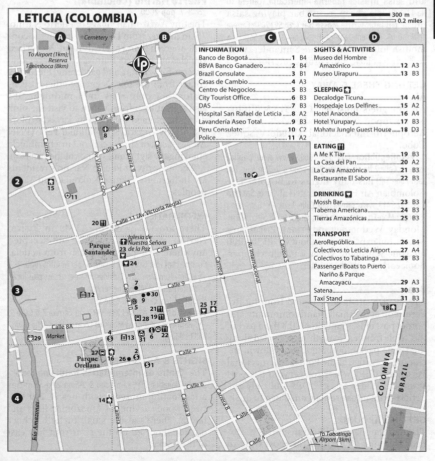

LETICIA (COLOMBIA)

0 _____ 300 m
0 _____ 0.2 miles

INFORMATION	
Banco de Bogotá	1 B4
BBVA Banco Ganadero	2 B4
Brazil Consulate	3 B1
Casas de Cambio	4 A3
Centro de Negocios	5 B3
City Tourist Office	6 B3
DAS	7 B3
Hospital San Rafael de Leticia	8 A2
Lavandería Aseo Total	9 B3
Peru Consulate	10 C2
Police	11 A2

SIGHTS & ACTIVITIES	
Museo del Hombre Amazónico	12 A3
Museo Uirapuru	13 B3

SLEEPING 🛏	
Decalodge Ticuna	14 A4
Hospedaje Los Delfines	15 A2
Hotel Anaconda	16 A4
Hotel Yurupary	17 B3
Mahatu Jungle Guest House	18 D3

EATING 🍴	
A Me K Tiar	19 B3
La Casa del Pan	20 A2
La Cava Amazónica	21 B3
Restaurante El Sabor	22 B3

DRINKING 🍷	
Mossh Bar	23 B3
Taberna Americana	24 B3
Tierras Amazónicas	25 B3

TRANSPORT	
AeroRepública	26 B4
Colectivos to Leticia Airport	27 A4
Colectivos to Tabatinga	28 B3
Passenger Boats to Puerto Nariño & Parque Amacayacu	29 A3
Satena	30 B3
Taxi Stand	31 B3

parillas (grilled meats) at great prices, this place is popular with locals and tourists alike. Wash your meal down with cold beer or freshly blended juices.

La Cava Amazónica (☎ 592 4935; Carrera 9 No 8-23; set meals COP$6000, mains COP$10,000-17,000; ◷ lunch & dinner) This open-air restaurant is a locals' lunchtime favorite. The set meals include huge portions of soup, salad, a meat dish and side of veggies, all for just COP$6000. It can get quite crowded during the weekday lunch rush.

DRINKING

Calle 8 has several bars and cafés, including **Tierras Amazónicas** (Calle 8 No 7-50), near Hotel Yurupary, a mellow spot that specializes in *aguardente* (high-proof sugarcane alcohol) and salsa music. **Taberna Americana** (Carrera 10 No 11-108) is a cheap, rustic bar playing salsa music till late, while **Mossh Bar** (☎ 592 7097; Carrera 10 No 10-08; ◷ 4pm-2am Tue-Thu, 4pm-4am Fri & Sat) is a modish joint facing Parque Santander, with red, white, black, and chrome interior.

GETTING THERE & AWAY
Air

All foreigners must pay COP$15,500 tourist tax upon arrival at Leticia's airport, Aeropuerto Internacional Alfredo Vásquez Cobo.

AeroRepública (☎ 592 7666; www.aerorepublica.com.co; Calle 7 No 10-36; ◷ 8am-noon & 2-6pm Mon-Fri, 8am-noon Sat) has daily flights to Bogotá. The Colombian Air Force–operated airline, **Satena** (☎ 592 5419; www.satena.com; Calle 9 s/n; ◷ 8am-noon & 2-6pm Mon-Fri, 8am-noon Sat), flies to Bogotá on Monday, Wednesday and Friday. Prices vary widely, but expect to pay about COP$300,000 for a one-way flight; Satena is usually cheaper. Book early for the best rates.

Boat

Passenger boats headed to and from Iquito, Peru, stop at the small island community and border post of Isla Santa Rosa, the third part of the 'triple frontier.' Everything is located along the single paved footpath through town, including the office of the Policía Internacional Peruviano (PIP), where you get your passport stamped. Water taxis (COP$4000) ply the Leticia–Santa Rosa route from dawn to dusk.

GETTING AROUND

The main mode of public transport is moto-taxi, charging COP$1000 for most trips in town, or COP$2000 to Tabatinga. (Hang on tight!) *Colectivos* to Tabatinga wait at the corner of Carrera 10 and Calle 8 (COP$2500) – in Tabatinga, they pass Porto da Feria, the turnoff for Porto Fluvial, the Polícia Federal post and the airport, before turning back.

A taxi to Leticia's airport runs COP$15,000; there's a stand on Carrera 10 between Calles 7 and 8. *Colectivos* to Leticia's airport leave from Parque Orellana (COP$1000). A taxi to Tabatinga's airport costs COP$20,000.

Fast passenger boats to Puerto Nariño (COP$22,000, two hours), with a stop at Parque Amacayacu (COP$21,000, 1½ hours) along the way, leave from a pier at the end of Calle 8 at 8am, 10am and 2pm on weekdays.

Puerto Nariño (Colombia)
☎ 8 / pop 2000

The tiny Amazonian village of Puerto Nariño, 75km upriver from Leticia, has taken the concept of green living to an art form. Motorized vehicles are banned. Rainwater is collected in cisterns for washing and gardening. Electricity comes from the town's energy-efficient generator, but only runs until midnight. It's also a great base from which to visit the pink dolphins of Lago Tarapoto by kayak, explore the nearby Amacayacu National Park (PNN Amacayacu), or simply chill out in a hammock, enjoying the sights and sounds of the Amazon.

The majority of Puerto Nariño's residents are indigenous Tikuna, Kokoma, and Yagua peoples.

INFORMATION

There are no banks or ATMs in Puerto Nariño, and credit cards are not accepted anywhere. Bring plenty of cash from Leticia.
Compartel (cnr Carrera 6 & Calle 5; per hr COP$2000; ◷ 8am-9pm Mon-Sat) Provides internet access plus local and international telephone service.
Hospital (cnr Carrera 4 & Calle 5)
Tourist office (☎ 313 235 3687; cnr Carrera 7 & Calle 5; ◷ 8am-noon & 2-5pm Mon-Fri) Located inside the town hall building.

SIGHTS & ACTIVITIES

The **Centro de Interpretación Natütama** (admission by donation; ◷ 8am-noon & 2-5pm Wed-Mon) has a fascinating museum with nearly 100 life-sized wood carvings of Amazonian flora and fauna. There's also a small turtle hatchery outside. Located on the riverfront just east of the docks.

Lago Tarapoto, 10km west of Puerto Nariño, is a beautiful jungle lake that is home to pink dolphins, manatees and massive Victoria Regia waterlilies. A half-day trip to the lake in a *peque-peque* (motorized canoe) can be organized from Puerto Nariño (COP$50,000 for up to four people). You can organize similar outings to **Parque Nacional Natural Amacayacu**, located a short distance downstream.

You can **hike** to several nearby indigenous villages including **San Martín** (three hours) and **20 de Julio** (30 minutes) by following the sidewalks leading out of town. For a bird's-eye view of the village, climb the **Mirador** (COP$5000, ⏱ 5am-5pm) tower, located at the top of Calle 4.

SLEEPING & EATING

our pick **Hotel Napú** (☎ 310 488 0998; Calle 4 No 5-72; olgabeco@yahoo.com; r per person COP$20,000-25,000) Our favorite hotel has the look and feel of a treehouse fort. The rooms are simple but comfy, with basic furnishings, fan and shared bathrooms. Try for rooms 7 and 8 of the back building, which share a balcony with hammocks overlooking the courtyard garden and jungle.

Casa Selva (☎ in Bogota 315 333 2796; casaselva-hotel@yahoo.es; Carrera 6 No 6-78; s/d/tr COP$112,000/ 134,000/186,000) A tall, handsome wood building two blocks up from the dock is the most luxurious option in town. The 12 tasteful rooms have bathroom, fan and balcony, surrounding a two-story courtyard and restaurant (mains COP$11,000).

Las Margaritas (Calle 6 No 6-80; set meals COP$6000-12,000; ⏱ breakfast, lunch & dinner) Hidden behind a picket fence under a huge *palapa* (thatched roof), Las Margaritas is the best restaurant in town. The huge set meals of the day include local specialties such as *pirarucú* and *carne asada* (grilled steak).

GETTING THERE & AWAY

High-speed boats to Puerto Nariño depart from Leticia's dock at 8am, 10am and 2pm daily (COP$23,000, two hours); return boats to Leticia depart at 7:30am, 11am and 4pm.

Purchase tickets at **Transportes Fluviales** (☎ 592 5999, Calle 8 No 11; ⏱ 7am-1pm) near the riverfront in Leticia. Boats can get very full, so buy your tickets early or the day before.

RIO JAVARI

The meandering Rio Javari provides Brazil and Peru with a border, and travelers with excellent opportunities to see the Amazon rain forest up close and undisturbed. A handful of jungle lodges offer accommodations and activities similar to those found elsewhere in the Amazon Basin, including forest walks, fishing, nighttime caiman-spotting, bird-watching, and dolphin-watching. It's also possible to visit indigenous settlements (though be forewarned they are not the 'uncontacted' sort many travelers imagine). Petru Popescu's book *Amazon Beaming* relates photographer Loren McIntyre's extraordinary experiences among one of the indigenous groups here. Prices vary according to the number of days and types of activities you schedule, as well as the season. In general, expect to pay US$75 to US$125 per day per person.

Operated by Amazon Jungle Trips, **Zacambú Lodge** (☎ 592 7377; amazonjungletrips@yahoo.com; Av Internacional 6-25, Leticia) is on Lake Zacambú, in a beautiful lake region on the Peruvian side of the Javari river. It's the closest of the lodges to the triple frontier – about 70km from Tabatinga, or three hours by motorboat. Accommodations are simple but comfortable, in hammocks or small rooms, with shared toilets. Most excursions are made by motorboat or canoe, for obvious reasons – the bird-watching is particularly good.

Reserva Natural Palmari (☎ in Leticia 592 4156; www.palmari.org) is another 20km upstream on the south bank of the river, overlooking a bend where pink and gray dolphins are often seen. A slew of activities and outings are possible, from trekking and canoeing to sport fishing and zip-lines up in the canopy. The lodge receives a number of large groups; you may want to ask how many people will be at the lodge when you are (and adjust your schedule accordingly).

Even further still, **Reserva Natural Heliconia** (☎ 311-508 5666; www.amazonheliconia.com; Calle 13 No 11-74) provides room and board in thatch-covered cabins, plus tours via boat or foot of the river, creeks and jungle. There are also organized visits to indigenous villages and special tours devoted to bird-watching and dolphin-watching.

RORAIMA

The tropical rain forest that blankets Roraima's southern half (bisected by the equator) gives way to broad savanna in the middle of the state, and remote and beautiful mountains in

the north. It includes most of the Brazilian territories of the Yanomami, one of the country's
largest surviving indigenous peoples. The state
capital, Boa Vista, still doesn't make the itinerary of most travelers, but has better and better
tour options every year. Roraima is home to
Monte Roraima, of course, but this intriguing
flat-topped mountain sits right on the Brazil–
Venezuela–Guyana border, and the best way
up is from the Venezuelan side.

BOA VISTA
☎ 0xx95 / pop 267,000

The state capital, a planned city on the banks
of the Rio Branco, is home to more than half of
Roraima's population. It's long been a transfer
point for travelers headed to Guyana or to
Venezuela's beautiful high plains, just three
hours north. The town itself lacks pizzazz,
but two quality tour outfits based here offer
excursions to the pristine and little-visited regions of Serra Grande and Serra de Tepequém.

Information
BOOKSTORES
Nobel (☎ 3621 3422; Av Glaycon de Paiva 789A;
🕙 9am-7pm Mon-Sat) Occasionally stocks English-
language guidebooks.

CONSULATES
Venezuela consulate (☎ 3623 9285; Av Benjamin
Constant 525E; 🕙 8am-2pm Mon-Fri)

EMERGENCY
Hospital Geral (p670) has a 24-hour emer-
gency room.
Ambulance (☎ 192)
Police (☎ 190)

INTERNET ACCESS
Nobel (☎ 3621 3422; Av Glaycon de Paiva 789A; per hr
R$3; 🕙 9am-7pm Mon-Sat)
Red Zone (cnr Rua Araújo Filho & Av Benjamin Constant;
per hr R$2; 🕙 9am-midnight)

MEDICAL SERVICES
Hospital Geral (☎ 3236 0326; Rua Recife 1581) Boa
Vista's main public hospital, located 2km from the center
of town toward the airport.
Yellow-fever vaccines (🕙 8am-noon & 2-6pm Mon-
Fri) Available for free at the airport clinic.

MONEY
Banco do Brasil (Av Glaycon de Paiva 56; 🕙 8am-2pm
Mon-Fri) Changes euros and US dollars.

Bradesco (cnr Av Sebastão Diniz & Rua Inácio Magalhães)
Reliable ATMs.
Gold & pawn shops (Av Benjamin Constant) Numerous
shops on this block change US, Venezuelan and Guyanese
currencies.

POST
Main post office (☎ 3621 3535; Praça do Centro Cívico;
🕙 8am-4:30pm Mon-Fri, 8am-noon Sat)

TRAVEL AGENCIES
Timbo Turismo (☎ 3224 4077; timbotur@osite.com
.br; Av Benjamin Constant at Rua Araújo Filho; 🕙 8am-
noon & 2-6pm Mon-Fri, 8am-noon Sat) Sells plane and
bus tickets.

Dangers & Annoyances
If you go to Praia Grande, be careful of stingrays, especially during low-water season. The
sting hurts like a mother; fortunately, rays
are quite skittish and you have to actually
step on one for it to sting you. Shuffle your
feet when entering or exiting the water –
the cloud of sand will scare them away – or
use a long stick to poke the shallow water in
front of you.

Also, while Orla Taumanan (p673) is well
lit and a popular watering hole at night, the
surrounding streets can be a bit seedy – be
alert walking home, or just take a cab.

Sights
PARQUE ANAUÁ &
MUSEU INTEGRADO DE RORAIMA
About 2.5km northwest of the center, the
vast grounds of **Parque Anauá** (Av Brigadeiro Eduardo
Gomes) contain gardens, a lake, a museum, an
amphitheater and various sporting facilities.
Inside the park, the **Museu Integrado de Roraima**
(admission free; 🕙 8am-6pm) has modest displays on
the state's archaeology, indigenous peoples,
wildlife and history.

PRAIA GRANDE
A tawny sandbar beach emerges on the far
bank of the Rio Branco, opposite Boa Vista,
during low water, roughly October to April.
Known as Praia Grande, it is indeed big and
beachy, and makes for a pleasant afternoon
visit. Its transitory existence means there is
no shade – bring an umbrella or consider
waiting until the afternoon. **Porto do Babazinho**
(☎ 3624 8382; Av Major Williams 1) offers ferry service
for R$4 round-trip, and can provide food
and drinks.

BOA VISTA

INFORMATION	
Banco do Brasil	**1** B2
Bradesco	**2** C2
Gold & Pawn Shops	**3** B2
Main Post Office	**4** C2
Nobel	**5** B2
Red Zone	**6** B2
Timbo Turismo	**7** B2
Venezuela Consulate	**8** C1

SIGHTS & ACTIVITIES	
Porto de Babazinho	**9** D1
Roraima Adventures	**10** C2

SLEEPING	
Aipana Plaza Hotel	**11** B2
Hotel Euzébio's	**12** B1
Hotel Ideal	**13** B2
Hotel Monte Líbano	**14** B2
Uiramutam Palace	**15** A1

EATING	
Bob's	**16** A1
La Gondola	**17** B2
Mister Quilo	**18** C2
Open-Air Food Court	**19** B1
Peixada Tropical	**20** A1

ENTERTAINMENT	
Orla Taumanan	**21** C3
S69	**22** B2

SHOPPING	
Centro de Artesanato	
Caxabmú	**23** C2

TRANSPORT	
Mini-Terminal Urbano	**24** B1
Municipal Bus Terminal	**25** C3

Activities & Tours

Porto do Babazinho (☎ 9111 3511; babarinhorr@yahoo
.com; Av Major Williams 1) is home-base for longtime
local guide Sebastião de Souza e Silva (aka
'Babazinho'), who leads and arranges a variety
of adventuresome outings, from windsurfing
lessons and rentals, to daylong and multiday
hiking, canoeing and animal-spotting excursions, all at reasonable rates.

Roraima Adventures (☎ 3624 9611; www.roraima
-brasil.com.br; Rua Coronel Pinto 86; ☺ 8am-noon & 2-6pm
Mon-Fri, 8am-noon Sat) offers professional multiday camping tours all over Roraima, including Serra do Tepequém and Mt Roraima in
Venezuela, and even into the Yanomami reserve (provided the proper permissions can
be secured).

Sleeping

Hotel Monte Líbano (☎ 8122 1220, 9124 0240; Av
Benjamin Constant 319 W; s/d with fan R$25/35, with air-con
R$35/45; ❄) The least worst of a string of cheap
hotels in this area, the Monte Líbano still has
drab rooms, grubby bathrooms and no free
breakfast. Rooms with air-con are slightly
better, and come with TVs, but then again

the only good reason to stay here is to save
every last real.

Hotel Ideal (☎ 3224 6342; Rua Araújo Filho 533; s/d/tr
R$45/55, with minibar R$50/60; ❄) Boa Vista's best
budget option, the Ideal's bright lobby and
dining area give way to tidy rooms with high
ceilings, TV and air-conditioning. Decor is
quite sparse, but the friendly service and convenient location more than make up for it.

Hotel Euzébio's (☎ 2121 0300; Rua Cecília Brasil 1517;
s/d standard R$65/90, superior R$100/120; ❄ ☎ ☎)
Standard rooms are clean but small; superiors
are bigger, more cheerful and come with hot
water, minibar and phone. All rooms have air-
con and TV. The swimming pool is a treat, and
frequent discounts make this place good value.
A bit removed from the center, but closer to
the appealing walkways and nighttime restaurants in the center of Av Capitan Ene Garcez.

Uiramutam Palace (☎ 3624 4700; www.uiramu
tam.com.br; Av Capitan Ene Garcez 427; s/d/tr standard
R$70/100/120, deluxe R$120/160/180; ❄ ☎ ☎)
Standard rooms here are awfully plain for
the price, but the deluxe units are larger and
cheerier, with spiffy bathrooms (think porcelain sinks and glass showers), flat-screen TVs,

THE AMAZON

and a 20% cash discount to boot. The pool is a welcome midafternoon diversion, notwithstanding the huge satellite dish peering up from one corner of the pool area.

Aipana Plaza Hotel (☎ 3224 4800; www.aipana plaza.com.br; west side of Praça do Centro Cívico; s/d/tr R$165/195/210; 🅿 🛜 🔊) The reception area of Boa Vista's fanciest hotel has leather sofas, modern paintings and sculptures and a hip lobby bar. Rooms are no less classy, with muted decor, slate floors, glass showers and

good beds. The well-maintained pool makes a nice escape from the heat.

Eating

our pick **La Gondola** (Av Benjamin Constant 35 W; self-service per kg R$18; ☺ lunch) Facing the plaza across a busy intersection, this smaller per-kilo place offers outdoor, fan-cooled or air-con dining areas, in addition to the typical per-kilo options: pasta, potatoes, roast chicken, grilled beef, rice, beans etc.

THE YANOMAMI

The Yanomami are one of the most populous indigenous peoples of Amazonia, and also among its most primitive, living a seminomadic life with stone implements, pottery, animal hides and plants in a remote area on the Brazil–Venezuela border. Despite their numbers – estimated at around 15,000 – they remained uncontacted until the 1950s, and then only occasionally until the 1970s. That's when the Brazilian government decided to build Hwy BR-210, abruptly dragging a Stone Age people into the 20th century. Predictably, the Yanomami began dying of measles, influenza and venereal diseases introduced through contact with the highway's construction workers. Several villages were wiped out.

A decade later, a gold rush sent some 40,000 miners swarming into Yanomami territory, polluting rivers and destroying the forest in the process. In 1988 the government attempted to strip the Yanomami of 70% of their traditional territory and open it to mining. It backed off the plan in the face of national and international uproar, but the plight of the Yanomami remained dire. Nearly a fifth of the tribe's population died between 1986 and 1993, mostly of disease.

In 1991 the Venezuelan government officially recognized its country's portion of the Yanomami territory as a special *índio* reserve. Brazil followed suit a month later, creating the 96,650-sq-km **Terra Indígena Yanomami**, Brazil's largest single *índio* territory. But conflicts continued: in 1993, a gang of goldminers used machetes and rifles to kill 16 Yanomami, including an infant. Four of the attackers were eventually convicted and jailed, but many more murders have gone uninvestigated.

The Yanomami are a slight people, with typical Amerindian features. The focal point of each community is the *yano*, a large round timber-and-thatch structure where each family has its own section facing onto an open central area used for communal dance and ceremony. Each family arranges its own area by slinging hammocks around a constantly burning fire that forms the center of family life.

Their diet includes monkey (a delicacy), tapir, wild pig and a variety of insects, plus fruits, yams, bananas and manioc. The Yanomami hold elaborate ceremonies and rituals and place great emphasis on intertribal alliances, primarily to minimize feuds. When nearby soil and hunting grounds are exhausted, the *yano* is dismantled and the village moves to a new site.

Disease is cured with shaman dances, healing hands and various herbs, including *yakoana* (a hallucinogenic herbal powder). When a tribe member dies, the body is hung from a tree until dry, then burned to ashes. The ashes are mixed with bananas, which are then eaten by friends and family of the deceased to incorporate and preserve the spirit.

Anthropologist Napoleon Chagnon lived with the Yanomami off and on for three decades and described them in his best-selling book *The Fierce People* as aggressive and living in a state of 'chronic warfare.' He received acclaim when the book was published in 1968, but his methods and findings came under increasing scrutiny over the years. In 2001, activist Patrick Tierny wrote *Darkness in El Dorado*, in which he accused Chagnon and a colleague of ethical breaches, from using gifts to pry information from subjects, to knowingly exacerbating a measles outbreak. The most serious accusations proved unfounded, but the controversy highlighted the ethical dilemmas inherent in studying isolated indigenous groups.

Mister Quilo (Rua Inácio Magalhães 346; per kg R$24, ☽ lunch & dinner) The tinted doors conceal a huge and perpetually busy dining area, with three levels, air-con machines blasting and a bevy of blue-shirted waitresses hustling to keep up with drink orders. Diners queue up for a large self-serve spread, including fresh grilled meats, pastas, and desserts.

Peixada Tropical (cnr Rua Ajuricaba & Rua Pedro Rodrigues; dishes for 2 R$35-50; ☎ lunch & dinner) Another popular open-air lunch spot serving fish in every way imaginable, from Portuguese fish stew to fried-up spicy, Bahian style.

A busy **open-air food court** (mains R$5-20; ☽ dinner) occupies part of the long narrow park between the split lanes of Av Capitan Ene Garcez. A slew of mom-and-pop restaurants have tables set up under a high awning, serving cheap tasty Brazilian fare. There's occasionally live music, but the lively, family-friendly ambience is the real draw here.

At the top of the same park is a restaurant quartet: a pizza joint, upscale Italian restaurant, midrange *churrascaria* (barbecued-meat restaurant), and Bob's, the ubiquitous burger chain. They occupy top and bottom floors of identical side-by-side buildings, and are open for lunch and dinner. Take your pick!

Entertainment

Boa Vista's recently refurbished waterfront, known as **Orla Taumanan**, has a handful of open-air beer gardens that fill up most weekend evenings and nights. The streets around the waterfront can get a little lonely, however – stay alert walking back to the hotel, or grab a cab.

S69 (cnr Rua Araújo Filho & Av NS da Consolata; ☽ midnight-6am Sat only) Boa Vista's most prominent gay club makes the most of its once-weekly schedule, with dancing and drinking until dawn. This is actually a GLS spot – *gay, lesbiana, e simpatizante* (gay, lesbian,and down straight people) – and foreigners are welcome.

Shopping

Centro de Artesanato Caxabmú (☎ 3623 1615; Rua Floriano Peixoto 158; ☽ 8am-6pm Mon-Sat) Two city blocks have been designated as pedestrian only, and are lined with stalls selling everything from handicrafts to cashew nuts.

Getting There & Away
AIR
Frequent promotions mean flying is often only slightly more expensive than the bus.

Gol (☎ 3224 5824; www.voegol.com.br; ☽ 11:30am-5:30pm & 10pm-4am)

Meta (☎ 3224 7490; www.voemeta.com.br; ☽ 8am-6pm Mon-Fri) Flights to Guyana and Suriname twice weekly.

TAM (☎ 3623 0049; www.tamairlines.com.br; ☽ 8am-10pm Mon-Fri, 8am-6pm Sat & Sun)

BUS
Eucatur (☎ 3623 1318) has five daily buses to Manaus (R$100, 12 hours, 9am, 6pm, 8pm and 9pm) including *semi-leito* service on the 7pm and 9pm departures. There are four daily buses to Pacaraíma on the Venezuela border (R$12, three hours, 7am, 7:30am, noon and 4pm); the 7:30am bus continues across the border to Santa Elena (R$10) all the way to Puerto La Cruz (R$100, 19 hours). You can also take a collective taxi to Pacaraíma, which costs R$30 but makes the trip in under three hours. A single Venezuela-bound bus passes Boa Vista once a day at 7:30am continuing to Santa Elena de Uairén (R$20, four to five hours), Puerto Ordaz (R$80, 14 hours) and Puerto La Cruz (R$100, 20 hours).

Amatur (☎ 3224 0004) operates daily buses to Bonfim on the Guyana border (R$15, 1½ hours, 7am, 10am, 2pm and 4:30pm). From there, you cross the border to Lethem, and catch a bus to Georgetown (R$95 from Boa Vista; 15 to 16 hours, Monday, Tuesday, Thursday, Friday and Sunday).

Getting Around
Around town, taxis marked 'Lotação' operate like buses, following fixed routes and carrying up to four passengers. The fare is R$2, or R$4 if the driver veers off the route to drop you at a given spot. Private cabs use meters, and can be pricey.

The airport is 3.5km northwest of the city center. To get there, you can take a 'Carana-Aeroporto' bus 206 (R$2) from the *rodoviária urbano* (municipal bus terminal) on Av Dr Silvio Botelho or across from the *mini-terminal urbano* at the top of Praça do Centro Cívico. Buses depart roughly every 30 to 90 minutes from 6am until 11:15pm; the schedule is reduced on weekends. Taxis to/from the airport and center charge R$25.

The **bus station** (Av das Guianas, Bairro São Vicente) is 2.5km southwest of the center. Several buses go there to/from the *rodoviária urbano* and the *mini-terminal urbano*, including '214-Jockei Clube' and '215-Nova Ciudad' (all

R$2, every 20 to 30 minutes). Catch any of the same buses back to the center; buses run from 5:30am to midnight every day. A private taxi from the center to the bus station costs about R$10, a *lotação* cab is R$2.50.

AROUND BOA VISTA
Bonfim & Lethem (Guyana)
Bonfim ☎ 0xx95 / pop 11,000
Lethem (Guyana) ☎ 072 / pop 900
The small town of Bonfim, 125km northeast of Boa Vista, is the stepping stone to Guyana. The Guyanese town of Lethem is about 5km west across the Rio Tacutu. Neither Bonfim nor Lethem is exactly pleasant, but Lethem is the better of the two; both have hotels in case you get stuck.

Arriving from Boa Vista, bus drivers usually wait for passengers to get exit stamps at the Polícia Federal before continuing the short distance further to the pier on the river. From there, a canoe across the river costs R$3, and Guyanese immigration is another 1.5km from there.

Pousada Fronteira (☎ 3552 1294; Rua Aluísio de Menezes 26, Bonfim; s/d US$27/35) is one of various

AROUND BOA VISTA

not-so-good options in Bonfim, with basic rooms and OK bathrooms.

See p673 for info on buses to Bonfim and continuing to Georgetown.

SANTA ELENA DE UAIRÉN (VENEZUELA)
☎ 0289 / pop 18,500
Santa Elena de Uairén (Santa Elena) is a dusty town located a few kilometers north of the only land-border crossing between Brazil and Venezuela. The town is higher and cooler than Boa Vista, and provides access to Venezuela's vast and beautiful Gran Sabana. The region is dotted with waterfalls and curious flat-topped mountains called *tepuis;* the largest and most famous *tepui* is Mt Roraima (see opposite), a spectacular natural monument and the spot where Brazil, Venezuela and Guyana meet.

Brazilian and Venezuelan immigration procedures are all dealt with at the border, locally known as La Línea, 15km south of Santa Elena (and about 1km apart from each other). Most travelers no longer need an advance visa to enter Venezuela – it can be issued on the spot on the border. Returning to Brazil, you'll need to show a valid yellow-fever vaccination card.

Orientation
Calle Bolívar is Santa Elena's main drag, with hotels, internet and shops. Where it intersects with Calle Urdaneta is called Cuatro Esquinas (Four Corners); this is the spot where moneychangers typically hang out. Turn right on Calle Urdaneta and you hit Plaza Bolívar, the town's central square; turn left and in a couple blocks you'll pass backpacker central – a cluster of hotels, eateries, and tour operators. At the end of the block is Av Perimetral, which runs along the edge of town.

Information
EMERGENCY
Ambulance, Fire, Police (☎ 171)

IMMIGRATION
Brazil Consulate (☎ 995 1256; Edificio Galeno, Calle Los Castanos, Urb Roraima del Casco Central; ☉ 8am-2pm Mon-Fri)

INTERNET ACCESS
Cafe Iruk (☎ Calle Bolívar; ☉ 9am-11pm Mon-Sat, 1-11pm Sun) Across from Hotel Panazarelli.

THE AMAZON

LAUNDRY
Lavandería Pereira (Calle Urdaneta)

MEDICAL SERVICES
Hospital Rosario Vera Zurita (Calle Icabarú) No phone; linked to 171 emergency services via radio. Basic services.

MONEY
In 2008, Venezuela adopted the *bolívar fuerte*, abbreviated BsF. At the time of research, the standard exchange rate was 4.30BsF per US$1, and 2.40BsF per Brazilian R$1. Brazilian reais, US dollars, and EU euros can easily and safely be exchanged with the many moneychangers at the corner of Calle Bolívar and Calle Urdaneta.

Banco Guyana (Plaza Bolívar)
Banco Industrial de Venezuela (Calle Bolívar) Fifty meters north of Hotel Augusta.

POST
Ipostel (Calle Urdaneta) Between Calles Bolívar and Roscio; the door had no sign at last check.

Sights & Activities
GRAN SABANA
Santa Elena is at the southern tip of the massive Parque Nacional Canaima (30,000 sq km). At its heart is the Gran Sabana, a high savanna dotted with stark flat-topped mountains called *tepuis*, and crisscrossed by rivers. Trips here include great vista points, swimming in natural pools and visiting spectacular waterfalls, including the 100m Salto Aponwao. Other options include whitewater rafting and visiting the town/region of El Paují, an interesting combination of natural attractions and counterculture community.

MT RORAIMA
The largest and highest of the *tepuis* is 2810m Mt Roraima, and climbing it is the reason most people come to Santa Elena. The standard trip is six days, including three spent exploring the wild 60-sq-km moonscape on top. Highlights up there include 'La Ventana' with terrific views; 'El Foso,' a round deep sinkhole with interior arches; and a series of freezing quartz-lined ponds called the 'Jacuzzis.' If a tour doesn't appeal, you can hire a guide and porters in the towns of San Francisco de Yuruaní (66km north of Santa Elena) or Paraitepui (26km east). Reaching the top requires no technical climbing, but you definitely should be in good shape. Mt

Roraima straddles Venezuela, Brazil and Guyana, but this is the only nonvertical route to the top.

Tours
All Santa Elena tour agencies run one-, two- or three-day jeep tours around the Gran Sabana, with visits to the most interesting sights, mostly waterfalls. Budget between 170BsF to 380BsF per person per day, depending on group size and whether it includes just guide and transportation or food and accommodation as well.

For most visitors, the main attraction is a Roraima tour, generally offered as an all-inclusive six-day package for 1200BsF to 1700BsF (you get what you pay for). The operators who organize this tour usually also rent out camping equipment and can provide transportation to Paraitepui, the starting point for the Roraima trek, for about 500BsF per jeep each way for up to six people. Check on specifics, including group size, hiker-to-guide ratio, and equipment quality before signing up for any Roraima tour.

Recommended local tour companies:
Adrenaline Expeditions (☎ 0424-970 7329; adrenalinexptours@hotmail.com) The literal sibling of the Ciudad Bolívar agency, it specializes in adventurous Gran Sabana trips.
Backpacker Tours (☎ 995-1415, 0414-886 7227; www.backpacker-tours.com; Calle Urdaneta) The local powerhouse, it has the most organized, best-equipped and most expensive tours of Roraima and the region. Also rents mountain bikes.
Mystic Tours (☎ 416 0558; www.mystictours.com.ve; Calle Urdaneta) Some of the least expensive tours to Roraima, and local tours with a new age bent.
Representaciones y Servicios Turísticos Francisco Alvarez (☎ 0414-385-2846; rstgransabana@hotmail.com; Bus Terminal) Personable and helpful, with regional tours and camping-equipment rentals.
Ruta Salvaje (☎ 995-1134; www.rutasalvaje.com; Av Mariscal Sucre) The standard tours, plus rafting trips and paragliding.

Sleeping
Posada Michelle (☎ 995 2017; hotelmichelle@cantv.net; Calle Urdaneta; s/d/tr/q 40/60/70/80BsF) The undisputed backpacker headquarters, this clean and surprisingly quiet pousada, between Calle Ikabarú and Av Perimetral, has 25 rooms with fans, hot water and a basic kitchen downstairs. Sweat-caked Roraima hikers can take advantage of half-day rest-and-shower (40BsF per

room) or shower-only (5BsF) rates before taking the night bus out. Bulletin boards on the front patio announce upcoming trips, if you're looking to join or fill out a group.

Posada Backpacker Tours (☎ 995 1415; www .backpacker-tours.com; Calle Urdaneta; s/d/tr 60/80/120BsF; 🖳 🛜) Affiliated with the recommended tour operator of the same name; rooms here are reasonably clean and comfortable, and there's a popular outdoor restaurant and internet cafe on-site. It's between Calle Ikabarú and Av Perimetral.

Hotel Lucrecia (☎ 995 1105; hotellucrecia@hotmail .com; Av Perimetral at Calle Las Apamates; s/d/tr 100/120/ 150BsF; 🕸 🖳 🛋) Fifteen aging but clean rooms face a nice garden area. The small pool is a treat, though it faces onto a somewhat busy road. The hotel is a bit further removed from the center than other hotels, but not inconveniently so. A good option if you really want air-conditioning.

Eating

Restaurant Michelle (☎ 995 1415; Calle Urdaneta; mains 17-22BsF; 🕑 lunch & dinner) Dig into huge portions at this popular Chinese restaurant, just two doors down from the hotel of the same name.

Alfredo's Restaurant (☎ 995 1628; Av Perimetral; pastas & pizzas 22-40BsF, mains 45-70BsF; 🕑 11am-3pm & 6-10pm Tue-Sun) One of the best restaurants in town, Alfredo's has a lengthy menu, gourmet meals and tortellini with ricotta and spinach that melts in your mouth. The filling lunch special is a bargain.

ServeKilo Nova Opção (Av Perimetral; buffet per kg 30BsF; 🕑 buffet 11am-4pm, mains 4-11pm) You'll think you're back in Brazil at this popular lunch spot. The large spread includes dishes from both sides of the border, including grilled meats and a few vegetarian options. When the heat drives you to drink, revitalize with a freshly blended juice.

Gran Sabana Deli (Calle Bolívar; pastries 8BsF; 🕑 6am-8pm Mon-Sat, 6am-noon Sun) Mammoth two-person sandwiches (35BsF) make good on-the-go sustenance.

Getting There & Away

AIR

Utica (☎ in Ciudad Bolívar 0285-632 6290) has flights most mornings to Ciudad Bolívar (600BsF), usually via Canaima (same price) on five-seater Cessnas. Buy tickets at the airport, 7km south of town. A taxi to or from the airport costs around 10BsF.

BUS

The bus terminal is on the Ciudad Guayana highway about 2km east of the town's center. There are no buses – catch a taxi (8BsF). Eight buses depart daily to Ciudad Bolívar (45BsF to 60BsF, 10 to 12 hours), all stopping at Ciudad Guayana.

There is no direct service from Santa Elena into Brazil. Instead, take a taxi across the border to the Pacaraíma bus terminal, where buses to Boa Vista (R$12, three to four hours) leave four times daily, and collective taxis leave whenever there are four passengers (R$25, two to three hours).

Entering Venezuela, you can easily walk the 300m from the Pacaraíma bus terminal to the **Brazilian border post** (🕑 8am-7:30pm). From there it's a sweaty 750m to the **Venezuelan post** (🕑 8am-6pm) – fortunately, taxis pass frequently and typically don't charge for a quick stop at Venezuelan immigration before continuing to Santa Elena.

Leaving Venezuela, taxis from Santa Elena to *la línea* (the border) charge the same as when arriving, though *por puesto* (collective) cabs may tag on a couple BsFs if you take long passing immigration. Be sure to confirm that they'll take you all the way to Brazilian immigration – some go only as far as the Venezuelan post.

RONDÔNIA

In 1943 President Getúlio Vargas created the Territory of Guaporé from chunks of Amazonas and Mato Grosso. In 1981 it became the state of Rondônia, named for Marechal Cândido Rondon, the enlightened and humane soldier who 'tamed' this region in the 1920s when he constructed a telegraph line linking it to the rest of Brazil. Rondon also founded the Serviço de Proteção ao Índio (SPI), predecessor of Funai (Fundação Nacional do Índio; government *índio* agency). He exhorted SPI agents to '*Morrer, se preciso for, matar nunca!*' ('Die, if necessary, but never kill!').

Policies later in the century were not so forward-thinking. In 1981 the Brazilian government, with help from the World Bank, launched an initiative to distribute land to poor settlers. Called Polonoreste, the project spawned a land rush, and Rondônia's population leapt from 111,000 in 1970 to 1.13 million in 1991. Environmental safeguards were flimsy, and about one-fifth of the state's primary virgin forest was cut down to make farmland. The rate of deforestation in the 1980s was equivalent to more than a football field a minute, for a whole decade.

Rondônia is a transition zone between dense Amazonian forests and cerrado, and despite its sad environmental past, it still has a rich diversity of fauna and flora.

Deforestation in Rondônia has dropped considerably from those highs, accounting for less than 10% of overall cutting in the Amazon, down from more than 15% in past years. However, in 2010, a Dutch study conducted in Rondônia showed that that small-time farmers, not medium or large-scale operations, are now the driving force behind deforestation in the state (and, presumably, the rest of the Amazon). Federal law stipulates that no more than 20% of any land grant may be cleared for farming or ranching; corporate farms have proved easier to police than smaller ones, who, the study found, clear as much as 50% of their forest plots. And while political pressure has proved effective against large argo-business, changing the practices of small-time farmers will require a far more nimble bureaucracy – never Brazil's strong point, especially in the Amazon.

PORTO VELHO
☎ 0xx69 / pop 383,500

Porto Velho is not high on anyone's list of favorite cities in the Amazon. It isn't one of the worst cities either, but few travelers find reason to linger long here. Charming or not, Porto Velho is a vital link in Brazil's agricultural economy, as soybeans and other products are shipped on huge barges from here up the Rio Madeira and transferred directly to ocean liners headed abroad. That same ride – albeit on a boat not a barge – draws some travelers up from Cuiabá and the Pantanal on the slow route to Manaus and the Amazon.

Information
EMERGENCY
Ambulance (☎ 192)
Emergency room (☎ 224 5225; Hospital Central, Rua Julio de Castiho 149)
Police (☎ 190)

INTERNET ACCESS
Amazon House (Av Pinheiro Machado at Rua José de Alencar; per hr R$3; ⏰ 8am-10:30pm Mon-Sat, 9am-10pm Sun)

PortoNet (Praça Rondón; per hr R$2; ⏰ 8am-10:30pm Mon-Fri, 1-10:20pm Sat, 5-10:30pm Sun)

LAUNDRY
Lavandería Mamoré (☎ 3221 3266; Av Pinheiro Machado 1455; per piece R$1.50-6; ⏰ 7:45am-6:15pm Mon-Sat) Quick and professional, but prices are ridiculously high. You can save a bit by forgoing ironing.

MEDICAL SERVICES
Drogaria Natal (Av Pinheiro Machado at Rua Julio de Castiho; ⏰ 7am-11pm Mon-Sat, 8am-10pm Sun) Large pharmacy and convenience store.
Hospital Central (☎ 3224 5225; Rua Julio de Castiho 149) Public hospital.
UNIMED (☎ 3216 6800; Rua Rio Madeira 1618) Private hospital.

MONEY
Bradesco has reliable ATMs, on Av Carlos Gomes and Av Sete de Setembro.
Casa de Câmbio Marco Aurélio (☎ 3221 4922; Rua José de Alencar 3353; ⏰ 8:30am-3pm Mon-Fri) Changes foreign currencies.

POST
Post office (☎ 217 3667; cnr Av Presidente Dutra & Av Sete de Setembro; ⏰ 8am-5pm Mon-Fri, 9am-noon Sat)

TOURIST INFORMATION
IBAMA (☎ 3223 2023; Av Jorge Teixeira 3559) Check here on progress toward opening nearby protected areas, including Lago do Cuniã (p681), for ecotourism. The office is 4km north of the center – bus 201 signed 'Hospital de Base via Aeroporto' passes here.

TRAVEL AGENCIES
Nossa Viagens e Turismo (☎ 3224 4777; Rua Tenreiro Aranha 2125) Sells plane tickets; one of many agencies around town.

Sights & Activities
MUSEU DA ESTRADA DE FERRO MADEIRA-MAMORÉ
The city's only real sight of interest, the **Museu da Estrada de Ferro Madeira-Mamoré** (Madeira-Mamoré Railway Museum; cnr Av Sete de Setembro & Av Farqhuar) was undergoing a major renovation at the time of research. A massive complex, it occupies several huge sheds that made up the original train station, and boasts an extensive collection of artifacts and memorabilia related to the infamous Madeira-Mamoré railway, including the US-built 'Colonel Church,' the first locomotive to run in Amazonia.

PORTO VELHO

INFORMATION		
Amazon House	1	B3
Bradesco	2	B3
Bradesco	3	B3
Casa de Câmbio Marco Aurélio	4	A2
Drogaria Natal	5	B2
Hospital Central	6	B3
Lavandaria Mamoré	7	C2
Nossa Viagens e Turismo	8	B3
PortoNet	9	B4
Post Office	10	B3

SIGHTS & ACTIVITIES		
Museu da Estrada de Ferro		
Madeira-Mamoré	11	A4

SLEEPING		
Hotel Central	12	B3
Hotel Tia Carmem	13	B3
Hotel Vila Rica	14	C3
Hotel Yara	15	B3
Vitória Palace Hotel	16	B3

EATING		
Caffé Restaurante	17	B3
Casa D'Italia	18	B2
Praça Rondón	19	B4
Remanso do Tucunaré	20	C4

DRINKING		
Buda's Bar	(see 21)	
Emporium	21	A3
Estação do Porto	(see 21)	
Food and Beer Stalls	22	A4
Praça Rondón	(see 19)	

ENTERTAINMENT		
Cine Rio	23	C3

SHOPPING		
Artes Brasil	24	A3

TRANSPORT		
Agência Amazonas	25	A4
Bus 201 to Bus Station &		
Airport	26	B3
Porto Cai n'Água	27	A4

RIVER TRIPS

The broad Rio Madeira forms the western boundary of Porto Velho. Measurements of the length of the mud-brown river usually include its main tributary, the Rio Mamoré, and *its* tributaries, which originate in the Bolivian Andes, making the Madeira 3200km long. With an average flow of 1.4 billion liters a minute, the Madeira has the sixth-greatest volume of all the world's rivers. It enters the Amazon River 150km downstream from Manaus.

From about 9am to 7pm daily, riverboats make 45-minute cruises along the Rio Madeira from the dock in front of the Madeira-Mamoré train station (R$7 per person). While not exactly thrilling, this is a reasonable way to idle away an hour or so – with luck you'll see a few pink dolphins. You can buy snacks and drinks on board.

Sleeping

Hotel Tia Carmem (☎ 3221 7910; Av Campos Sales 2895; s/d with fan & shared bathroom R$35/50, s with fan & bathroom R$40, s/d with air-con R$40/60, s/d with air-con & bathroom R$70/90; ⚙ ⚏) A reliable family-run budget choice, though beware the awful foam mattresses in some of the cheapest rooms. Service ranges from hands-off to a bit surly, akin to visiting your grumpy grandma's house. It's removed from the bustle of downtown, but is still an easy walk to and from nightlife on Av Pinheiro Machado. No breakfast on Sundays.

Vitória Palace Hotel (☎ 3221 9232; Rua Duque de Caxias 745; s/d with fan R$35/45, with air-con & minibar

R$75/85; ☒) A small step up from the Tia Carmem, with somewhat bigger rooms and more central location, but the same guesthouse ambience. Simple, tidy rooms have bathrooms (with hot water) and high ceilings for a bit more breathing space. They open right onto the dining area, however, which may annoy late sleepers.

Hotel Yara (☎ 3221 2127; Rua General Osório 255; s/d R$68/120; ☒ ☎) Ordinary, somewhat cramped rooms are nevertheless clean and reasonably comfortable. The double price seems excessive, but it's good value for solo travelers. The location isn't exactly charming, but it's safe and convenient to the bank, riverboat dock, and airport buses. Definitely the best option on Av Sete de Setembro.

Hotel Central (☎ 2181 2500; www.enter-net.com.br /hcentral; Rua Tenreiro Aranha 2472; s/d R$145/180; ☒ ☎) A classy modern hotel with comfortable rooms and prompt professional service. The location is a bit removed – and the street a bit lonely, especially at night – but that just makes getting here all the more comforting. The rates keep creeping up, making it less of a good-value place, but it's still a good upper-end choice.

Hotel Vila Rica (☎ 3224 3433; www.hotelvilarica.com. br; Av Carlos Gomes 1616; s/d R$245/390; ☒ ☐ ☎ ☒) Porto Velho's finest hotel has a spacious lobby, and excellent views from the upper floor rooms, though the rooms are a bit dated, especially for this price. A business center and swimming pool make this suitable for work or pleasure. On Saturdays, the hotel hosts the popular *Feijoada do Vila*, a huge lunch buffet (per plate R$35) that attracts travelers and Porto Velho's upper crust alike.

Eating

Praça Rondón (cnr Av Sete de Setembro & Av Presidente Dutra; ☾ 4-11pm) A handful of kiosks in the lower part of the plaza serve hot sandwiches, fresh juices and other light fare at street-cart prices. Afterward, migrate across the plaza to one of the outdoor bars for a tall beer at a plastic table.

our pick **Caffé Restaurante** (☎ 3224 3176; Av Carlos Gomes 1097; per kg R$25; ☾ lunch) Come here for the excellent lunch buffet. A wide selection of mains – from shepherds pie to fried fish – and a slew of sides and a refrigerated case full of succulent desserts are served in a nice and cool dining area. Popular with professionals, but perfectly affordable.

Casa D'Italia (cnr Rua Golçalves Dias & Av Pinheiro Machado; mains R$10-25; ☾ dinner Wed-Mon) The *rodízio* (smorgasbord) concept works perfectly well for Italian food: instead of skewers of meat, waiters rotate by with dishes of lasagna, pastas with red or cream sauces, and of course pizza of all sorts, including chocolate and banana pizzas for dessert. It's all-you-can-eat, but don't get greedy: you pay extra if you leave anything on your plate.

Remanso do Tucunaré (☎ 3221 2353; Av Brasília 1506; dishes R$16-40; ☾ lunch & dinner) Good fish dishes serve two easily; try a delicious *caldeirada de tucunaré* (river-fish stew) or *tambaquí* – big fish chunks boiled with onion and tomatoes in a souplike sauce, accompanied by rice.

Drinking & Entertainment

The corner of Av Pinheiro Machado and Av Presidente Dutra is the epicenter of Porto Velho's nightlife. Three bars in a row – Emporium, Estação do Porto and Buda's Bar serve up beer, mixed drinks, and a cool, bohemian-ish atmosphere that draws a mixed-age crowd. Weekends are busiest, of course, and occasionally feature live music. Further down Av Pinheiro Machado – to about Rua Goncalves – are several more small bars, restaurants and cafés, if you're looking for something bit mellower (or just a bite to eat).

If you don't feel like walking up to Av Pinheiro Machado, **Praça Rondón** (cnr Av Sete de Setembro & Av Presidente Dutra; ☾ 4-11pm) has a handful of restaurant-bars with tables set up in the plaza, where you can chill out over a cold beer or two.

For something a bit edgier, the riverbank area by the Madeira-Mamoré train station has a slew of outdoor stands serving beer, and a couple of floating docks that double as bars. Saturday and Sunday nights have live music and dancing; things can get a bit seedy as the night wears on, so definitely be alert.

Cine Rio (tickets R$10, R$4 Wed) is a one-screen theater located on the 2nd floor of Rio Shopping, a small mall on Av Carlos Gomes, between Rua Joaquim Nabuco and Av Brasília; at least five people are required to run the movie, and some nights a quorum is not to be had.

Shopping

Artes Brasil (☎ 3224 4774; Rua Euclides da Cunha 1952) The best items here are carved wooden animals, from pink dolphins to peacock b and ranging from keychain size to several feet long. The rest is fairly predictable *artesenato*, but still worth perusing. It faces the Mercado Central, a short distance from the railroad museum.

Getting There & Away

AIR

Porto Velho airport is 7km north of town. There are daily direct flights to and from Rio Branco, Manaus and Brasília, with onward connections from there. The small airport has Bradesco, HSBC and Banco de Brasil cash machines, a post office, rental-car agencies, an information desk and a strangely large food court. The airlines have offices in the airport only, and most ticketing changes require a trek out there.

Gol (☎ 3219 7491; www.voegol.com.br)

Ocean (☎ 3219 7472; www.oceanair.com.br)

TAM (☎ 3219 7508; www.tam.com.br)

TRIP (☎ 3225 7534, www.voetrip.com.br)

BOAT

Slow boats to Manaus via the Rio Madeira and Rio Amazonas (a 2½-day trip) leave twice weekly from Porto Cai n'Água at the end of Rua 13 de Maio. Departures are on Tuesday (arriving in Manaus on Friday morning) and Friday at (arriving on Monday morning) at 6pm. Tickets are R$150 for hammock, R$500 for a *camarote* (one to two people, fan, no bathroom) and R$600 for a suite (one to two people, air-con, private bathroom); all include three meals per day, the latter two get somewhat better meals, and lunch and dinner are delivered to your room. **Agência Amazonas** (☎ 3223 9743; ⏲ 7am-7pm Mon-Sat, 7am-11am Sun) is one of several ticket offices on Rua 13 de Maio near the port; ticket prices are negotiable, especially for groups. Most agencies can reserve good hammock spots for you, and even sell you a hammock (though you'll get better prices at the market); otherwise, arrive at the boat in the morning to secure a good place to hang your hammock. You can even arrive a day or two in advance, and stay for free on the boat before it departs (see the boxed text, p615).

BUS

The **bus station** (cnr Av Jorge Teixeira & Av Carlos Gomes) is 2km east of the center.

Real Norte (☎ 3225 2891) runs four daily buses to Rio Branco (R$55, eight hours) departing at 7am, noon, 9pm and midnight; the 10pm departure is direct. It also has service to Guajará-Mirim (R$40, six hours) at

---

UNCONTACTED

The idea of indigenous groups living deep in the rain forest, yet to be contacted by the outside world, is not as illusory as you might think. In fact, such groups exist all around the world, with the greatest number in the Brazilian Amazon. A 2007 report by Funai, Brazil's indigenous-affairs agency, estimates there are 67 uncontacted tribes (or 'isolated peoples') in the country, up from the previous estimate of 40.

Arriving at that number, and estimating how many people belong to each group, is obviously difficult, but not impossible. Contacted tribes often tell of uncontacted families living in remote areas of their territories. Occasionally members of an uncontacted group will emerge from the jungle, having left or been expelled from their land. Funai studied footprints, abandoned huts and other clues in its recent study. Experts believe most uncontacted groups have seen or even encountered non-*índios* – and have probably seen and heard airplanes – but choose to remain hidden.

Several uncontacted groups are believed to live in Rondônia, including at least three in the Uru-eu-Wau-Wau indigenous reserve, in the center of the state. The reserve suffers rampant illegal mining and logging, and uncontacted groups have retreated ever deeper into the forest. Rondônia also is home to an indigenous man believed to be the last member of an unknown tribe. He has refused all contact, despite being surrounded by pastures and plantations. When Funai arranged for a woman from a nearby tribe to meet him, and possibly reproduce, he chased away the would-be bride with bow and arrows. He is called the 'man in the hole' because he has a hole in his hut, protected by sharp spikes, where he hides when outsiders approach. In December 2009, he survived an attack by gunmen believed to be connected to nearby ranchers; no one has been arrested for the crime.

6am, 6:30am, 10am, 2pm, 6pm, 11:30pm and 1am; the 2pm and 1am departures are direct. Collective taxis also make the trip to Guajará-Mirim (per person R$40, four hours). The price is based on a minimum of four passengers; ask taxi drivers at the bus station.

Andorinha (☎ 3225 3025) has virtually identical services that go to Real Norte, including to Rio Branco (R$55, eight hours, four departures daily), Guajará-Mirim (ordinary/direct R$30/34, five hours, six departures daily) and Cuiabá (R$150, 22 hours, three departures daily).

Eucatur (☎ 3222 2233) offers long-distance service to destinations like Cuiabá (R$128, 24 hours, six departures daily), São Paulo (R$326, 48 hours, one departure daily) and Brasília (R$318, 40 hours, one departure daily).

Tekla (☎ 3225 2867) serves the glutton-for-punishment route, with buses to Imperitriz (R$380, 2½ to three days, one departure weekly) where you can connect to Belém.

Getting Around

Bus 201 (R$2), signed 'Hospital de Base via Aeroporto,' runs between the city center and the bus station and the airport, passing each roughly every hour. Pick it up at the bus station or airport terminal (in both cases, the stop is to your right as you leave the main doorways), or at designated stops along Av Sete de Setembro. A taxi between the bus station and town costs R$10; to or from the airport is R$26.50.

RESERVA EXTRATIVISTA DO LAGO DO CUNIÃ

This 558-sq-km reserve, created in 1999, lies 150km down the Rio Madeira from Porto Velho and is accessible only by river. It's Rondônia's largest fish-spawning ground (*pirarucu* and *aruanã* are among the species breeding here) and is renowned for its abundant bird life. Plans to open the reserve to tourism have been delayed by several years, as IBAMA completes required environmental studies. Contact **IBAMA** (☎ 3223 2023; eseccunia.ro@ibama.gov.br; Av Jorge Teixeira 3559) in Porto Velho to check the progress.

GUAJARÁ-MIRIM

☎ 0xx69 / pop 41,000

This low-key town on the Rio Mamoré came into existence as the southern terminus of

the Madeira-Mamoré railway. Both Guajará-Mirim and Bolivian Guayaramerín across the river are free-trade zones with a steady stream of shopping tourists.

Though exceedingly sleepy most of the year, Guajará-Mirim perks up in mid-August when it hosts its own **Boi-Bumbá festival**, a recreation of the huge bash of the same name held in Parantins, near Manaus, and which is itself an adaptation of the Bomba Meu Boi festival celebrated in São Luis and other parts of the Northeast. Guajará-Mirim's festival includes many of the same elements, including mock feuds between the 'Caprichosos' and 'Garantidos' (traditionally dressed in blue and red, respectively) and nighttime performances depicting the story of an ox that's killed and then resurrected. A R$5 admission is charged for some events.

Information

EMERGENCY

Emergency room (☎ 192; Hospital Regional, cnr Rua Marechal Deodoro & Av Costa Marques)

Police (☎ 190)

INTERNET ACCESS

TriboNet (Av 15 de Novembro; per hr R$1.75; ☼ 8am-midnight Mon-Fri, 1-11pm Sat-Sun) Fast connection.

Lan House Center (Av 15 de Novembro; per hr R$1.50; ☼ 9am-11pm) Across the street from the bus station.

MEDICAL SERVICES

Hospital Regional (☎ 3541 7129, toll-free 192; cnr Rua Marechal Deodoro & Av Costa Marques) You may have to wait a long time for service at this crowded public hospital.

Yellow-fever vaccinations (cnr Av Beira Rio; ☼ 7am-7pm Mon-Sat, 7am-noon Sun) Free of charge at the health post near the port.

MONEY

There are numerous moneychangers at the port in Guayaramerín (p684), on the Bolivian side.

Banco do Brasil (Av Mendonça Lima 388; ☼ 9am-2pm Mon-Fri) Exchanges US cash but not traveler's checks.

Bradesco (cnr Av Costa Marques) Reliable ATMs.

POST & TELEPHONE

Post office (☎ 3541 2777; cnr Av Presidente Dutra & Rua Marechal Deodoro; ☼ 8am-noon & 2-6pm Mon-Fri, 8am-noon Sat)

Posto Telefónico (☎ 3541 3991; Av 15 de Novembro 620; ☼ 8am-9pm) Sells telephone cards.

THE AMAZON

GUAJARÁ-MIRIM

0 / 300 m
0 / 0.2 miles

INFORMATION
Banco do Brasil.......................1 C2
Bolivia Consulate....................2 B3
Bradesco................................3 B2
Hospital Regional....................4 C3
Polícia Federal........................5 B2
Post Office.............................6 C3
Posto Telefónico.....................7 C2
Yellow Fever Vaccinations.......8 B3

SIGHTS & ACTIVITIES
Hurukunê-Wao.......................9 C3
Museu Histórico Municipal...10 B3

SLEEPING
Hotel Jamaica.......................11 C1
Hotel Mine-Estrela...............12 C2

EATING
Lanchonete e Pizzaria Pit
    Stop................................13 D2
Restaurante Oásis................14 C2

TRANSPORT
Boats to Forte Príncipe da
    Beira..............................15 B3
Guayaramerín Passenger
    Boat Ticket Office............16 B3
Passenger Boats to
    Guayaramerín..................17 B3
Vehicle Ferry to
    Guayaramerín..................18 B3

To Tribonet (100m);
Lan House Center (1.5km);
Bus Station (1.5km)

Cathedral

Rio Mamoré

To Pakaas Palafitas
Lodge (8km by river)

Sights & Activities
MUSEU HISTÓRICO MUNICIPAL
'Have animal, will stuff' seems to be the motto at Guajará-Mirim's **Museu Histórico Municipal** (cnr Av Constituição & Av 15 de Novembro; admission free; 8:30-11:30am & 2:30-5:30pm Mon-Fri, 8:30-11:30am Sat). Monkeys, falcons and anteaters are among the slew of birds and mammals stuffed (none too recently, it seems) and posed in a tree in the museum's foyer. Inside the main room, a stuffed anaconda is stretched the length of the main salon, while another is wrapped around a crocodile, also stuffed. A few other oddities, like conjoined-twin piglets preserved in formaldehyde, complete the bizarre natural history collection. The museum is housed in the old Madeira-Mamoré train station, and has some mildly interesting train memorabilia, and there are two genuine steam locomotives parked outside.

HURUKUNÊ-WAO
A small gallery and cultural center, **Hurukunê-Wao** (cnr Av Constituição & Travessa do Navigante; admission free; 8am-6pm Mon-Fri, 8am-noon Sat) is intended to highlight the art and culture of Rondônia's in-

digenous communities. At that it's partly successful, with a handful of informative displays and folk-art pieces mixed in with predictable tourist kitsch. It's attached to the local office of Funai, the federal *índio* affairs agency.

PAKAAS PALAFITAS LODGE
A visit to the upscale ecohotel **Pakaas Palafitas Lodge** (3541 3058; www.pakaas.com.br; all-day entry incl lunch R$40) is an agreeable way to spend the day. You can walk along the 2.5km of raised scenic trails, and book a canoe tour through nearby channels and flooded forest. Or just relax beside the beautiful pool, which overlooks a 'meeting of the waters,' like the larger and more famous one near Manaus, and enjoy a fine buffet lunch. A taxi to the lodge from town costs R$50.

Sleeping & Eating
Hotel Mine-Estrela (3541 1206; Av 15 de Novembro 460; s/d R$35/60;) Offers large basic rooms with cable TV, and a location that's convenient to restaurants, internet and passing taxis for getting to the port or bus station. By no means luxurious, but a reliable budget choice, especially if you're just passing through.

Hotel Jamaica (☎ 3541 3722; Av Leopoldo de Matos 755; s/d R$60/90; 🅿 🛜) Near the cathedral, this is one of Guajará-Mirim's best hotels, with excellent service and large comfortable rooms arranged along a long internal corridor and lobby. For not too much more than the Mine-Estrela, you are sure to have fresh sheets, a flat-screen TV and a well-supplied breakfast. Rooms vary in size; those in front are larger, but the rear units get less hallway traffic.

Pakaas Palafitas Lodge (☎ 3541 3058; www.pakaas.com.br; s/d with jungle view R$159/282, with river view R$200/355; 🅿 🖳 🛜) A memorable, locally owned jungle lodge about 30 minutes by taxi from Guajará-Mirim whose price includes all meals. Built on stilts, the lodge overlooks the confluence of the Mamoré and Pacaas rivers, which – one being white, the other black – form a stark 'meeting of the waters' like the one near Manaus. The best view is from the hotel's suspended pool – from the right angle, it looks like a meeting of *three* waters. The lodge has 28 comfortable chalets, and 2.5km of raised walkways through the surrounding forest – it's secondary growth, but home to many animals and birds. Guests can book various tours (R$90 to R$250 for one to five people), including nighttime caiman-spotting and canoeing through the flooded forest. Closed December 23 to January 2.

Lanchonete e Pizzaria Pit Stop (☎ 3541 4213; Av 15 de Novembro 620; dishes US$4-6; 🕑 dinner) A popular if somewhat sterile eatery serving decent pizzas. It has a huge wide-screen TV, so you're sure not to miss a moment of the latest *novela* or soccer game.

Restaurante Oásis (☎ 541 1621; Av 15 de Novembro 460; self-service per kg R$25; 🕑 lunch daily except Tue) This longtime favorite in Guajará-Mirim can be counted on for a tasty, well-prepared lunch buffet, including fresh grilled meats. The airy dining area gets some street noise, but is still a pleasant place for a midday break.

Getting There & Around

The **bus station** (☎ 541 2448; Av 15 de Novembro) is about 2km east of the center. There is no public transportation to the bus station; a taxi to or from the station to the center of town costs R$10. Your hotel receptionist can call a cab, or you may find some parked at the port, or at the park at Avs 15 de Novembro and Costa Marques. Simply waiting for one to pass can take a while, however.

Real Norte (☎ 3541 2302) runs six daily buses to Porto Velho (R$40, 5½ to 6½ hours) at 6:30am, 10am, 1pm, 2pm, 7pm and 11:55pm; the 1pm and 11:55pm departures are direct and about an hour quicker. There's just one bus to Rio Branco (R$49, nine hours, noon) with a transfer in Abunã.

Passenger boats sail up the Mamoré and Guaporé rivers from Guajará-Mirim to the Forte Príncipe da Beira (hammock including meals R$90, 40 hours) about every eight to 10 days. Return trips are the same frequency, but take about half as long. Ask about services at the moorings at the end of Av Dr Antônio da Costa. Fast boats can make the trip in about eight hours, but cost considerably more.

Occasional boats go up the Guaporé as far as Vila Bela da Santíssima Trindade in Mato Grosso.

TO/FROM BOLIVIA

Motorboats ferry passengers across the Rio Mamoré between Guajará-Mirim and Guayaramerín, Bolivia (B$2, 10 minutes). A minimum of 10 passengers is usually required, but boats often go with fewer. Mornings and afternoons are the busiest, and it's rare to wait more than 30 minutes at any time of the day. The port and **ticket office** (☎ 3541 7221; 🕑 24hr) in Guajará-Mirim are on Av Beira Rio, near the east end of Av 15 de Novembro. Moneychangers on the Bolivian side change reais and *bolivianos*.

Bolivia consulate (☎ 3541 8622; Av Beira Rio; 🕑 8:30am-12:30pm & 2-7pm Mon-Fri) Look for a Bolivian flag on the 2nd floor; the door is partway down a narrow passageway on the south side of the building.

Polícia Federal (☎ 3541 2437; cnr Av Presidente Dutra & Av Quintino Bocaiúva; 🕑 8am-noon & 2-6pm Mon-Fri) The immigration office is an unmarked door on Av Presidente Dutra, but you can use the main entrance on Av Quintino Bocaiúva after hours and on weekends.

GUAYARAMERÍN (BOLIVIA)

☎ 0xx855 / pop 36,000

Guayaramerín, on the Rio Mamoré opposite Guajará-Mirim, is a frontier town, river port, trading center and the start of a road to La Paz, the Bolivian capital, via Riberalta (90km away) and Rurrenabaque.

The town is so small you can walk just about anywhere, except to the bus terminal (2.5km south from the ferry terminal). Moto-taxis charge B$1 to B$3.

THE AMAZON

Information

Estudio Fotográfico Relieve (Av Beni; per hr B$6; telephone calls to USA & Europe B$4-6; ☽ 7:30am-9:30pm Mon-Sat, 7:30am-7pm Sat)

Hospital Guayaramerín (☎ 112, 885 3007, 885 3008; Calle Mamoré s/n) Basic medical services.

Internet M@s@s (Calle 25 de Mayo; per hr B$5; ☽ 9:30am-midnight)

Milán Cambio y Turismo (☎ 885 3400; Plaza Principal; ☽ 8:30am-noon & 2:30-6pm Mon-Fri, 8:30am-noon Sat) Changes US, Bolivian and Brazilian cash.

Moneychangers (Guayaramerín port) Change US, Bolivian and Brazilian cash.

Police (☎ 110; cnr Av Mariscal Santa Cruz & Calle 6 de Agosto)

Post office (Av Mariscal Santa Cruz s/n; ☽ 8am-noon & 2-5pm Mon-Fri, 8am-noon Sat)

Punto Entel (☎ 885 9076; Plaza Principal; internet per hr B$7, telephone calls to USA & Europe per min B$4; ☽ 7:30am-11pm)

Sleeping & Eating

ourpick Hotel Santa Ana (☎ 855 3900; Calle 25 de Mayo 611; s/d B$50/100) Operated by a cheerful elderly couple, this hotel offers simple affordable lodging. Rooms are basic but clean, and most open onto a sunny courtyard brimming with potted plants. No food service, but water and coffee are always available.

Hotel Anexo Plaza (☎ 855 3650; Av Mariscal Santa Cruz 19; s/d B$40/80) A good alternative if the Santa Ana is full, rooms here are tidy and simple, arranged on either side of a long outdoor corridor. Service is friendly and the location ideal, facing right onto the central plaza.

Hotel San Carlos (☎ 855 3555; Calle 6 de Agosto 347; s/d B$170/240; ▨ ☻ ▨) By far the most upmarket place in town, with an attitude and parking area full of SUVs to prove it. Guests can make use of a pool, restaurant and billiards table; rooms are a bit disappointing for the price – what's up with the old-school air-conditioning units? – but still a step above the competition.

ourpick Restaurant Un Gusto a Más (Calle 25 de Mayo; per kg R$12 or B$40; ☽ lunch & dinner Mon-Sat, lunch only Sun) Get Brazilian-style grub at Bolivian prices at this bright, popular eatery, run by a hard-working Bolivian-Brazilian family. The self-serve spread is modest but tasty, with dishes from both sides of the border, and the dining area is spacious and colorful.

Snack Antonella (Av Mariscal Santa Cruz; mains B$5-20; ☽ 8am-midnight) Serves simple meals in an eclectic dining area carved out of the family's home, and at wood tables set up on the sidewalk facing the plaza. It's mostly tortas, *salgados*, and other light fare but it also has fish and chicken dishes, served with rice, beans and salad.

Getting There & Away

AIR

Guayaramerín's small simple airport is on the eastern edge of town, and served by two airlines: **Aerocon** (☎ 885 5025, 885 5035, in Brazil 9264 7995; www.aerocon.bo; cnr Calle 25 de Mayo & Av 16 de Julio; ☽ 8am-12:30pm & 2-6:30pm Mon-Fri, 8am-12:30pm Sat) and **TAM** (☎ 885 3924, 885 3925; cnr Av 16 de Julio & Calle Sucre; ☽ 8am-noon & 3-5:30pm Mon-Fri, 8am-noon Sat). The latter is operated by the Bolivian military, and while it typically offers cheaper fares, it

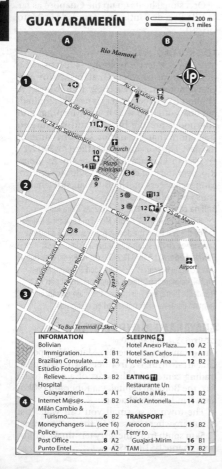

GUAYARAMERÍN

INFORMATION			SLEEPING 🛏		
Bolivian			Hotel Anexo Plaza.........**10** A2		
Immigration................**1** B1			Hotel San Carlos..........**11** A1		
Brazilian Consulate........**2** B2			Hotel Santa Ana.........**12** B2		
Estudio Fotográfico			**EATING 🍴**		
Relieve.......................**3** B2			Restaurante Un		
Hospital			Gusto a Más..............**13** B2		
Guayaramerín.............**4** A1			Snack Antonella...........**14** A2		
Internet M@s@s...........**5** B2			**TRANSPORT**		
Milán Cambio &			Aerocon.....................**15** B2		
Turismo.....................**6** B2			Ferry to		
Moneychangers.......(see 16)			Guajará-Mirim.........**16** B1		
Police........................**7** A1			TAM..........................**17** B2		
Post Office..................**8** B2					
Punto Entel.................**9** A2					

reportedly is not held to the same strict safety standards that the commercial airlines are. TAM airplanes also tend to be less modern and comfortable, as they are mostly repurposed military cargo planes.

Between them, there are several daily flights to Trinidad, with connections from there to La Paz, Santa Cruz, Cochbamba and elsewhere. If you are connecting, be sure to confirm the flight is the same day, lest you are stuck in Trinidad unexpectedly. At the time of research, a one-way ticket to Trinidad cost around B$600, and B$1235 to La Paz.

BOAT

Motorboats zip back and forth between Guayamerín and Guajará-Mirim (R$4, five minutes). There was no long-distance passenger-boat travel at the time of research, but in the past it has been possible to catch boats up the Rio Mamoré to Trinidad (hammock only, five to seven days) and beyond. Ask at the office of the Capitanía del Puerto for current information.

BUS & TAXI

Think twice about taking long-distance buses here, especially in the rainy season (roughly from November to April). Flooded roads and bridges can triple the estimated travel time, and two-, three- and even five-day epics are not uncommon. Most locals either fly or wait for the roads to clear. Depending on where you're headed, consider crossing into Brazil, where the roads are much better, and re-entering Bolivia closer to your destination.

The bus terminal is 2.5km from the river along Av Federico Román. A taxi to the terminal will cost you B$5.

TO/FROM BRAZIL

See p685 for information about boats between Bolivia and Brazil. For most non-US travelers, both countries offer 90-day tourist visas for free and on the spot. Americans, however, must obtain a five-year multi-entry visa, which costs US$130 in both countries; the Brazilian consulate claims it processes them in one to two days, while the Bolivians can take two weeks or more. You'll also need passport-size photos, yellow-fever vaccine and other items; needless to say, you're much better off having handled all this before arrival. Officials on both sides look for the other's exit stamp, so be sure to get one before crossing the river.

Bolivian immigration (☎ 855 4413, after hours 7395 2902; cnr Av Costañera & Calle Mariscal Santa Cruz; 🕒 8am-8pm Mon-Fri, 8am-noon Sat & Sun)
Brazilian consulate (☎ 855 3766; cnr Av 24 de Septiembre & Av Beni; 🕒 9am-noon & 2:30-5pm Mon-Fri)

GUAPORÉ VALLEY & CENTRAL RONDÔNIA
Forte Príncipe da Beira

Remote Forte Príncipe da Beira, beside the Rio Guaporé, 210km south of Guajará-Mirim, was constructed by the Portuguese between 1776 and 1783 to consolidate their hold on the lands east of the Guaporé and Mamoré against the Spanish. The star-shaped fort, one of only two ever constructed by Portugal in the Brazilian interior, has 10m-high walls and four corner bastions, each of which held 14 cannons. Today just one cannon remains. The walls, nearly 1km around, are surrounded by a moat and enclose the ruins of a chapel, armory, officers quarters and prison cells in which bored convicts scrawled poetic graffiti. Underground passageways lead from the fortress to the river. The fort was abandoned as a military post in 1889. Today Brazil maintains a garrison of around 70 soldiers beside the fort. There's also a village, Vila Príncipe da Beira, here.

The town of **Costa Marques** (population 7000), about 25km from the fort, is home to an attractive church, orchid park and a turtle nursery. Rooms at **Hotel Girassol Palácio** (☎ 3651 2215; Av Demétrio Melas 1796; s/d B$80/135; 🖳) have TV and come with free breakfast.

The road to Costa Marques is impassable from about November to April. **Real Norte** (☎ 3225 2891) offers seasonal service, usually connecting in Presidente Medici.

Reserva Extrativista Pedras Negras

About 240km upstream from Costa Marques, the **Reserva Extrativista Pedras Negras** has good opportunities for hiking, canoeing, and spotting rare orchids, macaws, toucans, caimans, deer, and river dolphins. There are also a few rural villages, dedicated mostly to rubber and Brazil-nut harvesting, that can be visited. A small lodge has two simple but comfortable cabins with hot water, mosquito screens, 24-hour electricity and beds or hammocks for up to 12 people.

The reserve is normally open from June 15 to November 15 only, due to heavy rainfall the rest of the year. The best months to go

THE AMAZON

are August to November, when river beaches are exposed. From September, turtle-nesting sites can be observed.

Visits to the reserve were suspended at the time of research, as a new agency was sought to manage them. Check with IBAMA in Porto Velho (p677) for the latest.

Parque Nacional de Pacaás Novos

This rugged, 7648-sq-km national park includes Rondônia's highest peak, Pico do Tracoá (1230m) and some spectacular waterfalls. Fauna includes jaguars, tapirs, giant anteaters, howler monkeys, and rare blue macaws. The park lies inside an *índio* reserve, Terra Indígena Uru-Eu-Wau-Wau. Ibama has plans to open the park to visitors, including constructing a research and visitors center, but as with other reserves in the state, the necessary studies have not been completed. Once again, check with IBAMA in Porto Velho for the latest.

ACRE

Present-day Acre was originally part of Bolivia, but by the end of the 19th century it was mostly populated by Brazilian *seringueiros*, spreading south from the Amazonas. In August 1902, Bolivia sent its army to assert control and was met by fierce resistance from the *seringueiros* in what is known here, a bit melodramatically, as the 'Acrean Revolution.' Bolivia eventually ceded the territory to Brazil in exchange for two million British pounds and a promise to build a railroad from the border to Porto Velho to facilitate Bolivian exports. (The railroad was never completed and some in Bolivia say the money was never paid.) The Brazilian government, however, had never really supported the upstart Acreans and refused to name Acre a state, designating it the nation's first 'federal territory' instead. Thus the 'autonomist' movement was born, a sometimes-armed conflict that took 60 years to be resolved.

Acre is the home state of martyred union and environmental leader Chico Mendes, and was a key battleground for battles over deforestation. Hundreds of union leaders, activists and ordinary workers died in the conflicts, including Mendes, who was assassinated in 1988. But thanks to those struggles, today a full third of the state is under environmental protection or designated as indigenous lands.

RIO BRANCO

☎ 0xx68 / pop 306,000

Rio Branco, the capital of Acre, was founded in 1882 by rubber-tappers on the banks of the Rio Acre. Once a brash, uneasy town, Rio Branco has transformed itself into a genuinely pleasant place, with several excellent cultural outlets and easy access to some interesting sites, including Xapuri, the hometown of the environmentalist Chico Mendes. Unfortunately for Rio Branco, few travelers make it here for the simple reason that it's not on the way to or from anywhere travelers commonly go.

Information

EMERGENCY

Emergency room (☎ 192, 3223 3080; Hospital Geral, cnr Av Nações Unidos & Rua Hugo Carneiro)
Police (☎ 190)

INTERNET ACCESS

Cyber Mapinguary (Rua Epaminondas Jácome; per hr R$2; ⏰ 8am-5pm Mon-Fri) Located on the 2nd floor of a small commercial center.
Viper.net (Av Ceará; per hr R$2; ⏰ 7am-8:30pm Mon-Sat, noon-8:30pm Sun)

MEDICAL SERVICES

Hospital Geral (☎ 192, 3223 3080; cnr Av Nações Unidos & Rua Hugo Carneiro)

MONEY

Banco do Brasil (Rua Porto Leal 85)
Bradesco (Rua Porto Leal 83)
HSBC (cnr Rua Rui Barbosa & Rua Marechal Deodoro)

POST

Post office (Rua Epaminondas Jácome 447; ⏰ 7am-4pm Mon-Fri, 8am-noon Sat)

TOURIST INFORMATION

Centro de Atendimento ao Turista (☎ 0800 647 3998; Praça Povos da Floresta; ⏰ 8am-6pm Mon-Sat, 4-9pm Sun) Not terribly helpful, but a good place to start. Otherwise, try asking at the Museu da Borracha, where staff are more used to encountering foreign tourists.

TRAVEL AGENCIES

Inácio's Tur (☎ 3214 7100; Inacio Palace Hotel, Rua Rui Barbosa 469; ⏰ 7:30am-noon & 2-6pm Mon-Fri, 7:30am-noon Sat) Sells plane tickets.

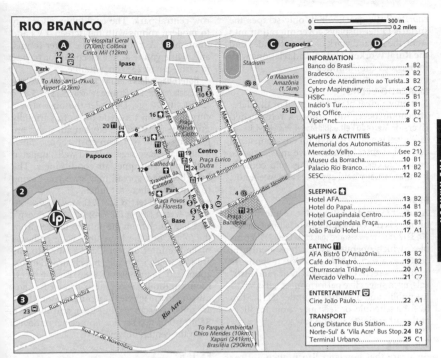

RIO BRANCO

0 ____ 300 m
0 ____ 0.2 miles

INFORMATION
Banco do Brasil.............................1 B2
Bradesco.......................................2 B2
Centro de Atendimento ao Turista.3 B2
Cyber Mapinguary.......................4 C2
HSBC...5 B1
Inácio's Tur..................................6 B1
Post Office....................................7 B2
Viper*net......................................8 C1

SIGHTS & ACTIVITIES
Memorial dos Autonomistas.........9 B2
Mercado Velho.....................(see 21)
Museu da Borracha.....................10 B1
Palacio Rio Branco.......................11 B2
SESC...12 B2

SLEEPING 🏠
Hotel AFA....................................13 B2
Hotel do Papai............................14 B1
Hotel Guapindaia Centro.............15 B1
Hotel Guapindaia Praça...............16 B1
João Paulo Hotel........................17 A1

EATING 🍴
AFA Bistrô D'Amazônia................18 B2
Café do Theatro...........................19 B2
Churrascaria Triângulo................20 A1
Mercado Velho............................21 C2

ENTERTAINMENT 🎭
Cine João Paulo...........................22 A1

TRANSPORT
Long Distance Bus Station...........23 A3
Norte-Sul & 'Vila Acre' Bus Stop.24 B2
Terminal Urbano.........................25 C1

THE AMAZON

Maanaim Amazônia (☎ 3223 3232; www.maainaim .amazonia.com; Hotel Imperador Galvez, Rua Santa Inês 401) Local tour operator offering everything from historical tours about Chico Mendes and the Acrean Revolution, to hiking and riverboat excursions.

Sights

PALACIO RIO BRANCO

Acre's first capital building, the imposing **Palacio Rio Branco** (☎ 3223 9241; Av Getúlio Vargas facing Praça Povos da Floresta; admission free; ☉ 8am-6pm Tue-Fri, 4-9pm Sat & Sun) is now mostly a tourist attraction. A maze of interconnected rooms contain interesting and well-done displays on prehistoric artifacts, indigenous communities, Chico Mendes and the Acrean Revolution. Docents are available for free guided tours, though you'll have to understand Portuguese. (Same goes for the all displays.)

MEMORIAL DOS AUTONOMISTAS

In its spiffy home just uphill from the Palacio Rio Branco, the **Memorial dos Autonomistas** (Autonomists Memorial; ☎ 3224 2133; Praça Eurico Dutra; admission free; ☉ 8am-6pm Tue-Fri, 4-9pm Sat & Sun) has a permanent display on the history of Acre's

battle for statehood – which is how 'autonomous' is meant here, as opposed to Acre's then-status as a federal territory, though not in pursuit of full independence – plus space for rotating art exhibits, typically paintings and sculptures by local artists. This is also the resting place of José Guiomard dos Santos and his wife; highly revered, Guiomard dos Santos served as federal administrator of Acre in the early 1940s and was later (by then a senator) the chief sponsor of the bill that eventually gave Acre its statehood. But blood runs thicker than water, especially in Acre – Guiomard, born in Minas Gerais, lost to Acre native José Augusto in the state's first gubernatorial election.

MUSEU DA BORRACHA

Housed in a beautifully restored mansion, the **Museu da Borracha** (Rubber Museum; ☎ 3224 6605; Av Ceará 1441; admission free; ☉ 8am-6pm Tue-Fri, 4-9pm Sat & Sun) has three small rooms with exhibits on the history of rubber-tapping. One room explains the extraction and processing of rubber, including the transition from using small axes (which killed the tree) to a tool called a *cabrita* (little goat), which only scrapes the surface. Other displays cover migration into Acre, the life and work of Chico Mendes and the Rural Workers Union, and relations with indigenous communities.

MERCADO VELHO

Not only a great place for a meal or that late-afternoon beer, Rio Branco's refurbished riverside **Mercado Velho** (Old Market; Praça Bandeira; admission free) is a favorite spot for city-sponsored cultural events, including live music, dance performances, poetry readings and comedy troupes, usually held evenings and weekends.

SESC

Another example of Rio Branco's unexpected hipness is the city's **SESC** (Serviço Social do Comercio; ☎ 3212 2828; www.sescacre.com.br; Av Brasil 713) complex, which operates as much as a cultural center as a social-services office. It sponsors lectures, screens creative film cycles and festivals, even stages live performances, all open to the public, and most free or under R$10. Stop by for a schedule, or keep an eye out for fliers at the other sights around town.

Sleeping

Be aware that hotels in Rio Branco are required to record the passport and visa information for all guests, as part of an effort by the federal police to stem illicit cross-border activity.

Hotel AFA (☎ 3224 1938; Rua Franco Ribeiro 99; s R$35-55, d R$50-80; ⊠) Standard rooms are a little rough around the edges, though some are quite large with windows facing the street. Otherwise, the newer deluxe rooms are decent value, with better beds, matching fixtures, even paintings on the walls. Next door is its sister-restaurant, AFA Bistro, one of the city's best per-kilo restaurants.

Hotel do Papai (☎ 3223 2044; cnr Rua Floriano Peixoto & Rua Rui Barbosa; s/d R$65/90; ⊠) A huge, sparsely decorated reception area gives way to smaller but equally sparse guestrooms, where high ceilings (and the lack of decor) lend an airy uncluttered feel, and the beds and bathrooms are aging, but clean. A reliable budget choice.

Hotel Guapindaia Praça (☎ 3224 7677; www .hoteisguapinda.com.br; Rua Rui Barbosa 354; s/d R$180/250; P ⊠ 🛜 🍴) You can't beat this newly refurbished hotel (formerly the Rio Branco Hotel) for its location, catercorner to a leafy plaza and just a block uphill from the city's nar-

row central park. The cool lobby gives way to modern rooms with flat-screen TVs and mini-splits. Ask for one of the larger rooms, and, while you're at it, a discount for paying in cash – up to 25% on a double.

Hotel Guapindaia Centro (☎ 3223 5747; www.hoteis guapindaia.com.br; Rua Floriano Peixoto 550; s R$75-85, d 125-140; P ⊠ 🛜) Don't let the busy street-corner location turn you off to this friendly midrange favorite; the city's main sights are just a block away. Clean crisp rooms, albeit a bit small, have sage-colored walls, updated bathrooms and quiet air-conditioners. The huge breakfast spread may save you having to stop somewhere for lunch.

João Paulo Hotel (☎ 3223 8933; www.joaopaulohotel .com.br; Av Ceará 2090; s/d R$83/145; ⊠ 🛜) It doesn't look like much from the outside, or even from the lobby, but the incredibly wide hallways make the interior feel like a castle. Rooms are a bit small, ironically, but clean and nicely appointed. Four suites (R$180) are the nicest rooms in Rio Branco. Guests receive free admission to the movie theater next door (there are only two screens, but hey), and there's a R$50 airport taxi service. Somewhat removed from the center, however.

Eating

Café do Theatro (☎ 3223 5862; cnr Av Brasil & Av Getúlio Vargas; dishes US$3-9; ⏱ 8am-9pm Tue-Sat, 4pm-midnight Sun) Part of the Memorial dos Autonomistas (see p687), this low-key café serves great coffee and light meals, including sandwiches and quiche. Daily specials (R$10 to R$18) are more substantial, and there's an extensive wine and cocktail menu. Under renovation when we passed through.

our pick **Mercado Velho** (Praça Bandeira; dishes R$6-20; ⏱ 7am-10pm) Dubbed the 'Old Market', this is in fact part of Rio Branco's newest and most successful urban renewal efforts. An old port building was transformed into a small, pleasant food court. Grilled beef, fried fish and other comfort foods are cooked up at clean booths. Eat inside or on benches overlooking the river.

Churrascaria Triângulo (☎ 3224 9265; Hotel Triângulo, Rua Floriano Peixoto 727; per kg R$28, rodízio R$28-30; ⏱ lunch & dinner, lunch only Sat) True, the ambience here is quite lacking – it's a hotel restaurant – but if you're famished and in the mood for meat, you are sure to get your fill here. The *rodízio* is sort of an all-you-can-eat meat buffet: waiters pass by your table with long skewers of fresh-grilled meats that you can sample as long as your stomach and chair hold up. It also includes all the self-serve side dishes you like, as if you'll have room.

AFA Bistrô D'Amazônia (☎ 3224 3936; Rua Franco Ribeiro 99; self-service per kg R$30; ☺ lunch) The name has changed but this unassuming bistro remains one of the best per-kilo lunch spots you'll find in the Amazonia. The city's professional classes pack in for fresh and original salad combinations, tender meat and fish dishes, and irresistible desserts. Sundays feature *frutas do mar* (seafood) and the price jumps to a hefty R$40 per kilo.

Entertainment

Praça Bandeira has a handful of outdoor restaurant-bars on the waterfront, between Av Gétulio Vargas and Rua Marechal Deodoro) overlooking the river. It's a popular place to nurse a few tall beers and contemplate the new pedestrian bridge, which at night is bathed in a hypnotic blue light.

Cine João Paulo (☎ 3223 3828; Av Ceará 2090; tickets Mon-Wed R$10, Thu-Sun R$14; shows start around 5pm) has two screens showing relatively recent Hollywood movies. Next to, and operated by, the João Paulo Hotel (guests get free passes).

Getting There & Away

Highway BR-364 is paved and well maintained between Rio Branco and Porto Velho, and as far as Sena Madureira, 170km beyond Rio Branco. Likewise, the road from Rio Branco to Brasiléia (235km) and Assis Brasil on the Peruvian border are also paved, and have year-round bus service. Beyond those corridors, however, most of Acre's roads are unpaved, and can be difficult or impassable during the rainy season, usually October to May (most of the year, that is). Boat and plane may be the only options during those times.

AIR

Rio Branco's small airport has daily flights to Porto Velho and Brasília (and onward connections from there) plus seasonal service to Cruzeiro do Sol.

Gol (☎ 0300 115 2121; airport)

TAM (☎ 4002 5700; airport)

Trip (☎ 0300 789 8747; airport)

BOAT

The Rio Acre is navigable all the way to the Peruvian border at Assis Brasil but there's

little river traffic (and none that follows a schedule). Headed the other direction, it's possible to catch a boat down the Rio Purus from the town of Boca do Acre, north of Rio Branco, theoretically all the way to Manaus. That said, if Manaus is your destination, there's much more frequent and reliable boat service on the Rio Madeiro, leaving from Porto Velho.

BUS

Real Norte (☎ 3224 4293; toll-free 0800 647 6666; www .realnorte.com.br) has service to Xapuri (R$19, 3½ hours, 6am and 1:45pm), Brasiléia (R$24, four hours, 6am, 6:30am, noon, 3pm, and 6pm), Assis Brasil (R$33.50, six hours, noon only), Guajará-Mirim (R$50, seven to eight hours, 11am only); and Porto Velho (R$55, seven to eight hours, 7am, 11am, 9pm, and 11pm). The road to Cruzeiro do Sol ($108, 19 hours) is passable only in July and August; otherwise, the only way to get there is to fly.

Eucatur (☎ 3244 2233) and **Andorinha** (☎ 3224 2233) each have morning departures to Brasília (R$275 to R$300, 50 to 55 hours) with onward connections from there.

Getting Around

Rio Branco has an efficient **terminal urbano** (city bus terminal; Rua Sergipe btwn Av Ceará & Rua Benjamin Constant), tucked into an area packed with street vendors. You pay your fare at a bank of turnstiles, and buses come and go from clearly marked platforms. You can board at bus stops around town as well; there's a handy one on Av Gétulio Vargas, near the Palacio Rio Branco.

The airport is located 22km west of town, on Hwy BR-364. A taxi to or from town costs an eye-popping R$70 to R$80. Some hotels have arrangements with taxis to charge 'only' R$50; it's normally for their own guests, but those staying elsewhere may be able to plead their case. Consider asking fellow passengers about sharing a ride; taxi drivers sometimes help pair people up. Alternatively, bus 304, signed as 'Custódio Freire' and/or 'Aeroporto,' runs between the airport and town about once an hour (R$2, one hour, 5am to 11pm).

The **long-distance bus station** (Av Uirapuru) is 1.25km southwest of the center, across the Rio Acre. At least three different city buses run between there and the center of town, including those marked 'Norte-Sul,' 'Taquarí' and 'Domoacir' (R$1.75, 25 minutes, every half hour). Catch them at either bus terminal or at the bus stop on Av Getúlio Vargas by the Palacio Rio Branco. A taxi to or from the city center costs R$15, a moto-taxi R$3.

AROUND RIO BRANCO
Parque Ambiental Chico Mendes

Only 52 hectares in size, of which roughly half is native forest, **Parque Ambiental Chico Mendes** (admission free) is nevertheless the most interesting park easily accessible to Rio Branco. A memorial to Chico Mendes stands near the entrance. The park also has a picnic area, a funny cast-iron treetop lookout, bike paths and a small zoo. Along the paths are theme huts representing different aspects of life in the region, including rubber tapping, a *maloca* (*índio* dwelling) and myths and legends. Some wildlife can be seen.

The park is located at Km 3 on Hwy AC-040, about 10km south of Rio Branco. To get here take a 'Vila Acre' bus from the *terminal urbano* of the stop on Av Getúlio Vargas (R$2, 45 minutes, every half hour).

Santo Daime Centers

There are several centers of the Santo Daime religious cult in and around Rio Branco, where it was founded in 1930 by Raimundo Irineu Serra (1892–1971), also known as Mestre Irineu. The cult's practices revolve around a sacred hallucinogenic drink called *ayahuasca*. Thursday is the group's holy day, and important ceremonies typically take place on the 15th and 30th of every month.

The ceremonial center at the cult's birthplace, called **Alto Santo**, is 7km from Rio Branco in Colônia Custódio Freire. You can reach it on an 'Irineu Serra' bus from the terminal urbano. A visitors center (of sorts) has been built there, next to Irineu Serra's tomb, though a visit here still requires a fair amount of simply asking around. Another community of Santo Daime followers, **Colônia Cinco Mil**, is 12km north of Rio Branco.

Although you can certainly just show up, it's ideal to try to find somebody from the community to organize your visit, especially if you're interested in witnessing or even participating in the group's ceremonies. The folks at the Museu da Borracha (p687) may be able to help, or at least point you in the right direction. You can reach the community by taxi (about R$30) or by catching a 'Porto Acre' bus along Hwy AC-010, which will drop you

at the turnoff for Colônia Cinco Mil, from which it's a 2.5km walk.

XAPURI
☎ 0xx68 / pop 15,000

This tidy little town of neat wooden houses along broad streets was home to environmental hero Chico Mendes. It lies about 12km northwest of Hwy BR-317, the main road between Rio Branco (241km away) and Brasiléia (74km away).

Information

Banco da Amazona (Rua C Bradão) Next to the gas station.

Tourist information kiosk (opp bus station; ☒ 7am-noon & 2-5pm Mon-Fri) Has more handicrafts that tourist information, but does have friendly attendants and a handy brochure about Xapuri.

Sights
CASA CHICO MENDES

Just across the street from the Fundação Chico Mendes, the teal and pink **Chico Mendes House** is just that: the simple wood house where Mendes, his wife and two children lived until his murder. This is also where he was killed; tours conducted by docents from the Chico Mendes Foundation (required) include a graphic description of the place and moment he was shot, with bloodstains still on the walls. Photos are not permitted inside the house, but outside is OK.

FUNDAÇÃO CHICO MENDES

The visitors center of the **Fundação Chico Mendes** (Chico Mendes Foundation; ☎ 3542 2651; admission free; ☒ 8am-noon & 2-6pm) contains wall-size photos of Chico Mendes with his wife and children, tapping rubber trees, and leading *empate*s – work stoppages designed to stop clear-cutting in the rain forest. There are some personal effects, including the blood-stained clothes and bath towel he had when he was murdered, and numerous awards given to Mendes, both before and after he died. Though interesting, you're sure to leave wishing there was more about the life and legacy of this seminal figure in workers' and environmental activism. Unfortunately, the foundation – which is headed by Mendes' widow and daughter, both of whom live in Rio Branco – does virtually no work beyond maintaining the modest visitors center, and Casa de Chico Mendes across the street.

MUSEU DO XAPURI

The modest but interesting **Museu do Xapuri** (Rua C Brandão; admission free; 8am-6pm Tue-Fri, 8:30am-5:30pm Sat, 9am-1pm Sun) covers the history of Acre and Xapuri, which was once a major hub for commercial activity, thanks to its location at the confluence of two rivers. Rubber, nuts, wood and other products were floated downstream to market, while roaming merchants (mostly Lebanese and Syrian, interestingly enough) used the waterways to peddle everything from shovels to perfume. Housed in an attractive mansion that served as the city hall from 1929 to 2000.

PRESERVATIVOS NATEX

Keeping hundreds of local rubber-tappers in business, **Preservativos Natex** (3542 6000, preservativosnatex.com.br; Estrada da Borracha Km 6; by appt) turns rubber into rubbers. The factory produces 100 million condoms per year, all for distribution by government health agencies. Around 700 families collect and sell latex to the factory, which was opened in 2008 with joint private and public backing. The company has been slow to open its facility to curious travelers, but is working with tourism officials to organize tours, which will include a short talk and a factory walk-through (complete with hair net and face mask) of the process, from liquid latex to willie warmer. Located on the road between Xapuri and the highway.

Sleeping & Eating

Pousada Floresta Viva (3542 2406; s/d R$35/75;)
The live-in owners of this hotel work elsewhere full time, and the cleaning person isn't around all the time; ask across the street if no one answers the door. Rooms are large and clean, and while newer than the Chapurys, they seem to have less character. Located about 150m from the bus terminal, and a block past Casa Chico Mendes.

Pousada das Chapurys (3542 2253; pousada _chapurys@hotmail.com; Rua Sadala Koury 1385; s/d/tr R$40/70/100;   ) A short walk from the bus terminal, this is the old standby of Xapuri's hotels, and still a pleasant and convenient place to stay. The friendly owners were close friends of Chico Mendes, and have photos and memorabilia in the hotel's dining area (as well as some fascinating stories). Rooms are large and comfortable, though showing their age.

Pousada Villa Verde (3542 3012; pousada-villa verde@hotmail.com; Rua Rodovaldo Nogueira 500; s/d R$55/85;

) Well worth the extra couple hundred meters you'll have to walk from the bus terminal, the Villa Verde has a huge leafy garden and just eight cozy rooms, all with aircon, comfortable beds and in-room internet. Some have private patios, and there's a small clean pool for cooling off. Speaking of cool, ask the owners about having a peek through their professional-grade telescope, housed in a shed-turned observatory on the hotel grounds.

ourpick **Pousada Ecológica Seringal Cachoeira** (3901-3017 3012; dm R$60, d R$130-190;   )
Twenty kilometers outside town is Seringal Cachoeira, where martyred union leader Chico Mendes first tapped rubber trees and collected Brazil nuts. It's still a working *seringal* (rubber forest) but a new lodge offers visitors cozy accommodations and excellent guided hikes. The most popular tour is a six-hour outing (beginning at 4am) for a real-life look at how trees are tapped, latex collected, and trails maintained. You may spot wildlife along the way, including monkeys, birds and insects, plus local flora, from medicinal plants to behemoth trees. Lodging is in dorms, 'chalets' or stand-alone 'suites' (with loft, patio, TV, even coffeemaker); all have air-con. Meals are served in the pousada's spacious main building. To get there, look for a turnoff 4km south of the Xapuri junction; it's another 16 km by dirt road from there. The pousada can arrange transport from Rio Branco; a taxi from Xapuri costs about R$70.

Pizzaria Tribos (3542 2531; Rua C Branbão; mains R$15-25; dinner) One of a handful of kiosks in a small park a block off the main plaza, Tribos serves up tasty pizzas at small outdoor tables and gets kudos for playing something other than *forró* or Brazilian pop (or simply blasting the TV). Select from one of the dozen or so usual suspects – shredded chicken, prosciutto, tuna, palm hearts – while head-bobbing to Maria Rita, Natiruts or some good ol' U2.

Bebum (Rua C Branbão) After pizza, you can migrate a few dozen meters down the park to this kiosk, a popular watering hole for Xapuri's young and restless.

Getting There & Away

Real Norte (3542 2384; toll-free 0800 647 6666; www .realnorte.com.br) has bus service from Xapuri to Rio Branco (R$19, 3½ hours) twice daily at 6am and 3:20pm. There's only one bus from Xapuri to Brasiléia (R$7, 1½ hours) departing at 9am. Alternatively, you can catch a

THE AMAZON

cab to the *trocamento* (junction) on Hwy BR-317 (R$10), where buses to Rio Branco pass at 7am, noon and 7pm, and to Brasiléia at 2:30pm, 5:30pm and 8:30pm.

BRASILÉIA
☎ 0xx68 / pop 20,500

The border town of Brasiléia is separated from Cobija, Bolivia, by the meandering Rio Acre

and Igarapé Bahia. There's precious little to do here, unless you're in the market for a computer or DVD player – for that, you can join the crowds crossing into Cobija to take advantage of the lower prices and a duty-free border.

Orientation

Hwy BR-317 from Rio Branco approaches Brasiléia from the southeast, through the adja-

---

CHICO MENDES & HIS LEGACY

In the mid-1970s an ambitious military government plan to tame the Amazon attracted a flood of developers, ranchers, logging companies and settlers into Acre, clear-cutting rubber and Brazil trees to make room for ranches. Francisco Alves Mendes Filho, better known as Chico Mendes, was a 30-something rubber-tapper, but one of few who could read and write, and had long taken an interest in improving the lives of fellow rubber-tappers, or *seringueiros*. In 1977, he cofounded the Sindicato dos Trabalhadores Rurais de Xapuri (Xapuri Rural Workers' Union) to defy the violent intimidation and dispossession practiced by the newcomers.

Mendes organized *empates* (stoppages), nonviolent human blockades to stop the clear-cutting. But Mendes was not initially an environmentalist – his motivation was to help rubber-tappers, whose livelihood happened to depend on a healthy, intact forest. Likewise, the environmental movement (largely based in the USA at the time) was focused on preserving 'virgin' forest, which it assumed to be empty of humans save a few *índio* tribes.

The joining of those groups – rubber-tappers and US environmentalists – was one of Mendes' key accomplishments. He convinced rubber-tappers to see themselves as stewards of the forest and allies of indigenous peoples. And he helped conceive of 'extractive reserves,' to this day an important means of protecting land and people there. He won numerous international awards in the process, including election to the UN Environment Organization's Global 500 Honor Roll in 1987.

Mendes' fame abroad made life increasingly dangerous at home. Killings of rural workers and activists, including priests and lawyers, jumped from single digits in the 1960s, to over a hundred in 1980, to nearly 500 between 1985 and 1987, according to Amnesty International.

In December 1988 he moved to establish his birthplace, Seringal Cachoeira, as an extractive reserve, defying a local rancher and strongman, Darly Alves da Silva, who claimed the land. Mendes had already denounced Silva to the police for threatening his life and for the murder of a union representative earlier that year. Mendes received innumerable death threats, but resisted the urging of colleagues to flee Acre state. On December 22, 1988, Mendes stepped onto the back porch of his home in Xapuri and was shot at close range by men hiding in the bushes. He staggered into the house, where his wife and children were watching TV, and bled to death.

Mendes' was the first of hundreds of murders to be thoroughly investigated and prosecuted, owing to the massive international reaction to his killing. Darly Alves da Silva and his son Darci Pereira da Silva were sentenced to 19 years in prison for ordering and committing the crime. Both da Silvas escaped from jail in 1993, apparently just walking free, suggesting complicity among the guards, but were recaptured in 1996, after another outcry, and returned to jail. The men completed their sentences in 2009; Darci reportedly lives in the Pantanal area, but Darly has remained in the area, and can be seen around Xapuri to this day.

Mendes' life and death brought unprecedented international attention to the environmental crisis in the Amazon. But activism on behalf of the forest and people who live there remains a dangerous undertaking. On February 12, 2005, a US-born nun named Dorothy Stang was gunned down in the small town of Anapú, in the soy and cattle country of Pará state. She was killed by men acting on the orders of a rancher Stang had accused of illegally clearing land. The rancher who ordered her killing was convicted in 2007 and sentenced to 30 years in prison. However, he is only the fourth such 'mastermind' to have been held to account for scores of murders that have taken place there, even since the assassination of Chico Mendes.

cent but independent town of Epitáciolândia. The Brasiléia bus station is just across a small bridge; from there it's a 300m walk (or R$5 taxi ride) to the center of town. If you do walk, bear right out of the bus terminal, and follow Rua Odilon Pratagi to Av Prefeito R Moreira, where most of the listings here are located.

A bridge over the Igarapé Bahia connects Epitáciolândia to Cobija, and is the official border crossing, with immigration offices for both countries nearby. A smaller, more convenient bridge spans the Rio Acre, making it possible to walk from one downtown to the other in just a few minutes. The smaller bridge – which is dedicated to Wilson Pinheiro, a rubber-tapper union president and friend of Chico Mendes who was assassinated in July 1980 – is at the end of Av Prefeito R Moriera; there is a customs post there, but no immigration officers.

Information

Banco das Amazonas (cnr Av Prefeito R Moreira & Rua Odilon Pratagi; 8am-1pm Mon-Fri) Has ATM and changes foreign cash.

Banco do Brasil (Av Prefeito R Moreira No 470) Has ATM.

No-name internet café (Rua Odilon Pratagi; per hr R$2; 8:30am-10pm) Two blocks from Pousada Las Palmeras.

Police (190, 3546 3207; Av Prefeito R Moreira No 456; 24hr)

Post office (Av Prefeito R Moreira btwn Banco das Amazonas & tourist information kiosk; 8am-noon & 2-5pm Mon-Fri)

Tourist information kiosk (Av Prefeito R Moreira near Restaurante Lili; 7am-6pm) Exceedingly unhelpful, more concerned with selling handicrafts than aiding visitors. You may find some worthwhile brochures here, however.

Sleeping & Eating

Pousada Orquidia Negra (9911 8967; Travessa 7 de Setembro 69; s/d R$45/65) Simple rooms have tile floors and clean bathrooms; a few have hot water and all are painted cheerful colors. The owner, who lives on-site with his family, worked alongside Chico Mendes, Wilson Pinheiro, and others back in the day, and has plenty of stories (many conspiratorial) for anyone who's interested.

Pousada Las Palmeras (3546 3284; Rua Odilon Pratagi at Av Geny Assis; s/d R$60/80;) Brasiléia's most appealing hotel has a variety of rooms, from narrow singles to spacious doubles, all with air-con, TV, minibar and hot water; the

breakfast is excellent. Newer units are spotless, although there's just no way to dress up faux-marble tile. Older ones have less tile and more character, but the amenities also creak and complain more. A wraparound covered passageway in front has chairs and sofas on one side, and breakfast area on the other.

Restaurant Lili (Av Prefeito R Moreira; lunch & dinner) Lunch is by weight (per kilo R$19), while dinner is R$7 per plate at the same self-serve buffet – a chance to hone your stacking skills. Pickings are reliable, if uninspired. Located near the tourist office.

Saborella (Rua Odilon Pratagi s/n; mains R$8-20; lunch daily, dinner Tue-Sun) Daily specials make ordering easy at this small restaurant, one of few genuinely agreeable places in town. Options are same-old, same-old – chicken, beef, sometimes fish, served with rice and beans – but are well prepared and usually served with a smile. Half-a-block from the bus station, and about 300m from the internet café.

Getting There & Away
BUS

The bus station is 500m from the listed hotels and the main commercial strip; a taxi in either direction costs R$5. **Real Norte** (3546 3257; www.realnorte.com.br) has five daily departures to Rio Branco (R$24, four hours, 6am, 11am, 2pm, 3pm and 6pm) plus service to Xapuri (R$7, two hours, 11am and 3:20pm) and Assis Brasil (R$9, two hours, 4pm). You can usually catch a collective taxi to any of the above as well; the fares are roughly double and you may need a minimum of four passengers, but the trip tends to be quicker and the driver will drop you at your hotel door.

TO/FROM PERU

Access to Peru is through the village of Assis Brasil, 110km west of Brasiléia. Once an adventure route, the road is now paved and has daily bus services. Complete Brazilian immigration procedures in Brasiléia, and Peruvian immigration at the border town of Iñapari.

Real Norte has bus services to Assis Brasil to/from Rio Branco and Brasiléia; see those sections (p689 and p693 respectively) for schedules and fares.

TO/FROM COBIJA (BOLIVIA)

You are free to cross back and forth between Cobija and Brasiléia without passing immigration, provided you're going for a short period. If you plan to continue inland, or stay longer than a couple days, you ought to clear immigration officially.

Bolivian immigration (☾ 8:30am-8:30pm) is on the main international bridge. In Brazil, the **Polícia Federal** (☎ 3546 3204; ☾ 24hr) handle immigration procedures; the office is in Epitáciolândia, just across the main international bridge. In Cobija, the **Brazilian consulate** (☾ 8am-1pm Mon-Fri) is a half-block from the main plaza, on Av General Rene Barrientos, next to the Banco Mercantil de Bolivia.

Remember that both Bolivia and Brazil have made visa requirements much stricter for US citizens, charging US$130 and taking a week or more to process the application. Most non-US travelers are issued with 90-day tourist visas on the spot, free of charge. Both countries require proof of yellow-fever vaccinations.

A Brazilian taxi from Brasiléia into Bolivia, with brief stops at the immigration offices, costs R$10 to R$15. A Bolivian cab charges R$5 for the same trip back.

COBIJA (BOLIVIA)

☎ 03 / pop 15,000

The capital of Bolivia's Pando department is the wettest spot in Bolivia, with 1770mm of precipitation annually. It is a hilly town on the banks of the Rio Acre, with a pleasant enough plaza but a somewhat gritty atmosphere. Prices in this section are listed in *bolivianos* (B$), which at the time of research

was trading at roughly R$1 to B$4, or US$1 to B$8. That doesn't mean you'll need Bolivian money right away, however. In Cobija you can use Brazilian reais to pay for just about everything.

Orientation

Crossing the smaller bridge from Brasiléia, turn left after the military base and make your way up to Cobija's main plaza, at the top of the hill. Coming from the main international bridge, Av Internacional extends 600m to Av 9 de Febrero. Turn right, and follow Av 9 de Febrero about 1.5km to the center of town.

Information

Internet Jandy (☎ 842 2921; Av 9 de Febrero 156; per hr B$5; ☾ 8am-midnight Mon-Sat, noon to 10pm Sun) A block downhill from Hotel Nanijo's.

Police (☎ 110)

Post office (ECOBOL; main plaza; ☾ 8am-noon & 3-7pm Mon-Fri, 9am-noon Sat)

Prodem (☎ 842 2800; Plaza Principal 186) ATM and currency exchange.

Sleeping & Eating

It is not customary in Bolivia to include free breakfast in room rates.

Hostería Sucre (☎ 842 3944; Sucre 56 near Suárez; s/d B$70/120) A block and a half from the plaza, this is a supremely friendly family-run place with clean, airy rooms, all with cable TV, bathroom and ceiling fan. Coffee and cold water available all day. It represents the best value at the lower end of the price scale.

Residencial Frontera (☎ 842 2740; Calle Beni s/n; B$100/120) The fan-cooled rooms here are small but clean; those with bathroom also have TVs. Though far from luxurious, the hotel is more comfortable than its drab exterior and reception area suggest.

GETTING TO BOLIVIA

Brazilian immigration procedures are handled at the Polícia Federal station in Epitáciolândia, while Bolivian border officials are at the main international bridge. Remember that both Bolivia and Brazil have made visa requirements much stricter for US citizens, charging US$130 and taking a week or more to process the application. Most non-US travelers are issued 90-day tourist visas on the spot, free of charge.

Hotel Nanijo's (☎ 842 2230; 6 de Agosto 147; s/d incl breakfast B$150/260; 🗷 🖭) This is Cobija's very first hotel, originally owned and operated by the city (which may explain the bland design and exterior). The inside has been renovated, however, making this one of Cobija's best hotels. Clean comfy rooms are freshly painted and sport modern TVs. Best of all, there's a large clean pool in the center courtyard that's perfect for cooling off on hot humid days. Breakfast is included in the price.

Esquina de la Abuela (☎ 842 2364; cnr Av Fernández Molina & Calle Sucre; dishes B$35-40; 🕑 8am-noon, 12:30-3pm & 7-11pm Mon-Fri, 9am-noon Sat) This friendly place has pleasant indoor and outdoor seating and standard meat and chicken fare. The morning service consists of *salteñas* (salty breakfast pastries) only.

Getting There & Away

AIR

Cobija's **airport** (☎ 842 2260) is 3km southeast of town on the Porvenir road. A taxi to/from the town center is B$15; there is no regular bus service. Flights in June, July, August, December and January get heavily booked, and advance reservations are almost always required in those months.

AeroSur (☎ 842 3050; www.aerosur.com; cnr Av Fernández Molina & Calle Teniente Coronel Cornejo; 🕑 8am-noon & 3-6pm Mon-Fri, 8am-noon Sat) has flights to La Paz (B$1050, 55 minutes) on Tuesday, Thursday and Saturday afternoons, with same-day connections to Santa Cruz and Cochabamba (both B$1250) and next-day connections for national and international destinations.

Aerocon (☎ 842 4575; www.aerocon.bo; Av Fernández Molina; 🕑 8am-12:30pm & 3pm-6:30pm Mon-Sat, open at airport Sun) has one daily flight to Trinidad (B$759, 1½ hours) with onward connections from there.

Amaszonas (☎ 842 3844; www.amaszonas.com; Av Fernández Molina) is just a block down from the other two airline offices and has daily service to Trinidad (B$759, 1½ hours) with connections to destinations throughout Bolivia, including Rurrenabaque (B$1525 total) and Santa Cruz (B$1050 total).

TAM (☎ 842 2267; road to airport; 🕑 8am-noon & 3-6pm Mon-Fri, 8am-noon Sat) has flights to La Paz on Monday, Wednesday and Friday at lower fares than other airlines. However, TAM is operated by the Bolivian military and some say it does not follow the same safety and maintenance guidelines that commercial airlines do.

BUS

Bus companies cluster at Km 2 of the road to the airport, just past the turnoff for Av Internacional and the main bridge to Brazil. Be aware that bus travel in this part of Bolivia is never deluxe, and can be especially arduous during the rainy season (roughly November to April). The roads are unpaved and there are numerous river crossings (four on the Cobija–Riberalta stretch alone). Travel times can easily double or triple due to mud and flooding. Prices and travel times are identical for all bus lines: to Riberalta (B$130, seven to 12 hours), Guayaramerín (B$140, nine to 14 hours), Trinidad (B$280, 24 to 36 hours), and La Paz (B$250, 48 to 72 hours).

Sindicato Unificado Guayaramerín (☎ 842 2703) and **Flota Vaca Diez** (☎ cell 7610 0319) both have service to Riberalta and Guayaramerín, departing Tuesday and Saturday. The former has an additional departure on Thursday.

Transpando (☎ 842 3831) and **Flota Cobija** (☎ 842 3588) go to Riberalta on Sunday, Monday, Wednesday and Friday. Transpando buses continue to Trinidad.

Flota Yugeña (☎ 842 2833) is the only line with service to La Paz, departing on Tuesday, Thursday and Saturday.

TO/FROM BRASILÉIA

You are free to make short trips back and forth between Cobija and Brasiléia, without passing immigration. For longer stays, it's a good idea to get your passport stamped; remember that you will be required to show a valid yellow-fever vaccination in order to enter (or re-enter) Brazil. See p694 for details on crossing between the two countries.

A taxi from Cobija into Brasiléia costs around B$15 or R$5, including stops at both countries' immigration offices. Moto-taxis charge the same around town, but are not allowed to carry passengers into Brazil. A taxi from Brazil into Bolivia costs R$10 to R$15.

Directory

CONTENTS

ACCOMMODATIONS

Brazilian accommodations range from battered, windowless cells to sumptuous, seaside guesthouses, with many possibilities in between. Nearly every pousada (guesthouse), hostel and hotel serves some form of *café da manha* (breakfast). In this book we note only when breakfast is not served. Private rooms with communal bathrooms are called *quartos*. Rooms with a private bathroom are *apartamentos*.

For our listings, hostels as well as guesthouses where dorm beds or double rooms cost less than R$80 are placed in the budget category. At the bottom end of this scale, cheap hotel rooms outside of major cities and resort areas sometimes cost as little as R$40/60 for a single/double. At that price expect a bare room with nothing but a bed and maybe a fan.

Midrange listings run from R$80 to R$200 and are usually comfortable but not stylish, with decent beds, air-conditioning, hot-water bathrooms and cable TV. The top end runs from R$200 and up. Here you'll find spacious digs, with maybe a veranda, a pool in back and other amenities. Many midrange and top-end hotels have safes in the rooms for storing valuables. Note that R$200 buys you a lot less in pricier haunts, such as Rio, Salvador and Búzios than it does at smaller, less-visited towns.

In tourist centers, especially Rio, it's wise to make reservations during July (school holidays), and from Christmas to Carnaval. The same holds for any vacation mecca (eg Búzios, Ilha Bela, Morro de São Paulo) on weekends, and anywhere during major festivals. For prime peak times (eg Carnaval), try to make contact months ahead. Many places allow you to book online, which can save you 30% or more. In Rio you can score discount rates by booking through reputable local outfits, such as www.ipanema.com and riocharm.com.br.

Camping

Camping has limited popularity in Brazil but is a viable alternative in some parts of the country for those wanting to explore national or state parks. Obviously, you'll need your own tent and other necessary gear. The biggest concern is safety. Many camping grounds are near urban areas and it's unwise to camp in these spots, unless trustworthy locals have assured you it's safe.

The **Camping Clube do Brasil** (Map p138; ☎ 0xx21-2532 0203; www.campingclube.com.br, in Portuguese;

BOOK YOUR STAY ONLINE

For more accommodations reviews and recommendations by Lonely Planet authors, check out the online booking service at www.lonelyplanet.com/hotels. You'll find the true, insider low-down on the best places to stay. Reviews are thorough and independent. Best of all, you can book online.

29th fl, Rua Senador Dantas 75, Centro, Rio de Janeiro) operates several dozen camping grounds as far apart as Fortaleza and Porto Alegre. Check its website for info.

Hostels

Youth hostels in Brazil are called *albergues da juventude*. The HI-affiliated **Federação Brasileira de Albergues da Juventude** (FBAJ; www.hostel.org.br) has more than 90 hostels in the country, most with links on the website. There are also scores of private hostels. Rio is by far the country's hostel capital, with more than three dozen at last count. Quality varies considerably, but they're generally good places to meet Brazilian and foreign travelers.

A dorm bed in a FBAJ hostel costs between R$20 and R$45 per person. At HI-hostels, nonmembers usually pay around 20% extra, but you can buy an HI guest card for R$40 at many hostels and at youth hostel association offices in Brazil.

Hotels

Brazil's hotels range from the good, modern and luxurious, to shabby and moldy. At the more expensive places, taxes of 15% are often added to the price. Always ask for prices, as they're often lower than posted prices. Also it never hurts to ask *'Tem desconto?'* ('Is there a discount?'), which might net a small saving. Prices typically rise by 30% to 40% during the high season, and room rates double or even triple during Carnaval and around New Year's Eve. Hotels in business-oriented cities such as São Paulo, Curitiba, Porto Alegre and Brasília usually give discounts for stays on weekends.

Jungle Lodges

One popular type of remote-area accommodations is the jungle lodge, which caters to tourists in or on the edge of the forest. Though sometimes pricey, you're paying for the experience of lodging in the rain forest, rather than amenities – which are midrange at best. All the same, some lodges do have options for different budgets, eg an area for hammocks and shared toilets, and an area with private rooms with en suites. Naturally, the setting is considerably more exotic as is the architecture (they're usually made of wood and often stand on stilts). The largest number of jungle lodges are found outside of Manaus.

Pousadas

A pousada typically means a small family-owned guesthouse, though some hotels call themselves 'pousadas' to improve their charm quotient. Rustic pousadas can cost as little as R$60/90 per single/double and as much as R$500 for a lavish double – breakfast is typically included in these rates.

Rental Accommodations

It's possible to rent holiday, short- or long-term apartments through a number of sources. Real-estate agencies in most large cities will be able to provide information on rentals for foreigners. The best bet is to speak to other foreigners in Brazil to get an idea of current prices, which vary from city to city. In the classified real-estate sections of newspapers, apartments are usually listed under *temporada* or *apartamentos para aluguel*. If you just want a room in someone else's house or apartment, look under *vaga* or *quarto*.

DIRECTORY

Generally, an apartment that costs R$300 per week in Belo Horizonte will cost you two to three times that in Rio or São Paulo.

ACTIVITIES

Mountains, coast and sea all provide great opportunities for fresh-air adventure. The Portuguese-language website **360 Graus** (http://360graus.terra.com.br) covers a host of activities: canyoning, paragliding, kitesurfing or wakeboarding to rafting, surfing, trekking, diving or mountain climbing.

Climbing

Climbing in Brazil is best from April to October. You can be on the beach and then one hour later be on a world-class climb, 300m above a city. Brazil has lots of fantastic climbs, ranging from beginner level to routes yet to be conquered. Within 40 minutes of central Rio de Janeiro, the hub of Brazilian climbing, are some 350 documented climbs. The national parks of Serra dos Órgãos (p207) and Itatiaia (p201) and Caparaó (p271) have some particularly good climbs. For climbing in Rio, see p152.

Diving & Snorkeling

The *mergulho* (diving) here doesn't match the Caribbean, but is worthwhile if you're keen.

CLIMBING VOCABULARY

Although most Brazilians in the clubs know some English, a little Portuguese helps smooth the way.

baudrie – harness
corda – rope
dar segurança – to belay
equipamento – equipment
estar preso – to be secured
fenda – crack
fita – webbing
grampo – bolt
mochila – backpack
mosquetão – carabiner
pó de magnésio – chalk powder
queda – a fall
rocha – rock
tomar uma vaca – to make a stupid mistake and fall
topo – summit; also *cume*
uma agarra – a hold
via – route; also *rota*

You can arrange diving excursions or rent equipment in Rio (p155). Good dive spots are Arraial do Cabo (p211); the Reserva Biológica do Avoredo (p354), near Porto Belo in Santa Catarina state; Boipeba (p470); Ponta do Seixas (p549), near João Pessoa in Paraíba; and Fernando de Noronha (p539), perhaps the country's finest diving spot.

You can find superb snorkeling on Fernando de Noronha (p539); there's decent snorkeling on boat trips from Morro de São Paulo (p467), Maceió (p507) and Maragogi (p518), and in the waters of the Parque Nacional Marinho de Abrolhos (p491); for something truly extraordinary, plan a snorkeling trip in the crystal-clear rivers around Bonito (p428).

Fishing

Fishing in the interior of Brazil is fantastic. The Rio Araguaia in Goiás and Tocantins states is known as a fishing paradise with a large variety of fish, including the pintado, dourado and the legendary tucunaré (peacock bass) – which unfortunately is heavily fished and faces declining numbers. Fishing for piranha is not undertaken by serious anglers, though is good fun. Fishing is brilliant in the Pantanal (p413) too, and is allowed from February to October.

Hang Gliding & Paragliding

It's easy – and fantastic – to hang glide *duplo* (double) in Rio (p154). Paragliding (*parapente*) can be set up, too. Another place you can double hang glide is Rio da Barra, near Trancoso (p486) in Bahia.

Hiking

Hiking in Brazil is highly popular. It's best done during the cooler months of April to October. During the summer, the tropical sun heats the rock to oven temperatures and turns the jungles into steamy saunas. If you plan to hike in the Amazon, aim to come when the water levels are low (roughly August to December); at other times the forest is flooded and virtually all your activities will be by canoe.

There are lots of great places to hike in Brazil, both in the national and state parks and along the coastline, and especially in the Southeast and South. Plenty of good hikes are mentioned in the regional chapters. Outstanding areas include the national parks of Chapada Diamantina (p497), Serra dos Órgãos (p207) and Itatiaia (p201), PN Chapada dos Veadeiros (p399) and Caparaó (p271), as well as the Parque Estadual Marumbi (p322), Parque Nacional Serra do Cipó (p265), the Cambará do Sul in the Serra Gaúcha in Rio Grande do Sul (p369) and the Serra de São José (p259), near Tiradentes.

Horseback Riding

In Minas Gerais you can ride stretches of the old gold road, the Estrada Real, or take a five-day horse trek from the state capital, Belo Horizonte, to its most famous historic town, Ouro Prêto. Accommodations options in the Pantanal (p413) also offer riding in this attractive area.

Kayaking & Canoeing

There are some great places to get out on the water, paddle in hand, and take in the great Brazilian landscape. Foremost among them is the Amazon, where you can arrange dugout-canoe trips with many tour operators (see p655). You can also go kayaking off Ilha Grande (p188), on the Lagoa da Conceição on Ilha de Santa Catarina (p344), on excursions in the Pantanal (p413), and from Itacaré (p473) and other beach destinations in the Northeast.

For a different aquatic experience, grab an inner tube and launch down the Rio Nhundiaquara (p322).

Surfing

Surfing is very popular, and several Brazilian professionals are usually to be found in the top 20 of the world rankings.

There's surf virtually all along the coast, with particularly good waves in the South. The best surf beaches are in Santa Catarina state and the Brazilian championships are held here at Praia da Joaquina (p344), on Ilha de Santa Catarina. São Francisco do Sul (p352), Ilha do Mel (p424), Ubatuba (p305), Ilhabela (p307), Maresias (p309) and the Boiçucanga area (p309) all serve up good waves.

There's also excellent surf just outside of Rio (see p154 and p153) and a within a day's travel of the city in Saquarema (p210), Búzios (p214) and Ilha Grande (p186). The waves are best in the Brazilian winter (from June to August).

On other beaches surfing is still a way of life – even in Espírito Santo state with its

---

SURFING VOCABULARY

Despite their reputation for aggressiveness in the water, once on land Brazilian surfers are fairly keen on meeting foreign surfers and hearing about their travels. Some are even willing to lend you a board if you ask politely.

body board – boogic board
onda – wave
Pode me emprestar sua prancha por favor? – Could I borrow your board please?
prancha – surfboard
quebrar – to break
surfista – surfer
Tem ondas? – Are there any waves?
Vamos pegar ondas. – Let's go surfing.
vento – wind

---

breaks of 1m to 3m – boogie boarding is popular too. Renting boards can be difficult outside of popular tourist areas, though. If you plan to do a lot of surfing in less traveled places, you'll need to bring your own board.

Further to the north, Itacaré (p473), Sítio (p466), Porto de Galinhas (p536) and Fernando de Noronha (p539) are among the better spots.

A curious event is the national *pororoca* (tidal bore) surf championship held at São Domingos do Capim (p618) at the time of the full moon nearest the March equinox. The waves here are formed by the tidal bore on a tributary of the Rio Amazonas, a long way from the ocean. Waves can reach a few meters in height.

Windsurfing

Windsurfing has caught on in Brazil. In Rio you can rent equipment at Barra da Tijuca, but there are better conditions, and again equipment to rent northeast of Rio at Búzios (p214). In São Paulo state there's good windsurfing at Ilhabela (p307) and around Boiçucanga (p309). But Brazil's hardcore windsurfing mecca can be found much further north, along the Ceará coast, northwest of Fortaleza, where constant, regular, strong trade winds blow from July to December. Jericoacoara (p578) is one of the best spots in the country for windsurfing. Near Fortaleza, the beaches of Praia do Futuro (p570) and Praia de Iracema (p570) are also popular spots.

TOP PICKS FOR CHILDREN & FAMILIES

With beautiful beaches and verdant rain forests, Brazil has some pretty obvious appeal for the younger set. For top kids' picks in Rio, see p158.

Coastal Highlights

Itaúnas State Park (p222; Espírito Santo) Nature-minded kids and adults alike will enjoy accompanying biologists on their daily trek down the beach to monitor sea turtle nests.

Ilha Grande (p186; west of Rio de Janeiro) A tropical rain-forest-covered island, an old abandoned prison, boat trips, snorkeling, lovely beaches, howler monkeys – and all of it completely free from traffic. What more could a kid (or a parent for that matter) want?

Balneário Camboriu (p353; Santa Catarina) This resort town has many attractions for kids, including an aerial tram, beaches, a roller coaster, with proximity to the Beto Carrero World amusement park (p353).

Porto Belo (p354; Santa Catarina) Another laid-back resort spot in the South, Porto Belo has lovely snorkeling, plus a scenic nature reserve and eco-museum at an island just offshore.

Maragogi (p518; Alagoas) A fine destination for snorkeling in natural pools off the coast.

Arraial d'Ajuda (p484; Bahia) This low-key beach-lovers town has the usual coastal attractions, plus you can rent a buggy for exploring sandy coastal paths around the area.

Jungle Highlights

Foz do Iguaçu & Around (p328; Paraná) The thundering waterfalls are quite family-friendly, with discount entrances for kids to the falls, and kids stay and eat free all over town; there are also various wildlife adventures, boating activities, plus the jaw-dropping falls themselves.

Serra Verde Express (p321; Paraná) This memorable train ride traverses lush forests with sweeping views down to the coast.

Jardim Zoológico (p291; São Paulo) Brazil's largest zoo is home to some 3000 animal species and is spread out over some 900 hectares, much of which is old-growth Mata Atlântica (Atlantic rain forest).

Ecoparque de Una (p479; Bahia) Take a guided walk along a 2km trail that includes several treetop canopy walkways in the wildlife-rich Atlantic rain forest.

Bonito (p428; Mato Grosso do Sul) One of nature's wondrous playgrounds, Bonito has caves, lush rain forests, treetop canopy walks and crystal-clear rivers that you snorkel/float idly down, taking in the array of amazing aquatic life.

Amazon Tree Climbing (p657; Manaus) A chance for folks of all ages to have an up-close look at the Amazon's magnificent rain forest canopy.

Jungle Lodges (p658) Many jungle lodges near Manaus are very accessible and offer fairly low-impact excursions, making them good for families with kids. High-water season may be best, as you do more canoeing than hiking. Black-water areas have far fewer mosquitoes and much lower risk of malaria.

Other Highlights

Inhotim Art Museum (p241; west of Belo Horizonte) Not your standard art museum, Inhotim has vast outdoor spaces where kids can roam free, and the exhibits are eclectic enough so that there's generally something for younger audiences to connect with.

Caldas Novas (p398; Goiás) This upmarket hot-springs resort is a kid friendly (but not so wallet-friendly) destination in the Central West complete with thermal pools and an extravagant water park.

Bosque da Ciência (p647; Manaus) and the **Museu Emílio Goeldi & Parque Zoobotánico** (p609; Belém) are two excellent places to see the animals of the Amazon.

BUSINESS HOURS

Most shops and government services (including post offices) are open from 9am to 6pm Monday to Friday and 9am to 1pm Saturday. Shopping malls usually stay open till 10pm Monday to Saturday, and some even open on Sunday (usually late, from 3pm to 9pm). Because many Brazilians have little free time during the week, Saturday morning is often spent shopping.

Restaurants usually open from noon till 2:30pm and from 6pm till 10pm; aside from juice stands and cafés. Few restaurants open for breakfast, but those that do generally serve it between 8am and 10:30am. Bars typically open 7pm to 2am – until 4am on weekends.

Banks, always in their own little world, are generally open from 9am or 10am to 2pm or 3pm Monday to Friday.

CHILDREN

Brazilians generally love well behaved children, who are welcome at nearly all hotels, cafés and restaurants. Many hotels let children stay free, although the age limit varies. Babysitters are readily available, and most restaurants will be able to provide high chairs. The common bond shared by all parents of all nationalities will often bring you that welcome extra personal contact and attention from Brazilians.

Apart from the obvious attractions for children of beaches, coasts and swimming pools in Brazil, you can also find excellent special attractions in many areas, such as amusement parks, zoos, aquariums, and train and boat rides (see the Index, p753).

Diapers (nappies) are widely available in Brazil, but you may not easily find creams, baby foods or familiar medicines if you are outside larger cities.

See p712 for information on special bureaucratic requirements for unaccompanied travelers under the age of 18.

CLIMATE CHARTS

For information about weather and seasonal patterns, see When to Go (p23).

COURSES

Aside from language instruction, very few courses are geared for foreigners. If you know a bit of Portuguese, you can join in classes of dance, percussion and capoeira. Rio and Salvador are the best places to find such activities.

For water sports, almost any of the surf and windsurf schools on Ilha da Santa Catarina can arrange English-speaking instructors; the scuba diving schools in Porto Belo also have instructors who speak English.

Cooking

You can learn how to prepare some iconic Brazilian dishes (moqueca, feijoada) and expert caipirinhas at a half-day class in English offered by Cook in Rio (see p157). Best of all, you get to enjoy the fruits of your labors. Another fine place for travelers to learn the art of Brazilian cooking is at the Academia de Cozinha e Outros Prazeres (p196) in Paraty.

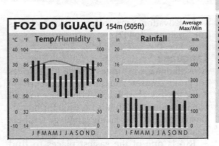

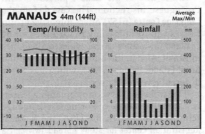

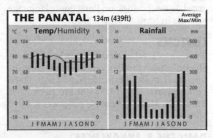

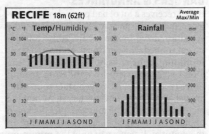

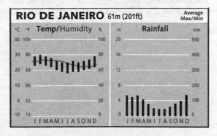

In Salvador, Senac offers cooking classes for foreigners (p447).

Language

Most language institutes charge high prices for group courses. You can often find a private tutor for less. Hostels are a good place to troll for instructors, with ads on bulletin boards posted by native-speaking language teachers available for hire.

Rio is one of the easiest places to find Portuguese instruction. The **Casa do Caminho Language Centre** (p157) offers intensive group classes with profits going toward the **Casa do Caminho** (www.casadocaminhobrasil.org) orphanages in Brazil. Also in Rio is the respected **Instituto Brasil-Estados Unidos** (p157), which has three different levels of classes.

The website, www.onestoplanguage.net, has a small database of Portuguese-language schools in Brazil. In the USA, the **National Registration Center for Study Abroad** (www.nrcsa .com) has information on Portuguese language schools in some Brazilian cities.

CUSTOMS

Travelers entering Brazil can bring in 2L of alcohol, 400 cigarettes, one personal computer, video and still camera. Newly purchased goods worth up to US$500 are permitted duty-free. Meat and cheese products are not allowed.

DANGERS & ANNOYANCES

Brazil receives a lot of bad press about its violence and high crime rate. While undoubtedly sensationalized by the media, some tourists do get robbed while in Brazil, and you'll want to minimize the risks of becoming a victim. Don't start your trip by wandering around touristy areas in a jet-lagged state soon after arrival: you'll be an obvious target. Accept the fact that you might be mugged, pickpocketed or have your bag snatched while you're in the country. If you carry only the minimum needed for the day (neither too much nor too little), and don't try to resist thieves, you're unlikely to come to any real harm. Other tips:

- Don't come to Brazil with jewelry, iPods, expensive watches and other items you'll worry about.
- Don't dress like a gringo. Avoid wearing baseball caps, shiny sunglasses and black socks (Brazilians, like North Americans, wear white socks with sneakers). Dress down in casual clothes that blend in. Bermuda shorts, T-shirts, a pair of Havaianas and other clothes bought in Brazil are a good choice.
- Keep small change handy so you don't have to flash a wallet to pay bus fare.
- Don't wear a backpack when heading out sightseeing.
- Don't wander around with a camera in view – keep it out of sight. Consider carrying it in a plastic bag from a local store. Disposable cameras are less worry.
- Before arriving in a new place, get a map or at least have a rough idea of the area's orientation. Use taxis to avoid walking through high-risk areas.
- Be alert and walk purposefully. Criminals will hone in on dopey, hesitant, disoriented-looking individuals.
- Use ATMs inside buildings. When using any ATM or exchanging money, be aware of those around you. Robbers sometimes watch these places looking for targets.
- Check the windows and doors of your room for security, and don't leave anything valuable lying around. If you consider your hotel to be reliable, place your valuables in its safe and get a receipt.
- If you're suspicious or uneasy about a situation, don't hesitate to make excuses and leave, change your route, or whatever else is needed to extricate yourself.
- Don't take anything to city beaches except your bathing suit, a towel and just enough money for food and drinks. No camera, no bag, no jewelry.
- Don't walk along empty or nearly empty streets or into deserted parks.
- Don't wander into the favelas (shantytowns) unless you're with a trustworthy guide who really knows the area.
- Never carry any more money than you need for the specific outing you're on, and keep it discreetly stashed away in a money belt, sock, secret pocket or shoe. But always have enough cash on hand to appease a mugger (R$40 or so).
- If you have the misfortune of being robbed, slowly hand over the goods. Thieves are only too willing to use their weapons if given provocation.
- If something is stolen from you, you can report it to the police, but it can be an enormous hassle just to get a police report for your insurance company. The

---

GOVERNMENT TRAVEL ADVICE

The following government websites offer travel advisories and information on the security situation in Brazil and elsewhere.

Australian Department of Foreign Affairs (☎ 1300 139 281; www.smarttraveller.gov.au)
British Foreign Office (☎ 0845-850-2829; www.fco.gov.uk/travel)
Canadian Department of Foreign Affairs (☎ 1-800-267 6788; www.dfait-maeci.gc.ca)
US State Department (☎ 1-888-407 4747; http://travel.state.gov)

---

tourist police are the best equipped to deal with foreigners, but are rare outside of Rio.

Scams & Robbery Techniques

One of the biggest scams to watch out for is people hacking into your bank account after you use an ATM machine. There have been many reports of this by travelers throughout Brazil. When withdrawing money, try to use machines inside banks that get a lot of pedestrian traffic and always hide the number pad when you're inputting your PIN.

Distraction is a common tactic employed by street thieves in Brazil and elsewhere around the world. The aim is to throw potential victims off guard so that they're easier prey. It may be something as simple as asking you for a cigarette or a light so that you slow down and take your attention off other people around you.

There have also been reports of druggings, including spiked drinks. While you're temporarily unconscious or semiconscious as a result of some noxious substance being slipped into your beverage, you're powerless to resist thieves. If you start to feel unaccountably dizzy, disoriented, fatigued, or just mentally vacant not long after imbibing, your drink may have been spiked. If you suspect this to be the case, call for help, quickly extricate yourself from the situation and try to get to a safe place – your hotel room.

Exercise *extreme* caution when someone you don't know and trust offers you a drink of *any* kind or even cigarettes, sweets etc. If the circumstances make you suspicious, the offer can be tactfully refused by claiming stomach or other medical problems.

CUT-RATE TOUR OPERATORS & TOUTS

In Manaus, Cuiabá and other parts of the Amazon and the Pantanal, there's a major problem with freelancers and shady operators selling cut-rate tours that turn out to be ecologically unsound, awful and/or unsafe. As a rule never book a tour (or even accept help) from someone who approaches you unsolicited at the airport or on the street. Go directly to the offices in town, or book on their website ahead of time. For more tips on avoiding Jungle Trip Scams and choosing tour operators, see p658 and p416.

EMBASSIES & CONSULATES
Brazilian Embassies & Consulates

The most important reason to contact your local Brazilian consulate is to inquire about visa matters; see p712 for more details.

Argentina (www.brasil.org.ar)
Australia (www.brasil.org.au)
Bolivia (www.brasil.org.bo)
Canada (www.consbrastoronto.org)
France (www.bresil.org)
Germany (www.brasilianische-botschaft.de)
Paraguay (www.embajadabrasil.org.py)
UK (www.brazil.org.uk)
Uruguay (www.brasil.org.uy)
USA (www.brasilemb.org)

Embassies & Consulates in Brazil

The embassies are all in Brasília, but many countries have consulates in Rio and São Paulo, and often other cities as well. For addresses in Brasília, SES stands for Setor de Embaixadas Sul.

Argentina Brasília (off Map p378; ☎ 0xx61-3364 7600; www.brasil.embajada-argentina.gov.ar; SHIS Quadra 2, Conj 01, Casa 19, Lago Sul, Brasília); Foz do Iguaçu (Map p329; ☎ 0xx45-3574 2969; Rua Dom Pedro II 28, Foz do Iguaçu; ✒ 10am-2:30pm Mon-Fri); Porto Alegre (☎ 0xx51-3321 1360; Rua Coronel Bordini 1033, Porto Alegre); Rio (Map p136; ☎ 0xx21-2553 1646; Praia de Botafogo 228, Room 201, Botafogo, Rio de Janeiro); São Paulo (☎ 0xx11-3284 1355; 9th fl, Av Paulista 1106, São Paulo)
Australia Brasília (Map p378; ☎ 0xx61-3226 3111; www.brazil.embassy.gov.au; SES, Av das Nações, Q 801, Conj K, Lota 7, Brasília); Rio (Map p138; ☎ 0xx21-3824 4624; 23rd fl, Av Presidente Wilson 231, Centro, Rio de Janeiro)

Bolivia Brasiléia (☎ 0xx61-3366-3432; SHIS, QL 19, Conj 13, Casa 19 Brasiléia; ☾ 8am-noon Mon-Fri); Brasília (off Map p378; ☎ 0xx61-3364-3362; SHIS, Q L-10, Conj 01, Casa 06, Lago Sul, Brasília); Corumbá (off Map p425; ☎ 0xx67-3231-5605; Rua Antônio Maria Coelho 881, Corumbá; ☾ 8:30am-1:30pm Mon-Fri); Guajará-Mirim (Map p682; ☎ 0xx69-3541 5876; 1st fl, Av Beira Rio 505, Guajará-Mirim; ☾ 8am-1:30pm Mon-Fri); Rio (☎ 0xx21-2551 1796; Room 101, Av Rui Barbosa 664, Botafogo, Rio de Janeiro)

Canada Brasília (Map p378; ☎ 0xx61-3424 5400; www .canadainternational.gc.ca; SES, Av das Nações, Q 803, l ote 16, Brasília); Rio (Map p134; ☎ 0xx21-2543 3004; 5th fl, Av Atlântica 1130, Copacabana, Rio de Janeiro); São Paulo (☎ 0xx11-5509 4321; 16th fl, Av Nações Unidas 12901, São Paulo)

Colombia Brasília (Map p378; ☎ 0xx61-3226 8897; www.embcol.org.br; SES, Av das Nações, Q 803, Lote 10, Brasília); Rio (☎ 0xx21-2552 6248; Room 101, Praia do Flamengo 284, Rio de Janeiro); Tabatinga (☎ 0xx92-3412 2597; Rua General Sampaio 623, Tabatinga)

France Brasília (Map p378; ☎ 0xx61-3222 3999; www .ambafrance-br.org; SES, Av das Nações, Q 801, Lote 04, Brasília); Rio (Map p138; ☎ 0xx21-3974 6699; 6th fl, Av Presidente Antônio Carlos 58, Rio de Janeiro)

Germany Brasília (Map p378; ☎ 0xx61-3442 7000; www.brasilia.diplo.de; SES, Av das Nações, Q 807, Lote 25, Brasília); Rio (☎ 0xx21-2554 0004; Rua Presidente Carlos de Campos 417, Laranjeiras, Rio de Janeiro)

Guyana Brasília (Map p378; ☎ 0xx61-3248 0874; SHIS Quadra 5, Conj 19, Casa 24, Brasília)

Ireland Rio honorary consulate (☎ 0xx21-2501 8455; Rua 24 de Maio 347, Riachuelo, Rio de Janeiro)

Israel Brasília (Map p378; ☎ 2105 0500; SES, Av das Nações, Q 809, Lote 38, Brasília)

Netherlands Brasília (Map p378; ☎ 0xx61-3961 3200; www.mfa.nl; SES, Av das Nações, Quadra 801, Lote 05, Brasília); Rio (☎ 0xx21-2157 5400; 10th fl, Praia de Botafogo 242, Rio de Janeiro)

New Zealand São Paulo (☎ 0xx11-3288 0307; 15th fl, Alameda Campinas 579, São Paulo)

Paraguay Brasília (Map p378; ☎ 0xx61-3242 3732; SES, Av das Nações, Quadra 811, Lote 42, Brasília); Foz do Iguaçu (Map p329; ☎ 0xx45-3523-2898; Rua Marechal Deodoro da Fonseca 901, Foz do Iguaçu; ☾ 8:30am-4:30pm Mon-Fri); Rio (☎ 0xx21-2553-2294; 2nd fl, Praia de Botafogo 242, Rio de Janeiro)

Peru Brasília (Map p378; ☎ 0xx61-3242 9933; www. embperu.org.br; SES, Av das Nações, Quadra 811, Lote 43, Brasília); Rio (☎ 0xx21-2551-9596; 2nd fl, Av Rui Barbosa 314, Flamengo, Rio de Janeiro)

Spain Brasília (Map p378; ☎ 0xx61-3244 2121; SES, Av das Nações, Quadra 811, Lote 44, Brasília); Rio (☎ 0xx21-2543 3200; Rooms 1601 & 1612, Rua Lauro Müller 116, Torre Rio Sul, Botafogo, Rio de Janeiro)

UK Brasília (Map p378; ☎ 0xx61-3329 2300; www .reinounido.org.br; SES, Av das Nações, Quadra 801, Conj K, Lote 08, Brasília); Rio (Map p136; ☎ 0xx21-2555 9600; 2nd fl, Praia do Flamengo 284, Flamengo, Rio de Janeiro); São Paulo (☎ 0xx11-3094 2700; 2nd fl, Rua Fereira de Arauja 741, Pinheiros, São Paulo)

Uruguay Brasília (Map p378; ☎ 0xx61-3322 1200; www .emburuguai.org.br; SES Av das Nações, Quadra 803, Lote 14, Brasília); Porto Alegre (☎ 0xx51-3224 3499; Rua Siqueira Campos 1171, Porto Alegre); Rio (☎ 0xx21-2553 6030; 6th fl, Praia de Botafogo 242, Rio de Janeiro)

USA Brasília (Map p378; ☎ 0xx61-3312 7000; www.embaixada-americana.org.br; SES, Av das Nações, Quadra 801, Lote 3, Brasília); Rio (Map p138; ☎ 0xx21-3823 2000; www.consuladodoseua-rio.org. br; Av Presidente Wilson 147, Rio de Janeiro); Salvador (☎ 0xx71-3113 2090; Salvador Trade Center, sala 1401, Torre Sul, Ave Tancredo Neves 1632, Salvador); São Paulo (Map p378; ☎ 0xx11-5186 7000; http://saopaulo .usconsulate.gov; Rua Henri Dunant 500, Chácara Santo Antônio, São Paulo)

Venezuela Boa Vista (Map p671; ☎ 0xx95-3623 9285; cnr Av Benjamin Constant & Rua Barão do Rio Branco; ☾ 8am-noon Mon-Fri); Brasília (Map p378; ☎ 0xx61-3322 1011; SES, Av das Nações, Quadra 803, Lote 13, Brasília); Manaus (☎ 0xx92-3233-6004; Rua Ferreira Pena 179, Centro, Manaus); Rio (☎ 0xx21-3552 6699; 5th fl, Praia de Botafogo 242, Rio de Janeiro)

FOOD

Check out Food & Drink (p85) for more details on Brazil's culinary breadth. Where we have divided our eatery reviews into different price ranges, you can expect a main course to cost less than R$12 in a budget eatery, R$12 to R$25 in a midrange one and more than R$25 in a top-end restaurant.

GAY & LESBIAN TRAVELERS

Brazilians are pretty laid-back when it comes to most sexual issues, and homosexuality is more accepted here than in any other part of Latin America. That said, the degree to which you can be out in Brazil varies greatly by region, and in some smaller towns discrimination is prevalent.

Rio is the gay capital of Latin America, though São Paulo and to a lesser extent Salvador also have lively scenes. Gay bars in Brazil are all-welcome affairs attended by GLS (Gays, Lesbians e Simpatizantes), a mixed heterosexual and homosexual crowd far more concerned with dancing and having a good time than anything else. For details on gay life in Rio de Janeiro, see p177.

There is no law against homosexuality in Brazil, and the age of consent is 18, the same as for heterosexuals. In Salvador the **Grupo Gay da Bahia** (Map p440; ☎ 0xx71-3322 2552; www.ggb.org.br, in Portuguese; Rua Frei Vicente 24, Pelourinho) is a gay lobbying group that provides assistance and information to the local gay and lesbian community.

Gay Travel Brasil (☎ 0xx21 3415-3126; www.gaytravelbrasil.com; Rua Sergipe 57, Rio de Janeiro), a gay-owned travel agency in Rio and São Paulo arranges customized trips, language instruction and cruises; staff also work with gay-owned and gay-friendly guesthouses and properties throughout Brazil.

The **Rio Gay Guide** (www.riogayguide.com) is an excellent resource for gay and lesbian travelers in Rio.

HOLIDAYS

April 19, the **Dia do Índio** (Indigenous Day), is not a national holiday, but it is marked by festivities in indigenous villages around the country. For major festivals in Brazil, see p28.

The official national holidays consist of the following:

New Year's Day January 1 – officially the Day of Universal Confraternization

Carnaval February/March – the two days before Ash Wednesday, which falls 46 days before Easter Sunday

Good Friday & Easter Sunday March/April

Tiradentes Day April 21 – in honor of Tiradentes (see p44)

May Day/Labor Day May 1

Corpus Christi Late May/June – 60 days after Easter Sunday

Independence Day September 7

Day of NS de Aparecida October 12 – holiday of Brazil's religious patron

All Souls' Day November 2

Proclamation of the Republic November 15

Christmas Day December 25

INSURANCE

A travel-insurance policy to cover theft, loss and medical problems is a good idea. The policies handled by STA Travel and other student travel organizations are usually good value. Some policies offer lower and higher medical-expense options; the higher ones are chiefly for countries, such as the USA, that have extremely high medical costs. There is a wide variety of policies available, so check the fine print.

Some policies specifically exclude 'dangerous activities,' which can include scuba diving, motorcycling and even hiking. Note that a locally acquired motorcycle license is not valid under some policies.

You may prefer a policy that pays doctors or hospitals directly rather than you having to pay on the spot and claim later. If you have to claim later, make sure you keep all documentation.

Some policies ask you to call back (reverse charges) to a center in your home country for immediate assessment of your problem.

Check that the policy covers ambulances or an emergency flight home.

INTERNET ACCESS

Many hostels, midrange hotels and top-end options in cities such as Rio, São Paulo and Salvador provide high-speed internet access from your room, and wi-fi is increasingly common. Internet cafés are also a good option for getting online, and these are widespread across the country. Most places in the South and Southeast charge between R$4 and R$8 an hour; elsewhere (Amazon, Northeast, Central West) charges typically run R$3 to R$5 per hour.

LEGAL MATTERS

If something is stolen from you, you can report it to the police. No big investigation is going to occur, but you will get a police report to give to your insurance company. The police, however, aren't always to be trusted. Brazilian police have on occasion planted drugs and stung gringos for bribes.

Speaking of drugs, the penalties for possession are harsh, and drugs provide a perfect excuse for some police to extract from you a fair amount of money; you don't want to end up in a Brazilian prison. If you are arrested, know that you have the right to remain silent, and that you are innocent until proven guilty. You also have a right to be visited by your lawyer or a family member.

Police checkpoints along the highways stop cars and buses at random. Some are even set up outside nightclubs to stop taxis and give the full pat down to club-goers on their way home (hint, don't carry anything!). Police along the coastal drive from Rio to Búzios and Rio to São Paulo are notorious for hassling young people and foreigners. Border areas are also a danger, particularly around the Bolivian border.

A large amount of cocaine is smuggled out of Bolivia and Peru through Brazil. Be very careful with drugs. If you're going to buy, don't buy from strangers and don't carry anything around with you.

Marijuana is plentiful in Brazil and very illegal. Nevertheless, it's widely used, and, like many other things in Brazil, everyone except the military and the police has a rather tolerant attitude towards it. Bahia seems to have the most open climate.

If you're coming from one of the Andean countries and have been chewing coca leaves, be especially careful to clean out your pack before arriving in Brazil. Sentences are stiff even for possession of coca leaves.

Because of the harsh penalties involved with possession or apparent possession, we advise you to stay away from it in any form.

MAPS

The best maps in Brazil are the Quatro Rodas series. These good regional maps (Norte, Nordeste etc) are available throughout Brazil. It also publishes the *Atlas Rodoviário* road atlas, useful if you're driving, as well as excellent street atlases for the main cities.

In the USA, **Omni Resources** (www.omnimap.com) is a good source of Brazil maps, publishing both paper maps as well as downloadable road maps for GPS. You can order online.

Good topographical maps are published by the **IBGE** (www.ibge.gov.br), the government geographical service, and the DSG, the army geographical service. Availability is erratic, but IBGE offices in most state capitals sell IBGE maps. Office locations can be found on the IBGE website. Telephone directories in many states include city maps.

MONEY

Brazil's currency is the real (hay-*ow;* often written R$); the plural is reais (hay-*ice*). One real is made up of 100 centavos. The real was introduced on a one-for-one parity with the US dollar in 1994; it experienced some fluctuations during its first decade, though since 2004 the real has proven to be a strong, stable currency. For exchange rates see the front cover of this book.

Banknotes are easy to distinguish from each other as they come in different colors with a different animal featured on each. There's a green one-real note (hummingbird), a blue two (hawksbill turtle), a violet five (egret), a scarlet 10 (macaw), a yellow 20 (lion-faced monkey), a golden-brown 50 (jaguar) and a blue 100 (grouper fish).

ATMs

ATMs are the easiest way of getting cash in big cities and are common. In many smaller towns, ATMs exist but don't always work for non-Brazilian cards. Make sure you have a four-digit PIN (longer PINs may not work). In general HSBC, Citibank, Banco do Brasil and Bradesco are the best ATMs to try (HSBC currently charges the lowest transaction fees). Look for the stickers on the machines that say Cirrus, Visa, or whatever system your card uses – though this may not mean the machine will necessarily work. Do take care when using ATMs; there have been a number of scams, where criminals have managed to hack into bank accounts of ATM users and subsequently drain them. See p703 for more info.

Bargaining

A little bargaining for hotel rooms should become second nature. Before you agree to take a room, ask for a better price. *'Tem desconto?'* (Is there a discount?) and *'Pode fazer um melhor preço?'* (Can you give a better price?) are the phrases to use. It's also possible to reduce the price if you state that you don't want a TV, private bathroom or air-con. There's sometimes a discount for paying *à vista* (cash).

You should also bargain when shopping in markets, and if you're about to ride in unmetered taxis arrange the price before departing.

Cash & Traveler's Checks

Cash might come in handy to keep on reserve, though you'll want to be exceptionally cautious when traveling with it. Traveler's checks, unfortunately, are impractical in Brazil, as few places will cash them and you won't receive very favorable exchange rates. You can try to change these in banks or in *casas de câmbio* (exchange offices). Banks have slower, more bureaucratic procedures but on the whole give better exchange rates (an exception being Banco do Brasil which charges R$40 commission for every traveler's check transaction). You'll usually get a 1% or 2% better exchange rate for cash than for traveler's checks. Checks, of course, have the advantage of being replaceable if lost or stolen.

Both cash and traveler's checks should be either in US dollars or euros, and Amex is easily the most recognized traveler's check. Thomas Cook, Barclays and Citibank traveler's checks are less widely accepted, but you should be able to cash them in large cities.

Credit Cards

You can use credit cards for many purchases and to make cash withdrawals from ATMs and banks. Visa is the most widely accepted card, followed by MasterCard. Amex and Diners Club cards are less useful. Visa cash advances are widely available, even in small towns with no other currency-exchange facilities; you'll need your passport, and the process can be time consuming, especially at the ubiquitous but bureaucratic Banco do Brasil. In Brazilian banks, generally it's preferable to deal with machines than to try to make contact with human beings. Credit-card fraud is extremely common in Brazil. Keep your card in sight at all times, especially in restaurants. Have them bring the portable machine to your table – don't give them your card.

Tipping

Workers in most services get tipped 10%. In restaurants the service charge will usually be included in the bill and is mandatory. If a waitperson is friendly and helpful you can give more. When the service charge is not included, a 10% tip is customary.

On jungle trips, it's customary to tip your guide at the end, and certainly appreciated if you can give a little to the assistant or boat operator(s).

There are many places where tipping is not customary but is a welcome gesture, and can make a big difference for low-wage earners such as hotel housekeepers. The local juice stands, bars, coffee corners, street and beach vendors are all tipped on occasion. Parking assistants receive no wages and are dependent on tips, usually R$2. Gas-station attendants, shoe shiners and barbers are also frequently tipped.

Most people round up taxi fares to the nearest real, but tipping is not expected.

PHOTOGRAPHY

Cameras will suffer on the road and they may get broken, lost or stolen. But there are so many good shots in Brazil that you'll kick yourself if you don't bring a camera along on your travels. If you're nervous about losing an expensive camera, disposable ones are readily available in most large cities.

Try not to carry a flashy camera bag – it may attract the attention of thieves – and make sure your equipment is insured.

Some Candomblé temples do not permit photography. Avoid taking photographs or a video in banks or near military bases or other sensitive areas.

Be respectful of the locals and always ask before taking photos – this applies to indigenous peoples in the Amazon, who may not feel comfortable being photographed or filmed.

Photographing in the rain forest is notoriously difficult. It pays to learn how to adjust the speed and aperture of your camera – even a digital point-and-shoot – to get the best shots in low light beneath the canopy.

Most cities have shops where you can download or print out digital images. Look for signs advertising Kodak, Fuji and other well-known brands. If you lose your camera, there are electronics stores just about everywhere. **Casa & Video** (www.casaevideo.com.br) has many branches in Rio state.

POST

Most post offices are open 9am to 6pm Monday to Friday, and Saturday morning. Airmail letters to the USA and Europe arrive in a week or so. For Australia, allow about two weeks.

Brazilian postal codes are five numbers followed by three; the first five are the code for the city, the others specify the location.

SHOPPING

Smart souvenir hunters can do well in Brazil, provided they know a little about Brazilian culture. Many people find the best souvenirs to be handicrafts, artwork, recorded music and fashion. Try to buy arts and crafts directly from the artist or artisan rather than giving most of your money to some guy simply because he has a storefront.

Glitzy, air-conditioned shopping malls – imaginatively called *shoppings* – are in every self-respecting medium-sized city, and São Paulo has scores of them. Browsing markets and small streetside stores yields, for better or worse, less predictable results.

Never buy products made from endangered plants or animals. In Brazil you may see souvenirs made from coral, turtle shell, rare bird feathers, caiman skin and bits of jaguar skin. Remember that these products are only sold because there is a tourist demand for them.

DIRECTORY

Art & Crafts

Although nearly everything can be found in Rio and São Paulo, there is a premium for moving craft and art pieces from the hinterland into the fancy stores of the big cities. Rio has excellent shopping (p180) at markets such as the Hippie Fair, the wild Feira Nordestina and the popular Babilônia Feira Hype. Among Rio's handicrafts shops (see p179), O Sol in Jardim Botânico, Pé de Boi in Botafogo and La Vareda in Santa Teresa, offer good selections.

Outside these big cities, your best bets for craftwork are artisan fairs – held on Saturday and Sunday in many cities – cooperative stores and government-run shops. The Northeast has a rich assortment of artistic items. Salvador and nearby Cachoeira are notable for their rough-hewn wood sculpture. Artisans in Fortaleza and the southeastern coast of Ceará specialize in fine lace. The interior of Pernambuco, in particular Caruaru, is famous for its wildly imaginative ceramic figurines.

Some Amazonian indigenous peoples now make artifacts such as bows, arrows, baskets, feather headdresses, carvings, pottery and beads specifically as commodities to sell. Some are very attractive, even if not quite the genuine article. Two excellent shops for authentic Amazonian/indigenous crafts, artwork and traditional items actually in the Amazon are Arariba (p631) in Alter do Chão and Galeria Amazônica (p653) in Manaus.

Gemstones

Gemstones are the most famous souvenir/luxury items from Minas Gerais. But if you're in the market for fine jewelry and precious stones, wait until you return to the big cities to make your purchases. Buy from a large and reputable dealer such as Amsterdam Sauer (p142) or H Stern (p142) in Rio. Stern is an international dealership based in Ipanema, and its reputation for quality and honesty is considered to be beyond reproach. It isn't a discount store, but its jewelry is less expensive in Brazil than at its outlets in other parts of the world.

Leather

Brazilian leather goods are moderately priced, but the leather isn't particularly supple. The better Brazilian shoes, belts, wallets, purses and luggage are sold in the upmarket shops of Ipanema and Leblon. Shoes are extremely good value, but many of the best are reserved for export, and larger sizes are difficult to find. Good-quality, cheap, durable, leather footballs with hand-stitched panels are sold all over Brazil in sporting-goods stores. (Inflated footballs should not be put in the cargo hold of a plane.)

In interior Pernambuco, the Sertanejos' curious traditional leather hats appeal to some travelers.

Music

Don't leave the country without buying some music. Rio has great music stores (p180), with plenty of used and new shops, places for DJs and open-air music markets. In other cities, your best bet for music may be the big malls. New-release CDs cost around R$30 in stores.

Brazil's variety of percussion, wind and string instruments make fun souvenirs and presents. You can often find inexpensive ones at craft markets as well as in music stores.

Other Purchases

Functional and decorative hammocks are available in cities throughout Amazonia. They're indispensable for travelers and make fine, portable gifts. A typical one-person hammock costs R$40 to R$70; a large *casal* (double) hammock might run around R$90.

Coffee-table picture books on Brazil, DVDs of Carnaval and of highlights of the national football team and Pelé in various World Cup matches are hawked in the streets of Copacabana – though better book selections are found in Ipanema bookshops.

Guaraná powder, a stimulant (said to be an aphrodisiac) derived from an Amazonian fruit, is sold by health stores, such as Rio's **Mundo Verde** (Map p134; ☎ 2257 3183; Av NS de Copacabana 630, Copacabana) and some pharmacies. In the Amazon region itself, there are plenty of shops and market stalls devoted to herbal and natural medicines. Belém's **Mercado Ver-o-Peso** (p608) and Manaus' Mercado Municipal Adolfo Lisboa (p653) are fascinating places to browse. One of Brazil's best food markets is the Mercado Municipal (p282).

A Brazilian *fio dental* (dental-floss bikini) is fun to have. Apart from this, Rio's Ipanema has dozens of shops selling stylish beachwear for men and women.

Candomblé stores are a good source of curios. They range from magical incense guaranteed to bring good fortune and increase sexual allure, wisdom and health to amulets and ceramic figurines of Afro-Brazilian gods.

SOLO TRAVELERS

On your own, you need to be alert about what's going on around you, and be particularly prudent about where you go. These are cardinal rules for solo female travelers.

Brazil is an excellent place to meet other travelers. There's a large network of hostels, and many towns that are particularly suited for meeting travel companions (Rio, Salvador and Jericoacoara topping the list). Language schools, group tours and volunteer work provide fine opportunities for mingling with travelers and locals.

Since double rooms often cost only slightly more than single ones, solo travelers face higher accommodations costs than others. If you're on a tight budget – or simply want to meet other travelers – the hostels are your best bet.

TELEPHONE
Domestic Calls

You can make domestic calls – intercity or local – from normal card pay phones on the street and in telephone offices. The phone cards you need are sold in denominations of 20, 50 and 90 units (costing between R$5 and R$20) by vendors, newsstands and anywhere you see advertising *cartões telefônicos.*

For calls within the city you're in, just slide the card into the phone, then check the read-out to see if it's given you proper credit, and dial the eight-digit number. Local fixed-line phone calls cost only a few units. For directory information, call ☎ 102.

For calls to other cities, you need to precede the number with 0, then the code of your selected carrier (see the boxed text, below), then the two or three digits representing the city area code. City codes are therefore usually given in the format 0xx digit digit, with the 'xx' representing the carrier code. A long-distance call usually eats up between five and 10 phonecard units per minute.

You need to include the city code (0xx digit digit) when calling to another city even if that city has the same city code as the one you're calling from.

To make a *chamada a cobrar* (intercity collect) call, stick a 9 in front of the 0xx. To make a local collect call, dial ☎ 9090 and then the number. A recorded message in Portuguese will ask you to say your name and the name of the state where you're calling from, after the beep.

International Calls

To phone Brazil from abroad, dial your international access code, then 55 (Brazil's country code), then the city code (omitting the initial 0xx), then the number.

BRAZILIAN CITY CODES & CARRIERS

Brazil has several rival long-distance telephone carriers. When making a long-distance call (either between cities or internationally), you have to select a carrier and include its two-digit *código de prestadora* (code) in the number you dial. Brazilian city codes are commonly quoted with an xx representing the carrier code, eg ☎ 0xx21 for Rio de Janeiro or ☎ 0xx71 for Salvador. You'll find city codes listed in this way beneath each city and many town heading in this book.

This construction may look complicated, but in practice it's straightforward. For one thing, you can use the main carriers, **Embratel** (☎ 21) or **Inteleg** (☎ 23) or **Oi Telemar** (☎ 31) for any call; for another, other major carriers usually have their names and codes widely displayed in their localities, particularly on public phones.

For example, to call from Rio de Janeiro to Fortaleza (city code ☎ 0xx85), in the state of Ceará, you dial 0 followed by 21 or 23 or 85 (the codes of the four carriers that cover both Rio and Ceará), followed by 85 for Fortaleza, followed by the number.

For an international call, dial 00 followed by either 21, 23 or 31 (the international carriers), followed by the country code, city code and number.

The following are Brazil's main carriers, which can be used calling to make intercity or international calls:

- Embratel   ☎ 21
- Inteleg   ☎ 23
- Oi Telemar   ☎ 31

The least-expensive way of calling abroad from Brazil is via **Skype** (www.skype.com), which you can access from internet cafés.

The cost of international calls from a traditional line in Brazil is pricey. Expect to pay a minimum of R$2 a minute and up to R$5 a minute to call internationally. Prices are about 20% lower during off-peak hours, which is typically from 8pm to 6am daily and all day Sunday.

To make an international call at your own expense, ordinary card pay phones – nicknamed *orelhões* (big ears; you'll soon understand why when you see one) – are of little use unless you have an international calling card.

If you don't have an international calling card, you can buy Embratel phonecards from newsstands and pharmacies (sold in denominations of R$20 to R$50). These have a bar on the back that you scratch off to reveal a code to enter along with the number you are calling. (Instructions are printed on the cards in English and Portuguese.) You can make calls from any phone. Rates are generally about R$2 to $4 a minute. Not all pay phones will work.

Another option is to find an internet or phone café, where you pay in cash after you finish talking (don't forget to establish the cost per minute before you call). Normally you'll be directed to a booth and will dial the call yourself. Country codes include the following:

Argentina ☎ 54
Australia ☎ 61
Bolivia ☎ 591
France ☎ 33
Germany ☎ 49
New Zealand ☎ 64
Paraguay ☎ 595
Peru ☎ 51
UK ☎ 44
USA & Canada ☎ 1
Venezuela ☎ 58

You can also make calls from your hotel or a private phone, but in hotels it's essential to attempt to establish beforehand what it will cost you. Hotels often charge astronomical rates.

For *a cobrar* (international collect) calls, dial ☎ 0800-703 2111 from any phone. Or try dialing the local operator (☎ 103 31 or 103 21) and asking to be transferred to a *telefonista internacional* (international operator). Since many operators do not speak English, you could experiment with some of the phrases in the boxed text, above.

USEFUL TELEPHONE PHRASES

I would like to make an international call to...
Quero fazer uma ligação internacional para...
I would like to reverse the charges.
Quero fazê-la a cobrar.
I am calling from a public (private) telephone in Rio de Janeiro. *Estou falando dum telefone público (particular) no Rio de Janeiro.*
My name is...   *Meu nôme é...*
The area code is...   *O código é...*
The number is...   *O número é...*

Be careful with services advertised by stickers on some phones announcing free calls to multilingual operators who can get you collect calls to the US or international credit-card calls. Make sure you establish the costs of any call before making it.

Cell (Mobile) Phones

Cell phones are ubiquitous throughout Brazil (103 million at last count). Known as a *celular* (often shortened to *cel*), a mobile phone has eight-digit numbers starting with a 9 or 8, and calls to them run through your phonecard units much faster than calls to regular numbers. Cell phones have city codes just like normal phone numbers (0xx digit digit), and if you're calling from another city you have to use them.

If you plan to use your own cell phone in Brazil, you have several options. To stay with your own carrier, and use roaming international minutes, you must have a 2G compatible device to 900 MHz/1800 MHz or a 3G compatible device to 2100 MHz frequencies that are used by the Brazilian network. Or, if you have an unlocked phone, you can purchase a prepaid SIM card in Brazil, and refill with extra minutes as needed. *Cartões pre-pago* (prepaid cards) to refill minutes are sold at newspaper kiosks throughout Brazil. Charges are high, typically running R$1.50 per minute for calls within Brazil. Brazil's major mobile carriers, offering the widest coverage, are Vivo, TIM and Claro. TIM generally has the best, most hassle-free service.

In several cities, you can rent a cell phone for around R$10 a day plus call charges, from agencies such as Rio-based **ConnectCom** (☎ 0xx21-2215 0002; www.connectcomrj.com.br).

TIME

Brazil has four time zones. Brasília time, which is GMT/UTC minus three hours, covers the whole of the Southeast (including Rio and São Paulo), South and Northeast regions, plus, in the Central West section, Distrito Federal (including Brasília) and the state of Goiás, and, in the Amazon, the states of Tocantins, Amapá and the eastern half of Pará.

The remainder of the Central West (Mato Grosso and Mato Grosso do Sul states) and the rest of the Amazon are one hour behind Brasília time (GMT/UTC minus four hours). The Fernando de Noronha archipelago, out in the Atlantic Ocean, 350km off Natal, is one hour *ahead* of Brasília time (GMT/UTC minus two hours).

Thus, when it's noon in London and 7am in New York, it should be 9am in most of Brazil, but 10am in Fernando de Noronha and 8am in Mato Grosso and the Amazon. We say 'should be' because daylight saving means that it usually isn't. Brazilian daylight-saving time runs from mid-October to mid-February, during which period clocks are advanced one hour – but only in the Southeast, South and Central West and the states of Bahia and Tocantins! And of course northern hemisphere daylight saving happens in the other half of the year, so in reality the time difference between Rio and New York is three hours in December and one hour in July. And the time difference between Rio and Manaus is three hours from October to February but two hours otherwise. Got that clear then?

Not surprisingly, Brazilians, as well as foreign travelers, sometimes don't know what time of day it is, and a lot of travelers have a few tales to tell about connections missed due to temporal ignorance.

Even when they do know the time, Brazilians can be somewhat lax regarding appointments. Don't be surprised, or angry, if they arrive a couple of hours later than expected.

TOILETS

Public toilets are not common but can be found at every bus station and airport and somewhere else in most cities and towns; there's usually an charge of around R$0.50 to R$1. Brazilians are generally nice about letting you use toilets in restaurants and bars. As in other Latin American countries, toilet paper isn't flushed. There's usually a nice smelly basket next to the toilet to put waste in.

TOURIST INFORMATION

Most tourist offices in Brazil are sponsored by individual states and municipalities. In many places, they have shoestring budgets that are chopped or maintained according to the whims (or feuds!) of regional and local politicians. Some tourist offices function only as a sinecure for politicians' relatives; others have dedicated, knowledgeable staff who care about tourism in their locality and are interested in providing information. Some offices are conveniently placed in the center of town; others are so far out of range that you'll spend an entire day getting there. Keep your sense of humor, prepare for potluck and don't expect too much!

Embratur (☎ 0xx61-3429 7777; www.braziltour.com; Setor Comercial Norte, Quadra 2, Bloco G, Brasília), the Brazilian tourism institute, has its headquarters in Brasília.

Outside of the country, Brazilian consulates and embassies (see p703) are able to provide limited tourist information, although the embassy in the UK actually has a dedicated tourist information section. Several Brazilian embassies and consulates provide useful tourist information on their websites.

TRAVELERS WITH DISABILITIES

Travelers in wheelchairs don't have an easy time in Brazil, but in the large cities there is a concerted effort to keep people mobile. Problems you'll encounter include immensely crowded public buses and restaurants with entrance steps. It pays to plan your trip through contact with some of the organizations listed following.

Rio is probably the most accessible city in Brazil for disabled travelers to get around, but that doesn't mean it's always easy. The metro system has electronic wheelchair lifts, but these aren't always operational. The streets and sidewalks along the main beaches have curb cuts and are wheelchair accessible but most other areas do not have cuts. Many restaurants also have entrance steps. For transport around Rio, contact **Coop Taxi** (Map p132; ☎ 0xx21-3295-9606).

Most of the newer hotels have wheelchair-accessible rooms, and some cable TV is closed-captioned.

Useful Organizations

The **Centro de Vida Independente** (Map p132; ☎ 0xx21-2512 1088; www.cvi-rio.org.br, in Portuguese;

DIRECTORY

Rua Marquês de São Vicente 225, Gávea) can provide advice for the disabled about travel in Brazil.

Those in the USA may like to contact the **Society for Accessible Travel & Hospitality** (SATH; ☎ 212-447 7284; www.sath.org). SATH's website is a good resource for disabled travelers. Another excellent website to check out is www.access -able.com.

VISAS & DOCUMENTS

Brazil has a reciprocal visa system, so if your home country requires Brazilian nationals to secure a visa, then you will need one to enter Brazil. At the time of writing, US, Canadian and Australian citizens need visas, but citizens of New Zealand, South Africa, the UK, Ireland and most other EU countries do not. Check with the Brazilian embassy or consulate in your home country before your trip.

Tourist visas are issued by Brazilian diplomatic offices. They are valid from the date you arrive in Brazil for a 90-day stay. They are renewable in Brazil for an additional 90 days. In most embassies and consulates, visas can be processed within 24 hours.

In many Brazilian embassies and consulates it takes only a couple of hours to issue a visa if you go in person (it's instant in some places), but the processing can take a couple of weeks or more if you do it by mail. You will normally need to present a passport valid for at least six months beyond your intended arrival date, a passport photograph, and a round-trip or onward ticket (or a photocopy of it) or a statement from a travel agent that you have it. If you don't have the ticketing requirements, having proof of means of support – such as credit cards or bank statements – may be acceptable.

If you decide to return to Brazil, your visa is valid for five years.

The fee for visas is also reciprocal. For most nationalities, a visa costs between US$20 and US$60, though for US citizens it's US$130 (which is what the US charges Brazilians for visas).

Applicants under 18 years of age who are traveling alone must also submit a notarized letter of authorization from a parent or legal guardian.

Business travelers may need a business visa. It's also valid for 90 days and has the same requirements as a tourist visa. You'll also need a letter on your company letterhead addressed to the Brazilian embassy or consulate, stating your business in Brazil, your arrival and

departure dates and your contacts. The letter from your employer must also assume full financial and moral(!) responsibility for you during your stay.

Depending on where you are coming from when you arrive in Brazil, you may need a yellow-fever vaccination certificate. On your arrival in Brazil, immigration officials sometimes ask to see your onward or return ticket and/or proof of means of support such as credit cards or traveler's checks.

Visa regulations change from time to time, and you should always get the latest information from your local Brazilian embassy or consulate (see p703).

Entry/Exit Card

On entering Brazil, all tourists must fill out a *cartão de entrada/saida* (entry/exit card); immigration officials will keep half, you keep the other. They will also stamp your passport and, if for some reason they are not granting you the usual 90-day stay in Brazil, the number of days will be written beneath the word *Prazo* on the stamp in your passport.

When you leave Brazil, the second half of the entry/exit card will be taken by immigration officials. Don't lose your card while in Brazil, as it could cause hassles and needless delays when you leave.

EXTENSIONS TO ENTRY/EXIT CARDS & VISAS

These are handled by Brazil's Polícia Federal (Federal Police), which has offices in the state capitals and border towns. You must apply before your entry/exit card or visa lapses, and don't leave it until the last minute. Tourist offices can tell you where the nearest Polícia Federal office is. When you go, dress nicely! Some Fed stations don't take kindly to people in shorts.

In most cases an extension seems to be pretty automatic, but sometimes you may not be given the full 90 days. The police may well require that you have a ticket out of the country and proof of sufficient funds, though this seems to be at the discretion of the officer. You may be told to complete a Documento de Arrecadeção de Receitas Federais (DARF; Federal Revenue Collection Document) form, which you have to buy from vendors outside the police station or from a *papelaria* (stationery shop). After filling it out, you must go to a bank and pay a fee of about R$100. You then return to the federal police with the DARF form stamped by the bank. The extension should then be routinely issued.

If you opt for the maximum 90-day extension and then leave the country before the end of that period, you cannot return until the full 90 days have elapsed. This doesn't usually apply to day trips across the border to towns such as Puerto Iguazú (Argentina) or Leticia (Colombia).

Passport

By law you must carry a passport with you at all times, but many travelers opt to carry a photocopy (preferably certified) when traveling about town and leave their passport securely locked up at their hotel. It's convenient to have extra passport photos for any documents or visas you may need to acquire in Brazil. Travelers from other South American countries can travel from country to country without a passport.

WOMEN TRAVELERS
Attitudes Toward Women

Depending on where they travel in Brazil, women traveling alone will experience a range of responses. In São Paulo, for example, where there are many people of European ancestry, foreign women without traveling companions will scarcely be given a sideways glance. In the more traditional rural areas of the Northeast, where a large percentage of the population is of ethnically mixed origin, blonde-haired and light-skinned women, especially those without male escorts, will certainly arouse curiosity.

Although machismo is an undeniable element in the Brazilian social structure, it is less overt than in Spanish-speaking Latin America. Perhaps because attitudes towards sex and pornography are quite liberal in Brazil, males feel little need to assert their masculinity or prove their prowess in the eyes of peers.

Flirtation – often exaggerated – is a prominent element in Brazilian male/female relations. It goes both ways and is nearly always regarded as amusingly innocent banter; no sense of insult, exploitation or serious intent should be assumed.

Safety Precautions

If you encounter unwelcome attention, you should be able to stop it by merely expressing displeasure.

Although most of Brazil is nearly as safe for women as for men, it's a good idea to keep a low profile in the cities at night and to avoid going alone to bars and nightclubs if you'd rather not chance your behavior being misinterpreted.

Similarly, women should not hitchhike alone or even in groups (even men or couples should exercise caution when hitching). Most importantly, the roughest areas of the North and West, where there are lots of men but few local women, should be considered off-limits by lone female travelers.

For health advice, see p731.

What to Wear

Once you've spent an hour or two in Copacabana or Ipanema, where some women run their errands wearing *fio dental* (dental floss – the famous skimpy bikini) you'll be aware that in some parts of Brazil, the dress guidelines aren't quite as strict as in others. What works in Rio will probably not be appropriate in a Northeastern city or in a Piauí backwater. It's best to adapt your clothing to local standards.

WORK

Brazil has high unemployment, and visitors who enter the country as tourists are not legally allowed to take jobs. It's not unusual for foreigners to find English-teaching work in language schools, though. The pay isn't great (if you hustle you can make around R$1500 a month), but you can still live on it. For this kind of work it's always helpful to speak some Portuguese, although some schools insist that only English be spoken in class. Private language tutoring may pay a little more, but you'll have to do some legwork to get students.

To find this type of work, log on to a Brazilian web server such as **Terra** (www.terra.com.br, in Portuguese) or **UOL** (www.radaruol.com.br, in Portuguese), and search for English academies. Also, look for 'Professor de Ingles' (English Teacher) in newspaper classified ads, and ask around at the language schools.

Volunteer Work

RíoVoluntário (☎ 0xx21-2262 1110; www.riovoluntario.org.br, in Portuguese), headquartered in Rio de Janeiro, supports several hundred volunteer organizations, from those involved in social work and the environment to health care. It's an excellent resource for finding volunteer work.

One notable volunteer organization you can get involved with is Rio-based **Iko Poran** (☎ 0xx21-2205-1365; www.ikoporan.org), which links the diverse talents of volunteers with needy organizations. Previous volunteers have worked as dance, music, art and language instructors, among other things. Iko Poran also provides housing for volunteers.

Elsewhere in Rio State, **Regua** (www.regua.co.uk; Reserva Ecológica de Guapi Assu) accepts volunteers from all over the world for reforestation and other conservation work. See also the boxed text, p208).

In the coastal enclave of Itacaré in Bahia, the Australian-owned **Brazil Trip Tour** (☎ 8157 5155; www.braziltriptour.com) is a recommended outfit that has opportunities for interested volunteers working in projects that they're most suited to – from teaching English to giving surf and other sporting classes.

The UK-based **Task Brasil** (www.taskbrasil.org.uk) is another laudable organization that places volunteers in Rio. Here, you'll have to make arrangements in advance and pay a fee that will go toward Task Brasil projects and your expenses as a volunteer.

The best website for browsing volunteer opportunities is **Action Without Borders** (www .idealist.org).

A little doorknocking can help you find volunteer work in Brazil. There's plenty of need, and many local welfare organizations will gladly find you some rewarding work. Ask around at churches and community centers.

International NGOs (nongovernmental organizations) work in all sorts of fields in Brazil, including environmental, medical and social-welfare projects. If you have some particular interest or skill, try contacting relevant organizations to volunteer your services.

Transportation

CONTENTS

GETTING THERE & AWAY

ENTERING THE COUNTRY

Most travelers start their Brazilian odyssey by flying into Rio, but the country has several other gateway airports as well as land borders with every country in South America except Chile and Ecuador.

AIR

Airports & Airlines

The most popular international gateways are Aeroporto Galeão (GIG) in Rio de Janeiro and São Paulo's Aeroporto Guarulhos (GRU). From both, connecting flights leave regularly to airports throughout the country. Salvador

---

THINGS CHANGE...

The information in this chapter is particularly vulnerable to change. Check directly with the airline or a travel agent to make sure you understand how a fare (and ticket you may buy) works and be aware of the security requirements for international travel. Shop carefully. The details given in this chapter should be regarded as pointers and are not a substitute for your own careful, up-to-date research.

(SSA) and Recife (REC) receive a few direct scheduled flights from Europe.

TAM is Brazil's main international carrier, with flights to New York, Miami, Paris, London, Lisbon and seven South American cities. The US Federal Aviation Administration has assessed TAM as Category 1, which means they are in compliance with international aviation standards.

Major airlines flying to/from Brazil are listed following. All phone numbers that begin with 0xx11 numbers are in São Paulo; numbers that begin with 0xx21 are in Rio; and numbers that begin with 4 can be called directly from any metropolitan area without prefixes. Some other airlines operating in South America are listed, p716. For Brazil's domestic carriers, see p719.

AIRLINES FLYING TO/FROM BRAZIL

Aerolíneas Argentinas (AR; ☎ 0800-707 3313; www.aerolineas.com.ar)

Aeroméxico (AM; ☎ 0xx11-3253 3888; www.aeromexico.com)

Air Canada (AC; ☎ 0xx11-3254 6600; www.aircanada.ca)

Air France (AF; ☎ 4003 9955; www.airfrance.com)

Alitalia (AZ; ☎ 0800-704 0206; www.alitalia.com)

American Airlines (AA; ☎ 4502 4000; www.aa.com)

Avianca (AV; ☎ 0xx21-2240 4413; www.avianca.com)

British Airways (BA; ☎ 4004 4440; www.britishairways.com)

Continental Airlines (CO; ☎ 0800-702 7500; www.continental.com)

COPA (CM; ☎ 0800-771 2672; www.copaair.com)

Delta Airlines (DL; ☎ 4003 2121; www.delta.com)

Gol (G3; ☎ 0300-115 2121; www.voegol.com.br)

Iberia (IB; ☎ 0xx11-3218 7130; www.iberia.com)

Japan Airlines (JL; ☎ 0xx11-3175 2270; www.jal.com)

KLM (KL; ☎ 0800-891 5024; www.klm.com)

Lan Chile (LA; ☎ 0800-761 0056; www.lan.com)

Lufthansa (LH; ☎ 0xx11-3048 5800; www.lufthansa.com)

Ocean Air (O6; ☎ 4004 4040; www.oceanair.com.br)

South African (SA; ☎ 0xx11-3065 5115; www.flysaa.com)

Swissair (LX; ☎ 0xx11-3049 2720; www.swiss.com)

TAM (KK; ☎ 4002 5700; www.tam.com.br)

TAP Air Portugal (TP; ☎ 0xx21-2131 7771; www.flytap.com)

United Airlines (UA; ☎ 0xx21-2217 1951; www.united.com)

Tickets

For high-season travel, roughly between mid-December and the end of February, tickets to Brazil cost about US$300 more than they do during the rest of the year.

INTERNATIONAL AIR PASSES

If you're combining travel in Brazil with other countries in southern South America, air passes can be decent value if you're covering a lot of ground in 30 days and don't mind a fixed itinerary. The TAM South America Airpass is valid for flights within Argentina, Bolivia, Brazil, Chile (except Easter Island), Paraguay, Peru, Uruguay and Venezuela. The cost is based on the number of standard air kilometres/miles you want to cover (prices range from US$339 to US$1236 for 3040km/1900 miles to 13,200km/8200 miles).

The Visit South America air pass offered by airlines of the **Oneworld Alliance** (www.oneworld.com) allows stops in more than 30 cities in 10 South American countries. Prices are calculated on a per flight, per distance basis (eg US$119 for 900km/560 miles, US$179 for 2050km/1280 miles and US$359 for 5600km/3500 miles).

The Gol Mercosul airpass is valid for travel on Gol's network, including routes between Brazil and Chile, Argentina, Paraguay, Uruguay, Peru and Bolivia. Fares are US$632 for four flights, US$772 for five flights; each additional flight is US$120.

For information on air passes for flights solely within Brazil, see p719.

IN BRAZIL

Rio de Janeiro is Brazil's most popular international gateway, and has many travel agents. For student fares, try the **Student Travel Bureau** (STB; ☎ 0xx21-2512 8577; www.stb.com.br; Rua Visconde de Pirajá 550, Ipanema), which has some 30 branches around the country. Discount agencies in São Paulo include **US Tour** (☎ 0xx11-3815 8262; www.ustour.com.br). Websites with cheap flights include www.passagembarata.net.

Australia & New Zealand

Lan Chile and several of its codeshare partners (including Qantas) fly from Sydney to São Paulo or Rio de Janeiro, stopping in Santiago, Chile; some flights also pass through Auckland. Round-trip fares start at A$3000. If you're planning a longer trip through Latin America, an open-jaw (into one city, out of another) or even an around-the-world ticket will be your best bet.

Canada

Airlines flying between Canada and Brazil include Canadian Airlines and Air Canada, but many routings are with US airlines, involving a change of planes in the US.

Continental Europe

A variety of European and Brazilian airlines fly direct to Rio and São Paulo. There are also less-frequent flights from Lisbon to destinations in the Northeast operated by TAP Air Portugal and its codeshare partners (including TAM). From Lisbon you can fly to Salvador, Recife, Fortaleza and Natal.

Fares are pretty similar from starting points across Western Europe, with fares to Rio or São Paulo starting at around €900, and usually several hundred euros more for most other destinations.

South America

In addition to flights between South American capitals and the major Brazilian cities, shortish cross-border flights provide alternatives to some overland routes into or out of Brazil. For more information on flights to other South American destinations, see the relevant sections of the towns and cities listed below.

Argentina Round-trip flights from Buenos Aires to Rio or São Paulo are available on Gol, TAM, British Airways or Aerolíneas Argentinas. Other flights from Buenos Aires go to Porto Alegre, Curitiba, Florianópolis and Puerto Iguazú in Argentina, a short cross-border hop from Foz do Iguaçu.

Bolivia Gol flies from Santa Cruz to Campo Grande. TAM and **Aerosur** (www.aerosur.com) fly from Santa Cruz to São Paulo. Inside Bolivia, Aerosur and **Aerocon** (www .aerocon.bo) fly from other Bolivian cities to Cobija, Guayaramerin and Puerto Suárez, across the border from the Brazilian towns of Brasiléia, Guajará-Mirim and Corumbá, respectively.

Chile Gol, TAM and Lan Chile fly between São Paulo and Santiago (Chile).

CLIMATE CHANGE & TRAVEL

Every form of transport that relies on carbon-based fuel generates CO_2, the main cause of human-induced climate change. Modern travel is dependent on aeroplanes and while they might use less fuel per kilometre per person than most cars, they travel much greater distances. It's not just CO_2 emissions from aircraft that are the problem. The altitude at which aircraft emit gases (including CO_2) and particles contributes significantly to their total climate change impact. The Intergovernmental Panel on Climate Change believes aviation is responsible for 4.9% of climate change – double the effect of its CO_2 emissions alone.

Lonely Planet regards travel as a global benefit. We encourage the use of more climate-friendly travel modes where possible and, together with other concerned partners across many industries, we support the carbon offset scheme run by ClimateCare. Websites such as climatecare.org use 'carbon calculators' that allow people to offset the greenhouse gases they are responsible for with contributions to portfolios of climate-friendly initiatives throughout the developing world. Lonely Planet offsets the carbon footprint of all staff and author travel.

Colombia Aero República and Satena fly from Bogotá to Leticia, from where you can walk, taxi or take a *combi* (minibus) across the border into Tabatinga, Brazil. Avianca and Gol fly direct from Bogotá to São Paulo. Flights to Rio usually stop in São Paulo as well.

The Guianas & Suriname A Brazilian regional airline, **Meta** (www.voemeta.com), flies from Georgetown (Guyana) and Paramaribo (Suriname) to Belém and Boa Vista. French Guiana carrier **Air Caraïbes** (www.aircaraibes.com) flies between Belém and Cayenne.

Paraguay TAM flies between São Paulo and Asunción (Paraguay) and Rio or São Paulo. Gol goes to Asunción from Curitiba as well.

Peru: TAM, Lan Chile, Taca and Gol fly from Lima to São Paulo.

Uruguay TAM, Gol and Pluna fly direct from Montevideo to São Paulo. Pluna also flies direct to Rio. Gol also flies direct from Montevideo to Porto Alegre.

Venezuela TAM flies direct from Caracas to São Paulo and Rio as well as via Manaus. Gol flies between Caracas and both Rio and São Paulo.

UK & Ireland

TAM and British Airways offer direct flights from London. Fares on average range from UK£750 to UK£900. You can often find cheaper fares on flights from Europe. At the time of writing, there were no direct flights from Ireland.

USA

Nonstop flights to Brazil arrive from New York, Los Angeles, Miami and Atlanta. Prices can range from US$800 to US$1200. If you don't want to arrive in Rio or São Paulo, you can also fly to Fortaleza and Recife, though you'll have to connect through São Paulo or Rio.

LAND

There's direct land access to Brazil from nine countries. Several border towns can also be reached by river from Bolivia or Peru – see p719 for details. If arriving overland from Colombia or Venezuela, you'll need to have a certificate of a yellow fever vaccine to enter Brazil (not to mention a visa!).

Bus

International buses travel between Brazil and Argentina, Paraguay and Uruguay, along decent roads. Prices of bus tickets between countries are substantially more than you'd pay if you took a bus to the border, crossed on foot and caught another on the other side, but you'll lose a lot of time that way. If arriving by bus, make sure your papers are in order. See p712 for information on visas and documents.

Car & Motorcycle

If you plan to take a vehicle into Brazil, see p721 for information on essential documents, road rules, and info on fuel and spare parts. At the border you will be asked to sign a bond called a *termo de responsabilidade*, which lists the owner's identification details and home address, destination, and description of the vehicle (make, model, year, serial number, color and tag number). You will also be asked to pay a bank guarantee (the amount to be determined by customs) and sign a statement agreeing that if you stay for more than 90 days, you will contact customs in the area where the entry was registered to apply for an extension for the permit. This must be presented to customs at the time of departure. If your vehicle overstays its permitted time in Brazil, it is liable to be seized and the bank guarantee forfeited. It's illegal to sell the vehicle in Brazil.

Border Crossings

ARGENTINA

The main border point used by travelers is Puerto Iguazú–Foz do Iguaçu, a 20-hour bus ride from Buenos Aires (see p332 for more information). Further south, you can cross from Paso de los Libres (Argentina) to Uruguaiana (Brazil), which is also served by buses from Buenos Aires.

Direct buses run between Buenos Aires and Porto Alegre (R$195, 18 hours) and Rio de Janeiro (R$325, 42 hours). Other destinations include Florianópolis (R$216, 25 hours), Curitiba (R$230, 34 hours) and São Paulo (R$285, 36 hours).

BOLIVIA

Brazil's longest border runs through remote wetlands and forests, and is much used by smugglers. The main crossings are at Corumbá, Cáceres, Guajará-Mirim and Brasiléia.

The busiest crossing is between Quijarro (Bolivia) and Corumbá (Brazil), which is a good access point for the Pantanal. Quijarro has a daily train link with Santa Cruz, Bolivia. Corumbá has bus connections with Bonito, Campo Grande, São Paulo, Rio de Janeiro and southern Brazil.

Cáceres, in Mato Grosso (Brazil) has a daily bus link with Santa Cruz (Bolivia) via the Bolivian border town of San Matías.

Guajará-Mirim (Brazil) is a short river crossing from Guayaramerín (Bolivia). Both

towns have onward bus links into their respective countries (Guayaramerín also has flights from there), but from late December to late February heavy rains can make the northern Bolivian roads a very difficult proposition.

Brasiléia (Brazil), a 4½-hour bus ride from Rio Branco, stands opposite Cobija (Bolivia), which has bus and plane connections into Bolivia. Bolivian buses confront the same wet-season difficulties.

CHILE

Although there is no border with Chile, direct buses run between Santiago and Brazilian cities (via Argentina) such as Porto Alegre (R$320, 36 hours), Curitiba (R$340, 54 hours), São Paulo (R$360, 54 hours) and Rio de Janeiro (R$370, 62 hours).

COLOMBIA

Leticia, on the Rio Amazonas in far southeast Colombia, is contiguous with Tabatinga, Brazil. You can cross the border by foot, Kombi van or taxi. From within Colombia, Leticia is only really accessible by air. Tabatinga is a quick flight (or a several-day Amazon boat ride) from Manaus or Tefé. See p653 for more details.

FRENCH GUIANA

The Brazilian town of Oiapoque, a rugged 560km bus ride (or a quick flight) from Macapá, stands across the Rio Oiapoque from St Georges (French Guiana). A road connects St Georges to the French Guiana capital, Cayenne, with minibuses shuttling between the two. (Get there early in the morning to catch one.) Another option is to fly directly from Belém to Cayenne, which if booked early enough can often be cheaper than ground transportation.

GUYANA & SURINAME

Lethem (southwest Guyana) is a short boat ride from Bonfim (Roraima, Brazil), a two-hour bus ride from Boa Vista. See p674 for details.

Overland travel between Suriname and Brazil involves first passing through either French Guiana or Guyana.

PARAGUAY

The major border crossing is Ciudad del Este–Foz do Iguaçu. Less convenient is the

---

BOLIVIAN ENTRY REQUIREMENTS

As of 2007, any US citizen entering Bolivia is required to have a visa, which costs US$135. Citizens from most other nations receive free 30-day entry. Although technically it's possible to obtain a visa at the border, it's wise to secure this beforehand – particularly if arriving overland as long delays are likely. Bolivian Immigration has a whole host of other requirements, including certificate of Yellow Fever vaccine, proof of financial solvency, and more. Visit www.bolivia-usa.org for the latest.

crossing between Pedro Juan Caballero–Ponta Porá. The latter gives access to the Pantanal. Direct buses run between Asunción and Brazilian cities such as Florianópolis (R$168, 22 hours), Curitiba (R$120, 14 hours), São Paulo (R$160, 20 hours) and Rio de Janeiro (R$210, 26 hours).

PERU
The only land access to Peru is via Iñapari, a five-hour minibus or truck ride north of Puerto Maldonado (Peru). This route is only open during the dry season. You wade across the Rio Acre between Iñapari and the small Brazilian town of Assis Brasil, a three- to four-hour bus or 4WD trip from Brasiléia.

URUGUAY
The crossing most used by travelers is Chuy-Chuí. This is actually one town, with the international border running down the middle of its main street. See p375 for details.

Other crossings are Río Branco–Jaguarão, Isidoro Noblia–Aceguá, Rivera–Santana do Livramento, Artigas–Quaraí and Bella Unión–Barra do Quaraí. Buses run between Montevideo and Brazilian cities such as Porto Alegre (R$170, 12 hours), Florianópolis (R$220, 18 hours) and São Paulo (R$295, 30 hours).

VENEZUELA
Roads from northern Venezuela go southeast to Ciudad Bolívar, Ciudad Guayana and Santa Elena de Uairén (p674), on the border near Pacaraíma, Brazil. From here, a paved road heads south to Boa Vista (215km) and Manaus (990km). Buses run to Manaus and Boa Vista from as far north as Venezuela's Puerto La Cruz. Santa Elena has buses to and from Caracas.

RIVER
Bolivia
From Trinidad in Bolivia you can reach Brazil by a boat trip of about five days down the Río Mamoré to Guayaramerín, opposite the Brazilian town of Guajará-Mirim (p685).

Peru
Fast passenger boats make the 400km trip (US$60 to US$90, eight to 10 hours) along the Rio Amazonas between Iquitos (Peru) and Tabatinga (Brazil). From Tabatinga you can continue 3000km down the river to its mouth. See p665 for more information.

GETTING AROUND

AIR
Because of the great distances in Brazil, the occasional flight can be a necessity, and may not cost much more than a long-haul bus journey. If you intend to take more than just a couple of flights, a Brazil Airpass (p719) will probably save you money. Book ahead if traveling during busy travel times – from Christmas to Carnaval, around Easter, July and August. Always reconfirm your flights, as schedules frequently change. See p720 for major air routes.

Airlines in Brazil
Brazil has two major national carriers, Gol and TAM, and many smaller regional airlines.
Brazil's main carriers:
Azul (☎ 0xx21-3296 2850; www.voeazul.com.br)
Gol (☎ 0800-280 0465; www.voegol.com.br)
Ocean Air (☎ 0300-789 8160; www.oceanair.com.br)
TAM (☎ 0800 570 5700; www.tam.com.br)
Trip (☎ 0800-789 8747; www.airtrip.com.br)
Varig (☎ 0xx11-4003 7000; www.varig.com.br)

Air Passes
A Brazil Airpass is a good investment if you're planning on covering a lot of ground in 30 days or less. Gol Airlines offers an air pass involving four/five domestic flights anywhere on its extensive network for US$532/672, and each additional flight costs US$120. TAM also offers an air pass, which gives you four flights for US$582 (US$532 if you fly TAM to Brazil). Additional flights cost U$160 each (US$120 if you fly TAM to Brazil).

Either of these passes must be purchased before you go to Brazil, and you have to book your air pass itinerary at the time you buy it – or possibly pay penalties for changing reservations. Many travel agents sell the air pass, as does the Brazilian travel specialist **Brol** (www.brol.com).

DOMESTIC DEPARTURE TAX
Embarkation tax on domestic flights ranges from R$8 to R$20, depending on the airport (the bigger the airport, the bigger the tax). If it isn't already included in the price of your ticket, you have to pay the tax in cash (reais) at check-in.

If for any reason you do not fly on an air-pass flight you have reserved, you should reconfirm all your other flights. Travelers have sometimes found that all their air-pass reservations had been scrubbed from the computer after they missed, or were bumped from, one flight.

Air Taxis

Many areas, especially Amazonia, feature air-taxi companies that will fly you anywhere their small planes can reach. You need to book the whole plane, and costs are high. Unfortunately these planes and the runways they land on aren't always maintained. You might think twice before booking one of these flights.

BICYCLE

You don't see many long-distance cyclists in Brazil. Crazy drivers who only respect vehicles larger than themselves, lots of trucks on the main roads spewing out unfiltered exhaust fumes, roads without shoulder room, long distances and the threat of theft are just some of the reasons for this. Long-distance cycling in Brazil is not recommended; it's a danger-ous thing to do.

If you're determined to tackle Brazil by bike, go over your bike with a fine-tooth comb be-fore leaving home and fill your repair kit with every imaginable spare part. There are several decent bike shops in Rio for buying equipment and gear – as well as renting bikes (which aver-age R$50 per day). See p154 for more details.

DOMESTIC AIR ROUTES

BOAT

The Amazon region is one of the last great bastions of passenger river travel in the world. Rivers still perform the function of highways throughout much of Amazonia, with passenger vessels of many shapes and sizes putt-putting up and down every river and creek that has anyone living near it. For more information on Amazonian River transportation, see p615.

Boats are also essential for getting around parts of the Pantanal and accessing islands and beaches along the Atlantic coast.

BUS

Bus services in Brazil are generally excellent. Departure times are usually strictly adhered to, and most of the buses are clean, comfortable and well-serviced Mercedes, Volvos and Scanias.

All major cities are linked by frequent buses – one leaves every 15 minutes from Rio to São Paulo during peak hours – and there are a surprising number of long-distance buses. Every big city, and most small ones, has at least one main long-distance bus station, known as a *rodoviária* (pronounced ho-do-vi-*ah*-ree-ya).

Bus service and road conditions vary by region. The South has the most and the best roads. Coastal highways are usually good; while the roads of Amazonia and the *sertão* (backlands of the Northeast) are quite bad. The Quatro Rodas *Atlas Rodoviário,* a very useful road atlas for any traveler, helpfully marks the worst stretches of road with lines of large Xs and classifies them as *estradas precárias*.

Brazil has numerous bus companies and the larger cities have several dozen rival agencies. Before buying a bus ticket from São Paulo or Rio de Janeiro to other destinations, be sure to shop around.

Classes

There are three main classes of long-distance bus. The ordinary *convencional* or *comum* is indeed the most common. It's fairly comfortable and usually has a toilet on board. An *executivo* is more comfortable (often with reclining seats), costs about 25% more and stops less often. A *leito* (overnight sleeper) can cost twice as much as a *comum* and is exceptionally comfortable. It has spacious, fully reclining seats with blankets and pillows, air-con, and more often than not, an attendant serving sandwiches, coffee, soda and *água mineral* (mineral water). If you don't mind missing the scenery, a *leito* can get you there in comfort and save you the additional cost of a hotel room.

With or without toilets, buses generally make pit stops every three or four hours. These stops are great places to meet other passengers, buy bizarre memorabilia, and load up on greasy plates of food.

Air-con on buses is sometimes strong; carry a light sweater or jacket to keep warm.

Costs

Bus travel throughout Brazil can be expensive; *convencional* fares average around R$8 to R$10 per hour. Sample fares from Rio are as follows: São Paulo (six hours), R$68/77/110 *convencional/executivo/leito;* Florianópolis (18 hours), R$176/199 *convencional/executivo;* Salvador (25 hours), R$225 *convencional;* Foz do Iguaçu (22 hours), R$210 *convencional;* Belém (52 hours), R$464 *convencional.*

Reservations

Usually you can go down to the bus station and buy a ticket for the next departing bus. If this is not the case (eg in Ouro Prêto), it will be mentioned in the relevant destination chapter. In general, though, it's a good idea to buy a ticket at least a few hours in advance or, if it's convenient, the day before departure. On weekends, holidays and from December to February, advance purchase is always a good idea. It's sometimes possible to buy bus tickets from travel agencies. Although they tack on a small commission, it will save you an extra trip out to the station. Ask at local tourist offices for agencies that sell bus tickets.

CAR & MOTORCYCLE

Especially in Rio, the anarchic side of the Brazilian personality emerges from behind the driver's wheel as lane dividers, one-way streets, sidewalks and pedestrians are disregarded.

Bringing Your Own Vehicle

All vehicles in Brazil must carry the registration document and proof of insurance. To take a vehicle in or out of Brazil, you might be asked for a *carnet de passage en douane,* which is kind of a vehicle passport, or a *libreta de pasos por aduana,* which is a booklet of customs passes; in practice these are not often required. Contact your local automobile association for details about all documentation.

Driver's License

Your home-country driver's license is valid in Brazil, but because local authorities probably won't be familiar with it, it's a good idea to carry an International Driver's Permit (IDP) as well. This gives police less scope for claiming that you are not driving with a legal license. IDPs are issued by your national motoring association and usually cost the equivalent of about US$10. It is illegal for foreigners to drive motorbikes in Brazil unless they have a Brazilian license.

Fuel & Spare Parts

Ordinary gasoline (called *combustível* or *gasolina*) costs around R$2.80 per liter. Travelers taking their own vehicles need to check in advance what spare parts and gasoline are likely to be available.

Hire

A small four-door car with insurance and unlimited kilometers costs around R$100 a day (R$130 with air-con). You can sometimes get discounts for longer rentals.

To rent a car you must be 25 years old (21 with some rental firms, including Avis), have a credit card in your name and a valid driver's license from your home country (not just an IDP).

Minimum insurance coverage is always tacked onto the cost of renting, though you can get extra protection (a wise idea) for another R$20 to R$40.

In Brazil, 4WD vehicles are hard to come by and can be quite expensive (over R$200 per day). Motorbike rental is even harder to find. Riders planning a long trip might have better luck purchasing a bike in the country and reselling it at the end of the trip.

Road Rules & Hazards

Brazil is a dangerous place to drive, with some 35,000 people killed in automobile accidents each year. Some roads are especially hazardous, such as the busy highways between Rio and São Paulo. This cult of speed is insatiable.

Owing to the danger of robbery, at night many motorists don't stop at red lights; they merely slow down. This is particularly common in São Paulo. In big cities, keep your windows closed and doors locked when stationary.

Driving at night is particularly hazardous; other drivers are more likely to be drunk and, at least in the Northeast and the interior, the roads are often poor and unreliable. Poorly banked turns are the norm. To save a bit of fuel, some motorists drive at night with their headlights turned to low-beam or turned off completely.

Brazilian speed bumps are quite prevalent. Always slow down as you enter a town.

Further headaches for drivers in Brazil are posed by poor signposting; impossible one-way systems; tropical rainstorms; drivers overtaking on blind corners; flat tires (common, but there are *borracheiros*, or tire repairers, stationed at frequent intervals along the roads); and, of course, the police pulling you over for bogus moving violations.

For security, choose hotels with off-street parking; most in the midrange and top-end range offer this option.

HITCHHIKING

Hitchhiking is never entirely safe in any country, and is not recommended. Travelers who decide to hitchhike should understand that they are taking a small but potentially serious risk. People who do choose to hitchhike will be safer if they travel in pairs and let someone know where they are planning to go.

Hitchhiking in Brazil, with the possible exception of the Pantanal and several other areas where it's commonplace among locals, is difficult. The Portuguese word for 'lift' is *carona*, so ask *'Pode dar carona?'* (Can you give us a lift?). The best way to hitchhike – practically the only way if you want rides – is to ask drivers when they're not in their vehicles, for example by waiting at a gas station or a truck stop. But even this can be difficult. It's polite to offer to pay for your share of the gas for your lift.

LOCAL TRANSPORTATION
Bus

Local bus services tend to be decent in Brazil. Since most Brazilians take the bus to work, municipal buses are usually frequent and their network of routes is comprehensive. Fares range from R$1.80 to R$2.30.

In most city buses, you get on at the front and exit from the back, though occasionally the reverse is true. Usually there's a money collector sitting at a turnstile just inside the entrance.

Crime can be a problem on buses. Don't take valuables onto the buses. See Dangers & Annoyances (p702) for more information.

Jumping on a local bus is one of the best ways to get to know a city. With a map and a few dollars you can get an overview of the town.

Metro

Both Rio and São Paulo have excellent metro systems with Rio's system being expanded for the 2016 Olympic Games. These metros are a safe, cheap and efficient way of exploring the cities. One-way fares cost around R$2.80.

Taxi

Taxi rides are reasonably priced, and are the best option for getting around cities at night. Taxis in cities usually have meters that start at R$4.30 and rise by something like R$3 per kilometre (more on nights and weekends). Occasionally, the driver will refer to a chart and revise slightly upwards. This reflects recent official hikes in taxi rates and the meter has not yet been adjusted.

In small towns, taxis often don't have meters, and you'll have to arrange a price – beforehand.

Some airports and bus stations have a system for you to purchase a fixed-price taxi ticket from a *bilheteria* (ticket office). At a few such places it's cheaper to go onto the street outside and find a cab that will take you for the meter fare or sometimes even less. If carrying valuables, however, the special airport taxi, or a radio taxi, can be a worthwhile investment.

If possible, orient yourself before taking a taxi, and keep a map handy in case you find yourself being taken on a wild detour. The worst place to get a cab is where the tourists are. In particular, don't get a cab near one of the expensive hotels. In Rio, for example, walk a block away from the beach at Copacabana to flag down a cab.

Moto-taxis (involving a ride on the back of a motorcycle) are another means of short-distance travel in places such as Rio.

TRAIN

Brazil's passenger-train services have been scaled down to almost nothing, though there are a few journeys well worthwhile taking. One outstanding trip goes from Curitiba to Paranaguá (see the boxed text, p321), descending the coastal mountain range with memorable views. The Belo Horizonte Vitória run (p241), via Santa Bárbara and Sabará, is also scenic.

Steam trains are affectionately known as Marias Fumaça (Smoking Marys), and several still run as tourist attractions. There's a 13km ride from São João del Rei to Tiradentes in Minas Gerais (see the boxed text, p257). Another pleasant short trip, this time by electric train, is the ride through the Serra da Mantiqueira of São Paulo state from Campos do Jordão to Santo Antônio do Pinhal, the highest stretch of track in the country (p313).

Health Dr David Goldberg

CONTENTS

Prevention is the key to staying healthy while abroad. Travelers who receive the recommended vaccines and follow commonsense precautions usually come away with nothing more dangerous than a little diarrhea.

Medically speaking, Brazil is part of tropical South America, which includes most of the continent except for the southernmost portion. The diseases found in this area are comparable to those found in tropical areas in Africa and Asia. Particularly important are mosquito-borne infections, including malaria, yellow fever and dengue fever, which are not a significant concern in temperate regions.

BEFORE YOU GO

INSURANCE
If your health insurer doesn't cover you for medical expenses incurred abroad, you'll need to get some extra travel insurance. Find out in advance if your travel insurer will make payments directly to providers or reimburse you later for overseas health expenditures.

RECOMMENDED VACCINATIONS
Since most vaccines don't produce immunity until at least two weeks after they're given, visit a physician four to eight weeks before departure. Ask your doctor for an International Certificate of Vaccination (otherwise known as the yellow booklet), which will list all the vaccinations you've received. This is mandatory for countries that require proof of yellow-fever vaccination upon entry, but it's a good idea to carry it wherever you travel.

MEDICAL CHECKLIST
Bring medications in their original containers, clearly labeled. A signed, dated letter from your doctor describing your medical conditions and medications (including their generic names) is a good idea. If carrying syringes or needles, take a physician's letter documenting their medical necessity.

INTERNET RESOURCES
There is a wealth of travel-health advice on the internet. For further information, the Lonely Planet website at www.lonelyplanet .com is a good place to start. The World Health Organization (WHO) publishes a superb book called *International Travel and Health,* which is revised annually and is available online at no cost (www.who.int/ith/). Another website of general interest is the MD Travel Health website at www.mdtravelhealth .com, which provides free, complete travel-health recommendations for every country and is updated daily.

It's usually a good idea to consult your government's travel-health website before departure, if one is available:
Australia www.dfat.gov.au/travel/
Canada www.phac-aspc.gc.ca
UK www.fco/en/travel-and-living-abroad/staying-safe/ health
US www.cdc.gov/travel/

FURTHER READING
For more detailed information on health matters, see *Healthy Travel Central & South America,* published by Lonely Planet. If you are traveling with children, Lonely Planet's *Travel with Children* provides useful advice. The *ABC of Healthy Travel* by E Walker et al is another valuable resource.

IN TRANSIT
DEEP VEIN THROMBOSIS (DVT)

Blood clots may form in the legs (deep vein thrombosis; DVT) during plane flights, chiefly because of prolonged immobility. The longer the flight, the greater the risk. Though most blood clots are reabsorbed uneventfully, some may break off and travel through the blood vessels to the lungs, where they could cause life-threatening complications.

The chief symptom of DVT is swelling or pain of the foot, ankle or calf, usually but not always on just one side. When a blood clot travels to the lungs, it may cause chest pain and difficulty breathing. Travelers with any of these symptoms should seek medical attention immediately.

To prevent DVT on long flights you should walk about the cabin, perform isometric compressions of the leg muscles (ie contract leg muscles while sitting), drink lots of fluids, and avoid alcohol and tobacco.

JET LAG & MOTION SICKNESS

Jet lag is common when crossing more than five time zones and can result in insomnia, fatigue, malaise or nausea. To avoid jet lag try drinking plenty of (nonalcoholic) fluids and eating light meals. Upon arrival, get exposure to natural sunlight and readjust your schedule (for meals, sleep etc) as soon as possible.

Antihistamines such as dimenhydrinate (Dramamine) and meclizine (Antivert, Bonine) are usually the first choice for treating motion sickness. Their main side effect is drowsiness. An herbal alternative is ginger, which works like a charm for some people.

IN BRAZIL
AVAILABILITY & COST OF HEALTH CARE

For an ambulance in Brazil, call ☎ 192, or an emergency number (listed following).

Good medical care is available in the larger cities, but may be difficult to find in rural areas. Medical care in Brazil may be extremely expensive. Most doctors and hospitals expect payment in cash, regardless of whether you have travel-health insurance.

The US embassy website at www.embaixada-americana.org.br has an extensive list of physicians, dentists, pharmacists, laboratories and

emergency services. If you're pregnant, be sure to check this site before departure to find the name of one or two obstetricians in the area you'll be visiting, just in case.

The **Einstein Hospital** (☎ emergencies 55-11-3747 0200, ambulance & air ambulance 0xx11-3747 1000/1100; Av Albert Einstein 627, Morumbi) in São Paulo is used by expatriates throughout Brazil, including US government personnel. English is also spoken at **Hospital Sírio-Libânes** (Map p281; ☎ information 0xx11-2344 8877, ambulance 0xx11-826 0111 or 926 0400; Rua da Adma Jafet 91, Bela Vista) in São Paulo.

If you develop a medical emergency while in Rio, the best hospital for foreigners is the **Clínica Galdino Campos** (Map p134; ☎ 0xx21-2548 9966; www.galdinocampos.com.br; Av NS de Copacabana 492, Copacabana; � 24hr). Here you'll find high-quality care and multilingual doctors (who even make house calls); and the clinic works with most international health plans and travel insurance policies.

If you develop a life-threatening medical problem, you'll probably want to be evacuated to a country with state-of-the-art medical care. Since this may cost tens of thousands of dollars, be sure you have insurance to cover this before you depart. You can find a list of medical-evacuation and travel-insurance companies on the US State Department website at www.travel.state.gov/medical.html.

Each Brazilian pharmacy has a licensed pharmacist. Most are well supplied. Many medications that require prescriptions in the US are available over the counter in Brazil. If you're taking medication on a regular basis, be sure you know its generic (scientific) name, since many pharmaceuticals go under different names in Brazil. Droga Raia is a large pharmacy chain; many stores are open 24 hours.

INFECTIOUS DISEASES
Cholera

Cholera is an intestinal infection acquired through ingestion of contaminated food or water. The main symptom is profuse, watery diarrhea, which may be so severe that it causes life-threatening dehydration. The key treatment is drinking oral rehydration solution. Antibiotics are also given (tetracycline or doxycycline), though quinolone antibiotics such as ciprofloxacin and levofloxacin are also effective.

Cholera sometimes occurs in Brazil, but it's rare among travelers. Cholera vaccine is no longer required, and is in fact no longer available in some countries, including the US, because the old vaccine was relatively ineffective and caused side effects. There are new vaccines that are safer and more effective, but they're not available in many countries and are only recommended for those at particularly high risk.

Dengue

Dengue fever is a viral infection found throughout South America. A large outbreak of dengue was reported from the Rio area in early 2002, ultimately affecting almost 800,000 people. Dengue is transmitted by aedes mosquitoes, which bite preferentially during the daytime and are usually found close to human habitations, often indoors. They breed primarily in artificial water containers, such as jars, barrels, cans, cisterns, metal drums, plastic containers and discarded tires. As a result, dengue is especially common in densely populated, urban environments.

Dengue usually causes flulike symptoms, including fever, muscle aches, joint pains, headaches, nausea and vomiting, often followed by a rash. The body aches may be quite uncomfortable, but most cases resolve uneventfully in a few days. Severe cases usually occur in children under the age of 15 who are experiencing their second bout of dengue infection.

There is no treatment for dengue fever except to take analgesics such as acetaminophen/paracetamol (Tylenol) and to drink plenty of fluids. Severe cases may require hospitalization for intravenous fluids and supportive care. There is no vaccine. The cornerstone of prevention is protection against insect bites (see p730).

Hepatitis A

Hepatitis A is the second most common travel-related infection (after traveler's diarrhea). It's a viral infection of the liver that is usually acquired by ingestion of contaminated water, food or ice, though it may also be acquired by direct contact with infected persons. The illness occurs throughout the world, but the incidence is higher in developing nations. Symptoms may include fever, malaise, jaundice, nausea, vomiting and abdominal pain. Most cases resolve without complications, though hepatitis A occasionally causes severe liver damage. There is no treatment.

The vaccine for hepatitis A is extremely safe and highly effective. If you get a booster six to 12 months later, it lasts for at least 10 years. You really should get it before you go to Brazil or any other developing nation. Because the safety of hepatitis A vaccine has not been established for pregnant women or children under the age of two, they should instead be given a gamma globulin injection.

Hepatitis B

Like hepatitis A, hepatitis B is a liver infection that occurs worldwide but is more common in developing nations. Unlike hepatitis A, the disease is usually acquired by sexual contact or by exposure to infected blood, generally through blood transfusions or contaminated needles. The vaccine is recommended only for long-term travelers (on the road more than six months) who expect to live in rural areas or have close physical contact with the local population. Additionally, the vaccine is recommended for anyone who anticipates sexual contact with the local inhabitants or a need for medical, dental or other treatments while abroad, especially transfusions or injections.

Hepatitis B vaccine is safe and highly effective. A total of three injections, however, is necessary to establish full immunity. Several countries added hepatitis B vaccine to the list of routine childhood immunizations in the 1980s, so many young adults are already protected.

Malaria

Malaria occurs in every South American country except Chile, Uruguay and the Falkland Islands. It's transmitted by mosquito bites, usually between dusk and dawn. The main symptoms are high spiking fevers, which may be accompanied by chills, sweats, headache, body aches, weakness, vomiting or diarrhea. Severe cases may involve the central nervous system and lead to seizures, confusion, coma and death.

Taking malaria pills is strongly recommended for forested areas within the nine states of the 'Legal Amazonia' region, including Acre, Amapá, Amazonas, Maranhão (western part), Mato Grosso (northern part), Pará (except Belém city), Rondônia, Roraima and Tocantins, and for urban areas within this region, including the cities of Porto Velho, Boa Vista, Macapá, Manaus, Santarém and Maraba. Transmission is greatest in remote jungle areas where mining, lumbering and agriculture occur and which have been settled for less than five years. Malaria risk is negligible outside the states of 'Legal Amazonia.' Travelers visiting only the coastal states from the horn to the Uruguay border and Iguaçu Falls do not need prophylaxis.

There is a choice of three malaria pills, all of which work about equally well. Mefloquine (Lariam) is taken once weekly in a dosage of 250mg, starting one to two weeks before arrival and continuing through the trip and for four weeks after return. The problem is that a certain percentage of people (the number is debatable) develop neuro-psychiatric side effects, which may range from mild to severe. Atovaquone/proguanil (Malarone) is a newly approved combination pill taken once daily with food starting two days before arrival and continuing through the trip and for seven days after departure. Side effects are typically mild. Doxycycline is a third alternative, but it may cause an exaggerated sunburn reaction.

In general, Malarone seems to cause fewer side effects than Lariam and is becoming more popular. The chief disadvantage is that it has to be taken daily. For longer trips, it's probably worth trying Lariam; for shorter trips, Malarone will be the drug of choice for most people.

Protecting yourself against mosquito bites is just as important as taking malaria pills (see p730), since none of the pills is 100% effective.

If you may not have access to medical care while traveling, you should bring along additional pills for emergency self-treatment, which you should take if you can't reach a doctor and you develop symptoms that suggest malaria, such as high spiking fevers. One option is to take four tablets of Malarone once daily for three days. Malarone should not be used for treatment, however, if you're already taking it for prevention. An alternative is to take 650mg of quinine three times daily and 100mg of doxycycline twice daily for one week. If you start self-medication, see a doctor at the earliest possible opportunity.

If you develop a fever after returning home, see a physician, as malaria symptoms may not occur for months.

Plague

The plague continues to occur among animals in the drier northern and eastern states, from Ceará south to Minas Gerais, but human cases are uncommon. Most occur in Bahia state. The infection is usually transmitted to humans by the bite of rodent fleas, typically when rodents die off. Symptoms include fever, chills, muscle aches and malaise, associated with the development of an acutely swollen, exquisitely painful lymph node, known as a bubo, most often in the groin. Most travelers are at extremely low risk of the plague. But if there's a chance you will have contact with rodents or their fleas, especially in the above areas, you should bring along a bottle of doxycycline, to be taken prophylactically during periods of exposure. Those less than eight years old or allergic to doxycycline should take trimethoprim-sulfamethoxazole instead. In addition, you should avoid areas containing rodent burrows or nests, never handle sick or dead animals, and follow the guidelines in this chapter for protecting yourself from insect bites (see p730).

Rabies

Rabies is a viral infection of the brain and spinal cord that is almost always fatal. The rabies virus is carried in the saliva of infected animals and is typically transmitted through an animal bite, though contamination of any break in the skin with infected saliva may result in rabies. Rabies occurs in all South American countries. In Brazil, most cases are reported from the extreme western Minas Gerais state and northeastern areas. Dog bites are the most common cause, but bites from other animals can also lead to rabies. In 2004 several dozen people in the Amazon died from rabies after being bitten by vampire bats.

Rabies vaccine is safe, but a full series requires three injections and is quite expensive. Those at high risk of rabies, such as animal handlers and spelunkers (cave explorers), should certainly get the vaccine. In addition, those at lower risk of animal bites should consider asking for the vaccine if they may be traveling to remote areas and may not have access to appropriate medical care if needed. The treatment for a possibly rabid bite consists of rabies vaccine with rabies immune globulin. It's effective, but must be given promptly. Most travelers don't need rabies vaccine.

All animal bites and scratches must be promptly and thoroughly cleansed with large amounts of soap and water and local health authorities contacted to determine whether or not further treatment is necessary.

Typhoid

Typhoid fever is caused by ingestion of food or water contaminated by a species of salmonella known as *Salmonella typhi*. Fever occurs in virtually all cases. Other symptoms may include headache, malaise, muscle aches, dizziness, loss of appetite, nausea and abdominal pain. Either diarrhea or constipation may occur. Possible complications include intestinal perforation, intestinal bleeding, confusion, delirium or (rarely) coma.

Unless you expect to take all your meals in major hotels and restaurants, typhoid vaccine is a good idea. It's usually given orally, but is also available as an injection. Neither vaccine is approved for use in children under the age of two.

The drug of choice for typhoid fever is usually a quinolone antibiotic such as ciprofloxacin (Cipro) or levofloxacin (Levaquin), which many travelers carry for treatment of traveler's diarrhea. However, if you self-treat for typhoid fever, you may also need to self-treat for malaria, since the symptoms of the two diseases may be indistinguishable.

Yellow Fever

Yellow fever is a life-threatening viral infection transmitted by mosquitoes in forested areas. The illness begins with flulike symptoms, which may include fever, chills, headache, muscle aches, backache, loss of appetite, nausea and vomiting. These symptoms usually subside in a few days, but one person in six enters a second, toxic phase characterized by recurrent fever, vomiting, listlessness, jaundice, kidney failure, and hemorrhage, leading to death in up to half of the cases. There is no treatment except for supportive care.

Yellow fever vaccine is strongly recommended for all travelers to Brazil, except those visiting only Rio de Janeiro, São Paulo, the central eastern area to the coast, and the coastal areas south of São Luís. Major outbreaks have recently been reported from Minas Gerais state, and additional cases occur elsewhere. Fatal cases of yellow fever among travelers who failed to get vaccinated are periodically reported. For an up-to-date map showing the distribution of yellow fever in Brazil, go to the Centers for Disease Control

(CDC) website at www.cdc.gov/ncidod/dobid/yellowfever/YF_Maps_Stats.html.

Proof of vaccination is required from all travelers arriving from a yellow fever-infected country in Africa or the Americas.

Yellow fever vaccine is given only in approved yellow fever vaccination centers, which provide validated International Certificates of Vaccination. The vaccine should be given at least 10 days before any potential exposure to yellow fever and remains effective for approximately 10 years. Reactions to the vaccine are generally mild and may include headaches, muscle aches, low-grade fevers or discomfort at the injection site. Severe, life-threatening reactions have been described but are extremely rare. In general, the risk of becoming ill from the vaccine is far less than the risk of becoming ill from yellow fever, and you're strongly encouraged to get the vaccine.

Taking measures to protect yourself from mosquito bites (see p730) is an essential part of preventing yellow fever.

Other Infectious Diseases

SCHISTOSOMIASIS

This is a parasitic infection acquired by skin exposure to contaminated fresh water; it occurs in almost all states of the Northeast, and two states (Minas Gerais and Espírito Santo) in the Southeast. When traveling in these areas, you should avoid swimming, wading, bathing or washing in bodies of fresh water, including lakes, ponds, streams and rivers. Salt water and chlorinated pools carry no risk of schistosomiasis.

TOXOPLASMOSIS

This has been reported from various areas, including northwestern Paraná state and northern Rio de Janeiro state. Most cases have been related to contaminated water supplies. Pregnant women should be particularly careful to avoid drinking unfiltered water, since toxoplasmosis may cause severe fetal illness. In nonpregnant people with normal immune systems, most cases of toxoplasmosis clear uneventfully.

CHAGAS' DISEASE

This parasitic infection is transmitted by triatomine insects (reduviid bugs), which inhabit crevices in the walls and roofs of substandard housing in South and Central America. In Brazil, the disease has been eliminated in every state except Bahia and Tocantins through an aggressive program of insecticide spraying. The triatomine insect drops its feces on human skin as it bites, usually at night. A person becomes infected when they unknowingly rub the feces into the bite wound or any other open sore. Chagas' disease is extremely rare in travelers. If you sleep in a poorly constructed house, especially one made of mud, adobe or thatch, however, you should be sure to protect yourself with a bed net and a good insecticide.

LEISHMANIASIS
Leishmaniasis occurs in the mountains and jungles of all South American countries except for Chile, Uruguay and the Falkland Islands. The infection is transmitted by sand flies, which are about one-third the size of mosquitoes. In Brazil, leishmaniasis has been reported from suburban areas in Rio de Janeiro and São Paulo. Most cases are limited to the skin, causing slowly growing ulcers over exposed parts of the body. The more severe type of leishmaniasis, which disseminates to the bone marrow, liver and spleen, occurs mainly in the Northeast. Leishmaniasis may be particularly severe in those with HIV. There is no vaccine. To protect yourself from sand flies, follow the same precautions as for mosquitoes (see p730), except that netting must be made of a finer mesh (at least 18 holes per 2.54cm or to the linear inch).

HANTAVIRUS PULMONARY SYNDROME
A rapidly progressive, life-threatening infection, hantavirus is acquired through exposure to the excretions of wild rodents. Most cases occur in those people who live in rodent-infested dwellings in rural areas. In Brazil, hantavirus infections are reported from the states of Minas Gerais, Santa Catarina and São Paulo.

ECHINOCOCCUS
This is a parasite that infects the liver, usually in people who work with sheep. Echinococcus infections occur chiefly in the southernmost part of the country.

BRUCELLOSIS
Brucellosis is an infection of domestic and wild animals that may be transmitted to humans through animal contact or by consumption of unpasteurized dairy products

from infected animals. In Brazil, most human cases are related to infected cattle. Symptoms include fever, malaise, depression, loss of appetite, headache, muscle aches and back pain. Complications may include arthritis, hepatitis, meningitis and endocarditis (heart-valve infection).

FASCIOLIASIS
This is a parasitic infection that is typically acquired by eating contaminated watercress grown in sheep-raising areas. Early symptoms may include fever, nausea, vomiting and painful enlargement of the liver.

ONCHOCERCIASIS
Also known as river blindness, onchocerciasis is caused by a roundworm that may invade the eye, leading to blindness. The infection is transmitted by black flies, which breed along the banks of rapidly flowing rivers and streams. In Brazil, onchocerciasis is reported among the indigenous Yanomami population living along the Venezuelan border, as well as in nearby tribes and non-*índios* visiting the area. Most cases occur near swift-flowing streams in densely forested highlands.

VENEZUELAN EQUINE ENCEPHALITIS
Transmitted by mosquitoes and causing brain inflammation, this form of encephalitis occurs sporadically.

'CATERPILLAR PLAGUE'
Cases were reported from the Amazon delta region between 1983 and 1985 and from southern Brazil in 1995. The disease is caused by contact with the larvae (caterpillars) of the butterfly *Lamonia achelous*, which secrete venom through their skins. The illness is characterized by high fever, bleeding from the nose and ears, kidney failure, and death. The caterpillar is found from December through March. The adult and pupal forms are harmless.

HIV/AIDS
HIV/AIDS is a danger in Brazil. An estimated 600,000 Brazilians carry the virus. Be sure to use condoms for all sexual encounters.

TRAVELER'S DIARRHEA
Traveler's diarrhea is defined as the passage of more than three watery bowel actions within 24 hours, plus at least one other symptom

HEALTH

such as fever, cramps, nausea, vomiting or feeling generally unwell. In over 80% of cases, traveler's diarrhea is caused by a bacteria and therefore responds promptly to treatment with antibiotics. Treatment with antibiotics will depend on your situation – how sick you are, how quickly you need to get better, where you are etc.

To prevent diarrhea, avoid tap water in suspect places unless it has been boiled, filtered or chemically disinfected (iodine tablets); be wary of dairy products that may contain unpasteurized milk; and be selective when eating food from street vendors.

Treatment consists of staying well hydrated. Drink plenty of fluids, preferably an oral rehydration solution like Gastrolite. Coconut water, which is loaded with electrolytes, is also good for rehydration. Antibiotics such as Norfloxacin, Ciprofloxacin or Azithromycin will kill the bacteria quickly.

Loperamide is just a 'stopper' and doesn't get to the cause of the problem. It can be helpful, for example, on a long bus ride. Don't take Loperamide if you have a fever or blood in your stools. Seek medical attention quickly if you do not respond to an appropriate antibiotic.

If diarrhea is bloody, persists for more than 72 hours or is accompanied by fever, shaking chills or severe abdominal pain, you should seek medical attention.

ENVIRONMENTAL HAZARDS
Animal Bites
Do not attempt to pet, handle or feed any animal, with the exception of domestic animals known to be free of any infectious disease. Most animal injuries are directly related to a person's attempt to touch or feed the animal.

Any bite or scratch from a mammal, including bats, should be promptly and thoroughly cleansed with large amounts of soap and water, followed by application of an antiseptic such as iodine or alcohol. The local health authorities should be contacted immediately for possible post-exposure rabies treatment, whether or not you've been immunized against rabies. It may also be advisable to start an antibiotic, since wounds caused by animal bites and scratches frequently become infected. One of the newer quinolones, such as levofloxacin (Levaquin), which many travelers carry in case of diarrhea, would be an appropriate choice.

Insect Bites & Stings
To prevent mosquito bites, wear long sleeves, long pants, hats and shoes (rather than sandals). Bring along a good insect repellent, preferably one containing DEET, which should be applied to exposed skin and clothing, but not to eyes, mouth, cuts, wounds or irritated skin. Products containing lower concentrations of DEET are as effective, but for shorter periods of time. In general, adults and children over the age of 12 should use preparations containing 25% to 35% DEET, which usually last about six hours. Children between two and 12 years of age should use preparations containing no more than 10% DEET, applied sparingly, which will usually last about three hours. Neurologic toxicity has been reported from DEET, especially in children, but appears to be extremely uncommon and generally related to overuse. DEET-containing compounds should not be used on children under the age of two.

Insect repellents containing certain botanical products, including oil of eucalyptus and soybean oil, are effective but last only 1½ to two hours. DEET-containing repellents are preferable for areas where there is a high risk of malaria or yellow fever. Products based on citronella are not effective.

For additional protection, you can apply permethrin to clothing, shoes, tents and bed nets. Permethrin treatments are safe and remain effective for at least two weeks, even when items are laundered. Permethrin should not be applied directly to skin.

Don't sleep with the window open unless there is a screen in the window frame. If sleeping outdoors or in accommodations that allow entry of mosquitoes, use a bed net, preferably treated with permethrin, with edges tucked in under the mattress. The mesh size should be smaller than 1.5mm. If the sleeping area is not otherwise protected, use a mosquito coil, which will fill the room with insecticide throughout the night. Repellent-impregnated wristbands are not effective.

Snake Bites
Snakes and leeches are a hazard in some areas of South America. In the event of a venomous snake bite, place the victim at rest, keep the bitten area immobilized and move the victim immediately to the nearest medical facility. Avoid tourniquets, which are no longer recommended.

Sun

To protect yourself from excessive sun exposure, you should stay out of the midday sun, wear sunglasses and a wide-brimmed sun hat, and apply sunscreen with SPF15 or higher, with both UVA and UVB protection. Sunscreen should be generously applied to all exposed parts of the body approximately 30 minutes before sun exposure and should be reapplied after swimming or vigorous activity. Travelers should also drink plenty of fluids and avoid strenuous exercise when the temperature is high.

Water

Tap water in Brazilian cities such as Rio and São Paulo is generally safe to drink – though many locals prefer purified or bottled water. In remote areas, tap water may be suspect. Many hotels and guesthouses filter their water – be sure to inquire about the status where you're staying. Vigorous boiling for one minute is the most effective means of water purification. At altitudes greater than 2000m (6500ft), boil for three minutes.

One simple method of purification: a handheld water purifier that uses ultraviolet light to purify water. A steripen – available online and in some camping stores – is a safe, effective and lightweight device for accomplishing this. Another option is to disinfect water with iodine pills. Instructions are usually enclosed and should be carefully followed. Or you can add 2% tincture of iodine to one quart or liter of water (five drops to clear water, 10 drops to cloudy water) and let stand for 30 minutes. If the water is cold, longer times may be required. The taste of iodinated water may be improved by adding vitamin C (ascorbic acid). Iodinated water should not be consumed for more than a few weeks. Pregnant women, those with a history of thyroid disease, and those allergic to iodine should not drink iodinated water.

A number of water filters are on the market. Those with smaller pores (reverse-osmosis filters) provide the broadest protection, but they are relatively large and are readily plugged by debris. Those with somewhat larger pores (microstrainer filters) are ineffective against viruses, although they remove other organisms. Manufacturers' instructions must be carefully followed.

TRAVELING WITH CHILDREN

In general, children under the age of nine months should not be brought to areas where yellow fever occurs, since the vaccine is not safe in this age group.

When traveling with young children, be particularly careful about what you allow them to eat and drink, because diarrhea can be especially dangerous in this age group and because the vaccines for hepatitis A and typhoid fever are not approved for use in children who are under the age of two years.

The two main malaria medications, Lariam and Malarone, may be given to children, but insect repellents must be applied in lower concentrations.

WOMEN TRAVELERS

Tampons and other sanitary items are widely available in most pharmacies, though you'll want to stock up before heading into rural areas. To avoid the risk of unwanted pregnancy, most pharmacies in Brazil stock the 'morning-after' pill (a pílula do dia seguinte), which costs about R$20.

You can find an English-speaking obstetrician near your location in Brazil by going to the US embassy website at www.embixada-americana.org.br. However, medical facilities will probably not be comparable to those in your home country. It's safer to avoid travel to Brazil late in pregnancy, so that you don't have to risk delivering there.

If pregnant, it's preferable to avoid areas where yellow fever occurs, since the vaccine is not safe during pregnancy.

For malaria-prevention measures, mefloquine (Lariam) is the safest during pregnancy.

Language

CONTENTS

Brazilians speak Portuguese, which looks similar to Spanish on paper but sounds completely different. You'll do quite well, though, if you speak Spanish when in Brazil. Brazilians will understand you, but you won't get much of what they say – so don't think studying Portuguese is a waste of time. Listen to language tapes and develop an ear for Portuguese – it's a beautiful-sounding language.

When the Portuguese arrived in 1500, an estimated 700 indigenous languages were spoken by Brazil's indigenous peoples. About 180 survive, 130 of them being considered endangered because they have fewer than 600 speakers. These indigenous languages, together with the various idioms and dialects spoken by the Africans brought in as slaves, extensively changed the Portuguese spoken by the early settlers.

Along with Portuguese, the Tupi-Guarani language, simplified and given a written form by the Jesuits, became a common language that was understood by the majority of the population. It was spoken by the general public until the middle of the 18th century, but its usage diminished with the great number of Portuguese gold-rush immigrants and a royal proclamation in 1757 prohibiting its use. With the expulsion of the Jesuits in 1759, Portuguese was established as the national language.

Nevertheless, many words from indigenous and African languages remain in the Brazilian Portuguese language of today. From Tupi-Guarani come lots of place names (such as Guanabara, Carioca, Tijuca and Niterói), animal names (such as piranha, *capivara* and *urubu*) and plant names (such as *mandioca*, *abacaxí*, *caju* and *jacarandá*). Words from African languages, mainly those from Nigeria and Angola, are used in Afro-Brazilian religious ceremonies (eg Orixá, Exú and Iansã), cooking (eg *vatapá*, *acarajé* and *abará*) and in general conversation (eg samba, mocambo and moleque).

In Brazil, body language also plays an important role in conversation. Brazilians accompany their speech with a rich body language, a sort of parallel dialogue. The thumbs up *tudo bem* is used as a greeting, or to signify 'OK' or 'Thank you.' The authoritative *não-não* finger-wagging is most intimidating when done right under someone's nose, but it's not a threat.

The sign of the *figa*, a thumb inserted between the first and second fingers of a clenched fist, is a symbol of good luck that has been derived from an African sexual charm. It's more commonly used as jewelry than in body language. To indicate *rápido* (speed and haste), thumb and middle finger snap while rapidly shaking the wrist – a gesture it often seems only Brazilians can make. If you don't want something (*não quero*), slap the back of your hands as if ridding yourself of the entire affair. Touching a finger to the lateral corner of the eye means 'I'm wise to you.'

Brazilians are easy to befriend, but the vast majority of them speak little or no English. This is changing, however, as practically all Brazilians in school are learning English. All the same, don't count on finding an English speaker, especially outside of the cities. The more Portuguese you speak, the more rewarding your stay will be, and locals will appreciate the effort.

LANGUAGE RESOURCES

An excellent pocket resource is Lonely Planet's *Brazilian Portuguese* phrasebook. In addition to covering most travel situations, the book will also provide much help in social situations. It includes an easy-to-follow grammar guide, a comprehensive section on food and dining, plus a two-way dictionary.

There's a growing selection of Portuguese language learning material. One of the best introductions is *Complete Portuguese: the Basics* by Living Language. The kit includes a course book, dictionary and CDs. The lessons are easy to follow and designed to get you speaking quickly.

For grammar, pick up a copy of *Essential Portuguese Grammar* by Alexander da Prista. Although it's old (published in 1966), this slim volume is still a gem, with clear and concise explanations of grammatical structures and the language in practice.

If you'd like to delve deeper into the language, and have the time to dedicate to a challenging self-study course, try the US Foreign Service Institute (FSI) series (see www.foreignserviceinstitute.com)

Combine these with a few old bossa nova albums, some Brazilian cinema (seek out a Walter Salles or Fernando Meirelles film) and some Jorge Amado novels, and you're ready for the next level of instruction – on the streets and beaches of Brazil.

PRONUNCIATION

Brazilian Portuguese pronunciation can be quite tricky for the uninitiated. The big shocker is that, generally, an **r** is pronounced like an 'h': so 'Rio' becomes 'hee·oh,' the currency 'real' is pronounced 'hay·ow' etc. In the same spirit of fun, a **t** (or **d**) followed by a vowel is pronounced 'ch' as in 'church' or 'j' as in 'judge', so the word *restaurante* is pronounced approximately as 'hess·to·roch.'

The letter **ç** is pronounced like an English 's'; the letter **x** as the 'sh' as in 'ship.' So 'Iguaçu' is 'ig·wa·soo' and 'Caxambu' 'ka·sham·boo.'

You'll know you've mastered Brazilian Portuguese pronunciation when you've successfully ordered one of the country's more popular beers, *Antarctica* (that's right, you say 'ant·okt·chee·kah'!).

In Brazil, accents, dialects and slang (*gíria*) vary regionally. The Carioca (from Rio) inserts the 'sh' sound in place of **s**. The *gaúcho* speaks a Spanish-sounding Portuguese, the Baiano (from Bahia) speaks slowly, and the accents of the Cearense (from Ceará) are often incomprehensible to outsiders.

Don't worry too much about pronunciation – if you read our pronunciation guides as if they were English, you'll be understood just fine throughout the country.

Vowel Sounds

a	as the 'u' in 'run', eg *camera*
a	as in 'father', eg *padre*
ai	as in 'aisle', eg *pai*
aw	as in 'saw', eg *nó*
ay	as in 'day', eg *lei*
e	as in 'bet', eg *cedo*
ee	as in 'bee', eg *fino*
o	as in 'go', eg *gato*
oo	as in 'moon', eg *azul*
ow	as in 'how', eg *saudades*
oy	as in 'boy', eg *noite*

A characteristic feature of Brazilian Portuguese is the use of nasal vowels. These are pronounced as if you're trying to produce the sound through your nose rather than your mouth. English also has nasal vowels to some extent – when you say 'sing' in English, the 'i' is nasalized by the 'ng.' In Brazilian Portuguese, written vowels that have a nasal consonant after them (**m** or **n**), or a tilde over them (eg **ã**), will be nasal. In our pronunciation guide, we've used 'ng' after nasal vowels to indicate a nasal sound.

Consonants

The following lists a few of the letters used in our pronunciation guide that represent the trickier Portuguese consonant sounds.

ly	as the 'lli' in 'million'
ny	as in 'canyon'
r	as in 'run'
rr	as in 'run' but stronger and rolled
zh	as the 's' in 'pleasure'

Word Stress

Word stress usually falls on the second-last syllable of a word, though there are exceptions. When a word ends in **-r** or is pronounced with a nasalized vowel, the stress falls on the last syllable. Another exception is that if a written vowel has an accent marked over it, the stress falls on the syllable containing that vowel.

In our pronunciation guides, we have indicated the stressed syllable with italics.

GENDER

Portuguese has masculine and feminine forms of nouns and adjectives. In this chapter, alternative endings are separated by a slash. Generally, 'o' indicates masculine and 'a' indicates feminine.

ACCOMMODATIONS

I'm looking for a ...
Estou procurando por ...   es·*to* pro·koo·*rang*·do porr ...
Where is a ...?
Onde tem ...?   *on*·de teng ...
   room
   um quarto   oom *kwarr*·to
   bed and breakfast
   uma pensão   oo·ma pen·*sowng*
   camping ground
   um local para   oom lo·*kow* pa·ra
    acampamento   a·kam·pa·*meng*·to
   guesthouse
   uma hospedaria   oo·ma os·pe·da·*ree*·a
   hotel
   um hotel   oom o·*tel*
   youth hostel
   um albergue   oom ow·*berr*·ge
   da juventude   da zhoo·veng·*too*·de

I'd like a ... room.
Eu gostaria um   e·oo gos·ta·*ree*·a oom
quarto de ...   *kwarr*·to de ...
   double
   casal   ka·*zow*
   single
   solteiro   sol·*tay*·ro
   twin
   duplo   *doo*·plo

What's the address?
Qual é o endereço?   kwow e o en·de·*re*·so
Do you have a ... room?
Tem um quarto de ...?   teng oom *kwarr*·to de ...
For (three) nights.
Para (três) noites.   pa·ra (tres) *noy*·tes
Does it include breakfast?
Inclui café da manhã?   eeng·kloo·ee ka·fe da ma·*nyang*
May I see it?
Posso ver?   po·so verr
I'll take it.
Eu fico com ele.   e·oo *fee*·ko kom e·lee

MAKING A RESERVATION
(for phone or email requests)

To ...	*Para ...*
From ...	*De ...*
Date	*Data*
I'd like to book ...	*Eu gostaria de fazer uma reserva ...* (see the list under 'Accommodations' for bed/room options)
in the name of ...	*no nome de ...*
for the nights of ...	*para os dias ...*
from ... to ...	*de ... até ...*
credit card ...	*cartão de credito ...*
number	*número*
expiry date	*data de vencimento*
Please confirm ...	*Por favor confirme ...*
availability	*a disponibilidade*
price	*o preço*

I don't like it.
Não gosto.   nowng *gos*·to
I'm leaving now.
Estou indo embora   es·*to* een·do em·*bo*·ra
agora.   a·*go*·ra

How much is it per ...?
Quanto custa por ...?   *kwan*·to *koos*·ta porr ...
   night
   noite   *noy*·te
   person
   pessoa   pe·*so*·a
   week
   semana   se·*ma*·na

Can I pay ...?
Posso pagar com ...?   *po*·so pa·*garr* kom ...
   by credit card
   cartão de crédito   karr·*towng* de *kre*·dee·to
   by traveler's check
   traveler cheque   tra·ve·ler *she*·kee

CONVERSATION & ESSENTIALS
Hello.
Olá.   o·*la*
Hi.
Oi.   oy
Good day.
Bom dia.   bong *dee*·a
Good evening.
Boa noite.   bo·a *noy*·te
See you later.
Até mais tarde.   a·*te* mais *tarr*·de

Goodbye.
Tchau.   chau
How are you?
Como vai?   ko·mo vai
Fine, and you?
Bem, e você?   beng e vo·se
I'm pleased to meet you.
Prazer em conhecê-lo.   pra·zerr eng ko·nye·se·lo (m)
Prazer em conhecê-la.   pra·zerr eng ko·nye·se·la (f)
Yes.
Sim.   seem
No.
Não.   nowng
Please.
Por favor.   por fa·vorr
Thank you (very much).
(Muito) obrigado/   *(mween·*to) o·bree·*ga·*do/
obrigada. (m/f)   o·bree·*ga·*da
You're welcome.
De nada.   de na·da
Excuse me.
Com licença   kom lee·seng·sa
Sorry.
Desculpa.   des·kool·pa
What's your name?
Qual é o seu nome?   kwow é o se·oo no·me
My name is ...
Meu nome é ...   me·oo no·me e ...
Where are you from?
De onde você é?   de ong·de vo·se e
I'm from ...
Eu sou (da/do/de) ...   e·oo so (da/do/de)
May I take a photo (of you)?
Posso tirar uma foto   po so tee rarr oo ma fo to
(de você)?   (de vo se)

DIRECTIONS
Where is ...?
Onde fica ...?   on·de fee·ka ...
Can you show me (on the map)?
Você poderia me   o·se po·de·ree·a me
mostrar (no mapa)?   mos·trarr (no ma·pa)
What's the address?
Qual é o endereço?   kwow é o en·de·re·so
How far is it?
Qual a distância   kwow a dees·tan·see·a
daqui?   da·kee
How do I get there?
Como é que eu chego lá?   ko·mo e ke e·oo she·go la

Turn ...	*Vire ...*	vee·re ...
at the corner	*à esquina*	a es·kee·na
at the traffic	*no sinal de*	no see·now de
lights	*trânsito*	tran·zee·to
left	*à esquerda*	a es·kerr·da
right	*à direita*	a dee·ray·ta
here	*aqui*	a·kee
there	*lá*	la
near ...	*perto ...*	perr·to ...
straight ahead	*em frente*	eng freng·te

SIGNS

Delegacia de Polícia	Police Station
Hospital	Hospital
Polícia	Police
Pronto Socorro	Emergency Department
Banheiro	Bathroom/Toilet
Não Tem Vaga	No Vacancy
Tem Vaga	Vacancy

north	norte	norr·te
south	sul	sool
east	leste	les·te
west	oeste	o·es·te

EATING OUT

breakfast	café da manhã	kaa·fe daa ma·nyang
lunch	almoço	ow·mo·so
dinner	jantar	zhang·taarr
snack	lanche	lang·she

The menu (in English), please.
O cardapio (em inglês), o kar·da·pyo eng eeng·gles
por favor. porr fa·vorr

What would you recommend?
O que você recomenda? o ke vo·se he·ko·meng·da

I'm a vegetarian.
Eu sou e·oo so
vegetariano/a. ve·zhe·ta·ree·a·no/a (m/f)

I'd like...
Queria... ke·ree·a...

Do you have...?
Tem... teng...

I'm full./I've eaten well.
Estou satisfeito/a. es·to sa·tees·fay·to/a (m/f)

The check, please.
A conta, por favor. a kong·ta porr fa·vorr

Cheers!
Saúde! sa·oo·de

For a food and drink glossary, see p92.

HEALTH

I'm ill.
Estou doente. es·to do·eng·te

I need a doctor (who speaks English).
Eu preciso de um médico e·oo pre·see·zo de oom me·dee·ko
(que fale inglês). (ke fa·le een·gles)

It hurts here.
Aqui dói. a·kee doy

I've been vomiting.
Estive vomitando. e·steev vo·mee·tan·do

I feel ...
Estou me sentindo ... es·to me seng·teeng·do ...
dizzy
tonto/tonta (m/f) tong·to/tong·ta
nauseous
enjoado/enjoada (m/f) eng·zho·a·do/en·zho·a·da

diarrhea	diarréia	dee·a·he·ee·a
fever	febre	fe·bre
nausea	náusea	now·ze·a
pain	dor	dorr

Where's the nearest ...?
Onde fica ...is perto? on·de fee·ka ... mais perr·to
(night) chemist
a farmácia (noturna) a farr·ma·see·a (no·toor·na)
dentist
o dentista o deng·tees·ta
doctor
o médico o me·dee·ko
hospital
o hospital o os·pee·tow
medical centre
a clínica médica a klee·nee·ka me·dee·ka

I'm allergic to ...
Tenho alergia à ... te·nyo a·lerr·zhee·a a ...
antibiotics
antibióticos an·tee·bee·o·tee·kos
aspirin
aspirina as·pee·ree·na
bees
abelhas a·be·lyas
peanuts
amendoims a·meng·do·eengs
penicillin
penicilina pe·nee·see·lee·na
antiseptic
anti-séptico an·tee·sep·tee·ko
contraceptives
anticoncepcionais an·tee·kon·sep·see·o·now
painkillers
analgésicos a·now·zhe·zee·ko

EMERGENCIES

Help!
Socorro! so·ko·ho

It's an emergency.
É uma emergência. e oo·ma e·merr·zheng·see·a

I'm lost.
Estou perdido/a. (m/f) es·to perr·dee·do/a

Where are the toilets?
Onde tem um on·de teng oom
banheiro? ba·nyay·ro

Go away!
Vai embora! vai eng·bo·ra

Call ...!
a doctor
um médico! oom me·dee·ko
an ambulance
uma ambulância oo·ma am·boo·lan·see·a
the police
a polícia a po·lee·see·a

LANGUAGE DIFFICULTIES

Do you speak English?
Você fala inglês?   vo·se fa·la een·gles
Does anyone here speak English?
Alguém aqui fala inglês?   ow·geng a·kee fa·la een·gles
Do you understand?
Você entende?   vo·se en·teng·de
I (don't) understand.
Eu (não) entendo.   e·oo (nowng) en·teng·do
What does ... mean?
O que quer dizer ...?   o ke kerr dee·zerr ...

Could you please ...?
Você poderia por favor ...? vo·se po·de·ree·a porr fa·vorr ...
  repeat that
  repetir isto   he·pe·teerr ees·to
  speak more slowly
  falar mais devagar   fa·larr mais de·va·garr
  write it down
  escrever num papel   es·kre·verr noom pa·pel

NUMBERS

0	zero	ze·ro
1	um	oom
2	dois	doys
3	três	tres
4	quatro	kwa·tro
5	cinco	seen·ko
6	seis	says
7	sete	se·te
8	oito	oy·to
9	nove	naw·ve
10	dez	dez
11	onze	ong·ze
12	doze	do·ze
13	treze	tre·ze
14	quatorze	ka·torr·ze
15	quinze	keen·ze
16	dezesseis	de·ze·says
17	dezesete	de·ze·se·te
18	dezoito	de·zoy·to
19	dezenove	de·ze·naw·ve
20	vinte	veen·te
21	vinte e um	veen·te e oom
22	vinte e dois	veen·te e doys
30	trinta	treen·ta
40	quarenta	kwa·ren·ta
50	cinquenta	seen·kwen·ta
60	sessenta	se·seng·ta
70	setenta	se·teng·ta
80	oitenta	oy·teng·ta
90	noventa	no·veng·ta
100	cem	seng
200	duzentos	doo·zeng·tos
1000	mil	mee·oo

ON THE BEACH

I can't swim.   *Eu não sei nadar.*
Can I swim here?   *Posso nadar aqui?*
Is it safe to swim   *É seguro nadar aqui?*
here?
What time is high/   *A que horas será a maré*
low tide?   *alta/baixa?*
How's the surf?   *Como estão as ondas?*
Where's a good place   *Onde tem um bom lugar*
to surf?   *para surfar?*
beach   *praia*
beach towel   *toalha de praia*
coast   *costa*
lifeguard   *salva-vidas*
rock   *pedra*
sand   *areia*
sea   *mar*
sunblock   *protetor solar*
wave   *onda*

QUESTION WORDS

Who?
Quem?   keng
What?
(O) Que?   (o) ke
When?
Quando?   kwang·do
Where?
Onde?   ong·de
Why?
Por que?   porr ke
Which/What?
Qual/Quais? (sg/pl) kwow kais

SHOPPING & SERVICES

I'd like to buy ...
Gostaria de comprar ...   gos·ta·ree·a de kom·prarr ...
I'm just looking.
Estou só olhando.   es·to so o·lyan·do
May I look at it?
Posso ver?   po·so verr
How much?
Quanto?   kwan·to
That's too expensive.
Está muito caro.   es·ta mweeng·to ka·ro
Can you lower the price?
Pode baixar o preço?   po·de ba·sharr o pre·so
Do you have something cheaper?
Tem uma coisa mais   teng oo·ma koy·za mais
barata?   ba·ra·ta
I'll give you (five reals).
Dou (cinco reais).   do (seen·ko he·ais)

LANGUAGE

I don't like it.
Não gosto.   nowng *gos*·to
I'll take it.
Vou levar isso.   vo le·*var* ee·so

Where is ...?
Onde fica ...?   on·de *fee*·ka ...
 an ATM
 um caixa automático   oom *kai*·sha ow·to·ma·tee·ko
 a bank
 o banco   o *ban*·ko
 a bookstore
 uma livraria   oo·ma lee·vra·*ree*·a
 the ... embassy
 a embaixada do/da ...   a eng·bai·*sha*·da do/da ...
 a foreign-exchange office
 uma loja de câmbio   oo·ma *lo*·zha de *kam*·bee·o
 a market
 o mercado   o merr·*ka*·do
 the police station
 a delegacia de polícia   a de·le·ga·*see*·a de po·*lee*·see·a
 a pharmacy/chemist
 uma farmácia   oo·ma far·*ma*·sya
 the post office
 o correio   o ko·*hay*·o
 a supermarket
 o supermercado   o soo·perr·merr·*ka*·do
 the tourist office
 a secretaria de turismo   a se·kre·ta·*ree*·a de too·*rees*·mo
 a laundrette
 uma lavanderia   oo·ma la·vang·de·*ree*·a

less	menos	*me*·nos
more	mais	mais
large	grande	*grang*·de
small	pequeno/a	pe·*ke*·no/a

What time does ... open?
A que horas abre ...?   a ke *aw*·ras *a*·bre ...
Do you have any others?
Você tem outros?   vo·*se* teng *o*·tros
How many?
Quantos/Quantas? (m/f)   *kwan*·tos/*kwan*·tas

Do you accept ...?
Vocês aceitam ...?   vo·*ses* a·*say*·tam ...
 credit cards
 cartão de crédito   karr·*towng* de *kre*·dee·to
 traveler's checks
 traveler cheques   tra·ve·*ler* *she*·kes

letter	uma carta	oo·ma *karr*·ta
parcel	uma	oo·ma
	encomenda	eng·ko·*meng*·da

I want to buy ...
Quero comprar ...   *ke*·ro kom·*prarr* ...
 an aerogram
 um aerograma   oom a·e·ro·*gra*·ma
 an envelope
 um envelope   oom eng·ve·*lo*·pe
 a phone card
 um cartão telefônico   oom kar·*towng* te·le·*fo*·nee·ko
 a postcard
 um cartão-postal   oom karr·*towng* pos·*tow*
 stamps
 selos   *se*·los

Where can I ...?
Onde posso ...?   on·de *po*·so ...
 change a traveler's check
 trocar traveler cheques   tro·*karr* tra·ve·*ler* *she*·kes
 change money
 trocar dinheiro   tro·*kar* dee·*nyay*·ro
 check my email
 checar meu e-mail   *she*·karr me·oo e·mail
 get internet access
 ter acesso à internet   terr a·*se*·so a een·terr·*ne*·tee

TIME & DATES
What time is it?
 Que horas são?   ke *aw*·ras sowng
It's (ten) o'clock.
 São (dez) horas.   sowng (des) *aw*·ras

now	agora	a·*go*·ra
this morning	esta manhã	es·ta ma·*nyang*
this afternoon	esta tarde	es·ta *tarr*·de
today	hoje	*o*·zhe
tonight	hoje à noite	*o*·zhe a *noy*·te
tomorrow	amanhã	a·ma·*nyang*
yesterday	ontem	*on*·teng

Monday	segunda-feira	se·*goon*·da·*fay*·ra
Tuesday	terça-feira	terr·sa·*fay*·ra
Wednesday	quarta-feira	kwarr·ta·*fay*·ra
Thursday	quinta-feira	keen·ta·*fay*·ra
Friday	sexta-feira	ses·ta·*fay*·ra
Saturday	sábado	*sa*·ba·doo
Sunday	domingo	do·*meen*·go

January	janeiro	zha·*nay*·ro
February	fevereiro	fe·ve·*ray*·ro
March	março	*marr*·so
April	abril	a·*bree*·oo
May	maio	*ma*·yo
June	junho	*zhoo*·nyo
July	julho	*zhoo*·lyo
August	agosto	a·*gos*·to

LANGUAGE

September	*setembro*	se·*teng*·bro
October	*outubro*	o·*too*·bro
November	*novembro*	no·*veng*·bro
December	*dezembro*	de·*zeng*·bro

TRANSPORT
Public Transport

Which ... goes	*Qual o ... que*	kwow o ... ke
to ...?	*vai para ...?*	vai *pa*·ra ...
boat	*barco*	*barr* ko
bus	*ônibus*	o·nee·*boos*
city/local bus	*ônibus local*	o·nee·*boos* lo·*kow*
ferry	*balsa*	*bal*·sa
inter-city bus	*ônibus inter-*	o·nee·*boos* een·
	urbano	terr oorr·*ba*·no
plane	*avião*	a·vee·*owng*
train	*trem*	treng

When's the ...	*Quando sai o ...*	*kwang*·do sai o ...
(bus)?	*(ônibus)?*	(o·nee·*boos*)
first	*primeiro*	pree·*may*·ro
last	*último*	*ool*·tee·mo
next	*próximo*	*pro*·see·mo

What time does it leave?
Que horas sai?   ke *aw*·ras sai
What time does it get to (Paraty)?
Que horas chega   ke *aw*·ras *she*·ga
em (Paraty)?   eng (pa·*ra*·tee)

A ... ticket	*Uma passagem*	oo·ma pa·*sa*·zhem
to (...)	*de ... para (...)*	de ... *pa*·ra (...)
1st-class	*primeira classe*	pree·*may*·ra *kla*·se
2nd-class	*segunda classe*	se·*goon*·da *kla*·se
one-way	*ida*	ee·da
round-trip	*ida e volta*	ee·da e *vol*·ta

How much is it?
Quanto é?   *kwan*·to e
Is this the bus to ...?
Este ônibus vai para ...? es·te o·nee·boos vai *pa*·ra ...?
Do I need to change?
Preciso trocar de trem?   pre·see·so tro·*karr* de treng
the luggage check room
o balcão de guarda   o bal·*kowng* de *gwarr*·da
volumes   vo·*loo*·me
a luggage locker
um guarda volume   oom *gwarr*·da vo·*loo*·me
Is this taxi free?
Este táxi está livre?   es·te tak·see es·*ta* lee·vre
Please put the meter on.
Por favor ligue o   porr fa·*vorr* lee·ge o
taxímetro.   tak·*see*·me·tro
How much is it to ...?
Quanto custa até ...?   kwan·to koos·ta a·*te* ...

JUNGLE EXCURSIONS

Does the tour include ...?
A excursão inclui ...?
Will we sleep in hammocks?
Iremos dormir em redes?
What is the breakdown of costs?
Como é dividido o custo?
Is the water level high or low?
O nível das águas esta alto ou baixo?
Does the boat have life jackets?
O barco tem coletes salva-vidas?
How long does it take to get there?
Quanto tempo leva para chegar lá?
Can we shop for food together?
Podemos ir comprar comida juntos?
Do you have fishing gear?
Você tem equipamento de pesca?
Is it safe to go there?
É seguro ir lá?
Will we see animals?
Iremos ver animais?

Are there ...?	*Lá tem ...?*
dangerous animals	*animais perigosos*
snakes	*cobras*
spiders	*aranhas*
lots of mosquitos	*muitos pernilongos*
accommodations	*alojamento*
canoe	*canoa*
food/drinks	*comida/bebida*
fuel	*combustível*
guides	*guias*
jungle	*selva/mata/floresta*

Please take me to (this address).
Me leve para este   me *le*·ve *pa*·ra es·te
endereço por favor.   en·de·*re*·so porr fa·*vorr*

Private Transport

I'd like to hire	*Gostaria de*	gos·ta·*ree*·a de
a/an ...	*alugar ...*	a·loo·*garr* ...
4WD	*um quatro*	oom *kwa*·tro
	por quatro	por *kwa*·tro
bicycle	*uma bicicleta*	oo·ma
		bee·see·*kle*·ta
car	*um carro*	oom ka·ho
motorbike	*uma motocicleta*	oo·ma mo·to·
		see·*kle*·ta

Is this the road to ...?
Esta é a estrada para ...?   es·*ta* e a es·*tra*·da *pa*·ra ...
(How long) Can I park here?
(Quanto tempo) Posso   (kwan·to teng·po) *po*·so
estacionar aqui?   es·ta·see·o·*narr* a·kee

ROAD SIGNS	
Entrada	Entrance
Estrada dê Preferência	Give Way
Mão Única	One-way
Pare	Stop
Pedágio	Toll
Proibido Entrar	No Entry
Rua Sem Saída	Dead End
Saída	Freeway Exit

Where's a gas/petrol station?
Onde tem um posto   on·de teng oom *pos*·to
de gasolina?   de ga·zo·*lee*·na
Please fill it up.
Enche o tanque, por   en·she o *tan*·ke porr
favor.   fa·*vorr*
I'd like ... liters.
Coloque ... litros.   ko·*lo*·ke ... *lee*·tros

diesel	diesel	*dee*·sel
ethanol	álcool	*ow*·kol
unleaded	gasolina	ga·zo·*lee*·na
	comum	ko·*moon*

The (car/motorbike) has broken down at ...
(O carro/A motocicleta) (o *ka*·ho/a mo·to·se·*kle*·ta)
quebrou em ...   ke·*bro* eng ...
The car won't start.
O carro não está   o *ka*·ho nowng *es*·ta
pegando.   pe·*gang*·do
I need a mechanic.
Preciso de um   pre·*see*·so de oom
mecânico.   me·*ka*·nee·ko
I've run out of gas/petrol.
Estou sem gasolina.   es·to seng ga·zo·*lee*·na
I've had an accident.
Sofri um acidente.   so·*free* oom a·see·*den*·te

Brazilian
Portuguese

Also available from Lonely Planet:
Brazilian Portuguese phrasebook

TRAVEL WITH CHILDREN
I need (a/an) ...
Preciso de ...
pre·*see*·zo de ...
Do you have (a/an) ...?
Aqui tem ...?
a·*kee* teng
   baby change room
   uma sala para trocar   oo·ma *sa*·la *pa*·ra tro·*karr*
   bebê   be·*be*
   baby seat
   um assento de criança   oom a·*seng*·to de kree·*an*·sa
   booster seat
   um assento de elevaçã   oom a·*seng*·to de e·le·va·*sowng*
   child-minding service
   um serviço de babá   oom serr·*vee*·so de ba·*ba*
   children's menu
   um cardápio para   oom kar·*da*·pee·o *pa*·ra
   criança   kree·*an*·sa
   (English-speaking) babysitter
   uma babá   oo·ma ba·*ba*
   (que fale ingles)   (ke *fa*·le een·*gles*)
   formula (milk)
   leite em pó (para bebê) *lay*·te (pa·ra be·*be*)
   high-chair
   uma cadeira de criança oo·ma ka·*day*·ra de kree·*an*·sa
   potty
   um troninho   oom tro·*nee*·nyo
   pusher/stroller
   um carrinho de bebê   oom ka·*hee*·nyo de be·*be*
   (disposable) nappies/diapers
   fraldas (descartáveis) *frow*·das (des·karr·*ta*·vays)

Do you mind if I breast-feed here?
Você se importa se eu   vo·*se* se eeng·*porr*·ta se *e*·oo
amamentar aqui?   a·ma·meng·*tarr* a·*kee*
Are children allowed?
É permitida a entrada   e perr·mee·*tee*·da a eng·*tra*·da
de crianças?   de kree·*an*·sas

Glossary

For a glossary of food and drink items, see p92. For some other useful words and phrases, see p732

afoxé – music of Bahia, which has strong African rhythms and close ties to Candomblé
albergue – lodging house or hostel
albergue da juventude – youth hostel
aldeia – originally a village built by Jesuits to convert *índios* to Christianity; now the term for any small, usually indigenous, village
andar – walk; also a floor of a multistory building
apartamento – hotel room with a private bathroom
apelido – nickname
arara – macaw
artesanato – handcrafted workmanship
ayahuasca – hallucinogenic drink
azulejos – Portuguese ceramic tiles with a distinctive blue glaze, often seen in churches

babaçu – versatile palm tree that is the basis of the rural economy in Maranhão
bairro – district
bandeirantes – bands of 17th- and 18th-century roaming adventurers who explored the vast Brazilian interior while searching for gold and *índios* to enslave; typically born of an *índio* mother and a Portuguese father
barraca – any stall or hut, including food and drink stands common at beaches, parks etc
bateria – rhythm section of a band, including the enormous ones in samba parades
beija-flor – literally 'flower kisser'; hummingbird; also the name of Rio's most famous samba school
berimbau – musical instrument that accompanies capoeira
bilheteria – ticket office
bloco – large group, usually numbering in the hundreds, of singing or drumming Carnaval revelers in costume, organized around a neighborhood or theme
boate – nightclub with a dance floor, sometimes featuring strippers; also *boîte*
bonde – cable car, tram or trolley
bossa nova – music that mixes North American jazz with Brazilian influences
boteco – small, open-air bar
boto – freshwater dolphin of the Amazon
Bumba Meu Boi – the most important festival in Maranhão, a rich folkloric event that revolves around a Carnavalesque dance/procession
bunda – African word for buttocks

caatinga – scrub vegetation of the *sertão*
Caboclo – literally 'copper-colored'; person of mixed Caucasian and *índio* ancestry
cachoeira – waterfall
camisinha – condom
Candomblé – Afro-Brazilian religion of Bahia
cangaceiros – legendary bandits of the *sertão*
capivara – capybara; the world's largest rodent, which looks like a large guinea pig and lives in the Pantanal
Capixaba – resident of Espírito Santo state
capoeira – martial art/dance developed by the slaves of Bahia
Carioca – resident of Rio de Janeiro
cartão telefônico – phonecard
casa de câmbio – money-exchange office
casa grande – big house or plantation owner's mansion
casal – married couple; double bed
chapada – tableland or plateau that divides a river basin
churrascaria – restaurant featuring barbecued meat
cidades históricas – historic colonial towns
Círio de Nazaré – Brazil's largest religious festival, which takes place in Belém
cobra – any snake
coronel – literally 'colonel'; rural landowner who typically controlled the local political, judicial and police systems; any powerful person
correio – post office

delegacia de polícia – police station

Embratur – Brazilian Tourist Board
engenho – sugar mill or sugar plantation
escolas de samba – large samba clubs that compete in the annual Carnaval parade
estalagem – inn
estrangeiro – foreigner
Exú – spirit that serves as messenger between the gods and humans in Afro-Brazilian religions

fantasia – Carnavalesque costume
favela – slum, shantytown
favelado – resident of a favela
fazenda – ranch or farm, usually a large landholding; also cloth, fabric
fazendeiro – estate owner
feira – produce market
ferroviária – train station
festa – party
Filhos de Gandhl – Bahia's most famous Carnaval *bloco*

fio dental – literally 'dental floss'; Brazil's famous skimpy bikini
Flamengo – Rio's most popular football team; also one of Rio's most populated areas
Fluminense – native of Rio state; also the football team that is Flamengo's main rival
forró – popular music of the Northeast, recently enjoying a wave of nationwide popularity
frevo – fast-paced, popular music from Pernambuco
frigobar – minibar
Funai – Fundação Nacional do Indio; government *índio* agency
Fusca – Volkswagen Beetle, Brazil's most popular car
futebol – football (soccer)
futevôlei – volleyball played without hands

gafieira – dance hall
garimpeiro – prospector or miner; originally an illegal diamond prospector
garimpo – mining camp
gaúcho – cowboy of southern Brazil
gringo – foreigner or person with light hair and complexion; can even refer to light-skinned Brazilians
gruta – grotto or cavern

hidrovia – aquatic freeway
hidroviária – boat terminal
hospedagem – cheap boardinghouse used by locals

Iemanjá – Afro-Brazilian goddess of the sea
igapó – flooded Amazon forest
igarapé – creek or small river in Amazonia
igreja – church
ilha – island
índio – indigenous person; translates as 'Indian'

jaburú – jabiru; a giant white stork of the Pantanal with a black head and a red band on its neck
jacaré – caiman
jangada – beautiful sailboat of the Northeast
jangadeiros – crews who use *jangadas*
jeito/jeitinho – possibly the most Brazilian expression, both a feeling and a form of action; from *dar um jeito*, meaning 'to find a way to get something done,' no matter how seemingly impossible, even if the solution may not be completely orthodox or legal
Jogo dos Búzios – Casting of Shells; type of fortune-telling performed by a *pai de santo* or *mãe de santo*

leito – sleeping berth
literatura de cordel – literally 'string literature'; popular literature of the Northeast
litoral – coastal region
luxo – deluxe or 'luxury' rooms

machista – male chauvinist
mãe de santo – female Afro-Brazilian spiritual leader
malandro do morro – vagabond; scoundrel from the hills; a popular figure in Rio's mythology
maloca – *índio* dwelling
Maracanã – football (soccer) stadium in Rio
mercado – market
mestiço – a person of mixed *índio* and European parentage
Mineiro – resident of Minas Gerais
moço/a – waiter or other service industry worker
morro – hill; a person or culture of the favelas
mulato/a – person of mixed black and white parentage

novela – soap opera; Brazil's most popular TV shows
NS – Nosso Senhor (Our Lord) or Nossa Senhora (Our Lady)

O Globo – Brazil's biggest media empire, with the prime national TV station and several newspapers and magazines
orixá – deity of the Afro-Brazilian religions

pagode – popular samba music
pai de santo – male spiritual leader in Afro-Brazilian religions
palácio – palace or large government building
palafita – stilt or a house built on stilts
pampas – grassy plains of the interior of southern Brazil
parque nacional – national park
pau brasil – now-scarce brazilwood tree; a red dye made from the tree that was the colony's first commodity
Paulista – resident of São Paulo state
Paulistano – resident of São Paulo city
PCB – Communist Party of Brazil
pensão – guesthouse
posta restante – poste restante
posto – post; lifeguard posts along Rio de Janeiro's beaches, used as names for different sections of beach
posto de gasolina – a gas (petrol) station
posto telefônico – telephone office
pousada – guesthouse
praça – plaza or town square
praia – beach
prefeitura – city or town hall
PT – Partido dos Trabalhadores (Worker's Party); Brazil's newest and most radical political party

quarto – hotel room without a bathroom
quente – hot
quilombo – community of runaway slaves
Quimbanda – black magic

rápido – fast
real – Brazil's unit of currency since 1994; plural reais
rede – hammock
rio – river

rodoferroviária – bus and train station
rodoviária – bus station

s/n – abbreviation for *sem número* (without number), used in some street addresses
sambista – samba composer or dancer
sambódromo – street with tiers of seating built for samba parades
senzala – slave quarters
serra – mountain range
Sertanejo – resident of the *sertão*
sertão – the drought-prone backlands of the Northeast
shopping – shopping mall

telefonista internacional – international telephone operator
Terra da Vera Cruz – Land of the True Cross; the original Portuguese name for Brazil
terreiro – Afro-Brazilian house of worship

travessa – lane
travesti – transvestite; a popular figure throughout Brazil, considered by some to be the national symbol
trem – train
trio elétrico – three-pronged electrical outlet; electrically amplified bands that play atop trucks
tropicalismo – important cultural movement centered in Bahia in the late 1960s
Tupi – indigenous people and language that predominated along the coast at the time of the European invasion

Umbanda – white magic, a mixture of Candomblé and spiritism

vaqueiro – cowboy of the Northeast
várzea – Amazonian floodplain

zona da mata – bushland just inside the *litoral* in the Northeastern states

The Authors

REGIS ST LOUIS
Coordinating Author, Rio de Janeiro City

Regis' longtime admiration for the Cidade Maravilhosa (Marvelous City) of Rio de Janeiro has led to his deep involvement with Brazil, both as a traveler and as a writer. Rio's vibrant music scene, its colorful *botecos* (small open-air bars) and samba clubs, and the alluring energy of the Cariocas are just a few of the reasons why he's returned so often over the past 10 years. Regis speaks both Portuguese and Spanish, and his articles on Brazil and Latin America have appeared in the *Chicago Tribune*, the *LA Times* and the *San Francisco Chronicle*, among other publications. He is also the coordinating author of Lonely Planet's *Rio de Janeiro* guide and *South America on a shoestring*. He splits his time between New York City and the tropics.

GARY CHANDLER
The Amazon

This was Gary's third time working on the Amazon chapter, and once again the mother of all rivers proved a mother to cover. In all, Gary took nine flights, a half-dozen overnight bus trips and countless boat rides; he made use of four different currencies, adjusted his watch three times and ate pizza with palm hearts on both sides of the equator. He managed to catch only two piranha, a tad shy of his 2007 record of three. Gary studied poetry and ethnic studies at UC Berkeley and has a master's degree in journalism from Columbia University. He currently lives in Colorado, USA, with his wife and fellow author Liza Prado, and their two young children.

GREGOR CLARK
Rio de Janeiro State, Espírito Santo, Minas Gerais

Gregor's passion for all things Brazilian dates back to his first Portuguese class at age 19, where he became enamored of Brazilians' exuberant vocal cadences. (Where else can you call a picnic 'peeky-neeky'?) During his many extended trips to Brazil since 1990, he's fallen in love with countless aspects of the country: the music, the food, the remarkable array of wild and beautiful places; but what always keeps him coming back for more is the warmth, enthusiasm and graciousness of Brazil's people. Gregor has written for Lonely Planet since 2000, contributing to books including those on California, Mexico and Uruguay. He lives with his wife and daughters in Vermont (USA).

LONELY PLANET AUTHORS

Why is our travel information the best in the world? It's simple: our authors are passionate, dedicated travelers. They don't take freebies in exchange for positive coverage so you can be sure the advice you're given is impartial. They travel widely to all the popular spots, and off the beaten track. They don't research using just the internet or phone. They discover new places not included in any other guidebook. They personally visit thousands of hotels, restaurants, palaces, trails, galleries, temples and more. They speak with dozens of locals every day to make sure you get the kind of insider knowledge only a local could tell you. They take pride in getting all the details right, and in telling it how it is. Think you can do it? Find out how at **lonelyplanet.com**.

AIMÉE DOWL
Paraná, Santa Catarina, Rio Grande do Sul

Aimée's first encounter with Brazil was the jungly and remote northern region bordering the Guianas, which she covered for Lonely Planet's *South America on a shoestring*. Research for this edition took her to Brazil's temperate and orderly southeastern corner, where she was caught without a sweater one downright chilly night in the Serra Gaúcha and without an umbrella under the showers of Iguaçu/Iguazú Falls. When she is not covering other South American countries for Lonely Planet, Aimée lives at a cool 2850m in Quito, Ecuador, and works as a freelance travel and culture writer. Her work has appeared in the *New York Times, Viajes, Ms Magazine, BBC History* and four Lonely Planet books.

BRIDGET GLEESON
Bahia, Sergipe & Alagoas

A great lover of the sea, coconuts and Jorge Amado, Bridget considered her trip to northeast Brazil a dream assignment – and after two snorkeling injuries and 200 mosquito bites, she still considers it so. Based in Buenos Aires, she's also lived in the Czech Republic and Nicaragua, and she's written about adventures both indoors and out – from camping in Chilean Patagonia and horseback riding in Argentina's lake region to the pleasures of Uruguayan wine and Mexico's boutique hotels. She was the author and a contributing photographer of Lonely Planet's *Buenos Aires Encounter II*; she also writes for *Delta Sky*, AOL Travel, Tablet Hotels and Mr & Mrs Smith.

ROBERT LANDON
São Paulo State

In 2002 Robert went to Brazil for one week, stayed two, returned home only to quit his job and sell all his worldly goods. A month later he was living in Copacabana, where he still lives today with his partner and two cats. Now fluent in Portuguese, he has spent extensive time in both São Paulo and the south of Brazil, as well as in Rio. A graduate of Stanford University and the University of California at Irvine, Robert has been a travel writer for almost 15 years, including a two-year stint in Paris. His work has appeared in *Dwell* magazine, the *Los Angeles Times*, the *Miami Herald*, the *Houston Chronicle* and the *San Jose Mercury News*.

KEVIN RAUB
Pernambuco, Paraíba & Rio Grande do Norte, Ceará, Piauí & Maranhão

Kevin Raub grew up in Atlanta, USA, and started his career as a music journalist in New York, working for *Men's Journal* and *Rolling Stone* magazines. The rock-and-roll lifestyle took its toll, so he needed an extended vacation and took up travel writing while ditching the States for Brazil. He lives in São Paulo, but relishes his escapes to the Northeast, where he met his wife and his dream island in Fernando de Noronha. This is his 10th Lonely Planet title.

THE AUTHORS

PAUL SMITH   Brasília, Goiás, Mato Grosso & Mato Grosso do Sul

From an early age, and with a vague and naive ambition to be the next David Attenborough, Paul dreamed of exploring the remotest areas of South America in search of wildlife. After spending two months at the Beni Biological Station as a student that dream started to come true, but with David Attenborough still going strong he changed his career plans, became a travel writer and moved to South America (Paraguay) permanently in 2003. While researching this edition Paul came face to face with a petulant pacu, got to grips with 'logical' addresses in Brasília and learnt that even if cerrado (savanna) fruits don't have English names, they *all* taste good!

Behind the Scenes

THIS BOOK

The 8th edition of *Brazil* was researched and written by Regis St Louis (coordinating author), Gary Chandler, Gregor Clark, Aimée Dowl, Bridget Gleeson, Robert Landon, Kevin Raub and Paul Smith. The Health chapter is based on text prepared by David Goldberg MD.

This guidebook was commissioned in Lonely Planet's Oakland office, and produced by the following:

Commissioning Editors Kathleen Munnelly, Suki Gear
Coordinating Editor Evan Jones
Coordinating Cartographer Amanda Sierp
Coordinating Layout Designer Carlos Solarte
Managing Editors Bruce Evans, Brigitte Ellemor
Managing Cartographers David Connolly, Alison Lyall
Managing Layout Designer Celia Wood
Assisting Editors Carolyn Boicos, Kim Hutchins, Jackey Coyle, Kate Daly, Gina Tsarouhas, Laura Gibb, Jeanette Wall
Assisting Cartographers Valeska Cañas, Andrew Smith, David Kemp
Cover Research Naomi Parker
Internal Image Research Sabrina Dalbesio
Language Content Annelies Mertens, Laura Crawford
Thanks to Indra Kilfoyle, Averil Robertson, Juan Winata, John Taufa, John Mazzocchi, Rebecca Lalor, Raphael Richards, Melanie Dankel, Katie Lynch, Frank Deim, Jim Hsu, Shahara Ahmed

THANKS
REGIS ST LOUIS

Warmest thanks (and congratulations) to commissioning editor Kathleen Munnelly and my co-authors for their dedication to all things *Brasileiro*. In Brazil, special thanks to Cristiano Nogueira, Cândida Botafogo, Marcelo Esteves, Marta & John Miller, Madson Araujo, Aurélio Curtim, Simone Theisen, Nelly Pager, Ricardo Hamond, John Tabor, Laurent Tran and Marcos Silviano do Prado. I'd also like to thank the folks at Riotur, the Caprichosos de Pilares friends who paraded with me during Carnaval and the Rocinha gang for fun during the technical rehearsal. Thanks also to the many travelers who wrote in with tips as well as Alison Lyall and all the Lonely Planet talent working behind the scenes. Many thanks to my wife Cassandra Loomis and our lovely daughters Magdalena and Genevieve.

GARY CHANDLER

Special thanks (and congratulations!) to Kathleen Munnelly, commissioning editor extraordinaire, for giving me another crack at the Amazon, and to Regis St Louis for his kind and able shepherding during research and writing. Thank you, too, to Suki Gear, Alison Lyall, Evan Jones, Kim Hutchins, and everyone at Lonely Planet for making this book great. In Manaus, I'm grateful to Antonio of

THE LONELY PLANET STORY

Fresh from an epic journey across Europe, Asia and Australia in 1972, Tony and Maureen Wheeler sat at their kitchen table stapling together notes. The first Lonely Planet guidebook, *Across Asia on the Cheap*, was born.

Travelers snapped up the guides. Inspired by their success, the Wheelers began publishing books to Southeast Asia, India and beyond. Demand was prodigious, and the Wheelers expanded the business rapidly to keep up. Over the years, Lonely Planet extended its coverage to every country and into the virtual world via lonelyplanet.com and the Thorn Tree message board.

As Lonely Planet became a globally loved brand, Tony and Maureen received several offers for the company. But it wasn't until 2007 that they found a partner whom they trusted to remain true to the company's principles of traveling widely, treading lightly and giving sustainably. In October of that year, BBC Worldwide acquired a 75% share in the company, pledging to uphold Lonely Planet's commitment to independent travel, trustworthy advice and editorial independence.

Today, Lonely Planet has offices in Melbourne, London and Oakland, with over 500 staff members and 300 authors. Tony and Maureen are still actively involved with Lonely Planet. They're traveling more often than ever, and they're devoting their spare time to charitable projects. And the company is still driven by the philosophy of *Across Asia on the Cheap*: 'All you've got to do is decide to go and the hardest part is over. So go!'

BEHIND THE SCENES

Amazon Antonio Jungle Tours, Gero and Pedro of Amazon Gero's Tours, Marinilda and Bruno of Malocas Jungle Lodge, Clive of Maguire's Guesthouse and Sofia at Juma Lodge. Thank you to Rodrigo at Instituto Mamirauá and Betinne of Guesthouse Multicultura, both in Tefé; to Neila at Areia Branca Ecotour in Alter do Chão; and of course to the many, many everyday Brazilians who helped with info, directions, patience and kindness along the away. To my brilliant and beautiful wife Liza; to our indescribably delightful daughter Eva; and to little Leo, lovely and new: thank you for everything.

GREGOR CLARK
Thanks to countless Brazilians whose thumbs-ups and warm smiles lighted my way (as always). Um abraço to Lena and Ricardo in Ouro Prêto, Alex and Maira in Diamantina, Bia and Beto in Tiradentes, José Milton in Serra da Bocaina, Bixão in Itaúnas, Dora in Arraial do Cabo, Wilson and Amanda in Guarapari, and Alba and Mariane in Caratinga. Special thanks to my commissioning editor Kathleen Munnelly, coordinating author Regis St Louis, and all the other great folks at Lonely Planet. And finally, enormous muriqui-style hugs to Gaen, Meigan and Chloe, who always make coming home the best part of the trip.

AIMÉE DOWL
Top billing goes to Kathleen Munnelly, whose confidence in my work has meant the world, and to Suki Gear, whose transition was seamless. Huge props go out to Regis St Louis, who has led me through the labyrinth three times. I am deeply indebted to my always punctual Portuguese linguistics coordinator, Vandrea. Thanks to Amy for friendship in Porto Alegre, the barefoot luggage hustlers on Ilha do Mel for wave advice, and endless, unnamable Floripans who pointed me toward the action. To Derek, who always sees the beauty flying and perched around us, even when obscured by the travesties of man, I dedicate this one, as with all of them, to you.

BRIDGET GLEESON
Thank you to the kind Brazilian people who welcomed me warmly wherever I went – particularly Fabio at the Maceió Hostel, Nestor at Pousada Caravelas in Morro de São Paulo (even though he's more Argentinian than Bahian) and the staff of Pousada O Ninho in Salvador. Great thanks to my mother, Margaret, a wonderful travel companion, and my dear sister Molly for joining me in Bahia to taste-test moquecas (Bahian fish stew) and agua de coco (coconut milk). I'm equally grateful to Rodolfo Diaz for educating me in the Portuguese language and waiting patiently for me at home. At Lonely Planet, I'm truly appreciative of Regis St Louis, Alison Lyall and especially Kathleen Munnelly for her professionalism and her willingness to give me some of the best assignments in South America.

ROBERT LANDON
Obrigadão first and foremost to Ann Williams and Igor for generously hosting me and sharing their first-hand knowledge; Thiago for tolerating my absence during research and presence during write-up; Noemia for her culinary talent; Kathleen Munnelly for her enthusiasm about São Paulo and choosing me to write about it; Regis St Louis for his patience and forbearance; and, finally, my mother for planting the travel bug in me in the first place (it sure wasn't my dad).

KEVIN RAUB
Special thanks to my wife, Adriana Schmidt, who first introduced me to the wonders of the Northeast and, once again, saved my ass on many occasions during research. At Lonely Planet, thanks to Kathleen Munnelly and Regis St Louis. On the road in Brazil: Maysa Provedello, Patricia Giglio, Chris Lipp, Mauricio Vilela, Fernanda Velloso, Roberta Rodrigues, Julien Jauneau, Hugo Vasconcelos, Todd Adamson, John Wolinan, Anushka Fowler, Paula Salles, Marcio Henandez, Anne Knapp, Buna and Monica, Edvaldo and Maria Luiza Baltazar, Alexandre Ugarte, Laura Dantas, Sergio Camara, Patrick and Ana Mueller, Fotosub, Gloria Wei, Cadu, Joab and Monica Marciel, Suene Ramalho, and Paul from the Netherlands for the cashews.

PAUL SMITH
Thanks to everybody I met on the road in Brasília, Goiás and the MGs. In particular Ailton Lara who showed me the wonders of Chapada dos Guimarães and took the author photo for me, Luis Octavio who made Bonito unforgettable and Joel Souza who was a great host in Cuiabá. Kevin and Gregor both offered valuable advice on how to handle Campo Grande, and Regis St Louis did his usual great job of keeping everybody sane. Congratulations to Kathleen Munnelly on her new arrival and thanks to everybody else behind the scenes too, especially Alison Lyall. Particular thanks to my wife Carol and beautiful baby son Shawn for making sure that, no matter how great a trip I have, it never beats coming home and seeing their smiling faces.

OUR READERS

Many thanks to the travelers who used the last edition and wrote to us with helpful hints, useful advice and interesting anecdotes:

A Heather Abel, Allie Ackerman, Joao Almeida, Tim Amphlett, Stephanie Andre, Leonardo Aritonang, Dominique Aubert **B** Heiko Baerschneider, Barbara Bansemer, Filippo Bedani, Ryan Bennett, Nuno Bernardo, Leanne Bird, Liz Bissett, Luis Bittencourt, Robert Blackie, Magnus Blomstedt, Yoann Borsato, Gry Bossen, Patrick Brady, Emma Brooks, Thomas Brooks, Mike Buser **C** Keith Camburn, Donald Cameron, Cecile Cannone, Corinne Cath, Drissia Chahma, Louise Chang, Helen Cheung, Anmol Chibber, David Clayton, Adele Cleaver, Gary Cobin, Timothy Crow **D** Rodolpho De Castro, Jelly De Jong, Graziella De Luis, Freddy De Mattos, Anibal De Nicola, Martijn De Rooi, Andre De Souza, Hector Del Olmo, Claudius Doceka, Maria Donnelly, Annette Doornbosch,

SEND US YOUR FEEDBACK

We love to hear from travelers – your comments keep us on our toes and help make our books better. Our well-traveled team reads every word on what you loved or loathed about this book. Although we cannot reply individually to postal submissions, we always guarantee that your feedback goes straight to the appropriate authors, in time for the next edition. Each person who sends us information is thanked in the next edition and the most useful submissions are rewarded with a free book.

To send us your updates – and find out about Lonely Planet events, newsletters and travel news – visit our award-winning website: **www.lonelyplanet.com/contact**.

Note: We may edit, reproduce and incorporate your comments in Lonely Planet products such as guidebooks, websites and digital products, so let us know if you don't want your comments reproduced or your name acknowledged. For a copy of our privacy policy visit www.lonelyplanet.com/privacy.

Sabine Dorn, Gene Draper, Josiane Droeghag, Luciana Drucker **E** Kristen Eder, Raphaelle Eytan **F** Abel Fagundes, Henry Faughnan, Thomas Fischer, Clarisse Fournes, Meredith Franklin, Chris French **G** Joël Gaboriau, Linda Glenn, Suzanne Godfrey, Nicki Goh, Nicolas Gouble, Roberta Gregoli **H** Rachel Hall, Matthew Hamilton, Annika Haraldsson Da Silva, Marcus Harbord, Pierre Harlay, Thomas Harper, Karen Hartley, Heleen Haverkort, Hans Heckel, Kir Heel, Lena Heijken, Conn Herriott, Amber Hoffman, Petra Hoffmann, Michelle Horn, Pip Hunter **J** Bruce Jay, Isabelle Johnson **K** Nikos Kazouris, Frederucj Kent, Sebastian Kernbaum, Susan Khalifah, Cynthia Kharoufeh, Rosie King, Jacek Kostyrko, Stefan Krueger, Corinne Kuipers **L** Réal Lambert, Eva Lecat, Danielle Lee, Stephen Lee, Stephane Legrand, Katrin Looser, Iain Loughnan, James Loxton, Haenen Luc, Atila Lvg **M** John Mac Lloyd, Matthew Maclean, Eloise Madden, Regina Maier, Lewis Martins, Louis Matalon, Carlos Menezes, Irene Messina, Seda Mollen, Tom Mollenkamp, Marina Moretti, Vincent Muraire, Val Murray, Emile Myburgh, Nate Myers **N** Guilherme Nunes **O** Marianna Olinger, Thais Oliveira, Hanan Beit On **P** Marcel Pace, Charlotte Padelsi, Kaven Paradis, Supaya Pasbo, Megan Passey, Mark Pery-Knox-Gore, David Peterson, Neil Pike, Vinícius Pimenta, Ada Pinkston, Nicky Pinto, Bryan Pitts, Tim Plaggenborg, Esther Postma, Dina Priess Dos Santos **R** Stéphane Raynaud, Steffen Reimlinger, Benjamin Remia, Evan Rieder, Anton Rijsdijk, Rik Roelofs, Valentina Rojas Loa Salazar, Patrick Roman, Royce Romberg, Sally Rosevear, David Rosler, Evan Ross, Mar Rosseneu, Toni Royo, Letizia Russo **S** Maike Schmidt, Wolfgang Schuler, David Seeberg Ravnskjær, Justina Southworth, Rodrigo Souza De Souza, Eduardo Stival, Sho Alexander Sugihara, Adam Sulkowski, Rembrandt Sutorius **T** Linda Techell, Fiona Teng, James Tubman **V** Laurent Vahl, Edwin Van Der Lem, Jana Van Der Schoot, Alexander Van Rijn, Mark Vander Meer, William Van-Ham, Barbara Vazquez, Bobbi Verdugo, Petra Versol, Kathryn Victor, Bernard Vixseboxse, Maria Vragova **W** Lindsay Walker, Sonia Washuus De Carvalho, Paul Wegmann, Uta Westerhüs, Don Wilks, Isabelle Willems, Danielle Wolbers, Ronald Wolff, Jim Woolam, Jane Wright **Y** Feyza Yazar, Froucke Ykema, Nadia Yoshioka, **Z** Foteini Zafeiriou, Tania Zulkoskey, Manuele Zunelli

ACKNOWLEDGMENTS

Many thanks to the following for the use of their content:

Globe on title page ©Mountain High Maps 1993 Digital Wisdom, Inc.

BEHIND THE SCENES

Index

INDEX

INDEX

000 Map pages
000 Photograph pages

INDEX

INDEX

GreenDex

GREENDEX

GREENDEX

MAP LEGEND

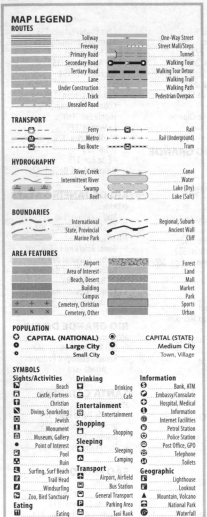

ROUTES

Tollway
Freeway
Primary Road
Secondary Road
Tertiary Road
Lane
Under Construction
Track
Unsealed Road

One-Way Street
Street Mall/Steps
Tunnel
Walking Tour
Walking Tour Detour
Walking Trail
Walking Path
Pedestrian Overpass

TRANSPORT

Ferry
Metro
Bus Route

Rail
Rail (Underground)
Tram

HYDROGRAPHY

River, Creek
Intermittent River
Swamp
Reef

Canal
Water
Lake (Dry)
Lake (Salt)

BOUNDARIES

International
State, Provincial
Marine Park

Regional, Suburb
Ancient Wall
Cliff

AREA FEATURES

Airport
Area of Interest
Beach, Desert
Building
Campus
Cemetery, Christian
Cemetery, Other

Forest
Land
Mall
Market
Park
Sports
Urban

POPULATION

◎ **CAPITAL (NATIONAL)**
● **Large City**
● Small City

◉ **CAPITAL (STATE)**
◉ **Medium City**
◉ Town, Village

SYMBOLS

Sights/Activities
Beach
Castle, Fortress
Christian
Diving, Snorkeling
Jewish
Monument
Museum, Gallery
Point of Interest
Pool
Ruin
Surfing, Surf Beach
Trail Head
Windsurfing
Zoo, Bird Sanctuary

Eating
Eating

Drinking
Drinking
Café

Entertainment
Entertainment

Shopping
Shopping

Sleeping
Sleeping
Camping

Transport
Airport, Airfield
Bus Station
General Transport
Parking Area
Taxi Rank

Information
Bank, ATM
Embassy/Consulate
Hospital, Medical
Information
Internet Facilities
Petrol Station
Police Station
Post Office, GPO
Telephone
Toilets

Geographic
Lighthouse
Lookout
Mountain, Volcano
National Park
Waterfall

LONELY PLANET OFFICES

Australia (Head Office)
Locked Bag 1, Footscray, Victoria 3011
☎ 03 8379 8000, fax 03 8379 8111

USA
150 Linden St, Oakland, CA 94607
☎ 510 250 6400, toll free 800 275 8555
fax 510 893 8572

UK
2nd fl, 186 City Rd,
London EC1V 2NT
☎ 020 7106 2100, fax 020 7106 2101

Contact
talk2us@lonelyplanet.com
lonelyplanet.com/contact

Published by Lonely Planet Publications Pty Ltd
ABN 36 005 607 983

© Lonely Planet 2010

© photographers as indicated 2010

Cover photograph: Macaw plumage detail. Brazil, South America/ Diego Lezama. Many of the images in this guide are available for licensing from Lonely Planet Images: lonelyplanetimages.com.

Printed by Toppan Security Printing Pte. Ltd.
Printed in Singapore.

MIX
Paper from
responsible sources
FSC
www.fsc.org
FSC™ C021741
